ing Centre

Mind and Cognition

BLACKWELL PHILOSOPHY ANTHOLOGIES

Each volume in this outstanding new series provides an authoritative and comprehensive collection of the essential primary readings from philosophy's main fields of study. Designed to complement the *Blackwell Companions to Philosophy* series, each volume represents an unparalleled resource in its own right, and will provide the ideal platform for course use.

Mind and Cognition
An Anthology

Second Edition

Edited by *William G. Lycan*

University of North Carolina

BLACKWELL
Publishers

Copyright © Blackwell Publishers Ltd 1990, 1999

First published 1990

Second edition published 1999

2 4 6 8 10 9 7 5 3 1

Blackwell Publishers Inc.
350 Main Street
Malden, Massachusetts 02148
USA

Blackwell Publishers Ltd
108 Cowley Road
Oxford OX4 1JF
UK

Library of Congress Cataloging-in-Publication Data

Mind and cognition: an anthology / edited by William G. Lycan. — 2nd ed.
    p.   cm. — (Blackwell philosophy anthologies; 8)
    Includes bibliographical references and index.
    ISBN 0–631–21204–3 (hardcover: alk. paper). — ISBN 0–631–20545–4 (pbk.: alk. paper)
    1. Mind and body.   2. Thought and thinking.
    3. Cognitive science. I. Lycan, William G.   II. Series.
  BF171.   M55 1999
  128'.2 — dc21   98–35450
                                                                    CIP

British Library Cataloguing in Publication Data

A CIP catalogue record for this book is available from the British Library

Typeset in 9 on 11 pt Ehrhardt by Pure Tech India Ltd, Pondicherry
http://www.puretech.com.
Printed in Great Britain by T.J. International , Padstow, Cornwall

This book is printed on acid-free paper

Contents

Contents

Contents

Contents

Contents

Contents

Preface to the Second Edition

I was surprised at how much revision has been required after just eight years; the philosophy of mind and cognition must be doing well.

Thanks to Steve Smith, of Blackwell Publishers, for urging and supporting a new edition, and especially to Sean McKeever for his extensive editorial help.

1998

Preface to the First Edition

In the past thirty years, the philosophy of mind has seen a massive shift of doctrine, of method, and of perspective. Characteristic of this shift is the unprecedented attention of philosophers of mind to science: not only to psychology and linguistics, but to computer science, evolutionary biology, and neuroscience as well. As a result, the mind–body problem is now better understood than at any previous point in human history – so I would contend and the contention is borne out by the contents of this anthology. That is not to claim consensus for any one solution to the mind–body problem, for (of course) none exists. It is to claim a fairish consensus on questions of what the going arguments do and do not show, what the live options are, and what is at stake.

The essays and excerpts collected here are themselves predominantly philosophical. I would rather have assembled a more eclectic gathering, to include works written by empirical scientists with no speculative parsnips to butter, but the presentation of a significant number of such pieces as an integrated whole would have required a book-length introductory survey. The reader will have to rely on my bibliographies and (better) on my authors' endnotes.

Even regarding philosophy alone, my choice of headings for the various Parts, and of the readings themselves, reflects my no doubt tendentious view of the field and of what has happened in the philosophy of mind since the 1960s. Others may see things differently, and I am sure others would have included different items in the bibliographies.

This volume's closest and most distinguished predecessor is Ned Block (ed.), *Readings in Philosophy of Psychology*, vols 1 and 2 (Cambridge, Mass.: Harvard University Press, 1980). I thank Block for his unselfish encouragement of my own project, and I urge every reader who has already purchased a copy of this anthology to buy Block's as well.

My greatest debts are to Stephan Chambers, of Blackwell Publishers, who suggested this anthology and has supported my work unstintingly, to Kim Sterelny for valuable discussions on choice of contents, and of course to the authors, especially to those who have contributed new or substantially revised essays.

I have written a brief synoptic introduction to each of the Parts. Citations in those introductions refer to items in the "Further reading" lists at the end of each introduction.

1990

Acknowledgments

The publisher and editor wish to thank the following for permission to reprint copyright material in this book:

D. M. Armstrong: for "The Causal Theory of the Mind" in *The Nature of Mind and Other Essays* (University of Queensland Press, 1980), to the publisher.

William Bechtel: for "The Case for Connectionism," in *Philosophical Studies*, 71 (1992), to the author and Kluwer Academic Publishers.

Ned Block: for " 'Qualia'-Based Objections to Functionalism," an excerpt from "Troubles with Functionalism," first published in *Perception and Cognition: Minnesota Studies in the Philosophy of Science*, volume IX, edited by W. Savage (University of Minnesota Press, 1978), to the author; for "Inverted Earth" in *Philosophical Perspectives, 4, Action Theory and Philosophy of Mind*, edited by James E. Tomberling (Ridgeview Publishing Company, 1990), to the author and publisher.

Patricia Smith Churchland and Terrence J. Sejnowski: for "Neural Representation and Neural Computation," in *Neural Connections, Mental Computations*, edited by L. Nadel, L. Cooper, P. Culicover, and R. M. Harnish (MIT Press, 1989), to the publisher.

Paul M. Churchland: for "Eliminative Materialism and the Propositional Attitudes," in *Journal of Philosophy*, LXXVIII, 2 (February 1981), to the author and publisher; (with Patricia Smith Churchland) for "Stalking the Wild Epistemic Engine," in *Noûs*, 17 (1983), to Blackwell Publishers, Inc.

Donald Davidson: for "Knowing One's Own Mind," in *Proceedings and Addresses of the American Philosophical Association*, volume 60, no. 3, to the author and publisher; for "Mental Events," in *Essays on Actions and Events* by Donald Davidson (1980), to Oxford University Press.

Martin Davies: for "The Mental Simulation Debate," in *Proceedings of the British Academy*, volume 83, *Objectivity, Simulation and the Unity of Consciousness: Current Issues in the Philosophy of Mind, edited by Christopher Peacock*, © The British Academy 1994, to the author and The British Academy.

Daniel C. Dennett: for "Real Patterns," in *Journal of Philosophy*, LXXXVII (January 1991), © 1991 The Journal of Philosophy, Inc., to the author and publisher; for "True Believers: The Internatinal Strategy and Why it Works," in *Scientific Explanation: Papers based on Herbert Spencer Lectures given in the University of Oxford*, edited by A. F. Heath (1981), © Oxford University Press 1981, to the author and publisher.

Michael Devitt: for "A Narrow Representational Theory of the Mind," in *Mind and Cognition: A Reader*, edited by William G. Lycan (Blackwell, 1990), to the author.

Jerry A. Fodor: for an extract from "The Appeal to Tacit Knowledge in Psychological Explanation," in *Journal of Philosophy*, LXV, 20 (October 24, 1968), to the author and publisher; for "A Theory of Content, II: The Theory," in *Theory of Content and Other Essays* by Jerry A. Fodor (MIT Press, 1990), to the author and publisher; for chapter 2, "Individualism and

Acknowledgments

Supervenience," in *Psychosemantics* by Jerry A. Fodor (MIT Press, 1987), © Bradford Books/MIT Press, to the publisher; for "Why There Still Has to Be a Language of Thought," in *Psychosemantics* by Jerry A. Fodor (MIT Press, 1987), to the publisher.

Tim Van Gelder: for "What Might Cognition Be, If Not Computation?" in *Journal of Philosophy*, XCII, 7 (July 1995), © 1995 The Journal of Philosophy, Inc., to the author and publisher.

Robert M. Gordon: for "Folk Psychology as Simulation," in *Mind and Language*, 1 (1986), © Blackwell Publishers Ltd, to the publisher.

Paul E. Griffiths: for "Modularity and the Psychoevolutionary Theory of Emotion," in *Biology and Philosophy*, 5 (1990), © 1990 Kluwer Academic Publishers, to the author and publisher.

Robert Van Gulick: for chapter 7, "Understanding the Phenomenal Mind: Are We All Just Armadillos? in *Consciousness: Psychological and Philosophical Essays*, edited by M. Davies and G. Humphreys (Blackwell, 1993), to the publisher.

Gilbert Harman: for "The Intrinsic Quality of Experience," in *Philosophical Perspectives, 4, Action Theory and Philosophy of Mind*, edited by James E. Tomberlin (1990), © Ridgeview Publishing Company, Atascadero, California, to the author and publisher.

John Heil: for "Privileged Access," from *Mind*, volume XCVII (1986), to the author and Oxford University Press.

Terence Horgan and James Woodward: for "Folk Psychology is Here to Stay," in *Philosophical Review*, 94, no. 2 (April 1985), © 1985 Cornell University, to the author and publisher.

Frank Jackson: for "Epiphenomenal Qualia," in *Philosophical Quarterly*, 32 (1982), © the Editors of The Philosophical Quarterly, to Blackwell Publishers Ltd.

Jaegwon Kim: for chapter 6, "Mental Causation," in *Philosophy of Mind* by Jaegwon Kim (Westview Press, 1996), © 1996 by Westview Press, to the author and publisher.

David Lewis for "What Experience Teaches," in *Proceedings of the Russellian Society*, edited by J. Copley-Coltheart (University of Sydney, 1988), to the publisher.

William G. Lycan: for "The Continuity of Levels of Nature," excerpted from chapters 4 and 5 of *Consciousness* (MIT Press, 1987), to the publisher.

Brian P. McLaughlin: for "Type Epiphenomenalism, Type Dualism, and the Causal Priority of the Physical," in *Philosophical Perspectives*, 3 (1989), to the author and Blackwell Publishers, Inc.

Ruth Garrett Millikan: for "Biosemantics," in *Journal of Philosophy*, 6 (June 1989), © 1989 The Journal of Philosophy, Inc., to the author and publisher.

Ronald Alan Nash: for "Cognitive Theories of Emotion," in *Nôus*, 23 (1989), © 1989 by Nôus Publications, to Blackwell Publishers, Inc.

U. T. Place: for "Is Consciousness a Brain Process?" in *British Journal of Psychology* (1956), © The British Psychological Society, to the author and publisher. (A slightly revised version of this paper appears in this volume, incorporating modifications presented by the author in a paper entitled "We needed the analytical–synthetic distinction to formulate mind-brain identity then: we still do," delivered at a conference on "Forty Years of Australian Materialism" at the University of Leeds in June 1997.)

Hilary Putnam: for "The Nature of Mental States," originally published as "Psychological Predicates" by Hilary Putnam, in *Art, Mind, and Religion*, edited by W. H. Capitan and D. D. Merrill, © 1967 by the University of Pittsburgh Press, to the publisher.

Elliott Sober: for "Putting the Function Back into Functionalism," excerpted from "Panglossian Functionalism and the Philosophy of Mind" by E. Sober, in *Synthese*, volume 64, no. 2 (1985), © 1986/1985 by D. Reidel Publishing Company, to Kluwer Academic Publishers.

Stephen P. Stich: for "Narrow Content Meets Fat Syntax," in *Meaning in Mind: Fodor and His Critics*, edited by Barry Loewer and Georges Rey (Blackwell, 1991), to the author and publisher; for "Dennett on Intentional Systems," in *Philosophical Topics*, 12 (1981), to the author; for "Autonomous Psychology and the Belief–Desire Thesis," in *Monist*, 61 (1978), © 1978, The Monist, La Salle, Illinois 61301, to the publisher.

Robert A. Wilson: for chapter 2, "An *a priori* Argument: The Argument from Causal Powers," in *Cartesian Psychology and Physical Minds* by Robert A. Wilson (1995), to the author and Cambridge University Press.

PART I

Ontology: The Identity Theory and Functionalism

Introduction

Until nearly midway through the present century, the philosophy of mind was dominated by a "first-person" perspective. Throughout history (though with a few signal exceptions), most philosophers have accepted the idea, made fiercely explicit by Descartes, that the mind is both better known than the body and metaphysically in the body's driver's-seat. Some accepted Idealism, the view that only mind really exists and that matter is an illusion; some held that although matter does truly exist, it is somehow composed or constructed out of otherwise mental materials; some granted that matter exists even apart from mind but insisted that mind is wholly distinct from matter and partially in control of matter. Philosophers of this last sort we shall call "Cartesian Dualists."

Dualism and Behaviorism

All the aforementioned philosophers agreed that (a) mind is distinct from matter (if any), and that (b) there is at least a theoretical *problem* of how we human subjects can know that "external," everyday physical objects exist, even if there are tenable solutions to that problem. We subjects are immured within a movie theater of the mind, though we may have some defensible ways of inferring what goes on outside the theater.

All this changed very suddenly in the 1930s, with the accumulated impact of Logical Positivism and the verification theory of meaning. *Intersubjective verifiability* became the criterion

both of scientific probity and of linguistic meaning itself. If the mind, in particular, was to be respected either scientifically or even as meaningfully describable in the first place, mental ascriptions would have to be pegged to publicly, physically testable verification-conditions. Science takes an intersubjective, "third-person" perspective on everything; the traditional first-person perspective had to be abandoned for scientific and serious metaphysical purposes.

The obvious verification-conditions for mental ascriptions are behavioral. How can the rest of us tell that you *are in pain* save by your wincing-and-groaning behavior in circumstances of presumable disorder, or that you *believe that broccoli will kill you* save by your verbal avowals and your nonverbal avoidance of broccoli? If the verification-conditions are behavioral, then the very meanings of the ascriptions, or at least the only facts genuinely described, are not inner and ineffable but behavioral. Thus Behaviorism as a theory of mind and a paradigm for psychology.

In psychology, Behaviorism took primarily a methodological form: Psychological Behaviorists claimed (i) that psychology itself is a science for the prediction and control of behavior, (ii) that the only proper data or observational input for psychology are behavioral, specifically patterns of physical responses to physical stimuli, and (iii) that *inner* states and events, neurophysiological or mental, are not proper objects of psychological investigation – neurophysiological states and events are the business of biologists, and mental states and events, so far as they exist at all, are not to be mentioned unless operationalized nearly to death. Officially, the Psychological Behaviorists made no metaphysical claims; minds and mental entities might exist for all they knew, but this was not to be presumed in psychological experiment or theorizing. Psychological theorizing was to consist, *à la* Logical Positivism, of the subsuming of empirically established stimulus–response generalizations under broader stimulus–response generalizations.

In philosophy, Behaviorism did (naturally) take a metaphysical form: chiefly that of Analytical Behaviorism, the claim that mental ascriptions simply *mean* things about behavioral responses to environmental impingements. Thus, "Edmund is in pain" means, not anything about Edmund's putative inner life or any episode taking place within Edmund, but that Edmund either is actually behaving in a wincing-and-groaning way or is disposed so to behave (in that he would so behave were something not keeping him from so doing). "Edmund believes that broccoli will kill him" means just that if asked, Edmund will assent to that proposition, and if confronted by broccoli, Edmund will shun it, and so forth.

But it should be noted that a Behaviorist metaphysician need make no claim about the meanings of mental expressions. One might be a merely Reductive Behaviorist, and hold that although mental ascriptions do not *simply mean* things about behavioral responses to stimuli, they are ultimately (in reality) made true just by things about actual and counterfactual responses to stimuli. (On the difference between "analytic" reduction by linguistic meaning and "synthetic" reduction by *a posteriori* identification, see the next section of this introduction.) Or one might be an Eliminative Behaviorist, and hold that there are no mental states or events at all, but only behavioral responses to stimuli, mental ascriptions being uniformly false or meaningless.

Any Behaviorist will subscribe to what has come to be called the "Turing Test." In response to the perennially popular question "Can machines think?", Alan Turing (1964) replied that a better question is that of whether a sophisticated computer could ever pass a battery of (verbal) behavioral tests, to the extent of fooling a limited observer into thinking it is human and sentient; if a machine did pass such tests, then the putatively further question of whether the machine really *thought* would be idle at best, whatever metaphysical ana-

lysis one might attach to it. Barring Turing's tendentious limitation of the machine's behavior to verbal as opposed to nonverbal responses, any Behaviorist, psychological or philosophical, would agree that psychological differences cannot outrun behavioral test; organisms (including machines) whose actual and counterfactual behavior is just the same are psychologically just alike.

Philosophical Behaviorism adroitly avoided a number of nasty objections to Cartesian Dualism (see Carnap 1932/33; Ryle 1949; Place, this volume; Smart 1959; Armstrong 1968, ch. 5; Campbell 1984), even besides solving the methodological problem of intersubjective verification: it dispensed with immaterial Cartesian egos and ghostly nonphysical events, writing them off as ontological excrescences. It disposed of Descartes's admitted problem of mind–body interaction, since it posited no immaterial, nonspatial causes of behavior. It raised no scientific mysteries concerning the intervention of Cartesian substances in physics or biology, since it countenanced no such intervention.

Yet some theorists were uneasy; they felt that in its total repudiation of the inner, Behaviorism was leaving out something real and important. When they voiced this worry, the Behaviorists often replied with mockery, assimilating the doubters to old-fashioned Dualists who believed in ghosts, ectoplasm, and/or the Easter Bunny. Behaviorism was the only (even halfway sensible) game in town. Nonetheless, the doubters made several lasting points against it. First, anyone who is honest and not anaesthetized knows perfectly well that he/she experiences and can introspect actual inner mental episodes or occurrences, that are neither actually accompanied by characteristic behavior nor are merely static hypothetical facts of how he/she would behave if subjected to such-and-such a stimulation. Place (this volume) speaks of an "intractable residue" of conscious mental states that bear no clear relations to behavior of any particular sort; see also Armstrong (1968, ch. 5) and Campbell (1984). Second, contrary to the Turing Test, it seems perfectly possible for two people to differ psychologically despite total similarity of their actual and counterfactual behavior, as in a Lockean case of "inverted spectrum"; for that matter, a creature *might* exhibit all the appropriate stimulus–response relations and lack mentation entirely (Campbell 1984; Fodor and Block 1972; Block 1981; Kirk 1974). Third, the Analytical Behaviorist's behavioral analyses of mental ascriptions seem adequate only so long as one makes substantive assumptions about the rest of the subject's *mentality* (Chisholm 1957, ch. 11; Geach 1957, p. 8; Block 1981), and so are either circular or radically incomplete as analyses of the mental generally.

So matters stood in stalemate between Dualists, Behaviorists and doubters, until the mid-1950s, when Place (this volume) and Smart (1959) proposed a middle way, an irenic solution.

The Identity Theory

According to Place and Smart, contrary to the Behaviorists, at least some mental states and events are genuinely inner and genuinely episodic after all. They are not to be identified with outward behavior or even with hypothetical dispositions to behave. But, contrary to the Dualists, the episodic mental items are not ghostly or nonphysical either. Rather, they are neurophysiological. They are identical with states and events occurring in their owners' central nervous systems; more precisely, every mental state or event is numerically identical with some such neurophysiological state or event. To be in pain is to have one's (for example) c-fibers, or possibly a-fibers, firing; to believe that broccoli will kill you is to have one's B_{bk}-fibers firing, and so on.

By making the mental entirely physical, this Identity Theory of the mind shared the Behaviorist advantage of avoiding the nasty objections to Dualism; but it also brilliantly accommodated the inner and the episodic as the Behaviorists did not. For according to the Identity Theory, mental states and events actually occur in their owners' central nervous systems; hence they are *inner* in an even more literal sense than could be granted by Descartes. The Identity Theory also thoroughly vindicated the idea that organisms could differ mentally despite total behavioral similarity, since clearly organisms can differ neurophysiologically in mediating their outward stimulus–response regularities. And of course the connection between a belief or a desire and the usually accompanying behavior is defeasible by other current mental states, since the connection between a B- or D-neural state and its normal behavioral effect is defeasible by other psychologically characterizable interacting neural states. The Identity Theory was the ideal resolution of the Dualist/Behaviorist impasse.

Moreover, there was a direct deductive argument for the Identity Theory, hit upon independently by David Lewis (1972) and D. M. Armstrong (1968, this volume). Lewis and Armstrong maintained that mental terms were *defined* causally, in terms of mental items' typical causes and effects. For example, "pain" *means* a state that is typically brought about by physical damage and that typically causes withdrawal, favoring, complaint, desire for cessation, and so on. (Armstrong claimed to establish this by straightforward "conceptual analysis"; Lewis held that mental terms are the theoretical terms of a commonsensical "folk theory" (see Part V below), and with the Positivists that all theoretical terms are implicitly defined by the theories in which they occur.) Now if by definition, pain is whatever state occupies a certain causal niche, and if, as is overwhelmingly likely, scientific research reveals that that particular niche is in fact occupied by such-and-such a neurophysiological state, it follows by the transitivity of identity that pain is that neurophysiological state; QED. Pain retains its conceptual connection to behavior, but also undergoes an empirical identification with an inner state of its owner. (An advanced if convolute elaboration of this already hybrid view is developed by Lewis (1980); for meticulous criticism, see Block (1978), Shoemaker (1981), and Tye (1983).)

Notice that although Armstrong and Lewis began their arguments with a claim about the meanings of mental terms, their Common-Sense Causal version of the Identity Theory itself was no such thing, any more than was the original Identity Theory of Place and Smart. Rather, all four philosophers relied on the idea that things or properties can sometimes be identified with "other" things or properties even when there is no synonymy of terms; there is such a thing as synthetic and *a posteriori* identity that is nonetheless genuine identity. While the identity of triangles with trilaterals holds simply in virtue of the meanings of the two terms and can be established by reason alone, without empirical investigation, the following identities are standard examples of the synthetic *a posteriori*, and were discovered empirically: clouds with masses of water droplets; water with H_2O; lightning with electrical discharge; the Morning Star with Venus; Mendelian genes with segments of DNA molecules; temperature (of a gas) with mean molecular kinetic energy. The Identity Theory was offered similarly, in a spirit of scientific speculation; one could not properly object that mental expressions do not mean anything about brains or neural firings.

So the Dualists were wrong in thinking that mental items are nonphysical but right in thinking them inner and episodic; the Behaviorists were right in their physicalism but wrong to repudiate inner mental episodes. Alas, this happy synthesis was too good to be true.

Machine Functionalism

In the mid-1960s Putnam (1960, this volume) and Fodor (1968) pointed out a presumptuous implication of the Identity Theory understood as a theory of "types" or *kinds* of mental items: that a mental state such as pain has *always and everywhere* the neurophysiological characterization initially assigned to it. For example, if the Identity Theorist identified pain itself with the firings of *c*-fibers, it followed that a creature of any species (earthly or science-fiction) could be in pain only if that creature *had* *c*-fibers and they were firing. But such a constraint on the biology of any being capable of feeling pain is both gratuitous and indefensible; why should we suppose that any organism must be made of the same chemical materials as we in order to have what can be accurately recognized as pain? The Identity Theorist had overreacted to the Behaviorists' difficulties and focused too narrowly on the specifics of biological humans' actual inner states, and in so doing they had fallen into species chauvinism.

Fodor and Putnam advocated the obvious correction: What was important was not its being *c*-fibers (*per se*) that were firing, but what the *c*-fiber firings were doing, what their firing contributed to the operation of the organism as a whole. The *role* of the *c*-fibers could have been performed by any mechanically suitable component; so long as that role was performed, the psychology of the containing organism would have been unaffected. Thus, to be in pain is not *per se* to have *c*-fibers that are firing, but merely to be in some state or other, of whatever biochemical description, that plays the same causal role as did the firings of *c*-fibers in the human beings we have investigated. We may continue to maintain that pain "tokens," individual instances of pain occurring in particular subjects at particular times, are strictly identical with particular neurophysiological states of those subjects at those times, viz., with the states that happen to be playing the appropriate roles; this is the thesis of "token identity" or "token physicalism." But pain itself, the kind, universal, or "type," can be identified only with something more abstract: the causal or functional role that *c*-fiber firings share with their potential replacements or surrogates. Mental state-types are identified not with neurophysiological types but with more abstract functional roles, as specified by state-tokens' causal relations to the organism's sensory inputs, motor outputs, and other psychological states.

Putnam compared mental states to the functional or "logical" states of a computer: just as a computer program can be realized or instantiated by any of a number of physically different hardware configurations, so a psychological "program" can be realized by different organisms of various physiochemical composition, and that is why different physiological states of organisms of different species can realize one and the same mental state-type. Where an Identity Theorist's type-identification would take the form, "To be in mental state of type *M* is to be in the neurophysiological state of type *N*," Putnam's Machine Functionalism (as I shall call it) has it that to be in *M* is to be merely in some physiological state or other that plays role *R* in the relevant computer program (that is, the program that at a suitable level of abstraction mediates the creature's total outputs given total inputs and so serves as the creature's global psychology). The physiological state "plays role *R*" in that it stands in a set of relations to physical inputs, outputs, and other inner states that matches one-to-one the abstract input/output/logical-state relations codified in the computer program.

The Functionalist, then, mobilizes three distinct levels of description but applies them all to the same fundamental reality. A physical state-token in someone's brain at a particular time has a neurophysiological description, but may also have a functional description relative to a machine program that the brain happens to be realizing, and it may further have a mental description if some mental state is correctly type-identified with the functional category it exemplifies. And so there is after all a sense in which "the mental" is distinct from "the physical": though there are no nonphysical substances or stuffs, and every mental token is itself entirely physical, mental characterization is not physical characterization, and the property of being a pain is not simply the property of being such-and-such a neural firing.

Cognitive Psychology

In a not accidentally similar vein, Psychological Behaviorism has almost entirely given way to "Cognitivism" in psychology. Cognitivism is roughly the view that (i) psychologists may and must advert to inner states and episodes in explaining behavior, so long as the states and episodes are construed throughout as physical, and (ii) human beings and other psychological organisms are best viewed as in some sense *information-processing* systems. As cognitive psychology sets the agenda, its questions take the form, "How does this organism receive information through its sense-organs, process the information, store it, and then mobilize it in such a way as to result in intelligent behavior?" During the 1960s, the cognitive psychologists' initially vague notion of "information processing" (inspired in large part by the popularity of "Information Theory" in regard to physical systems of communication) became the idea that organisms employ internal representations and perform computational operations on those representations; *cognition* became a matter of the rule-governed manipulation of representations much as it occurs in actual digital computers.

The working language of cognitive psychology is of course highly congenial to the Functionalist, for Cognitivism thinks of human beings as systems of interconnected functional components, interacting with each other in an efficient and productive way.

Artificial Intelligence and the Computer Model of the Mind

Meanwhile, researchers in computer science have pursued fruitful research programs based on the idea of intelligent behavior as the output of skillful information-processing given input. Artifical Intelligence (AI) is, roughly, the project of getting computing machines to perform tasks that would usually be taken to demand human intelligence and judgment. Computers have achieved some modest success in proving theorems, guiding missiles, sorting mail, driving assembly-line robots, diagnosing illnesses, predicting weather and economic events, and the like. A computer *just is* a machine that receives, interprets, processes, stores,

manipulates and uses information, and AI researchers think of it in just that way as they try to program intelligent behavior; an AI problem takes the form, "Given that the machine sees this as input, what must it already know and what must it accordingly do with that input in order to be able to . . . [recognize, identify, sort, put together, predict, tell us, etc.] . . . ? And how, then, can we start it off knowing that and get it to do those things?" So we may reasonably attribute such success as AI has had to self-conscious reliance on the information-processing paradigm.

This encourages the aforementioned idea that *human* intelligence and cognition generally are matters of computational information-processing. Indeed, that idea has already filtered well down into the everyday speech of ordinary people, among whom computer jargon is fairly common. This tentative and crude coalescing of the notions *cognition*, *computation*, *information*, and *intelligence* raises two general questions, one in each of two directions. First, to what extent might computers approximate minds? Second, to what extent do minds approximate computers?

The first question breaks down into three, which differ sharply and importantly from each other. (i) What intelligent tasks will any computer ever be able to perform? (ii) Given that a computer performs interesting tasks X, Y, and Z, does it do so *in the same way* that human beings do? (iii) Given that a computer performs X, Y, and Z and that it does so in the same way humans do, does that show that it has psychological and mental properties, such as (real) intelligence, thought, consciousness, feeling, sensation, emotion, and the like? Subquestion (i) is one of engineering, (ii) is one of cognitive psychology, and (iii) is philosophical; theorists' answers will depend accordingly on their commitments in these respective areas. But for the record let us distinguish three different senses or grades of "AI": AI in the weakest sense is cautiously optimistic as regards (i); it says these engineering efforts are promising and should be funded. AI in a stronger sense says that the engineering efforts can well serve as modelings of human cognition, and that their successes can be taken as pointers toward the truth about human functional organization. AI in the strongest sense favors an affirmative answer to (iii) and some qualified respect for the Turing Test: it says that if a machine performs intelligently *and* does so on the basis of a sufficiently human-like information-processing etiology, then there is little reason to doubt that the machine has the relevant human qualities of mind and sensation. (AI in the strongest sense is fairly strong, but notice carefully that it does not presuppose affirmative answers to either (i) or (ii).)

The opposite issue, that of assimilating minds to computers, is very close to the philosophical matter of Functionalism. But here too there are importantly distinct subquestions, this time two: (i) Do human minds work in very like the way computers do as computers are currently designed and construed; for example, using flipflops grouped into banks and registers, with an assembly language collecting individual machine-code operations into subroutines and these subroutines being called by higher-level manipulations of real-world information according to programmed rules? (ii) Regardless of architecture, can human psychological capacities be entirely captured by a third-person, hardware-realizable design of *some* sort that could in principle be built in a laboratory? Subquestion (i) is of great interest (see Parts III and IV below), but is not particularly philosophical. Subquestion (ii) is tantamount to the fate of Functionalism.

Anomalous Monism

Donald Davidson (this volume, 1973, 1974) took a more radical view of the split between the token identity thesis (for mental and neurophysiological states or events) and the Identity Theorists' type thesis. He gave a novel and ingenious argument for token identity, based on his "Principle of the Anomalism of the Mental": "There are no strict and deterministic laws on the basis of which mental events can be predicted and explained" (this volume). The argument is roughly that since mental events interact causally with physical events and causality requires strict laws, the mental events must have physical descriptions under which they are related to other physical events by strict laws.

But then Davidson used the same principle to argue that in the matter of type identification, mental events are even worse off than the Machine Functionalist had suggested: Since in fact, mental types are individuated by considerations that are nonscientific, distinctively humanistic, and in part normative, they will not coincide with any types that are designated in scientific terms, let alone neurophysiological types. Thus, there will be no interesting type-identification of mental states or events with anything found in any science. The latter conclusion is not entirely explicit in Davidson, for he leaves some slack in the "strictness" a law must have in order to count as a scientific law. But he has refused to grant that the generalizations afforded by a Functionalist psychology, in particular, would count as sufficiently strict, for they are infested by *ceteris paribus* qualifications that can never be discharged.

Critics have replied that Davidson's case against the Functionalist type-identification is unproven, for that identification is entirely consistent with his premises (Van Gulick 1980; Lycan 1981; Antony 1989). Moreover, either the *ceteris paribus* qualification eventually could be discharged by a completed Functionalist psychology, or if not, then there is no reason to doubt that the same is true of other special sciences, such as biology.

Other commentators have criticized Davidson's notion of "supervenient" causation (Johnston 1985; Kim 1985; and see Part V below.)

Homuncular Functionalism and Teleology

Machine Functionalism supposed that human brains may be described at each of three levels, the first two scientific and the third familiar and commonsensical. (1) Biologists would map out human neuroanatomy and provide neurophysiological descriptions of brain states. (2) Psychologists would (eventually) work out the machine program that was being realized by the lower-level neuroanatomy and would describe the same brain states in more abstract, computational terms. (3) Psychologists would also explain behavior, characterized in everyday terms, by reference to stimuli and to intervening mental states such as beliefs and desires, type-identifying the mental states with functional or computational states as they went. Such explanations would themselves presuppose nothing about neuroanatomy, since the relevant psychological/computational generalizations would hold regardless of what particular biochemistry might happen to be realizing the abstract program in question.

Machine Functionalism as described has more recently been challenged on each of a number of points, that together motivate a specifically teleological notion of "function" (Sober (this volume) speaks aptly of "putting the function back into Functionalism"):

(i) The Machine Functionalist still conceived psychological *explanation* in the Positivists' terms of subsumption of data under wider and wider universal generalizations. But Fodor (this volume), Cummins (1983), and Dennett (1978) have defended a competing picture of psychological explanation, according to which behavioral data are to be seen as manifestations of subjects' psychological capacities, and those capacities are to be explained by understanding the subjects as systems of interconnected components. Each component is a "homunculus," in that it is identified by reference to the function it performs, and the various homuncular components cooperate with each other in such a way as to produce overall behavioral responses to stimuli. The "homunculi" are themselves broken down into subcomponents whose functions and interactions are similarly used to explain the capacities of the subsystems they compose, and so again and again until the sub–sub–... components are seen to be neuroanatomical structures. (An automobile works – locomotes – by having a fuel reservoir, a fuel line, a carburetor, a combustion chamber, an ignition system, a transmission, and wheels that turn. If one wants to know how the carburetor works, one will be told what its parts are and how they work together to infuse oxygen into fuel; and so on.) Thus biologic and mechanical systems alike are hierarchically organized, on the principle of what computer scientists call "hierarchical control."

(ii) The Machine Functionalist treated functional "realization," the relation between an individual physical organism and the abstract program it was said to instantiate, as a simple matter of one-to-one correspondence between the organism's repertoire of physical stimuli, structural states, and behavior, on the one hand, and the program's defining input/state/output function on the other. But this criterion of realization was seen to be too liberal; since virtually anything bears a one–one correlation of some sort to virtually anything else, "realization" in the sense of mere one–one correspondence is far too easily come by (Block (1978), Lycan (1987, ch. 3)).

Some theorists have proposed to remedy this defect by imposing a teleological requirement on realization: a physical state of an organism will count as realizing such-and-such a functional description only if the organism has genuine organic integrity and the state plays its functional role properly *for* the organism, in the teleological sense of "for" and in the teleological sense of "function." The state must do what it does as a matter of, so to speak, its biological purpose.

(iii) Machine Functionalism's two-leveled picture of human psychobiology is unbiological in the extreme. Neither living things nor even computers themselves are split into a purely "structural" level of biological/physiochemical description and any one "abstract" computational level of machine/psychological description. Rather, they are all hierarchically organized at many levels, each level "abstract" with respect to those beneath it but "structural" or concrete as it realizes those levels above it. The "functional"/"structural" or "software"/"hardware" distinction is entirely relative to one's chosen level of organization. This relativity has repercussions for Functionalist solutions to problems in the philosophy of mind (Lycan 1987, ch. 5), and for current controversies surrounding Connectionism and neural modeling (see Part III of this volume).

(iv) The teleologizing of functional realization has helped functionalists to rebut various objections based on the "qualia" or "feels" or experienced phenomenal characters of mental states (Lycan 1981; Sober, this volume).

(v) Millikan (1984, this volume), Van Gulick (1980), Fodor (1984, 1990), Dretske, (1988), and others have argued powerfully that teleology must enter into any adequate analysis of the intentionality or aboutness of mental states such as beliefs and desires. According to the teleological theorists, a neurophysiological state should count as *a belief that broccoli will kill you*, and in particular as *about broccoli*, only if that state has the representing of broccoli as in some sense one of its psychobiological functions.

All this talk of teleology and biological function seems to presuppose that biological and other "structural" states of physical systems really have functions in the teleological sense. The latter claim is controversial to say the least. Some philosophers dismiss it as hilariously false, as a superstitious relic of primitive animism or Panglossian theism or at best the vitalism of the nineteenth century; others tolerate it but only as a useful metaphor; still others take teleological characterizations to be literally but only interest-relatively true, true *modulo* a convenient classificatory or interpretive scheme (Cummins 1975). Only a few fairly recent writers (Wimsatt 1972, Wright 1973, Millikan 1984, and a few others) have taken teleological characterizations to be literally and categorically true. This may seem to embarrass teleologized Functionalist theories of mind.

Yes and no. Yes, because if a Homuncular and/or Teleological Functionalist type-identifies mental items with teleologically characterized items, and teleological characterizations are not literally true, then mental ascriptions cannot be literally true either. Equivalently, if people really do have mental states and events, on their own and not merely in virtue of anyone's superstitious or subjective interpretation of them, but their physical states do not have objectively teleological functions, then mental states cannot be type-identified with teleological states.

Fortunately for the Teleological Functionalist there is now a small but vigorous industry whose purpose is to explicate biological teleology in naturalistic terms, typically in terms of etiology. For example, a trait may be said to have the function of doing *F* in virtue of its having been selected for because it did *F*; a heart's function is to pump blood because hearts' pumping blood in the past has given them a selection advantage and so led to the survival of more animals with hearts. Actually, no simple etiological explication will do (Cummins 1975, Boorse 1976, Bigelow and Pargetter 1987, Davies 1994), but philosophers of biology have continued to refine the earlier accounts and to make them into adequate naturalistic analyses of genuine function (Neander 1991, Godfrey-Smith 1994).

It should be noted that the correctness of type-identifying mental items with teleological items does not strictly depend on the objectivity or even the truth of teleological descriptions. For corresponding to each metaphysical view of teleology, including deflationary and flatly derisive ones, there is a tenable view of mind. Just as teleology may be a matter of interest-relative interpretation, so, after all, may mental ascriptions be

(see Part II of this volume). For that matter, just as teleology may be only metaphorical, fictional, or illusory, so may mental ascriptions be; some philosophers now hold that mental ascriptions are in the end false (see Part III). But we shall consider those possibilities in due course.

Chronic Problems

Functionalism, cognitive psychology considered as a complete theory of human thought, and AI in the strongest sense all inherit some of the same problems that earlier beset Behaviorism and the Identity Theory. These remaining problems fall into two main categories, respectively headed, by philosophers, "qualia" and "intentionality," both mentioned in the previous section.

The "quale" of a mental state or event is that state or event's *feel*, its introspectible "phenomenal character." Many philosophers have objected that neither Functionalist metaphysics nor cognitive psychology nor AI nor the computer model of the mind can explain, illuminate, acknowledge, or even tolerate the notion of *what it feels like* to be in a mental state of such-and-such a sort. Yet, say these philosophers, the feels are quintessentially mental – it is the feels that make the mental states the mental states they are. Something, therefore, must be drastically wrong with Functionalism, cognitive psychology, AI in the strongest sense, and the computer model of the mind. Such "qualia"-based objections and responses to them will be the topic of Part VI below.

"Intentionality" is a feature common to most mental states and events, particularly the "propositional attitudes," those cognitive and conative states that are described in everyday language with the use of "that"-clauses. One believes *that broccoli is lethal*, desires *that visitors should wipe their feet*, hopes *that the Republican candidate will win*, etc. Other propositional attitudes include thoughts, intentions, rememberings, doubts, wishes, and wonderings.

A "that"-clause contains what is itself grammatically a sentence; intuitively that internal sentence expresses the "content" of the belief, desire, or other attitude in question. This is because propositional attitudes *represent* actual or possible states of affairs. That indeed is what makes them propositional attitudes, and accordingly they are described in terms of their respective representational contents.

The objects and states of affairs upon which our propositional attitudes are directed may actually obtain, in the real world. But equally they may not: beliefs are often false, desires can be frustrated, hopes may be dashed. The attitudes may also be about "things" that do not exist: Sherlock Holmes, the Easter Bunny, the free lunch. Franz Brentano raised the question of how any purely physical entity or state could have the property of being about or "directed upon" a nonexistent state of affairs or object; that is not the sort of feature that ordinary, purely physical objects can have. Many philosophers, including Chisholm (1957), have argued that no purely physical account of a system or organism, human or computer, could explain Brentano's property. That difficulty for Functionalism et al. will be addressed in Parts IV and V.

In alluding to sensory states and to mental states with intentional content, we have said nothing specifically about the emotions. Since the rejection of Behaviorism, theories of mind have tended not to be applied directly to the emotions; rather, the emotions have been generally thought to be conceptually analyzable as complexes of more central

or "core" mental states, typically propositional attitudes such as belief and desire (and the intentionality of emotions has accordingly been traced back to that of attitudes). Kenny (1963) took this line, as do Armstrong (1968, ch. 8, sec. III), Solomon (1977), and Gordon (1987). However, there is a nascent literature on Functionalism and the emotions; see Part VII below.

It may be wondered whether materialist theories of the mind and/or functionalist theories in particular have any interesting implications for morality and ethics. Three materialists take this up explicitly: Smart (1963, ch. VIII), tries to exhibit a materialist basis for morals; Michael Levin (1979, ch. VII) addresses the specific charge that materialists cannot allow freedom of the will or whatever else may be necessary to make room for moral responsibility; Lycan (1985) explores some moral consequences of the computational view of the mind. A main purpose of Dennett (1978) is also to show why moral responsibility and the mental vernacular that supports it are possible despite Dennett's instrumentalist – sometimes fictionalist – treatment of the mental (see Part III of this volume).

Further Reading

Useful general works on theories of mind
Campbell, K. K. (1984) *Body and Mind* (2nd edn), University of Notre Dame Press.
Churchland, P. M. (1988) *Matter and Consciousness* (2nd edn), Bradford Books/MIT Press.
Braddon-Mitchell, D. and Jackson, F. (1996) *Philosophy of Mind and Cognition*, Blackwell Publishers.
Kim, J. (1996) *Philosophy of Mind*, Westview Press.
Rey, G. (1997) *Contemporary Philosophy of Mind*, Blackwell Publishers.

All five books contain very clear discussions of Dualism, Behaviorism, the Identity Theory, and Functionalism, as well as bibliographies. Churchland's takes up some of the newer developments in "neurophilosophy" (see Part III). See also McGinn, C. (1982) *The Character of Mind*, Oxford University Press; Smith, P. and Jones, O. R. (1986) *The Philosophy of Mind*, Cambridge University Press; Bechtel, W. (1988) *Philosophy of Mind: An Overview for Cognitive Science*, Laurence Erlbaum; Flanagan, O. (1991) *The Science of Mind*, Bradford Books/MIT Press; Graham, G. (1993) *Philosophy of Mind: An Introduction*, Blackwell Publishers. An excellent general reference work in the field is Guttenplan, S. (ed.) (1994) *A Companion to the Philosophy of Mind*, Blackwell Publishers.

Psychological Behaviorism
Skinner, B. F. (1933) *Science and Human Behavior*, Macmillan.
Chomsky, N. (1959) Review of B. F. Skinner's *Verbal Behavior*, *Language* 35, 26–58.
Behavioral and Brain Sciences 7, 4 (1984), a special issue on the "Canonical papers of B. F. Skinner." [See particularly Skinner's "Representations and misrepresentations," 655–65, his response to "Open peer commentary" on his article "Behaviorism at fifty."]

Analytical Behaviorism
Carnap, R. (1932/33) "Psychology in physical language," *Erkenntnis* 3, 107–42. [In the full text, Carnap considers possible objections at length.]
Hempel, C. G. (1949) "The logical analysis of psychology," in H. Feigl and W. Sellars (eds), *Readings in Philosophical Analysis*, Appleton Century Crofts.
Ryle, G. (1949) *The Concept of Mind*, Barnes and Noble.
Chisholm, R. M. (1957) *Perceiving*, Cornell University Press.
Geach, P. (1957) *Mental Acts*, Routledge & Kegan Paul.
Putnam, H. (1965) "Brains and behaviour," in R. J. Butler (ed.), *Analytical Philosophy, Part II*, Basil Blackwell.

Introduction

The Turing Test

Turing, A. M. (1964) "Computing machinery and intelligence," reprinted in A. R. Anderson (ed.), *Minds and Machines*, Prentice-Hall.

Gunderson, K. (1985) *Mentality and Machines* (2nd edn), University of Minnesota Press.

Block, N. J. (1981) "Psychologism and Behaviorism," *Philosophical Review* 90, 5–43.

Rosenberg, J. F. (1982) "Conversation and intelligence," in B. de Gelder (ed.), *Knowledge and Representation*, Routledge & Kegan Paul.

Dennett, D. C. (1985) "Can machines think?", in M. Shafto (ed.), *How We Know*, Harper & Row.

The Identity Theory

Smart, J. J. C. (1959) "Sensations and brain processes," *Philosophical Review* 68, 141–56.

Feigl, H. (1967) *The "Mental" and the "Physical": The Essay and a Postscript*, University of Minnesota Press.

Presley, C. F. (ed.) (1967) *The Identity Theory of Mind*, University of Queensland Press.

Borst, C. V. (ed.) (1970) *The Mind/Brain Identity Theory*, Macmillan.

The Common-Sense Causal Theory

Armstrong, D. M. (1968) *A Materialist Theory of the Mind*, Routledge & Kegan Paul.

Armstrong, D. M. (1981) "Epistemological foundations for a materialist theory of the mind," reprinted in *The Nature of Mind and Other Essays*. Cornell University Press.

Lewis, D. (1972) "Psychophysical and theoretical identifications," *Australasian Journal of Philosophy* 50, 249–58.

Nagel, T. (1970) "Armstrong on the mind," *Philosophical Review* 79, 394–403.

Pappas, G. (1977) "Armstrong's Materialism," *Canadian Journal of Philosophy* 7, 569–92.

Block, N. J. (1978) "Troubles with Functionalism," in W. Savage (ed.), *Perception and Cognition: Minnesota Studies in the Philosophy of Science*, vol. IX, University of Minnesota Press. [N.b., Block's section on Lewis is included in neither the short version of his paper reprinted in this volume nor that reprinted in his own anthology, *Readings in Philosophy of Psychology*, vol. 1 (Harvard University Press, 1980).]

Lewis, D. (1980) "Mad pain and Martian pain," in N. Block (ed.), *Readings in Philosophy of Psychology*, vol. 1, ibid.

Shoemaker, S. (1981) "Some varieties of Functionalism," *Philosophical Topics* 12, 93–119.

Tye, M. (1983) "Functionalism and Type Physicalism," *Philosophical Studies* 44, 161–74.

Hill, C. S. (1991) *Sensations: A Defense of Type Materialism*, Cambridge University Press.

Machine Functionalism

Putnam, H. (1960) "Minds and machines," in S. Hook (ed.), *Dimensions of Mind*, Collier Books.

Putnam, H. (1967) "The mental life of some machines," in H.-N. Castañeda (ed.), *Intentionality, Minds, and Perception*, Wayne State University Press.

Fodor, J. A. (1968) *Psychological Explanation*, Random House.

Kalke, W. (1969) "What is wrong with Fodor and Putnam's Functionalism?" *Noûs* 3, 83–94.

Rorty, R. (1972) "Functionalism, machines, and incorrigibility," *Journal of Philosophy* 69, 203–20.

Fodor, J. A. and Block, N. J. (1972) "What psychological states are not," *Philosophical Review* 81, 159–81.

Lycan, W. (1974) "Mental states and Putnam's Functionalist hypothesis," *Australasian Journal of Philosophy* 52, 48–62.

Cognitive Psychology

Johnson-Laird, P. N. and Wason, P. C. (1977) *Thinking: Readings in Cognitive Science*, Cambridge University Press.

Anderson, J. R. (1985) *Cognitive Psychology and its Implications* (2nd edn), W. H. Freeman.

Glass. A. L. and Holyoak, K. J. (1986) *Cognition* (2nd edn), Random House.

N. A. Stillings et al. (1987) *Cognitive Science: An Introduction*, Bradford Books/MIT Press.

D. N. Osherson et al. (eds) (1995) *An Invitation to Cognitive Science*, 2nd edn, especially vol. 3, *Thinking* (ed. by E. E. Smith and D. N. Osherson), Bradford Books/MIT Press.

Artificial Intelligence and the computer model of the mind

A. R. Anderson (ed.) (1964) *Minds and Machines*, Prentice Hall.

Hofstadter, D. (1979) *Gödel, Escher, Bach: An Eternal Golden Braid*, Basic Books. [See also Hofstadter, D. and Dennett, D. C. (eds) (1981) *The Mind's I: Fantasies and Reflections on Self and Soul*, Basic Books.]

Winston, P. H. (1984) *Artificial Intelligence* (2nd edn), Addison-Wesley.

Pylyshyn, Z. W. (1984) *Computation and Cognition: Toward a Foundation for Cognitive Science*, MIT Press.

Charniak, E. and McDermott, D. (1985) *Introduction to Artificial Intelligence*, Addison-Wesley.

Haugland, J. (1985) *Artificial Intelligence: The Very Idea*, Bradford Books/MIT Press.

Dennett, D. C. (1986) "The logical geography of computational approaches: a view from the East Pole," in M. Brand and R. M. Harnish (eds), *The Representation of Knowledge and Belief*, University of Arizona Press.

Johnson-Laird, P. (1988) *The Computer and the Mind*, Harvard University Press.

Haugland, J. (ed.) (1997) *Mind Design II: Philosophy, Psychology, Artificial Intelligence*, Bradford Books/MIT Press.

Anomalous Monism

Davidson, D. (1973) "The material mind," in P. Suppes, L. Henkin, and A. Joja (eds), *Logic, Methodology and Philosophy of Science*, vol. 4, North-Holland.

Davidson, D. (1974) "Psychology as philosophy," in S. C. Brown (ed.), *Philosophy of Psychology*, Macmillan.

Van Gulick, R. (1980) "Rationality and the anomalous nature of the mental," *Philosophical Research Archives* 7, 1404.

Lycan, W. (1981) "Psychological laws," *Philosophical Topics* 12, 9–38.

Johnston, M. (1985) "Why having a mind matters," in E. Lepore and B. McLaughlin (eds), *Actions and Events: Perspectives on the Philosophy of Donald Davidson*, Basil Blackwell.

Kim, J. (1985) "Psychophysical laws," in E. Lepore and B. McLaughlin (eds), *Actions and Events: Perspectives on the Philosophy of Donald Davidson*, Basil Blackwell.

Antony, L. (1989) "Anomalous Monism and the problem of explanatory force," in *Philosophical Review* 98, 153–87.

Homuncular Functionalism

Attneave, F. (1960) "In defense of homunculi," in W. Rosenblith (ed.), *Sensory Communication*, MIT Press.

Simon, H. (1969) "The architecture of complexity," in *The Sciences of the Artificial*, MIT Press.

Wimsatt, W. C. (1976) "Reductionism, levels of organization, and the mind–body problem," in G. Globus, G. Maxwell, and I. Savodnik (eds), *Consciousness and the Brain*, Plenum.

Dennett, D. C. (1978) *Brainstorms*, Bradford Books.

Haugeland, J. (1978) "The nature and plausibility of Cognitivism," *Behavioral and Brain Sciences* 1, 215–26.

Lycan, W. (1981) "Form, function, and feel," *Journal of Philosophy* 78, 24–50.

Cummins, R. (1983) *The Nature of Psychological Explanation*, Bradford Books/MIT Press.

Lycan, W. G. (1987) *Consciousness*, Bradford Books/MIT Press.

Teleological Functionalism

Dennett, D. C. (1969) *Content and Consciousness*, Routledge & Kegan Paul, chs III and IV.

Van Gulick, R. (1980) "Functionalism, Information and Content," *Nature and System*, 139–62; reprinted in the 1990 first edition of this anthology.

Fodor, J. A. (1984) "Semantics, Wisconsin Style," *Synthese* 59, 231–50.

Millikan, R. G. (1984) *Language, Thought, and Other Biological Categories*, Bradford Books/MIT Press.

Papineau, D. (1987) *Reality and Representation*, Basil Blackwell, ch. 4.

Fodor, J. A. (1980) "Psychosemantics," in the 1990 first edition of this anthology.

Dretske, F. (1988) *Explaining Behavior*, Bradford Books/MIT Press.

Naturalistic theories of teleology

Wimsatt, W. C. (1972) "Teleology and the logical structure of function statements," *Studies in History and Philosophy of Science* 3, 1–80.

Wright, L. (1973) "Functions," *Philosophical Review* 82, 139–68.

Cummins, R. (1975) "Functional analysis," *Journal of Philosophy* 72, 741–64.

Bennett, J. (1976) *Linguistic Behaviour*, Cambridge University Press, ch. 1.

Boorse, C. (1976) "Wright on functions," *Philosophical Review* 85, 70–86.

Bigelow, J. and Pargetter, R. (1987) "Functions," *Journal of Philosophy* 84, 181–96.

Neander, K. (1991) "Functions as Selected Effects: The Conceptual Analyst's Defense," *Philosophy of Science* 58, 168–84.

Davies, P. S. (1994) "Troubles for direct proper functions," *Noûs* 28, 363.

Godfrey-Smith, P. (1994) "A modern history theory of functions," *Noûs* 28, 344–62.

Emotions

Kenny, A. (1963) *Action, Emotion, and Will*, Routledge & Kegan Paul.

de Sousa, R. (1987) *The Rationality of Emotion*, Bradford Books/MIT Press.

Gordon, R. M. (1987) *The Structure of Emotions*, Cambridge University Press.

Solomon, R. (1977) *The Passions*, Doubleday.

Morality

Levin, M. (1979) *Metaphysics and the Mind–Body Problem*, Oxford University Press.

Lycan, W. (1985) "Abortion and the civil rights of machines," in N. T. Potter and M. Timmons (eds), *Morality and Universality*, D. Reidel.

Smart, J. J. C. (1963) *Philosophy and Scientific Realism*, Routledge & Kegan Paul.

1

The Identity Theory

Is Consciousness a Brain Process?

U. T. Place

The thesis that consciousness is a process in the brain is put forward as a reasonable scientific hypothesis, not to be dismissed on logical grounds alone. The conditions under which two sets of observations are treated as observations of the same process, rather than as observations of two independent correlated processes, are discussed. It is suggested that we can identify consciousness with a given pattern of brain activity, if we can explain the subject's introspective observations by reference to the brain processes with which they are correlated. It is argued that the problem of providing a physiological explanation of introspective observations is made to seem more difficult than it really is by the "phenomenological fallacy," the mistaken idea that descriptions of the appearances of things are descriptions of the actual state of affairs in a mysterious internal environment.

I Introduction

The view that there exists a separate class of events, mental events, which cannot be described in terms of the concepts employed by the physical sciences no longer commands the universal and unquestioning acceptance among philosophers and psychologists which it once did. Modern physicalism, however, unlike the materialism of the seventeenth and eighteenth centuries, is behavioristic. Consciousness on this view is either a special type of behavior, "sampling" or "running-back-and-forth" behavior as Tolman has it,[1] or a disposition to behave in a certain way, an itch, for example, being a temporary propensity to scratch. In the case of cognitive concepts like "knowing," "believing," "understanding," "remembering," and volitional concepts like "wanting" and "intending," there can be little doubt, I think, that an analysis in terms of dispositions to behave is fundamentally sound.[2] On the other hand, there would seem to be an intractable residue of concepts clustering around the notions of consciousness, experience, sensation, and mental imagery, where some sort of inner process story is unavoidable.[3] It is possible, of course, that a satisfactory behavioristic account of this conceptual residuum will ultimately be found. For our present purposes, however, I shall assume that this cannot be done and that statements about pains and twinges, about how things look, sound, and feel, about things dreamed of or pictured in the mind's eye, are statements referring to events and processes which are in some sense private or internal to the individual of whom they are predicated. The question I wish to raise is whether in making this assumption we are inevitably committed to a dualist position in which sensations and mental images form a separate category of processes over and above the physical and physiological processes with which they are known to be correlated. I shall argue that an acceptance of inner processes does not entail dualism and that the thesis that consciousness is a process in the brain cannot be dismissed on logical grounds.

14

II   The "Is" of Definition and the "Is" of Composition

I want to stress from the outset that in defending the thesis that consciousness is a process in the brain, I am not trying to argue that when we describe our dreams, fantasies, and sensations we are talking about processes in our brains. That is, I am not claiming that statements about sensations and mental images are reducible to or analyzable into statements about brain processes, in the way in which "cognition statements" are analyzable into statements about behavior. To say that statements about consciousness are statements about brain processes is manifestly false. This is shown (a) by the fact that you can describe your sensations and mental imagery without knowing anything about your brain processes or even that such things exist, (b) by the fact that statements about one's consciousness and statements about one's brain processes are verified in entirely different ways, and (c) by the fact that there is nothing self-contradictory about the statement "X has a pain but there is nothing going on in his brain." What I do want to assert, however, is that the statement "Consciousness is a process in the brain," although not necessarily true, is not necessarily false. "Consciousness is a process in the brain" in my view is neither self-contradictory nor self-evident; it is a reasonable scientific hypothesis, in the way that the statement "Lightning is a motion of electric charges" is a reasonable scientific hypothesis.

The all but universally accepted view that an assertion of identity between consciousness and brain processes can be ruled out on logical grounds alone derives, I suspect, from a failure to distinguish between what we may call the "is" of definition and the "is" of composition. The distinction I have in mind here is the difference between the function of the word "is" in statements like "A square is an equilateral rectangle," "Red is a color," "To understand an instruction is to be able to act appropriately under the appropriate circumstances," and its function in statements like "His table is an old packing case," "Her hat is a bundle of straw tied together with string," "A cloud is a mass of water droplets or other particles in suspension." These two types of "is" statements have one thing in common. In both cases it makes sense to add the qualification "and nothing else." In this they differ from those statements in which the "is" is an "is" of predication; the

statements "Toby is eighty years old and nothing else," "Her hat is red and nothing else," or "Giraffes are tall and nothing else," for example, are nonsense. This logical feature may be described by saying that in both cases both the grammatical subject and the grammatical predicate are expressions which provide an adequate characterization of the state of affairs to which they both refer.

In another respect, however, the two groups of statements are strikingly different. Statements like "A square is an equilateral rectangle" are necessary statements which are true by definition. Statements like "His table is an old packing-case," on the other hand, are contingent statements which have to be verified by observation. In the case of statements like "A square is an equilateral rectangle" or "Red is a color," there is a relationship between the meaning of the expression forming the grammatical predicate and the meaning of the expression forming the grammatical subject, such that whenever the subject expression is applicable the predicate must also be applicable. If you can describe something as red then you must also be able to describe it as colored. In the case of statements like "His table is an old packing-case," on the other hand, there is no such relationship between the meanings of the expressions "his table" and "old packing-case"; it merely so happens that in this case both expressions are applicable to and at the same time provide an adequate characterization of the same object. Those who contend that the statement "Consciousness is a brain process" is logically untenable, base their claim, I suspect, on the mistaken assumption that if the meanings of two statements or expressions are quite unconnected, they cannot both provide an adequate characterization of the same object or state of affairs: if something is a state of consciousness, it cannot be a brain process, since there is nothing self-contradictory in supposing that someone feels a pain when there is nothing happening inside his skull. By the same token we might be led to conclude that a table cannot be an old packing-case, since there is nothing self-contradictory in supposing that someone has a table, but is not in possession of an old packing-case.

III   The Logical Independence of Expressions and the Ontological Independence of Entities

There is, of course, an important difference between the table/packing-case and the consciousness/brain process case in that the statement "His table is an old packing-case" is a particular proposition which refers only to one particular case, whereas the statement "Consciousness is a process in the brain" is a general or universal proposition applying to all states of consciousness whatever. It is fairly clear, I think, that if we lived in a world in which all tables without exception were packing-cases, the concepts of "table" and "packing-case" in our language would not have their present logically independent status. In such a world a table would be a species of packing-case in much the same way that red is a species of color. It seems to be a rule of language that whenever a given variety of object or state of affairs has two characteristics or sets of characteristics, one of which is unique to the variety of object or state of affairs in question, the expression used to refer to the characteristics or set of characteristics which defines the variety of object or state of affairs in question will always entail the expression used to refer to the other characteristic or set of characteristics. If this rule admitted of no exception it would follow that any expression which is logically independent of another expression which uniquely characterizes a given variety of object or state of affairs must refer to a characteristic or set of characteristics which is not normally or necessarily associated with the object or state of affairs in question. It is because this rule applies almost universally, I suggest, that we are normally justified in arguing from the logical independence of two expressions to the ontological independence of the states of affairs to which they refer. This would explain both the undoubted force of the argument that consciousness and brain processes must be independent entities because the expressions used to refer to them are logically independent and, in general, the curious phenomenon whereby questions about the furniture of the universe are often fought and not infrequently decided merely on a point of logic.

The argument from the logical independence of two expressions to the ontological independence of the entities to which they refer breaks down in the case of brain processes and consciousness, I believe, because this is one of a relatively small number of cases where the rule stated above does not apply. These exceptions are to be found, I suggest, in those cases where the operations which have to be performed in order to verify the presence of the two sets of characteristics inhering in the object or state of affairs in question can seldom if ever be performed simultaneously. A good example here is the case of the cloud and the mass of droplets or other particles in suspension. A cloud is a large semi-transparent mass with a fleecy texture suspended in the atmosphere whose shape is subject to continual and kaleidoscopic change. When observed at close quarters, however, it is found to consist of a mass of tiny particles, usually water droplets, in continuous motion. On the basis of this second observation we conclude that a cloud is a mass of tiny particles and nothing else. But there is no logical connection in our language between a cloud and a mass of tiny particles; there is nothing self-contradictory in talking about a cloud which is not composed of tiny particles in suspension. There is no contradiction involved in supposing that clouds consist of a dense mass of fibrous tissue; indeed, such a consistency seems to be implied by many of the functions performed by clouds in fairy stories and mythology. It is clear from this that the terms "cloud" and "mass of tiny particles in suspension" mean quite different things. Yet we do not conclude from this that there must be two things, the mass of particles in suspension and the cloud. The reason for this, I suggest, is that although the characteristics of being a cloud and being a mass of tiny particles in suspension are invariably associated, we never make the observations necessary to verify the statement "That is a cloud" and those necessary to verify the statement "This is a mass of tiny particles in suspension" at one and the same time. We can observe the micro-structure of a cloud only when we are enveloped by it, a condition which effectively prevents us from observing those characteristics which from a distance lead us to describe it as a cloud. Indeed, so disparate are these two experiences that we use different words to describe them. That which is a cloud when we observe it from a distance becomes a fog or mist when we are enveloped by it.

IV   When Are Two Sets of Observations Observations of the Same Event?

The example of the cloud and the mass of tiny particles in suspension was chosen because it is one of the few cases of a general proposition involving what I have called the "is" of composition which does not involve us in scientific technicalities. It is useful because it brings out the connection between the ordinary everyday cases of the "is" of composition like the table/packing-case example and the more technical cases like "Lightning is a motion of electric charges" where the analogy with the consciousness/brain process case is most marked. The limitation of the cloud/tiny particles in suspension case is that it does not bring out sufficiently clearly the crucial problems of how the identity of the states of affairs referred to by the two expressions is established. In the cloud case the fact that something is a cloud and the fact that something is a mass of tiny particles in suspension are both verified by the normal processes of visual observation. It is arguable, moreover, that the identity of the entities referred to by the two expressions is established by the continuity between the two sets of observations as the observer moves towards or away from the cloud. In the case of brain processes and consciousness there is no such continuity between the two sets of observations involved. A closer introspective scrutiny will never reveal the passage of nerve impulses over a thousand synapses in the way that a closer scrutiny of a cloud will reveal a mass of tiny particles in suspension. The operations required to verify statements about consciousness and statements about brain processes are fundamentally different.

To find a parallel for this feature we must examine other cases where an identity is asserted between something whose occurrence is verified by the ordinary processes of observation and something whose occurrence is established by special procedures. For this purpose I have chosen the case where we say that lightning is a motion of electric charges. As in the case of consciousness, however closely we scrutinize the lightning we shall never be able to observe the electric charges, and just as the operations for determining the nature of one's state of consciousness are radically different from those involved in determining the nature of one's brain processes, so the operations for determining the occurrence of lightning are radically different from those involved in determining the occurrence of a motion of electric charges. What is it, therefore, that leads us to say that the two sets of observations are observations of the same event? It cannot be merely the fact that the two sets of observations are systematically correlated such that whenever there is lightning there is always a motion of electric charges. There are innumerable cases of such correlations where we have no temptation to say that the two sets of observations are observations of the same event. There is a systematic correlation, for example,

between the movement of the tides and the stages of the moon, but this does not lead us to say that records of tidal levels are records of the moon's stages or vice versa. We speak rather of a causal connection between two independent events or processes.

The answer here seems to be that we treat the two sets of observations as observations of the same event in those cases where the technical scientific observations set in the context of the appropriate body of scientific theory provide an immediate explanation of the observations made by the man in the street. Thus we conclude that lightning is nothing more than a motion of electric charges, because we know that a motion of electric charges through the atmosphere, such as occurs when lightning is reported, gives rise to the type of visual stimulation which would lead an observer to report a flash of lightning. In the moon/tide case, on the other hand, there is no such direct causal connection between the stages of the moon and the observations made by the man who measures the height of the tide. The causal connection is between the moon and the tides, not between the moon and the measurement of the tides.

V   The Physiological Explanation of Introspection and the Phenomenological Fallacy

If this account is correct, it should follow that in order to establish the identity of consciousness and certain processes in the brain, it would be necessary to show that the introspective observations reported by the subject can be accounted for in terms of processes which are known to have occurred in his brain. In the light of this suggestion it is extremely interesting to find that when a physiologist, as distinct from a philosopher, finds it difficult to see how consciousness could be a process in the brain, what worries him is not any supposed self- contradiction involved in such an assumption, but the apparent impossibility of accounting for the reports given by the subject of his conscious processes in terms of the known properties of the central nervous system. Sir Charles Sherrington has posed the problem as follows:

The chain of events stretching from the sun's radiation entering the eye to, on the one hand, the contraction of the pupillary muscles, and on the other, to the electrical disturbances in the brain-cortex are all straightforward steps in a sequence of physical "causation," such as, thanks to science, are intelligible. But in the second serial chain there follows on, or attends, the stage of brain-cortex reaction an event or set of events quite inexplicable to us, which both as to themselves and as to the causal tie between them and what preceded them science does not help us; a set of events seemingly incommensurable with any of the events leading up to it. The self "sees" the sun; it senses a two-dimensional disc of brightness, located in the "sky," this last a field of lesser brightness, and overhead shaped as a rather flattened dome, coping the self and a hundred other visual things as well. Of hint that this is within the head there is none. Vision is saturated with this strange property called "projection," the unargued inference that what it sees is at a "distance" from the seeing "self." Enough has been said to stress that in the sequence of events a step is reached where a physical situation in the brain leads to a psychical, which however contains no hint of the brain or any other bodily part . . . The supposition has to be, it would seem, two continuous series of events, one physico-chemical, the other psychical, and at times interaction between them.[4]

Just as the physiologist is not likely to be impressed by the philosopher's contention that there is some self-contradiction involved in supposing consciousness to be a brain process, so the philosopher is unlikely to be impressed by the considerations which lead Sherrington to conclude that there are two sets of events, one physico-chemical, the other psychical. Sherrington's argument, for all its emotional appeal, depends on a fairly simply logical mistake, which is unfortunately all too frequently made by psychologists and physiologists and not infrequently in the past by the philosophers themselves. This logical mistake, which I shall refer to as the "phenomenological fallacy," is the mistake of supposing that when the subject describes his experience, when he describes how things look, sound, smell, taste, or feel to him, he is describing the literal properties of objects and events on a peculiar sort of internal cinema or television screen, usually referred to in the modern psychological literature as the "phenomenal field." If we assume, for example, that when a subject reports a green after-image he is asserting the occurrence inside himself of an object which is literally green, it is clear that we have on our hands an entity for which there is no place in the world of physics. In the case of the green after-image there is no green object in the subject's environment corresponding to the description that he gives. Nor is there anything green in his brain; certainly there is nothing which could have emerged when he reported the appearance of the green after-image. Brain processes are not the sort of things to which color concepts can be properly applied.

The phenomenological fallacy on which this argument is based depends on the mistaken assumption that because our ability to describe things in our environment depends on our consciousness of them, our descriptions of things are primarily descriptions of our conscious experience and only secondarily, indirectly, and inferentially descriptions of the objects and events in our environments. It is assumed that because we recognize things in our environment by their look, sound, smell, taste, and feel, we begin by describing their phenomenal properties, i.e. the properties of the looks, sounds, smell, tastes, and feels which they produce in us, and infer their real properties from their phenomenal properties. In fact, the reverse is the case. We begin by learning to recognize the real properties of things in our environment. We learn to recognize them, of course, by their look, sound, smell, taste, and feel; but this does not mean that we have to learn to describe the look, sound, smell, taste, and feel of things before we can describe the things themselves. Indeed, it is only after we have learned to describe the things in our environment that we learn to describe our consciousness of them. We describe our conscious experience not in terms of the mythological "phenomenal properties" which are supposed to inhere in the mythological "objects" in the mythological "phenomenal field," but by reference to the actual physical properties of the concrete physical objects, events, and processes which normally, though not perhaps in the present instance, give rise to the sort of conscious experience which we are trying to describe. In other words when we describe the after-image as green, we are not saying that there is something, the after-image, which is green; we are saying that we are having the sort of experience which we normally have when, and which we have learned to describe as, looking at a green patch of light.

Once we rid ourselves of the phenomenological fallacy we realize that the problem of explaining introspective observations in terms of brain processes is far from insuperable. We realize that there is nothing that the introspecting subject says about his conscious experiences which is inconsistent with anything the physiologist might want to say about the brain processes which cause him to describe the environment and his consciousness of that environment in the way he does. When the subject describes his experience by saying that a light which is in fact stationary appears to move, all the physiologist or physiological psychologist has to do in order to explain the subject's introspective observations is to show that the brain process which is causing the subject to describe his experience in this way is the sort of process which normally occurs when he is observing an actual moving object and which therefore normally causes him to report the movement of an object in his environment. Once the mechanism whereby the individual describes what is going on in his environment has been worked out, all that is required to explain the individual's capacity to make introspective observations is an explanation of his ability to discriminate between those cases where his normal habits of verbal descriptions are appropriate to the stimulus situation and those cases where they are not, and an explanation of how and why, in those cases where the appropriateness of his normal descriptive habits is in doubt, he learns to issue his ordinary descriptive protocols preceded by a qualificatory phrase like "it appears," "seems," "looks," "feels," etc.[5]

Notes

1 E. C. Tolman, *Purposive Behaviour in Animals and Men* (Berkeley 1932).
2 L. Wittgenstein, *Philosophical Investigations* (Oxford 1953); G. Ryle, *The Concept of Mind* (1949).
3 Place, "The Concept of Heed," *British Journal of Psychology* XLV (1954), 243–55.
4 Sir Charles Sherrington, *The Integrative Action of the Nervous System* (Cambridge 1947), pp. xx–xxi.
5 I am greatly indebted to my fellow-participants in a series of informal discussions on this topic which took place in the Department of Philosophy, University of Adelaide, in particular to Mr C. B. Martin for his persistent and searching criticism of my earlier attempts to defend the thesis that consciousness is a brain process, to Professor D. A. T. Gasking, of the University of Melbourne, for clarifying many of the logical issues involved, and to Professor J. J. C. Smart for moral support and encouragement in what often seemed a lost cause.

2

Early Causal and Functionalist Views

The Causal Theory of the Mind

D. M. Armstrong

Is Philosophy Just Conceptual Analysis?

What can philosophy contribute to solving the problem of the relation to mind to body? Twenty years ago, many English-speaking philosophers would have answered: "Nothing beyond an analysis of the various mental *concepts*." If we seek knowledge of things, they thought, it is to science that we must turn. Philosophy can only cast light upon our concepts of those things.

This retreat from things to concepts was not undertaken lightly. Ever since the seventeenth century, the great intellectual fact of our culture has been the incredible expansion of knowledge both in the natural and in the rational sciences (mathematics, logic). Everyday life presents us with certain simple verities. But, it seems, through science and only through science can we build upon these verities, and with astonishing results.

The success of science created a crisis in philosophy. What was there for philosophy to do? Hume had already perceived the problem in some degree, and so surely did Kant, but it was not until the twentieth century, with the Vienna Circle and with Wittgenstein, that the difficulty began to weigh heavily. Wittgenstein took the view that philosophy could do no more than strive to undo the intellectual knots it itself had tied, so achieving intellectual release, and even a certain illumination, but no knowledge. A little later, and more optimistically, Ryle saw a positive, if reduced, role for philosophy in mapping the "log-ical geography" of our concepts: how they stood to each other and how they were to be analyzed.

On the whole, Ryle's view proved more popular than Wittgenstein's. After all, it retained a special, if much reduced, realm for philosophy where she might still be queen. There was better hope of continued employment for members of the profession!

Since that time, however, philosophers in the "analytic" tradition have swung back from Wittgensteinian and even Rylean pessimism to a more traditional conception of the proper role and tasks of philosophy. Many analytic philosophers now would accept the view that the central task of philosophy is to give an account, or at least play a part in giving an account, of the most general nature of things and of man. (I would include myself among that many.)

Why has this swing back occurred? Has the old urge of the philosopher to determine the nature of things by *a priori* reasoning proved too strong? To use Freudian terms, are we simply witnessing a return of what philosophers had repressed? I think not. One consideration that has had great influence was the realization that those who thought that they were abandoning ontological and other substantive questions for a mere investigation of concepts were in fact smuggling in views on the substantive questions. They did not acknowledge that they held these views, but the views were there; and far worse from their standpoint, the views imposed a form upon their answers to the conceptual questions.

For instance, in *The Concept of Mind* (1949), Gilbert Ryle, although he denied that he was a Behaviorist, seemed to be upholding an account of man and his mind that was extremely close to Behaviorism. Furthermore, it seemed in many cases that it was this view of the mind–body problem that led him to his particular analyses of particular mental concepts, rather than the other way around. Faced with examples like this, it began to appear that, since philosophers could not help holding views on substantive matters, and the views could not help affecting their analyses of concepts, the views had better be held and discussed explicitly instead of appearing in a distorted, because unacknowledged, form.

The swing back by analytic philosophers to first-order questions was also due to the growth of a more sophisticated understanding of the nature of scientific investigation. For a philosophical tradition that is oriented towards science, as, on the whole, Western philosophy is, the consideration of the *methods* of science must be an important topic. It was gradually realized that in the past scientific investigation had regularly been conceived in far too positivistic, sensationalistic, and observationalistic a spirit. (The influence of Karl Popper has been of the greatest importance in this realization.) As the central role of speculation, theory, and reasoning in scientific investigation began to be appreciated by more and more philosophers, the border-line between science and philosophy began to seem at least more fluid, and the hope arose again that philosophy might have something to contribute to first-order questions.

The philosopher has certain special skills. These include the stating and assessing of the worth of arguments, including the bringing to light and making explicit suppressed premises of arguments, the detection of ambiguities and inconsistencies, and, perhaps especially, the analysis of concepts. But, I contend, these special skills do not entail that the *objective* of philosophy is to do these things. They are rather the special *means* by which philosophy attempts to achieve further objectives. Ryle was wrong in taking the analysis of concepts to be the end of philosophy. Rather, the analysis of concepts is a means by which the philosopher makes his contribution to great general questions, not about concepts, but about things.

In the particular case of the mind–body problem, the propositions the philosopher arrives at need not be of a special nature. They perhaps might have been arrived at by the psychologist, the neurophysiologist, the biochemist or others, and, indeed, may be suggested to the philosopher by the results achieved or programs proposed by those disciplines. But the way that the argument is marshaled by a philosopher will be a special way. Whether this special way has or has not any particular value in the search for truth is a matter to be decided in particular cases. There is no *a priori* reason for thinking that the special methods of philosophy will be able to make a contribution to the mind–body problem. But neither is there an *a priori* reason for assuming that the philosopher's contribution will be valueless.

The Concept of a Mental State

The philosophy of philosophy is perhaps a somewhat joyless and unrewarding subject for reflection. Let us now turn to the mind–body problem itself, hoping that what is to be said about this particular topic will confirm the general remarks about philosophy that have just been made.

If we consider the mind–body problem today, then it seems that we ought to take account of the following consideration. The present state of scientific knowledge makes it probable that we can give a purely physicochemical account of man's body. It seems increasingly likely that the body and the brain of man are constituted and work according to exactly the same principles as those physical principles that govern other, non-organic, matter. The differences between a stone and a human body appear to lie solely in the extremely complex material set-up that is to be found in the living body and which is absent in the stone. Furthermore, there is rather strong evidence that it is the state of our brain that completely determines the state of our consciousness and our mental state generally.

All this is not beyond the realm of controversy, and it is easy to imagine evidence that would upset the picture. In particular, I think that it is just possible that evidence from psychical research might be forthcoming that a physicochemical view of man's brain could not accommodate. But suppose that the physicochemical view of the working of the brain is correct, as I take it to be. It will be very natural to conclude that mental states are not simply *determined* by corresponding states of the brain, but that they are actually *identical* with these brain-states, brain-states that involve nothing but physical properties.

The argument just outlined is quite a simple one, and it hardly demands philosophical skill to develop it or to appreciate its force! But although many contemporary thinkers would accept its conclusion, there are others, including many philosophers, who would not. To a great many thinkers it has seemed obvious *a priori* that mental states could not be physical states of the brain. Nobody would identify a number with a piece of rock: it is sufficiently obvious that the two entities fall under different categories. In the same way, it has been thought, a perception or a feeling of sorrow must be a different category of thing from an electrochemical discharge in the central nervous system.

Here, it seems to me, is a question to which philosophers can expect to make a useful contribution. It is a question about mental concepts. Is our concept of a mental state such that it is an intelligible hypothesis that mental states are physical states of the brain? If the philosopher can show that it is an *intelligible* proposition (that is, a non-self-contradictory proposition) that mental states are physical states of the brain, then the scientific argument just given above can be taken at its face value as a strong reason for accepting the truth of the proposition.

My view is that the identification of mental states with physical states of the brain is a perfectly intelligible one, and that this becomes clear once we achieve a correct view of the analysis of the mental concepts. I admit that my analysis of the mental concepts was itself adopted because it permitted this identification, but such a procedure is commonplace in the construction of theories, and perfectly legitimate. In any case, whatever the motive for proposing the analysis, it is there to speak for itself, to be measured against competitors, and to be assessed as plausible or implausible independently of the identification it makes possible.

The problem of the identification may be put in a Kantian way: "How is it possible that mental states should be physical states of the brain?" The solution will take the form of proposing an *independently plausible* analysis of the concept of a mental state that will permit this identification. In this way, the philosopher makes the way smooth for a first-order doctrine, which, true or false, is a doctrine of the first importance: a purely physicalist view of man.

The analysis proposed may be called the Causal analysis of the mental concepts. According to this view, the concept of a mental state essentially involves, and is exhausted by, the concept of a state that is *apt to be the cause of certain effects or apt to be the effect of certain causes.*

An example of a causal concept is the concept of poison. The concept of poison is the concept of something that when introduced into an organism causes that organism to sicken and/or die.[1] This is but a rough analysis of the concept the structure of which is in fact somewhat more complex and subtle than this. If *A* pours molten lead down *B*'s throat, then he may cause *B* to die as a result, but he can hardly be said to have poisoned him. For a thing to be called a poison, it is necessary that it act in a certain *sort* of way: roughly, in a biological as opposed to a purely physical way. Again, a poison can be introduced into the system of an organism and that organism fail to die or even to sicken. This might occur if an antidote were administered promptly. Yet again, the poison may be present in insufficient quantities to do any damage. Other qualifications could be made.

But the essential point about the concept of poison is that it is the concept of *that, whatever it is, which produces certain effects.* This leaves open the possibility of the *scientific identification* of poisons, of discovering that a certain sort of substance, such as cyanide, is a poison, and discovering further what it is about the substance that makes it poisonous.

Poisons are accounted poisons in virtue of their active powers, but many sorts of thing are accounted the sorts of thing they are by virtue of their *passive* powers. Thus brittle objects are accounted brittle because of the disposition they have to break and shatter when sharply struck. This leaves open the possibility of discovering empirically what sorts of thing are brittle and what it is about them that makes them brittle.

Now *if* the concepts of the various sorts of mental state are concepts of that which is, in various sorts of way, apt for causing certain effects and apt for being the effect of certain causes, then it would be a quite unpuzzling thing if mental states should turn out to be physical states of the brain.

The concept of a mental state is the concept of something that is, characteristically, the cause of certain effects and the effect of certain causes. What sort of effects and what sort of causes? The effects caused by the mental state will be certain patterns of behaviour of the person in that state. For instance, the desire for food is a state of a person or animal that characteristically brings about food-seeking and food-consuming behaviour by that person or animal. The causes of mental states will be objects and events in the person's environment. For instance, a sensation of green is the characteristic effect in a person of the action upon his eyes of a nearby green surface.

The general pattern of analysis is at its most obvious and plausible in the case of *purposes*. If a man's purpose is to go to the kitchen to get something to eat, it is completely natural to conceive of this purpose as a cause within him that brings about, or tends to bring about, that particular line of conduct. It is, furthermore, notorious that we are unable to characterize purposes *except* in terms of that which they tend to bring about. How can we distinguish the purpose to go to the kitchen to get something to eat from another purpose to go to the bedroom to lie down? Only by the different outcomes that the two purposes tend to bring about. This fact was an encouragement to Behaviorism. It is still more plausibly explained by saying that the concept of purpose is a causal concept. The further hypothesis that the two purposes are, in their own nature, different physical patterns in, or physical states of, the central nervous system is then a natural (although, of course, not logically inevitable) supplement to the causal analysis.

Simple models have great value in trying to grasp complex conceptions, but they are ladders that may need to be kicked away after we have mounted up by their means. It is vital to realize that the mental concepts have a far more complex logical structure than simple causal notions such as the concept of poison. The fact should occasion no surprise. In the case of poisons, the effect of which they are the cause is a gross and obvious phenomenon and the level of causal explanation involved in simply calling a substance "a poison" is crude and simple. But in the case of mental states, their effects are all those complexities of behavior that mark off men and higher animals from the rest of the objects in the world. Furthermore, differences in such behavior are elaborately correlated with differences in the mental causes operating. So it is only to be expected that the causal patterns invoked by the mental concepts should be extremely complex and sophisticated.

In the case of the notion of a purpose, for instance, it is plausible to assert that it is the notion of a cause within which drives, or tends to drive, the man or animal through a series of actions to a certain end-state. But this is not the whole story. A purpose is only a purpose if it works to bring about behavioral effects *in a certain sort of way*. We may sum up this sort of way by saying that purposes are *information-sensitive* causes. By this is meant that purposes direct behavior by utilizing *perceptions* and *beliefs*, perceptions and beliefs about the agent's current situation and the way it develops, and beliefs about the way the world works. For instance, it is part of what it is to be a purpose to achieve X that this cause will cease to operate, will be "switched off," if the agent perceives or otherwise comes to believe that X has been achieved.

At this point, we observe that an account is being given of that special species of cause that is a purpose in terms of *further* mental items: perceptions and beliefs. This means that if we are to give a purely causal analysis even of the concept of a purpose we also will have to give a purely causal analysis of perceptions and beliefs. We may think of man's behavior as brought about by the joint operation of two sets of causes: first, his purposes and, second, his perceptions of and/or beliefs about the world. But since perceptions and beliefs are quite different sorts of thing from purposes, a Causal analysis must assign quite different causal *roles* to these different things in the bringing about of behavior.

I believe that this can be done by giving an account of perceptions and beliefs as *mappings* of the world. They are structures within us that model the world beyond the structure. This model is created in us by the world. Purposes may then be thought of as driving causes that utilize such mappings.

This is a mere thumb-nail, which requires much further development as well as qualification. One point that becomes clear when that development is given is that just as the concept of purpose cannot be elucidated without appealing to the concepts of perception and belief, so the latter cannot be elucidated without appealing to the concept of purpose. (This comes out, for instance, when we raise Hume's problem: what marks off beliefs from the mere entertaining of the same proposition? It seems that we can only mark off beliefs as those mappings in the light of which we are prepared to *act*, that is, which are potential servants of our purposes.) The logical dependence of purpose on perception and belief, and of perception and belief upon purpose, is not circularity in definition. What it shows is that the corresponding concepts *must be introduced together or not at all*. In itself, there is nothing very surprising in this. Correlative or mutually implicated concepts are common enough: for instance, the concepts of husband and wife or the concepts of soldier and army. No husbands without wives or wives without husbands. No soldiers without an army, no army without soldiers. But if the concepts of purpose, perception, and belief are (i) correlative concepts and (ii) different species of purely causal concepts, then it is clear that they are far more complex in structure than a simple causal concept like poison. What falls under the mental concepts will be a complex and interlocking set of causal factors, which together are responsible for the "minded" behavior of men and the higher animals.

The working out of the Causal theory of the mental concepts thus turns out to be an extremely complex business. Indeed when it is merely baldly stated, the Causal theory is, to use the phrase of Imre Lakatos, a *research program* in conceptual analysis rather than a developed theory. I have tried to show that it is a hopeful program by attempting, at least in outline, a Causal analysis of all the main concepts in *A Materialist Theory of Mind* (1968); and I have supplemented the rather thin account given there of the concepts of belief, knowledge, and inferring in *Belief, Truth and Knowledge* (1973).

Two examples of mental concepts where an especially complex and sophisticated type of Causal analysis is required are the notions of introspective awareness (one sense of the word "consciousness") and the having of mental imagery. Introspective awareness is analyzable as a mental state that is a "perception" of mental states. It is a mapping of the causal factors themselves. The having of mental imagery is a sort of mental state that cannot be elucidated in *directly* causal terms, but only by resemblance to the corresponding perceptions, which *are* explicated in terms of their causal role.

Two advantages of the Causal theory may now be mentioned. First, it has often been remarked by philosophers and others that the realm of mind is a shadowy one, and that the nature of mental states is singularly elusive and hard to grasp. This has given aid and comfort to Dualist or Cartesian theories of mind, according to which minds are quite different sorts of thing from material objects. But if the Causal analysis is correct, the facts admit of another explanation. What Dualist philosophers have grasped in a confused way is that our direct acquaintance with mind, which occurs in introspective awareness, is an acquaintance with something that we are aware of only as something that is causally linked, directly or indirectly, with behavior. In the case of our purposes and desires, for instance, we are often (though not invariably) introspectively aware of them. What we are aware of is the presence of factors within us that drive in a certain direction. We are not aware of the intrinsic nature of the factors. This emptiness or gap in our awareness is then interpreted by Dualists as immateriality. In fact, however, if the Causal analysis is correct, there is no warrant for this interpretation and, if the Physicalist identification of the nature of the causes is correct, the interpretation is actually false.

Second, the Causal analysis yields a still more spectacular verification. It shows promise of explaining a philosophically notorious feature of all or almost all mental states: their *intentionality*. This was the feature of mental states to which Brentano in particular drew attention, the fact that they may point towards certain objects or states of affairs, but that these objects and states of affairs need not exist. When a man strives, his striving has an objective, but that objective may never be achieved. When he believes, there is something he believes, but what he believes may not be the case. This capacity of mental states to "point" to what does not exist can seem very special. Brentano held that intentionality set the mind completely apart from matter.

Suppose, however, that we consider a concept like the concept of poison. Does it not provide us with a miniature and unsophisticated model for the intentionality of mental states? Poisons are substances apt to make organisms sicken and die when the poison is administered. So it may be said that this is what poisons "point" to. Nevertheless, poisons may fail of their effect. A poison does not fail to be a poison because an antidote neutralizes the customary effect of the poison.

May not the intentionality of mental states, therefore, be in principle a no more mysterious affair, although indefinitely more complex, than the death that lurks in the poison? As an intermediate case between poisons and mental states, consider the mechanisms involved in a homing rocket. Given a certain setting of its mechanism, the rocket may "point" towards a certain target in a way that is a simulacrum of the way in which purposes point towards their objectives. The mechanism will only bring the rocket to the target in "standard" circumstances: many factors can be conceived that would "defeat" the mechanism. For the mechanism to operate successfully, some device will be required by which the developing situation is "mapped" in the mechanism (i.e. what course the rocket is currently on, etc.). This mapping is an elementary analogue of perception, and so the course that is "mapped" in the mechanism may be thought of as a simulacrum of the perceptual intentional object. Through one circumstance or another (e.g. malfunction of the gyroscope) this mapping may be "incorrect."

It is no objection to this analogy that homing rockets are built by men with purposes, who deliberately stamp a crude model of their own purposes into the rocket. Homing rockets might have been natural products, and non-minded objects that operate in a similar but far more complex way are found in nature. The living cell is a case in point.

So the Causal analyses of the mental concepts show promise of explaining both the transparency and the intentionality of mental states. One problem quite frequently raised in connection with these analyses, however, is in what sense they can be called "analyses." The welter of complications in which the so-called analyses are involved make it sufficiently obvious that they do not consist of *synonymous translations* of statements in which mental terms figure. But, it has been objected, if synonymous translations of mental statements are unavailable, what precisely can be meant by speaking of "analyses of concepts"?

I am far from clear what should be said in reply to this objection. Clearly, however, it does depend upon taking all conceptual analyses as claims about the synonymy of sentences, and that seems to be too simple a view. Going back to the case of poison: it is surely not an empirical fact, to be learnt by experience, that poisons kill. It is at the center of our notion of what poisons are that they have the power to bring about this effect. If they did not do that, they would not be properly called "poisons." But although this seems obvious enough, it is extremely difficult to give exact translations of sentences containing the word "poison" into other sentences that do not contain the word or any synonym. Even in this simple case, it is not at all clear that the task can actually be accomplished.

For this reason, I think that sentence translation (with synonymy) is too strict a demand to make upon a purported conceptual analysis. What more relaxed demand can we make and still have a conceptual analysis? I do not know. One thing that we clearly need further light upon here is the concept of a concept, and how concepts are tied to language. I incline to the view that the connection between concepts and language is much less close than many philosophers have assumed. Concepts are linked primarily with belief and thought, and belief and thought, I think, have a great degree of logical independence of language, however close the empirical connection may be in many cases. If this is so, then an analysis of concepts, although of course conducted *in* words, may not be an investigation *into* words. (A compromise proposal: analysis of concepts might be an investigation into some sort of "deep structure" – to use the currently hallowed phrase – which underlies the use of certain words and sentences.) I wish I were able to take the topic further.

The Problem of the Secondary Qualities

No discussion of the Causal theory of the mental concepts is complete that does not say something about the *secondary qualities*. If we consider such mental states as purposes and intentions, their "transparency" is a rather conspicuous feature. It is notorious that introspection cannot differentiate such states except in terms of their different objects. It is not so immediately obvious, however, that *perception* has this transparent character. Perception involves the experience of color and of visual extension; touch the experience of the whole obscure range of tactual properties, including tactual extension; hearing, taste, and smell the experience of sounds, tastes, and smells. These phenomenal qualities, it may be argued, endow different perceptions with different qualities. The lack of transparency is even more obvious in the case of bodily sensations. Pains, itches, tickles, and tingles are mental states, even if mental states of no very high-grade sort, and they each seem to involve their own peculiar qualities. Again, associated with different emotions it is quite plausible to claim to discern special emotion qualities. If perception, bodily sensation, and emotions involve qualities, then this seems to falsify a purely Causal analysis of these mental states. They are not mere "that whiches" known only by their causal role.

However, it is not at all clear how strong is the line of argument sketched in the previous paragraph. We distinguish between the intention and what is intended, and in just the same way we must distinguish between the perception and what is perceived. The intention is a mental state and so is the perception, but what is intended is not in general something mental and nor is what is perceived. What is intended may not come to pass, it is a merely intentional object, and the same may be said of what is perceived. Now in the case of the phenomenal qualities, it seems plausible to say that they are qualities not of the perception but rather of what is perceived. "Visual extension" is the shape, size, etc. that some object of visual perception is perceived to have (an object that need not exist). Color seems to be a quality of that object. And similarly for the other phenomenal qualities. Even in the case of the bodily sensations, the qualities associated with the sensations do not *appear* to be qualities of mental states but instead to be qualities of portions of our bodies: more or less fleeting qualities that qualify the place where the sensation is located. Only in the case of the emotions does it seem natural to place the quality on the mental rather than the object side: but then it is not so clear whether there really *are* peculiar qualities associated with the emotions. The different patterns of bodily sensations associated with the different emotions may be sufficient to do phenomenological justice to the emotions.

For these reasons, it is not certain whether the phenomenal qualities pose any threat to the Causal analysis of the mental concepts. But what a subset of these qualities quite certainly does pose a threat to, is the doctrine that the Causal analysis of the mental concepts is a step towards: Materialism or Physicalism.

The qualities of color, sound, heat and cold, taste and smell together with the qualities that appear to be involved in bodily sensations and those that may be involved in the case of the emotions, are an embarrassment to the modern Materialist. He seeks to give an account of the world and of man purely in terms of *physical* properties, that is to say in terms of the properties that the physicist appeals to in his explanations of phenomena. The Materialist is not committed to the *current* set of properties to which the physicist appeals, but he is committed to whatever set of properties the physicist in the end will appeal to. It is clear that such properties as color, sound, taste, and smell – the so-called "secondary qualities" – will never be properties to which the physicist will appeal.

It is, however, a plausible thesis that associated with different secondary qualities are properties that are respectable from a physicist's point of view. Physical surfaces *appear* to have color.

They not merely appear to, but undoubtedly do, emit light-waves, and the different mixtures of lengths of wave emitted are linked with differences in color. In the same way, different sorts of sound are linked with different sorts of sound-wave and differences in heat with differences in the mean kinetic energy of the molecules composing the hot things. The Materialist's problem therefore would be very simply solved if the secondary qualities could be identified with these physically respectable properties. (The qualities associated with bodily sensations would be identified with different sorts of stimulation of bodily receptors. If there are unique qualities associated with the emotions, they would presumably be identified with some of the physical states of the brain linked with particular emotions.)

But now the Materialist philosopher faces a problem. Previously he asked: "How is it possible that mental states could be physical states of the brain?" This question was answered by the Causal theory of the mental concepts. Now he must ask: "How is it possible that secondary qualities could be purely physical properties of the objects they are qualities of?" A Causal analysis does not seem to be of any avail. To try to give an analysis of, say, the quality of being red in Causal terms would lead us to produce such analyses as "those properties of a physical surface, whatever they are, that characteristically produce *red sensations* in us." But this analysis simply shifts the problem unhelpfully from property of surface to property of sensation. Either the red sensations involve nothing but physically respectable properties or they involve something more. If they involve something more, Materialism fails. But if they are simply physical states of the brain, having nothing but physical properties, then the Materialist faces the problem: "How is it possible that red sensations should be physical states of the brain?" This question is no easier to answer than the original question about the redness of physical surfaces. (To give a Causal analysis of red sensations as the characteristic effects of the action of red surfaces is, of course, to move round in a circle.)

The great problem presented by the secondary qualities, such as redness, is that they are *unanalyzable*. They have certain relations of resemblance and so on to each other, so they cannot be said to be completely simple. But they are simple in the sense that they resist any analysis. You cannot give any complete account of the concept of redness without involving the notion of redness itself. This has seemed to be, and still seems to many philosophers to be, an absolute bar to identifying redness with, say, certain patterns of emission of light-waves.

But I am not so sure. I think it can be maintained that although the secondary qualities *appear* to be simple, they are not in fact simple. Perhaps their simplicity is *epistemological* only, not ontological, a matter of our awareness of them rather than the way they are. The best model I can give for the situation is the sort of phenomena made familiar to us by the Gestalt psychologists. It is possible to grasp that certain things or situations have a certain special property, but be unable to analyze that property. For instance, it may be possible to perceive that certain people are all alike in some way without being able to make it clear to oneself what the likeness is. We are aware that all these people have a certain likeness to each other, but are unable to define or specify that likeness. Later psychological research may achieve a specification of the likeness, a specification that may come as a complete surprise to us. Perhaps, therefore, the secondary qualities are in fact complex, and perhaps they are complex characteristics of a sort demanded by Materialism, but we are unable to grasp their complexity in perception.

There are two divergences between the model just suggested and the case of the secondary qualities. First, in the case of grasping the indefinable likeness of people, we are under no temptation to think that the likeness is a likeness in some simple quality. The likeness is indefinable, but we are vaguely aware that it is complex. Second, once research has determined the concrete nature of the likeness, our attention can be drawn to, and we can observe individually, the features that determine the likeness.

But although the model suggested and the case of the secondary qualities undoubtedly exhibit these differences, I do not think that they show that the secondary qualities cannot be identified with respectable physical characteristics of objects. Why should not a complex property appear to be simple? There would seem to be no contradiction in adding such a condition to the model. It has the consequence that perception of the secondary qualities involves an element of illusion, but the consequence involves no contradiction. It is true also that in the case of the secondary qualities the illusion cannot be overcome within perception: it is impossible to see a colored surface as a surface emitting certain light-waves. (Though one sometimes seems to *hear* a sound as a vibration of the air.) But while this means that the identification of color and light-waves is a purely *theoretical* one, it still seems to be a possible one. And if the identification is a possible one, we have general scientific reasons to think it a *plausible* one.

The doctrine of mental states and of the secondary qualities briefly presented in this essay seems to me to show promise of meeting many of the traditional philosophical objections to a Materialist or Physicalist account of the world. As I have emphasized, the philosopher is not professionally competent to argue the positive case for Materialism. There he must rely upon the evidence presented by the scientist, particularly the physicist. But at least he may neutralize the objections to Materialism advanced by his fellow philosophers.

Note

1 "Any substance which, when introduced into or absorbed by a living organism, destroys life or injures health." (*Shorter Oxford Dictionary*, 3rd edn, rev., 1978.)

The Nature of Mental States

Hilary Putnam

The typical concerns of the Philosopher of Mind might be represented by three questions: (1) How do we know that other people have pains? (2) Are pains brain states? (3) What is the analysis of the concept *pain*? I do not wish to discuss questions (1) and (3) in this essay. I shall say something about question (2).[1]

I Identity Questions

"Is pain a brain state?" (Or, "Is the property of having a pain at time t a brain state?")[2] It is impossible to discuss this question sensibly without saying something about the peculiar rules which have grown up in the course of the development of "analytical philosophy" – rules which, far from leading to an end to all conceptual confusions, themselves represent considerable conceptual confusion. These rules – which are, of course, implicit rather than explicit in the practice of most analytical philosophers – are (1) that a statement of the form "being A is being B" (e.g., "being in pain is being in a certain brain state") can be *correct* only if it follows, in some sense, from the meaning of the terms A and B; and (2) that a statement of the form "being A is being B" can be philosophically *informative* only if it is in some sense reductive (e.g., "being in pain is having a certain unpleasant sensation" is not philosophically informative; "being in pain is having a certain behavior disposition" is, if true, philosophically informative). These rules are excellent rules if we still believe that the program of reductive analysis (in the style of the 1930s) can be carried out; if we don't, then they turn analytical philosophy into a mug's game, at least so far as "is" questions are concerned.

In this essay I shall use the term "property" as a blanket term for such things as being in pain, being in a particular brain state, having a particular behavior disposition, and also for magnitudes such as temperature, etc. – i.e., for things which can naturally be represented by one-or-more-place predicates or functors. I shall use the term "concept" for things which can be identified with synonymy-classes of expressions. Thus the concept *temperature* can be identified (I maintain) with the synonymy-class of the word "temperature".[3] (This is like saying that the number 2 can be identified with the class of all pairs. This is quite a different statement from the peculiar statement that 2 *is* the class of all pairs. I do not maintain that concepts *are* synonymy-classes, whatever that might mean, but that they can be identified with synonymy-classes, for the purpose of formalization of the relevant discourse.)

The question "What is the concept *temperature*?" is a very "funny" one. One might take it to mean "What is temperature? Please take my question as a conceptual one." In that case an answer might be (pretend for a moment "heat" and "temperature" are synonyms) "temperature is heat," or even "the concept of temperature is the same concept as the concept of heat." Or one might take it to mean "What are *concepts*, really? For example, what is 'the concept of temperature'?" In that case heaven knows what an "answer" would be. (Perhaps it would be the statement that concepts *can be identified with* synonymy-classes.)

Of course, the question "What is the property temperature?" is also "funny." And one way of interpreting it is to take it as a question about the concept of temperature. But this is not the way a physicist would take it.

The effect of saying that the property P_1 can be identical with the property P_2 only if the terms P_1, P_2 are in some suitable sense "synonyms" is, to all intents and purposes, to collapse the two notions of "property" and "concept" into a single notion. The view that concepts (intensions) *are* the same as properties has been explicitly advocated by Carnap (e.g., in *Meaning and Necessity*). This seems an unfortunate view, since "temperature is mean molecular kinetic energy" appears to be a perfectly good example of a true statement of identity of properties, whereas "the concept of temperature is the same concept as the concept of mean molecular kinetic energy" is simply false.

Many philosophers believe that the statement "pain is a brain state" violates some rules or norms of English. But the arguments offered are hardly convincing. For example, if the fact that I can know that I am in pain without knowing that I am in brain state S shows that pain cannot be brain state S, then, by exactly the same argument, the fact that I can know that the stove is hot without knowing that the mean molecular kinetic energy is high (or even that molecules exist) shows that it is *false* that temperature is mean molecular kinetic energy, physics to the contrary. In fact, all that immediately follows from the fact that I can know that I am in pain without knowing that I am in brain state S is that the concept of pain is not the same concept as the concept of being in brain state S. But either pain, or the state of being in pain, or some pain, or some pain state, might still be brain state S. After all, the concept of temperature is not the same concept as the concept of mean molecular kinetic energy. But temperature is mean molecular kinetic energy.

Some philosophers maintain that both "pain is a brain state" and "pain states are brain states" are unintelligible. The answer is to explain to these philosophers, as well as we can, given the vagueness of all scientific methodology, what sorts of considerations lead one to make an empirical reduction (i.e., to say such things as "water is H₂O," light is electromagnetic radiation," "temperature is mean molecular kinetic energy"). If, without giving reasons, he still maintains in the face of such examples that one cannot imagine parallel circumstances for the use of "pains are brain states" (or, perhaps, "pain states are brain states") one has grounds to regard him as perverse.

Some philosophers maintain that "P_1 is P_2" is something that can be true, when the "is" involved is the "is" of empirical reduction, only when the properties P_1 and P_2 are (a) associated with a spatiotemporal region; and (b) the region is one and the same in both cases. Thus "temperature is mean molecular kinetic energy" is an admissible empirical reduction, since the temperature and the molecular energy are associated with the same space-time region, but "having a pain in my arm is being in a brain state" is not, since the spatial regions involved are different.

This argument does not appear very strong. Surely no one is going to be deterred from saying that mirror images are light reflected from an object and then from the surface of a mirror by the fact that an image can be "located" three feet *behind* the mirror! (Moreover, one can always find *some* common property of the reductions one is willing to allow – e.g., temperature is mean molecular kinetic energy – which is not a property of some one identification one wishes to disallow. This is not very impressive unless one has an argument to show that the very purposes of such identification depend upon the common property in question.)

Again, other philosophers have contended that all the predictions that can be derived from the conjunction of neurophysiological laws with such statements as "pain states are such-and-such brain states" can equally well be derived from the conjunction of the same neurophysiological laws with "being in pain is correlated with such-and-such brain states," and hence (sic!) there can be no methodological grounds for saying that pains (or pain states) *are* brain states, as opposed to saying that they are *correlated* (invariantly) with brain states. This argument, too, would show that light is only correlated with electromagnetic radiation.

The mistake is in ignoring the fact that, although the theories in question may indeed lead to the same predictions, they open and exclude different *questions*. "Light is invariantly correlated with electromagnetic radiation" would leave open the questions "What is the light then, if it isn't the same as the electromagnetic radiation?" and "What makes the light accompany the electromagnetic radiation?" – questions which are excluded by saying that the light *is* the electromagnetic radiation. Similarly, the purpose of saying that pains are brain states is precisely to exclude from empirical meaningfulness the questions "What is the pain, then, if it isn't the same as the brain state?" and "What makes the pain accompany the brain state?" If there are grounds to suggest that these questions represent, so to speak, the wrong way to look at the matter, then those grounds are grounds for a theoretical identification of pains with brain states.

If all arguments to the contrary are unconvincing, shall we then conclude that it is meaningful (and perhaps true) to say either that pains are brain states or that pain states are brain states?

1 It is perfectly meaningful (violates no "rule of English," involves no "extension of usage") to say "pains are brain states."
2 It is not meaningful (involves a "changing of meaning" or "an extension of usage," etc.) to say "pains are brain states."

My own position is not expressed by either (1) or (2). It seems to me that the notions "change of meaning" and "extension of usage" are simply so ill-defined that one cannot in fact say *either* (1) or (2). I see no reason to believe that either the linguist, or the man-on-the-street, or the philosopher possesses today a notion of "change of meaning" applicable to such cases as the one we have been discussing. The *job* for which the notion of change of meaning was developed in the history of the language was just a *much* cruder job than this one.

But, if we don't assert either (1) or (2) – in other words, if we regard the "change of meaning" issue as a pseudo-issue in this case – then how are we to discuss the question with which we started? "Is pain a brain state?"

The answer is to allow statements of the form "pain is A," where "pain" and "A" are in no sense synonyms, and to see whether any such statement can be found which might be acceptable on empirical and methodological grounds. This is what we shall now proceed to do.

II   Is Pain a Brain State?

We shall discuss "Is pain a brain State?," then. And we have agreed to waive the "change of meaning" issue.

Since I am discussing not what the concept of pain comes to, but what pain is, in a sense of "is" which requires empirical theory-construction (or, at least, empirical speculation), I shall not apologize for advancing an empirical hypothesis. Indeed, my strategy will be to argue that pain is *not* a brain state, not on *a priori* grounds, but on the grounds that another hypothesis is more plausible. The detailed development and verification of my hypothesis would be just as Utopian a task as the detailed development and verification of the brain-state hypothesis. But the putting-forward, not of detailed and scientifically "finished" hypotheses, but of schemata for hypotheses, has long been a function of philosophy. I shall, in short, argue that pain is not a brain state, in the sense of a physical–chemical state of the brain (or even the whole nervous system), but another *kind* of state entirely. I propose the hypothesis that pain, or the state of being in pain, is a functional state of a whole organism.

To explain this it is necessary to introduce some technical notions. In previous papers I have explained the notion of a Turing Machine and discussed the use of this notion as a model for an organism. The notion of a Probabilistic Automaton is defined similarly to a Turing Machine, except that the transitions between "states" are allowed to be with various probabilities rather than being "deterministic." (Of course, a Turing Machine is simply a special kind of Probabilistic Automaton, one with transition probabilities 0, 1.) I shall assume the notion of a Probabilistic Automaton has been generalized to allow for "sensory inputs" and "motor outputs" – that is, the Machine Table specifies, for every possible combination of a "state" and a complete set of "sensory inputs," an "instruction" which determines the probability of the next "state," and also the probabilities of the "motor outputs." (This replaces the idea of the Machine as printing on a tape.) I shall also assume that the physical realization of the sense organs responsible for the various inputs, and of the motor organs, is specified, but that the "states" and the "inputs" themselves are, as usual, specified only "implicitly" – i.e., by the set of transition probabilities given by the Machine Table.

Since an empirically given system can simultaneously be a "physical realization" of many different Probabilistic Automata, I introduce the notion of a *Description* of a system. A Description of S where S is a system, is any true statement to the effect that S possesses distinct states $S_1, S_2 \ldots, S_n$ which are related to one another and to the motor outputs and sensory inputs by the transition probabilities given in such-and-such a Machine Table. The Machine Table mentioned in the Description will then be called the Functional Organization of S relative to that Description, and the S_i such that S is in state S_i at a given time will be called the Total State of S (at that time) relative to that Description. It should be noted that knowing the Total State of a system relative to a Description. Description involves knowing a good deal about how the system is likely to "behave," given various combinations of sensory inputs, but does *not* involve knowing the physical realization of the S_i as, e.g., physical–chemical states of the brain. The S_i, to repeat, are specified only *implicitly* by the Description – i.e., specified *only* by the set of transition probabilities given in the Machine Table.

The hypothesis that "being in pain is a functional state of the organism" may now be spelled out more exactly as follows:

1   All organisms capable of feeling pain are Probabilistic Automata.
2   Every organism capable of feeling pain possesses at least one Description of a certain kind (i.e., being capable of feeling pain *is* possessing an appropriate kind of Functional Organization.)
3   No organism capable of feeling pain possesses a decomposition into parts which separately possess Descriptions of the kind referred to in (2).
4   For every Description of the kind referred to in (2), there exists a subset of the sensory inputs such that an organism with that Description is in pain when and only when some of its sensory inputs are in that subset.

This hypothesis is admittedly vague, though surely no vaguer than the brain-state hypothesis in its present form. For example, one would like to know more about the kind of Functional Organization that an organism must have to be capable of feeling pain, and more about the marks that distinguish the subset of the sensory inputs referred to in (4). With respect to the first question, one can probably say that the Functional Organization must include something that resembles a "preference function," or at least a preference partial ordering, and something that resembles an "inductive logic" (i.e., the Machine must be able to "learn from experience"). (The meaning of these conditions, for Automata models, is discussed in my paper "The mental life of some machines".) In addition, it seems natural to require that the Machine possess "pain sensors," i.e., sensory organs which normally signal damage to the Machine's body, or dangerous temperatures, pressures, etc., which transmit a special subset of the inputs, the subset referred to in (4). Finally, and with respect to the second question, we would want to require at least that the inputs in the distinguished subset have a high disvalue on the Machine's preference function or ordering (further conditions are discussed in "The mental life of some machines"). The purpose of condition (3) is to rule out such "organisms" (if they can count as such) as swarms of bees as single pain-feelers. The condition (1) is, obviously, redundant, and is only introduced for expository reasons. (It is, in fact, empty, since everything is a Probabilistic Automaton under *some* Description.)

I contend, in passing, that this hypothesis, in spite of its admitted vagueness, is far *less* vague than the "physical–chemical state" hypothesis is today, and far more susceptible to investigation of both a mathematical and an empirical kind. Indeed, to investigate this hypothesis is just to attempt to produce "mechanical" models of organisms – and isn't this, in a sense, just what psychology is about? The difficult step, of course, will be to pass from models of *specific* organisms to a *normal form* for the psychological description of organisms – for this is what is required to make (2) and (4) precise. But this too seems to be an inevitable part of the program of psychology.

I shall now compare the hypothesis just advanced with (a) the hypothesis that pain is a brain state, and (b) the hypothesis that pain is a behavior disposition.

III   Functional State versus Brain State

It may, perhaps, be asked if I am not somewhat unfair in taking the brain-state theorist to be talking about *physical–chemical* states of the brain. But (a) these are the only sorts of states ever mentioned by brain-state theorists. (b) The brain-state theorist usually mentions (with a certain pride, slightly reminiscent of the Village Atheist) the incompatibility of his hypothesis with all forms of dualism and mentalism. This is natural if physical–chemical states of the brain are what is at issue. However, functional states of whole systems are something quite different. In particular, the functional-state hypothesis is *not* incompatible with dualism! Although it goes without saying that the hypothesis is "mechanistic" in its inspiration, it is a slightly remarkable fact that a system consisting of a body and a "soul," if such things there be, can perfectly well be a Probabilistic Automaton. (c) One argument advanced by Smart is that the brain-state theory assumes only "physical" properties, and Smart finds "nonphysical" properties unintelligible. The Total States and the "inputs" defined above are, of course, neither mental nor physical *per se*, and I cannot imagine a functionalist advancing this argument. (d) If the brain-state theorist does mean (or at least allow) states other than physical–chemical states, then his hypothesis is completely empty, at least until he specifies *what* sort of "states" he *does* mean.

Taking the brain-state hypothesis in this way, then, what reasons are there to prefer the functional-state hypothesis over the brain-state hypothesis? Consider what the brain-state theorist has to do to make good his claims. He has to specify a physical–chemical state such that *any* organism (not just a mammal) is in pain if and only if (a) it possesses a brain of a suitable physical–chemical structure; and (b) its brain is in that physical–chemical state. This means that the physical–chemical state in question must be a possible state of a mammalian brain, a reptilian brain, a mollusc's brain (octopuses are mollusca, and certainly feel pain), etc. At the same time, it must *not* be a possible (physically possible) state of the brain of any physically possible creature that cannot feel pain. Even if such a state can be found, it must be nomologically certain that it will also be a state of the brain of any extra-terrestrial life that may be found that will be capable of feeling pain before we can even entertain the supposition that it may *be* pain.

It is not altogether impossible that such a state will be found. Even though octopus and mammal are examples of parallel (rather than sequential) evolution, for example, virtually identical structures (physically speaking) have evolved in the eye of the octopus and in the eye of the mammal, notwithstanding the fact that this organ has evolved from different kinds of cells in the two cases. Thus it is at least possible that parallel evolution, all over the universe, might *always* lead to *one and the same* physical "correlate" of pain. But this is certainly an ambitious hypothesis.

Finally, the hypothesis becomes still more ambitious when we realize that the brain-state theorist is not just saying that *pain* is a brain state; he is, of course, concerned to maintain that *every* psychological state is a brain state. Thus if we can find even one psychological predicate which can clearly be applied to both a mammal and an octopus (say "hungry"), but whose physical–chemical "correlate" is different in the two cases, the brain-state theory has collapsed. It seems to me overwhelmingly probable that we can do this. Granted, in such a case the brain-state theorist can save himself by *ad hoc* assumptions (e.g., defining the disjunction of two states to be a single "physical–chemical state"), but this does not have to be taken seriously.

Turning now to the considerations *for* the functional-state theory, let us begin with the fact that we identify organisms as in pain, or hungry, or angry, or in heat, etc., on the basis of their *behavior*. But it is a truism that similarities in the behavior of two systems are at least a reason to suspect similarities in the functional organization of the two systems, and a much *weaker* reason to suspect similarities in the actual physical details. Moreover, we expect the various psychological states – at least the basic ones, such as hunger, thirst, aggression, etc. – to have more or less similar "transition probabilities" (within wide and ill-defined limits, to be sure) with each other and with behavior in the case of different species, because this is an artifact of the way in which we identify these states. Thus, we would not count an animal as *thirsty* if its "unsatiated" behavior did not seem to be directed toward drinking and was not followed by "satiation for liquid." Thus any animal that we count as capable of these various states will at least *seem* to have a certain rough kind of functional organization. And, as already remarked, if the program of finding psychological laws that are not species-specific – i.e., of finding a normal form for psychological theories of different species – ever succeeds, then it will bring in its wake a delineation of the kind of functional organization that is necessary and sufficient for a given psychological state, as well as a precise definition of the notion "psychological state." In contrast, the brain-state theorist has to hope for the eventual development of neurophysiological laws that are species-independent, which seems much less reasonable than the hope that psychological laws (of a sufficiently general kind) may be species-independent, or, still weaker, that a species-independent *form* can be found in which psychological laws can be written.

IV Functional State versus Behavior Disposition

The theory that being in pain is neither a brain state nor a functional state but a behavior disposition has one apparent advantage: it appears to agree with the way in which we verify that organisms are in pain. We do not in practice know anything about the brain state of an animal when we say that it is in pain; and we possess little if any knowledge of its functional organization, except in a crude intuitive way. In fact, however, this "advantage" is no advantage at all: for, although statements about how we verify that x is A may have a good deal to do with what the concept of being A comes to, they have precious little to do with what the property A is. To argue on the ground just mentioned that pain is neither a brain state nor a functional state is like arguing that heat is not mean molecular kinetic energy from the fact that ordinary people do not (they think) ascertain the mean molecular kinetic energy of something when they verify that it is hot or cold. It is not necessary that they should; what is necessary is that the marks that they take as indications of heat should in fact be explained by the mean molecular kinetic energy. And, similarly, it is necessary to our hypothesis that the marks that are taken as behavioral indications of pain should be explained by the fact that the organism is in a functional state of the appropriate kind, but not that speakers should *know* that this is so.

The difficulties with "behavior disposition" accounts are so well known that I shall do little more than recall them here. The difficulty – it appears to be more than "difficulty," in fact – of specifying the required behavior disposition except as "the disposition of X to behave as if X were in *pain*," is the chief one, of course. In contrast, we *can* specify the functional state with which we propose to identify pain, at least roughly, without using the notion of pain. Namely, the functional state we have in mind is the state of receiving sensory inputs which play a certain role in the Functional Organization of the organism. This role is characterized, at least partially, by the fact that the sense organs responsible for the inputs in question are organs whose function is to detect damage to the body, or dangerous extremes of temperature, pressure, etc., and by the fact that the "inputs" themselves, whatever their physical realization, represent a condition that the organism assigns a high disvalue to. As I stressed in "The mental life of some machines," this does *not* mean that the Machine will always *avoid* being in the condition in question ("pain"); it only means that the condition will be avoided unless not avoiding it is necessary to the attainment of some more highly valued goal. Since the behavior of the Machine (in this case, an organism) will depend not merely on the sensory inputs, but also on the Total State (i.e., on other values, beliefs, etc.), it seems hopeless to make any general statement about how an organism in such a condition *must* behave; but this does not mean that we must abandon hope of characterizing the condition. Indeed, we have just characterized it.[4]

Not only does the behavior-disposition theory seem hopelessly vague; if the "behavior" referred to is peripheral behavior, and the relevant stimuli are peripheral stimuli (e.g., we do not say anything about what the organism will do if its brain is operated upon), then the theory seems clearly false. For example, two animals with all motor nerves cut will have the same actual and potential "behavior" (viz., none to speak of); but if one has cut pain fibers and the other has uncut pain fibers, then one will feel pain and the other won't. Again, if one person has cut pain fibers, and another suppresses all pain responses deliberately due to some strong compulsion, then the actual and potential peripheral behavior may be the same, but one will feel pain and the other won't. (Some philosophers maintain that this last case is conceptually impossible, but the only evidence for this appears to be that *they* can't, or don't want to, conceive of it.)[5] If, instead of pain, we take some sensation the "bodily expression" of which is easier to suppress – say, a slight coolness in one's left little finger – the case becomes even clearer.

Finally, even if there *were* some behavior disposition invariantly correlated with pain (species-independently!), and specifiable without using the term "pain," it would still be more plausible to identify being in pain with some state whose pre-sence *explains* this behavior disposition – the brain state or functional state – than with the behavior disposition itself. Such considerations of plausibility may be somewhat subjective; but if other things *were* equal (of course, they aren't) why shouldn't we allow considerations of plausibility to play the deciding role?

V Methodological Considerations

So far we have considered only what might be called the "empirical" reasons for saying that being in pain is a functional state, rather than a brain state or a behavior disposition; viz., that it seems more likely that the functional state we described is invariantly "correlated" with pain, species-independently, than that there is either a physical–chemical state of the brain (must an organism have a *brain* to feel pain? perhaps some ganglia will do) or a behavior disposition so correlated. If this is correct, then it follows that the identification we proposed is at least a candidate for consideration. What of methodological considerations?

The methodological considerations are roughly similar in all cases of reduction, so no surprises need be expected here. First, identification of psychological states with functional states means that the laws of psychology can be derived from statements of the form "such-and-such organisms have such-and-such Descriptions" together with the identification statements ("being in pain is such-and-such a functional state," etc.). Second, the presence of the functional state (i.e., of inputs which play the role we have described in the Functional Organization of the organism) is not merely "correlated with" but actually explains the pain behavior on the part of the organism. Third, the identification serves to exclude questions which (if a naturalistic view is correct) represent an altogether wrong way of looking at the matter, e.g., "What *is* pain if it isn't either the brain state or the functional state?" and "What causes the pain to be always accompanied by this sort of functional state?" In short, the identification is to be tentatively accepted as a theory which leads to both fruitful predictions and to fruitful *questions*, and which serves to discourage fruitless and empirically senseless questions, where by "empirically senseless" I mean "senseless" not merely from the standpoint of verification, but from the standpoint of what there in fact *is*.

Notes

1 I have discussed these and related topics in the following papers: "Minds and machines," in *Dimensions
of Mind*, ed. Sidney Hook, New York, 1960, pp. 148–
79; "Brains and behavior," in *Analytical Philosophy*,
second series, ed. Ronald Butler, Oxford, 1965, pp.
1–20; and "The mental life of some machines," in
Intentionality, Minds, and Perception, ed. Hector-Neri
Castañeda, Detroit, 1967, pp. 177–200.

2 In this essay I wish to avoid the vexed question of the
relation between *pains* and *pain states*. I only remark
in passing that one common argument *against* identification of these two – viz., that a pain can be in one's
arm but a state (of the organism) cannot be in one's
arm – is easily seen to be fallacious.

3 There are some well-known remarks by Alonzo
Church on this topic. Those remarks do not bear
(as might at first be supposed) on the identification
of concepts with synonymy-classes as such, but rather
support the view that (in formal semantics) it is
necessary to retain Frege's distinction between the
normal and the "oblique" use of expressions. That is,
even if we say that the concept of temperature *is* the
synonymy-class of the word "temperature", we must
not thereby be led into the error of supposing that
"the concept of temperature" is synonymous with
"the synonymy-class of the word 'temperature'" –
for then "the concept of temperature" and "der
Begriff der Temperatur" would not be synonymous,
which they are. Rather, we must say that "the concept of temperature" *refers* to the synonymy-class of
the word "temperature" (on this particular reconstruction); but that class is *identified* not as "the
synonymy class to which such-and-such a word
belongs," but in another way (e.g., as the synonymy-class whose members have such-and-such a
characteristic use).

4 In the "Mental life of some machines" a further, and
somewhat independent, characteristic of the pain
inputs is discussed in terms of Automata models –
namely the spontaneity of the inclination to withdraw
the injured part, etc. This raises the question, which
is discussed in that paper, of giving a functional
analysis of the notion of a spontaneous inclination.
Of course, still further characteristics come readily to
mind – for example, that feelings of pain are (or seem
to be) *located* in the parts of the body.

5 Cf. the discussion of "super-spartans" in "Brains and
behavior."

3

Anomalous Monism

Mental Events

Donald Davidson

Mental events such as perceivings, rememberings, decisions, and actions resist capture in the nomological net of physical theory.[1] How can this fact be reconciled with the causal role of mental events in the physical world? Reconciling freedom with causal determinism is a special case of the problem if we suppose that causal determinism entails capture in, and freedom requires escape from, the nomological net. But the broader issue can remain alive even for someone who believes a correct analysis of free action reveals no conflict with determinism. *Autonomy* (freedom, self-rule) may or may not clash with determinism; *anomaly* (failure to fall under a law) is, it would seem, another matter.

I start from the assumption that both the causal dependence, and the anomalousness, of mental events are undeniable facts. My aim is therefore to explain, in the face of apparent difficulties, how this can be. I am in sympathy with Kant when he says,

it is as impossible for the subtlest philosophy as for the commonest reasoning to argue freedom away. Philosophy must therefore assume that no true contradiction will be found between freedom and natural necessity in the same human actions, for it cannot give up the idea of nature any more than that of freedom. Hence even if we should never be able to conceive how freedom is possible, at least this apparent contradiction must be convincingly eradicated. For if the thought of freedom contradicts itself or na-

ture . . . it would have to be surrendered in competition with natural necessity.[2]

Generalize human actions to mental events, substitute anomaly for freedom, and this is a description of my problem. And of course the connection is closer, since Kant believed freedom entails anomaly.

Now let me try to formulate a little more carefully the "apparent contradiction" about mental events that I want to discuss and finally dissipate. It may be seen as stemming from three principles.

The first principle asserts that at least some mental events interact causally with physical events. (We could call this the Principle of Causal Interaction.) Thus for example if someone sank the *Bismarck*, then various mental events such as perceivings, notings, calculations, judgments, decisions, intentional actions, and changes of belief played a causal role in the sinking of the *Bismarck*. In particular, I would urge that the fact that someone sank the *Bismarck* entails that he moved his body in a way that was caused by mental events of certain sorts, and that this bodily movement in turn caused the *Bismarck* to sink.[3] Perception illustrates how causality may run from the physical to the mental: if a man perceives that a ship is approaching, then a ship approaching must have caused him to come to believe that a ship is approaching. (Nothing depends on accepting these as examples of causal interaction.)

Though perception and action provide the most obvious cases where mental and physical events interact causally, I think reasons could be given for the view that all mental events ultimately, perhaps through causal relations with other mental events, have causal intercourse with physical events. But if there are mental events that have no physical events as causes or effects, the argument will not touch them.

The second principle is that where there is causality, there must be a law: events related as cause and effect fall under strict deterministic laws. (We may term this the Principle of the Nomological Character of Causality.) This principle, like the first, will be treated here as an assumption, though I shall say something by way of interpretation.[4]

The third principle is that there are no strict deterministic laws on the basis of which mental events can be predicted and explained (the Anomalism of the Mental).

The paradox I wish to discuss arises for someone who is inclined to accept these three assumptions or principles, and who thinks they are inconsistent with one another. The inconsistency is not, of course, formal unless more premises are added. Nevertheless it is natural to reason that the first two principles, that of causal interaction, and that of the nomological character of causality, together imply that at least some mental events can be predicted and explained on the basis of laws, while the principle of the anomalism of the mental denies this. Many philosophers have accepted, with or without argument, the view that the three principles do lead to a contradiction. It seems to me, however, that all three principles are true, so that what must be done is to explain away the appearance of contradiction; essentially the Kantian line.

The rest of this essay falls into three parts. The first part describes a version of the identity theory of the mental and the physical that shows how the three principles may be reconciled. The second part argues that there cannot be strict psychophysical laws; this is not quite the principle of the anomalism of the mental, but on reasonable assumptions entails it. The last part tries to show that from the fact that there can be no strict psychophysical laws, and our other two principles, we can infer the truth of a version of the identity theory, that is, a theory that identifies at least some mental events with physical events. It is clear that this "proof" of the identity theory will be at best

conditional, since two of its premises are unsupported, and the argument for the third may be found less than conclusive. But even someone unpersuaded of the truth of the premises may be interested to learn how they may be reconciled and that they serve to establish a version of the identity theory of the mental. Finally, if the argument is a good one, it should lay to rest the view, common to many friends and some foes of identity theories, that support for such theories can come only from the discovery of psychophysical laws.

I

The three principles will be shown consistent with one another by describing a view of the mental and the physical that contains no inner contradiction and that entails the three principles. According to this view, mental events are identical with physical events. Events are taken to be unrepeatable, dated individuals such as the particular eruption of a volcano, the (first) birth or death of a person, the playing of the 1968 World Series, or the historic utterance of the words, "You may fire when ready, Gridley." We can easily frame identity statements about individual events; examples (true or false) might be:

The death of Scott = the death of the author of *Waverley*.
The assassination of the Archduke Ferdinand = the event that started the First World War.
The eruption of Vesuvius in AD 79 = the cause of the destruction of Pompeii.

The theory under discussion is silent about processes, states, and attributes if these differ from individual events.

What does it mean to say that an event is mental or physical? One natural answer is that an event is physical if it is describable in a purely physical vocabulary, mental if describable in mental terms. But if this is taken to suggest that an event is physical, say, if some physical predicate is true of it, then there is the following difficulty. Assume that the predicate "x took place at Noosa Heads" belongs to the physical vocabulary; then so also must the predicate "x did not take place at Noosa Heads" belong to the physical vocabulary. But the predicate "x did or did not take place at Noosa Heads" is true of every event, whether mental or physical.[5] We might rule out predicates that are tautologically true of every event, but this will not help since every event is truly describable either by "x took place at Noosa Heads" or by "x did not take place at Noosa Heads." A different approach is needed.[6]

We may call those verbs mental that express propositional attitudes like believing, intending, desiring, hoping, knowing, perceiving, noticing, remembering, and so on. Such verbs are characterized by the fact that they sometimes feature in sentences with subjects that refer to persons, and are completed by embedded sentences in which the usual rules of substitution appear to break down. This criterion is not precise, since I do not want to include these verbs when they occur in contexts that are fully extensional ("He knows Paris," "He perceives the moon" may be cases), nor exclude them whenever they are not followed by embedded sentences. An alternative characterization of the desired class of mental verbs might be that they are psychological verbs as used when they create apparently nonextensional contexts.

Let us call a description of the form "the event that is M" or an open sentence of the form "event x is M" a *mental description* or a *mental open sentence* if and only if the expression that replaces "M" contains at least one mental verb essentially. (Essentially, so as to rule out cases where the description or open sentence is logically equivalent to one not containing mental vocabulary.) Now we may say that an event is mental if and only if it has a mental description, or (the description operator not being primitive) if there is a mental open sentence true of that event alone. Physical events are those picked out by descriptions or open sentences that contain only the physical vocabulary essentially. It is less important to characterize a physical vocabulary because relative to the mental it is, so to speak, recessive in determining whether a description is mental or physical. (There will be some comments presently on the nature of a physical vocabulary, but these comments will fall far short of providing a criterion.)

On the proposed test of the mental, the distinguishing feature of the mental is not that it is private, subjective, or immaterial, but that it exhibits what Brentano called intentionality. Thus intentional actions are clearly included in the realm of the mental along with thoughts, hopes, and regrets (or the events tied to these). What may seem doubtful is whether the criterion will include events that have often been considered paradigmatic of the mental. Is it obvious, for example, that feeling a pain or seeing an afterimage will

count as mental? Sentences that report such events seem free from taint of nonextensionality, and the same should be true of reports of raw feels, sense data, and other uninterpreted sensations, if there are any.

However, the criterion actually covers not only the havings of pains and afterimages, but much more besides. Take some event one would intuitively accept as physical, let's say the collision of two stars in distant space. There must be a purely physical predicate "Px" true of this collision, and of others, but true of only this one at the time it occurred. This particular time, though, may be pinpointed as the same time that Jones notices that a pencil starts to roll across his desk. The distant stellar collision is thus *the* event x such that Px and x is simultaneous with Jones's noticing that a pencil starts to roll across his desk. The collision has now been picked out by a mental description and must be counted as a mental event.

This strategy will probably work to show every event to be mental; we have obviously failed to capture the intuitive concept of the mental. It would be instructive to try to mend this trouble, but it is not necessary for present purposes. We can afford Spinozistic extravagance with the mental since accidental inclusions can only strengthen the hypothesis that all mental events are identical with physical events. What would matter would be failure to include bona fide mental events, but of this there seems to be no danger.

I want to describe, and presently to argue for, a version of the identity theory that denies that there can be strict laws connecting the mental and the physical. The very possibility of such a theory is easily obscured by the way in which identity theories are commonly defended and attacked. Charles Taylor, for example, agrees with protagonists of identity theories that the sole "ground" for accepting such theories is the supposition that correlations or laws can be established linking events described as mental with events described as physical. He says, "It is easy to see why this is so: unless a given mental event is invariably accompanied by a given, say, brain process, there is no ground for even mooting a general identity between the two."[7] Taylor goes on (correctly, I think) to allow that there may be identity without correlating laws, but my present interest is in noticing the invitation to confusion in the statement just quoted. What can "a given mental event" mean here? Not a particular, dated, event, for it would not make sense to speak of an individual event being "invariably accompanied" by another. Taylor is evidently thinking of events of a given *kind*. But if the only identities are of kinds of events, the identity theory presupposes correlating laws.

One finds the same tendency to build laws into the statement of the identity theory in these typical remarks:

> When I say that a sensation is a brain process or that lightning is an electrical discharge, I am using "is" in the sense of strict identity . . . there are not two things: a flash of lightning and an electrical discharge. There is one thing, a flash of lightning, which is described scientifically as an electrical discharge to the earth from a cloud of ionized water molecules.[8]

The last sentence of this quotation is perhaps to be understood as saying that for every lightning flash there exists an electrical discharge to the earth from a cloud of ionized water molecules with which it is identical. Here we have an honest ontology of individual events and can make literal sense of identity. We can also see how there could be identities without correlating laws. It is possible, however, to have an ontology of events with the conditions of individuation specified in such a way that any identity implies a correlating law. Kim, for example, suggests that Fa and Gb "describe or refer to the same event" if and only if $a = b$ and the property of being F = the property of being G. The identity of the properties in turn entails that $(x) (Fx \leftrightarrow Gx)$.[9] No wonder Kim says:

> If pain is identical with brain state B, there must be a concomitance between occurrences of pain and occurrences of brain state B. . . . Thus, a necessary condition of the pain-brain state B identity is that the two expressions "being in pain" and "being in brain state B" have the same extension. . . . There is no conceivable observation that would confirm or refute the identity but not the associated correlation.[10]

It may make the situation clearer to give a fourfold classification of theories of the relation between mental and physical events that emphasizes the independence of claims about laws and claims of identity. On the one hand there are those who assert, and those who deny, the existence of psychophysical laws; on the other hand there are those who say mental events are identical with physical and those who deny this. Theories are thus divided into four sorts: *Nomological monism*, which affirms that there are correlating laws and that the events correlated are one (materialists belong in this category); *nomological dualism*, which comprises various forms of parallelism, interactionism, and epiphenomenalism; *anomalous dualism*, which combines ontological dualism with the general failure of laws correlating the mental and the physical (Cartesianism). And finally there is *anomalous monism*, which classifies the position I wish to occupy.[11]

Anomalous monism resembles materialism in its claim that all events are physical, but rejects the thesis, usually considered essential to materialism, that mental phenomena can be given purely physical explanations. Anomalous monism shows an ontological bias only in that it allows the possibility that not all events are mental, while insisting that all events are physical. Such a bland monism, unbuttressed by correlating laws or conceptual economies, does not seem to merit the term "reductionism"; in any case it is not apt to inspire the nothing-but reflex ("Conceiving the *Art of the Fugue* was nothing but a complex neural event," and so forth).

Although the position I describe denies there are psychophysical laws, it is consistent with the view that mental characteristics are in some sense dependent, or supervenient, on physical characteristics. Such supervenience might be taken to mean that there cannot be two events alike in all physical respects but differing in some mental respect, or that an object cannot alter in some mental respect without altering in some physical respect. Dependence or supervenience of this kind does not entail reducibility through law or definition: if it did, we could reduce moral properties to descriptive, and this there is good reason to *believe* cannot be done; and we might be able to reduce truth in a formal system to syntactical properties, and this we *know* cannot in general be done.

This last example is in useful analogy with the sort of lawless monism under consideration. Think of the physical vocabulary as the entire vocabulary of some language L with resources adequate to express a certain amount of mathematics, and its own syntax. L' is L augmented with the truth predicate "true-in-L," which is "mental." In L (and hence L') it is possible to pick out, with a definite description or open sentence, each sentence in the extension of the truth predicate, but if L is consistent there exists no predicate of syntax (of the "physical" vocabulary), no matter how complex, that applies to all and only the true sentences of L. There can be no "psychophysical law" in the form of a biconditional, "(x) (x is true-in-L if and only if x is ϕ)" where "ϕ" is replaced by a "physical" predicate (a predicate of L). Similarly, we can pick out each mental event using the physical vocabulary alone, but no purely physical predicate, no matter how complex, has, as a matter of law, the same extension as a mental predicate.

It should now be evident how anomalous monism reconciles the three original principles. Causality and identity are relations between individual events no matter how described. But laws are linguistic; and so events can instantiate laws, and hence be explained or predicted in the light of laws, only as those events are described in one or another way. The principle of causal interaction deals with events in extension and is therefore blind to the mental–physical dichotomy. The principle of the anomalism of the mental concerns events described as mental, for events are mental only as described. The principle of the nomological character of causality must be read carefully: it says that when events are related as cause and effect, they have descriptions that instantiate a law. It does not say that every true singular statement of causality instantiates a law.[12]

II

The analogy just bruited, between the place of the mental amid the physical, and the place of the semantical in a world of syntax, should not be strained. Tarski proved that a consistent language cannot (under some natural assumptions) contain an open sentence "Fx" true of all and only the true sentences of that language. If our analogy were pressed, then we would expect a proof that there can be no physical open sentence "Px" true of all and only the events having some mental property. In fact, however, nothing I can say about the irreducibility of the mental deserves to be called a proof; and the kind of irreducibility is different. For if anomalous monism is correct, not only can every mental event be uniquely singled out using only physical concepts, but since the number of events that falls under each mental predicate may, for all we know, be finite, there may well exist a physical open sentence coextensive with each mental predicate, though to construct it might involve the tedium of a lengthy and uninstructive alterna-

tion. Indeed, even if finitude is not assumed, there seems no compelling reason to deny that there could be coextensive predicates, one mental and one physical.

The thesis is rather that the mental is nomologically irreducible: there may be *true* general statements relating the mental and the physical, statements that have the logical form of a law; but they are not *lawlike* (in a strong sense to be described). If by absurdly remote chance we were to stumble on a nonstochastic true psychophysical generalization, we would have no reason to believe it more than roughly true.

Do we, by declaring that there are no (strict) psychophysical laws, poach on the empirical preserves of science – a form of *hubris* against which philosophers are often warned? Of course, to judge a statement lawlike or illegal is not to decide its truth outright; relative to the acceptance of a general statement on the basis of instances, ruling it lawlike must be *a priori*. But such relative apriorism does not in itself justify philosophy, for in general the grounds for deciding to trust a statement on the basis of its instances will in turn be governed by theoretical and empirical concerns not to be distinguished from those of science. If the case of supposed laws linking the mental and the physical is different, it can only be because to allow the possibility of such laws would amount to changing the subject. By changing the subject I mean here: deciding not to accept the criterion of the mental in terms of the vocabulary of the propositional attitudes. This short answer cannot prevent further ramifications of the problem, however, for there is no clear line between changing the subject and changing what one says on an old subject, which is to admit, in the present context at least, that there is no clear line between philosophy and science. Where there are no fixed boundaries only the timid never risk trespass.

It will sharpen our appreciation of the anomological character of mental–physical generalizations to consider a related matter, the failure of definitional behaviorism. Why are we willing (as I assume we are) to abandon the attempt to give explicit definitions of mental concepts in terms of behavioral ones? Not, surely, just because all actual tries are conspicuously inadequate. Rather it is because we are persuaded, as we are in the case of so many other forms of definitional reductionism (naturalism in ethics, instrumentalism and operationalism in the sciences, the causal theory of meaning, phenomenalism, and so on – the catalogue of philosophy's defeats), that there is system in the failures. Suppose we try to say, not using any mental concepts, what it is for a man to believe there is life on Mars. One line we could take is this: when a certain sound is produced in the man's presence ("Is there life on Mars?") he produces another ("Yes"). But of course this shows he believes there is life on Mars only if he understands English, his production of the sound was intentional, and was a response to the sounds as meaning something in English; and so on. For each discovered deficiency, we add a new proviso. Yet no matter how we patch and fit the nonmental conditions, we always find the need for an additional condition (provided he *notices*, *understands*, etc.) that is mental in character.[13]

A striking feature of attempts at definitional reduction is how little seems to hinge on the question of synonymy between definiens and definiendum. Of course, by imagining counterexamples we do discredit claims of synonymy. But the pattern of failure prompts a stronger conclusion: if we were to find an open sentence couched in behavioral terms and exactly coextensive with some mental predicate, nothing could reasonably persuade us that we had found it. We know too much about thought and behavior to trust exact and universal statements linking them. Beliefs and desires issue in behavior only as modified and mediated by further beliefs and desires, attitudes and attendings, without limit. Clearly this holism of the mental realm is a clue both to the autonomy and to the anomalous character of the mental.

These remarks apropos definitional behaviorism provide at best hints of why we should not expect nomological connections between the mental and the physical. The central case invites further consideration.

Lawlike statements are general statements that support counterfactual and subjunctive claims, and are supported by their instances. There is (in my view) no nonquestion-begging criterion of the lawlike, which is not to say there are no reasons in particular cases for a judgment. Lawlikeness is a matter of degree, which is not to deny that there may be cases beyond debate. And within limits set by the conditions of communication, there is room for much variation between individuals in the pattern of statements to which various degrees of nomologicality are assigned. In all these respects, nomologicality is much like analyticity, as one might expect since both are linked to meaning.

"All emeralds are green" is lawlike in that its instances confirm it, but "all emeralds are grue" is not, for "grue" means "observed before time *t* and green, otherwise blue," and if our observations were all made before *t* and uniformly revealed green emeralds, this would not be a reason to expect other emeralds to be blue. Nelson Goodman has suggested that this shows that some predicates, "grue" for example, are unsuited to laws (and thus a criterion of suitable predicates could lead to a criterion of the lawlike). But it seems to me the anomalous character of "All emeralds are grue" shows only that the predicates "is an emerald" and "is grue" are not suited to one another: grueness is not an inductive property of emeralds. Grueness *is* however an inductive property of entities of other sorts, for instance of emerires. (Something is an emerire if it is examined before *t* and is an emerald, and otherwise is a sapphire.) Not only is "All emerires are grue" entailed by the conjunction of the lawlike statements "All emeralds are green" and "All sapphires are blue," but there is no reason, as far as I can see, to reject the deliverance of intuition, that it is itself lawlike.[14] Nomological statements bring together predicates that we know *a priori* are made for each other – know, that is, independently of knowing whether the evidence supports a connection between them. "Blue," "red," and "green" are made for emeralds, sapphires, and roses; "grue," "bleen," and "gred" are made for sapphalds, emerires, and emeroses.

The direction in which the discussion seems headed is this: mental and physical predicates are not made for one another. In point of lawlikeness, psychophysical statements are more like "All emeralds are grue" than like "All emeralds are green."

Before this claim is plausible, it must be seriously modified. The fact that emeralds examined before *t* are grue not only is no reason to believe all emeralds are grue; it is not even a reason (if we know the time) to believe *any* unobserved emeralds are grue. But if an event of a certain mental sort has usually been accompanied by an event of a certain physical sort, this often is a good reason to expect other cases to follow suit roughly in proportion. The generalizations that embody such practical wisdom are assumed to be only roughly true, or they are explicitly stated in probabilistic terms, or they are insulated from counterexample by generous escape clauses. Their importance lies mainly in the support they lend singular causal claims and related explanations of particular events. The support derives from the fact that such a generalization, however crude and vague, may provide good reason to believe that underlying the particular case there is a regularity that could be formulated sharply and without caveat.

In our daily traffic with events and actions that must be foreseen or understood, we perforce make use of the sketchy summary generalization, for we do not know a more accurate law, or if we do, we lack a description of the particular events in which we are interested that would show the relevance of the law. But there is an important distinction to be made within the category of the rude rule of thumb. On the one hand, there are generalizations whose positive instances give us reason to believe the generalization itself could be improved by adding further provisos and conditions stated in the same general vocabulary as the original generalization. Such a generalization points to the form and vocabulary of the finished law: we may say that it is a *homonomic* generalization. On the other hand there are generalizations which when instantiated may give us reason to believe there is a precise law at work, but one that can be stated only by shifting to a different vocabulary. We may call such generalizations *heteronomic*.

I suppose most of our practical lore (and science) is heteronomic. This is because a law can hope to be precise, explicit, and as exceptionless as possible only if it draws its concepts from a comprehensive closed theory. This ideal theory may or may not be deterministic, but it is if any true theory is. Within the physical sciences we do find homonomic generalizations, generalizations such that if the evidence supports them, we then have reason to believe they may be sharpened indefinitely by drawing upon further physical concepts: there is a theoretical asymptote of perfect coherence with all the evidence, perfect predictability (under the terms of the system), total explanation (again under the terms of the system). Or perhaps the ultimate theory is probabilistic, and the asymptote is less than perfection; but in that case there will be no better to be had.

Confidence that a statement is homonomic, correctible within its own conceptual domain, demands that it draw its concepts from a theory with strong constitutive elements. Here is the simplest possible illustration; if the lesson carries, it will be obvious that the simplification could be mended.

The measurement of length, weight, temperature, or time depends (among many other things, of course) on the existence in each case of a two–place relation that is transitive and asymmetric: warmer than, later than, heavier than, and so forth. Let us take the relation *longer than* as our example. The law or postulate of transitivity is this:

(L) $\mathrm{L}(x,y)$ and $\mathrm{L}(y,z) \rightarrow \mathrm{L}(x,z)$

Unless this law (or some sophisticated variant) holds, we cannot easily make sense of the concept of length. There will be no way of assigning numbers to register even so much as ranking in length, let alone the more powerful demands of measurement on a ratio scale. And this remark goes not only for any three items directly involved in an intransitivity: it is easy to show (given a few more assumptions essential to measurement of length) that there is no consistent assignment of a ranking to any item unless (L) holds in full generality.

Clearly (L) alone cannot exhaust the import of "longer than" – otherwise it would not differ from "warmer than" or "later than." We must suppose there is some empirical content, however difficult to formulate in the available vocabulary, that distinguishes "longer than" from the other two- place transitive predicates of measurement and on the basis of which we may assert that one thing is longer than another. Imagine this empirical content to be partly given by the predicate "$\mathrm{O}(x,y)$". So we have this "meaning postulate":

(M) $\mathrm{O}(x,y) \rightarrow \mathrm{L}(x,y)$

that partly interprets (L). But now (L) and (M) together yield an empirical theory of great strength, for together they entail that there do not exist three objects a, b, and c such that $\mathrm{O}(a,b)$, $\mathrm{O}(b,c)$, and $\mathrm{O}(c,a)$. Yet what is to prevent this happening if "$\mathrm{O}(x,y)$" is a predicate we can ever, with confidence, apply? Suppose we *think* we observe an intransitive triad; what do we say? We could count (L) false, but then we would have no application for the concept of length. We could say (M) gives a wrong test for length; but then it is unclear what we thought was the *content* of the idea of one thing being longer than another. Or we could say that the objects under observation are not, as the theory requires, *rigid* objects. It is a mistake to think we are forced to accept some one of these answers. Concepts such as that of length are sustained in equilibrium by a number of conceptual pressures, and theories of fundamental measurement are distorted if we force the decision, among such principles as (L) and (M): analytic or synthetic. It is better to say the whole set of axioms, laws, or postulates for the measurement of length is partly constitutive of the idea of a system of macroscopic, rigid, physical objects. I suggest that the existence of lawlike statements in physical science depends upon the existence of constitutive (or synthetic *a priori*) laws like those of the measurement of length within the same conceptual domain.

Just as we cannot intelligibly assign a length to any object unless a comprehensive theory holds of objects of that sort, we cannot intelligibly attribute any propositional attitude to an agent except within the framework of a viable theory of his beliefs, desires, intentions, and decisions.

There is no assigning beliefs to a person one by one on the basis of his verbal behavior, his choices, or other local signs no matter how plain and evident, for we make sense of particular beliefs only as they cohere with other beliefs, with preferences, with intentions, hopes, fears, expectations, and the rest. It is not merely, as with the measurement of length, that each case tests a theory and depends upon it, but that the content of a propositional attitude derives from its place in the pattern.

Crediting people with a large degree of consistency cannot be counted mere charity: it is unavoidable if we are to be in a position to accuse them meaningfully of error and some degree of irrationality. Global confusion, like universal mistake, is unthinkable, not because imagination boggles, but because too much confusion leaves nothing to be confused about and massive error erodes the background of true belief against which alone failure can be construed. To appreciate the limits to the kind and amount of blunder and bad thinking we can intelligibly pin on others is to see once more the inseparability of the question what concepts a person commands and the question what he does with those concepts in the way of belief, desire, and intention. To the extent that we fail to discover a coherent and plausible pattern in the attitudes and actions of others we simply forego the chance of treating them as persons.

The problem is not bypassed but given center stage by appeal to explicit speech behavior. For we could not begin to decode a man's sayings if we could not make out his attitudes towards his sentences, such as holding, wishing, or wanting them to be true. Beginning from these attitudes, we must work out a theory of what he means, thus simultaneously giving content to his attitudes and to his words. In our need to make him make sense, we will try for a theory that finds him consistent, a believer of truths, and a lover of the good (all by our own lights, it goes without saying). Life being what it is, there will be no simple theory that fully meets these demands. Many theories will effect a more or less acceptable compromise, and between these theories there may be no objective grounds for choice.

The heteronomic character of general statements linking the mental and the physical traces back to this central role of translation in the description of all propositional attitudes, and to the indeterminacy of translation.[15] There are no strict psychophysical laws because of the disparate commitments of the mental and physical schemes. It is a feature of physical reality that physical change can be explained by laws that connect it with other changes and conditions physically described. It is a feature of the mental that the attribution of mental phenomena must be responsible to the background of reasons, beliefs, and intentions of the individual. There cannot be tight connections between the realms if each is to retain allegiance to its proper source of evidence. The nomological irreducibility of the mental does not derive merely from the seamless nature of the world of thought, preference and intention, for such interdependence is common to physical theory, and is compatible with there being a single right way of interpreting a man's attitudes without relativization to a scheme of translation. Nor is the irreducibility due simply to the possibility of many equally eligible schemes, for this is compatible with an arbitrary choice of one scheme relative to which assignments of mental traits are made. The point is rather that when we use the concepts of belief, desire and the rest, we must stand prepared, as the evidence accumulates, to adjust our theory in the light of considerations of overall cogency: the constitutive ideal of rationality partly controls each phase in the evolution of what must be an evolving theory. An arbitrary choice of translation scheme would preclude such opportunistic tempering of theory; put differently, a right arbitrary choice of a translation manual would be of a manual acceptable in the light of all possible evidence, and this is a choice we cannot make. We must conclude, I think, that nomological slack between the mental and the physical is essential as long as we conceive of man as a rational animal.

III

The gist of the foregoing discussion, as well as its conclusion, will be familiar. That there is a categorial difference between the mental and the physical is a commonplace. It may seem odd that I say nothing of the supposed privacy of the mental, or the special authority an agent has with respect to his own propositional attitudes, but this appearance of novelty would fade if we were to investigate in more detail the grounds for accepting a scheme of translation. The step from the categorial difference between the mental and the physical to the impossibility of strict laws relating them is less common, but certainly not new. If there is a surprise, then, it will be to find the lawlessness of the mental serving to help establish the identity of the mental with that paradigm of the lawlike, the physical.

The reasoning is this. We are assuming, under the Principle of the Causal Dependence of the Mental, that some mental events at least are causes or effects of physical events; the argument applies only to these. A second Principle (of the Nomological Character of Causality) says that each true singular causal statement is backed by a strict law connecting events of kinds to which the events mentioned as cause and effect belong. Where there are rough, but homonomic, laws, there are laws drawing on concepts from the same conceptual domain and upon which there is no improving in point of precision and comprehensiveness. We urged in the last section that such laws occur in the physical sciences. Physical theory promises to provide a comprehensive closed system guaranteed to yield a standardized, unique description of every physical event couched in a vocabulary amenable to law.

It is not plausible that mental concepts alone can provide such a framework, simply because the mental does not, by our first principle, constitute a closed system. Too much happens to affect the mental that is not itself a systematic part of the mental. But if we combine this observation with the conclusion that no psychophysical statement is, or can be built into, a strict law, we have the Principle of the Anomalism of the Mental: there are no strict laws at all on the basis of which we can predict and explain mental phenomena.

The demonstration of identity follows easily. Suppose m, a mental event, caused p, a physical event; then under some description m and p instantiate a strict law. This law can only be physical, according to the previous paragraph. But if m falls under a physical law, it has a physical description; which is to say it is a physical event. An analogous argument works when a physical event causes a mental event. So every mental event that is causally related to a physical event is a physical event. In order to establish anomalous monism in full generality it would be sufficient to show that every mental event is cause or effect of some physical event; I shall not attempt this.

If one event causes another, there is a strict law which those events instantiate when properly described. But it is possible (and typical) to know of the singular causal relation without knowing the law or the relevant descriptions. Knowledge requires reasons, but these are available in the form of rough heteronomic generalizations, which are lawlike in that instances make it reasonable to expect other instances to follow suit without being lawlike in the sense of being indefinitely refinable. Applying these facts to knowledge of identities, we see that it is possible to know that a mental event is identical with some physical event without knowing which one (in the sense of being able to give it a unique physical description that brings it under a relevant law). Even if someone knew the entire physical history of the world, and every mental event were identical with a physical, it would not follow that he could predict or explain a single mental event (so described, of course).

Two features of mental events in their relation to the physical – causal dependence and nomological independence – combine, then, to dissolve what has often seemed a paradox, the efficacy of thought and purpose in the material world, and their freedom from law. When we portray events as perceivings, rememberings, decisions, and actions, we necessarily locate them amid physical happenings through the relation of cause and effect; but that same mode of portrayal insulates mental events, as long as we do not change the idiom, from the strict laws that can in principle be called upon to explain and predict physical phenomena.

Mental events as a class cannot be explained by physical science; particular mental events can when we know particular identities. But the explanations of mental events in which we are typically interested relate them to other mental events and conditions. We explain a man's free actions, for example, by appeal to his desires, habits, knowledge and perceptions. Such accounts of intentional behavior operate in a conceptual framework removed from the direct reach of physical law by describing both cause and effect, reason and action, as aspects of a portrait of a human agent. The anomalism of the mental is thus a necessary condition for viewing action as autonomous. I conclude with a second passage from Kant:

It is an indispensable problem of speculative philosophy to show that its illusion respecting the contradiction rests on this, that we think of man in a different sense and relation when we call him free, and when we regard him as subject to the laws of nature. . . . It must therefore show that not only can both of these very well coexist, but that both must be thought *as necessarily united* in the same subject.[16]

Notes

1 I was helped and influenced by Daniel Bennett, Sue Larson, and Richard Rorty, who are not responsible for the result. My research was supported by the National Science Foundation and the Center for Advanced Study in the Behavioral Sciences.

2 *Fundamental Principles of the Metaphysics of Morals*, trans. T. K. Abbott (London, 1909), pp. 75–6.

3 These claims are defended in my "Actions, reasons and causes," *The Journal of Philosophy*, LX (1963), pp. 685–700 and in "Agency," a paper in the proceedings of the November 1968 colloquium on Agent, Action, and Reason at the University of Western Ontario, London, Canada.

4 In "Causal relations," *The Journal of Philosophy*, LXIV (1967), pp. 691–703, I elaborate on the view of causality assumed here. The stipulation that the laws be deterministic is stronger than required by the reasoning, and will be relaxed.

5 The point depends on assuming that mental events may intelligibly be said to have a location; but it is an assumption that must be true if an identity theory is, and here I am not trying to prove the theory but to formulate it.

6 I am indebted to Lee Bowie for emphasizing this difficulty.

7 Charles Taylor, "Mind-body identity, a side issue?" *The Philosophical Review*, LXXVI (1967), p. 202.

8 J. J. C. Smart, "Sensations and brain processes," *The Philosophical Review*, LXVIII (1959), pp. 141–56. The quoted passages are on pp. 163–5 of the reprinted version in *The Philosophy of Mind*, ed. V. C. Chappell (Englewood Cliffs, NJ, 1962). For another example, see David K. Lewis, "An argument for the identity theory," *The Journal of Philosophy*, LXIII (1966), pp. 17–25. Here the assumption is made explicit when Lewis takes events as universals (p. 17, footnotes 1 and 2). I do not suggest that Smart and Lewis are confused, only that their way of stating the identity theory tends to obscure the distinction between particular events and kinds of events on which the formulation of my theory depends.

9 Jaegwon Kim, "On the psycho-physical identity theory," *American Philosophical Quarterly*, III (1966), p. 231.

10 Ibid., pp. 227–8. Richard Brandt and Jaegwon Kim propose roughly the same criterion in "The logic of the identity theory," *The Journal of Philosophy* LIV (1967), pp. 515–37. They remark that on their conception of event identity, the identity theory "makes a stronger claim than merely that there is a pervasive phenomenal–physical correlation" (p. 518). I do not discuss the stronger claim.

11 Anomalous monism is more or less explicitly recognized as a possible position by Herbert Feigl, "The 'mental' and the 'physical,'" in *Concepts, Theories and the Mind–Body Problem*, vol. II, *Minnesota Studies in the Philosophy of Science* (Minneapolis, 1958); Sydney Shoemaker, "Ziff's other minds," *The Journal of Philosophy*, LXII (1965), p. 589; David Randall Luce, "Mind–body identity and psycho-physical correlation," *Philosophical Studies*, XVII (1966), pp. 1–7; Charles Taylor, "Mind–body identity," p. 207. Something like my position is tentatively accepted by Thomas Nagel, "Physicalism," *The Philosophical Review*, LXXIV (1965), pp. 339–56, and briefly endorsed by P. F. Strawson in *Freedom and the Will*, ed. D. F. Pears (London, 1963), pp. 63–7.

12 The point that substitutivity of identity fails in the context of explanation is made in connection with the present subject by Norman Malcolm, "Scientific materialism and the identity theory," *Dialogue*, III (1964–5), pp. 123–4. See also my "Actions, reasons and causes," *The Journal of Philosophy*, LX (1963), pp. 696–9 and "The individuation of events" in *Essays in Honor of Carl G. Hempel*, ed. N. Rescher et al. (Dordrecht, 1969).

13 The theme is developed in Roderick Chisholm, *Perceiving* (Ithaca, NY, 1957), ch. 11.

14 This view is accepted by Richard C. Jeffrey, "Goodman's query," *The Journal of Philosophy*, LXII (1966), pp. 286 ff.; John R. Wallace, "Goodman, logic, induction," same journal and issue, p. 318, and John M. Vickers, "Characteristics of projectible predicates," *The Journal of Philosophy*, LXIV (1967), p. 285. On pp. 328–9 and 286–7 of these journal issues respectively Goodman disputes the lawlikeness of statements like "All emerires are grue." I

cannot see, however, that he meets the point of my "Emeroses by other names," *The Journal of Philosophy*, LXIII (1966), pp. 778–80.

15 The influence of W. V. Quine's doctrine of the indeterminacy of translation, as in ch. 2 of *Word and Object* (Cambridge, Mass., 1960), is, I hope, obvious. In § 45 Quine develops the connection between translation and the propositional attitudes, and remarks that "Brentano's thesis of the irreducibility of intentional idioms is of a piece with the thesis of indeterminacy of translation" (p. 221).

16 *Fundamental Principles*, p. 76.

4

Homuncular and Teleological Functionalism

An excerpt from "The Appeal to Tacit Knowledge in Psychological Explanation"

Jerry A. Fodor

Remember thee!
Ay, thou poor ghost, while memory holds a seat
In this distracted globe.

Hamlet, Act I, *Scene* V

In this essay I want to defend "intellectualist" accounts of mental competences and to suggest that, in attributing tacit knowledge to organisms, intellectualist theories exploit a legitimate form of nondemonstrative inference: the inference from like effects to like causes. In passing, I shall have a few things to say about the distinction between knowing how and knowing that.

Here is the way we tie our shoes:
There is a little man who lives in one's head. The little man keeps a library. When one acts upon the intention to tie one's shoes, the little man fetches down a volume entitled *Tying One's Shoes*. The volume says such things as: "Take the left free end of the shoelace in the left hand. Cross the left free end of the shoelace over the right free end of the shoelace . . . , etc."

When the little man reads the instruction "take the left free end of the shoelace in the left hand," he pushes a button on a control panel. The button is marked "take the left free end of a shoelace in the left hand." When depressed, it activates a series of wheels, cogs, levers, and hydraulic mechanisms. As a causal consequence of the functioning of these

mechanisms, one's left hand comes to seize the appropriate end of the shoelace. Similarly, *mutatis mutandis,* for the rest of the instructions.

The instructions end with the word "end." When the little man reads the word "end," he returns the book of instructions to his library.

That is the way we tie our shoes.

What is wrong with this explanation?

In the first place, the details are surely incorrect. For example, the action of the arm and hand in tying a shoelace cannot literally be accounted for on mechanical and hydraulic principles. We shall presumably need chemical and electrical systems as well and, among these, feedback devices to mediate hand/eye coordinations. We are not, then, to take the foregoing account as proposing a serious theory of the physics of shoe tying.

Second, some of the behaviors we have supposed to be involved in shoe tying are of considerable complexity. It would seem, for example, that there can be no *single* button marked "take the left free end of a shoelace in the left hand." Seizing a shoelace involves the production of a complicated pattern of behavior having a characteristic unity and complexity of its own. A serious theory of the behavioral integrations involved in tying one's shoes must explicate this complexity.

There is, then, a problem about when we are to represent a given form of behavior as "complex" and what the theoretical consequences of such a representation might be. We shall return to this problem presently. Prima facie, however, grasping a shoelace should be considered complex behavior, because doing so involves the production of motions that also play a role in other actions.

We might thus consider expanding the population in one's head to include subordinate little men who superintend the execution of the "elementary" behaviors involved in complex sequences like grasping a shoelace. When the little man reads "take the left free end of the shoelace in the left hand," we imagine him ringing up the shop foreman in charge of grasping shoelaces. The shop foreman goes about supervising that activity in a way that is, in essence, a microcosm of supervising tying one's shoe. Indeed the shop foreman might be imagined to superintend a detail of wage slaves, whose functions include: searching inputs for traces of shoelace, flexing and contracting fingers on the left hand, etc.

But these are matters of empirical detail. Psychologists too seek to carve nature at the joints: to assign to the operation of a single causal agent whatever aspects of behavior have a common etiology. So questions about how many little men there are and about what functions each little man superintends can be left to them. What this essay will be most concerned with is the philosophical opinion that there is something *methodologically* wrong with the sort of account I sketched.

It is alleged, for example, that this kind of explanation is viciously circular. And indeed there *would* be something wrong with an explanation that said, "*This* is the way we tie our shoes: we notify a little man in our head who does it for us." This account invites the question: "How does the little man do it?" but, *ex hypothesi*, provides no conceptual mechanisms for answering such questions.

But this sort of objection is irrelevant to the explanation I had envisaged. For my theory included a specification of instructions for tying one's shoes, and it was there that its explanatory power lay. In my story, appeals to the little man do not function as a way to avoid explaining how we tie our shoes. Rather the little man stands as a representative *pro tem* for psychological faculties which mediate the integration of shoe-tying behavior by applying information about how shoes are

tied. I know of no correct psychological theory that offers a specification of these faculties. Assigning psychological functions to little men makes explicit our inability to provide an account of the mechanisms that mediate those functions.

We refine a psychological theory by replacing global little men by less global little men, each of whom has fewer unanalyzed behaviors to perform than did his predecessors. Though it may look as though proceeding in this way invites the proliferation of little men *ad infinitum*, this appearance is misleading.

A completed psychological theory must provide systems of instructions to account for the forms of behavior available to an organism, and it must do so in a way that makes reference to no unanalyzed psychological processes. One way of clarifying the latter requirement is the following. Assume that there exists a class of *elementary* instructions which the nervous system is specifically wired to execute. Each elementary instruction specifies an *elementary operation*, and an elementary operation is one which the normal nervous system can perform but of which it cannot perform a proper part. Intuitively speaking, the elementary operations are those which have no theoretically relevant internal structure. Now to say an operation is elementary is to say that certain kinds of "how"-questions cannot arise about it. In particular, we cannot ask for instructions for performing it by performing some further sequences of operations. (It makes sense to ask how to spell "add" but not to ask how to spell "n".) So, given a list of elementary instructions for producing a type of behavior, we need no further instructions for carrying out the instructions on the list and no little men to supervise their execution. The nervous system carries out its complex operations in some way or other (i.e., by performing one or another sequence of elementary operations).

But the nervous system performs elementary operations in no *way* at all: it simply performs them. If every operation of the nervous system is identical with some sequence of elementary operations, we get around proliferating little men by constraining a completed psychological theory to be written in sequences of elementary instructions (or, of course, in abbreviations of such sequences).

We have been suggesting that the distinction between the homunculus and the instructions whose performances he supervises is the distinction between what psychologists understand about the etiology of behavior and what they do not. The paradigmatic psychological theory is a list of instructions for producing behavior. A constraint upon the vocabulary in which the instructions are formulated is that its terms designate only operations that are elementary for the organism in question. The little man's how-to books are, then, written in this vocabulary. Since, *ex hypothesi*, the nervous system *just is* a device for performing elementary operations, the more we know about the little man's library, the less we need to know about the little man.

Or, to vary the image, every box name in a computer flow chart is the name of a problem. If the computer is to simulate behavior, every box name will be the name of a psychological problem. The problem is to specify a sequence of instructions which

(a) will convert the input to the box into the output from the box, and
(b) can be written in a way that mentions only operations that are elementary for the organism whose behavior we are trying to simulate.

The problem is solved (an optimal simulation is achieved) when instructions are formulated which satisfy both these conditions and which meet the usual methodological constraints upon theories: simplicity, conservatism, coherence with theories in related sciences, etc.

Philosophers who don't like the kind of psychological explanations I have been discussing have hoped to get mileage out of the distinction between "knowing how" and "knowing that." They hold that intellectualist explanations fudge the distinction between knowing how to do something and knowing how the thing is done. In particular, such explanations assume that in doing a thing one knows how to do, one employs the information that the thing can be done in such and such a way. In effect, intellectualist theories undertake to explain each bit of knowledge-how by postulating some corresponding bit of knowledge-that. Thus intellectualist theories appear to blur an important distinction.

Ryle, for example, says "according to the (intellectualist) legend, whenever an agent does anything intelligently, his act is preceded and steered by another internal act of considering a regulative proposition appropriate to this practical problem."[1] But, he continues, this legend needs to be debunked.

The general assertion that all intelligent performance requires to be prefaced by the consideration of appropriate propositions rings unplausibly, even when it is apologetically conceded that the required consideration is often very swift and may go quite unmarked by the agent...the intellectualist legend is false and...when we describe a performance as intelligent, this does not entail the double operation of considering and executing. (Ibid., pp. 29–30)

The issue of consciousness lies athwart the issues about knowing how and knowing that. If the intellectualist says that, in tying one's shoes, one rehearses shoe-tying instructions to oneself, then the intellectualist is wrong on a point of fact. Children perhaps give themselves instructions when they tie their shoes, and new sailors tie bowlines to the dictates of a small inner voice. But an adult tying his shoes normally has other things to think about. Indeed thinking about tying one's shoes may get in the way of doing it. "Thus the native hue of resolution is sicklied o'er with the pale cast of thought...," etc.

Well, why doesn't the discussion end here? The intellectualist says we give ourselves instructions when we tie our shoes. But it is introspectively obvious that we normally do no such thing. Hence intellectualist accounts must be false.

One begins to see what is wrong with this argument when one notes that much of our behavior is responsive to internal and external stimuli we are unable to report. Psychologists are forever finding out surprising things about the etiology of our behavior, often by employing quite unsurprising methods of investigation.

For example: texture gradients, stereopsis, overlap, flow pattern, and other cues contribute to causally determining our visual estimates of depth. This is not a philosophical contention but a routine experimental finding. The significance of these sorts of variables can be demonstrated by untendentious employments of the method of differences. In a properly arranged experimental situation, any of these "cues" can make the difference between "seeing" depth and "seeing" a flat surface.

But, of course, no subject who is not himself sophisticated about psychology can *tell* you what cues determine his estimates of visual depth. It is a *discovery* that one responds to flow patterns in judging spatial relations, and there are, doubtless, many more such discoveries waiting to be made.

What is thus a matter of fact, and not of philosophy, is that the organism is unable to report a wide variety of its causal interactions with its environment. But it might well be argued that this fact does not demonstrate the methodological probity of intellectualist theories. For the intellectualist is required to say not just that there are causal interactions in which the organism is unconsciously involved, but also that there are unconscious processes of learning, storing, and applying rules which in some sense "go on" within the organism and contribute to the etiology of its behavior.

So, the anti-intellectualist argument could go like this: "Of course we are unconsciously affected by things like texture gradients, just as we are unconsciously affected by things like cosmic radiation. But intellectualists appeal to *unconscious mental operations*; and demonstrating unreportable causal agencies in perception provides no precedent for such an appeal."

The answer, surely, is this. If the story about the causal determination of depth estimates by texture gradients is true and if the central nervous system is the kind of organ most sensible people now think it is, then some of the things the central nervous system *does*, some of the physical transactions that take place in the central nervous system when we make estimates of depth, must satisfy such descriptions as "monitoring texture gradients," "processing information about texture gradients," "computing derivatives of texture gradients," etc. For, on one hand, varying texture gradients does, in fact, cause concomitant variation in depth estimates, and on the other, the central nervous system is the organ whose functioning mediates this causal relation. And it is a point of logic that the central nervous system *can* be the organ that medi-

ates the causal relation between texture gradients and depth estimates only if its operations satisfy the sort of descriptions mentioned above, since whatever physical system mediates our perception of depth must, *ipso facto*, perform whatever operations are nomologically necessary and sufficient for depth perception. If, then, our perceptions of depth are mediated by the central nervous system and if depth estimates vary as a function of the first derivative of texture gradients, then among the operations of the central nervous system must be some which satisfy such descriptions as "is computing the first derivative of texture gradient t".

But perhaps this shows only that the notion of some physical system mediating causal relations like the one between texture gradients and depth perception is somehow confused. For how *could* some bioelectrical exchange in my nervous system satisfy a description like "is processing information about texture gradients"? That is, how could an event which satisfies *that* sort of description also satisfy physiological descriptions like "is the firing of a phase sequence of neurons"?

But this is an odd question. Suppose someone were to ask "how *could* a contraction of the muscles of the heart count as the heart pumping the blood?" Well, we might explain, what the heart is doing when it contracts in that way is: forcing the blood through the arteries. Just so, what the nervous system is doing when it exhibits *that* pattern of firing is: computing the first derivative of a texture gradient. Of course this is not the sort of thing we find out just by looking at the heart (nervous system). To know this sort of thing is part of knowing how the circulatory (nervous) system works; hence it is to know something of what the heart (brain) does....

Note

1   *The Concept of Mind* (New York: Barnes & Noble, 1949), p. 31.

The Continuity of Levels of Nature
William G. Lycan

Contemporary Functionalism in the philosophy of mind began with a distinction between *role* and *occupant*. As we have seen, the seductive comparison of people (or their brains) to computing machines drew our attention to the contrast between a machine's program (abstractly viewed) and the particular stuff of which the machine happens to be physically made, that *realizes* the program. It is the former, not the latter, that interests us *vis-à-vis* the interpretation, explanation, prediction, and exploitation of the machine's "behavior"; people build computers to run programs, and use whatever physical materials will best lend themselves to that task.

The distinction between "program" and "realizing-stuff," or more familiarly "software" and "hardware," lend itself happily back to the philosophy of mind when Putnam and Fodor exposed the chauvinistic implications of the Identity Theory. What "*c*- fibers" and the like are doing could have been done – this role could have been performed – by some physiochemically different structure. And sure enough, if the same role were performed, the same functions realized, by silicon- instead of carbon-based neurochemistry, or if our individual neurons were replaced piecemeal by electronic prostheses that did the same jobs, then intuitively our mentality would remain unaffected. What matters is function, not functionary; program, not realizing-stuff; software, not hardware; role, not occupant. Thus the birth of Functionalism, and the distinction between "functional" and "structural" states or properties of an organism.

Functionalism is the only positive doctrine in all of philosophy that I am prepared (if not licensed) to kill for.[1] And I see the "role"/"occupant" distinction (some say obsessively) as fundamental to metaphysics. But I maintain that the *implementation* of that distinction in recent philosophy of mind is both wrong and pernicious. And my purpose in this chapter is to attack the dichotomies of "software"/"hardware," "function"/"structure" in their usual philosophical forms, and to exhibit some of the substantive confusions and correct some of the mistakes that have flowed from them.

The Hierarchy

Very generally put, my objection is that "software"/"hardware" talk encourages the idea of a bipartite Nature, divided into two levels, roughly the physiochemical and the (supervenient) "functional" or higher-organizational – as against reality, which is a multiple *hierarchy* of levels of nature, each level marked by nexus of nomic generalizations and supervenient on all those levels below it on the continuum.[2] See Nature as hier-

archically organized in this way, and the "function"/"structure" distinction *goes relative*: something is a role as opposed to an occupant, a functional state as opposed to a realizer, or vice versa, only *modulo* a designated level of nature. Let me illustrate.

Physiology and microphysiology abound with examples: *Cells* – to take a rather conspicuously functional term(!) – are constituted of cooperating teams of smaller items including membrane, nucleus, mitochondria, and the like: these items are themselves *systems* of yet smaller, still cooperating constituents. For that matter, still lower levels of nature are numerous and markedly distinct: the chemical, the molecular, the atomic, the (traditional) subatomic, the microphysical. Levels are nexus of interesting lawlike generalizations, and are individuated according to the types of generalizations involved. But cells, to look back upward along the hierarchy, are grouped into tissues, which combine to form organs, which group themselves into organ systems, which cooperate – marvelously – to comprise whole organ*isms* such as human beings. Organisms, for that matter, collect themselves into organized (*organ-ized*) groups. And there is no clear difference of kind between what we ordinarily think of as single organisms and groups of organisms that function corporately in a markedly singleminded way – "group organisms" themselves, we might say.[3]

Corresponding to this bottom–up aggregative picture of the hierarchical organization of Nature is the familiar top–down explanatory strategy.[4] If we want to know how wastes and toxins are eliminated from the bodies of humans, we look for and find an *excretory system* interlocked with the digestive and circulatory systems. If we look at that system closely we find (not surprisingly) that it treats water-soluble and nonsoluble wastes differently. We find in particular a *kidney*, which works on soluble wastes in particular. If we probe the details further, proceeding downward through the hierarchy of levels, we find the kidney divided into renal cortex (a filter) and medulla (a collector). The cortex is composed mainly of nephrons. Each nephron has a glomerulus accessed by an afferent arteriole, and a contractile muscular cuff to control pressure (the pressure pushes water and solutes through the capillary walls into Bowman's Capsule, leaving blood cells and the larger blood proteins stuck behind). Reabsorption and so on are explained in cellular terms, e.g., by the special properties of the epithelial cells that line the nephron's long tubule; those special properties are in turn explained in terms of the physical chemistry of the cell membranes.

The brain is no exception to this hierarchical picture of the organism and its organs. *Neurons* are cells, comprised of *somata* containing a nucleus and protoplasm, and fibers attached to those somata, which fibers have rather dramatically isolable functions; and we are told even of smaller functional items such as the ionic pumps, which maintain high potassium concentration inside. Neurons themselves are grouped into nerve nets and other structures, such as columnar formations, which in turn combine to form larger, more clearly functional (though not so obviously modular) parts of the brain. The auditory system is a fair example. There is evidence that the auditory cortex displays two-dimensional columnar organization:[5] columns of variously specialized cells arranged along one axis respond selectively to frequencies indicated by incoming impulses from the auditory nerve, while columns roughly orthogonal to these somehow coordinate input from the one ear with input from the other. The particular sensitivities of the specialized cells is to be explained in turn by reference to ion transfer across cell membranes, and so on down. For its own part, the auditory cortex interacts with other higher-level agencies – the thalamus, the superior colliculus, and other cortical areas – which interactions are highly structured.

Thus do an aggregative ontology and a top–down epistemology of nature collaborate. The collaboration has been eloquently argued for the science of psychology in particular, by Attneave (1960), Fodor (this volume), and Dennett (1978). I shall develop the point at some length, following Lycan (1981a).

Homuncular Functionalism

Dennett (1978, p. 80) takes his cue from the methodology of certain AI research projects.[6]

> The AI researcher *starts* with an intentionally characterized problem (e.g., how can I get a computer to *understand* questions of English?), breaks it down into subproblems that are also intentionally characterized (e.g., how do I get the computer to *recognize* questions, *distinguish* subjects from predicates, *ignore* irrelevant parsings?) and then breaks these problems

down still further until finally he reaches problem or task descriptions that are obviously mechanistic.

Dennett extrapolates this methodological passage to the case of human psychology, and I take it to suggest that we view a *person* as a corporate entity that corporately performs many immensely complex functions – functions of the sort usually called mental or psychological. A psychologist who adopts Fodor's and Dennett's AI-inspired methodology will describe this person by means of a flow chart, which depicts the person's immediately subpersonal agencies and their many and various routes of access to each other that enable them to cooperate in carrying out the purposes of the containing "institution" or organism that that person is. Each of the immediately subpersonal agencies, represented by a "black box" on the original flow chart, is in turn describable by its own flow chart, that breaks *it* into further, sub-subpersonal agencies that cooperate to fulfill *its* purposes, and so on. On this view, the psychological capacities of a person and the various administrative units of a corporate organization stand in functional hierarchies of just the same type and in just the same sense.

To characterize the psychologists' quest in the way I have is to see them as first noting some intentionally or otherwise psychologically characterized abilities of the human subject at the level of data or phenomena, and positing – as theoretical entities – the homunculi or subpersonal agencies that are needed to explain the subject's having those abilities. Then the psychologists posit further, smaller homunculi in order to explain the previously posited molar behavior of the original homunculi, etc., etc. It is this feature of the Attneave/Fodor/Dennett model that ingeniously blocks the standard Rylean infinite-regress objection to homuncular theories in psychology.[7] We explain the successful activity of one homunculus, not by idly positing a second homunculus within it that successfully performs that activity, but by positing *a team* consisting of several smaller, individually less talented and more specialized homunculi – and detailing the ways in which the team members cooperate in order to produce their joint or corporate output.

Cognitive and perceptual psychologists have a reasonably good idea of the sorts of subpersonal agencies that will have to be assumed to be functioning within a human being in order for that human being to be able to perform the actions and other functions that it performs. Dennett (1978, ch. 9) mentions, at the immediately subpersonal level, a "print-out component" or speech center,[8] a "higher executive or *Control* component," a "short-term memory store or buffer memory," a "perceptual analysis component," and a "prob-lem-solving component." And Dennett (1978, ch. 11) examines, in some clinical detail, a multi-leveled subpersonal structure that models the behavior that manifests human pain. "Behavior" here must be understood very richly, since Den-nett scrupulously takes into account, not just the usual sorts of behavior that are common coin among philosophical Behaviorists and the apostles of commonsense psychology, but subtler pheno-mena as well: very small differences in our phe-nomenological descriptions of pain; infrequently remarked phenomena such as the felt time lag between our feeling that we have been burned and our feeling the deep pain of the burn; and (most interesting from the Homunctionalist point of view) the grandly varied effects of a number of different kinds of anesthetics and other drugs on a patient's live and retrospective reports concerning pain. Considerations of these various sorts serve the psychologists (and Dennett) as vivid pointers toward complexities in the relevant functional organization of the CNS, indicating the distinct black-box components at various levels of institu-tional organization that we must represent in our hierarchically arranged flow diagrams – the kinds of receptors, inhibitors, filters, damping mechan-isms, triggers, and so on that we must posit – and the comparably various sorts of pathways that con-nect these components with each other and with the grosser functional components of their owners such as perceptual analyzers, information stores, and the speech center.

The homuncular approach, teleologically inter-preted, has many advantages. I shall recount them when I have said a bit more about teleology. In the meantime, I put my cards on the table as regards the general form of a type-identification of the mental with the not-so-obviously mental: I pro-pose to type-identify a mental state with the prop-erty of having such-and-such an institutionally characterized state of affairs obtaining in one (or more) of one's appropriate homunctional depart-ments or subagencies. (The subagencies are those that would be depicted in the flow charts asso-ciated with their owners at various levels of insti-tutional abstraction.) The same holds for mental events, processes, and properties. To be in pain of type T, we might say, is for one's sub- ... subpersonal ϕ-er to be in a characteristic state $S_T(\phi)$, or for a characteristic activity $A_T(\phi)$ to be going on in one's ϕ-er.

Homunculi and Teleology

It may be protested that the characterization "ϕ-er" and "$S_T(\phi)$" are themselves only implicitly defined by a teleological map of the organism, and that explications of them in turn would contain ultimately ineliminable references to other teleo-logically characterized agencies and states of the organism. This is plausible, but relatively harm-less. Our job as philosophers of mind was to explic-ate the mental in a reductive (and noncircular) way, and this I am doing, by reducing mental characterization to homuncular institutional ones, which are teleological characterizations at various levels of functional abstraction. I am not addition-ally required to reduce the institutional character-izations to "nicer," more structural ones; if there were a reduction of institutional types to, say, physiological types, then on Homunctionalism the Identity Theory would be true. Institutional *types* (at any given hierarchical level of abstraction) are irreducible, though I assume throughout that institutional *tokens* are reducible in the sense of strict identity, all the way down to the subatomic level.

In fact, the irreducibility of institutional types makes for a mark in favor of Homunctionalism as a philosophical theory of the mental. As Donald Davidson and Wilfrid Sellars have both observed, an adequate theory of mind must, among its other tasks, explain the existence of the mind–body problem itself; this would involve explaining why the mental *seems* so different from the physical as to occasion Cartesianism in the naive, why it has historically proved so difficult even for the soph-isticated to formulate a plausible reduction of the mental to the physical, and why our mental con-cepts as a family seem to comprise a "seamless whole," conceptually quite unrelated to the physiological or physical family.[9] Homunctional-ism provides the rudiments of such explanations. The apparent irreducibility of the mental is the genuine irreducibility of institutional types to the less teleological.[10] The difficulty of outlining a tenable reduction of the mental even to the institu-tional is due to our ignorance of the organizational workings of the institution itself at a sufficiently low level of abstraction. Nor is the irreducibility of institutional types to more physiological types an embarrassment, so long as our system of institutional categories, our system of physiological categories, and our system of physical categories are just alternative groupings of the same tokens.

Some philosophers might find the Homunctionalist "reduction" very cold comfort. Certainly it would bore anyone who antecedently understands teleological characterizations of things *in terms of* mental items such as desires or intentions. Of course, as the foregoing discussion implies, I do not understand teleological talk in that way; rather, I am taking mental types to form a small subclass of teleological types occurring for the most part at a high level of functional abstraction. But if so, then how *do* I understand the teleological?

On this general issue I have little of my own to contribute. I hope, and am inclined to believe, that the teleological characterizations that Homunctionalism requires can be independently explained in evolutionary terms. This hope is considerably encouraged by the work of Karl Popper, William Wimsatt, Larry Wright, Karen Neander, and other philosophers of biology;[11] I cannot improve on their technical discussions. However, I do want to make one theoretical point, and then offer one example to back it up.

The theoretical point is that the teleologicalness of characterizations is a matter of degree: some characterizations of a thing are more teleological than others. One and the same space-time slice may be occupied by a collection of molecules, a piece of very hard stuff, a metal strip with an articulated flange, a mover of tumblers, a key, an unlocker of doors, an allower of entry to hotel rooms, a facilitator of adulterous liaisons, a destroyer of souls. Thus, we cannot split our theory of nature neatly into a well-behaved, purely mechanistic part and dubious, messy vitalistic part better ignored or done away with. And for this reason we cannot maintain that a reduction of the mental to the teleological is no gain in ontological tractability; highly teleological characterizations, unlike naive and explicated mental characterizations, have the virtue of shading off fairly smoothly into (more) brutely physical ones.[12]

Let me give one illustration pertinent to psychology. Consider an organism capable of *recognizing faces* (to take one of Dennett's nice examples of a programmable psychological capacity). There is plenty of point to the question of *how* the organism

does its job; the creature might accomplish its face-recognizing by being built according to any number of entirely dissimilar functional plans. Suppose the particular plan it does use is as follows: It will accept the command to identify only when it is given as input a front view, right profile, or left profile. The executive routine will direct a *viewpoint locator* to look over the perceptual display, and the viewpoint locator will sort the input into one of the three possible orientation categories. The display will then be shown to the appropriate *analyzer*, which will produce as output a coding of the display's content. A *librarian* will check this coded formula against the stock of similarly coded visual reports already stored in the organism's memory; if it finds a match, it will look at the identification tag attached to the matching code formula and show the tag to the organism's *public relations officer*, who will give phonological instructions to the *motor subroutines* that will result in the organism's publicly and loudly pronouncing a name.

Knowing that this is the way in which our particular face-recognizer performs its job, we may want to ask for further details. We may want to know how the viewpoint locator works (is it a simple template?), or how the PR office is organized, or what kinds of subcomponents the analyzer employs. Suppose the analyzer is found to consist of a *projector*, which imposes a grid on the visual display, and a scanner, which runs through the grid a square at a time and produces a binary code number. We may go on to ask how the scanner works, and be told that it consists mainly of a light meter that registers a certain degree of darkness at a square and reports "0" or "1" accordingly; we may ask how the light meter works and be told some things about photosensitive chemicals, etc., etc. Now at what point in this descent through the institutional hierarchy (from *recognizer* to *scanner* to *light meter* to *photosensitive substance*, and as much further down as one might care to go) does our characterization stop being teleological, period, and start being purely mechanical, period? I think it is clear that there is no such point, but rather a finely grained continuum connecting the abstract and highly teleological to the grittily concrete and only barely teleological. And this is why the mental can *seem* totally distinct and cut off from the physiochemical without *being*, ontologically, any such thing.[13]

A final word about my reliance on barely explicated teleology: I do not claim that barely explicated

William G. Lycan

teleology is good or desirable. I do not like it at all, myself. My point is only that the mystery of the mental is *no greater than* the mystery of the heart, the kidney, the carburetor, or the pocket calculator. And as an ontological point it is a very comforting one.[14]

Advantages of the Teleological Approach

The reader will not have failed to notice that I take *function* very seriously and literally: as honest-to-goodness natural teleology.[15] The policy of taking "function" teleologically has some key virtues: (i) As we have seen, a teleological understanding of "function" helps to account for the perceived *seamlessness* of the mental, the interlocking of mental notions in a way that has nothing visibly to do with chemical and physical concepts.[16] (ii) By imposing a teleological requirement on the notion of functional realization, we avoid all the standard counterexamples to Machine Functionalism, and, I would claim, to any other version of Functionalism; see below. (iii) A teleological functionalism also helps us to understand the nature of biological and psychological *laws*, particularly in the face of Davidsonian skepticism about the latter (Lycan 1981b; Cummins 1983). (iv) If teleological characterizations are themselves explicated in evolutionary terms, then our capacities for mental states themselves become more readily explicable by final cause; it is more obvious why we have pains, beliefs, desires, and so on.[17] (v) The teleological view affords the beginnings of an account of *intentionality* that avoids the standard difficulties for other naturalistic accounts and in particular allows brain states and events to have *false* intentional content. Causal and nomological theories of intentionality tend to falter on this last task (see Lycan 1989).

I have argued above that we need a notion of teleology that comes in degrees, or at least allows for degrees of teleologicalness of characterization, and that we already have such a notion, hard as it may be to explicate – recall the examples of the face-recognizer and the key. Philosophers may differ among themselves as to the correct analysis of this degree notion of teleology – for my own part, I tend to see the degrees as determined by amenability to explanation by final cause, where explanation "by final cause" is reconstrued in turn as a sort of evolutionary explanation (though some

details of this remain to be worked out). But two main points are already clear: (i) At least for single organisms, degrees of teleologicalness of characterization correspond rather nicely to levels of nature.[18] And (ii) there is no single spot *either* on the continuum of teleologicalness or amid the various levels of nature where it is plainly natural to drive a decisive wedge, where descriptions of nature can be split neatly into a well-behaved, purely "structural," purely mechanistic mode and a more abstract and more dubious, intentional, and perhaps vitalistic mode – certainly not any spot that also corresponds to any intuitive distinction between the psychological and the merely chemical, for there is too much and too various biology in between.

My own panpsychist or at least panteleologic tendencies are showing now. Many tougher-minded philosophers will find them fanciful at best, and of course (in my lucid moments) I am prepared to admit that it is hard to see any use in regarding, say, *atomic*-level description as teleological to any degree;[19] certainly explanation-by-final-cause does not persist all the way down. *But*: unmistakably teleological characterization (description that is obviously teleological to some however small degree) persists *as far* down as could possibly be relevant to psychology (well below neuroanatomy, for example). And the *role/occupant* distinction extends much further down still. Thus the vaunted "function"/"structure" distinction as ordinarily conceived by philosophers fails to get a grip on human psychology where it lives. . . .

Everything I have said so far may seem dull and obvious. I hope it does. I am trying to call attention to what I consider a home truth about the structure of the physical world, because I think neglect of this truth, inattention to the hierarchical nature of Nature, has led to significant errors about consciousness and qualia. In what remains I shall briefly discuss a few.

Block (1981), Lycan (1987), and others have put forward various counterexample cases, designed to show that having a functional organization, however complex, is insufficient for hosting qualitative, phenomenal feely states; probably the best known and most discussed of these are Block's "homunculi-head" and "population of China" examples. If such counterexamples are to be rebutted, the Functionalist must exhibit some reasonable requirement that they fail to satisfy, despite their mimicking in one way or another the functional organization of a real sentient creature.

Homunctionalism teleologically understood does the trick with ease. For none of the systems imagined in the counterexamples is teleologically organized in anything like the right way; most are not even organisms at all (see Lycan 1987, chs 3 and 5).

Even if the puzzle cases fail to refute Homunctionalism, some problems of chauvinism and liberalism remain to be resolved. Whether or not Fodor and Block are right in suggesting that Putnam moved too far back toward Behaviorism in backing off from the Identity Theory, the Functionalist certainly bears the responsibility of finding a level of characterization of mental states that is neither so abstract or behavioristic as to rule out the possibility of inverted spectrum, etc., nor so specific and structural as to fall into chauvinism. Block himself goes on to argue that this problem is insoluble.

He raises the dilemma for the characterization of *inputs* and *outputs* in particular. Plainly, inputs and outputs cannot be characterized in human neural terms; this would chauvinistically preclude our awarding mental descriptions to machines, Martians, and other creatures who differ from us biologically, no matter what convincing credentials they might offer in defense of their sentience. On the other hand, inputs and outputs cannot be characterized in purely abstract terms (i.e., merely as "inputs" and "outputs"), since this will lead to the sort of ultraliberalism that Block has disparaged by means of his earlier examples and also by means of new ones, such as that of an economic system that has very complex inputs, outputs, and internal states but that certainly has no mental characteristics. Nor can we appeal to any particular sorts of interactions of the sentient being with its environment via inputs and outputs, since in a few cases (those of paralytics, brains *in vitro*, and the like) we want to award mental descriptions to objects that cannot succeed in interacting with their environments in any way. Block concludes,

> Is there a description of inputs and outputs specific enough to avoid liberalism, yet general enough to avoid chauvinism? I doubt that there is.
>
> Every proposal for a description of inputs and outputs I have seen or thought of is guilty of either liberalism or chauvinism. Though this

paper has focused on liberalism, chauvinism is the more pervasive problem.

> ...*there will be no physical characterizations that apply to all mental systems' inputs and outputs.* Hence, any attempt to formulate a functional description with physical characterizations of inputs and outputs will inevitably either exclude some [possible] systems with mentality or include some systems without mentality.
>
> ...On the other hand, as you will recall, characterizing inputs and outputs simply *as* inputs and outputs is inevitably liberal. I, for one, do not see how functionalism can describe inputs and outputs without falling afoul of either liberalism or chauvinism, or abandoning the original project of characterizing mentality in nonmental terms. I do not claim that this is a conclusive argument against functionalism. Rather, like the functionalist argument against physicalism, it is perhaps best construed as a burden of proof argument.

I am not sure how detailed a plan Block is demanding of the Functionalist here, though I have agreed that, on a mild-mannered understanding of "burden of proof," Block's challenge is one that the functionalist does bear the burden of meeting. The question is whether this burden is as prohibitively heavy as Block seems to assume. And there are at least three factors that I think lighten it considerably and give us some cause for optimism:

First, there is a line of argument that offers at least some slight positive reason or natural motivation for thinking that the dilemma of chauvinism and liberalism (either in regard to inputs and outputs or in regard to the inner states that the Functionalist identifies with our mental states) does admit a solution. It begins as a slippery-slope argument. Block has stated the dilemma very uncompromisingly, implying that one's only choices are (a) to characterize inputs and outputs physiologically and be a chauvinist, or (b) to characterize inputs and outputs "purely abstractly" and be a bleeding heart. But this brutal statement of the alternatives overlooks the fact...that functional abstraction is a matter of degree. Purely physiological characterization is an extreme, lying at the lower or "more structural" end of the spectrum; "purely abstract" characterization is the opposite extreme, lying at the higher or "more functional" end. Notice that...there are characterizations that are even *more* "structural" than physiological ones are, such as microphysical ones, relative to which physiological ones are "functional"; similarly, there are really more abstract characterizations than "input" and "output" themselves, such as "transfer," "motion," or even "occurrence." If it is true, as it seems to be, that "purely abstract" characterizations and physiological characterizations merely lie near the two ends of a continuum of functional abstraction, then it is reasonable to expect that there exists some intermediate level of abstraction that would yield characterizations that rules out the Bolivian economy, the Abnegonian Galaxy, the microbiology of the Everglades and their ilk, but would make room for human beings, molluscs, Martians, and brains *in vitro*. The truth lies (as it so often does) somewhere in between, and, depending on which aspect of which mental state interests one, not always at the same spot in between either. Wait and see what resources will be available at various intermediate levels.[20] . . .

Let us remember in addition (here is my second point in response to Block's challenge) that nothing forces us to assume that all the different kinds of mental states occur at the *same* level of functional abstraction. The intuitively "more behavioral" sorts of mental states, such as beliefs and desires and intentions, presumably occur at a relatively high level of abstraction, and this makes it easy for us to ascribe beliefs and desires and intentions to Martians whose overt behavior and very superficial psychology match ours; the same is true of highly "informational" mental activities such as remembering and (literal) computing. Intuitively, "less behavioral," more qualitative mental states probably occur at a much lower level of abstraction; sensings that have certain particular kinds of qualitative characters probably *are* quite specific to species (at least, we should not be very surprised to find out that this was so), and quite possibly our Martian's humanoid behavior *is* prompted by his having sensations (or possibly "schmensations") somewhat unlike ours, despite his superficial behavioral similarities to us.

I am not aware that anyone has ever explicitly defended Two-Levelism as such.[21] But Two-Levelism seems to be what lies directly behind such apparent dilemmas as Block's "problem of the inputs and the outputs."

Parallel considerations apply to the problem of intentionality. We think that a state of an organism is either an intentional state or not, period, and

then we wonder what the functional or institutional locus of intentionality might be. I do not think intentionality can be a *purely* functional property at all, for reasons that are now familiar,[22] but insofar as it is, I think we would do well to admit that intentionality itself comes in degrees.[23] The "marks" of intentionality or aboutness are none too clear, but what does seem clear upon reflection is that there is an intermediate level of functional characterization that offers a *kind* of directedness-upon-a-possibly-nonexistent-object-or-type that nevertheless falls short of the rich, full-blooded intentionality exhibited by the human mind. At this intermediate level, we speak systems-theoretically of "detectors," "scanners," "filters," "inhibitors," and the like, meaning these terms quite literally but without actually imputing *thought* or what might be called "occurrent" aboutness. But I must leave the development of these observations for another occasion.[24]

Third, it might be profitable for us simply to stand by the "purely abstract" characterization of inputs and outputs, throwing the whole problem of chauvinism and liberalism back onto our characterization of internal states and events. There are so many possibilities, so many different levels of abstraction in the functional hierarchy as it applies to the brain (many of which overlap and cut across each other), that it seems quite reasonable to expect there to be, for each mental state-type, some middle way between chauvinism and liberalism – not necessarily the *same* middle way for each state-type. It is simply an error to think that all mental phenomena must be functionally located at the same level, or that any single mental state must be localized entirely at one level. Regarding the "more functional," *nearly* behavioristic mental states, perhaps we would not even mind admitting that an economic system or the population of China could have such states (say, dispositional beliefs), if it were to come to that. And possibly at the least functional end of the continuum there are even mental state-types of which the Identity Theory is true, though it is hard to think of any mental state that is as "qualitative" as that.

The foregoing remarks suggest a final additional response to Block's "absent qualia" arguments, one that I think is virtually conclusive. Earlier I characterized Block's intuitive disquiet over Functionalism as being a matter of feeling the incongruity between the relationalness of Functionalist explications and the homogeneous, primitively *monadic* qualitative characters of their explicanda; I gather that this incongruity seems to him absolute. Notice that evidently he has no similar objection to the Identity Theory; like any other materialist, he would simply charge the Identity Theorist with chauvinism and raise no further complaint. After all, one of the theory's main advantages was its ability to account for the possibility of inverted spectrum or other inner variation despite outward conformity. But if we also accept my claim that Homunctional characterizations and physiological characterizations of states of persons reflect merely different levels of abstraction within a surrounding functional hierarchy or continuum, then we can no longer distinguish the Functionalist from the Identity Theorist in any absolute way. "Neuron," for example, may be understood either as a physiological term (denoting a kind of human cell) or as a (teleo-) functional term (denoting a relayer of electrical charge); on *either* construal it stands for an instantiable – if you like, for a role being played by a group of more fundamental objects. Thus, *even the Identity Theorist is a Functionalist* – one who locates mental entities at a very low level of abstraction. The moral is that if Block does want to insist that Functionalist psychology is stymied by a principled incongruity of the sort I have mentioned and that a philosophy of mind that explicates mental items in terms of relational roles or instantiables cannot in principle accommodate the intractable monadicity of qualia, then one would have to make the same charge against the Identity Theorist as well, and this, I trust, he feels no intuitive compulsion to do.[25] In fact, Block lets that Theory cop a plea of species chauvinism overall, and even allows that it is probably true of some mental properties.

There is an idea, brought on by blind Two-Levelism, that Functionalism differs somehow *conceptually or structurally* from the Identity Theory, in such a way as to incur different sorts of objections. As I have said, the Identity Theory is just an empirically special case of Functionalism, one that (implausibly) locates all mental states at the same very low level of institutional abstraction – the neuroanatomical. Thus there should be no purely conceptual or philosophical objections that apply to Functionalism that do not apply to the Identity Theory or vice versa, even if one is empirically less reasonable than the other. Yet philosophers such as Block have claimed to see such objections. If my doctrine of the continuity of nature is right, something must be wrong here;

for neuroanatomical terms are functional and so relational just as higher-organizational terms are, albeit at a lower level of abstraction. If there is a principled incongruity between relational characterization and the intrinsicness of phenomenal quality, and if that incongruity stymies Functionalism, then it should preclude the Identity Theory as well.[26]

Consider a second example of such an objection: Block further contends that Functionalism is unable to allow the possibility of "inverted spectrum" or other types of internally switched qualia unreflected even counterfactually in behavior – unable in a way that the Identity Theory is not, since the Identity Theory is *made to order* for representing cases of inverted qualia. But if my reflections on the continuity of levels of nature are right, something must be amiss here. And something is. Just as it is easy to imagine undetectably switched *neurophysiology* underlying inverted spectrum (see Lycan 1973), it is easy to imagine a switching of functional components more abstractly described (though doubtless there are limits to this, and quite possibly one could not ascend to a very much higher level of abstraction and keep the inversion behaviorally undetectable).

The truth of the matter is obscured by a pragmatic ambiguity in the notion of "inverted qualia," an ambiguity that I think has lent Block rhetorical aid even though it is far from subtle. To wit, there is a hidden parameter: "inverted" *with respect to what?* (Compare the correlative relation of *supervenience*: supervenient on what?) Traditionally, "inverted spectrum" has meant (color) qualia inverted with respect to actual and counterfactual input–output relations alone. Either from duty or by inclination, Analytical Behaviorists and Wittgensteinians denied the conceivability of *that* inversion, but most people's ordinary modal intuitions have favored it, and Identity and Functionalist theories alike have accommodated it with ease; it has never posed any threat to Functionalism. What would damage Functionalism is the conceivability of qualia inverted with respect to I–O relations *plus* internal functional organization. *This* inversion hypothesis is much stronger and more daring. Its possibility is controversial to say the least. Indeed, to assert it is simply to deny the truth of Functionalism – it is to say without argument that two organisms could differ in their qualitative states even though they were exactly alike in their entire global functional organization, *at whatever level of institutional abstraction is in question*. Of course there have been philosophers who have insisted without argument on the metaphysical possibility of organisms' differing in their qualitative states despite being *molecular* duplicates, for that matter, but such insistence has no intrinsic credibility even if the relevant theories of mind turn out in the end to be false. The possibility of spectrum inverted with respect to I–O relations alone is a well-entrenched and respectable though I suppose defeasible modal intuition; the possibility of spectrum inverted with respect to I–O relations *plus internal functional organization at however low a level of abstraction proponents feel it plausible to name* is anything but obvious and in conflict with some intuitively plausible supervenience theses.

(Some relationally minded theorists may find it natural to assume a certain *privileged* level of abstraction at the outset. For example, "*analytical* functionalists," or as I prefer to call them, commonsense relationalists, who hold that the *meanings of mental terms* are determined by the causal roles associated with those terms by common sense or "folk psychology," thereby deny themselves appeal to any level of functional organization lower than is accessible to common sense.[27] Folk psychology aside, the "High Church" computationalists[28] scorn appeal to human biology even within a purely *scientific* account of cognition and behavior, though their own chosen level of nature is none too clearly specified.[29] A theorist who cleaves to such a privileged level of organization may of course admit "inverted spectrum" relative to that chosen level, so long as he or she is willing to type-identify qualia with still lower-level items.[30]

Two Alternative Strategies

I have recommended one way of solving the problems of chauvinism and liberalism concerning qualia within a Functionalist ontology of the mental. There are alternative possible strategies. One alternative approach would be to bifurcate our view of the mental, by simply taking over the distinction between a mental state and its qualitative character, explicating the states in functional terms and the characters in rather broad physiological terms, tolerating the consequence that inverted spectrum or lesser interpersonal differences in qualia might be more prevalent than we think (viz., exactly as prevalent as are interpersonal

physiological differences of comparable magnitude).[31]

Pain would present a useful test case for this second suggested way of accommodating qualia. An interesting and distinctive thing about pain is that (unlike most other mental states) it has both a strongly associated behavior pattern *and* vivid introspectible feely properties. This means, on the present proposal, that pain states may receive *multileveled* analyses. For example (just to speculate a bit), we might end up wanting to classify any internal state of an organism that played pain's usual "gross" behavioral role (that of being caused by damage and producing withdrawal- *cum*-favoring) as being a pain, but to distinguish the feels of pains according to the states' physiological bases.[32] It would follow that, although mollusks and Martians have pains, their pains probably feel differently to them from the ways in which our pains feel to us. It would also follow that a state that feels like a pain state of mine might in a differently organized creature be a mental state of some kind other than pain; some philosophers may find this crassly counterintuitive.

Incidentally, the bifurcated view has become fairly popular in the past few years,[33] and is often expressed by saying that (e.g.) "pain itself is functional while its specific feel is neurophysiological." But the latter formulation again presupposes Two-Levelism. See the "functional"/"structural" distinction as level-relative, and the bifurcated theory collapses into a pointlessly specific version of the thesis (which I hope will become a truism) that mental states and their qualitative characters may well not be explicated in terms of the same level of nature (in particular, the locus of qualitative character may be lower in the hierarchy than that of the mental state generically considered). I emphatically agree with the latter thesis, as I have already indicated, but it is no competing *alternative* to Functionalism.

A third alternative approach suggests itself for the case of bodily sensations (though I doubt whether it could easily be applied to perceptual qualia). It is to suppose that feelings that seem phenomenally to be simple are actually complex and that the distinctive quale associated with a feeling of a certain type is really the coincidence or superimposition of a number of distinct, individually manageable homunctional features. I think this line, rather than that adumbrated in the foregoing paragraph, is the most plausible to take for the case of pain, because it is strongly suggested by the anesthesiological data collected and summarized by Dennett (1978, ch. 11). What these data seem to indicate is that chemically different anesthetics and analgesics disrupt subjects' normal "pain" subroutines at different functional junctures, eliciting from the subjects quite different verbal reports of their effects. Of a group of subjects suffering pain of roughly the same kind and intensity, one subgroup given drug *A* may report that the pain has diminished or gone away entirely, whereas a subgroup given drug *B* may report that although they know that the pain is still there, they cannot feel it; a subgroup given drug *C* may say that although they can still feel the pain just as intensely as ever, they do not *mind* any more; and so on. That some of these reports sound funny to us (they would be pooh-poohed as "unintelligible" by some Wittgensteinians) naturally reflects the fact that the subjects' normal inner workings are being disrupted, and their normal inner experience of pain being altered, by the drugs. What the drugs seem to be doing is *splitting off components* of the subjects' phenomenal experience of the pain, by splitting off component subsubroutines of its rather complicated functional basis. And if this is so, it follows that our phenomenal experience of pain *has* components – it is a complex, consisting (perhaps) of urges, desires, impulses, and beliefs, probably occurring at quite different levels of institutional abstraction. If these components can individually be split off from each other by drugs, then we may perform a *Gedankenexperiment* in which we hypothetically take a suffering subject, split off one component of his pain by administering drug *A*, then split off another component by administering drug *B*, and repeat

this process, eliciting reports as we go to keep track of how we are doing. It seems to me plausible to think that if we were to keep this up, disrupting one access pathway after another and eliminating the component urges, desires, and beliefs one by one, we would sooner or later succeed in eliminating the pain itself; it also seems that if we were to reverse the process – to begin restoring the pathways by withholding the various drugs one by one – the subject would necessarily come to feel the full-fledged pain again (provided his damaged tissues had not been repaired in the meantime). I believe this makes it reasonable to suppose that some (again) *multileveled* proper subsequence of the relevant complex of functional goings-on is both necessary and sufficient for the occurrence of the pain, contrary to the spirit of Block's antiliberalism.

I do not know how to make a conclusive choice among the three alternative approaches I have described, or what sorts of further evidence we might seek. I have run through some of the options only in order to show that the Homunctionalist has fairly rich resources that can be brought to bear both on the dilemma of chauvinism and liberalism and on the positive task of accounting for qualia. On the basis of these resources I believe we are entitled to conclude that Block's pessimism about qualia is unwarranted. . . .

If my continuity doctrine is obvious as stated, it has not been obvious enough to some of our leading philosophers of mind. I hope the foregoing demonstrations will also serve to make Homunctionalism all the more attractive as a theory of the mental.

Notes

1 I believe just as firmly in some form of act-utilitarianism in ethics, but the sacred principle of utility itself forbids my even telling you this, much less committing (detectable) murders in its name.

2 This multileveled hierarchical structure was noted and eloquently presented by Herbert A. Simon (1969); I do not know if the idea predates him. William C. Wimsatt has also written brilliantly on it (1976). Its application to psychology was first brought to my attention by Fodor (1968) and Dennett (this volume); see further references below.

3 I have in mind Lewis Thomas's (1974) discussion of insect societies and of the relation between

human beings and their own mitochondria. The mereology of "organisms" is highly interest-relative. Note well, we must grant a pluralism of different reductive relations between levels of nature; consider also the entirely tenable notion of the corporation as person (Biro 1981; French 1984; Brooks 1986).

4 For a rich exposition and defense of the strategy, see Cummins (1983). However, Richardson (1983) throws some fairly cold water.

5 For philosophically relevant discussion and references, see P. M. Churchland (1986) and P. S. Churchland (1986).

6 Dennett's main concern in the work containing the following passage is the explication of intentionality.

That concern is not mine here; I am interested only in homuncular breakdown *per se*.

7 In fact, as David Armstrong has pointed out to me, the present maneuver blocks a number of typical infinite-regress arguments in the philosophy of mind, including Ryle's complaint against volitional theories of deciding. Dennett himself wields it against "Hume's problem" regarding self-understanding representations (1978, pp. 122ff.).

8 For an actual hands-on homuncular breakdown of the speech center, see figure 1, p. 262 of Lycan (1984).

9 For stout insistence of this, see Davidson (1970).

10 Thus, Smart's example of the logic of "nation" statements' being different from the logic of "citizen" statements may have been more apropos than he imagined.

11 Popper (1972); Wimsatt (1972); Wright (1973); Millikan (1984); Neander (1981, 1983). Neander's evolutionary explication is the best I know. It is criticized with effect by E. Prior in an unpublished note and by Pargetter and Bigelow (1987); the truth seems to me to lie somewhere in between. Jonathan Bennett (1976) offers a different naturalistic approach to teleology due to Ann Wilbur MacKenzie (1972) (and in discussion has urged me to switch).

12 Characterizations of the contents of our space-time slice may thus be arranged in a continuum, from the least teleological to the most (highly) teleological. This continuum corresponds fairly neatly to the hierarchy of functional instantiation or realization. The molecules jointly realize, or play the role of, the piece of metal; the piece of metal plays the role of the key; the key serves as our door-unlocker; and so on. The prevalence of functional hierarchies of this kind, I believe, is what encourages ontological reduction and the idea that "everything is ultimately a matter of physics." On the relations between teleology viewed from an evolutionary perspective, functional hierarchies, ontology, and the methodology of scientific reduction, see again Wimsatt (1976). I have also profited from reading Mellick (1973), and see Matthen and Levy (1984).

13 As Jerry Fodor has pointed out to me in discussion, there is one tolerably clear distinction that a Two-Leveler might have in mind and that is absolute: it is the distinction between objects whose proper parts are essential to them and objects whose parts are not. For example, a bicycle's or even a tree's parts are replaceable, while a water molecule's parts perhaps are not (one might argue either that if the molecule were to lose one of its hydrogen or oxygen atoms it would not be *that* molecule or that without the right sorts of atoms it would not be a water molecule at all). I agree that this distinction is gen-

uine, and I expect it has some metaphysical importance. But it has no *psychological* importance. The level of chemistry is far too low in the institutional hierarchy to affect mentation; that is, if two neuro-anatomies are just the same even though they are realized by different chemicals, psychology is the same.

14 Amelie Rorty has suggested to me the Aristotelian idea of explaining an organism's component functions (more exactly, of explaining its-functions'-constituting-its-thriving) by reference to the suitability of those functions for the material conditions of the organism's species. This idea fits well with the etiological account of function that I tend to favor. Given a relatively undifferentiated mass of "lower" biological material at a much earlier evolutionary stage, how would it clump together and articulate itself in order to face the world at large in a more robust and less vulnerable way? Its own "structural" or "material" nature would enforce some answers and suggest still others, and given selection pressures of various now retrodictable sorts it is no surprise that many or most of these answers have been realized. If "function" is understood in evolutionary terms, then, function itself gets explained in this way, in terms of the propensities of the organism's material substratum. I take that explanation to complement, rather than to compete with, "downward-causation" explanations based in higher levels of nature (of the sort Wimsatt talks about). In fact, we get a sort of pincer movement: selection pressure from much higher levels interacting with bottom-up pressure from the nature and propensities of the particular chemical constitution of the pre-existing neighborhood, the two pressures jointly molding what lies between. But one might want to emphasize the bottom-up pressure at the expense of higher-level explanations. *In some sense* that emphasis has to be right, given supervenience of top on bottom, though it is tricky to work out all the different up–down interrelations there are.

Rorty points out (in correspondence) that full-scale multiple realizability must be distinguished from mere functional characterization of states of organisms, since detailed accounts of function tend to put strict requirements on realizing-stuff; there is a trade-off here. But I do not see that the Aristotelian bottom-up explanation strategy *per se* counts against multiple realizability. For the same functional answers or solutions might well be hit upon by chemically quite different bunches of primordial stuff. Rorty offers the example of *eating*: Computers do not eat, in any literal sense, and the earth does not ingest rain; multiple realizability fails even though the activity is functionally characterized. I want to make the same sort of rejoinder that I shall be making to an argument of Block's below: Of course computers and other (even biologic) entities do not eat; but there is an intermediate, more abstract characterization of eating itself – *holotropism* as it was called in my college biology classes – which excludes computers but includes lots of species biochemically quite different from ours; it has something to do with acquiring proteins very similar to one's own and physically homogenizing them and ingesting them and making them part of one without major rearrangement of amino acids or something of the sort – at any rate, it is a form of nourishment that is sharply distinguished from many other species' and is rather distinctive of our phylum or whatever. This point checks nicely with my usual idea of functional characterizations that hold for intermediate levels of nature and are neither too vague and general nor too chauvinistically species-bound.

15 Elliott Sober (this volume) praises this attitude as "putting the function back into functionalism"; cf. my remarks on p. 27 of Lycan (1981a) regarding Putnam and Fodor's pun on the word "function."

16 For details, see Lycan (1981b).

17 Why does pain hurt? Why could we not have a damage-signaling and repair-instigating system that was not uncomfortable? The answer is simple. Suppose I had just such a system, like the red warning light on my auto engine. Just as I habitually though irrationally ignore the warning light and vaguely hope it will go away, I would ignore a personal warning light if it did not intrinsically provide me with an urgent motive to do something about it.

18 Robert Van Gulick has presented me (in correspondence) with some meteorological and geological cases in which (apparent) degrees of teleologicalness do not follow levels of nature. Such cases are very much to the point, but I shall have to postpone going into them.

19 Ned Block, who violently disagrees with me on the present issues, once said (in conversation), "I'll give you *neurons* and *cells* and so on as functional, but when you come to *hydrogen* and *oxygen*, when you get right down to the level of *chemistry*, there's just nothing functional or teleological at all!" Oh, no? "Hydro-"*what*? "Oxy-"*what*? (The shot is a cheap one but immensely satisfying.)

20 "Wait till next year!" John Searle jeers in a different but very similar connection (1980). *Of course* wait till next year!

21 Save perhaps the "analytical functionalist," whose view I reject (see note 27).

22 Putnam (1975); Fodor (1980); Stich, this volume; Burge (1979); Lycan (1981c); . . .

23 This idea is anticipated in part by Dretske (1981). See also Van Gulick (this volume, 1982).

24 I would also observe that some current disputes within the cognitive science community are misconceived in the Two-Levelist way. For example, the "bottom-uppers" versus the "High-Church Computationalists" (see P. S. Churchland 1986, and Dennett 1986) and the New Connectionists versus the same (see Bechtel 1985). The New Connectionists in particular are a superb example of a biocomputational middle way. Somewhat in the same spirit is P. M. Churchland's (1986) "phase-space sandwich" model of sensorimotor coordination, based on Pellionisz and Llinas (1979, 1982); or rather, though *he* does not always think it in a mediating way, I count it as another feasible middle way *within the spirit of a properly teleologized functionalism.*

25 Wilfrid Sellars does. But that is another story . . .; see chapter 8 of Lycan (1987).

26 Block does not himself stress the relational/monadic contrast, but offers his differential intuitions raw; so he may remain unmoved by my foregoing *ad hominem* and simply insist that having a neurochemistry roughly like ours is a necessary condition for experiencing qualia, relational or not. Yet, I wonder, how could a *philosopher* know *that*? Is it aglow with the Natural Light?

27 I am indebted to Sydney Shoemaker for useful correspondence on this point. For my own part, I cannot accept analytical functionalism, for two reasons: (i) I reject the alternatively conceptual-analysis or implicit-definition theory of meaning on which that theory rests. (See Armstrong 1968 and Lewis 1972 for its two most explicit versions and defenses, and Lycan 1981b, especially note 10, for my alternative view of the semantics of mental terms; also, for a similar view, see Jacoby 1985.) (ii) I doubt that common sense or "folk psychology" contains enough information about mental entities to characterize their natures as richly as would be needed to avoid counterexample. Clothespin models of folk psychology would be pretty easy to come by, without the massive complexity and teleological organization that would warrant an ascription of real mentality.

28 The term is due to Dennett (1986).

29 Here I follow some recent writers in supposing that there are really any High Church Computationalists; I am not sure that any actual Functionalist has ever self-consciously intended the view. It is usually ascribed to Zenon Pylyshyn and Jerry Fodor, on the basis of some of their remarks about multiple realizability. Perhaps Ned Block does really hold it, or he would not continue to resist my case against Two-Levelism as begun in my 1981a.

30 See particularly (again) Bechtel (1985) and the references made therein.

31 Block hints on p. 460 that he might not find this suggestion entirely uncongenial. And see note 33.

32 This move would take some of the sting out of what I take to be an anti-Functionalist argument in David Lewis (1980).

33 Block hinted at this view, as I have mentioned. I developed the suggestion in Lycan (1981a), pp. 47–8. It has also been picked up by Hilary Putnam (1981), Sydney Shoemaker (1981), Patricia Kitcher (1982), Terence Horgan (1984), and Gregory Sheridan (1986) among others (Shoemaker calls its "selective parochialism").

References

Armstrong, D. M. (1968) *A Materialist Theory of the Mind*, Routledge & Kegan Paul.

Attneave, F. (1960) "In defense of homunculi," in W. Rosenblith (ed.), *Sensory Communication*, MIT Press.

Bechtel, P. W. (1985) "Contemporary connectionism: Are the new parallel distributed processing models cognitive or associationist?" *Behaviorism* 13, 53–61.

Bennett, J. (1976) *Linguistic Behaviour*, Cambridge University Press.

Bigelow, J. and Pargetter, R. (1987) "Functions," *Journal of Philosophy* 84, 181–96.

Biro, J. (1981) "Persons as corporate entities and corporations as persons," *Nature and System* 3, 173–80.

Block, N. J. (1981) "Psychologism and behaviorism," *Philosophical Review* 90, 5–43.

Brooks, D. H. M. (1986) "Group minds," *Australasian Journal of Philosophy* 64, 456–70.

Burge, T. (1979) "Individualism and the mental," in P. French, T. E. Uehling and H. Wettstein (eds), *Midwest Studies in Philosophy, vol. IV: Studies in Metaphysics*, University of Minnesota Press.

Churchland, P. M. (1986) "Some reductive strategies in cognitive neurobiology," *Mind* 95, 223–38.

Churchland, P. S. (1986) *Neurophilosophy*, Bradford Books/MIT Press.

Cummins, R. (1983) *The Nature of Psychological Explanation*, Bradford Books/MIT Press.

Davidson, D. (1970) "Mental events," in L. Foster and J. W. Swanson (eds), *Experience and Theory*, University of Massachusetts Press.

Dennett, D. C. (1978) *Brainstorms*, Bradford Books.

Dennett, D. C. (1986) "The logical geography of computational approaches: a view from the East Pole," in M. Brand and R. M. Harnish (eds), *The Representation of Knowledge and Belief*, University of Arizona Press.

Dretske, F. (1981) *Knowledge and the Flow of Information*, Bradford Books/MIT Press.

Fodor, J. A. (1980) "Methodological solipsism considered as a research strategy in cognitive psychology," *Behavioral and Brain Sciences* 3, 63–73.

French, P. (1984) *Collective and Corporate Responsibility*, Columbia University Press.

Horgan, T. (1984) "Functionalism, qualia, and the inverted spectrum," *Philosophy and Phenomenological Research* 44, 453–70.

Jacoby, H. (1985) "Eliminativism, meaning, and qualitative states," *Philosophical Studies* 47, 257–70.

Kitcher, P. (1982) "Two versions of the Identity Theory," *Erkenntnis* 17, 213–28.

Lewis, D. (1972) "Psychophysical and theoretical identifications," *Australasian Journal of Philosophy* 50, 249–58.

Lewis, D. (1980) "Mad pain and Martian pain," in N. Block (ed.), *Readings in Philosophy of Psychology*, vol. 1, Harvard University Press.

Lycan, W. (1973) "Inverted spectrum," *Ratio* 15, 315–19.

Lycan, W. (1981a) "Form, function, and feel," *Journal of Philosophy* 78, 24–50.

Lycan, W. (1981b) "Psychological laws," *Philosophical Topics* 12, 9–38.

Lycan, W. (1981c) "Toward a homuncular theory of believing," *Cognition and Brain Theory* 4, 139–59.

Lycan, W. (1984) *Logical Form in Natural Language*, Bradford Books/MIT Press.

Lycan, W. (1987) *Consciousness*, Bradford Books/MIT Press.

Lycan, W. (1989) "Ideas of representation," in *Mind, Value, and Culture: Essays in Honor of E. M. Adams* (edited by D. Weissbord), Ridgeview Publishing.

MacKenzie, A. W. (1972) "An analysis of purposive behavior," Cornell University doctoral dissertation.

Matthen, M. and Levy, E. (1984) "Teleology, error, and the human immune system," *Journal of Philosophy* 81, 351–71.

Mellick, D. (1973) "Behavioral strata," Ohio State University doctoral dissertation.

Millikan, R. G. (1984) *Language, Thought, and Other Biological Categories*, Bradford Books/MIT Press.

Neander, K. (1981) "Teleology in biology." Unpublished Xerox.

Neander, K. (1983) "Abnormal psychobiology," La Trobe University doctoral dissertation.

Pellionisz, A. and Llinas, R. (1979) "Brain modelling by tensor network theory and computer simulation. The cerebellum: distributed processor for predictive coordination," *Neuroscience* 4, 323–48.

Pellionisz, A. and Llinas, R. (1982) "Space-time representation in the brain. The cerebellum as a predictive space-time metric tensor," *Neuroscience* 7, 2,949–70.

Popper, K. (1972) "Of clouds and clocks: an approach to the problem of rationality and the freedom of man," in *Objective Knowledge: An Evolutionary Approach*, Oxford University Press.

Putnam, H. (1975) "The meaning of 'meaning'," in K. Gunderson (ed.), *Minnesota Studies in the Philosophy of Science, vol. 7: Language, Mind and Knowledge*, University of Minnesota Press.

Putnam, H. (1981) *Reason, Truth and History*, Cambridge University Press.

Richardson, R. (1983) "Computational models of mind." Unpublished monograph.

Searle, J. (1980) "Minds, brains and programs," *Behavioral and Brain Sciences* 3, 417–24.

Sheridan, G. (1983) "Can there be moral subjects in a physicalistic universe?" *Philosophy and Phenomenological Research* 43, 425–48.

Sheridan, G. (1986) "Selective parochialism and Shoemaker's argument for functionalism," typescript, Western Michigan University.

Shoemaker, S. (1981) "Some varieties of functionalism," *Philosophical Topics* 12, 93–119.

Simon, H. (1969) "The architecture of complexity," in *The Sciences of the Artificial*, MIT Press.

Thomas, L. (1974) *Lives of a Cell*, Bantam Books.

Van Gulick, R. (1982) "Mental representation – a functionalist view," *Pacific Philosophical Quarterly* 63, 3–20.

Wimsatt, W. C. (1972) "Teleology and the logical structure of function statements," *Studies in History and Philosophy of Science* 3, 1–80.

Wimsatt, W. C. (1976) "Reductionism, levels of organization, and the mind–body problem," in G. Globus, G. Maxwell, and I. Savodnik (eds), *Consciousness and the Brain*, Plenum.

Wright, L. (1973) "Functions," *Philosophical Review* 82, 139–68.

Putting the Function Back into Functionalism

Elliott Sober

Functionalism got off on the wrong foot. The problem was that *function* is ambiguous, and the doctrine was developed with the wrong meaning in mind. A mathematical function is a mapping from some objects to others; each input has a unique output. For example, we may talk about the plus function, wherein a pair of numbers is mapped on to their sum. On the other hand, there is the teleological concept of function – as when we say that the function of the heart is to pump blood. Corresponding to the first concept, there arose in the philosophy of mind a view I will call Turing Machine Functionalism. Corresponding to the second is the view I will call Teleological Functionalism. Functionalism as a solution to the mind/body problem should have been developed as a form of Teleological Functionalism. Instead, Functionalism usually was understood to mean Turing Machine Functionalism.

As a result of this early mis-step, functionalism is thought to face a number of decisive objections. I will argue that these objections dissolve, once Functionalism is understood teleologically. Not that this provides the mind/body problem with a solution, since the teleological idea has problems of its own. But if lessons are to be learned from the failure of theories, we must see what makes the best version of a theory fail.

Functionalism began as a reaction against the identity theory. Functionalism's negative insight was that psychological properties are not type-identical with physical properties. Psychological state types are multiply realizable (Putnam 1967; Block and Fodor 1972). But this claim about what psychological states are not had to be supplemented with some positive account of what the nature of psychological states is.

Functionalists found the beginning of a positive doctrine in their valve lifters and mouse traps (Fodor 1968). What makes a mouse trap a mouse trap is, roughly, that it plays a certain causal role. Given a free mouse as input, it produces a caught mouse as output. A particular functional state will bear certain cause and effect relationships to other states. Of course, the same is true of particular physical states; we can characterize what it is to be an acid in terms of the causal role that acidity plays (Lycan 1981). Functionalists hope to characterize psychological states in terms of their causal connections to behavior, to stimuli, and to other mental states. Only in so far as these provide substantive constraints on how psychological states are individuated does Functionalism become a nontrivial doctrine.

Quite distinct from this teleological idea – that the mind is a functional device just as a mouse trap is a functional device – lurked another suggestive idea. This is the thought that the mind is a computer. Here the idea is that for an individual to have various cognitive capacities is for the individual to have access to certain computer programs. To perceive something or to come to hold a particular belief is then understood as the execution of a series of computations.

This still does not count as even a candidate solution for the mind/body problem. If mental states are to be individuated computationally, how is one to understand the concept of computation? It is here that the idea behind Turing Machine Functionalism made its appearance. A computer computes by instantiating a machine table, which is just a function from inputs to outputs. The state the machine occupies determines what the machine should output and what state the machine should go into next.

The principle for individuating machine tables is the principle for individuating any mathematical function. Roughly, it is simply the requirement of an abstract isomorphism. When I successively add 1 to itself fourteen times, I am executing the "same" program that the ocean executes when it adds another layer of sand to the beach each day for a fortnight.

This Turing Machine development of the idea of Functionalism led to problems. Suppose we possess some psychological property P. Turing Machine Functionalism would have it that any individual will possess P precisely when it is abstractly isomorphic with us. It is rather clear, however, that this suggestion is neither necessary nor sufficient.

The lack of sufficiency is illustrated by an idea discussed by Davis (1974), Dennett (1978a, 1978b), and Block (1978), among others. Suppose a large group of people is paid to behave in a way that is structurally isomorphic to the way my brain behaves when I think "I want an ice cream." When one neuron sends a signal to another, one hireling hits another over the head with a hammer. The group of people is structurally isomorphic with my brain, yet I have the belief, while the group (presumably) does not.

The fact that structural isomorphism is not necessary for possessing the same psychological state is a point made by Block and Fodor (1972). What defeated the identity theory was that two individuals can be in the same mental state even though they are in different physical states. In just the same way, it seems possible for two individuals to be in the same mental state even though they're in different computational states. Two computers

can multiply 35 and 44 in very different ways. By analogy, two sentient beings might possess some of the same psychological properties even though their psychologies involve very different programs. The computer model of mind thereby suggests, surprisingly, that mental states are *not* to be identified with computational states.

Although these objections have seemed to be pretty decisive when applied to Turning Machine Functionalism, matters are different when Teleological Functionalism is considered instead. To see why, consider this analog to the mind/body problem: What is the relationship between the process of digestion and the physical processes of the body? What is the relationship between digestive states and properties and physical states and properties?

One possible suggestion is an identity theory: the processing of food does not consist in the operation of some immaterial substance on the food item. Rather, a perfectly down-to-earth physicochemical process is all that is involved. This idea would be a step forward from the idea that food contains a mysterious spiritual substance which is extracted for use by the organism by recondite spiritual machinery. On the other hand, the identity theory has some obvious limitations. Multiple realizability is just as much a property of digestion as it is of perception and cogitation. Other species digest food via physicochemical processes that differ markedly from those employed in our own species; in addition, it is not inconceivable that advanced computer automatons one day will forage for food and digest it, this being done in ways that will differ even more markedly from our own.

So the identity theory of digestion gives way to Functionalism. How should this latter doctrine be formulated? The Turing Machine version falls prey to the same problems mentioned above in the mind/body problem. Just as a group of people can be paid to abstractly mimic my thought processes, a group can be hired to abstractly mimic my digestive processes. But the group that does this mimicking is no more digesting than it is thinking. A better approach is the teleological version of Functionalism. Sameness of (teleological) function has nothing to do with sameness of abstract program. Two organisms can digest food in markedly different ways. There can be physical differences between their digestive processes, and there can be abstract differences between them too. For a system to engage in the process of digestion is for it to engage in a process that has a certain (teleological) function.

Another problem about Functionalism, related to the one just described of group mimicry, is clarified by a teleological approach. Instead of having a group of people hired for an hour or a day to abstractly mimic the micro-processes in my brain (or gut), let's imagine that a quite different relationship obtains between this group entity and me. Here I have in mind Block's (1978) idea of homunculus heads. Suppose my brain is removed and replaced by a radio transmitter and receiver. The various different input channels leading into the brain now have their signals sent to a group of people. Each individual mimics the behavior of one of my neurons. Some of these individuals are hooked up directly to the radio transmitter in my head; others are hooked up only to other individuals in the group; and still others transmit signals back to the receiver in my body, which then relays signals to the rest of my body, causing behavior.

In this case, the group entity is not merely engaged in abstract and inconsequential mimicry. Rather, the group is functioning as my prosthetic brain (see also Lycan 1979). They are to my normal psychological functioning what a kidney machine might be to my normal kidney function. When I use a kidney machine, my blood gets cleaned. In the homunculus case, my hook-up to the group allows perception and cognition to proceed. The cases are parallel.

There is a puzzle here, which arises from taking seriously the idea that brains in vats can have mental states. Although my brain allows my body to interact in various ways with the environment, this connection of brain to body appears to be inessential for my brain to occupy psychological states. Even if we grant that belief is a wide psychological state (as urged by Putnam (1975)), so that the individuation of beliefs depends on facts about the environment, not just on the mind's internal states, the point still remains: it seems implausible to insist that a brain in a vat would have no mental states whatever.

Now if this is true for normal brains when they are detached from their containing bodies, it presumably also must be true for artificial brains. In the previous example, a group of people provided me with an artificial brain. Let us now sever the connection of this group with my body, and instead connect the group to a computer which sends and receives signals, much as a computer might send and receive signals when connected to a brain in a vat. In this case, the group of people is not functioning as a mental organ for any organism; it is just a cog in a simulation experiment. Do we still want to say that the group has mental states?

Intuition strongly suggests that brains in vats have mental states. Perhaps intuition is less single-minded about what one should say about prosthetic brains that are not connected (or are not connected "in the right way") to the sorts of containing systems for which brains normally perform functions. I do not see this as a difficulty for Teleological Functionalism. The same questions arise for other artificial organs – especially ones that we might call "control devices."

A healthy heart regulates its own contractions. A pacemaker is a device for performing the same function. Pacemakers, let us suppose, can be surgically implanted or kept external to the patient and made to do their work by radio hook-up. In addition, a group of people could abstractly mimic the workings of a pacemaker; they also could themselves *be* a pacemaker, if suitably connected to someone's heart. However, as in the case of the group of people that is disconnected from any organism for whom they might provide a prosthetic brain, it might be difficult to decide what one should say about a device which *could* perform a function but does not, in virtue of its lack of connection with the "normal" sort of containing system. Is a device that is physically indistinguishable from a pacemaker, which is hooked up to a computer, engaged in coronary regulation? Well, there is clearly no heart that it is regulating. On the other hand, there seems to be a sense in which the device is engaged in regulatory activity.

I'm not going to suggest a principled way to answer such puzzles. My hunch is that sufficiently bizarre examples deserve to be viewed with suspicion and not elevated into test cases for theories. However, I do want to urge that the difficulty that functionalism faces here in the mind/body problem is really a more general problem about function ascription, construed teleologically. The fact that this difficulty arises, and has the logical contours it does, supports, rather than disconfirms, Teleological Functionalism.

Another criticism that has been leveled against Functionalism falls nicely into place when we substitute Teleological for Turing Machine Functionalism. This is Block's (1978) "problem of the inputs and the outputs." When functionalists describe the information processing procedures that you exploit when you form perceptual judgments, for example, they will characterize this set of procedures as a program, which has inputs and outputs. In the case of visual perception, we might want to describe the inputs physically in terms of patterns of light; the outputs might be described as the construction of a representation, which then may have effects on other representations and on behavior. Functionalism's negative insight, as Block has put it, is to avoid chauvinism. We shouldn't think that an organism with a mind must be just like us physically. But this lesson has relevance to how a functionalist should characterize inputs and outputs. There is no reason why perception or cogitation has to work via the kind of processing of light signals that we use in the case of vision, nor need perceptual representations be realized in the neuronal structures we happen to deploy. A functionalist should abstract away from such physical details.

How might this be done? If we abstract away from physical details too much, we will end up with a purely abstract specification of our own psychology, and we will be back to the problem of the group hired to engage in abstract mimicry. Block suspects that this problem is insoluble – a functionalist will either err on the side of chauvinism or on the side of liberalism, when it comes to determining the right description of the inputs and the outputs.

Teleological functionalism makes this problem look like it might be tractable. Again, let's consider digestion. We digest certain foods by way of certain physical processes. But digestion can and does proceed via other physical processes, and indeed, other organisms have diets markedly different from our own. Just as our perceptual contact with the world is mediated by some physical signals rather than others, so our energetic contact with the world is mediated by some tidbits rather than others. Perceiving and eating can be diverse in their mechanisms and diverse in what can serve as inputs. However, I do not see why this should spell doom for a functionalist theory of digestion. Despite the fact of multiple realizability, there seems to be something like a common core. Roughly speaking, it seems plausible to say that all digestion involves extracting energy from the environment. Although I have nothing substantive to say about what the function of the mind is, it is worth considering a (somewhat vague) answer to Block's question about inputs and outputs for the case of perception. Perception involves extracting information from the environment. Inputs are to be specified in terms of their information-bearing

properties. Light-packets are inessential, as are retinas and neurons. These merely constitute one among many physical realizations of what we call the perceptual process. It is up to science to give a detailed account of the process of information flow. My point is that I can't see any *a priori* reason why theorizing at this level of abstraction should be impossible.

At the same time, we must be alive to the possibility that science may not deliver theoretical characterizations of some of the very abstract and general properties deployed in common sense psychology. Perhaps "perception" will turn out to be too broad a category to be worth theorizing about. If so, it would be wrong to criticize a functionalist psychology for failing to provide a functionalist theory of perception as a general category. Rather, what might be more realistic is that there be various functionalist theor*ies* about different sorts of perception. In any event, how things will turn out is not for armchair philosophy to say. I conclude that Block's problem of the inputs and the outputs is as tractable as it needs to be, once Functionalism is construed teleologically.

Another problem for Functionalism derives from applying Putnam's (1975) ideas about meaning to psychological states like belief. Twin Earth thought-experiments suggest that two individuals can be physically identical and yet have different beliefs. Your term "water" refers to H_2O, whereas your twin's term "water" refers to XYZ. If Functionalism is understood as Turing Machine Functionalism, it looks like there can be no functionalist theory of belief. Your term "water" and your twin's term "water" have the same causal susceptibilities and powers. The presence of H_2O or XYZ under "normal" conditions will lead both of you to formulate the sentence "there is some water." And that sentence, when present in the "belief box," will lead to drinking, if you and your twin are thirsty.

This apparent failure of Functionalism to deal with non-narrow psychological states like belief will not be bothersome to those, like Block (1978) and Fodor (1980), who think that psychology is about narrow states only. But for "pluralists" like myself (see Sober 1982), who hold that narrow and wide properties of the organism both have a role to play in psychology, it is a matter of concern that Functionalism seems incapable of handling non-narrow states.

However, once again, matters change when Teleological Functionalism is considered. A simple fact about (teleological) functions is that what the function of something is depends on the kind of environment in which it is embedded (Wimsatt 1980). Two physically identical pieces of metal may have different functions, if they are placed in different machines. You have the concept of water; your twin has the concept of twin-water. How can the two of you have different concepts if you and your twin are physically identical? We might characterize the difference as a difference in function. Again, let me stress that I do not pretend to know what the function of any mental item is. But to illustrate the resources of Teleological Functionalism, I frame this conjecture: your term "water" has the function of representing water ($= H_2O$), whereas your twin's term functions to represent twin-water ($= XYZ$). A naturalistic theory of content faces the task of elaborating this bare suggestion; it remains to be seen how such a theory will fare. But as things now stand, I think that Functionalism has nothing to fear from non-narrow psychological states.

The last objection to Functionalism I will consider concerns qualia. It has been developed in various forms by Bradley (1964), Campbell (1970), and Block (1978), among others. The problem can be illustrated via the inverted spectrum problem. Suppose you and I are otherwise identical in our psychological characteristics, except that red things look green to you, while green things look red. I, on the other hand, am psychologically "normal." To me, green things look green and red things look red. When I look at a green thing (in normal lighting conditions, etc.), I go into state G, whereas you go into state R. When I look at a red thing, I go into state R, whereas you go into state G. The problem for Functionalism is this: Although your state G (R) and my state R (G) are qualitatively different, they appear to be causally the same. You are caused to go into R (G) by exactly the same things that cause me to go into G (R). And the effects of my being in state R (G) are precisely the same as the effects of your being in state G (R). For example, looking at a fire engine produces state R in me and state G in you; and my being in state R causes me (if other psychological dispositions are right) to say "yes" to the question "Is that thing red?", which is exactly what your being in state G causes. So the states differ psychologically, even though they do not differ in terms of their causal (functional) role. Hence, Functionalism cannot handle qualia.

Along with Block (1978), I will assume that "qualia realism" is true. There really could be a difference between your qualitative state and mine, even if this could not be detected in any of our outward behavior. My disagreement with Block concerns the issue of whether a qualia realist can be a functionalist.

To see why qualia realism need not be a problem for Functionalism, consider the following parody of the above argument:

> Imagine two very different computer programs that both take pairs of numbers as inputs and output the product of those numbers. These two programs are interchangeable in any larger, containing computer. Hence, Functionalism cannot characterize the difference between the two programs, since, by hypothesis, the two programs play identical causal roles.

The defect in this argument is that it fails to attend to what might be going on *inside* the programs. Although the two programs may be weakly equivalent, their internal processes may be functionally different.

Your qualia and mine differ, even though they appear to play the same causal roles. Does it follow that Functionalism cannot capture the difference between greenish qualia in me and reddish qualia in you? No, this does not follow, for it may be the case that there is lots of structure lurking within that distinguishes the two. Perhaps we experience qualia as simples, but that does not mean that they are simples. For all we know, there may be lots of complexity that a functionalist theory may identify and thereby make out a difference between your qualia and mine.

For this reason, I do not think we can conclude that Functionalism cannot handle qualia. The sticking point is the assumption that qualia are simples. In spite of this, I think there is a lesson we can draw from the problem of qualia, one which does point to a real limitation in Functionalism, even when that doctrine is given its strongest (teleological) formulation.

In any functionally organized system, whether it be the digestive system or the perceptual system, we should expect that there will be states or devices that are functionally equivalent. Not only is it true, as the functionalist realizes, that physically different states can be functionally equivalent. It also is the case that *psychologically different states can be identical in their psychological function.*

So my agreement with Block concerns a general point, rather than his specific conclusion about qualia. I see no compelling reason to think that Functionalism cannot handle qualia. However, it would surprise me if every psychological difference corresponds to a functional difference. This would constitute a mark of the mental, in that it would place the mind in an entirely different category from our other functional systems, like digestion and respiration.

Upon discovering that two traits have identical biological functions, biologists do not conclude that there is no biological difference between them. The Javanese rhinoceros has two horns, but the Africa rhino has only one. There is absolutely no reason to think that there is any difference in function here. Does it follow that there is no biological difference between having two horns and having only one? Likewise, upon discovering that a certain trait simply has no biological function, why should we stipulate that it is not a biological trait at all? Gould and Lewontin (1979) say that the human chin has no function; is it thereby not a biological item?

Biology encompasses a great many things. One salient fact about biological function is this: where there is functional organization, there also will be artifacts of functional organization – items that have no function at all. When objects are unified into a system, each having their separate functions, there will be fallout; there will be traits of the system and of the objects involved which do not themselves have functions, but which are merely consequences – artifacts – of the functions that do exist. Since biology studies not just the fact of functional organization, but also the consequences of functional organization, biology will study artifacts.

Psychologists study the functional organization of the perceptual and cognitive systems. But as with any system of objects, the existence of function pretty much guarantees the existence of artifacts. If psychologists study the consequences of functional organization, they will end up studying traits that have no psychological function. They also will wish to distinguish between traits that are functionally equivalent.

So my view is that Functionalism is a very bizarre doctrine, when taken as a claim about the identity conditions that attach to *every* psychological state. Functionalism seems to imagine that there is perfect economy – that every psychological state has its uniquely individuating psychological function. Following Gould and Lewontin (1979), I

call this assumption *Panglossian*; recall Dr Pangloss in Voltaire's *Candide*, who claimed that everything has a function, which it executes optimally. Panglossian Functionalism has the virtue of simplicity. But functional organization is more messy than this, perhaps necessarily so.

Since I have shamelessly plundered the concept of function in this essay, I should say a few words about how I have understood that shady idea. There is an extremely minimal interpretation of function, explicated by Cummins (1975), according to which everything has a function. The function of a part of a containing system is whatever that part does to contribute to the containing system's having whatever properties it has. The metaphor is that of the assembly line: the function of the components is whatever they do that allows the assembly line to do whatever it does. There is nothing wrong, on this view, with talking about the function of the heart's being to have a certain weight. The heart has a particular weight and thereby contributes to the body's being able to tip the scales at some, somewhat greater, weight. According to Cummins, there is nothing false about this ascription of function. It just doesn't strike us as very interesting. It will be clear that according to this analysis, there is no such thing as a thing's not having a function. Furthermore, any two devices with different effects of any kind will thereby have different functions. We can always find a function, and we can always find a difference in function.

I don't propose to argue that this analysis is false. However, within psychology, as in biology, we *do* want to be able to say that some items have no function, while other items have identical functions, even though there are obvious differences between them in their effects. What this means is that we must relativize our ascriptions of function to certain privileged states of the containing system. For example, if we want to say that the appendix has no function, we might put this point by saying that the appendix does not have a function as far as digestion is concerned. If we want to say that my red qualia and your green ones have the same function, this must mean that they have identical functions, as far as certain psychological processes are concerned.

Without such relativization and addition of detail, the claim that psychological states are functional states is incredibly trivial. Every psychological state has its causes and effects, and if we look carefully enough, we can always find a causal difference between any two different psychological states. Indeed, without relativization, Functionalism is perfectly compatible with the identity theory, since physical states also can be individuated in terms of their causal connections (Lycan 1981). On the other hand, once Functionalism is properly relativized, it becomes a suspect Panglossian doctrine. Not all biological states are individuated in terms of their biological functions. I expect no less of psychology.

Panglossian assumptions can be useful to a discipline, especially when the discipline is relatively young and theory is relatively undeveloped. The idea that every trait has a function and performs that function optimally has its uses in evolutionary theory, if only as a guide to asking questions (this is not to deny that the idea has been abused at times). But one sign that a functional theory has matured is that it is able to provide some independent source of evidence for whether a trait has a function and for whether two traits really are functionally equivalent.

In psychology and the philosophy of mind, Panglossian ideas arise in many contexts. I have explored just one of them here. Another that is worth mentioning is the status of the rationality assumption; many philosophers have held that ascribing beliefs to agents requires that they be viewed as rational. It has been held that this is not just a practical expedient but is an *a priori* requirement. My view is that it is a Panglossian simplification, useful but not inevitable for theorizing that has not sufficiently matured (Sober 1978, 1985).

As Panglossian assumptions steadily lose their grip in biology, a parallel problem in philosophy of biology becomes less interesting. What ever happened to vitalism and kindred theories about the relationship of biological states and properties to physical states and properties? It is a mistake to think that materialism (that is, a type/type identity theory) won the day. Functionalism's negative insight applies to biology no less than to psychology. Concepts like *fitness* and *predator* are not type-reducible to physical properties (Rosenberg 1978; Sober 1984b). I would suggest that we now have no adequate philosophical theory about the nature of biological states and properties as a category; I would add that this hyper-general question is not an interesting one in the first place. Progress in various areas of biology has removed the mystery that made the philosophical problem posed by vitalism seem so compelling. Separate biological theories circumscribe their own domains and characterize their own properties in a rather heterogeneous way. This biological analogy suggests that progress in the cognitive sciences, besides lossening the grip of Panglossian assumptions, will also change our perspective on some of the problems that functionalist ideas were invented to solve.

References

Block, N. (1978) "Troubles with functionalism," in W. Savage (ed.), *Perception and Cognition: Issues in the Foundations of Psychology: Minnesota Studies in the Philosophy of Science*, vol. ix, University of Minnesota Press.

Block, N. and Fodor, J. (1972) "What psychological states are not," *Philosophical Review* 81, 159–82.

Bradley, M. (1964) "Critical notice of Smart's 'Philosophy and Scientific Realism,'" *Australasian Journal of Philosophy* 71, 262–83.

Campbell, K. (1970) *Body and Mind*, New York: Doubleday.

Cummins, R. (1975) "Functional analysis," *Journal of Philosophy* 72, 741–64. Reprinted in Sober 1984a.

Davis, L. (1974) "Functional definitions and how it feels to be in pain." Unpublished manuscript.

Dennett, D. (1978a) "Towards a cognitive theory of consciousness," in *Brainstorms*, Montgomery, Vt: Bradford Books.

Dennett, D. (1978b) "Why you can't make a computer that feels pain," in *Brainstorms*, Montgomery, Vt: Bradford Books.

Fodor, J. (1968) *Psychological Explanation*, New York: Random House.

Fodor, J. (1980) "Methodological solipsism as a research strategy in cognitive psychology," *Behavior and Brain Sciences* 3, 63–100.

Gould, S. and Lewontin, R. (1979) "The spandrels of San Marco and the Panglossian paradigm: a critique of the adaptationist programme," *Proceedings of the Royal Society of London* B 205, 581–98. Reprinted in Sober 1984a.

Lycan, W. (1979) "A new Lilliputian argument against machine functionalism," *Philosophical Studies* 35, 279–87.

Lycan, W. (1981) "Form, function, and feel," *Journal of Philosophy* 78, 24–50.

Putnam, H. (1967) "Psychological predicates," in W. Capitan and D. Merrills (eds), *Art, Mind, and Religion*, University of Pittsburgh Press.

Putnam, H. (1975) "The meaning of 'meaning'," in K. Gunderson (ed.), *Minnesota Studies in the Philosophy of Science*, vol. 7, University of Minnesota Press.

Rosenberg, A. (1978) "The supervenience of biological concepts," *Philosophy of Science* 45, 368–86. Reprinted in Sober 1984a.

Sober, E. (1978) "Psychologism," *Journal for the Theory of Social Behavior* 8, 165–91.

Sober, E. (1982) "Rational biology and naturalistic biology, *Behavior and Brain Sciences* 5, 300–2.

Sober, E. (1984a) *Conceptual Issues in Evolutionary Biology: An Anthology*, MIT Press.

Sober, E. (1984b) *The Nature of Selection: Evolutionary Theory in Philosophical Focus*, MIT Press.

Sober, E. (1985) "Panglossian functionalism and the philosophy of mind," *Synthese* 64, 165–93.

Wimsatt, W. (1980) "Teleology and the logical structure of function statements," *Studies in the History and Philosophy of Science* 3, 1–80.

PART II

Instrumentalism

Introduction

The Identity Theorists and the Functionalists (Machine or Teleological) joined common sense and current cognitive psychology in understanding mental states and events both as *internal to human subjects* and as *causes*. Beliefs and desires in particular are thought to be caused by perceptual or other cognitive events and as in turn conspiring from within to cause behavior. If Armstrong's or Lewis's theory of mind is correct, this idea is not only commonsensical but a conceptual truth; if Functionalism is correct, it is at least a metaphysical fact.

In rallying to the inner-causal story, as we saw in the Introduction to Part I, the Identity Theorists and Functionalists broke with the Behaviorists, for Behaviorists did not think of mental items as entities, as inner, or as causes in any stronger sense than the bare hypothetical. Behaviorists either dispensed with the mentalistic idiom altogether, or paraphrased mental ascriptions in terms of putative responses to hypothetical stimuli. More recently, other philosophers have followed them in rejecting the idea of beliefs and desires as inner causes and in construing them in a more purely operational or instrumental fashion. Daniel Dennett, notoriously, denies that beliefs and desires are causally active inner states of people, and maintains instead that belief- and desire-ascriptions are merely calculational devices that happen to have predictive usefulness for a reason he goes on to explain. Such ascriptions are often objectively true, but not in virtue of describing inner mechanisms.

Thus Dennett has been an *instrumentalist* about propositional attitudes such as belief and desire. (An "instrumentalist" about *X*s is a theorist who claims that although sentences about "*X*s" are often true, they do not really describe entities of a special kind, but only serve to systematize more familiar phenomena. For example, we are all instrumentalists about "the average American homeowner," who is white, male, and the father of exactly 1.9 children.) To ascribe a "belief" or a "desire" is not to describe some segment of physical reality, Dennett says, but is more like moving a group of beads in an abacus.

In his collected works on "the intentional stance" (1978, 1987), Dennett offers basically five grounds for his rejection of the commonsensical inner-cause thesis. (i) He thinks it quite unlikely that any science will ever turn up any distinctive inner-causal mechanism that would be shared by all the possible subjects that had a particular belief. (ii) He offers numerous objections to "language-of-thought psychology," currently the most popular inner-cause theory. (iii) He compares the belief/desire interpretation of human beings to that of lower animals, chess-playing computers, and even lightning-rods, arguing that (a) in their case we have no reason to think of belief- and desire-ascriptions as other than mere calculational/predictive devices and (b) we have no more reason for the case of humans to think of belief- and desire-ascriptions as other than that. (iv) Dennett argues from the verification conditions of belief- and desire-ascriptions – basically a matter of extrapolating rationally from what a subject *ought* to believe and want in his/her circumstances – and then he boldly just identifies the truth-makers of those ascriptions with their verification-conditions, challenging inner-cause theorists to show why instrumentalism does not accommodate all the actual evidence. (v) He argues that in any case if a purely normative assumption (the "rationality assumption") is required for the licensing of an ascription, then the ascription cannot itself be a purely factual description of a plain state of affairs.

Stich (this volume, this Part) explores and criticizes Dennett's instrumentalism at length (perhaps oddly, Stich (1983) goes on to defend a view

nearly as deprecating as Dennett's, though clearly distinct from it). Dennett (1987) responds to Stich, bringing out more clearly the force of the "rationality assumption" assumption. Other critics of Dennett are listed in the bibliography.

More recently, in "Real patterns" (this volume), Dennett has moderated his original instrumentalism, emphasizing the reality and objectivity of the patterns in nature that make belief- and desire-ascriptions practically indispensable. At one point (pp. 113–14, n. 22), he even concedes that propositional attitudes can be causes, in a weak (non-"pinched") sense of "cause." (Cohen (1995) offers a nice critique of "Real patterns.")

Further Reading

Other Instrumentalist works

Dray, W. H. (1963) "The historical explanation of action reconsidered," in S. Hook (ed.), *Philosophy and History*, New York University Press.

Dennett, D. C. (1978) *Brainstorms*, Part I, Bradford Books.

Dennett, D. C. (1987) *The Intentional Stance*, Bradford Books/MIT Press.

Dennet's critics

Churchland, P. M. (1970) "The logical character of action explanations," *Philosophical Review* 79, 214–36.

Richardson, R. (1980) "Intentional realism or intentional instrumentalism?" *Cognition and Brain Theory* 3, 125–35.

Bechtel, P. W. (1985) "Realism, reason, and the intentional stance," *Cognitive Science* 9, 473–97.

Fodor, J. A. (1981) "Three cheers for propositional attitudes," in *Representations*, Bradford Books/MIT Press.

Stich, S. (1983) *From Folk Psychology to Cognitive Science*, Bradford Books/MIT Press.

Lycan, W. (1988) "Dennett's instrumentalism," *Behavioral and Brain Sciences*, 11, 518–19.

[And other contributions to the "Open peer commentary" in that issue on Dennett's precis of *The Intentional Stance*.]

Peacocke, C. (1983) *Sense and Content*, ch. 8, Oxford University Press.

Cohen, B. A. (1995) "Patterns lost: indeterminacy and Dennett's realism," *Pacific Philosophical Quarterly*, 76.

5

An Instrumentalist Theory

True Believers: The Intentional Strategy and Why it Works

Daniel C. Dennett

Death Speaks

There was a merchant in Baghdad who sent his servant to market to buy provisions and in a little while the servant came back, white and trembling, and said, Master, just now when I was in the market-place I was jostled by a woman in the crowd and when I turned I saw it was Death that jostled me. She looked at me and made a threatening gesture; now, lend me your horse, and I will ride away from the city and avoid my fate. I will go to Samarra and there Death will not find me. The merchant lent him his horse, and the servant mounted it, and he dug his spurs in its flanks and as fast as the horse could gallop he went. Then the merchant went down to the market-place and he saw me standing in the crowd, and he came to me and said, why did you make a threatening gesture to my servant when you saw him this morning? That was not a threatening gesture, I said, it was only a start of surprise. I was astonished to see him in Baghdad, for I had an appointment with him tonight in Samarra.

W. Somerset Maugham

In the social sciences, talk about *belief* is ubiquitous. Since social scientists are typically self-conscious about their methods, there is also a lot of talk about *talk about belief*. And since belief is a genuinely curious and perplexing phenomenon,

showing many different faces to the world, there is abundant controversy. Sometimes belief attribution appears to be a dark, risky, and imponderable business – especially when exotic, and more particularly religious or superstitious, beliefs are in the limelight. These are not the only troublesome cases; we also court argument and skepticism when we attribute beliefs to non-human animals, or to infants, or to computers or robots. Or when the beliefs we feel constrained to attribute to an apparently healthy, adult member of our own society are contradictory, or even just wildly false. A biologist colleague of mine was once called on the telephone by a man in a bar who wanted him to settle a bet. The man asked: "Are rabbits birds?" "No" said the biologist. "Damn!" said the man as he hung up. Now could he *really* have believed that rabbits were birds? Could anyone really and truly be attributed that belief? Perhaps, but it would take a bit of a story to bring us to accept it.

In all of these cases belief attribution appears beset with subjectivity, infected with cultural relativism, prone to "indeterminacy of radical translation" – clearly an enterprise demanding special talents: the art of phenomenological analysis, hermeneutics, empathy, *Verstehen*, and all that. On other occasions, normal occasions, when familiar beliefs are the topic, belief attribution looks as easy as speaking prose, and as objective and reliable as counting beans in a dish. Particularly when these straightforward cases are before us, it is quite plausible to suppose that *in principle* (if not yet in practice) it would be possible to confirm these simple, objective belief attributions by *finding something inside the believer's head* – by finding the beliefs themselves, in effect. "Look," someone might say, "You either believe there's milk in the fridge or you don't believe there's milk in the fridge" (you might have no opinion, in the latter case). But if you do believe this, that's a perfectly objective fact about you, and it must come down in the end to your brain's being in some particular physical state. If we knew more about physiological psychology we could in principle determine the facts about your brain state, and thereby determine whether or not you believe there is milk in the fridge, even if you were determined to be silent, or disingenuous on the topic. In principle, on this view physiological psychology could trump the results – or non-results – of any "black box" method in the social sciences that divines beliefs (and other mental features) by behavioral, cultural, social, historical, *external* criteria.

These differing reflections congeal into two opposing views on the nature of belief attribution, and hence on the nature of belief. The latter, a variety of *realism*, likens the question of whether a person has a particular belief to the question of whether a person is infected with a particular virus – a perfectly objective internal matter of fact about which an observer can often make educated guesses of great reliability. The former, which we could call *interpretationism* if we absolutely had to give it a name, likens the question of whether a person has a particular belief to the question of whether a person is immoral, or has style, or talent, or would make a good wife. Faced with such questions, we preface our answers with "Well, it all depends on what you're interested in," or make some similar acknowledgment of the relativity of the issue. "It's a matter of interpretation," we say. These two opposing views, so baldly stated, do not fairly represent any serious theorists' positions, but they do express views that are typically seen as mutually exclusive and exhaustive; the theorist must be friendly with one and only one of these themes.

I think this is a mistake. My thesis will be that while belief is a perfectly objective phenomenon (that apparently makes me a realist), it can be discerned only from the point of view of one who adopts a certain *predictive strategy*, and its existence can be confirmed only by an assessment of the success of that strategy (that apparently makes me an interpretationist).

First I will describe the strategy, which I call the intentional strategy, or adopting the intentional stance. To a first approximation, the intentional strategy consists of treating the object whose behavior you want to predict as a rational agent with beliefs and desires and other mental states exhibiting what Brentano and others call *intentionality*. The strategy has often been described before, but I shall try to put this very familiar material in a new light, by showing *how* it works, and by showing *how well* it works.

Then I will argue that any object – or as I shall say, any *system* – whose behavior is well predicted by this strategy is in the fullest sense of the word a believer. *What it is* to be a true believer is to be an *intentional system*, a system whose behavior is reliably and voluminously predictable via the intentional strategy. I have argued for this position before,[1] and my arguments have so far garnered few converts and many presumed counterexamples. I shall try again here, harder, and shall also deal with several compelling objections.

The Intentional Strategy and How it Works

There are many strategies, some good, some bad. Here is a strategy, for instance, for predicting the future behavior of a person: determine the date and hour of the person's birth, and then feed this modest datum into one or another astrological algorithm for generating predictions of the person's prospects. This strategy is deplorably popular. Its popularity is deplorable only because we have such good reasons for believing that *it does not work*.[2] When astrological predictions come true this is sheer luck, or the result of such vagueness or ambiguity in the prophecy that almost any eventuality can be construed to confirm it. But suppose the astrological strategy did in fact work well on some people. We could call those people *astrological systems* – systems whose behavior was, as a matter of fact, predictable by the astrological strategy. If there were such people, such astrological systems, we would be more interested than most of us in fact are in *how the astrological strategy works* – that is, we would be interested in the rules, principles, or methods of astrology. We could find out how the strategy works by asking astrologers, reading their books, and observing them in action.

But we would also be curious about *why* it worked. We might find that astrologers had no useful opinions about this latter question – they either had no theory of why it worked, or their theories were pure hokum. Having a good strategy is one thing; knowing why it works is another.

So far as we know, however, the class of astrological systems is empty, so the astrological strategy is of interest only as a social curiosity. Other strategies have better credentials. Consider the physical strategy, or physical stance: if you want to predict the behavior of a system, determine its physical constitution (perhaps all the way down to the microphysical level) and the physical nature of the impingements upon it, and use your knowledge of the laws of physics to predict the outcome for any input. This is the grand and impractical strategy of Laplace for predicting the entire future of everything in the universe, but it has more modest, local, actually usable versions. The chemist or physicist in the laboratory can use this strategy to predict the behavior of exotic materials, but equally the cook in the kitchen can predict the effect of leaving the pot on the burner too long. The strategy is not always practically available, but that it will always work *in principle* is a dogma of the physical sciences. (I ignore the minor complications raised by the subatomic indeterminacies of quantum physics.)

Sometimes, in any event, it is more effective to switch from the physical stance to what I call the design stance, where one ignores the actual (possibly messy) details of the physical constitution of an object, and, on the assumption that it has a certain design, predicts that it will behave *as it is designed to behave* under various circumstances. For instance, most users of computers have not the foggiest idea what physical principles are responsible for the computer's highly reliable, and hence predictable, behavior. But if they have a good idea of what the computer is designed to do (a description of its operation at any one of the many possible levels of abstraction), they can predict its behavior with great accuracy and reliability, subject to disconfirmation only in cases of physical malfunction. Less dramatically, almost anyone can predict when an alarm clock will sound on the basis of the most casual inspection of its exterior. One does not know or care to know whether it is spring wound, battery driven, sunlight powered, made of brass wheels and jewel bearings or silicon chips – one just assumes that it is designed so that the alarm will sound when it is set to sound, and it

is set to sound where it appears to be set to sound, and the clock will keep on running until that time and beyond, and is designed to run more or less accurately, and so forth. For more accurate and detailed design stance predictions of the alarm clock, one must descend to a less abstract level of description of its design; for instance, to the level at which gears are described, but their material is not specified.

Only the designed behavior of a system is predictable from the design stance, of course. If you want to predict the behavior of an alarm clock when it is pumped full of liquid helium, revert to the physical stance. Not just artifacts, but also many biological objects (plants and animals, kidneys and hearts, stamens and pistils) behave in ways that can be predicted from the design stance. They are not just physical systems but designed systems.

Sometimes even the design stance is practically inaccessible, and then there is yet another stance or strategy one can adopt: the intentional stance. Here is how it works: first you decide to treat the object whose behavior is to be predicted as a rational agent; then you figure out what beliefs that agent ought to have, given its place in the world and its purpose. Then you figure out what desires it ought to have, on the same considerations, and finally you predict that this rational agent will act to further its goals in the light of its beliefs. A little practical reasoning from the chosen set of beliefs and desires will in many – but not all – instances yield a decision about what the agent ought to do; that is what you predict the agent *will* do.

The strategy becomes clearer with a little elaboration. Consider first how we go about populating each other's heads with beliefs. A few truisms: sheltered people tend to be ignorant; if you expose someone to something he comes to know all about it. In general, it seems, we come to believe all the truths about the parts of the world around us we are put in a position to learn about. *Exposure to x,* that is, sensory confrontation with *x* over some suitable period of time, is the *normally sufficient* condition for knowing (or having true beliefs) about *x*. As we say, we come to *know all about* the things around us. Such exposure is only *normally* sufficient for knowledge, but this is not the large escape hatch it might appear; our threshold for accepting abnormal ignorance in the face of exposure is quite high. "I didn't know the gun was loaded," said by one who was observed to be present, sighted, and awake during the loading, meets with a variety of utter skepticism that only the most outlandish supporting tale could overwhelm.

Of course we do not come to learn or remember all the truths our sensory histories avail us. In spite of the phrase "know all about," what we come to know, normally, are only all the *relevant* truths our sensory histories avail us. I do not typically come to know the ratio of spectacle-wearing people to trousered people in a room I inhabit, though if this interested me, it would be readily learnable. It is not just that some facts about my environment are below my thresholds of discrimination or beyond the integration and holding-power of my memory (such as the height in inches of all the people present), but that many perfectly detectable, graspable, memorable facts are of no interest to me, and hence do not come to be believed by me. So one rule for attributing beliefs in the intentional strategy is this: attribute as beliefs all the truths relevant to the system's interests (or desires) that the system's experience to date has made available. This rule leads to attributing somewhat too much – since we all are somewhat forgetful, even of important things. It also fails to capture the false beliefs we are all known to have. But the attribution of false belief, *any* false belief, requires a special genealogy, which will be seen to consist in the main in true beliefs. Two paradigm cases: S believes (falsely) that *p*, because S believes (truly) that Jones told him that *p*, that Jones is pretty clever, that Jones did not intend to deceive him, ... etc. Second case: S believes (falsely) that there is a snake on the barstool, because S believes (truly) that he seems to see a snake on the barstool, is himself sitting in a bar not a yard from the barstool he sees, and so forth. The falsehood has to start somewhere; the seed may be sown in hallucination, illusion, a normal variety of simple misperception, memory deterioration, or deliberate fraud, for instance, but the false beliefs that are reaped grow in a culture medium of true beliefs.

Then there are the arcane and sophisticated beliefs, true and false, that are so often at the focus of attention in discussions of belief attribution. They do not arise directly, goodness knows, from exposure to mundane things and events, but their attribution requires tracing out a lineage of mainly good argument or reasoning from the bulk of beliefs already attributed. An implication of the intentional strategy, then, is that true believers mainly believe truths. If anyone could devise an

agreed-upon method of individuating and counting beliefs (which I doubt very much), we would see that all but the smallest portion (say, less than 10 percent) of a person's beliefs were attributable under our first rule.[3]

Note that this rule is a derived rule, an elaboration and further specification of the fundamental rule: attribute those beliefs the system *ought to have*. Note also that the rule interacts with the attribution of desires. How do we attribute the desires (preferences, goals, interests) on whose basis we will shape the list of beliefs? We attribute the desires the system *ought to have*. That is the fundamental rule. It dictates, on a first pass, that we attribute the familiar list of highest, or most basic, desires to people: survival, absence of pain, food, comfort, procreation, entertainment. Citing any one of these desires typically terminates the "Why?" game of reason giving. One is not supposed to need an ulterior motive for desiring comfort or pleasure or the prolongation of one's existence. Derived rules of desire attribution interact with belief attributions. Trivially, we have the rule: attribute desires for those things a system believes to be good for it. Somewhat more informatively, attribute desires for those things a system believes to be best means to other ends it desires. The attribution of bizarre and detrimental desires thus requires, like the attribution of false beliefs, special stories.

The interaction between belief and desire becomes trickier when we consider what desires we attribute on the basis of verbal behavior. The capacity to *express* desires in language opens the floodgates of desire attribution. "I want a two-egg mushroom omelette, some French bread and butter, and a half bottle of lightly chilled white Burgundy." How could one begin to attribute a desire for anything so specific in the absence of such verbal declaration? How, indeed, could a creature come to *contract* such a specific desire without the aid of language? Languages *enables* us to formulate highly specific desires, but it also *forces* us on occasion to commit ourselves to desires altogether more stringent in their conditions of satisfaction than anything we would otherwise have any reason to endeavour to satisfy. Since in order to get what you want you often have to say what you want, and since you often cannot say what you want without saying something more specific than you antecedently mean, you often end up giving others evidence – the very best of evidence, your unextorted word – that you desire things or states of affairs far more particular than would satisfy you – or better, than would have satisfied you, for once you have declared, being a man of your word, you acquire an interest in satisfying exactly the desire you declared and no other.

"I'd like some baked beans, please."

"Yes sir. How many?"

You might well object to having such a specification of desire demanded of you, but in fact we are all socialized to accede to similar requirements in daily life – to the point of not noticing it, and certainly not feeling oppressed by it. I dwell on this because it has a parallel in the realm of belief, where our linguistic environment is forever forcing us to give – or concede – precise verbal expression to convictions that lack the hard edges verbalization endows them with.[4] By concentrating on the *results* of this social force, while ignoring its distorting effect, one can easily be misled into thinking that it is *obvious* that beliefs and desires are rather like *sentences stored in the head*. Being language-using creatures, it is inevitable that we should often come to believe that some particular, actually formulated, spelled and punctuated sentence *is true*, and that on other occasions we should come to want such a sentence to *come true*, but these are special cases of belief and desire, and as such may not be reliable models for the whole domain.

That is enough, on this occasion, about the principles of belief and desire attribution to be found in the intentional strategy. What about the rationality one attributes to an intentional system? One starts with the ideal of perfect rationality and revises downwards as circumstances dictate. That is, one starts with the assumption that people believe all the implications of their beliefs, and believe no contradictory pairs of beliefs. This does not create a practical problem of clutter (infinitely many implications, for instance), for one is interested only in ensuring that the system one is predicting is rational enough to get to the particular implications that are relevant to its behavioral predicament of the moment. Instances of irrationality, or of finitely powerful capacities of inference, raise particularly knotty problems of interpretation, which I will set aside on this occasion.[5]

For I want to turn from the description of the strategy to the question of its use. Do people actually use this strategy? Yes, all the time. There may someday be other strategies for attributing belief and desire and for predicting behavior, but this is the only one we all know now. And

when does it work? It works with people almost all the time. Why would it *not* be a good idea to allow individual Oxford colleges to create and grant academic degrees whenever they saw fit? The answer is a long story, but very easy to generate. And there would be widespread agreement about the major points. We have no difficulty thinking of the reasons people would then have for acting in such ways as to give others reasons for acting in such ways as to give others reasons for . . . creating a circumstance we would not want. Our use of the intentional strategy is so habitual and effortless that the role it plays in shaping our expectations about people is easily overlooked. The strategy also works on most other mammals most of the time. For instance, you can use it to design better traps to catch those mammals, by reasoning about what the creature knows or believes about various things, what it prefers, what it wants to avoid. The strategy works on birds, and on fish, and on reptiles, and on insects and spiders, and even on such lowly and unenterprising creatures as clams (once a clam believes there is danger about, it will not relax its grip on its closed shell until it is convinced that the danger has passed). It also works on some artifacts: the chess-playing computer will not take your knight because it knows that there is a line of ensuing play that would lead to losing its rook, and it does not want that to happen. More modestly, the thermostat will turn off the boiler as soon as it comes to believe the room has reached the desired temperature.

The strategy even works for plants. In a locale with late spring storms you should plant apple varieties that are particularly *cautions* about *concluding* that it is spring – which is when they *want* to blossom, of course. It even works for such inanimate and apparently undesigned phenomena as lightning. An electrician once explained to me how he worked out how to protect my underground water pump from lightning damage: lightning, he said, always wants to find the best way to ground but sometimes it gets tricked into taking second-best paths. You can protect the pump by making another, better path more *obvious* to the lightning.

True Believers as Intentional Systems

Now clearly this is a motley assortment of "serious" belief attributions, dubious belief attributions, pedagogically useful metaphors, *façons de parler*, and perhaps worse: outright frauds. The next task would seem to be distinguishing those intentional systems that *really* have beliefs and desires from those we may find it handy to treat *as if* they had beliefs and desires. But that would be a Sisyphean labor, or else would be terminated by fiat. A better understanding of the phenomenon of belief begins with the observation that even in the worst of these cases, even when we are surest that the strategy works *for the wrong reasons*, it is nevertheless true that it does work, at least a little bit. This is an interesting fact, which distinguishes this class of objects, the class of *intentional systems*, from the class of objects for which the strategy never works. But is this so? Does our definition of an intentional system exclude any objects at all? For instance, it seems the lectern in this lecture room can be construed as an intentional system, fully rational, and believing that it is currently located at the center of the civilized world (as some of you may also think); and desiring above all else to remain at that center. What should such a rational agent so equipped with belief and desire do? Stay put, clearly, which is just what the lectern does. I predict the lectern's behavior, accurately, from the intentional stance, so is it an intentional system? If it is, anything at all is.

What should disqualify the lectern? For one thing, the strategy does not recommend itself in this case, for we get no predictive power from it that we did not antecedently have. We already knew what the lectern was going to do – namely nothing – and tailored the beliefs and desires to fit in a quite unprincipled way. In the case of people, or animals, or computers, however, the situation is different. In these cases often the only strategy that is at all practical is the intentional strategy; it gives us predictive power we can get by no other method. But, it will be urged, this is no difference in nature, but merely a difference that reflects upon our limited capacities as scientists. The Laplacean omniscient physicist could predict the behavior of a computer – or of a live human body, assuming it to be ultimately governed by the laws of physics – without any need for the risky, short-cut methods of either the design or intentional strategies. For people of limited mechanical aptitude, the intentional interpretation of a simple thermostat is a handy and largely innocuous crutch, but the engineers among us can quite fully grasp its internal operation without the aid of this anthropomorphizing. It may be true that the cleverest engineers find it practically imposs-

ible to maintain a clear conception of more complex systems, such as a time-sharing computer system or remote-controlled space probe, without lapsing into an intentional stance (and viewing these devices as asking and telling, trying and avoiding, wanting and believing), but this is just a more advanced case of human epistemic frailty. We would not want to classify these artifacts with the true believers – ourselves – on such variable and parochial grounds, would we? Would it not be intolerable to hold that some artifact, or creature, or person was a believer from the point of view of one observer, but not a believer at all from the point of view of another, cleverer observer? That would be a particularly radical version of interpretationism, and some have thought I espoused it in urging that belief be viewed in terms of the success of the intentional strategy. I must confess that my presentation of the view has sometimes invited that reading, but I now want to discourage it. The decision to adopt the intentional stance is free, but the facts about the success or failure of the stance, were one to adopt it, are perfectly objective.

Once the intentional strategy is in place, it is an extraordinarily powerful tool in prediction – a fact that is largely concealed by our typical concentration on the cases in which it yields dubious or unreliable results. Consider, for instance, predicting moves in a chess game. What makes chess an interesting game, one can see, is the *un*predictability of one's opponent's moves, except in those cases where moves are "forced" – where there is *clearly* one best move – typically the least of the available evils. But this unpredictability is put in context when one recognizes that in the typical chess situation there are very many perfectly legal and hence available moves, but only a few – perhaps half a dozen – with anything to be said for them, and hence only a few high probability moves according to the intentional strategy. Even where the intentional strategy fails to distinguish a single move with a highest probability, it can dramatically reduce the number of live options.

The same feature is apparent when the intentional strategy is applied to "real world" cases. It is notoriously unable to predict the exact purchase and sell decisions of stock traders, for instance, or the exact sequence of words a politician will utter when making a scheduled speech, but one's confidence can be very high indeed about slightly less specific predictions: that the particular trader *will not buy utilities today*, or that the politician *will side with the unions against his party*, for example. This inability to predict fine-grained descriptions of actions, looked at another way, is a source of strength for the intentional strategy, for it is this neutrality with regard to details of implementation that permits one to exploit the intentional strategy in complex cases, for instance, in *chaining predictions*.[6] Suppose the US Secretary of State were to announce he was a paid agent of the KGB. What an unparalleled event! How unpredictable its consequences! Yet in fact we can predict dozens of not terribly interesting but perfectly salient consequences, and consequences of consequences. The President would confer with the rest of the Cabinet, which would support his decision to relieve the Secretary of State of his duties pending the results of various investigations, psychiatric and political, and all this would be reported at a news conference to people who would write stories that would be commented upon in editorials that would be read by people who would write letters to the editors, and so forth. None of that is daring prognostication, but note that it describes an arc of causation in space-time that could not be predicted under *any* description by any imaginable practical extension of physics or biology.

The power of the intentional strategy can be seen even more sharply with the aid of an objection first raised by Robert Nozick some years ago. Suppose, he suggested, some beings of vastly superior intelligence – from Mars, let us say – were to descend upon us, and suppose that we were to them as simple thermostats are to clever engineers. Suppose, that is, that they did not *need* the intentional stance – or even the design stance – to predict our behavior in all its detail. They can be supposed to be Laplacean super-physicists, capable of comprehending the activity on Wall Street, for instance, at the microphysical level. Where we see brokers and buildings and sell orders and bids, they see vast congeries of subatomic particles milling about – and they are such good physicists that they can predict days in advance what ink marks will appear each day on the paper tape labeled 'Closing Dow Jones Industrial Average.' They can predict the individual behaviors of all the various moving bodies they observe without ever treating any of them as intentional systems. Would we be right then to say that from *their* point of view we really were not believers at all (any more than a simple thermostat)? If so, then our status as believers is nothing objective, but rather something in the eye of the beholder –

provided the beholder shares our intellectual limitations.

Our imagined Martians might be able to predict the future of the human race by Laplacean methods, but if they did not also see us as intentional systems, they would be *missing something* perfectly objective: the *patterns* in human behavior that are describable from the intentional stance, and only from that stance, and which support generalizations and predictions. Take a particular instance in which the Martians observe a stock broker deciding to place an order for 500 shares of General Motors. They predict the exact motions of his fingers as he dials the phone, and the exact vibrations of his vocal cords as he intones his order. But if the Martians do not see that indefinitely many *different* patterns of finger motions and vocal cord vibrations – even the motions of indefinitely many different individuals – could have been substituted for the actual particulars without perturbing the subsequent operation of the market, then they have failed to see a real pattern in the world they are observing. Just as there are indefinitely many ways of *being a spark plug* – and one has not understood what an internal combustion engine is unless one realizes that a variety of different devices can be screwed into these sockets without affecting the performance of the engine – so there are indefinitely many ways of *ordering 500 shares of General Motors*, and there are societal sockets in which one of these ways will produce just about the same effect as any other. There are also societal pivot points, as it were, where which way people go depends on whether they *believe that p*, or *desire A*, and does not depend on any of the other infinitely many ways they may be alike or different.

Suppose, pursuing our Martian fantasy a little further, that one of the Martians were to engage in a predicting contest with an Earthling. The Earthling and the Martian observe (and observe each other observing) a particular bit of local physical transaction. From the Earthling's point of view, this is what is observed. The telephone rings in Mrs Gardner's kitchen. She answers, and this is what she says: "Oh, hello dear. You're coming home early? Within the hour? And bringing the boss to dinner? Pick up a bottle of wine on the way home, then, and drive carefully." On the basis of this observation, our Earthling predicts that a large metallic vehicle with rubber tyres will come to a stop in the drive within one hour, disgorging two human beings one of whom will be holding a paper bag containing a bottle containing an alcoholic fluid. The prediction is a bit risky, perhaps, but a good bet on all counts. The Martian makes the same prediction, but has to avail himself of much more information about an extraordinary number of interactions of which, so far as he can tell, the Earthling is entirely ignorant. For instance, the deceleration of the vehicle at intersection A, five miles from the house, without which there would have been a collision with another vehicle – whose collision course had been laboriously calculated over some hundreds of meters by the Martian. The Earthling's performance would look like magic! How did the Earthling know that the human being who got out of the car and got the bottle in the shop would get back in? The coming true of the Earthling's prediction, after all the vagaries, intersections, and branches in the paths charted by the Martian, would seem to anyone bereft of the intentional strategy as marvelous and inexplicable as the fatalistic inevitability of the appointment in Samarra. Fatalists – for instance, astrologers – believe that there is a pattern in human affairs that is inexorable, that will impose itself *come what may*, that is, no matter how the victims scheme and second-guess, no matter how they twist and turn in their chains. These fatalists are wrong, but they are *almost* right. There *are* patterns in human affairs that impose themselves, not quite inexorably but with great vigor, absorbing physical perturbations and variations that might as well be considered random; these are the patterns that we characterize in terms of the beliefs, desires, and intentions of rational agents.

No doubt you will have noticed, and been distracted by, a serious flaw in our thought-experiment: the Martian is presumed to treat his Earthling opponent as an intelligent being like himself, with whom communication is possible, a being with whom one can make a wager, against whom one can compete. In short, a being with beliefs (such as the belief he expressed in his prediction) and desires (such as the desire to win the prediction contest). So if the Martian sees the pattern in one Earthling, how can he fail to see it in the others? As a bit of narrative, our example could be strengthened by supposing that our Earthling cleverly learned Martian (which is transmitted by X-ray modulation) and disguised himself as a Martian, counting on the species-chauvinism of these otherwise brilliant aliens to permit him to pass as an intentional system while not giving away the secret of his fellow human

beings. This addition might get us over a bad twist in the tale, but might obscure the moral to be drawn: namely, the unavoidability of the intentional stance with regard to oneself and one's fellow intelligent beings. This unavoidability is itself interest-relative; it is perfectly possible to adopt a physical stance, for instance, with regard to an intelligent being, oneself included, but not to the exclusion of maintaining at the same time an intentional stance with regard to oneself at a minimum, and one's fellows *if* one intends, for instance, to learn what they know (a point that has been powerfully made by Stuart Hampshire in a number of writings). We can perhaps suppose our super-intelligent Martians fail to recognize *us* as intentional systems, but we cannot suppose them to lack the requisite concepts.[7] If they observe, theorize, predict, communicate, they view *themselves* as intentional systems.[8] Where there are intelligent beings the patterns must be there to be described, whether or not we care to see them.

It is important to recognize the objective reality of the intentional patterns discernible in the activities of intelligent creatures, but also important to recognize the incompleteness and imperfections in the patterns. The objective fact is that the intentional strategy *works as well as it does*, which is not perfectly. No one is perfectly rational, perfectly unforgetful, all-observant, or invulnerable to fatigue, malfunction, or design imperfection. This leads inevitably to circumstances beyond the power of the intentional strategy to describe, in much the same way that physical damage to an artifact, such as a telephone or an automobile, may render it indescribable by the normal design terminology for that artifact. How do you draw the schematic wiring diagram of an audio amplifier that has been partially melted, or how do you characterize the program state of a malfunctioning computer? In cases of even the mildest and most familiar cognitive pathology – where people seem to hold contradictory beliefs, or to be deceiving themselves, for instance – the canons of interpretation of the intentional strategy fail to yield clear, stable verdicts about which beliefs and desires to attribute to a person.

Now a *strong* realist position on beliefs and desires would claim that in these cases the person in question really does have some particular beliefs and desires which the intentional strategy, as I have described it, is simply unable to divine. On the milder sort of realism I am advocating, there is no fact of the matter of exactly which beliefs and desires a person has in these degenerate cases, but this is not a surrender to relativism or subjectivism, for *when* and *why* there is no fact of the matter is itself a matter of objective fact. On this view one can even acknowledge the *interest relativity* of belief attributions, and grant that given the different interests of different cultures, for instance, the beliefs and desires one culture would attribute to a member might be quite different from the beliefs and desires another culture would attribute to that very same person. But supposing that were so in a particular case, there would be the further facts about *how well* each of the rival intentional strategies worked for predicting the behavior of that person. We can be sure in advance that no intentional interpretation of an individual will work to perfection, and it may be that two rival schemes are about equally good, and better than any others we can devise. That this is the case is itself something about which there can be a fact of the matter. The objective presence of one pattern (with whatever imperfections) does not rule out the objective presence of another pattern (with whatever imperfections).

The bogey of radically different interpretations with equal warrant from the intentional strategy is theoretically important – one might better say metaphysically important – but practically negligible once one restricts one's attention to the largest and most complex intentional systems we know: human beings.[9]

Until now I have been stressing our kinship to clams and thermostats, in order to emphasize a view of the logical status of belief attribution, but the time has come to acknowledge the obvious differences, and say what can be made of them. The perverse claim remains: *all there is* to being a true believer is being a system whose behavior is reliably predictable via the intentional strategy, and hence *all there is* to really and truly believing that *p* (for any proposition *p*) is being an intentional system for which *p* occurs as a belief in the best (most predictive) interpretation. But once we turn our attention to the truly interesting and versatile intentional systems, we see that this apparently shallow and instrumentalistic criterion of belief puts a severe constraint on the internal constitution of a genuine believer, and thus yields a robust version of belief after all.

Consider the lowly thermostat, as degenerate a case of an intentional system as could conceivably hold our attention for more than a moment. Going along with the gag we might agree to grant it the

capacity for about half a dozen different beliefs and fewer desires – it can believe the room is too cold or too hot, that the boiler is on or off, and that if it wants the room warmer it should turn on the boiler, and so forth. But surely this is imputing too much to the thermostat; it has no concept of heat or of a boiler, for instance. So suppose we *de-interpret* its beliefs and desires: it can believe the *A* is too *F* or *G*, and if it wants the *A* to be more *F* it should do *K*, and so forth. After all, by attaching the thermostatic control mechanism to different input and output devices, it could be made to regulate the amount of water in a tank, or the speed of a train, for instance. Its attachment to a heat-sensitive "transducer" and a boiler is too impoverished a link to the world to grant any rich semantics to its belief-like states.

But suppose we then enrich these modes of attachment. Suppose we give it more than one way of learning about the temperature, for instance. We give it an eye of sorts that can distinguish huddled, shivering occupants of the room, and an ear so that it can be told how cold it is. We give it some facts about geography so that it can conclude that it is probably in a cold place if it learns that its spatiotemporal location is Winnipeg in December. Of course giving it a visual system that is multi-purpose and general – not a mere shivering-object detector – will require vast complications of its inner structure. Suppose we also give our system more behavioral versatility: it chooses the boiler fuel, purchases it from the cheapest and most reliable dealer, checks the weatherstripping and so forth. This adds another dimension of internal complexity; it gives individual belief-like states *more to do*, in effect, by providing more and different occasions for their derivation or deduction from other states, and by providing more and different occasions for them to serve as premises for further reasoning. The cumulative effect of enriching these connections between the device and the world in which it resides is to enrich the semantics of its dummy predicates, *F* and *G* and the rest. The more of this we add, the less amenable our device becomes to serving as the control structure of anything other than a room temperature maintenance system. A more formal way of saying this is that the class of indistinguishably satisfactory models of the formal system embodied in its internal states gets smaller and smaller as we add such complexities; the more we add, the richer or more demanding or specific the semantics of the system, until eventually we reach systems for which a *unique* semantic interpretation is *practically* (but never *in principle*) dictated.[10] At that point we say this device (or animal, or person) has beliefs *about heat*, and *about this very room*, and so forth, not only because of the system's *actual* location in, and operations on, the world, but because we cannot imagine another niche in which it could be placed *where it would work*.

Our original simple thermostat had a state we called a belief about a particular boiler, to the effect that it was on or off. Why about *that* boiler? Well, what *other* boiler would you want to say it was about? The belief is about the boiler because it is *fastened* to the boiler.[11] Given the actual, if minimal, causal link to the world that happened to be in effect, we could endow a state of the device with *meaning* (of a sort) and *truth conditions*, but it was altogether too easy to substitute a different minimal link and completely change the meaning (in this impoverished sense) of that internal state. But as systems become perceptually richer and behaviorally more versatile, it becomes harder and harder to make substitutions in the actual links of the system to the world without changing the organization of the system itself. If you change its environment, it will *notice*, in effect, and make a change in its internal state in response. There comes to be a two-way constraint of growing specificity between the device and the environment. Fix the device in any one state and it demands a *very* specific environment in which to operate properly (you can no longer switch it easily from regulating temperature to regulating speed or anything else); but at the same time, if you do not *fix* the state it is in, but just plonk it down in a changed environment, its sensory attachments will be sensitive and discriminative enough to respond appropriately to the change, driving the system into a new state, in which it will operate effectively in the new environment. There is a familiar way of alluding to this tight relationship that can exist between the organization of a system and its environment: you say that the organism continuously *mirrors* the environment, or that there is a *representation* of the environment in – or implicit in – the organization of the system.

It is not that we attribute (or should attribute) beliefs and desires only to things in which we find internal representations, but rather that when we discover some object for which the intentional strategy works, we endeavor to interpret some of its internal states or processes as internal representations. What makes some internal feature of a thing a representation could only be its role in regulating the behavior of an intentional system.

Now the reason for stressing our kinship with the thermostat should be clear. There is no magic moment in the transition from a single thermostat to a system that *really* has an internal representation of the world around it. The thermostat has a minimally demanding representation of the world, fancier thermostats have more demanding representations of the world, fancier robots for helping around the house would have still more demanding representations of the world. Finally you reach us. We are so multifariously and intricately connected to the world that almost no substitution is possible – though it is clearly imaginable in a thought-experiment. Hilary Putnam imagines the planet Twin Earth, which is just like Earth right down to the scuff marks on the shoes of the Twin Earth replica of your neighbor, but which differs from Earth in some property that is entirely beneath the thresholds of your capacities to discriminate. (What they call water on Twin Earth has a different chemical analysis.) Were *you* to be whisked instantaneously to Twin Earth and exchanged for your Twin Earth replica, you would never be the wiser – just like the simple control system that cannot tell whether it is regulating temperature, speed, or volume of water in a tank. It is easy to devise radically different Twin Earths for something as simple and sensorily deprived as a thermostat, but your internal organization puts a much more stringent demand on substitution. Your Twin Earth and Earth must be virtual replicas or you will change state dramatically on arrival.

So which boiler are *your* beliefs about, when you believe the boiler is on? Why, the boiler in your cellar (rather than its twin on Twin Earth, for instance). What *other* boiler would your beliefs be about? The *completion* of the semantic interpretation of your beliefs, fixing the *referents* of your beliefs, requires, as in the case of the thermostat, facts about your actual embedding in the world. The principles, and problems, of interpretation that we discover when we attribute beliefs to people are the *same* principles and problems we discover when we look at the ludicrous, but blessedly simple, problem of attributing beliefs to a thermostat. The differences are of degree, but nevertheless of such great degree that understanding the internal organization of a simple intentional system gives one very little basis for understanding the internal organization of a complex intentional system, such as a human being.

Why Does the Intentional Strategy Work?

When we turn to the question of *why* the intentional strategy works as well as it does, we find that the question is ambiguous, admitting of two very different sorts of answers. If the intentional system is a simple thermostat, one answer is simply this: the intentional strategy works because the thermostat is well designed; it was designed to be a system that could be easily and reliably comprehended and manipulated from this stance. That is true, but not very informative, if what we are after are the actual features of its design that explain its performance. Fortunately, however, in the case of a simple thermostat those features are easily discovered and understood, so the other answer to our *why* question, which is really an answer about *how the machinery works*, is readily available.

If the intentional system in question is a person, there is also an ambiguity in our question. The first answer to the question of why the intentional strategy works is that evolution has designed human beings to be rational, to believe what they ought to believe and want what they ought to want. The fact that we are products of a long and demanding evolutionary process guarantees that using the intentional strategy on us is a safe bet. This answer has the virtues of truth and brevity, and on this occasion the additional virtue of being an answer Herbert Spencer would applaud, but it is also strikingly uninformative. The more difficult version of the question asks, in effect, how the machinery which Nature has provided us works. And we cannot yet give a good answer to that question. We just do not know. We do know how the *strategy* works, and we know the easy answer to the question of why it works, but knowing these does not help us much with the hard answer.

It is not that there is any dearth of doctrine, however. A Skinnerian behaviorist, for instance, would say that the strategy works because its imputations of beliefs and desires are shorthand, in effect, for as yet unimaginably complex descriptions of the effects of prior histories of response and reinforcement. To say that someone wants some ice cream is to say that in the past the ingestion of ice cream has been reinforced in him by the results, creating a propensity under certain background conditions (also too complex to describe) to engage in ice-cream-acquiring behavior. In the absence of detailed knowledge of those historical facts we can nevertheless make shrewd guesses on inductive grounds; these guesses are embodied in our intentional stance claims. Even if all this were true, it would tell us very little about the way such propensities were regulated by the internal machinery.

A currently more popular explanation is that the account of how the strategy works and the account of how the mechanism works will (roughly) *coincide*: for each predictively attributable belief, there will be a functionally salient internal state of the machinery, decomposable into functional parts in just about the same way the sentence expressing the belief is decomposable into parts – that is, words or terms. The inferences we attribute to rational creatures will be mirrored by physical, causal processes in the hardware; the *logical* form of the propositions believed will be copied in the *structural* form of the states in correspondence with them. This is the hypothesis that there is a *language of thought* coded in our brains, and our brains will eventually be understood as symbol-manipulating systems in at least rough analogy with computers. Many different versions of this view are currently being explored, in the new research program called cognitive science, and provided one allows great latitude for attenuation of the basic, bold claim, I think some version of it will prove correct.

But I do not believe that this is *obvious*. Those who think that it is obvious, or inevitable, that such a theory will prove true (and there are many who do), are confusing two different empirical claims. The first is that intentional stance description yields an objective, real pattern in the world – the pattern our imaginary Martians missed. This is an empirical claim, but one that is confirmed beyond skepticism. The second is that this real pattern is *produced* by another real pattern roughly isomorphic to it within the brains of intelligent creatures. Doubting the existence of the second real pattern is not doubting the existence of the first. There *are* reasons for believing in the second pattern, but they are not overwhelming. The best simple account I can give of the reasons is as follows.

As we ascend the scale of complexity from simple thermostat, through sophisticated robot, to human being, we discover that our efforts to design systems with the requisite behavior increasingly run foul of the problem of *combinatorial explosion*. Increasing some parameter by, say, 10 percent – 10 percent more inputs, or more degrees of freedom in the behavior to be controlled, or more words to be recognized, or whatever – tends to increase the internal complexity of the system being designed by orders of magnitude. Things get out of hand very fast and, for instance, can lead to computer programs that will swamp the largest, fastest machines. Now somehow the brain has solved the problem of combinatorial explosion. It is a gigantic network of billions of cells, but still finite, compact, reliable, and swift, and capable of learning new behaviors, vocabularies, theories, almost without limit. Some elegant, *generative*, indefinitely extendable principles of

representation must be responsible. We have only one model of such a representation system: a human language. So the argument for a language of thought comes down to this: what else could it be? We have so far been unable to imagine any plausible alternative in any detail. That is a good enough reason, I think, for recommending as a matter of scientific tactics that we pursue the hypothesis in its various forms as far as we can.[12] But we will engage in that exploration more circumspectly, and fruitfully, if we bear in mind that its inevitable rightness is far from assured. One does not well understand even a true empirical hypothesis so long as one is under the misapprehension that it is necessarily true.[13]

Notes

1 "Intentional systems," *Journal of Philosophy* (1971). "Conditions of personhood," in *The Identities of Persons* (ed. A. Rorty), University of California Press (1975). Both reprinted in *Brainstorms*, Montgomery Vt, Bradford (1978). "Three kinds of intentional psychology," in *Mind, Psychology and Reductionism* (ed. R. A. Healey), Cambridge University Press (1981).

2 *Pace* Paul Feyerabend, whose latest book, *Science in a Free Society*, New Left Books, London (1978), is heroically open-minded about astrology.

3 The idea that most of anyone's beliefs *must* be true seems obvious to some people. Support for the idea can be found in works by Quine, Putnam, Shoemaker, Davidson, and myself. Other people find the idea equally incredible – so probably each side is calling a different phenomenon belief. Once one makes the distinction between belief and opinion (in my technical sense – see "How to change your mind," in *Brainstorms*, ch. 16), according to which opinions are linguistically infected, relatively sophisticated cognitive states – *roughly*, states of betting on the truth of a particular, formulated sentence, one can see the near triviality of the claim that most beliefs are true. A few reflections on peripheral matters should bring it out. Consider Democritus, who had a systematic, all-embracing, but (let us say, for the sake of argument) entirely false physics. He had things *all wrong*, though his views held together and had a sort of systematic utility. But even if every *claim* that scholarship permits us to attribute to Democritus (either explicit or implicit in his writings) is false, these represent a vanishingly small fraction of his *beliefs*, which include both the vast numbers of humdrum standing beliefs he must have had (about which house he lived in, what

to look for in a good pair of sandals, and so forth), and also those occasional beliefs thatcame and went by the millions as his perceptual experience changed.

But, it may be urged, this isolation of his humdrum beliefs from his science relies on an insupportable distinction between truths of observation and truths of theory; all Democritus's beliefs are theory-laden, and since his theory is false, they are false. The reply is as follows: Granted that all observation beliefs are theory-laden, why should we choose Democritus's *explicit*, sophisticated theory (couched in his *opinions*) as the theory with which to burden his quotidian observations? Note that the least theoretical compatriot of Democritus also had myriads of theory-laden observation beliefs – and was, in one sense, none the wiser for it. Why should we not suppose their observations are laden with the same theory? If Democritus forgot his theory, or changed his mind, his observational beliefs would be *largely* untouched. To the extent that his sophisticated theory played a discernible role in his routine behavior and expectations and so forth, it would be quite appropriate to couch his humdrum beliefs in terms of the sophisticated theory, but this will not yield a *mainly false* catalog of beliefs, since so few of his beliefs wil be affected. (The effect of theory on observation is nevertheless often underrated. See Paul Churchland, *Scientific Realism and the Plasticity of Mind*, Cambridge University Press (1979), for dramatic and convincing examples of the tight relationship that can sometimes exist between theory and experience.) (The discussion in this note was distilled from a useful conversation with Paul and Patricia Churchland and Michael Stack.)

4 See my *Content and Consciousness*, Routledge & Kegan Paul, London (1969), pp. 184–5, and "How to change your mind," in *Brainstorms*.

5 See *Brainstorms*, and "Three kinds of intentional psychology." See also C. Cherniak, "Minimal rationality," *Mind*, (1981), and my response to Stephen Stich's "Headaches," in *Philosophical Books* (1980).

6 See "On giving libertarians what they say they want," in *Brainstorms*.

7 A member of the audience in Oxford pointed out that if the Martian included the Earthling in his physical stance purview (a possibility I had not explicitly excluded), he would not be surprised by the Earthling's prediction. He would indeed have predicted exactly the pattern of X-ray modulations produced by the Earthling speaking Martian. True, but as the Martian wrote down the results of his calculations, his prediction of the Earthling's prediction would appear, word by Martian word, as on a Ouija board, and what would be baffling to the Martian was how this chunk of mechanism, the Earthling predictor dressed up like a Martian, was able to yield this *true* sentence of Martian when it was so informationally isolated from the events the Martian needed to know of in order to make his own prediction about the arriving automobile.

8 Might there not be intelligent beings who had no use for communicating, predicting, observing . . . ? There might be marvelous, nifty, invulnerable entities lacking these modes of action, but I cannot see what would lead us to call them *intelligent*.

9 John McCarthy's analogy to cryptography nicely makes this point. The larger the corpus of cipher text, the less chance there is of dual, systematically unrelated decipherings. For a very useful discussion of the principles and presuppositions of the intentional stance applied to machines – explicitly including thermostats – see McCarthy's "Ascribing mental qualities to machines," in *Philosophical Perspectives on Artificial Intelligence* (ed. Martin Ringle), Humanities Press (1979).

10 Patrick Hayes explores this application of Tarskian model theory to the semantics of mental representation in "The naive physics manifesto" in *Expert Systems in the Micro-Electronic Age* (ed. D. Michie), Edinburgh University Press.

11 This idea is the ancestor in effect of the species of different ideas lumped together under the rubric of *de re* belief. If one builds from this idea towards its scions one can see better the difficulties with them, and how to repair them.

12 The fact that all *language of thought* models of mental representation so far proposed fall victim to combinatorial explosion in one way or another should temper one's enthusiasm for engaging in what Fodor aptly calls "the only game in town."

13 This essay was written during a Fellowship at the Center for Advanced Study in the Behavioral Sciences. I am grateful for financial support provided by the National Endowment for the Humanities, the National Science Foundation (BNS 78–24671), and the Alfred P. Sloan Foundation.

Dennett on Intentional Systems

Stephen P. Stich

During the last dozen years, Daniel Dennett has been elaborating an interconnected – and increasingly influential – set of views in the philosophy of mind, the philosophy of psychology, and those parts of moral philosophy that deal with the notions of freedom, responsibility, and personhood. The central unifying theme running through Dennett's writings on each of these topics is his concept of an *intentional system*. He invokes the concept to "legitimize" mentalistic predicates (*Brainstorms*, p. xvii),[1] to explain the theoretical strategy of cognitive psychology and artificial intelligence, and, ultimately, to attempt a reconciliation between "our vision of ourselves as responsible, free, rational agents, and our vision of ourselves as complex parts of the physical world

of science" (*BS*, p. x). My goal in this essay is to raise some doubts about the "intentional coin" (*BS*, p. xviii) with which Dennett proposes to purchase his moral and "mental treasures." Since I aim to offer a critique of Dennett's views, it is inevitable that much of what I say will be negative in tone. But this tone should not be misconstrued. It is my view that Dennett's theories are of great importance and will shape discussion in the philosophy of mind for decades to come. Moreover, I think that much of what Dennett says is close to being true. If we reconstruct his notion of an intentional system to eliminate its instrumentalism and its unfortunate infatuation with idealized rationality, we can use the result to give a better account of common-sense mentalistic notions, and also to give a clearer and more tenable account of the strategy of cognitive science. Toward the end of this essay I will sketch the outlines of such a "derationalized" cousin to Dennett's idea of an intentional system.

I

In explaining the idea of an intentional system, Dennett's recurrent illustration is the chess-playing computer. There are, he urges, three quite different stances we might "adopt in trying to predict and explain its behavior" (*BS*, p. 237).

First there is the *design stance*. If one knows exactly how the computer's program has been designed...one can predict the computer's designed response to any move one makes. One's prediction will come true provided only that the computer performs as designed, that is, without breakdown....The essential feature of the design stance is that we make predictions solely from knowledge or assumptions about the system's design, often without making any examination of the innards of the particular object.

Second, there is what we may call the *physical stance*. From this stance our predictions are based on the actual state of the particular system, and are worked out by applying whatever knowledge we have of the laws of nature. ...One seldom adopts the physical stance in dealing with a computer just because the number of critical variables in the physical constitution of a computer would overwhelm the most prodigious human calculator....Attempting to give a physical account or prediction of the chess playing computer would be a pointless and herculean labor, but it would work in principle. One could predict the response it would make in a chess game by tracing out the effects of the input energies all the way through the computer until once more type was pressed against paper and a response was printed.

There is a third stance one can adopt toward a system, and that is the *intentional stance*. This tends to be the most appropriate when the system one is dealing with is too complex to be dealt with effectively from the other stances. In the case of a chess playing computer one adopts this stance when one tries to predict its response to one's move by figuring out what a good or

reasonable response would be, given the information the computer has about the situation. Here one assumes not just the absence of malfunction but the rationality of the design or programming as well.

Whenever one can successfully adopt the intentional stance toward an object, I call that object an *intentional* system. The success of the stance is of course a matter settled pragmatically, without reference to whether the object *really* has beliefs, intentions, and so forth; so whether or not any computer can be conscious, or have thoughts or desires, some computers undeniably *are* intentional systems, for they are systems whose behavior can be predicted, and most efficiently predicted, by adopting the intentional stance towards them. (*BS*, pp. 237–8; for a largely identical passage, cf. *BS*, pp. 4–7.)

So *any* object will count as an intentional system if we can usefully predict its behavior by assuming that it will behave *rationally*. And what is it to behave rationally? Here, Dennett suggests, the full answer must ultimately be provided by a new sort of theory, *intentional–system theory*, which will provide us with a *normative* account of rationality. This new theory "is envisaged as a close kin of – and overlapping with – such already existing disciplines as epistemic logic, decision theory and game theory, which are all similarly abstract, normative and couched in intentional language" (*TK*, p. 19). Of course, we already have some "rough and ready principles" of rationality which we can and do press into service pending a more detailed normative theory:

1   A system's beliefs are those it *ought to have*, given its perceptual capacities, its epistemic needs, and its biography. Thus in general, its beliefs are both true and relevant to its life....
2   A system's desires are those it ought to have, given its biological needs and the most practicable means of satisfying them. Thus [naturally evolved] intentional systems desire survival and procreation, and hence desire food, security, health, sex, wealth, power, influence, and so forth, and also whatever local arrangements tend (in their eyes – given their beliefs) to further these ends in appropriate measure....
3   A system's behavior will consist of those acts that *it would be rational* for an agent with those beliefs and desires to perform. (*TK*, pp. 8–9)

Obviously these three principles are very rough and ready indeed. However, we also have a wealth of more detailed common-sense principles that anchor our intuitive notion of rationality. Some of these, in turn, are systematized and improved upon by existing theories in logic, evolutionary biology, and decision theory. But though the intentional–system theorist can count on some help from these more developed disciplines, he still has a great deal of work to do. Neither singly nor severally do these disciplines tell us what beliefs a given organism or system ought to have, what desires it ought to have, or how it should act, given the beliefs and desires it has. Dennett has no illusions on the point. He portrays intentional-system theory – the general normative theory of rationality – as a discipline in its infancy. When the course of our argument requires some substantive premises about what it would be rational for a system to believe or do, we can follow Dennett's lead and let our common-sense intuitions be our guide.

I have been stressing the role of a normative theory of rationality in Dennett's account of the intentional stance. But there is a second, equally important, component in his view. According to Dennett, when we describe an organism or an artifact as an intentional system, we are making no commitments about the internal physical work-ings of the system. *Nor are we saying anything about the design or program of the system.* Just as a single program or design description is compatible with indefinitely many physical realizations, so too a single intentional description is compatible with indefinitely many different programs or design descriptions. To view an object as an intentional system we must attribute to it a substantial range of beliefs and desires – the beliefs and desires it would be rational for such an object to have, given its nature and history. However, we need not assume that the beliefs and desires attributed cor-respond in any systematic way to internal states characterized either physically or functionally. Dennett makes the point vividly with the example of two robots each designed to be identical to a given person, Mary, when viewed from the inten-tional stance. The first robot, Ruth, "has internal processes which 'model' Mary's as closely as you like" (*BS*, p. 105). It is functionally identical to Mary, though the two may be quite different phys-ically. Since Mary and Ruth share a common design or program, they will behave identically. Thus any beliefs and desires we attribute to

Mary we may attribute also to Ruth, and the attributions will be equally useful in predicting their behavior. The second robot, Sally, has a program which is input–output equivalent to Ruth's, though it uses a quite different computa-tional strategy. "Sally may not be a very good psychological model of Mary," since "Sally's response delays, errors and the like may not match Mary's." But at the level of common-sense descriptions of actions, all three will behave alike. ". . . the ascription of all Mary's beliefs and desires (etc.) to Sally will be just as predictive as their ascription to Ruth so far as prediction of action goes" (*BS*, p. 105). So when we adopt the intentional stance, Mary, Ruth, and Sally are indistinguishable.

Dennett, then, is a self-professed instrumental-ist about the beliefs and desires we ascribe to an object when we adopt the intentional stance toward it. ". . . the beliefs and other intentions of an intentional system need [not] be *represented* 'within' the system in any way for us to get a purchase on predicting its behavior by ascribing such intentions to it" (*BS*, p. 277). Rather, these "putative . . . states" can be relegated "to the role of idealized fictions in an action-predicting, action-explaining calculus" (*BS*, p. 30). For Dennett, the belief and desire states of an intentional system are not what Reichenbach calls "illata – posited theoretical entities." Rather they are "abstracta – calculation bound entities or logical constructs" (*TK*, p. 13). Their status is analogous to the lines in a parallelogram of forces (*TK*, p. 20). Of course, it is conceivable that some objects which are usefully treated as intentional systems really do have internal states that correspond to the beliefs and desires ascribed to them in an intentional characterization. As some writers have suggested, there might be functionally distinct neural belief and desire stores where each belief and desire is inscribed in an appropriate neural code. Dennett, however, thinks this is not likely to be true for people, animals, and other familiar intentional systems.[2] Be this as it may, the import-ant point in the present context is that when we describe an object in intentional-system terms, we are quite explicitly *not* making any commitment about its workings, beyond the minimal claim that whatever the mechanism causally responsible for the behavior may be, it must be the sort of mechanism which will produce behavior generally predictable by assuming the intentional stance.

This completes my sketch of Dennett's notion of intentional systems. Let us now consider what Dennett wants to do with the notion. The principal project Dennett has in mind for intentional systems is "legitimizing" (*BS*, p. xvii), or providing a sort of "conceptual reduction" (*TK*, p. 30) of various notions in common-sense or folk psychology. The sort of legitimizing Dennett has in mind is explained by analogy with Church's Thesis. Church proposed that the informal, intuitive mathematical concept of an "effective" procedure be identified with the formal notion of a recursive (or Turing-machine computable) function. The proposal "is not provable, since it hinges on the intuitive and unformalizable notion of an effective procedure, but it is generally accepted, and it provides a very useful reduction of a fuzzy-but-useful mathematical notion to a crisply defined notion of apparently equal scope and greater power" (*BS*, p. xviii; cf. also *TK*, p. 30). It is Dennett's hope to provide the same sort of legitimization of the notions of folk psychology by showing how these notions can be characterized in terms of the notions of intentional-system theory. ". . . the claim that every mental phenomenon alluded to in folk psychology is *intentional-system-characterizable* would, if true, provide a reduction of the mental as ordinarily understood – a domain whose boundaries are at best fixed by mutual acknowledgement and shared intuition – to a clearly defined domain of entities, whose principles of organization are familiar, relatively formal and systematic, and entirely general" (*TK*, pp. 30–1).

All this sounds reasonable enough – an exciting project, if Dennett can pull it off. The effort looks even more intriguing when we note how broadly Dennett intends to cast his net. It is his aim to show not only that such "program receptive" (*BS*, p. 29) features of mentality as belief and desire are intentional-system-characterizable, but also that "program resistant features of mentality" like pain, dreams, mental images, and even free will are "captured in the net of intentional systems" (*BS*, p. xviii). But a dark cloud looms on the horizon, one that will continue to plague us. In much of his work Dennett exhibits an exasperating tendency to make bold, flamboyant, fascinating claims in one breath, only to take them back, or seem to, in the next. Thus, scarcely a page after proclaiming his intention to show that a broad range of common-sense mental phenomena are intentional-system-characterizable and thus legitimized, Dennett proclaims himself to be an eliminative materialist concerning these very same phenomena. Beliefs, desires, pains, mental images, experiences – as these are ordinarily understood – "are not good theoretical entities, however well entrenched" (*BS*, p. xx) the terms "belief," "pain," etc. may be in the habits of thought of our society. So "we legislate the putative items right out of existence" (*BS*, p. xx). How are we to make sense of this apparent contradiction?

There is, I think, a plausible – and uncontradictory – interpretation of what Dennett is up to. The problem he is grappling with is that the fit between our intuitive folk-psychological notions and the intentional-system characterizations he provides for them is just not as comfortable as the fit between the intuitive notion of effective mathematical procedure and the formal notion of Turing computability. Our folk-psychological concepts, "like folk productions generally," are complex, messy, variegated, and in danger of incoherence (*TK*, p. 16). By contrast, notions characterized in terms of intentional-system theory are – it is to be hoped – coherent, sharply drawn and constructed with a self-conscious eye for their subsequent incorporation into science (*TK*, p. 6). The intentional-system analysans are intended to be improvements on their analysanda. What they give us is not an "anthropological" (*TK*, p. 6) portrait of our folk notions (warts and all), but rather an improved version of "the parts of folk psychology worth caring about" (*TK*, p. 30). So Dennett is an eliminative materialist about mental phenomena alluded to in warts-and-all folk psychology; what are intentional-system-characterizable are not the notions of folk psychology, but rather related successor concepts which capture all that's worth caring about.

But now what are we to make of the claim that the intentional system *Ersätze* capture all that's worth caring about in folk psychology: What *is* worth caring about? Dennett concedes that an "anthropological" study of unreconstructed folk notions which includes "whatever folk actually include in their theory, however misguided, incoherent, gratuitous some of it may be," (*TK*, p. 6) would be a perfectly legitimate endeavor. Folk theory may be myth, "but it is a myth we live in, so it is an 'important' phenomenon in nature" (*TK*, p. 6).[3] However, Dennett does not share the anthropologist's (or the cognitive simulator's) interest in the idiosyncrasies and contradictions embedded in our folk notions. What is of interest to him, he strongly suggests, is "the proto-scientific quest": "an attempt to prepare folk theory for subsequent incorporation into or reduction to the rest of science," eliminating "all that is false or ill-founded" (*TK*, p. 6). If matters stopped there, we could parse Dennett's "all that's worth caring about" as "all that's worth caring about for the purposes of science." But matters do not stop there. To see why, we will have to take a detour to survey another central theme in Dennett's thinking.

As we have noted, a basic goal of Dennett's theory is to reconcile "our vision of ourselves as responsible, free, rational agents, and our vision of ourselves as complex parts of the physical world of science" (*BS*, p. x). The conflict that threatens between these two visions is a perennial philosophical preoccupation:

> the validity of our conceptual scheme of moral agents having dignity, freedom and responsibility stands or falls on the question: can men ever be truly said to have beliefs, desires, intentions? If they can, there is at least some hope of retaining a notion of the dignity of man; if they cannot, if men never can be said truly to want or believe, then surely they never can be said truly to act responsibly, or to have a conception of justice, or to know the difference between right and wrong. (*BS*, pp. 63–4)

Yet many psychologists, most notoriously Skinner, have denied that people have beliefs, desires, and other mental states.[4] This threat to our view of ourselves as moral agents does not arise only from rabid behaviorism. Dennett sees it lurking also in certain recently fashionable philosophical theories about the nature of mental states. Consider, for example, the type–type identity theory which holds that every mental-state type is to be identified with a physical-state type – a brain state characterized in physicochemical terms. What if it should turn out that there simply is *no* physical-state type that is shared by all beings to whom we commonly attribute the belief that snow is white? If we hang on to the type–type identity theory, then this very plausible empirical finding would seem to entail that there is no such mental state as believing that snow is white. Much the same result threatens from those versions of functionalism which hold that "each mental type is identifiable as a functional type in the language of Turing machine description" (*BS*, p. xvi). For "there is really no more reason to believe you and I 'have the same program' in *any* relaxed and abstract sense, considering the differences in our

nature and nurture, than that our brains have identical physico-chemical descriptions" (*BS*, p. xvi). So if we adhere to functionalism, a plausible result in cognitive psychology – the discovery that people do not have the same programs – threatens to establish that people do not have beliefs at all.[5]

We can now see one of the principal virtues of Dennett's instrumentalism about intentional systems. Since describing an object as an intentional system entails nothing whatever about either the physicochemical nature or the functional design of the mechanism that causes the object's behavior, neither neurophysiology nor "subpersonal cognitive psychology" (which studies the functional organization or program of the organism) could possibly show that the object was not an intentional system. Thus if beliefs and desires (or some respectable *Ersätze*) can be characterized in terms of intentional-system theory, we need have no fear that advances in psychology or brain science might establish that people do not really have beliefs and desires. So the viability of our "conceptual scheme of moral agents" is sustained, in this quarter at least.[6]

Now, finally, it is clear how Dennett's preoccupation with moral themes bears on his eliminative materialism. Recall that Dennett proposes to trade our ungainly folk-psychological notions for concepts characterized in terms of intentional systems. The claim is not that the new concepts are identical with the old, but that they are *better*. They are clearer, more systematic, free from the incoherence lurking in folk notions, *and they capture everything in folk psychology that is worth caring about.* One of the things worth caring about, for Dennett, is the suitability of the clarified notions for incorporation into science. However, if he is to succeed in insulating our moral worldview from the threat posed by scientific psychology, then there is obviously something else Dennett must count as worth caring about. The new concepts built from intentional-system notions must be as serviceable as the older folk notions in sustaining our vision of ourselves as persons.

II

In this section I want to examine just how well Dennett's intentional system *Ersätze* mirror the notions of folk psychology. My focus will be on the "program receptive" notions of belief and desire, concepts which should be easiest to purchase "with intentional coin," and my claim will be that the fit between our common-sense notions and Dennett's proffered replacements is a very poor one.[7] Of course, Dennett does not maintain that the fit is perfect, only that intentional-system theory preserves "the parts of folk psychology worth caring about" (*TK*, p. 30). This is the doctrine I am concerned to challenge. On my view, the move to an intentional-system-characterized notion of belief would leave us unable to say a great deal that we wish to say about ourselves and our fellows. Moreover, the losses will be important ones. If we accept Dennett's trade, we will have no coherent way to describe our cognitive shortcomings nor the process by which we may learn to overcome them. Equally unwelcome, the thriving scientific study of the strengths and weaknesses of human reasoning would wither and die, its hypotheses ruled literally incoherent. What is more, the instrumentalism of Dennett's intentional-system notions seems to fly in the face of some deeply rooted intuitions about responsibility and moral agency. Throughout most of what follows, I will cleave to the fiction that we already have a tolerably well worked out normative theory of rationality, or could readily build one, though in the closing pages I will offer some skeptical thoughts about how likely this fiction is.

I begin with the problems posed by irrationality. An intentional system, recall, is an ideally rational system; it believes, wants, and does just what it ought to, as stipulated by a normative theory of rationality. People, by contrast, are not ideally rational, and therein lies a devastating problem for Dennett. If we were to adopt his suggestion and trade up to the intentional-system notions of belief and desire (hereafter IS belief and IS desire), then we simply would not be able to say all those things we need to say about ourselves and our fellows when we deal with each other's idiosyncrasies, shortcomings, and cognitive growth.

Consider belief. Presumably no system *ought* to hold contradictory beliefs, and all systems *ought* to believe all the logical truths, along with all the logical consequences of what they believe (cf. *BS*, pp. 11, 20, 44; *TK*, p. 11). But people depart from this ideal in a variety of ways. We generally fail to believe *all* logical consequences of our beliefs – sometimes because the reasoning required would be difficult, and sometimes because we simply fail to take account of one or more of our beliefs. Suppose, for example, that an astronaut set the controls incorrectly and has sent his craft into a perilous spin. One possible explanation of his mistake would be that the on-board computer was down, and he had to hand-calculate the setting for the controls. He made a mistake in the calculation, and thus came to have a mistaken belief about what the setting should be. Another possibility is that, although he knew the craft was in the gravitational field of a nearby asteroid – indeed he could see it through the window – he simply forgot to take this into account in figuring out where the control should be set. There is nothing in the least paradoxical about these explanations. We offer similar explanations all the time in explaining our own actions and those of other people. Indeed, since these explanations are so intimately bound up with our notions of excuse and blame, quick-wittedness, absent-mindedness and a host of others, it boggles the mind to try imagining how we would get on with each other if we resolved to renounce them. But if, following Dennett, we agree to swap the folk notion of belief for the intentional-system notion, then renounce them we must. It simply makes no sense to attribute inferential failings or inconsistent beliefs to an ideally rational system.

Our intuitive grasp on the notion of rational desire is rather more tenuous than our grasp on the analogous notion for belief. Still, there seem to be many cases in which we want to ascribe desires to people which are not rational on any plausible reading of that term. Jones is a successful writer, in good health, with many friends and admirers. But he says he wants to die, and ultimately takes his own life. Smith has a dreadful allergy to chocolate, and he knows it. One taste and he is condemned to a week of painful, debilitating hives. But he *really* wants that chocolate bar at the checkout counter. After staring at it for a minute, he buys it and gobbles it down. Brown collects spiders. They are of no economic value, and he doesn't even think they are very pretty. But it is his hobby. He wants to add to his collection a specimen of a species found only in the desert. So, despite his dislike of hot weather, he arranges to spend his vacation spider hunting in Nevada. By my lights, both Jones's desire and Smith's are simply irrational. As for Brown, "irrational" seems much too strong. Yet it is certainly implausible to say that he *ought* to want that spider. So, on Dennett's account, it is not a rational desire. But idealized intentional systems have all and only the desires they ought to have. Thus if we trade the common-sense notion of want for Dennett's IS want, we simply will not be able to say that Brown wants the spider or that Jones wants to die.

The existence of examples like the ones I have been sketching is not news to Dennett. From his earliest paper on intentional systems to his most recent, he has struggled with analogous cases. Unfortunately, however, he is far from clear on what he proposes to do about them. As I read him, there are two quite different lines that he proposes; I will call them the *hard line* and the *soft line*. Neither is carefully spelled out in Dennett's writings, and he often seems to endorse both within a single paper. Once they have been sharply stated, I think it will be clear that neither line is tenable.

The Hard Line

The hard line sticks firmly with the idealized notion of an intentional system and tries to minimize the importance of the gap between IS beliefs and IS desires and their folk-psychological namesakes. The basic ploy here is to suggest that when folk psychology ascribes contradictory beliefs to people or when it insists that a person does not believe some of the consequences of his beliefs, folk psychology undermines its own usefulness and threatens to lapse into incoherence. When this happens, we are forced back to the design stance or the physical stance:

> The presumption of rationality is so strongly entrenched in our inference habits that when our predictions [based on the assumption] prove false, we at first cast about for adjustments in the information possession conditions (he must not have heard, he must not know English, he must not have seen x, . . .) or goal weightings, before questioning the rationality of the system as a whole. In extreme cases personalities may prove to be so unpredictable from the intentional stance that we abandon it, and if we have accumulated a lot of evidence in the meanwhile about the nature of response patterns in the individual, we may find that a species of design stance can be effectively adopted. This is the fundamentally different attitude we occasionally adopt toward the insane. (*BS*, pp. 9–10)

Here, surely, Dennett is *just wrong* about what we do when predictions based on idealized rationality prove false. When a neighborhood boy gives me the wrong change from my purchase at his lemon-

ade stand, I do not assume that he believes quarters are only worth 23 cents, nor that he wants to cheat me out of the 2 cents I am due. My *first* assumption is that he is not yet very good at doing sums in his head. Similarly, when a subject working on one of Wason and Johnson-Laird's deceptively difficult reasoning tasks gets the wrong answer, we are not likely to assume that he didn't understand the instructions, nor that he didn't want to get the right answer. Our *first* assumption is that he blew it; he made a mistake in reasoning.[8] What misleads Dennett here is that he is focusing on cases of counterintuitive or unfamiliar cognitive failings. When someone seems to have made a mistake we can't readily imagine ourselves ever making, we do indeed begin to wonder whether he might perhaps have some unanticipated beliefs and desires. Or if a person seems to be making enormous numbers of mistakes and ending up with a substantial hoard of bizarre beliefs, we grow increasingly reluctant to ascribe beliefs and desires to him at all. Perhaps we count him among the insane. These facts will assume some importance later on. But they are of little use to the hard-line defense of intentional systems. For it is in the diverse domain of more or less familiar inferential shortcomings that common sense most readily and usefully portrays people as departing from an idealized standard of rationality.

Dennett frequently suggests that we cannot coherently describe a person whose beliefs depart from the idealized standard:

> Conflict arises . . . when a person falls short of perfect rationality, and avows beliefs that either are strongly disconfirmed by the available empirical evidence or are self-contradictory or contradict other avowals he has made. If we lean on the myth that a man is perfectly rational, we must find his avowals less than authoritative: "You *can't* mean – understand – what you're saying!"; if we lean on his right as a speaking intentional system to have his word accepted, we grant him an irrational set of beliefs. Neither position provides a stable resting place, for, as we saw earlier, *intentional explanation and prediction cannot be accommodated either to breakdown or to less than optimal design, so there is no coherent intentional description of such an impasse.* (*BS*, 20; last emphasis added)[9]

In the paper from which the quote is taken, Dennett uses "intentional description," "intentional explanation," and the like for both common-sense belief-desire accounts and idealized intentional system accounts. The ambiguity this engenders is crucial in evaluating his claim. On the idealized intentional systems reading it is a tautology that "there is no coherent intentional description of such an impasse." But on the common-sense reading it is simply false. There is nothing at all incoherent about a (common-sense) intentional description of a man who has miscalculated the balance in his checking account!

The fact that folk psychology often comfortably and unproblematically views people as departing from the standard of full rationality often looms large in cases where questions of morality and responsibility are salient. Consider the case of Oscar, the engineer. It is his job to review planned operations at the factory and halt those that might lead to explosion. But one day there is an explosion and, bureaucracy being what it is, three years later Oscar is called before a board of inquiry. Why didn't he halt the hazardous operation? It looks bad for Oscar, since an independent expert has testified that the data Oscar had logically entail a certain equation, and it is a commonplace amongst competent safety engineers that the equation is a sure sign of trouble. But Oscar has an impressive defense. Granted the data he had entails the equation, and granted any competent engineer would know that the equation is a sign of trouble. But at the time of the accident neither Oscar nor anyone else knew that the data logically entailed the equation. It was only six months after the accident that Professor Brain at Cambridge proved a fundamental theorem needed to show that the data entail the equation. Without knowledge of the theorem, neither Oscar nor anyone else could be expected to believe that the data entail the equation.

At several places Dennett cites Quine as a fellow defender of the view that the ascription of inconsistent beliefs is problematic.

> To echo a theme I have long cherished in Quine's work, all the evidence – behavioral *and internal* – we acquire for the correctness of one of these ascriptions is not only evidence against the other, but the best sort of evidence. (*R*, p. 74)

However, Dennett misconstrues Quine's point. What Quine urges is not that *any* inconsistency is evidence of bad translation (or bad belief ascription), but rather that *obvious* inconsistency is a sign that something has gone wrong. For Quine, unlike

Dennett, sees translation (and belief ascription) as a matter of putting ourselves in our subject's shoes. And the self we put in those shoes, we are too well aware, departs in many ways from the standard of optimal rationality. The point can be made vividly by contrasting Oscar, our safety engineer, with Otto, a lesser functionary. Otto is charged with the responsibility of memorizing a list of contingency plans: if the red light flashes, order the building evacuated; if the warning light goes on, turn the big blue valve; if the buzzer sounds, alert the manager. Now suppose that while he is on duty the red light flashes but Otto fails to order an evacuation. There is a strong prima facie case that Otto is to be held responsible for the consequences. Either he failed to see the light (he was asleep or not paying due attention), or he did not memorize the contingency plans as he was obligated to, or he has some sinister motive. But, and this is the crucial point, it will be no excuse for Otto to claim that he had memorized the plan, saw the light, and was paying attention, but it just never occurred to him to order the evacuation. It is in these cases of apparently blatant or "incomprehensible" irrationality that we hunt first for hidden motives or beliefs. For, absent these, the subject must be judged irrational in a way we cannot imagine ourselves being irrational; and it is this sort of irrationality that threatens the application of our common-sense notions of belief and desire.

In Dennett's writings there are frequent hints of a second strategy for defending the hard line, a strategy which relies on an evolutionary argument. He cheerfully concedes that he has "left [his] claim about the relation between rationality and evolutionary considerations so open-ended that it is hard to argue against efficiently" (*R*, p. 73). Still, I think it is important to try wringing some arguments out of Dennett's vague meditations on this topic. As I read him, Dennett is exploring a pair of ideas for showing that the gap between IS notions and folk notions is much smaller than some have feared. If he can show this, the hard line will have been vindicated.

The first idea is suggested by a passage (*BS*, pp. 8–9) in which Dennett asks whether we could adopt the intentional stance toward exotic creatures encountered on an alien planet. His answer is that we could, provided "we have reason to suppose that a process of natural selection has been in effect..." (*BS*, p. 8). The argument seems to be that natural selection favors true beliefs, and thus will favor cognitive processes which generally yield true beliefs in the organism's natural environment. So if an organism is the product of natural selection, we can safely assume that most of its beliefs will be true, and most of its belief-forming strategies will be rational. Departures from the normative standard required by the intentional stance will be few and far between.

For two quite different reasons, this argument is untenable. First, it is simply not the case that natural selection favors true beliefs over false ones. What natural selection does favor is beliefs which yield selective advantage. And there are many environmental circumstances in which false beliefs will be more useful than true ones. In these circumstances, natural selection ought to favor cognitive processes which yield suitable false beliefs and disfavor processes which yield true beliefs. Moreover, even when having true beliefs is optimal, natural selection may often favor a process that yields false beliefs most of the time, but which has a high probability of yielding true beliefs when it counts. Thus, for example, in an environment with a wide variety of suitable foods, an organism may do very well if it radically over-generalizes about what is inedible. If eating a certain food caused illness on a single occasion, the organism would immediately come to believe (falsely, let us assume) that all passingly similar foods are poisonous as well. When it comes to food poisoning, *better safe than sorry* is a policy that recommends itself to natural selection.[10]

The second fault in the argument I am attributing to Dennett is a subtle but enormously important one. As stated, the argument slips almost unnoticeably from the claim that natural selection favors cognitive processes which yield true beliefs in the natural environment to the claim that natural selection favors *rational* belief-forming strategies. But, even if the first claim were true, the second would not follow. There are many circumstances in which inferential strategies which from a normative standpoint are patently invalid will nonetheless generally yield the right answer. The social-psychology literature is rich with illustrations of inferential strategies which stand subjects in good stead ordinarily but which subjects readily overextend, with unhappy results.[11]

So long as we recognize a distinction between a normative theory of inference or decision making and a set of inferential practices which (in the right environment) generally get the right (or selectively useful) answer, it will be clear that the two need

not, and generally do not, coincide. However, in a number of places Dennett seems to be suggesting that there really *is* no distinction here, that by "normative theory of inference and decision" he simply *means* "practices favored by natural selection." This move is at the core of the second idea I see in Dennett for using evolutionary notions to buttress the hard line (cf. *R*, pp. 73–4). And buttress it would! For it would then become *tautologous* that naturally evolved creatures are intentional systems, believing, wanting, and doing what they ought, save when they are malfunctioning. Yet Dennett will have to pay a heavy price for turning the hard line into a tautology. For if *this* is what he means by "normative theory of belief and decision," then such established theories as deductive and inductive logic, decision theory, and game theory are of no help in assessing what an organism "ought to believe." Natural selection, as we have already noted, sometimes smiles upon cognitive processes that depart substantially from the canons of logic and decision theory. So these established theories and our guesses about how to extend them will be of no help in assessing what an intentional system should believe, desire, or do. Instead, to predict from the intentional stance we should need a detailed study of the organism's physiology, its ecological environment, and its history. But predicting from the intentional stance, characterized in *this* way, is surely not to be recommended when we "doubt the practicality of prediction from the design or physical stance" (*BS*, p. 8). Nor, obviously, does *this* intentional stance promise to yield belief and desire attributions that are all but coextensive with those made in common sense.

This is all I shall have to say by way of meeting the hard line head on. I think it is fair to conclude that the hard line simply cannot be maintained. The differences separating the IS notions of belief and desire from their common-sense counterparts are anything but insubstantial. Before turning to Dennett's soft line, we should note a further unwelcome consequence of rejecting folk psychology in favor of intentional-system theory. During the last decade, cognitive psychologists have become increasingly interested in studying the strengths and foibles of human reasoning. There is a substantial and growing literature aimed at uncovering predictable departures from normative standards of reasoning and decision making, almost all of it implicitly or explicitly cast in the idiom of folk psychology.[12] Were we to replace folk notions with their intentional-system analogs, we should have to conclude that all of this work lining the boundaries of human rationality is simply incoherent. For, as Dennett notes, "the presuppositions of intentional explanation...put prediction of *lapses* in principle beyond its scope..." (*BS*, p. 246).[13]

The Soft Line

In contrast with the hard line, which tries to minimize the size or importance of the difference between folk and IS notions, the soft line acknowledges a substantial and significant divergence. To deal with the problems this gap creates, the soft line proposes some fiddling with the idealized notion of an intentional system. The basic idea is that once we have an idealized theory of intentional systems in hand, we can study an array of variations on the idealized theme. We can construct theories about "imperfect intentional systems" (the term is mine, not Dennett's) which have specified deficiences in memory, reasoning power, etc. And we can attempt to determine empirically which imperfect intentional system best predicts the behavior of a particular subject or species. Rather than assuming the intentional stance toward an organism or person, we may assume one of a range of "imperfect intentional stances," from which it will make sense to ascribe a less than fully rational set of beliefs and desires. From these various stances we can give intentional descriptions of our cognitive shortcomings and elaborate an empirical science which maps the inferential strengths and weaknesses of humans and other creatures. We can also legitimize our folk-psychological descriptions of ourselves – protecting "personhood from the march of science" (*R*, p. 75) – by appeal to the imperfect-intentional-system theory which best predicts our actual behavior. But *genuine* intentional-system theory (*sans phrase*) would have a definite pride of place among these theories of imperfect intentional systems. For all of the latter would be variations on the basic IS framework.

Dennett, with his disconcerting penchant for working both sides of the street, never flatly endorses the soft line, though it is clear that he has pondered something like it:

Consider a set *T* of transformations that take beliefs into beliefs. The problem is to determine the set T_s for each intentional system *S*, so that if we know that *S* believes *p*, we will be able to determine other things that *S* believes by seeing what the transformations of *p* are for T_s. If *S* were ideally rational, every valid transformation would be in T_s; *S* would believe every logical consequence of every belief (and, ideally, *S* would have no false beliefs). Now we know that no actual intentional system will be ideally rational; so we must suppose any actual system will have a *T* with less in it. But we also know that, to qualify as an intentional system at all, *S* must have a *T* with some integrity; *T* cannot be empty. (*BS*, p. 21)

In the next few sentences, however, Dennett expresses qualms about the soft line:

What rationale could we have, however, for fixing some set between the extremes and calling it *the* set for belief (for *S*, for earthlings, for ten-year-old-girls)? This is another way of asking whether we could replace Hintikka's normative theory of belief with an empirical theory of belief, and, if so, what evidence we would use. "Actually," one is tempted to say, "people do believe contradictions on occasion, as their utterances demonstrate; so any adequate logic of belief or analysis of the concept of belief must accommodate this fact." But any attempt to *legitimize* human fallibility in a theory of belief by fixing a permissible level of error would be like adding one more rule to chess: an Official Tolerance Rule to the effect that any game of chess containing no more than *k* moves that are illegal relative to the other rules of the game is a legal game of chess. (*BS*, p. 21)

In a more recent paper, Dennett sounds more enthusiastic about the soft line:

Of course we don't all sit in the dark in our studies like mad Leibnizians rationalistically excogitating behavioral predictions from pure, idealized concepts of our neighbors, nor do we derive all our readiness to attribute desires to a careful generation of them from the ultimate goal of survival.... Rationalistic generation of attributions is augmented and even corrected on occasion by empirical generalizations about belief and desire that guide our attributions and are learned more or less inductively.... I grant the existence of all this naturalistic generalization, and its role in the normal calculation of folk psychologists – i.e., all of us. . . . *I would insist, however, that all this empirically obtained lore is laid over a fundamental generative and normative framework that has the features I have described.* (*TK*, pp. 14–15, last emphasis added)

Whatever Dennett's considered view may be, I think the soft line is clearly preferable to the hard line. Indeed, the soft line is similar to a view that I have myself defended.[14] As a way of focusing in on my misgivings about the soft line, let me quickly sketch my own view and note how it differs from the view I am trying to foist on Dennett. Mine is an effort squarely situated in what Dennett calls "the anthropological quest" (*TK*, p. 6). I want to describe as accurately as possible just what we are up to when we engage in the "folk practice" of ascribing beliefs to one another and dealing with one another partly on the basis of these ascriptions. My theory is an elaboration on Quine's observation that in ascribing beliefs to others "we project ourselves into what, from his remarks and other indications, we imagine the speaker's state of mind to have been, and then we say what, in our language, is natural and relevant for us in the state thus feigned" (*Word and Object*, p. 219). As I see it, when we say *S believes that p* we are saying that *S* is in a certain sort of functionally characterized psychological state, viz., a "belief state." The role of the "content sentence", *p*, is to specify *which* belief state it is. If we imagine that we ourselves were now to utter *p* in earnest, the belief we are attributing to *S* is one *similar* (along specified dimensions) to the belief which would cause our own imagined assertion. One of the dimensions of similarity that figures in belief ascription is the pattern of inference that the belief states in question enter into. When the network of potential inferences surrounding a subject's belief state differs substantially from the network surrounding our own belief that *p*, we are reluctant to count the subject's belief as a belief *that p*. Thus we will not have any comfortable way of ascribing content to the belief states of a subject whose inferential network is markedly different from ours. Since we take ourselves to approximate rationality, this explains the fact, noted by Dennett, that intentional description falters in the face of egregious irrationality. It also explains the fact, missed by Dennett, that familiar irrationality – the sort we know ourselves to be guilty of – poses no problem for folk psychology.

A full elaboration of my theory would be a long story, out of place here. What is important for our present purposes is to note the differences between my account and what I have been calling Dennett's soft line. These differences are two. First, my story does not portray folk psychology as an *instrumentalist* theory. Belief states are *functional* states which can and do play a role in the causation of behavior. Thus folk psychology is not immune from the advance of science. If it turns out that the human brain does not have the sort of functional organization assumed in our folk theory, then there are no such things as beliefs and desires. Second, the notion of idealized rationality plays *no role at all* in my account. In ascribing content to belief states, we measure others not against an idealized standard but against ourselves. It is in virtue of this Protagorean parochialism that the exotic and the insane fall outside the reach of intentional explanation.

So much for the difference between my view and Dennett's. Why should mine be preferred? There are two answers. First, I think it is simply wrong that we ordinarily conceive of beliefs and desires in instrumentalist terms – as abstracta rather than illata. It is, however, no easy task to take aim at Dennett's instrumentalism, since the target refuses to stay still. Consider:

Folk psychology is *instrumentalistic* . . . Beliefs and desires of folk psychology . . . are abstracta. (*TK*, p. 13)

It is not particularly to the point to argue against me that folk psychology is *in fact* committed to beliefs and desires as distinguishable, causally interacting *illata*; what must be shown is that it ought to be. The latter claim I will deal with in due course. The former claim I *could* concede without embarrassment to my overall project, but I do not concede it, for it seems to me that the evidence is quite strong that our ordinary notion of belief has next to nothing of the concrete in it. (*TK*, p. 15)

The *ordinary* notion of belief no doubt does place beliefs somewhere midway between being *illata* and being *abstracta*. (*TK*, p. 16)

In arguing for his sometimes instrumentalism Dennett conjures the sad tale of Pierre, shot dead by Jacques in Trafalgar Square. Jacques is apprehended on the spot by Sherlock; Tom reads about it in the *Times* and Boris learns of it in *Pravda*. Now Jacques, Sherlock, Tom and Boris have had remarkably different experiences – to say nothing of their earlier biographies and future prospects – but there is one thing they share: they all believe that a Frenchman has committed a murder in Trafalgar Square. They did not all *say* this, not even "to themselves"; *that proposition* did not, we can suppose, "occur to" any of them, and even if it had, it would have had entirely different import for Jacques, Sherlock, Tom and Boris. (*TK*, p. 15)

Dennett's point is that while all four men believe that a Frenchman committed a murder in Trafalgar Square, their histories, interests, and relations to the deed are so different that they could hardly be thought to share a single, functionally characterizable state. This is quite right, but it does not force us to view beliefs as abstracta. For if, as my theory insists, there is a *similarity* claim embedded in belief ascriptions, then we should expect these ascriptions to be both vague and sensitive to pragmatic context. For Jacques and Boris both to believe that a Frenchman committed a murder in Trafalgar Square, they need not be in the very same functional state, but only in states that are sufficiently similar for the communicative purposes at hand.

As Dennett notes, one need not be crucially concerned with what "folk psychology is in fact committed to." Since he aims to replace folk psychology with intentional-system notions, it would suffice to show that the instrumentalism of these latter notions is no disadvantage. But here again I am skeptical. It is my hunch that our concept of ourselves as moral agents simply will not sit comfortably with the view that beliefs and desires are mere computational conveniences that correspond in no interesting way to what goes on inside the head. I cannot offer much of an argument for my hunch, though I am encouraged by the fact that Dennett seems to share the intuition lying behind it:

Stich accurately diagnoses and describes the strategic role I envisage for the concept of an intentional system, permitting the claim that human beings are genuine believers and desirers to survive almost any imaginable discoveries in cognitive and physiological psychology, thus making our status as moral agents well nigh invulnerable to scientific disconfirmation. Not "in principle" invulnerable, for in a science-fiction mood we can imagine startling discoveries (e.g., some "people" are organic puppets remotely controlled by Martians) that would upset any particular home truths about believers and moral agenthood you like.... (*R*, p. 73)

Now if our concept of moral agenthood were really compatible with the intentional-system construal of beliefs and desires, it is hard to see why the imagined discovery about Martians should be in the least unsettling. For, controlled by Martians or not, organic puppets are still intentional systems in perfectly good standing. So long as their behavior is usefully predictable from the intentional stance, the transceivers inside their heads sanction no skepticism about whether they really have IS beliefs and IS desires. But Dennett is right, of course. We would not count his organic puppets as believers or moral agents. The reason, I submit, is that the morally relevant concept of belief is not an instrumentalistic concept.

The second reason for preferring my line to Dennett's soft line is that the idea of a *normative* theory of beliefs and desires, which is central to Dennett's view, plays no role in mine. And this notion, I would urge, is one we are best rid of. Recall that from the outset we have been relying on rough and ready intuitions about what an organism ought to believe, desire, and do, and assuming that these intuitions could be elaborated and systematized into a theory. But I am inclined to think that this assumption is mistaken. Rather, it would appear that the intuitions Dennett exploits are underlain by a variety of different ideas about what an organism ought to believe or desire, ideas which as often as not pull in quite different directions. Sometimes it is an evolutionary story which motivates the intuition that a belief or desire is the one a well-designed intentional system should have. At other times intuitions are guided by appeal to logic or decision theory. But as we have seen, the evolutionary account of what an organism ought to believe and desire just will not do for Dennett, since it presupposes an abundance of information about the ecological niche and physiological workings of the organism. Nor is there any serious prospect of elaborating logic and decision theory into a suitably general account of what an organism ought to believe and desire. Indeed, apart from a few special cases, I think our intuitions about what an organism ought to believe and desire are simply nonexistent. The problem is not merely that we lack a worked-out normative theory of belief and desire; it runs much deeper. For in general we have no idea what such a normative theory would be telling us. We do not really know what it *means* to say that an organism *ought to have* a given belief or desire. Consider some examples:

Ought Descartes to have believed his theory of vortices?

Ought Nixon to have believed that he would not be impeached?

Ought William James to have believed in the existence of a personal God?

Should all people have perfect memories, retaining for life all beliefs save those for which they later acquire negative evidence?

In each of these cases our grasp of what the question is supposed to *mean* is at best tenuous. The prospects of a *general theory* capable of answering all of them in a motivated way are surely very dim. Worse still, the general theory of intentional systems that Dennett would have us work toward must tell us

not only what *people* in various situations ought to believe, but also what other animals ought to believe. Ought the frog to believe that there is an insect flying off to the right? Or merely that there is some food there? Or perhaps should it only have a conditional belief: if it flicks its tongue in a certain way, something yummy will end up in its mouth? Suppose the fly is of a species that causes frogs acute indigestion. Ought the frog to believe this? Does it make a difference how many fellow frogs he has seen come to grief after munching on similar bugs? A normative theory of desire is, if anything, more problematic. Should I want to father as many offspring as possible? Should the frog?

To the extent that these questions are obscure, the notion of a normative theory of belief and desire is obscure. And that obscurity in turn infects much of what Dennett says about intentional systems and the intentional stance. Perhaps Dennett can dispel some of the mystery. But in the interim I am inclined to think that the normatively appropriate attitude is the skepticism I urged in my opening paragraph.[15]

Notes

1 References to Dennett's writings will be identified in parentheses in the text. I will use the following abbreviations:
   BS = Daniel Dennett, *Brainstorms* (Montgomery, Vt: Bradford Books, 1978).
   TK = Daniel Dennett, "Three kinds of intentional psychology," in *Reduction, Time, and Reality* (ed. R. A. Healey), Cambridge University Press, 1981.
   R = Daniel Dennett, "Reply to Professor Stich," *Philosophical Books*, 21, 2 (April, 1980).
   TB = Daniel Dennett, "True believers: the intentional strategy and why it works," reprinted in this volume above.

2 For his arguments on this point, cf. "Brain writing and mind reading," (*BS*, pp. 39–50) and "A cure for the common code," (*BS*, pp. 90–108).

3 This "anthropological quest," when pursued systematically is the business of the cognitive simulator. Cf., for example, Roger Shank and Robert Abelson, *Scripts, Plans, Goals and Understanding* (Hillsdale, NJ: Lawrence Erlbaum Associates, 1977); also Aaron Sloman, *The Computer Revolution in Philosophy* (Atlantic Highlands, NJ: Humanities Press, 1978), ch. 4.

4 Skinner often muddies the waters by claiming to offer "translations" of common-sense mentalistic terms into the language of behaviorism. But, as Dennett and others have noted (*BS*, pp. 53–70), these "translations" generally utterly fail to capture the meaning or even the extension of the common-sense term being "translated."

5 For an elaboration of the point, cf. Thomas Nagel, "Armstrong on the mind," *Philosophical Review*, 79 (1970), pp. 394–403.

6 An entirely parallel strategy works for those other common-sense mental phenomena which Dennett takes to be essential to our concept of ourselves as persons – e.g., consciousness (*BS*, p. 269). If we can give an acceptable intentional system *Ersatz* for the folk-psychological notion of consciousness, we need have no fear that advances in science will threaten our personhood by showing that the notion of consciousness is otiose in the causal explanation of our behavior.

7 For some qualms about Dennett's treatment of "program resistant" features of mentality like pains, see my "Headaches," *Philosophical Books*, April 1980.

8 Cf. P. C. Wason and P. N. Johnson-Laird, *The Psychology of Human Reasoning: Structure and Content* (London: Batsford, 1972).

9 For parallel passages, cf. *TB*, p. 19; *R*, p. 74; *BS*, p. 22.

10 For a detailed discussion of some examples and further references, cf. H. A. Lewis, "The argument from evolution," *Proceedings of the Aristotelian Society*, supplementary vol. LIII, 1979; also my "Could man be an irrational animal?" *Synthese* 64 (1985), 115–35.

11 Cf. Richard Nisbett and Lee Ross, *Human Inference* (Englewood Cliffs, NJ: Prentice-Hall, 1980).

12 E.g., Nisbett and Ross, *Human Inference*, and Wason and Johnson-Laird, *Psychology of Human Reasoning*, along with the many studies cited in these books.

13 Dennett appends the following footnote to the quoted sentence: "In practice we predict lapses at the intentional level ("You watch! He'll forget all about your knight after you move the queen") on the basis of loose-jointed inductive hypotheses about individual or widespread human frailties. These hypotheses are expressed in intentional terms, but if they were given rigorous support, they would in the process be recast as predictions from the design or physical stance" (*BS*, p. 246). So the scientific study of intentionally described inferential short-comings can aspire to no more than "loose-jointed hypotheses" in need of recasting. But cf. *TK*, pp. 11–12, where Dennett pulls in his horns a bit.

14 In "On the ascription of content," in A. Woodfield (ed.), *Thought and Object* (Oxford University Press, 1982).

15 I have learned a good deal from the helpful comments of Bo Dahlbom, Robert Cummins, Philip Pettit, and Robert Richardson.

Real Patterns

Daniel C. Dennett

Are there really beliefs? Or are we learning (from neuroscience and psychology, presumably) that, strictly speaking, beliefs are figments of our imagination, items in a superseded ontology? Philosophers generally regard such ontological questions as admitting just two possible answers: either beliefs exist or they do not. There is no such state as quasi existence; there are no stable doctrines of semirealism. Beliefs must either be vindicated along with the viruses or banished along with the banshees. A bracing conviction prevails, then, to the effect that when it comes to beliefs (and other mental items) one must be either a realist or an eliminative materialist.

1 Realism About Beliefs

This conviction prevails in spite of my best efforts over the years to undermine it with various analogies: are *voices* in your ontology?[1] Are *centers of gravity* in your ontology?[2]

It is amusing to note that my analogizing beliefs to centers of gravity has been attacked from both sides of the ontological dichotomy, by philosophers who think it is simply obvious that centers of gravity are useful fictions, and by philosophers who think it is simply obvious that centers of gravity are perfectly real:

The trouble with these supposed parallels . . . is that they are all strictly speaking *false*, although they are no doubt useful simplifications for many purposes. It is false, for example, that the gravitational attraction between the Earth and the Moon involves two point masses; but it is a good enough first approximation for many calculations. However, this is not at all what Dennett really wants to say about intentional states. For he insists that to adopt the intentional stance and interpret an agent as acting on certain beliefs and desires is to discern a pattern in his actions which is genuinely there (a pattern which is missed if we instead adopt a scientific stance): Dennett certainly does not hold that the role of intentional ascriptions is merely to give us a useful approximation to a truth that can be more accurately expressed in non-intentional terms.[3]

Compare this with Fred Dretske's[4] equally confident assertion of realism:

I am a realist about centers of gravity. . . . The earth obviously exerts a gravitational attraction on *all* parts of the moon – not just its center of gravity. The *resultant* force, a vector sum, acts through a point, but this is something quite different. One should be very clear about what centers of gravity are *before* deciding whether to be literal about them, *before* deciding whether or not to be a center-of-gravity realist. (Ibid., p. 511)

Dretske's advice is well-taken. What are centers of gravity? They are mathematical points –

abstract objects or what Hans Reichenbach called *abstracta* – definable in terms of physical forces and other properties. The question of whether abstract objects are real – the question of whether or not "one should be a realist about them" – can take two different paths, which we might call the metaphysical and the scientific. The metaphysical path simply concerns the reality or existence of abstract objects generally, and does not distinguish them in terms of their scientific utility. Consider, for instance, the *center of population* of the United States. I define this as the mathematical point at the intersection of the two lines such that there are as many inhabitants north as south of the latitude, and as many inhabitants east as west of the longitude. This point is (or can be) just as precisely defined as the center of gravity or center of mass of an object. (Since these median strips might turn out to be wide, take the midline of each strip as the line; count as inhabitants all those within the territorial waters and up to twenty miles in altitude – orbiting astronauts do not count – and take each inhabitant's navel to be the determining point, etc.) I do not know the center of population's current geographic location, but I am quite sure it is west of where it was ten years ago. It jiggles around constantly, as people move about, taking rides on planes, trains, and automobiles, etc. I doubt that this abstract object is of any value at all in any scientific theory, but just in case it is, here is an even more trivial abstract object: Dennett's lost sock center: the point defined as the center of the smallest sphere that can be inscribed around all the socks I have ever lost in my life.

These abstract objects have the same metaphysical status as centers of gravity. Is Dretske a realist about them all? Should we be? I do not intend to pursue this question, for I suspect that Dretske is – and we should be – more interested in the scientific path to realism: centers of gravity are real because they are (somehow) *good* abstract objects. They deserve to be taken seriously, learned about, used. If we go so far as to distinguish them as *real* (contrasting them, perhaps, with those abstract objects which are *bogus*), that is because we think they serve in perspicuous representations of real forces, "natural" properties, and the like. This path brings us closer, in any case, to the issues running in the debates about the reality of beliefs.

I have claimed that beliefs are best considered to be abstract objects rather like centers of gravity. Smith considers centers of gravity to be useful fictions while Dretske considers them to be useful

(and hence?) real abstractions, and each takes his view to constitute a criticism of my position. The optimistic assessment of these opposite criticisms is that they cancel each other out; my analogy must have hit the nail on the head. The pessimistic assessment is that more needs to be said to convince philosophers that a mild and intermediate sort of realism is a positively attractive position, and not just the desperate dodge of ontological responsibility it has sometimes been taken to be. I have just such a case to present, a generalization and extension of my earlier attempts, via the concept of a *pattern*. My aim on this occasion is not so much to prove that my intermediate doctrine about the reality of psychological states is right, but just that it is quite possibly right, because a parallel doctrine is demonstrably right about some simpler cases.

We use folk psychology – interpretation of each other as believers, wanters, intenders, and the like – to predict what people will do next. Prediction is not the only thing we care about, of course. Folk psychology helps us understand and empathize with others, organize our memories, interpret our emotions, and flavor our vision in a thousand ways, but at the heart of all these is the enormous predictive leverage of folk psychology. Without its predictive power, we could have no interpersonal projects or relations at all; human activity would be just so much Brownian motion; we would be baffling ciphers to each other and to ourselves – we could not even conceptualize our own flailings. In what follows, I shall concentrate always on folk-psychological prediction, not because I make the mistake of ignoring all the other interests we have in people aside from making bets on what they will do next, but because I claim that our power to *interpret* the actions of others depends on our power – seldom explicitly exercised – to predict them.[5]

Where utter patternlessness or randomness prevails, nothing is predictable. The success of folk-psychological prediction, like the success of any prediction, depends on there being some order or pattern in the world to exploit. Exactly where in the world does this pattern exist? What is the pattern a pattern *of*?[6] Some have thought, with Fodor, that the pattern of belief must in the end be a pattern of structures in the brain, formulae written in the language of thought. Where else could it be? Gibsonians might say the pattern is "in the light" – and Quinians (such as Donald Davidson and I) could almost agree: the pattern is discernible in agents' (observable) behavior when we subject it to "radical interpretation" (Davidson) "from the intentional stance" (Dennett).

When are the elements of a pattern real and not merely apparent? Answering this question will help us resolve the misconceptions that have led to the proliferation of "ontological positions" about beliefs, the different grades or kinds of realism. I shall concentrate on five salient exemplars arrayed in the space of possibilities: Fodor's industrial-strength Realism (he writes it with a capital "R"); Davidson's regular strength realism; my mild realism; Richard Rorty's milder-than-mild irrealism, according to which the pattern is *only* in the eyes of the beholders, and Paul Churchland's eliminative materialism, which denies the reality of beliefs altogether.

In what follows, I shall assume that these disagreements all take place within an arena of common acceptance of what Arthur Fine[7] calls NOA, the natural ontological attitude. That is, I take the interest in these disagreements to lie not in differences of opinion about the ultimate metaphysical status of physical things or abstract things (e.g., electrons or centers of gravity), but in differences of opinion about whether beliefs and other mental states are, shall we say, *as real as* electrons or centers of gravity. I want to show that mild realism is the doctrine that makes the most sense when what we are talking about is real patterns, such as the real patterns discernible from the intentional stance.[8]

In order to make clear the attractions and difficulties of these different positions about patterns, I shall apply them first to a much simpler, more readily visualized, and uncontroversial sort of pattern.

2 The Reality of Patterns

Consider the six objects in figure 5.1 (which I shall call *frames*).

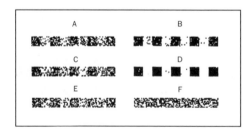

Figure 5.1

We can understand a frame to be a finite subset of data, a window on an indefinitely larger world of further data. In one sense $A-F$ all display different patterns; if you look closely you will see that no two frames are exactly alike ("atom-for-atom replicas," if you like). In another sense, $A-F$ all display the same pattern; they were all made by the same basic process, a printing of ten rows of ninety dots, ten black dots followed by ten white dots, etc. The overall effect is to create five equally spaced black squares or bars in the window. I take it that this pattern, which I shall dub *bar code*, is a real pattern if anything is. But some random (actually pseudo-random) "noise" has been allowed to interfere with the actual printing. The noise ratio is as follows:

A: 25%
B: 10%
C: 25%
D: 1%
E: 33%
F: 50%

It is impossible to see that F is not purely (pseudo-) random noise; you will just have to take my word for it that it was actually generated by the same program that generated the other five patterns; all I changed was the noise ratio.

Now, what does it mean to say that a pattern in one of these frames is real, or that it is really there? Given our privileged information about how these frames were generated, we may be tempted to say that there is a single pattern in all six cases – even in F, where it is "indiscernible." But I propose that the self-contradictory air of "indiscernible pattern" should be taken seriously. We may be able to make some extended, or metaphorical, sense of the idea of indiscernible patterns (or invisible pictures or silent symphonies), but in the root case a pattern is "by definition" a candidate for pattern *recognition*. (It is this loose but unbreakable link to observers or perspectives, of course, that makes "pattern" an attractive term to someone perched between instrumentalism and industrial-strength realism.)

Fortunately, there is a standard way of making these intuitions about the discernibility-in-principle of patterns precise. Consider the task of transmitting information about one of the frames from one place to another. How many bits of information will it take to transmit each frame? The least efficient method is simply to send the "bit map," which identifies each dot *seriatim* ("dot one is black, dot two is white, dot three is white, …").

For a black-and-white frame of 900 dots (or pixels, as they are called), the transmission requires 900 bits. Sending the bit map is in effect verbatim quotation, accurate but inefficient. Its most important virtue is that it is equally capable of transmitting any pattern or any particular instance of utter patternlessness.

Gregory Chaitin's[9] valuable definition of mathematical randomness invokes this idea. A series (of dots or numbers or whatever) is random if and only if the information required to describe (transmit) the series accurately is *incompressible:* nothing shorter than the verbatim bit map will preserve the series. Then a series is not random – has a pattern – if and only if there is some more efficient way of describing it.[10] Frame *D*, for instance, can be described as "ten rows of ninety: ten black followed by ten white, etc., *with the following exceptions:* dots 57, 88, ..." This expression, suitably encoded, is much shorter than 900 bits long. The comparable expressions for the other frames will be proportionally longer, since they will have to mention, verbatim, more exceptions, and the degeneracy of the "pattern" in *F* is revealed by the fact that its description in this system will be no improvement over the bit map – in fact, it will tend on average to be trivially longer, since it takes some bits to describe the pattern that is then obliterated by all the exceptions.

Of course, there are bound to be other ways of describing the evident patterns in these frames, and some will be more efficient than others – in the precise sense of being systematically specifiable in fewer bits.[11] Any such description, if an improvement over the bit map, is the description of a real pattern in the data.[12]

Consider bar code, the particular pattern seen in *A–E*, and almost perfectly instantiated in *D*. *That* pattern is quite readily discernible to the naked human eye in these presentations of the data, because of the particular pattern-recognition machinery hard-wired in our visual systems – edge detectors, luminance detectors, and the like. But the very same data (the very same streams of bits) presented in some other format might well yield no hint of pattern to us, especially in the cases where bar code is contaminated by salt and pepper, as in frames *A* through *C*. For instance, if we broke the 900-bit series of frame *B* into 4-bit chunks, and then translated each of these into hexadecimal notation, one would be hard pressed indeed to tell the resulting series of hexadecimal digits from a random series, since the hexadecimal

chunking would be seriously out of phase with the decimal pattern – and hence the "noise" would not "stand out" as noise. There are myriad ways of displaying any 900-bit series of data points, and not many of them would inspire us to concoct an efficient description of the series. Other creatures with different sense organs, or different interests, might readily perceive patterns that were imperceptible to us. The patterns would be *there* all along, but just invisible to *us*.

The idiosyncracy of perceivers' capacities to discern patterns is striking. Visual patterns with axes of vertical symmetry stick out like sore thumbs for us, but if one simply rotates the frame a few degrees, the symmetry is often utterly beyond noticing. And the "perspectives" from which patterns are "perceptible" are not restricted to variations on presentation to the sense modalities. Differences in knowledge yield striking differences in the capacity to pick up patterns. Expert chess players can instantly perceive (and subsequently recall with high accuracy) the total board position in a real game, but are much worse at recall if the same chess pieces are randomly placed on the board, even though to a novice both boards are equally hard to recall.[13] This should not surprise anyone who considers that an expert speaker of English would have much less difficulty perceiving and recalling

The frightened cat struggled to get loose.

than

Te ser.ioghehnde t srugfcalde go tgtt ohle

which contains the same pieces, now somewhat disordered. Expert chess players, unlike novices, not only know how to *play* chess; they know how to *read* chess – how to see the patterns at a glance.

A pattern exists in some data – is real – if *there is* a description of the data that is more efficient than the bit map, whether or not anyone can concoct it. Compression algorithms, as general-purpose pattern describers, are efficient ways of transmitting exact copies of frames, such as *A–F*, from one place to another, but our interests often favor a somewhat different goal: transmitting *inexact* copies that nevertheless preserve "the" pattern that is important to us. For some purposes, we need not list the exceptions to bar code, but only transmit the information that the pattern is bar code with *n* percent noise. Following this strategy, frames *A* and *C*, though discernibly different under careful inspection, count as *the same pattern*, since what matters to us is that the pattern is bar code with 25 percent noise, and we do not care which particular noise occurs, only that it occurs.

Sometimes we are interested in not just ignoring the noise, but eliminating it, improving the pattern in transmission. Copy-editing is a good example. Consider the likely effect thes santince wull hive hod on tha cupy adutor whu preparis thas mone-scrupt fur prunteng. *My* interest in this particular instance is that the "noise" be transmitted, not removed, though I actually do not care exactly *which* noise is there.

Here then are three different attitudes we take at various times toward patterns. Sometimes we care about exact description or reproduction of detail, at whatever cost. From this perspective, a real pattern in frame A is *bar code with the following exceptions: 7, 8, 11, ...* At other times we care about the noise, but not where in particular it occurs. From this perspective, a real pattern in frame A is *bar code with 25 percent noise.* And sometimes, we simply tolerate or ignore the noise. From this perspective, a real pattern in frame A is simply: *bar code.* But is bar code really there in frame A? I am tempted to respond: Look! You can see it with your own eyes. But there is something more constructive to say as well.

When two individuals confront the same data, they may perceive different patterns in them, but since we can have varied interests and perspectives, these differences do not all count as disagreements. Or in any event they should not. If Jones sees pattern α (with n percent noise) and Brown sees pattern β (with m percent noise) there may be no ground for determining that one of them is right and the other wrong. Suppose they are both using their patterns to bet on the next datum in the series. Jones bets according to the "pure" pattern α, but budgets for n percent errors when he looks for odds. Brown does likewise, using pattern β. If both patterns are real, they will both get rich. That is to say, so long as they use their expectation of deviations from the "ideal" to temper their odds policy, they will do better than chance – perhaps very much better.

Now suppose they compare notes. Suppose that α is a simple, easy-to-calculate pattern, but with a high noise rate – for instance, suppose α is bar code as it appears in frame E. And suppose that Brown has found some periodicity or progression in the "random" noise that Jones just tolerates, so

that β is a much more complicated description of pattern-superimposed-on-pattern. This permits Brown to do better than chance, we may suppose, at predicting when the "noise" will come. As a result, Brown budgets for a lower error rate – say only 5 percent. "What you call noise, Jones, is actually pattern," Brown might say. "Of course there is still *some* noise in my pattern, but my pattern is better – more real – than yours! Yours is actually just a mere appearance." Jones might well reply that it is all a matter of taste; he notes how hard Brown has to work to calculate predictions, and points to the fact that he is getting just as rich (or maybe richer) by using a simpler, sloppier system and making more bets at good odds than Brown can muster. "My pattern is perfectly real – look how rich I'm getting. If it were an illusion, I'd be broke."

This crass way of putting things – in terms of betting and getting rich – is simply a vivid way of drawing attention to a real, and far from crass, trade-off that is ubiquitous in nature, and hence in folk psychology. Would we prefer an extremely compact pattern description with a high noise ratio or a less compact pattern description with a lower noise ratio? Our decision may depend on how swiftly and reliably we can discern the simple pattern, how dangerous errors are, how much of our resources we can afford to allocate to detection and calculation. These "design decisions" are typically not left to us to make by individual and deliberate choices; they are incorporated into the design of our sense organs by genetic evolution, and into our culture by cultural evolution. The product of this design evolution process is what Wilfrid Sellars[14] calls our *manifest image*, and it is composed of folk physics, folk psychology, and the other pattern-making perspectives we have on the buzzing blooming confusion that bombards us with data. The ontology generated by the manifest image has thus a deeply pragmatic source.[15]

Do these same pragmatic considerations apply to the scientific image, widely regarded as the final arbiter of ontology? Science is supposed to carve nature at the joints – at its *real* joints, of course. Is it permissible in science to adopt a carving system so simple that it makes sense to tolerate occasional misdivisions and consequent mispredictions? It happens all the time. The ubiquitous practice of using idealized models is exactly a matter of trading off reliability and accuracy of prediction against computational tractability. A particularly elegant and handy oversimplification may under some circumstances be irresistible. The use of Newtonian rather than Einsteinian mechanics in most mundane scientific and engineering calculations is an obvious example. A tractable oversimplification may be attractive even in the face of a high error rate; considering inherited traits to be carried by single genes "for" those traits is an example; considering agents in the marketplace to be perfectly rational self-aggrandizers with perfect information is another.

3 Patterns in Life

The time has come to export these observations about patterns and reality to the controversial arena of belief attribution. The largish leap we must make is nicely expedited by pausing at a stepping-stone example midway between the world of the dot frames and the world of folk psychology: John Horton Conway's Game of Life. In my opinion, every philosophy student should be held responsible for an intimate acquaintance with the Game of Life. It should be considered an essential tool in every thought-experimenter's kit, a prodigiously versatile generator of philosophically important examples and thought-experiments of admirable clarity and vividness. In *The Intentional Stance* I briefly exploited it to make a point about the costs and benefits of risky prediction from the intentional stance,[16] but I have since learned that I presumed too much familiarity with the underlying ideas. Here, then, is a somewhat expanded basic introduction to Life.[17]

Life is played on a two-dimensional grid, such as a checkerboard or a computer screen; it is not a game one plays to win; if it is a game at all, it is solitaire. The grid divides space into square cells, and each cell is either ON or OFF at each moment. Each cell has eight neighbors: the four adjacent cells north, south, east, and west, and the four diagonals: northeast, southeast, southwest, and northwest. Time in the Life world is also discrete, not continuous; it advances in ticks, and the state of the world changes between each tick according to the following rule:

Each cell, in order to determine what to do in the next instant, counts how many of its eight neighbors is ON at the present instant. If the answer is exactly two, the cell stays in its present state (ON or OFF) in the next instant. If the answer is exactly three, the cell is ON in the next instant whatever its current state. Under all other conditions the cell is OFF.

The entire physics of the Life world is captured in that single, unexceptioned law. While this is the fundamental law of the "physics" of the Life world, it helps at first to conceive this curious physics in biological terms: think of cells going ON as births, cells going OFF as deaths, and succeeding instants as generations. Either overcrowding (more than three inhabited neighbors) or isolation (less than two inhabited neighbors) leads to death. By the scrupulous application of this single law, one can predict with perfect accuracy the next instant of any configuration of ON and OFF cells, and the instant after that, and so forth. In other words, the Life world is a toy world that perfectly instantiates Laplace's vision of determinism: given the state description of this world at an instant, we finite observers can perfectly predict the future instants by the simple application of our one law of physics. Or, in my terms, when we adopt the physical stance toward a configuration in the Life world, our powers of prediction are perfect: there is no noise, no uncertainty, no probability less than one. Moreover, it follows from the two-dimensionality of the Life world that nothing is hidden from view. There is no back-stage; there are no hidden variables; the unfolding of the physics of objects in the Life world is directly and completely visible.

There are computer simulations of the Life world in which one can set up configurations on the screen and then watch them evolve according to the single rule. In the best simulations, one can change the scale of both time and space, alternating between close-up and bird's-eye view. A nice touch added to some color versions is that ON cells (often just called pixels) are color-coded by their age; they are born blue, let us say, and then change color each generation, moving through green to yellow to orange to red to brown to black and then staying black unless they die. This permits one to see at a glance how old certain patterns are, which cells are co-generational, where the birth action is, and so forth.[18]

One soon discovers that some simple configurations are more interesting than others. In addition to those configurations which never change – the "still lifes" such as four pixels in a square – and

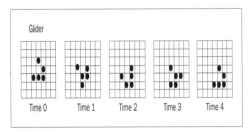

Figure 5.2   (from Poundstone, *The Recursive Universe*)

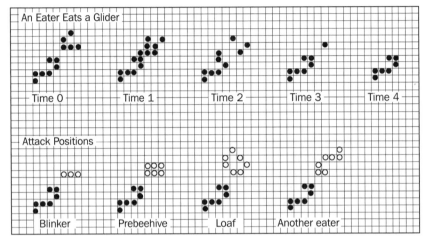

Figure 5.3

those which evaporate entirely – such as any long diagonal line segment, whose two tail pixels die of isolation each instant until the line disappears entirely – there are configurations with all manner of periodicity. Three pixels in a line make a simple flasher, which becomes three pixels in a column in the next instant, and reverts to three in a line in the next, *ad infinitum*, unless some other configuration encroaches. Encroachment is what makes Life interesting: among the periodic configurations are some that swim, amoeba-like, across the plane. The simplest is the *glider*, the five-pixel configuration shown taking a single stroke to the southeast in figure 5.2. Then there are the eaters, the puffer trains, and space rakes, and a host of other aptly named denizens of the Life world that emerge in the ontology of a new level, analogous to what I have called the design level. This level has its own language, a transparent foreshortening of the tedious descriptions one could give at the physical level. For instance:

An eater can eat a glider in four generations. Whatever is being consumed, the basic process is the same. A bridge forms between the eater and its prey. In the next generation, the bridge region dies from overpopulation, taking a bite out of both eater and prey. The eater then repairs itself. The prey usually cannot. If the remainder of the prey dies out as with the glider, the prey is consumed. (Ibid., p. 38)

Note that there has been a distinct ontological shift as we move between levels; whereas at the physical level there is no motion, and the only individuals, cells, are defined by their fixed spatial location, at this design level we have the motion of persisting objects; it is one and the same glider that has moved southeast in figure 5.2, changing shape as it moves, and there is one less glider in the world after the eater has eaten it in figure 5.3. (Here is a warming-up exercise for what is to follow: should we say that there is *real* motion in the Life world, or only *apparent* motion? The flashing pixels on the computer screen are a paradigm case, after all, of what a psychologist would call apparent motion. Are there *really* gliders that move, or are there just patterns of cell state that move? And if we opt for the latter, should we say at least that these moving patterns are real?)

Notice, too, that at this level one proposes generalizations that require "usually" or "provided nothing encroaches" clauses. Stray bits of debris from earlier events can "break" or "kill" one of the objects in the ontology at this level; their *salience as real things* is considerable, but not guaranteed. To say that their salience is considerable is to say that one can, with some small risk, ascend to this design level, adopt its ontology, and proceed to predict – sketchily and riskily – the behavior of larger configurations or systems of configurations, without bothering to compute the physical level. For instance, one can set oneself the task of designing some interesting supersystem out of the "parts" that the design level makes available. Surely the most impressive triumph of this design activity in the Life world is the proof that a working model of a universal Turing machine can in principle be constructed in the Life plane! Von Neumann had already shown that in principle a two-dimensional universal Turing machine could be constructed out of cellular automata, so it was "just" a matter of "engineering" to show how, in principle, it could be constructed out of the simpler cellular automata defined in the Life world. Glider streams can provide the tape, for instance, and the tape reader can be some huge assembly of eaters, gliders, and other bits and pieces. What does this huge Turing machine look like? Poundstone calculates that the whole construction, a self-reproducing machine incorporating a universal Turing machine, would be on the order of 10^{13} pixels.

Displaying a 10^{13}-pixel pattern would require a video screen about 3 million pixels across at least. Assume the pixels are 1 millimeter square (which is very high resolution by the standards of home computers). Then the screen would have to be 3 kilometers (about two miles) across. It would have an area about six times that of Monaco.

Perspective would shrink the pixels of a self-reproducing pattern to invisibility. If you got far enough away from the screen so that the entire pattern was comfortably in view, the pixels (and

even the gliders, eaters and guns) would be too tiny to make out. A self-reproducing pattern would be a hazy glow, like a galaxy. (Ibid., pp. 227–8)

Now, since the universal Turing machine can compute any computable function, it can play chess – simply by mimicking the program of any chess-playing computer you like. Suppose, then, that such an entity occupies the Life plane, playing chess against itself. Looking at the configuration of dots that accomplishes this marvel would almost certainly be unilluminating to anyone who had no clue that a configuration with such powers could exist. But from the perspective of one who had the hypothesis that this huge array of black dots was a chess-playing computer, enormously efficient ways of predicting the future of that configuration are made available. As a first step one can shift from an ontology of gliders and eaters to an ontology of symbols and machine states, and, adopting this higher design stance toward the configuration, predict its future *as* a Turing machine. As a second and still more efficient step, one can shift to an ontology of chess-board positions, possible chess moves, and the grounds for evaluating them; then, adopting the intentional stance toward the configuration, one can predict its future *as* a chess player performing intentional actions – making chess moves and trying to achieve checkmate. Once one has fixed on an interpretation scheme, permitting one to say which configurations of pixels count as which symbols (either, at the Turing machine level, the symbols "0" or "1," say, or at the intentional level, "*QxBch*" and the other symbols for chess moves), one can use the interpretation scheme to predict, for instance, that the next configuration to emerge from the galaxy will be such-and-such a glider stream (the symbols for "*RxQ*", say). There is risk involved in either case, because the chess program being run on the Turing machine may be far from perfectly rational, and, at a different level, debris may wander onto the scene and "break" the Turing machine configuration before it finishes the game.

In other words, real but (potentially) noisy patterns abound in such a configuration of the Life world, there for the picking up if only we are lucky or clever enough to hit on the right perspective. They are not *visual* patterns but, one might say, *intellectual* patterns. Squinting or twisting the page is not apt to help, while posing fanciful interpretations (or what W. V. Quine would call

Daniel C. Dennett

"analytical hypotheses") may uncover a goldmine. The opportunity confronting the observer of such a Life world is analogous to the opportunity confronting the cryptographer staring at a new patch of cipher text, or the opportunity confronting the Martian, peering through a telescope at the Superbowl Game. If the Martian hits on the intentional stance – or folk psychology – as the right level to look for pattern, shapes will readily emerge through the noise.

4 The Reality of Intentional Patterns

The scale of compression when one adopts the intentional stance toward the two-dimensional chess-playing computer galaxy is stupendous: it is the difference between figuring out in your head what white's most likely (best) move is versus calculating the state of a few trillion pixels through a few hundred thousand generations. But the scale of the savings is really no greater in the Life world than in our own. Predicting that someone will duck if you throw a brick at him is easy from the folk-psychological stance; it is and will always be intractable if you have to trace the photons from brick to eyeball, the neurotransmitters from optic nerve to motor nerve, and so forth.

For such vast computational leverage one might be prepared to pay quite a steep price in errors, but in fact one belief that is shared by all of the representatives on the spectrum I am discussing is that "folk psychology" provides a description system that permits highly reliable prediction of human (and much nonhuman) behavior.[19] They differ in the explanations they offer of this predictive prowess, and the implications they see in it about "realism."

For Fodor, an industrial-strength Realist, beliefs and their kin would not be real unless the pattern dimly discernible from the perspective of folk psychology could also be discerned (more clearly, with less noise) as a pattern of structures in the brain. The pattern would have to be discernible from the different perspective provided by a properly tuned *syntactoscope* aimed at the purely formal (nonsemantic) features of Mentalese terms written in the brain. For Fodor, the pattern seen through the noise by everyday folk psychologists would tell us nothing about reality, unless it, and the noise, had the following sort of explanation: what we discern from the perspective of folk psychology is the net effect of two processes: an

ulterior, hidden process wherein the pattern exists quite pure, overlaid, and partially obscured by various intervening sources of noise: performance errors, observation errors, and other more or less random obstructions. He might add that the interior belief-producing process was in this respect *just* like the process responsible for the creation of frames *A–F*. If you were permitted to peer behind the scenes at the program I devised to create the frames, you would see, clear as a bell, the perfect bar-code periodicity, with the noise thrown on afterward like so much salt and pepper.

This is often the explanation for the look of a data set in science, and Fodor may think that it is either the only explanation that can ever be given, or at any rate the only one that makes any sense of the success of folk psychology. But the rest of us disagree. As G. E. M. Anscombe[20] put it in her pioneering exploration of intentional explanation, "if Aristotle's account [of reasoning using the practical syllogism] were supposed to describe actual mental processes, it would in general be quite absurd. The interest of the account is that it describes an order which is there whenever actions are done with intentions..." (ibid., p. 80).

But how *could* the order be there, so visible amidst the noise, if it were not the direct outline of a concrete orderly process in the background? Well, it *could* be there thanks to the statistical effect of very many concrete minutiae producing, as if by a hidden hand, an approximation of the "ideal" order. Philosophers have tended to ignore a variety of regularity intermediate between the regularities of planets and other objects "obeying" the laws of physics and the regularities of rule-following (that is, rule-*consulting*) systems.[21] These intermediate regularities are those which are preserved under selection pressure: the regularities dictated by principles of good design and hence homed in on by self-designing systems. That is, a "rule of thought" may be much more than a mere regularity; it may be a *wise* rule, a rule one would design a system by if one were a system designer, and hence a rule one would expect self-designing systems to "discover" in the course of settling into their patterns of activity. Such rules no more need be explicitly represented than do the principles of aerodynamics that are honored in the design of birds' wings.[22]

The contrast between these different sorts of pattern-generation processes can be illustrated. The frames in figure 5.1 were created by a hard-edged process (ten black, ten white, ten black,...)

obscured by noise, while the frames in figure 5.4 were created by a process almost the reverse of that: the top frame shows a pattern created by a normal distribution of black dots around means at $x = 10, 30, 50, 70$, and 90 (rather like Mach bands or interference fringes); the middle and bottom frames were created by successive applications of a very simple contrast enhancer applied to the top frame: a vertical slit "window" three pixels high is thrown randomly onto the frame; the pixels in the window vote, and majority rules. This gradually removes the salt from the pepper and the pepper from the salt, creating "artifact" edges such as those discernible in the bottom frame. The effect would be more striking at a finer pixel scale, where the black merges imperceptibly through grays to white but I chose to keep the scale at the ten-pixel period of bar code. I do not mean to suggest that it is impossible to tell the patterns in figure 5.4 from the patterns in figure 5.1. Of course it is possible; for one thing, the process that produced the frames in figure 5.1 will almost always show edges at exactly $10, 20, 30, \ldots$ and almost never at $9, 11, 19, 21, \ldots$ while there is a higher probability of these "displaced" edges being created by the process of figure 5.4 (as a close inspection of figure 5.4 reveals). Fine tuning could of course reduce these probabilities, but that is not my point. My point is that *even if* the evidence is substantial that the discernible pattern is produced by one process rather than another, it can be rational to ignore those differences and use the simplest pattern description (e.g., *bar code*) as one's way of organizing the data.

Fodor and others have claimed that an interior language of thought is the best explanation of the hard edges visible in "propositional attitude psychology." Churchland and I have offered an alternative explanation of these edges, an explanation for which the process that produced the frames in figure 5.4 is a fine visual metaphor. The process that produces the data of folk psychology, we claim, is one in which the multidimensional complexities of the underlying processes are projected *through linguistic behavior*, which creates an appearance of definiteness and precision, thanks to the discreteness of words.[23] As Churchland[24] puts it, a person's declarative utterance is a "one-dimensional *projection* – through the compound lens of Wernicke's and Broca's areas onto the idiosyncratic surface of the speaker's language – a one-dimensional projection of a four- or five-dimensional 'solid' that is an element in his true kinematic state" (ibid., p. 85).

Fodor's industrial-strength Realism takes beliefs to be things in the head – just like cells and blood vessels and viruses. Davidson and I both like Churchland's alternative idea of propositional-attitude statements as indirect "measurements" of a reality diffused in the behavioral dispositions of the brain (and body).[25] We think beliefs are quite real enough to call real just so long as belief talk measures these complex behavior-disposing organs as predictively as it does. What do we disagree about? As John Haugeland[26] has pointed out, Davidson is more of a realist than I am, and I have recently tracked down the source of this disagreement to a difference of opinion we have about the status of Quine's principle of indeterminacy of translation, which we both accept.

For Davidson, the principle is not the shocker it is often taken to be; in fact, it is well-nigh trivial – the two different translation manuals between which no fact of the matter decides are like two different scales for measuring temperature.

We know there is no contradiction between the temperature of the air being 32° fahrenheit and 0° celsius; there is nothing in this "relativism" to show that the properties being measured are not "real". Curiously, though, this conclusion has repeatedly been drawn.... Yet in the light of the considerations put forward here, this comes to no more than the recognition that more than one set of one person's utterances might be equally successful in capturing the contents of someone else's thoughts or speech. Just as numbers can capture all the empirically significant relations among weights or temperatures in infinitely many ways, so one person's utterances can capture all the significant features of another person's thoughts and speech in different ways.

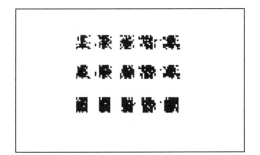

Figure 5.4

Daniel C. Dennett

This fact does not challenge the "reality" of the attitudes or meanings thus reported.[27]

On Davidson's view, no substantive disagreements emerge from a comparison of the two description schemes, and so they can quite properly be viewed as competing descriptions of the same reality.

I think this is a flawed analogy. A better one is provided by the example of "rival" descriptions of patterns-with-noise. Consider two rival intentional interpretations of a single individual; they agree on the general shape of this individual's collection of beliefs (and desires, etc), but because of their different idealizations of the pattern, they do not agree point-for-point. Recalling a famous analogy of Quine's[28] and extending it beyond radical translation to radical interpretation (as Davidson and I both wish to do), we get the image in figure 5.5.

To the left we see Brown's intentional interpretation of Ella; to the right, Jones's interpretation. Since these are intentional interpretations, the pixels or data points represent beliefs and so forth, not (for instance) bits of bodily motion or organs or cells or atoms, and since these are rival intentional interpretations of a single individual, the patterns discerned are not statistical averages (e.g., "Democrats tend to favor welfare programs") but personal cognitive idiosyncracies (e.g., "She thinks she should get her queen out early"). Some of the patterns may indeed be simple observed periodicities (e.g., "Ella wants to talk about football on Mondays") but we are to understand the pattern to be what Anscombe called the "order which is there" in the rational coherence of a person's set of beliefs, desires, and intentions.

Notice that here the disagreements can be substantial – at least before the fact: when Brown and Jones make a series of predictive bets, they will not always make the same bet. They may *often* dis-

agree on what, according to their chosen pattern, will happen next. To take a dramatic case, Brown may predict that Ella will decide to kill herself; Jones may disagree. This is not a trivial disagreement of prediction, and in principle this momentous difference may emerge in spite of the overall consonance of the two interpretations.

Suppose, then, that Brown and Jones make a series of predictions of Ella's behavior, based on their rival interpretations. Consider the different categories that compose their track records. First, there are the occasions where they agree and are right. Both systems look good from the vantage point of these successes. Second, there are the occasions where they agree and are wrong. Both chalk it up to noise, take their budgeted loss and move on to the next case. But there will also be the occasions where they disagree, where their systems make different predictions, and in these cases sometimes (but not always) one will win and the other lose. (In the real world, predictions are not always from among binary alternatives, so in many cases they will disagree and both be wrong.) When one wins and the other loses, it will look to the myopic observer as if one "theory" has scored a serious point against the other, but when one recognizes the possibility that both may chalk up such victories, and that there may be no pattern in the victories which permits either one to improve his theory by making adjustments, one sees that local triumphs may be insufficient to provide any ground in reality for declaring one account a closer approximation of the truth.

Now, some might think this situation is *always* unstable; eventually one interpretation is bound to ramify better to new cases, or be deducible from some larger scheme covering other data, etc. That might be true in many cases, but – and this, I think, is the central point of Quine's indeterminacy thesis – it need not be true in all. *If* the strategy of intentional-stance description is, as Quine says, a "dramatic idiom" in which there is ineliminable use of idealization, and if Fodor's industrial-strength Realism is thus not the correct explanation of the reliable "visibility" of the pattern, such radical indeterminacy is a genuine and stable possibility.

This indeterminacy will be most striking in such cases as the imagined disagreement over Ella's suicidal mindset. If Ella does kill herself, is Brown shown to have clearly had the better intentional interpretation? Not necessarily. When Jones chalks up his scheme's failure in this instance to a

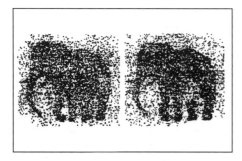

Figure 5.5

bit of noise, this is no more ad hoc or unprincipled than the occasions when Brown was wrong about whether Ella would order the steak not the lobster, and chalked those misses up to noise. This is not at all to say that an interpretation can never be shown to be just wrong; there is plenty of leverage within the principles of intentional interpretation to refute particular hypotheses – for instance, by forcing their defense down the path of Pickwickian explosion ("You see, she didn't believe the gun was loaded because she thought that those bullet-shaped things were chocolates wrapped in foil, which was just a fantasy that occurred to her because...."). It *is* to say that there could be two interpretation schemes that were reliable and compact predictors over the long run, but that nevertheless disagreed on crucial cases.

It might seem that in a case as momentous as Ella's intention to kill herself, a closer examination of the details just prior to the fatal moment (if not at an earlier stage) would have to provide additional support for Brown's interpretation at the expense of Jones's interpretation. After all, there would be at least a few seconds – or a few hundred milliseconds – during which Ella's decision to pull the trigger got implemented, and during that brief period, at least, the evidence would swing sharply in favor of Brown's interpretation. That is no doubt true, and it is *perhaps* true that had one gone into enough detail earlier, all this last-second detail could have been predicted – but to have gone into *those* details earlier would have been to drop down from the intentional stance to the design or physical stances. From the intentional stance, these determining considerations would have been invisible to both Brown and Jones, who were both prepared to smear over such details as noise in the interests of more practical prediction. Both interpreters concede that they will make false predictions, and moreover, that when they make false predictions there are apt to be harbingers of misprediction in the moments during which the *dénouement* unfolds. Such a brief swing does not constitute refutation of the interpretation, any more than the upcoming misprediction of behavior does.

How, then, does this make me less of a realist than Davidson? I see that there could be two different systems of belief attribution to an individual which differed *substantially* in what they attributed – even in yielding substantially different predictions of the individual's future behavior –

and yet where no deeper fact of the matter could establish that one was a description of the individual's *real* beliefs and the other not. In other words, there could be two different, but equally real, patterns discernible in the noisy world. The rival theorists would not even agree on which parts of the world were pattern and which were noise, and yet nothing deeper would settle the issue.[29] The choice of a pattern would indeed be up to the observer, a matter to be decided on idiosyncratic pragmatic grounds. I myself do not see any feature of Davidson's position that would be a serious obstacle to his shifting analogies and agreeing with me. But then he would want to grant that indeterminacy is not such a trivial matter after all.[30]

What then is Rorty's view on these issues? Rorty wants to deny that any brand of "realism" could *explain* the (apparent?) success of the intentional stance. But since we have already joined Fine and set aside the "metaphysical" problem of realism, Rorty's reminding us of this only postpones the issue. Even someone who has transcended the scheme/content distinction and has seen the futility of correspondence theories of truth must accept the fact that *within* the natural ontological attitude we sometimes explain success by correspondence: one does better navigating off the coast of Maine when one uses an up-to-date nautical chart than one does when one uses a road map of Kansas. Why? Because the former accurately represents the hazards, markers, depths, and coastlines of the Maine coast, and the latter does not. Now why does one do better navigating the shoals of interpersonal relations using folk psychology than using astrology? Rorty might hold that the predictive "success" we folk-psychology players relish is itself an artifact, a mutual agreement engendered by the egging-on or consensual support we who play this game provide each other. He would grant that the game has no rivals in popularity, due – in the opinion of the players – to the power it gives them to understand and anticipate the animate world. But he would refuse to endorse this opinion. How, then, would he distinguish this popularity from the popularity among a smaller coterie of astrology?[31] It is undeniable that astrology provides its adherents with a highly articulated system of patterns that they *think* they see in the events of the world. The difference, however, is that no one has ever been able to get rich by betting on the patterns, but only by selling the patterns to others.

Rorty would have to claim that this is not a significant difference; the rest of us, however, find abundant evidence that our allegiance to folk psychology as a predictive tool can be defended in coldly objective terms. We agree that there is a real pattern being described by the terms of folk psychology. What divides the rest of us is the nature of the pattern, and the ontological implications of that nature.

Let us finally consider Churchland's eliminative materialism from this vantage point. As already pointed out, he is second to none in his appreciation of the power, to date, of the intentional stance as a strategy of prediction. Why does he think that it is nevertheless doomed to the trash heap? Because he anticipates that neuroscience will eventually – perhaps even soon – discover a pattern that is so clearly superior to the noisy pattern of folk psychology that everyone will readily abandon the former for the latter (except, perhaps, in the rough-and-tumble of daily life). This might happen, I suppose. But Churchland here is only playing a hunch, a hunch that should not be seen to gain plausibility from reflections on the irresistible forward march of science. For it is not enough for Churchland to suppose that in principle, neuro-scientific levels of description will explain more of the variance, predict more of the "noise" that bedevils higher levels. This is, of course, bound to be true in the limit – if we descend all the way to the neurophysiological "bit map." But as we have seen, the trade-off between ease of use and immun-ity from error for such a cumbersome system may make it profoundly unattractive.[32] If the "pattern" is scarcely an improvement over the bit map, talk of eliminative materialism will fall on deaf ears – just as it does when radical eliminativists urge us to abandon our ontological commitments to tables and chairs. A truly general-purpose, robust system of pattern description more valuable than the intentional stance is not an impossibility, but any-one who wants to bet on it might care to talk to me about the odds they will take.

What does all this show? Not that Fodor's industrial-strength Realism must be false, and not that Churchland's eliminative materialism must be false, but just that both views are gratuitously strong forms of materialism – presumptive theses way out in front of the empirical support they require. Rorty's view errs in the opposite direction, ignoring the impressive empirical track record that distinguishes the intentional stance from the astrological stance. Davidson's intermediate position, like mine, ties reality to the brute existence of pattern, but David-son has overlooked the possibility of two or more *conflicting* patterns being superimposed on the same data – a more radical indeterminacy of translation than he had supposed possible. Now, once again, is the view I am defending here a sort of instrument-alism or a sort of realism? I think that the view itself is clearer than either of the labels, so I shall leave that question to anyone who still finds illumination in them.

Notes

Thanks to Kathleen Akins, Akeel Bilgrami, Donald David-son, Barbara Hannan, Douglas Hofstadter, Norton Nelkin, W. V. O. Quine, Richard Rorty, George Smith, Peter Suber, Stephen White, and the MIT/Tufts philosophy of psychology discussion group for the discussions that provoked and shaped this essay.

1 *Content and Consciousness* (Boston: Routledge & Kegan Paul, 1969), ch. 1.
2 "Three kinds of intentional psychology," in R. Hea-ley, ed., *Reduction, Time and Reality* (New York: Cambridge, 1981); and *The Intentional Stance* (Cam-bridge: MIT, 1987).
3 Peter Smith, "Wit and chutzpah," review of *The Inten-tional Stance* and Jerry A. Fodor's *Psychosemantics*, *Times Higher Education Supplement* (August 7, 1988), p. 22.
4 "The stance stance," commentary on *The Intentional Stance*, in *Behavioral and Brain Sciences*, XI (1988): 511–12.

5 R. A. Sharpe, in "Dennett's journey towards panpsy-chism," *Inquiry*, XXXII (1989): 233–40, takes me to task on this point, using examples from Proust to drive home the point that "Proust draws our atten-tion to possible lives and these possible lives are various. But in none of them is prediction of para-mount importance" (p. 240). I agree. I also agree that what makes people interesting (in novels and in real life) is precisely their unpredictability. But that unpredictability is only interesting against the back-drop of routine predictability on which all inter-pretation depends. As I note in *The Intentional Stance* (p. 79) in response to a similar objection of Fodor's, the same is true of chess: the game is interesting only because of the unpredictability of one's opponent, but that is to say: the intentional stance can usually eliminate *only* 90 percent of the legal moves.

6 Norton Nelkin, "Patterns," forthcoming.

7 *The Shaky Game: Einstein Realism and the Quantum Theory* (Chicago: University Press, 1986); see esp. p. 153n., and his comments there on Rorty, which I take to be consonant with mine here.

8 See *The Intentional Stance*, pp. 38–42, "Real patterns, deeper facts, and empty questions."

9 "Randomness and mathematical proof," *Scientific American*, CCXXXII (1975): 47–52.

10 More precisely: "A series of numbers is random if the smallest algorithm capable of specifying it to a computer has about the same number of bits of information as the series itself" (Chaitin, p. 48). This is what explains the fact that the "random number generator" built into most computers is not really properly named, since it is some function describable in a few bits (a little subroutine that is called for some output whenever a program requires a "random" number or series). If I send you the description of the pseudo-random number generator on my computer, you can use it to generate exactly the same infinite series of random-seeming digits.

11 Such schemes for efficient description, called compression algorithms, are widely used in computer graphics for saving storage space. They break the screen into uniformly colored regions, for instance, and specify region boundaries (rather like the "paint by numbers" line drawings sold in craft shops). The more complicated the picture on the screen, the longer the compressed description will be; in the worst case (a picture of confetti randomly sprinkled over the screen) the compression algorithm will be stumped, and can do no better than a verbatim bit map.

12 What about the "system" of pattern description that simply baptizes frames with proper names (*A* through *F*, in this case) and tells the receiver which frame is up by simply sending "*F*? This looks much shorter than the bit map until we consider that such a description must be part of an entirely general system. How many proper names will we need to name all possible 900-dot frames? Trivially, the 900-bit binary number, 11111111....To send the "worst-case" proper name will take exactly as many bits as sending the bit map. This confirms our intuition that proper names are maximally inefficient ways of couching generalizations ("Alf is tall and Bill is tall and...").

13 A. D. de Groot, *Thought and Choice in Chess* (The Hague: Mouton, 1965).

14 *Science, Perception and Reality* (Boston: Routledge & Kegan Paul, 1963).

15 In "Randomness and perceived randomness in evolutionary biology," *Synthese*, XLIII (1980): 287–329, William Wimsatt offers a nice example (p. 296): while the insectivorous bird tracks individual insects, the anteater just averages over the ant-infested area; one might say that, while the bird's

manifest image quantifies over insects, "ant" is a mass term for anteaters. See the discussion of this and related examples in my *Elbow Room* (Cambridge: MIT, 1984), pp. 108–10.

16 *The Intentional Stance*, pp. 37–9.

17 Martin Gardner introduced the Game of Life to a wide audience in two columns in *Scientific American* in October, 1970, and February, 1971. William Poundstone, *The Recursive Universe: Cosmic Complexity and the Limits of Scientific Knowledge* (New York: Morrow, 1985), is an excellent exploration of the game and its philosophical implications. Two figures from Poundstone's book are reproduced here with kind permission from the author and publisher.

18 Poundstone (ibid.) provides simple BASIC and IBM-PC assembly language simulations you can copy for your own home computer, and describes some of the interesting variations.

19 To see that the opposite poles share this view, see Fodor, *Psychosemantics* (Cambridge: MIT, 1987), ch. 1, "Introduction: the persistence of the attitudes"; and Paul Churchland, *Scientific Realism and the Plasticity of Mind* (New York: Cambridge, 1979), esp. p. 100: "For the P-theory [folk psychology] is in fact a marvelous intellectual achievement. It gives its possessor an explicit and systematic insight into the behaviour, verbal and otherwise, of some of the most complex agents in the environment, and its overall prowess in that respect remains unsurpassed by anything else our considerable theoretical efforts have produced."

20 *Intention* (New York: Blackwell, 1957).

21 A notable early exception is Sellars, who discussed the importance of just this sort of regularity in "Some reflections on language games," *Philosophy of Science*, XXI (1954): 204–28. See especially the subsection of this classic paper, entitled "Pattern governed and rule obeying behavior," reprinted in Sellars's *Science, Perception and Reality*, pp. 324–7.

22 Several interpreters of a draft of this article have supposed that the conclusion I am urging here is that beliefs (or their contents) are *epiphenomena* having no causal powers, but this is a misinterpretation traceable to a simplistic notion of causation. If one finds a predictive pattern of the sort just described one has *ipso facto* discovered a causal power – a difference in the world that makes a subsequent difference testable by standard empirical methods of variable manipulation. Consider the crowd-drawing power of a sign reading "Free Lunch" placed in the window of a restaurant, and compare its power in a restaurant in New York to its power in a restaurant in Tokyo. The intentional level is obviously the right level at which to predict and explain such causal powers; the sign more reliably produces a particular belief in one population of perceivers than in the other, and variations in the

color of typography of the sign are not as predictive of variations in crowd-drawing power as are variations in (perceivable) meaning. The fact that the regularities on which these successful predictions are based are efficiently capturable (only) in intentional terms and are not derived from "covering laws" does not show that the regularities are not "causal"; it just shows that philosophers have often relied on pinched notions of causality derived from exclusive attention to a few examples drawn from physics and chemistry. Smith has pointed out to me that here I am echoing Aristotle's claim that his predecessors had ignored final causes.

23 See my discussion of the distinction between beliefs and (linguistically infected) *opinions;* in *Brainstorms* (Montgomery, Vt: Bradford, 1978), ch. 16, and in "The illusions of realism," in *The Intentional Stance*, pp. 110–16.

24 "Eliminative materialism and the propositional attitudes," *The Journal of Philosophy,* LXXVIII, 2 (February 1981): 67–90, esp. p. 85.

25 Churchland introduces the idea in *Scientific Realism and the Plasticity of Mind*, pp. 100–7. My adoption of the idea was in "Beyond belief," in A. Woodfield, ed., *Thought and Object* (New York: Oxford, 1982), repr. as ch. 5 of *The Intentional Stance*. Davidson's guarded approval is expressed in "What is present to the mind?" read at the Sociedad Filosófica Ibero Americana meeting in Buenos Aires, 1989.

26 See the discussion of Haugeland's views in the last chapter of *The Intentional Stance*, "Mid-term examination: compare and contrast," pp. 348–9.

27 Davidson, "What is present to the mind?" (ms.), p. 10.

28 "Different persons growing up in the same language are like different bushes trimmed and trained to take the shape of identical elephants. The anatomical details of twigs and branches will fulfill the elephantine form differently from bush to bush, but the overall outward results are the same." *Word and Object* (Cambridge: MIT, 1960), p. 8.

29 Cf. "The abilities of men and machines," in *Brainstorms*, where I discuss two people who agree exactly on the future behavior of some artifact, but impose different Turing-machine interpretations of it. On both interpretations, the machine occasionally "makes errors" but the two interpreters disagree about which cases are the errors. (They disagree about which features of the object's behavior count as signal and which as noise.) Which Turing machine is it really? This question has no answer.

30 Andrej Zabludowski seems to me to have overlooked this version of indeterminacy in "On Quine's indeterminacy doctrine," *Philosophical Review,* XCVIII (1989): 35–64.

31 Cf. my comparison of "the astrological stance" to the intentional stance, *The Intentional Stance*, p. 16.

32 As I have put it, physical-stance predictions trump design-stance predictions, which trump intentional-stance predictions – but one pays for the power with a loss of portability and a (usually unbearable) computational cost.

PART III

Eliminativism and Neurophilosophy

Introduction

We saw that Dennett's instrumentalism broke fairly radically with common sense and with philosophical tradition in denying that propositional attitudes such as belief and desire are real inner causal states of people. But Dennett concedes – indeed urgently insists – that belief- and desire-ascriptions are true, and objectively true, nonetheless. Other philosophers have taken a less conciliatory, still more radically uncommonsensical view: that mental ascriptions are not true after all, but are simply *false*. Common sense is just mistaken in supposing that people believe and desire things, and perhaps in supposing that people have sensations and feelings, disconcerting as that nihilistic claim may seem.

Following standard usage, let us call the nihilistic claim "Eliminative Materialism," or "Eliminativism" for short. It is important to note a customary if unexpected alliance between the Eliminativist and the token physicalist: the Eliminativist, the Identity Theorist, and the Functionalist all agree that mental items are, *if anything*, real inner causal states of people. They disagree only on the empirical question of whether any real neurophysiological states of people do in fact answer to the commonsensical mental categories of "folk psychology." Eliminativists praise Identity Theorists and Functionalists for their forthright willingness to step up and take their empirical shot. Both Eliminativists and token physicalists scorn the Instrumentalist's sleazy evasion. (But Eliminativists agree with Instrumentalists that Functionalism is a pipe dream, and Functionalists agree with Instrumentalists that mental ascriptions are often true and obviously so. The three views form an Eternal Triangle of a not uncommon sort.)

Paul Feyerabend (1963a, 1963b) was the first to argue openly that the mental categories of folk psychology simply fail to capture anything in physical reality and that everyday mental ascriptions are therefore false. (Rorty (1965) took a notoriously Eliminativist line also, but following Wilfrid Sellars tried to soften its nihilism; Lycan and Pappas (1972) argued that the softening served only to collapse Rorty's position into incoherence.) Feyerabend attracted no great following, presumably because of his view's outrageous flouting of common sense. But Eliminativism was resurrected by Paul Churchland (this volume) and others, and defended in more detail.

Churchland argues mainly from the poverty of "folk psychology"; he claims that historically, when other primitive theories such as alchemy have done as badly on scientific grounds as folk psychology has, they have been abandoned and rightly so. Patricia Churchland (1986, this volume (with Terrence Sejnowski)) emphasizes the comparative scientific reality and causal efficacy of neuroanatomical mechanisms: given the scientific excellence of neurophysiological explanation and the contrasting diffuseness and type-irreducibility of folk psychology, why should we suppose even for a minute, much less automatically, that the platitudes of folk psychology express truths?

Introduction

Patricia Churchland's intense interest in neurophysiology and her distrust of the categories of folk psychology are matched within a sector of the AI community, in an equally intense upsurge of "neural modeling." In particular, what is called "Connectionism" or Parallel Distributed Processing ("PDP" for short; McClelland et al. 1986) is an AI research program that diverges from the standard deployment of "rules and representations" (see Part IV of this volume) and from the idea of linear or monotonic theorem-proving from a pre-loaded database. PDP employs (in practice, only simulates) an array of "units," each unit connected by ligatures to other units and each having an "activation potential" that is directly affected by the potentials of adjoining units; the obvious, and intended, allusion is to the brain's neural nets. Some units are designated as inputs, others as outputs; the rest are "hidden," and mysteriously regulate output given input according to various algorithms. A major focus of PDP research is on *learning over time*; connectionist networks are good at learning pattern-recognition tasks, notably when their activation algorithms work by back-propagation of error.

"Connectionism" as described is an engineering approach within AI. But during the 1980s the term caught on among both psychologists and philosophers, and is now often used neologistically, as naming (a) a psychological theory, roughly that such-and-such behavioral capacities are explained by connectionist architecture actually realized in organisms' brains, or (b) a philosophical contention reminiscent of Ryle, roughly that intelligent human capacities, thinking, and rationality are somehow holistically emergent from connectionist architecture in the brain rather than being a matter of the manipulation of internal beliefs or other representations according to rules.

Some philosophers take connectionism in one or another of its several senses to refute or at least embarrass the idea that human cognition is a matter of hosting internal representational states such as beliefs and desires. But, logically speaking, connectionism seems entirely compatible with representationalism (Bechtel, 1988; Smolensky 1988), and arguably it is *an instance of* representationalism (Fodor and Pylyshyn in *Cognition* (1988); Lycan (1991); but see Bechtel (this volume)).

Further debate over connectionism concerns whether connectionist models can adequately perform tasks or reproduce cognitive features that do not seem to suit a connectionist network's associative style of learning and classifying. For example, Fodor and Pylyshyn (in *Cognition* (1988)) pointed out that human language understanding exhibits a property called "systematicity": Anyone who understands one sentence of a natural language (say, "John loves Mary") will invariably understand any sentence containing the same words with a closely related grammatical structure ("Mary loves John"). But, Fodor and Pylyshyn argued, connectionist modeling cannot explain systematicity (that is, unless it does so by implementing a classical "rules and representations" architecture). Clark (1989), Braddon-Mitchell and Fitzpatrick (1990), Smolensky (1991), and others have replied on the connectionists' behalf; the discussion rages on (Fodor and McLaughlin 1990; Chalmers 1990; McLaughlin 1993; Hadley 1994).

It has been questioned whether connectionist models do in fact outperform classical models even at the sorts of pattern-recognition task for which they are famous; see, e.g., McLaughlin and Warfield (1994).

A more recent sort of neural modeling takes its cue from the mathematics of dynamical systems theory (Van Gelder, this volume). On this view, cognition is explained in terms of trajectories through high-dimensional state spaces, described by differential equations. Just as it is controversial whether connectionist modeling is a serious rival to the classical "rules and representations" approach, so is it controversial whether the dynamical systems view is a serious rival to connectionism.

Further Reading

Classical eliminativism

Feyerabend, P. (1963a) "Materialism and the mind–body problem," *Review of Metaphysics* 17, 49–67.

Feyerabend, P. (1963b) "Mental events and the brain," *Journal of Philosophy* 60, 295–6.

Quine, W. V. (1966) "On mental entities," reprinted in *The Ways of Paradox and Other Essays*, Random House.

Rorty, R. (1965) "Mind–body identity, privacy, and categories," *Review of Metaphysics* 19, 24–54.

Lycan, W. and Pappas, G. (1972) "What is eliminative materialism?" *Australasian Journal of Philosophy* 50 149–59.

Current eliminativism
Churchland, P. M. (1979) *Scientific Realism and the Plasticity of Mind*, Cambridge University Press.
Dennett, D. C. (1982) "How to study consciousness empirically, or: Nothing comes to mind," *Synthese* 53, 159–80.
Bricke, J. (1984) "Dennett's eliminative arguments," *Philosophical Studies* 45, 413–30.
Churchland, P. S. (1986) *Neurophilosophy*, Bradford Books/MIT Press, section 9.6.
Baker, L. R. (1988) *Saving Belief*, Princeton University Press.
Churchland, P. M. *A Neurocomputational Perspective*, Bradford Books/MIT Press.
Ramsey, W., Stich, S., and Garon, J. (1990) "Connectionism, eliminativism, and the future of folk psychology," in W. Ramsey, S. P. Stich, and D. Rumelhart (eds), *Philosophy and Connectionist Theory*, Laurence Erlbaum Associates.
[See also the defenses of "folk psychology" cited in the Introduction to Part VI.]

Connectionism
McClelland, J., Rumelhart, D., and the PDP Research Group (eds) (1986) *Parallel Distributed Processing: Explorations in the Microstructure of Cognition*, Bradford Books/MIT Press.
Smolensky, P. (1988) "On the proper treatment of connectionism," *Behavioral and Brain Sciences* 11, 1–23. [Accompanied by multifarious "Open Peer Commentary."]
Cognition (1988) vol. 28: special issue on connectionism. Reissued as S. Pinker and J. Mehler (eds), *Connections and Symbols*, MIT Press, 1988. [Especially Fodor and Pylyshyn, "Connectionism and cognitive architecture: a critical analysis," 3–71.]
Horgan, T. and Tienson, J. (eds) (1988) *Spindel Conference 1987: Connectionism and the Philosophy of Mind. Southern Journal of Philosophy*, supplement to vol. 26.
Bechtel, W. (1988) "Connectionism and the philosophy of mind: an overview," in Horgan and Tienson (1988),

Spindel Conference 1987; reprinted in the 1990 first edition of this anthology.
Bechtel, W. and Abrahamsen, A. (1991) *Connectionism and the Mind: An Introduction to Parallel Processing in Networks*, Blackwell Publishers.
Clark, A. (1989) *Microcognition: Philosophy, Science, and Parallel Distributed Processing*, Bradford Books/MIT Press.
Clark, A. (1993) *Associative Engines*, Bradford Books/MIT Press.
Braddon-Mitchell, D. and Fitzpatrick, J. (1990) "Explanation and the language of thought," *Synthese* 83, 3–29.
Chalmers, D. (1990) "Syntactic transformations on distributed representations," *Connection Science* 2, 53–62.
Fodor, J. A. and McLaughlin, B. (1990) "Connectionism and the problem of systematicity: why Smolensky's solution doesn't work," *Cognition* 35, 183–204.
Smolensky, P. (1991) "Connectionism, constituency and the language of thought," in B. Loewer and G. Rey (eds), *Meaning in Mind: Fodor and His Critics*, Blackwell Publishers.
Ramsey, W., Stich, S. P., and Rumelhart, D. (eds) (1991) *Philosophy and Connectionist Theory*, loc. cit.
Davis, S. (ed.) (1992) *Connectionism: Theory and Practice*, Oxford University Press. [On the systematicity issue, see particularly J. Elman's paper in that volume, "Grammatical structure and distributed representations."]
McLaughlin, B. (1993) "The connectionism/classicism battle to win souls," *Philosophical Studies* 71, 163–90.
Hadley, R. (1994) "Systematicity in connectionist language learning," *Mind and Language* 9, 247–71.
McLaughlin, B. and Warfield, T. (1994) "The allure of connectionism reexamined," *Synthese* 101, 365–400.
Churchland, P. M. (1995) *The Engine of Reason, the Seat of the Soul*, Bradford Books/MIT Press.
Horgan, T. and Tienson, J. (1996) *Connectionism and the Philosophy of Psychology*, Bradford Books/MIT Press.

The dynamical systems approach
Port, R. F. and Van Gelder, T. (eds), *Mind as Motion: Explorations in the Dynamics of Cognition*, Bradford Books/MIT Press.

6

Current Eliminativism

Eliminative Materialism and the Propositional Attitudes

Paul M. Churchland

Eliminative materialism is the thesis that our common-sense conception of psychological phenomena constitutes a radically false theory, a theory so fundamentally defective that both the principles and the ontology of that theory will eventually be displaced, rather than smoothly reduced, by completed neuroscience. Our mutual understanding and even our introspection may then be reconstituted within the conceptual framework of completed neuroscience, a theory we may expect to be more powerful by far than the common-sense psychology it displaces, and more substantially integrated within physical science generally. My purpose in this essay is to explore these projections, especially as they bear on (1) the principal elements of common-sense psychology: the propositional attitudes (beliefs, desires, etc.), and (2) the conception of rationality in which these elements figure.

This focus represents a change in the fortunes of materialism. Twenty years ago, emotions, qualia, and "raw feels" were held to be the principal stumbling blocks for the materialist program. With these barriers dissolving,[1] the locus of opposition has shifted. Now it is the realm of the intentional, the realm of the propositional attitude, that is most commonly held up as being both irreducible to and ineliminable in favor of anything from within a materialist framework. Whether and why this is so, we must examine.

Such an examination will make little sense, however, unless it is first appreciated that the relevant network of common-sense concepts does indeed constitute an empirical theory, with all the functions, virtues, *and perils* entailed by that status. I shall therefore begin with a brief sketch of this view and a summary rehearsal of its rationale. The resistance it encounters still surprises me. After all, common sense has yielded up many theories. Recall the view that space has a preferred direction in which all things fall; that weight is an intrinsic feature of a body; that a force-free moving object will promptly return to rest; that the sphere of the heavens turns daily; and so on. These examples are clear, perhaps, but people seem willing to concede a theoretical component within common sense only if (1) the theory and the common sense involved are safely located in antiquity, and (2) the relevant theory is now so clearly false that its speculative nature is inescapable. Theories are indeed easier to discern under these circumstances. But the vision of hindsight is always 20/20. Let us aspire to some foresight for a change.

1 Why Folk Psychology is a Theory

Seeing our common-sense conceptual framework for mental phenomena as a theory brings a simple and unifying organization to most of the major topics in the philosophy of mind, including the explanation and prediction of behavior, the semantics of mental predicates, action theory, the other-minds problem, the intentionality of mental states, the nature of introspection, and the mind–body problem. Any view that can pull this lot together deserves careful consideration.

Let us begin with the explanation of human (and animal) behavior. The fact is that the average person is able to explain, and even predict, the behavior of other persons with a facility and success that is remarkable. Such explanations and predictions standardly make reference to the desires, beliefs, fears, intentions, perceptions, and so forth, to which the agents are presumed subject. But explanations presuppose laws – rough and ready ones, at least – that connect the explanatory conditions with the behavior explained. The same is true for the making of predictions, and for the justification of subjunctive and counterfactual conditionals concerning behavior. Reassuringly, a rich network of common-sense laws can indeed be reconstructed from this quotidean commerce of explanation and anticipation; its principles are familiar homilies; and their sundry functions are transparent. Each of us understands others, as well as we do, because we share a tacit command of an integrated body of lore concerning the lawlike relations holding among external circumstances, internal states, and overt behavior. Given its nature and functions, this body of lore may quite aptly be called "folk psychology."[2]

This approach entails that the semantics of the terms in our familiar mentalistic vocabulary is to be understood in the same manner as the semantics of theoretical terms generally: the meaning of any theoretical term is fixed or constituted by the network of laws in which it figures. (This position is quite distinct from logical behaviorism. We deny that the relevant laws are analytic, and it is the lawlike connections generally that carry the semantic weight, not just the connections with overt behavior. But this view does account for what little plausibility logical behaviorism did enjoy.)

More importantly, the recognition that folk psychology is a theory provides a simple and decisive solution to an old skeptical problem, the problem of other minds. The problematic conviction that another individual is the subject of certain mental states is not inferred deductively from his behavior, nor is it inferred by inductive analogy from the perilously isolated instance of one's own case. Rather, that conviction is a singular *explanatory hypothesis* of a perfectly straightforward kind. Its function, in conjunction with the background laws of folk psychology, is to provide explanations/pre-

dictions/understanding of the individual's continuing behavior, and it is credible to the degree that it is successful in this regard over competing hypotheses. In the main, such hypotheses are successful, and so the belief that others enjoy the internal states comprehended by folk psychology is a reasonable belief.

Knowledge of other minds thus has no essential dependence on knowledge of one's own mind. Applying the principles of our folk psychology to our behavior, a Martian could justly ascribe to us the familiar run of mental states, even though his own psychology were very different from ours. He would not, therefore, be "generalizing from his own case."

As well, introspective judgments about one's own case turn out not to have any special status or integrity anyway. On the present view, an introspective judgment is just an instance of an acquired habit of conceptual response to one's internal states, and the integrity of any particular response is always contingent on the integrity of the acquired conceptual framework (theory) in which the response is framed. Accordingly, one's *introspective* certainty that one's mind is the seat of beliefs and desires may be as badly misplaced as was the classical man's *visual* certainty that the star-flecked sphere of the heavens turns daily.

Another conundrum is the intentionality of mental states. The "propositional attitudes," as Russell called them, form the systematic core of folk psychology; and their uniqueness and anomalous logical properties have inspired some to see here a fundamental contrast with anything that mere physical phenomena might conceivably display. The key to this matter lies again in the theoretical nature of folk psychology. The intentionality of mental states here emerges not as a mystery of nature, but as a structural feature of the concepts of folk psychology. Ironically, those same structural features reveal the very close affinity that folk psychology bears to theories in the physical sciences. Let me try to explain.

Consider the large variety of what might be called "numerical attitudes" appearing in the conceptual framework of physical science: "...has a mass$_{kg}$ of n", "...has a velocity of n", "...has a temperature$_K$ of n", and so forth. These expressions are predicate-forming expressions: when one substitutes a singular term for a number into the place held by "n", a determinate predicate results.

More interestingly, the relations between the various "numerical attitudes" that result are precisely the relations between the numbers "contained" in those attitudes. More interesting still, the argument place that takes the singular terms for numbers is open to quantification. All this permits the expression of generalizations concerning the lawlike relations that hold between the various numerical attitudes in nature. Such laws involve quantification over numbers, and they exploit the mathematical relations holding in that domain. Thus, for example,

$$(1) \ (x)(f)(m)[((x \text{ has a mass of } m)$$
$$\& \ (x \text{ suffers a net force of } f))$$
$$\supset (x \text{ accelerates at } f/m)]$$

Consider now the large variety of propositional attitudes: "…believes that p", "…desires that p", "…fears that p", "…is happy that p", etc. These expressions are predicate-forming expressions also. When one substitutes a singular term for a proposition into the place held by "p", a determinate predicate results, e.g., "…believes that Tom is tall." (Sentences do not generally function as singular terms, but it is difficult to escape the idea that when a sentence occurs in the place held by "p", it is there functioning as or like a singular term. On this, more below.) More interestingly, the relations between the resulting propositional attitudes are characteristically the relations that hold between the propositions "contained" in them, relations such as entailment, equivalence, and mutual inconsistency. More interesting still, the argument place that takes the singular terms for propositions is open to quantification. All this permits the expression of generalizations concerning the lawlike relations that hold among propositional attitudes. Such laws involve quantification over propositions, and they exploit various relations holding in that domain. Thus, for example,

$$(2) \ (x)(p)[(x \text{ fears that } p) \supset (x \text{ desires that } \sim p)]$$
$$(3) \ (x)(p)[(x \text{ hopes that } p) \ \& \ (x \text{ discovers that } p)$$
$$\supset (x \text{ is pleased that } p)]$$
$$(4) \ (x)(p)(q)[((x \text{ believes that } p) \ \& \ (x \text{ believes}$$
$$\text{that } (\text{if } p \text{ then } q))) \supset (\text{barring confusion,}$$
$$\text{distraction, etc., } x \text{ believes that } q)]$$

$$(5) \ (x)(p)(q)[((x \text{ desires that } p) \ \& \ (x \text{ believes that}$$
$$(\text{if } q \text{ then } p)) \& \ (x \text{ is able to bring it}$$
$$\text{about that } q)) \supset (\text{barring conflicting}$$
$$\text{desires or preferred strategies, } x \text{ brings it}$$
$$\text{about that } q)]^3$$

Not only is folk psychology a theory, it is so *obviously* a theory that it must be held a major mystery why it has taken until the last half of the twentieth century for philosophers to realize it. The structural features of folk psychology parallel perfectly those of mathematical physics; the only difference lies in the respective domain of abstract entities they exploit – numbers in the case of physics, and propositions in the case of psychology.

Finally, the realization that folk psychology is a theory puts a new light on the mind–body problem. The issue becomes a matter of how the ontology of one theory (folk psychology) is, or is not, going to be related to the ontology of another theory (completed neuroscience); and the major philosophical positions on the mind–body problem emerge as so many different anticipations of what future research will reveal about the intertheoretic status and integrity of folk psychology.

The identity theorist optimistically expects that folk psychology will be smoothly *reduced* by completed neuroscience, and its ontology preserved by dint of transtheoretic identities. The dualist expects that it will prove *ir*reducible to completed neuroscience, by dint of being a nonredundant description of an autonomous, nonphysical domain of natural phenomena. The functionalist also expects that it will prove irreducible, but on the quite different grounds that the internal economy characterized by folk psychology is not, in the last analysis, a law-governed economy of natural states, but an abstract organization of functional states, an organization instantiable in a variety of quite different material substrates. It is therefore irreducible to the principles peculiar to any of them.

Finally, the eliminative materialist is also pessimistic about the prospects for reduction, but his reason is that folk psychology is a radically inadequate account of our internal activities, too confused and too defective to win survival through intertheoretic reduction. On his view it will simply be displaced by a better theory of those activities.

Which of these fates is the real destiny of folk psychology, we shall attempt to divine presently. For now, the point to keep in mind is that we shall be exploring the fate of a theory, a systematic, corrigible, speculative *theory*.

2   Why Folk Psychology Might (Really) Be False

Given that folk psychology is an empirical theory, it is at least an abstract possibility that its principles are radically false and that its ontology is an illusion. With the exception of eliminative materialism, however, none of the major positions takes this possibility seriously. None of them doubts the basic integrity or truth of folk psychology (hereafter, "FP"), and all of them anticipate a future in which its laws and categories are conserved. This conservatism is not without some foundation. After all, FP does enjoy a substantial amount of explanatory and predictive success. And what better grounds than this for confidence in the integrity of its categories?

What better grounds indeed? Even so, the presumption in FP's favor is spurious, born of innocence and tunnel vision. A more searching examination reveals a different picture. First, we must reckon not only with FP's successes, but with its explanatory failures, and with their extent and seriousness. Second, we must consider the long-term history of FP, its growth, fertility, and current promise of future development. And third, we must consider what sorts of theories are *likely* to be true of the etiology of our behavior, given what else we have learned about ourselves in recent history. That is, we must evaluate FP with regard to its coherence and continuity with fertile and well-established theories in adjacent and overlapping domains – with evolutionary theory, biology, and neuroscience, for example – because active coherence with the rest of what we presume to know is perhaps the final measure of any hypothesis.

A serious inventory of this sort reveals a very troubled situation, one which would evoke open skepticism in the case of any theory less familiar and dear to us. Let me sketch some relevant detail. When one centers one's attention not on what FP can explain, but on what it cannot explain or fails even to address, one discovers that there is a very great deal. As examples of central and important mental phenomena that remain largely or wholly mysterious within the framework of FP, consider the nature and dynamics of mental illness, the faculty of creative imagination, or the ground of intelligence differences between individuals. Consider our utter ignorance of the nature and psychological functions of sleep, that curious state in which a third of one's life is spent. Reflect on the common ability to catch an outfield fly ball on the run, or hit a moving car with a snowball. Consider the internal construction of a 3-D visual image from subtle differences in the 2-D array of stimulations in our respective retinas. Consider the rich variety of perceptual illusions, visual and otherwise. Or consider the miracle of memory, with its lightning capacity for relevant retrieval. On these and many other mental phenomena, FP sheds negligible light.

One particularly outstanding mystery is the nature of the learning process itself, especially where it involves large-scale conceptual change, and especially as it appears in its pre-linguistic or entirely nonlinguistic form (as in infants and animals), which is by far the most common form in nature. FP is faced with special difficulties here, since its conception of learning as the manipulation and storage of propositional attitudes founders on the fact that how to formulate, manipulate, and store a rich fabric of propositional attitudes is itself something that is learned, and is only one among many acquired cognitive skills. FP would thus appear constitutionally incapable of even addressing this most basic of mysteries.[4]

Failures on such a large scale do not (yet) show that FP is a false theory, but they do move that prospect well into the range of real possibility, and they do show decisively that FP is *at best* a highly superficial theory, a partial and unpenetrating gloss on a deeper and more complex reality. Having reached this opinion, we may be forgiven for exploring the possibility that FP provides a positively misleading sketch of our internal kinematics and dynamics, one whose success is owed more to selective application and forced interpretation on our part than to genuine theoretical insight on FP's part.

A look at the history of FP does little to allay such fears, once raised. The story is one of retreat, infertility, and decadence. The presumed domain of FP used to be much larger than it is now. In primitive cultures, the behavior of most of the elements of nature were understood in intentional terms. The wind could know anger, the moon jealousy, the river generosity, the sea fury, and so forth. These were not metaphors. Sacrifices were made and auguries undertaken to placate or divine the changing passions of the gods. Despite its sterility, this animistic approach to nature has dominated our history, and it is only in the last two or three thousand years that we have restricted FP's literal application to the domain of the higher animals.

Even in this preferred domain, however, both the content and the success of FP have not advanced sensibly in two or three thousand years. The FP of the Greeks is essentially the FP we use today, and we are negligibly better at explaining human behavior in its terms than was Sophocles. This is a very long period of stagnation and infertility for any theory to display, especially when faced with such an enormous backlog of anomalies and mysteries in its own explanatory domain. Perfect theories, perhaps, have no need to evolve. But FP is profoundly imperfect. Its failure to develop its resources and extend its range of success is therefore darkly curious, and one must query the integrity of its basic categories. To use Imre Lakatos's terms, FP is a stagnant or degenerating research program, and has been for millennia.

Explanatory success to date is of course not the only dimension in which a theory can display virtue or promise. A troubled or stagnant theory may merit patience and solicitude on other grounds; for example, on grounds that it is the only theory or theoretical approach that fits well with other theories about adjacent subject matters, or the only one that promises to reduce to or be explained by some established background theory whose domain encompasses the domain of the theory at issue. In sum, it may rate credence because it holds promise of theoretical integration. How does FP rate in this dimension?

It is just here, perhaps, that FP fares poorest of all. If we approach *Homo sapiens* from the perspective of natural history and the physical sciences, we can tell a coherent story of his constitution, development, and behavioral capacities which encompasses particle physics, atomic and molecular theory, organic chemistry, evolutionary theory, biology, physiology, and materialistic neuroscience. That story, though still radically incomplete, is already extremely powerful, outperforming FP at many points even in its own domain. And it is deliberately and self-consciously coherent with the rest of our developing world picture. In short, the greatest theoretical synthesis in the history of the human race is currently in our hands, and parts of it already provide searching descriptions and explanations of human sensory input, neural activity, and motor control.

But FP is no part of this growing synthesis. Its intentional categories stand magnificently alone, without visible prospect of reduction to that larger corpus. A successful reduction cannot be ruled out, in my view, but FP's explanatory impotence and long stagnation inspire little faith that its categories will find themselves neatly reflected in the framework of neuroscience. On the contrary, one is reminded of how alchemy must have looked as elemental chemistry was taking form, how Aristotelean cosmology must have looked as classical mechanics was being articulated, or how the vitalist conception of life must have looked as organic chemistry marched forward.

In sketching a fair summary of this situation, we must make a special effort to abstract from the fact that FP is a central part of our current *lebenswelt*, and serves as the principal vehicle of our interpersonal commerce. For these facts provide FP with a conceptual inertia that goes far beyond its purely theoretical virtues. Restricting ourselves to this latter dimension, what we must say is that FP suffers explanatory failures on an epic scale, that it has been stagnant for at least twenty-five centuries, and that its categories appear (so far) to be incommensurable with or orthogonal to the categories of the background physical science whose long-term claim to explain human behavior seems undeniable. Any theory that meets this description must be allowed a serious candidate for outright elimination.

We can of course insist on no stronger conclusion at this stage. Nor is it my concern to do so. We are here exploring a possibility, and the facts demand no more, and no less, than that it be taken seriously. The distinguishing feature of the eliminative materialist is that he takes it very seriously indeed.

3 Arguments Against Elimination

Thus the basic rationale of eliminative materialism: FP is a theory, and quite probably a false one; let us attempt, therefore, to transcend it.

The rationale is clear and simple, but many find it uncompelling. It will be objected that FP is not, strictly speaking, an *empirical* theory; that it is not false, or at least not refutable by empirical considerations; and that it ought not or cannot be transcended in the fashion of a defunct empirical theory. In what follows we shall examine these objections as they flow from the most popular and best-founded of the competing positions in the philosophy of mind: functionalism.

An antipathy toward eliminative materialism arises from two distinct threads running through contemporary functionalism. The first thread concerns the *normative* character of FP, or at least of that central core of FP which treats of the propositional attitudes. FP, some will say, is a characterization of an ideal, or at least praiseworthy mode of internal activity. It outlines not only what it is to have and process beliefs and desires, but also (and inevitably) what it is to be rational in their administration. The ideal laid down by FP may be imperfectly achieved by empirical humans, but this does not impugn FP as a normative characterization. Nor need such failures seriously impugn FP even as a descriptive characterization, for it remains true that our activities can be both usefully and accurately understood as rational *except for* the occasional lapse due to noise, interference, or other breakdown, which defects empirical research may eventually unravel. Accordingly, though neuroscience may usefully augment it, FP has no pressing need to be displaced, even as a descriptive theory; nor could it be replaced, *qua* normative characterization, by any descriptive theory of neural mechanisms, since rationality is defined over propositional attitudes like beliefs and desires. FP, therefore, is here to stay.

Daniel Dennett has defended a view along these lines.[5] And the view just outlined gives voice to a theme of the property dualists as well. Karl Popper and Joseph Margolis both cite the normative nature of mental and linguistic activity as a bar to their penetration or elimination by any descriptive/materialist theory.[6] I hope to deflate the appeal of such moves below.

The second thread concerns the *abstract* nature of FP. The central claim of functionalism is that the principles of FP characterize our internal states in a fashion that makes no reference to their intrinsic nature or physical constitution. Rather, they are characterized in terms of the network of causal relations they bear to one another, and to sensory circumstances and overt behavior. Given its abstract specification, that internal economy may therefore be realized in a nomically heterogeneous variety of physical systems. All of them may differ,

even radically, in their physical constitution, and yet at another level, they will all share the same nature. This view, says Fodor, "is compatible with very strong claims about the ineliminability of mental language from behavioral theories."[7] Given the real possibility of multiple instantiations in heterogeneous physical substrates, we cannot eliminate the functional characterization in favor of any theory peculiar to one such substrate. That would preclude our being able to describe the (abstract) organization that any one instantiation shares with all the other. A functional characterization of our internal states is therefore here to stay.

This second theme, like the first, assigns a faintly stipulative character to FP, as if the onus were on the empirical systems to instantiate faithfully the organization that FP specifies, instead of the onus being on FP to describe faithfully the internal activities of a naturally distinct class of empirical systems. This impression is enhanced by the standard examples used to illustrate the claims of functionalism – mousetraps, valve-lifters, arithmetical calculators, computers, robots, and the like. These are artifacts, constructed to fill a preconceived bill. In such cases, a failure of fit between the physical system and the relevant functional characterization impugns only the former, not the latter. The functional characterization is thus removed from empirical criticism in a way that is most unlike the case of an empirical theory. One prominent functionalist – Hilary Putnam – has argued outright that FP is not a corrigible theory at all.[8] Plainly, if FP is construed on these models, as regularly it is, the question of its empirical integrity is unlikely ever to pose itself, let alone receive a critical answer.

Although fair to some functionalists, the preceding is not entirely fair to Fodor. On his view the aim of psychology is to find the *best* functional characterization of ourselves, and what that is remains an empirical question. As well, his argument for the ineliminability of mental vocabulary from psychology does not pick out current FP in particular as ineliminable. It need claim only that *some* abstract functional characterization must be retained, some articulation or refinement of FP perhaps.

His estimate of eliminative materialism remains low, however. First, it is plain that Fodor thinks there is nothing fundamentally or interestingly wrong with FP. On the contrary, FP's central conception of cognitive activity – as consisting in the manipulation of propositional attitudes – turns up as the central element in Fodor's own theory on the nature of thought (*The Language of Thought*). And second, there remains the point that, whatever tidying up FP may or may not require, it cannot be displaced by any naturalistic theory of our physical substrate, since it is the abstract functional features of his internal states that make a person, not the chemistry of his substrate.

All of this is appealing. But almost none of it, I think, is right. Functionalism has too long enjoyed its reputation as a daring and *avant garde* position. It needs to be revealed for the short-sighted and reactionary position it is.

4 The Conservative Nature of Functionalism

A valuable perspective on functionalism can be gained from the following story. To begin with, recall the alchemists' theory of inanimate matter. We have here a long and variegated tradition, of course, not a single theory, but our purposes will be served by a gloss.

The alchemists conceived the "inanimate" as entirely continuous with animated matter, in that the sensible and behavioral properties of the various substances are owed to the ensoulment of baser matter by various spirits or essences. These nonmaterial aspects were held to undergo development, just as we find growth and development in the various souls of plants, animals, and humans. The alchemist's peculiar skill lay in knowing how to seed, nourish, and bring to maturity the desired spirits enmattered in the appropriate combinations.

On one orthodoxy, the four fundamental spirits (for "inanimate" matter) were named "mercury," "sulphur," "yellow arsenic," and "sal ammoniac." Each of these spirits was held responsible for a rough but characteristic syndrome of sensible, combinatorial, and causal properties. The spirit mercury, for example, was held responsible for certain features typical of metallic substances – their shininess, liquefiability, and so forth. Sulphur was held responsible for certain residual features typical of metals, and for those displayed by the ores from which running metal could be distilled. Any given metallic substance was a critical orchestration principally of these two spirits. A similar story held for the other two spirits, and among the four of them a certain domain of physical features and transformations was rendered intelligible and controllable.

The degree of control was always limited, of course. Or better, such prediction and control as the alchemists possessed was owed more to the manipulative lore acquired as an apprentice to a master, than to any genuine insight specified by the theory. The theory followed, more than it dictated, practice. But the theory did supply some rhyme to the practice, and in the absence of a developed alternative it was sufficiently compelling to sustain a long and stubborn tradition.

The tradition had become faded and fragmented by the time the elemental chemistry of Lavoisier and Dalton arose to replace it for good. But let us suppose that it had hung on a little longer – perhaps because the four-spirit orthodoxy had become a thumb-worn part of everyman's common sense – and let us examine the nature of the conflict between the two theories and some possible avenues of resolution.

No doubt the simplest line of resolution, and the one which historically took place, is outright displacement. The dualistic interpretation of the four essences – as immaterial spirits – will appear both feckless and unnecessary given the power of the corpuscularian taxonomy of atomic chemistry. And a reduction of the old taxonomy to the new will appear impossible, given the extent to which the comparatively toothless old theory cross-classifies things relative to the new. Elimination would thus appear the only alternative – *unless* some cunning and determined defender of the alchemical vision has the wit to suggest the following defense.

Being "ensouled by mercury," or "sulphur," or either of the other two so-called spirits, is actually a *functional* state. The first, for example, is defined by the disposition to reflect light, to liquefy under heat, to unite with other matter in the same state, and so forth. And each of these four states is related to the others, in that the syndrome for each varies as a function of which of the other three states is also instantiated in the same substrate. Thus, the level of description comprehended by the alchemical vocabulary is abstract: various material substances, suitably "ensouled," can display the features of a metal, for example, or even of gold specifically. For it is the total syndrome of occurrent and causal properties which matters, not the corpuscularian details of the substrate. Alchemy, it is concluded, comprehends a level of organization in reality distinct from and irreducible to the organization found at the level of corpuscularian chemistry.

This view might have had considerable appeal. After all, it spares alchemists the burden of defending immaterial souls that come and go; it frees them from having to meet the very strong demands of a naturalistic reduction; and it spares them the shock and confusion of outright elimination. Alchemical theory emerges as basically all right! Nor need they appear too obviously stubborn or dogmatic in this. Alchemy as it stands, they concede, may need substantial tidying up, and experience must be our guide. But we need not fear its naturalistic displacement, they remind us, since it is the particular orchestration of the syndromes of occurrent and causal properties which makes a piece of matter gold, not the idiosyncratic details of its corpuscularian substrate. A further circumstance would have made this claim even more plausible. For the fact is, the alchemists *did* know how to make gold, in this relevantly weakened sense of "gold," and they could do so in a variety of ways. Their "gold" was never as perfect, alas, as the "gold" nurtured in nature's womb, but what mortal can expect to match the skills of nature herself?

What this story shows is that it is at least possible for the constellation of moves, claims, and defenses characteristic of functionalism to constitute an outrage against reason and truth, and to do so with a plausibility that is frightening. Alchemy is a terrible theory, well-deserving of its complete elimination, and the defense of it just explored is reactionary, obfuscatory, retrograde, and wrong. But in historical context, that defense might have seemed wholly sensible, even to reasonable people.

The alchemical example is a deliberately transparent case of what might well be called "the functionalist strategem," and other cases are easy to imagine. A cracking good defense of the phlogiston theory of combustion can also be constructed along these lines. Construe being highly phlogisticated and being dephlogisticated as functional states defined by certain syndromes of causal dispositions; point to the great variety of natural substrates capable of combustion and calxification; claim an irreducible functional integrity for what has proved to lack any natural integrity; and bury the remaining defects under a pledge to contrive improvements. A similar recipe will provide new life for the four humors of medieval medicine, for the vital essence or archeus of premodern biology, and so forth.

If its application in these other cases is any guide, the functionalist strategem is a smokescreen for the preservation of error and confusion. Whence derives our assurance that in contemporary journals the same charade is not being played out on behalf of FP? The parallel with the case of alchemy is in all other respects distressingly complete, right down to the parallel between the search for artificial gold and the search for artificial intelligence!

Let me not be misunderstood on this last point. Both aims are worthy aims: thanks to nuclear physics, artificial (but real) gold is finally within our means, if only in submicroscopic quantities; and artificial (but real) intelligence eventually will be. But just as the careful orchestration of superficial syndromes was the wrong way to produce genuine gold, so may the careful orchestration of superficial syndromes be the wrong way to produce genuine intelligence. Just as with gold, what may be required is that our science penetrate to the underlying *natural* kind that gives rise to the total syndrome directly.

In summary, when confronted with the explanatory impotence, stagnant history, and systematic isolation of the intentional idioms of FP, it is not an adequate or responsive defense to insist that those idioms are abstract, functional, and irreducible in character. For one thing, this same defense could have been mounted with comparable plausibility no matter *what* haywire network of internal states our folklore had ascribed to us. And for another, the defense assumes essentially what is at issue: it assumes that it is the intentional idioms of FP, plus or minus a bit, that express the *important* features shared by all cognitive systems. But they may not. Certainly it is wrong to assume that they do, and then argue against the possibility of a materialistic displacement on grounds that it must describe matters at a level that is different from the important level. This just begs the question in favor of the older framework.

Finally, it is very important to point out that eliminative materialism is strictly *consistent* with the claim that the essence of a cognitive system resides in the abstract functional organization of its internal states. The eliminative materialist is not committed to the idea that the correct account of cognition *must* be a naturalistic account, though he may be forgiven for exploring the possibility. What he does hold is that the correct account of cognition, whether functionalistic or naturalistic, will bear about as much resemblance to

FP as modern chemistry bears to four-spirit alchemy.

Let us now try to deal with the argument, against eliminative materialism, from the normative dimension of FP. This can be dealt with rather swiftly, I believe.

First, the fact that the regularities ascribed by the intentional core of FP are predicated on certain logical relations among propositions is not by itself grounds for claiming anything essentially normative about FP. To draw a relevant parallel, the fact that the regularities ascribed by the classical gas law are predicated on arithmetical relations between numbers does not imply anything essentially normative about the classical gas law. And logical relations between propositions are as much an objective matter of abstract fact as are arithmetical relations between numbers. In this respect, the law

(6) $(x)(p)(q)[(x$ believes that $p)$ $\&(x$ believes
$$\supset \text{(barring that (if } p \text{ then } q)))$$
$$\text{confusion, distraction, etc.,}$$
$$x \text{ believes that } q)]$$

is entirely on a par with the classical gas law

(7) $(x)(P)(V)(\mu)[((x$ has a pressure $P)$ $\&$
$$(x \text{ has a volume } V) \& (x \text{ has a}$$
$$\text{quantity } \mu)) \supset \text{(barring very high}$$
$$\text{pressure or density, } x \text{ has a}$$
$$\text{temperature of } PV/\mu R)]$$

A normative dimension enters only because we happen to *value* most of the patterns ascribed by FP. But we do not value all of them. Consider

(8) $(x)(p)[((x$ desires with all his heart that $p)$
$$\& (x \text{ learns that } \sim p))$$
$$\supset \text{(barring unusual strength of character,}$$
$$x \text{ is shattered that } \sim p)]$$

Moreover, and as with normative convictions generally, fresh insight may motivate major changes in what we value.

Second, the laws of FP ascribe to us only a very minimal and truncated rationality, not an ideal rationality as some have suggested. The rationality characterized by the set of all FP laws falls well short of an ideal rationality. This is not surprising.

We have no clear or finished conception of ideal rationality anyway; certainly the ordinary man does not. Accordingly, it is just not plausible to suppose that the explanatory failures from which FP suffers are owed primarily to human failure to live up to the ideal standard it provides. Quite to the contrary, the conception of rationality it provides appears limping and superficial, especially when compared with the dialectical complexity of our scientific history, or with the ratiocinative virtuosity displayed by any child.

Third, even if our current conception of rationality – and more generally, of cognitive virtue – is largely constituted within the sentential/propositional framework of FP, there is no guarantee that this framework is adequate to the deeper and more accurate account of cognitive virtue which is clearly needed. Even if we concede the categorial integrity of FP, at least as applied to language-using humans, it remains far from clear that the basic parameters of intellectual virtue are to be found at the categorial level comprehended by the propositional attitudes. After all, language use is something that is learned, by a brain already capable of vigorous cognitive activity; language use is acquired as only one among a great variety of learned manipulative skills; and it is mastered by a brain that evolution has shaped for a great many functions, language using being only the very latest and perhaps the least of them. Against the background of these facts, language use appears as an extremely peripheral activity, as a species-specific mode of social interaction which is mastered thanks to the versatility and power of a more basic mode of activity. Why accept, then, a theory of cognitive activity that models its elements on the elements of human language? And why assume that the fundamental parameters of intellectual virtue are or can be defined over the elements at this superficial level?

A serious advance in our appreciation of cognitive virtue would thus seem to *require* that we go beyond FP, that we transcend the poverty of FP's conception of rationality by transcending its propositional kinematics entirely, by developing a deeper and more general kinematics of cognitive activity, and by distinguishing within this new framework which of the kinematically possible modes of activity are to be valued and encouraged (as more efficient, reliable, productive, or whatever). Eliminative materialism thus does not imply the end of our normative concerns. It implies only that they will have to be reconstituted at a more revealing level of understanding, the level that a matured neuroscience will provide.

What a theoretically informed future might hold in store for us, we shall now turn to explore. Not because we can foresee matters with any special clarity, but because it is important to try to break the grip on our imagination held by the propositional kinematics of FP. As far as the present section is concerned, we may summarize our conclusions as follows. FP is nothing more and nothing less than a culturally entrenched theory of how we and the higher animals work. It has no special features that make it empirically invulnerable, no unique functions that make it irreplaceable, no special status of any kind whatsoever. We shall turn a skeptical ear then, to any special pleading on its behalf.

5 Beyond Folk Psychology

What might the elimination of FP actually involve – not just the comparatively straightforward idioms for sensation, but the entire apparatus of propositional attitudes? That depends heavily on what neuroscience might discover, and on our determination to capitalize on it. Here follow three scenarios in which the operative conception of cognitive activity is progressively divorced from the forms and categories that characterize natural language. If the reader will indulge the lack of actual substance, I shall try to sketch some plausible form.

First suppose that research into the structure and activity of the brain, both fine-grained and global, finally does yield a new kinematics and correlative dynamics for what is now thought of as cognitive activity. The theory is uniform for all terrestrial brains, not just human brains, and it makes suitable conceptual contact with both evolutionary biology and non-equilibrium thermodynamics. It ascribes to us, at any given time, a set or configuration of complex states, which are specified within the theory as figurative "solids" within a four- or five-dimensional phase space. The laws of the theory govern the interaction, motion, and transformation of these "solid" states within that space, and also their relations to whatever sensory and motor transducers the system possesses. As with celestial mechanics, the exact specification of the "solids" involved and the exhaustive accounting of all dynamically relevant adjacent "solids" is not practically possible, for many reasons, but here also it turns out that the obvious approximations we fall back on yield excellent explanations/predictions of internal change and external behavior, at least in the short term. Regarding long-term activity, the theory provides powerful and unified accounts of the learning process, the nature of mental illness, and variations in character and intelligence across the animal kingdom as well as across individual humans.

Moreover, it provides a straightforward account of "knowledge," as traditionally conceived. According to the new theory, and declarative sentence to which a speaker would give confident assent is merely a one-dimensional *projection* – through the compound lens of Wernicke's and Broca's areas onto the idiosyncratic surface of the speaker's language – a one-dimensional projection of a four- or five-dimensional "solid" that is an element in his true kinematical state. (Recall the shadows on the wall of Plato's cave.) Being projections of that inner reality, such sentences do carry significant information regarding it and are thus fit to function as elements in a communication system. On the other hand, being *sub*dimensional projections, they reflect but a narrow part of the reality projected. They are therefore *un*fit to represent the deeper reality in all its kinematically, dynamically, and even normatively relevant respects. That is to say, a system of propositional attitudes, such as FP, must inevitably fail to capture what is going on here, though it may reflect just enough superficial structure to sustain an alchemylike tradition among folk who lack any better theory. From the perspective of the newer theory, however, it is plain that there simply are no law-governed states of the kind FP postulates. The real laws governing our internal activities are defined over different and much more complex kinematical states and configurations, as are the normative criteria for a developmental integrity and intellectual virtue.

A theoretical outcome of the kind just described may fairly be counted as a case of elimination of one theoretical ontology in favor of another, but the success here imagined for systematic neuroscience need not have any sensible effect on common practice. Old ways die hard, and in the absence of some practical necessity, they may not die at all. Even so, it is not inconceivable that some segment of the population, or all of it, should become intimately familiar with the vocabulary required to characterize our kinematical states, learn the laws governing their interactions and behavioral projections, acquire a facility in their first-person ascription, and displace the use of FP altogether, even in the marketplace. The demise of FP's ontology would then be complete.

We may now explore a second and rather more radical possibility. Everyone is familiar with Chomsky's thesis that the human mind or brain contains innately and uniquely the abstract structures for learning and using specifically human natural languages. A competing hypothesis is that our brain does indeed contain innate structures, but that those structure have as their original and still primary function the organization of perceptual experience, the administration of linguistic categories being an acquired and additional function for which evolution has only incidentally suited them.[9] This hypothesis has the advantage of not requiring the evolutionary saltation that Chomsky's view would seem to require, and there are other advantages as well. But these matters need not concern us here. Suppose, for our purposes, that this competing view is true, and consider the following story.

Research into the neural structures that fund the organization and processing of perceptual information reveals that they are capable of administering a great variety of complex tasks, some of them showing a complexity far in excess of that shown by natural language. Natural languages, it turns out, exploit only a very elementary portion of the available machinery, the bulk of which serves far more complex activities beyond the ken of the propositional conceptions of FP. The detailed unraveling of what that machinery is and of the capacities it has makes it plain that a form of language far more sophisticated than "natural" language, though decidedly "alien" in its syntactic and semantic structures, could also be learned and used by our innate systems. Such a novel system of communication, it is quickly realized, could raise the efficiency of information exchange between brains by an order of magnitude, and would enhance epistemic evaluation by a comparable amount, since it would reflect the underlying structure of our cognitive activities in greater detail than does natural language.

Guided by our new understanding of those internal structures, we manage to construct a new system of verbal communication entirely distinct from natural language, with a new and more powerful combinatorial grammar over novel elements forming novel combinations with exotic properties. The compounded strings of this alternative system – call them "übersätze" – are not evaluated as true or false, nor are the relations between them remotely analogous to the relations of entailment, etc., that hold between sentences. They display a different organization and manifest different virtues.

Once constructed, this "language" proves to be learnable; it has the power projected; and in two generations it has swept the planet. Everyone uses the new system. The syntactic forms and semantic categories of so-called "natural" language disappear entirely. And with them disappear the propositional attitudes of FP, displaced by a more revealing scheme in which (of course) "übersatzenal attitudes" play the leading role. FP again suffers elimination.

This second story, note, illustrates a theme with endless variations. There are possible as many different "folk psychologies" as there are possible differently structured communication systems to serve as models for them.

A third and even stranger possibility can be outlined as follows. We know that there is considerable lateralization of function between the two cerebral hemispheres, and that the two hemispheres make use of the information they get from each other by way of the great cerebral commissure – the corpus callosum – a giant cable of neurons connecting them. Patients whose commissure has been surgically severed display a variety of behavioral deficits that indicate a loss of access by one hemisphere to information it used to get from the other. However, in people with callosal agenesis (a congenital defect in which the connecting cable is simply absent), there is little or no behavioral deficit, suggesting that the two hemispheres have learned to exploit the information carried in other less direct pathways connecting them through the subcortical regions. This suggests that, even in the normal case, a developing hemisphere *learns* to make use of the information the cerebral commissure deposits at its doorstep. What we have then, in the case of a normal human, is two physically distinct cognitive systems (both capable of independent function) responding in a systematic and learned fashion to exchanged information. And what is especially interesting about this case is the sheer amount of information exchanged. The cable of the commissure consists of $\approx$ 200 million neurons,[10] and even if we assume that each of these fibres is capable of one of only two possible states each second (a most conservative estimate), we are looking at a channel whose information capacity is $> 2 \times 10^8$ binary bits/second. Compare this to the < 500 bits/second capacity of spoken English.

Now, if two distinct hemispheres can learn to communicate on so impressive a scale, why shouldn't two distinct brains learn to do it also? This would require an artificial "commissure" of some kind, but let us suppose that we can fashion a workable transducer for implantation at some site in the brain that research reveals to be suitable, a transducer to convert a symphony of neural activity into (say) microwaves radiated from an aerial in the forehead, and to perform the reverse function of converting received microwaves back into neural activation. Connecting it up need not be an insuperable problem. We simply trick the normal processes of dendritic arborization into growing their own myriad connections with the active microsurface of the transducer.

Once the channel is opened between two or more people, they can learn (*learn*) to exchange information and coordinate their behavior with the same intimacy and virtuosity displayed by your own cerebral hemispheres. Think what this might do for hockey teams, and ballet companies, and research teams! If the entire population were thus fitted out, spoken language of any kind might well disappear completely, a victim of the "why crawl when you can fly?" principle. Libraries become filled not with books, but with long recordings of exemplary bouts of neural activity. These constitute a growing cultural heritage, an evolving "Third World," to use Karl Popper's terms. But they do not consist of sentences or arguments.

How will such people understand and conceive of other individuals? To this question I can only answer, "In roughly the same fashion that your right hemisphere 'understands' and 'conceives of' your left hemisphere – intimately and efficiently, but not propositionally!"

These speculations, I hope, will evoke the required sense of untapped possibilities, and I shall in any case bring them to a close here. Their function is to make some inroads into the aura of inconceivability that commonly surrounds the idea that we might reject FP. The felt conceptual strain even finds expression in an argument to the effect that the thesis of eliminative materialism is incoherent since it denies the very conditions presupposed by the assumption that it is meaningful. I shall

close with a brief discussion of this very popular move.

As I have received it, the reductio proceeds by pointing out that the statement of eliminative materialism is just a meaningless string of marks or noises, unless that string is the expression of a certain *belief*, and a certain *intention* to communicate, and a *knowledge* of the grammar of the language, and so forth. But if the statement of eliminative materialism is true, then there are no such states to express. The statement at issue would then be a meaningless string of marks or noises. It would therefore *not* be true. Therefore it is not true. Q.E.D.

The difficulty with any nonformal reductio is that the conclusion against the initial assumption is always no better than the material assumptions invoked to reach the incoherent conclusion. In this case the additional assumptions involve a certain theory of meaning, one that presupposes the integrity of FP. But formally speaking, one can as well infer, from the incoherent result, that this theory of meaning is what must be rejected. Given the independent critique of FP leveled earlier, this would even seem the preferred option. But in any case, one cannot simply assume that particular theory of meaning without begging the question at issue, namely, the integrity of FP.

The question-begging nature of this move is most graphically illustrated by the following analog, which I owe to Patricia Churchland.[11] The issue here, placed in the seventeenth century, is whether there exists such a substance as *vital spirit*. At the time, this substance was held, without significant awareness of real alternatives, to be that which distinguished the animate from the inanimate. Given the monopoly enjoyed by this conception, given the degree to which it was integrated with many of our other conceptions, and given the magnitude of the revisions any serious alternative conception would require, the following refutation of any antivitalist claim would be found instantly plausible.

The anti-vitalist says that there is no such thing as vital spirit. But this claim is self-refuting. The speaker can expect to be taken seriously only if his claim cannot. For if the claim is true, then the speaker does not have vital spirit and must be *dead*. But if he is dead, then his statement is a meaningless string of noises, devoid of reason and truth.

The question-begging nature of this argument does not, I assume, require elaboration. To those moved by the earlier argument, I commend the parallel for examination.

The thesis of this essay may be summarized as follows. The propositional attitudes of folk psy-chology do not constitute an unbreachable barrier to the advancing tide of neuroscience. On the contrary, the principled displacement of folk psy-chology is not only richly possible, it represents one of the most intriguing theoretical displace-ments we can currently imagine.

Notes

An earlier draft of this paper was presented at the Uni-versity of Ottawa, and to the *Brain, Mind, and Person* colloquium at SUNY, Oswego. My thanks for the sug-gestions and criticisms that have informed the present version.

1 See Paul Feyerabend, "Materialism and mind–body problem," *Review of Metaphysics* XVII.I, 65 (Septem-ber 1963), 49–66; Richard Rorty, "Mind–body iden-tity, privacy, and categories," *Journal of Metaphysics*, XIX.I, 73 (September 1965), 24–54; and my *Scientific Realism and the Plasticity of Mind* (New York: Cam-bridge, 1979).

2 We shall examine a handful of these laws presently. For a more comprehensive sampling of the laws of folk psychology see my *Scientific Realism and the Plasticity of Mind*, ch. 4. For a detailed examination of the folk principles that underwrite action explana-tions in particular, see my "The logical character of action explanations," *Philosophical Review* LXXIX, 2 (April 1970), 214–36.

3 Staying within an objectual interpretation of the quantifiers, perhaps the simplest way to make sys-tematic sense of expressions like ⌜x believes that p⌝ and closed sentences formed therefrom is just to construe whatever occurs in the nested position held by "p", "q", etc. as there having the function of a singular term. Accordingly, the standard connectives, as they occur between terms in that nested position, must be construed as there functioning as operators that form compound singular terms from other sin-gular terms, and not as sentence operators. The com-pound singular terms so formed denote the appropriate compound propositions. Substitutional quantification will of course underwrite a different interpretation, and there are other approaches as well. Especially appealing is the prosentential approach of Dorothy Grover, Joseph Camp, and Nuel Belnap, "A prosentential theory of truth," *Philosophical Studies* XXVII, 2 (February 1975), 73–

125. But the resolution of these issues is not vital to the present discussion.

4 A possible response here is to insist that the cognitive activity of animals and infants is linguaformal in its elements, structures, and processing right from birth. J. A. Fodor, in *The Language of Thought* (New York: Crowell, 1975), has erected a positive theory of thought on the assumption that the innate forms of cognitive activity have precisely the form here denied. For a critique of Fodor's view, see Patricia Churchland, "Fodor on language learning," *Synthese* XXXVIII, 1 (May 1978), 149–59.

5 Most explicitly in "Three kinds of intentional psychology," in R. A. Healy (ed.), *Reduction, Time and Reality* (Cambridge University Press, 1981), but this theme of Dennett's goes all the way back to his "Intentional systems," *Journal of Philosophy*, LXVIII, 4 (Feb. 25, 1971), 87–106; reprinted in his *Brainstorms* (Montgomery, Vt.: Bradford Books, 1978).

6 Popper, *Objective Knowledge* (New York: Oxford, 1972); with J. Eccles, *The Self and Its Brain* (New York: Springer Verlag, 1978). Margolis, *Persons and Minds* (Boston: Reidel, 1978).

7 *Psychological Explanation* (New York: Random House, 1968), p. 116.

8 "Robots: machines or artificially created life?", *Jour-nal of Philosophy*, LXI, 21 (Nov. 12, 1964), 668–91, pp. 675, 681ff.

9 Richard Gregory defends such a view in "The gram-mar of vision," *Listener* LXXXIII, 2133 (February 1970), 242–6; reprinted in his *Concepts and Mechan-isms of Perception* (London: Duckworth, 1975), pp. 622–9.

10 M. S. Gazzaniga and J. E. LeDoux, *The Integrated Mind* (New York: Plenum Press, 1975).

11 "Is determinism self-refuting?", *Mind* 90 (1981), 99–101.

7

Neurophilosophy and Connectionism

Neural Representation and Neural Computation

Patricia Smith Churchland and Terrence J. Sejnowski

The types of representation and the styles of computation in the brain appear to be very different from the symbolic expressions and logical inferences that are used in sentence-logic models of cognition. In this essay we explore the consequences that brain-style processing may have on theories of cognition. Connectionist models are used as examples to illustrate neural representation and computation in the pronouncing of English text and in the extracting of shape parameters from shaded images. Levels of analysis are not independent in connectionist models, and the dependencies between levels provide an opportunity to co-evolve theories at all levels. This is a radical departure from the *a priori*, introspection-based strategy that has characterized most previous work in epistemology.

1   How do we Represent the World?

The central epistemological question, from Plato on, is this: *How is representation of a world by a self possible?* So far as we can tell, there is a reality existing external to ourselves, and it appears that we do come to represent that reality, and sometimes even to know how its initial appearance to our senses differs from how it actually is. How is this accomplished, and how is knowledge possible? How is science itself possible?

The dominant philosophical tradition has been to try to resolve the epistemological puzzles by invoking mainly intuition and logic to figure out such things as the organization of knowledge, the nature of the "mirroring" of the outer world by the inner world, and the roles of reason and inference in the generation of internal models of reality. Epistemology thus pursued was the product of "pure reason," not of empirical investigation, and thus epistemological theories were believed to delimit the necessary conditions, the absolute foundations, and the incontrovertible presuppositions of human knowledge. For this *a priori* task – a task of reflective understanding and pure reason – empirical observations by psychologists and neurobiologists are typically considered irrelevant, or at least incapable of effecting any significant correction of the *a priori* conclusions. Plato, Descartes, and Kant are some of the major historical figures in that tradition; some contemporary figures are Chisholm (1966), Strawson (1966), Davidson (1974), and McGinn (1982). It is safe to say that most philosophers still espouse the *a priori* strategy to some nontrivial extent.

In a recent departure from this venerable tradition of *a priori* philosophy, some philosophers have argued that epistemology itself must be informed by the psychological and neurobiological data that bear upon how in fact we represent and model the world. First articulated in a systematic and powerful way by Quine (1960),[1] this new "naturalism" has begun to seem more in keeping with evolutionary and biological science and to promise more testable and less speculative answers.

If, as it seems, acquiring knowledge is an essentially biological phenomenon, in the straightforward sense that it is something our brains do, then there is no reason to expect that brains should have evolved to have *a priori* knowledge of the true nature of things: not of fire, not of light, not of the heart and the blood, and certainly not of knowledge or of its own microstructure and microfunction. There are, undoubtedly, innate dispositions to behave in certain ways, to believe certain things, and to organize data in certain ways, but innateness is no guarantee of truth, and it is the truth that *a priori* reflections are presumed to reveal. Innate beliefs and cognitive structure cannot be assumed to be either optimal or true, because all evolution "cares" about is that the internal models enable the species to survive. Satisficing is good enough. It is left for science to care about the truth (or perhaps empirical adequacy), and the theories science generates may well show the inadequacies of our innately specified models of external reality. Even more dramatically, they may show the inadequacy of our model of our internal reality – of the nature of our selves.

The *a priori* insights of the Great Philosophers should be understood, therefore, not as The Absolute Truth about how the mind-brain must be, but as articulations of the *assumptions* that live deep in our collective *conception* of ourselves. As assumptions, however, they may be misconceived and empirically unsound, or at least they may be open to revision in the light of scientific progress. The possibility of such revision does not entail that the assumptions are ludicrous or useless. On the contrary, they may well be very important elements in the theoretical scaffolding as neurobiology and psychology inch their way toward empirically adequate theories of mind-brain function. The methodological point is that in science we cannot proceed with no theoretical framework, so even intuitive folk theory is better than nothing as the scientific enterprise gets underway.

In addition to asking how the self can know about the external reality, Kant asked: How is representation of a *self* by a knowing self possible? One of his important ideas was that the nature of the internal world of the self is no more unmediated or *given* than is knowledge of the external world of physical objects in space and time. A modern version of this insight says: Just as the inner thoughts and experiences may represent but not *resemble* the outer reality, so the inner thoughts may represent but not resemble the inner reality of which they are the representation. This idea, taken with Quine's naturalism, implies that if we want to know how we represent the world – the external world of colored, moving objects, and the internal world of thoughts, consciousness, motives, and dreams – the scientific approach is likely to be the most rewarding. Inner knowledge, like outer knowledge, is conceptually and theoretically mediated – it is the result of complex information processing. Whether our intuitive understanding of the nature of our inner world is at all adequate is an empirical question, not an *a priori* one.

If empirical results are relevant to our understanding of how the mind-brain represents, it is also entirely possible that scientific progress on this frontier will be as revolutionary as it has been in astronomy, physics, chemistry, biology, and geology. With this observation comes the recognition that it may reconfigure our current assumptions about knowledge, consciousness, representations, and the self at least as much as Copernicus and Darwin reconfigured our dearest assumptions about the nature of the universe and our place in it. Our intuitive assumptions, and even what seems phenomenologically obvious, may be misconceived and may thus undergo reconfiguration as new theory emerges from psychology and neurobiology.

Philosophers – and sometimes psychologists, and occasionally even neuroscientists – generally make one of two responses to the naturalists' conception of the status of our self-understanding:

1   Philosophy is an *a priori* discipline, and the fundamental conceptual truths about the nature of the mind, of knowledge, of reason, etc. will come only from *a priori* investigations. In this way, philosophy sets the bounds for science – indeed, the bounds of sense, as Strawson (1966) would put it. In a more extreme vein, some existentialist philosophers would claim that the naturalistic approach is itself symptomatic of a civilizational neurosis: the infatuation with science. On this view, the scientific approach to human nature is deeply irrational. Mandt (1986, p. 274) describes the existentialist criticism as follows: "That scientific modes of thought have become paradigmatic indicates the degree to which traditional modes of human life and experience

have disintegrated, plunging civilization into a nihilistic abyss."

2   Even if a naturalistic approach is useful for some aspects of the nature of knowledge and representation, the neurosciences in particular are largely irrelevant to the enterprise. Neuroscience may be fascinating enough in its own right, but for a variety of reasons it is irrelevant to answering the questions we care about concerning cognition, representation, intelligent behavior, learning, consciousness, and so forth. Psychology and linguistics might actually be useful in informing us about such matters, but neurobiology is just off the book.

2   Why is Neurobiology Dismissed as Irrelevant to Understanding How the Mind Works?

2.1   The traditional problem

In its traditional guise, the mind–body problem can be stated thus: Are mental phenomena (experiences, beliefs, desires, etc.) actually phenomena of the physical brain? Dualists have answered No to this question. On the dualist's view, mental phenomena inhere in a special, nonphysical substance: the mind (also referred to as the soul or the spirit). The mind, on the dualist's theory, is the ghost in the machine; it is composed not of physical material obeying physical laws but of soul-stuff, or "spooky" stuff, and it operates according to principles unique to spooky stuff.

The most renowned of the substance dualists are Plato and Descartes, and, more recently, J. C. Eccles (1977) and Richard Swinburne (1986). Because dualists believe the mind to be a wholly separate kind of stuff or entity, they expect that it can be understood only in its own terms. At most, neuroscience can shed light on the *interaction* between mind and body, but not on the nature of the mind itself. Dualists consequently see psychology as essentially independent of neurobiology, which, after all, is devoted to finding out how the *physical* stuff of the nervous system works. It might be thought a bonus of dualism that it implies that to understand the mind we do not have to know much about the brain.

Materialism answers the mind–body question (Are mental states actually states of the physical brain?) in the affirmative. The predominant arguments for materialism draw upon the spectacular failure of dualism to cohere with the rest of ongoing science. And as physics, molecular biology, evolutionary biology, and neuroscience have progressed, this failure has become more rather than less marked. In short, the weight of empirical evidence is against the existence of special soul-stuff (spooky stuff). (For a more thorough discussion of the failures of substance dualism, see P. S. Churchland 1986.) Proponents of materialism include Hobbes (in the seventeenth century), B. F. Skinner (1957, 1976), J. J. C. Smart (1959), W. V. O. Quine (1960), D. C. Dennett (1978), and P. M. Churchland (1988).

Despite the general commitment to materialism, there are significant differences among materialists in addressing the central question of how best to explain psychological states. Strict behaviorists, such as Skinner, thought that explanations would take the form of stimulus–response profiles *exclusively*. Supporting this empirical hypothesis with a philosophical theory, philosophical behaviorists claimed that the mental terminology itself could be analyzed into sheerly physicalistic language about dispositions to behave. (For discussion, see P. M. Churchland 1988). Curiously, perhaps, the behaviorists (both empirical and philosophical) share with the dualists the conviction that it is not necessary to understand the workings of the brain in order to explain intelligent behavior. On the behaviorists' research ideology, again we have a bonus: In order to explain behavior, *we do not have to know anything about the brain.*

In contrast to behaviorism, identity theorists (Smart 1959; Enc 1983) claimed that mental states, such as visual perceptions, pains, beliefs, and drives, were in fact identical to states of the brain, though it would of course be up to neuroscience to discover precisely what brain states were in fact identical to what mental states. On the research ideology advocated by these materialists, explanation of behavior will have to refer to inner representations and hence to what the brain is doing.

2.2   The contemporary problem: theory dualism

Many philosophers who are materialists to the extent that they doubt the existence of soul-stuff nonetheless believe that psychology ought to be essentially autonomous from neuroscience, and that neuroscience will not contribute significantly to our understanding of perception, language use, thinking, problem solving, and (more generally) cognition. Thus, the mind–body problem in its contemporary guise is this: Can we get a *unified* science of the mind–brain? Will psychological theory reduce to neuroscience?

A widespread view (which we call theory dualism) answers No to the above question. Typically, three sorts of reasons are offered:

(a) *Neuroscience is too hard.* The brain is too complex; there are too many neurons and too many connections, and it is a hopeless task to suppose we can ever understand complex higher functions in terms of the dynamics and organization of neurons.

(b) *The argument from multiple instantiability.* Psychological states are functional states and, as such, can be implemented (instantiated) in diverse machines (Putnam 1967; Fodor 1975; Pylyshyn 1984). Therefore, no particular psychological state, such as believing that the earth is round or that $2 + 2 = 4$, can be identified with exactly this or that machine state. So no functional (cognitive) process can be reduced to the behavior of particular neuronal systems.

(c) *Psychological states have intentionality.* That is, they are identified in terms of their semantic content; they are "about" other things; they represent things; they have logical relations to one another. We can think about objects in their absence, and even of nonexistent objects. For example, if someone has the belief that Mars is warmer than Venus, then that psychological state is specified as the state it is in terms of the sentence "Mars is warmer than Venus," which has a specific meaning (its content) and which is logically related to other sentences. It is a belief *about* Mars and Venus, but it is not caused by Mars or Venus. Someone might have this belief because he was told, or because he deduced it from other things he knew. In cognitive generalizations states are related semantically and logically, whereas in neurobiological generalizations states can only be *causally* related. Neurobiological explanations cannot be sensitive to the logical relations between the contents of cognitive states, or to meaning or "aboutness." They respond only to *causal* properties. Neurobiology, therefore, cannot

do justice to cognition, and thus no reduction is possible.

2.3   What is wrong with theory dualism?

In opposition to theory dualists, reductionists think we ought to strive for an integration of psychological and neurobiological theory. Obviously, a crucial element in the discussion concerns what is meant by "reduction"; hence, part of what must first be achieved is a proper account of what sort of business intertheoretic reduction is.

Roughly, the account is this: Reductions are *explanations* of phenomena described by one theory in terms of the phenomena described by a more basic theory. Reductions typically involve the co-evolution of theories over time, and as they co-evolve one theory is normally revised, corrected, and modified by its co-evolutionary cohort theory at the other level. This revisionary interaction can, and usually does, go both ways: from the more basic to the less basic theory and vice versa. It is important to emphasize the modification to theories as they co-evolve, because sometimes the modification is radical and entails massive reconfiguration of the very categories used to describe the phenomena. In such an event, the very data to be explained may come to be redescribed under pressure from the evolving theories. Examples of categories that have undergone varying degrees of revision, from the minor to the radical, include impetus, caloric, gene, neuron, electricity, instinct, life, and very recently, excitability (in neurons) (Schaffner 1976; P. M. Churchland 1979; Hooker 1981).

Because reductionism is frequently misunderstood, it is necessary to be explicit about what is *not* meant. First, seeking reductions of macro-level theory to micro level does not imply that one must first know everything about the elements of the micro theory before research at the macro level can be usefully undertaken. Quite the reverse is advocated – research should proceed at all levels of the system, and co-evolution of theory may enhance progress at all levels. Data from one level *constrain* theorizing at that level and at other levels. Additionally, the reduction of theories does *not* mean that the reduced phenomena somehow disappear or are discredited. The theory of optics was reduced to the theory of electromagnetic radiation, but light itself did not disappear, not did it become disreputable to study light at the macro level.

Nor was the reduced theory cast out as useless or discredited; on the contrary, it was and continues to be useful for addressing phenomena at a higher level of description. As for the phenomenon, it is what it is, and it continues to be whatever it is as theories are reduced or abandoned. Whether a category is ultimately rejected or revised depends on its scientific integrity, and that is, of course, determined empirically. (For more detail on intertheoretic reduction, see P. S. Churchland 1986.)

Given this brief account of reduction as a backdrop, an outline of how the reductionist answers the theory dualist goes as follows:

(a) Neuroscience *is* hard, but with many new techniques now available, an impressive body of data is available to constrain our theories, and a lot of data are very suggestive as to how neural networks function. (See Sejnowski and Churchland, in press.) We have begun to see the shape of neurobiological answers to functional questions, such as how information is stored, how networks learn, and how networks of neurons represent.

(b) High-level states are multiply instantiable. So what? If, in any given species, we can show that particular functional states are identical to specific neuronal configurations (for example, that being in REM sleep is having a specified neuronal state, or that one type of learning involves changing synaptic weights according to a Hebb rule), that will be sufficient to declare a reduction relative to that domain (Richardson 1979; Enc 1983; P. S. Churchland 1986; section 3 below). Very pure philosophers who cannot bring themselves to call these perfectly respectable domain-relative explanations "reductions" are really just digging in on who gets to use the word. Moreover, it should be emphasized that the explanation of high-level cognitive phenomena will not be achieved directly in terms of phenomena at the lowest level of nervous-system organization, such as synapses and individual neurons. Rather, the explanation will refer to properties at higher structural levels, such as networks or systems. Functional properties of networks and systems will be explained by reference to properties at the next level down, and so on. What we envision is a chain of explanations linking higher to next-lower levels, and so on down

the ladder of structural levels. (See Sejnowski and Churchland, in press.) Aspects of individual variation at the synaptic and cellular levels are probably invisible at the systems level, where similarity of larger-scale emergent properties, such as position in a high-dimensional parameter space, is critical in identifying similarity of information-processing function (Sejnowski et al. 1988). A theory of how states in a nervous system represent or model the world will need to be set in the context of the evolution and development of nervous systems, and will try to explain the interactive role of neural states in the ongoing neurocognitive economy of the system. Nervous systems do not represent all aspects of the physical environment; they selectively represent information a species needs, given its environmental niche and its way of life. Nervous systems are programmed to respond to certain selected features, and within limits they learn other features through experience by encountering examples and generalizing. Cognitive neuroscience is now beginning to understand how this is done (Livingstone 1988; Goldman-Rakic 1988; Kelso et al. 1986). Although the task is difficult, it now seems reasonable to assume that the "aboutness" or "meaningfulness" of representational states is not a spooky relation but a neurobiological relation. As we come to understand more about the dynamical properties of networks, we may ultimately be able to generate a theory of how human language is learned and represented by our sort of nervous system, and thence to explain language-dependent kinds of meaning. Because this answer is highly cryptic and because intentionality has often seemed forever beyond the reach of neurobiology, the next section will focus on intentionality: the theory dualist's motivation, and the reductionist's strategy.

3 Levels, Intentionality, and the Sentence-logic Model of the Mind

3.1 *Sentential attitudes and the computer metaphor*

Two deep and interrelated assumptions concerning the nature of cognition drive the third anti-reductionist argument:

1   Cognition essentially involves representations and computations. Representations are, in general, symbolic structures, and computations are, in general, rules (such as rules of logic) for manipulating those symbolic structures.

2   A good model for understanding mind-brain functions is the computer – that is, a machine based on the same logical foundations as a Turing machine and on the von Neumann architecture for a digital computer. Such machines are ideally suited for the manipulation of symbols according to rules. The computer metaphor suggests that the mind-brain, at the information-processing level, can be understood as a kind of digital computer, the problem for cognitive psychology is to determine the program that our brains run.

The motivating vision here is that cognition is to be modeled largely on language and logical reasoning; having a thought is, functionally speaking, having a sentence in the head, and thinking is, functionally speaking, doing logic, or at least running on procedures very like logic. Put thus baldly, it may seem faintly ridiculous, but the theory is supported quite plausibly by the observation that beliefs, thoughts, hopes, desires, and so forth are essential in the explanation of cognition, and that such states are irreducibly semantic because they are identified in virtue of their content sentences. That is, such states are always and essentially beliefs that p, thoughts that p, or desires that p, where for "p" we substitute the appropriate sentence, such as "Nixon was a Russian spy" or "Custard is made with milk". Such cognitive states – the so-called sentential attitudes – are the states they are in virtue of the sentences that specify what they are about. Moreover, a content sentence stands in specific logical and semantic relations to other sentences. The state transitions are determined by semantic and logical relations between the content sentences, not by casual relations among states neurobiologically described. Thus, cognitive states have *meaning* (that is, content, or intentionality), and it might be argued that it is precisely in virtue of their meaningfulness that they play the role in cognition that they do.

The fundamental conception is, accordingly, well and truly rooted in folk psychology, the body of concepts and everyday lore by means of which we routinely explain one another's behavior by invoking sentential attitudes (Stich 1983; P. M. Churchland 1988) – for example, Smith paid for the vase because he believed that his son had dropped it and he feared that the store owner would be angry. In these sorts of intentional explanations, the basic unit of representation is the sentence, and state transitions are accomplished through the following of rules: deductive inference, inductive inference, and assorted other rules.

Extending the framework of folk psychology to get an encompassing account of cognition in general, this approach takes it that thinking, problem solving, language use, perception, and so forth will be understood as we determine the sequence of sentences corresponding to the steps in a given information-processing task; that is, as we understand the mechanics of sentence crunching. According to this research paradigm, known as sententialism, it is the task of cognitive science to figure out what programs the brain runs, and neuroscience can then check these top-down hypotheses against the wetware to see if they are generally possible. (See especially Fodor 1975, 1981; Pylyshyn 1984.)

3.2   Is cognition mainly symbol manipulation in the language of thought?

Although this view concerning the nature of cognition and the research strategy for studying the cognition may be appealing (where much of the appeal is derived from the comfortable place found for folk psychology), it suffers from major defects. Many of these defects have been discussed in detail by Anderson and Hinton (1981), by P. S. Churchland (1986), and in various chapters of McClelland and Rumelhart (1986). A summary will call them to mind:

1   Many cognitive tasks, such as visual recognition and answering simple true-or-false questions, can be accomplished in about half a second. Given what we know about conduction velocities and synaptic delays in neurons, this allows about 5 milliseconds per computational step, which means that there is time for only about 100 steps. For a sequential program run on a conventional computer, 100 steps is not going to get us remotely close to task completion. Feldman and Ballard (1982) call this the hundred-step rule.

2   Anatomically and physiologically, the brain is a parallel system, not a sequential von Neumann machine. The neural architecture is highly

interconnected. Neurons such as Purkinje cells may have upwards of 80,000 input connections, and neurons in cerebral cortex can have upwards of 10,000 output connections (Anderson and Hinton 1981; Pellionisz and Llinas 1982; Sejnowski 1986).

3   However information is stored in nervous systems, it appears to be radically unlike information storage in a digital computer, where storage and processing are separated and items are stored in memory according to addressable *locations*. In nervous systems, information seems to be stored in the connections between the same neurons that process the information. There does not appear to be a distinct storage location for each piece of stored information, and information is content addressable rather than location addressable. Information storage is probably at least somewhat distributed rather than punctuate, since memories tend to be degraded with damage to the system rather than selectively wiped out one by one.

4   A task may fall gracefully to one architecture and not to another. Certain kinds of tasks, such as numerical calculation, fall gracefully to a von Neumann architecture, but others, such as learning or associative memory, do not. Things we humans find effortless (such as facial recognition and visual perception) are tasks which artificial intelligence has great difficulty simulating on a von Neumann architecture, whereas things we find "effortful" (such as simple proofs in the propositional calculus or mathematic calculations) are straightforward for a digital computer (Anderson and Hinton 1981; Rumelhart, Hinton, and McClelland 1986). This suggests that the computational style of nervous systems may be very unlike that suited to von Neumann architectures.

5   The hardware/software analogy fails for many reasons, the most prominent of which are that nervous systems are plastic and that neurons continually change as we grow and learn. Related, perhaps, is the observation that nervous systems degrade gracefully and are relatively fault tolerant. A von Neumann machine is rigid and fault intolerant, and a breakdown of one tiny component disrupts the machine's performance.

6   The analogy between levels of description in a conventional computer (such as the hardware/software distinction) and levels of explanation

in nervous systems may well be profoundly misleading. Exactly how many levels of organization we need to postulate in order to understand nervous-system function is an empirical question, and it may turn out that there are many levels between the molecular and the behavioral. In nervous systems we may already discern as distinct descriptive levels the molecule, the membrane, the cell, the circuit, networks, maps, brain systems, and several levels of behavior (from the reflexive to the highest levels of cognition). Other levels may come to be described as more is discovered about the nature of nervous systems. As is discussed below, the properties at one level may constrain the kind of properties realizable at another level.

7   Nonverbal animals and infraverbal humans present a major problem for the sentence-logic theory of cognition: How is their cognition accomplished? On the sentence-logic theory of cognition, either their cognition resembles the human variety (and hence involves symbol manipulation according to rules, and a language of thought replete with a substantial conceptual repertoire) or their cognitive processes are entirely different from the usual human ones. Neither alternative is remotely credible. The first lacks any evidence. At best, its defense is circular; it helps to save the theory. The second alternative entails a radical discontinuity in evolution – sufficiently radical that language-of-thought cognition is a bolt from the blue. This implies that evolutionary biology and developmental neurobiology are mistaken in some fundamental respects. Since neither alternative can be taken seriously, the hypothesis itself has diminished credibility.

If cognition, then, is *not*, in general, to be understood on the sentence-logical model, the pressing questions then are these: How *does* the brain represent? How do nervous systems model the external world of objects in motion and the internal world of the nervous system itself? And when representations do stand in semantic and logical relations to one another, how is this achieved by neural networks? How is the semantic and logical structure of language – as we both comprehend and speak – represented in the brain? According to the rejected model, we postulate an internal organization – a language of thought – with the very same structure and organization as language. But if that model is rejected, what do we replace it with?

These are, of course, *the* central questions, and getting answers will not be easy. But the difficulty should not make the language-of-thought hypothesis more appealing. In certain respects, the current scientific state of a general theory of representation is analogous to the science of embryology in the nineteenth century. The development of highly structured, complex, fully formed organisms from eggs and sperm is a profoundly amazing thing. Faced with this mystery, some scientists concluded that the only way to explain the emergence of a fully structured organism at birth was to join the ancients in assuming that the structure was already there. Hence the homuncular theory of reproduction, which claimed that a miniature but complete human already exists in the sperm and merely expands during its tenure in the womb.

We now know that there *is* structure in the sperm (and the egg) – not in the form of a miniature, fully structured organism, but mainly in the form of DNA – a molecule that looks not at *all* like a fully formed human. Thus, the structure of the cause does not resemble the structure of the effect. Accordingly, the homuncular theorists were right in supposing that the highly structured neonate does not come from *nothing*, but they were wrong in looking for a structural resemblance between cause and effect. It was, of course, terribly hard to imagine the nature of the structural organization that enables development yet in no way resembles the final product. Only through molecular biology and detailed work in embryology have we begun to understand how one kind of structure can, through intermediate mechanisms, yield another, very different kind of structure.

The parallel with cognitive neurobiology is this: The neuronal processes underlying cognition have a structure of some kind, but almost certainly it will not, in general, look anything like the semantic/logic structure visible in overt language. The organizational principles of nervous systems are what permit highly complex, structured patterns of behavior, for it is certain that the behavioral structure does not emerge magically from neuronal chaos. As things stand, it is very hard to imagine what those organizational principles could look like, and, just as in genetics and embryology, we can find answers only by framing hypotheses and doing experiments.

Instead of starting from the old sentence-logic model, we model information processing in terms of *the trajectory of a complex nonlinear dynamical system in a very high-dimensional space*. This structure does not resemble sentences arrayed in logical sequences, but it is potentially rich enough and complex enough to yield behavior capable of supporting semantic and logical relationships. We shall now explore what representing looks like in a particular class of nonlinear dynamical systems called connectionist models.

4   Representation in Connectionist Models

As the name implies, a connectionist model is characterized by connections and differential strengths of connections between processing units. Processing units are meant to be rather like neurons, and communicate with one another by signals (such as firing rate) that are numerical rather than symbolic. Connectionist models are designed to perform a task by specifying the architecture: the number of units, their arrangement in layers and columns, the patterns of connectivity, and the weight or strength of each connection (figures 7.1 and 7.2). These models have close ties with the computational level on which the task is

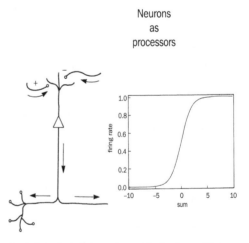

Figure 7.1   Left: Schematic model of a neuron-like processing unit that receives synapse-like inputs from other processing units. Right: Nonlinear sigmoid-shaped transformation between summed inputs and the output "firing rate" of a processing unit. The output is a continuous value between 0 and 1.

specified, and with the implementation level on which the task is physically instantiated (Marr 1982). This species of network models should properly be considered a class of algorithms specified at various levels of organization – in some cases at the small-circuit level, in other cases at the system level. Both the task description and the neural embodiment are, however, crucially important in constraining the class of networks that will be explored. On the one hand the networks have to be powerful enough to match human performance of the computational tasks, and on the other hand they have to be built from the available materials. In the case of the brain, that means neurons and synapses; in the case of network models, that means neuron-like processing units and synapse-like weights.

Digital computers are used to simulate neural networks, and the network models that can be simulated on current machines are tiny in comparison with the number of synapses and neurons in the mammalian brain. The networks that have been constructed should be understood, therefore, as small parts of a more complex processing system whose general configuration has not yet been worked out, rather than as simulations of a whole system. To avoid misunderstanding, it should be emphasized that connectionist models cannot yet support a full cognitive system. To begin to reach that goal will require both a computing technology capable of supporting more detailed simulations and a more complete specification of the nervous system.

Granting these limitations, we may nonetheless be able to catch a glimpse of what representations might look like within the parallel-style architecture of the brain by taking a look inside a connectionist network. The place to look is in the dynamics of the system; that is, in the patterns of activity generated by the system of interconnected units. This approach has its roots in the work of previous generations of researchers – primarily the Gestalt school of psychology and D. O. Hebb (1949), who developed many ideas about learning and representation in neural assemblies. Only recently, however, has sufficient computer power been available to explore the consequences of these ideas by direct simulation, since the dynamics of massively parallel nonlinear networks is highly computation intensive. Parallel-network models are now being used to explore many different aspects of perception and cognition (McClelland and Rumelhart 1986; Feldman and Ballard 1982;

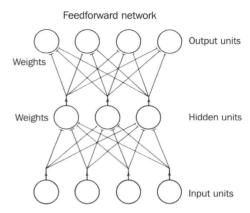

Feedforward network

Output units

Weights

Weights

Hidden units

Input units

Figure 7.2 Schematic model of a three-layered network. Each input unit makes connections with each of the hidden units on the middle layer, which in turn projects to each of the output units. This is feedforward architecture in which information provided as an input vector flows through the network, one layer at a time, to produce an output vector. More complex architectures allow feedback connections from an upper to a lower layer and lateral interactions between units within a layer.

Cognitive Science, special issue, vol. 9, 1985) but in this essay we shall focus on two representative examples. The first is NETtalk, perhaps the most complex network model yet constructed, which learns to convert English text to speech sounds (Sejnowski and Rosenberg 1987, 1988). The second is a network model that computes surface curvatures of an object from its gray-level input image. NETtalk will be used primarily to illustrate two things: how a network can learn to perform a very complex task without symbols and without rules to manipulate symbols, and the differences between local and distributed representations.

Connectionist models can be applied on a large scale to model whole brain systems or, on a smaller scale, to model particular brain circuits. NETtalk is on a large scale, since the problem of pronunciation is constrained mainly by the abstract cognitive considerations and since its solution in the brain must involve a number of systems, including the visual system, the motor-articulatory system, and the language areas. The second example is more directly related to smaller brain circuits used in visual processing; the representational organization achieved by the network model can be related to the known representational organization in visual cortex.

In the models reviewed here, the processing units sum the inputs from connections with other processing units, each input weighted by the strength of the connection. The output of each processing unit is a real number that is a nonlinear function of the linearly summed inputs. The output is small when the inputs are below threshold, and it increases rapidly as the total input becomes more positive. Roughly, the activity level can be considered the sum of the postsynaptic potentials in a neuron, and the output can be considered its firing rate (figure 7.1).

4.1 Speech processing: text to speech

In the simplest NETtalk system[2] there are three layers of processing units. The first level receives as input letters in a word: the final layer yields the elementary sounds, or phonemes (table 7.1); and

an intervening layer of "hidden units," which is fully connected with the input and output layers, performs the transformation of letters to sounds (figure 7.3). On the input layer, there is *local representation* with respect to letters because single units are used to represent single letters of the alphabet. Notice, however, that the representation could be construed as *distributed* with respect to *words*, inasmuch as each word is represented as a pattern of activity among the input units. Similarly, each phoneme is represented by a pattern of activity among the output units, and phonemic representation is therefore distributed. But each output unit is coded for a particular *distinctive feature* of the speech sound, such as whether the phoneme was voiced, and consequently each unit is local with respect to distinctive features.

NETtalk has 309 processing units and 18,629 connection strengths (weights) that must be

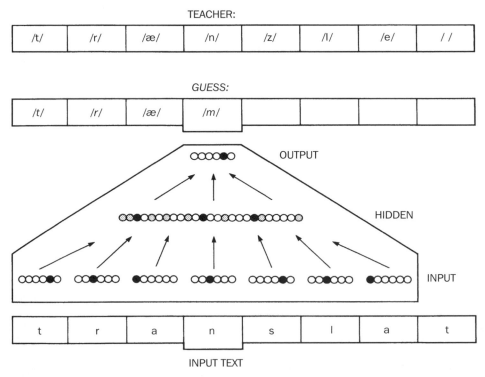

Figure 7.3 Schematic drawing of the NETtalk network architecture. A window of letters in an English text is fed to an array of 203 input units arranged in 7 groups of 29 units each. Information from these units is transformed by an intermediate layer of 80 hidden units to produce a pattern of activity in 26 output units. The connections in the network are specified by a total of 18,629 weight parameters (including a variable threshold for each unit). During the training, information about the desired output provided by the Teacher is compared with the actual output of the network, and the weights in the network are changed slightly so as to reduce the error.

specified. The network does not have any initial or built-in organization for processing the input or (more exactly) mapping letters on to sounds. All the structure emerges during the training period. The values of the weights are determined by using the "back-propagation" learning algorithm developed by Rumelhart, Hinton, and Williams (1986). (For a review of network learning algorithms, see Hinton 1988 and Sejnowski 1988.) The strategy exploits the calculated error between the *actual* values of the processing units in the output layer and the *desired* values, which is provided by a training signal. The resulting error signal is propagated from the output layer backward to the input layer and used to adjust each weight in the network. The network learns, as the weights are changed, to minimize the mean squared error over the training set of words. Thus, the system can be characterized as following a path in weight space (the space of all possible weights) unitil it finds a minimum (figure 7.4). The important point to be illustrated, therefore, is this: The network processes information by nonlinear dynamics, not by manipulating symbols and accessing rules. It learns by gradient

Table 1 Symbols for phonemes used in NETtalk.

Symbol	Phoneme	Symbol	Phoneme
/a/	father	/C/	chin
/b/	bet	/D/	this
/c/	bought	/E/	bet
/d/	debt	/G/	sing
/e/	bake	/I/	bit
/f/	fin	/K/	sexual
/g/	guess	/L/	bottle
/h/	head	/M/	absym
/i/	Pete	/N/	button
/k/	Ken	/O/	boy
/l/	let	/Q/	quest
/m/	met	/R/	bird
/n/	net	/S/	shin
/o/	boat	/T/	thin
/p/	pet	/U/	book
/r/	red	/W/	bout
/s/	sit	/X/	excess
/t/	test	/Y/	cute
/u/	lute	/Z/	leisure
/v/	vest	/@/	bat
/w/	wet	/!/	Nazi
/x/	about	/#/	examine
/y/	yet	/*/	one
/z/	zoo	/|/	logic
/A/	bite	/^/	but

descent in a complex interactive system, not by generating new rules (Hinton and Sejnowski 1986).

The issue that we want to focus on next is the structural organization that is "discovered" by the network, in virtue of which it succeeds in converting letters to phonemes and manages to pronounce, with few errors, the many irregularities of English. If there are no rules in the network, how is the transformation accomplished? Since a trained network can generalize quite well to new words, some knowledge about the pattern of English pronunciation must be contained inside the network. Although a representational organization was imposed on the input and output layers, the network had to create new, internal representations in the hidden layer of processing units. How did the network organize its "knowledge"? To be more accurate: How did the equivalence class of networks organize its knowledge? (Each time the network was started from a random set of weights, a different network was generated.)

The answers were not immediately available, because a network does not leave an explanation of its travels through weight space, nor does it

Gradient descent in weight space

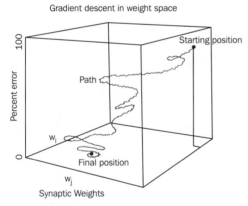

Figure 7.4 Schematic drawing of a path followed in weight space as the network finds a minimum of the average error over the set of training patterns. Only two weights of many thousands are shown. The learning algorithm only ensures convergence to a local minimum, which is often a good solution. Typically, many sets of weights are good solutions, so the network is likely to find one of them from a random starting position in weight space. The learning time can be reduced by starting the network near a good solution; for example, the pattern of connections can be limited to a geometry that reduces the number of variable weights that must be searched by gradient descent.

provide a decoding scheme when it reaches a resting place. Even so, some progress was made by measuring the activity pattern among the hidden units for specific inputs. In a sense, this test mimics at the modeling level what neurophysiologists do at the cellular level when they record the activity of a single neuron to try to find the effective stimulus that makes it respond. NETtalk is a fortunate "preparation," inasmuch as the number of processing units is relatively small, and it is possible to determine the activity patterns of all the units for all possible input patterns. These measurements, despite the relatively small network, did create a staggering amount of data, and then the puzzle was this: How does one find the order in all these data?

For each set of input letters, there is a pattern of activity among the hidden units (figure 7.5). The first step in the analysis of the activity of the hidden units was to compute the average level of activity for each letter-to-sound correspondence. For example, all words with the letter c in the middle position yielding the hard-c sound /k/ were presented to the network, and the average

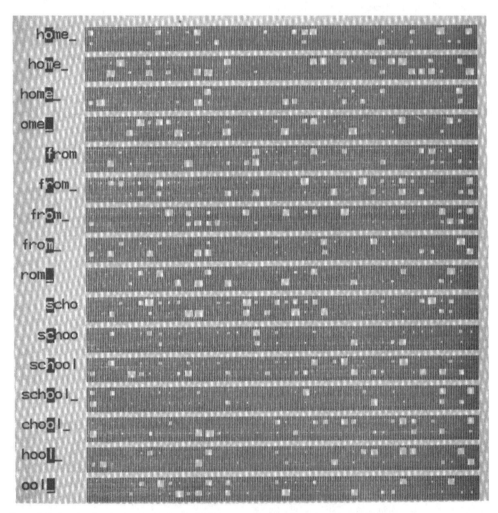

Figure 7.5 Levels of activation in the layer of hidden units for a variety of words. The input string in the window of seven letters is shown to the left, with the target letter emphasized. The output from the network is the phoneme that corresponds to the target letter. The transformation is accomplished by 80 hidden units, whose activity levels are shown to the right in two rows of 40 units each. The area of each white square is proportional to the activity level. Most units have little or no activity for a given input, but a few are highly activated.

level of activity was calculated. Typically, about 15 of the 80 hidden units were very highly activated, and the rest of the hidden units had little or no activity. This procedure was repeated for each of the 79 letter-to-sound correspondences. The result was 79 vectors, each vector pointing in a different direction in the 80-dimensional space of average hidden-unit activities. The next step was to explore the relationship among the vectors in this space by cluster analysis. It is useful to conceive of each vector as the internal code that is used to represent a specific letter-to-sound correspondence; consequently, those vectors that clustered close together would have similar codes.

Remarkably, all the vectors for vowel sounds clustered together, indicating that they were represented in the network by patterns of activity in units that were distinct from those representing the consonants (which were themselves clustered together). (See figure 7.6.) Within the vowels, all the letter-to-sound corespondences that used the letter a were clustered together, as were the vectors of e, i, o, and u and the relevant instances of y. This was a very robust organizational scheme that occurred in all the networks that were analyzed, differences in starting weights notwithstanding. The coding scheme for consonants was more variable from network to network, but as a general rule the clustering was based more on similarities in sounds than on letters. Thus, the labial stops /p/ and /b/ were very close together in the space of hidden-unit activities, as were all the letter-to-sound corespondences that result in the hard-c sound /k/.

Other statistical techniques, such as factor analysis and multidimensional scaling, are also being applied to the network, and activity patterns from individual inputs, rather than averages over classes, are also being studied (Rosenberg 1988). These statistical techniques are providing us with a detailed description of the representation for single inputs as well as classes or input–output pairs.

Several aspects of NETtalk's organization should be emphasized:

1 The representational organization visible in the trained-up network is not programmed or coded into the network; it is found by the network. In a sense it "programs" itself, by virtue of being connected in the manner described and having weights changed by experience according to the learning algorithm. The dynamical properties of this sort of system are such that the network will settle into the displayed organization.

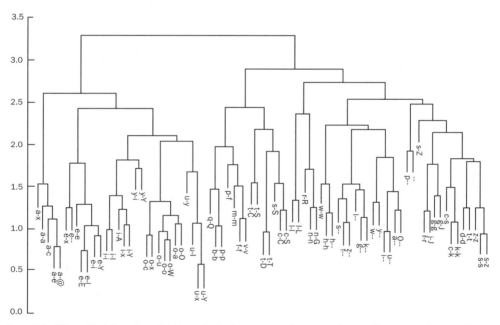

Figure 7.6 Hierarchical clustering of hidden units for letter-to-sound correspondences. The vectors of average hidden unit activity for each correspondence ("l-p" for letter l and phoneme p) were successively merging from right to left in the binary tree. The scale at the top indicates the Euclidean distance between the clusters. (From Sejnowski and Rosenberg 1987.)

2   The network's representation for letter-to-sound correspondences is neither local nor completely distributed; it is somewhere in between. The point is, each unit participates in more than one correspondence, and so the representation is not local, but since it does not participate in all correspondences, the representation is not completely distributed either.

3   The representation is a property of the collection of hidden units, and does not resemble sentence-logic organization.

4   The organization is structured, which suggests that emergent subordinate and superordinate relations might be a general principle of network organization that could be used as input for other networks assigned other tasks if NETtalk were embedded in a larger system of networks.

5   General properties of the hierarchical organization of letter-to-sound correspondences emerged only at the level of groups of units. This organization was invariant across all the networks created from the same sample of English words, even where the processing units in distinct networks had specialized for a different aspect of the problem.

6   Different networks created by starting from different initial conditions all achieved about the same level of performance, but the detailed response properties of the individual units in the networks differed greatly. Nonetheless, all the networks had similar functional clusterings for letter-to-sound correspondence (figure 7.6). This suggests that single neurons code information relative to other neurons in small groups or assemblies (Hebb 1949).

The representational organization in NETtalk may illustrate important principles concerning network computation and representation, but what do they tell us about neural representations? Some of the principles uncovered might be generally applicable to a wide class of tasks, but it would be surprising if the details of the model bore any significant resemblance to the way reading skills are represented in the human nervous system. NETtalk is more of a demonstration of certain network capacities and properties than a faithful model of some subsystem of the brain, and it may be a long time before data concerning the human neurobiology of reading become available. Nevertheless, the same network techniques that were used to explore the language domain can be applied to problems in other domains, such as vision, where much more is known about the anatomy and the physiology.

4.2   Visual processing: computing surface curvature from shaded images

The general constraints from brain architecture touched on in section 3 should be supplemented, wherever possible, by more detailed constraints from brain physiology and anatomy. Building models of real neural networks is a difficult task, however, because essential knowledge about the style of computation in the brain is not yet available (Sejnowski 1986). Not only is the fine detail (such as the connectivity patterns in neurons in cerebral cortex) not known, but even global-level knowledge specifying the flow of information through different parts of the brain during normal function is limited. Even if more neurophysiological and neuroanatomical detail were available, current computing technology would put rather severe limits on how much detail could be captured in a simulation. Nevertheless, the same type of network model used in NETtalk could be useful in understanding how information is coded within small networks confined to cortical columns. The processing units in this model will be identified with neurons in the visual cortex.

Ever since Hubel and Wiesel (1962) first reported that single neurons in the cat visual cortex respond better to oriented bars of light and to dark/light edges than to spots of light, it has been generally assumed, or at least widely hoped, that the function of these neurons is to detect boundaries of objects in the world. In general, the inference from a cell's response profile to its function in the wider information-processing economy is intuitively very plausible, and if we are to have any hope of understanding neural representations we need to start in an area – such as visual cortex – where it is possible to build on an impressive body of existing data. The trouble is, however, that many functions are consistent with the particular response properties of a neuronal population. That a cell responds optimally to an oriented bar of light is compatible with its having lots of functions other than detecting object boundaries, though the hypothesis that it serves to detect boundaries does tend to remain intuitively compelling. To see that our intuitions might really mislead us as we try to infer function from response profiles, it would be useful if we could demonstrate this point concretely. In what follows we shall show how the same response properties could in fact serve in the processing of visual information about the regions of a surface between boundaries rather than about the boundaries themselves.

Boundaries of objects are relatively rare in images, yet the preponderance of cells in visual cortex respond preferentially to oriented bars and slits. If we assume that all those cells are detecting boundaries, then it is puzzling that there should be so many cells whose sole function is to detect boundaries when there are not many boundaries to detect. It would, therefore, seem wasteful if, of all the neurons with oriented fields, only a small fraction carried useful information about a particular image. Within their boundaries, most objects have shaded or textured surfaces that will partially activate these neurons. The problem, accordingly, is this: Can the information contained in a population of partially activated cortical neurons be used to compute useful information about the three-dimensional surfaces between the boundaries of objects in the image?

One of the primary properties of a surface is its curvature. Some surfaces, such as the top of a table, are flat, and have no intrinsic curvature. Other surfaces, such as cylinders and spheres, are curved, and around each point on a surface the degree of curvature can be characterized by the direction along the surface of maximum and minimum curvature. It can be shown that these directions are always at right angles to each other, and the values are called the *principle curvatures* (Hilbert and Cohn-Vossen 1952). The principal curvatures and the orientation of the axes provide a complete description of the local curvature.

One problem with extracting the principal curvatures from an image is that the gray-level shading depends on many factors, such as the direction of illumination, the reflectance of the surface, and the orientation of the surface relative to the viewer. Somehow our visual system is able to separate these variables and to extract information about the shape of an object independent of these other variables. Pentland (1984) has shown that a significant amount of information about the curvature of a surface is available locally. Can a network model be constructed that can extract this information from shaded images?

Until recently it was not obvious how to begin to construct such a network, but network learning algorithms (see above) provide us with a powerful method for creating a network by giving it examples of the task at hand. The learning algorithm is being used in this instance simply as a design tool to see whether some network can be found that performs the task. Many examples of simple surfaces (elliptic paraboloids) were generated and presented to the network. A set of weights was indeed found with this procedure that, independent of the direction of illumination, extracted the principal curvatures of three-dimensional surfaces and the direction of maximum curvature from shaded images (Lehky and Sejnowski 1987).

The input to the network is from an array of on-center and off-center receptive fields similar to those of cells in the lateral geniculate nucleus. The output layer is a population of units that conjointly represent the curvatures and the broadly tuned direction of maximum curvature. The units of the intermediate layer, which are needed to perform the transformation, have oriented receptive fields, similar to those of simple cells in the visual cortex of cats and monkeys that respond optimally to oriented bars and edges (figure 7.7). It is important to emphasize that these properties of the hidden units were not put into the network directly but emerged during training. The system "chose" these properties because they are useful in performing a particular task. Interestingly, the output units, which were required to code information about the principal curvatures and principal orientations of surfaces, had properties, when probed with bars of light, that were similar to those of a class of complex cells that are end-stopped (Lehky and Sejnowski 1988). The surprising thing, given the plausible receptive-field-to-function inference rule, is that the function of the units in the network is not to detect boundary contours, but to extract curvature information from shaded images.

What the shape-from-shading network demonstrates is that we cannot directly infer function from receptive field properties. In the trained-up network, the hidden units represent an intermediate transformation for a computational task quite different from the one that has been customarily ascribed to simple cells in visual cortex – they are used to determine shape from shading, not to detect boundaries. It turns out, however, that the hidden units have *receptive fields similar to those of simple cells in visual cortex*. Therefore, bars and edges as receptive-field properties do not necessarily mean that the cell's function is to detect bars and edges in objects; it might be to

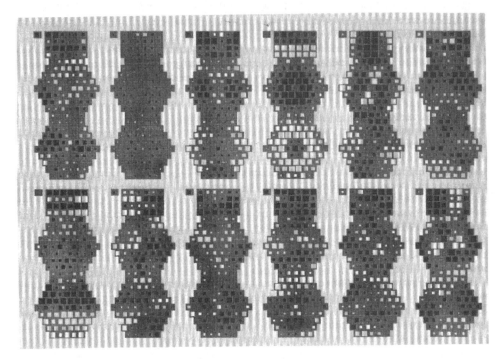

Figure 7.7 Hinton diagram showing the connection strengths in a network that computes the principal curvatures and direction of minimum curvature from shaded images in a small patch of the visual field corresponding roughtly to the area represented in a cortical column. There are 12 hidden units which receive connections from the 122 inputs and project to each of the 23 output units. The diagram shows each of the connection strengths to and from the hidden units. Each weight is represented by one square, the area of which is proportional to the magnitude of the weight. The color is white if the weight is excitatory and black if it is inhibitory. The inputs are two hexagonal arrays of 61 processing units each. Each input unit has a concentric on-center (top) or off-surround (bottom) receptive field similar to those of principal cells in the lateral geniculate nucleus. The output consists of 24 units that conjointly represent the direction of maximum curvature (six columns) and principal curvature (four rows: two for each principal curvature). Each of the 12 hidden units is represented in the diagram in a way that reveals all the connections to and from the unit. Within each of the 12 gray background regions, the weights from the inputs are shown on the bottom and the weights to the output layer are shown above. To the left of each hidden unit, the lone square gives the threshold of the unit, which was also allowed to vary. Note that there emerged two different types of hidden units as revealed by the "projective field." The six units in the bottom row and the fourth and fifth from the left in the top row were mainly responsible for providing information about the direction of minimum curvature, while others were responsible for computing the signs and magnitudes of the two principal curvatures. The curvature-selective units could be further classified as convexity detectors (top row, third from left) or elongation filters (top row, second and sixth from left).

detect curvature and shape, as it is in the network model, or perhaps some other surface property such as texture. The general implication is that there is no way of determining the function of each hidden unit in the network simply by "recording" the receptive-field properties of the unit. This, in turn, implies that, despite its intuitive plausibility, the receptive-field-to-function inference rule is untenable.

The function of a unit is revealed only when its *outputs* – its "projective field" (Lehky and Sej-

nowski 1988) – are also examined. It is the projective field of a unit that provides the additional information needed to interpret the unit's computational role in the network. In the network model the projective field could be examined directly, but in real neural networks it can only be inferred indirectly by examining the next stage of processing. Whether or not curvature is directly represented in visual cortex, for example, can be tested by designing experiments with images of curved surfaces.

4.3   Next-generation networks

NETtalk and the shape-from-shading network are important examples because they yield clues to how the nervous system can embody models of various domains of the world. Parallel-network modeling is still in a pioneering stage of development. There are bound to be many snags and hitches, and many problems yet undreamt of will have to be solved. At this stage, the representational structure of networks has not yet been explored in detail, nor is it known how well the performance of network models will scale with the number of neurons and the difficulty of the task. (That is, will representations and computations in a cortical column with 200,000 neurons be similar to those in a model network comprising only a few hundred processing units?)

Moreover, taken literally as a model of functioning neurons, back-propagation is biologically implausible, inasmuch as error signals cannot literally be propagated back down the very same axon the signal came up. Taken as a *systems-level* algorithm, however, back-propagation may have a realization using feedback projections that do map on to neural hardware. Even squarely facing these cautionary considerations, the important thing is that something with this sort of character at least lets us see what representational structure – good, meaty, usable structure – could *look like* in a neuronal network.

Temporal chaining of sequences of representations is probably a prominent feature of many kinds of behavior, and it may turn out to be particularly important for language acquisition and use. It is conceivable that structured sequences – long, temporally extended sequences – are the elements of an abstract sort of neural state space that enable humans to use language. Sereno (1986) has suggested something along these lines, pointing out that DNA, as a spatially extended sequence of nucleotides, allows for encoding; by analogy, one may envision that the development of mechanisms for generating temporally extended sequences of neuronal (abstract) structures may allow for a kind of structured behavior (that is, language) that short sequences do not allow for. (See also MacKay 1987; Dehaene et al. 1987.)

One promising strategy will be to try first to unscramble the more fundamental kinds of representing accomplished by nervous systems, shelving until later the problem of complex representations

such as linguistic representations. To solve such problems, the solutions discovered for simpler representations may be crucial. At the most basic level, there appears to be an isomorphism between cell responses and external events (for example, cells in visual cortex responding to bars of light moving in a specific direction). At higher levels the receptive-field properties change (Allman et al. 1985; Andersen 1987), and it may be that the lower-level isomorphism gives way to more complicated and dynamic network effects. Motivation, planning, and other factors may, at this level, have roles in how a representation is generated. At still higher levels, still other principles may be operative. Once we understand the nature of representing in early sensory processing, as we have indeed begun to do, and go on to address the nature of representations at more and more abstract levels, we may finally be able to address how learning a language yields another kind of representation, and how symbols can be represented in neural networks. Whatever the basic principles of language representation, they are not likely to be utterly unrelated to the way or ways that the nervous system generates visual representations or auditory representations, or represents spatial maps and motor planning. (On semantic relations in connectionist models, see Hinton 1981, 1986.)

5   Dogmas and Dreams: George Boole, Ramon y Cajal, David Marr

The connectionist models discussed are valuable for the glimpse of representational and computational space that they provide, for it is exactly such glimpses that free us from the bonds of the intuitive conceptions of representations as language-like and computation as logic-like. They thus free us from what Hofstadter (1982) called the *Boolean Dream*, where all cognition is symbol-manipulation according to the rules of logic.

Equally important, they also free us from what we call the *Neurobiologists' Dream* (perhaps, with all due respect, it might be called Cajal's Dream), which is really the faith that the answers we seek will be manifest once the fine-grain details of each neuron (its morphology, physiology, and connections) are revealed – these models also teach the tremendously important lesson that *system properties are not accessible at the single-unit level*. In a system, what we need to know is how the elements in large sets of elements interact over time. Until we have new physiological techniques for supplying data of that sort, building network models is a method of first resort.

To be really useful, a model must be biologically constrained. However, exactly which biological properties are crucial to a model's utility and which can be safely ignored until later are matters that can be decided only by hunches until a mature theory is in place. Such "bottom-up" constraints are crucial, since computational space is immensely vast – too vast for us to be lucky enough to light on the correct theory simply from the engineering bench. Moreover, the brain's solutions to the problems of vision, motor control, and so forth may be far more powerful, more beautiful, and even more simple than what we engineer into existence. This is the point of Orgel's Second Rule: Nature is more ingenious than we are. And we stand to miss all that power and ingenuity unless we attend to neurobiological plausibility. The point is, *evolution has already done it*, so why not learn how that stupendous machine, our brain, actually works?

This observation allows us to awake from *Marr's Dream* of three levels of explanation: the computational level of abstract problem analysis, the level of the algorithm, and the level of physical implementation of the computation. In Marr's view, a higher level was independent of the levels below it, and hence computational problems could be analyzed independent of an understanding of the algorithm that executes the computation, and the algorithmic problem could be solved independent of an understanding of the physical implementation. Marr's assessment of the relations between levels has been reevaluated, and the dependence of higher levels on lower levels has come to be recognized.

The matter of the interdependence of levels marks a major conceptual difference between Marr and the current generation of connectionists. Network models are not independent of either the computational level or the implementational level; they depend in important ways on constraints from all levels of analysis. Network models show how knowledge of brain architecture can contribute to the devising of likely and powerful algorithms that can be efficiently implemented in the architecture of the nervous system and may alter even how we construe the computational problems.

On the heels of the insight that the use of constraints from higher up and lower down matters

tremendously, the notion that there are basically *three* levels of analysis also begins to look questionable. If we examine more closely how the three levels of analysis are meant to map on to the organization of the nervous system, the answer is far from straightforward.

To begin with, the idea that there is essentially one single implementational level is an oversimplification. Depending on the fineness of grain, research techniques reveal structural organization at many strata: the biochemical level; then the levels of the membrane, the single cell, and the circuit; and perhaps yet other levels, such as brain subsystems, brain systems, brain maps, and the whole central nervous system. But notice that at each structurally specified stratum we can raise the functional question: What does it contribute to the wider, functional business of the brain?

This range of structural organization implies, therefore, that the oversimplification with respect to implementation has a companion oversimplification with respect to computational descriptions. And indeed, on reflection it does seem most unlikely that a single type of computational description can do justice to the computational niche of diverse structural organization. On the contrary, one would expect distinct task descriptions corresponding to distinct structural levels. But if there is a ramifying of task specifications to match the ramified structural organization, this diversity will probably be reflected in the ramification of the *algorithms* that characterize how a task is accomplished. And this, in turn, means that the notion of *the* algorithmic levels is as oversimplified as the notion of *the* implementation level.

Similar algorithms were used to specify the network models in NETtalk and the shape-from-shading network, but they have a quite different status in these two examples. On this perspective of the levels of organization, NETtalk is a network relevant to the *systems* level, whereas the shape-from-shading network is relevant to the *circuit* level. Since the networks are meant to reflect principles at entirely different levels of organization, their implementations will also be at different scales in the nervous system. Other computational principles may be found to apply to the single cell or to neural maps.

Once we look at them closely, Marr's three *levels of analysis* and the brain's *levels of organization* do not appear to mesh in a very useful or satisfying manner. So poor is the fit that it may be doubted whether levels of analysis, *as conceived by Marr*, have much methodological significance. Accordingly, in light of the flaws with the notion of *independence*, and in light of the flaws with the *tripartite* character of the conception of levels, it seems that Marr's dream, inspiring though it was for a time, must be left behind.

The vision that inspires network modeling is essentially and inescapably interdisciplinary. Unless we explicitly theorize above the level of the single cell, we will never find the key to the order and the systematicity hidden in the blinding minutiae of the neuropil. Unless our theorizing is geared to mesh with the neurobiological data, we risk wasting our time exploring some impossibly remote, if temporarily fashionable, corner of computational space. Additionally,

without the constraints from psychology, ethology, and linguistics to specify more exactly the parameters of the large-scale capacities of nervous systems, our conception of the functions for which we need explanation will be so woolly and tangled as to effectively smother progress.

Consequently, cross-disciplinary research, combining constraints from psychology, neurology, neurophysiology, linguistics, and computer modeling, is the best hope for the co-evolution that could ultimately yield a unified, integrated science of the mind-brain. It has to be admitted, however, that this vision is itself a dream. From within the dream, we cannot yet reliably discern what are the flaws that will impede progress, what crucial elements are missing, or at which points the vague if tantalizing hunches might be replaced by palpable results.

Notes

1   An earlier exploration of these ideas is to be found in Kenneth Craik's book *The Nature of Explanation* (Cambridge University Press, 1943).

2   NETtalk networks can differ in how input letters and output phonemes are represented, and in the number and arrangement of hidden units.

References

Allman, J., Miezin, F., and McGuniness E. (1985) "Stimulus specific responses from beyond the classic receptive field." *Annual Review of Neuroscience* 8: 407–30.

Andersen, R. A. (1987) "The role of posterior parietal cortex in spatial perception and visual–motor integration." In *Handbook of Physiology – The Nervous System V*, ed. V. B. Mountcastle, F. Plum, and S. R. Geiger.

Anderson, J. A. and Hinton, G. E. (1981) "Models of information processing in the brain." In Hinton and Anderson 1981.

Chisholm, R. M. (1966) *Theory of Knowledge*. Englewood Cliffs, NJ: Prentice-Hall.

Churchland, P. M. (1979) *Scientific Realism and the Plasticity of Mind*. Cambridge University Press.

Churchland, P. M. (1988) *Matter and Consciousness* (revised edition). Cambridge, Mass.: MIT Press.

Churchland, P. S. (1986) *Neurophilosophy: Toward a Unified Science of the Mind-Brain*. Cambridge, Mass.: MIT Press.

Davidson, D. (1974) "On the very idea of a conceptual scheme." *Proceedings and Addresses of the American Philosophical Association* 47: 5–20.

Dehaene, S., Changeux, J.-P., and Nadal, J.-P. (1987) "Neural networks that learn temporal sequences by selection." *Proceedings of the National Academy of Sciences* 84: 2727–31.

Dennett, D. C. (1978) *Brainstorms: Philosophical Essays on Mind and Psychology*. Cambridge, Mass.: MIT Press.

Eccles, J. C. (1977) Part II of K. Popper, *The Self and Its Brain*. Berlin: Springer-Verlag.

Enc, B. (1983) "In defense of the identity theory." *Journal of Philosophy* 80: 279–98.

Feldman, J. A. and Ballard, F. H. (1982) "Connectionist models and their properties." *Cognitive Science* 6: 205–54.

Fodor, J. A. (1975) *The Language of Thought*. New York: Crowell. (Paperback edition: Cambridge, Mass.: MIT Press, 1979.)

Fodor, J. A. (1981) *Representations*. Cambridge, Mass.: MIT Press.

Goldman-Rakic, P. S. (1987) "Circuitry of primate prefrontal cortex and regulation of behavior by representational memory." In *Handbook of Physiology – The Nervous System V*, ed. V. B. Mountcastle, F. Plum, and S. R. Geiger.

Hebb, D. O. (1949) *Organization of Behavior*. New York: Wiley.

Hilbert, J. and Cohn-Vossen, S. (1952) *Geometry and the Imagination*. New York: Chelsea.

Hinton, G. E. (1981) "Implementing semantic networks in parallel hardware." In Hinton and Anderson 1981.

Hinton, G. E. (1986) "Learning distributed representations of concepts." In *Proceedings of the Eighth Annual Conference of the Cognitive Science Society*. Hillsdale, NJ: Erlbaum.

Hinton, G. E. (1988) "Connectionist learning procedures." *Artificial Intelligence*, in press.

Hinton, E. E. and Anderson, J. A. (eds) (1981) *Parallel Models of Associative Memory*. Hillsdale, NJ: Erlbaum.

Hinton, G. E. and Sejnowski, T. J. (1986) "Learning and relearning in Boltzmann machines." In McClelland and Rumelhart 1986.

Hofstadter, D. R. (1982) "Artificial intelligence: Subcognition as computation." *Technical Report No. 132*, Computer Science Department, Indiana University.

Hooker, C. A. (1981) "Toward a general theory of reduction. Part I: Historical and scientific setting. Part II: Identity in reduction. Part III: Cross-categorical reduction." *Dialogue* 20: 38–59, 201–36, 496–529.

Hubel, D. H. and Wiesel, T. N. (1962) "Receptive fields, binocular interaction and functional architecture in cat's visual cortex." *Journal of Physiology* 160: 106–54.

Kelso, S. R., Ganong, A. H., and Brown, T. H. (1986) "Hebbian synapses in hippocampus." *Proceedings of National Academy of Sciences* 83: 5326–30.

Lehky, S. and Sejnowski, T. J. (1987) "Extracting 3-D curvatures from images using a neural model." *Society for Neuroscience Abstracts* 13: 1451.

Lehky, S. and Sejnowski, T. J. (1988) "Neural network model for the representation of surface curvature from images of shaded surfaces." In *Organizing Principles of Sensory Processing*, ed. J. Lund, Oxford University Press.

Livingstone, M. S. (1988) "Art, illusion, and the visual system." *Scientific American* 258: 78–85.

McClelland, J. L. and Rumelhart, D. E. (1986) *Parallel Distributed Processing: Explorations in the Microstructure of Cognition*. Cambridge, Mass.: MIT Press.

McGinn, C. (1982) *The Character of Mind*. Oxford: Oxford University Press.

MacKay, D. (1987) *The Organization and Perception of Action*. Berlin: Springer-Verlag.

Mandt, A. J. (1986) "The triumph of philosophical pluralism? Notes on the transformation of academic philosophy." *Proceedings and Addresses of the American Philosophical Association* 60: 265–77.

Marr, D. (1982) *Vision*. San Francisco: Freeman.

Pellionisz, A. and Llinas, R. (1982) "Space-time representation in the brain. The cerebellum as a predictive space-time metric tensor." *Neuroscience* 7: 2249–70.

Pentland, A. P. (1984) "Local shading analysis." *IEEE Transactions: Pattern Analysis and Machine Intelligence* 6: 170–87.

Putnam, H. (1967) "The nature of mental states." In *Arts, Mind and Religion*, ed. W. H. Capitan and D. D. Merrill (University of Pittsburgh Press). Reprinted in H. Putnam, *Mind, Language and Reality: Philosophical Papers*, vol. 2 (Cambridge University Press, 1975).

Pylyshyn, Z. (1984) *Computation and Cognition*, Cambridge, Mass.: MIT Press.

Quine, W. V. O. (1960) *Word and Object*. Cambridge, Mass.: MIT Press.

Richardson, R. (1979) "Functionalism and reductionism." *Philosophy of Science* 46: 533–58.

Rosenberg, C. R. (1988) Ph.D. thesis, Princeton University.

Rumelhart, D. E., Hinton, G. E., and McClelland, J. L. (1986) "A general framework for parallel distributed processing." In McClelland and Rumelhart 1986.

Rumelhart, D. E., Hinton, G. E., and Williams, R. J. (1986) "Learning internal representations by error propagation." In McClelland and Rumelhart 1986.

Schaffner, K. F. (1976) "Reductionism in biology: prospects and problems." In *PSA Proceedings 1974* ed. R. S. Cohen, C. A. Hooker, A. C. Michalos, and J. W. Van Evra. Dordrecht: Reidel.

Sejnowski, T. J. (1986) "Open questions about computation in cerebral cortex." In McClelland and Rumelhart 1986.

Sejnowski, T. J. (1988) "Neural network learning algorithms." In *Neural Computers*, ed. R. Eckmiller and C. von der Malsberg, Berlin: Springer-Verlag.

Sejnowski, T. J. and Churchland, P. S. (In press) "Brain and cognition." In *Foundations of Cognitive Science*, ed. M. I. Posner, Cambridge, Mass.: MIT Press.

Sejnowski, T. J. and Rosenberg, C. R. (1987) "Parallel networks that learn to pronounce English text." *Complex Systems* I: 145–68.

Sejnowski, T. J. and Rosenberg, C. R. (1988) "Learning and representation in connectionist models." In *Perspective in Memory Research and Training*, ed. M. Gazzaniga, Cambridge, Mass.: MIT Press.

Sejnowski, T. J., Koch, C., and Churchland, P. S. (1988) "Computational neuroscience." *Science*, 241, pp. 1299–1306.

Sereno, M. (1986) "A program for the neurobiology of mind." *Inquiry* 29: 217–40.

Skinner, B. F. (1957) *Verbal Behavior*. New York: Appleton-Century-Crofts.

Skinner, B. F. (1976) *About Behaviorism*. New York: Knopf.

Smart, J. J. C. (1959) "Sensations and brain processes." *Philosophical Review* 68: 141–56.

Stich, S. P. (1983) *From Folk Psychology to Cognitive Science: The Case Against Belief*. Cambridge, Mass.: MIT Press.

Strawson, P. F. (1966) *The Bounds of Sense: An Essay on Kant's Critique of Pure Reason*. London: Methuen.

Swinburne, R. (1986) *The Evolution of the Soul*. Oxford: Oxford University Press.

The Case for Connectionism

William Bechtel

1 Introduction

When artificial intelligence began to emerge as a research endeavor in the middle of this century, two approaches vied with one another. Seymour Papert (1988) has characterized these as the natural and the artificial sisters. The natural sister sought to design networks of simple neuron-like processing devices which could perform cognitive tasks. (The term *connectionist* was applied to these networks, presumably to emphasize the fact that the behavior of these networks resulted not from units which independently performed significant cognitive activities, but from the way many simple units were linked together.) The artificial sister designed computer programs to perform cognitive tasks. These programs specify rules for manipulating symbolic representations: accordingly, this approach is often referred to as the *rules and representations* or *symbol processing* approach. (For brevity, I will refer to it as the *symbolic* approach.) Typically the natural sister focused on more basic cognitive tasks such as those involved in perceptual processing (thus, Rosenblat (1962) referred to his devices as *perceptrons*), while the artificial sister pursued high-level cognitive tasks such as those involving reasoning (e.g., chess playing). According to Papert's tale, the two sisters got along well until a rich suitor appeared. Lord DARPA. In the competition for this suitor the natural sister had to be slain and the deed was done by none other than Papert himself who, together with Marvin Minsky, wrote *Perceptrons* (Minsky and Paper 1969). In that book they showed that there were classes of tasks which perceptrons could not solve. Fortunately in Papert's tale (although unfortunately for Papert's position) the dead do not stay dead and in the 1980s the natural sister reemerged (coincidentally just before the rich suitor's benefactor was to fall on hard times?) in the guise of the *new connectionism*.

Papert's account exaggerates the demise of the research tradition initiated by Rosenblat and others. Much serious work was accomplished with connectionist networks during the supposedly dark ages of the 1970s and early 1980s by researchers such as James Anderson, Teuvo Kohonen, and Stephen Grossberg. In contrast with the symbolic approach, however, the connectionist approach did not experience a period of explosive growth during this period. Its period of explosive growth was delayed until the late 1980s. The explosion at this time can be attributed to a variety of factors. One was a sense of frustration with some of the undesirable features of symbolic approaches such as the need to specify rules for all processes and the rigidity of rule processing systems. (Some of these undesirable features have been ameliorated with the advent of newer symbolic modeling strategies, such as use of numeric parameters attached to rules and representations. See Anderson (1983) and Newell (1989).) A second factor was the introduction of learning algorithms such as back-propagation (Rumelhart, Hinton, and Williams 1986) and the Boltzmann training procedure (Ackley, Hinton, and Sejnowski 1985) that overcame the limitations of the perceptron model. Finally, a not insignificant factor was simply the increasing availability of computer resources adequate to solve the equations that describe the behavior of networks. The computational requirements grow rapidly once one expands beyond very simple networks and without the availability of von Neumann or symbolic processing devices to perform the computations, it would be nearly impossible to perform any significant connectionist modeling.

In this essay my task is to present the case for connectionism as an approach to artificial intelligence. My approach will be first to provide a very elementary introduction to connectionist modeling for those with little or no previous exposure to connectionism. That will be followed by a short section sketching the potential of connectionism to expand our conception of cognition beyond that which is current in philosophy and is exhibited in symbolic approaches to cognitive modeling. I will then turn to one of the more serious objections that has been raised by the symbolic tradition against connectionism as an approach to cognitive modeling, and present a connectionist strategy for answering that challenge. Finally, I will take up a standard objection to the symbol processing account of cognition specifically and to AI in general, and argue that connectionism may have the resources to overcome that objection. Before I pursue this endeavor, however, a qualification is in order. I view the connectionist systems that are being explored today as exemplars of a much broader class of dynamical systems. The points I make on behalf of connectionist systems are not intended to defend connectionism *per se*, but to recommend an expansion of artificial intelligence and cognitive science to include the development of nonlinear dynamical systems of various sorts to model cognitive performance.

2   A Brief Overview of Connectionism

The key to the behavior of connectionist networks is the way in which the activation values of units are determined. Figure 1 illustrates one approach. In this case we assign three units (labeled 1–3) activation values. The input each of these provides to Unit 4 is equal to the product of the unit's own activation and the weight of the connection linking it with Unit 4. This product is summed over all of the units feeding Unit 4 to generate the net input to Unit 4. An equation is then

used to determine the activation of Unit 4; in this case the frequently used logistic function is employed.

To illustrate how such simple processing could result in performance of a cognitive task, I will consider a relatively simple network which was used to generate the proper phonemic representation of the past tense of English verbs from the phonemic representation of the present tense. What makes this task challenging is that while the past tense of most verbs is formed in one of three regular ways – by adding to the verb stem either /ed/ (*add → added*), /d/ (*play → played*) or /t/ (*walk → walked*) – some verbs take an irregular past test (*is → was*). This task was originally modeled by Rumelhart and McClelland (1986), whose simulation was critiqued by Pinker and Prince (1988). (See Bechtel and Abrahamsen (1991) for discussion and evaluation of that controversy.) Subsequently, Plunkett and Marchman (1991) have constructed an alternative simulation that addressed many of the earlier objections and provides a clear example of how a feedforward network performs such tasks. They developed an artificial vocabulary of 500 three-phoneme words. Each phoneme is represented on six of the 18 input

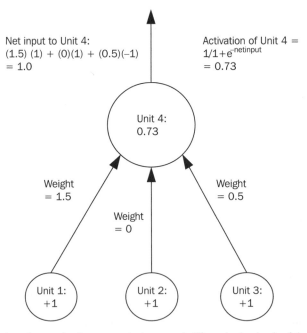

Net input to Unit 4:
(1.5) (1) + (0)(1) + (0.5)(−1)
= 1.0

Activation of Unit 4 =
$1/1 + e^{-netinput}$
= 0.73

Unit 4:
0.73

Weight
= 1.5

Weight
= 0

Weight
= 0.5

Unit 1:
+1

Unit 2:
+1

Unit 3:
+1

Figure 7.8   An illustration of processing in a connectionist network. The activation levels of the four units are shown beneath their labels. The weights on the three connections leading to Unit 4 are also shown. The Netinput to Unit 4 is determined by multiplying the activation of each feeding unit by the weight on the connection and summing across the three feeding units. The activation of Unit 4 is then determined according to the logistic activation function.

units; these units encode whether the phoneme is a vowel or consonant, is voiced or unvoiced, and the manner and place of articulation (figure 7.9). Activation is passed along weighted connections to 30 hidden units, and from them to 20 output units, on which representations of the past-tense is to be generated. Eighteen of the units serve the same function as they do on the input layer, while the remaining two units encode the possible regular endings. Most of the vocabulary items form the past tense in one of the three regular ways. Some, however, were assigned irregular forms (either arbitrary mappings such as found in the English *go → went*, identity mappings as in *hit → hit*, and vowel change mappings as in *run → ran*).

Training the network involved activating the phonemic representation of a verb on the input layer and letting it generate an output by successive application of the procedure outlined above. The activation of a given output unit is then compared with the target activation for that unit, and the difference constitutes a measure of error. The back-propagation learning algorithm (Rumelhart, Hinton, and Williams, 1986) uses the derivative of the error with respect to the activation of the unit to guide changing the weights in the network in such a way as to generate a smaller error when the same input pattern is presented in the future. Plunkett and Marchman demonstrated not only that this network could learn to generate the proper past tense for the words in their vocabulary, but also that the learning showed some important similarities to the way children learned the English past tense. The network was initially trained on a set that included a large number of irregular words. Then additional words, including a smaller percentage of irregulars, were gradually added to the training set. Like children, the network first learned the correct form for the irregulars in its corpus, but subsequently overgeneralized the regular form and applied it to some irregular forms (thus producing, using an English example, *comed* instead of *came*) before learning the proper form of all verbs.

This example illustrates what are known as *feedforward* networks, since inputs are supplied on one layer, and activations are fed from there through possible hidden layers to an output layer. There

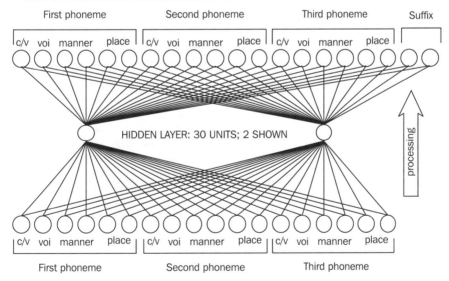

OUTPUT LAYER: PHONOLOGICAL FEATURE REPRESENTATION OF PAST TENSE FORM

Figure 7.9 Three-layer feedforward network used in Plunkett and Marchman's (1991) simulation of learning the past tense of English verbs. The input units encode representations of the three phonemes of the present tense of the artificial words used in this simulation, while the output units encode the three phonemes employed in the past tense form and the suffixes (/d/, /ed/, or /t/) used on regular verbs. Each input unit is connected to each of the 30 hidden units and so spreads activation to those units in proportion to its activation and the weight on the connection. Likewise, all hidden units are connected to every output unit.

are other designs which involve more interaction of units (a unit might, for instance, receive an input from a unit to which it also supplied an input), but the examples of connectionist models I present in this essay all employ the relatively simpler design of feed-forward networks. With this as a brief introduction to connectionist modeling, I will now turn to some of the implications of the connectionist approach to cognitive modeling, focusing on how it differs from the symbolic approach, how it can hope to respond to challenges raised by proponents of the symbolic approach, and how it promises to overcome one of the serious liabilities of the symbolic approach.

3 Expanding the Conception of Cognition

It is a truism to say that the subject matter of cognitive science is cognition. But for this to be informative, one must say what one means by *cognition*. Within philosophy, the traditional answer to that question is that cognition, or thinking, involves something like logical inference. One view, to which no one quite subscribes, is that the rules of deductive logic are, or should be, the rules governing thinking. The obvious problem with this approach is that thinking often leads us to conclusions that are not derivable from the premises. Thus, minimally, we would have to add inductive and abductive logic to deductive logic if we want to make a connection between thinking and logic.

Philosophers have generally not attempted to work out a detailed account of how the kind of manipulation of propositions involved in logic could account for human thinking. This has been the business of cognitive scientists, some of whom have accepted the linkage between thought and logic. Some early efforts in modeling cognition stayed close to the formalisms used in symbolic logic, representing pieces of knowledge in propositional formats and developing computer programs that would manipulate these propositions in a formal manner (Black 1968; Kintsch 1974). One of the things that cognitive scientists have clearly recognized is that the simple propositional representation of information is too impoverished to model cognition. Thus, one of the major advances in cognitive science in the 1970s was the introduction of larger-scale structures for representing knowledge, such as frames, scripts, and schemas

(Rumelhart 1975; Minsky 1975; Shank and Abelson 1977).

Even as researchers in cognitive science enriched the tools contributed by philosophy, however, most continued to accept a basic assumption that had been contributed by philosophy. For philosophers, linguistic representation of information has been primary. Knowledge is represented in sentences, and justification of knowledge has required the production of arguments showing that the sentences in question were true. In a critical manner, the *linguistic turn* in philosophy set language up as an autonomous representational system. Instead of looking to structures in nature and their interactions, the strategy for solving philosophical problems involved analyzing linguistic facts or relations. The deductive-nomological model of explanation that has been so influential in philosophy of science is one consequence of this tradition. There have been attempts to resist the hegemony of linguistic representation within philosophy. Gilbert Ryle (1949) emphasized *knowing how*, and argued that it was far more basic than propositional knowledge or *knowing that*. Hubert Dreyfus (1979), drawing upon Continental philosophers, emphasized the importance of embodiment for a cognitive system. Currently some philosophers of science (e.g., Darden 1991) have begun to emphasize the role of diagrams in presenting scientific information. But the linguistic conception of knowledge remains dominant even today.

One of the reasons for the dominance of the linguistic paradigm in cognitive science has been that the main tool for modeling cognitive processes, programs designed to run on von Neumann machines, function by storing information in propositional formats and operating upon those stored representations. This approach to modeling cognition has given rise to a rather unusual question: is a properly programmed computer literally a mind? In most areas where computer modeling or simulation is performed, the computer is viewed as solving equations that characterize how the system in question operates; the simulation will thus predict how the system will behave in various circumstances. But in the case of simulations of cognitive functions, some theorists have claimed that the programmed computer is working on the same representations as the human mind, and thus could be considered a mind itself.

This approach to cognitive modeling also assumes that any cognitive task involves operating upon the sort of representations that can be constructed in computer languages. While this has worked reasonably well for some problem solving tasks such as chess playing and medical diagnosis, it has worked less well for modeling other activities such as perception and motor control. It has proven far more difficult to develop adequate scene analyzers or systems for controlling robot movement than to solve problems of medical diagnosis.

One strategy is to deny that these are *cognitive* problems. But this move, I contend, unduly limits the use of the word *cognitive* and restricts the focus of cognitive science. It also may provide us a very misleading conception of how we deal with most of the tasks confronting us. Many of these tasks are ones performed as well by intralinguistic animals: they too must determine where they are in an environment, recognize what objects are around them, determine courses of actions likely to satisfy goals, and determine how to perform these actions. It is a reasonable starting point in cognitive modeling to assume that we perform these tasks in the same manner as intralinguistic animals.

It is because connectionist systems do not operate by performing logical inferences, but by having dynamical systems undergo changes of state, that they offer a way to broaden the conception of cognition. Connectionist models exhibit properties which make them reasonable tools to use in modeling such basic cognitive tasks as pattern recognition and categorization. For example, they perform pattern classification by imposing similarity metrics on input spaces; this permits them to classify new inputs as belonging to the same categories as others on which they have already been trained. They learn this similarity metric through performing tasks; it does not have to be provided by the simulation designer and can in fact change as a result of further experience. Thus, connectionism permits the expansion of the domain of the cognitive beyond that of logical reasoning. A fair question, of course, is why we should so expand the domain of the cognitive. Here I can only offer two quick and dirty answers. First, there is reason to construe logical reasoning as itself a process of pattern recognition (Bechtel and Abrahamsen 1991). Think for a moment what it is you teach students in a basic logic course! Students learn both the patterns that constitute the basic valid and invalid logical forms and the patterns of putting simple inferences together into proofs. Second, a reasonably natural way to characterize cognitive processes is as that set of processes

which occur in organisms that makes it possible for them to acquire information from their environment and produce action in their environment. If this consists more generally in recognizing and evaluating patterns in the environment than in performing logical inferences on linguistically encoded information, then we ought to expand the conception of the cognitive to include these processes.

4 Accounting for the Productivity and Systematicity of Thought

Advocates of the symbol processing tradition may respond to the above suggestions by arguing that, while it is well and good to attend to some of the basic components of cognition (although they may be reluctant to characterize these processes as *cognitive*), cognition does manifest features that cannot be accounted for in connectionist networks. These require a symbolic system. The most developed and general (i.e., not limited to pointing out the deficits in particular connectionist models) argument to this effect is due to Fodor and Pylyshyn (1988; see also Fodor and McLaughlin 1991). They argue that like language, thought is productive and systematic. *Productivity* refers to the capacity to always generate a new sentence or a new thought beyond those that have already appeared in any given corpus. *Systematicity*, with respect to language, refers to the fact that any language that can encode certain sentences will automatically be able to encode a variety of related sentences. For example, as a result of being able to encode the sentence

Mary loves the florist

English can also encode the sentence

The florist loves Mary.

Thought, Fodor and Pylyshyn contend, also shows systematicity: any cognitive system that can think one of these sentences will also be able to think the other.

Fodor and Pylyshyn argue that symbolic systems are able to account for the productivity and systematicity of language because they employ a compositional syntax for their internal representations and build the meaning of compound structures from that of the components in accord with

| red | blue | green | brown | square | triangle | circle |

Figure 7.10 An illustration of the problem facing connectionist representations that do not employ a compositional syntax. The units for *red*, *blue*, *square*, and *circle* are all active, but there is no way to indicate whether it is the circle or square that is red.

these syntactic rules. Symbolic systems assume an internal language of thought (Fodor 1975). Fodor and Pylyshyn's challenge to connectionism is that what count as representations in most connectionist models are not built up according to compositional rules and so are not themselves syntactically structured in a manner that permits structure-sensitive processing rules to be applied to them. The reason is that activation patterns in networks can only represent the presence or absence of features or objects, not relations between those features. Multiple units being on, for example, can indicate that multiple features are present, but it cannot indicate whether the features are instantiated in one object, or in many. For example, if in the set of units pictured in figure 7.10 units representing features for *red*, *blue circle*, and *square* are active, one cannot tell whether the circle is being represented as red or blue, and similarly for the square.

How should connectionists respond to Fodor and Pylyshyn's challenge? Many connectionists have struggled with this question. One strategy pursued by some connectionists is to develop symbolic systems within connectionist architectures. Thus, Touretzky (1990) has attempted to implement LISP in a connectionist system and Touretzky and Hinton (1988) implemented a simplified production system. To these approaches, Fodor and Pylyshyn can respond that it is the symbolic system which is being implemented that gives the system its *cognitive* character; the implementation itself is not a cognitivist's concern. Connectionists pursuing these strategies, however, argue that the distinction between the cognitive architecture and its implementation is not as sharp as Fodor and Pylyshyn make out. They insist that the connectionist implementation is relevant to cognitive questions insofar as it provides the system with some important characteristics of cognitive systems.

In *Connectionism and the Mind* Abrahamsen and I termed the Touretzky strategy the *compatibilist* response. While the compatibilist strategy may be useful for technological purposes, as an approach

for accounting for human cognition it faces the same theoretical challenges as the classical symbolic program. Among these challenges, one of the most serious is to explain how such a system could have evolved. A production system architecture, like a language of thought model, is fundamentally a syntactic processing system without intrinsic semantics. What selection forces would have led to the gradual evolution of an internal syntactic processor? In *Connectionism and the Mind* we contrasted the compatibilist approach with two other approaches, which we termed the *approximationist approach* and the *external symbol approach*. These approaches support one another and together offer a much more plausible scenario for the evolution of the cognitive system. The core claim of the approximationist approach is that the performance of the human cognitive system, at least on some tasks, is sufficiently like that of a symbolic system so that a symbolic system might approximate its performance. But the approximationists insist that the symbolic system is only an approximation of the real cognitive system, which operates without the use of syntactically structured internal representations upon which formal operations can be performed (see Smolensky 1988). This approach avoids some of the problems of the compatibilist approach since it does not posit an internal syntactic processor but only a system whose behavior, on occasions, can be approximated by a system employing syntactic principles. What this approach requires to answer the evolutionary question fully is an account of what selection forces could have led it to develop patterns of behavior that could be approximated by a symbol processing device. The external symbol approach advances a solution to that problem, and a rather radical way of answering Fodor and Pylyshyn.

The key to the external symbol approach is to move formal symbols, which adhere to syntactic rules, out of the head and locate them in the environment of the system. Rumelhart, Smolensky, McClelland, and Hinton (1986) offer one example of how a system might use external symbols. To do arithmetic problems that are at all complex, such as multiplication of one three-digit number by another, we write the numbers on paper in a canonical form. (The use of canonical form is extremely important – a large part of the problem students face in mastering such a task is to learn that it is important to adhere to the conventions of the canonical form.) Once this is done, a complex task is decomposed into simple tasks – multiplying two one-digit numbers, and sometimes adding a carry to that. This is a task that can be performed using memorized answers or a rather simple connectionist network that carries out pattern recognition. Using such external symbols radically reduces the demands upon the cognitive system. What exists inside the cognitive system is not an internal representation of these external symbols, but an ability to extract information from them and to produce symbol strings which adhere to the syntactic rules that characterize properly formed strings.

In the case of language, the external symbols are, for the language learner, generally sounds or manual signs. One thing to note about such symbols is that they *afford* composition since they can be strung together in a linear sequence. Different communities can develop different systems for stringing these symbols together (systems that depend not just on word order, but also on case markings, another feature afforded by such symbols). The key claim of the external symbol approach is that a cognitive system must learn the particular concatenation scheme employed in the language community in which it exists. The suggestion here that grammar might be learned goes against a classical argument of Chomsky's (1968) that the stimulus is too impoverished to permit such learning. But some of the bite of that argument is removed if we consider how long it in fact takes human cognitive systems to learn a first language. It takes children a considerable period of time just to learn the proper production of these external signs. (According to Liebermann (1992) it is not until children are more than ten years old that they fully master the phonemics of their native language.) During the early part of their second year of life, though, they typically develop the ability to produce reasonably recognizable approximations of the adult form of some words in what will be their native language, and begin to use these words in proper contexts. Several more months elapse before children begin to put words together (this is often preceded by a period in which they

put words together with gestures). Gradually children begin to produce sentences with more complex grammatical structures, but it takes them several years to master many of the complex grammatical structures found in natural languages.

In the previous paragraph I have focused on the productive use of language, but in fact children begin to comprehend linguistic structures before they exhibit them in their own production. This makes it far more difficult to study how children are learning the linguistic devices of their native language. One must attend carefully to the child's comprehension of particular sentences in which the meaning depends upon correctly interpreting the syntactic devices of the language. But a focus on comprehension does suggest a principle that might govern learning the linguistic devices of a language: a cognitive system might learn a linguistic device when it becomes clear that there is information encoded by that device that is relevant for the activities of the system. Much of the information of a language is in fact encoded in the semantics of the content words comprising sentences. By being able to decode the main content words of the sentence (as well as the intonation with which the sentence was uttered), one can figure out what the sentence likely meant. It is for this reason that for many decades Broca's aphasics appeared to have intact language comprehension while they exhibit severe deficits in language production. With further investigation, it became clear that they faced severe comprehension deficits when the correct interpretation of the sentence depended upon closed-class vocabulary (syntactic indicator words such as prepositions). Further investigation (Bradley, Garrett, and Zurif 1980) revealed that while they could comprehend closed-class vocabulary, they processed these words much more slowly than normal subjects. They processed them at the speed as open-class vocabulary, not at the more accelerated speed normally exhibited with closed-class vocabulary. Apparently proper decoding of the syntactic structures of a language requires faster, automatic processing of closed-class vocabulary, so that the analysis of these words is complete before content words are fully processed. But Friederici (1992) argues that children do not manifest this adult pattern until the beginning of the second decade of life. If in fact children do take an extended period of time to learn to decode and to use syntactic devices, it may be that these abilities could be mastered by a network that interacts with external symbols.[1]

The question facing the external symbol approach is whether a system that lacks an internal representational system with composition syntax and semantics could nonetheless learn to extract information appropriately from linguistic representations that employ syntactic devices and could learn to produce properly structured linguistic representations. While there are no comprehensive simulations that show this is possible, there are at least some connectionist simulations that suggest that it is. One approach is to train a network to extract from an English sentence an assignment of the proper thematic roles for the concepts mentioned in the sentence. Thus, the network might be given as input the sentence

The juvenile delinquent broke the window with a brick.

The network would then be required to determine that the agent is the juvenile delinquent, the action is breaking, the patient is the window, and the instrument is the brick. This is not a trivial task. The same case role information could have been encoded in the sentence:

The window was broken by the juvenile delinquent with a brick.

The subject of the second sentence has the same thematic role as the direct object of the first sentence, etc.

One of the problems in designing a network to perform this task is to determine how to present the input to the network. An early simulation used a single set of input nodes, some of which were predesignated for the grammatical subject of the sentence, others for the verb, etc. (McClelland and Kawamoto 1986). This strategy, unfortunately, artificially limits the grammatical variability of the input sentences and so undercuts some of the potential for productivity in the linguistic input. One of the factors that makes for productivity in natural languages is that the length of sentences is not bounded; through a variety of devices, most notably dependent clauses, we can always expand the length of sentences. Thus, ideally we should present the input to the network sequentially. With simple feedforward nets, however, this presents a problem. The proper interpretation of any given word in a sentence depends not only on its intrinsic meaning, but also on how it is related to

other words in a sentence. Some means is required to insure that the interpretation of a given word is properly constrained by those preceding and following it. One technique for achieving this that has now been widely used involves feedback information from previous processing cycles when subsequent words in the sentence are presented. Modifying a design of Michael Jordan (1986), Jeffrey Elman (1990) introduced what he calls a *recurrent network*. In a recurrent network the output of hidden layer units is fed back as part of the next input (see figure 7.11). In a standard feedforward network, the representation on the hidden units provides an intermediate representation of the problem. In a recurrent network, the pattern on the hidden units is sensitive both to the new input and the pattern of representation of hidden units in the previous processing cycle. Since the previous pattern was also sensitive to the one before that, the network becomes sensitive to information over a much longer duration. Although there is no explicit representation of the state of the hidden units two cycles previously, the current representation on the hidden units will be sensitive to that representation. The trace of earlier states degrades over cycles, but is enough to enable the network to be responsive to modestly long dependencies.

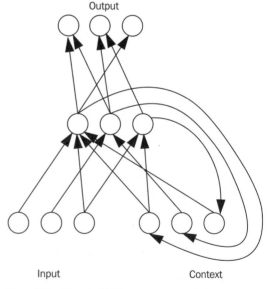

Figure 7.11 Elman's (1990) recurrent network. Patterns generated on hidden units during one cycle of processing are copied onto the context units, and from there provide part of the input on the next cycle.

The following example illustrates how a recurrent network can become sensitive to prior context. The network is to learn to provide the designated output number for each number in the following three five-number sequences:

Sequence 1		Sequence 2		Sequence 3	
Input	Output	Input	Output	Input	Output
1	1	4	2	2	4
2	2	3	4	5	3
3	3	1	3	1	5
4	4	5	1	4	1
5	5	2	5	3	2

It is significant that the same input number can appear in any of the three sequences. Hence, if the input is the number 3, the proper output might be 3, 4, or 2 depending on what preceded it in the sequence. In both the second and third input set, 3 is preceded by 4. In order to arrive at the correct response, the network must be sensitive to the fact that in the second sequence the 4 was the beginning while in the third it was preceded by a 1. To show that recurrent networks can provide such sensitivity, I employed a network of five input units, three hidden units, and five output units. Each of the input and output units represented one of the five numbers. The activations of these hidden units on a given cycle were reentered into the network as part of the input in the next cycle. During training the three sequences were fed to the network sequentially; to mark the divisions between the sequences, an input pattern of all 1's was employed, during which no recurrent input was reentered. Although many epochs of training were required, the network successfully learned to generate the proper output sequence for each input sequence.

St. John and McClelland (1990) employed a recurrent network in a sentence processing task. Sentences were presented to the network one word at a time and the task for the network was to match thematic roles and filters. One of the sentences used in their simulation was:

The schoolgirl spread something with a knife.

The available thematic roles were:

agent, action, patient, instrument, co-agent, co-patient, location, adverb, and recipient.

When queried as to the agent, the network should answer *schoolgirl*, and it should answer *knife* when queried as to instrument. If queried with *spread* it should respond with action. In addition to specifying the actual filler, the network was also trained to respond with a number of features of the filler, such as *person*, *adult*, *child*, *male*, or *female* for agents.

In their simulation, St. John and McClelland employed a rather complex network (see figure 7.12), which can be analyzed into two parts. The lower part is designed to create a *sentence gestalt* of the sentence that is being input. The sentence is input one word at a time, and the sentence gestalt constructed from the previously input words is supplied along with the new word. These activities are processed through a set of hidden units and generate the sentence gestalt on the designated units. St. John and McClelland did not specify the target sentence gestalt for each input sentence; rather, the network developed its own sentence gestalt representations as it performed the subsequent task of specifying case role and filler. This

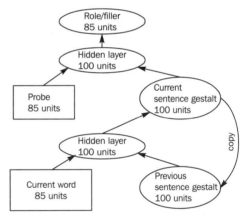

Figure 7.12 St. John and McClelland's network for determining thematic roles and fillers from sentences presented one word at a time. The two rectangular boxes indicate input units. The input on the Probe units specifies either a thematic role or the filler; on the output units the network is to provide the appropriate combination of thematic role and filler. The sentence is input one word at a time on the current word input units. This pattern is processed through a set of hidden units to create a current sentence gestalt. When a subsequent word is presented, the current sentence gestalt is copied onto the previous sentence gestalt and provides part of the input. This recurrent connection serves to provide the network a representation of the part of the sentence that has already been input.

was done by the upper part of the network. To perform this task, another input was supplied, called a *probe*, which together with the sentence gestalt would provide input to a further set of hidden units, which would in turn activate the output units. After the network has developed its sentence gestalt in response to the first word of the sentence, a probe is supplied for each role and filler for the whole sentence, and the error on the output units is used to train the network. Then the second word of the sentence is presented, and the procedure is repeated. Thus, from the very first word of the sentence the network is required to guess at all the role/filler combinations for the whole sentence. It is this training procedure which accounts for a significant part of the network's ability to learn syntactic and semantic relationships between words.

St. John and McClelland trained the network on a corpus of over 22,000 sentences describing 120 different events. Multiple sentences can be constructed for each event since there are different words that can be used for the same entity or action (e.g., *someone*, *adult*, and *bus driver* can all be used to designate the bus driver), and not all components of the event must be mentioned in each sentence (e.g., if the bus driver is eating, the instrument may be included or omitted). The events are constructed from frames associated with the 14 verbs in the vocabulary (four of which could also be used in the passive). The procedures used to construct the events made some events far more likely than others, exposing the network to a number of rather sexist stereotypes. For example, the bus driver (always a male) is described as eating steak more frequently than soup, and is generally portrayed as eating with gusto, while the teacher (always a female) more commonly eats soup and does so daintily, 330,000 random sentence trials were presented to the network during training. The network learned to make correct thematic role/filler assignments to the active sentences more quickly, but at this point also began to make correct assignments for the passive sentences.

The network was able to process a wide variety of sentences. In some cases, such as "The schoolgirl stirred the kool-aid with a spoon," the semantics was sufficient to determine the thematic role/filler assignments. But in a passive sentence such as "The bus driver was given the rose by the teacher" the syntax is crucial. (To insure that the network was relying on syntactic information, it

was trained with equal numbers of instances of the bus driver giving a rose to the teacher, and the teacher giving a rose to the bus driver.) The network also made correct thematic role/filler assignments in ambiguous sentences such as "The pitcher hit the bat with the bat," in sentences in which concepts were not explicitly instantiated such as "The schoolgirl spread something with a knife," and in sentences in which role fillers were not explicitly mentioned such as "The teacher ate the soup" (instrument not specified). One of the more interesting abilities the network exhibited was its ability to revise earlier assignments when information later in the sentence required it. In the sentence "The adult ate the steak with daintiness" the network must supply the individual for the general category *adult*. When only "The adult ate" has been input, the network assigns equal response values to bus driver and teacher as agents and to steak and soup as patients. But after the word "steak" is input, it judges bus driver and steak to be the two most likely fillers, since the bus driver is described far more often as eating steak. The network at this point also supplies the filler *gusto* for the adverb role. Supplying "daintiness" as input, however, brings a reversal. Now not only does *daintiness* surpass *gusto* in activation strength, but *teacher* receives more activation than *bus driver*. While *steak* receives more activation that *soup*, *steak* declines in activation and *soup* increases. The network is thus able to update its interpretation of previous information as new information becomes available to it.

What is interesting about this simulation from my perspective is that, while clearly sensitive to the grammatical structure in the input sentence (as evidenced by the fact that it was able to extract information that was encoded using the grammar), the network does not build up an internal representation of the sentence as a grammatically structured entity. The representation the network has formed on the units designated "sentence gestalt" represents the information encoded in the sentence or anticipated from what was encoded in the sentence. The network *knows how* to extract information from grammatically structured sentences, but in order to do this it does not have to have an internal representation of the sentence upon which computations can be performed. Does this suffice for giving the network productivity and systematicity? Clearly there are many limitations to this simulation. Because of the manner in which the output to queries was encoded, it was not possible to test this network's abilities to process complex grammatical constructions such as embedded clauses. But some appreciation of the network's productivity and systematicity is found in the manner in which the network was able to respond to sentences on which it had not been trained. In a separate simulation, St. John and McClelland developed a corpus of 2,000 sentences using ten names of people, ten verbs, and both active and passive structures. 1,750 of the sentences were used as the training set; the performance of the network was then evaluated on the remaining 250. The network was 97 per cent correct on these remaining sentences. Thus, the network was able to perform, in at least a limited manner, a task requiring it to process novel sentences (productivity) that used the same components as sentences it had already learned, but with different syntactic relations between them (thus showing systematicity).

Can a network of this sort handle the full corpus of English? It would certainly have to be more complex to accommodate such things as relative clauses and compound subjects or predicates. Moreover, the network will probably be severely impoverished in mastering more complex sentences if it lacks knowledge of the world which linguistic structures describe (see next section). Only further research will show whether a more complex simulation could succeed in exhibiting the requisite productivity and systematicity to master a natural language. In addressing this question, however, we should be careful not to exaggerate human ability. In written prose we can retrace our steps as necessary when dealing with extremely complex sentences. In oral communication, however, we often make mistakes in comprehending complex sentences in which the correct interpretation depends on specific grammatical cues. What is desired is a network that can deal as well with linguistic structures as competent human language users can, not a network that can manifest the full competence in language identified in linguistic theories.

To return to the central issue of this section, the basic strategy for answering Fodor and Pylyshyn is to agree that the cognition of adult humans who have mastered a natural language does exhibit a significant degree of productivity and systematicity. My claim, against Fodor and Pylyshyn, is that this is due to the system having adapted to the use of external symbols, those of the natural language, and having put these symbols to use. Languages, as cultural products, have evolved devices providing compositional syntax and semantics; humans, in learning these languages, have developed capacities for decoding information encoded using the compositional syntax and semantics of the language, and for producing properly structured strings of these languages. If the internal processing does not require a system with compositional syntax or semantics, however, then it is possible that a connectionist system will prove adequate for modeling human capacities when it has learned to work with an external symbol system. The key to my proposal is to view the human cognitive system as having adapted to a linguistic environment and to find the source of productivity and systematicity in the external symbols of the language.

Two final issues need to be considered in this answer to Fodor and Pylyshyn. First, it is clear that adult speakers of a language can think to themselves using language. As Vygotsky (1962) and others have argued, however, this is a capacity which is developed after the child first learns to use language to communicate with others. I would contend that this capacity still employs, in an important sense, external symbols. Silent speech generates a string of symbols which we *hear* with an *inner ear*. Just as it now appears that mental imagery relies on the same neural processes as visual image processing (Farrah 1988), it seems plausible that inner speech employs the same neural processes involved in actual speech production and comprehension. Thus, the language system may produce and process symbols much as if they were actually produced as physical sounds. Second, Fodor and Pylyshyn argue that productivity and systematicity are features of thought itself, not just linguistically mediated thought. Fodor (1987) claims that gray cat, for example, thinks systematically. This is a claim, however, for which evidence is required. I would not be surprised that gray cat could think "I will chase that mouse" but not be able to think "The mouse will chase me." (Of course, on my account gray cat would not think these thoughts using a linguistic medium. Thinking would involve being sensitive to this information and using it to guide other activities, including purely cognitive ones.) There is evidence that learning languages changes our brains, and it may be that learning languages makes our thinking far more productive and systematic than it would be if we lacked language. Thus, we may exhibit forms of systematicity that a non-language using organism would not.

William Bechtel

5 Accounting for the Intentionality of Cognition

Having proposed a strategy for answering one of the major objections lodged against connectionism, I will turn in this last section to showing how connectionism might fare better than the symbolic approach with respect to one of the major objections that has been made against the symbolic approach. This is that it cannot account for the meaning of the symbols used in its models. These symbols are purely formal structures which are operated on by formal rules. They lack real semantics. What is called *semantics* in the course of symbolic modeling is purely formal; the system has a set of rules connecting one symbol with others in particular ways. But these symbols are never connected to things in the world. This has been called the *symbol grounding problem* (Harnad 1990) or the problem of *original intentionality* (Searle 1980). Searle's Chinese room argument is meant to show that these symbols lack any *aboutness*: a system could learn to manipulate a set of symbols in all the right ways without ever knowing what the symbols are about. Searle claims that this is totally unlike human cognition: when we think about something or say something, we know what our thought or utterance is about.

In presenting his argument, Searle considers a number of replies that researchers in artificial intelligence might make. One of the most promising of these is the *robot* reply according to which the computer program is hooked up to a robot so that its inputs come from the sensors of the robot and its outputs manipulate the motor controls of the robot. But Searle contends that adding a robot to a programmed computer does nothing to generate aboutness or intentionality. He simply re-employs the same thought experiment:

Suppose that instead of the computer inside the robot, you put me inside the room and, as in the original Chinese case, you give me more Chinese symbols with more instructions in English for matching Chinese symbols to Chinese symbols and feeding back Chinese symbols to the outside. Suppose, unknown to me, some of the Chinese symbols that come to me come from a television camera attached to the robot and other Chinese symbols that I am giving out serve to make the motors inside the robot move the robot's legs or arms. It is important

to emphasize that all I am doing is manipulating formal symbols: I know none of these other facts. (1980, p.420)

The force of Searle's reply is that there is nothing about the symbols the computer uses that makes them about the objects that the robot is engaging.

What gives Searle's response to the robot reply its plausibility is that the symbols used by the cognitive engine are, in a crucial sense, *autonomous* from the things represented by them. As a result of the robot's encounter with the world, some additional symbols might be transduced and provided as input to the system, and other symbols will be transduced into system outputs. But the set of symbols itself will not be changed. Therefore, any other environment which was isomorphic to the current one in terms of what was transduced across the sensory and motor thresholds would make no difference to the internal system, and hence there is nothing that makes the internal symbols be about this environment rather than some other.

One strategy for overcoming this limitation of symbolic systems is to allow internal representations to be shaped by the inputs and outputs of the system so that they become part of the system's adaptation to its environment. This is not generally possible in a symbolic system due to the sharp differentiation between representation and processes operating on that representation. But that distinction is not made in connectionist systems, raising the possibility that a connectionist system will not suffer the same deficiency. The key to the connectionist solution is to view the symbols in connectionist models as adapting to their environments. They are thus about their environments in at least as strong a sense as biological traits are *adapted* to features of their niches.

What count as representations in connectionist systems are patterns of activation on sets of units. The patterns of activation on the input and output units are typically engineered by the network designer and there is no opportunity for modifying these (but see Miikkulainen and Dyer 1990). But if there are hidden units within the system, and the system learned to perform its task by changing the weights on its connections, then the patterns of activation on the hidden units in the system will be adjusted so as to facilitate performing that task. If the task depends on picking out information about the inputs to the network, then the network will not only develop its own ways of categorizing the inputs, but also of representing them. Hinton (1986) illustrated this with a network he designed to answer questions about relations in two-isomorphic family trees. Its input specified one person in the family and a relationship, and it was trained to respond with the name or names of the people who stood in that relation. The input and output layers encoded each person and each relationship with a single unit, but the hidden units developed a different representation. For instance, two units identified the input person in terms of nationality, two others in terms of generation. Thus, the network re-represented each individual in terms of these distinctions. It was not taught this alternative way of representing individuals; rather, the network created this representation to facilitate solving the task of identifying the person(s) who stood in the appropriate relation to this person.

Hinton's simulation shows how networks create their own representations on hidden units. These representations are part of the adaptation the network undergoes as it is trained to perform a task. These patterns are not arbitrary and could not easily be reinterpreted otherwise. For this reason, Searle's objections seem less compelling. However, the plausibility of this as an answer to Searle is compromised by the fact that the actual input and output patterns used by the network were encoded and assigned intentional interpretations. This makes the intentionality of the whole network dependent upon the intentional interpretation the network designer assigned to the input and output units. If, however, the network were guiding a robot, and its *survival* or *reproduction* depended upon its success in learning how to maneuver in that environment, then the attribution of intentionality to the representation used by the network may seem more compelling since they would not be directly inherited from the network designer.

Nolfi, Elman, and Parisi (1990) have developed a simple simulation of this sort. Their goal was to show how learning and evolution can work together. They began this simulation with very simple connectionist networks (figure 7.13) that function as model organisms that traverse a landscape in which there are designated food sites. The networks have four input units, and two of which specify the angle and distance of the nearest food site, and two of which specify the action the network last took. These actions are the product of the two output units, which can direct the unit to halt (00), move right (01), move left (10), and move

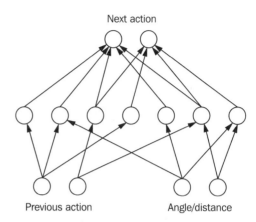

Next action

Previous action   Angle/distance

Figure 7.13   The network constituting the simple organism in Nolfi, Elman, and Parisi's (1990) first simulation. The two input units on the left specify the previous action, which is equivalent to the output on the previous cycle. The two input units on the right specify the angle and location of the nearest food site. This network undergoes no learning.

forward (11). In between the inputs and output are seven hidden units. In the first simulation there was no learning by the organisms; rather, changes in behavior were determined simply by evolution. One hundred organisms were created by assigning random weights to the connections. The organisms navigated a 10 cell × 10 cell environment, with some cells containing food. Figure 7.14 shows a typical trajectory. Each organism lived for 20 epochs, each epoch consisting of a set of 50 actions in 5 different environments (for a total of 5,000 actions); at the end of its life the number of food squares it encountered was summed. The 20 organisms acquiring the most food were allowed to reproduce; five new copies of each were created and weights were changed by a small random amount. After 50 generations the organisms evolved so as to find many more food squares. Figure 7.15 shows the path taken by a typical organism in the fiftieth generation. The selection procedure has clearly led to the development of organisms that visit more food sites.

One way to construe the selection process is as imposing demands on the organisms which, from the organism's point of view might be construed as needs. For food to really serve as a need or goal, though, the organism must be able to take actions to promote its ability to acquire food. That is where learning comes into the story. To combine learning with evolutionary adjustment, Nolfi et al.

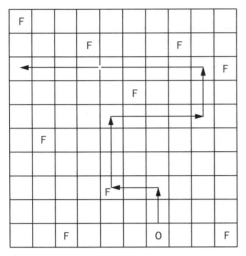

Figure 7.14 a typical trajectory through an envoron-
ment of an organism in the first generation. The 20
networks visiting the most food sites during a generation
are selected for reproduction, which consists in creating
five copies to part of the subsequent generation.

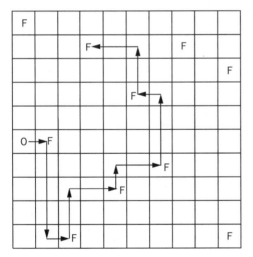

Figure 7.15 A typical trajectory through an environment of an organism in the fiftieth generation.

provided a *second* set of output units (see figure
7.16). These units were designed to *predict* what
the sensory input (angle and distance of nearest
food site) would be after the movement. This
information will certainly be available to the organism after its action (indeed, it is part of the input
the organism receives on the next epoch); hence, it
is realistic to think that the organism could learn to

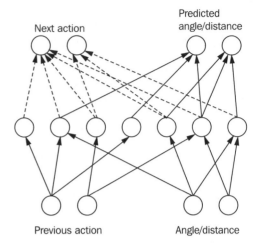

Figure 7.16 The network constituting the simple organism in Nolfi, Elman, and Parisi's (1990) second simulation. Two additional output units are employed, on
which the organism is to predict the angle and distance
of the nearest food site after it performs its actions. This
is information that the organism will, of course, receive as
input after the action. The connections from the hidden
units to these output units, and from all the input units to
the hidden units, are subject to learning through application of the back-propagation algorithm.

make better predictions. Therefore, the error
between the prediction and what the next sensory
input turned out to be was used to change the
weights leading to these units and from the input
units to the hidden units. (The weights from the
hidden units to the motor output units were fixed
by evolution and not subject to learning.) This
learning procedure was applied during the life
cycle of each organism, and organisms were
selected for reproduction in the same manner as
in the preceding simulation. When it became
time to reproduce, the new organisms were based
on the *original* weights of the preceding generation, not those acquired by learning (hence, no
inheritance of acquired characteristics). These
weights were altered randomly to a slight degree
and a new generation was created that could begin
learning.

The primary question Nolfi et al. were investi-
gating was how evolution and learning affected
each other. Their basic result was that learning
during the lifetime of an organism led to much
better performance even when organisms in subsequent generations could not benefit directly
from that learning since they started over with
small variations of the weights their parents had

at the beginning of training. Nolfi et al.'s explanation of how selective reproduction and learning interact to produce better organisms even when the consequences of learning are not inherited is that what learning provides is a means for determining which organism will most likely benefit from random mutation on its weights. An organism that gains from learning is one that has a set of initial weights which, on the basis of small changes during learning, will produce even better results. Then variation and selective retention is also able to produce more fit organisms. An organism that does not gain from learning is one whose weights are such that small changes will not produce any benefits. That organism may have found a local maximum in weight space and small changes in weights introduced by variation and selective retention will not produce further benefits. For my purposes, however, there is another aspect of the coupling between learning and evolution that is more noteworthy. Evolution imposed needs on the organism, and learning has facilitated the organism's satisfying those needs. While labeling the task a food searching task is clearly simply a ruse, since the organism gains nothing from the food squares, nonetheless, there is a task of visiting certain squares that is imposed on the organism by the selection procedure, and this has governed the way in which the organism has represented its environment.

It is also noteworthy that the organism does not receive feedback for learning about what is an optimal food-acquisition strategy, but rather simply feedback about whether it has correctly predicted its next sensory input. Thus, learning to perform one task on which an organism is very likely to receive feedback information (predict the future appearance of the environment) improved performance on another task (food acquisition) for which no direct learning signal is possible. What makes this possible is the fact that the two tasks rely on related information: the information needed to predict the future appearance of the environment is correlated with the information needed to find food in the environment. Why this should be the case can be seen by considering a case in which the nearest food location is at an angle of 90°. This is information that should both lead to a decision to turn right and an expectation that after one does, the food will be at approximately 0°. Both the outputs specifying actions and those predicting future angle/distance of food need to group the input patterns into similarity

groups, and the same similarity groups subserve both tasks. A natural question to ask at this point is what precisely is being represented on the hidden units. Nolfi et al. do not report an analysis of the pattern of representation on these units, so we cannot describe their semantics. It seems likely that the representation on the hidden units will be highly distributed, but that a cluster analysis will show that situations that require similar actions and then result in similar new angle/distance input patterns will result in very similar patterns of representation on the hidden units. It is in this way that learning to perform one task will facilitate an organism's performance of another task and thus subserve that goal.

Nolfi et al.'s simulation does employ representations of its environment, but they seem far from arbitrary. One representation could not equally well serve the function of another one. In this respect, the link between the representation and that which it represents (similarity groups among the input patterns with respect to the tasks the network must perform) has been strengthened. In a situation such as this, Searle's Chinese room argument will seem far less compelling. Insofar as both the procedures for handling the representations, and the representations themselves are being developed as the network learns its task, the network is adapting to its environment. Since there are no fixed structures, it is not clear what role Searle could play in simulation. There are no representations he can manipulate according to predefined rules. The only level at which he could function is at the level of determining the behavior of the various individual units, since the rules governing their behaviors remain constant. But insofar as the representational functions are not fixed for each unit, but are changing as the network is learning, there is no sense in which Searle would thereby be manipulating representations without understanding them. He would be performing operations at a subrepresentational level, and there is no reason to think that processes at this level should have any content or understanding.

There remains, however, a sense in which Searle's objection may seem to be telling. We do seem to know what we are thinking about when we have internal representations, but a simple connectionist network does not. But I would suggest that this is not due to the intrinsic intentionality of our internal states, but to something else. In addition to learning to recognize patterns and behave in accord with them, we have learned a natural language. If we assume for a moment that our cognitive system is a connectionist network (or better, a collection of them), then before we learn a language we have already learned to categorize a good deal of our environment and govern our actions in accord with those categorizations. Language is (in part) a social device for categorizing information about the environment; by learning that categorization system we are able to acquire information not readily available to us as individuals. It is therefore worthwhile for us to learn to use the external symbols of a language. This involves, in part, coordinating them with our already developed strategies for categorizing our environment. Such coordination need not involve any one-to-one mapping or translation from internal representations to linguistic representations. Rather, it only need involve developing the ability to use external symbols in ways that help facilitate behaviors already partially determined by internal representations (see Bechtel 1993).

Once we have learned to use these external symbols, we can then use them to communicate our thoughts. Again, this is not taken to involve a translation of an internal structure into a linguistic structure. I have argued elsewhere (Bechtel and Abrahamsen 1993) that our characterization of people in folk psychological vocabulary of beliefs and desires does not ascribe particular internal states to people but provides more global characterizations of how people relate to their environments (what information they possess and what outcomes they will work towards). All that is required here is the ability to use language in ways that characterize our overall states of belief and desire. The story of how we come to do this is complex, and I cannot go into it here. But the point I want to make can now be presented. Original intentionality is an illusion generated by the fact that we have two systems for characterizing our relations to our environment: our own cognitive system, together with whatever internal representations it employs, and the external representational system of language. We can characterize our own adaptedness to our environment through our use of language, and our adaptedness to our environment is coordinated with our use of language. We have two systems that are adapted to our environment, and it is our ability to use one to describe the other that makes it seem like our representations directly attach to features of our

environment. Underlying this ability is the capacity of the mental system to represent the environment. A major advantage of using connectionist systems to model cognitive processes is that their representations adapt to the features of the environment they need to represent and thus are about them in a far stronger sense than symbolic representations.

6   Conclusion

As a result of developments during the 1980s, connectionism has returned to the scene as a framework for cognitive modeling. To my mind, the greatest contribution of connectionism is to open up the possibilities for cognitive modeling beyond systems designed to implement logical reasoning. The current incarnations of connectionist systems are unlikely to offer final solutions. Rather, they are exemplars of nonlinear dynamical systems. The challenge is to determine whether such systems can provide understanding of how cognitive tasks are performed. In part I have urged that connectionism may help us expand the conception of what is cognitive, and many cognitive tasks may be better modeled with non linear dynamical systems than with logic systems. As a strategic matter, connectionism would likely be better served if it simply explored cognitive tasks to which it is well-suited even as these take us beyond the traditional domain of the cognitive. The symbolic tradition, however, has issued a challenge: connectionism must also explain the productivity and systematicity of thought or it is not even a candidate cognitive model. I have argued that these are not properties of thought *per se*, but of thought by language-using systems. I have proposed, therefore, that connectionists may be able to account for these features of thought by showing how a system without internal syntactic representations might learn to extract information from syntactically encoded language and produce properly structured language. Finally, I have proposed that connectionism may be in a position to answer an objection lodged against symbolic systems, namely, that it cannot explain the intentionality of thought. There is, thus, reason to hope that connectionism can both overcome the objections raised by proponents of the symbolic tradition and solve problems inherent in that tradition, making it a fruitful framework to use in modeling cognitive performance.

Note

1 There is no need for a connectionist to insist on a strong empiricist position that rejects nativism. The human mind may well come with systems predisposed to learning language. What is important for the connectionist who rejects the compatibilist approach is to claim that this capacity not involve use of linguistically structured internal representations of the external symbols.

References

Ackley, D. H., Hinton G. E., and Sejnowski, T. J. (1985) "A learning algorithm for Boltzmann machines." *Cognitive Science* 9, pp. 147–69.

Anderson, J. R. (1993) *The Architecture of Cognition.* Cambridge, Mass.: Harvard University Press.

Bechtel. W. (1993) "Decomposing intentionality: perspectives on intentionality drawn form language research with two species of chimpanzees." *Biology and Philosophy* 8, pp. 1–32.

Bechtel, W. and Abrahamsen, A. (1991) *Connectionism and the Mind: An Introduction to Parallel Processing in Networks.* Oxford: Basil Blackwell.

Bechtel, W. and Abrahamsen, A. (1993) "Connectionism and the future of folk psychology." In R. Burton (ed.) *Minds: Natural and Artificial*, pp. 69–100. Albany: SUNY Press.

Black, F. (1968) "A deductive question-answering system." In M. Minsky (ed.) *Semantic Information Processing*, pp. 354–402. Cambridge, Mass.: MIT Press.

Bradley, D. M., Garrett, M., and Zurif, E. (1980) "Syntactic deficits in Broca's aphasia." In D. Caplan (ed.) *Biological Studies of Mental Processes*, pp. 269–87. Cambridge, Mass.: MIT Press.

Chomsky, N. (1968) *Language and Mind.* New York: Harcourt, Brace, Jovanovich.

Darden, L. (1991) *Theory Change in Science: Strategies from Mendelian Genetics.* Oxford: Oxford University Press.

Dreyfus, H. L. (1979) *What Computers Can't Do: The Limits of Artificial Intelligence*, 2nd edition. New York: Harper & Row.

Elman, J. L. (1990) "Finding structure in time." *Cognitive Science* 14, pp. 179–212.

Farrah, M. (1988) "Is visual perception really visual? Overlooked evidence from neuropsychology." *Psychological Review* 95, pp. 307–17.

Fodor, J. A. (1975) *The Language of Thought.* New York: Crowell.

Fodor, J. A. (1987) *Psychosemantics: The Problem of Meaning in the Philosophy of Mind.* Cambridge, Mass.: MIT Press.

Fodor, J. A. and McLaughlin, B. P. (1990) "Connectionism and the problem of systematicity: why Smolensky's solution doesn't work." *Cognition* 35, pp. 183–204.

Fodor, J. A. and Pylyshyn, Z. W. (1988) "Connectionism and cognitive architecture: a critical analysis." *Cognition* 28, pp. 3–71.

Friederici, A. (1992) "Neuropsychological aspects of language development and language use." Paper presented at conference on Biological and Cultural Aspects of Language Development, Zentrum für interdisziplinäre Forschung, Universität Bielefeld.

Harnad, S. (1990) "The symbol grounding problem." *Physical D* 42, pp. 335–46.

Jordan, M. (1986) "Attractor dynamics and parallelism in a connectionist sequential machine." *Proceedings of the Eighth Annual Conference of the Cognitive Science Society.* Hillsdale, NJ: Lawrence Erlbaum.

Kintsch, W. (1974) *The Representation of Meaning in Memory.* Hillsdale, NJ: Lawrence Erlbaum.

Lieberman, P. (1992) "Uniquely human: the evolution of speech, thought, and selfless behavior." Paper presented at conference on Biological and Cultural Aspects of Language Developement, Zentrum für interdisziplinäre Forschung, Universität Bielefeld.

McClelland, J. L. and Kawamoto, A. (1986) "Mechanisms of sentence processing: assigning roles to constituents." In J. L. McClelland, D. E. Rumelhart, and the PDP Research Group, *Parallel Distributed Processing: Explorations in the Microstructure of Cognition, Vol. 2: Psychological and Biological Models.* Cambridge, Mass.: MIT Press.

Miikkulainen, R. and Dyer, M. G. (1989) "A modular neural network architecture for sequential paraphrasing of script-based stories." Technical Report UCLA-A1-89-02, Artificial Intelligence Laboratory, Computer Science Department, University of California, Los Angeles, Los Angeles, CA 90024.

Minsky, M. A. (1975) "A framework for knowledge representation." In P. H. Winston (ed.) *The Psychology of Computer Vision*, pp. 211–77. New York: McGraw Hill.

Minsky, M. A. and Papert, S. (1969) *Perceptrons.* Cambridge, Mass.: MIT Press.

Newell, A. (1989) *Unified Theories of Cognition.* Cambridge, Mass.: Harvard University Press.

Nolfi, S., Elman, J. L., and Parisi, D. (1990) "Learning and evolution in neutral networks." Technical report 9019, Center for Research in Language, University of California, San Diego.

Papert, S. (1988) "One AI or many?" *Daedalus* 117, pp. 1–14.

Pinker, S. and Prince, A. (1988) "On language and connectionism: analysis of a parallel distributed processing model of language acquisition." *Cognition* 28, pp. 73–193.

Plunkett, K. and Marchman, V. (1991) "U-shaped learning and frequency effects in a multi-layered perception: implications for child language acquisition." *Cognition* 38, pp. 1–60.

Rosenblat, R. (1959) *The Principle of Neurodynamics*. New York: Spartan.

Rumelhart, D. E. (1975) "Notes on a schema for stories." In D. G. Bobrow and A. M. Collins (eds) *Representations and Understanding*. New York: Academic.

Rumelhart, D. E. and McClelland, J. L. (1986) "On learning the past tense of English verbs." In J. L. McClelland, D. E. Rumelhart, and the PDP Research Group, *Parallel Distributed Processing: Explorations in the Microstructure of Cognition, Vol. 2: Psychological and Biological Models*, pp. 216–71. Cambridge, Mass.: MIT Press.

Rumelhart, D. E., Hinton, G. E., and Williams, R. J. (1986) "Learning internal representations by error propagation." In D. E. Rumelhart, J. L. McClelland, and the PDP Research Group, *Parallel Distributed Processing: Explorations in the Microstructure of Cognition, Vol. 1: Foundations*, pp. 318–62. Cambridge, Mass.: MIT Press.

Rumelhart, D. E., Smolensky, P., McClelland, J. L., and Hinton, G. E. (1986) "Schemas and sequential thought processes in PDP model." In J. L. McClelland, D. E. Rumelhart, and the PDP Research Group, *Parallel Distributed Processing: Explorations in the Microstructure of Cognition, Vol. 2: Psychological and Biological Models*. Cambridge, Mass.: MIT Press.

Ryle, G. (1949) *The Concept of Mind*. New York: Barnes and Noble.

Schank, R. C. and Abelson, R. (1977) *Scripts, Plans, Goals, and Understanding*. Hillsdale, NJ: Lawrence Erlbaum.

Searle, J. R. (1980) "Minds, brains, and programs." *The Behavioral and Brain Sciences* 78, pp. 720–33.

Smolensky, P. (1988) "On the proper treatment of connectionism." *Behavioral and Brain Sciences* 11, pp. 1–74.

St. John, M. F. and McClelland, J. L. (1990) "Learning and applying contextual constraints in sentence comprehension." *Artificial Intelligence* 46, pp. 217–57.

Touretzky, D. S. (1990) "BoltzCONS: dynamic symbol structures in a connectionist network." *Artificial Intelligence* 46, pp. 5–46.

Touretzky, D. S. and Hinton, G. E. (1988) "A distributed connectionist production system." *Cognitive Science* 12, pp. 423–66.

Vygotsky, L. S. (1962) *Language and Thought*. Cambridge, Mass.: MIT Press.

What Might Cognition Be, If Not Computation?

Tim Van Gelder

What is cognition? Contemporary orthodoxy maintains that it is computation: the mind is a special kind of computer, and cognitive processes are the rule-governed manipulation of internal symbolic representations. This broad idea has dominated the philosophy and the rhetoric of cognitive science – and even, to a large extent, its practice – ever since the field emerged from the postwar cybernetic melee. It has provided the general framework for much of the most well-developed and insightful research into the nature of mental operation. Yet, over the last decade or more, the computational vision has lost much of its luster. Although work within it continues apace, a variety of difficulties and limitations have become increasingly apparent, and researchers across cognitive science and related disciplines have been casting around for other ways to understand cognitive processes. Partly as a result, there are now many research programs which, one way or another, stand opposed to the traditional computational approach; these include connectionism, neurocomputational approaches, ecological psychology, situated robotics, synergetics, and artificial life.

These approaches appear to offer a variety of differing and even conflicting conceptions of the nature of cognition. It is therefore an appropriate time to step back and reconsider the question: What general arguments are there in favor of the idea that cognitive processes must be specifically *computational* in nature? In order properly to address this question, however, we must first address another: What are the alternatives? What *could* cognition be, if it were *not* computation of some form or other?

There are at least two reasons why this second question is important. First, arguments in favor of some broad hypothesis are rarely, if ever, completely general. They tend to be arguments not for *A* alone, but rather in favor of *A* as opposed to *B*, and such arguments often fail to support *A* as opposed to *C*. For example, one of the most powerful early considerations raised in favor of the computational conception of cognition was the idea that intelligent behavior requires sophisticated internal representations. While this clearly supported the computational conception against a behaviorism which eschewed such resources, however, it was no use against a connectionism which helped itself to internal representations, though rather different in kind than the standard symbolic variety.

The second reason we need to ask what alternatives there may be is that one of the most influential arguments in favor of the computational view is the claim that there is simply no alternative. This is sometimes known as the "*what else could it be?*" argument.[1] As Allen Newell[2] recently put it:

> although a small chance exists that we will see a new paradigm emerge for mind, it seems unlikely to me. Basically, there do not seem to be any viable alternatives. This position is not surprising. In lots of sciences we end up where there are no major alternatives around to the particular theories we have. Then, all the interesting kinds of scientific action occur inside the major view. It seems to me that we are getting rather close to that situation with respect to the computational theory of mind. (Ibid., p. 56)

This essay describes a viable alternative. Rather than computers, cognitive systems may be dynamical systems; rather than computation, cognitive processes may be state-space evolution within these very different kinds of systems. It thus disarms the "what else could it be?" argument, and advances the broader project of evaluating competing hypotheses concerning the nature of cognition. Note that achieving these goals does not require decisively establishing that the dynamical hypothesis is true. That would require considerably more space than is available here, and to attempt it now would be hopelessly premature anyway. All that must be done is to describe and motivate the dynamical conception sufficiently to show that it does in fact amount to an alternative conception of cognition, and one which is currently viable, as far as we can now tell.

A fruitful way to present the dynamical conception is to begin with an unusual detour, via the early industrial revolution in England, circa 1788.

1 The Governing Problem

A central engineering challenge for the industrial revolution was to find a source of power that was reliable, smooth, and uniform. In the latter half of the eighteenth century, this had become the problem of translating the oscillating action of the steam piston into the rotating motion of a flywheel. In one of history's most significant technological achievements, Scottish engineer James Watt designed and patented a gearing system for a rotative engine. Steam power was no longer limited to pumping; it could be applied to any machinery that could be driven by a flywheel. The cotton industry was particularly eager to replace its horses and water wheels with the new engines. High-quality spinning and weaving required, however, that the source of power be highly uniform, that is, there should be little or no variation in the speed of revolution of the main driving flywheel. This is a problem, since the speed of the flywheel is affected both by the pressure of the steam from the boilers, and by the total workload being placed on the engine, and these are constantly fluctuating.

It was clear enough how the speed of the flywheel had to be regulated. In the pipe carrying steam from the boiler to the piston there was a throttle valve. The pressure in the piston, and so the speed of the wheel, could be adjusted by turning this valve. To keep engine speed uniform, the throttle valve would have to be turned, at just the right time and by just the right amount, to cope with changes in boiler pressure and workload. How was this to be done? The most obvious solution was to employ a human mechanic to turn the valve as necessary. This had a number of drawbacks, however: mechanics required wages, and were often unable to react sufficiently swiftly and accurately. The industrial revolution thus confronted a second engineering challenge: design a device which can automatically adjust the throttle valve so as to maintain uniform speed of the flywheel despite changes in steam pressure or workload. Such a device is known as a *governor*.

Difficult engineering problems are often best approached by breaking the overall task down into simpler subtasks, continuing the process of decomposition until one can see how to construct devices that can directly implement the various component tasks. In the case of the governing problem, the relevant decomposition seems clear. A change need only be made to the throttle valve if the flywheel is not currently running at the correct speed. Therefore, the first subtask must be to measure the speed of the wheel, and the second subtask must be to calculate whether there is any discrepancy between the desired speed and the actual speed. If there is no discrepancy, no change is needed, for the moment at least. If there is a discrepancy, then the governor must determine by how much the throttle valve should be adjusted to bring the speed of the wheel to the desired level. This will depend, of course, on the current steam pressure, and so the governor must measure the current steam pressure and then on that basis calculate how much to adjust the valve. Finally, of course, the valve must be adjusted. This overall sequence of subtasks must be carried out as often as necessary to keep the speed of the wheel sufficiently close to the desired speed.

A device that can solve the governing problem would have to carry out these various subtasks repeatedly in the correct order, and so we can think of it as obeying the following algorithm:

1 Measure the speed of the flywheel.
2 Compare the actual speed against the desired speed.
3 If there is no discrepancy, return to step 1. Otherwise,
   a. measure the current steam pressure;
   b. calculate the desired alteration in steam pressure;
   c. calculate the necessary throttle valve adjustment.
4 Make the throttle valve adjustment. Return to step 1.

There must be some physical device capable of actually carrying out each of these subtasks, and so we can think of the governor as incorporating a tachometer (for measuring the speed of the wheel); a device for calculating the speed discrepancy; a steam pressure meter; a device for calculating the throttle valve adjustment; a throttle valve adjuster; and some kind of central executive to handle sequencing of operations. This conceptual breakdown of the components of the governor may even correspond to its actual breakdown; that is, each of these components may be implemented by a distinct, dedicated physical device. The engineering problem would then reduce to the (presumably much simpler) problem of constructing the various components and hooking them together so that the whole system functions in a coherent fashion.

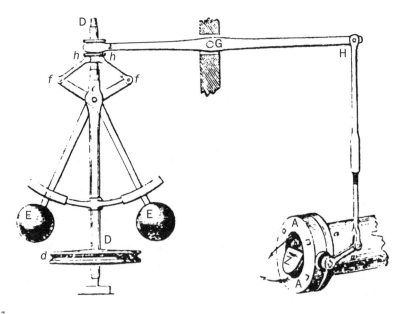

Figure 7.17

Now, as obvious as this approach now seems, it was not the way the governing problem was actually solved. For one thing, it presupposes devices that can swiftly perform some quite complex calculations, and although some simple calculating devices had been invented in the seventeenth century, there was certainly nothing available in the late eighteenth century that could have met the demands of a practical governor.

The real solution, adapted by Watt from existing windmill technology, was much more direct and elegant. It consisted of a vertical spindle geared into the main flywheel so that it rotated at a speed directly dependent upon that of the flywheel itself (see figure 7.17). Attached to the spindle by hinges were two arms, and on the end of each arm was a metal ball. As the spindle turned, centrifugal force drove the balls outward and hence upward. By a clever arrangement, this arm motion was linked directly to the throttle valve. The result was that as the speed of the main wheel increased, the arms raised, closing the valve and restricting the flow of steam; as the speed decreased, the arms fell, opening the valve and allowing more steam to flow. The engine adopted a constant speed, maintained with extraordinary swiftness and smoothness in the presence of large fluctuations in pressure and load.

It is worth emphasizing how remarkably well the centrifugal governor actually performed its task. This device was not just an engineering hack employed because computer technology was unavailable. *Scientific American* claimed in 1858 that an American variant of the basic centrifugal governor, "if not absolutely perfect in its action, is so nearly so, as to leave in our opinion nothing further to be desired."

But why should any of this be of any interest in the philosophy of cognitive science? The answer may become apparent as we examine a little more closely some of the differences between the two governors.

2   Two Kinds of Governors

The two governors described in the previous section are patently different in construction, yet they both solve the same control problem, and we can assume (for purposes of this discussion) that they both solve it sufficiently well. Does it follow that, deep down, they are really the same kind of device, despite superficial differences in construction? Or

are they deeply different, despite their similarity in overt performance?

It is natural to think of the first governor as a computational device; one which, as part of its operation computes some result, namely, the desired change in throttle valve angle. Closer attention reveals that there is in fact a complex group of properties here, a group whose elements are worth teasing apart.

Perhaps the most central of the computational governor's distinctive properties is its dependence on representation. Every aspect of its operation, as outlined above, deals with representations in some manner or other. The very first thing it does is measure its environment (the engine) to obtain a symbolic representation of current engine speed. It then performs a series of operations on this and other representations, resulting in an output representation, a symbolic specification of the alteration to be made in the throttle valve; this representation then causes the valve adjusting mechanism to make the corresponding change. This is why it is appropriately described as computational (now in a somewhat narrower sense): it literally computes the desired change in throttle valve by manipulating symbols according to a schedule of rules. Those symbols, in the context of the device and its situation, have meaning, and the success of the governor in its task is owed to its symbol manipulations being in systematic accord with those meanings. The manipulations are discrete operations which necessarily occur in a determinate sequence; for example, the appropriate change in the throttle valve can only be calculated after the discrepancy between current and desired speeds has been calculated. At the highest level, the whole device operates in a cyclic fashion: it first measures (or "perceives") its environment; it then internally computes an appropriate change in throttle valve; it then effects this change ("acts" on its environment). After the change has been made and given time to affect engine speed, the governor runs through whole the cycle again ... and again. ... Finally, notice that the governor is homuncular in construction. Homuncularity is a special kind of breakdown of a system into parts or components, each of which is responsible for a particular subtask. Homuncular components are ones that, like departments or committees within bureaucracies, interact by communication (that is, by passing meaningful messages). Obviously, the representational and computational nature of the governor is essential to its homuncular construction: if the system as a whole did not operate by manipulating representations, it would not be possible for its components to interact by communication.

These properties – representation, computation, sequential and cyclic operation, and homuncularity – form a mutually interdependent cluster; a device with any one of them will standardly possess others. Now, the Watt centrifugal governor does not exhibit this cluster of properties as a whole, nor any one of them individually. As obvious as this may seem, it deserves a little detailed discussion and argument, since it often meets resistance, and some useful insights can be gained along the way.

Since manipulable representations lie at the heart of the computational picture, the nonrepresentational nature of the centrifugal governor is a good place to start. There is a common and initially quite attractive intuition to the effect that the angle at which the arms are swinging is a representation of the current speed of the engine, and it is because the arms are related in this way to engine speed that the governor is able to control that speed. This intuition is misleading, however; arm angle and engine speed are of course intimately related, but the relationship is not representational. There are a number of powerful arguments favoring this conclusion. They are not based on any unduly restrictive definition of the notion of representation; they go through on pretty much any reasonable characterization, based around a core idea of some state of a system which, by virtue of some general representational scheme, stands in for some further state of affairs, thereby enabling the system to behave appropriately with respect to that state of affairs.[4]

A useful criterion of representation – a reliable way of telling whether a system contains them or not – is to ask whether there is any explanatory utility in describing the system in representational terms. If you really can make substantially more sense of how a system works by concretely describing various identifiable parts or aspects of it as representations in the above sense, that is the best evidence you could have that the system really does contain representations. Conversely, if describing the system as representational lets you explain nothing over and above what you could explain before, why on earth suppose it to be so? Note that very often representational descriptions do yield substantial explanatory benefits. This is certainly true for pocket calculators, and main-

stream cognitive science is premised on the idea that humans and animals are like that as well. A noteworthy fact about standard explanations of how the centrifugal governor works is, however, that they never talk about representations. This was true for the informal description given above, which apparently suffices for most readers; more importantly, it has been true of the much more detailed descriptions offered by those who have actually been in the business of constructing centrifugal governors or analyzing their behavior. Thus, for example, a mechanics manual for construction of governors from the middle of the last century, Maxwell's original dynamical analysis (see below), and contemporary mathematical treatments all describe the arm angle and its role in the operation of the governor in nonrepresentational terms. The reason, one might reasonably conclude, is that the governor contains no representations.

The temptation to treat the arm angle as a representation comes from the informal observation that there is some kind of correlation between arm angle and engine speed; when the engine rotates at a certain speed, the arms will swing at a given angle. Now, supposing for the moment that this is an appropriate way to describe their relationship, it would not follow that the arm angle is a representation. One of the few points of general agreement in the philosophy of cognitive science is that mere correlation does not make something a representation. Virtually everything is correlated, fortuitously or otherwise, with something else; to describe every correlation as representation is to trivialize representation. For the arm angle to count, in the context of the governing system alone, as a representation, we would have to be told what else about it justifies the claim that it is a representation.

But to talk of some kind of correlation between arm angle and engine speed is grossly inadequate, and once this is properly understood, there is simply no incentive to search for this extra ingredient. For a start, notice that the correlation at issue only obtains when the total system has reached its stable equilibrium point, and is immediately disturbed whenever there is some sudden change in, for example, the workload on the engine. At such times, the speed of the engine quickly drops for a short period, while the angle of the arms adjusts only at the relatively slow pace dictated by gravitational acceleration. Yet, even as the arms are falling, more steam is entering the piston, and hence the device is already working;

indeed, these are exactly the times when it is most crucial that the governor work effectively. Consequently, no simple correlation between arm angle and engine speed can be the basis of the operation of the governor.

The fourth and deepest reason for supposing that the centrifugal governor is not representational is that, when we fully understand the relationship between engine speed and arm angle, we see that the notion of representation is just the wrong sort of conceptual tool to apply. There is no doubt that at all times the arm angle is in some interesting way related to the speed of the engine. This is the insight which leads people to suppose that the arm angle is a representation. Yet appropriately close examination of this dependence shows exactly why the relationship cannot be one of representation. For notice that, because the arms are directly linked to the throttle valve, the angle of the arms is at all times determining the amount of steam entering the piston, and hence at all times the speed of the engine depends in some interesting way on the angle of the arms. Thus, arm angle and engine speed are at all times both determined by, and determining, each other's behavior. As we shall see below, there is nothing mysterious about this relationship; it is quite amenable to mathematical description. Yet it is much more subtle and complex than the standard concept of representation can handle, even when construed as broadly as is done here. In order to describe the relationship between arm angle and engine speed, we need a more powerful conceptual framework than mere talk of representations. That framework is the mathematical language of dynamics, and in that language, the two quantities are said to be coupled. The real problem with describing the governor as a representational device, then, is that the relation of representing – something standing in for some other state of affairs – is too simple to capture the actual interaction between the governor and the engine.

If the centrifugal governor is not representational, then it cannot be computational, at least in the specific sense that its processing cannot be a matter of the rule-governed manipulation of symbolic representations. Its noncomputational nature can also be established another way. Not only are there no representations to be manipulated, there are no distinct manipulatings that might count as computational operations. There are no discrete, identifiable steps in which one representation gets transformed into another. Rather, the system's entire operation is smooth and continuous; there is no possibility of nonarbitrarily dividing its changes over time into distinct manipulatings, and no point in trying to do so. From this, it follows that the centrifugal governor is not sequential and not cyclic in its operation in anything like the manner of the computational governor. Since there are no distinct processing steps, there can be no sequence in which those steps occur. There is never any one operation that must occur before another one can take place. Consequently, there is nothing cyclical about its operation. The device has, to be sure, an "input" end (where the spindle is driven by the engine) and an "output" end (the connection to the throttle valve). But the centrifugal governor does not follow a cycle where it first takes a measurement, then computes a throttle valve change, then makes that adjustment, then takes a measurement, and so on. Rather, input, internal activity, and output are all happening continuously and at the very same time, much as a radio is producing music at the very same time as its antenna is receiving signals.

The fact that the centrifugal governor is not sequential or cyclic in any respect points to yet another deep difference between the two kinds of governor. There is an important sense in which time does not matter in the operation of the computational governor. There is, of course, the minimal constraint that the device must control the engine speed adequately, and so individual operations within the device must be sufficiently fast. There is also the constraint that internal operations must happen in the right sequence. Beyond these, however, there is nothing that dictates when each internal operation takes place, how long it takes to carry it out, and how long elapses between each operation. There are only pragmatic implementation considerations: which algorithms to use, what kind of hardware to use to run the algorithms, and so forth. The timing of the internal operations is thus essentially arbitrary relative to that of any wider course of events. It is as if the wheel said to the governing system: "Go away and figure out how much to change the valve to keep me spinning at 100 rpm. I don't care how you do it, how many steps you take, or how long you take over each step, as long as you report back within (say) 10 milliseconds."

In the centrifugal governor, by contrast, there is simply nothing that is temporally unconstrained in this way. There are no occurrences whose timing is arbitrary relative to the operation of the engine. All behavior in the centrifugal governor happens in the very same real time frame as change in the speed of the flywheel. We can sum up the point this way: the two kinds of governor differ fundamentally in their temporality, and the temporality of the centrifugal governor is essentially that of the engine itself.

Finally, it need hardly be labored that the centrifugal governor is not a homuncular system. It has parts, to be sure, and its overall behavior is the direct result of the organized interaction of those parts. The difference is that those parts are not modules interacting by communication; they are not like little bureaucratic agents passing representations among themselves as the system achieves the overall task.

3 Conceptual Frameworks

In the previous section, I argued that the differences in nature between the two governors run much more deeply than the obvious differences in mechanical construction. Not surprisingly, these differences in nature are reflected in the kind of conceptual tools that we must bring to bear if we wish to understand the operation of these devices. That is, the two different governors require very different conceptual frameworks in order to understand how it is that they function as governors, that is, how they manage to control their environment.

In the case of the computational governor, the behavior is captured in all relevant detail by an algorithm, and the general conceptual framework we are bringing to bear is that of mainstream computer science. Computer scientists are typically concerned with what you can achieve by stringing together, in an appropriate order, some set of basic operations: either how best to string them together to achieve some particular goal (programming, theory of algorithms), or what is achievable in principle in this manner (computation theory). So we understand the computational governor as a device capable of carrying out some set of basic operations (measurings, subtractings, etc.), and whose sophisticated overall behavior results from nothing more than the complex sequencing of these basic operations. Note that there is a direct correspondence between elements of the governor (the basic processing steps it goes through) and elements of the algorithm which describes its operation (the basic instructions).

The Watt centrifugal governor, by contrast, cannot be understood this way at all. There is nothing in that device for any algorithm to lock onto. Very different conceptual tools have always been applied to this device. The terms in which it was described above, and indeed by Watt and his peers, were straightforwardly mechanical: rotations, spindles, levers, displacements, forces. Last century, more precise and powerful descriptions became available, but these also have nothing to do with computer science. In 1868, the physicist James Clerk Maxwell[5] made a pioneering extension of the mathematical tools of dynamics to regulating and governing devices. The general approach he established has been standard ever since. Though familiar to physicists and control engineers, it is less so to most cognitive scientists and philosophers of mind, and hence is worth describing in a little detail.

The key feature of the governor's behavior is the angle at which the arms are hanging, for this angle determines how much the throttle value is opened or closed. Therefore, in order to understand the behavior of the governor, we need to understand the basic principles governing how arm angle changes over time. Obviously, the arm angle depends on the speed of the engine; hence we need to understand change in arm angle as a function of engine speed. If we suppose for the moment that the link between the governor and the throttle value is disconnected, then this change is given by the differential equation:

$$\frac{d^2\theta}{dt^2} = (n\omega)^2 \cos\theta \sin\theta - \frac{g}{l}\sin\theta - r\frac{d\theta}{dt}$$

Where θ is the angle of arms, n is a gearing constant, ω is the speed of engine, g is a constant for gravity, l is the length of the arms, and r is a constant of friction at hinges.[6] This nonlinear, second-order differential equation tells us the instantaneous acceleration in arm angle, as a function of what the current arm angle happens to be (designated by the state variable θ), how fast arm angle is currently changing (the derivative of θ with respect to time, $d\theta/dt$) and the current engine speed (ω). In other words, the equation tells us how change in arm angle is changing, depending on the current arm angle, the way it is changing already, and the engine speed. Note that in the system defined by this equation, change over time occurs only in arm angle θ (and its derivatives). The other quantities (ω, n, g, l, and r) are assumed to stay fixed, and are called parameters. The particular values at which the parameters are fixed determine the precise shape of the change in θ. For this reason, the parameter settings are said to fix the dynamics of the system.

This differential equation is perfectly general and highly succinct: it is a way of describing how the governor behaves for any arm angle and engine speed. This generality and succinctness comes at a price, however. If we happen to know what the current arm angle is, how fast it is changing, and what the engine speed is, then from this equation all we can figure out is the current instantaneous acceleration. If we want to know at what angle the arms will be in a half-second, for example, we need to find a solution to the general equation – that is, an equation that tells us what values θ takes as a function of time, which satisfies the differential equation. There are any number of such solutions, corresponding to all the different behavioral trajectories that the governor might exhibit, but these solutions often have important general properties in common; thus, as long as the parameters stay within certain bounds, the arms will always eventually settle into a particular angle of equilibrium for that engine speed; that angle is known as a *point attractor*.

Thus far I have been discussing the governor without taking into account its effect on the engine, and thereby indirectly on itself. Here, the situation gets a little more complicated, but the same mathematical tools apply. Suppose we think of the steam engine itself as a dynamical system governed by a set of differential equations, one of which gives us some derivative of engine speed as a function of current engine speed and a number of other variables and parameters:

$$\frac{d^n\omega}{dt^n} = F(\omega, \ldots, \tau, \ldots)$$

One of these parameters is the current setting of the throttle value, τ, which depends directly on the governor arm angle θ. We can thus think of θ as a parameter of the engine system, just as engine speed ω is a parameter of the governor system. (Alternatively, we can think of the governor and steam engine as comprising a single dynamical system in which both arm angle and engine speed are state variables.) This relationship, known as *coupling*, is particularly interesting and subtle. Changing a parameter of a dynamical system changes its total dynamics (that is, the way its

state variables change their values depending on their current values, across the full range of values they may take). Thus, any change in engine speed, no matter how small, changes not the state of the governor directly, but rather the way the state of the governor *changes*, and any change in arm angle changes the way the state of the engine changes. Again, however, the overall system (coupled engine and governor) settles quickly into a point attractor, that is, engine speed and arm angle remain constant. Indeed, the remarkable thing about this coupled system is that under a wide variety of conditions it always settles swiftly into states at which the engine is running at a particular speed. This is of course exactly what is wanted: coupling the governor to the engine results in the engine running at a constant speed.

In this discussion, two very broad, closely related sets of conceptual resources have (in a modest way) been brought into play. The first is dynamical modeling, that branch of applied mathematics which attempts to describe change in real-world systems by describing the states of the system numerically and then writing equations that capture how these numerical states change over time. The second set of resources is dynamical systems theory, the general study of dynamical systems considered as abstract mathematical structures. Roughly speaking, dynamical modeling attempts to understand natural phenomena as the behavior of real-world realizations of abstract dynamical systems, whereas dynamical systems theory studies the abstract systems themselves. There is no sharp distinction between these two sets of resources, and for our purposes they can be lumped together under the general heading of dynamics.

4 Morals

This discussion of the governing task suggests a number of closely related lessons for cognitive science:

1 Various different kinds of systems, fundamentally different in nature and requiring very different conceptual tools for their understanding, can subserve sophisticated tasks – including interacting with a changing environment – which may initially appear to demand that the system have knowledge of, and reason about, its environment. The governing problem is one

simple example of such a task; it can be solved either by a computational system or by a non-computational dynamical system, the Watt centrifugal governor.

2   In any given case, our sense that a specific cognitive task *must* be subserved by a (generically) computational system may be due to deceptively compelling preconceptions about how systems solving complex tasks must work. Many people are oblivious to the possibility of a noncomputational, dynamical solution to the governing problem, and so all-too-readily assume that it must be solved in a computational manner. Likewise, it may be that the basically computational shape of most mainstream models of cognition results not so much from the nature of cognition itself as it does from the shape of the conceptual equipment that cognitive scientists typically bring to bear in studying cognition.

3   Cognitive systems may in fact be *dynamical* systems, and cognition the behavior of some (noncomputational) dynamical system. Perhaps, that is, cognitive systems are more relevantly similar to the centrifugal governor than they are similar either to the computational governor, or to that more famous exemplar of the broad category of computational systems, the Turing machine.

In what follows, the first and third of these points will be elaborated in just enough detail to substantiate the basic claim of this essay, that there is in fact a currently viable alternative to the computational conception of cognition. As a first step toward doing that, however, I shall briefly describe an example of dynamical research in cognitive science, in order to provide what might seem to be no more than rank speculation with a little healthy flesh.

5   An Example of Dynamical Research

Consider the process of coming to make a decision between a variety of options, each of which has attractions and drawbacks. This is surely a high-level cognitive task, if anything is. Psychologists have done endless experimental studies determining how people choose, and produced many mathematical models attempting to describe and explain their choice behavior. The dominant approach in modeling stems from the classic

expected-utility theory and statistical decision theory as originally developed by John von Neumann and Oskar Morgenstern. The basic idea here is that an agent makes a decision by selecting the option that has the highest expected utility, which is calculated in turn by combining some formal measure of the utility of any given possible outcome with the probability that it will eventuate if the option is chosen. Much of the work within the classical framework is mathematically elegant and provides a useful description of optimal reasoning strategies. As an account of the actual decisions people reach, however, classical utility theory is seriously flawed; human subjects typically deviate from its recommendations in a variety of ways. As a result, many theories incorporating variations on the classical core have been developed, typically relaxing certain of its standard assumptions, with varying degrees of success in matching actual human choice behavior. Nevertheless, virtually all such theories remain subject to some further drawbacks:

1   They do not incorporate any account of the underlying motivations that give rise to the utility that an object or outcome holds at a given time.

2   They conceive of the utilities themselves as static values, and can offer no good account of how and why they might change over time, and why preferences are often inconsistent and inconstant.

3   They offer no serious account of the deliberation process, with its attendant vacillations, inconsistencies, and distress; and they have nothing to say about the relationships that have been uncovered between time spent deliberating and the choices eventually made.

Curiously, these drawbacks appear to have a common theme; they all concern, one way or another, *temporal* aspects of decision making. It is worth asking whether they arise because of some deep structural feature inherent in the whole framework which conceptualizes decision-making behaviour in terms of calculating expected utilities.

Notice that utility-theory based accounts of human decision making ("utility theories") are deeply akin to the computational solution to the governing task. That is, if we take such accounts as not just describing the outcome of decision-making behavior, but also as a guide to the structures and processes that underlie such behavior,[7] then there are basic structural similarities to the computational governor. Thus, utility theories are straightforwardly computational; they are based on static representations of options, utilities, probabilities, and so on, and processing is the algorithmically specifiable internal manipulation of these representations to obtain a final representation of the choice to be made. Consequently, utility theories are strictly sequential; they presuppose some initial temporal stage at which the relevant information about options, likelihoods, and so on, is acquired; a second stage in which expected utilities are calculated; and a third stage at which the choice is effected in actual behavior. And, like the computational governor, they are essentially atemporal; there are no inherent constraints on the timing of the various internal operations with respect to each other or change in the environment.

What we have, in other words, is a model of human cognition which, on one hand, instantiates the same deep structure as the computational governor, and on the other, seems structurally incapable of accounting for certain essentially temporal dimensions of decision-making behavior. At this stage, we might ask: What kind of model of decision-making behavior we would get if, rather, we took the *centrifugal* governor as a prototype? It would be a model with a relatively small number of continuous variables influencing each other in real time. It would be governed by nonlinear differential equations. And it would be a model in which the agent and the choice environment, like the governor and the engine, are tightly interlocked.

It would, in short, be rather like the *motivational oscillatory theory* (MOT) modeling framework described by mathematical psychologist James Townsend.[8] MOT enables modeling of various qualitative properties of the kind of cyclical behaviors that occur when circumstances offer the possibility of satiation of desires arising from more or less permanent motivations; an obvious example is regular eating in response to recurrent natural hunger. It is built around the idea that in such situations, your underlying motivation, transitory desires with regard to the object, distance from the object, and consumption of it are continuously evolving and affecting each other in real time; for example, if your desire for food is high and you are far from it, you will move toward it (that is, z changes), which influences your satiation and so your desire. The framework thus includes variables for the current state of motivation, satiation,

preference, and action (movement), and a set of differential equations describe how these variables change over time as a function of the current state of the system.[9]

MOT stands to utility theories in much the same relation as the centrifugal governor does to the computational governor. In MOT, cognition is not the manipulation of symbols, but rather state-space evolution in a dynamical system. MOT models produce behavior which, if one squints while looking at it, seems like decision making – after all, the agent will make the move which offers the most reward, which in this case means moving toward food if sufficiently hungry. But this is decision making without decisions, so to speak, for there never are in the model any discrete internal occurrences that one could characterize as decisions. In this approach, decision making is better thought of as the behavior of an agent under the influence of the pushes and pulls that emanate from desirable outcomes, undesirable outcomes, and internal desires and motivations; in a quasi-gravitational way, these forces act on the agent with strength varying as a function of distance.

The MOT modeling framework is a special case of a more general (and rather more complex) dynamical framework which Townsend and Jerome Busemeyer[10] call "decision field theory." That framework allows faithful modeling of a wide range of behaviors more easily recognizable as decision making as studied within the traditional research paradigm; indeed, their claim is that decision field theory "covers a broader range of phenomena in greater detail" than classical utility theories, and even goes beyond them by explaining in a natural way several important paradoxes of decision making, such as the so-called "common consequence effect" and "common ratio effect." The important point for immediate purposes, however, is that the general decision field theory works on the same fundamental dynamical principles as MOT. There is thus no question that at least certain aspects of human high-level cognitive functioning can be modeled effectively using dynamical systems of the kind that can be highlighted by reference to the centrifugal governor.

Thus far, all I have done is to use the governing problem as a means of exploring some of the deep differences between computational and noncomputational solutions to complex tasks, drawn out some suggestive implications for cognitive science, and used the Busemeyer and Townsend work to illustrate the claim that high-level cognitive processes can in fact be modeled using noncomputational, dynamical systems. But these moves do not really describe an alternative to the computational conception so much as just gesture in that general direction. What we need now is a sharper characterization of the dynamical conception of cognition, and some reason to suppose that the dynamical conception really is viable as a general alternative.

6 Three Conceptions of Cognitive Systems

At the outset of this essay, I suggested that in order properly to evaluate the computational conception of cognition, we really need to know what viable alternatives there are (if any). Moreover, ideally, we would have some understanding of what the entire range of alternatives is, for only this way can we be sure that the candidates we are entertaining are in fact the most relevant. In other words, we need to be able to see the computational conception and its alternatives as options within a common field which contains all relevant possibilities.

Fortunately, the easiest way to present a sharpened characterization of the dynamical approach is in fact to sketch a common field within which can be situated, if not every conceivable option, at least the current main contenders – the computational, connectionist, and dynamical conceptions. The common field is the "space" of all state-dependent systems. A (concrete) state-dependent system is a set of features or aspects of the world which change over time interdependently, that is, in such a way that the nature of the change in any member of the system at a given time depends on the state of the members of the system at that time.[11] The most famous example from the history of science is, of course, the solar system: the positions and momentums of the sun and various planets are constantly changing in a way that always depends, in a manner captured in the laws first laid down by Newton, on what they happen to be. Another example is the Watt centrifugal governor, as described above: its future arm angles are determined by its current arm angle (and current rate of change of arm angle) according to its differential equation. And for our purposes, another particularly important category is that of computers: systems whose states are basically configurations of symbols and whose state at time $t + 1$ is

always determined according to some rule by their state at time t.

Consider two centrifugal governors that are identical in all relevant physical detail. These devices will respond in exactly the same way to a given engine speed; that is, their arm angles will pass through exactly the same sequences of positions over time. These two concrete systems share an abstract structure in their behavior. This structure can be distilled out, and its general properties studied, independently of any particular mechanical device. This mathematical structure is an example of an abstract state-dependent system. Generally speaking, concrete systems belong to the real world; they exist in time, and have states that change over time. Abstract systems, on the other hand, exist only in the timeless and changeless realm of pure mathematical form. They can be regarded as having three components: a set of entities (for example, the real numbers) constituting "states"; a set (for example, the integers) corresponding to points of "time", and a rule of evolution which pairs states with times to form sequences or trajectories. Thus, even if no centrifugal governor had ever been invented, mathematicians could study the abstract state-dependent system (or rather, family of systems)

$$\left\langle R^2, R, \frac{d^2\theta}{dt^2} = (n\omega)^2 \cos\theta \sin\theta - \frac{g}{l} \sin\theta - r\frac{d\theta}{dt} \right\rangle$$

where $(\theta, d\theta/dt)$ picks out points in R^2 (two dimensional Euclidean space) and the differential equation determines sequences of such points.

Abstract state-dependent systems can be realized ("made real") by particular parts (sets of aspects) of the real, physical world, as when a particular centrifugal governor realizes the abstract system just specified. An abstract system is realized by some part of the world when we can systematically classify its states (for example, by measurement) such that the sequences of states the concrete system undergoes is found to replicate the sequences specified by the abstract model. In fact, in order to count as a system at all, any concrete object must realize some abstract system or other (but not vice versa).

Now, when cognitive scientists come to study cognitive systems, whose basic nature is a matter for empirical investigation, they often proceed by providing models. Generally speaking, a model is another entity which is either better understood already, or somehow more amenable to exploration, and which is similar in relevant respects to the explanatory target. Scientific models are either concrete objects, or – more commonly – abstract mathematical entities; very often, they can be understood as state-dependent systems. If a model is sufficiently good, then we suppose that it somehow captures the nature of the explanatory target. What does this mean? Well, if the model is an abstract state-dependent system, then we suppose that the target system realizes the abstract system, or one relevantly like it. If the model is a concrete system, then we suppose that the model and the target system are systems of the same kind, in the sense that they both realize the same abstract system (or relevantly similar systems). Thus, even when providing a concrete model, what the scientist is really interested in determining is the abstract structure in the behavior of the target system.

There is a vast range of abstract state-dependent systems. Schools of thought which differ over the nature of cognition can be seen as differing over which of these abstract systems are realized by cognitive systems; or, put differently, as differing over *where* in the range of all possible systems the best models of cognition are to be found. So we can understand everyone as agreeing that cognitive systems are state-dependent systems of some kind, but as disagreeing as to which more particular category of state-dependent systems they belong. As will be explained below, this disagreement by no means exhausts the differences between the various schools of thought. Their differing commitments as to the relevant category of systems do, however, constitute a kind of core difference, around which their other differences can be organized.

1 *The computational hypothesis.* In one of the most well-known presentations of the computational conception of cognition, Newell and Herbert Simon[12] hypothesized that "physical symbol systems contain the necessary and sufficient means for general intelligent action," where a physical symbol system is "a machine that produces through time an evolving collection of symbol structures." Bearing this in mind, as well as other well-known characterizations of essentially the same target (for example, John Haugeland's definition of computers as interpreted automatic formal systems, and various paradigm examples of computational systems such as Turing machines, pocket calculators, and classic AI systems such as Newell and Simon's GPS, Terry Winograd's

SHRDLU, and Doug Lenat's CYC)[13] we can characterize the computational subcategory of state-dependent systems as follows: (abstract) computational systems are abstract state-dependent systems whose states are constituted in part by configurations of symbol types, whose time set is the integers (or some equivalent set), and whose rule of evolution specifies sequences of such configurations. A concrete computational system – a computer – is any system realizing an abstract computational system. In order to realize such a system, some chunk of the actual world must realize the sequences of configurations of symbol types specified by the abstract system. This means that, at any given time, it must contain an appropriate configuration of *tokens* of the symbol types, and it must change sequentially from one such configuration to another in accordance with the rule of evolution.

For example, consider a particular abstract Turing machine, Minsky's four symbol, seven head-state universal Turing machine defined by the following machine table:[14]

	1	2	3	4	5	6	7
Y	_L1	_L1	YL3	YL4	YR5	YR6	_R7
_		_L1	YR2	HALT	YR5	YL3	AL3	YR6
1	1L2	AR2	AL3	1L7	AR5	AR6	1R7
A	1L1	YR6	IL4	1L4	1R5	1R6	_R2

This table dictates the specific symbol manipulations that take place in the machine. (Thus, the first square tells us that, if the head is currently in state 1 and the symbol in the cell over which the head is positioned is a "Y", then change that symbol to a "_" (blank), move left, and "change" head state to state 1.) This machine constitutes the abstract state-dependent system, represented

$$< \{< s, p, h >\}, I, F >$$

where each total state of the system at a given time is itself a triple made up of a configuration of symbol types s (corresponding to the contents of the entire tape), a head position with respect to that configuration (p), and a head state (h). The rule of evolution F specifies sequences of total states of the system by specifying what the next (or successor) total state will be given the current total state; hence an appropriate time set for this system is the integers (I). F is essentially equivalent to the machine table above, though the machine table specifies local manipulations rather than transformations from one total state to another. The rule can be obtained by reformulation of the machine table; the result is simple in form but too ungainly to be worth laying out here.[15] Note that a computation, from this perspective, is a sequence of transitions from one total state of the computational system to another; or, in other words, a matter of *touring* the system's symbolic state space.

A general form of the computational hypothesis, then, is that cognitive systems such as people are computational systems in the sense just defined, and that cognition is the behavior of such systems, that is, sequences of configurations of symbols. An alternative form is that for any given cognitive process, the best model of that process will be drawn from the computational subcategory of systems.

Although, as mentioned above, their primary interest is in the abstract structure of the target phenomenon, for various reasons researchers in this approach standardly provide a concrete model: an actual computer programmed so that (hopefully) it realizes the same (or a relevantly similar) abstract computational system as is realized by the cognitive systems under study. If the concrete model appears able to perform actual cognitive tasks in much the way people do, then the hypothesis that people are such systems is supported. One reason to provide a concrete model is that the abstract systems themselves are too complex to be studied by purely analytical means. In order to determine whether the model has the right properties, the theorist lets a concrete version run from a variety of starting points (initial conditions), and observes its behavior. Another reason for providing a concrete model is that, given the complexity of the abstract systems, it is very difficult actually to discover that structure except through an iterative procedure of constructing a concrete model, testing it, making improvements, and so on.

2 *The dynamical hypothesis.* Recall that one suggestion coming out of the discussion of the centrifugal governor was that an interesting alternative to the computational conception is that cognitive systems may be *dynamical* systems. In order to characterize this position as an alternative within the current framework, we need a definition of dynamical systems as a subcategory of state-dependent systems, a definition which is as useful as possible in clarifying differences among various approaches to the study of cognition.

The centrifugal governor is a paradigm example of a dynamical system. Perhaps the most pertinent contrast between it and the computational governor is that the states through which it evolves are not configurations of symbols but rather numerically measurable arm angles and rates of change of arm angle. Generalizing this feature, and, of course, looking over the shoulder at other textbook examples of dynamical systems and the kind of systems that are employed by dynamicists in cognitive science, we can define dynamical systems as state-dependent systems whose states are numerical (in the abstract case, these will be numbers, vectors, etc.; in the concrete case, numerically measurable quantities) and whose rule of evolution specifies sequences of such numerical states.

The rule of evolution in the case of the centrifugal governor was a differential equation. In general, a differential equation is any equation involving a function and one or more of its derivatives; informally, for current purposes, it can be thought of as an equation that tells you the instantaneous rate of change of some aspect of the system as a function of the current state of other aspects of the system. Since our interest is in cognition as processes that occur in time, we assume that the function is one of time (for example, $\theta(t)$) and that any derivative involved is with respect to time (for example, $d\theta/dt$). Because differential equations involve derivatives, they presuppose continuity; hence the "time" set in an abstract dynamical system is standardly R, the real numbers. Dynamical systems governed by differential equations are a particularly interesting and important subcategory, not least because of their central role in the history of science.[16] But dynamical systems in the general sense just defined might also be governed by difference equations, which specify the state of the system at time $t+1$ in terms of its state at time t:

$$s_{t+1} = F(s_t)$$

and determine sequences of states, or trajectories, by repeated application or iteration. The "time" set for abstract systems defined by difference equations is standardly the integers. For example, one of the most-studied families of dynamical systems is that defined by the difference equation known as the logistic map.[17]

$$< R, I, x_{t+1} = ax_t(1 - x_t) >$$

where *a* is a parameter; each possible value of *a* makes the rule different and hence defines a distinct system.

A concrete dynamical system, of course, is any concrete system that realizes an abstract dynamical system. The realization relationship here is quite different than in the computational case, however. Rather than configurations of tokens of symbol types, the concrete dynamical system is made up of quantities changing in a way that corresponds to the numerical sequences specified by the rule of evolution. This correspondence is set up by measuring the quantities, that is, by using some yardstick to assign a number to each quantity at any given point in time. For example, in the case of the centrifugal governor we set up a correspondence between the actual device and the abstract mathematical system by using the "degrees" yardstick to assign a number (for example, 45) to the angle of the arm at each point in time.

The dynamical hypothesis in cognitive science, then, is the exact counterpart to the computational hypothesis: cognitive systems such as people are *dynamical* systems in the sense just laid out, and cognition is state-space evolution in such systems. Alternatively, dynamicists are committed to the claim that the best model of any given cognitive process will turn out to be drawn from the dynamical subcategory of state-dependent systems.

As in the computational case, although the theorist's primary goal is to identify the relevant abstract structure, it is often necessary in practice to explore particular concrete models. It tends to be difficult, however, to set up and explore the behavior of a concrete dynamical system with the right properties. Fortunately, there is a convenient alternative: program (that is, physically configure) a computer (a concrete computational system) so that it produces sequences of symbol-configurations which *represent* points in the state trajectories of the abstract dynamical model under consideration. In such a situation, the computer does not itself constitute a model of the cognitive process, since it does not contain numerically measurable aspects changing over time in the way that aspects of the target system are hypothesized to be changing. That is, the computer does not realize the abstract dynamical model; rather, it *simulates* it.

3 *The connectionist hypothesis*. Broadly speaking, connectionists in cognitive science are those who try to understand cognition using connectionist models, which are typically characterized along something like the following lines:

> Connectionist models are large networks of simple parallel computing elements, each of which carries a numerical *activation value* which it computes from the values of neighboring elements in the network, using some simple numerical formula. The network elements, or *units*, influence each other's values through connections that carry a numerical strength, or *weight*. The influence of each unit *i* on unit *j* is the activation value of unit *i* times the strength of the connection from *i* to *j*.[18]

In order to comprehend connectionism within the current framework, we need to characterize connectionist models as a particular subcategory of state-dependent systems. It is clear from the description just given, however, that all connectionist models are dynamical systems in the sense of the previous section. If the network has *n* neural units, then the state of the system at any given time is just an *n*-dimensional vector of activation values, and the behavior of the network is a sequence of such vectors determined by the equations that update unit activation values. There are, of course, innumerable variations on this basic structure, and much connectionist work consists in exploring such variations in order to find a good model of some particular cognitive phenomenon.

Why then is connectionism not simply the same thing as the dynamical conception? There are two reasons, one discussed in this section, the other in the next. The first is that connectionist models are only a particular subcategory of the wider class of dynamical systems. The core connectionist hypothesis, that the best model of any given cognitive process will be a connectionist model, is thus best regarded as a more specific version of the wider dynamical hypothesis. There are plenty of dynamical systems that are *not* connectionist networks, and plenty of dynamicists in cognitive science who are not connectionists (for example, Busemeyer and Townsend in the work described above).

What then makes a dynamical system a connectionist system? Roughly, it should conform to the Smolensky characterization above. What this means in terms of species of dynamical state-dependent systems can be seen by examining a typical connectionist system, and noting those basic features which contrast with, for example, the centrifugal governor or the MOT model. Connectionist researchers Sven Anderson and Robert Port[19] used the following quite typical abstract connectionist dynamical system as a model of certain aspects of auditory pattern recognition:

$$\left\langle R^n, R, \frac{dy_i}{dt} = -\tau_i y_i(t) + \frac{1}{1 + e - \left(\sum_j w_{ij} y_j + I_i(t) + \theta_i \right)} \right\rangle$$

The network had n neural units, each with a real activation value y_i. Hence its states were points in an n-dimensional space of real numbers, that is, elements of R^n; its time set was R, and its evolution equation was the differential equation given (in schema form) above, which specifies the instantaneous rate of change in each y_i as a function of its current value, a decay parameter (τ_i), the activation of other units (y_i), the connection weights (w_{ij}), any external input (I_i), and a threshold or bias term (θ_i). For current purposes it is not necessary fully to understand this "simple numerical formula" or the behavior of the system as a whole. Of significance here are three closely related properties of connectionist systems that it illustrates. Connectionist systems are typically:

High-dimensional: connectionist networks standardly contain tens, or even hundreds or more, of neural units, each corresponding to a dimension of the state space. This makes them considerably larger in dimension than systems found in many other standard dynamical investigations in cognitive science, other sciences such as physics, and pure mathematics.

Homogeneous: connectionist networks are homogeneous in the sense that they are made up of units that all have basically the same form; or, as Randy Beer has put the point, which are just parametric variations on a common theme. Thus, in the system above, a single equation schema suffices to describe the behavior of every unit in the network, with just the particular parameter values being specific to each unit.

"Neural": connectionist systems are made up of units which are connected with others and which adjust their activation as a function of their total input, that is, of the summed weighted activations of other units. This structural property is reflected in the form of the evolution equations for connectionist models. Thus, the connectionist equation schema above includes the term $\Sigma w_{ij} y_j$ which stands for the summed input to a unit. The defining equations

of connectionist systems always include a term of this general kind.

None of these properties obtains in the case of the centrifugal governor, nor in the case of the MOT model described above; both, therefore, count as good examples of nonconnectionist dynamical systems.

4 *Hypotheses and worldviews.* Thus far, the differences between the computationalist, dynamicist, and connectionist conceptions of cognition have been described simply in terms of differing commitments as to where in the space of state-dependent systems the best models of cognition are likely to be found. Yet each of these approaches is much more richly textured than this implies; they can and should be compared and contrasted in other ways as well.

At this point, the discussion of schools of thought in cognitive science connects with the earlier discussion of the governing problem. Recall that one suggestion emerging there was that cognitive systems may in fact be more similar to the centrifugal governor than to the computational governor. Recall also that the two kinds of governor were found to contrast at two distinct "levels" – that of basic properties (representation, computation, cyclic, etc.) and that of relevant conceptual framework; and that there was a kind of natural fit between these levels. It turns out that this fit is really three-way: if you have a computational state-dependent system, it naturally implements a system that is representational, sequential, cyclic, homuncular, and so on, and the most appropriate conceptual framework to bring to bear on a system that is computational at both these levels is, of course, that of computer science and mainstream computational cognitive science. Computationalists in cognitive science do not merely select models from a particular region of the space of abstract state-dependent systems; they also make strong presuppositions about the basic overall structure of cognitive systems and they use corresponding tools in thinking about how cognitive systems work.

In other words, taking cognitive systems to be state-dependent systems that proceed from one configuration of symbols to the next is part and parcel of a general vision of the nature of cognitive systems. For computationalists, the cognitive system is basically the brain, which is a kind of control unit located inside a body which in turn is located in an external environment. The cognitive system interacts with the outside world via its more direct interaction with the body. Interaction with the environment is handled by sensory and motor transducers, whose function is to translate between the purely physical events in the body and the environment and the symbolic states that are the medium of cognitive processing. The sense organs convert physical stimulation into elementary symbolic representations of events in the body and in the environment, and the motor system converts symbolic specifications of actions into movements of the muscles. Cognitive episodes take place in a cyclic and sequential fashion; first there is sensory input to the cognitive system, then the cognitive system algorithmically manipulates symbols, coming up with an output which then causes movement of the body; then the whole cycle begins again. Internally, the cognitive system has a modular, hierarchical construction; at the highest level, there are modules corresponding to vision, language, planning, and so on, and each of these modules breaks down into simpler modules for more elementary tasks. Each module replicates in basic structure the cognitive system as a whole; thus, they take symbolic representations as inputs, algorithmically manipulate those representations, and deliver a symbolic specification as output. Note that because the cognitive system traffics only in symbolic representations, the human body and the physical environment can be dropped from consideration; it is possible to study the cognitive system as an autonomous, bodiless, and worldless system whose function is to transform input representations into output representations.

In short, in the computational vision, cognitive systems are the computational governor writ large. Of course, there are innumerable variants on the basic computational picture; any one might diverge from the standard picture in some respects, but still remain generically computational in nature (for example, symbolic models that utilize some measure of parallel processing).

The dynamical conception of cognition likewise involves interdependent commitments at three distinct levels, but stands opposed to the computational conception in almost every respect. The core dynamical hypothesis – that the best models of any given cognitive process will specify sequences, not of configurations of symbol types, but rather of numerical states – goes hand in hand with a conception of cognitive systems not as devices that transform symbolic inputs into symbolic outputs but rather as complexes of continuous, simultaneous, and mutually determining change, for which the tools of dynamical modeling and dynamical systems theory are most appropriate. In this vision, the cognitive system is not just the encapsulated brain; rather, since the nervous system, body, and environment are all constantly changing and simultaneously influencing each other, the true cognitive system is a single unified system embracing all three. The cognitive system does not interact with the body and the external world by means of the occasional static symbolic inputs and outputs; rather, interaction between the inner and the outer is best thought of as a matter of coupling, such that both sets of processes continually influencing each other's direction of change. At the level at which the mechanisms are best described, cognitive processing is not sequential and cyclic, for all aspects of the cognitive system are undergoing change all the time. Any sequential character in cognitive performance is the high-level, overall trajectory of change in a system whose rules of evolution specify not sequential change but rather simultaneous mutual co-evolution.

Where does connectionism fit into all this? Perched somewhere in the middle. Recall that connectionist models are dynamical systems, but that there are reasons not simply to assimilate the connectionist and dynamical conceptions. The first was that connectionist models are really a quite specific kind of dynamical system. What we can now add is that although many connectionists are thoroughly dynamical in their general vision of the nature of cognitive systems, many others attempt to combine their connectionist dynamical substrates with an overall conception of the nature of cognitive systems which owes more to the computational worldview. Thus, consider "good old fashioned connectionism": standard, layered-network back-propagation connectionism of the kind that became fashionable with the well-known 1986 volumes. A classic exemplar is David Rumelhart and James McClelland's[20] past-tense learning model. In this kind of work, underlying systems that are basically dynamical in nature are configured so as sequentially to transform static input representations into output representations. They retain much of the basic structure of the computational picture, changing some ingredients (in particular, the nature of the representations) but retaining others. Connectionism of this kind can be regarded as having taken up a half-way house between the computational and dynamical conceptions, combining ingredients from both in what may well turn out to be an unstable mixture. If this is right, we should expect as time goes on that such connectionist models will increasingly give way either to implementations of generically computational conceptions of cognition, or to models that are more thoroughly dynamical.

7 Is the Dynamical Conception Viable?

In order soundly to refute the "what else could it be?" argument, a proposed alternative must be viable, that is, plausible enough that it is reasonably deemed an open empirical question whether the orthodox approach, or the alternative, is the more correct.

One measure of the viability of an approach is whether valuable research can be carried out within its terms. On this measure, the dynamical approach is certainly in good health. Dynamical theories and models have been or are being developed of a very wide range of aspects of cognitive functioning, from (so-called) low-level or peripheral aspects such as brain function, perception, and motor control, to (so-called) central or higher aspects such as language and decision making, and through to related areas such as psychiatry and social psychology. As already mentioned, a good deal of connectionist work falls under the dynamical banner, and this work alone would qualify the dynamical approach as worth taking seriously. But there are nonconnectionist dynamical models of numerous aspects of cognition, and their ranks are swelling. In a number of fields under the broader umbrella of cognitive science, dynamics provides the dominant formal framework within which particular theories and models are developed: these include neural modeling, autonomous agent ("animat") research, ecological psychology, and, increasingly, developmental psychology.[21]

Of course, it is quite possible that a research program is flourishing, and yet there be deep reasons why it will eventually prove inadequate, either in general or with respect to particular aspects of cognition. (Consider behaviorism in its hey-day, for example.) In evaluating the plausibility of an alternative, we should also consider whether there are known *general* considerations that either strongly support – or, perhaps more importantly, stand opposed to – that approach.

Many considerations have been raised in favor of the computational conception of cognition, and, given the deep differences between the approaches, each might appear to constitute an argument against the dynamical alternative. It is not possible adequately to address all (or even any) such arguments here, but I shall briefly comment on two of the most powerful, in order to reveal not the weakness but rather something of the potential of the dynamical approach.

Cognition is distinguished from other kinds of complex natural processes (such as thunderstorms, subatomic processes, etc.) by at least two deep features: on one hand, a dependence on knowledge; and distinctive kinds of complexity, as manifested most clearly in the structural complexity of natural languages. One challenge for cognitive scientists is to understand how a physical system might exhibit these features.

The usual approach to explaining the dependence on knowledge is to suppose that the system contains internal structures that represent that knowledge. Further, the most powerful known way of doing this is to use symbolic representations, manipulated by some computational system. Insofar as the dynamical approach abjures representation completely, or offers some less powerful representational substitute, it may seem doomed.

While the centrifugal governor is clearly a nonrepresentational dynamical system, and while it was argued above that representation figures in a natural cluster of deep features that are jointly characteristic of computational models, in fact there is nothing preventing dynamical systems from incorporating some form of representation; indeed, an exciting feature of the dynamical approach is that it offers opportunities for dramatically reconceiving the nature of representation in cognitive systems, even within a broadly noncomputational framework. A common strategy in dynamical modeling is to assign representational significance to some or all of the state variables or parameters (for example, see the Townsend and Busemeyer decision field theory model described above, or consider a connectionist network in which units stand for features of the domain). While representations of this kind may be exactly what is needed for some cognitive modeling purposes, they do not have the kind of combinatorial structure that is often thought necessary for other aspects of high-level cognition. Within the conceptual repertoire of dynamics, however, there is a vast range of entities and structures that might be harnessed into representational roles; individual state variables and parameters are merely the simplest of them. For example, it is known how to construct representational schemes in which complex contents (such as linguistic structures) are assigned in a recursive manner to points in the state space of a dynamical system, such that the representations form a fractal structure of potentially infinite depth, and such that the behavior of the system can be seen as transforming representations in ways that respect the represented structure.[22] Yet even these methods are doing little more than dipping a toe into the pool of possibilities. For example, representations can be trajectories or attractors of various kinds, or even such exotica as transformations of attractor arrangements as a system's control parameters change.[23] Dynamicists are actively exploring how these and other representational possibilities might be incorporated into cognitive models, without buying the rest of the computational worldview. Consequently, while the dynamical approach is certainly a long way from having actual solutions to most concrete problems of knowledge representation, it clearly holds sufficient promise to maintain its current viability as an alternative.

What, then, about arguments that are based on the distinctive complexity of human cognition? Perhaps the most common, and probably the most persuasive argument of this kind focuses on the complexity of sentences of natural language. It begins from the observation that any proficient language user can understand and produce an effectively unbounded number of distinct sentences, and proceeds to note that these sentences can manifest phenomena such as repeated embedding and dependencies over arbitrarily long distances. If we attempt to describe languages with this kind of complexity by means of a grammar (a finite set of rules for combining a finite set of primitive elements into complex structures), we find they can only be compactly specified by grammars more powerful than so-called "regular" or "phrase-structure" grammars. If we then ask what kind of computational device is capable of following the rules of these grammars to recognize or produce such sentences, the answer is that they can only be implemented on machines more powerful than finite-state machines, such as push-down automata or linear-bounded automata. Therefore, human cognitive systems must be one of these more powerful computational systems.

A crucial question, then, is whether there is reason to believe that dynamical systems, with their numerical states and rules of evolution defined over them, are capable of exhibiting this order of complexity in behavior. The investigation of the "computational" power of dynamical systems, especially in the form of neural networks, is a relatively new topic, but there is already a sizable literature and results available indicate a positive answer. For example, J. P. Crutchfield and K. Young[24] have studied the complexity of the behavior in certain nonlinear dynamical systems "at the edge of chaos" (that is, at settings of parameters close to those settings which would produce genuinely chaotic behavior). If passing through a particular region of the state space is counted as producing a symbol, then allowing the system to run produces a sequence of symbols. It turns out that the complexity of these sequences is such that describing them requires an indexed context-free grammar. This means that the system is producing behavior of the same broad order of complexity as many believe natural language to possess.

Similarly, Jordan Pollack[25] has studied the ability of connectionist dynamical systems to recognize languages (that is, to indicate whether or not any given sequence belongs to the language). In his networks, the system bounces around its numerical state space under the influence of successive inputs corresponding to symbols in the sequence to be recognized. A well-formed sequence is regarded as successfully recognized if the system ends up in a particular region after exposure to the whole sentence, while ending up in some other region for non-well-formed sequences. Pollack (among others) has found that there are networks that can recognize nonregular languages, and in fact can learn to have this ability, via a novel form of induction in language learning, involving bifurcations in system dynamics which occur as the weights in the network gradually change.

More generally, it is clear that nonlinear dynamical systems can not only match but exceed the complexity of behavior of standard computational systems such as Turing machines.[26] Of course, this alone by no means establishes that cognitive systems are, or are more likely to be, dynamical systems than computational systems. It does establish that the dynamical approach is not automatically ruled out by these kinds of complexity considerations. What kind of system humans in fact are is therefore a question only to be resolved by means of patient and detailed modeling.

So much for defenses of viability. What positive reasons are there to think that the dynamical approach is actually on the right track? Again, space does not allow serious treatment of these arguments, but some are at least worth mentioning. In practice, an important part of the appeal of the dynamical approach is that it brings to the study of cognition tools that have proved so extraordinarily successful in so many other areas of science. But what is there about *cognition*, in particular, which suggests that it will be best understood dynamically?

One central fact about natural cognitive processes is that they always happen *in time*, which means not merely that, like any physical process including ordinary digital computation, they occupy some extent of actual time, but that details of *timing* (durations, rates, rhythms, etc.) are critical to a system that operates in a real body and environment. As we saw above, dynamics is all about describing how processes happen in time, while computational models are inherently limited in this respect. Cognition also has other general features for which a dynamical approach appears particularly well-suited. For example, it is a kind of complex behavioral organization that is emergent from the local interactions of very large numbers of (relatively) simple and homogenous elements. It is pervaded by both continuous and discrete forms of change. At every level, it involves multiple, simultaneous, interacting processes. Dynamics is a natural framework for developing theories that account for such features. Further, that within which cognition takes place (the brain, the body, and the environment) demand dynamical tools in their description. A dynamical account of cognition promises to minimize difficulties in understanding how cognition systems are real biological systems in constant, intimate dependence on, or interaction with, their surrounds.[27]

A final way to underpin the viability of the dynamical conception is to place it and the computational conception in broad historical perspective. Computationalism, as cognitive science orthodoxy, amounts to a sophisticated instantiation of the basic outlines of a generically Cartesian picture of the nature of mind. Conversely, the prior grip that this Cartesian picture has on how most people think about mind and cognition makes the computational conception intuitively attractive to many people. This would be unobjectionable if the Cartesian conception was basically sound. But the upshot of philosophical evaluation of the Car-

tesian framework over the last three centuries, and especially this century, is that it seriously misconceives mind and its place in nature. Cognitive scientists tend to suppose that the primary respect in which Descartes was wrong about mind was in subscribing to an interactionist dualism, that is, that doctrine that mind and body are two distinct substances that causally interact with one another. Already by the eighteenth century, however, the inadequacy of this particular aspect of Cartesianism had been repeatedly exposed, and thoroughgoing brain-based materialisms had been espoused by philosophers such as Thomas Hobbes and Julien Offray de La Mettrie. Some of the greatest achievements of twentieth-century philosophy of mind have been the exposing of various other, more subtle, pervasive, and pernicious epistemological and ontological misconceptions inherent in the Cartesian picture. These misconceptions are very often retained even when substance dualism is rejected in favor of some brain-based materialism, such as functionalism in its various guises.

For current purposes, one of the most important anti-Cartesian movements is the one spearheaded by Gilbert Ryle in Anglo-American philosophy and Martin Heidegger in "Continental" philosophy.[28] Its target has been the generically Cartesian idea that mind is an inner realm of representations and processes, and that mind conceived this way is the causal underpinning of our intelligent behavior. This movement comprises at least three major components, all intimately interrelated. The first is a relocating of mind. The Cartesian tradition is mistaken in supposing that mind is an inner entity of any kind, whether mind-stuff, brain states, or whatever. Ontologically, mind is much more a matter of what we *do* within environmental and social possibilities and bounds. Twentieth-century anti-Cartesianism thus draws much of mind out, and in particular outside the skull. The second component is a reconceiving of our fundamental relationship to the world around us. In the Cartesian framework, the basic stance of mind toward the world is one of representing and thinking about it, with occasional, peripheral, causal interaction via perception and action. It has been known since Bishop Berkeley that this framework had fundamental epistemological problems. It has been a more recent achievement to show that escaping these epistemological problems means reconceiving the human agent as essentially embedded in, and skillfully coping with, a changing world; and that representing and thinking about the world is secondary to and dependent upon such embeddedness.[29] The third component is an attack on the supposition that the kind of behaviors we exhibit (such that we are embedded in our world and can be said to have minds) could ever be causally explained utilizing only the generically Cartesian resources of representations, rules, procedures, algorithms, and so on. A fundamental Cartesian mistake is, as Ryle variously put it, to suppose that practice is accounted for by theory; that knowledge how is explained in terms of knowledge that; or that skill is a matter of thought. That is, not only is mind not to be found wholly inside the skull; cognition, the inner causal underpinning of mind, is not to be explained in terms of the basic entities of the Cartesian conception of mind.

My concern here is not to substantiate these claims or the post-Cartesian conception of the person to which they point;[30] it is simply to make the computational conception of cognition seem less than inevitable by pointing out that serious doubt has been cast upon the philosophical framework in which it is embedded. Orthodox computational cognitive science has absorbed some of the important lessons of seventeenth-century reactions to Cartesianism, but so far has remained largely oblivious to the more radical twentieth-century

critiques. Conversely, if we begin with a thoroughly post-Cartesian approach, the dynamical account of cognition will, in many ways, be immediately attractive. The post-Cartesian conception rejects the model of mind as an atemporal representer and, like the dynamical approach to cognition, emphasizes instead the ongoing, real-time interaction of the situated agent with a changing world. The post-Cartesian agent is essentially temporal, since its most basic relationship to the world is one of skillful coping; the dynamical framework is a therefore natural choice since it builds time in right from the very start. The post-Cartesian agent manages to cope with the world without necessarily representing it; a dynamical approach suggests how this might be possible by showing how the internal operation of a system interacting with an external world can be so subtle and complex as to defy description in representational terms – how, in other words, cognition can *transcend* representation. In short, from the philosophical perspective that has managed to overcome the deep structures of the Cartesian worldview, the dynamical approach looks distinctly appealing; the Watt governor is preferable to the Turning machine as a landmark for models of cognition.

Notes

Criticism and advice from numerous people helped improve this paper, but special acknowledgment is due to Robert Port, John Haugeland, and James Townsend. Audiences at the University of Illinois/Chicago, the New Mexico State University, Indiana University, the Australian National University, the University of New South Wales, Princeton University, Lehigh University, and the University of Sküvde were suitably and helpfully critical of earlier versions.

1 This title may have been first used in print by John Haugeland in "The nature and plausibility of cognitivism," *Behavioral and Brain Sciences*, I (1978): 215–26.

2 "Are there alternatives?" in W. Sieg, ed., *Acting and Reflecting* (Boston: Kluwer, 1990).

3 The Watt centrifugal governor for controlling the speed of a steam engine – from J. Farey, *A Treatise on the Steam Engine: Historical, Practical, and Descriptive* (London: Longman, Rees, Orme, Brown, and Green, 1827).

4 This broad characterization is adapted from Haugeland, "Representational Genera," in W. Ramsey, S. P. Stich, D. E. Rumelhart (eds), *Philosophy and Connectionist Theory* (Hillsdale, NJ: Erlbaum, 1991), pp. 61–89.

5 "On governors," *Proceedings of the Royal Society*, XVI (1868): 270–83.

6 Edward Beltrami, *Mathematics for Dynamical Modeling* (Boston: Academic, 1987), p. 163.

7 See, for example, J. W. Payne, J. R. Bettman, and E. J. Johnson, "Adaptive strategy selection in decision making," *Journal of Experimental Psychology: Learning, Memory, Cognition*, XIV (1988): 534–52.

8 See "A neuroconnectionistic formulation of dynamic decision field theory," in D. Vickers and P. L. Smith (eds), *Human Information Processing: Measures, Mechanisms, and Models* (Amsterdam: North Holland, 1988); and "Don't be fazed by PHASER: beginning exploration of a cyclical motivational system," *Behavior Research Methods, Instruments and Computers*, XXIV (1992): 219–27.

9 The equations, with rough and partial translations into English, are:

$$\frac{dx}{dt} = M - m - c$$

(The change in motivation depends on how the current levels of motivation and of consumption compare with some standard level of motivation, M.)

$$\frac{dx}{dt} = \left[\frac{1}{z_1^2 + z_2^2 + a} + 1 \right] \cdot m$$

(The change in one's *preference* for the goal will depend on current motivation and one's distance from the object of preference.)

$$\frac{dc}{dt} = (x + C - c) \cdot \left[\frac{b}{z_1^2 + z_2^2 + r} \right]$$

(The change in consumption will depend on the level of preference, the level of consumption, and the distance from the object of preference.)

$$\frac{dz_1}{dt} = -x \cdot z_1 \qquad \frac{dz_2}{dt} = -x \cdot z_2$$

(How one moves towards or away from the object depends on one's current level of preference for the object.) See "Don't Be Fazed by PHASER" for an accessible and graphic introduction to the behaviors defined by these equations.

10 "Decision field theory: a dynamic-cognitive approach to decision making in an uncertain environment," *Psychological Review*, C (1993): 432–59; an accessible overview is given in "Dynamic representation of decision making," in R. Port and myself, eds, *Mind as Motion: Explorations in the Dynamics of Cognition* (Cambridge: MIT, 1995).

11 The notion of a *state-dependent* system is a generalization of that of a *state-determined* system (see Ross Ashby, *Design for a Brain* (London: Chapman and Hall, 1952)) to allow for systems in which the relation between change and current state is stochastic rather than deterministic.

12 "Computer science as empirical inquiry: symbols and search," in Haugeland, ed., *Mind Design* (Cambridge: MIT, 1981): pp. 35–66, here p.40.

13 See Haugeland, *Artificial Intelligence: The Very Idea* (Cambridge: MIT, 1985); Newell and Simon, "GPS, a program that simulates human thought," in E. A. Feigenbaum and J. Feldman, eds, *Computers and Thought* (New York: McGraw-Hill, 1963); Terry Winograd, *Understanding Natural Language* (New York: Academic, 1972); D. B. Lenat and R. V. Guha, *Building Large Knowledge-based Systems: Representation and Inference in the CYC Project* (Reading, Mass. Addison-Wesley, 1990).

14 See Marvin Minsky, *Computation: Finite and Infinite Machines* (Englewood Cliffs, NJ: Prentice-Hall, 1967).

15 See Marco Giunti, *Computers, Dynamical Systems, Phenomena and the Mind*, Ph.D. Dissertation (Indiana University, 1991).

16 See M. Hirsch, "The dynamical systems approach to differential equations," *Bulletin of the American Mathematical Society*, XI (1984): 1–64.

17 For extensive discussion, see R. L. Devaney, *An Introduction to Chaotic Dynamical Systems* (Menlo Park, CA: Cummings, 1986).

18 Paul Smolensky, "On the proper treatment of connectionism," *Behavioral and Brain Sciences*, XI (1988): 1–74, here p. 1.

19 "A network model of auditory pattern recognition," *Technical Report* XI (Indiana University Cognitive Science Program, 1990).

20 "On learning the past tenses of English verbs," in McClelland and Rumelhart (eds), *Parallel Distributed Processing: Explorations in the Microstructure of Cognition, Volume II: Psychological and Biological Models* (Cambridge, Mass.: MIT, 1986), pp. 216–68.

21 Rather than cite individual examples, I merely list here some overviews or collections that the interested reader can use as a bridge into the extensive realm of dynamical research on cognition. A broad sampling of current research is contained in *Mind as Motion: Explorations in the Dynamics of Cognition*; this book contains guides to a much larger literature. An excellent illustration of the power and scope of dynamical research, in a neural network guise, is S. Grossberg (ed), *Neural Networks and Natural Intelligence* (Cambridge, Mass.: MIT, 1988). R. Serra and G. Zanarini, *Complex Systems and Cognitive Processes* (Berlin: Springer, 1990) presents an overview of a variety of dynamical systems approaches in artificial intelligence research. For the role of dynamics in developmental psychology, see Esther Thelen and Linda Smith, *A Dynamics Systems Approach to the Development of Cognition and Action* (Cambridge, Mass.: MIT, 1993) and *Dynamic Systems in Development: Applications* (Cambridge, Mass.: MIT, 1993). Hermann Haken, *Synergetic Computers and Cognition: A Top-down Approach to Neural Nets* (Berlin: Springer, 1991) provides an introduction and overview to the "synergetic" form of the dynamical approach.

22 See, for example, Jordan Pollack, "Recursive distributed representations," *Artificial Intelligence*, XLVI (1990): 77–105.

23 See, for example, Jean Petitot, "Morphodynamics and attractor syntax," in *Mind as Motion: Explorations in the Dynamics of Cognition*.

24 See J. P. Crutchfield and K. Young, "Computation at the onset of chaos," in W. H. Zurek (ed.), *Complexity, Entropy, and the Physics of Information, SFI Studies in the Sciences of Complexity, Volume VIII* (Reading, Mass: Addison-Wesley, 1990).

25 "The induction of dynamical recognizers," *Machine Learning*, VII (1991): 227–52.

26 See, for example, Hava Siegelmann and Eduardo Sontag, "Analog computation via neural networks,"

Theoretical Computer Science, CXXX, 1 (1994): 331–60.

27 For more detailed treatment of these and other arguments, see Port and my "It's about time: an overview of the dynamical approach to cognition," in *Mind as Motion: Explorations in the Dynamics of Cognition*.

28 See Ryle, *The Concept of Mind* (Chicago: University of Chicago Press, 1984); Heidegger, *Being and Time*, John Macquarrie and Edward Robinson, trans.

(New York: Harper, 1962); and Hubert Dreyfus, *Being-in-the-World: A Commentary on Heidegger's Being and Time, Division 1* (Cambridge, Mass.: MIT, 1991).

29 See Charles Guignon, *Heidegger and the Problem of Knowledge* (Indianapolis: Hackett, 1983).

30 Dreyfus, *What Computers Still Can't Do: A Critique of Artificial Reason* (Cambridge, Mass.: MIT, 1992) is excellent in this regard.

PART IV

The "Language of Thought" Hypothesis

Introduction

In the introductions to previous parts we have alluded to the intentionality, aboutness or representational character of beliefs and desires, their "directedness upon objects." "Brentano's Problem," as Field (1978) calls it, is to explain how a purely physical system or organism can be in states having such features.

A key point to note is that intentional or representational features are *semantical* features: beliefs are *true*, or false; they *entail* or imply other beliefs; they are (it seems) composed of concepts and depend for their truth on a match between their internal structures and the way the world is; in particular their "aboutness" is very naturally regarded as a matter of mental *referring*. Some philosophers, most notably Sellars (1963), Fodor (1975, 1981, this volume), and Field (1978), have taken this semanticity of beliefs as a strong clue to the nature of intentionality itself, suggesting that beliefs and thoughts have their intentionality in virtue of properties they share with other semantically characterized items, the sentences of public natural languages.

Sellars argued (against the Behaviorists) that people's intentional states are indeed inner and are indeed representations. They are physical states of the central nervous system. Nonetheless (*contra* Brentano) they are physical states *that have semantical properties*. They have those properties in virtue of the functional roles they play in their owners' behavioral economies, closely analogous to the inferential roles that corresponding linguistic tokens play in public, entirely physical lan-

guage-games. To put the thesis slightly more formally: for a subject S to think or "occurrently believe" that P is for there to be a state of S's central nervous system that bears the semantic content that P; the state bears that content in much the same sense and in much the same way that a sentence of English or another natural language means that P. Let us call this the Representational Theory of thinking.

It is tempting to gloss the Representational Theory by speaking of a "language of thought," and its leading proponents have given in to that temptation. Fodor argues that representation and the inferential manipulation of representations require a medium of representation, no less in human subjects than in computers. Computers employ machine languages of various kinds; it is reasonable to posit one or more human "machine languages" in which human thought and cognition take place. On the other hand, there are obvious disanalogies between private thought and public speech, so if we are to take Representationalism seriously we must specify, in at least a preliminary way, what similarities are being claimed.

On the Representationalist's behalf, let us say that physically realized thoughts and mental representations are "linguistic" in the following sense: (i) They are composed of parts and are syntactically structured; (ii) their atomic parts refer to or denote things and properties in the world; (iii) their meanings as wholes are determined by the semantical properties of their atomic parts together with the grammatical rules that have generated their overall syntactic structures; (iv) they have truth-conditions, and accordingly truth-values determined by the way the world is; (v) they bear logical relations of entailment or implication to each other. Thus, according to the Representational Theory: human beings have systems of physical states that serve as the elements of a lexicon or vocabulary, and human beings (somehow) physically realize rules that combine strings of those elements into configurations having the complex representational contents that common sense associates with the propositional attitudes. And that is why thoughts and beliefs are true or false just as English sentences are, though a "language of thought" (Mentalese, or Brainese) may differ sharply in its grammar from any natural language.

The arguments for the Representational Theory take a number of impressively different forms (most recently, Fodor 1981, 1987; Lycan 1981, 1993; Devitt and Sterelny 1987, Sterelny (1990)). Though they are formidable, the theory has also come in for a good deal of criticism in recent years, and there too the arguments take a number of impressively different forms. Some leading objections are these:

1 Chisholm (1972) and others have pointed out that the meanings of natural-language sentences are conventional, and so depend on the beliefs and intentions of human speakers. Beliefs and intentions are propositional attitudes. How, then, without circularity or regress, can attitude content be explicated in terms of meaning in the public-linguistic sense?

2 Dennett (1978) argues on several grounds that the idea of "sentences in the head," implemented as inscriptions scrawled in brain chalk upon a brain blackboard, is fanciful, not to say grotesque. (Though his target seems to be a stronger and more outlandish version of Representationalism than the one sketched above.)

3 Churchland and Churchland (this volume) contend that the "language of thought" idea is distinctly *unbiological*. When one recalls that human beings are card-carrying members of the animal kingdom and that we have evolved in the usual way by natural selection, our linguistic abilities, and our cognitive functions on any highly linguisticized account of them, seem to be an evolutionary afterthought at best, and a tiny fragment of the psychology

that actually gets us around in the world. P. S. Churchland (1986) and P. M. Churchland (1986) compellingly depict a brain that works by connectionist networking (see the introduction to Part III above) and by physically hard-wired coordinate transformation, not by digital-computer-like inferential computation over syntactically structured sentences or logical formulas.

4 While public language is (again) conventional in each of several ways, there is obviously nothing social or conventional about the workings of the brain. The "reference" of the alleged language-of-thought's vocabulary items must be natural. The English word "dog" is an arbitrary vocable socially attached by the English-speaking community to dogs, but the Mentalese word for "dog" must somehow be naturally connected to dogs, without human intervention. That is a bit hard to swallow.

5 Fodor himself (1975) argues, with reservations but without shame, that if the "language of thought" story is correct so far, then Mentalese concepts must also be *innate* in a very strong sense: every normal child must naturally and at a very early age develop every concept to which he or she can ever afterward attach a public word of a natural language. (But Devitt and Sterelny (1987) safely block this outrageous implication.)

6 If thoughts and beliefs can be about Margaret Thatcher or about Santa Claus because the neurophysiological states that realize them somehow semantically refer to Margaret Thatcher or Santa Claus, and if the neurophysiological states do their semantical referring in virtue of some physical, functional or otherwise naturalistic property they have, what is that property? We may imagine that our thoughts of Thatcher stand in some historical relation to Thatcher herself, but our thoughts of Santa Claus do not stand in any historical relation to Santa Claus himself, for he does not exist. Nor, in trying to say what it is in virtue of which some neurophysiological state "refers to" anything, may we invoke unexplicated propositional attitudes or representational content, and that proves to be a biting constraint.

The attempt to find any naturalistic property or relation with which noncircularly to identify "mental reference" has come to be called the problem of "psychosemantics," following Fodor (1987, 1990). It admits of several basic lines of approach, reconcilable though distinct in origin.

The first is the "Causal–Historical" approach, in the spirit of Kripke (1972) and Putnam (1975), according to which a mental/brain item M refers to a thing X just in case X figures appropriately in M's etiology. Practitioners of this approach cash the word "appropriately" in any number of hopeful ways; any successful way will have to account for reference to *nonexistent* things, no small task in itself and multiply hard given that one may not, on pain of circularity, invoke unexplicated propositional-attitude contents. See, e.g., Devitt (1981).

A second approach has been called "indicator" semantics (Stampe (1977), Dretske (1981), Stalnaker (1984)). On that view, a mental token refers in virtue of its nomic connection to an environmental entity or state of affairs; for example, a state might be said to mean or represent that P iff its subject nomically could not, or perhaps just would not, be in that state unless P. But the troubles with this view are obvious: First, how then is it possible for a state to *mis*represent? There seems to be no provision for a representation to be false.

At this point "indicator" theorists tried restricting, idealizing, or teleologizing the indicator relation (e.g., Dretske 1981, 1988). But then the problem of misrepresentation turned into what is called the "Disjunction Problem": Suppose a theorist allows that "cow" tokens can be deployed in response to cats rather than cows, but only under non-ideal, abnormal, etc., conditions. Then that theorist must find some independent reason to insist that the token really is a "cow" representation rather than a *cow or cat* representation which is always tokened accurately.

A second objection to "indicator" semantics is that a vast range of beliefs and thoughts are about things other than physically present environmental events: mathematics, literature, philosophy, religion. The "indicator" view gives no hint as to how such topics are just as ready objects of thought as are nearby cows and cats.

More sophisticated teleological theorists (as mentioned in the introduction to Part I) have pushed on in the face of these difficulties. In particular, they seek to secure full generality: human mental states can be about anything, but so far as the external world is concerned, no individual brain state can have more than a few psychobiological functions at a time; how can neurophysiological states be about anything but food, shelter, predators, and opposite-sexed conspecifics? Fodor (1990) was the first teleological theorist to solve that problem – however inadequately, and however quickly he repudiated the details of that solution (in a book (1987) of the sardonically identical title). Millikan (this volume) pursues this approach.

Dissatisfied with teleology, Fodor (1987, this volume) devised a variation on "indicator" semantics that he calls the "asymmetric dependence" theory. His idea is roughly that although both cats and cows can cause "cow" tokens, the "cow" tokens mean *cow* rather than *cat* or *cow or cat* because "there being cat-caused 'cow' tokens depends on there being cow- caused 'cow' tokens, but not the other way around". (Alternately, "'Cow' means *cow* because but that cow tokens carry information about cows, they wouldn't carry information about anything.")

A fifth style of psychosemantics is the "two-factor" approach advocated by Block and others. But its exposition needs some background that will not be developed until the introduction to Part V.

The problem of psychosemantics is further exacerbated by a resounding discovery of Hilary Putnam's, later exploded by Fodor into an enormous and very fruitful literature that goes under the label of "methodological solipsism." Putnam and Fodor's thesis will be taken up in the introduction to Part V below.

Further Reading

For the standard works on intentionality and "Brentano's Problem" previous to the 1970s, see A. Marras (ed.) (1972) *Intentionality, Mind, and Language*, University of Illinois Press.

Defending the "language of thought"
Sellars, W. (1963) *Science, Perception and Reality*, Routledge & Kegan Paul.

Sellars, W. (1981) "Mental events," *Philosophical Studies* 39, 325–45.

"The Rosenthal–Sellars correspondence on intentionality," published in Marras 1972, ibid.

Harman, G. (1973) *Thought*, Princeton University Press.

Rosenberg, J. F. (1974) *Linguistic Representation*, D. Reidel.

Fodor, J. A. (1975) *The Language of Thought*, Harvester Press.

Fodor, J. A. (1981) *Representations*, Bradford Books/ MIT Press.

Field, H. (1978) "Mental representation," *Erkenntnis* 13, 9–61.

Lycan, W. (1981) "Toward a homuncular theory of believing," *Cognition and Brain Theory* 4, 139–59; reprinted with revisions in his *Judgement and Justification*, Cambridge University Press, 1988.

Sterelny, K. (1990) *The Representational Theory of Mind: An Introduction*, Blackwell Publishers.

Lycan, W. (1993) "A deductive argument for the representational theory of thinking," *Mind and Language* 8, 404–22.

Attacking the "language of thought"

Chisholm, R. M. (1972) Contributions to "The Chisholm–Sellars correspondence on intentionality," reprinted in Marras 1972, ibid.

Marras, A. (1973) "On Sellars' linguistic theory of conceptual activity," *Canadian Journal of Philosophy* 2, 471–83.

Dennett, D. C. (1978) "Brain writing and mind reading" and "A cure for the common code," both reprinted in *Brainstorms*, Bradford Books.

Harman, G. (1978) "Is there mental representation?" in *Minnesota Studies in the Philosophy of Science, Vol. IX*, University of Minnesota Press. [Second thoughts.]

Churchland, P. S. (1980) "Language, thought, and information processing," *Noûs* 14, 147–70.

Loar, B. (1983) "Must beliefs be sentences?" in P. Asquith and T. Nickles (eds), *Proceedings of the PSA*, 1982, East Lansing, Michigan. [There are replies by Fodor and Harman.]

Churchland, P. M. (1986) "Some reductive strategies in neurobiology," *Mind* 95, 279–309.

Churchland, P. S. (1986) *Neurophilosophy*, Bradford Books/MIT Press.

Schiffer, S. (1987) *Remnants of Meaning*, Bradford Books / MIT Press.

Stalnaker, R. (1990) "Mental content and linguistic form," *Philosophical Studies* 58, pp. 000–146.

Developing psychosemantics

Kripke, S. (1972) "Naming and necessity," in D. Davidson and G. Harman (eds), *Semantics of Natural Language*, D. Reidel.

Putnam, H. (1975) "The meaning of 'meaning'," in K. Gunderson (ed.), *Minnesota Studies in the Philosophy of Science, Vol. 7: Language, Mind and Knowledge*, University of Minnesota Press. [The Kripke and Putnam essays propose a causal-historical account of public linguistic meaning, but the account has been extrapolated by others to cover the "language of thought" as well.]

Stampe, D. (1977) "*Towards a causal theory of linguistic representation*," in P. French, T. E. Uehling, and H. Wettstein (eds), *Midwest Studies in Philosophy, Vol. II*, University of Minnesota Press.

Loar, Brain (1981) *Mind and Meaning*, Cambridge University Press.

Fodor, J. A. (1986) "Why Paramecia don't have mental representations," in P. French, T. E. Uehling, and H. Weinstein (eds), *Midwest Studies in Philosophy X: Studies in the Philosophy of Mind*, University of Minnesota Press.

Devitt, M. and Sterelny, K. (1987) *Language and Reality*, Bradford Books/MIT Press.

Dretske, F. (1981) *Knowledge and the Flow of Information*, Bradford Books/MIT Press.

Dretske, F. (1988) *Explaining Behavior*, Bradford Books / MIT Press.

Papineau, D. (1988) *Reality and Representation*, Blackwell Publishers.

Cummins, R. (1989) *Meaning and Mental Representation*, Bradford Books/MIT Press.

Fodor, J. A. (1990) "Psychosemantics," in the 1990 first edition of this anthology.

Bilgrami, A. (1992) *Belief and Meaning*, Blackwell Publishers.

Fodor, J. A. (1994) *The Elm and The Expert*, Bradford Books/MIT Press.

Cummins, R. (1996) *Representations, Targets, and Attitudes*, Bradford Books/MIT Press.

8

Defending the "Language of Thought"

Why There Still Has to Be a Language of Thought

Jerry A. Fodor

"But why," Aunty asks with perceptible asperity, "does it have to be a *language*?" Aunty speaks with the voice of the Establishment, and her intransigence is something awful. She is, however, prepared to make certain concessions in the present case. First, she concedes that there are beliefs and desires and that there is a matter of fact about their intentional contents; there's a matter of fact, that is to say, about which proposition the intentional object of a belief or a desire is. Second, Aunty accepts the coherence of physicalism. It may be that believing and desiring will prove to be states of the brain, and if they do that's OK with Aunty. Third, she is prepared to concede that beliefs and desires have causal roles and that overt behavior is typically the effect of complex interactions among these mental causes. (That Aunty was raised as a strict behaviorist goes without saying. But she hasn't been quite the same since the sixties. Which of us has?) In short, Aunty recognizes that psychological explanations need to postulate a network of causally related intentional states. "But why," she asks with perceptible asperity, "does it have to be a *language*?" Or, to put it more succinctly than Aunty often does, what − over and above mere Intentional Realism − does the Language of Thought Hypothesis buy? That is what this discussion is about.[1]

A prior question: What − over and above mere Intentional Realism − does the language of Thought Hypothesis *claim*? Here, I think, the situation is reasonably clear. To begin with, LOT wants to construe propositional-attitude tokens as relations to symbol tokens. According to standard formulations, to believe that *P* is to bear a certain relation to a token of a symbol which means that *P*. (It is generally assumed that tokens of the symbols in question are neural objects, but this assumption won't be urgent in the present discussion.) Now, symbols have intentional contents and their tokens are physical in all the known cases. And − *qua* physical − symbol tokens are the right sorts of things to exhibit causal roles. So there doesn't seem to be anything that LOT wants to claim *so far* that Aunty needs to feel uptight about. What, then, exactly is the issue?

Here's a way to put it. Practically everybody thinks that the *objects* of intentional states are in some way complex: for example, that what you believe when you believe that John is late for dinner is something composite whose elements are − as it might be − the concept of John and the concept of being late for dinner (or − as it might be − John himself and the property of being late for dinner). And, similarly, what you believe when you believe that *P & Q* is also something composite, whose elements are − as it might be − the proposition that *P* and the proposition that *Q*.

But the (putative) complexity of the *intentional object* of a mental state does not, of course, entail the complexity of the mental state itself. It's here

199

that LOT ventures beyond mere Intentional Realism, and it's here that Aunty proposes to get off the bus. LOT claims that *mental states* – and not just their propositional objects – *typically have constituent structure.* So far as I can see, this is the *only* real difference between LOT and the sorts of Intentional Realism that even Aunty admits to be respectable. So a defense of LOT has to be an argument that believing and desiring are typically structured states.

Consider a schematic formulation of LOT that's owing to Stephen Schiffer. There is, in your head, a certain mechanism, an *intention box.* To make the exposition easier, I'll assume that every intention is the intention to make some proposition true. So then, here's how it goes in your head, according to this version of LOT, when you intend to make it true that *P.* What you do is, you put into the intention box a token of a mental symbol that *means* that *P.* And what the box does is, it churns and gurgles and computes and causes and the outcome is that you behave in a way that (*ceteris paribus*) makes it true that *P.* So, for example, suppose I intend to raise my left hand (I intend to make true the proposition that I raise my left hand). Then what I do is, I put in my intention box a token of a mental symbol that means "I raise my left hand." And then, after suitable churning and gurgling and computing and causing, my left hand goes up. (Or it doesn't, in which case the *ceteris paribus* condition must somehow not have been satisfied.) Much the same story would go for my intending to become the next king of France, only in that case the gurgling and churning would continue appreciably longer.

Now, it's important to see that although this is *going* to be a Language of Thought story, it's not a Language of Thought story yet. For so far all we have is what Intentional Realists *qua* Intentional Realists (including Aunty *qua* Aunty) are prepared to admit: viz., that there are mental states that have associated intentional objects (for example, the state of having a symbol that means, "I raise my left hand" in my intention box) and that these mental states that have associated intentional objects also have causal roles (for example, my being in one of these states causes my left hand to rise). What makes the story a Language of Thought story, and not just an Intentional Realist story, is the idea that these mental states that have content also have syntactic structure – constituent structure in particular – that's appropriate to the content that they have. For example, it's compatible with the story I told

above that what I put in the intention box when I intend to raise my left hand is a *rock*; so long as it's a rock that's semantically evaluable. Whereas according to the LOT story, what I put in the intention box has to be something like a *sentence*; in the present case, it has to be a formula which contains, *inter alia*, an expression that denotes me and an expression that denotes my left hand.

Similarly, on the merely Intentional Realist story, what I put in the intention box when I intend to make it true that I raise my left hand and hop on my right foot might also be a rock (though not, of course, the same rock, since the intention to raise one's left hand is not the same as the intention to raise one's left hand and hop on one's right foot). Whereas according to the LOT story, if I intend to raise my left hand and hop on my right foot, I must put into the intention box a formula which contains, *inter alia*, a subexpression that means *I raise my left hand* and a subexpression that means *I hop on my right foot.*

So then, according to the LOT story, these semantically evaluable formulas that get put into intention boxes typically contain semantically evaluable subformulas as constituents; moreover, they can *share* the constituents that they contain, since, presumably, the subexpression that denotes "foot" in "I raise my left foot" is a token of the same type as the subexpression that denotes "foot" in "I raise my right foot." (Similarly, *mutatis mutandis*, the "*P*" that expresses the proposition *P* in the formula "*P*" is a token of the same type as the "*P*" that expresses the proposition *P* in the formula "*P & O*".) If we wanted to be slightly more precise, we could say that the LOT story amounts to the claims that (1) (some) mental formulas have mental formulas as parts; and (2) the parts are "transportable": the same parts can appear in *lots* of mental formulas.

It's important to see – indeed, it generates the issue that this discussion is about – that Intentional Realism doesn't logically require the LOT story; it's no sort of *necessary* truth that only formulas – only things that have syntactic structure – are semantically evaluable. No doubt it's puzzling how a rock (or the state of having a rock in your intention box) could have a propositional object; but then, it's no less puzzling how a formula (or the state of having a formula in your intention box) could have a propositional object. It is, in fact, approximately equally puzzling how *anything* could have a propositional object, which is to say that it's puzzling how Intentional Realism could be true. For better or for worse, however, Aunty and I are both assuming that Intentional Realism *is* true. The question we're arguing about isn't, then, whether mental states have a semantics. Roughly, it's whether they have a syntax. Or, if you prefer, it's whether they have a *combinatorial* semantics: the kind of semantics in which there are (relatively) complex expressions whose content is determined, in some regular way, by the content of their (relatively) simple parts.

So here, to recapitulate, is what the argument is about: Everybody thinks that mental states have intentional objects; everybody thinks that the intentional objects of mental states are characteristically complex – in effect, that propositions have parts; everybody thinks that mental states have causal roles; and, for present purposes at least, everybody is a functionalist, which is to say that we all hold that mental states are individuated, at least in part, by reference to their causal powers. (This is, of course, implicit in the talk about "intention boxes" and the like: To be – metaphorically speaking – in the state of having such-and-such a rock in your intention box is just to be – literally speaking – in a state that is the normal cause of certain sorts of effects and/or the normal effect of certain sorts of causes.) What's at issue, however, is the internal structure of these functionally individuated states. Aunty thinks they have none; only the *intentional objects* of mental states are complex. I think they constitute a language; roughly, the syntactic structure of mental states mirrors the semantic relations among their intentional objects. If it seems to you that this dispute among Intentional Realists is just a domestic squabble, I agree with you. But so was the Trojan War.

In fact, the significance of the issue comes out quite clearly when Aunty turns her hand to cognitive architecture; specifically to the question "What sorts of relations among mental states should a psychological theory recognize?" It is quite natural, given Aunty's philosophical views, for her to think of the mind as a sort of directed graph; the nodes correspond to semantically evaluable mental states, and the paths correspond to the causal connections among these states. To intend, for example, that $P \& Q$ is to be in a state that has a certain pattern of (dispositional) causal relations to the state of intending that P and to the state of intending that Q. (E.g., being in the first state is normally causally sufficient for being in the second and third.) We could diagram this relation in the familiar way illustrated in figure 8.1.

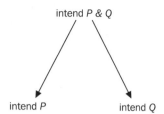

Figure 8.1

NB: in this sort of architecture, the relation between – as it might be – intending that $P \& Q$ and intending that P is a matter of *connectivity* rather than *constituency*. You can see this instantly when you compare what's involved in intending that $P \& Q$ on the LOT story. On the LOT story, intending that $P \& Q$ requires having a sentence in your intention box – or, if you like, in a register or on a tape – one of whose parts is a token of the very same type that's in the intention box when you intend that P, and another of whose parts is a token of the very same type that's in the intention box when you intend that Q.

So, it turns out that the philosophical disagreement about whether there's a Language of Thought corresponds quite closely to the disagreement, current among cognitive scientists, about the appropriate architecture for mental models. If propositional attitudes have internal structure, then we need to acknowledge constituency – as well as causal connectivity – as a fundamental relation among mental states. Analogously, arguments that suggest that mental states have constituent structure *ipso facto* favor Turing/Von Neumann architectures, which can compute in a language whose formulas have transportable parts, as against associative networks, which by definition cannot. It turns out that dear Aunty is, of all things, a New Connectionist Groupie. If she's in trouble, so are they, and for much the same reasons.[2]

In what follows I propose to sketch three reasons for believing that cognitive states – and not just their intentional objects – typically have constituent structure. I don't suppose that these

Figure 8.2

arguments are knockdown; but I do think that, taken together, they ought to convince any Aunty who hasn't a *parti pris*.

First, however, I'd better 'fess up to a metaphysical prejudice that all three arguments assume. I don't believe that there are intentional mechanisms. That is, I don't believe that contents *per se* determine causal roles. In consequence, it's got to be possible to tell the whole story about mental causation (the whole story about the implementation of the generalizations that belief/desire psychologies articulate) *without referring to the intentional properties of the mental states that such generalizations subsume*. Suppose, in particular, that there is something about their causal roles that requires token mental states to be complex. Then I'm assuming that it does *not* suffice to satisfy this requirement that these mental states should have *complex intentional objects*.

This is not, by the way, any sort of epiphenomenalism; or if it is, it's patently a harmless sort. There are plenty of cases in the respectable sciences where a law connects a pair of properties, but where the properties that the law connects *don't figure in the story about how the law is implemented*. So, for example, it's a law, more or less, that tall parents have tall children. And there's a pretty neat story about the mechanisms that implement that law. But the property of *being tall* doesn't figure in the story about the implementation; all that figures in that story is *genetic* properties. You got something that looks like figure 8.2, where the arrows indicate routes of causation.

The moral is that even though it's true that psychological laws generally pick out the mental states that they apply to by specifying the intentional contents of the states, it *doesn't* follow that intentional properties figure in psychological mechanisms.[3] And while I'm prepared to sign on for counterfactual-supporting intentional generalizations, I balk at intentional causation. There are two reasons I can offer to sustain this prejudice (though I suspect that the prejudice goes deeper than the reasons). One of them is technical and the other is metaphysical.

Technical reason: If thoughts have their causal roles in virtue of their contents *per se*, then two thoughts with identical contents ought to be identical in their causal roles. And we know that this is wrong; we know that causal roles *slice things thinner* than contents do. The thought that P, for example, has the same content as the thought that $\sim\sim P$ on any notion of content that I can imagine defend-

ing; but the effects of entertaining these thoughts are nevertheless not guaranteed to be the same. Take a mental life in which the thought that $P \,\&\, (P \to Q)$ immediately and spontaneously gives rise to the thought that Q; there is *no* guarantee that the thought that $\sim\sim P \,\&\, (P \to Q)$ immediately and spontaneously gives rise to the thought that Q in that mental life.

Metaphysical reason: It looks as though intentional properties essentially involve relations between mental states and *merely possible* contingencies. For example, it's plausible that for a thought to have the content THAT SNOW IS BLACK is for that thought to be related, in a certain way, to the possible (but nonactual) state of affairs in which snow is black; viz., it's for the thought to be true just in case that state of affairs obtains. Correspondingly, what distinguishes the content of the thought that snow is black from the content of the thought that grass is blue is differences among the truth values that these thoughts have in possible but nonactual worlds.

Now, the following metaphysical principle strikes me as plausible: the causal powers of a thing are not affected by its relations to merely possible entities; only relations to *actual* entities affect causal powers. It is, for example, a determinant of my causal powers that I am standing on the brink of a high cliff. But it is *not* a determinant of my causal powers that I am standing on the brink of a possible-but-nonactual high cliff; I can't throw myself off one of *those*, however hard I try.[4]

Well, if this metaphysical principle is right, and if it's right that intentional properties essentially involve relations to nonactual objects, then it would follow that intentional properties are not *per se* determinants of causal powers, hence that there are no intentional mechanisms. I admit, however, that that is a fair number of ifs to hang an intuition on.

OK, now for the arguments that mental states, and not just their intentional objects, are structured entities.

1 A Methodological Argument

I don't, generally speaking, much like methodological arguments; who wants to win by a TKO? But in the present case, it seems to me that Aunty is being a little unreasonable even by her own lights. Here is a plausible rule of nondemonstrative inference that I take her to be at risk of breaking:

Principle P: Suppose there is a kind of event c1 of which the normal effect is a kind of event e1; and a kind of event c2 of which the normal effect is a kind of event e2; and a kind of event c3 of which the normal effect is a complex event e1 & e2. Viz.:

c1→e1
c2→e2
c3→e1 & e2

Then, *ceteris paribus*, it is reasonable to infer that c3 is a complex event whose constituents include c1 and c2.

So, for example, suppose there is a kind of event of which the normal effect is a bang and a kind of event of which the normal effect is a stink, and a kind of event of which the normal effect is that kind of a bang and that kind of a stink. Then, according to P, it is *ceteris paribus* reasonable to infer that the third kind of event consists (*inter alia*) of the co-occurence of events of the first two kinds.

You may think that this rule is arbitrary, but I think that it isn't; P is just a special case of a general principle which untendentiously requires us to prefer theories that *minimize accidents*. For, if the etiology of events that are e1 and e2 does not somehow include the etiology of events that are e1 but not e2, then it must be that there are *two* ways of producing e1 events; and the convergence of these (*ex hypothesi*) distinct etiologies upon events of type e1 is, thus far, unexplained. (It won't do, of course, to reply that the convergence of two etiologies is only a very *little* accident. For in principle, the embarrassment *iterates*. Thus, you can imagine a kind of event c4, of which the normal effect is a complex event e1 & e6 & e7; and a kind of event c5, of which the normal effect is a complex event e1 & e10 & e12 . . . etc. And now, if P is flouted, we'll have to tolerate a *four*-way accident. That is, barring P – and all else being equal – we'll have to allow that theories which postulate four kinds of causal histories for e1 events are just as good as theories which postulate only one kind of causal history for e1 events. It is, to put it mildly, hard to square this with the idea that we value our theories for the generalizations they articulate.)

Well, the moral seems clear enough. Let c1 be intending to raise your left hand, and e1 be raising your left hand; let c2 be intending to hop on your right foot, and e2 be hopping on your right foot; let c3 be intending to raise your left hand and hop on your right foot, and e3 be raising your left hand

and hopping on your right foot. Then the choices are: *either* we respect P and hold that events of the c3 type are complexes which have events of type c1 as constituents, *or* we flout P and posit two etiologies for e1 events, the convergence of these etiologies being, thus far, accidental. I repeat that what's at issue here is the complexity of mental events and not merely the complexity of the propositions that are their intentional objects. P is a principle that constrains etiological inferences, and – according to the prejudice previously confessed to – the intentional properties of mental states are *ipso facto not* etiological.

But we're not home yet. There's a way out that Aunty has devised; she is, for all her faults, a devious old dear. Aunty could accept P but deny that (for example) raising your left hand counts as *the same sort of* event on occasions when you *just* raise your left hand as it does on occasions when you raise your left hand while you hop on your right foot. In effect, Aunty can avoid admitting that *intentions* have constituent structure if she's prepared to deny that *behavior* has constituent structure. A principle like P, which governs the assignment of etiologies to complex events, will be vacuously satisfied in psychology if no behaviors are going to count as complex. But Aunty's back is to the wall; she is, for once, constrained by vulgar fact. Behavior does – very often – exhibit constituent structure, and that it does is vital to its explanation, at least as far as anybody knows. Verbal behavior is the paradigm, of course; everything in linguistics, from phonetics to semantics, depends on the fact that verbal forms are put together from recurrent elements; that, for example, [oon] occurs in both "Moon" and "June". But it's not just verbal behavior for whose segmental analysis we have pretty conclusive evidence; indeed, it's not just *human* behavior. It turns out, for one example in a plethora, that bird song is a tidy system of recurrent phrases; we lose "syntactic" generalizations of some elegance if we refuse to so describe it.

To put the point quite generally, psychologists have a use for the distinction between segmented behaviors and what they call "synergisms." (Synergisms are cases where what appear to be behavioral elements are in fact "fused" to one another, so that the whole business functions as a unit; as when a well-practiced pianist plays a fluent arpeggio.) Since it's empirically quite clear that not all behavior is synergistic, it follows that Aunty may not, in aid of her philosophical prejudices, simply help herself to the contrary assumption.

Now we *are* at home. If, as a matter of fact, behavior is often segmented, then principle P requires us to prefer the theory that the causes of behavior are complex over the theory that they aren't, all else being equal. And all else *is* equal to the best of my knowledge. For if Aunty has any *positive* evidence against the LOT story, she has been keeping it very quiet. Which wouldn't be at all like Aunty, I assure you.[5]

Argument 2: Psychological Processes (Why Aunty Can't Have Them for Free)

In the cognitive sciences mental symbols are the rage. Psycholinguists, in particular, often talk in ways that make Aunty simply livid. For example, they say things like this: "When you understand an utterance of a sentence, what you do is construct a *mental representation* [*sic*, emphasis mine] of the sentence that is being uttered. To a first approximation, such a representation is a parsing tree; and this parsing tree specifies the constituent structure of the sentence you're hearing, together with the categories to which its constituents belong. Parsing trees are constructed left to right, bottom to top, with restricted look ahead..." and so forth, depending on the details of the psycholinguist's story. Much the same sort of examples could be culled from the theory of vision (where mental operations are routinely identified with transformations of structural descriptions of scenes) or, indeed, from any other area of recent perceptual psychology.

Philosophical attention is hereby directed to the logical form of such theories. They certainly look to be quantifying over a specified class of mental objects: in the present case, over parsing trees. The usual apparatus of ontological commitment – existential quantifiers, bound variables, and such – is abundantly in evidence. So you might think that Aunty would argue like this: "When I was a girl, ontology was thought to be an *a priori* science; but now I'm told that view is out of fashion. If, therefore, psychologists say that there are mental representations, then I suppose that there probably are. I therefore subscribe to the Language of Thought hypothesis." That is not, however, the way that Aunty actually does argue. Far from it.

Instead, Aunty regards Cognitive Science in much the same light as Sodom, Gomorrah, and Los Angeles. If there is one thing that Aunty believes in her bones, it is the ontological promiscuity of psychologists. So in the present case, although psycholinguists may *talk as though* they were professionally committed to mental representations, Aunty takes that to be *loose* talk. Strictly speaking, she explains, the offending passages can be translated out with no loss to the explanatory/predictive power of psychological theories. Thus, an ontologically profligate psycholinguist may speak of perceptual processes that construct a parsing tree; say, one that represents a certain utterance as consisting of a noun phrase followed by a verb phrase, as in figure 8.3.

But Aunty recognizes no such processes and quantifies over no such trees. What she admits instead are (1) the utterance under perceptual analysis (the "distal" utterance, as I'll henceforth call it) and (2) a mental process which eventuates in the distal utterance being *heard as* consisting of a noun phrase followed by a verb phrase. Notice that this ontologically purified account, though it recognizes mental states with their intentional contents, does not recognize mental representations. Indeed, the point of the proposal is precisely to emphasize as live for Intentional Realists the option of postulating representational mental states and then crying halt. If the translations go through, then the facts which psychologists take to argue for mental representations don't actually do so; and if those facts don't, then maybe nothing does.

Well, but *do* the translations go through? On my view, the answer is that some do and others don't, and that the ones that don't make the case for a Language of Thought. This will take some sorting out.

Mental representations do two jobs in theories that employ them. First, they provide a canonical notation for specifying the intentional contents of mental states. But second, mental symbols constitute domains over which *mental processes* are defined. If you think of a mental process – exten-

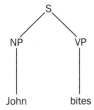

Figure 8.3

sionally, as it were – as a sequence of mental states each specified with reference to its intentional content, then mental representations provide a mechanism for the construction of these sequences; they allow you to get, in a mechanical way, from one such state to the next *by performing operations on the representations.*

Suppose, for example, that this is how it goes with English wh-questions: Such sentences have two constituent structures, one in which the questioned phrase is in the object position, as per figure 8.4, and one in which the questioned phrase is in the subject position, as per figure 8.5. And suppose that the psycholinguistic story is that the perceptual analysis of utterances of such sentences requires the assignment of these constituent structures in, as it might be, reverse order. Well, Aunty can tell *that* story *without* postulating mental representations; *a fortiori* without postulating mental representations that have constituent structure. She does so by talking about *the intentional contents of the hearer's mental states* rather than the mental representations he constructs. "The hearer," Aunty says, "starts out by representing the distal utterance as having "John" in the subject position and a questioned NP in the object position; and he ends up by representing the distal utterance as having these NPs in the reverse configuration. Thus we see that when it's *properly* construed, claims about "perceiving as" are all that talk about mental representation ever really comes to." Says Aunty.

But in saying this, it seems to me that Aunty goes too fast. For what *doesn't* paraphrase out this way is the idea that the hearer gets from one of these representational states to the other *by moving a piece of the parsing tree* (e.g., by moving the piece that represents "who" as a constituent of the type NP2). This untranslated part of the story isn't, notice, about what intentional contents the hearer entertains or the order in which he entertains them. Rather, it's about the mechanisms that mediate

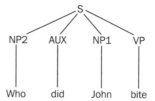

Figure 8.5

the transitions among his intentional states. Roughly, the story says that the mechanism of mental state transitions is *computational*; and if the story's true, then (a) there must *be* parsing trees to define the computations over, and (b) these parsing trees need to have a kind of structure that will sustain talk of moving part of a tree while leaving the rest of it alone. In effect, they need to have constituent structure.

I must now report a quirk of Aunty's that I do not fully understand: she refuses to take seriously the ontological commitments of computational theories of mental processes. This is all the more puzzling because Aunty is usually content to play by the following rule: given a well-evidenced empirical theory, either you endorse the entities that it's committed to or you find a paraphrase that preserves the theory while dispensing with the commitments. Aunty holds that this is simply good deportment for a philosopher; and I, for once, agree with her completely. So, as we've seen, Aunty has a proposal for deontologizing the computational story about which state understanding a sentence is: she proposes to translate talk about trees in the head into talk about hearing utterances under descriptions, and that seems to be all right as far as it goes. But it doesn't go far enough, because the ontological commitments of psychological theories are inherited not just from their account of mental states but also from their account of mental processes and the computational account of mental processes would appear to be *ineliminably* committed to mental representations construed as structured objects.

The moral, I suppose, is that if Aunty won't bite the bullet, she will have to pay the piper. As things stand now, the cost of not having a Language of Thought is not having a theory of thinking. It's a striking fact about the philosophy of mind that we've indulged for the last fifty years or so that it's been quite content to pony up this price. Thus, while an eighteenth-century Empiricist – Hume, say – took it for granted that a theory of cognitive

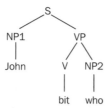

Figure 8.4

processes (specifically, Associationism) would have to be the cornerstone of psychology, modern philosophers – like Wittgenstein and Ryle and Gibson and Aunty – *have* no theory of thought to speak of. I do think this is appalling; how can you seriously hope for a good account of belief if you have no account of belief *fixation*? But I don't think it's entirely surprising. Modern philosophers who haven't been overt behaviorists have quite generally been covert behaviorists. And while a behaviorist can recognize mental states – which he identifies with behavioral dispositions – he has literally no use for cognitive processes such as causal trains of thought. The last thing a behaviorist wants is mental causes ontologically distinct from their behavioral effects.

It may be that Aunty has not quite outgrown the behaviorist legacy of her early training (it's painfully obvious that Wittgenstein, Ryle, and Gibson never did). Anyhow, if you ask her what she's prepared to recognize in place of computational mental processes, she unblushingly replies (I quote): "Unknown Neurological Mechanisms." (I think she may have gotten that from John Searle, whose theory of thinking it closely resembles.) If you then ask her whether it's not sort of unreasonable to prefer no psychology of thought to a computational psychology of thought, she affects a glacial silence. Ah well, there's nothing can be done with Aunty when she stands upon her dignity and strikes an Anglo-Saxon attitude – except to try a different line of argument.

Argument 3: Productivity and Systematicity

The classical argument that mental states are complex adverts to the productivity of the attitudes. There is a (potentially) infinite set of – for example – belief-state types, each with its distinctive intentional object and its distinctive causal role. This is immediately explicable on the assumption that belief states have combinatorial structure; that they are somehow built up out of elements and that the intentional object and causal role of each such state depends on what elements it contains and how they are put together. The LOT story is, of course, a paradigm of this sort of explanation, since it takes believing to involve a relation to a syntactically structured object for which a compositional semantics is assumed.

There is, however, a notorious problem with productivity arguments. The facts of mortality being what they are, not more than a finite part of any mental capacity ever actually gets exploited. So it requires idealization to secure the crucial premise that mental capacities really *are* productive. It is, for example, quite possible to deny the *productivity* of thought even while admitting that people are forever thinking new things. You can imagine a story – vaguely Gibsonian in spirit – according to which cognitive capacity involves a sort of "tuning" of the brain. What happens, on this view, is that you have whatever experiences engender such capacities, and the experiences have Unknown Neurological Effects (these Unknown Neurological Effects being mediated, it goes without saying, by the corresponding Unknown Neurological Mechanisms), and the upshot is that you come to have a very large – but finite – number of, as it were, *independent* mental dispositions. E.g., the disposition to think that the cat is on the mat on some occasions; and the disposition to think that 3 is prime on other occasions; and the disposition to think that secondary qualities are epiphenomenal on other occasions...and so forth. New occasions might thus provoke novel thoughts; and yet the capacity to think wouldn't have to be productive. In principle it could turn out, after a lot of thinking, that your experience catches up with your cognitive capacities so that you actually succeed in thinking everything that you are able to. It's no good saying that you take this consequence to be absurd; I agree with you, but Aunty doesn't.

In short, it needs productivity to establish that thoughts have combinatorial structure, and it needs idealization to establish productivity; so it's open to Somebody who doesn't want to admit productivity (because, for example, She doesn't like LOT) simply to refuse to idealize. This is, no doubt, an empirical issue in the very long run. Scientific idealization is demonstrably appropriate if it eventually leads to theories that are independently well confirmed. But vindication in the very long run is a species of cold comfort; perhaps there's a way to get the goodness out of productivity arguments *without* relying on idealizations that are plausibly viewed as tendentious.

Here's how I propose to argue:

a   There's a certain property that linguistic capacities have in virtue of the fact that natural languages have a combinatorial semantics.

b Thought has this property too.

c So thought too must have a combinational semantics.

Aunty, reading over my shoulder, remarks that this has the form of affirmation of the consequent. So be it; one man's affirmation of the consequent is another man's inference to the best explanation.

The property of linguistic capacities that I have in mind is one that inheres in the ability to understand and produce sentences. That ability is – as I shall say – *systematic*: by which I mean that the ability to produce/understand some of the sentences is *intrinsically* connected to the ability to produce/understand many of the others. You can see the force of this if you compare learning a language the way we really do learn them with learning a language by memorizing an enormous phrase book. The present point isn't that phrase books are finite and can therefore exhaustively describe only nonproductive languages; that's true, but I've sworn off productivity arguments for the duration of this discussion, as explained above. The point that I'm now pushing is that you can learn *any part* of a phrase book *without learning the rest*. Hence, on the phrase book model, it would be perfectly possible to learn that uttering the form of words "Granny's cat is on Uncle Arthur's mat" is the way to say that Granny's cat is on Uncle Arthur's mat, and yet have no idea how to say that it's raining (or, for that matter, how to say that Uncle Arthur's cat is on Granny's mat). I pause to rub this point in. I know – to a first approximation – how to say "Who does his mother love very much?" in Korean; viz., *ki-iy emma-ka nuku-lil mewu saranna-ci*? But since I did get this from a phrase book, it helps me not at all with saying anything else in Korean. In fact, I don't know how to say anything else in Korean; I have just shot my bolt.

Perhaps it's self-evident that the phrase book story must be wrong about language acquisition because a speaker's knowledge of his native language is never like that. You don't, for example, find native speakers who know how to say in English that John loves Mary but don't know how to say in English that Mary loves John. If you did find someone in such a fix, you'd take that as presumptive evidence that he's not a native English speaker but some sort of a tourist. (This is one important reason why it is so misleading to speak of the block/slab game that Wittgenstein describes in paragraph 2 of the *Investigations* as a "complete primitive language"; to think of languages that way is precisely to miss the systematicity of linguistic capacities – to say nothing of their productivity.)

Notice, by the way, that systematicity (again like productivity) is a property of sentences but not of words. The phrase book model really *does* fit what it's like to learn the *vocabulary* of English, since when you learn English vocabulary you acquire a lot of basically *independent* dispositions. So you might perfectly well learn that using the form of words "cat" is the way to refer to cats and yet have no idea that using the form of words "deciduous conifer" is the way to refer to deciduous conifers. My linguist friends tell me that there are languages – unlike English – in which the lexicon, as well as the syntax, is productive. It's candy from babies to predict that a native speaker's mastery of the vocabulary of such a language is always systematic. Productivity and systematicity run together; if you postulate mechanisms adequate to account for the one, then – assuming you're prepared to idealize – you get the other automatically.

What sort of mechanisms? Well, the alternative to the phrase book story about acquisition depends on the idea, more or less standard in the field since Frege, that the sentences of a natural language have a combinatorial semantics (and, *mutatis mutandis*, that the lexicon does in languages where the lexicon is productive). On this view, learning a language is learning a perfectly general procedure for determining the meaning of a sentence from a specification of its syntactic structure together with the meanings of its lexical elements. Linguistic capacities *can't help but* be systematic on this account, because, give or take a bit, the very same combinatorial mechanisms that determine the meaning of any of the sentences determine the meaning of all of the rest.

Notice two things:

First, you can make these points about the systematicity of language without idealizing to astronomical computational capacities. *Productivity* is involved with our ability to understand sentences that are a billion trillion zillion words long. But *systematicity* involves facts that are much nearer home: such facts as the one we mentioned above, that no native speaker comes to understand the form of words "John loves Mary" except as he *also* comes to understand the form of words "Mary loves John." Insofar as there are "theory neutral" data to constrain our speculations about language, this surely ought to count as one of them.

Second, if the systematicity of linguistic capacities turns on sentences having a combinatorial semantics, the fact that sentences have a combinatorial semantics turns on their having constituent structure. You can't construct the meaning of an object out of the meanings of its constituents unless it *has* constituents. The sentences of English wouldn't have a combinatorial semantics if they weren't made out of recurrent words and phrases.

OK, so here's the argument: linguistic capacities are systematic, and that's because sentences have constituent structure. But cognitive capacities are systematic too, and that must be because *thoughts* have constituent structure. But if thoughts have constituent structure, then LOT is true. So I win and Aunty loses. Goody!

I take it that what needs defending here is the idea that cognitive capacities are systematic, *not* the idea that the systematicity of cognitive capacities implies the combinatorial structure of thoughts. I get the second claim for free for want of an alternative account. So then, how do we know that cognitive capacities are systematic?

A fast argument is that cognitive capacities must be *at least* as systematic as linguistic capacities, since the function of language is to express thought. To understand a sentence is to grasp the thought that its utterance standardly conveys; so it wouldn't be possible that everyone who understands the sentence "John loves Mary" also understands the sentence "Mary loves John" if it weren't that everyone who can *think the thought* that John loves Mary can also think the thought that Mary loves John. You can't have it that language expresses thought *and* that language is systematic unless you also have it that thought is as systematic as language is.

And that is quite sufficiently systematic to embarrass Aunty. For, of course, the systematicity of thought does *not* follow from what Aunty is prepared to concede: viz., from mere Intentional Realism. If having the thought that John loves Mary is just being in one Unknown But Semantically Evaluable Neurological Condition, and having the thought that Mary loves John is just being in another Unknown But Semantically Evaluable Neurological Condition, then it is – to put it mildly – not obvious why God couldn't have made a creature that's capable of being in one of these Semantically Evaluable Neurological conditions but not in the other, hence a creature that's capable of thinking one of these thoughts but not

the other. But if it's compatible with Intentional Realism that God could have made such a creature, then Intentional Realism doesn't explain the systematicity of thought; as we've seen, Intentional Realism is exhausted by the claim that there *are* Semantically Evaluable Neurological Conditions.

To put it in a nutshell, what you need to explain the systematicity of thought appears to be Intentional Realism *plus* LOT. LOT says that having a thought is being related to a structured array of representations; and, presumably, to have the thought that John loves Mary is *ipso facto* to have access to the same representations, and the same representational structures, that you need to have the thought that Mary loves John. So *of course* anybody who is in a position to have one of these thoughts is *ipso facto* in a position to have the other. LOT explains the systematicity of thought; mere Intentional Realism doesn't (and neither, for *exactly* the same reasons, does Connectionism). Thus I refute Aunty and her friends!

Four remarks to tidy up:

First: This argument takes it for granted that systematicity is *at least sometimes* a contingent feature of thought; that there are *at least some cases* in which it is logically possible for a creature to be able to entertain one but not the other of two content-related propositions.

I want to remain neutral, however, on the question whether systematicity is *always* a contingent feature of thought. For example, a philosopher who is committed to a strong "inferential role" theory of the individuation of the logical concepts might hold that you can't, in principle, think the thought that (*P* or *Q*) unless you are able to think the thought that *P*. (The argument might be that the ability to infer (*P* or *Q*) from *P* is *constitutive of having* the concept of disjunction.) If this claim is right, then – to that extent – you don't need LOT to explain the systematicity of thoughts which contain the concept OR; it simply *follows from* the fact that you can think that (*P* or *Q*) that you can also think that *P*.

Aunty is, of course, at liberty to try to explain *all* the facts about the systematicity of thought in this sort of way. I wish her joy of it. It seems to me perfectly clear that there could be creatures whose mental capacities constitute a proper subset of our own; creatures whose mental lives – viewed from our perspective – appear to contain gaps. If inferential role semantics denies this, then so much the worse for inferential role semantics.

Second: It is, as always, essential not to confuse the properties of the attitudes with the properties of their objects. I suppose that it *is* necessarily true that the *propositions* are "systematic"; i.e., that if there is the proposition that John loves Mary, then there is also the proposition that Mary loves John. But that necessity is no use to Aunty, since it doesn't explain the systematicity of our capacity to *grasp* the propositions. What LOT explains – and, to repeat, mere Intentional Realism does not – is a piece of our empirical psychology: the *de facto*, contingent connection between our ability to think one thought and our ability to think another.

Third: Many of Aunty's best friends hold that there is something very special about language; that it is only when we come to explaining linguistic capacities that we need the theoretical apparatus that LOT provides. But in fact, we can kick the ladder away: we don't need the systematicity of language to argue for the systematicity of thought. All we need is that it is on the one hand true, and on the other hand not a *necessary* truth, that whoever is able to think that John loves Mary is *ipso facto* able to think that Mary loves John.

Of course, Aunty has the option of arguing the *empirical* hypothesis that thought is systematic only for creatures that speak a language. But think what it would mean for this to be so. It would have to be quite usual to find, for example, animals capable of learning to respond selectively to a situation such that *a R b*, but quite unable to learn to respond selectively to a situation such that *b R a* (so that you could teach the beast to choose the picture with the square larger than the triangle, but you couldn't for the life of you teach it to choose the picture with the triangle larger than the square). I am not into rats and pigeons, but I once had a course in Comp Psych, and I'm prepared to assure you that animal minds aren't, in general, like that.

It may be partly a matter of taste whether you take it that the minds of animals are *productive*; but it's about as empirical as anything can be whether they are systematic. And – by and large – they are.

Fourth: Just a little systematicity of thought will do to make things hard for Aunty, since, as previously remarked, mere Intentional Realism is compatible with there being no systematicity of thought at all. And this is just as well, because although we can be sure that thought is somewhat systematic, we can't perhaps, be sure of just how systematic it is. The point is that if we are unable to think the thought that *P*, then I suppose we

must also be unable to think the thought that we are unable to think the thought that *P*. So it's at least arguable that to the extent that our cognitive capacities are *not* systematic, the fact that they aren't is bound to escape our attention. No doubt this opens up some rather spooky epistemic possibilities; but, as I say, it doesn't matter for the polemical purposes at hand. The fact that there are *any* contingent connections between our capacities for entertaining propositions is remarkable when rightly considered. I know of no account of this fact that isn't tantamount to LOT. And neither does Aunty.

So we've found at least three reasons for preferring LOT to mere Intentional Realism, and three reasons ought to be enough for anybody's Aunty. But is there any general moral to discern? Maybe there's this one:

If you look at the mind from what has recently become the philosopher's favorite point of view, it's the semantic evaluability of mental states that looms large. What's puzzling about the mind is that anything *physical* could have satisfaction conditions, and the polemics that center around Intentional Realism are the ones that this puzzle generates. On the other hand, if you look at the mind from the cognitive psychologist's viewpoint, the main problems are the ones about mental processes. What puzzles psychologists is belief fixation – and, more generally, the contingent, causal relations that hold among states of mind. The characteristic doctrines of modern cognitive psychology (including, notably, the idea that mental processes are computational) are thus largely motivated by problems about mental causation. Not surprisingly, given this divergence of main concerns, it looks to philosophers as though the computational theory of mind is mostly responsive to technical worries about mechanism and implementation; and it looks to psychologists as though Intentional Realism is mostly responsive to metaphysical and ontological worries about the place of content in the natural order. So, deep down, what philosophers and psychologists really want to say to one another is, "Why do you care so much about *that*?"

Now as Uncle Hegel used to enjoy pointing out, the trouble with perspectives is that they are, by definition, *partial* points of view; the Real problems are appreciated only when, in the course of the development of the World Spirit, the limits of perspective come to be transcended. Or, to put it less technically, it helps to be able to see the whole elephant. In the present case, I think the whole elephant looks like this: The key to the nature of cognition is that mental processes preserve semantic properties of mental states; trains of thought, for example, are generally truth preserving, so if you start your thinking with true assumptions you will generally arrive at conclusions that are also true. The central problem about the cognitive mind is to understand how this is so. And my point is that neither the metaphysical concerns that motivate Intentional Realists nor the problems about implementation that motivate cognitive psychologists suffice to frame this issue. To see this issue, you have to look at the problems about content and the problems about process *at the same time*. Thus far has the World Spirit progressed.

If Aunty's said it once, she's said it a hundred times: Children should play nicely together and respect each other's points of view. I do think Aunty's right about that.

Notes

1   Aunty's not the only one who'd like to know; much the same question has been raised by Noam Chomsky, John Searle, Brian Loar, David Israel, Jon Barwise and John Perry, and Tyler Burge, to name just a few. Aunty and I are grateful to all of the above for conversations which led to the present reflections. Also to Ned Block for characteristically perceptive comments on an earlier draft.

2   Do not be misled by the fact that the *node labels* in associative networks are composed of transportable constituents; the labels play no part in the theory. Cf. Fodor (in press) where this point is made twelve thousand eight hundred and fifteen times.

    By the way, it isn't the *associative* part of "associative network" that's at issue here. Classical Associationists – Hume, say – held that mental representations have transportable constituents and, I suppose, a combinatorial semantics: the mental image of a house contains, as proper parts, mental images of proper parts of houses. Hume is therefore on my side of the argument as against Aunty and the New Connectionists. The heart of the issue – to repeat the text – is whether you need *both* constituency *and* connectivity as basic relations among the semantically evaluated mental objects, or whether you can make do with connectivity alone.

3   In *From Folk Psychology to Cognitive Science*, Stich wrings his hands a lot about how I could hold that the counterfactual-supporting generalizations of psychology are uniformly intentional *and also hold* the "solipsistic" principle that mental operations are computational (viz., formal/syntactic). "How is it possible for Fodor to have it both ways, for him to urge *both* that cognitive generalizations apply to mental states in virtue of their content' and that 'only *non*-semantic properties of mental representations can figure in determining which mental operations apply to them'?" (p. 188).

    But there's no contradiction. The vocabulary required to articulate the characteristic laws of a special science is – almost invariably – different from the vocabulary required to articulate the mechanisms by which these laws are sustained, the theory of the mechanisms being pitched – to put it crudely – one level down. So the typical *laws* of psychology are intentional, and the typical *operations* of psychological mechanisms are computational, and everything's fine except that Stich has missed a distinction.

4   Notice – by contrast – that relations to nonactual entities can perfectly well be *constitutive of* causal powers: the solubility of this salt consists in such facts as that if there *were* water here, the salt would dissolve in it. The point in the text, then, is that though relations to nonactual objects can figure in the analysis of a causal power, they can't be among its causal determinants. Nothing – causal powers included – can be an effect of a merely possible cause. (I'm grateful to Georges Rey for helping me to get this sorted out.)

5   It remains open to Aunty to argue in the following relatively subtle sort of way: "All right, so principle P requires that the causes of complex behaviors should themselves be complex. But that still doesn't show that there's a Language of Thought, because the required complex causal objects could be the *propositional attitude states themselves* rather than the (putative) formulas of this (putative) mental language. *Believing that P & Q is itself a complex state* of which the simple parts are the state of believing that P and the state of believing that Q." In effect, Aunty could try conceding that propositional attitudes are *complex* but denying that they are, in the relevant respect, *relational*.

    This, however, will not do. Believing that P is *not* a constituent of, for example, believing that P or Q (or of believing that if P then Q . . . etc.); for it is perfectly possible to believe that P or Q (or that if P then Q) and not to believe that P. For similar reasons the required notion of constituency can't be defined over the *causal roles* of the attitudes, either. Thus, the causal role of believing that P is not a constituent of the causal role of believing that *P* or *Q* since, for example, the effects of believing that it will snow in August are categorically different from – and are not included among – the effects of believing that either it will snow in August or it won't.

See Fodor (1981) *circa* p. 30, and Fodor (1983) where these sorts of observations are parlayed into yet another argument for LOT. (I do wish that Aunty would read my stuff occasionally!)

References

Fodor, J. A. (in press) "Information and association," *Notre Dame Journal of Formal Logic*.

Fodor, J. A. (1981) *Representations*, Bradford Books/ MIT Press.

Fodor, J. A. (1983) "Reply to Brian Loar's 'Must beliefs be sentences?'," in P. Asquith and T. Nickles (eds), *Proceedings of the Philosophy of Science Association for 1982*, East Lansing, Michigan.

Stich, S. P. (1983) *From Folk Psychology to Cognitive Science*, Bradford Books/MIT Press.

9

Attacking the "Language of Thought"

Stalking the Wild Epistemic Engine
Paul M. Churchland and Patricia Smith Churchland

Introduction

In some manner, devolving from Evolution's blind trials and blunders, densely crowded packets of excitable cells inevitably come to represent the world. The conglomeration which is the human brain standardly evolves an awesomely complex world-representation in short order and on the basis of scanty input. Less distinguished beasts such as slugs and sloths are presumed to have world-representations which are less rich, or anyhow, different. It is perhaps salutary here to bear in mind that some animals have sensory detectors where we are stony blind. Pigeons have tiny ferro-magnets for detecting the earth's magnetic field; rattlesnakes have infra-red detectors; electric fish have organs which discern small variations in electric fields, and so on (Bullock et al. 1977). It is remarkable also that in the human case the world-representation evolves, and it evolves not only during the lifetime of one human brain, but across the life-spans of collections of brains. But *how* can a brain be a world-representer? How can brains change so that some of their changes consist in learning about the world? How are representations used by a brain such that the output yields purposive and intelligent behavior?

Broadly speaking, research on the question of how the mind-brain works follows one of two methodological colors. The first is in substantial degree part of the rationalist tradition, emphasizing the linguistic and rule-following aspect of cognition, and is now prominently represented by

cognitive/computational psychology, or by a substantial movement within that field (see especially Fodor 1975, 1978a, 1980; Pylyshyn 1980). The second is naturalistic in character, and is part of the tradition containing such thinkers as de la Mettrie, Darwin, Helmholtz, and Hebb, and is the guiding framework for most neuroscientists and physiological psychologists. On closer inspection, the distinction fuzzes and smears at border spots, but the general contrasts are distinct enough. Which approach, if any, will succeed in treeing answers is an empirical question, and in recent work (see Churchland, P. M. 1979, 1980, 1981, 1981; Churchland, P. S. 1980a, 1980b, 1982) we have argued that the odds favor the naturalistic approach. In this we turn to semantic questions, and confess at the outset to some trepidation. For one thing, semantics is a tar-baby. It is difficult to handle without becoming horribly stuck, and worse, once stuck, it is difficult to avoid the conviction that one is embraced by a verity. Additionally, the bounds of the essay exact brevity of presentation, and there are places where we have had to be ruthlessly synoptic.

Unadorned, the gist of the essay is twofold. The first and more familiar point is that computational psychology should seek a wider conception of cognitive processes than is embodied in a sentential/rationalistic model. The second point, however, is our main concern. We argue that, because computational psychology is quite properly methodologically solipsistic (we will explain what this means shortly), it cannot provide, and should not be expected to provide, a theory of how a representational system *hooks up to the world*. Insofar, it cannot explain how the representing creature survives and flourishes in the environment the creature is struggling to represent. To make good this deficit, we probe the possibilities for a naturalistic strategy. But first, a few remarks are needed on the contrast between naturalistic and non-naturalistic approaches.

Simplifying to the very bone, the dominant hypotheses of the rationalist version of computational psychology are as follows.

(a) The paradigm of the information-bearing or representational state is the propositional attitude, where the object of the attitude (its content) is a sentence.

(b) In cognitive activity, the transitions between representational states are a function of the logical relations holding between the *contents* of those states.

(c) Such representations, and the transitions between them, can thus be modeled or realized in a computer. (Dennett 1978; Fodor 1975; Haugeland 1981; Pylyshyn 1980.)

Church's Thesis says that whatever is computable is Turing computable. Assuming, with some safety, that what the mind-brain does is computable, then it can in principle be simulated by a computer. So what needs to be done is to figure out the program that mimics what cognitive organisms do. Fortunately, goes the rationale (and here is where we start to disagree), the essentially correct basis for devising that program can be found in the propositional attitudes of folk psychology. Extensions and innovations are to be expected, but folk psychological characterizations of the nature of representational structures are fundamentally correct. This is providential, since it means that part of the theory sought is already in hand, and moreover the work can be done without so much as opening a skull and implanting an electrode, and no one has to feed the animals and clean the cages. For those who are squeamish about looking nature in her occasionally noisome face, this assurance of remoteness comes as a relief.

A different strategy inspires the naturalist. The naturalist is moved by two large-scale intellectual visions: the evolution of complex nervous systems from simpler nervous systems, and secondly, the displacement of primitive theories, and their ontologies, by more encompassing and more powerful theories. Enthusiasm for the computational strategy is gutted by the observation that folk theories about the way one or other part of the universe works have typically lost out in the competition for explanatory space. They have, in the light of new theories, been revealed as misdirected, narrow, animistic, and misconceived in varying degrees – despite their having passed as uncontestable truths of common sense for eons. The history of science is littered with the dry bones of folk theory. Even as folk theories of the nature of fire, of the sky, of matter, of heat, of light, of space, of life, of numbers, of weather and climate, of birth and death and disease – even as these folk theories have succumbed to the sharper tooth and fleeter foot of modern biology, chemistry, physics, etc., so it would not be surprising to find folk psychology primitive and inadequate in competition with newer theories of how the mind-brain works. We do not say folk psychology *must* be as inadequate as, say, alchemy, but only that it would be astonishing if it alone amongst folk theories happened to be good enough to survive. A far, far more complex and devious object of wonder than heat or light, the brain is unlikely to have been adequately groped by folk theory in the misty dawn of emerging verbalization (Churchland, P. M. 1981).

In loosening the grip of the bonds of common sense psychology, the naturalist suggests we view ourselves as epistemic engines (Churchland, P. M. 1979). Call an epistemic engine any device that exploits a flow of environmental energy, and the information it already contains, to produce more information, and to guide movement. So far as natural (wild) epistemic engines are concerned, survival depends on a fit between the information contained and the world it inhabits. For example, a simple bottom creature who has sensory neurons which happen to be responsive to changes in magnetic field will not benefit from such responses unless the changes are related to its feeding, fleeing, fighting, or reproducing. The choice of the word "engine" is more apt than might be supposed, since its original meaning is "naive intelligence" or "mother wit," and is the source of "ingenuity." The planet abounds with a wondrous profusion of epistemic engines; building nests and bowers, peeling bark, dipping for termites, hunting wildebeests, and boosting themselves off the planet altogether. The human brain is but one result of Evolution's blind maunderings, and like other creatures with a nervous system, we too are epistemic engines. Accordingly, cast within the naturalist's framework, the problem consists in figuring out how epistemic engines work.

In considering the problem, the naturalists suggest we dethrone language as the model for the structure and dynamics of representational activity generally. Representations – information-bearing structures – did not emerge of a sudden with the evolution of verbally competent animals. As Sellars (1980) remarks, "the generic concept of a representation admits of many gradations between primitive systems and the sophisticated systems on which philosophers tend to concentrate" (p. 15). Whatever information-bearing structures humans enjoy, such structures have evolved from simpler structures, and such structures are part of a *system* of information-bearing structures and structure-manipulating processes. If we want to understand how epistemic engines work, we might have to understand simpler system first, and that means we cannot avoid penetrating the skull, implanting electrodes, and looking nature full in the face.

The Formality Condition: Epistemic Engines are Syntactic Engines

The central insight of computational psychology is that intentional and purposive behaviour is the outcome of mental states and operations, where a mental state is characterized as standing in a relation to a representation, and where mental operations are defined over representations. Computers are formal machines, in the sense that they operate on symbols in virtue of the form of the symbol, not in virtue of how the symbol may be interpreted. As Fodor (1980) puts it:

> Formal operations are the ones that are specified without reference to the semantic properties of representations, as, e.g., truth, reference, or meaning.

The basic point can be put in the following way: the machine goes from one state to another because it is caused to do so. If the machine treats two tokens differently, it will be because they have a formal difference in virtue of which the machine can discriminate them, and if they are formally indistinguishable, then the machine cannot distinguish them either.

The *formality condition* says that cognitive states are type-distinct only if the representations which constitute their objects are formally distinct. Fodor

(1980) has argued that computational psychology should honor the formality condition. This yields the position known as *methodological solipsism*: the causal explanation of cognitive processes must proceed without reference to whatever semantic properties our cognitive states may or may not have. So far as cognitive activity is concerned, semantics enters the picture inessentially, and only insofar as it has a purely syntactic image.

The question spawned by this methodological point is this: what *is* the semantics which has a syntactic image (i.e., syntactic stand-ins for semantic features)? The question is more approachable and familiar if put this way: what criteria of ascribing content to mental states specify content which has a syntactic image, and what criteria fail to specify content?

P. M. Churchland (1979) and Stich (1981) have made the observation that ascription of beliefs and desires (and propositional attitudes generally) to others is fundamentally akin to translation. Stich has developed the point, showing that when I ascribe the belief that p to Trudeau, this is to be analyzed roughly as saying that Trudeau has a mental state which is like the one I would be in were I to sincerely say this: p. Without tarrying over the niceties, notice that the ascription is a *similarity* judgment, and that it makes ineliminable reference to oneself and *to one's own representational system*. In that respect, such ascriptions are observer relative. Deepening his analysis, Stich has then convincingly argued that like similarity judgments in other domains, these similarity judgments (e.g. belief ascriptions) vary as a function of *which* criteria are used, and that a hodge-podge of criteria jockey for position. Depending on purpose, context, and sundry other considerations, one criterion may be preferred to another, and application of different critiera may well give conflicting descriptions of what Trudeau believes. Sometimes sameness of natural-kind-reference is made to count (cf. Putnam 1975), sometimes it is not. Sometimes conceptual role counts more, sometimes ideological similarity counts, sometimes linguistic practice figures in (see Burge 1979), sometimes social practice takes precedence over conceptual role and so on (see Stich 1981, 1983).

The question raised earlier can now be asked again: if computational psychology is to abide by the formality condition, which way of ascribing content will specify content which has a syntactic stand-in? Evidently the criterion which counts beliefs as different if the references are different will not do. Stich's own view, and we concur, is that the best choice will be the criterion which specifies similarity in terms of functional role (which he calls "narrow causal role," and is close enough to "conceptual role"). The point here is this: if what is wanted in computational psychology are generalizations describing routes from input to output, and the only semantic features relevant are features the machine can detect, then the semantic content of representations must be fixed by their conceptual role, by their narrow causal role, because that is what co-varies with differences in a representation's intrinsic formal structure. This kind of content we call *translational content*, since similarity of conceptual role is what faithful translation attempts to capture. Thus, when I ascribe to Trudeau the belief that dopamine is a neurotransmitter, I am saying that Trudeau stands in the belief-relation to a representation that plays the same inferential/causal/functional role in his representational system that "Dopamine is a neurotransmitter" (or its internal analog) plays in *my* representational system (see Sellars 1981). A translational mapping has been postulated between Trudeau and me. Notice that the relation is not between Trudeau's representations and some part of *the world*, but between Trudeau's representational system and *my representational system*.

Already it will be evident that a computational psychology which confines its semantics to conceptual role semantics will depart from folk psychology in certain minor ways. That is surely inevitable and part of what progress here requires. It is also important to mention that Stich argues that for a scientific psychology, even translational content is too much semantics, and that the semantics will have to be laundered out altogether. His worry here stems from the fact that the description of content is observer-relative. He finds this troublesome because for one thing, to the extent that another organism's representational system diverges from mine, I cannot ascribe content (translational content is what we are confined to now) to the other's representations. If the generalizations of cognitive psychology require specification of content, then the generalizations will be incapable of reaching cases where content specification is uncertain. Most obviously this happens in the case of preverbal children, humans from different cultures, humans with brain damage, and as well, the entire animal kingdom. Such a psychology threatens to be a psychology of Me-and-My-Friends, and chartered provincialism is a methodo-

logical *faux pas*. Hence Stich's (1983) attempt to see if computational psychology can define operations over uninterpreted syntactic objects.

We are convinced that computational psychology should honor the formality condition. Moreover, P. M. Churchland (1980) has argued that methodological solipsism can be derived from entirely naturalistic assumptions. The brain is evidently a syntactic engine, for a neuron cannot know the distant causal ancestry or the distant causal destiny of its input and outputs. An activated neuron causes a creature to withdraw into its shell not because such activation represents the presence of a predator – though it may indeed represent this – but because that neuron is connected to the withdrawal muscles, and because its activation is of the kind that causes them to contract. The "semantic" content of the state, if any, is causally irrelevant. What does adherence to the formality condition signify for the research program of computational psychology? It means, for one thing, that questions about how mental states hook up to the world are questions it simply shelves as not within its proper province. On the one hand this is fine, but on the other it means that a completed computational psychology is nonetheless a radically *incomplete* theory of how humans work. For if it has nothing whatsoever to say about how representational systems represent features in the world, it has left out a crucial part of the theory. It is like a genetic theory which tells us how genes produce phenotypic traits, but which throws up its hands on the matter of the relation between the traits and the world the organism inhabits.

Permit us to milk the point briefly. Organisms are syntactic engines. Yet via the nervous system an organism exhibits behavior suited to its surroundings. For example, honey bees remove dead bees from the hive, a herring gull chick pecks its mother's bill for food, a person drinks polio vaccine. Now even if computational psychology did dope out the internal cognitive program, it would still seem miraculous that a person's being in a certain state, syntactically described as say, I-P38, is followed by his drinking polio vaccine, rather than by his moving his rook or by his firing his bazooka or what have you (see also Fodor 1978b). The point is that *it seems* that brains do what they do in virtue of the referents of their assorted states, inasmuch as there is a stupendously good fit between representational systems and the world. Of course if I should specify the content of

Trudeau's state by saying he intends to drink polio vaccine, I am specifying the *translational content*; I am saying his representational system is like mine, and his hooks up to the world the way mine does, *whatever way that is*. And that is no *theory* of the way representational systems hook up to the world.

Perhaps this can all be avoided by saying that mind-brain states have intrinsic of-ness or original intentionality or ultimate aboutness, call it what you will. To some it may seem a plain, observable fact that epistemic engines – fancy ones anyhow – operate on states with intrinsic of-ness. It may even be conjectured that this is what makes mental states mental. The suggestion, to the extent that it makes sense, is unappealing. For one thing, it gives up just when things get particularly exciting. And it is a bit like explaining the nature of life by citing "original vitality," or the nature of neuronal responsiveness by citing "original excitability," and, insofar, it is a way of trumping up a virtue out of being stumped. Moreover, the exasperating thing about "plain facts" is that they often turn out to be neither plain nor factual. Intrinsic of-ness is an illusion, like intrinsic up-ness or intrinsic down-ness.

Another possibility here will be to base a theory of how representations hook up to the world on the idea that the content of a subject's mental state is linked to truth conditions for the content sentence. The analysis of "Jones knows the meaning of p" in terms of "Jones knows what conditions could make p true" is the basis. While there is more to be said here, our simple response is that this strategy will not work because it connects internal aspects of Jones's representational system – namely *his taking* (believing, etc.) the meaning to be thus and such with *his taking* the truth conditions to be thus and such – and hence does not clear the fence and tell us anything whatever about how representational systems hook up to the world.

A more promising suggestion addresses the *causal* relations that hold between representations and states of the world. For example, it may be that a specific representation R_1 occurs in a creature's "perceptual belief-register" only when something in its environment is F. We could thus ascribe "$(\exists x)(Fx)$" as R_1's propositional content. Other representations may be similarly keyed to other aspects of the environment, and we can thus ascribe content to each of them. This would constitute the first stage of a theory which would then go on to develop a wider account of how representations less tightly keyed to the environment

acquire content (see, e.g., Stampe 1972; Dretske 1981).

For perceptually sensitive representations, one can indeed ascribe propositional content in this way, and on the basis of real causal connections with the world. We call content thus ascribed *calibrational content* since this procedure is just another instance of calibrating an instrument of measurement or detection. The states of living creatures do indeed carry systematic information about the environment, in virtue of their law-governed connections with it.

Our enthusiasm for this approach to how representations hook up to the world must be dimmed, however, by three serious problems. First, it is very difficult to see how to make the jump from ascribing content to representations at the sensory periphery to assigning content to the dominant mass of representations not so conveniently tied to aspects of the environment.

Second, and more important, even for perceptual representations, the contents assigned in this way are not identical with their more familiar translation contents. These two kinds of content can and often do diverge radically. A Neanderthal's representation might have the calibrational content, "The wind is producing atmospheric resonances," but have the translational content, "The Storm god is howling at us." An Aristotelean's representation might have the calibrational content, "The planet beneath me has a non-zero angular momentum," but have the translational content, "The crystal sphere above me is turning." A Puritan's representation might have the calibrational content, "She is epileptic," but have the translational content, "She is possessed by Satan." In general, calibrational contents do nothing to reflect how the representing creature happens to conceive of things. This approach fails to explicate how our familiar *translational* contents hook up with the world.

Third, and equally important, the dynamic or functional properties of a representation, within one's overall cognitive economy, are not determined by its calibrational content, but by its "formal" or "structural" properties. An account of how a representational system hooks up to the world should make some contact with the system's behavior over time, but calibrational content is dynamically irrelevant. This is just the thesis of methodological solipsism showing itself again.

In sum, a causal approach must disappoint some of our original expectations regarding a general account of how epistemic, representing creatures "hook up" to the world. But we should not despair immediately. Perhaps it is those original expectations that need schooling. Perhaps we should not expect that all epistemic creatures must have representations that are somehow like sentences, and that a satisfactory account of the important hook-ups must address the relation between singular terms and things, the relation between predicates and properties, and the relation between sentences and states of affairs. Perhaps we should not expect this even for ourselves. Let us explore the problem without making these assumptions.

Neuroscience: Calibrational and Computational

In its bones, neuroscience is also solipsistic; it must honor the formality condition. How then does neuroscience expect to deal with the question of how representational systems hook up to the world? For if it sees the brain as syntactic, then it does seem miraculous that a sequence of events in a herring gull's brain results in its asking for food, or a sequence in a bee's brain results in its taking a particular flight path to nectar-heavy blossoms.

In the case of such animals as bees and slugs, we confidently expect to be able to defrock the mystery by giving evolutionary/neurobiological/neuroethological explanations. The idea is to treat the organism's nervous system as something which evolution calibrates (i.e., as something which, by random mutation and on random selection, is tuned to measure, via the excitable cells, certain features in the environment). When responses involved in measuring such features happen to be linked to motor responses relevant to survival, then the probability is enhanced that the organism's genes will be passed on. Bees are "calibrated," by natural selection, to detect oleic acid, and are tuned to produce a motor sequence which results in their lugging its source (dead bees) out of the hive. Herring gull chicks are calibrated to detect small red spots on moving objects (this picks out their mother's bill), and are tuned to peck at them, which results in their being fed. The neuronal story of how this works is not beyond us, and for simple creatures ascription of calibrational content to states of their humble nervous system is well underway.

What then of complex organisms such as humans? The story which defrocks the miracle in the case of the bees and the herring gull is relatively simple, in that their behavior is essentially fixed-action-pattern stuff. The story which defrocks the miracle in the case of persons will be much harder to ferret out. For here the enigma ramifies because these organisms are spectacular learners. Seemingly, they learn about the world, though in the syntactic spirit one would say, roughly, that their syntactic organization is fancied up with the end result that they do new things, where some of those things enhance their survival chances. The miracle now is how the syntactic engine ends up as advantageously tuned as it is. How is it that the fancy organisms "make hypotheses die in their stead"? And learn to become increasingly proficient at doing so? How is it that a syntactic engine evolved so that certain of its states seem to have intentionality? How can a person come to have an I-P38 state such that this state typically causes it to drink polio vaccine? Not, evidently, in virtue of evolution's *directly* selecting for a match between I-P38 states and drinking polio vaccine but rather, one guesses, in virtue of evolution's selecting "learner–planner rigmaroles." If the person acquires new concepts, that is, of course, a syntactical affair, but what is the causal story in virtue of which it can invent concepts which surpass the old when what is on the receiving end of the predictions are events in the world? The miracle is that the organism has become so "well-tuned" that it seems to have *an evolving world-picture*, rather as though the organism has tricked up an analog of the evolutionary process itself.

Here then the job for neurobiology and neuroethology is Herculean, but the bets are that the story for complex organisms will build on the more basic story of calibrational semantics for simpler organisms, following the steps of evolution itself. The backbone of what we are calling *calibrational content* is the observation that there are reliable, regular, standardized relations obtaining between specific neural responses on the one hand, and *types* of states in the world. The notion exploits the fact that specific neural responses are regularly caused by types of state in the organism's normal environment. Inching closer to a working definition, we suggest the following:

A state S of a system O contains the calibrational content P if and only if O would not be in S unless P, with some high degree of probability n/m.

For example, normally the receptor cells of the rattlesnake's pit organ respond only if there is a warm object within half a meter or so of the pit. That is, with very high probability, the receptors are not excited unless there is a warm object in the vicinity. The probability is less than 1 because receptors might be caused to respond by oddball things, such as an ethologist's injecting a drug into the pit, or by malfunction, as when the tired old receptors of a senescent rattlesnake fire spontaneously. In any case, these occurrences are rare. Crudely formalized, we can say, where x ranges over the relevant receptor cells and y ranges over objects in the environment:

(1) (x) (Excited $[x] \rightarrow$ (Prob$(\exists y)$(Warm$[y]$) $= 0.98$).

Moreover, given the snake's environment, there is a decent probability, let us say, 0.7, that the warm object is warm-blooded prey, such as a rabbit, mouse, etc. The probability is less than 1 because the pit receptors can be excited by something warm which is not the customary comestible – like a sun-heated rock, or a smoldering ember. The probability will vary with night and day, being higher at night, and of course it will plummet if the snake is put in an ethologist's laboratory filled with light bulbs and kettles. But assume his standard environment. Then we can crudely formalize the relation between warmth and food:

(2) (x)(Warm$[x] \rightarrow$ (Prob(Food$[x]$)) $= 0.7$.

Accordingly, the excitation of receptors is a moderately reliable indicator of the presence of food; $0.7 \times 0.98 = 0.686$. In a primitive infrared engine, an excited cell may be a sign for warm blooded prey often enough that it can rely on that simple connection to guide its motor response. In fact of course evolution cranks up the probability as it stumbles on better correlations between neural responses and food, but some of the fine tuning of responses will not be at the sensory periphery, but will be deeper in the neural network. The rattlesnake is eminently better tuned than the simple infrared engine. Information from the pit organ is sent to the optic tectum in a two-stage relay, and in the tectum there is integration of visual and infrared information. Some tectal cells, for example, respond with a brief high-frequency burst of impulses only when there is a *small, moving, warm* object nearby, where the visual system

provides the movement date, and the infrared system provides the temperature date. In particular, these cells do not respond to hot rocks (Newman and Hartline 1982). These cells represent small, moving, warm objects – their excited state contains calibrational content to the effect that there are small, moving warm objects nearby. Of these deeper cells, we might now say, again crudely:

(3) (x) Excited$[x] \supset$ Prob$(\exists y)$(Small$[y]$ & Moving$[y]$ & Warm$[y]$) $= 0.98$))

where x ranges over the relevant tectal cells, and y ranges over objects. Now in the rattlesnake's environment, the probability is, say 0.97, that small, moving warm objects are mice, so we can say with high probability $(0.98 \times 0.97 = 0.95)$ that the relevant cells would not be excited unless there were mice in the snake's vicinity. Excitation of these cells represents the presence of mice nearby.

The "computations" executed by the preceding system are of course trivial, and yet the story provides us with a useful conception of the snake's representational attunement to certain aspects of its environment, a conception which helps explain how the snake survives and flourishes. And none of the story ascribes representations with a sentence-like syntax, or talks about the reference of terms or the meaning of predicates.

But what of more talented creatures, creatures whose computational activities are more broadly directed and more intricately constituted? In particular, what of creatures in whom *learning* is a major element in their progressive attunement to the environment? In such cases, are we not forced to postulate an entire *system* of representations, manipulable by the creature? It seems that we are. But here we must resist our parochial impulses concerning the structure of such a system. In the first place, *such a system need not and almost certainly will not be monolithic or uniform at all.* More likely, we possess an integrated hierarchy of quite different computational/representational systems, facing very different problems and pursuing quite different strategies of solution. Why should we expect the representational systems used by the visual system, the auditory system, the proprioceptive system, and the motor system all to be the same? Even the cytoarchitecture of the relevant brain areas is different for each of these cognitive subsystems.

Will *some* subsystem of this functional mosaic display the familiar structures of human language? In humans, presumably yes, though other species need not possess it. And even in humans it may play a relatively minor role in our overall cognitive activities, serving a mainly social function. The bulk of cognition may take place in other subsystems, and follow principles inapplicable in the linguistic domain. What those other representational systems are, and how they are knit together to form human cognition, these are empirical questions, begging empirical answers. Lesion studies from neurology are one source of answers: the accidental destruction of isolated brain areas leaves people with isolated and often very curious cognitive deficits. The direct examination of active neural networks is another, though here animal studies must dominate. The computer simulation of proposed representational systems will also be invaluable, if it is neurophysiologically guided, since computers will allow us to defeat the problems of sheer functional complexity in the systems we discover. Research is well-established in all three of these areas, and it wants only our attention.

Our conclusion is that computational psychology cannot afford to embrace a principle of categorical aloofness from or methodological disdain for neuroscience, for at least two reasons. First, if we want to know how cognitive creatures hook up to the world they inhabit, neuroscience holds out the best hope for an enlightening account. And second, even if we restrict our concern to the brain's abstract computational activities, empirical neuroscience will provide authoritative data on just what those activities are, and on their many varieties. In particular, neuroscience holds out the best hope for understanding the individual evolutionary process we call *learning*, since the elements of variation, and the mechanisms of selection, whatever they are, are there under the skull, awaiting our exploration. A truly informed story of how the human cognitive system hooks up to the world must await their discovery and examination.

Note

This research was supported by a grant from the Social Sciences and Humanities and Research Council of Canada, no. 410–81–0182.

References

Bullock, T. H., Orkand, R., and Grinnel, A. (1977) *Introduction to Nervous Systems*, San Francisco: W. H. Freeman.

Burge, Tyler (1979) "Individualism and the mental," in P. A. French, T. E. Uehling, and H. K. Wettstein (eds), *Midwest Studies in Philosophy, Vol. IV*, Minneapolis: University of Minnesota Press.

Churchland, Paul M. (1979) *Scientific Realism and the Plasticity of Mind*, Cambridge: Cambridge University Press.

Churchland, Paul M. (1980) "In defense of naturalism," *Behavioral and Brain Sciences* 3: 74–5.

Churchland, Paul M. (1981) "Eliminative materialism and the propositional attitudes," *Journal of Philosophy* 78: 67–90.

Churchland, Paul M. (1982) "Is *Thinker* a natural kind?" *Dialogue* 21: 223–38.

Churchland, Patricia S. (1980a) "A perspective on mind-brain research," *Journal of Philosophy*, 77: 185–207.

Churchland, Patricia S. (1980b) "Neuroscience and psychology: should the labor be divided," *Behavioral and Brain Sciences* 3: 133.

Churchland, Patricia S. (1982) "Mind-brain reduction: new light from philosophy of science," *Neuroscience* 7: 1041–7.

Dennett, Daniel (1978) "Artificial Intelligence as philosophy and as psychology," *Brainstorms*, Cambridge, Mass.: MIT Press/Bradford.

Dennett, Daniel (1981) "Three kinds of intentional psychology," in R. Healey (ed.), *Reduction, Time and Reality*, Cambridge: Cambridge University Press: 37–61.

Dretske, Fred I. (1981) *Knowledge and the Flow of Information*, Cambridge, Mass.: MIT Press/Bradford.

Fodor, Jerry A. (1975) *The Language of Thought*, New York: Thomas Y. Crowell.

Fodor, Jerry A. (1978a) "Computation and reduction," in C. Wade Savage (ed.), *Minnesota Studies in the Philosophy of Science, Vol. 9*, Minneapolis: University of Minnesota Press; reprinted in his *Representations*, Cambridge, Mass.: MIT Press/Bradford; 146–74.

Fodor, Jerry A. (1978b) "Tom Swift and his procedural grandmother," *Cognition*; reprinted in his *Representa-*

tions, Cambridge, Mass.: MIT Press/Bradford, 1981: 204–24.

Fodor, Jerry A. (1980) "Methodological solipsism considered as a research strategy in cognitive psychology," *Behavioral and Brain Sciences* 3; reprinted in his *Representations*, Cambridge, Mass MIT Press/Bradford 1981: 225–53.

Haugeland, John (1981) "Semantic engines: an introduction to mind design," *Mind Design*, Cambridge, Mass.: MIT Press/Bradford: 1–34.

Newman, Eric A. and Hartline, Peter H. (1982) "The infrared 'vision' of snakes," *Scientific American* 246: 116–27.

Pellionisz, A. and Llinas, R. (1979) "Brain modeling by tensor network theory and computer simulation: distributed processor for predictive coordination," *Neuroscience* 4: 323–48.

Putnam, Hilary (1975) "The meaning of 'meaning'," in Keith Gunderson (ed.), *Minnesota Studies in the Phi-losophy of Science, Vol. 7*, Minneapolis: University of Minnesota Press: 131–93.

Pylyshyn, Zenon (1980) "Computation and cognition: issues in the foundations of cognitive science," *Behavioral and Brain Sciences* 3: 111–32.

Sellars, Wilfrid (1980) "Behaviorism, language, and meaning," *Pacific Philosophical Quarterly* 61: 3–25.

Sellars, Wilfrid (1981) "Mental events," *Philosophical Studies* 39: 325–45.

Stampe, Dennis W. (1972) "Toward a causal theory of linguistic representation", in French, Uehling, and Wettstein (eds), *Midwest Studies in Philosophy, Vol. 2*, Minneapolis: University of Minnesota Press: 82–102.

Stich, Stephen P. (1981) "On the ascription of content," in Andrew Woodfield (ed.), *Thought and Object*, Oxford: Clarendon Press: 153–206.

Stich, Stephen P. (1983) *Folk Psychology and Cognitive Science: The Case Against Belief*, Cambridge, Mass.: MIT Press/Bradford.

10

Psychosemantics

Biosemantics

Ruth Garrett Millikan

Causal or informational theories of the semantic content of mental states which have had an eye on the problem of false representations have characteristically begun with something like this intuition. There are some circumstances under which an inner representation has its represented as a necessary and/or sufficient cause or condition of production. That is how the content of the representation is fixed. False representations are to be explained as tokens that are produced under other circumstances. The challenge, then, is to tell what defines certain circumstances as the content-fixing ones.

I

Note that the answer cannot be just that these circumstances are *statistically* normal conditions. To gather such statistics, one would need to delimit a reference class of occasions, know how to count its members, and specify description categories. It would not do, for example, just to average over conditions-in-the-universe-any-place-any-time. Nor is it given how to carve out relevant description categories for conditions on occasions. Is it "average" in the summer for it to be (precisely) between 80° and 80.5° Fahrenheit with humidity 87 percent? And are average conditions those which obtain on at least 50 percent of the occasions, or is it 90 percent? Depending on how one sets these parameters, radically different conditions are "statistically normal." But the

notion of semantic content clearly is not relative, in this manner, to arbitrary parameters. The content-fixing circumstances must be *nonarbitrarily* determined.

A number of recent writers have made an appeal to teleology here, specifically to conditions of normal function or well-functioning of the systems that produce inner representations. Where the represented is *R* and its representation is "R," under conditions of well-functioning, we might suppose, only *R*s can or are likely to produce "Rs." Or perhaps "R" is a representation of *R* just in case the system was designed to react to *R*s by producing "Rs." But this sort of move yields too many representations. Every state of every functional system has normal causes, things that it is a response to in accordance with design. These causes may be proximate or remote, and many are disjunctive. Thus, a proximate normal cause of dilation of the skin capillaries is certain substances in the blood, more remote causes include muscular effort, sunburn, and being in an overheated environment. To each of these causes the vascular system responds by design, yet the response (a red face), though it may be a natural sign of burn or exertion or overheating, certainly is not a representation of that. If not every state of a system represents its normal causes, which are the states that do?

Jerry Fodor[1] has said that, whereas the content of an inner representation is determined by some sort of causal story, its status *as* a representation is determined by the functional organization of the part of the system which uses it. There is such a thing, it seems, as behaving like a representation without behaving like a representation of anything in particular. What the thing is a representation of is then determined by its cause under content-fixing conditions. It would be interesting to have the character of universal I-am-a-representation behavior spelled out for us. Yet, as Fodor well knows, there would still be the problem of demonstrating that there was only one normal cause per representation type.

A number of writers, including Dennis Stampe,[2] Fred Dretske,[3] and Mohan Matthen,[4] have suggested that what is different about effects that are representations is that their function is, precisely, to represent, "indicate," or "detect." For example, Matthen says of (fullfledged) perceptual states that they are "state[s] that [have] the function of *detecting* the presence of things of a certain type..." (ibid., p.20). It does not help to be told that inner representations are things that have representing (indicating, detecting) as their function, however, unless we are also told what kind of activity representing (indicating, detecting) is. Matthen does not tell us how to naturalize the notion "detecting." If "detecting" is function of a representational state, it must be something that the state effects or produces. For example, it cannot be the function of a state to have been produced in response to something. Or does Matthen mean that it is not the representational states themselves, but the part of the system which produces them, which has the function of detecting? It has the function, say, of producing states that correspond to or covary with something in the outside world? But, unfortunately, not every device whose job description includes producing items that vary with the world is a representation producer. The devices in me that produce calluses are supposed to vary their placement according to where the friction is, but calluses are not representations. The pigment arrangers in the skin of a chameleon, the function of which is to vary the chameleon's color with what it sits on, are not representation producers.

Stampe and Dretske do address the question what representing or (Dretske) "detecting" is. Each brings in his own description of what a natural sign or natural representation is, then assimilates *having the function of representing R* to being a natural sign or representer of *R* when the system functions normally. Now, the production of natural signs is undoubtedly an accidental side effect of normal operation of many systems. From my red face you can tell that either I have been exerting myself, or I have been in the heat, or I am burned. But the production of an accidental side effect, no matter how regular, is not one of a system's functions; that goes by definition. More damaging, however, it simply is not true that representations must carry natural information. Consider the signals with which various animals signal danger. Nature knows that it is better to err on the side of caution, and it is likely that many of these signs occur more often in the absence than in the presence of any real danger. Certainly there is nothing incoherent in the idea that this might be so, hence that many of these signals do not carry natural information concerning the dangers they signal.

II

I fully agree, however, that an appeal to teleology, to function, is what is needed to fly a naturalist theory of content. Moreover, what makes a thing into an inner representation is, near enough, that its function is to represent. But, I shall argue, the way to unpack this insight is to focus on representation *consumption*, rather than representation production. It is the devices that *use* representations which determine these to be representations and, at the same time (contra Fodor), determine their content. If it really is the function of an inner representation to indicate its represented, clearly it is not just a natural sign, a sign that you or I looking on might interpret. It must be one that functions as a sign or representation *for the system itself*. What is it then for a system to use a representation *as* a representation?

The conception of function on which I shall rely was defined in my *Language, Thought, and Other Biological Categories*[5] and defended in "In defense of proper functions"[6] under the label "proper function." Proper functions are determined by the histories of the items possessing them; functions that were "selected for" are paradigm cases.[7] The notions "function" and "design" should not be read, however, as referring only to origin. Natural selection does not slack after the emergence of a structure but actively preserves it by acting against the later emergence of less fit structures. And structures can be preserved due to performance of new functions unrelated to the forces that originally shaped them. Such functions are "proper functions," too, and are "performed in accordance with design."

The notion "design" should not be read – and this is very important – as a reference to innateness. A system may have been designed to be altered by its experience, perhaps to learn from its experience in a prescribed manner. Doing what it has learned to do in this manner is then "behaving in accordance with design" or "functioning properly."[8]

My term "normal" should be read normatively, historically, and relative to specific function. In the first instance, "normal" applies to explanations. A "normal explanation" explains the performance of a particular function, telling how it was (typically) historically performed on those (perhaps rare) occasions when it was properly performed. Normal explanations do not tell, say, why it has been common for a function to be performed; they are not statistical explanations. They cover only past times of actual performance, showing how these performances were entailed by natural law, given certain conditions, coupled with the dispositions and structures of the relevant functional devices.[9] In the second instance, "normal" applies to conditions. A "normal condition for performance of a function" is a condition, the presence of which must be mentioned in giving a full normal explanation for performance of that function. Other functions of the same organism or system may have other normal conditions. For example, normal conditions for discriminating colors are not the same as normal conditions for discriminating tastes, and normal conditions for seeing very large objects are not the same as for seeing very small ones. It follows that "normal conditions" must not be read as having anything to do with what is typical or average or even, in many cases, at all common. First, many functions are performed only rarely. For example, very few wild seeds land in conditions normal for their growth and development, and the protective colorings of caterpillars seldom actually succeed in preventing them from being eaten. Indeed, normal conditions might almost better be called "historically optimal" conditions. (If normal conditions for proper functioning, hence survival and proliferation, were a statistical norm, imagine how many rabbits there would be in the world.) Second, many proper functions only need to be performed under rare conditions. Consider, for example, the vomiting reflex, the function of which is to prevent (further) toxification of the body. A normal condition for

performance of this function is presence, specifically of poison in the stomach, for (I am guessing) it is only under that condition that this reflex has historically had beneficial effects. But poison in the stomach certainly is not an average condition. (Nor, of course, is it a normal condition for other functions of the digestive system.)[10]

If it is actually one of a system's functions to produce representations, as we have said, these representations must function as representations for the system itself. Let us view the system, then, as divided into two parts or two aspects, one of which produces representations for the other to consume. What we need to look at is the consumer part, at what it is to use a thing *as* a representation. Indeed, a good look at the consumer part of the system ought to be all that is needed to determine not only representational status but representational content. We argue this as follows. First, the part of the system which consumes representations must understand the representations proffered to it. Suppose, for example, that there were abundant "natural information" (in Dretske's[11] sense) contained in numerous natural signs all present in a certain state of a system. This information could still not serve the system *as* information, unless the signs were understood by the system, and, furthermore, understood as bearers of whatever specific information they, in fact, do bear. (Contrast Fodor's notion that something could function like a representation without functioning like a representation of anything in particular.) So there must be something about the consumer that *constitutes* its taking the signs to indicate, say, *p*, *q*, and *r* rather than *s*, *t*, and *u*. But, if we know what constitutes the consumer's *taking* a sign to indicate *p*, what *q*, what *r*, etc., then, granted that the consumer's takings are in some way systematically derived from the structures of the signs so taken, we can construct a semantics for the consumer's language. Anything the signs may indicate *qua* natural signs or natural information carriers then drops out as entirely irrelevant; the representation-producing side of the system had better pay undivided attention to the language of its consumer. The sign producer's function will be to produce signs that are true *as the consumer reads the language.*

The problem for the naturalist bent on describing intentionality, then, does not concern representation production at all. Although a representation always is something that is produced by a system whose proper function is to make that representation correspond by rule to the world, what the rule of correspondence is, what gives definition to this function, is determined entirely by the representation's consumers.

For a system to use an inner item as a representation, I propose, is for the following two conditions to be met. First, unless the representation accords, *so* (by a certain rule), with a represented, the consumer's normal use of, or response to, the representation will not be able to fulfill all of the consumer's proper functions in so responding – not, at least, in accordance with a normal explanation. (Of course, it might still fulfill these functions by freak accident, but not in the historically normal way.) Putting this more formally, that the representation and the represented accord with one another, so, is a normal condition for proper functioning of the consumer device as it reacts to the representation.[12] Note that the proposal is not that the content of the representation rests on the function of the representation or of the consumer, on what these do. The idea is not that there is such a thing as behaving like a representation of X or as being treated like a representation of X. The content hangs only on there being a certain condition that would be *normal* for performance of the consumer's functions – namely, that a certain correspondence relation hold between sign and world – whatever those functions may happen to be. For example, suppose the semantic rules for my belief representations are determined by the fact that belief tokens in me will aid the devices that use them to perform certain of their tasks in accordance with a normal explanation for success only under the condition that the forms or "shapes" of these belief tokens correspond, in accordance with said rules, to conditions in the world. Just what these user tasks are need not be mentioned.[13]

Second, represented conditions are conditions that vary, depending on the *form* of the representation, in accordance with specifiable correspondence rules that give the semantics for the relevant *system* of representation. More precisely, representations always admit of significant transformations (in the mathematical sense), which accord with transformations of their corresponding representeds, thus displaying significant articulation into variant and invariant aspects. If an item considered as compounded of certain variant and invariant aspects can be said to be "composed" of these, then we can also say that every representation is, as such, a member of a representational system

having a "compositional semantics." For it is not that the represented condition is itself a normal condition for proper operation of the representation consumer. A certain correspondence between the representation and the world is what is normal. Coordinately, there is no such thing as a representation consumer that can understand only one representation. There are always other representations, composed other ways, saying other things, which it could have understood as well, in accordance with the same principles of operation. A couple of very elementary examples should make this clear.[14]

First, consider beavers, who splash the water smartly with their tails to signal danger. This instinctive behavior has the function of causing other beavers to take cover. The splash means danger, because only when it corresponds to danger does the instinctive response to the splash on the part of the interpreter beavers, the consumers, serve a purpose. If there is no danger present, the interpreter beavers interrupt their activities uselessly. Hence, that the splash corresponds to danger is a normal condition for proper functioning of the interpreter beavers' instinctive reaction to the splash. (It does not follow, of course, that it is a usual condition. Beavers being skittish, most beaver splashes possibly occur in response to things not in fact endangering the beaver.) In the beaver splash semantic system, the time and place of the splash varies with, "corresponds to," the time and place of danger. The representation is articulate: properly speaking, it is not a splash but a splash-at-a-time-and-a-place. Other representations in the same system, splashes at other times and places, indicate other danger locations.

Second, consider honey bees, which perform "dances" to indicate the location of sources of nectar they have discovered. Variations in the tempo of the dance and in the angle of its long axis vary with the distance and direction of the nectar. The interpreter mechanisms in the watching bees – these are the representation consumers – will not perform their full proper functions of aiding the process of nectar collection in accordance with a normal explanation, unless the location of nectar corresponds correctly to the dance. So, the dances are representations of the location of nectar. The full representation here is a dance-at-a-time-in-a-place-at-a-tempo-with-an-orientation.

Notice that, on this account, it is not necessary to assume that most representations are true.

Many biological devices perform their proper functions not on the average, but just often enough. The protective coloring of the juveniles of many animal species, for example, is an adaptation passed on because *occasionally* it prevents a juvenile from being eaten, though most of the juveniles of these species get eaten anyway. Similarly, it is conceivable that the devices that fix human beliefs fix true ones not on the average, but just often enough. If the true beliefs are functional and the false beliefs are, for the most part, no worse than having an empty mind, then even very fallible belief-fixing devices might be better than no belief-fixing devices at all. These devices might even be, in a sense, "designed to deliver some falsehoods." Perhaps, given the difficulty of designing highly accurate belief-fixing mechanisms, it is actually advantageous to fix too many beliefs, letting some of these be false, rather than fix too few beliefs. Coordinately, perhaps our belief-consuming mechanisms are carefully designed to tolerate a large proportion of false beliefs. It would not follow, of course, that the belief consumers are designed to *use* false beliefs, certainly not that false beliefs can serve all of the functions that true ones can. Indeed, surely if none of the mechanisms that used beliefs ever cared at all how or whether these beliefs corresponded to anything in the world, beliefs would not be functioning as representations, but in some other capacity.

Shifting our focus from producing devices to consuming devices in our search for naturalized semantic content is important. But the shift from the *function* of consumers to *normal conditions* for proper operation is equally important. Matthen, for example, characterizes what he calls a "quasi-perceptual state" as, roughly, one whose job is to cause the system to do what it must do to perform its function, given that it is in certain circumstances, which are what it represents. Matthen is thus looking pretty squarely at the representation consumers, but at what it is the representation's job to get these consumers to do, rather than at normal conditions for their proper operation. As a result, Matthen now retreats. The description he has given of quasi-perceptual states, he says, cannot cover "real perception such as that which we humans experience. Quite simply, there is no such thing as *the* proper response, or even a range of functionally appropriate responses, to what perception tells us" ("Biological functions," p. 20).[15] On the contrary, representational content rests not on univocity of consumer function but on same-

ness of normal conditions for those functions. The same percept of the world may be used to guide any of very many and diverse activities, practical or theoretical. What stays the same is that the percept must correspond to environmental configurations in accordance with the same correspondence rules for each of these activities. For example, if the position of the chair in the room does not correspond, so, to my visual representation of its position, that will hinder me equally in my attempts to avoid the chair when passing through the room, to move the chair, to sit in it, to remove the cat from it, to make judgments about it, etc. Similarly, my belief that New York is large may be turned to any of diverse purposes, but those which require it to be a *representation* require also that New York indeed be large if these purposes are to succeed in accordance with a normal explanation for functioning of my cognitive systems.

III

We have just cleanly bypassed the whole genre of causal/informational accounts of mental content. To illustrate this, we consider an example of Dretske's. Dretske tells of a certain species of northern hemisphere bacteria which orient themselves away from toxic oxygen-rich surface water by attending to their magnetosomes, tiny inner magnets, which pull toward the magnetic north pole, hence pull down (ibid.). (Southern hemisphere bacteria have their magnetosomes reversed.) The function of the magnetosome thus appears to be to effect that the bacterium moves into oxygen-free water. Correlatively, intuition tells us that what the pull of the magnetosome represents is the whereabouts of oxygen-free water. The direction of oxygen-free water is not, however, a factor in *causing* the direction of pull of the magnetosome. And the most reliable natural information that the magnetosome carries is surely not about oxygen-free water but about distal and proximal causes of the pull, about the direction of geomagnetic or better, just plain magnetic, north. One can, after all, easily deflect the magnetosome away from the direction of lesser oxygen merely by holding a bar magnet overhead. Moreover, it is surely a function of the magnetosome to respond to that magnetic field, that is part of its normal mechanism of operation, whereas responding to oxygen density is not. None of this makes any sense on a causal or informational approach.

But on the biosemantic theory it does make sense. What the magnetosome represents is only what its *consumers* require that it correspond to in order to perform *their* tasks. Ignore, then, how the representation (a pull-in-a-direction-at-a-time) is normally produced. Concentrate, instead, on how the systems that react to the representation work, on what these systems need in order to do their job. What they need is only that the pull be in the direction of oxygen-free water at the time. For example, they care not at all how it came about that the pull is in that direction; the magnetosome that points toward oxygen-free water quite by accident and not in accordance with any normal explanation will do just as well as one that points that way for the normal reasons. (As Socrates concedes in the *Meno*, true opinion is just as good as knowledge so long as it stays put.) What the magnetosome represents then is univocal; it represents only the direction of oxygen-free water. For that is the only thing that corresponds (by a compositional rule) to it, the absence of which would matter – the absence of which would disrupt the function of those mechanisms which rely on the magnetosome for guidance.

It is worth noting that what is represented by the magnetosome is not proximal but distal; no proximal stimulus is represented at all. Nor, of course, does the bacterium perform an inference from the existence of the proximal stimulus (the magnetic field) to the existence of the represented. These are good results for a theory of content to have, for otherwise one needs to introduce a derivative theory of content for mental representations that do not refer, say, to sensory stimulations, and also a foundationalist account of belief fixation. Note also that, on the present view, representations manufactured in identical ways by different species of animal might have different contents. Thus, a certain kind of small swift image on the toad's retina, manufactured by his eye lens, represents a bug, for that is what it must correspond to if the reflex it (invariably) triggers is to perform its proper functions normally, while exactly the same kind of small swift image on the retina of a male hoverfly, manufactured, let us suppose, by a nearly identical lens, represents a passing female hoverfly, for that is what it must correspond to if the female-chasing reflex it (invariably) triggers is to perform its proper functions normally. Turning the coin over, representations with the same content may be normally manufactured in a diversity of ways, even in the same species. How many different ways do you

have, for example, of telling a lemon or your spouse? Nor is it necessary that any of the ways one has of manufacturing a given representation be especially reliable ways in order for the representation to have determinate content. These various results cut the biosemantic approach off from all varieties of verificationism and foundationalism with a clean, sharp knife.

IV

But perhaps it will be thought that belief fixation and consumption are not biologically proper activities, hence that there are no normal explanations, in our defined sense, for proper performances of human beliefs. Unlike bee dances, which are all variations on the same simple theme, beliefs in dinosaurs, in quarks, and in the instability of the dollar are recent, novel, and innumerably diverse, as are their possible uses. How could there be anything *biologically* normal or abnormal about the details of the consumption of such beliefs?

But what an organism does in accordance with evolutionary design can be very novel and surprising, for the more complex of nature's creatures are designed to learn. Unlike evolutionary adaptation, learning is not accomplished by *random* generate-and-test procedures. Even when learning involves trial and error (probably the exception rather than the rule), there are principles in accordance with which responses are selected by the system to try, and there are specific principles of generalization and discrimination, etc., which have been built into the system by natural selection. How these principles normally work, that is, how they work given normal (i.e., historically optimal) environments, to produce changes in the learner's nervous system which will effect the furthering of ends of the system has, of course, an explanation – the normal explanation for proper performance of the learning mechanism and of the states of the nervous system it produces.

Using a worn-out comparison, there is an infinity of functions which a modern computer mainframe is capable of performing, depending upon its input and on the program it is running. Each of these things it can do, so long as it is not damaged or broken, "in accordance with design," and to each of these capacities there corresponds an explanation of how it would be activated or fulfilled normally. The human's mainframe takes, roughly, stimulations of the afferent nerves as input, both to program and to run it.[16] It responds, in part, by developing concepts, by acquiring beliefs and desires in accordance with these concepts, by engaging in practical inference leading ultimately to action. Each of these activities may, of course, involve circumscribed sorts of trial and error learning. When conditions are optimal, all this aids survival and proliferation in accordance with an historically normal explanation – one of high generality, of course. When conditions are not optimal, it may yield, among other things, empty or confused concepts, biologically useless desires, and false beliefs. But, even when the desires are biologically useless (though probably not when the concepts expressed in them are empty or confused), there are still biologically normal ways for them to get fulfilled, the most obvious of which require reliance on true beliefs.[17]

Yet how do we know that our contemporary ways of forming concepts, desires, and beliefs do occur in accordance with evolutionary design? Fodor, for example, is ready with the labels "pop Darwinism" and "naive adaptationism" to abuse anyone who supposes that our cognitive systems were actually selected for their belief and desire using capacities.[18] Clearly, to believe that every structure must have a function would be naive. Nor is it wise uncritically to adopt hypotheses about the functions of structures when these functions are obscure. It does not follow that we should balk at the sort of adaptationist who, having found a highly complex structure that quite evidently is currently and effectively performing a highly complex and obviously indispensable function, then concludes, *ceteris paribus*, that this function has been the most recent historical task stabilizing the structure. To suspect that the brain has not been preserved for thinking with or that the eye has not been preserved for seeing with – to suspect this, moreover, in the absence of any alternative hypotheses about causes of the stability of these structures – would be totally irresponsible. Consider: nearly every human behavior is bound up with intentional action. Are we really to suppose that the degree to which our behaviors help to fulfill intentions, and the degree to which intentions result from logically related desires plus beliefs, is a sheer coincidence – that these patterns are irrelevant to survival and proliferation or, though relevant, have had no stabilizing effect on the gene pool? But the only alternative to biological design, in our sense of "design," is sheer coin-cidence, freak accident – unless there is a ghost running the machine!

Indeed, it is reasonable to suppose that the brain structures we have recently been using in developing space technology and elementary particle physics have been operating in accordance with the very same general principles as when prehistoric man used them for more primitive ventures. They are no more performing new and different functions or operating in accordance with new and different principles nowadays than are the eyes when what they see is television screens and space shuttles. Compare: the wheel was invented for the purpose of rolling ox carts, and did not come into its own (pulleys, gears, etc.) for several thousand years thereafter, during the industrial revolution. Similarly, it is reasonable that the cognitive structures with which man is endowed were originally nature's solution to some very simple demands made by man's evolutionary niche. But the solution nature stumbled on was elegant, supremely general, and powerful, indeed; I believe it was a solution that cut to the very bone of the ontological structure of the world. That solution involved the introduction of representations, inner and/or outer, having a subject/predicate structure, and subject to a negation transformation. (Why I believe that that particular development was so radical and so powerful has been explained in depth in LTOBC, chapters 14–19. But see also section V.6 below.)

V

One last worry about our sort of position is voiced by Daniel Dennett[19] and discussed at length by Fodor.[20] Is it really plausible that bacteria and paramecia, or even birds and bees, have inner representations in the same sense that we do? Am I really prepared to say that these creatures, too, have mental states, that they think? I am not prepared to say that. On the contrary, the representations that they have must differ from human beliefs in at least six very fundamental ways.[21]

(1) *Self-representing elements*. The representations that the magnetosome produces have three significant variables, each of which refers to itself. The time of the pull refers to the time of the oxygen-free water, the locale of the pull refers to the locale of the oxygen-free water, and the direction of pull refers to the direction of oxygen-free water. The beaver's splash has two self-referring

variables: a splash at a certain time and place indicates that there is danger at that same time and place. (There is nothing necessary about this. It might have meant that there would be danger at the nearest beaver dam in five minutes.) Compare the standard color coding on the outsides of colored markers: each color stands for itself. True, it may be that sophisticated indexical representations such as percepts and indexical beliefs also have their time or place or both as significant self-representing elements, but they also have other significant variables that are not self-representing. The magnetosome does not.

(2) *Storing representations.* Any representation the time or place of which is a significant variable obviously cannot be stored away, carried about with the organism for use on future occasions. Most beliefs are representations that can be stored away. Clearly this is an important difference.

(3) *Indicative and imperative representations.* The theory I have sketched here of the content of inner representations applies only to indicative representations, representations which are supposed to be determined by the facts, which tell what is the case. It does not apply to imperative representations, representations which are supposed to determine the facts, which tell the interpreter what to do. Neither do causal-informational theories of content apply to the contents of imperative representations. True, some philosophers seem to have assumed that having defined the content of various mental symbols by reference to what causes them to enter the "belief box," then when one finds these same symbols in, say, the "desire box" or the "intention box," one already knows what they mean. But how do we know that the desire box or the intention box use the same representational system as the belief box? To answer that question we would have to know what constitutes a desire box's or an intention box's using one representational system rather than another which, turned around, is the very question at issue. In LTOBC and "Thoughts without laws; cognitive science with content,"[22] I developed a parallel theory of the content of imperative representations. Very roughly, one of the proper functions of the consumer system for an imperative representation is to help *produce* a correspondence between the representation and the world. (Of course, this proper function often is not performed.) I also argued that desires and intentions are imperative representations.

Consider, then, the beaver's splash. It tells that there is danger here now. Or why not say, instead, that it tells other nearby beavers what to do now, namely, to seek cover? Consider the magnetosome. It tells which is the direction of oxygen-free water. Or why not say, instead, that it tells the bacterium which way to go? Simple animal signals are invariably both indicative and imperative. Even the dance of the honey bee, which is certainly no simple signal, is both indicative and imperative. It tells the worker bees where the nectar is; equally, it tells them where to go. The step from these primitive representations to human beliefs is an enormous one, for it involves the separation of indicative from imperative functions of the representational system. Representations that are undifferentiated between indicative and imperative connect states of affairs directly to actions, to specific things to be done in the face of those states of affairs. Human beliefs are not tied directly to actions. Unless combined with appropriate desires, human beliefs are impotent. And human desires are equally impotent unless combined with suitable beliefs.[23]

(4) *Inference.* As indicative and imperative functions are separated in the central inner representational systems of humans, they need to be reintegrated. Thus, humans engage in practical inference, combining beliefs and desires in novel ways to yield first intentions and then action. Humans also combine beliefs with beliefs to yield new beliefs. Surely nothing remotely like this takes place inside the bacterium.

(5) *Acts of identifying.* Mediate inferences always turn on something like a middle term, which must have the same representational value in both premises for the inference to go through. Indeed, the representation consumers in us perform many functions that require them to use two or more overlapping representations together, and in such a manner that, unless the represented corresponding to these indeed have a common element, these functions will not be properly performed. Put informally, the consumer device *takes* these represented elements to be the same, thus indentifying their representational values. Suppose, for example, that you intend to speak to Henry about something. In order to carry out this intention you must, when the time comes, be able to recognize Henry in perception as the person to whom you intend to speak. You must identify Henry as represented in perception with Henry as represented in your intention. Activities that involve the coordinated use of representations from different sensory modalities, as in the case of eye–hand coordination,

visual–tactile coordination, also require that certain objects, contours, places, or directions, etc., be identified as the same through the two modalities. Now, the foundation upon which modern representational theories of thought are built depends upon a denial that what is thought of is ever placed before a naked mind. Clearly, we can never know what an inner representation represents by a direct comparison of representation to represented. Rather, acts of identifying are our ways of "knowing what our representations represent." The bacterium is quite incapable of knowing, in this sense, what its representations are about. this might be a reason to say that it does not understand its own representations, not really.

(6) *Negation and propositional content.* The representational system to which the magnetosome pull belongs does not contain negation. Indeed, it does not even contain contrary representations, for the magnetosome cannot pull in two directions at once. Similarly, if two beavers splash at different times or places, or if two bees dance different dances at the same time, it may well be that there is indeed beaver danger two times or two places and that there is indeed nectar in two different locations.[24] Without contrariety, no conflict, of course and more specifically, no contradiction. If the law of noncontradiction plays as significant a role in the development of human concepts and knowledge as has traditionally been supposed, this is a large difference between us and the bacterium indeed.[25] In LTOBC, I argued that negation, hence explicit contradiction, is dependent upon subject-predicate, that is, propositional, structure and vice versa. Thus, representations that are simpler also do not have propositional content.

In sum, these six differences between our representations and those of the bacterium, or Fodor's paramecia, ought to be enough amply to secure our superiority, to make us feel comfortably more endowed with mind.

Notes

1 "Banish discontent," in Jeremy Butterfield, ed., *Language, Mind and Logic* (New York: Cambridge, 1986), pp. 1–23; *Psychosemantics: The Problem of Meaning in the Philosophy of Mind* (Cambridge, Mass.: MIT, 1987).

2 "Toward a causal theory of representation," in Peter French, Theodore Uehling Jr, Howard Wettstein, eds, *Contemporary Perspectives in the Philosophy of Language* (Minneapolis: Minnesota University Press, 1979), pp. 81–102.

3 "Misrepresentation," in Radu Bogdan, ed., *Belief: Form, Content, and Function* (New York: Oxford, 1986), pp. 17–36.

4 "Biological functions and perceptual content," *The Journal of Philosophy* LXXXV, 1 (January 1988): 5–27.

5 Cambridge, Mass.: MIT Press, 1984 (hereafter LTOBC).

6 *Philosophy of Science*, LVI, 2 (June 1989): 288–302.

7 An odd custom exists of identifying this sort of view with Larry Wright, who does not hold it. See my "In defense of proper functions." Natural selection is not the only source of proper functions. See LTOBC, chs 1 and 2.

8 See LTOBC; and "Truth rules, hoverflies, and the Kripke–Wittgenstein Paradox," *The Philosophical Review* (forthcoming).

9 This last clarification is offered to aid Fodor ("On there not being an evolutionary theory of content" [hereafter NETC], forthcoming), who uses my term "Normal" (here I am not capitalizing it but the idea has not changed) in a multiply confused way, making a parody of my views on representation. In this connection, see also nn. 13 and 17.

10 "Normal explanation" and "normal condition for performance of a function," along with "proper function," are defined with considerable detail in LTOBC. The reader may wish, in particular, to consult my discussion of normal explanations for performance of "adapted and derived proper functions," for these functions cover the functions of states of the nervous system which result in part from learning, such as states of human belief and desire.

11 *Knowledge and the Flow of Information* (Cambridge: MIT, 1981).

12 Strictly, this normal condition must derive from a "most proximate normal explanation" of the consumer's proper functioning. See LTOBC, ch. 6, where a more precise account of what I am here calling "representations" is given under the heading "intentional icons."

13 In this particular case, one task is, surely, contributing, in conformity with certain general principles or rules, to practical inference processes, hence to the fulfillment of current desires. So, if you like, all beliefs have the *same* proper function. Or, since the rules or principles that govern practical inference dictate that a belief's "shape" determines what other inner representations it may properly be combined with to form what products, we could say that each belief has a *different* range of proper functions. Take your pick. Cf. Fodor, "Information and

representation," in Philip Hanson, ed., *Information, Language, and Cognition* (Vancouver: British Columbia University Press, 1989); and NETC.

14   These examples are of representations that are not "inner" but out in the open. As in the case of inner representations, however, they are produced and consumed by mechanisms designed to cooperate with one another; each such representation stands intermediate between two parts of a single biological system.

15   Dretske (in "Misrepresentation," p. 28) and David Papineau [in *Reality and Representation* (New York: Blackwell Publishers, 1987), p. 67 ff.] have similar concerns.

16   This is a broad metaphor. I am not advocating computationalism.

17   A word of caution. The normal conditions for a desire's fulfillment are not necessarily fulfillable conditions. In general, normal conditions for fulfillment of a function are not quite the same as conditions which, when you add them and stir, always effect proper function, because they may well be impossible conditions. For example, Fodor, in "Information and representation" and NETC, has questioned me about the normal conditions under which his desire that it should rain tomorrow will perform its proper function of *getting* it to rain. Now, the biologically normal way for such a desire to be fulfilled is exactly the same as for any other desire: one has or acquires true beliefs about how to effect the fulfillment of the desire and acts on them. Biologically normal conditions for fulfillment of the desire for rain thus include the condition that one has true beliefs about how to make it rain. Clearly this is an example in which the biological norm fails to accord with the statistical norm: most desires

about the weather are fulfilled, if at all, by biological accident. It may even be that the laws of nature, coupled with my situation, prohibit my having any true beliefs about how to make it rain; the needed general condition cannot be realized in the particular case. Similarly, normal conditions for proper function of beliefs in impossible things are, of course, impossible conditions: these beliefs are such that they cannot correspond, in accordance with the rules of mentalese, to conditions in the world.

18   *Psychosemantics* and NETC.

19   *Brainstorms* (Montgomery, Vt: Bradford Books, 1978).

20   "Why paramecia don't have mental representations," in P. French, T. Uehling Jr, and H. Wettstein (eds), *Midwest Studies in Philosophy, X* (Minneapolis: Minnesota University Press, 1986), pp. 3–23.

21   Accordingly, in LTOBC I did not call these primitive forms "representations" but "intentional signals" and, for items like bee dances, "intentional icons," reserving the term "representation" for those icons, the representational values of which must be identified if their consumers are to function properly – see V.5 below.

22   *The Philosophical Review*, XLV, 1 (1986): 47–80.

23   Possibly human intentions are in both indicative and imperative mood, however, functioning simultaneously to represent settled facts about one's future and to direct one's action.

24   On the other hand, the bees cannot go two places at once.

25   In LTOBC, I defend the position that the law of noncontradiction plays a crucial role in allowing us to develop new methods of mapping the world with representations.

A Theory of Content

Jerry A. Fodor

"...the appeal to teleologically Normal conditions doesn't provide for a univocal notion of intentional content...it's just not true that Normally caused intentional states *ipso facto* mean whatever causes them. So we need a nonteleological solution of the disjunction problem. So be it." So the first part of this discussion concluded. But that did rather beg the question against the guy who holds that *there isn't going to be a solution of the disjunction problem* because there are no intentional states, and hence no matters of fact about the disjunctiveness, or otherwise, of their intentional contents. What you need, to put the matter brutally, is one thing; what

you are likely to get is quite another. What on earth would a naturalistic and nonteleological theory of content be like?

This rest of this essay explores and extends an approach to the disjunction problem that I first sketched in *Psychosemantics* (1987) and in "Information and representation" (forthcoming). This solution is broadly within the tradition of informational approaches to content[1] but it does not equate what a symbol means with the information that its tokens carry; and it does not try to solve the disjunction problem by distinguishing type one situations (those in which whatever causes a symbol to be tokened is *ipso facto* in its extension) from type two situations (those in which symbols are allowed to be caused by things that they don't apply to.)[2] In the second respect, at least, it differs from all the other treatments of the disjunction problem that I've seen in the literature.

I must acknowledge at the outset the existence of what seems to be quite an impressive consensus – among the maybe six or eight people who care about these matters – that my way of doing the disjunction problem won't work. But Granny says I'm not to be disconsolate; Rome wasn't deconstructed in a day, she says. Accordingly, I now propose to run through more or less all of the objections to my treatment of the disjunction problem that I've heard of, and a few that I've dreamed up. Partly this is to show you that I am not disconsolate; partly it is to try to convince you that my story actually copes pretty well with the putative counterexamples; and partly it's to provide an opportunity to refine and deepen the theory.

Asymmetric Dependence (and Teleology for Almost the Last Time)

Errors raise the disjunction problem, but the disjunction problem isn't really, deep down, a problem about error. What the disjunction problem is really about deep down is the difference between *meaning* and *information*. Let's start with this.

Information is tied to etiology in a way that meaning isn't. If the tokens of a symbol have two kinds of etiologies, it follows that there are two kinds of information that tokens of that symbol carry. (If some "cow" tokens are caused by cows and some "cow" tokens aren't, then it follows that some "cow" tokens carry information about cows and some "cow" tokens don't). By contrast, *the meaning of a symbol is one of the things that all of its tokens have in common, however they may happen to be caused.* All "cow" tokens mean *cow*; if they didn't they wouldn't be "cow" tokens.

So, information follows etiology and meaning doesn't, and that's why you get a disjunction problem if you identify the meaning of a symbol with the information that its tokens carry. Error is merely illustrative; it comes into the disjunction problem only because it's so plausible that the false tokens of a symbol have a different kind of causal history (and hence carry different information) than the true ones. But there are other sorts of examples of etiological heterogeneity (including representation in thought) and they produce disjunction problems too.

To put the same point another way, solving the disjunction problem requires not a theory of *error* but a theory of *meaning*; if a theory of meaning is any good, the conditions for disjunctive meaning should fall out as a special case (see the discussion in Fodor, forthcoming). If one is sympathetic to the Skinner-Dretske tradition, the trick in constructing such a theory is to explain how the meaning of a symbol can be insensitive to the heterogeneity of the (actual and possible) causes of its tokens even though, on the one hand, meaning is supposed somehow to reduce to information and, on the other hand, information varies with etiology.

You can now see what's *really* wrong with teleological theories of content. The heart of a teleological theory is the idea that "in Normal circumstances" the tokens of a symbol can have only *one kind* of cause – viz., the kind of cause that fixes meaning. (Normally, only cows cause "cows," so the teleological story goes.) But surely this underestimates what one might call the *robustness* of meaning: In actual fact, "cow" tokens get caused in *all sorts* of ways, and they all mean *cow* for all of that. Solving the disjunction problem and making clear how a symbol's meaning could be so insensitive to variability in the causes of its tokenings are really two ways of describing the same undertaking. If there's going to be a causal theory of content, there has to be some way of picking out *semantically relevant* causal relations from all the other kinds of causal relations that the tokens of a symbol can enter into. And we'd better not do this by implicitly denying robustness – e.g., by idealizing to contexts of etiological homogeneity.

Well, then, how *are* we to do it? Here's a first approximation to the proposal that I favor: Cows cause "cow" tokens, and (let's suppose) cats cause "cow" tokens. But "cow" means *cow* and not *cat* or *cow or cat* because *there being cat-caused "cow" tokens depends on there being cow-caused "cow" tokens, but not the other way around.* "Cow" means *cow* because, as I shall henceforth put it, noncow-caused "cow" tokens are *asymmetrically dependent upon* cow-caused "cow" tokens. "Cow" means *cow* because *but that "cow" tokens carry information about cows, they wouldn't carry information about anything.*

Notice that this sort of story has the desirable property of not assuming that there are such things as type one situations; in particular, it doesn't assume that there are circumstances – nomologically possible and naturalistically and otherwise non-question-beggingly specifiable – in which it's semantically necessary that only cows cause "cows." Nor does it assume that there are nonques-tion-beggingly specifiable circumstances in which it's semantically necessary that *all* cows would cause "cows."[3] All that's required for "cow" to mean *cow*, according to the present account, is that some "cow" tokens should be caused by (more precisely, that they should carry information about) cows, and that noncow-caused "cow" tokens should depend asymmetrically on these.

Teleological theories say that what's special about false tokens is that they can't happen when circumstances are Normal; if it's supposed that things actually are Normal some of the time (as, indeed, it must be if the theory is historical/Dar-winian) it follows that some of the time what's said (or thought) can't but be true. By contrast, the theory I'm selling says that false tokens can happen whenever they like; only if *they* happen, so too must tokenings of other kinds: No noncow-caused "cow"s without cow-caused "cow"s; false tokens are metaphysically dependent on true ones.[4] Since the satisfaction of the asymmetric depend-ence condition is compatible with any amount of heterogeneity in the causal history of "cow" tokens, this way of solving the disjunction problem is compatible with meaning being arbitrarily robust.[5]

This story also has the desirable property of being naturalistic in the sense discussed in chapter 3. It's atomistic ("cow"s could be asymmetrically dependent on cows in a world in which no other asymmetric dependencies obtain) and it's physi-calistic (you can say what asymmetric dependence is without resort to intentional or semantic idiom).[6] But despite its having these desirable properties, the proposal I've just sketched is *only* a first approximation. As it stands there's lots to be said against it. Before we commence to look at the problems, however, I have three prefatory remarks I want to make: a shortish one about a doctrine that you might call "pansemanticism," a longish one about ontology, and then a very short one about who has the burden of argument.

Pansemanticism

Here's a clash of intuitions for you.

On the one hand:

> ...symbols and mental states both have repres-entational *content*. And nothing else does that belongs to the causal order: not rocks, or worms or trees or spiral nebulae...the main joint busi-ness of the philosophy of language and the phi-losophy of mind is the problem of representation...How can anything manage to be *about* anything; and why is it that only thoughts and symbols succeed? (Me, in *Psycho-semantics*, 1987, p. xi)

And on the other hand:

> Clouds *mean* rain. Spots of a certain kind *mean* measles...In all such cases there is a lawlike or nomological regularity connecting one type of situation with another. Instances of these regu-larities are cases in which one situation means something or carries information about another: and, of course, in such cases there need be neither minds nor symbols used by minds. (Israel 1987, p. 3; emphasis his)

In fact, the idea that meaning is just *everywhere* is a natural conclusion to draw from informational analyses of content. If, after all, meaning reduces (more or less)[7] to reliable causal covariance, then since there is patently a lot of reliable causal covar-iance around, it looks to follow that there must be a lot of meaning around too. And the intuition that "means" is univocal – and means *carries informa-tion about* – in "smoke" means *smoke*' and 'smoke means fire' is close to the heart of information-based semantics.

But this can't be right. If it were, then (since "carries information about" is transitive) it would follow that "smoke" means *fire*; which it doesn't. On the asymmetric dependence account, by con-trast, this sort of case comes out all right. "Smoke" tokens carry information about fire (when they're caused by smoke that's caused by fire). But they don't *mean* fire because their dependence on fire is asymmetrically dependent on their dependence on smoke. Break the *fire* → *smoke* connection, and the *smoke* → "*smoke*" connection remains intact; our using "smoke" in situations where there's fire doesn't depend on smoke's carrying information about fire. But break the *smoke* → "*smoke*" con-nection and the *fire* → "*smoke*" connection goes too; our using "smoke" in situations where there's fire does depend on "smoke" 's carrying informa-tion about smoke.

There is, in short, a lot less meaning around than there is information. That's because all you need for information is reliable causal covariance, whereas for meaning you need (at least) asymmetric dependence too. Information is ubiquitous but not robust; meaning is robust but not ubiquitous. So much for pansemanticism.

Ontology

As I remarked in chapter 3, I assume that if the generalization that Xs cause Ys is counterfactual supporting, then there is a "covering" law that relates the property of being X to the property of being a cause of Ys: counterfactual supporting causal generalizations are (either identical to or) backed by causal laws, and laws are relations among properties. So, what the story about asymmetric dependence comes down to is that "cow" means *cow* if (i) there is a nomic relation between the property of being a cow and the property of being a cause of "cow" tokens; and (ii) if there are nomic relations between other properties and the property of being a cause of "cow" tokens, then the latter nomic relations depend asymmetrically upon the former.

Ontologically speaking, I'm inclined to believe that it's bedrock that the world contains properties and their nomic relations; i.e., that truths about nomic relations among properties are deeper than – and hence are not to be analyzed in terms of – counterfactual truths about individuals. In any event, *epistemologically* speaking, I'm quite certain that it's possible to know that there is a nomic relation among properties but not have much idea which counterfactuals are true in virtue of the fact that the relation holds. It is therefore, *methodologically* speaking, probably a bad idea to require of philosophical analyses that are articulated in terms of nomic relations among properties that they be, as one says in the trade, "cashed" by analyses that are articulated in terms of counterfactual relations among individuals.

This methodological point is one about which I feel strongly. So much so that I am prepared to succumb to a digression. Here come several paragraphs about how a philosopher can get into trouble by taking it for granted that truths about laws need to be analyzed by, or into, counterfactual truths.

The context is Kripke's critical discussion (1982) of dispositional accounts of rule following. According to such accounts, meaning *plus* by "+" is analyzed in terms of a disposition to "respond with the sum of [the] two numbers" when asked things like "What's m + n?" Kripke says this sort of analysis won't do because we have no such dispositions: our computational powers are finite; we make mistakes; and so forth. To which he imagines his interlocutor replying that: "... the trouble arises solely from too crude a notion of disposition: *ceteris paribus* notions of dispositions, not crude and literal notions, are the ones standardly used in philosophy and in science." So what's imagined is, in effect, a dispositional story about rule following that is backed by an appeal to the performance/competence distinction.

But, according to Kripke, that won't do either. For "... how should we flesh out the *ceteris paribus* clause? Perhaps [by invoking counterfactuals] as something like: If my brain had been stuffed with sufficient extra matter to grasp large enough numbers, and if it were given enough capacity to perform such a large addition ... [etc.] ..., then given an addition problem involving two large numbers m and n, I would respond with their sum ... But how can we have any confidence of this? How in the world can I tell what would happen if my brain were stuffed with extra brain matter. ... Surely such speculation should be left to science fiction writers and futurologists. We have no idea what the results of such experiments would be. They might lead me to go insane ... [and so forth]."

Apparently Kripke assumes that we can't have reason to accept that a generalization defined for idealized conditions is lawful unless we can specify the counterfactuals which would be true if the idealized conditions were to obtain. It is, however, hard to see why one should take this methodology seriously. For example: God only knows what would happen if molecules and containers actually met the conditions specified by the ideal gas laws (molecules are perfectly elastic; containers are infinitely impermeable; etc.); for all *I* know, if any of these things were true, the world would come to an end. After all, the satisfaction of these conditions is, presumably, *physically impossible* and who knows what would happen in physically impossible worlds?

But it's not required, in order that the ideal gas laws should be in scientific good repute, that we know anything like all of what would happen if there really were ideal gasses. All that's required is that we know (e.g.) that if there were ideal gasses, then, *ceteris paribus*, their volume would vary inversely with the pressure upon them. And *that* counterfactual *the theory itself tells us is true.*[8]

Similarly, if there are psychological laws that idealize to unbounded working memory, it is not required in order for *them* to be in scientific good repute that we know all of what would happen if working memory really were unbounded. All we need to know is that, if we did have unbounded memory, then, *ceteris paribus*, we would be able to compute the value of $m + n$ for arbitrary m and n.[9] And that counterfactual the theory itself tells us is true.

Similarly again, we can know that there are asymmetric dependencies among nomic relations between properties without knowing much about which counterfactuals these asymmetric dependencies make true. All we need to know is that if the nomic relation between $P1$ and $P2$ is asymmetrically dependent on the nomic relation between $P3$ and $P4$, then, *ceteris paribus*, breaking the relation between $P3$ and $P4$ would break the relation between $P1$ and $P2$. And that counterfactual the theory itself tells us is true. As per above.

Having gotten all that off my chest, I shall join the crowd and talk counterfactuals from time to time, *faut de mieux*. And, since it's widely supposed that talk about counterfactuals itself translates into talk about possibilia, I shall sometimes equate "there is a nomic dependence between the property of being a Y and the property of being a cause of Xs" with " Ys cause Xs in all (nearby? see below) nomologically possible worlds". But I am not happy about any of this; it seems to me to be just the sort of reductive move that is always blowing up in philosophers' faces. I suspect, in particular, that some of the troubles we're about to survey stem not from there being anything wrong with the proposal that content rests on asymmetrical dependencies among nomological relations, but rather from there being everything wrong with the assumption that claims about nomological relations need counterfactual/possible world translations.[10]

Who Has the Burden of Argument

The theory of meaning that I'm going to propose is elaborated largely in terms of subjunctive conditionals. It has this in common with all informational theories of meaning; it's in the nature of such theories to claim that a symbol means such-and-such because *if there were* instances of such-and-such they *would cause* tokenings of the symbol. So it may occur to you, in the course of these proceedings, to object as follows: "Why should I believe that the counterfactuals that are being invoked are true? Why should I believe that if there actually were such-and-suches they actually would cause symbol tokenings in the ways that your theory requires?"

The answer is: Don't forget, this stuff is supposed to be philosophy. In particular, it's an attempt to solve Brentano's problem by showing that there are naturalistically specifiable, and atomistic, sufficient conditions for a physical state to have an intentional content. In *that* context, I get to *stipulate* the counterfactuals. It's enough if I can make good the claim that *"X" would mean* such and such if so and so *were to be* the case. It's not also incumbent upon me to argue that since *"X" does* mean such and such, so and so *is* the case. That is, solving Brentano's problem requires giving sufficient conditions for intentionality, not *necessary* and sufficient conditions. So, if you want to argue with the metaphysical conclusions of this essay you've got to construct a world where my counterfactuals are all in place but where *"X"* doesn't mean what I say it does. Fair enough; let's see one.

OK, now to business.

To begin with, not an objection, but something more like a vague discomfort: *Even if you can get the theory to cope with the examples, I don't see why the theory should be true; I don't see why asymmetric dependence should, as it were, make the difference between information and content.*

Let's start by forgetting about the naturalization problem (we'll return to it in a couple of paragraphs). I want to make it seem plausible that asymmetric dependence might have deep roots in the analysis of semantical phenomena when the phenomena are viewed commonsensically, outside the context of metaphysical issues about reduction. And let's, for the moment, talk about linguistic rather than mental representation in order to keep the facts as much as possible out in the open. So, then:

We have, I suppose, a variety of practices with respect of the linguistic expressions we use. And I suppose it's plausible that these practices aren't all on a level; some of them presuppose others in the sense that some work only because others are in place. For a banal example, there's the business of having people paged. How it works is: Someone calls out "John" and, if everything goes right, John comes. Why John? I mean, why is it *John* that you get when you call out "John"? Well, because the practice is that the guy who is to come is the guy whose name is the vocable that is called. This much, surely, is untendentious.

Notice that you have to invoke the practice of naming to specify the practice of paging. So the practice of paging is parasitic on the practice of naming; you couldn't have the former but that you have the latter. But not, I suppose, vice versa? Couldn't you have the practices that are constitutive of naming (so that, for example, the convention is that "John is pink" is true if it's the person whose name is "John" that is pink) even if there were no practice of paging people by calling out their names? I take it to be plausible that you could, so I take it to be plausible that paging is *asymmetrically* dependent on naming.

Oh, no doubt, I could have an arrangement with my dog according to which my dog comes when I whistle; and this though the sound that I make when I whistle for my dog isn't, of course, my dog's name. But here learning the language game really *is* just training. The whistling works because there's a *pre*arrangement between me and my dog; I've taught the dog what to do when I make that noise. By contrast, I can page John by calling his name without this sort of prearrangement. When a convention of naming is in place, there's room for a practice of paging that is perfectly abstract: Anyone who has a name can be paged just by calling his name.

So, the *productivity* of the paging arrangement depends on there being a convention of naming. Similarly, *mutatis mutandis*, for the productivity of the practice in virtue of which I bring you a slab when you say "bring me a slab." That it's one of *those* things that you get when you say this has essentially to do with those being the kinds of things that are *called* "slabs" (with its being the case, for example, that those are the kinds of things that have to be pink if "slabs are pink" is true.) But not, surely, vice versa; surely the practices in virtue of our pursuit of which "is a slab" means *is a slab* could be in place even if there were no convention of bringing slabs when they're called for. So then it's plausible that the cluster of practices that center around bringing things when they're called for is asymmetrically dependent on the cluster of practices that fix the extensions of our predicates.

These kinds of considerations show one of the ways that asymmetric dependence gets a foothold in semantic analysis: Some of our linguistic practices presuppose some of our others, and it's plausible that practices of *applying* terms (names to their bearers, predicates to things in their extensions) are at the bottom of the pile.[11] But what, precisely, has all this got to do with robustness and with the relation between information and content? The idea is that, although tokens of "slab" that request slabs carry no information about slabs (if anything, they carry information about wants; viz., the information that a slab is wanted), still, *some* tokens of "slab" presumably carry information about slabs (in particular, the tokens that are used to predicate slabhood of slabs do); and, but for there being tokens of "slab" that carry information about slabs, I couldn't get a slab by using "slab" to call for one. My "slab" requests are thus, in a certain sense, *causally dependent on slabs even though there are no slabs in their causal histories.* But they're not, of course, causally dependent on slabs in the way that (according to informational semantics) my "slab" predications are. So then there are *two* semantically relevant ways that "slab" tokens can be causally dependent on slabs consonant with their meaning *slab*: by being "slab" tokens that are caused by slabs, and by being "slab" tokens that are asymmetrically dependent upon "slab" tokens that are caused by slabs. Equivalently: By being "slab" tokens that carry information about slabs, and by being "slab" tokens that asymmetrically depend upon "slab" tokens that carry information about slabs.

So far so good; we can see how asymmetric dependencies among our linguistic practices might explain how a token of "slab" could mean *slab* even when, as in the case of slab requests, it's a want rather than a slab that causes the tokening; and how a token of "John" could mean *John* even though, if it's used to page John, it's caused not by John but by his absence. Which is to say that we can see something of the connection between asymmetric dependence and robustness.

But, of course, as it stands none of this is of any use to a reductionist. For, in these examples, we've been construing robustness by appeal to asymmetric dependencies among *linguistic practices*. And linguistic *practices* depend on linguistic *policies*; the asymmetric dependence of my pagings on my namings comes down to my undertaking that, *ceteris paribus*, I will call out "John" only when the man I want to come is the one whom I undertake that I will use "John" to name; and so forth. Since, however, being in pursuit of a policy is being in an intentional state, how could asymmetric dependence among linguistic practices help with the naturalization problem?

The first point is that words can't have their meanings *just* because their users undertake to pursue some or other linguistic policies; or, indeed, just because of any purely *mental* phenomenon, anything that happens purely "in your head." Your undertaking to call John "John" doesn't, all by itself, make "John" a name of John. How could it? For "John" to be John's name, there must be some sort of *real relation* between the name and its bearer; and intentions don't, *per se*, establish real relations. This is because, of course, intentions are (merely) intentional; you can intend that there be a certain relation between "John" and John and yet there may be no such relation. *A fortiori*, you can intend that there be a certain *semantical* relation between "John" and John – that the one should name the other, for example – and yet there may be no such relation. Mere undertakings connect nothing with nothing; "intentional relation" is an oxymoron. For there to be a relation between "John" and John, something has to happen *in the world*. That's part of what makes the idea of a *causal* construal of semantic relations so attractive. (And it's also, I think, what's right about Wittgenstein's "private language" argument. Though, as I read the text, he has it muddled up with irrelevant epistemology. For "John" to mean *John*, something has to happen in the world. It doesn't follow that for "John" to mean John someone has to be in a position to *tell* that that thing has happened.)

Linguistic policies don't make semantic relations; but maybe they make *causal* relations, and maybe causal relations make semantic relations. This, anyhow, is a hope by which informational semantics lives. I pursue a policy according to which I use "is a slab" to predicate slabhood, and a policy according to which I use "bring a slab" to request slabs, and a policy according to which the second of these practices is asymmetrically dependent on the first. My pursuing these policies is my being in a certain complex mental state, and my being in that mental state has causal consequences: in particular it has the consequence that there is a certain pattern of causal relations between slabs and my tokenings of "is a slab;" and that there is a certain (very different) pattern of causal relations between slabs and my tokenings of "bring a slab;" and that the second pattern of causal relations is asymmetrically dependent on the first.

Now maybe we can kick away the ladder. Perhaps the policies *per se* aren't what matters for semantics; maybe all that matters is the patterns of causal dependencies that the pursuit of the policies give rise to. That one kind of causal relation between "slab"s and slabs should depend asymmetrically upon another kind of causal relation between "slab"s and slabs might be enough to explain the robustness of "slab" tokenings, *however* the relations are sustained. (Cf. a doctrine of Skinner's cited with approval in Chapter 3: semantics depends on a "functional relation" – a relation of nomic dependence – between symbols and their denotata. How this relation is mediated – e.g., that it is neurologically mediated, or for that matter, psychologically mediated – isn't part of the *semantical* story.)

The point is, if the asymmetric dependence story about robustness can be told just in terms of symbol–world causal relations, then we can tell it *even in a context where the project is naturalization*. No doubt, it's the linguistic policies of speakers that give rise to the asymmetric causal dependencies in terms of which the conditions for robustness are defined; but the conditions for robustness *quantify over* the mediating mechanisms, and so can be stated without referring to the policies; hence their compatibility with naturalism.

At a minimum, nobody who is independently committed to the reduction of semantic relations to causal ones should boggle at this way of accommodating the facts about robustness. Informational theories, for example, define "information" in just this sort of way: i.e., they appeal to reliable covariances while quantifying over the causal mechanisms by which these covariances are sustained. By doing so, they explain why information (indeed, why the very *same* information) can be transmitted over so many different kinds of channels.

Well, similarly, if it's the causal patterns themselves that count, rather than the mechanisms whose operations give rise to them, then perhaps our *mental* representations can be robust just in virtue of asymmetric dependencies among the causal patterns that our concepts enter into.[12] That is, perhaps there could be mechanisms which sustain asymmetric dependencies among the relations between mental representations and the world, even though, patently, we have no policies with respect to the tokenings of our mental representations. If that were so, then the conditions for the robustness of linguistic expressions and the conditions for the robustness of mental representations might be *identical* even though, of course, the mechanisms in virtue of whose operations the two sorts of symbols satisfy the conditions for robustness would be very, very different. Some races are won by sailboats and some are won by steamboats, and the mechanisms whose operation eventuates in winning the two sorts of races are very, very different. But the conditions for winning quantify over the mechanisms and are the same for both sorts of races; however you are driven, all you have to do to win is come in first (on corrected time, to be sure).

So much for some of the intuitions that are running the show. Now let's see to the counter-examples.

1 *First objection*: "What about 'unicorn'? It seems implausible that nonunicorn-caused 'unicorn' tokens should depend on unicorn-caused 'unicorn' tokens since, as you may have noticed, there are many of the former but none of the latter."

First reply: That's one of the reasons why I want to do the thing in terms of nomic relations among properties rather than causal relations among individuals. I take it that there can be nomic relations among properties that aren't instantiated; so it can be true that the property of being a unicorn is nomologically linked with the property of being a cause of "unicorn"s *even if there aren't any unicorns*. Maybe this cashes out into something like *there wouldn't be nonunicorn-caused "unicorn" tokens but that unicorns would cause "unicorn" tokens if there were any unicorns*. And maybe *that* cashes out into something like: *there are nonunicorn-caused "unicorn" tokens in worlds that are close to us only if there are unicorn-caused "unicorn" tokens in worlds that are close to them*. But this is very approximate. For example, I suppose that "unicorn" is an (uninstantiated) kind term. It will become clear later, when we worry about doppelgängers of things that are in the extensions of kind terms, that this entails that, *ceteris paribus*, no world in which only nonunicorns cause "unicorns" can be a close to ours as some world in which only unicorns do. And anyhow, for reasons previously set out, I am not an enthusiast for such translations.

Two subsidiary points should be noticed. First, this way of compensating for the lack of unicorns won't work if the lack of unicorns is *necessary* (e.g., nomologically or metaphysically necessary). For,

in that case, it's not a law that if there were unicorns they would cause "unicorn" tokens; laws aren't made true by vacuous satisfactions of their antecedents. Similar lines of argument suggest what appears to be quite a strong consequence of the asymmetric dependence story: *no* primitive symbol can express a property that is necessarily uninstantiated. (There can't, for example, be a primitive symbol that expresses the property of being a round square).

One would think that a theory that makes so strong a claim should be pretty easy to test. Not so, however, in the present case. For one thing, the notion of primitiveness that's at issue here isn't entirely clear. You could, presumably, have a *syntactically* primitive symbol[13] that means *is a round square* so long as it is "introduced by" a definition. Whatever, precisely, *that* may mean. In short, although the claim that all necessarily uninstantiated properties may be expressed by complex symbols looks to rule out a lot of possibilities, I, for one, can't think of any way to decide whether it's true. Suggestions are gratefully solicited.

2 *Second objection*: Why doesn't "horse" mean *small horse*, seeing that, after all, if horses cause "horses" it follows that small horses cause "horses?"

Second reply: That's another reason why I want to do the thing in terms of nomic relations among properties rather than causal relations among individuals. Being struck by lightning caused the death of the cow. The bolt that killed the cow was the fourth that Tuesday, so being struck by the fourth bolt on that Tuesday caused the death of the cow; "cause" is transparent to that sort of substitution. But though it's true (given the assumptions) that being struck by the fourth bolt on Tuesday killed the cow, the law that "covered" that causal transaction applies to cows and lightning bolts *qua* cow and lightning bolts (or, perhaps, *qua* organisms and electrical discharges?); it was because it was a lightning bolt – and not because it was the fourth such bolt that Tuesday – that its hitting the cow caused the cow to die.

Well, similarly in the semantic case. Small horses cause "horse"s if horses do; but nothing follows as to the identity of the properties involved in the law that covers these causal transactions (except that small horses must be in the extension of the one and token "horse"s in the extension of the other). As it turns out, routine application of the method of differences suggests that it must be the property of *being a horse* and not the property of *being a small horse* that is connected with the property of *being a cause of "horse" tokens* since many things that have the first property have the third despite their lack of the second: large horses and medium horses simply spring to mind. (Similar considerations explain why "horse" means *horse* rather than, as it might be, *animal*; consider this a take-home assignment.)

3 *Third objection* (suggested independently by Steven Wagner, Tim Maudlin, and Scott Weinstein, in reverse chronological order):
Aha! But how about this: Consider, on the one hand, Old Paint (hereinafter OP) and, on the other hand, all the horses except Old Paint (hereinafter HEOPs). It's plausible that OP wouldn't cause "horse"'s except that HEOPs do; and it's also plausible that HEOPs would cause "horse"'s even if OP didn't. So OP's causing "horse"'s is asymmetrically dependent on HEOPs causing "horse"'s; so "horse" means *all the horse except Old Paint*.

Third reply: This is a third reason why I want to do it in terms of nomic relations among properties rather than causal relations among individuals. In what follows, I will often have claims to make about what happens when you break the connection between Xs and "X"s. In thinking about these claims *it is essential* to bear in mind that 'break the connection between Xs and "X"s' is always shorthand for 'break the connection between the property in virtue of which Xs cause "X"s and the property of being a cause of "X"s.' In the present case, *by stipulation* the property in virtue of which OP causes "horse"'s is the property of *being a horse*. But if you break the connection between *that* property and the property of being a cause of "horse"'s, then the connection between HEOPs and "horse"'s fails too (since, of course, HEOPs are causes of "horse"'s not in virtue of being HEOPs, but in virtue of being horses).

So OP's causing "horse"'s is not, after all, asymmetrically dependent on HEOPs causing "horse"'s, and the counterexample fails.

Next worry: Does asymmetric dependence really solve the disjunction problem?

Asymmetric dependence finds *a* difference between, on the one hand, false tokens, representation in thought, and the like and, on the other hand, symbol tokens that are caused by things that they apply to. But is it the *right* difference? Does it, for example, explain why it's only in the case of the latter sort of tokenings that etiology determines meaning? I now propose to look rather closely at some worries about how the asymmetric dependence story copes with the disjunction problem.

4 *Baker's objection*: Here is a passage from a critical discussion of asymmetric dependence in a recent paper by Lynne Rudder Baker (1989).

> Let us consider this account in light of a particular case. Suppose that, although there are many ordinary cats around, a certain person, *S*, learns a particular Mentalese symbol solely from artifacts (say, Putnam's robot-cats) that impinge on sensory surfaces in exactly the same way as cats. Now (for the first time) *S* sees a real cat.... How should Fodor interpret the cat-caused token? ... There seem to be three possibilities...

none of which, Baker thinks, is tolerable. These are:

(a) the token means *cat* and is thus true of the cat. But this can't be right because "...if there is any asymmetric dependence, it goes the other way. *S*'s present disposition to apply 'cat' to a real cat depends upon her corresponding current disposition to apply it to robot-cats."

(b) the token means *robot-cat* and is thus false of the cat. But this can't be right since it ignores relevant counterfactuals. Specifically, it ignores the fact that – although only robots did cause *S*'s "cats" – cats *would* have caused them if *S* had happened to encounter any. "...the [counterfactual supporting] correlation is between tokens of a certain type and (cats or robot-cats). It is simply an accident that the actual causes of *S*'s early representations were all robot cats..."

This is a form of argument I accept; see the discussion of Dretske's "learning period" account of the disjunction problem in Chapter 3.

(c) the token means *robot-cat or cat* and is thus true of the cat. But this can't be right because it "...just rekindles the disjunction problem ....[Moreover, on this account] both the cat-caused and the robot-caused tokens are veridical after all – even when S, on subsequently discovering the difference between cats and robot-cats, exclaims, 'I mistook that robot for a cat!' [Option C] seems to preclude saying that S made an error. We would have to say that her mistake was to think that she had made a mistake, and try … to find some way to make sense of her 'second-order' mistake." (All quotes from ms. pp. 6–8, passim).

So none of the three options is any good. So there must be something wrong with the way the asymmetric dependence story treats the disjunction problem. What to do then, what to do?

For reasons that will become clear when we discuss the *echt* Twin Earth problem (the one about H_2O and XYZ), Baker's case is in certain important respects underdescribed. However, given just the information that she provides and the choices that she offers, I opt for (c); that first "cat"[14] token means *cat or robot* and is thus true of the cat that it's applied to.[15] I am pleased to be able to tell you that at least one other philosopher shares this intuition. Fred Dretske somewhere considers the following variant of a Twin Earth example: There are both H_2O and XYZ on Twin Earth, but, just fortuitously, some speaker of the local dialect learns "water" only from ostensions of samples of H_2O. Dretske's intuition (and mine) is that this speaker's tokens of "water" mean H_2O *or* XYZ; in this case, though not in the standard Twin cases, the fact that the speaker would have called XYZ samples "water" counts for determining the extension that term has in his mouth. Since Baker's cat/robot case seems to be much the same sort of example, I take it that Dretske would share my view that "cat" means *cat or robot-cat* in the circumstances that Baker imagines.[16]

How good are the objections Baker raises against this analysis? Baker says that to opt for (c) "rekindles the disjunction problem," but I don't see that that is so: It is OK for *some* predicates to be disjunctive as long as not all of them are. One can perfectly consistently hold, on the one hand, that "cat" means *robot or cat* when it's *accidental* that you learned it just from robot-cats; while denying, on the other hand, that it would mean *cat or robot* if you had learned it in a world where all you *could* have learned it from were robot-cats (e.g., because there aren't any cats around.) Similarly, Dretske can consistently hold that "water" is true of H_2O or XYZ in the case he describes while agreeing that it is true of H_2O and false of XYZ in the case that Putnam describes.

But what of S's sense, on subsequently discovering the difference between robots and cats, that she used to be mistaken when she applied "cats" to robots? If her "cat" tokens meant *cat or robot*, then they were true of *both* the cats and the robots that she applied them to. Is she, then, mistaken to suppose that she used to be mistaken? There is, I think, an easy answer and an interesting answer.

Easy answer: S used not to distinguish between cats and robots; her indiscriminate application of the same term to both was a symptom of her failure to distinguish between them. Not distinguishing between cats and robots was a serious mistake (by S's current lights. And, of course, by ours).

Interesting answer: This depends on formulating the disjunction problem a little more carefully than one usually needs to. A typical instance of the disjunction problem is: "Why does the extension of 'cat' not contain both cats and rats, assuming that both cats and rats cause 'cat's?" This isn't quite the same as: "Why doesn't 'cat' *mean cat or rat* given that both cats and rats cause 'cats'?" The difference makes a difference in Baker's case.

Suppose that option (c) is right. Then, if S used to use "cat" in the way that Baker imagines, cats and robots were both in its extension. But this doesn't, of course, imply that S used "cat" to express the disjunctive concept CAT OR ROBOT (i.e., to mean *cat or robot*). Quite the contrary, S *couldn't* have used "cat" to express that concept because, by assumption, she didn't *have* that concept. Nobody can have the concept CAT OR ROBOT unless he has the constituent concepts CAT and ROBOT; which by assumption, S didn't.

So, then, what concept *did* S use "cat" to express according to option (c)? There just isn't any way to say; English provides only a disjunctive formula (viz., the expression "cat or robot") to pick out the extension {cats U robots}, and this disjunctive formula expresses a disjunctive concept (viz., the concept CAT OR ROBOT), hence not the concept that S had in mind. (Rather similar arguments show that English won't let you say what "water" means in the mouth of my Twin Earth twin; and, *mutatis mutandis*, that English$_2$ won't let my twin say what "water" means in my mouth.)

Now we can see what mistake S used to make when she applied "cat" to robots. No doubt what she said when she did so was something true. But she said it because she took it that the robots that she called "cats" had a certain nondisjunctive property which they shared with everything else in the set {cats U robots}. By her present lights, by contrast, *there is no such property*. By her present lights, the only property that cats and robots share *qua* cats and robots is the disjunctive property of BEING A CAT OR A ROBOT. So, by her present lights, when she used to say "cat" of robots (or of cats for that matter) she was saying something true, but she was saying it *for the wrong reason*. Hence her present (well-founded) intuition that there was some sort of mistake underlying her usage.

Given all this, I take it that Baker's case doesn't refute the asymmetric dependence account of content.

5 *Indeterminacy*. We saw in Chapter 3 that teleological solutions to the disjunction problem have the following nasty habit: Teleology goes soft just when you need it most; you get indeterminacies of function in just the cases where you would like to appeal to function to resolve indeterminacies of content.

In the notorious frog and bug case, for example, one would think that a good theory of content should decide – and should give some reasons for deciding – whether the intentional objects of the frog's snaps are flies or little-black-things (in effect, whether the content of the frog's mental state is 'there's a fly' or 'there's a fly-or-bee-bee').[17] But, on inspection, the teleological story about content fails to do so. To recapitulate the argument I gave in Chapter 3: You can say why snapping is a good thing for frogs to do given their situation, whichever way you describe what they snap *at*. All that's required for frog snaps to be functional is that they normally succeed in getting the flies into the frogs; and, so long as the little black dots in the frog's Normal environment *are* flies, the snaps do this equally well on either account of their intentional objects. The mathematics of survival come out precisely the same either way. (This is the sort of thing that makes philosophers feel – incorrectly but understandably – that, deep down, *content makes no difference*. First Darwinism, then nihilism when Darwinism fails; a career familiar enough from nineteenth century moral theory.)

The asymmetric dependence story, by contrast, decides the case. The frog's snaps at flies are asymmetrically dependent on its snaps at little black dots. So it is black dots, not flies, that frogs snap at. (*De dicto*, of course; *de re* it's true both that frogs snap at little black dots *and* that they snap at flies since Normally flies are the only little black dots that frogs come across.)

Three subsidiary objections now need to be considered. To wit:

(i) "What makes you so sure that the counterfactuals are the way that you're assuming? Who says that the fly snaps are asymmetrically dependent on the black-dot snaps and not vice versa?"

Strictly speaking, this is a sort of question I do not feel obliged to answer; it suffices, for the present metaphysical purposes, that there are naturalistically specifiable conditions, not known to be false, such that *if* they obtain there is a matter of fact about what the frog is snapping at. (See above, the discussion of who has the burden of argument.) However, just this once:

The crucial observation is that frogs continue to snap at (and ingest) bee-bees even when they have plenty of evidence that the bee-bees that they're snapping at aren't flies. That is: frogs continue to snap at dots in worlds where there are dots but no flies; but they don't snap at flies in worlds where there are flies but no dots.[18] (In fact, frogs won't even snap at *dead* flies; it's *moving* black dots they care about.) I take it that this strongly suggests that either there is no nomic relation between the property of being-a-fly and the property of being-a-cause-of-frog-snaps, or that, if there is such a relation, it depends asymmetrically upon the nomic relation between the property of being-a-black-dot and the property of being-a-cause-of-fly-snaps.

So far as I can tell, there's nothing special here; just a routine employment of the method of differences.

(ii) "Doesn't asymmetric dependence capitulate to the argument from illusion? If the intentional object of the frog's fly-snaps is little black dots when (*de re*) the frog snaps at flies, then maybe the intentional object of my fly-swats is little black dots when (*de re*) I swat at flies. If the fact that frogs sometimes snap at little black dots that aren't flies means that they haven't got a FLY-concept, doesn't the fact that I sometimes swat at little black dots that aren't flies mean that I haven't got a FLY-concept either?"

The relevant consideration isn't however, *just* that frogs sometimes go for bee-bees; it's that they are prepared to go on going for bee-bees *forever*. Sometimes I swat at mere fly-appearances; but usually I only swat if there's a fly. Sometimes Macbeth starts at mere dagger appearances; but most of the time he startles only if there's a dagger. What Macbeth and I have in common – and what distinguishes our case from the frog's – is that *though he and I both make mistakes, we are both in a position to recover.*[19] By contrast, frogs *have no way at all* of telling flies from bee-bees. If you think of frog snaps at black dots as *mistaken* when the black dots are bee-bees, then such mistakes are *nomologically necessary* for the frog; and this not just in the weakish sense that it's a law that black dots elicit snaps if flies do in *this* world, but also in the stronger sense that black dots elicit snaps if flies do in *all* relevant worlds where the frog's psychological constitution is the same as here.

There is no world compatible with the perceptual mechanisms of frogs in which they can avoid mistaking black dots for flies. Whereas even if, freakishly, I mistake all the dagger appearances I actually come across for daggers; and even if, still more freakishly, I never do recover from any of these mistakes, still, that would be an *accident* since it is nomologically consonant with the way that I'm constructed that I should distinguish daggers from dagger appearances some of the time. But it is *not* nomologically consonant with the way that frogs are constructed that they should ever distinguish black dots from flies.

So Macbeth and I have dagger detectors and not dagger-or-dagger-appearance detectors but frogs have black-dot detectors and not fly detectors.

Here, then, is an interesting consequence of the present story about content: An organism can't have a kind of symbol which it *necessarily* misapplies, i.e., which it misapplies in every world compatible with its psychology. Suppose that Xs look a lot like Ys; suppose they look enough like Ys that S-tokens are quite often applied to them. Still, if S means Y and not X, then (according to the theory) there *must* be worlds, consonant with the organism's psychology in *this* world, in which S- tokens are applied to Ys but withheld from Xs. (And, of course, the asymmetric dependence condition requires that, *ceteris paribus*, some such worlds are nearer to ours than any worlds in which S-tokens are applied to Xs but withheld from Ys; see sections 8 and 10 below). The bottom line is that it's impossible for frogs to have FLY

concepts but not impossible for *us* to have FLY concepts. This is because it's consonant with our psychology, but not with theirs, to sometimes distinguish flies from bee-bees.

This consequence constrains robustness. There are, after all, some mistakes that can't be made; viz., mistakes from which it is nomologically impossible to recover, consonant with the character of one's psychology. To this extent, the asymmetric dependence story is an attenuated sort of verificationism. I think that perhaps it captures what's *true* about verificationism; but, of course, I would think that.[20]

(iii) "How do you avoid saying that frogs are really snapping at their retinas?"

The point about black dots was that (we're assuming) in the frog's ecology, "is a black dot" is a description Normally true of flies. So our problem was to choose – from among the descriptions that flies Normally satisfy when frogs snap at them – the descriptions that frogs snap at them under. There may, however, be Xs other than flies, and Fs other than being a black dot, such that flies getting snapped at by frogs is asymmetrically dependent on Xs being F. If there are such, the question would arise: Why aren't Xs that are Fs the intentional objects of fly snaps?

For example: it's presumably a law that no fly gets snapped at except as some proximal projection of the fly produces some state of excitation of the retina of the frog; a retinal excitation that is, in turn, causally implicated in producing the snap. Moreover, it's plausible that such states of retinal excitation would be sufficient for causing frog snaps even if they (the excitations) weren't produced by proximal projections of flies. If all this true, then the frog's fly-elicited fly snaps are asymmetrically dependent on these states of retinal excitation. So why aren't the excitation states the intentional objects of the frog's snaps?

I don't know what the story is with frogs, but in the general case there is no reason at all to suppose that the causal dependence of perceptual states on distal objects is asymmetrically dependent on the causal dependence of *specific arrays of proximal stimuli* on the distal objects; e.g., that there are specifiable sorts of proximal traces that a cow has to leave on pain of the cow $\rightarrow$ COW connection failing. On the contrary, in the usual case there are a heterogeneity of proximal arrays that will eventuate in cow perception, and there's a good reason for this: Since – due to the laws of optics, *inter alia* – cows are mapped one–many onto their proximal projections, the mechanisms of perception – constancy, bias, sharpening, and the like – must map the proximal projections many – one onto tokenings of COW. Given the vast number of ways that cows may impinge upon sensory mechanisms, a perceptual system which made COW tokenings intimately dependent upon specific proximal projections wouldn't work as a cow-spotter.

It might still be said, however, that the dependence of cow thoughts on distal cows is asymmetrically dependent on their dependence on *disjunctions* of proximal cow projections; distal cows wouldn't evoke COW tokens but that they project proximal whiffs or glimpses or snaps or crackles or...well, or what? Since, after all, cow spotting can be mediated by theory to any extent you like, the barest whiff or glimpse of cow can do the job for an observer who is suitably attuned. Less, indeed, than a whiff or glimpse; a mere ripple in cow-infested waters may suffice to turn the trick. On the present view, cow thoughts do *not*, of course, owe their intentional content to the belief systems in which they are embedded; what determines their content is simply their asymmetric causal dependence on cows. But it is quite compatible with this that belief systems should *mediate* these semantically salient causal dependencies. They can form links in the causal chain that runs from cows to COW tokens, just as instruments of observation form links in the causal chain that runs from galaxies to GALAXY tokens.[21] To the extent that this is so, just about *any* proximal display might mediate the relation between cows and cow-thoughts for some cow-thinker or other on some or other cow-spotting occasion.

So barring appeals to *open* disjunctions, it seems likely that there is just no way to specify an array of proximal stimulations upon which the dependence of cow-thoughts upon cows is asymmetrically dependent. And here's where I quit.[22] I mean, it does seem to me that the price of intentional univocality is holding that primitive intentional states can't express open disjunctions. The idea might be that, on the one hand, content depends on *nomic* relations among properties and, on the other, nothing falls under a law by satisfying an *open* disjunction (open disjunctions aren't projectible). Like the prohibition against primitive symbols that express impossible properties, this strikes me as a very strong consequence of the present semantical

theory; but not an embarrassment because not obviously false.[23]

6 *What about the logical vocabulary?* I don't know what about the logical vocabulary. Since I think that Kripke's objection fails (see above), I'm inclined to think that maybe there is *no* objection to the idea that "+", "and", "all" and the like have the meanings they do because they play a certain causal role in the mental lives of their users. This would, of course, be to accept a distinction in kind between the logical and the nonlogical vocabularies. (The semantics for the former would be a kind of "use" theory, whereas the semantics for the latter would depend on nomic, specifically mind-world, relations.) Gilbert Harman somewhere suggests that to be a logical word *just is* to be the sort of word of which a use-theory of meaning is true. That proposal strikes me as plausible.

You may wonder how anybody who claims to be implacably opposed to inferential role semantics can have the gall to identify the meaning of a logical word with its use. Answer: the trouble with use theories is that they invite holism by well-known paths of argument (see Chapter 3 above and, more extensively, *Psychosemantics*, Chapter 3). But these holistic arguments depend on the acknowledged impossibility of *defining* most terms (specifically, on the impossibility of distinguishing defining from merely nomic biconditionals). It is therefore unclear that they apply to the logical vocabulary since terms in the logical vocabulary generally *are* definable: Anything counts as meaning *plus* that expresses a function from the numbers m, n to $m + n$; anything counts as meaning *and* that expresses a function from propositions to truth values and assigns *true* to P, Q iff it assigns *true* to $P\&Q$.

Correspondingly, it is arguably a sufficient condition for a speaker's meaning *plus* by "+" that, *ceteris paribus*, he takes "$m + n$" to designate the sum of m and n; a sufficient condition for a speaker's meaning *and* by "and" that, *ceteris paribus*, he takes "P and Q" to be true iff he takes "P" to be true and "Q" to be true; and so forth. (Relations like "taking to express," "taking to be true" – which, on this construal, hold between symbol users and symbols they use – would have to receive a causal/dispositional reconstruction if circularity is to be avoided. But there are familiar proposals for wedding functionalist construals of these relations to functional role theories of content: Thus, a speaker means *and* by "and" iff, *ceteris paribus*, he has "*P* and *Q*" in his belief box iff he has "*P*" in his belief box and he has "*Q*" in his belief box. In the case of logical vocabulary, I know of no principled reason why some such proposal shouldn't be endorsed.)

7 *What about predicates that express abstractions (like "virtuous")?* All predicates express properties, and all properties are abstract. The semantics of the word "virtuous," for example, is determined by the nomic relation between the property of being a cause of tokens of that word and the property of being virtuous. It isn't interestingly different from the semantics of "horse."

8 *Block's problem.* The following characteristically insightful objection was pointed out to me by Ned Block in the following conversation; I suppose I'm grateful to him.

> Look, your theory comes down to: "cow" means *cow* and not *cat* because, though there are nomologically possible worlds in which cows cause "cow"s but cats don't, there are no nomologically possible worlds in which cats cause "cow"s but cows don't. But such face plausibility as this idea may have depends on equivocating between two readings of "cow." In fact, there's a dilemma: If you mean by "cow" something like *the phonological/orthographic sequence #cˆoˆw#*, then there's just no reason at all to believe the claim you're making. For example, there is surely a possible world in which cows don't cause #cˆoˆw#s but trees do, viz., *the world in which #cˆoˆw# means tree*. So, if when you write "cow" what you mean is #cˆoˆw#, then it clearly can't be nomologically necessary in order for "cow" to mean *cow* that nothing causes "cow"s in worlds where cows don't.
>
> Notice that it does no good to protest that the asymmetric dependence condition is supposed to be sufficient but not necessary for content. There is *no* orthographic/phonetic sequence "*X*" which mightn't mean *tree* in some nomologically possible world or other, whatever "*X*" happens to mean here. Given the conventionality of meaning, there couldn't be. It follows that there is no orthographic/phonetic sequence "*X*" the nomologically possibility of tokenings of which is dependent on "*X*"'s being caused by *X*s. So there is no such sequence that satisfies your sufficient condition for meaning *X*. A sufficient condition for content that *nothing* satis-

fies needn't much concern Brentano. Or us.

It wouldn't, of course, be a way out of this to amend the proposal to read "#cˆoˆw# means *cow* only if, in every world in which you break the cow → #cˆoˆw# connection, *either* nothing causes #cˆoˆw#s, *or* #cˆoˆw# doesn't mean *cow*." For, though that would indeed exclude the unwanted cases, it would do so by appealing to a semantical condition and would therefore be circular. Well, for the same sort of reason it's also no good arguing that, in the world imagined, tokens of #cˆoˆw# don't count as tokens of the (viz., *our*) word "cow"; i.e., to read "cow" in "cow's are asymmetrically dependent on cows" as naming the *word* "cow" rather than the orthographic/phonological sequence #cˆoˆw#. For, that would be to appeal implicitly to a semantical construal of the conditions for type identifying words. Barring circularity, the orthographic/phonological construal of "same word" is accessible to a naturalistic semantics, but the semantical construal of "same word" is not.

So, to put it in a nutshell, if you read "cow" orthographically/phonologically the claim that "cow" means *cow* because "cow"s are asymmetrically dependent on cows is false; and if you read "cow" morphemically the claim that "cow" means *cow* because "cow"s are asymmetrically dependent on cows is circular. Either way, it's a claim that seems to be in trouble.

This is a pretty nifty line of argument. Just the same, I think the problem it raises is actually only technical.

Block is, of course, perfectly right that for the purposes of a naturalistic semantics the only non-question-begging reading of "cow" is #cˆoˆw#. Henceforth be it so read. However, the asymmetric dependence proposal is that *all else being equal*, breaking cow → "cow" breaks X → "cow" for all X.[24] Correspondingly – to put the point intuitively – what's wrong with Block's argument is that all else *isn't* equal in the worlds that he imagines. To get those worlds, you need to suppose *not only* that cow → "cow" is broken, *but also and independently* that tree → "cow" is in force. It's this independent supposition that violates the "all else equal" clause.

Here's a way to make the same point in terms of possibilia. If you put in "all else equal," then what the theory requires is *not* that cows cause "cow"s in *every* nomologically possible world where Xs cause cows. Rather, what's required is just that there be worlds where cows cause "cows" and noncows don't; and that they be nearer to our world than any world in which some noncows cause "cows" and no cows do. Notice that, on this formulation of the asymmetric dependence condition, the nomological possibility of Block's world where #cˆoˆw# means *tree* is compatible with "cow" meaning (and hence being asymmetrically dependent upon) cows in our world. At least, it is on the intuitively plausible assumption that worlds that are just like ours except that it's the case that cows don't cause "cow"s are *ipso facto* nearer to us than worlds that are just like ours except that it's both the case that cows don't cause "cows" *and* that trees do.

Let's do this one more time: To get the nearest semantically relevant world to here, you break cow → "cow". All the X → "cow" relations that nomically depend on cow → "cow" will, of course, go too, since to say that X → "cow" is nomically dependent on cow → "cow" is to say that [not (X → "cow") unless (cow → "cow")] is nomologically necessary. What the present theory claims is that, in the world that's just like ours except that cow → "cow" and everything nomologically dependent on it are gone, X → "cow" is false for all X (where, to repeat, "cow" is read as #cˆoˆw#.) Well, if this is what you mean by "the nearest possible world in which cow → 'cow' is gone," then, clearly, Block's world doesn't qualify. To get to Block's world, you have to both break cow → "cow" and stipulate tree → "cow." So the nomological possibility of Block's world is compatible with "cow" meaning *cow* according to the present version of the asymmetric dependence criterion. So everything would seem to be OK.

Corollary: Suppose that, in *this* world, there happens to be a language L in which "cow" (viz., #cˆoˆw#) means *tree*. Presumably *our* (English-speakering) use of "cow" for cows is causally independent of L's use of "cow" for trees. So, then, the nearest world to ours in which cow → "cow" goes (taking with it everything that's nomically dependent on it) still has tree → "cow" intact; and the nearest world to ours in which tree → "cow" goes (taking with it everything that's nomically dependent on it) still has cow → "cow" intact. But by assumption (specifically, by the assumption that only L and English use #cˆoˆw#), in the nearest world in which *both* cow → "cow" *and* tree → "cow" goes for every X. So, for every X, either X → "cow" depends on

cow → "cow" or X → "cow" depends on tree → "cow," neither of which depends upon the other. So, if there is a language in which "cow" means *cow* and a language in which "cow" means *tree*, then there are two different ways in which tokens of "cow" satisfy the asymmetric dependence condition. So "cow" (viz., #cˆoˆw#) is ambiguous. This is, I take it, the intuitively correct solution.

Next objection?

9 *Why doesn't "WATER" mean the same as "H_2O"?* After all, it's plausible that they express the same property; in which case, it presumably follows that neither concept is asymmetrically dependent on the other.

Actually, I'm inclined to think that "WATER" *does* mean the same as "H_2O." What doesn't follow – and isn't true – is that having the concept WATER is the same mental state as having the concept H_2O. (I.e., it's not the case that concepts are individuated by their contents. For a discussion of this sort of distinction, see Chapter 6). Would you, therefore, kindly rephrase your objection?

OK. Why, given that they express the same property, is having the concept WATER not the same mental state as having the concept H_2O?

Reply: Because you can't have the concept H_2O without having the concept HYDROGEN and you can have the concept WATER without having the concept HYDROGEN; as, indeed, is evident from the fact that the (Mentalese) expression "H_2O" has internal lexico-syntactic structure.

10 *Do the Twin Cases.* Tell me why "water" doesn't mean XYZ. And don't tell me that "water" does mean XYZ; XYZ isn't even in its extension.

I suppose the worry is that an English speaker exposed to XYZ would call it "water," and the truth of this counterfactual suggests that there's a nomic dependence between the property of being a cause of "water" tokens and the disjunctive property of being H_2O or XYZ. Since, according to the present proposal, content arises from such nomic dependencies, the problem is to explain why H_2O is, but XYZ is not, in the extension of "water." (Less precisely, it's to explain why "water" doesn't mean something disjunctive.)

The thing to keep your eye on is this: It's built into the way that one tells the Twin Earth story that it's about kind- terms (*mutatis mutandis*, kind-concepts). In particular, it's part of the story about "water" being a kind-term that English speakers intended it to apply to all and only stuff of the same (natural) kind as paradigmatic local samples (and similarly for "water2" as it's used by speakers of English2.) *A fortiori*, it's part of "water" and "water2" being kind-terms that speakers intend *not* to apply them to anything that is distinguishably *not* of the same kind as their local samples. (There are, of course, sorts of expressions with perfectly kosher semantics whose uses are not controlled by these sorts of intentions, that are therefore not used to pick out natural kinds, and whose extensions are therefore disjunctive in the sense that things of more than one natural kind belong to them. The expression "stuff sort of like water" is, I suppose, one such.)

My point is that the intention to use "water" only of stuff of the same kind as the local samples has the effect of making its applications to XYZ asymmetrically dependent on its applications to H_2O *ceteris paribus*. Given that people are disposed to treat "water" as a kind term (and, of course, given that the local samples are all in fact H_2O) it follows that – all else equal – they would apply it to XYZ only when they would apply it to H_2O; specifically, they would apply it to XYZ only when they *mistake* XYZ for H_2O; only when (and only because) they can't tell XYZ and H_2O apart. Whereas, given a world in which they *can* tell XYZ and H_2O apart (and in which their intentions with respect to "water" are the same as they are in *this* world), they will continue to apply "water" to H_2O and refrain from applying it to XYZ.

Notice that worlds in which speakers intend to use "water" as a kind-term and XYZ is distinguishable from H_2O are "nearby" relative to worlds in which speakers do not intend to use "water" as a kind-term and XYZ is distinguishable from H_2O. So the possibilities play out like this:

- In nearby worlds where XYZ *can't* be distinguished from H_2O, if you break the H_2O/"water" connection you lose the XYZ/"water" connection and vice versa.
- In nearby worlds where XYZ *can* be distinguished from XYZ, if you break the H_2O/"water" connection you lose the XYZ/"water" connection, but *not* vice versa.

So, *ceteris paribus*, there are nearby worlds where you get the H_2O/"water" connection without the XYZ/"water" connection, but no nearby worlds

where you get the XYZ/"water" connection without the H_2O/"water" connection. I.e., it's nomologically possible for the XYZ/water connection to fail without the H_2O/water connection failing, but not vice versa. So applications of "water" to XYZ are asymmetrically dependent on applications of "water" to H_2O. So "water" means H_2O and not XYZ in the conditions that the Twin Earth story imagines; just as the standard intuitions require.[25]

So much for H_2O and XYZ. It may be useful, by way of summary, to bring together what I've said about the unicorn worry, the Baker worry, and the H_2O/XYZ worry, since all three involve cases where a semantic theory is required to make intuitively correct determinations of the extension of a term with respect to merely possible entities.

To begin with, you can now see why I said that the Baker example (about cats and robot-cats) was underdescribed. In the *echt* Twin cases, it's always assumed that the speaker intends the word in question to be a natural kind-term, and the speaker's having this intention has the effect of making the semantically relevant asymmetric dependencies true of his use of the word. In Baker's case, by contrast, we know that the speaker eventually comes to apply "cat" to cats and not to robots, but we *don't* know whether this is in virtue of a previous standing disposition to use "cat" as a kind-term. Baker doesn't say, so I've assumed that the speaker had no such standing disposition. So Baker's "cat" means *cat or robot* because, on the one hand, S would (indeed, does) use "cat" for either; and, on the other, there's nothing in Baker's description of the case that suggests a mechanism (such as an intention to use "cat" as a kind-term) that would make the use for the robots asymmetrically dependent upon the use for the cats (or vice versa).

"Unicorn" means unicorn because you can have lawful relations among uninstantiated properties (and people would apply "unicorn" to unicorns if there were any). By contrast, "water" means water (and not XYZ) because, although people would use "water" of XYZ if there were any (XYZ is supposed to be indistinguishable from H_2O) nevertheless, they have a settled policy of using "water" as a kind-term (of using it only for substances actually of the same kind as water), and their adherence to this policy makes their use of "water" for XYZ asymmetrically dependent on their use of "water" for H_2O: there's a break in the XYZ/"water" connection *without* a break in the H₂O/"water" connection in nearby world where H_2O is distinguishable from XYZ. (If, however, you don't like this story about why "water" doesn't mean XYZ, I'll tell you a different one presently.)

11 *Absolutely last objection.* But *how could* asymmetric dependence be sufficient for content? Surely you can have cases where one nomic relation is asymmetrically dependent on another but where there is no *semantical* relation at issue?

Well, maybe, but I've only been able to think of two candidates: asymmetric dependencies that arise from causal chains and asymmetric dependencies that involve nomic relations at different levels of analysis. And what's striking about both these cases is that the asymmetric dependencies they generate aren't the right kind to produce robustness. Since mere stipulation can ensure that only asymmetric dependencies that do produce robustness count for semantic purposes, neither of these kinds of cases poses a real threat to my story. Let's have a look at this.

Interlevel relations: Suppose you have a case where a microlevel law $(B \rightarrow C)$ provides the mechanism for a macrolevel law $(A \rightarrow D)$ (in the way that, for example, Bernoulli's law provides the mechanism for laws about airfoils). Then it might be that the $A \rightarrow D$ law is asymmetrically dependent on the $B \rightarrow C$ law. You might get this if, for example, $B \rightarrow C$ is necessary but not sufficient to sustain $A \rightarrow D$; in that case, breaking the $B \rightarrow C$ connection would break the $A \rightarrow D$ connection in all nomologically possible worlds, but there might be nomologically possible worlds in which the $A \rightarrow D$ connection goes even though the $B \rightarrow C$ connection is intact. Since it is, to put it mildly, not obvious that C has to mean B in such cases, it seems that asymmetric dependence isn't sufficient for content after all.

Reply: The point of appeals to asymmetric dependence in theories of content is to show how tokens of the same type could have heterogeneous causes compatible with their all meaning the same thing; i.e., it's to show how robustness is possible. Correspondingly, if a sufficient condition for content is going to be fashioned in terms of asymmetric dependence, it must advert to the dependence of one causal law *about "X" tokens* upon another causal law *about "X" tokens*. But the sort of asymmetric dependencies that interlevel cases generate don't meet this condition. What we

have in these cases is a law that governs the tokening of one thing (Ds in the example) that's dependent on a law that governs the tokening of some other thing (Cs in the example). This sort of asymmetric dependence doesn't produce robustness, so it's not semantically relevant.

Causal chains: We discussed these in a slightly different context when we asked why the frog's retinal irradiations are not the intentional objects of its fly-snaps: The causal link between distal stimuli and mental representations is mediated by (and thus depends asymmetrically upon) causal links between proximal stimuli and mental representations. In that example, we were given a state whose intentional object was assumed to be one of its causes, and the question was *which* one. The present issue is slightly different: Since causal chains give rise to a species of asymmetrical dependence, and since every event belongs to some causal chain or other, how are we to avoid concluding that everything means something? Pansemanticism gone mad.

Short form: Suppose As (*qua As*) cause Bs (*qua Bs*), and Bs (*qua Bs*) cause Cs (*qua Cs*), and assume that As are sufficient but not necessary for the Bs. Then the law $A \rightarrow C$ is asymmetrically dependent on the law $B \rightarrow C$. Why doesn't it follow that Cs mean B?

Answer: Because, although the causal chain makes the $A \rightarrow C$ connection asymmetrically depend on the $B \rightarrow C$ connection, the dependence of Cs on Bs that it engenders is not *ipso facto* robust, and content requires not just causal dependence but robustness too. The dependence of Cs on Bs is *robust only if there are non-B-caused Cs*. But the causal chain $A \rightarrow B \rightarrow C$, engenders an asymmetric dependence in which *all the A-caused Cs are also B-caused*. So the asymmetric dependence of $A \rightarrow C$ on $B \rightarrow C$ doesn't satisfy the conditions on robustness; so it's not semantically relevant.

But suppose we have both $A \rightarrow B \rightarrow C$ and $D \rightarrow B \rightarrow C$.

(i) C still doesn't mean B because every C is B-caused and robustness fails.

(ii) C doesn't mean A because Cs being caused by non-As doesn't depend on Cs being caused by As (i.e., you don't get $X \rightarrow C$ relations that are asymmetrically dependent on $A \rightarrow C$ relations). An analogous argument shows that C doesn't mean D either.

(iii) *C doesn't mean (A or D)* because *X*-caused *C*s that are asymmetrically dependent on *A*- or *D*-caused *C*s are *ipso facto* asymmetrically dependent on *B*-caused *C*s. Intuitively, what's wanted is that "*X*" means *X* only if *X*s are the *only* sorts of things on which *X*s are robustly dependent. Take-home problem: Formulate the asymmetric dependence condition to make this the case.

All that this technical fooling around shows is that if we stipulate that asymmetric dependence engenders content only if it produces robustness,

then perhaps we can avoid Crazy Pansemanticism: the doctrine that everything means something. But, of course, some causal chains – viz., the ones that do meet conditions for information and robustness – will, *ipso facto*, meet the present conditions for content. So, the really interesting question is whether meeting the conditions for information and robustness really *is* meeting the conditions for content. We'll return to this at the end.

So much for all the objections I've been able to think of.

Acknowledgments

I want to express a special indebtedness to Paul Boghossian for very helpful conversations on these topics and for having caught a bad mistake in an earlier draft of this essay. Literally dozens of other people have made suggestions I've found illuminating. They include all, but not only, the following (and I hereby apologize to anyone I have left out): Louise Antony, Lynne Baker, Ned Block, Dan Dennett, Michael Devitt, Joe Levine, Barry Loewer, Tim Maudlin, Brian McLaughlin, Georges Rey, Steve Wagner, and many graduate students at Rutgers and CUNY.

Notes

1 A variant of the theory that I'll discuss near the end departs significantly from the letter of informational semantics, though perhaps less significantly from its spirit.
2 For the type one/type two distinction, see chapter 3.
3 Compare *Psychosemantics* (1987), in which I took it for granted – wrongly, as I now think – that an information-based semantics would have to specify such circumstances. As far as I can tell, I assumed this because I thought that any informational theory of content would have to amount to a more or less hedged version of "all and only cows cause 'cow's'". This, too, was a failure to take semantic robustness sufficiently seriously. It's no more plausible that there are nonquestion-beggingly specifiable situations in which it's semantically necessary that all cows cause "cows" than that there are such situations in which, necessarily, only cows do. How *could* there be circumstances in which the content of a thought guarantees that someone will think it?
4 As are all other "nonlabeling" uses of a symbol. See Fodor (forthcoming).
5 Well, *almost* arbitrarily robust; see below.
6 Though not, of course, without resort to intentional (with-an-"s") idiom. The asymmetric dependence story is up to its ears in Realism about properties, relations, laws, and other abstracta. Whether this sort of Realism prejudices a semantic theory's claim to be physicalistic – and whether, if it does, it *matters*

whether a semantic theory is physicalistic – are questions of some interest; but not ones that I propose to take on here. Suffice it that *naturalism*, as I understand the term, needn't imply *materialism* if the latter is understood as denying independent ontological status to abstract entities.
7 The caveat is because informational semanticists rarely straight out identify "meaning that..." with "carrying the information that..." (though Isreal seems to be right on the edge of doing so in the passage cited in the text). Dretske, for example, adds constraints intended to ensure that the information carried should be *perfectly* reliable, and that it should be "digitally" encoded (this is Dretske's way of ensuring that "dog" means *dog* rather than *animal*.) Also, the Stanford theorists generally allow that information can be generated by reliable relations other than causal ones (e.g., entailment relations). These considerations don't, however, affect the point in the text.
8 As Georges Rey remarks, "The viability of a *ceteris paribus* clause depends not upon the actual specification or realizability of the idealization, but rather upon whether the apparent exceptions to the law to which it is attached can be explained as due to independently specifiable interference. It is a check written on the banks of independent theories, which is only as good as those theories and *their* independent evidence can make it. So the question...is not

(247)

whether the *ceteris paribus* clause can be replaced, but rather: Can all the errors be explained as independent interference?" (Rey, ms.) It's worth spelling out an implication of Rey's point: To know what, in general, the consequence of satisfying a *ceteris paribus* condition would be, we would have to know what would happen if none of the sources of "independent interference" were operative. And to know *that*, we'd have to know, at a minimum, what the sources of independent interference *are*; we'd have to know which other laws can interact with the *ceteris paribus* law under examination. But, of course, it's never possible to know (much) of this under the conditions actually operative in scientific theory construction; what interactions between L and other laws are possible depends not just on how L turns out, but also on *how the rest of science turns out*.

9   This counterfactual is, of course, by no means vacuous. It claims, in effect, that our capacities to add are bounded *only* by the limitations of our working memory; in particular, they aren't bounded *by what we know about how to add numbers*. Such claims are, to put it mildly, often nonobvious. For example, as of this date nobody knows whether it's true that, but for memory constraints, a normal English speaker could parse every sentence of his language. ("Garden path" sentences appear to offer counterexamples.) As it turns out, the resolution of some rather deep issues in linguistics depend on this question.

10   For example, Steven Wagner's "Theories of mental representation" (ms) criticizes one version of the view I'll be proposing by remarking that it "has the *wildly* implausible consequence that there are worlds remotely like ours in which cows could not be mistaken for horses." In fact, what I hold is only that if "cow" means *cow* and not *horse* then it must be nomologically possible to tell any cow from a horse; which doesn't sound all *that* wild after all. (Actually, there's a version of my story that requires still less; see the discussion of verificationism below.) You get the consequence that Wagner denounces only if you conjoin my story about semantics to the story about modals that says that if P is nomologically possible, then there is a world in which it's the case that P. So much the worse for that story about modals.

11   To be sure, this can't be the *only* way that asymmetric dependence gets its foothold. For example: if, as I'm claiming, the use of linguistic symbols to effect mislabelings, false predications, and the like is asymmetrically dependent on their being applied correctly, that asymmetry can't arise from linguistic practices in anything like the way that the asymmetric dependence of pagings on namings does; there's a *convention* for paging, but not for mislabeling. And, of course, we have no linguistic practices (no conventions) at all with respect to our mental

representations. Patience, dear Reader; all in good time.

12   I'll use "concept" ambiguously; sometimes it refers to a mental representation (thus following psychological usage) and sometimes to the intension of a mental representation (thus following philosophical usage). The context will often make clear which reading is at issue. When I wish to name a concept, I'll use the corresponding English word in caps; hence, "COW" for the concept cow.

13   Roughly, a symbol is syntactically primitive iff it has no semantically evaluable proper parts.

14   Baker raises her problem for tokens of Mentalese, but nothing turns on this, and English is easier to spell.

15   There may be readers who demand a semantics that makes the first "cat" token come out false (i.e., who demand that it mean *robot-cat*). I beg a temporary suspension of their disbelief. We'll see further on how the theory could be revised to accommodate them.

16   I think these sorts of cases throw some interesting side light on the standard Twin Earth examples. It's usual in the literature to take the moral of the Twin cases to be the significance of context in determining content: "Water" means H_2O because there isn't any XYZ on earth. But Dretske's case opens the possibility of super-Twins: creatures who have not only type-identical neural structures, but who also share a context (in some reasonable sense), but whose intentional states nevertheless differ in content: the extension of A's term "water" includes XYZ and the extension of B's term "water" does not because it's fortuitous for A but not for B that he has encountered no samples of XYZ.

Apparently, then, the content of your term may differ from the content of mine if there's something that prevents tokens of your term from being caused by instantiations of a property whose instantiations could (i.e., really could, not just nomologically possibly could) cause tokenings of mine. This might be true even of two creatures who live in the same world if, as it happens, they live in different parts of the wood. If the nearest XYZ to me is so far away that I can't possibly get there in a lifetime, then, I suppose, "water" means something nondisjunctive in my mouth. Whereas, if the nearest XYZ to you is so close that it's just an accident that you haven't come across any, then, I suppose, "water" does mean something disjunctive in yours.

Does any of this matter? If so, to what?

17   The hyphens are because nobody could think that the frog has the disjunctive concept FLY OR BEE BEE (just as nobody could think that S has the disjunctive concept CAT OR ROBOT CAT in the Baker case discussed above). The issue, rather, is whether the frog has the concept FLY or the

concept of a certain visible property which, *de facto*, flies and bee bees both exhibit.

18 It's crucial that this claim be read *synchronically* since, presumably, frogs wouldn't develop a disposition to snap at black dots in worlds where the black dots have *never* been flies. The semantically relevant sort of asymmetric dependence is a relation among an organism's *current* dispositions. Take real-world frogs and put them in possible worlds where the black dots are bee-bees and they'll snap away, happy as the day is long. But real-world frogs in possible worlds where the flies aren't black dots are *ipso facto* snapless.

19 Cf: "Is this a dagger which I see before me.../ Come, let me clutch thee. / I have thee not, and yet I see thee still. / Art thou not, fatal vision, sensible / To feeling as to sight? or art thou but / A dagger of the mind, a false creation, / Proceeding from the heat-oppressed brain?" Macbeth's morals were, no doubt, reprehensible, but his epistemology was spot on.

20 I've thus far made a point of not distinguishing two theses: (a) if *X* and *Y* are distinct concepts, then there must be a world in which *x*s but not *y*s cause "*X*"s; (b) if *X* and *Y* are distinct concepts *and xs and ys both cause "X"s* in this *world* then there must be a world in which *x*s but not *y*s cause "*X*"s. The (b) story is markedly less verificationist than the (a) story and some philosophers may prefer it on that ground. We'll come to this presently; but suffice it for now that both stories say the same things about what frogs snap at and about what Macbeth means by "dagger."

21 For further discussion of the analogy between the function of theories and of instruments of observa-tion in mediating the symbol/world relations upon which content depends, see chapter 3 (especially n.4); also Fodor, *Psychosemantics*, chapter 4.

22 The case is a little different when states of the central nervous system (as opposed, e.g., to retinal states) are proposed as the intentional objects of the thoughts that cows causally occasion. I suppose it might turn out that there are specifiable, *non*disjunctive states of the brain upon whose tokening the connection of cow-occasioned thoughts to cows asymmetrically depend. Such a discovery would not, however, require us to say that the intentional object of one's cow thoughts are brain states. Rather, we could simply take the brainstate tokens to be tokens of the Mentalese term for cow.

23 I say that one *might* rule out proximal referents for mental representations by appeal to the principle that open disjunctions aren't projectible. But one could also take the high ground and rule them out by stipulation: just as primitive symbols aren't allowed to express necessarily uninstantiated properties, so too they aren't allowed to express proximal properties. If this seems arbitrary, remember that we're looking for (naturalistically) *sufficient* conditions for representation.

24 And not vice versa. But where the asymmetry of the dependence is not germane to the point at issue I'll leave this clause out to simplify the exposition.

25 I take it that, but for the talk about intentions and policies, the same sort of line applies to kind-concepts. What makes something a kind-concept, according to his view, is what it tracks in worlds where instances of the kind to which it applies are distinguishable from instances of the kinds to which it doesn't.

References

Baker, Lynn (1989) "On a causal theory of Content." *Philosophical Perspectives*, 3. Atascadero, CA: Ridgeview Publishing.

Boghossian. P (1989) "Review of Colin McGinn's *Wittgenstein on Meaning*." *Philosophical Review*, 1, 83-4.

Cummins, R. (1989) "Representation and covariation." In S. Silvers (ed.), *Representation*, 40 (Philosophical Studies Series, Dordrecht: Kluwer).

Dretske, F. (1981) *Knowledge and the Flow of Information*. Cambridge, MA: MIT Press.

Fodor, J. A. (1981) "The current status of the innateness controversy." In *Representations*. Cambridge, MA: MIT Press.

Fodor, J. A. (1987) *Psychosemantics*. Cambridge, MA: MIT Press.

Fodor, J. A. (Forthcoming) "Information and representation."

Israel, D. (1987) *The Role of Propositional Objects of Belief in Action*. CSLI Monograph Report No. CSLI-87-72. Palo Alto: Standford University.

Kripke, S. (1982) *Wittgenstein on Rules and Private Language*. Cambridge, MA: Harvard University Press.

Rey, G. (Unpublished) "Concepts, stereotypes and individual psychology: sketch of a framework."

Wagner, S. (Unpublished) "Theories of mental representation."

PART V

The Status of "Folk Psychology"

Introduction

In Part III above we were introduced to the somewhat strange idea that mental terms and mental entities themselves are at risk. Sellars, Feyerabend, and Quine in the 1960s first urged the "theory" theory, as Morton (1980) calls it; that is, the idea that mental terms are the theoretical terms of a folk science. After an understandable period of incredulity, the "theory" theory became widely accepted. But the "theory" theory leads in a disconcerting direction: if the only reason we have for accepting the existence of mental entities is the utility and presumed truth of folk psychology, and if folk psychology should turn out to be largely *false* or seriously infirm in some other way, as scientific theories and especially folk theories often do, then presumably some version of Eliminativism is correct.

We have already looked (in Part III above) at some Eliminativist arguments. In this Part we shall turn to a special issue regarding propositional attitude content, the issue of "methodological solipsism" in Putnam's (1975) phrase, and examine its consequences for the probity of folk psychology. After that, we shall touch briefly on each of three or four other recent debates concerning folk psychology.

Methodological Solipsism

Suppose for the sake of argument that we attribute representational content to the internal states of computers – as in real life we do, however, anthropomorphically. A computer sometimes thinks this or wants that; at the very least, it computes this or computes that: the GNP of Monaco, the outcome of the coming Presidential election, the balance of our checking account or whatever.

Now, to take a key example of Jerry Fodor's (1980): it is quite possible that two computers, programmed by entirely different users for entirely different purposes, should happen to run physically in parallel. They might go through precisely the same sequence of electrical currents and flipflop settings and yet have their outputs interpreted differently by their respective users, especially if what they write to their screens is all in numerical form. One of them would naturally and correctly be described as figuring out the GNP of Monaco, while the other would just as naturally and correctly be described as figuring out the batting averages of New York Yankees then and now. The point, plain enough when we think about it, is simply that *what* a machine is computing is not fully determined by the physical or even the abstract-functional operations that are going on entirely inside the machine. What the machine is computing depends to some extent on something outside the machine itself – users' intentions, causal-historical chains (see Part IV above), teleology, interpretation by observers, or just the convenience of the beholder.

The point is not particularly surprising. But Putnam (1975) drew a broader conclusion that was developed to startling effect by Fodor (1980) and by Stich (this volume, this Part): as it is with computers, so it is with humans. The representational content of a human subject's propositional attitudes is underdetermined by even the total state of that subject's head. Putnam's "Twin Earth" and indexical examples show that, surprising at it may seem, two human beings could be molecule-for-molecule alike and still differ in their beliefs and desires, depending on various factors in their spatial and historical environments. (For dissent, however, see Searle (1983).)

Philosophers now distinguish between "narrow" properties, those that are determined by a subject's intrinsic physical composition, and "wide" properties, those that are not so determined.

The thesis that attitude contents are "wide" raises serious problems about the vaunted role of propositional attitudes in the explaining of behavior, and attendant questions for psychology (Fodor 1980; Stich, this volume, this Part). But for our purposes in this Part, the main question is this: if the representational content of a propositional attitude depends on factors outside the physical boundary of its owner's skin, what are those factors, and more importantly, can we still suppose that the attitude contents are genuine properties of the owner/subject. The specter of Elimination reappears; perhaps it is not really, objectively true of people that they believe this or desire that.

The question of what the environmental factors actually are is just the question of psychosemantics again (Part IV above). But what about the ontological status of people's beliefs and desires themselves? There are several different possibilities.

1   The external semantical interpretation of an organism's internal physical/functional states is entirely up for grabs: any interpretation that suits anyone's convenience is good enough, and if two interpreters' interpretations conflict, neither is correct to the exclusion of the other. (Schiffer (1981) discusses this possibility sympathetically, and construes Quine's famous doctrine of the "indeterminacy of translation" as getting at this position.) If we fall in with this view, we can hardly call it a hard fact that a subject believes one thing rather than another.

2   The semantical interpretation of beliefs is not up for grabs; it is at least loosely determined by various contextual factors, and some interpretations are correct while others are just wrong. But the contextual factors in question are intolerably vague and messy and social and interest-infested – quite unsuitable for incorporation into any genuine science. To ascribe the belief that P to someone is no more scientific, explanatory, or useful than is calling something "nice." (2) is the position of Stich (1983).

3   The semantical interpretation of beliefs is loosely determined by various contextual factors, and some interpretations are correct while others are just wrong, and this is what it is for the subject to believe one thing rather than another. Some complex causal–historical and/ or teleological feature of the subject's environment (cf. the introduction to Part IV) makes it objectively true that the subject believes so-and-so rather than such-and-such, whether or not the feature is scientifically interesting or well-behaved. (Lycan (1981, 1987) staunchly defends this view.)

4   There is nothing messy, interest-relative etc. about the contextual factors in question, even though they extend outside the skin boundary. They are a matter of *simple* nomological or teleological fact. This position is endorsed by "indicator" semanticists among others (Dretske, Stampe, Stalnaker).

The first position, (1), is essentially an Eliminative view, and certainly flouts the folk-psychological thesis that propositional attitudes *qua* propositional attitudes are real causal constituents of the world; (2) allows that attitude ascriptions may be true (however interest-infested), and consequently that people do believe one thing rather than another, but still rejects the folk-psychological view that the attitudes genuinely cause behavior; (3) and (4) are entirely compatible with folk psychology; (1) and (2) differ from each other, it seems, only in degree, so the real issue so far is that of whether (2) or (3) is more plausible.

First Reverberations of the "Narrow"/ "Wide" Distinction

Stephen Stich ("Autonomous psychology and the belief–desire thesis," this volume) argues from the wideness of beliefs and desires that most such contentful states cannot be invoked in a genuinely explanatory psychological theory, and that, therefore, most or many of our everyday singular causal statements that specify beliefs or desires as causes of actions are without foundation. Horgan and Woodward (this volume) defend folk psychology

Introduction

against both Churchland (this volume, Part III) and Stich; Burge (1986) also contends that existing psychological theories make entirely legitimate appeal to "wide" states of subjects.

Block (1986) and Devitt (this volume) strike middle ways between Stich and Burge, agreeing with Stich that psychological explanation (or much of it) must be narrow but insisting that there is a suitably narrow notion of belief- and desire content that resists Stich's general skepticism about content. Loar (1988) offers a different variation on the same line. Stich ("Narrow content meets fat syntax," this volume) responds that even if there is such a thing as narrow content, it will not serve the purposes for which it was designed. And recently, Stich (1996) has criticized and abandoned his original arguments.

Intentional Causation

Davidson (this volume, Part I) and Stich between them have raised the issue of how mental states and events can be said to cause physical ones, such as (most notably) human actions. This issue really splits into two, which I shall label accordingly.

"Supervenient causation": Given that mental events do not *as such* fall under the laws that underpin mind-to-world causation – or indeed, on Davidson's view, under any laws at all – how can they in propria persona be said to cause actions and other physical events at all? Jaegwon Kim (1989, 1993, 1995, this volume) appeals to principles of "explanatory exclusion" and "causal closure" to argue that such causation raises the specter of action-at-a-distance. McLaughlin (this volume) blocks at least one route to that conclusion.

"Wide causation": Given that ordinary propositional-attitude content is wide, how can it be said (as perhaps it is by common sense) that propositional attitudes cause behavior in virtue of their contents? For surely it is only their narrow functional properties that are internal to the subject, doing the actual causal work. Fodor (this volume, this Part) defends this line of argument. He also takes it as motivation for a notion of narrow content, since commonsensical honor can be satisfied if we suppose that propositional attitudes cause behavior in virtue at least of their narrow contents. Wilson (this volume) retorts that the argument against wide causation is unconvincing in the first place.

It should be noted that neither problem – of supervenient causation or of wide causation – is specific to the mind. Supervenient causation pervades nature, and many sciences besides the social and behavioral sciences appeal to wide causation (e.g., biology and even astronomy); see McClamrock (1995) and Wilson (1995). Thus, it is something of an historical oddity that the two issues should have been pursued mainly under the rubric of the philosophy of mind. (Though I believe Kim (1995) means to contest that.)

Self-Knowledge

If propositional-attitude content is wide, then how can we know by introspection what we believe, desire, or hope for? For presumably we can introspect only what is in our heads, not causal-historical and other extracalvarian factors. Davidson (this volume, this Part) raises that question, and tries to defuse it by rejecting the view that "to have a thought is to have an object 'before the mind'." Burge (1988) and Heil (this volume) argue, less drastically, that the problem is illusory because second-order states of introspective awareness inherit their own contents from the wide contents of the first-order attitudes they are about. The issue has received much subsequent discussion.

The "Theory" Theory vs. the Simulation Theory

Irrespective of "narrow"/"wide" issues, the "theory" theory of mental ascriptions has recently been challenged by a putative competitor, the "Simulation" theory advocated by Heal (1986), Gordon (this volume), and Goldman (1989). According to the latter view, the picture of mental states as posits hypothesized to explain and predict other people's behavior is mistaken. Rather, in order to explain and predict others' behavior, we imagine being in their circumstances and imagine our own ensuing mental and behavioral responses, adjusting where necessary for known differences between our subjects' psychologies and our own. On Goldman's view, which Gordon calls the "'model' model," this amounts to running a simulation, an off-line exercise of our own psychological mechanisms. (But Gordon himself de-emphasizes off-line processing. Davies (this volume) explores the consequences of that difference.) In any case, the Simulationist denies that the epistemology of mental ascriptions is as the "theory" theorist would have it.

It is not clear how extensively the Simulation view does compete or conflict with the "theory" theory, for that depends on what the "theory" theory is taken to be a theory *of* or about. There are a number of importantly different candidates for explanandum:

(a) The semantics of mental terms. The "theory" theory holds that mental terms have semantics of the same type as do scientific-theoretical terms generally.

(b) The metaphysics of the corresponding entities. The "theory" theory holds that mental states are theoretical entities, unobserved causes of observed physical events.

(c) The (if you like) basic epistemic security of mental states and events. The "theory" theory holds that mental ascriptions are not only individually fallible, but globally so: *contra* the Analytical Behaviorists, such ascriptions *might* all be false.

(d) The more detailed epistemology of mental entities. The "theory" theory holds that they are, or are exactly as if they were, posited for explanatory purposes, and that what justifies them is (always or primarily) inference to the best explanation.

(e) The actual mature psychology of mental ascription. The "theory" theory is naturally understood as implying that we arrive at our mental ascriptions through a process of explanatory hypothesis formation.

(f) The developmental psychology of mental ascription. Some Simulation theorists and some neutral parties have taken to regarding empirical developmental evidence as relevant to the general debate between Simulation and the "theory" theory.

To date, the "theory" theory is unopposed by the Simulation theory in areas (a), (b), and (c), for the Simulation theory is entirely compatible with the "theory" view of semantics, metaphysics, and basic epistemic security, and does not even suggest competing alternatives. (And historically, it was only those three areas to which the "theory" theory was addressed by its progenitors.) So the Simulation theorist who claims to dispute the "theory" theory in any or all of those areas needs to come up with a specific competitor.

Just as the Simulationist really has no interest in areas (a)–(c), the "theory" theorist has no official interest in area (f), developmental psychology, for no philosopher of my acquaintance has made any actual developmental claims (however much "theory" theorists might *welcome* indirect confirmation from developmental psychology). So there is no substantive debate between the "theory" theory and Simulation in area (f) either. (Similar remarks apply in particular to the burgeoning "Theory of Mind" literature in psychology, on which see, e.g., Astington (1993); Carruthers and Smith (1995); and Davies and Stone (1995).)

Area (e) is uncertain. The "theory" theory can understandably be construed as making a claimabout actual psychological processes, whether or not any of its authors had actually made that claim. Each professed "theory" theorist must decide whether to take the field in regard to (e), and whichever does must confront the Simulation theorist's apparently conflicting empirical data.

That leaves (d), and in that area there is indisputably real debate. A *pure* "theory" theory holds that mental ascriptions are always causal hypotheses justified by inference to the best explanation; the Simulation theorist insists to the contrary that all or most of them are instead justified by the off-line simulation technique. Of course, the truth may well be somewhere in between.

Further Reading

General works

Greenwood, J. (ed.) (1991) *The Future of Folk Psychology*, Cambridge University Press.

Christensen, S. M. and Turner, D. R. (eds) (1993) *Folk Psychology and the Philosophy of Mind*, Lawrence Erlbaum Associates.

"Methodological solipsism"

Putnam, H. (1975) "The meaning of 'meaning'," in K. Gunderson (ed.), *Minnesota Studies in the Philosophy of Science, Vol. 7: Language, Mind and Knowledge*, University of Minnesota Press.

Fodor, J. A. (1980) "Methodological solipsism considered as a research strategy in cognitive psychology," *Behavioral and Brain Sciences* 3, 63–73, as well as the Open Peer Commentaries on Fodor's article in the same issue and Elliott Sober's later commentary in vol. 5 (1982), 300–2.

Burge, T. (1979) "Individualism and the mental," in P. French. T. E. Uehling, and H. Wettstein (eds), *Midwest Studies in Philosophy IV: Studies in Metaphysics*, University of Minnesota Press.

Stich, S. (1983) *From Folk Psychology to Cognitive Science. The Case Against Belief*, Bradford Books/ MIT Press.

Reverberations of the "narrow"/"wide" distinction

Lycan, W. (1981) "Toward a homuncular theory of believing," *Cognition and Brain Theory* 4, 139–59.

Schiffer, S. (1981) "Truth and the theory of content," in H. Parret and J. Bouveresse (eds), *Meaning and Understanding*, Walter de Gruyter.

Dennett, D. C. (1982) "Beyond belief," in A. Woodfield (ed.), *Thought and Object*, Oxford University Press.

McGinn, C. (1982) "The structure of content," in A. Woodfield (ed.), *Thought and Object*.

Putnam, H. (1983) "Computational psychology and interpretation theory," reprinted in *Realism and Reason: Philosophical Papers*, vol. 3, Cambridge University Press; and (1988) in *Representation and Reality*, Bradford Books/MIT Press.

Owens, J. (1983) "Functionalism and propositional attitudes," *Noûs* 17, 529–49.

Fodor, J. A. (1987) *Psychosemantics*, Bradford Books/ MIT Press.

Loar, B. (1988) "Social content and psychological content," in R. H. Grimm and D. D. Merrill (eds), *Contents of Thought*, University of Arizona Press.

Owens, J. (1987) "In defense of a different doppelganger," *Philosophical Review* 96: 521–54.

Baker, L. R. (1988) *Saving Belief*, Princeton University Press.

Stalnaker, R. (1991) "Narrow content," in C. Anderson and J. Owens (eds) *Propositional Attitudes*, Stanford University Press.

Block, N. (1991) "What narrow content is not," in B. Loewer and G. Rey (eds) *Meaning in Mind: Fodor and His Critics*, Blackwell Publishers.

Fodor, J. A. (1991) "A modal argument for narrow content," *Journal of Philosophy* 88, 5–26.

Egan, F. (1991) "Must psychology be individualistic?" *Philosophical Review* 100: 179–203.

Defending folk psychology

Morton, A. (1980) *Frames of Mind*. Oxford University Press. [Not a defense of folk psychology *qua* empirical theory; Morton christens and criticizes the "theory" theory of folk psychology.]

von Eckardt, B. (1984) "Cognitive psychology and principled skepticism," *Journal of Philosophy* 81, 67–88.

Kitcher, P. (1984) "In defense of intentional psychology," *Journal of Philosophy* 81, 89–106.

Wilkes, K. (1984) "Pragmatics in science and theory in common sense," *Inquiry* 27: 339–61.

Wilkes, K. (1991) "The relationship between scientific psychology and common sense psychology," *Synthese* 89: 15–39. Reprinted in Christensen and Turner, op. cit.

Fodor, J. A. (1987) *Psychosemantics*, loc. cit.

Dennett, D. C. (1987) *The Intentional Stance*, Bradford Books/MIT Press.

Lycan, W. G. (1988) *Judgment and Justification*, Cambridge University Press.

Lycan, W. G. (1997) "Folk psychology and its liabilities," in M. Carrier and P. K. Machamer (eds), *Mindscapes: Philosophy, Science, and the Mind*, University of Pittsburgh Press.

Block, N. J. (1986) "Advertisement for a semantics for psychology," in P. French, T. E. Uehling, and H. Wettstein (eds), *Midwest Studies X: Studies in the Philosophy of Mind*, University of Minnesota Press.

Burge, T. (1986) "Individualism and psychology," *Philosophical Review* 95, 3–45.

Baker, L. R. (1995) *Explaining Attitudes*, Cambridge University Press.

Stich, S. (1996) *Deconstructing the Mind*, Oxford University Press.

Mental causation

Heil, J. and Mele, A. (eds) (1993) *Mental Causation*, Oxford University Press. [Contains many fine essays.]

Kim, J. (1989) "Mechanism, purpose, and explanatory exclusion," in J. E. Tomberlin (ed.), *Philosophical Perspectives, 3: Philosophy of Mind and Action Theory*, Ridgeview Publishing.

Kim, J. (1993) "The non-reductivist's troubles with mental causation," in J. Heil, and A. Mele (eds), *Mental Causation*, Oxford University Press.

Kim, J. (1995) "Mental causation: what? Me worry?" in E. Villanueva (ed.), *Content*, Ridgeview Publishing.

Tomberlin, J. E. (ed.) (1997) *Philosophical Perspectives, 11: Mind, Causation, and World*, Ridgeview Publishing. [Contains a useful symposium on Kim's work.].

LePore, E. and Loewer, B. (1987) "Mind matters," *Journal of Philosophy* 84: 630–42.

Dretske, F. (1988) *Explaining Behavior*, Bradford Books/ MIT Press.

Dretske, F. (1993) "Mental events as structuring causes of behavior," in J. Heil, and A. Mele (eds), *Mental Causation*, Oxford University Press.

Jackson, F. and Pettit, P. (1988) "Functionalism and broad content," *Mind* 97: 381–400.

Horgan, T. (1989) "Mental Quasation," in Tomberlin, op. cit.

Stalnaker, R. (1989) "On what's in the head," in Tomberlin, op. cit.

Fodor, J. A. (1989) "Making mind matter more," *Philosophical Topics* 17: 59–79.

Introduction

Block, N. (1990) "Can the mind change the world?," in G. Boolos (ed.), *Meaning and Method: Essays in Honor of Hilary Putnam*, Cambridge University Press.

Antony, L. (1991) "The causal relevance of the mental," *Mind and Language* 6: 295–327.

Segal, G. and Sober, E. (1991) "The causal efficacy of content," *Philosophical Studies* 63: 1–30.

Yablo, S. (1992) "Mental causation," *Philosophical Review* 101: 245–80.

Heil, J. (1992) *The Nature of True Minds*, Cambridge University Press.

Peacocke, C. (1993) "Externalist explanation," *Proceedings of the Aristotelian Society* 93: 203–30.

McClamrock, R. (1995) *Existential Cognition*, University of Chicago Press.

Wilson, R. A. (1995) *Cartesian Psychology and Physical Minds*, Cambridge University Press.

Jacob, P. (1997) *What Minds Can Do*, Cambridge University Press.

Self-knowledge

Burge, T. (1988) "Individualism and self-knowledge," *Journal of Philosophy* 85: 649–53.

Boghossian, P. (1989) "Content and self-knowledge," *Philosophical Topics* 17: 5–26.

Warfield, T. (1992) "Privileged self-knowledge and externalism are compatible," *Analysis* 52: 232–7.

Falvey, K. and Owens, J. (1994) "Externalism, self-knowledge, and skepticism," *Philosophical Review* 103: 107–37.

Georgalis, N. (1994) "Asymmetry of access to intentional states," *Erkenntnis* 40: 185–211.

The Simulation theory

Heal, J. (1986) "Replication and functionalism," in J. Butterfield (ed.), *Language, Mind and Logic*, Cambridge University Press.

Goldman, A. (1989) "Interpretation psychologized," *Mind and Language* 4: 161–85.

Davies, M. and Stone, T. (eds) (1995a) *Folk Psychology: The Theory of Mind Debate*, Blackwell Publishers.

[Reprints the original Heal, Gordon, and Goldman papers among others.]

Davies, M. and Stone, T. (eds) (1995b) *Mental Simulation: Evaluations and Applications*, Blackwell Publishers.

The "Theory of Mind" literature

Astington, J. W. (1993) *The Child's Discovery of the Mind*, Harvard University Press.

Carruthers, P. and Smith, P. (eds) (1995) *Theories of Theories of Mind*, Cambridge University Press.

11

Attacking "Folk Psychology"

Autonomous Psychology and the Belief–Desire Thesis

Stephen P. Stich

A venerable view, still very much alive, holds that human action is to be explained at least in part in terms of beliefs and desires. Those who advocate the view expect that the psychological theory which explains human behavior will invoke the concepts of belief and desire in a substantive way. I will call this expectation *the belief–desire thesis*. Though there would surely be a quibble or a caveat here and there, the thesis would be endorsed by an exceptionally heterogeneous collection of psychologists and philosophers ranging from Freud and Hume, to Thomas Szasz and Richard Brandt. Indeed, a number of philosophers have contended that the thesis, or something like it, is embedded in our ordinary, workaday concept of action.[1] If they are right, and I think they are, then insofar as we use the concept of action we are *all* committed to the belief–desire thesis. My purpose in this essay is to explore the tension between the belief–desire thesis and a widely held assumption about the nature of explanatory psychological theories, an assumption that serves as a fundamental regulative principle for much of contemporary psychological theorizing. This assumption, which for want of a better term I will call the *principle of psychological autonomy*, will be the focus of the first of the sections below. In the second section I will elaborate a bit on how the belief–desire thesis is to be interpreted, and try to extract from it a principle that will serve as a premise in the argument to follow. In the third

section I will set out an argument to the effect that large numbers of belief–desire explanations of action, indeed perhaps the bulk of such explanations, are incompatible with the principle of autonomy. Finally, in the last section, I will fend off a possible objection to my argument. In the process, I will try to make clear just why the argument works and what price we should have to pay if we were resolved to avoid its consequences.

1 The Principle of Psychological Autonomy

Perhaps the most vivid way of explaining the principle I have in mind is by invoking a type of science fiction example that has cropped up with some frequency in recent philosophical literature. Imagine that technology were available which would enable us to duplicate people. That is, we can build living human beings who are atom for atom and molecule for molecule replicas of some given human being.[2] Now suppose that we have before us a human being (or, for that matter, any sort of animal) and his exact replica. What the principle of autonomy claims is that these two humans will be psychologically identical, that any psychological property instantiated by one of these subjects will also be instantiated by the other.

Actually, a bit of hedging is needed to mark the boundaries of this claim to psychological identity.

First, let me note that the organisms claimed to be psychologically identical include any pair of organisms, existing at the same time or at different times, who happen to be atom for atom replicas of each other. Moreover, it is inessential that one organism should have been built to be a replica of the other. Even if the replication is entirely accidental, the two organisms will still be psychologically identical.

A caveat of another sort is needed to clarify just what I mean by calling two organisms "psychologically identical." For consider the following objection: "The original organism and his replica do not share *all* of their psychological properties. The original may, for example, remember seeing the Watergate hearings on television, but the replica remembers no such thing. He may think he remembers it, or have an identical "memory trace," but if he was not created until long after the Watergate hearings, then he did not see the hearings on television, and thus he could not remember seeing them." The point being urged by my imagined critic is a reasonable one. There are many sorts of properties plausibly labeled "psychological" that might be instantiated by a person and not by his replica. Remembering that p is one example, knowing that p and seeing that p are others. These properties have a sort of "hybrid" character. They seem to be analyzable into a "purely psychological" property (like seeming to remember that p, or believing that p) along with one or more nonpsychological properties and relations (like p being true, or the memory trace being caused in a certain way by the fact that p). But to insist that "hybrid" psychological properties are not psychological properties at all would be at best a rather high handed attempt at stipulative definition. Still, there is something a bit odd about these hybrid psychological properties, a fact which reflects itself in the intuitive distinction between "hybrids" and their underlying "purely psychological" components. What is odd about the hybrids, I think, is that we do not expect them to play any role in an explanatory psychological theory. Rather, we expect a psychological theory which aims at explaining behavior to invoke only the "purely psychological" properties which are shared by a subject and its replicas. Thus, for example, we are inclined to insist it is Jones's *belief* that there is no greatest prime number that plays a role in the explanation of his answering the exam question. He may, in fact, have *known* that there is no greatest prime number. But even if he did not

know it, if, for example, the source of his information had himself only been guessing, Jones's behavior would have been unaffected. What knowledge adds to belief is psychologically irrelevant. Similarly the difference between really remembering that p and merely seeming to remember that p makes no difference to the subject's behavior. In claiming that physical replicas are psychologically identical, the principle of psychological autonomy is to be understood as restricting itself to the properties that can play a role in explanatory psychological theory. Indeed, the principle is best viewed as a claim about what sorts of properties and relations may play a role in explanatory psychological theory. If the principle is to be observed, then the only properties and relations that may legitimately play a role in explanatory psychological theories are the properties and relations that a subject and its replica will share.

There is another way to explain the principle of psychological autonomy that does not appeal to the fanciful idea of a replica.... Jaegwon Kim has explicated and explored the notion of one class of properties *supervening* upon another class of properties.[3] Suppose S and W are two classes of properties, and that S# and W# are the sets of all properties constructible from the properties in S and W respectively. Then, following Kim, we will say that the family S of properties supervenes on the family W of properties (with respect to a domain D of objects) just in case, necessarily, any two objects in D which share all properties in W# will also share all properties in S#. A bit less formally, one class of properties supervenes on another if the presence or absence of properties in the former class is completely determined by the presence or absence of properties in the latter.[4] Now the principle of psychological autonomy states that the properties and relations to be invoked in an explanatory psychological theory must be supervenient upon the *current, internal physical* properties and relations of organisms (i.e., just those properties that an organism shares with all of its replicas).

Perhaps the best way to focus more sharply on what the autonomy principle states is to look at what it rules out. First, of course, if explanatory psychological properties and relations must supervene on *physical* properties, then at least some forms of dualism are false. The dualist who claims that there are psychological (or mental) properties which are not nomologically correlated with physical properties, but which nonetheless must be invoked in an explanation of the organism's behavior, is denying that explanatory psychological states supervene upon physical states. However, the autonomy principle is not inimical to all forms of dualism. Those dualists, for example, who hold that mental and physical properties are nomologically correlated need have no quarrel with the doctrine of autonomy. However, the principle of autonomy is significantly stronger than the mere insistence that psychological states supervene on physical states.[5] For autonomy requires in addition that certain physical properties and relations are psychologically irrelevant in the sense that organisms which differ *only* with respect to those properties and relations are psychologically identical.[6] In specifying that only "current" physical properties are psychologically relevant, the autonomy principle decrees irrelevant all those properties that deal with the history of the organism, both past and future. It is entirely possible, for example, for two organisms to have quite different physical histories and yet, at a specific pair of moments, to be replicas of one another. But this sort of difference, according to the autonomy principle, can make no difference from the point of view of explanatory psychology. Thus remembering that p (as contrasted with having a memory trace that p) cannot be an explanatory psychological state. For the difference between a person who remembers that p and a person who only seems to remember that p is not dependent on their current physical state, but only on the history of these states. Similarly, in specifying that only *internal* properties and relations are relevant to explanatory psychological properties, the autonomy principle decrees that relations between an organism and its external environment are irrelevant to its current (explanatory) psychological state. The restriction also entails that properties and relations of external objects cannot be relevant to the organism's current (explanatory) psychological state. Thus neither my seeing that Jones is falling nor my knowing that Ouagadougou is the capital of Upper Volta can play a role in an explanatory psychological theory, since the former depends in part on my relation to Jones, and the latter depends in part on the relation between Ouagadougou and Upper Volta.

Before we leave our discussion of the principle of psychological autonomy, let us reflect briefly on the status of the principle. On Kim's view, the belief that one set of properties supervenes on another "is largely, and often, a combination of metaphysical convictions and methodological considerations."[7] The description seems particularly apt for the principle of psychological autonomy. The autonomy principle serves a sort of regulative role in modern psychology, directing us to restrict the concepts we invoke in our explanatory theories in a very special way. When we act in accordance with the regulative stipulation of the principle we are giving witness to the tacit conviction that the best explanation of behavior will include a theory invoking properties supervenient upon the organism's current, internal physical state.[8] As Kim urges, this conviction is supported in part by the past success of theories which cleave to the principle's restrictions, and in part by some very fundamental metaphysical convictions. I think there is much to be learned in trying to pick apart the various metaphysical views that support the autonomy principle, for some of them have implications in areas quite removed from psychology. But that is a project for a different paper.

2 The Belief–Desire Thesis

The belief–desire thesis maintains that human action is to be explained, at least in part, in terms of beliefs and desires. To sharpen the thesis we need to say more about the intended sense of *explain*, and more about what it would be to explain action *in terms of beliefs and desires*. But before trying to pin down either of these notions, it will be useful to set out an example of the sort of informal belief–desire explanations that we commonly offer for our own actions and the actions of others.

Jones is watching television; from time to time he looks nervously at a lottery ticket grasped firmly in his hand. Suddenly he jumps up and rushes toward the phone. Why? It was because the TV announcer has just announced the winning lottery number, and it is the number on Jones's ticket. Jones believes that he has won the lottery. He also believes that to collect his winnings he must contact the lottery commission promptly. And, needless to say, he very much wants to collect his winnings.

Many theorists acknowledge that explanations like the one offered of Jones rushing toward the phone are often true (albeit incomplete) explanations of action. But this concession alone does not commit the theorist to the belief–desire thesis as I will interpret it here. There is considerable controversy over how we are to understand the "because" in "Jones rushed for the phone because he believed he had won the lottery and he wanted…" Some writers are inclined to read the "because" literally, as claiming that Jones's belief and his desire were the *causes* (or among the causes) of his action. Others offer a variety of non-causal accounts of the relation between beliefs and desires on the one hand and actions on the other.[9] However, it is the former, "literal," reading that is required by the belief–desire thesis as I am construing it.

To say that Jones's belief that he had won the lottery was among the causes of his rushing toward the phone is to say of one specific event that it had among its causes one specific state. There is much debate over how such "singular causal statements" are to be analyzed. Some philosophers hold that for a state or event S to be among the causes of an event E, there must be a law which somehow relates S and E. Other philosophers propose other accounts. Even among those who agree that singular causal statements must be subsumed by a law, there is debate over how this notion of subsumption is to be understood. At the heart of this controversy is the issue of how much difference there can be between the properties invoked in the law and those invoked in the description of the event if the event is to be an instance of the law.[10] Given our current purposes, there is no need to take a stand on this quite general metaphysical issue. But we will have to take a stand on a special case of the relation between beliefs, desires, and the psychological laws that subsume them. The belief–desire thesis, as I am viewing it, takes seriously the idea of developing a psychological theory couched in terms of beliefs and desires. Thus, in addition to holding that Jones's action was caused by his belief that he had won the lottery and his desire to collect his winnings, it also holds that this singular causal statement is true in virtue of being subsumed by laws which specify nomological relations among beliefs, desires, and action.[11]

There is one further point that needs to be made about my construal of the belief–desire thesis. If the thesis is right, then action is to be explained at least in part by appeal to laws detailing how beliefs, desires, and other psychological states effect action. But how are we to recognize such laws? It is, after all, plainly not enough for a theory simply to invoke the terms "belief" and "desire" in its

laws. If it were, then it would be possible to convert any theory into a belief–desire theory by the simple expedient of replacing a pair of its theoretical terms with the terms "belief" and "desire." The point I am laboring is that the belief–desire thesis must be construed as the claim that psychological theory will be couched in terms of beliefs and desires *as we ordinarily conceive of them*. Thus to spell out the belief–desire thesis in detail would require that we explicate our intuitive concepts of belief and desire. Fortunately, we need not embark on that project here.[12] To fuel the arguments I will develop in the following section, I will need only a single, intuitively plausible, premise about beliefs.

As a backdrop for the premise that I need, let me introduce some handy terminology. I believe that Ouagadougou is the capital of Upper Volta, and if you share my interest in atlases then it is likely that you have the same belief. Of course, there is also a perfectly coherent sense in which your belief is not the same as mine, since you could come to believe that Bobo Dioulasso is the capital of Upper Volta, while my belief remains unchanged. The point here is the obvious one that beliefs, like sentences, admit of a type–token distinction. I am inclined to view belief tokens as states of a person. And I take a state to be the instantiation of a property by an object during a time interval. Two belief states (or belief tokens) are of the same type if they are instantiations of the same property and they are of different types if they are instantiations of different properties.[13] In the example at hand, the property that both you and I instantiate is *believing that Ouagadougou is the capital of Upper Volta*.

Now the premise I need for my argument concerns the identity conditions for belief properties. Cast in its most intuitive form, the premise is simply that if a particular belief of yours is true and a particular belief of mine is false, then they are not the same belief. A bit more precisely: If a belief token of one subject differs in truth value from a belief token of another subject, then the tokens are not of the same type. Given our recent account of belief states, this is equivalent to a sufficient condition for the non-identity of belief properties: If an instantiation of belief property p_1 differs in truth value from an instantiation of belief property p_2 then p_1 and p_2 are different properties. This premise hardly constitutes an analysis of our motion of sameness of belief, since we surely do not hold belief tokens to be of the same type if they merely have the same truth value. But no matter.

There is no need here to explicate our intuitive notion of belief identity in any detail. What the premise does provide is a necessary condition on any state counting as a belief. If a pair of states can be type identical (i.e., can be instantiations of the same property) while differing in truth value, then the states are not beliefs as we ordinarily conceive of them.

Before putting my premise to work, it might be helpful to note how the premise can be derived from a quite traditional philosophical account of the nature of beliefs. According to this account, belief is a relation between a person and a proposition. Two persons have the same belief (instantiate the same belief property) if they are belief-related to the same proposition. And, finally, propositions are taken to be the vehicles of truth, so propositions with different truth values cannot be identical. Given this account of belief, it follows straightforwardly that belief tokens differing in truth value differ in type. But the entailment is not mutual, so those who, like me, have some suspicions about the account of belief as a relation between a person and a proposition are free to explore other accounts of belief without abandoning the intuitively sanctioned premise that differences in truth value entail difference in belief.

3 The Tension between Autonomy and the Belief–Desire Thesis

In this section I want to argue that a certain tension exists between the principle of psychological autonomy and the belief–desire thesis. The tension is not, strictly speaking, a logical incompatibility. Rather, there is an incompatibility between the autonomy principle and some assumptions that are naturally and all but universally shared by advocates of the belief–desire thesis. The additional assumptions are that singular causal statements like the ones extractable from our little story about Jones and the lottery ticket are often true. Moreover, they are true because they are subsumed by laws which invoke the very properties which are invoked in the characterization of the beliefs and desires. A bit less abstractly, what I am assuming is that statements like "Jones's belief that he had won the lottery was among the causes of his rushing toward the phone" are often true; and that they are true in virtue of being subsumed by laws invoking properties like *believing that he had just won the lottery*. The burden of my argument is that if we accept the principle of autonomy, then these assumptions must be rejected. More specifically, I will argue that if the autonomy principle is accepted then there are large numbers of belief properties that cannot play a role in an explanatory psychological theory. My strategy will be to examine four different cases, each representative of a large class. In each case we will consider a pair of subjects who, according to the autonomy principle, instantiate all the same explanatory psychological properties, but who have different beliefs. So if we accept the principle of psychological autonomy, then it follows that the belief properties our subjects instantiate cannot be explanatory psychological properties. After running through the examples, I will reflect briefly on the implications of the argument for the belief–desire thesis.

Case 1: Self-referential beliefs[14]

Suppose, as we did earlier, that we have the technology for creating atom for atom replicas of people. Suppose, further, that a replica for me has just been created. I believe that I have tasted a bottle of Chateau d'Yquem, 1962. Were you to ask me whether I had ever tasted a d'Yquem, 1962, I would likely reply, "Yes, I have." An advocate of the belief–desire thesis would urge, plausibly enough, that my belief is among the causes of my utterance. Now if you were to ask my replica whether he had ever tasted a d'Yquem, 1962, he would likely also reply, "Yes, I have." And surely a belief–desire theorist will also count my replica's belief among the causes of *his* utterance. But the belief which is a cause of my replica's utterance must be of a different type from the one which is a cause of my utterance. For his belief is false; he has just been created and has never tasted a d'Yquem, nor any other wine. So by the premise we set out in section 2, the belief property he instantiates is different from the one I instantiate. Yet since we are replicas, the autonomy principle entails that we share all our explanatory psychological properties. It follows that the property of believing that I have tasted a Chateau d'Yquem, 1962, cannot be one which plays a role in an explanatory psychological theory. In an obvious way, the example can be generalized to almost all beliefs about oneself. If we adhere to the principle of autonomy, then beliefs about ourselves can play no role in the explanation of our behavior.

Case 2: Beliefs about one's spatial and temporal location

Imagine, to vary the science fiction example, that cryogenics, the art of freezing people, has been perfected to the point at which a person can be frozen, stored, then defrosted, and at the end of the ordeal be atom for atom identical with the way he was at the beginning of the freezing process. Now suppose that I submit myself to cryogenic preservation this afternoon, and, after being frozen, I am transported to Iceland where I am stored for a century or two, then defrosted. I now believe that it is the twentieth century and that there are many strawberry farms nearby. It would be easy enough to tell stories which would incline the belief–desire theorists to say that each of these beliefs is serving as a cause of my actions. I will leave the details to the reader's imagination. On being defrosted, however, I would presumably still believe that it is the twentieth century and that there are many strawberry farms nearby. Since my current beliefs are both true and my future beliefs both false, they are not belief tokens of the same type, and do not instantiate the same belief property. But by hypothesis, I am, on defrosting, a replica of my current self. Thus the explanatory psychological properties that I instantiate cannot have changed. So the belief property I instantiate when I now believe that it is the twentieth century cannot play any role in an explanatory psychological theory. As in the previous case, the example generalizes to a large number of other beliefs involving a subject's temporal and spatial location.

Case 3: Beliefs about other people

In several papers Hilary Putnam has made interesting use of the following fanciful hypothesis.[15] Suppose that in some distant corner of the universe there is a planet very much like our own. Indeed, it is so much like our own that there is a person there who is my doppelganger. He is atom for atom identical with me and has led an entirely parallel life history. Like me, my doppelganger teaches in a philosophy department, and like me has heard a number of lectures on the subject of proper names delivered by a man called "Saul Kripke." However, his planet is not a complete physical replica of mine. For the philosopher called "Saul Kripke" on that planet, though strikingly similar to the one called by the same name on

our planet, was actually born in a state they call "South Dakota," which is to the north of a state they call "Nebraska." By contrast, our Saul Kripke was born in Nebraska – our Nebraska, of course, not theirs. But for reasons which need not be gone into here, many people on this distant planet, including my doppelganger, hold a belief which they express by saying "Saul Kripke was born in Nebraska." Now I also hold a belief which I express by saying "Saul Kripke was born in Nebraska." Now I also hold a belief which I express by saying "Saul Kripke was born in Nebraska." However, the belief I express with those words is very different from the belief my doppelganger expresses using the same words, so different, in fact, that his belief is false while mine is true. Yet since we are doppelgangers the autonomy principle dictates that we instantiate all the same explanatory psychological properties. Thus the belief property I instantiate in virtue of believing that Saul Kripke was born in Nebraska cannot be a property invoked in an explanatory psychological theory.

Case 4: Natural kind predicates

In Putnam's doppelganger planet stories, a crucial difference between our planet and the distant one is that on our planet the substance which we call "water," which fills our lakes, etc. is in fact H_2O, while on the other planet the substance they call "water" which fills their lakes, etc. is in fact some complex chemical whose chemical formula we may abbreviate XYZ. Now imagine that we are in the year 1700, and that some ancestor of mine hears a story from a source he takes to be beyond reproach to the effect that when lizards are dipped in water, they dissolve. The story, let us further suppose, is false, a fact which my ancestor might discover to his dismay when attempting to dissolve a lizard. For the belief–desire theorist, the unsuccessful attempt has as one of its causes the belief that lizards dissolve in water. Now suppose that my ancestor has a doppelganger on the far off planet who is told an identical sounding story by an equally trustworthy racanteur. However, as it happens that story is true, for there are lizards that do dissolve in XYZ, though none will dissolve in H_2O. The pattern should by now be familiar. My ancestor's belief is false, his doppelganger's is true. Thus the belief tokens instantiate different belief properties. But since *ex hypothesi* the people holding the beliefs are physically identical, the belief properties they instantiate cannot function in an explanatory psychological theory.[16]

This completes my presentation of cases. Obviously, the sorts of examples we have looked at are not the only ones susceptible to the sort of arguments I have been using. But let us now reflect for a moment on just what these arguments show. To begin, we should note that they do *not* show the belief–desire thesis is false. The thesis, as I have construed it here, holds that there are psychological laws which invoke various belief and desire properties and which have a substantive role to play in the explanation of behavior. Nothing we have said here would suffice to show that there are no such laws. At best, what we have shown is that, if we accept the principle of psychological autonomy, then a large class of belief properties cannot be invoked in an explanatory psychological theory. This, in turn, entails that many intuitively sanctioned singular causal statements which specify a belief as a cause of an action cannot be straightforwardly subsumed by a law. And it is just here, I think, that our argument may serve to undermine the belief–desire thesis. For the plausibility of the thesis rests, in large measure, on the plausibility of these singular causal statements. Indeed, I think the belief–desire thesis can be profitably viewed as the speculation that these intuitively sanctioned singular causal statements can be cashed out in a serious psychological theory couched in terms of beliefs and desires. In showing that large numbers of these singular causal statements cannot be cashed out in this way, we make the speculation embodied in the belief–desire thesis appear idle and unmotivated. In the section that follows, I will consider a way in which an advocate of the belief–desire thesis might try to deflect the impact of our arguments, and indicate the burden that this escape route imposes on the belief–desire theorist.

4 A Way Out and Its Costs

Perhaps the most tempting way to contain the damage done by the arguments of the previous section is to grant the conclusions while denying their relevance to the belief–desire thesis. I imagine a critic's objection going something like this: "Granted, if we accept the autonomy principle, then certain belief properties cannot be used in explanatory theories. But this does nothing to diminish the plausibility of the belief–desire thesis, because the properties you have shown incompa-

tible with autonomy are the *wrong kind* of belief properties. All of the examples you consider are cases of *de re* beliefs, none of them are *de dicto* beliefs. But those theorists who take seriously the idea of constructing a belief–desire psychological theory have in mind a theory invoking *de dicto* beliefs and desires. *De re* beliefs are a sort of hybrid; a person has a *de re* belief if he has a suitable underlying *de dicto* belief, *and* if he is related to specific objects in a certain way. But it is only the underlying *de dicto* belief that will play a role in psychological explanation. Thus your arguments do not cast any serious doubt on the belief–desire thesis."[17]

Before assessing this attempt to protect the belief–desire thesis, a few remarks on the *de dicto*/*de re* distinction are in order. In the recent philosophical discussion of *de re* and *de dicto* beliefs, the focus has been on the logical relations among various sorts of belief attributions. Writers concerned with the issue have generally invoked a substitution criterion to mark the boundary between *de dicto* and *de re* belief attributions. Roughly, a belief attribution of the form

S believes that p

is *de re* if any name or other referring expression within p can be replaced with a co-designating term without risk of change of truth value; otherwise the attribution is *de dicto*.[18]

But now given this way of drawing the *de re*/*de dicto* distinction, my imagined critic is simply wrong in suggesting that all of the examples used in my arguments are cases of *de re* belief. Indeed, just the opposite is true; I intend all of the belief attribution in my examples to be understood in the *de dicto* sense, and all my arguments work quite as well when they are read in this way. Thus, for example, in Case 3 I attribute to myself the belief that Saul Kripke was born in Nebraska. But I intend this to be understood in such a way that

Stich believes ϕ was born in Nebraska

might well be false if ϕ were replaced by a term which, quite unbeknownst to me, in fact denotes Saul Kripke.

There is, however, another way the critic could press his attack that sidesteps my rejoinder. Recently, a number of writers have challenged the substitutional account of the *de dicto*/*de re* distinction. The basic idea underlying their challenge is that the term "*de re*" should be used for all belief attributions which intend to ascribe a "real" relation of some sort between the believer and the object of his belief. The notion of a real relation is contrasted with the sort of relation that obtains between a person and an object when the object happens to satisfy some description that the person has in mind.[19] Burge, for example, holds that "a *de dicto* belief is a belief in which the believer is related only to a completely expressed proposition (*dictum*)," in contrast to a *de re* belief which is "a belief whose correct ascription places the believer in an appropriate, *nonconceptual, contextual* relation to the objects the belief is about."[20] Thus, if Brown believes that the most prosperous Oriental rug dealer in Los Angeles is an Armenian, and if he believes it simply because he believes all prosperous Oriental rug dealers are Armenian, but has no idea who the man may be, then his belief is *de dicto*. By contrast, if Brown is an intimate of the gentleman, he may have the *de re* belief that the most prosperous Oriental rug dealer in Los Angeles is an Armenian. The sentence

> Brown believes that the most prosperous Oriental rug dealer in Los Angeles is an Armenian.

is thus ambiguous, since it may be used either in the *de re* sense to assert that Brown and the rug dealer stand in some "appropriate, nonconceptual, contextual relation" or in the *de dicto* sense which asserts merely that Brown endorses the proposition that the most prosperous rug dealer in Los Angeles (whoever he may be) is an Armenian.

The problem with the substitutional account of the *de dicto*/*de re* distinction is that it classifies as *de dicto* many belief attributions which impute a "real" relation between the believer and the object of his belief. In many belief attributions the names or definite descriptions that occur in the content sentence do a sort of double duty. First, they serve the function commonly served by names and descriptions; they indicate (or refer to) an object, in this case the object to which the believer is said to be related. The names or descriptions in the content sentence *also* may serve to indicate how the believer conceives of the object, or how he might characterize it. When a name or description serving both roles is replaced by a codesignating expression which does *not* indicate how the believer conceives of the object, then the altered attribution (interpreted in the "double duty" sense) will be false. Thus the substitutional

account classifies the original attribution as *de dicto*, despite its imputation of a "real" relation between believer and object.[21]

Now if the *de dicto*/*de re* distinction is drawn by classifying as *de re* all those belief attributions which impute a "real" relation between believer and object, then the critic conjured in the first paragraph of this section is likely right in his contention that all of my arguments invoke examples of *de re* beliefs. Indeed, the strategy of my arguments is to cite an example of a *de re* (i.e., "real" relation") belief, then construct a second example in which the second believer is a physical replica of the first, but has no "real relation" to the object of the first believer's belief. However, to grant this much is not to grant that the critic has succeeded in blunting the point of my arguments.

Let me begin my rejoinder with a fussy point. The critic's contentions were two: first, that my examples all invoked *de re* belief properties; second, that *de re* belief properties are hybrids and are analyzable into *de dicto* belief properties. The fussy point is that even if both the critic's contentions are granted, the critic would not quite have met my arguments head on. The missing premise is that *de dicto* belief properties (construed now according to the "real relation" criterion) are in fact compatible with the principle of psychological autonomy. This premise may be true, but the notion of a "real" relation, on which the current account of *de dicto* belief properties depends, is sufficiently obscure that it is hard to tell. Fortunately, there is a simple way to finesse the problem. Let us introduce the term *autonomous beliefs* for those beliefs that a subject must share with all his replicas; and let us use the term *non-autonomous* for those beliefs which a subject need not share with his replica.[22] More generally, we can call any property which an organism must share with its replicas an *autonomous property*. We can now reconstrue the critic's claims as follows:

1   All the examples considered in section 3 invoke non-autonomous belief properties.
2   Non-autonomous belief properties are hybrids, analyzable into an underlying autonomous belief property (which can play a role in psychological explanation) plus some further relation(s) between the believer and the object of his belief.

On the first point I naturally have no quarrel, since a principal purpose of this essay is to show that a large class of belief properties are non-autonomous. On the second claim, however, I would balk, for I am skeptical that the proposed analysis can in fact be carried off. I must hasten to add that I know of *no argument* sufficient to show that the analysis is impossible. But, of course, my critic has no argument either. Behind my skepticism is the fact that no such analysis has ever been carried off. Moreover, the required analysis is considerably more demanding than the analysis of *de re* belief in terms of *de dicto* belief, when the distinction between the two is drawn by the substitutional criterion. For the class of autonomous beliefs is significantly smaller than the class of *de dicto* beliefs (characterized substitutionally).[23] And the most impressive attempts to reduce *de re* beliefs to *de dicto* plainly will not be of much help for the analysis my critic proposes.[24] But enough, I have already conceded that I cannot prove my critic's project is impossible. What I do hope to have established is that the critic's burden is the burden of the belief–desire theorist. If the reduction of non-autonomous beliefs to autonomous beliefs cannot be carried off, then there is small prospect that a psychological theory couched in terms of beliefs and desires will succeed in explaining any substantial part of human behavior.

A final point. It might be argued that, however difficult the analysis of non-autonomous beliefs to autonomous ones may be, it must be possible to carry it off. For, the argument continues, a subject's non-autonomous beliefs are determined in part by the autonomous psychological properties he instantiates and in part by his various relations to the objects of the world. Were either of these components suitably altered, the subject's non-autonomous beliefs would be altered as well. And since non-autonomous beliefs are jointly determined by autonomous psychological properties and by other relations, there must be some analy-sis, however complex, which specifies how this joint determination works. Now this last claim is not one I would want to challenge. I am quite prepared to grant that non-autonomous beliefs admit of some analysis in terms of autonomous psychological properties plus other relations. But what seems much more doubtful to me is that the autonomous properties invoked in the analysis would be *belief properties*. To see the reasons for my doubt, let us reflect on the picture suggested by the examples in section 3. In each case we had a pair of subjects who shared all their autonomous properties though their non-autonomous beliefs differed in truth value. The difference in truth value, in turn, was rooted in a difference in reference; the beliefs were simply about different persons, places, or times. In short, the beliefs represented different states of affairs. If the non-autonomous belief properties of these examples are to be analyzed into autonomous psychological properties plus various historical or external relations, then it is plausible to suppose that the autonomous psychological properties do not determine a truth value, an appropriate reference, or a represented state of affairs. So the state of exhibiting one (or more) of these autonomous properties itself has no truth value, is not referential, and does not represent anything. And this, I would urge, is more than enough reason to say that it is not a belief at all. None of this amounts to an *argument* that non-autonomous beliefs are not analyzable into autonomous ones. Those who seek such an analysis are still free to maintain that there will be at least one autonomous belief among the autonomous properties in the analysans of each non-autonomous belief property. But in the absence of an argument for this claim, I think few will find it particularly plausible. The ball is in the belief–desire theorist's court.[25,26]

Appendix

A bit more needs to be said about the premise urged at the end of section 2. The premise, it will be recalled, was this:

> If a belief token of one subject differs in truth value from a belief token of another subject, then the tokens are not of the same type.

A number of helpful critics have pointed out to me that we actually have a variety of intuitively sanc-tioned ways to decide when two belief tokens are of the same type. Moreover, some of these patently violate my premise. Thus, for example, if Jones and Smith each believes that he will win the next presidential election, there would be no intuitive oddness to the claim that Jones and Smith have the same belief. Though, of course, if Jones's belief is true, Smith's belief is false. It would be equally natural in this case to say that Jones and Smith have different beliefs. So I cannot rest my premise on our intuitive judgments; the intuitions will not bear the weight.

I think the best way of defending the premise is to make clear how it is related to a certain view (actually a category of views) about what beliefs are. The views I have in mind all share two features in common:

(i) they take belief to be a relation between a believer and a type of abstract object;

(ii) they take the abstract objects to be representational – that is, the abstract objects are taken to picture the world as being a certain way, or to claim that some state of affairs obtains. Thus the object, along with the actual state of the believer's world, determines a truth value.

For example, certain theorists take belief to be a relation between a person and a proposition; a proposition, in turn, determines a truth value for every possible world – truth for those worlds in which it is true and falsity for those worlds in which it is false. A person's belief is true if the proposition is true in his or her world. Rather more old fashioned is the theory which holds belief to be a relation between a person and an image or a mental picture. The belief is true if and only if the mental picture correctly depicts the believer's world.

Now on views such as these which take belief to be a relation between a person and an abstract object, the most natural way of determining when a pair of belief tokens are of the same type is by appeal to the abstract objects. A pair of subjects' belief tokens are of the same type when the subjects are related to the same abstract object. Thus when subjects are in the same possible world, their belief tokens are of the same type only if they are identical in truth value. And this, in effect, was the premise advanced in section 2. The thesis of this essay is best taken to be that the principle of psychological autonomy is in conflict with the belief–desire thesis, *when beliefs are construed as in (i) and (ii)*. Let me add a final observation. A number of theorists have taken belief to be a relation between a person and a sentence or sentence-like object. For example, in *The Language of Thought* (Crowell 1975) Jerry Fodor holds that belief is a relation between a person and a sentence in "the language of thought." It is interesting to ask whether a theory like Fodor's is at odds with the principle of psychological autonomy. The answer, I think, turns on whether the sentences in the language of thought are taken to have truth values, and whether their referring expressions are taken to determine a referent in a given world, independent of the head in which they happen to be inscribed. If sentences in the language of thought are taken to be analogous to Quine's eternal sentences, true or false in a given world regardless of who utters them or where they may be inscribed, then Fodor's view will satisfy (i) and (ii) and will run head on into the principle of psychological autonomy. For Fodor, I suspect, this would be argument enough to show that the sentences in the language of thought are not eternal.

Notes

1 The clearest and most detailed elaboration of this view that I know of is to be found in Goldman (1970). The view is also argued in Brandt and Kim (1963), and in Davidson (1963). However, Davidson does not advocate the belief–desire thesis as it will be construed below (cf. n. 11).

2 Cf. Putnam (1973 and 1975).

3 Kim (1978).

4 Kim's account of supervenience is intentionally noncommittal on the sort of necessity invoked in the definition. Different notions of necessity will yield different, though parallel, concepts of supervenience.

5 This weaker principle is discussed at some length in Kim (1977).

6 Note, however, that physical properties that are irrelevant in this sense may nonetheless be *causally* related to those physical properties upon which psychological properties supervene. Thus they may be "psychologically relevant" in the sense that they may play a role in the explanation of how the organism comes to have some psychological property.

7 Kim (1978).

8 It has been my experience that psychologists who agree on little else readily endorse the autonomy principle. Indeed, I have yet to find a psychologist who did not take the principle to be obviously true Some of these same psychologists also favored the sort of belief–desire explanations of action that I will later argue are at odds with the autonomy principle. None, however, was aware of the incompatibility, and a number of them vigorously resisted the contention that the incompatibility is there.

9 For a critique of these views, cf. Goldman (1970, chapter 3); Alston (1967b).

10 For discussion of these matters, see Kim (1973). Kim defends the view that the property invoked in the description must be identical with the one invoked in the law. For a much more liberal view see Davidson (1967).

11 Thus Davidson is not an advocate of the belief–desire thesis as I am construing it. For on his view, though beliefs and desires may be among the causes of actions, the general laws supporting the causal claims are not themselves couched in terms of beliefs and desires (cf. Davidson 1970). But David-son's view, though not without interest, is plainly idiosyncratic. Generally, philosophers who hold that beliefs and desires are among the causes of behavior also think that there are psychological laws to be found (most likely probabilistic ones) which are stated in terms of beliefs and desires. Cf., for example, Hempel (1965, pp. 463–87), Alston (1967a and 1967b); Goldman (1970, chapters 3 and 4).

We should also note that much of recent psychology can be viewed as a quest for psychological laws couched in terms of beliefs and/or desires. There is, for example, an enormous and varied literature on problem solving (cf. Newell and Simon 1972) and on informal inference (cf. Nisbett and Ross 1980) which explores the mechanisms and environmental determinants of belief formation. Also, much of the literature on motivation is concerned with uncovering the laws governing the formation and strength of desires (cf. Atkinson 1964).

12 For an attempt to explicate our informal concepts of belief and desire in some detail, see Stich (1983).

13 For more on this way of viewing states and events, cf. Kim (1969 and 1976). I think that most everything I say in this essay can be said as well, though not as briefly, without presupposing this account of states and events.

14 The examples in Case 1 and Case 2, along with my thinking on these matters, have been influenced by a pair of important papers by Castañeda (1966 and 1967).

15 Putnam (1973 and 1975).

16 We should note that this example and others invoking natural kind words work only if the extension of my ancestor's word "water" is different from the extension of the word "water" as used by my ancestor's doppelganger. I am inclined to agree with Putnam that the extensions are different. But the matter is controversial. For some support of Putnam's view, see Kripke (1972) and Teller (1977); for an opposing view cf. Zemach (1976). Incidentally, one critic has expressed doubt that my doppelganger and I could be physically identical if the stuff called "water" on the far off planet is actually XYZ. Those who find the point troubling are urged to construct a parallel example using kinds of material not generally occurring within people.

17 The idea that *de dicto* beliefs are psychologically more basic is widespread. For a particularly clear example, see Armstrong (1973, pp. 25–31). Of the various attempts to analyze *de re* beliefs in terms of *de dicto* beliefs, perhaps the best known are to be found in Kaplan (1968) and Chisholm (1976).

18 The substitutional account of the *de re/ de dicto* distinction has a curious consequence that has been little noted. Though most belief sentences of the form

  S believes that Fa

can be used to make either *de re or de dicto* attributions, the substitutional account entails that some can only be used to make *de re* attributions. Consider, for example.

  (i) Quine believes that the Queen of England is a turtle.

The claim of course, is false. Indeed, it is *so* false that it could not be used to make a *de dicto* belief attribution. For in all likelihood, there is *no* name or definite description ϕ denoting Elizabeth II such that

Quine believes that ϕ is a turtle

is true. Thus "Quine believes that the Queen of England is a turtle" is false and cannot be turned into a truth by the replacement of "the Queen of England" by a codesignating expression. So on the substitutional account, this sentence can be used to make only *de re* attributions. A parallel problem besets Quine's well known substitutional account of a *purely referential position* (Quine 1960, pp. 142ff.). In (i) the position occupied by "the Queen of England" can only be regarded as purely referential.

19 For more on the distinction between "real" relations and mere "satisfaction" relations, cf. Kim (1977).

20 Burge (1977, pp. 345 and 346); last emphasis added.

21 For more on this "double duty" view of the role of names and descriptions in content sentences, see Loar (1972).

22 Of course when the notion of a "real relation" has been suitably sharpened it might well turn out that the autonomous/non-autonomous distinction coincides with the "real relation" version of the *de dicto/ de re* distinction.

23 For example, when I say, "I believe that Kripke was born in Nebraska," I am attributing to myself a belief which is substitutionally *de dicto*, but not autonomous.

24 Kaplan's strategy, for example, will be of no help, since his analysans are, for the most part, non-autonomous substitutionally *de dicto* belief sentences. Cf. Kaplan (1968) and Burge (1977, pp. 350ff).

25 I am indebted to Robert Cummins, Jaegwon Kim, William Alston, and John Bennett for their helpful comments on the topics discussed in this essay.

26 After completing this essay, I was delighted to discover a very similar view in Perry (1979). Fodor (1980) defends a version of the principle of psychological autonomy.

References

Alston, W. P. (1967a) "Motives and motivation," *The Encyclopedia of Philosophy*, New York.

Alston, W. P. (1967b) "Wants, actions and causal explanations," in H. N. Castañeda (ed.) *Intentionality, Minds and Perception*, Detroit.

Armstrong, D. M. (1973) *Belief, Truth and Knowledge*, Cambridge.

Atkinson, J. W. (1964) *An Introduction to Motivation*, New York.

Brandt, R. B. and Kim, Jaegwon (1963) "Wants as explanations of actions," *Journal of Philosophy* LX, 425–35.

Burge, T. (1977) "Belief de re," *Journal of Philosophy* LXXIV, 338–62.

Castañeda, H. N. (1966). "'He': a study in the logic of self-consciousness," *Ratio*, 8, 130–57.

Castañeda, H. N. (1967) "Indicators and quasi-indicators," *American Philosophical Quarterly* 4, 85–100.

Chisholm, R. (1976) *Person and Object*, LaSalle, Ill.

Davidson, D. (1963) "Actions, reasons, and causes," *Journal of Philosophy* LX, 685–700.

Davidson, D. (1967) "Causal relations," *Journal of Philosophy* LXIV, 691–703.

Davidson, D. (1970) "Mental events," in L. Foster and J. W. Swanson (eds), *Experience and Theory*, Amherst.

Fodor, J. (1980) "Methodological solipsism considered as a research strategy in cognitive psychology," *Behavioral and Brain Sciences* 3, 63–73.

Goldman, A. (1970) *A Theory of Human Action*, Englewood Cliffs.

Hempel, C. G. (1965) *Aspects of Scientific Explanation*, New York.

Kaplan, D. (1968) "Quantifying in," *Synthese*, 19, 178–214.

Kim, J. (1969) "Events and their descriptions: some considerations," in N. Rescher et al. (eds), *Essays in Honor of C. G. Hempel*, Dordrecht, Holland.

Kim, J. (1973) "Causation, nomic subsumption and the concept of event," *Journal of Philosophy*, LXX, 217–36.

Kim, J. (1976) "Events as property-exemplifications," in M. Brand and D. Walton (eds), *Action Theory*, Dordrecht, Holland.

Kim, J. (1977) "Perception and reference without causality," *Journal of Philosophy*, 74, 606–20.

Kim, J. (1978) "Supervenience and nomological incommensurables." *American Philosophical Quarterly* 15, 2, 149–56.

Kripke, S. (1972) "Naming and necessity," in D. Davidson and G. Harman (eds), *Semantics and Natural Language*, Dordrecht, Holland.

Loar, B. (1972) "Reference and propositional attitudes," *Philosophical Review*, LXXX, 43–62.

Newell, A. and Simon, H. A. (1972) *Human Problem Solving*, Englewood Cliffs.

Nisbett, R. and Ross, L. (1980) *Human Inference: Strategies and Shortcomings of Social Judgment*, Prentice-Hall.

Perry, J. (1979) "The problem of the essential indexical," *Noûs*, 13, 3–21.

Putnam, H. (1973). "Meaning and reference," *Journal of Philosophy* LXX, 699–711.

Putnam, H. (1975) "The meaning of 'meaning'," in K. Gunderson (ed.), *Language, Mind and Knowledge*, Minneapolis.

Quine, W. V. O. (1960) *Word and Object*, Cambridge.

Stich, S. (1983) *From Folk Psychology to Cognitive Science*, Bradford Books/MIT Press.

Teller, P. (1977) "Indicative introduction," *Philosophical Studies* 31, 173–95.

Zemach, E. (1976) "Putnam's theory on the reference of substance terms," *Journal of Philosophy* LXXXIII, 116–27.

12

Defending "Folk Psychology"

Folk Psychology is Here to Stay

Terence Horgan and James Woodward

Folk psychology is a network of principles which constitutes a sort of common-sense theory about how to explain human behavior. These principles provide a central role to certain propositional attitudes, particularly beliefs and desires. The theory asserts, for example, that if someone desires that p, and this desire is not overridden by other desires, and he believes that an action of kind K will bring it about that p, and he believes that such an action is within his power, and he does not believe that some other kind of action is within his power and is a preferable way to bring it about that p, then *ceteris paribus*, the desire and the beliefs will cause him to perform an action of kind K. The theory is largely functional, in that the states it postulates are characterized primarily in terms of their causal relations to each other, to perception and other environmental stimuli, and to behavior.

Folk psychology (henceforth FP) is deeply ingrained in our common-sense conception of ourselves as persons. Whatever else a person is, he is supposed to be a rational (at least largely rational) *agent* – that is, a creature whose behavior is systematically caused by, and explainable in terms of, his beliefs, desires, and related propositional attitudes. The wholesale rejection of FP, therefore, would entail a drastic revision of our conceptual scheme. This fact seems to us to constitute a good prima facie reason for not discarding FP too quickly in the face of apparent difficulties.

Recently, however, FP has come under fire from two quarters. Paul Churchland (1981) has argued that since FP has been with us for at least twenty-five centuries, and thus is not the product of any deliberate and self-conscious attempt to develop a psychological theory which coheres with the account of *Homo sapiens* which the natural sciences provide, there is little reason to suppose that FP is true, or that humans undergo beliefs, desires, and the like. And Stephen Stich (1983) has argued that current work in cognitive science suggests that no events or states posited by a mature cognitive psychology will be identifiable as the events and states posited by FP; Stich maintains that if this turns out to be the case, then it will show that FP is radically false, and that humans simply do not undergo such mental states as beliefs and desires.

In this essay we shall argue that neither Churchland nor Stich has provided convincing reasons for doubting the integrity of FP. Much of our discussion will be devoted to showing that they each employ an implausibly stringent conception of how FP would have to mesh with lower-level theories in order to be compatible with them. We do not deny the possibility that FP will fail to be compatible with more comprehensive theories; this would happen, for instance, if the correct theoretical psychology turned out to be a version of radical Skinnerian behaviorism. But we maintain that there is no good reason to suppose that it will *actually* happen.

Before proceeding, several preliminaries. First, we shall use the rubric "event" in a broad sense, to include not only token changes, but also token states and token processes. Thus, nonmomentary folk-psychological token states will count as mental events, in our terminology.

Second, we shall take FP to consist of two components: a set of *theoretical principles*, and an *existential thesis*. Many or all of the theoretical principles may be expected to have the general form exemplified by the example in our opening paragraph; that is, they are universal closures of conditional formulas.[1] As such they do not carry any existential import, since they might all be vacuously true. The existential thesis of FP, on the other hand, is the assertion that generally our everyday folk-psychological descriptions of people are true, and that humans generally do undergo the folk-psychological events that we commonly attribute to them. We take it that Churchland and Stich are arguing primarily against the existential thesis of FP; i.e., they are claiming that our everyday folk-psychological ascriptions are radically false, and that there simply do not exist such things as beliefs, desires, and the rest. Thus their argument, as we understand it, leaves open the possibility that the theoretical principles of FP are true but merely vacuously so.

Third, we are not necessarily claiming that FP is fully correct in every respect, or that there is no room to correct or improve FP on the basis of new developments in cognitive science or neuroscience. Rather, we are claiming that FP's theoretical principles are *by and large* correct, and that everyday folk-psychological ascriptions are often true.

Fourth, we want to dissociate ourselves from our currently influential strategy for insulating FP from potential scientific falsification – viz., the instrumentalism of Daniel Dennett (1978, 1981). He says, of beliefs and desires, that these "putative ... states" can be relegated "to the role of idealized fictions in an action-predicting, action-explaining calculus" (1978, p. 30). They are not what Reichenbach calls "illata – posited theoretical entities"; instead, he maintains, they are "abstracta – calculation-bound entities or logical constructs" (1981, p. 13), whose status is analogous to components in a parallelogram of forces (1981, p. 20). In short, he evidently holds that they are instrumentalistic fictions, and hence that they are compatible with virtually anything we might discover in cognitive science or neuroscience. We reject Dennett's instrumentalism. We maintain that FP, in addition to providing a useful framework for prediction, also provides genuine *causal explanations*. Although an instrumentalistic attitude toward the intentional idioms of FP is compatible

with the mere predictive use of these idioms, it simply is not compatible with their explanatory use, or with talk of beliefs and desires as causes. Accordingly, FP requires a defense more vigorous than Dennett's instrumentalism.

I

Churchland's (1981) argument against the compatibility of FP and neuroscience rests on three considerations. First "FP suffers explanatory failures on an epic scale" (p. 76). Second, "it has been stagnant for at least twenty-five centuries" (p. 76). And third, "its intentional categories stand magnificently alone, without any visible prospect of reduction" to neuroscience (p. 75). Irreducibility is the main consideration, and it is allegedly reinforced by the other two points: "A successful reduction cannot be ruled out, in my view, but FP's explanatory impotence and long stagnation inspire little faith that its categories will find themselves neatly reflected in the framework of neuroscience" (p. 75).

Let us consider each of Churchland's three points in turn. In elaboration of the first point, he writes:

> As examples of central and important mental phenomena that remain largely or wholly mysterious within the framework of FP, consider the nature and dynamics of mental illness, the faculty of creative imagination ... the nature and psychological functions of sleep ... the common ability to catch an outfield fly ball on the run ... the internal construction of a 3-D visual image ... the rich variety of perceptual illusions ... the miracle of memory ... the nature of the learning process itself ... (p. 173)

There are at least two important respects in which this passage is misleading. First, while FP itself may have little to say about the matters Churchland mentions, theories based on concepts deriving from FP have a good deal to say about them. For example, cognitive psychologists have developed extensive and detailed theories about visual perception, memory, and learning that employ concepts recognizably like the folk-psychological concepts of belief, desire, judgment, etc.[2] The versions of attribution theory and cognitive dissonance theory considered below in connection with Stich are important cases of theories of this kind.

That all such theories are unexplanatory is most implausible, and in any case requires detailed empirical argument of a sort Churchland does not provide.

Secondly, Churchland's argument seems to impose the *a priori* demand that any successful psychological theory account for a certain pre-established range of phenomena, and do so in a unified way. Arguments of this general type deserve to be treated with skepticism and caution. The history of science is full of examples in which our pretheoretical expectations about which phenomena it is reasonable to expect a theory to account for or group together have turned out to be quite misleading. For example, the demand was frequently imposed on early optical theories that they account for facts which we would now recognize as having to do with the physiology or psychology of vision; this had a deleterious effect on early optical theorizing. Similar examples can readily be found in the history of chemistry.[3]

The general point is that reasonable judgments about which phenomena a theory of some general type should be expected to account for require considerable theoretical knowledge; when our theoretical knowledge is relatively primitive, as it is with regard to many psychological phenomena, such judgments can go seriously astray. There is no good reason, *a priori*, to expect that a theory like FP, designed primarily to explain common human actions in terms of beliefs, desires, and the like, should also account for phenomena having to do with visual perception, sleep, or complicated muscular coordination. The truth about the latter phenomena may simply be very different from the truth about the former.

What about Churchland's second argument, viz., that FP has remained stagnant for centuries? To begin with, it seems to us at least arguable that FP has indeed changed in significant and empirically progressive ways over the centuries, rather than stagnating. For example, it is a plausible conjecture that Europeans in the eighteenth or nineteenth centuries were much more likely to explain human behavior in terms of character types with enduring personality traits than twentieth century Europeans, who often appeal instead to "situational" factors. (Certainly this difference is dramatically evident in eighteenth and twentieth century literature; contrast, say, Jane Austen and John Barth.)[4] Another example of empirically progressive change, perhaps, is the greater willingness, in contemporary culture, to appeal to unconscious beliefs and motivations.

Another reason to question the "empirical unprogressiveness" argument is that cognitive psychological theories employing belief-like and desire-like events have led to a number of novel and surprising predictions, which have been borne out by experiment. (We discuss some pertinent examples below. For other striking cases the reader is referred to Nisbett and Ross (1980).) Yet Churchland seems to argue as though the (alleged) empirical unprogressiveness of FP is a good reason for taking any theory modeled on FP to be false.[5] This is rather like arguing that any sophisticated physical theory employing central forces must be false on the grounds that the ordinary person's notions of pushing and pulling have been empirically unprogressive.

Furthermore, the standard of "empirical progressiveness" is not very useful in assessing a theory like FP anyway. The typical user of FP is interested in applying a pre-existing theory to make particular causal judgments about particular instances of human behavior, not in formulating new causal generalizations. He is a consumer of causal generalizations, not an inventor of them. In this respect he resembles the historian, the detective, or the person who makes ordinary singular causal judgments about inanimate objects. It is not appropriate, we submit, to assess these activities using a standard explicitly designed to assess theories that aim at formulating novel causal generalizations.

This point emerges clearly when one realizes that much of the implicit theory behind many ordinary (but nonpsychological) particular causal judgments has presumably changed very slowly, if at all, over the past thousand years. Both we and our ancestors judge that the impact of the rock caused the shattering of the pot, that the lack of water caused the camel to die, that a very sharp blow on the head caused A's death, that heat causes water to boil, etc. None of these judgments are part of a (swiftly) empirically progressive theory, yet it seems ludicrous to conclude (on those grounds alone) that they are probably false. A similar point can be made about much (although by no means all) of the implicit causal theory employed by historians. These examples serve to remind us that not all folk theorizing is now regarded as radically false.

This brings us to Churchland's third, and most fundamental, argument for the alleged incommensurability of FP with neuroscience: viz., the likely irreducibility of the former to the latter. An ideal intertheoretic reduction, as he describes it, has two main features:

First, it provides us with a set of rules – "correspondence rules" or "bridge laws," as the standard vernacular has it – which effect a mapping of the terms of the old theory (T_o) onto a subset of the expressions of the new or reducing theory (T_n). These rules guide the application of those selected expressions of T_n in the following way: we are free to make singular applications of those expressions in all those cases where we normally make singular applications of their correspondence-rule doppelgangers in T_o . . .

Second, and equally important, a successful reduction ideally has the outcome that, under the term mapping effected by the correspondence rules, the central principles of T_o (those of semantic and systematic importance) are mapped onto general sentences of T_n that are *theorems* of T_n. (1979, p.81)

We certainly agree that an ideal, or approximately ideal, reduction of FP to natural science would be *one* way of salvaging FP. And we also agree that such a reduction – indeed, even a species-specific reduction – is an unlikely prospect, given that FP is at least twenty-five centuries old and hence obviously was not formulated with an eye toward smooth term-by-term absorption into twentieth-century science. (A non-species-specific reduction is even less likely, because if FP is true of humans then it can equally well be true of Martians whose physicochemical composition is vastly different from our own – so different that there are no theoretically interesting physical descriptions that can subsume both the physicochemical properties which "realize" FP in humans and the corresponding physicochemical properties in Martians.)

But even if FP cannot be reduced to lower-level theories, and even if lower-level theories can themselves provide a marvelous account of the nature and behavior of *Homo sapiens*, it simply does not follow that FP is radically false, or that humans do not undergo the intentional events it posits. Churchland's eliminative materialism is not the only viable naturalistic alternative to reductive materialism. Another important alternative is the nonreductive, noneliminative materialism of Donald Davidson (1970, 1973, 1974).

Davidson advocates a thesis which asserts that every concrete mental event is identical to some concrete neurological event, but which does not assert (indeed, denies) that there are systematic bridge laws linking mental event-*types*, or properties, with neurological event-types. He calls this view *anomalous monism*; it is a form of monism because it posits psychophysical identities, and it is "anomalous" because it rejects reductive bridge laws (or reductive type–type identities).[6]

The availability of anomalous monism as an alternative to reductive materialism makes it clear that even if FP is not reducible to neuroscience, nevertheless the token mental events posited by FP might well exist, and might well bear all the causal relations to each other, to sensation, and to behavior which FP says they do.

Churchland never mentions Davidson's version of the identity theory – a very odd fact, given its enormous influence and its obvious relevance to his argument. Instead he argues directly from the premise that FP probably is false. So his argument is fallacious, in light of token–token identity theory as an alternative possible account of the relation between FP and neuroscience. He is just mistaken to assume that FP must be reducible to neuroscience in order to be compatible with it.

II

Let us now consider Stich's reasons for claiming that FP probably will not prove compatible with a developed cognitive science (henceforth CS). Unlike Churchland, Stich does not assume that FP must be reducible to more comprehensive lower-level theories in order to be compatible with them. We shall say more presently about the way he thinks FP must fit with these theories.

Stich offers two arguments against the compatibility of FP and CS; we shall examine these in this section and the next. The first argument purports to show that the overall causal organization of the cognitive system probably does not conform with the causal organization which FP ascribes to it. The argument runs as follows. Events which satisfy a given sortal predicate of the form "... is a belief that p" are supposed to have typical behavioral effects of both verbal and nonverbal kinds. On the verbal side, the events in this class are ones which typically cause the subject, under appropriate elicitation conditions, to utter an assertion that p. On the nonverbal side, these events are ones which, in combination with a subject's other beliefs, desires, and the like, typically cause the subject to perform those actions which FP says are appropriate to the combination of that belief with those other propositional attitudes. But recent experimental evidence suggests, according to Stich, that the psychological events which control nonverbal behavior are essentially independent of those which control verbal behavior – and hence that the cognitive system simply does not contain events which, taken singly, occupy the causal role which FP assigns to beliefs. If these experimental results prove generalizable, and if CS subsequently develops in the direction of positing separate, largely independent, cognitive subsystems for the control of verbal and nonverbal behavior respectively, then we will be forced to conclude, argues Stich, that there are no such things as beliefs.

One of his central empirical examples is a study in attribution theory, performed by Storms and Nisbett (1970). He describes its first phase this way:

> Storms and Nisbett . . . asked insomniac subjects to record the time they went to bed and the time they finally fell asleep. After several days of record keeping, one group of subjects (the "arousal" group) was given a placebo pill to take fifteen minutes before going to bed. They were told that the pill would produce rapid heart rate, breathing irregularities, bodily warmth and alertness, which are just the typical symptoms of insomnia. A second group of subjects (the "relaxation" group) was told that the pills would produce the opposite symptoms: lowered heart rate, breathing rate, body temperature and alertness. Attribution theory predicts that the arousal group subjects would get to sleep *faster* on the nights they took the pills, because they would attribute their symptoms to the pills rather than to the emotionally laden thoughts that were running through their minds. It also predicts that subjects in the relaxation group will take *longer* to get to sleep. Since their symptoms persist despite having taken a pill intended to relieve the symptoms, they will infer that their emotionally laden thoughts must be particularly disturbing to them. And this belief will upset them further, making it all that much harder to get to sleep. Remarkably enough, both of these predictions were borne out. Arousal group subjects got to

sleep 28 percent faster on the nights they took the pill, while relaxation subjects took 42 percent longer to get to sleep. (Stich 1983, p. 232)

What Stich finds particularly significant is the second phase of this study. After the completion of the initial insomnia experiments, the members of the arousal group were informed that they had gotten to sleep more quickly after taking the pill, and the members of the relaxation group were informed that they had taken longer to fall asleep. They were asked *why* this happened, and Nisbett and Wilson report the following pattern of responses:

> Arousal subjects typically replied that they usually found it easier to get to sleep later in the week, or that they had taken an exam that had worried them but had done well on it and could now relax, or that problems with a roommate or girlfriend seemed on their way to resolution. Relaxation subjects were able to find similar sorts of reasons to explain their increased sleeplessness. When subjects were asked if they had thought about the pills at all before getting to sleep, they almost uniformly insisted that after taking the pills they had completely forgotten about them. When asked if it had occurred to them that the pill might be producing (or counteracting) the arousal symptoms, they reiterated their insistence that they had not thought about the pills at all after taking them. Finally, the experimental hypothesis and the postulated attribution process were described in detail. Subjects showed no recognition of the hypothesized process and . . . made little pretense of believing that *any* of the subjects could have gone through such processes. (Nisbett and Wilson, 1977, p. 238)

It is very likely, given the data from the first phase of the study, that the cognitive mechanisms which controlled the subjects' verbal responses in the second phase were largely distinct from the cognitive mechanisms which influenced their actual sleep patterns. And in numerous other studies in the literature of attribution theory and cognitive dissonance theory, the data support a similar conclusion: the mechanisms which control an initial piece of nonverbal behavior are largely distinct from the mechanisms which control the subject's subsequent verbal accounts of the reasons for that behavior.[7]

Stich, if we understand his argument correctly, draws three further conclusions. (1) In cases of the sort described, there is no cogent and consistent way to ascribe beliefs and desires; for FP typically attributes both verbal and nonverbal behavioral effects to particular beliefs and desires, but in these cases the cognitive causes of the nonverbal behavior are distinct from the cognitive causes of the verbal behavior, and hence neither kind of cause can comfortably be identified with a belief or desire. (2) It is likely that *in general* our verbal behavior is controlled by cognitive mechanisms different from those that control our nonverbal behavior; for the Storms–Nisbett pattern emerges in a broad range of studies in attribution theory and dissonance theory. From (1) and (2) he concludes: (3) It is likely that FP is radically false; that is, that humans do not undergo beliefs and desires.

We do not dispute the contention that in a surprising number of cases, as revealed by studies in attribution theory and dissonance theory, the mental states and processes which cause an initial item of nonverbal behavior are distinct from the states and processes which cause a subject's subsequent remarks about the etiology of that behavior. But we deny that either (1) or (2) is warranted by this contention. And without (1) or (2), of course the argument for (3) collapses.

Consider (1). Is there really a problem in consistently ascribing beliefs, desires, and other folk-psychological states in light of the phenomena described in the Storms–Nisbett study, for instance? No. For we can appeal to *unconscious* beliefs, desires, and inferences. Although FP asserts that beliefs and desires *normally* give rise to their own verbal expression under appropriate elicitation conditions, it does not assert this about unconscious beliefs and desires. On the contrary, part of what it means to say that a mental event is unconscious is that it lacks the usual sorts of direct causal influence over verbal behavior. Thus we have available the following natural and plausible folk-psychological account of the subjects' behavior in the Storms–Nisbett study; their initial nonverbal behavior was caused by unconscious beliefs and inferences, whereas their subsequent verbal behavior was caused by distinct, conscious, beliefs about the likely causes of their initial nonverbal behavior. In short, FP does not break down in such cases, because one has the option – the natural and plausible option – of positing unconscious folk-psychological causes.

There is a temptation, we realize, to identify FP with "what common sense would say," and to take the fact that the Storms–Nisbett results confute our common-sense expectations as automatically falsifying some component of FP. But this temptation should be resisted. Common sense would not postulate the relevant unconscious beliefs and desires. But once we *do* postulate them, perhaps on the basis of rather subtle nonverbal behavioral evidence, FP seems to yield the *correct* predictions about how the subjects will perform in Storms and Nisbett's study.

Indeed, as we understand the views of psychologists like Storms, Nisbett, and Wilson who cite such studies as evidence that verbal and nonverbal behavior often are under separate cognitive controls, this appeal to unconscious folk-psychological causes is precisely the theoretical move *they* are making concerning such cases. Attribution theory and cognitive dissonance theory give center stage to folk-psychological notions like desire and belief. Accordingly, the dual control thesis is nothing other than the folk-psychological thesis just stated: it is the claim that unconscious beliefs and inferences cause the subjects' initial nonverbal behavior, whereas distinct conscious beliefs (which constitute hypotheses about the causes of their original behavior) cause their subsequent verbal behavior.[8] Notice how Stich himself, in the above-quoted passage, describes the first phase of the Storms–Nisbett study. "Attribution theory," he says, "predicts that subjects in the relaxation group will *infer* that their emotionally laden thoughts must be particularly disturbing to them. And this *belief* will upset them further..." (emphasis ours). Now Stich may have in mind a way of reinterpreting these claims so that the notions of belief and inference they employ are very different from the FP-notions, but in the absence of such a reinterpretation, his contention that beliefs and belief-generating mechanisms cannot be cogently ascribed to subjects like those of Storms and Nisbett is quite unfounded.

Our construal of the dual-control thesis assumes, of course, that it makes sense to speak of beliefs and other mental events as unconscious. But Storms, Nisbett, and Wilson claim quite explicitly that there can be nonverbal behavioral criteria which warrant the ascription of beliefs and other mental events even when a subject's verbal behavior appears inconsistent with the existence of such events.[9]

It may well be that the appeal to these criteria – and to unconscious beliefs and inferences generally – constitutes an extension and partial modification of traditional FP; but even if it does, this is hardly a wholesale rejection of folk-psychological notions. On the contrary, the very naturalness of the appeal to unconscious folk-psychological causes reflects the fact that the overall causal architecture posited by FP remains largely intact even when we introduce the conscious/unconscious distinction.

So conclusion (1) should be rejected. This means that even if (2) were accepted, FP would not necessarily be undermined. But conclusion (2) should be rejected in any case. From the fact that unconscious mental mechanisms control our nonverbal behavior in a surprising number of cases, one may not reasonably infer that *in general* our verbal and nonverbal behavior are under separate cognitive control. The findings of attribution theory and dissonance theory, although they do caution us against excessive confidence in our ability to know ourselves, fall far short of establishing such a sweeping conclusion. In this connection it is useful to examine the remarks of Timothy Wilson (unpublished), a leading advocate of the idea of "dual cognitive control" over verbal and nonverbal behavior respectively. Stich makes much of Wilson's position, which he construes as the radical thesis that our own statements concerning the mental events that cause our nonverbal behavior are virtually *never* caused by those mental events themselves. But this is a mistaken interpretation, in our judgment. Wilson articulates his proposal this way:

> In essence the argument is that there are two mental systems: One which mediates behavior (especially unregulated behavior), is largely nonconscious, and is perhaps, the older of the two systems in evolutionary terms. The other, perhaps newer system, is largely conscious, and its function is to attempt to verbalize, explain, and communicate mental states. As argued earlier, people often have direct access to their mental states, and in these cases the verbal system can make direct and accurate reports. When there is limited access, however, the verbal system makes inferences about what these processes and states might be. (pp. 18–19)

It seems clear from this passage that Wilson is not suggesting that *in general* our utterances about our mental events are generated by cognitive events other than those mental events themselves. Rather, he is acknowledging that people often have direct conscious access to the mental causes of their behavior, and that at such times these states typically cause accurate reports about themselves. Only where access is limited, where the events are not conscious, are our subsequent utterances caused by inferences about likely mental causes rather than by the mental events themselves.[10]

Wilson goes on to suggest that it will typically be events that are results of considerable processing which will be relatively inaccessible to the agent, and that "more immediate states" (such as precognitive states) may be much more accessible (p. 39). Moreover, there are many cases which do seem to involve complex processing in which people exhibit integrated verbal and nonverbal behavior in a way that seems difficult to understand if the systems controlling verbal and nonverbal behavior are entirely independent. Consider engaging in some complicated task while explaining to someone else what you are doing – as in working logic problems on the blackboard as one lectures. It is hard to see how such an integrated performance is possible if the actor has no access to the beliefs which cause the nonverbal portion of his behavior (other than via after-the-fact inferences).

We conclude, then, that neither conclusion (1) nor conclusion (2) is warranted by the kinds of psychological studies Stich cites, and hence that his "dual-control" argument against FP is not successful.

III

The "dual-control" argument does not presuppose any particular conception of how FP must be related to CS in order for the two theories to be compatible. Stich's second argument for the incompatibility of FP and CS, however, does rest upon such a conception. In particular, he requires that beliefs, desires, and the like should be identical with "naturally isolable" parts of the cognitive system; he calls this the *modularity* principle.

Stich does not attempt to make this principle precise, but instead leaves the notion of natural isolability at the intuitive level. Accordingly, we too shall use this notion without explication; we think the points we shall make are applicable under any reasonable construal.

Stich argues that FP probably fails to satisfy the modularity principle *vis-à-vis* CS, and hence that there probably are no such events as beliefs, desires, and the like. He focuses on recent trends within CS concerning the modeling of human memory. Some early models of memory organization, he points out, postulate a distinct sentence or sentence-like structure for each memory. These models are clearly modular, he says, because the distinct sentence-like structures can be identified with separate beliefs. Another sort of model, motivated largely by the desire to explain how people are able to locate information relevant to a given task at hand, treats memory as a complex network of nodes and labeled links, with the nodes representing concepts and the links representing various sorts of relations among concepts. Stich regards network models as "still quite far over to the modular end of the spectrum," however, because in a network model it is generally unproblematic to isolate the part of the network which would play the causal role characteristic of a given belief (1983, p. 239).

But in recent years, he points out, several leading theorists have become quite skeptical about highly modular models, largely because such models do not seem capable of handling the enormous amount of nondeductive inference which is involved in language use and comprehension. Citing Minsky (1981) as an example, Stich writes:

In a...recent paper Minsky elaborates what he calls a "Society of Mind" view in which the mechanisms of thought are divided into many separate "specialists that communicate only sparsely" (p. 95). On the picture Minsky suggests, none of the distinct units or parts of the mental model "have meanings in themselves" (p. 100) and thus none can be identified with individual beliefs, desires, etc. Modularity – I borrow the term from Minsky – is violated in a radical way since meaning or content emerges only from "great webs of structure" (p. 100) and no natural part of the system can be correlated with "explicit" or verbally expressible beliefs. (1983, p. 241)

If Minsky's "Society of Mind" view is the direction that CS will take in the future, then presumably modularity will indeed be violated in a radical way.

We are quire prepared to acknowledge that CS may well become dramatically nonmodular, and hence that the modularity principle may well end up being refuted empirically.[11] Indeed, if one considers the relation between FP and neuroscience – or even the relation between CS and neuroscience, for that matter – one would expect modularity to be violated in an even more dramatic way. There are tens of billions of neurons in the human central nervous system, and thousands of billions of synaptic junctures; so if the "naturally isolable" events of neuroscience are events like neuron firings and intersynaptic transfers of electrical energy, then it is entirely likely that the naturally isolable events of both FP and CS will involve "great webs of structure" neurally – that is, great conglomerations of naturally isolable neural events.

So if modularity is really needed in order for FP-events to exist and to enter into causal relations, then the failure of modularity would indeed spell big trouble for the proffered compatibility of FP with lower-level theories. In fact, it also would spell big trouble for the proffered compatibility of *cognitive science* with lower-level theories like neuroscience; thus Stich's style of argument appears to prove more than he, as an advocate of CS, would like it to prove! And indeed, the demand for modularity even spells big trouble for the compatibility of *neuroscience* with physics–chemistry; for, if the natural-kind predicates of physics–chemistry are predicates like "...is an electron" and "...is a hydrogen atom," then it is most unlikely that entities falling under neuroscientific natural-kind terms like "...is a neuron" will also fall under physicochemical natural-kind terms. Rather, neurons and neuron firings are entities which, from the physicochemical point of view, involve "great webs of structure."

We point out these generalizations of Stich's argument because we think they make clear the enormous implausibility of the modularity principle as an intertheoretic compatibility condition. Surely objects like neurons, or events like neuron firings, don't have to be "naturally isolable" from the perspective of fundamental physics–chemistry in order to be compatible with it; rather, it is enough that they be fully decomposable into naturally isolable *parts*. Similarly, cognitive–psychological events don't have to be naturally isolable from the perspective of neuroscience in order to be compatible with it; again, it is enough that these events are decomposable into naturally isolable parts.[12]

The situation is exactly the same, we submit, for folk-psychological events in relation to the events of CS. Perhaps Minsky is right, and the role of a belief (say) is typically played by a vast, highly gerrymandered, conglomeration of CS-events. This doesn't show that the belief doesn't exist. On the contrary, all it shows is that the belief is an enormously *complex* event, consisting of numerous CS-events as parts.[13] After all, we expect those CS-events, in turn, to consist of numerous neurological events as parts; and we expect those neurological events, in their turn, to consist of numerous physicochemical events as parts.

Stich never attempts to justify the modularity principle as a compatibility condition, just as Churchland never attempts to justify the demand for reducibility. Thus Stich's modularity argument suffers the same defect as Churchland's reducibility argument: viz., it rests upon an unsubstantiated, and implausibly strong, conception of how FP must mesh with more comprehensive lower-level theories in order to be compatible with them. (It is important to note, incidentally, that even though Stich does not demand reducibility, still in a certain way his notion of intertheoretic fit is actually *stronger* than Churchland's notion. For, even a reductionist need not require that entities falling under higher-level natural-kind sortals should be naturally isolable from the lower-level perspective. A reductionist does require that there should be biconditional bridge laws correlating the higher-level sortals with open sentences of the lower-level theory, but these lower-level open sentences can be quite complex, rather than being (say) simple natural-kind sortal predicates.)

Although Stich offers no explicit rationale for the modularity principle, perhaps he is influenced by the following line of thought:

The propositional attitudes of FP involve a relation between a cognizer and a sentence-like "internal representation" (Fodor 1975, 1978; Field 1978; Lycan 1981). If FP is true, then part of the task of CS is to explain the nature of these internal representations. But CS cannot do this unless internal representations fall under its natural-kind predicates, or at any rate are *somehow* "naturally isolable" within the cognitive system. And if Minsky's "Society of Mind" approach is the direction CS will take in the future, then this requirement will not be met. Hence if the events of FP do not obey the modularity principle *vis-à-vis* CS, then FP must be radically false.

One reason we have for rejecting this line of reasoning is that we doubt whether propositional attitudes really involve internal representations – or whether they have "objects" at all (cf. note 1). Furthermore, if Minsky's approach did become the general trend in CS, then presumably this fact too would tend to undermine the claim that sentence-like representations are involved in the propositional attitudes – just as his approach already tends to undermine the claim that such representations are involved in the nondeductive inference that underlies the use and comprehension of language.

Moreover, even if the internal-representation view is correct, and even if part of the task of CS is to give an account of these representations, approaches like Minsky's would not necessarily render CS incapable of accomplishing this task. For it might turn out that the "atoms" of CS are the components of Minsky's Society of Minds, and that CS also posits complex, sentence-like "molecules" constructed from these "atoms." The molecules might be *very* complex, and highly gerrymandered. If so, then they won't count as naturally isolable components of the cognitive system when that system is viewed from the atomic perspective; however, they *will* count as naturally isolable from the higher, molecular perspective. (We think it more likely, however, that if the "Society of Minds" approach proves generalizable within CS, then the result will be a widespread rejection of the mental-representation view of propositional attitudes – a view which, as we said, we think is mistaken anyway.)

Another way one might try to defend the modularity principle is by appeal to Davidsonian considerations involving the role of laws in causality. One might argue (i) that FP contains no strict laws, but only so-called "heteronomic" generalizations (Davidson 1970, 1974); (ii) that two events are related as cause and effect only if they have descriptions which instantiate a strict law (Davidson 1967); and (iii) that event-descriptions which instantiate a strict law of a given theory must pick out events that are naturally isolable from the perspective of that theory. From these three claims, plus the assumption that folk-psychological events enter into causal relations, the modularity principle seems to follow.[14]

But suppose an event c causes an event e, where c and e both are naturally isolable from the perspective of FP. Suppose that c is fully decomposable into events which respectively satisfy the sortal predicates $F_1 \ldots F_m$ of an underlying homonomic theory T, and hence that these component-events all are naturally isolable from the perspective of T; suppose also that these events jointly satisfy a (possibly quite complex) description D_1 of T which specifies their structural interconnection. Likewise, suppose that e is fully decomposable into events which respectively satisfy the sortal predicates $G_1 \ldots G_n$ of T, and hence that these component-events all are naturally isolable from the perspective of T; suppose also that these component-events jointly satisfy a description D_2 of T which specifies their structural interconnection. Now even if c and e do not have natural-kind descriptions under which they themselves instantiate a strict law of T, nevertheless the strict laws of T might jointly entail an assertion of the following form:

For any event x, if x is fully decomposable into events $x_1 \ldots x_m$ such that $D_1(x_1 \ldots x_m)$ and $F_1(x_1)$, $F_2(x_2)$, and $\ldots F_m(x_m)$, then x will be followed by an event y that is fully decomposable into events $y_1 \ldots y_n$ such that $D_2(y_1 \ldots y_n)$ and $G_1(y_1)$, $G_2(y_2)$, and $\ldots$ and $G_n(y_n)$.

We see no reason why the causal relation between c and e cannot rest upon a regularity of this form. One either can call such regularities strict laws, in which case claim (iii) above will be false; or else one can reserve the term "strict law" for the relatively simple nomic postulates of a homonomic theory, rather than the set of logical consequences of those postulates – in which case claim (ii) above will be false. Either way, the Davidson-inspired argument for the modularity principle has a false premise. (Incidentally, we do not mean to attribute the argument to Davidson himself, since we doubt whether he would accept claim (iii).)

IV

We have been arguing that FP-events might well be identical with arbitrarily complex, highly gerrymandered, CS-events which themselves are not naturally isolable relative to CS, but instead are fully decomposable into *parts* which have this feature. Of course, if FP-events really do exist, then they will have to accord with the causal architecture of FP; that is, they will have to be causally related to each other, to sensation, and to behavior in the ways that FP says they are. Indeed, as functionalists in philosophy of mind have so

often stressed, the causal or functional principles of FP are crucial to the very individuation of FP-events; what makes a given event count (say) as a token belief-that-p is, to a considerable extent, the fact that it occupies the causal role which FP assigns to tokens of that belief-type.[15]

So if our nonmodular picture of the relation between FP and CS is to be plausible, it is essential that complex, gerrymandered events can properly be considered causes, even if they involve "great webs of structure" relative to lower-level theory. While a detailed discussion must be beyond the scope of this essay, a brief consideration of the causal status of complex events will help to clarify our argument.

Let us say that an event e *minimally* causes an event f just in case e causes f and no proper part of e causes f. We want to advance two claims about minimal causation, each of which will receive some support below. First, even if an event e is a genuine cause of an event f, nevertheless f also might be caused by some event which is a proper part of e; thus e might be a genuine cause of f without being a minimal cause of f. Second, if e causes not only f but also some other event g, then it might be that the part of e which minimally causes f is different from the part of e which minimally causes g.[16]

These two facts are important because they make it relatively easy for events to exist which satisfy the causal principles of FP. If FP attributes both the event f and the event g to a single cause e at time t, and in fact there are distinct (though perhaps partially overlapping) events e_1 and e_2 such that e_1 minimally causes f (at t) and e_2 minimally causes g (at t), this does not necessarily falsify FP. For, e might well have both e_1 and e_2 as *parts*; indeed, it might well have as parts all those events which minimally cause (at t) one or another of the various events which FP says are effects (at t) of e. As long as this complex event is itself the effect of whatever prior events FP says are e's causes, the event will be (identical with) e.

The upshot is that FP could very easily turn out to be true, even if modularity is dramatically violated. Not only can FP-events be complex and highly gerrymandered, with numerous naturally isolable CS-events as parts, but any given FP-event e can cause its effects in a conglomerative manner, with different effects having different parts of e as their respective minimal causes.[17]

V

Perhaps it will be objected that our analysis is too permissive; that unless we adopt Stich's modularity condition, over and above the requirement that FP-events conform to the causal architecture which FP assigns to them, we impose no nontrivial constraints on the truth conditions of upper-level causal claims; that is, we allow such claims to come out true regardless of the character of the theory that underlies them. We shall conclude by considering this objection.

It is clear that some underlying theories are inconsistent with the truth of some upper-level causal claims. For example, if the world is anything like the way our current chemistry and physics describe it, then possession by the devil cannot be a cause of any psychological disorders, and loss of phlogiston cannot be a cause of the chemical changes undergone by metals when they oxidize. To consider a case which is closer to home, it seems clear that if we are Skinnerian creatures – that is, creatures whose behavior is fully described and explained by the basic principles of Skinnerian psychology – then folk-psychological claims postulating beliefs, desires, and the like as among the causes of our behavior cannot be true.

The worry under consideration is that our nonmodular approach to intertheoretic compatibility is so liberal that it would allow claims of the above sort to come out true even though they seem clearly inconsistent with underlying theory. We shall argue that this worry is ill-founded.

It will be helpful to distinguish two different conceptions or expectations regarding the epistemic role of a radical failure of fit or integration between an upper-level theory and an underlying theory. On the first conception one thinks of this failure of fit as an important epistemic route to the falsity of the upper-level theory, where that falsity may not be obvious otherwise. The idea is that even if direct evidence at the upper level does not clearly point to the falsity of an upper-level theory (and indeed may even seem to support this theory), nonetheless we can detect the falsity of the upper-level theory by noting its failure to fit in some appropriate way with some underlying theory which we have strong reason to believe is true. Clearly, both Stich and Churchland argue in accordance with this conception.

We find more plausible an importantly different conception of the epistemic significance of failure of fit between an upper-level and a lower-level theory. We do not deny, of course, that lower-level theories can be incompatible with upper-level theories. We do doubt, however, whether it is common or typical that one can know that an upper-level theory is false only by noting its failure to fit with a true underlying theory. More typically, when an upper-level theory is false there is direct evidence for this fact, independently of the failure of fit. The incompatibility arises not because of a failure of modularity, but rather because there simply are no events – either simple or complex – which have all the features which the upper-level theory attributes to the events it posits. Crudely put, the idea is that while various theories of juvenile delinquency or learning behavior can be inconsistent with neurophysiological theories or with physical theories, the former are *likely* to be confirmable or disconfirmable by the sorts of evidence available to sociologists and psychologists. It will be rare for a theory to be supported by a very wide range of evidence available to the sociologist or the psychologist and yet turn out to be radically false (because its ontology fails to mesh properly with that of some underlying theory). So our conception suggests a greater epistemological autonomy for upper-level disciplines like psychology than does a conception of intertheoretic compatibility which incorporates a modularity condition.

We have emphasized this epistemological point because it bears directly on worries about the permissiveness of our nonmodular conception. While our approach is by no means trivial in the sense that it allows every upper-level theory to be compatible with every underlying theory, it is permissive and deflationary in that, at least for a wide variety of cases, considerations of fit will not play the sort of independent normative role which they would play under a modularity requirement.

With this in mind, let us return to the examples with which we began this section. Consider first the case of possession by the devil. Like other causally explanatory notions, the notion of possession by the devil is to be understood, in large measure, in terms of the role it plays in a network of causal relations. Possession by the devil causes or may cause various kinds of pathological behavior. Such effects may be diminished or eliminated by the use of appropriate religious ceremonies (for example, prayers or exorcism). When behavior is due to possession by the devil, there is no reason to suppose that it will be affected by other forms of treatment (drugs, nutritional changes, psychotherapy, etc.). The state of possession is itself the effect of the activities of a being who has many other extraordinary powers.

Now if an event of possession by the devil (call it d) is to be a cause of a certain bit of behavior (for example, jabbering incoherently), then d must, on our analysis, be identifiable with some event (call it e) describable in terms of the predicates of our underlying theory; and it must be the case that, given this identification, at least most of the other causal generalizations in which d is held to figure, according to the theory of devil-possession, should come out true. (Although our conception of intertheoretic fit countenances failures of modularity, it does insist that the identifications we make preserve the "causal architecture" of the upper-level theory.) We submit that no matter how large and complex one makes the event e with which one proposes to identify d, and no matter how willing one may be to regard proper parts of e as causally efficacious, there is simply *no* plausible candidate for e which, given our present physical and chemical theory, will make the network of causal claims associated with possession by the devil come out mainly true. That is, there is simply no event e, however complex, which is linked by law to various forms of behavior associated with possession, which is inefficacious in producing such behavior when exorcism is used, which is shown by law to be produced by an agency having the properties of the devil, and so forth.

This example illustrates the general epistemological claim made above. In effect, we have argued that causal claims about possession by the devil are false not because of sophisticated considerations having to do with modularity (or with "smoothness of reduction"), but because the causal architecture associated with possession by the devil is radically mistaken; nothing stands in the network of causal relations with various other events in the way that possession by the devil is supposed to. We can see this immediately by noting that the falsity of claims attributing causal efficacy to devil-possession is, so to speak, directly discoverable without considerations having to do with chemistry, physics, or biology. If one were to run suitably controlled experiments, then presumably one would quickly discover that exorcism does not affect devil-possession type behavior, that certain other therapies do, and so forth.[18]

A similar set of observations seems relevant in connection with the allegation that our approach would permit causal claims about beliefs to be true even if we are Skinnerian creatures. FP asserts that beliefs, desires, and other propositional attitudes are related to one another in many and various ways, over and above their causal relations to sensation and behavior. Skinnerian theory, on the other hand, denies that we need to postulate such richly interacting internal events in order to explain behavior, and it also denies that such events exist at all. Rather, the Skinnerian claims that the causal chains leading from environmental "stimulus" to behavioral "response" are largely isolated from one another, rather like the various parallel non-interacting communication-channels in a fiber-optics communications line; thus, whatever internal events are involved in any particular stimulus–response pairing will not bear very many significant causal relations to the internal events that are involved in other stimulus–response pairings; that is, the Skinnerian claims that as a matter of empirical fact, the generalizations linking stimuli and behavior are so simple and straightforward that they are incompatible with the existence of internal events which interact in the rich way which folk-psychological events are supposed to interact with one another. So if the Skinnerian is right, then there simply are no internal events, in humans or in other organisms, which bear all the causal relations to sensation, to behavior, and to one another which FP assigns to beliefs, desires, and the like. Thus our nonmodular conception of intertheoretic fit would indeed be violated if humans should turn out to be mere Skinnerian creatures. Accordingly, this conception is not unduly permissive after all.

This example also illustrates the epistemological claims made above. It is satisfaction of the "causal architecture" of FP, by some set of (possibly complex) events in the central nervous system, which is crucial to the truth of FP. Hence if we are Skinnerian creatures, so that the causal architecture assumed by FP is not instantiated in us by any events either simple or complex, then presumably this fact will show up at the level of a relatively coarse-grained analysis of our molar behavior. Simulus–response laws that are incompatible with the causal architecture of FP will be discoverable, and will be usable to explain and predict the full range of human behavior. Hence it will not be the case that FP seems to be largely true, according to the best available coarse-grained evidence, and yet turns out to be false merely because of failure to fit properly with some underlying theory.

The upshot, then, is that our approach seems exactly as permissive as it should be, and this fact speaks in its favor; by contrast, a modular conception of intertheoretic fit seems excessively strict, since it is unmotivated and it denies higher-level theories an adequate degree of epistemological autonomy. So, given (i) the notable failure, to date, of behaviorist-inspired psychology's efforts to unearth stimulus–response laws which are applicable to human behavior generally and which undercut the causal architecture of FP, (ii) the fact that folk-psychological notions seem to lie at the very heart of cognitivist theories like attribution theory and cognitive dissonance theory, and (iii) the fact that FP serves us very well in the everyday explanation and prediction of behavior, it seems very hard to deny that in all probability, folk psychology is here to stay.[19,20,21]

Notes

1 Actually, we regard the example in the first paragraph as a schema which yields a whole range of instances when various sentences are substituted for the letter "p" and various sortal predicates are substituted for the dummy phrase "of kind K." (The word "someone," though, functions as a quantificational term; under appropriate regimentation, it would go over into a universal quantifier whose scope is the whole schema.) We prefer to think of predicates of the form "... believes that p" as what Quine (1970) calls *attitudinatives* – i.e., complex one-place predicates constructed by appending a predicate-forming operator ("believes that") to a sentence. On this view, propositional attitudes have no "objects," since they are not relational states. For further discussion see Horgan (1989).

2 For visual perception, see e.g., Gregory (1970).

3 For example, eighteenth-century chemical theories attempted to explain such properties of metals as their shininess and ductility by appeal to the same factors which were also thought to explain the compound-forming behavior of metals. Chemical theories such as Lavoisier's focused just on compounds, and orginally were criticized for their failure to provide also a unified explanation of metallic shininess and ductility.

4 For some striking evidence that situational theories are more empirically adequate, and hence that this change has been a progressive one, see Nisbett and Ross (1980).

5 Thus his critical remarks on Fodor (1975), and in general on cognitive psychological theories that take information to be stored in sentential form; cf. Churchland (1981, pp. 78ff.).

6 In order to elevate anomalous monism into a full-fledged version of materialism, one must add to it an account of the metaphysical status of mental state-types (properties) *vis-à-vis* physicochemical state-types. The appropriate doctrine, we think, is one also propounded by Davidson (1970, 1974): viz., that mental properties are *supervenient* upon physical ones. Several philosophers recently have developed this idea, arguing that materialism should incorporate some sort of supervenience thesis. Cf. Kim (1978, 1982); Haugeland (1982); Horgan (1981b, 1982b); and Lewis (1983). Also see the papers collected in the Spindel issue of *The Southern Journal of Philosophy*, 22, 1984.

7 For surveys of the relevant literature, see Nisbett and Wilson (1977), and Wilson (unpublished).

8 At any rate, this is what the dual-control thesis amounts to as regards the Storms–Nisbett study. Other kinds of mental events besides beliefs and inferences might sometimes be involved too.

9 See, for instance, Wilson (unpublished), pp. 7ff.

10 Still, one can understand why Stich would be led to attribute the radical dual-control thesis to Wilson, even though Wilson evidently does not actually hold this view. Stich quotes from what evidently was an earlier version of the above-quoted passage, wherein Wilson said that the function of the verbal system "is to attempt to verbalize, explain and communicate what is occurring in the unconscious system." Admittedly, this earlier wording suggests that in verbalizing our mental states we *never* have conscious access to those states. But the present passage, with its explicit acknowledgment of frequent conscious access, evidently cancels this suggestion, along with any implicit commitment to the radical dual-control thesis.

11 Although we think it quite possible that CS will become nonmodular at its most fundamental levels, we also believe that certain higher-level branches of theoretical psychology probably not only will remain modular, but will continue to employ the concepts of FP itself. Attribution theory is a case in point. (By a "higher-level" psychological theory we mean one which posits events that are wholes whose parts are the events posited by "lower-level" psychological theories. More on this below.)

12 It is worth noting another respect in which Stich's (and Churchland's) arguments seem to lead to sweeping and implausibly strong conclusions. Much formal theory in the social sciences involves ascribing to individual actors states which are recognizably like, or recognizably descended from, the FP

notions of belief and desire. Within economic and game theory, for example, individual actors are thought of as having indifference curves, utility schedules, or preference orderings over various possible outcomes, and beliefs about the subjective probabilities of these outcomes. Within economic theories of voting or political party behavior, similar assumptions are made. Even among theorists of voting behavior who reject the "economic" approach, typically there are appeals to voters' beliefs and attitudes to explain behavior. (See, for example, Campbell et al. 1960.) Clearly, if Stich's modularity requirement and Churchland's smoothness of reduction requirement are not satisfied by the FP notions of belief and desire, then they are unlikely to be satisfied by the notions of utility, degree of belief, and so forth employed by such theories. Thus Stich and Churchland seem to have produced general arguments which, if cogent, would show – quite independently of any detailed empirical investigation of the actual behavior of markets, voters, etc. – that all these theories must be false, at least on their most natural interpretation.

13 A complex event of the relevant kind might be a mereological sum, or *fusion*, of simpler events; alternatively, it might be an entity distinct from this event-fusion. We shall take no stand on this matter here. (The issue is closely related to the question whether an entity like a ship is identical with the fusion of its physical parts, or is instead an entity distinct from this fusion, with different intra-world and transworld identity conditions.) To our knowledge, the most explicit and well-developed theory of parts and wholes for events is that of Thompson (1977); event-fusions are the only kinds of complex events she explicitly countenances.

14 This Davidsonian argument was suggested to us by Stich himself, in conversation.

15 But as the famous case of Twin Earth (Putnam 1975) seems to show, an event's causal role is not the only factor relevant to its folk-psychological individuation. Our doppelgangers on Twin Earth don't undergo tokens of the type *believing that water is good to drink*, even though they do undergo events that are functionally indistinguishable from our own token beliefs that water is good to drink. The trouble is that the stuff they call "water" isn't water at all. Cf. Burge (1979).

16 While a full defense of these claims must be beyond the scope of this essay, we think they are required for the truth of many causal statements in contexts where highly developed and precise formal theories are not available. Consider the claims (a) that application of a certain fertilizer causes plants to increase in mean height, and also causes them to increase in leaf width; (b) that following a certain study routine R causes an increase in SAT verbal scores, and also causes an increase in SAT mathematical scores; or

(c) that certain childrearing practices cause an increase in the incidence of juvenile delinquency in certain populations. There is an enormous literature detailing complex and ingenious statistical techniques for testing such claims. (Fisher (1935) is an early classic, inspired largely by problems connected with testing claims like (a); and many books on "causal modeling," like Blalock (1971), discuss procedures that are relevant to (b) and (c).) These techniques might well establish that the three claims are true. Yet the cases described in (a), (b), and (c) can easily fail to be minimal causes; the fertilizer will commonly be a mixture, containing compounds which are inert, or which have other effects on the plant besides those mentioned in (a); and it seems implausible to suppose that every feature or detail of study routine R or childrearing practice C is causally necessary for the above effects. (Typically, we have no practical way of determining what the minimal causes in such cases are.) Thus (a) can be true even though the fertilizer is a mixture of several distinct compounds, one of which causes increase in height (but not increase in leaf width) while the other causes increase in leaf width (but not height). Similarly, (b) can be true even though different aspects of study routine R are responsible for the increases in math and in verbal scores. (See Thomson (1977) for further defense of the claim that genuine causes don't have to be minimal causes.)

17 The point about conglomerative causation is also relevant to Stich's dual-control argument against FP. Even if verbal and nonverbal behavior should turn out to have largely separate minimal causes, FP could be true anyway; for, FP-events might be complexes of the minimal causes, and these complex events might be genuine causes (albeit nonminimal causes) of both the verbal and the nonverbal behavior. (We should stress, however, that we are *not* claiming that if the dual-control thesis is true, then whenever a subject is in some state B of his nonverbal behavioral system and some state V of his verbal system, it will always be possible, consistently with FP, to ascribe to him some single folk-psychological cause of both his verbal and nonverbal behavior. Whether this will be possible depends upon the specific states V and B and upon the behavior they cause. In the Storms–Wilson insomnia experiment, for example, the state B (subjects' attribution of their symptoms to pills) which causes the arousal group to fall asleep is not merely distinct from the state V which causes their verbal behavior (denial that the above attribution had anything to do with their falling asleep); but in addition, these two states cannot, consistently with the causal principles embodied in FP, be treated as components of some single belief.)

18 Of course, it might be that some cases of exorcism appear to be efficacious, but this is only because they

involve certain features which are also cited by other, more secular, theories (e.g., reassuring the "possessed" person, giving him attention, etc.). Establishing this can require ingenuity in experimental design, but poses no problem in principle. It is just false that we could never obtain direct experimental evidence (distinct from considerations of modularity or failure of fit) that would make it rational to reject the claim that exorcism is efficacious in itself, by virtue of dislodging the devil.

19 Although we have assumed throughout that folk-psychological events are complex events consisting of lower-level events as their parts, we want to acknowledge that it may be possible to defend the compatibility of FP and CS without this assumption. Jaegwon Kim (1966, 1969, 1973) holds that an event is an entity consisting in the instantiation of a property by an object at a time, and that mental events consist in the instantiation of mental properties by individuals at times. Under this approach, it is unclear whether lower-level events can sensibly be treated as parts of FP-events. Nevertheless, an advocate of Kim's theory of events still might be able to argue that FP-events exist and bear all the causal relations to one another that FP says they do. For he might be able to argue that these events are supervenient upon groups of lower-level events, and that supervenience transmits causal efficacy. Cf. Kim (1979, 1982, 1984).

20 Throughout this essay we have assumed, as is usual, that if everyday folk-psychological statements are

indeed true, then there really exist folk-psychological mental events – that is, token desires, token beliefs, and so forth. In fact, however, one of us (Horgan) thinks there are good reasons for denying the existence of events in general; cf. Horgan (1978, 1981a, 1982a). Horgan also thinks that if physicochemical events exist, then normally there will be numerous classes of physicochemical events from within someone's head which jointly meet all the causal conditions which would qualify a given class for identification with the class consisting of that person's folk-psychological mental events; and he takes this to indicate that even if psysicochemical events exist, and even if garden-variety folk-psychological statements (including statements about mental causation) are often true, nevertheless there really are no such entities as mental events; cf. Horgan and Tye (1985). We believe that the essential points of the present essay can be reformulated in a way which does not require the existence of mental events (even if physicochemical events are assumed to exist), and also in a way which does not require the existence of any events at all. But our objective here has been the more limited one of defending FP within the framework of the ontology of events which is widely taken for granted in contemporary philosophy of mind.

21 We thank Stephen Stich, William Tolhurst, and Michael Tye for helpful comments on an earlier version of this essay.

References

Blalock, H. (ed.) (1971) *Causal Models in the Social Sciences*, New York, Aldine.

Burge, T. (1979) "Individualism and the mental," in P. French, T. Uehling, and H. Wettstein (eds), *Midwest Studies in Philosophy*, vol. 4, *Studies in Epistemology*, Minneapolis, University of Minnesota Press.

Campbell, A., Converse, P., Miller, W., and Stokes, D. (1960) *The American Voter*, New York, John Wiley & Sons.

Churchland, P. (1979) *Scientific Realism and the Plasticity of Mind*, New York, Cambridge University Press.

Churchland, P. (1981) "Eliminative materialism and propositional attitudes," *Journal of Philosophy*, 78.

Davidson, D. (1967) "Causal relations," *Journal of Philosophy*, 64.

Davidson, D. (1970) "Mental events," in L. Foster and J. Swanson (eds), *Experience and Theory*, London, Duckworth.

Davidson, D. (1973). "The material mind," in P. Suppes et al. (eds), *Logic, Methodology, and the Philosophy of Science*, vol. 4, Amsterdam, North-Holland.

Davidson, D. (1974) "Psychology as philosophy," in S. C. Brown (ed.), *Philosophy of Psychology*, New York, Harper & Row.

Dennett, D. (1978) *Brainstorms*, Cambridge, Mass., Bradford.

Dennett, D. (1981) "Three kinds of intentional psychology," in R. Healey (ed.), *Reduction, Time, and Identity*, New York, Cambridge University Press.

Field, H. (1978) "Mental representation," *Erkenntnis*, 13.

Fisher, R. (1935) *The Design of Experiments*, Edinburgh, Oliver and Boyd.

Fodor, J. (1975) *The Language of Thought*, New York, Thomas Y. Crowell.

Fodor, J. (1978) "Propositional attitudes," *The Monist*, 61.

Gregory, R. (1970) *The Intelligent Eye*, New York, McGraw-Hill.

Haugeland, J. (1982) "Weak supervenience," *American Philosophical Quarterly*, 19.

Horgan, T. (1978) "The case against events," *Philosophical Review*, 87.

Horgan, T. (1981a) "Action theory without actions," *Mind*, 90.

Horgan, T. (1981b) "Token physicalism, supervenience, and the generality of physics," *Synthese*, 34.

Horgan, T. (1982a) "Substitutivity and the causal connective," *Philosophical Studies*, 42.

Horgan, T. (1982b) "Supervenience and microphysics," *Pacific Philosophical Quarterly*, 63

Horgan, T. (1989) "Attitudinatives," *Linguistics and Philosophy* 12, 133–65.

Horgan, T. and Tye, M. (1985) "Against the token identity theory," in E. LePore and B. McLaughlin (eds), *Essays on Actions and Events*, Blackwell Publishers.

Kim, J. (1966) "On the psycho-physical identity theory," *American Philosophical Quarterly*, 3.

Kim, J. (1969) "Events and their descriptions: some considerations," in N. Rescher et al. (eds), *Essays in Honor of Carl G. Hempel*, Dordrecht, Reidel.

Kim, J. (1973) "Causation, nomic subsumption, and the concept of event," *Journal of Philosophy*, 70.

Kim, J. (1978) "Supervenience and nomological incommensurables," *American Philosophical Quarterly*, 15.

Kim, J. (1979) "Causality, identity, and supervenience in the mind-body problem," *Midwest Studies in Philosophy*, 4.

Kim, J. (1982) "Psychophysical supervenience," *Philosophical Studies*, 41.

Kim, J. (1984) "Supervenience and supervenient causation," *Southern Journal of Philosophy*, 22.

Lewis, D. (1983) "New work for a theory of universals," *Australasian Journal of Philosophy*, 61.

Lycan, W. (1981) "Toward a homuncular theory of believing," *Cognition and Brain Theory*, 4.

Minsky, M. (1981) "K-Lines: a theory of memory," in D. Norman (ed.), *Perspectives on Cognitive Science*, Norwood, NJ, Ablex.

Nisbett, R. and Ross, L. (1980) *Human Inference: Strategies and Shortcomings of Social Judgment*, Englewood Cliffs, NJ, Prentice-Hall.

Nisbett, R. and Wilson, T. (1977) "Telling more than we can know: verbal reports on mental processes," *Psychological Review*, 84.

Putnam, H. (1975) "The meaning of 'meaning'," in K. Gunderson (ed.), *Language, Mind, and Knowledge, Minnesota Studies in the Philosophy of Science*, 7, Minneapolis, University of Minnesota Press.

Quine, W. V. O. (1970) *Philosophy of Logic*, Englewood Cliffs, NJ, Prentice-Hall.

Stich, S. (1983) *From Folk Psychology to Cognitive Science: The Case Against Belief*, Cambridge, Mass. Bradford.

Storms, M. and Nisbett, R. (1970) "Insomnia and the attribution process," *Journal of Personality and Social Psychology*, 2.

Thomson, J. (1977) *Acts and Other Events*, Ithaca, NY, Cornell.

Wilson, T. (unpublished) "Strangers to ourselves: the origins and accuracy of beliefs about one's own mental states."

13

The Debate Over Narrow and Wide Content

A Narrow Representational Theory of the Mind

Michael Devitt

1 Introduction

Cognitive science contains two sharply different lines of thought about thought. We might call them "the Folk Line" and "the Revisionist Line."

The general inspiration for the Folk Line is folk theory or, less pretentiously, folk opinion about the mind. More particularly, the inspiration is the folk view that people have thoughts with rich representational and semantic properties; in particular, people have mental states with truth-conditional content. Cognitive psychology must explain the interaction of thoughts with each other and the world by laws that advert to these semantic properties: psychology must be "wide."[1] Many who have joined in the debate follow the Folk Line. I suspect that many others do also. In my view, it has been most persuasively argued by Tyler Burge (1986).

The general inspiration for the Revisionist Line is the functionalist theory of the mind. More particularly, the inspiration is the arguments for "methodological solipsism" and autonomous psychology, and the analogy between the mind and a computer. Revisionists frequently hold that cognitive psychology must explain the interaction of mental states with each other and the world by laws that advert only to formal or syntactic properties, not to truth-conditional ones. They hold sometimes that the semantics for psychology

must be functional-(conceptual-)role semantics; psychology must be "narrow."[2]

It might seem appropriate for the Revisionists to take their disagreement with the Folk further: mental states do not have truth-conditional contents at all. For, if we do not need those contents for psychology, there seems no principled reason for supposing that mental states have them. Some Revisionists have taken this position, or at least toyed with it. Some have suggested that there are nonpsychological reasons for believing in truth conditions. Finally, some have simply assumed that mental states have truth conditions without confronting the question of why we should think they have.

My main concern is not with these variations but rather with the Revisionist Line on psychology. However, I will make some passing remarks that bear on them.

Stephen Stich's "Syntactic Theory of the Mind" ("STM"; see Stich [this volume, this Part]) seems to be a clear example of the Revisionist Line:

> cognitive states . . . can be systematically mapped to abstract syntactic objects in such a way that causal interactions among cognitive states, as well as causal links with stimuli and behavioral events, can be described in terms of the syntactic properties and relations of the abstract objects to which the cognitive states are mapped. (1983, p. 149)

The substantive and empirically exacting part of the theory consists in a set of generalizations which detail causal interactions among stimuli, B- and D-states [STM analogues of beliefs and desires], and behavioral events by appeal to the syntactic structure of the wffs to which they are mapped. (1983, p. 154)

A similar view has been urged by Hartry Field (1978, pp. 100–2) and Stephen Schiffer (1981, pp. 214–15).

It is natural to take many writings of Jerry Fodor and Zenon Pylyshyn as powerful defenses of the Revisionist Line. Fodor urges the "formality condition" which is definitive of "the computational theory of the mind" ("CTM"):

mental processes have access only to formal (nonsemantic) properties of the mental representations over which they are defined. (1980a, p. 63)

Pylyshyn endorses this condition (1980a, pp. 111–15; 1980b, pp. 158–61). He believes that "cognition *is* a type of computation" (1984, p. xiii). Since CTM is about mental processes, it seems to be about the lawlike generalizations of psychology: it seems to agree with Stich that these laws may advert only to syntactic properties. CTM has been taken this way by friend and foe alike.[3] However, this is not the way Fodor and Pylyshyn take it. They think that psychological laws will advert to full truth-conditional contents. This leads Stich to accuse Fodor of trying to "have it both ways" (1983, p. 188): the intentional talk of folk psychology on the one hand, and the formality condition on the other. Fodor thinks that he can have it both ways because CTM is concerned with a different level from that of the laws: the level of their implementation (1987, pp. 139–40, 166n.). CTM certainly does suggest a claim about a level of physical implementation, as we shall see (section 2). However, it is largely concerned with a psychological level, which Fodor thinks of as between the physical and the folk-psychological. I think that this *is* an attempt to have it both ways, but I shall not argue that here.[4] My interest is in CTM construed as a doctrine like STM that is revisionist about the laws of psychology; an example of the Revisionist Line.

I think that there is a great deal of confusion in the debate between the Folk and the Revisionist. When properly understood, methodological solipsism and the computer analogy do support a position that diverges from the Folk Line. However, the position may not be revisionist or eliminativist at all, and if it is, it is not disturbingly so. As a result, it is not open to the criticisms that Burge and others have aimed at the Revisionist Line. My diagnosis of most of the confusion and error in this debate is: too little attention to inputs (stimuli) and outputs (behavior).

I shall briefly describe a theory of the mind that ascribes a meaning or content to mental states that is not truth-conditional and hence is less than the Folk Line requires (section 4). However, the meaning is proto-truth-conditional and so is more than the Revisionist Line usually seems to allow. What is crucial about this meaning for my argument is that it goes beyond syntax: it includes links to sensory inputs. Whilst acknowledging the force of methodological solipsism and the computer analogy (section 3), I shall argue that we need to ascribe this much meaning for psychology (section 5). I shall then argue that this much meaning is sufficient for psychology (section 6).

The theory is a narrow representational theory of the mind, a narrow RTM. There have been signs of it elsewhere.[5] However, it has not been adequately distinguished from others, and hence its significance for the debate between Revisionist and Folk has not been brought out.

2 "Syntactic" and "Formal"

What precisely is the Revisionist Line? Much of the confusion in the debate comes from the absence of a clear answer to this question. I have described the Line as the view that psychology adverts only to the formal or syntactic properties of a representation; or, that it adverts only to the narrow properties of a functional-(conceptual-)role semantics not the wide ones of a truth-conditional semantics. Sometimes the properties needed for psychology are described as "nonsemantic" (for example by Fodor above). Sometimes psychology is said to treat representations as "meaningless" (Field 1978, p. 101) or "uninterpreted" (Schiffer 1981, pp. 214–15). These various descriptions reflect a jumble of different ideas that are best kept distinct.

I want to define a Revisionist doctrine using the term "syntactic." I am anxious to diminish the confusion and so I shall start by trying to be very clear about what I mean by that term. I think that my meaning is the standard one – outside this debate at least – and hence that the doctrines I define are appropriate ways to understand the most frequent statements of the Revisionist Line.

"Syntactic" is often treated in this debate as if it were a near-synonym of "formal." This is appropriate enough given the use of "formal" in logic. However, it is worth noting that there is an ordinary use of "formal" which would make the treatment quite inappropriate.

In this ordinary sense, formal properties are fairly "brute-physical" ones that are *intrinsic* to a symbol; for example, the shape of a letter, the pattern of on–off switches in a computer, or the array of neurons in the brain. If "formal" had the brute-physical sense in statements of CTM,[6] then there would be a straightforward way to understand CTM as concerned with a different level from folk psychology, a level of the physical realization of psychological states (cf. section 1 above). CTM would then be a physicalist doctrine (a false one if the arguments of this essay are sound). However, it would not be concerned with a psychological level, which is contrary to what Fodor and Pylyshyn claim for it and to the way it has been universally taken.

"Syntax" refers to properties that are quite different from the above brute-physical ones. It refers to properties a symbol has in virtue of its role in relation to other symbols in the language. These properties are the ones that bear on the construction of some symbols out of others. They are studied in the field known as "Syntax" (Chomsky 1957, p. 11). They are functional and *extrinsic* to the symbol.[7] Being a name,[8] being a one-place predicate, and being a sentence, are examples of such properties.[9]

I shall bring out my meaning of "syntactic" by likening it to the logicians' technical use of "formal." This use arises from the notions of a *formal language* and a *formal system*. It is very different from the above "ordinary" use.

> *A formal system* is like a game in which tokens are manipulated according to rules, in order to see what configurations can be obtained. (Haugeland 1985, p. 48)

Chess is a good example of such a system. In a realization of the system, a token of any type – for example, a pawn or a bishop – is, of course, a physical entity of a certain form in the above ordinary sense. It is usually important that tokens of each type differ in their brute-physical properties from those of any other type but, beyond that, it does not matter what form the tokens have in the ordinary sense. So far as the system is concerned, all that matters about a token is its role in the system. To be a token of a particular type is simply to be covered in a certain way by the rules. So a pawn is a pawn, however it is physically realized, because it plays the role of a pawn in the game. It is common to call types or properties, like *being a pawn*, "formal." Such properties abstract from the brute-physical properties of any realization of the system; that is, from the formal properties in the earlier ordinary sense. They are functional, structural, or relational properties. Note finally that nothing outside the system has any bearing on these properties. In particular, meaning is irrelevant to them.

The contrast between this sort of formal property and the earlier sort might be brought out as follows. Properties of the earlier sort characterize the "shape" of *an object*; they are intrinsic to the object. Properties of the present sort characterize the "shape" of *a structure of objects*; they are intrinsic to the structure but not to any object.

Some formal systems are or contain languages. Such a language consists of a set of basic symbols classified into various types – for example names, variables, one-place predicates, a conjunction symbol – together with *formation* rules for combining symbols of various types to form other symbols (such as sentences). The system containing the language also includes *transformation* rules for moving from some symbols to others as in an inference. Properties like *being a name* are just like *being a pawn*: they are functional. They are properties that a token has not in virtue of its brute-physical make-up but in virtue of its role in the system. So what matters to *being a conjunction symbol* is not whether a token looks like "&" or ".", but that it is governed by certain rules. Such properties of tokens in a formal language are also commonly called "formal."[10] And, of course, any meaning a token may have is irrelevant to its having one of these properties.[11]

It is important to note a feature of this sort of system that distinguishes it from chess: it is concerned with sameness and difference of types *within the basic types*. Thus it matters to the transformation rules not only whether a token is a name but also whether it is a token of the *same name* type as, or of a *different name* type from, another token. Consider, for example, the transformation rule *modus ponens*, which we might express:

> Given both a conditional and its antecedent, derive its consequent.

What is meant by "its antecedent"? It means, of course, a token of the same type as that of the token that is the antecedent of the conditional. But it means this not merely in the sense that the token must also be a sentence. The token has to be a token of the *same* sentence type as the token antecedent; that is, it has to have the same structure and have tokens of the same name type, predicate type, etc., occupying that structure. For example, if the conditional is a token of "F$a \rightarrow$ Fb," then what is referred to by "its antecedent" is a token of "Fa." So *relations of sameness and difference* of sentence type, name type, predicate type, etc., are also formal relations of the system. However – and this is especially important in what follows – the *properties of being a certain* sentence type, *being a certain* name type, *being a certain* predicate type, etc., are not formal properties, because such properties play no role in the system.

Of course, a token may *be* of a certain sentence type, name type, etc.; for example, it may be of the name type that refers to Reagan. But this property is irrelevant to the system and so is not a formal property. Word meaning is semantic not formal. A token may also be of a certain shape type; for example, it may be shaped like "*a*." But this property is relevant only to the realization of the system and so is not a formal property in this technical sense; it is a formal property in the ordinary sense.

The formal properties of symbols in a formal language, in the technical sense, are clearly just like the earlier-described syntactic properties of symbols in a natural language; and formal relations are just like syntactic relations. Indeed, formal properties and relations are often called "syntactic," most notably by Carnap (1937).[12] These are the properties and relations I shall be referring to by "syntactic."

In sum, a symbol has its syntactic properties and relations solely in virtue of its relations to others in a system of symbols; it has them solely in virtue of the system's *internal* relations.

3 Arguments for the Revisionist Line

I take it that my remarks about "syntactic" and "formal" are standard and hence that there is nothing eccentric about my use of "syntactic." So it is appropriate to take the many statements of Revisionism using "syntactic" and "formal" to be aptly captured by the following doctrine (with "syntactic" understood as above):

> SYNTACTIC PSYCHOLOGY: The laws of mental processes advert only to the syntactic properties of representations.

Further, I think that it is because Revisionism has been understood as SYNTACTIC PSYCHOLOGY that it has seemed so *excitingly* radical to its proponents and so *dangerously* radical to its opponents.

Do the arguments offered for Revisionism support SYNTACTIC PSYCHOLOGY? These arguments are familiar and so I shall be brief in my description of them.

The argument from the computer analogy. It is argued that we should take the computer analogy seriously and so see thought processes as computational. Now computational processes are defined syntactically; they are "syntactic operations over symbolic expressions" (Pylyshyn 1980a, p. 113); they are "both *symbolic* and *formal*" (Fodor 1980a, p. 64). So we should see thought processes as defined syntactically. A typical example of a law that satisfies this requirement might be one for *modus ponens* inferences:

> Whenever a person believes both a conditional and its antecedent, she tends to infer its consequent.

This law is, of course, reminiscent of the rule *modus ponens* for a formal system discussed in the last section. We saw then that all the properties and relations adverted to in such rules are syntactic.

This may seem to be an argument for SYNTACTIC PSYCHOLOGY. However, it is an argument only if we overlook a vital distinction: the distinction between thought processes and mental processes in general. The mental processes that concern (cognitive) psychology come in three sorts, as our initial quotes from Stich brought out (section 1):

(i)   processes from thoughts to thoughts;

(ii)   processes from sensory inputs to thoughts;

(iii) processes from thoughts to behavioral outputs.

What I have been calling "thought processes" are mental processes of sort (i): inferential processes. Computation is indeed a good analogy for those and so provides a good reason for taking them as syntactic. But since the literature provides no reason to believe that a computer's input and output processes are analogous to (ii) and (iii), we have been given no reason to believe that (ii) and (iii) are syntactic. The argument from the computer analogy supports not SYNTACTIC PSYCHOLOGY but rather the much more modest

SYNTACTIC THOUGHT PROCESSES: The laws of thought processes advert only to the syntactic properties of representations.

The argument has no bearing on whether the laws of mental processes in general have to advert to semantic properties or contents.

Not only is there no argument for the more extensive computer analogy required to support SYNTACTIC PSYCHOLOGY, that analogy seems very unlikely. The problem is that computers do not have transducers anything like those of humans and do not produce behavior in anything like the way humans do. Computers move from symbolic input via symbolic manipulation (computation) to symbolic output. Humans, in contrast, move from largely nonsymbolic sensory stimulation via symbolic manipulation (thinking) to largely nonsymbolic action. Any interpretation a computer's symbols have, *we* give them. However, it is plausible to suppose that a human's symbols have a particular interpretation in virtue of their perceptual causes, whatever we theorists may do or think about them. Furthermore, it is because of those links to sensory input that a symbol has its distinctive role in causing action. I shall be arguing for this later (section 5).

Participants in the debate about the mind are strangely uninterested in the distinction between thought processes and mental processes in general. The problem is not that they are unaware of the distinction: typically discussions will start with what amounts to an acknowledgment of the distinction – as, for example, in the quotes from Stich. The problem is that from then on all processes except thought processes tend to be ignored. Thought processes are treated as if they were representative of them all. Fodor is particularly striking in this respect. He begins his discussion of CTM by distinguishing the three sorts of process (1987, p.12). Yet a few pages later, in a passage important enough to be displayed, he describes "the nature of mental processes" in a way that applies only to thought processes.[13] Despite this, there is every sign that he takes CTM to cover all mental processes (see, for example, 1987, p.139).[14]

The argument from methodological solipsism and psychological autonomy. In psychology, we are concerned to explain why, given stimuli at her sense organs, a person evinced certain behavior. Only something that is entirely supervenient on what is inside her skin – on her intrinsic internal physical states, particularly her brain – could play the required explanatory role between peripheral input and output. Environmental causes of her stimuli and effects of her behavior are beside the psychological point. The person and all her physical, even functional, duplicates must be psychologically the same, whatever their environments. Mental states must be individuated according to their role within the individual, without regard to their relations to an environment. All of this counts against the Folk view that a thought's property of having a wide meaning, or truth conditions, is relevant to psychology. For that property is *not* supervenient on what is inside the person's skin. It *does* depend on relations to the environment because it depends on referential links. And Putnam's Twin Earth discussion has brought out that duplicates may *not* share wide meanings; that is the point of the slogan, "meanings just ain't in the head" (1975, p. 227).[15] Psychology should advert only to meanings that are determined by what is in the head, or, at least, inside the skin; it should advert only to narrow meaning.

This argument is open to question, as we shall see (section 6). For the moment, assume that it is good. Then it establishes that truth-conditional properties are irrelevant to psychology. The point to be made now is that the argument does *not* establish SYNTACTIC PSYCHOLOGY. Let us take for granted that syntactic properties are relevant to psychology. The argument does not establish that *only* syntactic properties are relevant. To establish that we need the further premise that there are no other non-truth-conditional properties that are relevant. To my knowledge, *no argument for this premise has ever been given*. I shall argue that the premise is false (section 5).

Similarly, the argument from methodological solipsism does not establish that only "nonsemantic" properties are relevant, nor that representations are "meaningless" or "uninterpreted" so far as psychology is concerned, unless "nonsemantic," "meaningless," and "uninterpreted" simply *mean* non-truth-conditional. I am as enthusiastic as anyone about truth-conditional semantics, but surely the question whether it is the *right* semantics is an empirical one, not something to be settled by definition.

Though the Revisionist Line is most frequently urged using "syntactic" and "formal" it is sometimes urged, often in the same breath, as a case for functional-(conceptual-)role, or narrow meaning (or content), in psychology.[16] Yet this version of the Line is very different from SYNTACTIC PSYCHOLOGY as we shall see (section 4). Briefly, syntax involves only the relations between representations, whereas functional-role meaning also involves the relations between representations and stimuli. Syntactic roles are not the only functional roles that go into narrow meaning.

Insofar as the argument from methodological solipsism is good, I think that it does support the case for functional-role semantics.[17] The narrow RTM I shall be urging proposes such a semantics for psychology. For proto-truth-conditional meaning is a type of functional-role meaning and does supervene on what is inside the skin; so it is a type of narrow meaning.

Now it may be that when Revisionists talk of "syntactic" or "formal" properties, they mean to refer to some sort of narrow meaning (or content). This is certainly suggested sometimes by the company the talk keeps. If this is what is meant, my only objection to the talk is that it is very misleading, for reasons to be brought out (section 4). However, understood in this way, Revisionism does not seem nearly so radical. Indeed, I shall argue that the proper form of it is hardly radical at all (section 6).

In sum, the argument from the computer analogy establishes SYNTACTIC THOUGHT PROCESSES but not SYNTACTIC PSYCHOLOGY. The argument from methodological solipsism may establish the irrelevance of truth-conditional properties to psychology but it does not establish that only syntactic ones are relevant. So it does not establish SYNTACTIC PSYCHOLOGY either. I shall argue that SYNTACTIC PSYCHOLOGY is false (section 5).

4 Narrow Psychology

According to the narrow RTM that I shall urge, the meaning (or content) that must be ascribed for the purposes of psychology can be abstracted from wide truth-conditional meaning. So first I need to consider the nature of that meaning. In so doing, I will draw on the semantics described and (partly) explained in *Language and Reality*.[18] However, many of the details of that semantics are irrelevant to our present concerns.

The initial idea is that the core of the meaning of a sentence – whether a public one or a mental sentence in thought – is its property of having certain truth conditions. We need to explain that property. The most plausible explanation is in terms of the syntactic structure of the sentence and the referential properties of its parts. We must then explain syntax and reference. Syntax is a matter of functional role (section 2). But how are we to explain reference? I think that three sorts of theory are possible and that very likely each sort has some application.

Description theories are one sort. They were once popular for proper names but are more plausible for terms like "bachelor" and "pediatrician." According to a description theory, the reference of a term is determined by the reference of certain other terms with which it is associated by speakers. Though such a theory may well be true of some terms it could not be true of all terms, for it is *essentially incomplete* as an explanation of reference. It explains the reference of one term by appealing to the reference of others. How then is the reference of those other terms to be explained? Perhaps we can use description theories again. This process cannot, however, go on for ever: there must be some terms whose referential properties are not parasitic on those of others. Otherwise, language as a whole is cut loose from the world. Description theories pass the referential buck. But the buck must stop somewhere.

In the light of Twin Earth and Putnam's slogan, it seems plausible to suppose that the referential buck stops with terms covered by "pure-causal" theories of reference. Pure-causal theories seem to be suggested for natural-kind terms and names by Putnam (1975), Saul Kripke (1980), and Keith Donnellan (1972). According to such a theory, the reference of a term is determined by direct causal links to external reality.

The third sort of theory of reference is a mixture of the other two, a "descriptive-causal" theory. In my view, it is the most plausible theory for proper names and natural-kind terms. According to it, the reference of a term is determined partly by direct causal links to external reality and partly by the reference of certain other terms with which it is associated by speakers.

How does word meaning relate to reference? For Frege a word's *meaning* was (roughly) a "mode of presentation" of its referent (1952, p. 57). I think Frege was right about that but not about the nature of the mode. We should identify a word's meaning with the sort of mechanism that, according to our theories of reference, explains its reference.[19] This mechanism may include descriptive associations. It must include causal links to reality, for the reference of any term is determined either by its own direct causal links, or by those of terms on which it referentially depends.

The truth-conditional meaning explained in this way is clearly wide, for it partly depends on causal links that are "outside the skin." If we abstract from those outside links, we are left with "proto-truth-conditional" meaning. This meaning is narrow in that it is entirely supervenient on the intrinsic inner states of the thinker. It is the inner, functional-role *part* of wide meaning. It is what I shall mean in future by "narrow meaning."

Narrow meaning (or content) is very rich. Not only does it include all the functional roles that determine the syntactic structure of sentences, but also the inner functional roles that partly determine the reference of words.[20] The latter roles are what is left of wide word meaning when the extracranial links are subtracted. The roles constitute narrow word meanings. Those meanings are functions taking external causes of peripheral stimuli as arguments to yield wide (referential) meanings as values.[21] *Narrow word meaning is (mostly) not a matter of syntax.* That is crucial to distinguishing my narrow RTM from SYNTACTIC PSYCHOLOGY.

Consider a term that is covered by a pure-causal theory. Its reference depends on its direct causal link to external reality. If we abstract from the part of that link that is external to the subject, we are left with the functional-role connections between peripheral stimuli and the term. This inner link is not negligible; it is the inner processing that must take place if a representation is to take referential advantage of the causal action of the world on the subject. The link, together with the term's syntactic category, determines the term's narrow meaning.

A pure-causal term's narrow meaning involves much more than its syntactic properties. Terms have their syntactic properties solely in virtue of their relations to other terms *within* the symbol system (section 2). Pure-causal terms have their narrow semantic properties largely in virtue of their relations to stimuli, which are *outside* the system. It is in virtue of these relations to stimuli that a token has the nonsyntactic property of *being a certain* term type within a syntactic category. Thus, consider the terms "echidna" and "platypus," which are clearly in the same category, and suppose that they are pure-causal terms (which I doubt). There is a relation of difference between them that is syntactic (section 2). However, what makes something an "echidna" token, and not a "platypus" token, is that it is links to echidna-ish stimuli. That is what gives the term the narrow meaning of "echidna" in particular. These links to stimuli are not in any way syntactic.

The same applies to part of the narrow meaning of a descriptive-causal term. For that part of its meaning is determined in the same way as the meaning of a pure-causal term. The other part of its narrow meaning depends on associations with other terms just as does all of the narrow meaning of a term covered by a description theory. At first sight, these meanings may seem to be syntactic. For the association of a term with other terms is plausibly seen as a syntactic relation. However, that association is only the first step in determining the term's reference. It simply passes the referential buck to the other terms. If the buck is to stop, the explanation must ultimately be of terms relying for their reference, fully or partly, on direct causal links to external reality. These links, as I have just noted, are not syntactic. So to the extent that the narrow meaning of a descriptive, or descriptive-causal, term is dependent on these links, that link is not syntactic.

Every part of the narrow meaning of every term involves functional-role links between the term and peripheral stimuli. Narrow word meaning is largely determined by relations that are not syntactic.

The theory I have been sketching differs from almost all others in not being holist. It is not holist in two respects. (i) It does not subscribe to the main tenet of holism: the meaning of any term depends on the meaning of every term. According to description and descriptive-causal theories, the meaning of a term does depend on others, but not on all others. This departure from holism requires an argument. I shall not give the argument, because the departure has no significance for this essay. I make the departure only because I think that the main tenet is, despite its popularity, implausible, underargued, and destructive of cognitive psychology.

(ii) The theory is not holist about the links between language and the world, and language and stimuli. The meanings of pure-causal and descriptive-causal terms depend immediately on causal links to particular parts of reality via particular stimuli. This aspect of a term's meaning, narrow and wide, is almost entirely independent of the meaning of any other term and so yields a striking departure from holism. I think that this departure is significant to this essay. However, I shall not argue for it because the contrary view is wildly implausible and, so far as I know, completely unsupported. For the contrary view is that the world contributes unselectively to meaning, so that echidna sightings have no more to do with the meaning of "echidna" than with the meanings of "oyster," "elephant," "telephone," "pediatrician," and "Alpha Centauri."[22]

In sum, a truth-conditional theory of wide meaning (or content) must include an explanation of a sentence's property of having certain truth conditions. This explanation will justify the ascription of a narrow functional-role meaning (or content) to the sentence: we simply abstract from the extra-cranial links referred to in the explanation. Narrow sentence meaning depends on narrow word meaning, and that is mostly not a matter of syntax.

The narrow RTM that I urge claims that narrow meaning is all that is required for psychology (I take narrow meaning, and also wide meaning, to include syntactic properties on the ground that syntactic properties partly constitute them):

NARROW PSYCHOLOGY: The laws of mental processes advert only to the narrow semantic properties of representations.

This doctrine, unlike SYNTACTIC PSYCHOLOGY, allows psychological laws to advert to narrow word meanings as well as the syntactic properties of sentences.

The contrast between this doctrine and the Folk Line can be brought out neatly by the following statement of that Line:

WIDE PSYCHOLOGY: The laws of mental processes advert to the wide semantic properties of representations.

In the last section I indicated that Revisionists sometimes seem to have a doctrine like NARROW PSYCHOLOGY in mind in their talk of "syntactic" and "formal" properties. If so, their talk shows a Humpty-Dumptyish contempt for the conventions of language (and even Humpty Dumpty *told us* what he meant by "glory"). Narrow word meanings cannot be captured syntactically, in any ordinary sense of that term. Nor are they like the formal properties of symbols in a formal system.[23] However, in so far as Revisionists are urging NARROW PSYCHOLOGY, I have no quarrel with them.

This section began with a semantics that ascribes truth-conditional contents to sentences, yet it ends by claiming that we do not need such contents for psychology. In introducing the Revisionist Line (section 1), I pointed out that such a claim raises a question: what *do* we need those contents for? This question is not so pressing for NARROW PSYCHOLOGY as for SYNTACTIC PSYCHOLOGY, because the former unlike the latter comes so close to truth-conditional content (as Hartry Field has pointed out to me).[24] Nevertheless, it would be nice to have an answer to the question. I think we have. We need truth-conditional content for *linguistics*.[25] Folk are interested in sentences not only to explain behavior but also to learn about the world (Field 1972, pp. 370–1). What properties do sentences have that make them thus interesting? They have truth-conditional content (Devitt and Sterelny 1987, pp. 169–71).

5   The Necessity of Narrow Meaning

I shall argue for NARROW PSYCHOLOGY in two steps. First, in this section, I shall argue that psychological laws must advert to narrow semantic properties *at least*. This is an argument against SYNTACTIC PSYCHOLOGY. In the next section, I shall argue that psychological laws must advert to narrow semantic properties at *most*. This is an argument against WIDE PSYCHOLOGY.

It is important to see that the disagreement with SYNTACTIC PSYCHOLOGY is not a boring verbal one over whether we should *call* the further properties that may be required for psychology "semantic," "meanings," or "contents." I do so, because I can see no reason for not doing so, but nothing hinges on that. The disagreement is over whether the further properties are required, whatever they are called.

Psychology seeks laws covering the three types of mental processes:

(i)   processes from thoughts to thoughts;
(ii) processes from sensory inputs to thoughts;
(iii) processes from thoughts to behavioral outputs.

According to SYNTACTIC PSYCHOLOGY, all these laws advert only to syntactic properties. I agree about the laws for (i), and so I agree with SYNTACTIC THOUGHT PROCESSES. I disagree about the laws for (ii) and (iii).

SYNTACTIC PSYCHOLOGY differs from SYNTACTIC THOUGHT PROCESSES in being too sweeping: it covers mental processes that are not thought processes. It differs from NARROW PSYCHOLOGY in being too restrictive about psychological laws: it does not allow them to advert to narrow meanings.

Laws for (ii) have to explain the fact that a particular sensory stimulus affects some thoughts and not others; for example, it may lead to certain beliefs being formed and others dropped, but leave the vast majority of beliefs unchanged. Suppose that the stimulus is the sight of Ron riding and that the only effect of this is the formation of the belief "Fa". How could that formation possibly be explained if we follow SYNTACTIC PSYCHOLOGY and ascribe to "Fa" only syntactic properties like being a one-place predicate, and syntactic relations like being different from "Fb," "Ga," "Gb," etc.? Why should the stimulus lead to "Fa" rather than any of these other beliefs, each of which is also a one-place predication and different from the others? A stimulus has a distinctive role in thought formation (which is not to say, of course, that a stimulus is ever sufficient – irrespective of other thoughts – for the formation of a thought). Syntax alone cannot explain that distinctive role.

WIDE PSYCHOLOGY has an explanation. Mental sentences don't have just syntax, they have wide meaning. "Fa" means that Ron is riding, whereas, say, "Fb" means that Maggie is riding, "Ga" means that Ron is kicking, and "Gb" means that Maggie is kicking. With the help of these properties of the mental sentences, we have some hope of finding the required laws. These laws will build on the idea that experience of Ron tends to affect thoughts that refer to Ron and not Maggie; that experience of riding tends to affect thoughts that refer to riding not kicking; and so on.

According to NARROW PSYCHOLOGY, we do not need this recourse to wide meaning to get our laws. However, we do need a recourse to the narrow part of this meaning. Talk of the syntax of the mental sentences is quite inadequate because syntax does not include links to sensory stimuli. By adverting to the links of "Ron" and "riding" to stimuli, we can hope to find laws about the roles of those sorts of stimuli in affecting thoughts containing the terms.[26]

A similar story holds for laws for (iii). These must explain the fact that a thought led to certain behavior and not others. Suppose that the behavior is the opening of a gate in the path of the mounted Ron, and that the belief that led to this is "Fa". How could the role of this belief possibly be explained if we ascribe to it only syntactic properties? Why should that belief lead to this behavior rather than clearing Maggie's vicinity of kickable objects, or whatever? A thought has a distinctive role in producing behavior (which is not to say, of course, that a thought is ever sufficient – irrespective of other thoughts – for a piece of behavior.) Syntax alone cannot explain that distinctive role.

WIDE PSYCHOLOGY's explanation is that "Fa" means that Ron is riding and not, for example, that Maggie is kicking. We have some hope then of finding laws that build on the idea that thoughts about Ron tend to lead to behavior that affects Ron and not Maggie; that thoughts about riding tend to lead to behavior that affects riding and not kicking. NARROW PSYCHOLOGY does not go that far. The narrow meaning of each term in a mental sentence includes links to certain sorts of stimuli. As a result, we can hope to find laws about the role of thoughts containing the term in bringing about certain sorts of behavior.

It may be objected that this criticism of SYNTACTIC PSYCHOLOGY rests on an unargued assumption that laws for (ii) and (iii) must advert to the *composition* of mental sentences; briefly, it assumes that the laws must be compositional. For it assumes that the way to supply what SYNTACTIC PSYCHOLOGY is alleged to miss is to include the links of *words* to stimuli. So differences between beliefs are to be explained partly in terms of syntax and partly in terms of word meaning. Yet if the laws for (ii) and (iii) need advert only to the input and output links of mental sentences *as a whole*, then it is not obvious that SYNTACTIC PSYCHOLOGY misses anything.

In discussing an objection by Patricia Churchland, Stich gives the following examples (1983, pp. 178–9) of the sorts of laws for (ii) and (iii) that his STM might contemplate:[27]

(12) For all subjects S, when an elephant comes into view, S will typically come to have a sequence of symbols, E, in his B-store.

(14) For all subjects S, if S has D-state R (i.e., if S has the sequence of symbols R in his D-store), and if S has no stronger incompatible D-states, then S will raise his arm.

So the response to my criticism might be that the only laws for (ii) and (iii) that we need are along these lines. Yet these do not advert to the composition of symbol sequences, nor indeed to any semantic property of the sequences.

(12) and (14) are certainly not the only laws that we *need*; they are not at the right theoretical level. This is indicated by the fact that psychology would require indefinitely many such laws to cope with the indefinitely many possible stimuli for, and behavioral outcomes of, beliefs. At best, (12) and (14) are low-level laws that are *applications* of higher level laws for (ii) and (iii) that we need.

Aside from that, the import of these laws is unclear. How are the symbol sequences E and R to be specified? They can't be specified by their "shape" (specified formally, in the ordinary sense; section 2), for that would take us outside psychology. (Futher, any shape can realize any symbol.) Merely specifying the syntactic properties and relations of the sequences will not do. For example, it will not be sufficient to say only that E has the syntactic properties and relations of "There is an elephant in front of me." Those properties and relations are insufficient to distinguish E appropriately from many other symbol sequences brought about by quite different stimuli; for example, the sequence T referred to in

(12)* For all subjects S, when a tiger is on top of S, S will typically come to have a sequence of symbols, T, in his B-store.

The differences between E and T are psychologically very significant, for E and T will lead to quite different behavior. We must say what the differences are. Very likely they have identical syntactic structures. They will still, of course, differ syntactically: they are different sentence types. But this difference clearly won't explain the differences in what E and T dispose S to do. For that we need to say what sentence type E is and what one T is; we need accounts of their natures. And those natures are not a matter of syntax (section 2). Could we not say simply that E is linked to the elephant input and T to the tiger input? So (12) and (12)* are explanatory of the very natures of E and T. I think that this is what we would have to say.

If we do say this we are abandoning the strict letter of SYNTACTIC PSYCHOLOGY, because we are assigning nonsyntactic properties to mental sentences for psychological purposes. On my usage, these properties constituted by links to input are meanings or contents of the mental states. So (12) determines that E as a whole has a certain meaning.

Despite this, if we could find the laws of which (12) and (14) are applications, and those laws were adequate for our theoretical purposes, then SYNTACTIC PSYCHOLOGY would seem only a little bit wrong. A desperately crude attempt at the law for (12) might be as follows:[28]

For all subjects S, sequences of symbols Q input types I, if the meaning of Q depends on I and S is presented with instance of I, then S will typically come to have Q in his B-store.

The meanings of sentences adverted to in this law are nothing more than are explained in the applications of the law. The meanings are not, as it were, something additional to the applications. So they might seem hardly worth mentioning. It is only when we see that laws for (ii) and (iii) have to advert to the meanings of parts of the sentences, meanings explained to a degree independently of the applications, that we see how badly wrong SYNTACTIC PSYCHOLOGY is. To see this we must show that the laws are compositional.

Note first that *according to* SYNTACTIC PSYCHOLOGY laws for (i) are compositional: they advert to the syntactic structure of thoughts. There is something paradoxical about the view that the "meaning" that accrues to a thought in virtue of its syntax is compositional, but that what accrues to it in virtue of its links to stimuli is not. There is something paradoxical about the view that laws for (i) are compositional, but laws for (ii) and (iii) are not. This apparent paradox indicates which way we should go.

Consider laws for (iii). The distinctive potential role of each thought in producing behavior must depend on the thought's causal relation to particular sorts of stimuli. E's role differs from T's because it is linked to elephantish stimuli not tigerish ones. This example suggest the following simple account of the dependency on stimuli: a thought linked to a certain sort of stimulus tends to produce a certain sort of behavior. This account is far too simple. Such a mental state would be a mere input–output function of the sort dear to behaviorist hearts. There would be no basis for ascribing even a syntax to it and no point in calling it a thought at all. A thought is something that *interacts with other thoughts* in inferences. Its causal relation to stimuli – hence its distinctive potential for behavior – must be partly via its relation to other thoughts in its history. But how can a thought pass on to another a link to stimuli? It cannot pass on all its links. That would lead to the following: belief B1 is linked to input I1; B2 to I2; B3 is inferred from B1 and B2 and so is linked to I1 and I2. Yet consider this example:

All police officers are corrupt
Dee Dee is a police officer
So, Dee Dee is corrupt.

The distinctive role of the belief that Dee Dee is corrupt is determined by the links of *parts of* each premise to stimuli. The links of each premise to police officers is beside the point. In some cases, a belief that plays a role in an inference contributes no stimulus to the distinctive role of the conclusion:

All A are B
All B are C
All C are D
So, all A are D

It seems clear that thoughts pass on their links to stimuli *at the level of their terms*.

I take it then that in considering what beliefs are likely to cause what behavior – laws for (iii) – we have to advert to the links of the terms in the beliefs to stimuli. These laws must be compositional.

The case for the compositionality of laws for (ii) is harder. These laws cover noninferential belief formations. My picture is as follows. Each term in a mental sentence, either directly, or indirectly via its association with other terms, has links to certain sorts of stimuli as part of its meaning. The way the term is linked depends on which theory of reference covers it (section 4). The link will be direct if

it is a pure-causal term. It will be partly direct, and partly indirect via its association with other terms, if it is a descriptive-causal term. It will be entirely indirect if it is a descriptive term. For terms that are causal or descriptive-causal, and thus have direct links to stimuli, we can hope to find laws about the roles of those sorts of stimuli in affecting thoughts containing those sorts of term. The laws will capture the idea that stimulus from Ron tends to affect beliefs containing a term with a certain sort of narrow meaning; and stimulus from someone riding tends to affect beliefs containing a term with another sort of meaning. So the laws will capture the idea that the combination of stimuli provided by Ron riding will tend to produce the narrow belief that we would ordinarily describe widely as the belief that Ron is riding.

A desperately crude example of what we might hope for as a law for (ii) is as follows:

For all subjects S, names N, descriptive-causal one-place predicates P, input types I1 and I2, if the meaning of N depends on I1 and that of P on I2, and S is presented with instances of I1 and I2 together, then S will typically come to stand in the believing relation to a sentence with N as subject and P as predicate.

This is the compositional alternative to the earlier similarly crude noncompositional law.

A difficulty in producing a more convincing rejection of the possibility of noncompositional laws for (ii) is that the same causal interactions that have a role in belief formation are likely to be having a role in determining the meaning of a term. Perhaps the strongest case for the compositionality of laws for (ii) comes from the fact that they have to be unified with the compositional laws for (i) and (iii).

Stich, in his response to Churchland, is comforted by his doubts that there are any satisfactory laws for (ii) and (iii) to be found (above the level of (12) and (14) perhaps). His doubts arise from his prediction that the laws will collapse into vacuity; the terms to which they will apply will be defined as the ones to which they apply (1983, pp. 180–1). But there is no more danger of vacuity here than anywhere in science. Our theory of tigers does not become vacuous because, in some sense, tigers are "defined" as what the theory applies to. In any case, if we cannot find satisfactory laws, that would not save SYNTACTIC PSYCHOLOGY. Rather, it would destroy cognitive psychology altogether.

I conclude my case against SYNTACTIC PSYCHOLOGY by considering some remarks of Pylyshyn. He gives the example of Mary running out of a smoke-filled building. Why did she run out? WIDE PSYCHOLOGY has an answer, central to which is the attribution to Mary of the belief that the building is on fire. She might have come by this belief in various ways: by hearing the utterance, "the building is on fire"; by hearing the fire alarm; by smelling smoke; indeed, by experiencing any event interpretable (given the appropriate beliefs) as entailing that the building is on fire. Pylyshyn argues against Stich's STM that leaving Mary's mental sentences

> as uninterpreted formal symbols begs the question of why these particular expressions should arise under what would seem (in the absence of interpretation) like a very strange collection of diverse circumstances, as well as the question of why these symbols should lead to building-evacuation behavior as opposed to something else. (1980b, p. 161)

Pylyshyn's second question about building-evacuation behavior is just the same as mine about laws for (iii). His first question about belief formation is different but related to mine about laws for (ii).

Stich's response to Pylyshyn is striking. He dismisses Pylyshyn's attempted answers as vacuous, but *makes no attempt to offer nonvacuous answers himself* (1983, p. 176). Yet Pylyshyn's questions are very good ones that demand answers. What I have been arguing is that it is impossible for SYNTACTIC PSYCHOLOGY to provide answers.

We are a very long way from having plausible candidate laws for (ii) and (iii), as the crudity of the laws proposed above indicates. So we cannot expect anyone to provide detailed answers to Pylyshyn's questions. Pylyshyn thinks that the answers must be sought by appealing to the truth-conditional interpretations of the symbols. I think that we achieve the desired level of generality by appealing to less.

I have already indicated how NARROW PSYCHOLOGY offers the hope that we can arrive at laws for (iii) by making use of the links to stimuli that partly constitute word meaning. Such laws would answer Pylyshyn's second question. Consider now Pylyshyn's first question about the several paths to the one thought. Laws for (ii) alone

might go a long way to answer this. To take a crude example, suppose that the meaning of "fire" is tied to both the sight of flames and the smell of smoke. Then we might hope for laws predicting beliefs involving "fire," sometimes the same belief, from the sight of flames and from the smell of smoke. But, of course, the variety of paths becomes much richer when we take account of the fact that a thought can be inferred from other thoughts. The meaning of any term in those other thoughts is also linked to certain stimuli. We can then hope for laws for (ii) explaining the formation of one of these thoughts following stimuli. With the help of laws for (i), we can explain how that thought joined with others to lead by inference to the original thought. Thus we open up the possibility of indefinitely many paths from stimuli to the one thought.

In sum, we need narrow meaning, at least, to have a hope of coming up with the laws for (ii) and (iii). We need it also to answer Pylyshyn's questions. SYNTACTIC PSYCHOLOGY is not only unargued (section 3) but also false.

6 The Sufficiency of Narrow Meaning

We have completed the first step of my argument for NARROW PSYCHOLOGY: psychology needs narrow meaning *at least*. The next step is to argue that psychology needs narrow meaning *at most*. This conclusion differs from WIDE PSYCHOLOGY. It may also differ from folk psychology. However, I doubt this and so doubt that NARROW PSYCHOLOGY is revisionist or eliminativist. And if it is, it is not disturbingly so. So, part of my aim in arguing for NARROW PSYCHOLOGY is to make it seem moderate.

WIDE PSYCHOLOGY holds that psychological laws must advert to wide semantic properties. The argument against this has already been given: the argument from methodological solipsism and psychological autonomy (section 3). The key to this argument is the claim that the states we need to posit for psychological explanation must supervene on the intrinsic internal physical states of the organism; roughly, on the brain. Burge points out that many seem to think that this claim is implied by the following principles:

> events in the external world causally affect the mental events of a subject only by affecting the subject's bodily surfaces;...nothing (not

excluding mental events) causally affects behavior except by affecting (causing or being a causal antecedent of causes of) local states of the subject's body. (1986, p. 15)

Yet the claim does not follow from these principles of local causation. For these principles are quite compatible with mental states being *individuated* in terms of their relations to the environment (pp. 16–17). States that are so individuated do not supervene on the brain alone: they partly supervene on the brain's external relations.

Burge gives some nice examples of relational individuation: continents in geology; lungs in biology. Indeed, relational individuation serves many explanatory purposes. It pervades the social sciences: someone is a capitalist in virtue of her economic relations. Think also of the parts of a car: something is an accelerator partly in virtue of its relations to the engine. Closer to home, think of syntactic properties: something is a conjunction symbol in virtue of its role within a language (section 2). In general, relational individuation is to be found wherever functional/structural explanations are appropriate. Such explanations do not go against principles of local causation like those above.

So I agree with Burge's objection. What then is left of the argument from methodological solipsism? Though the argument may often appear to rest on the mistaken inference above, I do not think that it really does. It is possible to draw boundaries anywhere and to look for explanations of the characteristics and peripheral behavior of the bounded entity or system in terms of what goes on within the boundary. I think that underlying the argument is the strong conviction that a scientifically appropriate boundary for explaining the behavior of an organism is its skin. It is by stopping at that point that we shall get the appropriate laws. I share this conviction.

Of course, if the argument against WIDE PSYCHOLOGY is understood in this way, it does not look very conclusive: the proof of the pudding seems to lie very much in the eating. But such is life.

Opposition to WIDE PSYCHOLOGY usually raises objections that start from the following questions:

1   How is narrow content to be ascribed in a psychological explanation?
2   How is behavior to be described so that it is open to psychological explanation?

Question (2) is particularly pressing given what I have just conceded to Burge. If behavior is described in ways that refer to things outside the skin, as it is by the folk, then it will have to be explained by mental states that refer to such things also.[29] The appropriate boundary for psychology will not be the skin. It is convenient to set these questions aside for a moment.

I shall try to support the above-mentioned conviction by describing NARROW PSYCHOLOGY in more detail. I shall be particularly concerned to show how little, if at all, NARROW PSYCHOLOGY is revisionist. I see this as strong support for NARROW PSYCHOLOGY, for conservatism is a theoretical virtue.[30]

Cognitive psychology seems to be concerned with mental states that purport to represent a world which is external to the mind and toward which the organism's behavior is directed. It is of the essence of those mental states – thoughts – that they do purport to represent a world. The Revisionist Line has usually seemed to deny this, and SYNTACTIC PSYCHOLOGY certainly does deny it. This is an important factor in making Revisionism seem so implausible to many. However, NARROW PSYCHOLOGY does not deny the importance of representation. It simply claims that psychology does not care *which* entities the organism, as a result of its external links to the environment, is actually representing; indeed, it does not care whether there really are such entities. What matters is only how the world seems from the point of view of the organism. The nature of a mental state is indeed "outward-looking." It just does not matter to psychology which world, if any, the state actually "sees."

WIDE PSYCHOLOGY is inspired by folk psychology. Yet it is not *obvious* that the latter is WIDE. The main reason for concluding that it *is* WIDE is that ordinary ascription of thought, which is the folk way of explaining behavior, always seems to take account of reference. So it is part of the truth conditions of an ascription, whether it is construed transparently or opaquely, that the thinker's representation refers to the objects and properties picked out by the content sentence of the ascription. In brief, the folk taxonomize thoughts widely. This reason is rather far from sufficient for the conclusion.

The first problem is that though an ordinary thought ascription may be a psychological *explanation*, it is not a psychological *law*. And WIDE PSYCHOLOGY is about laws. It is hard to be confident where folk stand on psychological laws, for they seem not to talk or think much about them.

The second problem is that it is unclear how much of the ascribed content the folk take to be psychological. Folk ascribe thoughts not only for psychological purposes but also to learn about the world (section 4). This dual purpose raises the possibility that the folk do not regard all the content they ascribe as relevant to the explanation of behavior. Futher, an explanation of behavior is always of an organism in a particular natural and social context. Perhaps the folk find it convenient to bring some of these contextual features into the explanation even though they do not regard them as *psychologically* relevant; they might be regarded as sociologically relevant, for example. So, thought ascriptions may be several-ways hybrid. To discover which parts the folk think are psychological, we would need to know which parts fall under folk psychological laws. That brings us back to the first problem. In sum, the folk taxonomy of thoughts is not merely psychological. And there is no simple way to read off folk psychology from the nature of thought ascriptions.

In so far as we have any evidence of the nature of folk psychological laws – which is not very far – I suggest that it favors the view that the folk are for NARROW rather than for WIDE PSYCHOLOGY.

Consider thoughts involving demonstratives and pronouns (briefly, "demonstratives"). Suppose that Raelene reaches for her gun. To explain this behavior we ascribe to her the belief that that is a man with a knife who means her no good. This ascription seems to require that Raelene have a thought about the man indicated, and so seems to be wide. What law do folk think the explanation comes under? If the folk have any law in mind, it is unlikely that the law is wide, so far as the demonstrative is concerned. Thus, suppose Gail reaches for her gun in a similar situation to Raelene, but one involving a different man. To explain Gail's behavior, we ascribe to her the belief that that is a man with a knife who means her no good. Then surely the folk would regard this belief as the same as Raelene's for the purpose of psychological explanation (thus using a narrow taxonomy for beliefs instead of the above-noted transparent and opaque taxonomies exemplified in thought ascriptions). They would think that even the lowest level laws that cover Raelene's belief will also cover Gail's; the different references of "that" are psychologically irrelevant. The laws will be concerned only with the functional-role properties of "that" which remain constant as the external links of the organism to the environment change; in that respect, the laws will be narrow. Indeed, if Raelene and Gail were alike in the other relevant respects, the folk would think that the explanations of their behaviors were the same.

In sum, if folk have psychological laws for demonstrative thoughts, it is likely that the laws, so far as the demonstratives are concerned, are narrow. In any case, I take it as obvious that the law should be thus narrow. Where does WIDE PSYCHOLOGY stand on this? It would be uncharitable to suppose that it disagrees. When people urge the importance of wide meaning to psychology, we should not suppose that they intend to include demonstratives. They do not think that the laws for these advert to the extracranial links, varying from context to context, that determine a demonstrative's reference.

The folk, WIDE and NARROW PSYCHOLOGY may agree on demonstratives, but they do not on proper names. Suppose that the Englishmen Jeremy and Nigel have functionally identical thoughts about different Australian philosophers called "Bruce." To avoid assuming that the two philosophers look alike, let us suppose that Jeremy and Nigel have not met the philosophers but have gained their names by reference borrowing. According to NARROW PSYCHOLOGY, the lowest level psychological laws covering Jeremy's thought will also cover Nigel's. For the laws will advert only to the narrow meanings they share. According to WIDE PSYCHOLOGY, in contrast, the lowest level laws for Jeremy and Nigel must differ because the laws advert to wide meanings that depend on reference and the thoughts of Jeremy and Nigel differ in reference. Where do the folk stand? Once again it is hard to say. However, the evidence surely shows them leaning toward NARROW PSYCHOLOGY, because it seems as if they would count Jeremy's and Nigel's beliefs the same for the purposes of explaining and predicting relevant behavior (a narrow taxonomy again); for example, in explaining or predicting their remarks about "Bruce" whilst having cocktails; or their actions when finally meeting an Australian philosopher called "Bruce."

Whatever the case with the folk, the claim that the reference of "Bruce" is irrelevant to psychological explanation is very plausible.

We have gone quite a way in our discussion of NARROW PSYCHOLOGY and revisionism – we have covered the many parts of thought involving demonstratives and names – without resorting to fantasies about Twin Earth or brains in a vat. There is nothing fantastic about Raelene, Gail, Jeremy, and Nigel.[31] However, if we want to go further, covering natural-kind terms for example, we have to resort to these fantasies. For these terms do not, as a matter of ordinary fact, normally vary in reference with changes in context without concomitant changes in their inner functional role. We need the fantasies to show that reference is irrelevant to their psychological role. Whether this conclusion is contrary to folk wisdom is again unclear, for insofar as the folk have constructed psychological laws they have not been worried about fantasies. What would they say if we were to worry them? My guess is that they would come down on the side of NARROW PSYCHOLOGY.

It is common to argue against wide meaning in psychology by noting that we want the one explanation to cover all functional duplicates; to cover, for example, Oscar, Twin Oscar, and brain-in-the-vat Oscar. This may seem a rather uninteresting demand since there probably are no functional duplicates. However, what we really want is that the explanation should cover all organisms that are functionally alike *in the respects relevant to the explanation*. Thus, Raelene and Gail may be relevantly alike in the above situation even though otherwise quite different. Similarly, Jeremy and Nigel.

On the matter of laws, I have suggested that there may be nothing revisionist about NARROW PSYCHOLOGY at all. If I am wrong about this, and the folk are committed to wide psychological laws, I hope to have shown that the revisionism of NARROW PSYCHOLOGY is not in any way shocking: the folk would be only a little bit wrong.

On the matter of explanations, NARROW PSYCHOLOGY claims that, for the purposes of psychology, these need not advert to the referential properties of thoughts. This does not mean that the folk are wrong to advert to these properties in their thought ascriptions. There is more to life than psychology. There is nothing wrong with hybrid ascriptions.

It is time to return to the two questions we set aside that are prompted by opposition to WIDE PSYCHOLOGY. The first was:

1 How is narrow content to be ascribed in a psychological explanation?

Behind this question usually lies an objection along the following lines. "Our language is truth-conditional. So we are unable to express any narrow contents in our language. If we cannot express them, we cannot ascribe them. So narrow contents are indescribable and useless for explaining behavior." Despite its apparent popularity, this objection has little force, in my view.

As it stands, the objection must be faulty. A scientific proposal should not be rejected on the ground that we do not already have the linguistic resources to put it into effect. Consider, for example, such a response to Einstein's proposal of the Theory of Relativity. Language must adapt to science, not constrain it. If there is any force to the objection it is this: the linguistic changes required by the proposal for psychology are so radical as to cast grave doubt on the wisdom of the proposal.

The changes are not radical. We already have linguistic devices for ascribing wide content; for example:

Raelene believes that that is a man with a knife who means her no good.

This ascription makes the referential properties of each part of the appropriate thought relevant to the truth of the ascription. If we want to ascribe only narrow content – the content relevant to psychology – we need to bracket off the links outside the skin that go into determining those referential properties. This we can easily do. Let "*" be such a bracketing device, exemplified in the following ascription:

Raelene believes* that that is a man with a knife who means her no good.

The "*" indicates that only the narrow meaning of the content clause is relevant to the ascription. It is not obvious that we also need to be able to *express* narrow content, but if we do, the same device will serve.

A protest can be expected "We don't understand these *ascriptions." I think we understand them as well, or as badly, as we understand ordinary ascriptions.

If I am right in my earlier claim that the folk sometimes use a narrow taxonomy of thoughts, they have *already* caught on to the idea that *ascriptions rest on. In any case, it would be easy to *teach someone to use* *ascriptions with the help of ideas like those mentioned in this discussion. Thus, it is easy to grasp that the truth of the *ascription to Raelene does not depend on her representing the particular person picked out by the speaker's "that"; we are abstracting from that. It is sufficient that she be representing someone demonstratively; or even that it be for her as if she is. In this respect, we already understand or could easily come to understand *ascriptions.

In another respect, we understand *ascriptions badly: we do not have a *worked out semantic theory* of them. But in this respect, we are no better off with ordinary ascriptions.[32] And it is a feature of this proposal that any theory we have of ordinary ascriptions is *ipso facto* a theory of *ascriptions. For the latter ascribe what the former do minus a bit.

*Ascriptions are necessary if we want our explanation to be strictly and solely psychological; an explanation falling under the laws of psychology. But, as I have pointed out, there is no harm in not being so strict, particularly in the marketplace; hybrid explanations are OK. So there is nothing wrong in continuing to explain behavior in a folk-theoretic way, making reference to wide content.

The other question we set aside was as follows:

2 How is behavior to be described so that it is open to psychological explanation?

Behind this question usually lies an objection along the following lines.

> Opponents of WIDE PSYCHOLOGY seem to have in mind that behavior should be construed as mere bodily movement. "But this construal has almost no relevance to psychology as it is actually practiced." Psychology attempts to explain *actions*, which are behaviors intentionally described. For example (Burge 1986, p. 11): "she picked up the apple, pointed to the square block, tracked the moving ball, smiled at the familiar face, took the money instead of the risk."

This objection raises a deep point, not just for the Revisionist Line on thought but for the functionalist theory of the mind in general. Ned Block has pointed out that "functionalism . . . has typically insisted that characterizations of mental states should contain descriptions of inputs and outputs

in *physical* language" (1978, pp. 263–4). At least it has insisted on the descriptions being nonmental. The motivation for this is clear: to reduce the mental to something nonmental. Block criticizes this approach on the ground that it is chauvinistic (pp. 314–17). There is a deeper problem with it. What psychological laws explain is not behavior described as neural impulses, as mere bodily movements, or as any other brute-physical event. These descriptions are at the wrong level, the level of psychological *implementation*. The level that yields the interesting generalizations of psychology requires that the behavior be treated as an action.[33] This goes against the demands of old-fashioned reductionism, but so much the worse for that reductionism. Functionalism often seems not to have fully grasped its own message about explanatory levels.

The laws linking thoughts to input and outputs must advert to certain properties of thoughts, inputs, and outputs. I have argued that the appropriate properties for thoughts are not merely syntactic (section 5). The present point is that the ones appropriate for outputs are not brute-physical.

According to NARROW PSYCHOLOGY, just as we do not need wide-semantic properties for thoughts, we do not need fully intentional ones for output: "proto-intentional" ones will do. To bring behavioral outputs under psychological laws, the outputs must be seen as goal-directed and as actions. However, we can see them in this way whilst abstracting from the particular contexts that are referred to in intentional descriptions and that are effected by actions. For example, the saga of Raelene may end with an action that we would ordinarily describe as "her shooting that man." But for strictly psychological purposes, it does not matter that it was that particular man that she shot. Our language does not have a way of setting aside that fact, but we can easily introduce one using "*" again.[34] And, once again, there is no harm in not being so strict: in giving a description that makes the behavior open to a hybrid explanation, part psychological and part sociological.[35]

7 Conclusions

The Revisionist Line about psychology frequently urges a doctrine that is most naturally understood as

SYNTACTIC PSYCHOLOGY: The laws of mental processes advert only to the syntactic properties of representations.

This doctrine is not supported by any of the arguments offered for Revisionism. The argument from the computer analogy supports a doctrine that is only about thought processes:

SYNTACTIC THOUGHT PROCESSES: The laws of thought processes advert only to the syntactic properties of representations.

This doctrine does not cover the processes linking inputs to thoughts, and thoughts to outputs. The argument from methodological solipsism, modified to take account of Burge's criticisms, goes against

WIDE PSYCHOLOGY: The laws of mental processes advert to the wide semantic properties of representations,

but it does not support SYNTACTIC PSYCHOLOGY. Rather, it supports

NARROW PSYCHOLOGY: The laws of mental processes advert only to the narrow semantic properties of representations.

This doctrine allows psychology to advert to narrow word meanings, which are (mostly) not syntactic.

I argue that we need to advert to narrow meanings, at least, in the laws linking inputs to thoughts, and thoughts to output. SYNTACTIC PSYCHOLOGY is not only not supported by argument, it is false.

I complete my argument for NARROW PSYCHOLOGY by adding to the above case against WIDE PSYCHOLOGY: psychology needs narrow meaning at most. Though WIDE PSYCHOLOGY is encouraged by folk psychological explanations, I argue that it is unlikely that folk psychology is WIDE. For WIDE PSYCHOLOGY is about laws, not explanations, and the little evidence we have suggests that the folk lean toward narrow laws. Even if they don't, the revisionism of NARROW PSYCHOLOGY should not be disturbing. It does not pose serious problems for the description of content and behavior.

The narrow meaning I urge is obtained from wide truth-conditional meaning by abstracting from referential links that lie outside the skin. Though wide meaning is not needed for psychology, I claim that it is needed for linguistics. One semantic theory will do for psychology and linguistics.

Notes

1 On the terminology, "wide" and "narrow," see Putnam (1975, pp. 220–2); Field (1978, pp. 102–4).
2 I shall not be taking account of the extreme eliminativism of Paul and Patricia Churchland (1983).
3 For example, Baker (1986, p. 41); Demopoulos (1980); Kitcher (1985, p. 89); LePore and Loewer (1986, pp. 598–9); McGinn (1982, p. 208); Schiffer (1981, pp. 214–15); Stich (1980, p. 97).
4 But see my in press c.
5 White (1982); Kitcher (1985, p. 87); Devitt (1984a, pp. 81–3, 100–1; 1984b, pp. 387, 395–6); Devitt and Sterelny (1987, p. 166). The idea started for me with my reaction (1981, pp. 156–7) to Hartry Field's conceptual-role semantics (1977).
6 There are some passages in Fodor that seem to suggest this sense (1980a, p. 64; 1980b, p. 106). See also the following comments, with which Fodor largely agrees: Haugeland (1980, pp. 81–2); Rey (1980, p. 91). But see below.

7 This is the deep truth in the structuralist tradition in linguistics. For the deep falsehood, particularly in the French version, see Devitt and Sterelny (1987, ch. 13).
8 I do not mean to suggest that properties like being a name may not *also* be semantic.
9 Mostly, it seems clear that Fodor has in mind a functional sense for both "formal" and "syntactic" (1985, p. 93; 1987, pp. 18–19, 156n). In comments on Fodor (1980a), Loar distinguishes the two senses and takes Fodor to intend the functional one (1980, p. 90). See also Pylyshyn (1980a, pp. 111–15). Some write as if they are uninterested in the distinction: Baker (1986, p. 27); Block (1986, p. 616).
10 This usage relates to that of "logical form." To say that these properties are formal is not, of course, to make a claim about what "name" and "conjunction symbol" "ordinarily mean"; doubtless their ordinary meaning is partly semantic. It is to say what they mean in discussing a formal language.

11 For more on the matter of the last three paragraphs, see e.g., Haugeland (1978, pp. 5–10, 21–2; 1985, pp. 4, 50–2, 58–63, 100–3).

12 It is natural to think of syntactic properties as a subclass of formal properties (in the senses specified): they are the formal properties of *symbols* (but not, say, of pawns). However, Haugeland extends "syntactic" to cover all formal properties (1985, p. 100).

13 "Mental processes are causal sequences of tokenings of mental representations" (1987, p. 17).

14 For another example of a swift move from mental processes to thought processes, see Block (1986, p. 628).

15 Searle (1983) argues against Putnam that meanings are in the head. See Devitt (in press, a) for a response.

16 For example, Field (1978, pp. 100–1); Fodor (1980b, p. 102); Stich (1983, pp. 190–1). See also Baker, a critic of Revisionism (1986, p. 27).

17 Of the usual solipsistic sort. Harman urges a non-solipsistic functional-role semantics (1982, 1983).

18 Devitt and Sterelny (1987). See also Devitt (1981).

19 This view of word meaning goes against the theory of "direct reference," which is often associated with the causal theory of reference. I have, in effect, argued against this association repeatedly, to no apparent avail (e.g. 1980, and 1985, pp. 222–3). I am trying again; in press b.

20 In this respect my narrow meaning differs from the functional-role factor proposed by "two-factor" theorists. Those theorists tend to treat this factor as if it were unrelated to the truth-conditional factor; see, e.g., McGinn (1982, pp. 211, 230); Loar (1982, p. 280–2; 1983, p. 629).

21 Note that narrow word meanings do not determine *reference* to the peripheral stimuli, because the words do not refer to the stimuli (cf. McDermott 1986). The *theory* of the word's reference to *external reality* refers to the stimuli.

22 Do holists believe the contrary view? According to Fiona Cowie (1987), it is very difficult to tell because the holists typically do not address the issue (a striking example of inattention to inputs). However, they usually write *as if* they believed the view. My approach to holism, reflected in these two paragraphs, owes a lot to Cowie.

23 A Revisionist's claim to have meant by "only syntactic properties" *only syntactic properties, or narrow semantic properties needed to explain behavior*, might be compared with a vegetable grower's claim to have meant by "only natural fertilizers" *only natural fertilizers, or artificial fertilizers needed to keep vegetables alive.*

24 So I worried too much about the question in *Realism and Truth* (1984a, chapter 6).

25 This goes against the common view that linguistics is part of psychology: Devitt and Sterelny (in press).

26 McDermott also emphasizes that the laws require that there be some semantically significant link between thoughts and stimuli, but he wrongly thinks that this entails that the thoughts be about stimuli (1986, pp. 281–3).

27 Though it seems that Stich even has doubts about laws along these lines (1983, p. 180).

28 For a suggestion along these lines, see Field (1978, p. 102).

29 Fodor confronts a difficulty like this in an interesting argument against Burge. Fodor argues that we should not individuate a mental state in terms of its relations to an environment because those relations are irrelevant to its *causal powers* (1987, pp. 33–4). The difficulty is that the individuation of causal powers depends on the individuation of their output. So if behavior is individuated relationally, mental states will be too (pp. 34–8). Fodor's solution to this difficulty is to insist that causal powers are always individuated nonrelationally; hence those of mental states are; hence behavior is (pp. 38–42). This not only begs the question against Burge, it seems quite wrong; think, for example, of the causal powers of a capitalist.

30 Despite this, I think that Burge goes a bit too far in his sermon against philosophical revisionism in general, and the imposition of philosophically motivated methodological constraints on psychology in particular (1986, pp. 17–22). Burge gives insufficient weight to the critical and unifying concerns that are proper to philosophy.

31 Given my earlier remarks about how thoughts are taxonomized, I must then disagree with Fodor (who is agreeing with Burge) when he says: "the differences between the way that [commonsense and psychologically appropriate] taxonomies carve things up only show in funny cases" like Twin Earth fantasies (1987, p. 159n.). Any taxonomy of thoughts that takes account of reference differs rather extensively from the one appropriate for psychology. And most, though I think not all, ordinary taxonomies do take account of reference.

32 My own best attempt at a theory is 1984b.

33 On this see Fodor (1987, pp. 8–10). Later, Fodor nicely mocks the tendency of functionalists to brush this problem under the carpet: "Since I am very busy just now, please do not ask me what 'inputs' and 'outputs' are" (p. 68). Interestingly enough, even Stich finds "no reason to expect" that "a purely physical description of movements" (1983, p. 169) will be the sort we want for psychology.

34 Both Fodor (1987, pp. 36–44) and Stich (1983, pp. 166–70) think that many folk-psychological descriptions of behavior are unsuitable for psychology. However, Stich seems to think that *some* ordinary descriptions – for example, "successfully performing a weld" (p. 168) – are suitable. Fodor does not think this, but neither does emphasize the con-

sequence: that the taxonomy of behavior for psychology will require a new linguistic device.

35 This essay grew from one called "The need for truth" which I gave at the following places in the period December 1986 to January 1987: University of Maryland; University of Connecticut; University of Vermont; University of Cincinnati; Northwestern University; University of California, San Diego.

Earlier versions were part of a seminar I gave to faculty and students at the University of Sydney from July to October 1987. The essay has benefited from all these experiences. I am indebted also to at least the following for comments: John Bacon, John Bigelow, Ned Block, Fiona Cowie, Hartry Field, Jerry Fodor, Denise Gamble, Bill Lycan, Joseph Tolliver, Kim Sterelny, and Stephen Stich.

References

Asquith, P. D. and Nickles, T. (eds) (1983) *PSA 1982*, vol. 2. East Lansing, Mich.: Philosophy of Science Association.

Baker, Lynne Rudder (1986) "Just what do we have in mind?", in French, Uehling, and Wettstein (eds) (1986), pp. 25–48.

Block, Ned (1978) "Troubles with Functionalism," in Savage (ed.) (1978), pp. 261–325; reprinted in Block (1981a), pp. 268–305.

Block, Ned (ed.) (1981a) *Readings in Philosophy of Psychology*, vol. 1. Cambridge, Mass.: Harvard University Press.

Block, Ned (ed.) (1981b) *Reading in Philosophy of Psychology*, vol. 2. Cambridge, Mass.: Harvard University Press.

Block, Ned (1986) "Advertisement for a semantics for psychology," in French, Uehling, and Wettstein (eds) (1986), pp. 615–78.

Burge, Tyler (1986) "Individualism and psychology," *Philosophical Review* 95, 3–45.

Carnap, Rudolf (1937) *The Logical Syntax of Language*. New York: Harcourt, Brace.

Chomsky, Noam (1957) *Syntactic Structures*. The Hague: Mouton & Co.

Churchland, Patricia S. and Churchland, Paul M. (1983) "Stalking the wild epistemic engine," *Noûs* 17, 5–20. Reprinted in this volume.

Cowie, Fiona (1987) "Meaning holism." Unpublished BA Thesis, University of Sydney.

Davidson, Donald and Harman, Gilbert (eds) (1972) *Semantics of Natural Language*. Dordrecht: Reidel.

Demopoulos, William (1980) "A remark on the completeness of the computational model of mind," *Behavioral and Brain Sciences* 3, 135.

Devitt, Michael (1980) "Brian Loar on singular terms," *Philosophical Studies* 37, 271–80.

Devitt, Michael (1981) *Designation*. New York: Columbia University Press.

Devitt, Michael (1984a) *Realism and Truth*. Oxford: Basil Blackwell; Princeton: Princeton University Press.

Devitt, Michael (1984b) "Thoughts and their ascription," in P. A. French, T. E. Uehling Jr, and H. K. Wettstein (eds) *Midwest Studies in Philosophy, Volume IX: Causation and Causal Theories*. Minneapolis: University of Minnesota Press, pp. 385–420.

Devitt, Michael (1985) "Critical notice of *The Varieties of Reference*, Gareth Evans," *Australasian Journal of Philosophy* 63, 216–32.

Devitt, Michael (in press a) "Meanings just ain't in the head," in George Boolos (ed.) *Method, Reason and Language: Essays in Honor of Hilary Putnam*. Cambridge: Cambridge University Press.

Devitt, Michael (in press b) "Against direct reference," in French, Uehling, and Wettstein (eds) *Midwest Studies in Philosophy, Volume XIV: Contemporary Perspectives in the Philosophy of Language II*. Notre Dame: University of Notre Dame Press.

Devitt, Michael (in press c) "Why Fodor can't have it both ways," in Barry Loewer and Georges Rey (eds) *Meaning in Mind: Fodor and His Critics*, Cambridge, Mass.: MIT Press.

Devitt, Michael and Sterelny, Kim (1987) *Language and Reality: An Introduction to the Philosophy of Language*. Oxford: Backwell Publishers.

Devitt, Michael and Sterelny, Kim (in press) "What's wrong with 'the Right View,'" in J. E. Tomberlin (ed.) *Philosophical Perspectives, Volume III: Philosophy of Mind and Action Theory*.

Donnellan, Keith (1972) "Proper names and identifying descriptions," in Davidson and Harman (eds) (1972), pp. 356–79.

Field, Hartry (1972) "Tarski's theory of truth," *Journal of Philosophy* 69, 347–75.

Field, Hartry (1977) "Logic, meaning, and conceptual role," *Journal of Philosophy* 74, 379–409.

Field, Hartry (1978) "Mental representation," *Erkenntnis* 13, 9–61; reprinted with Postscript in Block (1981b), pp. 78–114 (page references are to Block).

Fodor, Jerry A. (1980a) "Methodological solipsism considered as a research strategy in cognitive psychology," *Behavioral and Brain Sciences* 3, 63–73.

Fodor, Jerry A. (1980b) "Methodological solipsism: replies to commentators," *Behavioral and Brain Sciences* 3, 99–109.

Fodor, Jerry A. (1985) "Fodor's guide to mental representation: the intelligent auntie's vademecum," *Mind* 94, 76–100.

Fodor, Jerry A. (1987) *Psychosemantics: The Problem of Meaning in the Philosophy of Mind*. Cambridge, Mass.: MIT Press.

Frege, Gottlob (1952) *Translations from the Philosophical Writings of Gottlob Frege*, Peter Geach and Max Black (eds). Oxford: Basil Blackwell.

French, Peter A., Uehling, Theodore E. Jr, and Wettstein, Howard K. (eds) (1986) *Midwest Studies in Philosophy, Volume X: Studies in the Philosophy of Mind*. Minneapolis: University of Minnesota Press.

Harman, Gilbert (1982) "Conceptual role semantics," *Notre Dame Journal of Formal Logic* 28, 242–56.

Harman, Gilbert (1983) "Beliefs and concepts: comments on Brian Loar," in Asquith and Nickles (eds) (1983).

Haugeland, John (1978) "The nature and plausibility of cognitivism," *Behavioral and Brain Sciences* 1, 215–26; reprinted in Haugeland (ed.) (1981) pp. 243–81 (page references are to Haugeland 1981).

Haugeland, John (1980) "Formality and naturalism," *Behavioral and Brain Sciences* 3, 81–2.

Haugeland, John (ed.) (1981) *Mind Design: Philosophy, Psychology, Artificial Intelligence*. Cambridge, Mass.: MIT Press.

Haugeland, John (1985) *Artificial Intelligence: The Very Idea*. Cambridge, Mass.: MIT Press.

Kitcher, Patricia (1985) "Narrow taxonomy and wide functionalism," *Philosophy of Science* 52, 78–97.

Kripke, Saul (1980) *Naming and Necessity*. Cambridge, Mass.: Harvard University Press. [A corrected version of an article of the same name (plus an appendix) in Davidson and Harman (1972), together with a new preface.]

LePore, Ernest and Loewer, Barry (1986) "Solipsistic semantics," in French, Uehling, and Wettstein (eds) (1986), pp. 595–614.

Loar, Brain (1980) "Syntax, functional semantics, and referential semantics," *Behavioral and Brain Sciences* 3, 89–90.

Loar, Brain (1982) "Conceptual role and truth-conditions," *Notre Dame Journal of Formal Logic* 23, 272–83.

Loar, Brian (1983) "Must beliefs be sentences?" in Asquith and Nickles (eds) (1983), pp. 627–43.

McDermott, Michael (1986) "Narrow content," *Australasian Journal of Philosophy* 64, 277–88.

McGinn, Colin (1982) "The structure of content," in Woodfield (ed.) (1982), pp. 207–58.

Putnam, Hilary (1975) *Mind, Language and Reality: Philosophical Papers*, vol. 2. Cambridge: Cambridge University Press.

Pylyshyn, Z. (1980a) "Computation and cognition: issues in the foundations of cognitive science," *Behavioral and Brain Sciences* 3, 111–32.

Pylyshyn, Z. (1980b) "Cognitive representation and the process–architecture distinction," *Behavioral and Brain Sciences* 3, 154–69.

Pylyshyn, Z. (1984) *Computation and cognition*. Cambridge, Mass.: Bradford Books/MIT Press.

Rey, Georges (1980) "The formal and the opaque," *Behavioral and Brain Sciences* 3, 90–2.

Savage, C. Wade (1978) *Minnesota Studies in the Philosophy of Science, Volume IX: Perception and Cognition: Issues in the Foundations of Psychology*. Minneapolis: University of Minnesota Press.

Schiffer, Stephen (1981) "Truth and the theory of content," in Herman Parret and Jacques Bouveresse (eds) *Meaning and Understanding*. Berlin: Walter de Gruyter, pp. 204–22.

Searle, John R. (1983) *Intentionality: An Essay in the Philosophy of Mind*. Cambridge: Cambridge University Press.

Stich, Stephen P. (1980) "Paying the price for methodological solipsism," *Behavioral and Brain Sciences* 3, 97–8.

Stich, Stephen P. (1983) *From Folk Psychology to Cognitive Science: The Case Against Belief*. Cambridge, Mass.: MIT Press.

White, Stephen L. (1982) "Partial character and the language of thought," *Pacific Philosophical Quarterly* 63, 347–65.

Woodfield, A. (ed.) (1982) *Thought and Object*. Oxford: Clarendon Press.

Narrow Content Meets Fat Syntax

Stephen P. Stich

SSV: *[Still Small Voice – could it be the voice of conscience?] I do believe you've gone over to Steve Stich. Have you no conscience?*
Answer: *There, there; don't fret! What is emerging here is, in a certain sense, a "no content" account of narrow content; but it is nevertheless also a fully intentionalist account... In effect I'm prepared to give Stich everything except what he wants.*
Fodor, Psychosemantics

1 Introduction

A bit over a decade ago I published a paper in which I argued that Putnam's much discussed Twin Earth thought experiments posed a problem for the view that a psychological theory aimed at explaining human behavior will invoke common sense intentional concepts like belief and desire.[1] That argument relied on a pair of premises. The first, which I (perhaps infelicitously) called the *principle of psychological autonomy* maintains that any state or property properly invoked in a psychological explanation should supervene on the current, internal, physical state of the organism. Thus, a pair of Putnamian doppelgangers, being molecule for molecule replicas of one another, must share all the same explanatory psychological states and properties. The second premise was that commonsense intentional properties, properties like *believing that Eisenhower played golf* (or *having a belief the content that Eisenhower played golf*) and *believing that water is wet* (or *having a belief with the content that water is wet*) do not supervene on a person's current, internal, physical state. For want of a better label, I'll call this the *Autonomy* argument.

The first premise of the Autonomy argument was one that I took to be intuitively obvious and widely shared. Thus I offered little by way of support. The second premise seemed to be a straightforward consequence of the usual intuitions about Twin Earth style thought experiments. According to those intuitions, the belief that my doppelganger expresses when he says "Eisenhower played golf" is not *about* Eisenhower, the man whose hand I almost got to shake during the 1956 presidential election; it is about some other statesman in a far off corner of the universe. Thus the truth conditions of my belief and my doppelganger's are different. But it is plausible to suppose that on the conception of content implicit in commonsense psychology, belief tokens that are about different people and that have different truth conditions must have different contents. So my doppelganger and I do not both have beliefs with the content that Eisenhower played golf.

This argument was part of a larger project. Influenced by Quine, I have long been suspicious about the integrity and scientific utility of the commonsense notions of meaning and intentional content. This is not, of course, to deny that the intentional idioms of ordinary discourse have their uses, nor that these uses are important. But, like Quine, I view ordinary intentional locutions as projective context sensitive, observer relative, and essentially dramatic.[2] They are not the sorts of locutions we should welcome in serious scientific discourse. For those who are share this Quinean skepticism, the sudden flourishing of cognitive psychology in the 1970s posed something of a problem. On the account offered by Fodor and other observers, the cognitive psychology of that

period was exploiting both the ontology and the explanatory strategy of commonsense psychology. It proposed to explain cognition and certain aspects of behavior by positing beliefs, desires, and other psychological states with intentional content, and by couching generalizations about the interactions among those states in terms of their intentional content.[3] If this was right, then those of us who would banish talk of content in scientific settings would be throwing out the cognitive psychological baby with the intentional bath water. On my view, however, this account of cognitive psychology was seriously mistaken. The cognitive psychology of the 1970s and early 1980s was not positing contentful intentional states, nor was it adverting to content in its generalizations. Rather, I maintained, the cognitive psychology of the day was "really a kind of logical syntax (only psychologized)."[4] Moreover, it seemed to me that there were good reasons why cognitive psychology not only did not but *should* not traffic in intentional states. One of these reasons was provided by the Autonomy argument.

During the last decade, that argument and similar arguments offered by other writers have attracted a fair amount of attention, very little of it favorable.[5] Some critics have focused on the first premise, and have argued that explanatory psychology need not, and does not, restrict itself to states and properties that organisms and their doppelgangers share.[6] Others have focused on the second premise, with some arguing that commonsense psychology does not insist that beliefs with different truth conditions differ in content, or at least that it does not do so consistently, while others challenged the intuition that the beliefs of doppelgangers on Earth and Twin Earth differ in truth conditions.[7] I think each of these objections raises serious issues, and each merits a detailed reply. But in the present essay I'll say very little about them. My focus here will be on quite a different reaction to the Autonomy argument – a reaction which grants both premises of the argument. This reaction concedes that the *commonsense* notion of intentional content will not play a role in scientific psychology. But it insists that *another* notion of intentional content will be central to psychology. For this second, more technical, and less commonsensical notion of content, it is not the case that if a pair of belief tokens differ in truth conditions, or in what they are about, then they also differ in content. Thus Twin Earth cases and others of their ilk will not show that *this* sort of content does not supervene on the current internal state of the organism. Though my doppelganger and I have beliefs that are about different people (or stuff) and thus have different truth conditions, those beliefs may still have the same content, when content is construed in this new way. Since the ordinary notion of content determines truth conditions – typically conditions in the world beyond the head – while the new technical notion does not, the new notion has been dubbed *narrow content*; the old commonsense notion is often said to be *broad* or *wide*. There are various lines along which the narrow content response to the Autonomy argument can be developed.[8] But, as is appropriate in a volume focused on Fodor, the line I propose to explore is the one that Fodor follows. In section 3.1, I'll give a quick overview of Fodor's account of narrow content.

An objection often urged against the notion of narrow content is that it is not really a species of content at all.[9] One reason for this suspicion is that while it is generally easy to *say* what the (ordinary, broad) content of a belief is, there often seems no way at all to say what the narrow content of a belief is. Narrow content appears to be "radically inexpressible." However, I will argue that this suspicion is mistaken. Indeed, in section 3.2 I will sketch a straightforward way in which readily available resources can be used to construct a vocabulary for attributing narrow content. Of course, this alone is not enough to show that narrow content really is a kind of content, properly so-called. And I must confess that I'm not at all sure what it *would* take to show that narrow content is, or isn't, really a kind of content. So I propose to leave that question to be debated by those who think they understand it. As I see it, the major objection to narrow content, as Fodor develops the notion, is that it is very unlikely to be of any more use to psychology than the commonsense notion of broad content. If we taxonomize mental states by their narrow content, there are going to be lots of psychological generalizations that we are not going to be able to state. My argument for this claim is set out in section 3.3.

That argument presupposes a certain conception of the cognitive mind – a conception that portrays the mind as analogous to a kind of computer. Though very familiar, this picture of the mind has never been without its critics, and with the recent flowering of connectionism it has become particularly controversial. However, in the present essay I don't propose to challenge the

picture. Since Fodor himself has long been one of its most eloquent advocates, I will simply accept it, if only for argument's sake. In order to launch my argument against narrow content, it will be necessary to sketch in parts of the picture with somewhat more detail than is usually provided. This is the project I'll pursue in section 2.

Before getting on to any of this, however, we would do well to get a bit clearer about the issue that is in dispute. In the article in which I first set out the Autonomy argument, and in various subsequent publications, my "official" thesis was that serious scientific psychology should not invoke commonsense intentional notions like belief and desire. The official thesis certainly does not entail that beliefs, desires, and other propositional attitudes do not exist,[10] nor even that commonsense psychology is not "pretty close to being true"[11] – though it is, of course, consistent with these claims. But it is these claims that are at the heart of Fodor's concern. On his view, "if commonsense intentional psychology really were to collapse, that would be, beyond comparison, the greatest intellectual catastrophe in the history of our species...." (*PS*: xii). This leaves us with a rather delicate question. Just what would it take to show that commonsense intentional psychology had collapsed? Nobody thinks that *all* of commonsense psychology is going to turn out to be correct. Indeed, Fodor cheerfully concedes that "a lot of what common sense believes about the attitudes must surely be false (a lot of what common sense believes about *anything* must surely be false)" (*PS*: 15). He also concedes that "you can't make respectable science out of the attitudes as commonsensically individuated" (*PS*: 30). The "identity conditions for mental states" that "we need, when doing psychology" are not going to be "those that common sense prefers" (*PS*: 30). If all of this is not enough to undermine commonsense psychology and its intentional ontology, one might well wonder how much more it will take. Fortunately, Fodor tells us. He stipulates that a psychological theory will count as "endorsing" commonsense propositional attitudes "just in case it postulates states (entities, events, whatever) satisfying the following conditions:

(i)   They are semantically evaluable.
(ii) They have causal powers.
(iii) The implicit generalizations of commonsense belief/desire psychology are largely true of them.

"In effect," Fodor tells us, "I am assuming that (i)–(iii) are the essential properties of the attitudes. This seems to me intuitively plausible; if it doesn't seem intuitively plausible to you, so be it. Squabbling about intuitions strikes me as vulgar" (*PS*: 10)

I am not at all sure whether my intuitions agree with Fodor's here; indeed, I'm not even sure I *have* any intuitions about the essential properties of the attitudes. But no matter. This book is for Fodor; I'll play by his rules. What I propose to argue is that most of the implicit generalizations of commonsense psychology are not likely to turn out to be true of the states posited by psychological theories that cleave to the computational paradigm. So Fodor loses on (iii). Moreover, on at least one plausible reading of what it is to be "semantically evaluable," these states are not semantically evaluable either. Thus Fodor loses on (i) too. Whether or not we accept Fodor's intuitions about what is essential to the attitudes, this should be enough to show that propositional attitude psychology is in trouble.

2 The Computational Paradigm

My goal in this section is to provide a brief sketch of a familiar story about the cognitive mind. Since the basic outline is so well known, I will devote most of my attention to clarifying the ontological underpinnings of this account and the taxonomic strategies it exploits. Much of what I say in this section is based on the rather more detailed account I developed in *From Folk Psychology to Cognitive Science*. Since talk of *states* and the various ways in which they get taxonomized or individuated is going to be of some importance in what follows, I'll begin by making a few proposals about how this talk should be construed. So far as I can see, nothing in the arguments to follow depends on the details. We just need *some* systematic way of talking about states. Most any sensible proposal would do.

As I propose we view them, states are the instantiation of a *property* by an *object* during a *time interval*.[12] There are, of course, venerable disputes about what sorts of things properties are.[13] But for present purposes I propose to be quite permissive. Near enough, I'll count any open sentence with a reasonably clear extension as specifying a property. That raises the notorious question of when two open sentences specify the

same property. Fortunately, this is not a question for which we will need any fully general answer. All we'll need is the weak principle that open sentences with different extensions specify different properties.

On the view I'm recommending, states count as *particulars* with a more or less definite location in space and time. States also admit of what might be called an *essential* classification into types. A pair of states are of the same *essential type* if and only if they are instantiations of the same property. Although each state has only one essential type, states, like other particulars, can be grouped into nonessential types in an endless variety of ways. A type of state is simply a category of particulars, and we have specified a type when we have set out conditions for membership in the category. Though we are conceiving of states as particulars, it will sometimes be convenient to use the word "state" to talk about a type or category of states, or the property that members of a category have in common. When ambiguity threatens, I'll use "state token" to refer to particulars and "state type" to refer to categories or types.

So much for states. Let me turn, now, to the story about the mind that I have been calling the *computational paradigm*. The central assumption of the story is that the cognitive mind can be viewed as a particular kind of computer – that the mind is, in Fodor's phrase, "a syntax-driven machine" (*PS*: 20). On this view, each cognitive state token is a brain state token – its essential type is determined by some neurophysiological property or other. However, these neurophysiological state tokens can also be viewed as having syntactic structure in something like the same way that sentence tokens in a natural or formal language have a syntactic structure. That is, each cognitive state token can be viewed as belonging to a syntactic type (or having a "syntactic form"), just as each inscription of a sentence in English or in first order predicate calculus can be viewed as having a syntactic form. Cognitive processes consist of temporal sequences of these syntactically structured states. The reason that the cognitive mind can be thought of as a kind of computer is that the mechanism that controls these cognitive processes is "sensitive solely to syntactic properties" (*PS*: 19).

This account of the cognitive mind as a computer or a "syntactic engine" has become very familiar in recent years. But, as Michael Devitt notes in a recent article,[14] the account is very easy to misconstrue. Often, when offering quick sketches of the mind-as-computer story, writers will conjure the image of a "belief box" and a "desire box" inside the head in which syntactically structured sentence-like entities are stored. For vividness, it may even be suggested that the sentences be thought of as well formed formulas of some familiar formalized language.[15] But, as Devitt notes, this image invites us to think of the syntactic properties of cognitive state tokens (the properties in virtue of which they fall into one or another syntactic category) as *intrinsic* or "brute physical" properties – properties that we could detect if we looked at the appropriate bits of the brain in isolation, much as we could see whether an inscription in a "belief box" had the shape: (x) $Fx \rightarrow Gx$. If we think of the syntactic properties of mental states in this way, then it would make perfectly good sense to suppose that in certain brains syntactically structured states might be stored in the "belief box," though the mechanisms which control cognitive processes are *not* sensitive to the syntax. But, along with Devitt, I would urge that this is just the wrong way to conceive of things. Mental state tokens are brain state tokens. But the properties in virtue of which mental state tokens are classified into syntactic categories are not intrinsic features of those brain states; they are not features which depend exclusively on the shape or form or "brute physical" properties of the states. Rather, the syntactic properties of mental states are relational or functional properties – they are properties that certain states of the brain have in virtue of the way in which they causally interact with various other states of the system. To put the point in a slightly different way, we would have no reason to view brain states as syntactically structured unless that structure can be exploited in capturing generalizations about the workings of mind/brain's mechanisms. Attributing syntactic structure to brain state tokens – assigning them to syntactic types – is justified only if some interesting set of causal interactions among those tokens is isomorphic to formal relations among abstract syntactic objects. Here is how I elaborated on this theme in *From Folk Psychology to Cognitive Science*:

> The basic idea ... is that the cognitive states whose interaction is (in part) responsible for behavior can be systematically mapped to abstract syntactic objects in such a way that causal interactions among cognitive states, as

well as causal links with stimuli and behavioral events, can be described in terms of the syntactic properties and relations of the abstract objects to which the cognitive states are mapped. More briefly, the idea is that causal relations among cognitive states mirror formal relations among syntactic objects. If this is right, then it will be natural to view cognitive state tokens as tokens of abstract syntactic objects ...

The theorist's job in setting out [this sort of] cognitive theory can be viewed as having three parts. First, he must specify a class of [abstract] syntactic objects ... and do so in a way which assigns a formal or syntactic structure to each of these objects ...

Second, the theorist hypothesizes that for each organism covered by the theory, there exists a set of state types whose tokens are causally implicated in the production of behavior. He also hypothesizes that there is a mapping from these state types to syntactic objects in the specified class. Several observations about these hypotheses are in order. First, the theorist need say very little about the essential nature of the state tokens which are causally implicated in the production of behavior. Presumably they are physical states of the brain, and thus the properties which constitute their essential types are neurological properties ... Second, in asserting the existence of the mapping, the order of the quantifiers is of some importance. The theorist is not claiming that the mapping is the same for each subject, but only that for each subject there is a mapping. So in different subjects, quite different neurological state types may be mapped to a given syntactic object. These ... two points ... are in the spirit of functionalism, which stresses the possibility of multiple realizations of mental states ...

The third part of [this kind of] cognitive theory ... is a specification of the theory's generalizations. The core idea ... is that generalizations detailing causal relations among the hypothesized neurological states are to be specified indirectly via the formal relations among the syntactic objects to which the neurological states are mapped. Similarly, generalizations specifying causal relations between stimuli and neurological states will identify the neurological states not by adverting to their essential neurological types but, rather, by adverting to the syntactic objects to which the neurological types are mapped. Ditto for generalizations specifying causal relations between neurological states and behavior.[16]

As Devitt rightly points out, there is a certain tension in this passage that emerges when we ask how we would go about determining whether a pair of brain state tokens in two different people (or in one person at two different times) are tokens of the same syntactic type. One criterion for the syntactic type identity of tokens would require only that the tokens' patterns of causal interactions *with other tokens* be pretty much the same, so both patterns could be captured by the same formal relations among the appropriate system of syntactic objects. A more stringent criterion would require not only that the tokens' patterns of causal interactions with each other be the same, but also that their patterns of causal interaction with *stimuli* and *behavior* be pretty much the same as well. Since the terms "broad" and "narrow" have been appropriated for distinguishing kinds of content, I will call these two standards for determining the syntactic type of a hypothesized brain state token *skinny* and *fat* respectively. Though my writing has sometimes been less than clear on the point, it has always been my intention to invoke *fat syntax* in typing mental state tokens. When Fodor describes the mind as a "syntax-driven machine" it is not clear whether the standard of syntactic type individuation he has in mind is fat or skinny. In what follows, I'll assume that the syntactic types exploited in computational theories of the mind are fat, not skinny, though most of my argument will work either way.

3 Narrow Content

So much for the computational paradigm. Let's now return to the Autonomy argument, and Fodor's strategy for dealing with it. Since the notion of "narrow" content plays a central role in that strategy, I'll start with a sketch of how Fodor proposes to construct the notion. Once that's been done, I'll set out a pair of reasons for doubting that Fodor's notion of narrow content will do what he wants. One of these, I'll argue, is pretty easy to handle. The other is not.

3.1 Mental states, we are supposing, are states of the brain. And, while their essential type is neurophysiological, they can also be classified into all sorts of other categories. One such categorization, provided by commonsense psychology, is to type mental state tokens by their content. The problem posed by the Autonomy argument is that the taxonomy imposed by ordinary, "broad" content does not supervene on a person's current, internal, physical properties. So while those states in Fodor's brain which count as beliefs and those in Twin-Fodor's brain which count as beliefs are neurophysiologially the same, they may well differ in content. This difference in content, Fodor notes, must be due to differences in the world around them and their relations to that world.

> Presumably . . . there's something about the relation between Twin-Earth and Twin-Me in virtue of which his "water"-thoughts are about XYZ even though my water-thoughts are not. Call this condition that's satisfied by (Twin-Me, Twin-Earth) condition C (because it determines the *Context* of his "water"-thoughts). (*PS*: 48)

Fodor's proposal for constructing a notion of narrow content is to start with the taxonomy provided by the ordinary, broad, truth-condition determining notion of content, and subtract out the contribution of the contextual conditions, like condition C, that "anchor" it.[17] One way of thinking of the narrow content of a thought is that it is what remains of the broad content when we "take away the anchoring conditions" (*PS*: 51). But Fodor cautions against taking this subtraction picture too literally. A better way of thinking of narrow content, he suggests, is to view the narrow content of a thought as a function (in the mathematical sense – a mapping) from contexts to broad contents. Since broad contents determine truth conditions, narrow contents will determine mappings from contexts to truth conditions. "Two [narrow] thought contents are identical only if they effect the same mapping of thoughts and contexts onto truth conditions" (*PS*: 48). Thus the thought tokens that lead both Fodor and Twin-Fodor to say "Water is wet" have the same narrow content, since they would have the same broad content if they were embedded in the same context.

> Short of a miracle the following counterfactual must be true: Given the neurological identity between us, in a world where I am in my Twin's context, my "water"-thoughts are about XYZ iff his are. (And, of course, vice versa: in a world in which my Twin is in my context . . . it must

be that his water-thoughts are about H_2O iff mine are.) (*PS*: 48)

3.2 One complaint about this notion of narrow content, the one that Fodor suspects "*really* bugs people" (*PS*: 50), is that it seems impossible to say what the narrow content of a thought is. Fodor and Twin-Fodor have thought tokens with the same narrow content. But what is it that they both think? What is the narrow content of those thoughts? It can't be *that water is wet*, since Twin-Fodor doesn't think that. Nor can it be *that XYZ is wet*, since Fodor doesn't think that. It seems that "narrow content is radically inexpressible" (*PC*: 50). If this is right, however, it is hard to see how narrow content could serve the purpose for which it is intended. Recall that narrow content was supposed to provide a species of content-based taxonomy that would be useful in scientific psychology. If we insist, as Fodor does, that the states and properties invoked in scientific psychology must supervene on physiological states and properties, then psychological generalizations cannot invoke broad content. An alternative strategy is to couch those generalizations in terms of narrow content. But if narrow content is "radically inexpressible" it would appear that psychology's generalizations could never be stated.[18]

Fodor's response to this problem is to suggest that while we can't *express* the narrow content of the thought that he and his Twin share, we can "sneak up on the shared content by *mentioning*" an appropriate English expression – in this case presumably the sentence: "Water is wet." But in offering this response I think Fodor seriously understates the case to be made for his notion of narrow content. We can do more than "sneak up" on the narrow content of a mental state; we can explicitly introduce a way of talking about it. The central idea is very simple. Expressions of the form: "—— believes that p" are predicates whose extension in any possible world is the class of people who believe that p in that world. Given these predicates along with the notion of a doppelganger, we can introduce expressions of the form "—— believes that [p]" (think of it as "bracketed" belief) whose extensions in any possible world include everyone in that world who believes that p, along with all of their doppelgangers. Similarly, expressions of the form "—— has the (broad) content that p" are predicates whose extension in any possible world included the class of brain state tokens whose broad content is p. Here we can

introduce expressions of the form "—— has the (narrow) content that [p]" whose extension in any possible world includes the class of brain state tokens whose (broad) content is p, along with the physically identical tokens in all doppelgangers of people who harbor tokens whose broad content is p.[19] These "bracketed" predicates are no less clear and no less systematic than the broad-content predicates on which they are based.

This strategy for talking about narrow content has what might at first seem to be a curious feature. In some cases the extension of "—— has the (narrow) content that [p]" and the extension of "—— has the (narrow) content that [q]" are going to be the same even though "p" and "q" are replaced by sentences that differ in reference and truth value. Consider, for example, a version of Putnam's aluminum/molybdenum story. In the southern province of a certain English-speaking country, pots are typically made of aluminum, and this fact is known to a southerner, (Southern)Sam, who knows very little else about aluminum. In the northern province, pots are typically made of molybdenum. But in the north, molybdenum is called "aluminum." (Northern)Sam, who is (Southern)Sam's doppelganger, has a belief which he expresses with the words "Pots are typically made of aluminum," though of course given the standard intuitions in these cases, the belief token he is expressing has the (broad) content that pots are typically made of molybdenum. Now what about the narrow content of the belief (Northern) Sam expresses? Since that belief has the (broad) content that pots are typically made of molybdenum, it has the (narrow) content that [pots are typically made of molybdenum]. But since it is neurophysiologically identical to (Southern) Sam's belief whose (broad) content is that pots are typically made of aluminum, it also has the (narrow) content that [pots are typically made of aluminum]. Similarly, the belief token that (Southern)Sam expresses when the says "Pots are typically made of aluminum" has both narrow (or bracketed) contents. There is nothing particularly surprising about any of this. The device we've introduced for attributing narrow contents exploits the expressions we would use in attributing broad contents and expands their extensions in a systematic way. It is to be expected that in some cases two of these enlarged extensions will coincide.[20]

The conclusion I would draw here is that the putative "radical inexpressibility" of narrow content is not a problem that Fodor need worry much about. It is easy enough to devise locutions for attributing narrow content to cognitive states, and these locutions can be used to state psychological generalizations in much the same way that locutions attributing broad content can.

3.3 As I see it, the real problem with narrow content does not derive from our inability to talk about it, and thus state generalizations in terms of it. Rather, the problem is that if the computational paradigm sketched in section 2 is on the right track, then many of the true generalizations – many of those that actually describe mental processes – are not going to be statable in terms of narrow content. The taxonomy of mental states imposed by narrow content is going to be both too coarse and too ill-behaved to exploit in a serious scientific psychology. Perhaps the best way to see why a narrow content taxonomy is too coarse is to compare three taxonomic schemes: the one imposed by fat syntax, the one imposed by broad content, and the one imposed by narrow content.

Each mental state token is a brain state token; its "essential" type will be specified neurophysiologically, and still count as tokens of the same fat syntactic type, provided that they have basically the same pattern of causal connections with stimuli, with behavior, and with other appropriate brain states. It's also worth noting that if there is pair of neurophysiologically identical states embedded in a pair of neurophysiologically identical organisms, and if one of these states is in a fat syntactic category, the other will always be in the same fat syntactic category. Fat syntax supervenes on physiology. Our commonsense intuitions about broad content provide another scheme for classifying brain state tokens. The lesson to be learned from Twin Earth, and from Burge's thought experiments, is that classification by broad content turns on physical, historical, and linguistic *context*. Thus broad content does not supervene on physiology, and in this respect its taxonomic categories slice too finely; it sometimes puts an organism and its doppelganger in different categories. Narrow content provides a third strategy for classifying brain state tokens, one which starts with broad content but ignores context. Thus, despite the terminological oddness, the categories of narrow content are larger than those imposed by a broad content taxonomy. Moreover, like fat syntax, narrow content supervenes on physiology.

All of this might lead one to suppose that the taxonomies imposed by narrow content and fat syntax *coincide*. That is, it might lead one to think that a pair of brain state tokens in a pair of individuals will be of the same fat syntactic type if and only if they have the same narrow content. However, this is all but certain to be a mistake. If we ignore the vagueness of the narrow content taxonomy, a theme to which I'll return shortly, then it may be the case that sameness of fat syntax guarantees sameness of narrow content ("plus or minus a bit," as Fodor might say).[21] But on almost any plausible reading, the categories imposed by a narrow content taxonomy are much larger than those imposed by fat syntax. Thus sameness of narrow content does not guarantee sameness of fat syntax.

The literature is full of examples that illustrate this mismatch. Perhaps the most obvious examples involve people with unusual or defective perceptual systems. To take an extreme case, consider Helen Keller. If Ms Keller were to be told by a trusted informant that there is a fat cat in the room, she would come to believe that there is a fat cat in the room. That is, she would acquire a brain state which functions like a belief and which has the (broad) content that there is a fat cat in the room. Similarly, if I were told by a trusted informant that there is a fat cat in the room, I would acquire a brain state which functions like a belief and which has the (broad) content that there is a fat cat in the room. Thus both Ms Keller's brain state and mine would have the (narrow) content that [there is a fat cat in the room]. But surely those two states differ radically in their fat syntax. There are all sorts of perceptual stimuli (both visual and auditory) that would cause me, but not Ms Keller, to acquire the belief that [there is a fat cat in the room]. And states whose patterns of causal interaction with stimuli differ substantially do not share the same fat syntax. Much the same point could be made, though perhaps less dramatically, with examples of people with other perceptual anomalies, both real, like color blindness, and imagined.[22]

In the Helen Keller example, differences in fat syntax are due to differences in the way stimuli affect mental states. But there are also cases in which differences in syntactic type are engendered by differences in the way mental states interact with *each other*. Some people are logically acute; it is plausible to suppose that the mechanism underlying their reasoning makes many valid inferences and few invalid ones. Other people are significantly less acute; their mental mechanism makes many fewer valid inferences and many more invalid ones. On a syntactic taxonomy – *even a skinny syntactic taxonomy* – the states being manipulated by these mechanisms are of different syntactic types. But in many such cases the intuitive commonsense taxonomy of broad content classifies the states being manipulated as having the same (broad) content. And, of course, states with the same broad content have the same narrow content. In addition to these normal interpersonal differences in inferential capacities, there are also lots of pathological cases, some real and some imagined, in which people reason in ways very different from the way I reason, but where commonsense psychology is still comfortable in attributing the same broad content.[23] Here too, syntax and narrow content will diverge.

What I have been arguing is that there are major differences between a taxonomy based on narrow content and one based on fat syntax (or skinny syntax, for that matter). In many cases the syntactic taxonomy will be substantially more fine grained, and will draw substantially more distinctions, than the narrow content taxonomy. There are lots of examples in which a pair of belief state tokens will differ in their fat syntax though not in their narrow content. The reason this is important is that, along with Fodor, I have been assuming that the cognitive mind is "syntactic engine" and that the mechanism controlling cognitive processes is "sensitive solely to syntactic properties." But if this is right, then the generalizations that describe cognitive processes will be stable in syntactic terms, and these will typically be more fine grained than generalizations statable in terms of narrow content. The generalizations of a computational theory will describe different patterns of causal interaction for cognitive states with different fat syntax, even though in many cases those states will have the same narrow content. So if the computational paradigm is the right one, then many of the generalizations that describe the mind's workings are simply not going to be stable in terms of narrow content.

Throughout this section I have been writing as though the broad content taxonomy provided by commonsense psychology is reasonably clear and stable, and thus that predicates of the form "—— has the (broad) content that p" have a reasonably well defined extension. However, there is good reason to doubt that this is so. Following Quine's

lead, a number of writers have assembled cases which seem to show that commonsense intuitions about the extensions of such predicates are highly context sensitive. Whether or not a state can be comfortably classified as having the content that p depends, to a significant degree, on the context in which the question arises.[24] I have developed an account of the tacit principle underlying commonsense content attribution which views them as a sort of similarity judgment. This account explains their context sensitivity, and various other phenomena as well. But whether or not my explanation of the phenomena is correct, I am inclined to think that the data speak for themselves. By varying the context in which the question is asked, we can get competent users of commonsense psychology to judge that a particular cognitive state token clearly has the content that p, or that it clearly does not. If this is right, it provides yet another reason for thinking that the generalizations of a serious scientific psychology will not be stable in the taxonomic categories provided by narrow content. For the categories of a narrow content taxonomy are simply the categories of a broad content taxonomy extended to meet the demands of the principle of autonomy. But the broad content taxonomy of commonsense psychology is too vague, too context-sensitive, and too unstable to use in a serious scientific theory. *Narrow* content inherits all of these deficits.

4 Keeping Score

Toward the end of section I, I quoted the three conditions that, on Fodor's view, would have to be met by the states a psychological theory postulates, if that theory is to count as "endorsing" the propositional attitudes, and thus avoiding the "catastrophe" that would ensue "if commonsense intentional psychology really were to collapse." It's time to ask which of those conditions are likely to be met. Along with Fodor, I'll assume, as I have been all along, that the computational paradigm is correct, and that the mind is "a syntax driven machine" whose operations are "sensitive solely to syntactic properties."

The third condition on Fodor's list is that "the implicit generalizations of commonsense belief/ desire psychology" must be "largely true" of the states postulated by the psychological theory in question. Presumably, Fodor's hope went something like this:

The generalizations of commonsense psychology are couched in terms of (broad) content. But the Twin Earth examples show that "you can't make respectable science out of the attitudes as commonsensically individuated" (*PS*: 30). Very well, then, we'll move to narrow content, since, unlike broad content, narrow content supervenes on physiology. Given any commonsense generalization about tokens of the belief that p, there will be a parallel narrow generalization – a generalization about the tokens of the belief that [p]. And that latter generalization will be scientifically respectable.

To satisfy Fodor's third condition, however, it is not sufficient that the narrow analogues of broad content generalizations be scientifically respectable. Most of them must also be true. Now if the mind really is a syntax driven machine, and if syntactic categories can be matched up, near enough, with the categories of narrow content, then it looks like we're home free. But the burden of my argument in 3.3 was that syntactic and narrow content taxonomies will not match up, because the latter is both too coarse and too ill-behaved. If the computational paradigm is correct, I argued, then many of the generalizations that describe the mind's workings are not going to be stable in terms of narrow content. If that's right, then Fodor's third condition will not be satisfied.

Let's turn, now, to Fodor's first condition: that the states a psychological theory postulates must be "semantically evaluable." How well do we fare on this one if the computational paradigm is correct? I am inclined to think that here again the ill-behaved context sensitivity of semantic taxonomies poses real problems. If it is indeed the case that by varying the context of the question we can get competent users of commonsense psychology to judge that a particular cognitive state token clearly has the content that p, or that it clearly does not, then it's hard to see how even the tokens, let alone the types posited by a serious, computational, scientific psychology will be "semantically evaluable."

One final point. Suppose I am wrong about the mismatch between syntactic and narrow content taxonomies; suppose that the generalizations of a scientifically solid psychology really can be stated in terms of narrow content. Would it then follow that the states postulated by such a theory are "semantically evaluable"? Fodor himself seems ambivalent. Consider the following:

> If you mean by content what can be semantically evaluated, then what my water-thoughts share with Twin "water"-thoughts *isn't* content...We can't say...what Twin thoughts have in common. This is because what can be said is ipso facto semantically evaluable; and what Twin-thoughts have in common is ipso facto not. (*PS*: 50); the emphasis is Fodor's)

But, of course, what Fodor's water-thoughts share with Twin "water"-thoughts, what "Twin-thoughts have in common," *is* narrow content. So in this passage Fodor seems to admit – indeed insist – that narrow content is *not* semantically evaluable. Elsewhere he is even more explicit:

> You can have narrow content without functional-role semantics because *narrow contents aren't semantically evaluable*; only wide contents have conditions of satisfaction. (*PS*: 83; the emphasis is Fodor's)

Still, perhaps this is just a debater's point. For in several other passages Fodor notes that narrow content "is semantically evaluable relative to a context" (*PS*: 51). And perhaps this is all that is required to satisfy his first condition. There's no need to decide the point since, as I see it, the real problem with narrow content is not that it fails to be "semantically evaluable" (whatever that might come to) but that it fails to match up with the syntactic taxonomy of a computational psychology.

The remaining item on Fodor's list of conditions is that the states posited by a psychological theory must "have causal powers." On this one Fodor wins easily. If the computational paradigm is on the right track, then the syntactically taxonomized states posited by a correct computational theory are sure to have causal powers.

By my count, the score against Fodor – and against intentional psychology – is two to one.[25]

Notes

1 Stich (1978). For the details of Putnam's thought experiment, see Putnam (1975a).

2 Quine has urged this view of the propositional attitudes in many places. See, for example Quine

(1960: 219). For some elaboration on these themes, see Stich (1982); Stich (1983: chs 4–6); Gordon (1986); and Levin (1988).

3 See, for example, Fodor, (1975a: ch. 1); Fodor (1987d); Fodor (1980c); Fodor (1981d: "Introduction"; and Fodor (1987d: ch. 1).

4 The quote is from Fodor (1978b). For my account of the explanatory strategy of cognitive psychology, *circa* 1980, see Stich (1983: chs 7–9). Perhaps this is the place to say that when I talk of the cognitive psychology of the 1970s and early 1980s, what I have in mind is pre-connectionist cognitive psychology. The qualification is important since, on my view, neither Fodor's account of cognitive theorizing nor my syntactic account will mesh comfortably with the connectionist paradigm. For some elaboration of this point, see Ramsey, Stich, and Garon (1990).

5 For similar arguments, see Stack (unpublished); Putnam (1978); and Putnam (1983).

6 See, for example, Burge (1979); Burge (1986); Kitcher (1985); Owens (1987); Baker (1987a).

7 Loar (1987a); Lycan (1988: 76–79); Dow (in preparation).

8 See, for example, Block (1986); Dennett (1982); Devitt (1989a); Dow (in preparation); Loar (1987a).

9 See, for example, Owens (1987) and Baker (1987b).

10 On this point see Stich (1983: ch. 11 sec. 1).

11 Fodor, (1987d: x). Subsequent references to Fodor's *Psychosemantics* will be referred to as *PS* in the text.

12 My account of states is modeled on Kim's account of events. See Kim (1969) and Kim (1976).

13 See, for example, Armstrong (1978).

14 Devitt (1989a).

15 For a particularly vivid and influential example of the Belief Box metaphor, see Schiffer (1981).

16 Stich (1983: 149–51).

17 "I learned 'anchors' at Stanford," Fodor tells us. "It is a very useful term despite – or maybe because of – not being very well defined" (*PS*: 49).

18 I owe this way of making the point to Warren Dow. See Dow (in preparation). A similar point is made by Baker (1987a).

19 Something rather like this was suggested very briefly in Stich (1983: 192, n.). More recently, similar ideas have been developed by Valerie Walker (in press) and Michael Devitt (1989a). Perhaps I should add that I do not take my suggestion to be in competition with Fodor's strategy for "sneaking up on" narrow content; mine is just a bit more explicit. Indeed, were I to develop my definition more carefully, and without riding roughshod over the fine distinction between use and mention, it would be obvious that my story, like Fodor's, enables us to talk about narrow content by *mentioning* sentences.

20 This note is for afficionados only. I have argued that (Northern)Sam's belief falls within the extension of both

(i) "—— has the (narrow) content that [pots are typically made of molybdenum]",

and

(ii) "—— has the (narrow) content that [pots are typically made of aluminum]."

But it does not follow that (i) and (ii) are coextensive. For consider the case of an expert in the North, someone who knows a great deal about how to distinguish aluminum from molybdenum and who also (broadly) believes that pots are typically made of molybdenum. Plainly, his belief is in the extension of (i). Is it also in the extension of (ii)? Not unless he has a doppelganger whose belief has the (broad) content that pots are typically made of aluminum. But if he has a doppelganger in the South, it is not at all clear that his doppelganger would (broadly) believe that pots are typically made of aluminum. More likely, the relevant mental state of the expert's Southern doppelganger would be so anomalous that it would have no broad content at all. For unless the story is told in a pretty strange way, you *can't*

(a) be the doppelganger of an expert on aluminum and molybdenum who broadly believes that pots are typically made of molybdenum,

(b) live in a world in which pots are typically made of aluminum,

(c) (broadly) believe that pots are typically made of aluminum.

To see the point, imagine that the Northern expert can distinguish the two metals by touch and sight, and ask what his Southern doppelganger would say when confronting the aluminum pots that are typical in his environment.

21 Fodor (1980c: 240).

22 For detailed examples along these lines, see Stich (1983: 66–8) and Stich (1982: 185–8).

Kenneth Taylor has suggested that the objection I am urging against Fodor dissolves if we focus more steadfastly on Fodor's "official" account of narrow content which takes the narrow content of a thought to be a *function* from contexts to broad contents. On my account of narrow content, any two thoughts with the same broad content must have the same narrow content. But, Taylor urges, if we view the narrow content of a thought as a function from contexts to broad contents, then it is entirely possible that Ms Keller's thought and mine do not have the same narrow content. For there might be some contexts in which Ms Keller's thought and mine did not have the same broad content, and if this is possible, then on the function account of narrow content our thoughts do not have the same narrow content.

I am inclined to think that the function account of narrow content is more than a bit obscure. For I am not at all clear about what a *context* is; nor am I sure how we are supposed to play the game of imagining people and their thoughts embedded in other contexts. Consider the example in the text. Is Ms Keller's context different from mine? If so, what would it be for me to be in her context? Would I have to have her handicaps? Would I have to have had the same biography? The mind boggles.

But even if we suppose these questions can be answered in some coherent and principled way, I doubt the answers will do Fodor much good. To avoid the objection I am urging, it will have to be the case that the taxonomy generated by the function account of narrow content coincides with the taxonomy generated by fat syntax. And I see no reason to think this will be the case. Certainly, Fodor has offered no argument for this claim. Moreover, if as Taylor suggests, Ms Keller's belief and mine have different narrow contents on the function account, it is hard to see why the same will not be true of the beliefs of other people who broadly believe that there is a fat cat in the room, but who differ from me less radically than Ms Keller does. However, if this is the case, then the function account of narrow content runs the risk of individuating much too finely. Only doppelgangers will have thoughts with the same narrow content.

23 For some examples, see Stich (1983: 68–72). For examples of a rather different sort, see Cherniak (1986). For another example, see Dennett (1981b: 54–5).

24 See, for example, Stich (1982: 180–203), where I describe the phenomenon as the "pragmatic sensitivity" of belief attributions. See also Stich (1983: 90–110). Much the same moral can be drawn from Dennett's examples of the use of intentional notions to describe trees and his example of the young child who asserts that Daddy is a doctor. For the first, see Dennett (1981a: 22); for the second, see Dennett (1969: 183).

25 I am indebted to many people for much useful conversation on these matters. Those I can recall are Daniel Dennett, Michael Devitt, Warren Dow, Jerry Fodor, Gary Hardcastle, Patricia Kitcher, Kenneth Taylor, and Valerie Walker. I hope the others will accept my thanks anonymously. Special thanks are due to Warren Dow for his helpful comments on an earlier version of this essay.

14

Supervenient Causation

Mental Causation

Jaegwon Kim

Causal relations involving mental events are among the familiar facts of everyday experience. My fingers are busily dancing about on the computer keyboard because I want to write about mental causation. The word "because" connecting my want and the movements of my fingers is naturally taken to express a causal connection: My want causes my fingers to move. And we can causally explain the movements of my fingers – for example, why they hit the keys "m," "e," "n," "t," "a," and "l" in succession – by invoking my desire to type the word "mental." This is a case of *mental-to-physical* causation. There are two other kinds of causal relations in which mental events figure: *physical-to-mental* and *mental-to-mental* causation. Sensations are among the familiar examples that involve causal relations of the physical-to-mental kind: Severe burns cause pains, irradiations of the retinas cause visual sensations, and food poisoning can cause sensations of nausea. Instances of mental-to-mental causation are equally familiar. We often believe one thing (say, that we had better take an umbrella to work) because we believe another thing (say, that it is going to rain later today). This is a case in which a belief causes another belief. The belief that you have won a fellowship to graduate school may cause a feeling of joy and satisfaction, which may in turn cause you to want to call your parents. On a grander scale, it is human knowledge and desire that built the pyramids of Egypt and the Great Wall of China; produced the glorious music, literature, and other artworks of our forebears; built

our great cities; detonated nuclear bombs; and caused holes in the ozone layer. Our mental events are intricately woven into the complex mosaic of causal relations of our world. At least that is the way things seem.

But how is it possible for the mind to cause a change in a material body? Through what mechanism or process does a mental event manage to initiate, or insert itself into, a causal chain of physical events? How is it possible that a chain of physical and biological events and processes terminates, suddenly and magically, in a full-blown conscious experience, with its vivid colors, smells, and sounds? Think of your total sensory experience right now – visual, tactual, auditory, olfactory, and so on: How is it possible for all this to arise out of the electrochemical processes in the gray matter of your brain?

Agency and Mental Causation

An agent is someone with the capacity to perform *actions*. In this sense, we are all agents: We do such things as turning on the stove, heating water in the kettle, making coffee, and entertaining a friend. These are actions that we perform; they are unlike "mere happenings" that involve us, like sweating on a hot day in the sun, shuddering because of the cold, and growing hair and fingernails.

What do these actions involve? Consider my heating water in the kettle. This must at least involve my *causing* the water in the kettle to rise in temperature. It probably involves more than that: If I ask you to heat the stew pot and you then inadvertently turn on the wrong burner and heat the water in the kettle, it would be correct to say that I caused the temperature of the water to rise but incorrect (or at least odd) to say that I heated the water. In any case, why did I heat the water? I did so to make coffee. That is, I *wanted* to make coffee and *believed* that I needed hot water to make coffee (and, to be boringly detailed, I believed that by heating the water in the kettle I could get hot water). Our beliefs and desires guide our actions, and we appeal to them to explain why we do what we do.

We may consider the following schema as the fundamental principle that connects desire, belief, and action:

[The desire–belief–action principle (DBA)] If S desires something and believes that doing A will help secure it, S will do A.

As stated, DBA is too strong. For one thing, we often choose not to act on our desires, and sometimes we change or get rid of them when we realize that pursuing them is too costly, leading to consequences that we do not want. For example, you wake up in the middle of the night and want a glass of milk, but the thought of getting out of bed in the chilly winter night talks you out of it. For another, even when we try to act on our desires and relevant beliefs about the means needed to realize them, we may find ourselves physically incapable of doing A; it may be that when you have finally overcome your aversion to getting out of your bed, you find yourself chained to your bed! To save DBA, various things can be done to weaken it; we can add further conditions to the antecedent of DBA (e.g., the condition that there are no other conflicting desires) or weaken the consequent (e.g., by turning it into a probability or tendency statement[1] or adding the all-purpose hedge "*ceteris paribus*").

The belief–desire pair that is related to an action in accordance with DBA can be called a "reason" for that action. What the exceptions to DBA we have just considered show is that an agent may have a reason, a "good" reason, to do something but fail to do it. Sometimes there may be more than one belief–desire pair that is related to a given action, as specified by DBA: In addition to your desire for a glass of milk, you heard a suspicious noise from downstairs and wanted to check it out. Let us suppose that you finally did get out of your bed to venture down the stairway. Why did you do

that? What explains it? It is possible that you went downstairs because you thought you really ought to check out the noise and that your desire for a drink of milk had no role in it? If so, it is your desire to check the source of the noise, not your desire for milk, that explains why you went downstairs in the middle of the night. It would be correct for you to say, "I went downstairs because I wanted a glass of milk." We can also put the point this way: Your desire to check out the noise and your desire for milk were both *reasons for* going downstairs, but the first, not the second, was the *reason for which* you did what you did, namely, a *motivating reason*. And it is "reason for which," not mere "reason for," that explains the associated action. But what precisely is the difference between them? That is, what distinguishes explanatory reason from nonexplanatory reasons?

An influential answer defended by Donald Davidson[2] is the simple thesis that a reason for which an action is done is one that *causes* it. That is, what makes a reason for an action an explanatory reason is its role in the causation of that action. Thus, on Davidson's view, the crucial difference between my desire to check out the noise and my desire for a glass of milk lies in the fact that the former, not the latter, caused my action of going downstairs. This makes explanation of action by reasons, namely, "rationalizing explanation," a species of causal explanation: Reasons explain actions in virtue of being their causes.

If this is correct, it follows that agency is possible only if mental causation is possible. For an agent is someone who is able to act for reasons and whose actions can be explained and evaluated in terms of the reasons for which he acted. And this entails that reasons, that is, mental states like beliefs, desires, and emotions, must be able to cause us to do what we do. Since what we do includes bodily motions, this means that agency – at least human agency – presupposes the possibility of mental-to-physical causation. Somehow your beliefs and desires must cause your limbs to move in appropriate ways so that in half a minute you find your whole body displaced from your bedroom to the kitchen downstairs.

Mental Causation, Mental Realism, Epiphenomenalism

As already noted, sensations involve the causation of mental events by physical processes. In fact, the very idea of perceiving something – say, seeing a tree – involves the idea that the object seen is a cause of an appropriate perceptual experience. For suppose that there is a tree in front of you and that you are having a visual experience of the sort you would be having if your retinas were stimulated by the light rays reflected by the tree. But you would not be seeing *this* tree if there were a holographic image of a tree interposed between you and the tree that was exactly as the tree would look from where you stand. You would be seeing the holographic image of a tree, not the real tree. This difference, too, seems to be a causal one: Your perceptual experience is caused by the holographic image, not by the tree.

Perception is our only window to the world; without it we could know nothing about what goes on around us. If, therefore, perception necessarily involves mental causation, there could be no knowledge of the world without mental causation. Moreover, a significant part of our knowledge of the world is based on experimentation, not mere observation. Experimentation differs from passive observation in that it requires our active intervention in the natural course of events; we carefully design and deliberately set up the experimental conditions and then observe the outcome. This means that experimentation presupposes mental-to-physical causation and is impossible without it. Much of our knowledge of causal relations – in general, knowledge of what happens under what conditions – is based on experimentation, and such knowledge is crucial not only as a basis for our theoretical knowledge of the world but also as a guide to our practical decision-making. We must conclude, then, that if the mind cannot causally affect physical events and processes, neither practical knowledge required to inform our decisions nor theoretical knowledge that yields an understanding of the world is likely to be available.

Mental-to-mental causation, too, is involved in human knowledge. Consider the process of inferring one proposition from another. Suppose someone asks you, "Is the number of planets odd or even?" If you are like most people, you would probably proceed as follows: "Well, how many planets are there? Nine, and nine is an odd number. So there are an odd number of planets." You have just inferred the proposition that there are an odd number of planets from the proposition that there are nine planets and have accepted the former on the basis of this inference. This process evidently involves mental causation: Your belief

that the number of planets is odd was caused by your belief that there are nine planets. Inference is one way in which beliefs can generate other beliefs. A brief reflection makes it evident that most of our beliefs are generated by other beliefs we hold, and "generation" here could only mean causal generation. It follows, then, that all three types of mental causation – mental-to-physical, physical-to-mental, and mental-to-mental – are implicated in the possibility of human knowledge.

Epiphenomenalism is the thesis that although all mental events are caused by physical events, mental events are only "epiphenomena," that is, events without powers to cause any other event. Mental events are effects of physical processes, but they do not in turn cause anything else, being powerless to affect physical events or even other mental events; they are the absolute termini of causal chains. Think of a moving car and the series of shadows it casts as it moves: The shadows are caused by the moving car but have no effect on the car's motion. Nor are the shadows at different instants causally connected: The car shadow at a given instant t is caused not by the car shadow an instant earlier but by the car itself at t. A person who can only observe the moving shadows but not the car may very well be led to impute causal relations between the successive shadows, but he would be mistaken. Similarly, you may think that the pain in your tooth has caused your desire to take aspirin, but that, according to epiphenomenalism, would be a mistake: Your toothache and your desire for aspirin are both caused by brain events, which themselves may be causally connected, but the two mental events are not related as cause to effect any more than two successive car shadows. The apparent regularities that we observe in mental events, the epiphenomenalist will argue, do not represent genuine causal connections; like the regularities characterizing the moving shadows of a car or the successive symptoms of a disease, they are merely reflections of the real causal processes at a more fundamental level.

These are the claims of epiphenomenalism. Few philosophers have been self-professed epiphenomenalists, although there are those whose views appear to lead to such a position. We are more likely to find epiphenomenalist thinking among the scientists who do research in neurophysiology. They are apt to treat mentality, especially consciousness, as a mere shadow or afterglow thrown off by the complex neural processes going on in the brain; these physical/biological processes are what at bottom do all the pushing and pulling to keep the human organism properly functioning. How should we respond to this epiphenomenalist stance on the status of mind? Samuel Alexander, a noted emergentist during the early twentieth century, commented on epiphenomenalism with the following biting remark:

> [Epiphenomenalism] supposes something to exist in nature which has nothing to do, no purpose to serve, a species of noblesse which depends on the work of its inferiors, but is kept for show and might as well, and undoubtedly would in time, be abolished.[3]

Alexander is saying that if epiphenomenalism is true, mentality has no work to do and hence is entirely useless, and this renders it pointless to recognize it as something real. Our beliefs and desires would have no role in causing our decisions and actions and would be powerless to explain them; our perception and knowledge would have nothing to do with our artistic creations and technological inventions. *Being real and having causal powers go hand in hand; to deprive the mental of causal potency is in effect to deprive it of its reality.*

It is important to see that what Alexander has said is not an *argument against* epiphenomenalism: It only points out, in a stark and forceful way, what accepting epiphenomenalism means. We should also remind ourselves that the epiphenomenalist does not reject the reality of mental causation altogether; she only denies mind-to-body and mind-to-mind causation, not body-to-mind causation. In this sense, she gives the mental a well-defined place in the causal structure of the world; the mental, for her, is causally integrated into the world. But one who denies mental causation *tout court* treats the mental as both causeless and effectless. To a person holding such a view, mental events are in total causal isolation from the rest of the world, even from other mental events; each mental event is a solitary island unto itself, with no connection to anything else. Its existence would be entirely inexplicable since it has no cause, and it would make no difference to anything else since it has no effect. It would be a mystery how the existence of such things could be known to us. As Alexander declares, they could just as well be "abolished" – that is, regarded as nonexistent. On this line of reasoning, therefore, the reality of mental causation is equivalent to the reality of the mental itself.

Cartesian Interactionism

So why not grant the mind full causal powers, among them the power to influence bodily processes? This would save the reality of the mental and recognize what after all is so manifestly evident to common sense. And that is just what Descartes tried to do with his thesis that minds and bodies, even though they are substances of very different sorts, are in intimate causal commerce with each other. In fact, he thought that there was a specific site within the human body where the mind was in direct causal interaction with the body; in the *Sixth Meditation* he wrote:

> The mind is not immediately affected by all parts of the body, but only by the brain, or perhaps just by one small part of the brain .... Every time this part of the brain is in a given state, it presents the same signals to the mind, even though the other parts of the body may be in a different condition at the time... For example, when the nerves in the foot are set in motion in a violent and unusual manner, this motion, by way of the spinal cord, reaches the inner parts of the brain, and there gives the mind its signal for having a certain sensation, namely the sensation of a pain as occurring in the foot. This stimulates the mind to do its best to get rid of the cause of the pain, which it takes to be harmful to the foot.[4]

In the *Passions of the Soul*, Descartes identified the pineal gland as the "seat of the soul," the locus of direct mind–body interaction. This gland, Descartes maintained, could be moved directly by the soul, thereby moving the "animal spirits," which would then transmit the causal influence to appropriate parts of the body:

> And the activity of the soul consists entirely in the fact that simply by willing something it brings it about that the little gland to which it is closely joined moves in the manner required to produce the effect corresponding to this desire.[5]

In the case of physical-to-mental causation, this process is reversed: Disturbances in the animal spirits surrounding the pineal gland make the gland move, which in turn causes the mind to experience appropriate sensations and perceptions.

For Descartes, then, each of us is a "union" or "intermingling" of a mind and a body in direct causal interaction.

Few will quarrel with Descartes's acknowledgement of the reality of mind–body interaction or his wish to give an account of it. The only question, one that has troubled many thoughtful readers of Descartes for centuries, is how such interaction is possible – how the "mingling" or "union" of an immaterial soul with some bodily organ is possible – within the framework of Descartes's substance dualism. Descartes was immediately challenged by Pierre Gassendi, among others:

> But you still have to explain how that "joining and, as it were, intermingling" . . . can apply to you if you are incorporeal, unextended and indivisible. If you are no larger than a point, how are you joined to the entire body, which is so large? How can you be joined even to the brain, or a tiny part of it, since . . . no matter how small it is, it still has size or extension? If you wholly lack parts, how are you intermingled . . . with the particles of this region? For there can be no intermingling between things unless the parts of each of them can be intermingled. And if you are something separate, how are you compounded with matter so as to make up a unity?[6]

The Cartesian soul has no extension in space: Either it is entirely outside space, or, at best, it occupies a geometric point in space. How, Gassendi is asking, can such a thing "mingle" or "unite" with a material object, something with countless spatial parts? Could the two things mingle in the sense that they causally interact? But as Princess Elizabeth of Bohemia wondered, how can "man's soul, being only a thinking substance, . . . determine animal spirits so as to cause voluntary actions"?[7]

You want to raise your arm, and your arm goes up. Presumably, nerve impulses reaching appropriate muscles in your arm made those muscles contract, and that's how the arm went up. And these nerve signals presumably originated in the activation of certain neurons in your brain. What caused these neurons to fire? We now have a quite detailed understanding of the process that leads to the firing of a neuron, in terms of complex electrochemical processes involving ions in the fluid inside and outside a neuron, differences in voltage across cell membranes, and so forth. All in all we seem to have a pretty good picture of the processes

at this microlevel on the basis of the known laws of physics, chemistry, and biology. If the immaterial mind is going to cause a neuron to emit a signal (or prevent it from doing so), it must somehow intervene in these electrochemical processes. But how could that happen? At the very interface between the mental and the physical where direct and unmediated mind–body interaction takes place, the nonphysical mind must somehow influence the state of some molecules, perhaps by electrically charging them or nudging them this way or that way. Is this really conceivable? Surely the working neuroscientist does not believe that to have a complete understanding of these complex processes she needs to include in her account the workings of immaterial souls and how they influence the molecular processes involved. Perhaps we will never fully understand all the details of these processes, but our ignorance surely must be ignorance of further physical/biological facts, not of some facts about the operations of an immaterial soul. Even if the idea of a soul's influencing the motion of a molecule (let alone a whole pineal gland) were coherent, the postulation of such a causal agent would seem neither necessary nor helpful in understanding why and how our limbs move.

Psychophysical Laws and "Anomalous Monism"

The expulsion of minds as substantival entities perhaps makes it easier to understand the possibility of mental causation. For we would no longer have to contend with the question how immaterial souls with no physical characteristics – no bulk, no mass, no energy, no electric charge, perhaps no location in space – could causally influence, and be influenced by, material objects and processes. As we saw, few people now regard minds as substances of a special nonphysical sort, and mental events and processes are now standardly viewed as occurring in certain complex physical systems like biological organisms, not immaterial minds. The problem of mental causation, therefore, is now formulated in terms of two kinds of events, mental and physical, not in terms of two types of substances: How is it possible for a mental event to cause, or to be caused by, a physical event? Or in terms of properties: How is it possible for an instantiation of a mental property to cause a physical property to be instantiated, or vice versa?

But why is this supposed to be a "problem"? We don't usually think that there is a special philosophical problem about, say, chemical events causally influencing biological processes or a nation's economic and political conditions causally influencing each other. So what is it about mentality and physicality that makes causal relations between them a philosophical problem? For substance dualism, it is, at bottom, the extreme heterogeneity of minds and bodies that makes causal relations between them prima facie problematic. Given that mental substances have now been expunged, aren't we home free with mental causation? The answer is that certain other assumptions that demand our respect present prima facie obstacles to the possibility of mental causation.

One such assumption centers on the question whether there are *laws connecting mental phenomena with physical phenomena* that are needed to underwrite causal connections between them. Donald Davidson's celebrated "anomalism of the mental" states that there can be no such laws.[8] A principle connecting laws and causation that is widely, if not universally, accepted is this: *Causally connected events must instantiate a law.* If heating a metallic rod causes its length to increase, there must be a general law connecting events of the first type and events of the second type; that is, there must be a law stating that the heating of a metallic rod is generally followed by an increase in its length. But if causal connections require laws and there are no laws connecting mental events with physical events, it would seem to follow that there could be no mental–physical causation. This line of reasoning will be examined in more detail below. But is there any reason to doubt the existence of laws connecting mental and physical phenomena?

In earlier chapters we often assumed that there are lawlike connections between mental and physical events; you surely recall the stock example of pains and C-fiber excitations. The psychoneural identity theory, as we saw, assumes that each type of mental event is lawfully correlated with a type of physical event. Talk of "physical realization" of mental events, too, presupposes that there are lawlike connections between a mental event of a given kind and its diverse physical realizers; for a physical realizer of a mental event must at least be lawfully sufficient for the occurrence of that mental event. Now, Davidson's claim about the nonexistence of psychophysical laws is restricted to intentional mental events and states ("propositional attitudes"), those with propositional content, like beliefs, desires, and intentions, and doesn't touch nonintentional mental events and states, like pains, itches, and mental images. Why does Davidson think that there can be no laws connecting, say, beliefs with physical events? Doesn't – in fact, shouldn't – every mental event have a neural substrate, that is, a neural state that, as a matter of law, suffices for its occurrence?

Before we take a look at Davidson's argument, let us consider some examples. Take the belief that it's inappropriate for the president to get a $200 haircut. How reasonable is it to expect to find a neural substrate for this belief? Is it at all plausible to think that all and only people who have this belief share a certain specific neural state? It makes perfectly good sense to try to find neural correlates for pains, hunger sensations, visual images, and the like, but somehow it doesn't seem to make much sense to look for the neural correlates of mental states like our sample belief or for such things as your sudden realization that your philosophy paper is due tomorrow, your hope that airfares to California will be lower after Christmas, and the like. Is it just that these mental states are so complex that it is very difficult, perhaps impossible, for us to discover their neural bases? Or is it the case that they are simply not the sort of state for which neural correlates could exist and that it makes no sense to look for them?

There is another line of consideration for being skeptical about psychophysical laws, and this has to do with the way we individuate mental states. If you are like most people, you don't know the difference between birches and beeches – that is, when you are confronted by a birch (or a beech), you cannot tell whether it is a birch or a beech. But you've heard your gardener talk about the birches in your backyard, and you believe what he says. And you are apt to utter sentences like "The birches in my yard are pretty in the fall," "Birches are nice trees to have if you have a large yard," and the like. On the basis of these utterances, we may attribute to you the belief that there are birches in your backyard, that birches are pretty in the fall, and so on. Now imagine the following counterfactual situation: Everything is identical with the story that was just told except that in this contrary-to-fact situation the words "birch" and "beech" have exchanged their meanings. That is, in the counterfactual situation, "birch" means beech, and "beech" means birch; and when your gardener, in the counterfactual situation, talks to you about the trees he calls "birches," he is talking about beeches. Now, when you utter sentences like "The birches in my yard are pretty in the fall" in this counterfactual situation, we must attribute to you not the belief that the birches in your yard are pretty in the fall but rather the belief that the birches in your yard are pretty in the fall. That is so not because you in the counterfactual world are different from you in the actual world in any intrinsic respect but because in that other world the linguistic practice in your community is different. Since "birch" means beech in that world, when you utter the word "birch" in that world, we must take you to be talking about beeches, even though nothing about you is different. (Remember that you learned to use the word "birch" from your gardener.) What all this means is that what content a given belief of yours has – for example, whether your belief is about beeches or birches – depends, at least in part but crucially, on external factors, conditions outside your skin – in this instance the linguistic practices of the community of which you are a member. That is, belief content is individuated externally, not purely internally. This in turn implies that it will not be possible to find regular, lawlike relationships between your brain states, which are entirely internal to your body, on the one hand, and beliefs as individuated by their content, on the other. If this is the case, it would be fruitless to try to discover neural correlates for beliefs....

These considerations are not intended as conclusive arguments for the impossibility of psychophysical laws but only to dispel, or at least weaken, the strong presumption we are apt to hold that there must "obviously" be such laws since mentality depends on what goes on in the brain. It is now time to turn to Davidson's famous but difficult argument against psychophysical laws, which will be presented here only in outline; for a full appreciation of the argument, you are urged to consult the original sources.[9]

A crucial premise of Davidson's argument is the thesis that the ascription of intentional states, like beliefs and desires, is regulated by certain *principles of rationality*, principles to ensure that the total set of such states ascribed to a subject will be as rational and coherent as possible. This is why, for example, we refrain from attributing to a person flatly and obviously contradictory beliefs – even when the sentences uttered have the surface logical form of a contradiction. When someone replies, "Well, I do and don't" when asked, "Do you like Ross Perot?" we do not take her to be

expressing a literally contradictory belief, the belief that she both likes and does not like Perot; rather, we take her to be saying something like "I like some aspects of Perot (say, his economic agenda), but I don't like certain other aspects (say, his international policy)." If she were to insist: "No, I don't mean that; I really both do and don't like Perot, period," we wouldn't know what to make of her utterance; perhaps her "and" doesn't mean what the English "and" means. We cast about for some consistent interpretation of her meaning because an interpreter of a person's speech and mental states is under the mandate that an acceptable interpretation must make her come out with a consistent and reasonably coherent set of beliefs – as coherent and rational as evidence permits. When we fail to come up with a consistent interpretation, we are likely to blame our unsuccessful interpretive efforts rather than accuse our subject of harboring explicitly inconsistent beliefs. We also attribute to a subject beliefs that are obvious logical consequences of beliefs already attributed to him. For example, if we have ascribed to a person the belief that Boston is less than 50 miles from Providence, we would, and should, ascribe to him the belief that Boston is less than 60 miles from Providence, the belief that Boston is less than 70 miles from Providence, and countless others. We do not need independent evidence for these further belief attributions; if we are not prepared to attribute any one of these further beliefs, we should be prepared to withdraw the original belief attribution as well. Our concept of belief does not allow us to say that someone believes that Boston is within 50 miles of Providence but doesn't believe that it is within 60 miles of Providence – unless we are able to give an intelligible explanation of how this could happen in the particular case involved. This principle, which requires that the set of beliefs be "closed" under obvious logical entailment, goes beyond the simple requirement of consistency in a person's belief system; it requires the belief system to be coherent as a whole – it must in some sense hang together, without unexplained gaps. In any case, Davidson's thesis is that the requirement of rationality and coherence[10] is of the essence of the mental – that is, it is constitutive of the mental in the sense that it is exactly what makes the mental mental.

But it is clear that the physical domain is subject to no such requirement; as Davidson says, the principle of rationality and coherence has "no echo" in physical theory. But suppose that we have laws connecting beliefs with brain states; in particular, suppose we have laws that specify a neural substrate for each of our beliefs – a series of laws of the form "N occurs to a person at t if and only if B occurs to that person at t," where N is a neural state and B is a belief with a particular content (e.g., the belief that there are birches in your yard). If such laws were available, we could attribute beliefs to a subject, *one by one*, independently of the constraints of the rationality principle. For in order to determine whether she has a certain belief B, all we need to do would be to ascertain whether B's neural substrate N is present in her; there would be no need to check whether this belief makes sense in the context of her other beliefs or even what other beliefs she has. In short, we could read her beliefs off her brain. Thus, neurophysiology would preempt the rationality principle, and the practice of belief attribution would no longer need to be regulated by the rationality principle. By being connected by law with neural state N, belief B becomes hostage to the constraints of physical theory. On Davidson's view, as we saw, the rationality principle is constitutive of mentality, and beliefs that have escaped its jurisdiction can no longer be considered mental states. If, therefore, belief is to retain its identity and integrity as a mental phenomenon, its attribution must be regulated by the rationality principle and hence cannot be connected by law to a physical substrate.

Let us assume that Davidson has made a plausible case for the impossibility of psychophysical laws (we may call his thesis "psychophysical anomalism") so that it is worthwhile to explore its consequences. One question that was raised earlier is whether it might make mental causation impossible. Here the argument could go like this: Causal relations require laws, and this means that causal relations between mental events and physical events require psychophysical laws, laws connecting mental and physical events. But psychophysical anomalism holds that there can be no such laws, whence it follows that there can be no causal relations between mental and physical phenomena. Davidson, however, is a believer in mental causation; he explicitly holds that mental events sometimes cause, and are caused by, physical events. This means that Davidson must reject the argument just sketched that attempts to derive the nonexistence of mental causation from the nonexistence of psychophysical laws. How could he do that?

What Davidson disputes in this argument is its first step, namely, the inference from the premise that *causation requires laws* to the conclusion that *psychophysical causation requires psychophysical laws*. Let's look into this in some detail. To begin, what is it for one event c to cause another event e? This holds, on Davidson's view, only if the two events instantiate a law, in the following sense: c falls under a certain event kind (or description) F, e falls under an event kind G, and there is a law connecting events of kind F with events of kind G (as cause to effect). This is in essence the widely accepted nomological model of causation: Causal connections must be supported, or subsumed, by laws. Suppose, then, that a particular mental event, m, causes a physical event, p. This means, according to the nomological conception of causation, that for some event kinds, C and E, m falls under C and p falls under E, and there is a law that connects events of kind C with events of kind E. This makes it evident that laws connect individual events only as they fall under kinds (or descriptions). Thus, when psychophysical anomalism says that there are no psychophysical laws, what it says is that there are no laws connecting mental *kinds* with physical *kinds*. So what follows is only that *if mental event m causes physical event p, the kinds, C and E, under which m and p respectively fall and that are connected by law, must both be physical kinds*. In particular, C, under which mental event m falls, cannot be a mental kind or description; it must be a physical one. This means that m is a physical event! For an event is mental or physical according to whether it falls under a mental kind or a physical kind. But this "or" is not exclusive; m, being a mental event, must fall under a mental kind, but that does not prevent it from falling under a physical kind as well. This argument applies to all mental events that are causally related to physical events, and there appears to be no reason not to think that every mental event has some causal connection, directly or via a chain of other events, with a physical event. All such events, on Davidson's argument, are physical events.[11]

That is Davidson's "anomalous monism." It's a monism because it claims that all events, mental events included, are physical events (you will recall this as "token physicalism"). Moreover, it is physical monism that does not require psychophysical laws; in fact, as we just saw, it is based on the nonexistence of such laws. Davidson's world, then, looks like this: It consists exclusively of physical objects and physical events, but some physical events (and presumably some physical objects, too) also fall under mental kinds (or have mental properties) and therefore are mental events. Laws connect physical kinds and properties, thereby generating causal connections among individual events, and these causal nexus are what gives structure to the world.

Property Epiphenomenalism and the Causal Efficacy of Mental Properties

One of the premises from which Davidson derives anomalous monism is the claim that mental events are causes and effects of physical events. On anomalous monism, however, to say that a mental event m is a cause of a physical event p (p may be mental or physical) amounts only to this: m has a physical property Q such that an appropriate law connects Q (or events with property Q) with some physical property P of p. Since no laws exist that connect mental and physical properties, purely physical laws must do all the causal work, and this means that individual events can enter into causal relations only because they possess physical properties that figure in laws. Consider an example: Your desire for a drink of water causes you to turn on the tap. On the nomological model of causation, this requires a law that subsumes the two events, your desire for a drink of water and your turning on the tap. However, psychophysical anomalism says that this law must be a physical law, since there are no laws connecting mental-event kinds with physical-event kinds. Hence, your desire for a drink of water must be redescribed physically – that is, an appropriate physical property of your desire must be identified – before it can be brought under a law. In the absence of psychophysical laws, therefore, it is the physical properties of mental events that determine, wholly and exclusively, what causal relations they enter into. In particular, the fact that your desire for a drink of water is a desire for a drink of water – that is, the fact that it is an event of this mental kind – seems to have no bearing at all on its causation of your turning on the tap. What actually does the causal work is its physical properties – perhaps the fact that it is a neural event of a certain kind.

It seems, then, that under anomalous monism mental properties are causal idlers with no work to do. To be sure, anomalous monism is not epiphenomenalism in the classic sense, since mental events are allowed to be causes of other events. The point is that it is an epiphenomenalism about *mental properties* – we may call it "mental property epiphenomenalism"[12] – in that it renders mental properties and kinds causally irrelevant. At least it has nothing to say about how mental properties might be causally relevant, while affirming that every event that enters into a causal relation does so on account of its physical properties. To make this vivid: If you were to redistribute mental properties over the events of this world any way you please – you might even remove them entirely from all events, making them purely physical – that would not alter the network of causal relations of this world in the slightest way; it would not add or subtract a single causal relation anywhere in the world!

This shows the great importance of properties in the debate over mental causation: It is the causal efficacy of mental properties that we need to vindicate and give an account of. With mental substances out of the picture, there are only mental properties left to play any causal role, whether these are construed as properties of events or of objects. If mentality is to do any causal work, it must be the case that having a given mental property rather than another, or having it rather than not having it, must make a causal difference; it must be the case that an event, because it has a certain mental property (e.g., being a desire for a drink of water), enters into a causal relation (e.g., it causes you to look for a water fountain) that it would otherwise not have entered into.

Thus, the challenge posed by Davidson's psychophysical anomalism is to answer the following question: How can anomalous mental properties, properties that are not fit for laws, be causally efficacious properties? It would seem that there are only two ways of responding to this challenge: First, we may try to reject its principal premise, namely, psychophysical anomalism, by finding faults with Davidson's argument and then offering plausible reasons for thinking that there are indeed laws connecting mental and physical properties; second, we may try to show that the nomological conception of causality – in particular as it is understood by Davidson – is not the only concept of causality and that there are alternative conceptions of causation on which mental properties, though anomalous, could still be causally efficacious. Let us explore the second possibility.

Can Counterfactuals Help?

There indeed is an alternative approach to causation that on the face of it does not seem to require laws, and this is the counterfactual account of causation. According to this approach, to say that event *c* caused event *e* is to say that if *c* had not occurred, *e* would not have occurred. The idea that a cause is the *sine qua non* condition, or *necessary* condition, of its effect is a similar idea. This approach has much intuitive plausibility. The overturned space heater caused the house fire. Why do we say that? Because if the space heater had not overturned, the fire would not have occurred. What is the basis of saying that the accident was caused by a sudden braking on a rain-slick road? Because we think that if the driver had not suddenly stepped on his brakes on the wet road, the accident would not have occurred. In such cases we seem to depend on counterfactual ("what if") considerations rather than laws. Especially if you insist on exceptionless "strict laws," as Davidson appears to, we obviously are not in possession of such laws to support these perfectly ordinary and familiar causal claims. The situation seems the same when mental events are involved: There is no mystery about why I think that my desire for a drink of water caused me to step into the dark kitchen last night and stumble over the sleeping dog. I think that because I believe the evidently true counterfactual "If I had not wanted a drink of water last night, I wouldn't have gone into the kitchen and stumbled over the dog." In confidently making these ordinary causal or counterfactual claims, we seem entirely unconcerned about the question whether there are laws about wanting a glass of water and stumbling over a sleeping dog. Even if we were to reflect on such questions, we would be undeterred by the unlikely possibility that such laws exist or can be found. To summarize, then, the idea is this: We know that mental events, in virtue of their mental properties, can, and sometimes do, cause physical events because we can, and sometimes do, know appropriate psychophysical counterfactuals to be true. And mental causation is possible because such counterfactuals are sometimes true.

Does this solve the problem of mental causation? Before you embrace it as a solution, you should consider the following line of response. If "*c* caused *e*" just *means* "If *c* had not occurred, *e* would not have occurred," neither could "ground" the other; that is, neither could be offered as an explanation of how the other can be true. That George is an unmarried adult male cannot in any sense be a ground for, or explain, George's being a bachelor. Here there is a single fact expressed in two trivially equivalent ways. The same goes, on the counterfactual approach, for "My desire for a drink of water caused my walking into the kitchen" and "If I had not wanted a drink of water, I would not have walked into the kitchen." If we are concerned about how the first could be true, then we should be equally concerned about how the second could be true. For the two sentences express the same fact. So at this stage the counterfactual approach itself amounts to nothing more than a reaffirmation of faith in the reality of mental causation.

The counterfactualist will likely retort as follows: The counterfactual account goes beyond a mere reaffirmation of mental causation, for it opens up the possibility of accounting for mental causation in terms of an account of how mental–physical counterfactuals can be true. To show that there is a special problem about mental causation, you must show that there is a special problem about the truth of these counterfactuals. Moreover, by adopting the counterfactual strategy, we divorce mental causation from contentious questions about psychophysical laws.

This reply is fair enough. So are there special problems about these psychophysical counterfactuals? There are many philosophical puzzles and difficulties surrounding counterfactuals, especially about their "semantics" – that is, conditions under which counterfactuals can be evaluated as true or false. There are two main approaches to counterfactuals: (1) the nomic-derivational approach and (2) the possible-world approach. On the nomic-derivational approach, a counterfactual conditional, "If *P* were the case, *Q* would be the case," is true just in case the consequent, *Q*, of the conditional can be logically derived from its antecedent, *P*, when taken together with laws and, possibly, auxiliary statements of conditions holding on the occasion.[13] Consider an example: "If this match had been struck, it would have lighted." This counterfactual is true since (let us assume) its consequent "the match lighted" can be derived from its antecedent "the match was struck" in conjunction with the law "Whenever a dry match is struck in the presence of oxygen it lights" taken together with the auxiliary statements "The match was dry" and "There was oxygen present."

It should be immediately obvious that on this analysis of counterfactuals, the counterfactual account of mental causation won't make the problem of mental causation go away. For the truth of the psychophysical counterfactuals, like "If I had not wanted to check out the strange noise, I would not have gone downstairs" and "If Jones's C-fibers had been activated, she would have felt pain," would require laws that would enable the derivation of the physical consequents from their psychological antecedents (or vice versa), and it is difficult to see how any laws could serve this purpose unless they were psychophysical laws, laws connecting mental with physical phenomena. On the nomic-derivational approach, therefore, the problem of psychophysical laws arises all over again.

So let us consider the possible-world approach to counterfactuals. In a simplified form, it says this: The counterfactual "If P were the case, Q would be the case" is true just in case Q is true in the world in which P is true and that, apart from P's being true there, is as much like the actual world as possible (to put it another way: Q is true in the closest P-world).[14] In other words, to see whether or not this counterfactual is true, we go through the following steps: Since this is a counterfactual, its antecedent, P, is false in the actual world. We must go to a possible world ("world" for short) in which P is true and see if Q is also true there. But there are many worlds in which P is true – that is, there are many P-worlds – and in some of these Q will be true and in others false. So which P-world should we pick in which to check on Q? The answer: Pick that P-world which is the most similar, or the closest, to the actual world. The counterfactual "If P were true, Q would be true" is true if Q is true in that world; it is false otherwise.

Let's see how this works with the counterfactual "If this match had been struck, it would have lighted." In the actual world, the match wasn't struck; so suppose that the match was struck (this means, go to a world in which the match was struck), but keep other conditions the same as much as possible. Certain other conditions must also be altered under the counterfactual supposition that the match was struck: For example, in the actual world the match lay motionless in the matchbox and there was no disturbance in the air in its vicinity, so these conditions have to be changed to keep the world consistent as a whole. However, we need not, and should not, change

the fact that the match was dry and the fact that sufficient oxygen was present in the ambient air. So in the world we have picked, the following conditions, among others, obtain: The match was struck, it was dry, and oxygen was present in the vicinity. The counterfactual is true if and only if the match lighted in that world. Did the match light in that world? In asking this question, we are asking which of the following two worlds is closer to the actual world:[15]

W_1: The match was struck; it was dry; oxygen was present; the match lighted.

W_2: The match was struck; it was dry; oxygen was present; the match did not light.

We would judge, it seems, that of the two W_1 is closer to the actual world. But why do we judge this way? Because, it seems, we believe that in the actual world there is a lawful regularity to the effect that when a dry match is struck in the presence of oxygen it ignites, and W_1, but not W_2, respects this regularity. So in judging that this match, which in fact was dry and bathed in oxygen, would have lighted if it had been struck, we seem to be making crucial use of the law just mentioned. If in the actual world dry matches, when struck, seldom or never light, there seems little question that we would go for W_2 as the closer world and declare the counterfactual "If this match had been struck, it would have lighted" to be false. It is difficult to see what else could be involved in our judgment that W_1, not W_2, is the world that is closer to the actual world other than these considerations of lawful regularities.

Consider a psychophysical counterfactual: "If Brian had not wanted to check out the noise, he wouldn't have gone downstairs." Suppose that we take this counterfactual to be true, and on that basis we judge that Brian's desire to check out the noise caused him to go downstairs. Consider the following two worlds:

W_3: Brian didn't want to check out the noise; he didn't go downstairs.

W_4: Brian didn't want to check out the noise; he went downstairs anyway.

If W_4 is closer to the actual world than W_3 is, that would falsify our counterfactual. So why should we think that W_3 is closer than W_4? In the actual world, Brian wanted to check out the noise and went downstairs. As far as these two particular facts are concerned, W_4 evidently is closer to the actual world than W_3 is. So why would we hold W_3 to be closer and hence the counterfactual to be true? The only plausible answer, again, seems to be this: We know, or believe, that there are certain lawful regularities and propensities governing Brian's wants, beliefs, and so on, on the one hand and his behavior patterns, on the other, and that given the absence of a desire to check out a suspicious noise in the middle of the night, along with other conditions prevailing at the time, his not going downstairs at that particular time fits these regularities better than the supposition that he would have gone downstairs at that time. We consider such regularities and propensities to be reliable and lawlike and commonly appeal to them in assessing counterfactuals, even though we have only the vaguest idea about the details that we would need to know to state them in an explicit and precise way.

Again, the centrality of psychophysical laws to mental causation is apparent. Although there is room for further discussion on this point, it seems at least plausible that considerations of lawful regularities governing mental and physical phenomena are crucially involved in the evaluation of psychophysical counterfactuals of the sort that can ground causal relations between the mental and the physical. We need not know the details of such regularities, but we must believe that they exist and know their rough content and shape to be able to evaluate these counterfactuals as true or false. So are we back where we started, with Davidson and his argument for the impossibility of psychophysical laws?

Not exactly, fortunately. Because the laws involved need not be laws of the kind Davidson has in mind – what he sometimes calls "strict laws." These are exceptionless, explicitly articulated laws that form a closed and comprehensive theory, like the fundamental laws of physics. Rather, the laws involved in evaluating these counterfactuals – indeed, laws on the basis of which we make causal judgments in much of science as well as in daily life – are rough-and-ready generalizations tacitly qualified by escape clauses ("*ceteris paribus*," "under normal conditions," in the absence of interfering conditions," etc.) and apparently immune to falsification by isolated negative instances. Laws of this type, often called *ceteris paribus* laws, seem to satisfy the usual criteria of

lawlikeness: As we saw, they seem to have the power to ground counterfactuals, and our credence in them is enhanced as we see them confirmed in more and more instances. Their logical form, verification conditions, and their efficacy in explanations and predictions are not well understood, but it seems beyond question that they are the essential staple that sustains and nourishes our causal discourse.

Does the recognition that causal relations involving mental events are supported by these "nonstrict," *ceteris paribus* laws solve the problem of mental causation? It does enable us to get around the anomalist difficulty raised by Davidsonian considerations – at least temporarily. We can see, though, that even this difficulty has not been fully resolved. For it may well be that these nonstrict laws are possible only if strict laws are possible and that where there are no underlying strict laws that can explain them or otherwise ground them, they remain only rough, fortuitous correlations, their lawlike appearance perhaps only illusory.

We have thus far discussed various issues about mental causation that arise from the widely accepted thesis that causal relations require backing by laws and the apparent implication of this requirement that if there is to be mind–body causation, there must be laws connecting mental and physical properties. This, however, is not the only source of difficulties for mental causation. We turn to others in the sections to follow.

The Extrinsicness of Mental States

Computers compute with 0s and 1s. Suppose you have a computer running a certain program, say, a program that monitors the inventory of a supermarket. Given a string of 0s and 1s as input (a can of Campbell's tomato soup has just been scanned by the optical scanner at a checkout station), the computer will go through a series of computations and emit an output (the count of Campbell's tomato soup cans in stock has been adjusted, etc.). Thus, the input string of 0s and 1s represents a can of Campbell's tomato soup being sold, and the output string of 0s and 1s represents the amount of Campbell's tomato soup still in stock. When the manager checks the computer for a report on the available stock of Campbell's tomato soup, the computer "reports" that the present stock is such and such, and it does so *because* "it has been told" (by the checkout scanners) that twenty-five cans have been sold so far today. And this "because" is naturally understood as signifying a causal relation.

But we also know that it makes no difference to the computer what the strings of 0s and 1s *mean*. If the input string had meant the direction and speed of wind at the local airport or the identification code of an employee or even if it had meant nothing at all, the computer would have gone through exactly the same computational process and produced the same output string. In this case the output string, too, would have meant something else, but what is clear is that the "meanings," or "representational contents," of these 0s and 1s are in the eye of the computer programmer or user, not something that is involved in the computational process. Give the computer the same string of 0s and 1s as input, and it will go through the same computational process every time and give you the same output. The semantics of these strings is irrelevant to computation; what matters is their shape, that is, their syntax. The computer is a "syntactic engine," not a "semantic engine"; it's driven by the shapes of symbols, not their meanings.

According to an influential view of psychology (known as the "computational theory of mind" or "computationalism"), mental processes are best viewed as computational processes on internal mental representations. On this view, constructing a psychological theory is like writing a computer program; such a theory will specify for each appropriate input (say, a sensory stimulus) the computational process that a cognizer will undergo to produce a certain output (say, the visual detection of an edge). But what the argument of the preceding paragraph seems to show is that on the computational view of psychology, the meanings, or contents, of internal representations make no difference to psychological processes. Suppose a certain internal representation, i, represents the state of affairs S (say, that there are horses in the field); having S as its representational content, or meaning, is the semantics of i. But if we suppose, as is often done on the computational model, that internal representations form a languagelike system, i must also have a syntax, or formal structure. So if our considerations are right, it is the syntax of i, not its semantics, that determines the course of the computational process involving i. The fact that i means that there are horses in the field rather than, say, that there are lions in the field, is of no causal relevance to what other representations issue from

i. The computational process that i initiates will be wholly determined by i's syntactic shape. But this is to say that the *contents* of our beliefs and desires and of other propositional attitudes have no causal relevance for psychology; it is only their syntax that makes a difference to what they cause.

This difficulty is independent of computationalism and can be seen to arise for any broadly physicalist view of mentality. Assume that beliefs and desires and other intentional states are neural states (this only assumes token physicalism, the thesis that every instance, or "token," of a mental state is a physical "token" state, and not the reductionist type physicalism). Each such state, in addition to being a neural state with biological/physical properties, has a specific content (e.g., that water is wet or that Bill Clinton is left-handed). That a given state has the content it has is a *relational*, or *extrinsic*, *property* of that state; for the fact that your belief is about water or about Clinton is in part determined by your causal-historical association with water and Clinton. Let us consider what this means and why it is so.

Suppose there is in some remote region of this universe another planet ("twin earth") that is exactly like our earth except for the following fact: On twin earth there is no water, that is, no H_2O, but an observably indistinguishable chemical substance, XYZ, fills the lakes and oceans there, comes out of the tap in twin-earthian homes, and so on. Each of us has a doppelganger there who is an exact molecular duplicate of us (let us ignore the inconvenient fact that your twin there has XYZ molecules in her body where you have H_2O molecules in your body). On twin earth, people speak twin English, which is just like English, except for the fact that the twin-earthian "water" means XYZ, not water, and when twin earthians utter sentences containing the expression "water," they are talking about XYZ, not water. Thus, twin earthians have thoughts about XYZ, where earthians have thoughts about water, and when you believe that water is wet, your twin-earthian doppelganger has the belief that XYZ is wet, even though you and she are molecule-for-molecule duplicates. And when you think that Bill Clinton is left-handed, your twin thinks that the twin-earthian Bill Clinton (he is the president of the twin-earth United States) is left-handed. And so on. The differences in earthian and twin-earthian beliefs (and other intentional states) are due not to internal physical or mental differences but rather to their relationship to the different objects and conditions in their environment, including their past interactions with them. Content properties, therefore, are extrinsic, not intrinsic, properties of your internal states; they depend on your causal history and your relationships to the particular objects and events in your surroundings. States that have the same intrinsic properties – the same neural/physical properties – may have different contents if they are embedded in different environments. Further, an identical internal state that lacks an appropriate relationship to the external world may have no representational content at all.

But isn't it plausible to suppose that behavior causation is "local" and depends only on the intrinsic neural/physical properties of these states, not their extrinsic relational properties? Someone whose momentary neural/physical state is exactly identical with yours will emit the same behavior, say, raise the right arm, whether or not her brain state has the same content as yours or even if it had no content at all, as long as her state is identical with yours in all intrinsic neural/physical details. This raises doubts about the causal relevance of contents: The properties of our mental states involved in behavior causation are plausibly expected to be local and intrinsic, but contents of mental states are relational and extrinsic (and perhaps also historical). This, then, is another problem of mental causation; it challenges us to answer the question "How can extrinsic mental properties be causally efficacious in behavior causation?"

Various attempts have been made to reconcile the extrinsicness of contents with their causal efficacy, but it is fair to say that none of the available proposals offers a perspicuous and wholly adequate solution to this problem. The problem has turned out to be a highly complex one involving many issues in metaphysics, philosophy of language, and philosophy of science. We now turn to our third, and last, problem of mental causation.

The Causal Closure of the Physical Domain

Suppose, then, that we have somehow overcome the difficulties arising from the possible anomalousness and extrinsicness of mental properties. We are still not home free: There is a further challenge to mental causation that we must con-

front, one that arises from the principle, embraced by most physicalists, that the physical domain is *causally closed*. What does this mean? Pick any physical event, say, the decay of a uranium atom or the collision of two stars in distant space, and trace its causal ancestry or posterity as far as you would like; the principle of causal closure of the physical domain says that this will never take you outside the physical domain. Thus, no causal chain involving a physical event will ever cross the boundary of the physical into the nonphysical: If x is a physical event and y is a cause or effect of x, then y, too, must be a physical event. Another (somewhat weaker) way of putting the point would be this: If a physical event has a cause at time t, it has a physical cause at t. Thus, if the closure principle, in either form, holds, to explain the occurrence of a physical event we never need to go outside the physical domain.

Contrast this with the Cartesian picture: According to Cartesian interactionist dualism, a causal chain starting with a physical event could very well leave the physical domain and enter the mental domain (physical-to-mental causation), meander there for a while (mental-to-mental causation), and then return to the physical domain (mental-to-physical causation). This means that mental and physical events occur as links in the same causal chain and that to give a full causal explanation of why a physical event occurred, we sometimes have to go outside the physical domain and look for its mental cause. It follows, then, that *on Cartesian dualism there can be no complete physical theory of the physical domain*. To explain some physical events, you must go outside the physical realm and appeal to nonphysical causal agents and laws governing their behavior! Complete physics would in principle be impossible, even as an idealized goal. On the Cartesian model, the mental domain would not be closed either, and neither physics nor psychology could be pursued independently of the other.

Most physicalists will find the Cartesian model unacceptable if not incoherent; they accept the causal closure of the physical not only as a fundamental metaphysical doctrine but as an indispensable methodological presupposition of the physical sciences. If you reject it, you are buying into the Cartesian picture, a picture that no physicalist could tolerate. For it depicts the mental domain as an ontological equal of the physical domain; the two domains coexist side by side, causally interacting with each other, and there is no reason to call such a position physicalism rather than mentalism. Any physicalist must acknowledge the primacy of the physical in some robust sense, and the violation of the physical causal closure undermines that primacy.

If the causal closure of the physical domain is to be respected, it seems prima facie that mental causation must be ruled out – unless mental events and properties are somehow brought into the physical domain. But if they are part of the physical domain, doesn't that mean that they *are* physical properties and events? If so, that would be reductionism pure and simple. But this is a prospect that most philosophers, including many physicalists, find uncomfortable; they want to hold that although only physical things and events exist in this world, certain complex physical systems (e.g., biological organisms) and events (e.g., neural events) can have physically irreducible mental properties. Is there, then, a way of bringing the mental close enough to the physical so that the causal closure principle is not violated and yet not fully into it, so that the dreaded reductionism is avoided?

Mind–Body Supervenience and Causal/Explanatory Exclusion

As we have seen, functionalists think of mental properties as "physically realized," and that makes mental properties almost physical but not quite (or so functionalists think). We also saw how the functionalist conception of mental properties as second-order properties having physical properties as their realizers gives rise to difficulties in explaining the causal powers of mental properties. Let us here focus on another aspect of the functionalist conception shared by many nonfunctionalists as well: the idea that mental properties are *supervenient* on physical properties. Mind–body supervenience is the thesis that any two things, or events, that are exactly alike in all physical respects cannot differ in mental respects. That is to say, there can be no mental difference unless there is a physical difference. The idea that each mental-event or -state kind has a neural substrate or correlate, too, is a form of mind–body supervenience: It assumes that if two organisms are in identical neural states, they cannot be in different mental states. We can think of the neural substrate of mental property M as its "supervenience base"

or "base property," that is, the physical base on which it supervenes. Note the following points about supervenience thus conceived: (1) If N is a neural state on which mental property M supervenes, then N is a sufficient condition for the occurrence of M (that is, as a matter of law, whenever an organism is in N, it is in M);[16] (2) M can have multiple supervenience bases, $N_1, N_2, \ldots$, each of which is sufficient to give rise to M (this is analogous to the functionalist idea of multiple realizability of the mental); (3) M is distinct from each of its many bases, $N_1, N_2, \ldots$.

According to some philosophers, mind–body supervenience gives us the right kind of physicalism: It respects the primacy of the physical by giving a clear sense to the idea that the physical determines the mental. Without the instantiations of appropriate physical properties, no mental property can be instantiated, and what particular mental properties are instantiated depends wholly on what physical properties happen to be instantiated. And yet, in view of (3) above, mental properties remain distinct from their physical base properties. But does mind–body supervenience help with mental causation? Does it bring the mental close enough to the physical to allow mind–body causation and yet manage to avoid mind–body reductionism?

The sharp and sudden pain I felt in my elbow caused me to wince. Mind–body supervenience says that the pain has a supervenience base, a certain neural state N. (We can also think of N as the pain's neural substrate or realizer.) So the situation looks like thzis:

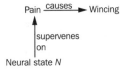

If neural state N is a supervenience base for pain, it is lawfully sufficient for pain. If, therefore, pain is a sufficient cause of wincing, there seems ample reason to conclude that N, too, is causally sufficient for wincing (by the transitivity of nomic/causal sufficiency). That is, there seems to be an excellent reason for thinking that N is a cause of wincing. On the standard nomological conception of causation, this conclusion is inescapable. Thus, we now have the following picture:

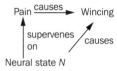

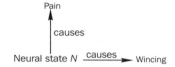

Does this mean that the wincing has *two distinct causes*, the pain and neural state N? This seems not credible. For that would mean that the wincing is *causally overdetermined*; in fact, it would follow that all cases of mental causation are cases of overdetermination, which is difficult to believe. And it doesn't make sense to think of the pain as an intermediate link in a causal chain starting from N and terminating at the wincing; for the pain and the occurrence of N are perfectly simultaneous, and it makes no sense to think of a causal chain or mechanism leading from N to the pain. The former supervenes on, or is realized by, N, not caused by it.

In this situation, moreover, the causal role of the pain is in danger of preemption by N. This is "the problem of causal/explanatory exclusion": For any single event, there can be no more than a single sufficient cause, or causal explanation, unless it is a case of causal overdetermination.[17] If we trace the causal chain backward from the wincing, we are likely to reach N first, not the pain. It is incoherent to think that the pain somehow directly, without an intervening chain of physiological processes, acted on certain muscles, causing them to contract; that would be telekinesis, a strange form of action at a distance! If the pain is to have a causal role here, it must somehow ride piggyback on the causal chain from N to the wincing. It is implausible in the extreme to think that there might be two independent causal paths here, one from N to the wincing and the other from the pain to the wincing.

Given these considerations, how could we fit the pain into this causal picture? We now see that the diagram above presents an unstable picture: The causal relations it depicts are not together coherent, and we must somewhat redraw the diagram to get a coherent picture of the situation. What are the options?

1   *The epiphenomenalist model.* This treats the pain as an epiphenomenon of neural state N, denying it a causal role in the production of the wincing. N taken by itself is a full cause of it. The following diagram represents this proposal.

We have already discussed the viability of epiphenomenalism as a solution to the mind–body problem.

2   *The model of supervenient causation.* This approach views the pain's claim as a cause of the wincing *as consisting in* its supervenience on neural state N, which causes a certain physiological event on which the wincing supervenes. More generally, it takes causal processes at the microlevel as fundamental and considers causal processes at the macrolevel as dependent, or supervenient, on those at the microlevel. The following diagram represents this approach:

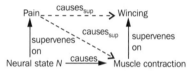

In this diagram "causes$_{sup}$" is to be read "superveniently causes" or "is a supervenient cause of"; the broken arrows represent this relation. As the diagram indicates, the pain supervenes on N and the wincing supervenes on the contraction of a certain group of muscles; the pain's causation of wincing consists in its supervenience base N's causing the muscle contraction, which is the supervenience base of the wincing. The latter causal relation is fully physical, and we are supposing here that there is no special problem about physical causation. Further, we may speak of the pain as a supervenient cause of the wincing as well, since its supervenience base causes it. In general, then, an instantiation of a property is a supervenient cause of an event in virtue of the fact that its supervenience base causes that event.

How does this differ from the epiphenomenalist model? What is the difference between saying that the pain is an epiphenomenon of N and saying that the pain is a supervenient cause? An advocate of the present approach will point out, first of all, as has been noted, that it is wrong to think of pain as a cpausal effect of N; although the pain depends on

N for its existence, this dependence is not happily viewed as causal – it isn't as though the pain is brought about by N through an intervening causal chain (what would such a causal chain look like?). The dependence involved is more like the way the rigidity of a steel rod depends on its molecular structure than the way the expansion of its length depends on its being heated. Second, it will be pointed out that this model of supervenient causation applies to all macrocausal relations, not just those involving mental causes. Heating this kettle of water causes the water to boil. How does this happen? The increase in the water temperature is supervenient on certain molecular processes (something like the water molecules' moving with increasing velocities), and these molecular processes causally lead to violent ejections of water molecules into the air, upon which the macrophenomenon, the boiling, supervenes. This means that mental events as supervenient causes are as causally robust as macrophysical phenomena, that is, the familiar physical phenomena of daily experience. The fact that macrocausation is implemented at the microlevel doesn't show, the advocate of this approach will argue, that macrophenomena are robbed of their causal efficacy. If the mental can be shown to have a causal status equal to that of macrophysical phenomena, why isn't that a suffi-cient vindication of their causal relevance and effi-cacy?[18]

3 *The reductionist model.* The simplest solution, and in many ways the most elegant one, is reductionism. The reductionist identifies pain with neural state N. Since pain $= N$, there is here only one cause of the wincing, and all the puzzles with our original triangular diagram vanish. And pain of course has all the causal powers of N, and its causal powers are fully vindicated. The following diagram represents the reductionist proposal:

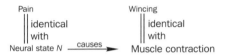

The fact that reductionism delivers the simplest solution to the problem of mental causation is probably the best argument in favor of it. But it may not be a sufficient argument, for reductionism has been rejected by a majority of philosophers of mind for what they take to be compelling reasons. We will look into the issues concerning reductive and nonreductive physicalism in a later chapter as well as some further issues involving mental causation.

Further Reading

Donald Davidson's "Mental events," "Psychology as philosophy," and "The material mind," all reprinted in his *Essays on Actions and Events* (New York: Oxford University Press, 1980), are the sources of anomalous monism. See Jaegwon Kim, "Psychophysical laws," in Kim, *Supervenience and Mind* (Cambridge: Cambridge University Press, 1993), for an explication and analysis of Davidson's argument for the anomalism of the mental. On the problem of mental causation associated with anomalous monism, see Ernest Sosa, "Mind–Body interaction and supervenient causation," *Midwest Studies in Philosophy* 9 (1984): 271–81; Louise Antony, "Anomalous monism and the problem of explanatory force," *Philosophical Review* 98 (1989): 153–8. Davidson's response is contained in his "Thinking causes," in *Mental Causation*, ed. John Heil and Alfred Mele (Oxford: Clarendon Press, 1993). This volume also contains rejoinders to Davidson by Kim, Sosa, and Brian McLaughlin, as well as a number of other interesting papers on mental causation.

For counterfactual-based accounts of mental causation, see Ernest LePore and Barry Loewer, "Mind mat-ters," *Journal of Philosophy* 84 (1987): 630–42; Terence Horgan, "Mental quausation," *Philosophical Perspectives* 3 (1989): 47–76.

On mental causation and wide and narrow content, see Fred Dretske, *Explaining Behavior* (Cambridge Mass.: MIT Press, 1988); Tyler Burge, "Individualism and causation in psychology," *Pacific Philosophical Quarterly* 70 (1989): 303–22.

On supervenience and mental causation, see Jaegwon Kim, "Epiphenomenal and supervenient causation," in Kim, *Supervenience and Mind*; Brian McLaughlin, "Event supervenience and supervenient causation," *Southern Journal of Philosophy* 22 (1984), the Spindel Conference Supplement: 71–92; Peter Menzies, "Against causal reductionism," *Mind* 97 (1988): 551–74; Gabriel Segal and Elliott Sober, "The causal efficacy of content," *Philosophical Studies* 63 (1991): 1–30; Stephen Yablo, "Mental causation," *Philosophical Review* 101 (1992): 245–80; Cynthia Macdonald and Graham Macdonald, "Introduction: supervenient causation," in *Philosophy of Psychology*, ed. Cynthia Macdonald and Graham Mac-donald (Oxford: Blackwell Publishers, 1995). Yablo's paper is also useful on the issue of causal/explanatory exclusion. John Heil's *The Nature of True Minds* (Cambridge: Cambridge University Press, 1992), ch. 4,

includes an interesting and wide-ranging discussion of mental causation.

Notes

1 For a systematic development of this approach, see J. W. Atkinson and D. Birch, *The Dynamics of Action* (New York: Wiley, 1970).

2 In Donald Davidson, "Actions, reasons, and causes," reprinted in his *Essays on Actions and Events* (New York: Oxford University Press, 1980). For important noncausal approaches, see G. H. von Wright, *Explanation and Understanding* (Ithaca, NY: Cornell University Press, 1971); George M. Wilson, *The Intentionality of Human Action* (Stanford: Stanford University Press, 1989); Carl Ginet, *On Action* (Cambridge: Cambridge University Press, 1990).

3 Samuel Alexander, *Space, Time, and Deity* (London: Macmillan, 1920), vol. 2, p. 8.

4 René Descartes, *The Philosophical Writings of Descartes*, vol. 1, eds. John Cottingham, Robert Stoothoff, and Dugald Murdoch (Cambridge: Cambridge University Press, 1985), pp. 59–60.

5 René Descartes, *The Passions of the Soul* I, 41, in ibid., vol. 2, p. 343.

6 Ibid., p. 238.

7 *The Essential Descartes*, ed. Margaret Wilson (New York: New American Library, 1969), p. 373.

8 More precisely, Davidson's claim is that there are no "strict laws" connecting psychological and physical phenomena. He now explicitly allows the existence of nonstrict psychophysical laws, qualified by *ceteris paribus* clauses. See his "Thinking causes" in *Mental Causation*, ed. John Heil and Alfred Mele (Oxford: Clarendon Press, 1993). The present discussion is not intended as an exact exegesis of Davidson's position.

9 See Davidson's "Mental events," "Psychology as philosophy," and "The material mind," all reprinted in *Essays on Actions and Events*. For an interpretive reconstruction of Davidson's argument, see Jaegwon Kim, "Psychophysical laws," in Kim, *Supervenience and Mind* (Cambridge: Cambridge University Press, 1993).

10 This is a form of what is often called "the principle of charity"; Davidson also requires that an interpretation of a person's belief system must make her beliefs come out largely *true*.

11 In "Mental Events" Davidson defends the stronger thesis that there are no laws at all about mental phenomena, whether psychophysical or purely psychological, and it is his view that the laws (or "strict laws," as he calls them) can be found only in basic physics. A sharp-eyed reader will have noticed that Davidson's argument here requires this stronger thesis, since the argument as it stands leaves open the possibility that the two causally connected events *m* and *p* instantiate a purely psychological law.

12 Brian McLaughlin calls it "type epiphenomenalism" in his "Type epiphenomenalism, type dualism, and the causal priority of the physical," *Philosophical Perspectives* 3 (1989): 109–36.

13 See Ernest Nagel, *The Structure of Science* (New York: Harcourt, Brace & World, 1961), ch. 4; J. L. Mackie, "Counterfactuals and causal laws," in *Analytic Philosophy*, ed. R. J. Butler (Oxford: Blackwell Publishers, 1962).

14 For fuller statements of this approach, see Robert Stalnaker, "A theory of conditionals," reprinted in *Conditionals*, ed. Frank Jackson (Oxford: Oxford University Press, 1991); David Lewis, *Counterfactuals* (Cambridge, Mass.: Harvard University Press, 1973).

15 These worlds are very much underdescribed, of course; we are assuming that the worlds are roughly the same in other respects.

16 If some mental states are "extrinsic" in the sense of the preceding section, they are likely to fail to supervene on local neural states. The present discussion may be considered restricted to those mental states that do supervene on neural states.

17 See Jaegwon Kim, "Mechanism, purpose, and explanatory exclusion," in Kim, *Supervenience and Mind*.

18 For further discussion, see Jaegwon Kim, "Epiphenomenal and supervenient causation," in Kim, *Supervenience and Mind*; also Brian McLaughlin, "Event supervenience and supervenient causation," *Southern Journal of Philosophy* 22 (1984), the Spindel Conference Supplement: 71–92; Peter Menzies, "Against causal reductionism," *Mind* 97 (1988): 551–74; Gabriel Segal and Elliott Sober, "The causal efficacy of content," *Philosophical Studies* 63 (1991): 1–30.

Type Epiphenomenalism, Type Dualism, and the Causal Priority of the Physical

Brian P. McLaughlin

1 Two Kinds of Epiphenomenalism

Sixty-three years ago, C. D. Broad distinguished two kinds of epiphenomenalism. He said:

> Epiphenomenalism may be taken to assert one of two things. (1) That certain events which have physiological characteristics have *also* mental characteristics ... And that an event which has mental characteristics never causes another event in virtue of its mental characteristics, but only in virtue of its physiological characteristics. Or (2) that no event has both mental and physiological characteristics; but that the complete cause of any event which has mental characteristics is an event or set of events which has physiological characteristics. And that no event which has mental characteristics is a cause–factor in the causation of any other event whatever, whether mental or physiological. (1925, p. 472)

(The inserted numerals are mine.) The following distinction is inspired by Broad's (1) and (2) respectively:

> *Type Epiphenomenalism* (Type-E). (a) Events can be causes in virtue of falling under physical types, but (b) events cannot be causes in virtue of falling under mental types.
> *Token Epiphenomenalism* (Token-E). (i) Physical events can cause mental events, but (ii) mental events cannot cause anything.

The "cannot" here is that of at least causal impossibility; and "event" is used in a broad sense that includes states as well as changes.

Both types of epiphenomenalism deny the mental a place in the causal order, though in different ways. Token-E implies that mental events cannot have causal efficacy: in no causally possible world does a mental event cause anything. Type-E implies that events cannot have causal efficacy *qua* mental: in no causally possible world does an

event cause anything in virtue of falling under a mental type. Thus, while according to Token-E, mental events cannot be causes, according to Type-E, mental event types are not, so to speak, causal powers.

Conjunct (ii) of Token-E implies conjunct (b) of Type-E: if mental events cannot be causes, then events cannot be causes in virtue of falling under mental types. (The reason is obvious: if an event can cause something in virtue of falling under a mental type, then an event can be both a cause and a mental event.) The converse, however, may well not hold: (b) may well not imply (ii). It will not if a mental event can cause something in virtue of falling under a nonmental event type. For, then, mental events can be causes, even if they cannot be causes *qua* mental.

But suppose that mental events can participate in causal relations in virtue of falling under nonmental types. Then, one can coherently reject Token-E while embracing Type-E. Indeed, in the past twenty years or so, a variety of views of the mental have been proposed that deny Token-E but either assert or are silent about Type-E: for example, certain functionalist views of the mental, Donald Davidson's Anomalous Monism (Davidson 1980e), Keith Cambell's "new" epiphenomenalism (Cambell 1970, ch. 6), and James Cornman's neutral monism (Cornman 1981, pp. 234–42). These views arguably imply that mental events are causes in virtue of falling under physical event types; and they either leave open whether, or deny that, events can be causes in virtue of falling under mental types. The question of whether Type-E is true arises even for those who reject Token-E.

2 The Problematic

Recent debates about epiphenomenalism have been about Type-E, rather than about Token-E. Indeed, it is fair to say that in the last decade or so discussions of the so-called mind–body problem have focused on whether Type-E is true. And the issues involved are related to such hotly debated issues as the status of "folk psychology" and the possibility of an intentional science. So I shall focus in what follows on Type-E.

It is not my aim, however, to determine whether Type-E is true. My primary aim is far more limited: I want to consider whether certain claims that are alleged to imply Type-E in fact imply it. I shall first present the claims in question, and then cite a secondary aim.

The claims are these:

Physical Comprehensiveness. It is causally necessary that when two events causally interact, they do so in virtue of falling under physical event types.
Type Dualism. There are mental event types, and no mental event type is identical with a physical event type.

My primary concern is whether Physical Comprehensiveness and Type Dualism imply Type-E. Of course, Physical Comprehensiveness implies (a) of Type-E, the claim that events can participate in causal relations in virtue of falling under physical event types. So what is at issue is whether Physical Comprehensiveness and Type Dualism jointly imply (b), the claim that events cannot participate in causal relations in virtue of falling under mental types.

Let us say that an event type is *causal* iff in some causally possible world an event token participates in a causal relation in virtue of falling under it. And let us say that an event type is *epiphenomenal* iff it is not causal. According to Type-E, then, at least some physical event types are causal while all mental event types are epiphenomenal. The primary issue, then, boils down to this:

(Q) Do Physical Comprehensiveness and Type Dualism exclude the existence of causal mental event types?

I shall argue in due course that the answer to (Q) is "no." One can hold Physical Comprehensiveness and Type Dualism without, thereby, being committed to Type-E. My primary aim is to show this.

Of course, if Physical Comprehensiveness and Type Dualism imply (ii) of Token-E, then they imply (b) of Type-E. Physical Comprehensiveness implies that it is causally necessary that every

event that participates in a causal relation is a physical event. But Physical Comprehensiveness and Type Dualism do not, however, imply (ii) if a mental event can be identical with a physical event. I sympathize with the Davidsonian view that a concrete event can be both mental and physical. This issue has been much discussed, and I have nothing to add here to that discussion. I shall simply assume in what follows that mental events can be physical.

Even if Physical Comprehensiveness and Type Dualism do not imply (ii), however, the question remains whether they imply (b). Question (Q) has emerged in recent literature mainly, though not exclusively, in connection with Davidson's views about psychophysical causal interaction. Davidson (see, e.g., 1980a) has long been an opponent of Token-E,[1] but he has been silent about Type-E. Despite this silence, it has been fairly widely charged that his doctrines of the Anomalism of the Mental and the Principle of the Nomological Character of Causality (described below in section 4) commit him to it.[2] I shall leave open whether they do. But I shall, however, attempt to undermine a central premise in the leading argument that they do. This is my secondary aim.

So much, then, by way of setting out the problematic. Six sections remain. In section 3, I discuss Type-E. In 4, I discuss the Anomalism of the Mental and the Principle of the Nomological Character of Causality. In 5, I present the central argument that the doctrines imply that all mental event types are epiphenomenal. In 6, I digress and discuss some responses that have been made to the claim that Davidson is committed to Type-E.[3] In 7, I try to cast doubt on a central premise of the argument in question. Finally, in 8, I try to make a case that Physical Comprehensiveness and Type Dualism do not imply Type-E.

3 Type Epiphenomenalism

Type-E is, perhaps, a less familiar doctrine than Token-E; so let us consider Type-E in more detail.

To begin, it is fairly widely held that the relata of the causal relation are event tokens but that they participate in causal relations in virtue of falling under event types. The idea is that while event tokens participate in causal transactions, such transactions must be *grounded* or *backed* by appropriate type-type relations. There is no received view about what sorts of type-type relations count as appropriate for grounding singular causal transactions. But whatever view is correct, an event type is causal iff it participates in a causation grounding relationship. So, Type-E is true iff at least some physical event types enter into causation grounding relationships and no mental event type does.

We need not decide here what sorts of type-type relations are singular causation grounding. But, to help fix our ideas, let us consider a leading view. According to nomic subsumption views of causation, events causally interact in virtue of instantiating event types that are nomologically related. On this view, causation requires laws that are such that if events fall under them, the events, thereby, count as causally related.[1] Such laws are *causal* laws. An analysis of the notion of a *causal* law would specify the features in virtue of which a law is such that when events fall under it, they, thereby, count as causally related. Whether a non-circular analysis of the notion is possible need not concern us here. The point to note for present purposes is just this: given a nomic subsumption view of causation, if Type-E is true, then physical event types do and mental event types do not figure in the causal laws of this world.

Suppose, then, that a nomic subsumption view of causation is correct. Then, figuring as a partial or complete cause-factor in a causal law suffices being a causal event type. To elaborate, if an event type C figures in a causal law as a *complete* cause-factor for the realization of a type E, then it is a causal law that whenever C is realized, E is, and C, thereby, counts as a causal event type. Suppose that an event type C figures in a causal law as a *partial* cause-factor for the realization of an event type E. Then, there is a condition D such that (i) the realization of D logically requires the realization of C and (ii) the realization of D nomologically suffices for the realization of E. For example, suppose it is a causal law that whenever F and G are realized, then H is. Then, the joint realization of F and G (in the same circumstance) nomologically suffices for the realization of H. So, F figures in the law in question as a partial cause-factor for the realization of H, and thereby counts as a causal event type. Suppose that it is a causal law that whenever F is realized, then, *ceteris paribus*, H is. (Events count as falling under a *ceteris paribus* law, of course, only if the *ceteris paribus* condition is satisfied in the circumstances of their occurrence.) Then, F figures as a partial cause-factor in the

ceteris paribus law for the realization of H. And F, thereby, counts as a causal event type.

Finally, suppose that *only* nomological relationships between types count as causation grounding. (As we shall see in section 7, this implies but is not implied by a nomic subsumption view of causation.) Then, Type-E is true iff there are physical causal laws and no mental event type is a partial or complete cause-factor in a causal law. So much, then, by way of presenting a leading view of causation grounding relations.

Following Broad, I used the locution "in virtue of" in formulating Type-E. While widely used in philosophical literature, the locution admittedly calls for explication. So, I shall close this section with a partial explication of it.

What is it, for instance, for some x to A in virtue of B-ing? I suggest the following initial answer: x As in virtue of B-ing iff that x Bs makes it true that x As. But this just shifts the burden to explicating "make it true that." So let us consider the in virtue of relation in more detail.

To begin, let us note some of its modal properties. If x As in virtue of B-ing, then either x's B-ing suffices for x's A-ing or else x's B-ing is necessary for something, x's C-ing, that occurs on the occasion in question and that suffices for x's A-ing. X can A in virtue of B-ing, however, even if B-ing is not required for A-ing. For example, one can live in New Jersey in virtue of living in New Brunswick, even though living in New Brunswick is not required for living in New Jersey. Likewise, a macro-property P might be realized in virtue of the realization of a micro-property $m(P)$, even if P is "multiply realizable" at the microlevel in question, and so the realization of $m(P)$ is not required for P's realization.

The in virtue of relation cannot be understood in modal terms alone. If x As in virtue of B-ing, then there must be an *appropriate explanatory connection* between x's A-ing and x's B-ing. As Quine has correctly noted "in virtue of" "is almost 'because of'" (1974, pp. 8–9).[5] Indeed, statements employing "in virtue of" imply statements employing "because." If Tim lives in New Jersey in virtue of living in New Brunswick, then he counts as living in New Jersey because he lives in New Brunswick. If an object has a certain temperature T in virtue of having a certain mean-kinetic energy E, then it counts as having T because it has E. Similarly, if two events are causally related in virtue of falling under certain event types, then they count as causally related because they fall under the types in question. Thus we sometimes explain why something counts as *A-ing* by citing the fact that it *B*s, or why a group of things count as *A-ing* by citing the fact that they *B*s. I suggest that: *x As* in virtue of *B-ing* if *x* counts as *A-ing* because *x Bs*. The kind of explanatory connection involved can vary. In the micro–macro case, it is something like "material causation," while in the case of event types and singular (efficient) causal transactions, it is something like "formal causation." In any case, a full explication of the in virtue of relation is a topic for a theory of explanation and need not be pursued further here.[6]

So much, then, by way of explicating Type-E. Turn to the doctrines of Davidson that are alleged to imply it.

4 The Davidsonian Doctrines Alleged to Imply Type-E

They are:

The Anomalism of the Mental. There are no strict psychological or psychophysical laws.[7]
The Principle of the Nomological Character of Causality. If events are causally related, they fall under a strict law.

It is uncertain what Davidson intends the modal status of these doctrines to be. But, for the sake of argument, I shall follow Davidson's critics in taking the intended modal force of the doctrines to be that of logical (or analytical, or conceptual) necessity.

Both doctrines employ the notion of a strict law. How to understand the notion is a topic for Davidsonian scholarship. I have discussed it at length elsewhere (McLaughlin 1985). But as will become clear, nothing will turn here on the details of what makes a law strict. Some remarks will, however, help to fix our ideas.

Davidson holds that laws are true, counterfactual supporting generalizations that are confirmable by their positive instances. He characterizes the notion of a strict law in terms of the notion of a closed comprehensive theory (1980e, p. 219, and pp. 223–4; and 1980f, p. 230). A theory *T* is *closed* iff events within the domain of *T* causally interact only with other events within the domain of *T*. A theory *T* is *comprehensive* only if whenever an event within its domain participates in a causal interaction, that interaction is subsumed by some law of *T*. Let us say that a set of terms is the *minimal*

vocabulary of a closed comprehensive theory iff it is the vocabulary of such a theory and no proper subset of it is. The notion of a strict law can be understood, then, as follows: a law is a *strict* law iff it is couched solely in the minimal vocabulary of a closed comprehensive theory or it can be derived via bridge laws from laws couched solely in such a vocabulary (cf. McLaughlin, 1985, pp. 342–8).[8] One of the main ideas underlying The Principle of the Nomological Character of Causality (hereafter, "The Principle of Causality") is that whenever two events are causally related, their causal interaction is subsumed by a law that is a nonredundant part of a comprehensive system of laws. According to Davidson, such a system will be couched in the minimal vocabulary of a closed comprehensive theory or in terms reducible to the terms of such a theory.

Davidson claims that physics *promises* to be closed and comprehensive (1980e, pp. 223–4). The idea is, I take it, that an ideally completed physics would be closed and comprehensive. (Hereafter, I shall drop the qualifier "ideally completed"). If so, laws couched in its minimal vocabulary and laws derivable from such laws by means of bridge laws would be strict. Moreover, Davidson explicitly claims that *most of science* employs non-strict laws (1980c, p. 219). He holds that *only* the vocabulary of physics is the minimal vocabulary of a closed comprehensive theory; and he doubts that even the vocabulary of biology can be reduced via bridge laws to terms in such a vocabulary, though he acknowledges that he does not know how to show this (Davidson 1980c, p. 241). (He maintains that he can show, however, that mental terms do not reduce via bridge laws to terms in such a vocabulary; but whether he can show that need not concern us here.)[9] Suppose that, indeed, only the vocabulary of physics is the minimal vocabulary of a closed comprehensive theory. Then, all strict laws are either laws of physics or derivable from such laws via bridge laws.

In any case, be all this as it may, it should be mentioned that The Principle of Causality and the claim that all strict laws are physical laws together imply that every event that participates in a causal relation with a physical event is a physical event. (Thus they imply that the physical is causally closed: physical events causally interact only with other physical events.) And the Anomalism of the Mental (hereafter, "Anomalism") and this version of token physicalism constitute Davidson's doctrine of Anomalous Monism (see McLaughlin

1985). This is the doctrine that (a) every event that causally interacts with a physical event is a physical event and that (b) there are no strict psychological or psychophysical laws. So much, then, by way of presenting Davidson's views.

Of course, whether The Principle of Causality and Anomalism are true is a question beyond the scope of this essay. My concern here is not with their truth, but rather with whether they jointly imply Type-E.

5   The Central Argument

One finds in the critical literature on the Davidsonian views in question a family of arguments that Anomalism and The Principle of Causality imply Type-E. One argument in the family is this: Anomalism implies Type Dualism. The Principle of Causality implies Physical Comprehensiveness. Type Dualism and Physical Comprehensiveness imply Type-E. So, Anomalism and The Principle of Causality imply Type-E. I won't challenge the claims that The Principle of Causality implies Physical Comprehensiveness and that Anomalism implies Type Dualism. But it should be noted that Physical Comprehensiveness and Type Dualism seem far more widely held than Anomalism and The Principle of Causality. And if former doctrines do indeed imply Type-E, commitment to Type-E would be fairly widespread even among realists about the mental. Consider Fodor's popular account (1974, and 1979 "Introduction") of the relationship between the special sciences and physical theory. On this account, it is causally necessary that whenever events within the domain of a special science causally interact, they do so in virtue of falling under some physical causal law or other. Moreover, Fodor maintains that nomic properties of the special sciences are typically not identical with nomic properties of physical theory. If Physical Comprehensiveness and Type Dualism implied Type-E, then Fodor's account of the special sciences would imply that nomic properties of the special sciences are typically epiphenomenal. It would follow that the laws of the special sciences are typically noncausal.[10] (This shocking conclusion should tip one off that something is rotten in Denmark.)

In the final section of the essay, I shall, as I mentioned earlier, challenge the claim that Type Dualism and Physical Comprehensiveness imply Type-E. The point to note now is that even if they

do *not* imply Type-E, Anomalism and The Principle of Causality still might. For even if strict laws must be physical laws, The Principle of Causality *logically* requires subsumption under a physical law, while Physical Comprehensiveness only causally requires subsumption under a physical law. In this section, I want to examine an argument in the family of arguments in question that is *specifically aimed* at proponents of Anomalism and The Principle of Causality. (Once we see why this argument fails, we will be in a position to see why Physical Comprehensiveness and Type Dualism do not imply Type-E.)

Before explicitly stating the argument in question, it is useful to turn first to some philosophers who charge Davidson with commitment to Type-E. I shall present a large sample of characteristic passages in which he is so charged. The reasons why I present a large sample will emerge in section 6, where I argue that the responses that have been made to Davidson's critics are inadequate; so please bear with me.

Ted Honderich (1982, p. 62) says that a "causally relevant property" is a property in virtue of which an event can enter into a causal relationship. He espouses a principle he calls "the Principle of the Nomological Character of Causally Relevant Properties," which asserts that only *nomic* properties are causally relevant. According to Honderich, The Principle of Causality implies this principle; and this principle together with Anomalism excludes there being causally relevant mental properties. Citing a debt to Honderich, Frederick Stoutland says:

> Davidson's view amounts to the claim that events are causes only in virtue of their having certain properties – namely, properties which figure in causal laws – nomic properties. His view that all causal laws are physical means that only *physical* properties are nomic. A reason cannot, therefore, cause an action in virtue of its psychological properties, for those are nonnomic; there are no nomological ties between the psychological and the physical. But if a reason causes an action only in virtue of its physical properties, then the psychological as psychological has no causal efficacy. (1985, p. 53)

Essentially the same concerns lead Jaegwon Kim to say that given Anomalism and The Principle of Causality, an event's

> causal powers are wholly determined by the physical description or characteristic that holds

for it; for it is under its physical description that it may be subsumed under a causal law. And Davidson explicitly denies any possibility of a nomological connection between an event's mental description and its physical description that could bring the mental into the causal picture. (1984b, p. 267)

He claims that Davidson "fails to provide an account of psychophysical causation in which the mental *qua mental* has any real causal role to play" (1984b, p. 267). Kim initiates his discussion of Davidson's position by saying that it is "strikingly similar" to Broad's version (1) of epiphenomenalism (quoted at the outset of the essay),[11] according to which "an event which has mental characteristics never causes another event in virtue of its mental characteristics, but only in virtue of its physiological characteristics." I take it that Kim holds that for the mental *qua* mental to have "a real causal role to play," at least some mental properties would have to be properties in virtue of which events can be causes. And he holds that The Principle of Causality and Anomalism imply that no mental property can be such a property. Similarly, Ernest Sosa says:

assuming the anomalism of the mental, though my extending my hand is, in a certain sense, caused by my sudden desire to quench my thirst, it is not caused by my desire qua desire but only by my desire qua *neurological* event of a certain sort. (1984, p. 278)

According to Sosa (1984, p. 279), an event, *c*, *qua* possessor of some property *P*, causes an event *e*, *qua* possessor of some property *Q*, only if *P* and *Q* figure in a law of the sort that can ground causal relations. And he holds that given The Principle of Causality and Anomalism, no event can cause another *qua* possessor of a mental property. Finally, Mark Johnston remarks that:

According to anomalous monism if there are mental properties or types none of them figure in laws. (In the formal mode, no mental predicate figures in any statement of law.) (1985, p. 423)

And he holds that, given The Principle of Causality and Anomalism, the *truth* of any singular causal statement can be "accounted for" only by laws that relate physical properties. He concludes

from this that "There is then a clear sense in which, according to anomalous monism, no mental properties are causally relevant" (1985, p. 424). This completes my sample survey.

(These authors speak of properties rather than event types. But nothing turns on this. Let us say that the property of being an event of a certain type is causal iff the event type is causal. And let us mean by a "mental property," a property of falling under a mental event type. So, given our broad use of "event type," the property of being a belief that water is wet, for example, counts as a mental property.)

The leading argument that emerges here is this: The Principle of Causality implies that only nomic properties are causal. Anomalism implies that no mental properties are nomic. So Anomalism and the Principle of Causality imply that no mental properties are causal, that is, that mental properties are epiphenomenal.

It should be noted first of all, however, that The Principle of Causality and Anomalism are claims about *strict* laws. As I have argued elsewhere (McLaughlin 1985, pp. 342–8), understanding the distinction between strict and non-strict laws is essential to understanding The Principle of Causality and Anomalism. In every paper in which Davidson discusses Anomalism, and in all of his published replies to commentaries on those papers, he is careful to distinguish strict laws from non-strict laws (see 1980c, pp. 240–1; 1980e, p. 219; 1980f, pp. 230–1; 1980g, p. 250). While all strict laws are laws, not all laws are strict. However the notion of a strict law is to be understood, it is compatible with Anomalism that there are non-strict psychological and psychophysical laws. And if there are, then there are nomic mental properties. So The Principle of Causality and Anomalism do not themselves exclude the existence of nomic mental properties.

Indeed, Davidson explicitly claims that there are psychological laws (see, e.g., 1980g, p. 250). He says, however, that such laws, "unlike those of physics, cannot be sharpened without limit, cannot be turned into the strict laws of a science closed within its area of application" (1980g, p. 250). Moreover, he holds that there are psychophysical laws, but that they are either only "roughly true" or "insulated from counterexample by generous escape clauses" (1980e, p. 219). And he says that "psychophysical generalizations must be treated as irreducibly statistical in character, in contrast to sciences where in principle exceptions can be taken care of by refinements couched in a homogenous vocabulary" (1980c, p. 240).[12] If I understand him, Davidson holds that there are non-strict psychological and psychophysical laws. But whether or not he holds this, as I said, it is compatible with Anomalism and The Principle of Causality that there are such laws.

Davidson's critics, for the most part, ignore his distinction between strict and non-strict laws. [13] The leading reason is, I suspect, this: they hold that even if it is compatible with The Principle of Causality and Anomalism that some mental properties are nomic, it is incompatible with these doctrines that there are *causal* mental properties. For, they hold, I suspect, that The Principle of Causality commits Davidson to the view that non-strict laws, if there are such, cannot be *causal* laws. Recall that, by stipulation, a causal law is a law such that if events fall under it, they, thereby, count as causally related. The critics maintain that the Principle of Causality implies that only strict laws are causal laws in this sense. If so, the existence of non-strict psychological or psychophysical laws is indeed irrelevant to whether there are causal mental properties or types. For non-strict nomological relationships will, then, not be causation grounding. It is for this reason, I suspect, that the distinction between strict and non-strict laws is so often ignored.

Even if Anomalism does not exclude the existence of nomic mental properties, it excludes the existence of strictly nomic mental properties. And if only strict laws are causation grounding, then only strictly nomic properties are causal. The argument under consideration, then, can be recast so as to make explicit reference to strictly nomic properties. Pedantically, it can be recast as follows:

(I) (p1) The Principle of Causality implies that only strictly nomic properties are causal.

(p2) Anomalism implies that no mental property is a strictly nomic property.

(c) Thus, The Principle of Causality and Anomalism imply that no mental property is a causal property (i.e., that mental properties are epiphenomenal).

Premise (p2) is true. I shall argue in due course, however, that (p1) is false and so that (I) is unsound.

A point should be stressed here, however, to avert possible misunderstanding: nothing I say in

arguing that (p1) is false will turn on the distinction between strict and non-strict laws. While understanding this distinction is essential to understanding Anomalism and The Principle of Causality, it is *not* essential to understanding why (p1) is false. Nothing will turn on my having recast the premises of the argument in terms of strictly nomic properties. For The Principle of Causality does not even imply that only *nomic* properties are causal. Even if there are neither strictly nomic nor non-strictly nomic mental properties, that fact and The Principle of Causality would not exclude the existence of causal mental properties or types. For it is compatible with The Principle of Causality that events can participate in causal relations in virtue of instantiating non-nomic properties. Premise (p1) implies this: The Principle of Causality implies that only nomic properties are causal. And this weaker claim is also false. More about this in section 7.

6 Some Would-be Defenses of Davidson

Let us first consider some recent responses to the charge that Davidson is committed to Type-E. (This section can be skipped without losing the thread of my argument against (p1).)

Norman Melchert (1986, pp. 267–74) defends Davidson by claiming that Davidson denies there are mental properties. Presumably, Melchert holds that since Davidson denies this, he does not hold that mental properties are epiphenomenal. It should be added that it is far from certain whether, when push comes to shove, Davidson thinks there are *any* properties at all, mental or physical. But conjunct (b) of Type-E does not imply that there are mental properties. It implies that if there are mental properties, they are epiphenomenal. And that concerns some friends of properties.

Moreover, Davidson (e.g., 1980e, pp. 210–11) holds that events can satisfy mental descriptions or open sentences, that mental predicates can be true of events. Nothing of relevance in what follows essentially turns on whether they are true of events in virtue of the fact that the events' have the properties expressed by the predicates. As Davidson's critics recognize, their argument can be recast in the formal mode for those with scruples about countenancing properties. It can be recast this way: The Principle of Causality implies that events can participate in causal relations only in virtue of satisfying strictly nomic descriptions. Anomalism implies that no mental description is strictly nomic. So The Principle of Causality and Anomalism imply that no event can participate in a causal relation in virtue of satisfying a mental description.

Turn, then, to a different reply to Davidson's critics. Ernest LePore and Barry Loewer claim that the charge of epiphenomenalism leveled by Honderich, Stoutland, Kim, Sosa, and Johnston, among others,

> rests on a simple, but perhaps not obvious, confusion. The confusion is between two ways in which properties of an event c may be said to be causally relevant and irrelevant. (1987, p. 634)

Abbreviating "Anomalous Monism" as AM, and treating The Principle of Causality as a subthesis of Anomalous Monism, they say:

> The heart of our response to the claim that AM is committed to epiphenomenalism is this: AM entails that mental features are causally irrelevant$_1$, but does not entail that they are causally irrelevant$_2$. (1987, pp. 635–6)

They claim that properties F and G are causally relevant$_1$ to c's causing e just in case c's having F and e's having G *makes it the case* that c causes e (1987, pp. 634–5). The notion of causal relevance$_2$ is introduced as follows: "Relevance$_2$ is a relation among c, one of its properties F, e, and one of its properties G. It holds when c's being F brings it about that e is G" (1987, p. 635). They explicate this last notion by appeal to certain kinds of counterfactual dependency relationships. And they say: "AM is compatible with there being counterfactual dependencies between events in virtue of their mental properties" (1987, p. 641). They hold that Anomalism and The Principle of Causality are consistent with the claim that mental properties can be causally relevant$_2$. It is in this way, they maintain, that, on Davidson's view, "mind can matter."

The charge made by Honderich, Stoutland, Kim, Sosa, and Johnston does not, however, rest on a confusion between causal relevance$_1$ and causal relevance$_2$. These authors do not deny that mental properties can be causally relevant$_2$. Rather, as the earlier quotes reveal, they deny that mental properties can be causally relevant$_1$. Recall that properties F and G are causally relevant$_1$ to c's causing e iff c's having F and e's

having G makes it the case that c causes e. The critics in question all essentially argue that Anomalism and The Principle of Causality imply that an event's having a mental property cannot *make it the case* that it causes another: it is in this way, they claim, that "mind cannot matter" on Davidson's view. If an event c causes an event e in virtue of c's having F and e's having G, then c's having F and e's having G makes it the case that c causes e. So if mental properties cannot be relevant$_1$ to any singular causal transaction, then they are not causal properties. Thus in conceding that on Davidson's view, mental properties are invariably irrelevant$_1$, LePore and Loewer, thereby, concede that mental properties are epiphenomenal in the sense at issue.

Let us see why LePore and Loewer maintain that Davidson is committed to the causal irrelevance$_1$ of mental properties. First, they hold that, given that he holds The Principle of Causality, he is committed to the following: c's having F and e's having G makes it the case that c causes e only if F and G figure in a strict law (1987, p. 631). So they hold that The Principle of Causality implies that relevant$_1$ properties must be strictly nomic. And they hold that Anomalism implies that mental properties cannot be strictly nomic. So, they hold that Anomalism and The Principle of Causality imply that mental properties cannot be relevant$_1$. As we saw, if a property cannot be relevant$_1$, then it is not a causal property. LePore and Loewer are thus committed to the view that Anomalism and The Principle of Causality imply Type-E for essentially the reasons stated in argument (I). If I am right that (p1) of (I) is false, then LePore and Loewer fail to show that Davidson is committed to the irrelevance$_1$ of mental properties.

Of course, it may well be that mental properties can be relevant$_2$. But, be this as it may, as LePore and Loewer acknowledge, relevance$_2$ does not suffice for relevance$_1$. They should be viewed as attempting to mitigate severity of the charge of Type-E rather than as attempting to refute it. Their main point seems to be that while Davidson cannot hold that mental properties can be properties in virtue of which events participate in causal relations, he can hold that mental properties can be causally relevant$_2$; and that that should satisfy realists about the mental. Whether Lepore and Loewer succeed in mitigating the severity of the charge that Davidson is committed to Type-E is, however, not my concern here.[14] My concern is with whether the charge can be made to stick.

7 Premise (P1) Examined

Consider, once again, premise (p1): The Principle of Causality implies that only strictly nomic properties are causal. I am unaware of any argument for (p1) in the literature. So let us start by addressing the following question: Why might one think (p1) is true?

To begin, recall The Principle of Causality: if events are causally related, then they fall under a strict law. As I mentioned, Davidson's critics take the modal force of this claim to be that of logical (or analytical, or conceptual) necessity. (Hereafter, to avoid prolixity, I shall, for the most part, drop "analytical" and "conceptual.") They understand the principle to be stating a logically necessary singular causation-making property: namely, the property of falling under a strict law. Thus, they understand The Principle of Causality to state that it is logically necessary that if events are causally related, they are so in virtue of falling under a strict law. Whether Davidson intends The Principle of Causality to be understood in this way is, I think, doubtful. (He nowhere, for instance, speaks of events being causally related *in virtue of* falling under strict laws.) But, for the sake of argument, let us understand The Principle of Causality in the way in question. If I understand proponents of (I), then, they take The Principle of Causality (so understood) to imply this:

Exclusion Principle. Events are causally related *only* in virtue of falling under strict laws.

Of course, the Exclusion Principle implies that only strictly nomic properties are causal. So if The Principle of Causality implies the Exclusion Principle, it implies that too. On the other hand, if The Principle of Causality does not imply the Exclusion Principle, it leaves open whether properties other than strictly nomic properties can be causal. Premise (p1) is true, then, iff The Principle of Causality implies the Exclusion Principle. I shall now try to make a case that it does not.

By an "*A*-making property," let us mean a property in virtue of which something is A. Then, of course, if a logically necessary *A*-making property is *ipso facto* the only *A*-making property, then The Principle of Causality indeed implies the Exclusion Principle. However, as I shall argue shortly, it is not the case that a property is *ipso facto* the only *A*-making property if it is a logically

necessary *A*-making property. Of course, showing this would not *demonstrate* that The Principle of Causality does not imply the Exclusion Principle. But I think that the assumption that a logically necessary *A*-making property is *ipso facto* the only *A*-making property lies behind the view that The Principle of Causality implies the Exclusion Principle. It is hard to see what other reason one might think that the former principle, *by itself*, implies the latter. So I shall try to undermine the claim that The Principle of Causality implies the Exclusion Principle by arguing that the assumption in question is false.

For starters, note that it is not the case that a necessary *A*-making property is *ipso facto* the only *A*-making property. If one lives in New Jersey, then one does so in virtue of living in some county of New Jersey. But it is not the case that one can live in New Jersey only in virtue of living in a county of New Jersey. For one can live in New Jersey in virtue of living in a city of New Jersey. To take an example involving metaphysical necessity, suppose that if something has a certain temperature T, then it has it in virtue of having a certain mean-kinetic energy E. This would not imply that something can have T only in virtue of having E. For this is compatible with something having T in virtue of having a property that is not identical with the property of having E. There may be some micro property $m(E)$ whose realization counts as the realization of E, but whose realization is not required for E's realization. For E may be multiply realizable at the level of $m(E)$. Yet something could have a certain temperature T in virtue of having $m(E)$. To take an example involving logical (or analytical, or conceptual) necessity, if one is a brother, then one is so in virtue of being a male sibling. But one can be a brother in virtue of possessing a property that is not identical with the property of being a male sibling. For example, the property of being a male with a sister is not identical with the property in question, and one can be a brother in virtue of being a male with a sister. Thus, being a male sibling is not the only brother-making property, despite the fact that it is a logically necessary brother-making property. To belabor the point, on standard accounts of basic actions, if one acts, then one does so in virtue of performing some basic action or other. But there are non-basic actions, and one can of course act in virtue of performing one. We see, then, that even if B is a logically (or analytically, or conceptually) necessary *A*-making property, it does not follow that B is the only A-making property. I contend that The Principle of Causality leaves open whether falling under a strict law is the only singular causation making property. The Principle of Causality does not imply the Exclusion Principle. The former principle does not itself exclude the existence of causal properties that are not strictly nomic. A proponent of The Principle of Causality can consistently hold, for instance, that the fact that two events are subsumed by a certain non-strict law makes it the case that they are causally related; that is, a proponent can consistently hold this provided that events are subsumed by the non-strict law only if they are subsumed by some strict law or other.

Indeed, The Principle of Causality does not even exclude the existence of non-nomic causal properties. For it leaves open whether there are non-nomological causation grounding relations. The Principle of Causality does not imply that only strict laws are causation grounding, or even that only laws are causation grounding. What it implies, rather, is that whenever events are causally related in virtue of falling under a causation grounding relation, they are causally related in virtue of falling under some strict law or other. (It is easy to see why: if two events instantiate a causation grounding relationship, then they are causally related. And, given The Principle of Causality, if two events are causally related, they fall under some strict law or other.)

A general point should be noted. According to nomic subsumption views of causation, events are causally related iff they fall under a causal law. Such views do not, however, thereby, imply that only causal laws are causation grounding. It is compatible with such views that falling under a causal law is not the only causation-making property. Nomic subsumption views do not, for example, exclude the possibility that there are certain kinds of counterfactual dependency relationships that can ground singular causal transactions. But such views imply that if events participate in a causal transaction in virtue of participating in a counterfactual dependency relationship, then participating in that relationship requires falling under some causal law or other. Nomic subsumption views do not imply that all causal properties or event types are nomic. What they imply, rather, is that if an event participates in a causal relation in virtue of having a certain property, then the event participates in the relation in virtue of having some nomic property or other. And this leaves open whether an event can participate in a causal relation in virtue of having a non-nomic property.

To sum up my main point, then: The Principle of Causality does not by itself imply the Exclusion Principle. So, (p1) is false. And since it is, (I) is unsound.

Now what type-type relations ground singular causal relations is a question for the theory of causation. Davidson does not attempt to offer a complete answer to it. For, as we have seen, The Principle of Causality leaves open whether there are causation grounding relationships that are not strictlaws. The only requirement that The Principle of Causality imposes on such type-type relations is that whenever they are instantiated by events, some strict law or other is instantiated by the events.

We need not decide here how Davidson might provide a complete account of causal properties. Nevertheless, it is instructive to ask how a proponent of Anomalism and The Principle of Causality might defend the claim that there are causal mental properties. One natural suggestion is that he or she might first claim that a property is a causal property in virtue of and only in virtue of figuring as a partial or complete cause factor in a causal law. Recall that Anomalism does not exclude there being mental properties that figure in non-strict laws. A proponent of the Principle of Causality and of Anomalism might then try to argue that Type-E is false on the grounds that some mental properties figure in non-strict causal laws.[15] For if a mental property figures in a non-strict causal law, it is a causal property. Moreover, as we saw, The Principle of Causality is compatible with the claim that there are non-nomic causal properties. So it is also open to a proponent of The Principle of Causality and of Anomalism to try to argue that there are non-nomic, but causal, mental properties.

Of course, if a proponent of the Principle of Causality and of Anomalism rejects the Exclusion Principle, and so maintains that there are indeed causation grounding type-type relations that are not strict laws, he or she must *argue* that when events instantiate such relations, they instantiate some strict law or other. An argument for the Principle of Causality would yield such an argument. For, given The Principle of Causality, if causation requires falling under a strict law, then falling under a causation grounding relationship requires falling under a strict law. But the point is that if there are causation grounding relationships that are not strict laws, an argument for The Principle of Causality must show that such relationships require the instantiation of some strict law or other in order to be instantiated. It would have to be argued that causation grounding relationships that are not strict laws (say, non-strict causal laws) are *non-basic* causation grounding relationships in that they require the instantiation of some distinct causation grounding relationship (a strict law) in order to be instantiated.

The point to underscore, however, is that Davidson's position on causation is more flexible than his critics acknowledge. As we saw, The Principle of Causality does not imply the Exclusion Principle. In seeing this, we see that Davidson is relieved of a burden. For while he must defend The Principle of Causality, he need not defend the Exclusion Principle. And that is all to the good since the latter principle at least seems widely implausible: it would, for instance, count most of the nomic properties of the special sciences as epiphenomenal. To be sure, The Principle of Causality is also open to challenge. But a defense of this principle need not be burdened with a defense of the Exclusion Principle. And any plausible defense of The Principle of Causality would, I believe, allow for causation grounding relationships that are not strict laws. Any such defense would, then, proceed, in part, by showing why such relationships require the instantiation of a strict law to be instantiated. Whether and how this can be done must, however, be left open here.

Finally, it is worthwhile making the obvious point that even if (I) is unsound, The Principle of Causality and Anomalism might, in conjunction with certain (at least causally) necessary truths about causal properties, imply Type-E. For example, despite the fact that The Principle of Causality is compatible with the existence of non-strict causal laws and Anomalism is compatible with the existence of psychological and psychophysical laws, it *may* of course be the case that the doctrines in question in conjunction with certain necessary truths about causal properties imply that there are no psychological or psychophysical *causal* laws. But to show that this *is* indeed the case, it would have to be shown that the Exclusion Principle follows from the doctrines and the truths in question.[16] My main point is that The Principle of Causality does not itself imply the Exclusion Principle. From the fact that falling under a strict law is a logically necessary causation making property,

it does not follow that it is the only causation making property. And by arguing that (I) is unsound, I hope to have hit the ball into the other court. As I mentioned at the outset, I leave open whether Davidson is committed to Type-E. But if he is, he is not so committed for the reasons given in (I). His position on causation has more flexibility than his critics acknowledge.[17]

8   Return to Question Q

My primary concern in this essay, recall, is to see whether the epiphenomenality of mental properties is implied by the following claims:

> *Physical Comprehensiveness.* It is causally necessary that when events are causally related, they are so in virtue of falling under physical event types.
> *Type Dualism.* There are mental event types, and no mental event type is identical with a physical event type.

Thus, recall our earlier question:

(Q) Do Physical Comprehensiveness and Type Dualism exclude the existence of causal mental event types?

The answer to this question is "yes" iff Physical Comprehensiveness implies that only physical event types are causal. For suppose that it does. Then, given Type Dualism, no mental type is causal. Suppose Physical Comprehensiveness does not imply that only physical types are causal. Then, even granting Type Dualism, it remains an open question whether there are causal mental types. So the answer to (Q) turns on whether Physical Comprehensiveness implies that only physical types are causal.

It should be easy to see now that Physical Comprehensiveness does not imply this. As we saw earlier, a logically necessary A-making property is not *ipso facto* the only A-making property. It follows that a causally necessary A-making property is not *ipso facto* the only A-making property. Even if following under a causation grounding physical type-type relation is causally necessary for one event to cause another, it does not follow that only physical type-type relations are causation grounding. What follows, rather, is that causation grounding relationships are either physical or, by causal necessity, require for their realization the realization of some physical causation grounding relationship or other. But an event type can, by causal necessity, require for its realization the realization of a physical event type without itself being a physical event type. This is so even if, for instance, the event type must be realized *in virtue* of the realization of some physical type. For an event type may be multiply realizable by physical types and not be identical with any physical type. Physical Comprehensiveness is compatible with events participating in causal relations in virtue of falling under nonphysical types. So Physical Comprehensiveness and Type Dualism do not exclude the existence of causal mental properties. The answer to (Q) is, in a word, "no." One can hold Physical Comprehensiveness and Type Dualism without, thereby, being committed to denying that mental events can be causes or that they can be so *qua* mental.

To be sure, a proponent of Physical Comprehensiveness and Type Dualism who rejects the claim that only physical properties are causal properties must *argue* that nonphysical causation grounding relationships *causally* require the realization of some physical causation grounding relationship or other for their realization. But how this

might be argued need not concern us here. I want to close, however, by suggesting that at least the following relationship holds between physical properties and any causal property:

Causal Priority of the Physical. For any causally possible world *w*, and for any causally possible world *w′*, if all and only the same physical properties exist in each, then all and only the same causal properties exist in each.

(Of course, a property can exist in a world without being exemplified in that world.) Given this, what nonphysical causal properties, if any, there are in a causally possible world is fixed by the physical properties of that world. But this leaves open whether there are nonphysical causal properties. Thus, suppose that the nomic properties of some special science fail to be identical with physical properties. It would not follow that the nomic properties of the special science are epiphenomenal, even if the Causal Priority of the Physical and Physical Comprehensiveness hold. Even given the truth of the doctrines in question, the laws of the special science in question may be *causal* laws, laws *in virtue of* which events participate in causal relations.[18,19]

Notes

1 See LePore and McLaughlin (1985) for a detailed discussion of Davidson's view that reasons are causes and that rationalization is a species of causal explanation.

2 The literature is vast, but see especially Stoutland (1976, 1985); Honderich (1982, 1983); Kim (1984); Sosa (1984); and Johnston (1985).

3 I discuss Melchert (1986) and LePore and Loewer (1987).

4 On some views of causal laws, falling under a causal law does not suffice for being causally related, other conditions must be satisfied. For example, the events must be appropriately spatio-temporally related in ways that need not be specified in a causal law. For a discussion of this issue, see Kim's discussion of the "pairing problem" (Kim, 1973). For present purposes, we can ignore the issue.

5 Quine (1974, pp. 9–12) thinks "because" and "in virtue of" are intentional connectives of some sort, and, of course, he shies away from such connectives.

6 Frank Jackson (1977, ch. one) treats "in virtue of" as expressing a two-placed relation. I favor treating it as a nonstandard sentential connective; but I shall continue here to put matters in the material rather than

the formal mode. It should be noted, however, that the reader can choose his or her preferred way of treating "because" – as a relation or as a nonstandard connective – and treat "in virtue of" likewise.

7 Davidson explicitly restricts his discussion of the psychological to the propositional attitudes (belief, desire, intention, and the like). And so what is at issue is whether he is committed to the view that propositional attitude types are epiphenomenal. But I shall not mention this again, since it does not matter for the points I make below.

8 Two points are in order. First, I provided only a necessary condition for a theory's being comprehensive. Any statement of necessary and sufficient conditions for comprehensiveness must, I believe, invoke the notion of a *maximally explicit* law (see McLaughlin 1985, pp. 342–8). But I do not attempt such a statement here since doing so would take me too far afield of my central concerns in this essay. Second, while Davidson takes laws to be true generalizations of a certain sort, I have been treating laws as singular relations between event types. But nothing will turn on this difference in what follows. As we shall see in section 6, the central issues here can be recast in the formal mode. Suffice it for now to note that if laws

are understood to be singular relations between event types, then the above account of strict law can be recast as an account of what makes a statement expressing a law the expression of a strict law.

9　I examine Davidson's *argument* for the claim that all strict laws are physical and point out some gaps in the argument in McLaughlin (1985, pp. 348–60); but it is not my concern here whether in fact all strict laws are physical.

10　Fodor (1987b) maintains that the special sciences employ causal laws, laws that can back or ground singular causal relations.

11　I owe the Broad quotation to Kim.

12　As I mentioned in note 7, Davidson restricts his discussion of the psychological to the propositional attitudes. So a point should be noted here so as to avert possible misunderstanding. I am not suggesting that Davidson takes the vocabulary of the propositional attitudes to be a promising one for a scientific psychology. Davidson gives reasons for doubting the prospects of a scientific propositional attitude psychology in (1980c). For present purposes, suffice it to note that a scientific psychology *may* have to be framed in other terms. In any case, this alone is no reason to doubt that there are nonstrict laws that invoke propositional attitudes. And Davidson does not, I think, doubt that there are.

13　One possible exception is Stoutland (1985, 51–3), though he does not actually speak of strict and nonstrict laws.

14　But I do not think that they succeed in this either. To see why, consider the following. First of all, they define relevance$_2$ (1987, p. 635) as follows: c's being F brings it about that e is G iff (1) c causes e, (2) c is F and e is G, (3) if c were not F, then e would not be G, and (4) c's being F and e's being G are logically and metaphysically independent. And they note that (1)–(4) would have to be supplemented to handle preemption and overdetermination. (Note by the way that any essential property of c will be causally relevant$_2$ to e's being G, provided (1) and (4) hold, and barring preemption and overdetermination.) Embracing a Lewis–Stalnaker view of counterfactuals, they hold that the sort of counterfactual cited in (3) is true iff in all the most similar worlds to the actual world it fails to be the case that c (or a counterpart of c) is F. And they correctly note that there are two ways that it may fail to be the case in a world that c (or a counterpart of c) is F. One way is if c (or a counterpart of c) occurs but is not F. Another way is if c fails to occur altogether (and no counterpart of c occurs). Given this and some quite plausible assumptions, however, mental properties can be relevant$_2$ if and only if mental events can be causes. The implication from left to right is, of course, trivial: given that relevance$_2$ requires that conditions (1) and (2) be satisfied, if mental properties can be relevant$_2$, mental events can be causes.

On two plausible assumptions, we can establish the implication from right to left. The first assumption is that if a mental event m causes a physical event p, then barring overdetermination and preemption, if m had not occurred, p would not have occurred. The second is that it *can* happen that all the most similar worlds to ours in which it failed to be the case that c (or a counterpart of c) is M are worlds in which c fails to occur (and no counterpart of c occurs). Given these assumptions, mental properties can be relevant$_2$ if mental events can be causes. I won't pursue how LePore and Loever might try to revise their definition to avoid this since, for one thing, I am uncertain what intuitive notion they are attempting to capture. For another, I am not concerned here with whether the severity of the charge of Type-E can be mitigated.

15　LePore and Loewer respond to Honderich at one point by claiming that Davidson can allow that there are non-strict causal laws (1987, pp. 637–8). However, Honderich and the other critics in question seem to hold that if a law is causal, then the properties it invokes can be causally relevant$_1$ to a singular causal transaction: for falling under a causal law makes it the case the events are causally related. LePore and Loewer do not think that Davidson can hold that there are non-strict causal laws in *this* sense. Rather, they hold that Davidson can hold that there are psychological and psychophysical *ceteris paribus* generalizations that are true, counterfactual supporting, and confirmable by their positive instances. But Davidson's critics need not deny this. LePore and Loewer's disagreement with Davidson's critics, on this point at least, is, I believe, merely verbal.

16　As I say below, it seems enormously plausible that causal properties must supervene on physical properties. It is, of course, an open question whether psychophysical supervenience is compatible with Anomalism (see Kim 1984; Sosa 1984; and McLaughlin 1985). I think that these claims are compatible since I think that psychophysical supervenience does *not* imply the existence of *strict* psychophysical laws. But this issue is beyond the scope of this essay.

17　Moreover, as I said at the outset, I leave open here whether Type-E is true. A wide variety of arguments have been offered for Type-E. And I have not even mentioned here what I take to pose the most serious threat of Type-E. If content fails to supervene on what's in the head, the question of whether intentional mental properties are epiphenomenal naturally arises. Suffice it to say that I think this threat too can be answered, but I leave that for another occasion. (For attempts to respond to this threat see Fodor (1987a) and Dretske (1988)

18　Of course, one would like to see an explanation of why the Causal Priority of the Physical holds, but I leave that for another occasion.

19   In addition to the help that I have cited above, I wish to thank the following for helpful discussions and/or useful comments on prior drafts: Gerald Barnes, Jerry Fodor, Gary Gleb, Jaegwon Kim, Ernest LePore, Barry Loewer, Tim Maudlin, Bradford Petrie, and the late William L. Stanton. I owe special thanks to Terence Horgan.

References

Broad, C. D. (1925) *The Mind and Its Place in Nature*, London.

Cambell, Keith (1970) *Body and Mind*, New York.

Cornman, James (1981) "A nonreductive identity theory about mind and body," in *Reason and Responsibility*, Belmont, California, Joel Feinberg ed.

Davidson, Donald (1980) *Essays on Actions and Events*, New York, Oxford.

Davidson, Donald (1980a) "Actions, reasons, and causes," reprinted in Davidson (1980).

Davidson, Donald (1980b) "Causal relations," reprinted in Davidson (1980).

Davidson, Donald (1980c) "Comments and replies," reprinted in Davidson (1980).

Davidson, Donald (1980d) "Hempel on explaining action," reprinted in Davidson (1980).

Davidson, Donald (1980e) "Mental events," reprinted in Davidson (1980).

Davidson, Donald (1980f) "Psychology as philosophy," reprinted in Davidson (1980).

Davidson, Donald (1980g) "The material mind," reprinted in Davidson (1980).

Dretske, Frederick (1988) *Explaining Behavior*, Cambridge, Bradford.

Fodor, Jerry, 1974, "The special sciences (or: the disunity of science as a working hypothesis)," *Synthese*, 28, 97–117.

Fodor, Jerry (1975) *The Language of Thought*, Cambridge, Mass., MIT.

Fodor, Jerry (1987a) *Psychosemantics*, Cambridge, Mass., MIT.

Fodor, Jerry (1987b) "Making mind matter more," presented at the Eastern Division Meetings of the American Philosophy Association as a commentary on LePore and Loewer (1987).

Honderich, Ted (1982) "The argument for anomalous monism," *Analysis*, XLII, 59–64.

Honderich, Ted (1983) "Anomalous monism: a reply to Smith," *Analysis*, XLIII.

Horgan, Terence (1981) "Token physicalism, supervenience, and the generality of physics," *Synthese*, 49.

Jackson, Frank (1977) *Perception: A Representative Theory*, Cambridge, Cambridge University Press.

Johnston, Mark (1985) "Why having a mind matters," LePore and McLaughlin (1985).

Kim, Jaegwon (1973) "Causation, nomic subsumption, and the concept of event," *Journal of Philosophy*, LXX, 217–30.

Kim, Jaegwon (1984a) "Concepts of supervenience," *Philosophy and Phenomenological Research*, XLV, 153–76.

Kim, Jaegwon (1984b) "Epiphenomenal and supervenient causation," *Midwest Studies in Philosophy*, 9, P. French, T. Uehling, Jr, and H. Wettstein, eds, Minneapolis, University of Minnesota Press.

Kim, Jaegwon (1987) " 'Strong' and 'global' supervenience revisited," *Philosophy and Phenomenological Research*, X:VIII, 315–26.

LePore, Ernest and Loewer, Barry (1987) "Mind matters," *Journal of Philosophy*, LXXXIV, 630–41.

LePore, Ernest and McLaughlin, Brian (1985) *Actions and Events: Perspectives on the Philosophy of Donald Davidson*, Blackwell Publishers.

LePore, Ernest and McLaughlin, Brian (1985) "Actions, reasons, causes, and intentions," in LePore and McLaughlin (1985).

McLaughlin, Brian (1985) "Anomalous monism and the irreducibility of the mental," in LePore and McLaughlin (1985).

McLaughlin, Brian (1983) "Event supervenience and supervenient causation," *Spindel Conference, Southern Journal of Philosophy*, 22.

Melchert, Norman (1986) "What's wrong with anomalous monism," *Journal of Philosophy*, LXXX, 265–74.

Quine, W. V. O. (1974) *The Roots of Reference*, La Salle, Ill. Open Court.

Smith, Peter (1984) "Anomalous monism and epiphenomenalism: a reply to Honderich," *Analysis*, XLIV.

Sosa, Ernest (1984) "Mind–body interaction and supervenient causation," *Midwest Studies in Philosophy*, IX, 276–81.

Stanton, William L. (1983) "Supervenience and psychological law in anomalous monism," *Pacific Philosophical Quarterly*, 64, 74–6.

Stoutland, Fred (1976) "The causation of behavior," *Essays On Wittgenstein in Honor of G. H. von Wright, Atca Philosophica Fennica*.

Stoutland, Fred (1985) "Davidson on intentional behavior," in LePore and McLaughlin (1985).

15

Wide Causation

Individualism and Supervenience

Jerry A. Fodor

After the Beardsley exhibit at the V & A, walking along that endless tunnel to South Kensington Station, I thought, why this is "behavior" – and I had said, perhaps even written: "where does 'behavior' begin and end?"

Barbara Pym

I beg your indulgence. I am about to tell you two stories that you've very probably heard before. Having once told you the stories, I will then spend most of this chapter trying to puzzle out what, if anything, they have to do either with commonsense belief/desire explanation or with RTM [the Representational Theory of Mind]. The conclusion will be: not much. That may sound pretty dreary, but I've been to parties that were worse; and there's a sort of excuse in the following consideration: the two stories I'm about to tell you have been at the center of a great lot of recent philosophical discussion. Indeed, contrary to the conclusion that I am driving toward, it is widely held that one or both stories have morals that tend to undermine the notion of content and thereby raise problems for propositional-attitude-based theories of mind.

Since these stories are so well known, I shall tell them in abbreviated form, entirely omitting the bits about the shaggy dog.

The Putnam story. Is there anyone who hasn't heard? There's this place, you see, that's just like here except that they've got XYZ where we've got H₂O. (XYZ is indistinguishable from H₂O by any causal test, though of course one could tell them apart in the chemical laboratory.) Now, in this place where they have XYZ, there's someone who's just like me down to and including his neurological microstructure. Call this guy Twin-Me. The intuition we're invited to share is that, in virtue of the chemical facts and in spite of the neurological ones, the form of words "water is wet" means something different in his mouth from what it does in mine. And, similarly, the content of the thought that Twin-Me has when he thinks (*in re* XYZ, as one might say) that water is wet is different from the content of the thought that I have when I think that water is wet *in re* H₂O. Indeed, the intuition we're invited to share is that, strictly speaking, Twin-Me can't have the thought that water is wet at all.

The Burge story. The English word "brisket," according to the Funk & Wagnalls *Standard Desk Dictionary* and other usually reliable authorities, means "the breast of an animal, esp. of one used as food" (from the Old French "bruschet," in case you were wondering). Imagine a guy – call him Oscar – who speaks English all right but who suffers from a ghastly misapprehension: Oscar believes that only certain food animals – only beef, say – have brisket; pork, according to Oscar's mistaken worldview, is *ipso facto* brisketless.

First intuition: Oscar, despite his misapprehension, can perfectly well have brisket-beliefs, brisket-desires, brisket-fears, brisket-doubts, brisket-qualms, and so forth. In general: If the butcher can bear attitude *A* toward the proposition that brisket is *F*, so too can Oscar. Of course, Oscar differs from the butcher – and other speakers of the prestige dialect – in that much of what Oscar believes about brisket is false. The point, however, is that Oscar's false belief that pork isn't brisket is nevertheless a brisket-belief; it *is brisket* that Oscar believes that pork brisket isn't (if you see what I mean). From which it follows that Oscar "has the concept" BRISKET – whatever exactly that amounts to.

Now imagine an Oscar-Twin; Oscar2 is molecularly identical to Oscar but lives in a language community (and talks a language) which differs from English in the following way. In that language the phonetic form "brisket" does apply only to breast of beef; so whereas what Oscar believes about brisket is false, what Oscar2 believes about brisket2 is true.

Second intuition: Oscar2 doesn't have brisket-attitudes; it would be wrong for us – us speakers of English, that is – to say of Oscar2 that his wants, beliefs, yearnings, or whatever are ever directed toward a proposition of the form: '...brisket ....' For Oscar2, unlike his molecularly identical twin Oscar, doesn't have the concept BRISKET; he has the concept BRISKET2 (= brisket of beef, as *we* would say).

So much for the stories. Now for the ground rules: Some philosophers are inclined to claim about the Putnam story that Twin-Me actually *is* just like Me; that it's wrong to think that Twin-Me hasn't got the concept WATER. Analogously, some philosophers are inclined to say that Oscar actually is just like Oscar2; that it's wrong to think that Oscar has the concept BRISKET. (Indeed, if your theory of language is at all "criteriological," you quite likely won't be prepared to have the intuitions that Putnam and Burge want you to have. Criteriological theories of language aren't fashionable at present, but I've noticed that the fashions tend to change.) Anyhow, for purposes of discussion I propose simply to grant the intuitions. If they're real and reliable, they're *worth* discussing; and if they're not, there's no great harm done.

Second, I will assume that the Burge story shows that whatever exactly the moral of the Putnam story is, it isn't specific to terms (/concepts) that denote "natural kinds." In fact, I'll assume that the Burge story shows that if the Putnam story raises *any* problems for the notion of content, then the problems that it raises are completely general and affect all content-bearing mental states.

Third, I will assume that what's at issue in the Putnam and Burge stories is something about how propositional attitudes are individuated; and that

the intuitions Putnam and Burge appeal to suggest that the attitudes are in some sense individuated with respect to their *relational* properties. (Thus, my Twin's water2-beliefs are supposed to differ in content from my water-beliefs, and what's supposed to account for the difference is the chemical composition of the stuff *in our respective environments*. Analogously, Oscar's brisket-beliefs are supposed to differ in content from Oscar2's brisket2-beliefs, and what's supposed to account for the difference is what the form of words "is brisket" applies to *in their respective language communities*.)

Brian Loar, in a recent, important paper (1988), has argued that these concessions may be too generous. Loar points out that the standard interpretation of the Twin cases takes for granted that if, for example, the predicate "believes that water is..." applies to me but not to my Twin, and the predicate "believes that water2 is..." applies to my Twin but not to me, then it follows that the content of my belief differs in some respect from the content of my Twin's. In effect, according to Loar, Putnam and Burge assume that you can infer identities and differences in beliefs from corresponding identities and differences in the "that..." clauses that are used to ascribe them; and Loar gives grounds for doubting that such inferences are invariably sound. I think Loar may well be right about this, but I propose to ignore it. It's interesting to see what would follow from assuming that people situated the way that the Twins and the Oscars are *ipso facto* believe different things, whether or not the Burge/Putnam intuitions actually show that they do.

In aid of which, I shall talk as follows: Standards of individuation according to which my beliefs differ in content from my Twin's (and Oscar's differ from Oscar2's) I'll call "relational." Conversely, if attitudes are individuated in such fashion that my beliefs and my Twin's are identical in content, then I'll say that the operative standards are "nonrelational." It's going to turn out, however, that this terminology is a little coarse and that relational individuation *per se* isn't really the heart of the matter. So when more precision is wanted, I'll borrow a term from Burge; standards of individuation according to which my Twin and I are in the same mental state are "individualistic."

OK, now: What do the Burge and Putnam stories show about the attitudes?

Supervenience

Here's a plausible answer: At a minimum they show that propositional attitudes, as common sense understands them, don't supervene on brain states. To put it roughly: States of type X supervene on states of type Y iff there is no difference among X states without a corresponding difference among Y states. So, in particular, the psychological states of organisms supervene on their brain states iff their brains differ whenever their minds differ. Now, the point about Me and Twin-Me (and about Oscar and Oscar2) is that although we have different propositional attitudes, our brains are identical molecule-for-molecule; so it looks like it just follows that our attitudes don't supervene upon our brain states. But it's arguable that any scientifically useful notion of psychological state ought to respect supervenience; mind/brain supervenience (and/or mind/brain identity) is, after all, the best idea that anyone has had so far about how mental causation is possible. The moral would appear to be that you can't make respectable science out of the attitudes as commonsensically individuated.

I'm actually rather sympathetic to this line of thought; I think there *is* an issue about supervenience and that it does come out that we need, when doing psychology, other identity conditions for mental states than those that common sense prefers. This doesn't bother me much, because (a) redrawing these boundaries doesn't jeopardize the major claim on which the vindication of the attitudes as explanatory constructs depends – viz., that scientific psychological explanation, like commonsense belief/desire explanation, is committed to states to which semantic and causal properties are simultaneously ascribable; and (b) I think it's quite easy to see how the required principles of individuation should be formulated.

All that will take some going into. For starters, however, there's this: It needs to be argued that there *is* any problem about supervenience to be solved. Contrary to first impressions, that doesn't just fall out of the Burge and Putnam stories. Here's why: to get a violation of supervenience, you need not just the relational individuation of mental states; you also need *the nonrelational individuation of brain states*. And the Twin examples imply only the former.

To put the same point minutely differently: My brain states are type-identical to my Twin's only if you assume that such relational properties as, for example, *being a brain that lives in a body that lives in a world where there is XYZ rather than H_2O in the puddles*, do *not* count for the individuation of brain states. But why should we assume that? And, of course, if we *don't* assume it, then it's just not true that my Twin and I (or, *mutatis mutandis*, Oscars 1 and 2) are in identical brain states; and it's therefore not true that they offer counterexamples to the supervenience of the attitudes.

("Fiddlesticks! For if brain states are individuated relationally, then they will themselves fail to supervene on states at the next level down; on molecular states, as it might be.")

"Fiddlesticks back again! You beg the question by assuming that *molecular* states are nonrelationally individuated. Why shouldn't it be relational individuation all the way down to quantum mechanics?")

You will be pleased to hear that I am not endorsing this way out of the supervenience problem. On the contrary, I hope the suggestion that brain states should be relationally individuated strikes you as plain silly. Why, then, did I suggest it?

Well, the standard picture in the recent philosophical literature on cognitive science is the one that I outlined above: The Burge and Putnam stories show that the commonsense way of individuating the attitudes violates supervenience; by contrast, the psychologist individuates the attitudes nonrelationally ("narrowly," as one sometimes says), thereby preserving supervenience but at the cost of requiring an individualistic (/"nonrelational"/"narrow") notion of content. Philosophers are then free to disagree about whether such a notion of content actually can be constructed. Which they do. Vehemently.

This standard understanding of the difference between the way that common sense construes the attitudes and the way that psychology does is summarized as follows:

Commonsense Taxonomy (Pattern A)
1. Individuates the attitudes relationally; hence, assumes a nonindividualistic notion of content.
2. Distinguishes: my beliefs from my Twin's, Oscar's beliefs from Oscar2's.
3. Individuates brain states nonrelationally; therefore:
4. Violates supervenience.[1]

Psychological Taxonomy (Pattern B)
1. Individuates the attitudes nonrelationally; hence, assume a narrow notion of content.

2 Identifies: my beliefs with my Twin's, Oscar's beliefs with Oscar2's.
3 Individuates brain states nonrelationally; therefore:
4 Preserves supervenience.

One can imagine quite a different reaction to the Twin examples, however. According to this revisionist account, psychology taxonomizes the attitudes precisely the same way that common sense does: Both follow pattern A; both assume principles of individuation that violate supervenience. And so much the worse for supervenience. This, if I understand him right, is the line that Burge himself takes;[2] in any event, it's a line that merits close consideration. If psychology individuates the attitudes relationally, then it is no more in need of a narrow notion of content than common sense is. It would save a lot of nuisance if this were true, since we would not then have the bother of cooking up some narrow notion of content for psychologists to play with. It would also disarm philosophers who argue that cognitive science is in trouble because it needs a notion of narrow content *and can't have one*, the very idea of narrow content being somehow incoherent.

Alas, there is always as much bother as possible; the revisionist reading cannot be sustained. It turns out that the considerations that militate for the nonrelational individuation of mental states (hence, for preserving supervenience at the cost of violating the commonsense taxonomy) are no different from the ones that militate for the nonrelational individuation of brain states, molecular states, and such. This becomes evident as soon as one understands the source of our commitment to nonrelational taxonomy in these latter cases.

All this takes some proving. I propose to proceed as follows: First, we'll consider why we think that brain states and the like should be individuated nonrelationally. This involves developing a sort of metaphysical argument that individuation in science is *always individualistic*. It follows, of course, that the scientific constructs of psychology must be individualistic too, and we'll pause to consider how the contrary opinion could ever have become prevalent. (It's here that the distinction between "nonrelational" and "individualistic" individuation is going to have some bite.) We will then be back exactly where we started: Common sense postulates a relational taxonomy for the attitudes; psychology postulates states that have content but are individualistic; so the ques-

tion arises what notion of content survives this shift in criteria of individuation. It will turn out – contrary to much recent advertisement – that this question is not really very hard to answer. The discussion will therefore close on an uncharacteristic note of optimism: The prospects for a scientifically defensible intentional psychology are, in any event, no worse now than they were before the discovery of XYZ; and brisket is a red herring.

Causal Powers

I have before me this gen-u-ine United States ten cent piece. It has precisely two stable configurations; call them "heads" and "tails." (I ignore dimes that stand on their edges; no theory is perfect.) What, in a time of permanent inflation, will this dime buy for me? Nothing less than control over the state of every physical particle in the universe.

I define "is an H-particle at t" so that it's satisfied by a particle at t iff my dime is heads-up at t. Correspondingly, I define "is a T-particle at t" so that it's satisfied by a particle at t iff my dime is tails-up at t. By facing my dime heads-up, I now bring it about that every particle in the universe is an H-particle...thus! And then, by reversing my dime, I change every particle in the universe into a T-particle...thus! And back again...thus! (Notice that by defining H and T predicates over objects at an appropriately higher level, I can obtain corresponding control over the state of every *brain* in the universe, changing H-brain states into T-brain states and back again just as the fancy takes me.) With great power comes great responsibility. It must be a comfort for you to know that it is a trained philosopher whose finger is on the button.

What is wrong with this egomaniacal fantasy? Well, in a certain sense, nothing; barring whatever problems there may be about simultaneity, "is H at t" and "is T at t" are perfectly well defined predicates and they pick out perfectly well defined (relational) properties of physical particles. Anybody who can get at my dime can, indeed, affect the distribution of these properties throughout the universe. It's a matter of temperament whether one finds it fun to do so.

What *would* be simply mad, however, would be to try to construct a particle physics that acknowledges *being an H-particle* or *being a T-particle* as part of its explanatory apparatus. *Why* would that be mad? Because particle physics, like every other branch of science, is in the business of causal explanation; and whether something is an *H*-(*T*-) particle *is irrelevant to its causal powers*. I don't know exactly what that means; but whatever it means, I'm morally certain that it's true. I propose to wade around in it a bit.

Here are some things it seems to me safe to assume about science: We want science to give causal explanations of such things (events, whatever) in nature as can be causally explained.[3] Giving such explanations essentially involves projecting and confirming causal generalizations. And causal generalizations subsume the things they apply to in virtue of the causal properties of the things they apply to. Of course.

In short, what you need in order to do science is a taxonomic apparatus that distinguishes between things insofar as they have *different* causal properties, and that groups things together insofar as they have the *same* causal properties. So now we can see why it would be mad to embrace a taxonomy that takes seriously the difference between *H*-particles and *T*-particles. All else being equal, *H*-particles and *T*-particles have identical causal properties; whether something is an *H*-(*T*) particle is irrelevant to its causal powers. To put it a little more tensely, if an event *e* is caused by *H* particle *p*, then that same event *e* is also caused by *p* in the nearest nomologically possible world in which *p* is *T* rather than *H*. (If you prefer some other way of construing counterfactuals, you are welcome to substitute it here. I have no axes to grind.) So the properties of being *H* (*/T*) are taxonomically irrelevant for purposes of scientific causal explanation.

But similarly, *mutatis mutandis*, for the properties of being *H* and *T brain* states. And similarly, *mutatis mutandis*, for the properties of being *H* and *T mental states. And similarly, mutatis mutandis, for the property of being a mental state of a person who lives in a world where there is XYZ rather than H₂O in the puddles.* These sorts of differences in the relational properties of psychological (/brain/particle) states are irrelevant to their causal powers; hence, irrelevant to scientific taxonomy.

So, to summarize, if you're interested in causal explanation, it would be mad to distinguish between Oscar's brain states and Oscar2's; their brain states have identical causal powers. That's why we individuate brain states individualistically. And if you are interested in causal explanation, it would be mad to distinguish between Oscar's mental states and Oscar2's; their mental states have identical causal powers. But common sense deploys a taxonomy that *does* distinguish between the mental states of Oscar and Oscar2. So the commonsense taxonomy won't do for the purposes of psychology. Q.E.D.[4]

I can, however, imagine somebody not being convinced by this argument. For the argument depends on assuming that the mental states of Twins do in fact have the same causal powers, and I can imagine somebody denying that this is so. Along either of the two following lines:

First line: "Consider the effects of my utterances of the form of words "Bring water!" Such utterances normally eventuate in somebody bringing me water – viz., in somebody bringing me H₂O. Whereas, by contrast, when my Twin utters "Bring water!" what he normally gets is water2 – viz., XYZ. So the causal powers of my water-utterances do, after all, differ from the causal powers of my Twin's "water"-utterances. And similarly, *mutatis mutandis*, for the causal powers of the mental states that such utterances express. And similarly, *mutatis mutandis*, for the mental states of the Oscars in respect of brisket and brisket2."

Reply: This will not do; identity of causal powers has to be assessed *across* contexts, not *within* contexts.

Consider, if you will, the causal powers of your biceps and of mine. Roughly, our biceps have the *same* causal powers if the following is true: *For any thing x and any context C, if you can lift x in C, then so can I; and if I can lift x in C, then so can you.* What is, however, *not* in general relevant to comparisons between the causal powers of our biceps is this: that there is a thing *x* and a pair of contexts *C* and *C'* such that you can lift *x* in *C* and I can not lift *x* in *C'*. Thus suppose, for example, that in *C* (a context in which this chair is not nailed to the floor) you can lift it; and in *C'* (a context in which this chair *is* nailed to the floor) I cannot lift it. That eventuality would give your biceps nothing to crow about. Your biceps – to repeat the moral – have cause for celebration only if they can lift *x*'s *in contexts in which my biceps can't.*

Well, to return to the causal powers of the water-utterances (/water-thoughts) of Twins: It's true that when I say "water" I get water and when my Twin says "water" he gets XYZ. But that's irrelevant to the question about identity of causal powers, *because these utterances (/thoughts) are being imagined to occur in different contexts (mine* occur in a context in which the local potable is H_2O, his occur in a context in which the local potable is XYZ). What *is* relevant to the question of identity of causal powers is the following pair of counterfactuals: (a) If his utterance (/thought) had occurred in my context, it *would have had* the effects that my utterance (/thought) did have; and (b) if my utterance (/thought) had occurred in his context, it *would have had* the effects that his utterance (/thought) did have. For our utterances (/thoughts) to have the same causal powers, both of those counterfactuals have to be true. But both of those counterfactuals *are* true, since (for example) if I had said "Bring water!" on Twin-Earth, it's XYZ that my interlocutors would have brought; and if he had said "Bring water!" here, his interlocutors would have brought him H_2O.

This line of argument no doubt assumes that I *can* say "Bring water!" on Twin-Earth – that my being on Twin-Earth doesn't *ipso facto* change my dialect to English2 (and, *mutatis mutandis*, convert my concept *water* into the concept *water2*). But although I've heard it suggested that mental states construed nonindividualistically are easily bruised and don't "travel," the contrary assumption would in fact seem to be secure. The standard intuition about "visiting" cases is that if, standing on Twin-Earth, I say "That's water" about a puddle of XYZ, then what I say is *false*. Which it wouldn't be if I were speaking English2.

So, OK so far; we have, so far, no reason to suppose that the causal powers of my Twin's mental states are different from the causal powers of mine. On the contrary, since the causal subjunctives about the two states are the same, it must be that they have the *same* causal powers and thus count as the same state by what we're taking to be the relevant typological criteria.

Second line: "Maybe the causal powers of the mental states of Twins are always the same when their effects are *non*intentionally individuated. But consider their effects as intentionally described; consider, in particular, the *behavioral* consequences of the mental states of Oscar and Oscar2. (I assume, here and throughout, that the interesting relations between behaviors and states of mind are typically causal. Philosophers have denied this, but they were wrong to do so.) Oscar's thoughts and desires sometimes eventuate in his *saying* such things as that he prefers brisket to, as it might be, hamburger; Oscar's thoughts sometimes lead to his evincing brisket-eating preferences and brisket-purchasing behavior; and so forth. Whereas

Oscar2 never does any of these things. Oscar2 may, of course, say that he likes brisket2; and he may evince brisket2 preferences; and he may, when appropriately stimulated (by, for example, a meat counter), behave brisket2-purchasingly.[5] And, of course, when he says and does these things with brisket2 in mind, he may produce precisely the same bodily *motions* as his counterpart produces when he says and does the corresponding things with brisket in mind. But all that shows is that behaving isn't to be identified with moving one's body; a lesson we ought to have learned long ago."

There's another aspect of this line of reply that's worth noticing: Independent of the present metaphysical issues, anybody who takes the Burge/Putnam intuitions to be decisive for the individuation of the attitudes has a strong motive for denying that Oscar's and Oscar2's behavior (or Mine and My Twin's) are, in general, type-identical. After all, behavior is supposed to be the result of mental causes, and you would generally expect different mental causes to eventuate in correspondingly different behavioral effects. By assumption the Twins' attitudes (and the two Oscars') differ a lot, so if these very different sorts of mental causes nevertheless invariably converge on identical behavioral effects, that would seem to be an accident on a very big scale. The way out is obviously to deny that the behavioral effects *are* identical; to insist that the commonsense way of identifying behaviors, like the commonsense way of identifying the attitudes, goes out into the world for its principles of individuation; that it depends essentially on the relational properties of the behavior. (Burge – who would, of course, accept this conclusion on independent grounds – nevertheless objects that the present sort of argument misunderstands the function of his and Putnam's thought experiments: Since the examples concern the description of circumstances presumed to be counterfactual, the likelihood or otherwise of such circumstances *actually occurring* is not, according to Burge, a relevant consideration. (See Burge 1986.) But this misses a point of methodology. We do, of course, want to tell the right story about how counterfactual circumstances should be described *qua* counterfactual. But we *also* want to tell the right story about how such circumstances should be described if they were real. The present intuition is that, were we actually to encounter Twins, what we should want to say of them is *not* that their quite different mental states have somehow managed to converge on the same behaviors; we *can* imagine examples that we'd want to describe that way, but Twins aren't among them. Rather, what we'd want to say about Twins is just that the (putative) *differences* between their minds are reflected, in the usual way, by corresponding differences between their behaviors. But we *can* say this only if we *are* prepared to describe their behaviors as different. So again it turns out that anyone who counts in a way that distinguishes the minds of Twins should also count in a way that distinguishes their acts.)

In short, Barbara Pym's question "Where does 'behavior' begin and end?" is one that needs to be taken seriously in a discussion of the causal powers of mental states. Claiming, as indeed I have been doing, that my mental states and my Twin's are identical in causal powers begs that question; or so, in any event, the objection might go.

First reply: If this argument shows that my mental state differs from my Twin's, it's hard to see why it doesn't show that our brain states differ too. My Twin is in a brain state that eventuates in his uttering the form of words "Bring water." I am in a brain state that eventuates in my uttering the form of words "Bring water." If our uttering these forms of words counts as our behaving differently, then it looks as though our brain states differ in their behavioral consequences, hence in their causal powers, hence in the state types of which they are tokens. (Similarly, *mutatis mutandis*, for our quantum mechanical states.) But I thought we agreed a while back that it would be grotesque to suppose that brain states that live on Twin-Earth are *ipso facto* typologically distinct from brain states that live around here.

Second reply: Notice that corresponding to the present argument for a taxonomic distinction between my mental state and my Twin's, there is the analogous argument for distinguishing H-particles from T-particles. Here's how it would sound: "Being H rather than T does affect causal powers after all; for H-particles enter into H-particle interactions, and no T-particle does. H-particle interactions may, of course, *look* a lot like T-particle interactions – just as Oscar2's brisket2-eating behaviors look a lot like Oscar's brisket-eating behaviors, and just as my water-requests sound a lot like my Twin's requests for XYZ. Philosophers are not, however, misled by mere appearances; we see where the eye does not."

The least that all this shows is how taxonomic and ontological decisions intertwine: You can save classification by causal powers, come what may, by fiddling the criteria for event identity. To classify by causal powers is to count no property as taxonomically relevant unless it affects causal powers. But x's having property P affects x's causal powers just in case x wouldn't have caused the same events had it not been P. But of course, whether x would have caused the same events had it not been P depends a lot on which events you count as the same and which you count as different. In the present case, whether the difference between being H and being T affects a particle's causal powers depends on whether the very same event that *was* an interaction of H-particles *could have been* an interaction of T particles. (Perhaps it goes without saying that the principle that events are individuated by their causes and effects is perfectly useless here; we can't apply it unless we already know whether an event that *was* caused by an H-particle could have had *the same cause* even if it had been the effect of a T-particle.)

Could it be that this is a dead end? It looked like the notion of taxonomy by causal powers gave us a sort of *a priori* argument for individualism and thus put some teeth into the idea that a conception of mental state suitable for the psychologist's purposes would have to be interestingly different from the commonsense conception of a propositional attitude. But now it appears that the requirement that states with identical causal powers ought *ipso facto* to be taxonomically identical can be met *trivially* by anyone prepared to make the appropriate ontological adjustments. Yet surely there has to be something wrong here; because it's false that two events could differ just in that one involves H-particles and the other involves T-particles; and it's false that H-particles and T-particles differ in their causal powers; and – as previously noted – it would be *mad* to suggest saving the supervenience of the propositional attitudes by individuating brain states relationally. Moreover, it is very plausible that all these intuitions hang together. The question is: What on earth do they hang *on*?

I hope I have managed to make this all seem very puzzling; otherwise you won't be impressed when I tell you the answer. But in fact the mystery is hardly bigger than a bread box, and certainly no deeper. Let's go back to the clear case and trace it through.

If H-particle interactions are *ipso facto* different events from T-particle interactions, then H-particles and T-particles have different causal powers.

But if *H*-particles and *T*-particles have different causal powers, then the causal powers – not just certain of the relational properties, mind you, but *the causal powers* – of every physical particle in the universe depend on the orientation of my gen-u-ine United States ten cent piece. That includes, of course, physical particles that are a long way away; physical particles on Alpha Centauri, for example. And *that's* what's crazy, because while such relational properties as being *H* or being *T* can depend on the orientation of my dime *by stipulation*, how on Earth could the *causal powers* of particles on Alpha Centauri depend on the orientation of my dime? Either there would have to be a causal mechanism to mediate this dependency, or it would have to be mediated by a fundamental law of nature; and there aren't any such mechanisms and there aren't any such laws. *Of course* there aren't.

So, then, to avoid postulating impossible causal mechanisms and/or impossible natural laws, we will have to say that, all else being equal, *H*-particle interactions are *not* distinct events from *T*-particle interactions; hence, that *H*-particles and *T*-particles do *not* differ in their causal powers; hence, that the difference between being an *H*-particle and being a *T*-particle does *not* count as taxonomic for purposes of causal explanation. which is, of course, just what intuition tells you that you *ought* to say.

Exactly the same considerations apply, however, to the individuation of mental states.[6] If every instance of brisket-chewing behavior *ipso facto* counts as an event distinct in kind from any instance of brisket2-chewing behavior, then, since brisket-cravings cause brisket-chewings and brisket2-cravings don't, Oscar's mental state differs in its causal powers from Oscar2's. But then there must be some mechanism that connects the causal powers of Oscar's mental states with the character of the speech community he lives in *and that does so without affecting Oscar's physiology* (remember, Oscar and Oscar2 are molecularly identical). But there is no such mechanism; you *can't* affect the causal powers of a person's mental states without affecting his physiology. That's not a conceptual claim or a metaphysical claim, of course. It's a contingent fact about how God made the world. God made the world such that the mechanisms by which environmental variables affect organic behaviors run via their effects on the organism's nervous system. Or so, at least, all the physiologists I know assure me.

Well then, in order to avoid postulating crazy causal mechanisms, we shall have to assume that brisket chewings are not *ipso facto* events distinct from chewings of brisket2; hence, that brisket cravings do not *ipso facto* have different causal powers from brisket2 cravings; hence, that for purposes of causal explanation Oscar's cravings count as mental states of the same kind as Oscar2's.

There is, I think, no doubt that we do count that way when we do psychology; Ned Block has a pretty example that makes this clear. He imagines a psychologist (call her Psyche – the *P* is silent, as in *P*smith) who is studying the etiology of food preferences, and who happens to have both Oscar and Oscar2 in her subject population. Now, on the intuitions that Burge invites us to share, Oscar and Oscar2 have different food preferences; what Oscar prefers to gruel is brisket, but what Oscar2 prefers to gruel is brisket2. Psyche, being a proper psychologist, is of course interested in sources of variance; so the present case puts Psyche in a pickle. If she discounts Oscar and Oscar2, she'll be able to say – as it might be – that there are two determinants of food preference: 27.3 percent of the variance is genetic and the remaining 72.7 percent is the result of early training. If, however, she counts Oscar and Oscar2 in, and if she counts their food preferences the way Burge wants her to, then she has to say that there are *three* sources of variance: genetic endowment, early training, *and linguistic affiliation*. But surely it's *mad* to say that linguistic affiliation is *per se* a determinant of food preference; how *could* it be?[7]

I think it's perfectly clear how Psyche ought to jump: she ought to say that Oscar and Oscar2 count as having *the same* food preferences and therefore do not constitute counterexamples to her claim that the determinants of food preference are exhausted by genes and early training. And the previous discussion makes clear just *why* she ought to say this: if Oscar and Oscar2 have different food preferences, then there must be some difference in the causal powers of their mental states – psychological taxonomy is taxonomy *by* causal powers. But if there is such a difference, then there must be some mechanism which can connect the causal powers of Oscar's mental states with the character of his linguistic affiliation *without affecting his physiological constitution*. But there is no such mechanism; the causal powers of Oscar's mental states supervene on his physiology, just like the causal powers of your mental states and mine.

So, then, to bring this all together: You can affect the relational properties of things in all sorts of ways – including by stipulation. But for one thing to affect the causal powers of another, there must be a mediating law or mechanism. It's a mystery what this could be in the Twin (or Oscar) cases; not surprisingly, since it's surely plausible that the only mechanisms that *can* mediate environmental effects on the causal powers of mental states are neurological. The way to avoid making this mystery is to count the mental states – and, *mutatis mutandis*, the behaviors – of Twins (Oscars) as having the same causal powers, hence as taxonomically identical.

So much for the main line of the argument for individualism. Now just a word to bring the reader up to date on the literature.

In a recent paper (1986), Burge says that reasoning of the sort I've been pursuing "is confused. The confusion is abetted by careless use of the term 'affect,' conflating causation with individuation. Variations in the environment that do not vary the impacts that causally 'affect' the subject's body may 'affect' the individuation of the... intentional processes he or she is undergoing.... It does not follow that the environment causally affects the subject in any way that circumvents its having effects on the subject's body" (p. 16). But it looks to me like that's precisely what *does* follow, assuming that by "causally affecting" the subject Burge means to include determining the causal powers of the subject's psychological states. You can't both individuate behaviors Burge's way (viz., *non*locally) and hold that the causal powers of mental states are locally supervenient. When individuation is *by* causal powers, questions of individuation and causation don't divide in the way that Burge wants them to.

Consider the case where my Twin and I both spy some water (viz., some H_2O). My seeing the stuff causes me to say (correctly) "That's water!" His seeing the stuff causes him to say (incorrectly) "That's water2!" (His saying this sounds just like my saying "That's water!" of course.) These saying count as *different behaviors* when you individuate behaviors Burge's way; so the behavioral effects of seeing water are different for the two of us; so the causal powers of the state of seeing water are different depending on which of us is in it. And this difference is uniquely attributable to differences in the contextual background; aside from the contextual background, my Twin and I are identical for present purposes. So if you individuate

behavior Burge's way, differences in contextual background effect differences in the causal powers of mental states without having correspondingly different "effects on the subject's body"; specifically, on his neural structure. But is Burge seriously prepared to give up the local supervenience of causal powers? *How could* differences of context affect the causal powers of one's mental states without affecting the states of one's brain?

Burge can say, if he likes, that mind/brain supervenience be damned; though, as I keep pointing out, if mind/brain supervenience goes, the intelligibility of mental causation goes with it. Or he can save mind/brain supervenience by going contextual on *neurological* individuation. (As, indeed, he appears to be tempted to do; see his footnote 18. Here both intuition and scientific practice clearly run against him, however.) But what he can't do is split the difference. If supervenience be damned for individuation, it can't be saved for causation. Burge says that "local causation does not make more plausible local individuation" (p.16), but he's wrong if, as it would seem, "local causation" implies local supervenience of causal powers. Local causation *requires* local individuation when so construed. You can have contextual individuation if you insist on it. But you can't have it for free. Etiology suffers.

Well, if all this is as patent as I'm making it out to be, how could anyone ever have supposed that the standards of individuation appropriate to the psychologist's purposes are other than individualistic? I cast no aspersions, but I have a dark suspicion; I think people get confused between methodological *individualism* and methodological *solipsism*. A brief excursus on this topic, therefore, will round off this part of the discussion.

Methodological individualism is the doctrine that psychological states are individuated *with respect to their causal powers*. Methodological solipsism is the doctrine that psychological states are individuated *without respect to their semantic evaluation*.[8]

Now, the semantic evaluation of a mental state depends on certain of its relational properties (in effect, on how the state corresponds to the world). So we could say, as a rough way of talking, that solipsistic individuation is *nonrelational*. But if we are going to talk that way, then *it is very important* to distinguish between solipsism and individualism. In particular, though it's a point of definition that solipsistic individuation is nonrelational, there is nothing to stop principles of individuation from being simultaneously relational and individualistic. *Individualism does not prohibit the relational individuation of mental states*; it just says that no property of mental states, relational or otherwise, counts taxonomically unless it affects causal powers.

Indeed, individualism couldn't rule out relational individuation *per se* if any of what I've been arguing for up till now is true. I've taken it that individualism is a completely general methodological principle in science; one which follows simply from the scientist's goal of causal explanation and which, therefore, all scientific taxonomies must obey. By contrast, it's patent that taxonomic categories in science are *often* relational. Just as you'd expect, relational properties can count taxonomically whenever they affect causal powers. Thus "being a planet" is a relational property *par excellence*, but it's one that individualism permits to operate in astronomical taxonomy. For whether you are a planet affects your trajectory, and your trajectory determines what you can bump into; so whether you're a planet affects your causal powers, which is all the individualism asks for. Equivalently, the property of being a planet is taxonomic because there are causal laws that things satisfy in virtue of being planets. By contrast, the property of living in a world in which there is XYZ in the puddles is *not* taxonomic because there are *no* causal laws that things satisfy in virtue of having *that* property. And similarly for the property of living in a speech community in which people use "brisket" to refer to brisket of beef. The operative consideration is, of course, that where there are no causal laws about a property, having the property – or failing to have it – has no effect on causal powers.[9]

To put the point the other way around, solipsism (construed as prohibiting the relational taxonomy of mental states) is unlike individualism in that it *couldn't conceivably* follow from any *general* considerations about scientific goals or practices. "Methodological solipsism" is, in fact, an empirical theory about the mind: it's the theory that mental processes are computational, hence syntactic. I think this theory is defensible; in fact, I think it's true. But its defense can't be conducted on *a priori* or metaphysical grounds, and its truth depends simply on the facts about how the mind works. Methodological solipsism differs from methodological individualism in both these respects.

Well, to come to the point: If you happen to have confused individualism with solipsism (and if you take solipsism to be the doctrine that psychological taxonomy is nonrelational), then you might try arguing against individualism by remarking that the psychologist's taxonomic apparatus is, often enough, nonsolipsistic (viz., that it's often relational). As, indeed, it is. Even computational ("information flow") psychologists are professionally interested in such questions as, "Why does this organism have the computational capacities that it has?"; "Why does its brain compute this algorithm rather than some other?"; or even, "Why is this mental process generally truth preserving?" Such questions often get answered by reference to relational properties of the organism's mental state. See, for example, Ullman, (1979), where you get lovely arguments that run like this: *This perceptual algorithm is generally truth preserving because the organism that computes it lives in a world where most spatial transformations of objects are rigid. If the same algorithm were run in a world in which most spatial transformations were not rigid, it wouldn't be truth preserving, and the ability to compute it would be without survival value. So, presumably, the organism wouldn't have this ability in such a world.* These sorts of explanations square with *individualism*, because the relational facts they advert to affect the causal powers of mental states; indeed, they affect their very existence. But naturally, explanations of this sort – for that matter, *all* teleological explanations – are *ipso facto* nonsolipsistic. So *if* you have confused solipsistic (viz., nonrelational) taxonomies with individualistic taxonomies (viz., taxonomies by causal powers), then you *might* wrongly suppose that the affection psychologists have for teleological explanation argues that they – like the laity – are prone to individuate mental states nonindividualistically. But it doesn't. And they aren't.

I repeat the main points in a spirit of recapitulation. There are two of them; one is about the methodology of science, and one is about its metaphysics.

Methodological point: Categorization in science is characteristically taxonomy by causal powers. Identity of causal powers is identity of causal consequences across nomologically possible contexts.

Metaphysical point: Causal powers supervene on local microstructure. In the psychological case, they supervene on local neural structure. We abandon this principle at our peril; mind/brain supervenience (/identity) is our only plausible account of how mental states could have the casual powers that they do have. On the other hand, given what causal *powers* are, preserving the principle constrains the way that we individuate causal *consequences*. In the case of the behavioral consequences of the attitudes, it requires us to individuate them in ways that violate the commonsense taxonomy. So be it.

Well, I've gotten us where I promised to: back to where we started. There is a difference between the way psychology individuates behaviors and mental states and the way common sense does. At least there is if you assume that the Burge/Putnam intuitions are reliable.[10] But this fact isn't, in and of itself, really very interesting; scientific taxonomy is forever cross-cutting categories of everyday employment. For that matter, the sciences are forever cross-cutting one another's taxonomies. Chemistry doesn't care about the distinction between streams and lakes; but geology does. Physics doesn't care about the distinction between bankers and butchers; but sociology does. (For that matter, physics doesn't care about the distinction between the Sun and Alpha Centauri either; sublime indifference!) None of this is surprising; things in Nature overlap in their causal powers to various degrees and in various respects; the sciences play these overlaps, each in its own way.

And, for nonscientific purposes, we are often interested in taxonomies that cross-cut causal powers. Causal explanation is just one human preoccupation among many; individualism is a constitutive principle of science, not of rational taxonomy *per se*. Or, to put it a little differently – more in the material mode – God could make a genuine electron, or diamond, or tiger, or person, because being an electron or a diamond or a tiger or a person isn't a matter of being the effect of the right kind of causes; rather, it's a matter of being the cause of the right kind of effects. And similarly, I think, for all the other natural kinds. Causal powers are decisively relevant to a taxonomy of natural kinds because such taxonomies are organized in behalf of causal explanation. Not all taxonomies have that end in view, however, so not all taxonomies classify by causal powers. Even God couldn't make a gen-u-ine United States ten cent piece; only the US Treasury Department can do that.

You can't, in short, make skepticism just out of the fact that the commonsense way of taxonomizing the mental differs from the psychologist's way. You might, however, try the idea that disagreement between the commonsense taxonomy and the scientific one matters more in psychology than it does elsewhere *because psychology needs the commonsense notion of mental content*. In particular, you might try the idea that the notion of mental content doesn't survive the transition from the layman's categories to the scientist's. I know of at least one argument that runs that way. Let's have a look at it.

What we have – though only by assumption, to be sure – is a typology for mental states according to which my thoughts and my Twin's (and Oscar's thoughts and Oscar2's) have identical contents. More generally, we have assumed a typology according to which the physiological identity of organisms guarantees the identity of their mental states (and, *a fortiori*, the identity of the contents of their mental states). All this is entailed by the principle – now taken to be operative – that the mental supervenes upon the physiological (together with the assumption – which I suppose to be untendentious – that mental states have their contents essentially, so that typological identity of the former guarantees typological identity of the latter). All right so far.

But now it appears that even if the physiological identity of organisms ensures the identity of their mental states and the identity of mental states ensures the identity of contents, *the identity of the contents of mental states does not ensure the identity of their extensions*: my thoughts and my Twin's – like Oscar's and Oscar2's – *differ in their truth conditions*, so it's an accident if they happen to have the same truth values. Whereas what makes my water-thoughts true is the facts about H_2O, what makes my Twin's "water"-thoughts true is the facts about XYZ. Whereas the thought that I have – when it runs through my head that water is wet – is true iff H_2O is wet, the thought that he has – when it runs through his head that "water" is wet – is true iff XYZ is wet. And it's an accident (that is, it's just contingent) that H_2O is wet iff XYZ is. (Similarly, what I'm thinking about when I think: *water*, is different from what he's thinking about when he thinks: "*water*"; he's thinking about XYZ, but I'm thinking about H_2O. So the denotations of our thoughts differ.) Hence the classical – Putnamian – formulation of the puzzle about Twins: If mental state supervenes upon physiology, then thoughts don't have their truth conditions essentially; two tokens of the *same* thought can have *different* truth conditions, hence different truth values. If thoughts are in the head, then content doesn't determine extension.

That, then, is the "Twin-Earth Problem." Except that so far it *isn't* a problem; it's just a handful of intuitions together with a commentary on some immediate implications of accepting them. If that were *all*, the right response would surely be "So what?" What connects the intuitions and their implications with the proposal that we give up on propositional-attitude psychology is a certain *Diagnosis*. And while a lot has been written about the intuitions and their implications, the diagnosis has gone largely unexamined. I propose now to examine it.

Here's the Diagnosis: "Look, on *anybody's* story, the notion of content has got to be at least a little problematic. For one thing, it seems to be a notion proprietary to the information sciences, and *soi-disant* 'emergents' bear the burden of proof. At a minimum, if you're going to have mental contents, you owe us some sort of account of their individuation.

"Now, prior to the Twin-Earth Problem, there *was* some sort of account of their individuation; you could say, to a first approximation, that identity of content depends on identity of extension. No doubt that story leaked a bit: Morning-Star thoughts look to be different in content from the corresponding Evening-Star thoughts, even though their truth conditions are arguably the same. But at least one could hold firmly to this: "Extension supervenes on content; no difference in extension without some difference in content." Conversely, it was a *test* for identity of content that the extensions had to come out to be the same. And that was the *best* test we had; it was the one source of evidence about content identity that seemed surely reliable. Compare the notorious wobbliness of intuitions about synonymy, analyticity, and the like.

"But now we see that *it's not true after all* that difference of extension implies difference of content; so unclear are we now about what content-identity comes to – hence, about what identity of propositional attitudes comes to – that we can't even assume that typologically identical thoughts will always be true and false together. The consequence of the psychologist's insistence on preserving supervenience is that we now have no idea at all what criteria of individuation for propositional attitudes might be like; hence, we have no idea at all what counts as *evidence* for the identity of propositional attitudes.

"Short form: Inferences from difference of extension to difference of content used to bear almost all the weight of propositional-attitude attribution. That was, however, a frail reed, and now it has broken. The Twin-Earth Problem *is* a problem, *because it breaks the connection between extensional identity and content identity*."

Now, the Twin-Earth intuitions are fascinating, and if you care about semantics you will, no doubt, do well to attend to them. But, as I've taken pains to emphasize, you need the Diagnosis to connect the intuitions about Twins to the issues about the status of belief/desire psychology, and – fortunately for those of us who envision a psychology of propositional attitudes – the Diagnosis rests on a quite trivial mistake: *The Twin-Earth examples don't break the connection between content and extension; they just relativize it to context.*

Suppose that what you used to think, prior to Twin-Earth, is that contents are something like functions from thoughts to truth conditions: given the content of a thought, you know the conditions under which that thought would be true. (Presumably a truth condition would itself then be a function from worlds to truth values: a thought that has the truth condition *TC* takes the value *T* in world *W* iff *TC* is satisfied in *W*. Thus, for example, in virtue of its content the thought that it's raining has the truth condition *that it's raining* and is thus true in a world iff it's raining in that world.) I hasten to emphasize that if you don't – or didn't – like that story, it's quite all right for you to choose some other; my point is going to be that if you liked any story of even remotely that kind before Twin-Earth, you're perfectly free to go on liking it now. For even if all the intuitions about Twin-Earth are right, and even if they have all the implications that they are said to have, extensional identity still constrains intentional identity because *contents still determine extensions relative to a context*. If you like, contents are functions from contexts and thoughts onto truth conditions.

What, if anything, does that mean? Well, it's presumably common ground that there's something about the relation between Twin-Earth and Twin-Me in virtue of which his "water"-thoughts are about XYZ even though my water-thoughts are not. Call this condition that's satisfied by {Twin-Me, Twin-Earth} condition *C* (because it determines the *Context* of his "water"-thoughts). Similarly, there must be something about the relation between me and Earth in virtue of which my water-thoughts are about H_2O even though my Twin's "water"-thoughts are not. Call this condition that is satisfied by {me, Earth} condition C'. I don't want to worry, just now, about the problem of how to articulate conditions C and C'. Some story about constraints on the causal relations between H_2O tokenings and water-thought tokenings (and between XYZ tokenings and "water"-thought tokenings) would be the obvious proposal; but it doesn't matter much for the purposes now at hand. Because we *do* know this: Short of a miracle, it must be true that if an organism shares the neurophysical constitution of my Twin *and satisfies* C, it follows that its thoughts and my Twin's thoughts share their truth conditions. For example, short of a miracle the following counterfactual must be true: Given the neurological identity between us, in a world where I am in my Twin's context my "water"-thoughts are about XYZ iff his are. (And, of course, vice versa: In a world in which my Twin is in my context, given the neurological identity between us, it must be that his water-thoughts are about H_2O iff mine are.)

But now we have an extensional identity criterion for mental contents: Two thought contents are identical only if they effect the same mapping of thoughts and contexts onto truth conditions. Specifically, your thought is content-identical to mine only if in every context in which your thought has truth condition T, mine has truth condition T and vice versa.

It's worth reemphasizing that, by this criterion, my Twin's "water"-thoughts are intentionally identical to my water-thoughts; they have the same contents even though, since their contexts are *de facto* different, they differ, *de facto*, in their truth conditions. In effect, what we have here is an extensional criterion for "narrow" content. The "broad content" of a thought, by contrast, is what you can semantically evaluate; it's what you get when you specify a narrow content *and fix a context*.

We can now see why we ought to reject both of the following two suggestions found in Putnam (1979): That we consider the extension of a term (/concept/thought) to be an independent component of its "meaning vector"; and that we make do, in our psychology, with stereotypes *instead of* contents. The first proposal is redundant, since, as we've just seen, contents (meanings) determine extensions given a context. The second proposal is unacceptable, because unlike contents, stereotypes *don't* determine extensions. (Since it's untenden-

tious that stereotypes supervene on physiology, the stereotypes for real water and Twin-water must be identical; so if stereotypes did fix extensions, my Twin's "water"-thoughts would have the same extension as mine.) But, as the Diagnosis rightly says, we need an extension determiner as a component of the meaning vector, because we rely on "different extension → different content" for the individuation of concepts.

"Stop, stop! I have an objection."

Oh, good! Do proceed.

"Well, since on your view your water-thoughts are content-identical to your Twin's, I suppose we may infer that the English word 'water' has the same intension as its Tw-English homonym (hereinafter spelled 'water2')."

We may.

"But if 'water' and 'water2' have the same intensions, they must apply to the same things. So since 'water2' applies to XYZ, 'water' applies to XYZ too. It follows that XYZ must *be* water (what else could it mean to say that 'water' applies to it?). But, as a matter of fact, XYZ *isn't* water; only H_2O is water. Scientists discover essences."

I don't know whether scientists discover essences. It may be that philosophers make them up. In either event, the present problem doesn't exist. The denotation of "water" is determined not just by its meaning but by its context. But the context for English "anchors" "water" to H_2O just as, *mutatis mutandis*, the context for Tw-English anchors "water2" to XYZ. (I learned "anchors" at Stanford; it is a very useful term despite – or maybe because of – not being very well defined. For present purposes, an expression is anchored iff it has a determinate semantic value.) So then, the condition for "x is water" to be true requires that x be H_2O. Which, by assumption, XYZ isn't. So English "water" doesn't apply to XYZ (though, of course, Tw-English "water" does). OK so far.

And yet... and yet! One seems to hear a Still Small Voice – could it be the voice of conscience? – crying out as follows: "You say that 'water' and its Tw-English homonym mean the same thing; well then, *what* do they mean?"

How like the voice of conscience to insist upon the formal mode. It might equally have put its problem this way: "What *is* the thought such that when I have it its truth condition is that H_2O is wet and when my Twin has it its truth condition is that XYZ is wet? What is the concept *water* such that it denotes H_2O in this world and XYZ in the next?" I suspect that this – and not Putnam's puzzle about individuation – is what *really* bugs people about narrow content. The construct invites a question which – so it appears – we simply don't have a way of answering.

But conscience be hanged; it's not the construct but the question that is ill advised. What the Still Small Voice wants me to do is utter an English sentence which expresses just what my "water"-thoughts have in common with my Twin's. Unsurprisingly, I can't do it. That's because the content that an English sentence expresses is *ipso facto anchored* content, hence *ipso facto not* narrow.

So, in particular, *qua* expression of English, "water is wet" is anchored to the wetness of water (i.e., of H_2O) just as, *qua* expression of Tw-English, "water2 is wet" is anchored to the wetness of water2 (i.e., of XYZ). And of course, since it is anchored to water, "water is wet" doesn't – can't – express the narrow content that my water-thoughts share with my Twin's. Indeed, if you mean by content what can be semantically evaluated, then what my water-thoughts share with Twin "water"-thoughts *isn't* content. Narrow content is radically inexpressible, because it's only content *potentially*; it's what gets to *be* content when – and only when – it gets to be anchored. We can't – to put it in a nutshell – *say* what Twin thoughts have in common. This is because what can be said is *ipso facto* semantically evaluable; and what Twin-thoughts have in common is *ipso facto* not.

Here is another way to put what is much the same point: You have to be sort of careful if you propose to co-opt the notion of narrow content for service in a "Griceian" theory of meaning. According to Griceian theories, the meaning of a sentence is inherited from the content of the propositional attitude(s) that the sentence is conventionally used to express. Well, that's fine so long as you remember that it's *anchored* content (that is, it's the content of anchored attitudes), and hence not narrow content, that sentences inherit. Looked at the other way around, when we use the content of a sentence to specify the content of a mental state (viz., by embedding the sentence to a verb of propositional attitude), the best we can do – in principle, *all* we can do – is avail ourselves of the content of the sentence *qua* anchored; for it's only *qua* anchored that sentences *have* content. The corresponding consideration is relatively transparent in the case of demonstratives. Suppose the thought "I've got a sore toe" runs through your head and also runs through mine; what's the content that these thoughts share? Well, you can't say what it is by using the sentence "I've got a sore toe," since, whenever you use that sentence, the "I" automatically gets anchored to you. You can, however, sneak up on the shared content by *mentioning* that sentence, as I did just above. In such cases, mentioning a sentence is a way of abstracting a form of words from the consequences of its being anchored.

One wants, above all, to avoid a sort of fallacy of subtraction: "Start with anchored content; take the anchoring conditions away, and you end up with a *new sort of content*, an unanchored content; a *narrow* content, as we say." (Compare: "Start with a bachelor; take the unmarriedness away, and you end up with a *new sort of bachelor*, a married bachelor; a *narrow* bachelor, as we say.") Or rather, there's nothing wrong with talking that way, so long as you don't then start to wonder *what the narrow content of – for example – the thought that water is wet could be*. Such questions can't be answered in the nature of things; so, in the nature of things, they shouldn't be asked.[11] People who positively *insist* on asking them generally get what they deserve: phenomenalism, verificationism, "procedural" semantics, or skepticism, depending on temperament and circumstance.

"But look," the SSV replies, "if narrow content isn't really content, then in what sense do you and your Twin have any water-thoughts in common at all? And if the form of words 'water is wet' doesn't express the narrow content of Twin water-thoughts, how can the form of words 'the thought that water is wet' succeed in picking out a thought that you share with your Twin?"

Answer: What I share with my Twin – what supervenience *guarantees* that we share – is a mental state that is semantically evaluable relative to a context. Referring expressions of English can therefore be used to pick out narrow contents via their *hypothetical* semantic properties. So, for example, the English expression "the thought that water is wet" can be used to specify the narrow content of a mental state that my Twin and I share (even though, *qua* anchored to H_2O, it doesn't, of course, *express* that content). In particular, it can be used to pick out the content of my Twin's "water"-thought via the truth conditions that it *would have had* if my Twin had been plugged into my world. Roughly speaking, this tactic works because the narrow thought that water is wet is the *unique* narrow thought that yields the truth condition H_2O *is wet* when anchored to my context and the truth condition *XYZ is wet* when anchored to his.

You can't, in absolute strictness, express narrow content; but as we've seen, there are ways of sneaking up on it.

SSV: "By that logic, why don't you call the narrow thought you share with your Twin 'the thought that water2 is wet'? After all, that's the 'water-thought' that you would have had if you had been plugged into your Twin's context (and that he *does* have in virtue of the fact that he *has* been plugged into his context). Turn about is fair play."

Answer: (a) "The thought that water2 is wet" is an expression of Tw-English; I don't speak Tw-English. (b) The home team gets to name the intension; the actual world has privileges that merely counterfactual worlds don't share.

SSV: "What about if you are a brain in a vat? What about then?"

Answer: If you are a brain in a vat, then you have, no doubt, got serious cause for complaint. But it may be some consolation that brains in vats have no special *semantical* difficulties according to the present account. They are, in fact, just special cases of Twins.

On the one hand, a brain in a vat instantiates the same function from contexts to truth conditions that the corresponding brain in a head does; being in a vat does not, therefore, affect the narrow content of one's thoughts. On the other hand, it *may* affect the *broad* content of one's thoughts; it may, for example, affect their truth conditions. That would depend on just which kind of brain-in-a-vat you have in mind; for example, on just what sorts of connections you imagine there are between the brain, the vat, and the world. If you imagine a brain in a vat that's hooked up to *this* world, and hooked up *just* the same way one's own brain is, then – of course – that brain shares one's thought-contents *both* narrow *and* broad. Broad content supervenes on neural state together with connections to context. It had better, after all; a skull is a kind of vat too.

SSV: "But if a brain is a function from contexts to truth conditions, and if a vat can be a context, then when a brain in a vat thinks 'water is wet' the truth condition of its thought will be (not something about H_2O or XYZ but) something about its vat. So it will be thinking something *true*. Which violates the intuiton that the thoughts of brains in vats have to be *false* thoughts."

Answer: You're confused about your intuitions. What they really tell you isn't that the thoughts of brains in vats have to be false; it's that being in a vat wouldn't stop a brain from having the very thoughts that you have now. And that intuition is *true*, so long as you individuate thoughts narrowly. It's tempting to infer that if a brain has your thoughts, and has them under conditions that would make your thoughts false, then the thoughts that the brain is having must be false too. But to argue this way is exactly to equivocate between the narrow way of individuating thoughts and the broad way.

SSV: "Mental states are supposed to cause behavior. How can a function cause anything?"

Answer: Some functions are implemented in brains; and brains cause things. You can think of a narrow mental state as determining an equivalence class of mechanisms, where the criterion for being in the class is *semantic*.

SSV: "I do believe you've gone over to Steve Stich. Have you no conscience? Do you take me for a mere expository convention?"

Answer: There, there; don't fret! What is emerging here is, in a certain sense, a "no content" account of narrow content; but it is nevertheless also a fully intentionalist account. According to the present story, a narrow content is *essentially* a function from contexts onto truth conditions; different functions from contexts onto truth conditions are *ipso facto* different narrow contents. It's hard to see what more you could want of an intentional state than that it should have semantic properties that are intrinsic to its individuation. In effect, I'm prepared to give Stich everything except what he wants. (See Stich, 1983.)

Now, sleep conscience!

What I hope this chapter has shown is this: Given the causal explanation of behavior as the psychologist's end in view, he has motivation for adopting a taxonomy of mental states that respects supervenience. However, the psychologist needs a way to reconcile his respect for supervenience with the idea that the extension of a mental state constrains its content; for he needs to hold onto the argument from *difference* of extension to *difference* of content. When it comes to individuating mental states, that's the best kind of argument he's got, just as Putnam says. It turns out, however, that it's not hard to reconcile respecting supervenience with observing extensional constraints on content, because you can relativize the constraints to context: given a context, contents are different if extensions are. There isn't a shred of evidence to suggest that this principle is untrue – surely the Twin cases provide no such evidence – or that it constrains content attributions any less well than the old, unrelativized account used to do. The point to bear in mind is that if "difference in extension → difference in intension" substantively constrains the attribution of propositional attitudes, then so too does this same principle when it is relativized to context. *The Moral*: If the worry about propositional attitudes is that Twin-Earth shows that contents don't determine extensions, the right thing to do is to *stop worrying*.

So it looks as though everything is all right. Super: Let, you might suppose, rejoicing be unconstrained. But if you do suppose that, that's only because you've let the Twin problems distract you from the hard problems.[12]

Notes

1 If, however, Loar (1988) is right, then the common-sense taxonomy actually fits pattern B; i.e., common sense and psychology both individuate the attitudes narrowly and both respect supervenience.

So far as I know, nobody has explicitly endorsed the fourth logically possible option – viz., that commonsense taxonomy is narrow and psychological taxonomy relational – though I suppose Skinner and his followers may implicitly hold some such view.

2 Notice that taking this line wouldn't commit Burge to a violation of *physicalism*; the differences between the attitudes of Twins and Oscars supervene on the (*inter alia*, physical) differences between their worlds. Or rather, they do assuming that the relevant differences between the linguistic practices in Oscar's speech community and Oscar2's are physicalistically specifiable. (I owe this caveat to James Higginbotham.)

3 No need to dogmatize, however, There may be scientific enterprises that are not – or not primarily – interested in causal explanation; natural history, for example. And in these sciences it is perhaps not identity and difference of causal powers that provide the criterion for taxonomic identity. But either propositional-attitude psychology is in the business of causal explanation or it is out of work.

To put it at a minimum, if there is so much as a presumption of scientific utility in favor of a taxonomy by causal powers, then if – as I'm arguing – the causal powers of the mental states of Twins are *ipso facto* identical, then there is a corresponding presumption in favor of the utility of narrow individuation in psychology.

4 The implication is that commonsense attitude attributions aren't – or rather, aren't *solely* – in aid of causal explanation; and this appears to be true. One reason why you might want to know what Psmith believes is in order to predict how he will behave. But another reason is that beliefs are often true, so if you know what Psmith believes, you have some basis for inferring how the world is. The relevant property of Psmith's beliefs for this latter purpose, however, is not their causal powers but something like *what information they transmit* (see Dretske, 1981). And, quite generally, what information a thing transmits depends on relational properties of the thing which may not affect its causal powers. My utterance "water is wet" has, let's say, the same causal powers as my Twin's; but – assuming that both utterances are true – one transmits the information that H_2O is wet and the other transmits the information that XYZ is.

It is, I think, the fact that attitude ascriptions serve both masters that is at the bottom of many of their logical peculiarities; of the pervasiveness of opacity/transparency ambiguities, for example.

5 Since all brisket2 is brisket (though not vice versa), every brisket2 purchase is a brisket purchase. This, however, is a consideration not profoundly relevant to the point at issue.

6 This is a little unfair – but, I think, *only* a little. There is, after all, *no causal relation at all* between my coin and the particles on Alpha Centauri whose causal powers its orientation is alleged to affect. Whereas, by contrast, there is supposed to be a causal relation between my Twin's "water"-thoughts and XYZ puddles (*mutatis mutandis*, between my water-thoughts and H_2O puddles) in virtue of which the thoughts refer to the stuff that they do. Similarly, it might be supposed that the semantic effects of linguistic coaffiliation require causal relations among the members of the language community so affected. (Though maybe not; it's sometimes suggested that the mere existence of experts in my language community shapes the contents of my mental states, whether or not there's a causal chain that connects us.)

But this hardly seems enough to meet the present worry, which isn't that my coin affects particles "at a distance," but that such relations as there are between the coin and the particles *aren't the right kind* to affect the causal powers of the latter. The point is that just specifying that *some causal relation or other* obtains isn't enough to plug this hole. Effects on causal powers require mediation by laws and/or mechanisms; and, in the Twin cases, there are no such mechanisms and no such laws.

If you are inclined to doubt this, notice that for any causal relation that holds between my mental states and the local water puddles, there must be a corresponding relation that holds between my *neurological* states and the local water puddles; a sort of causal relation into which, by assumption, my Twin's neurological states do not enter. Despite which, the intuition persists that my neurological states and my Twin's are taxonomically identical. Why? Because the difference in the causal *histories* of our brain states is not of the right sort to effect a difference in the causal *powers* of our brains. And *qua* scientific, neurological taxonomy groups *by* causal powers.

Parallelism of argument surely requires us to hold that the differences between the causal histories of the mental states of Twins are not of the right sort to effect differences in the causal powers of their minds. And, *qua* scientific, *psychological* taxonomy groups by causal powers too.

7   Burge points out (personal communication) that the Oscars' food preferences *don't* differ if you individuate *de re*; i.e., that brisket and gruel are such that *both Oscars* prefer the former to the latter (a fact that Psyche could establish by testing them on samples). But I don't see that this helps, since it seems to me thoroughly implausible that linguistic affiliation *per se* determines food preferences *de dicto*.

If it does, that opens up new vistas in nonintrusive therapy. For example, it looks as though we can relieve Oscar's unnatural craving for brisket just by changing the linguistic background – viz., by getting his colinguals to talk English2 instead of English. Whereas it used to seem that we'd be required to operate on *Oscar*: desensitization training, depth therapy, Lord knows what all else.

Psyche and I find this sort of consequence preposterous, but no doubt intuitions differ. That's why it's nice to have a principle or two to hone them on.

8   More precisely, methodological solipsism is a doctrine not about individuation in psychology at large but about individuation in aid of the psychology of mental processes. Methodological solipsism constrains the ways mental processes can specify their ranges and domains: They can't apply differently to mental states just in virtue of the truth or falsity of the propositions that the mental states express. And they can't apply differently to concepts depending on whether or not the concepts denote. (See Fodor, *MS*.) This is, however, a nicety that is almost always ignored in the literature, and I shan't bother about it here.

9   In published comments on an earlier version of this chapter, Martin Davies (1986) remarks that what I say about being a planet "seems to be in tension with the insistence that causal powers must be compared across contexts or environments. For it cannot be the case *both* that a planet has characteristic causal powers and not merely those of a physically similar chunk of matter that is not a planet, *and* that causal powers have to be compared across contexts or environments quite generally." But – to put it roughly – this confuses the question whether *being a planet* is taxonomic (which it is; two things that differ in *that* property *ipso facto* differ in their effects in many contexts) with the question whether *being this piece of rock* is taxonomic (which it isn't; two things that differ in *that* property do not thereby differ in their effects in *any* context).

Once again: A difference between properties *P* and *P1* can affect causal powers (can be taxonomic) only when there is a situation *S* such that the instantiation of *P* in *S* has, *ipso facto*, different effects from the instantiation of *P1* in *S*. By this criterion, the difference between *being a planet* and *not being a planet* affects causal powers because there are situations in which something that's a planet has, *ipso facto*, different effects from something that isn't. By contrast, the difference (in content) between the thought that water is wet and the thought that water2 is wet does *not* affect the causal powers of tokens of these thoughts: there are *no* situations in which one thought has, *ipso facto*, different effects than the other. So, in particular, if I am transported to Twin-Earth, all else being left unchanged, then if I have the thought that water is wet in a situation where my Twin's thought that water2 is wet has consequence *C*, then my thought has consequence *C* in that situation too. (Compare a real – taxonomically relevant – difference in content; e.g., the difference between my thought that water is toxic and your thought that it's potable. Tokens of these thoughts differ in their consequences in *all sorts* of situations.)

10   It is, however, worth echoing an important point that Burge makes; the differences between the way that these taxonomies carve things up only show in funny cases. In practically all the cases that anybody actually encounters outside philosophical fantasies, the states that one is tempted to count as token beliefs that *P* share not just the causal powers that psychologists care about but also the relational background to which the commonsense taxonomy is sensitive. This enormous *de facto* coextension is part of the argument that the psychologist's story really is a vindication of the commonsense belief/desire theory.

11   Since you by the narrow content construct at the cost of acknowledging a certain amount of inexpressibility, it may be some consolation that *not* buying the narrow content construct also has a certain cost in inexpressibility (though for quite a different sort of reason, to be sure). So, suppose you think that Twin-Earth shows that content doesn't determine extension and/or that content doesn't supervene on physiology. So, you have no use for narrow content. Still there's the following question: When my Twin thinks "water2 is wet," how do you say, in English,

what he is thinking? Not by saying "water2 is wet," for that's a sentence of Tw-English; and not by saying "water is wet," since, on the present assumptions, whatever "water2" means, it's something different from what "water" means; not by saying "XYZ is wet," since my Twin will presumably take "water2 is XYZ" to say something informative; something, indeed, which he might wish to deny. And not, for sure, by saying H$_2$O is wet,' since there isn't any H$_2$O on Twin-Earth, and my Twin has never so much as heard of the stuff. It looks like the meaning of "water2 is wet" is *inexpressible* in English. And of course, the same thing goes – only the other way "round – for expressing the meaning of "water" in Tw-English.

12 Much the same treatment of Twin examples as the one I propose here was independently suggested by White, 1982.

My indebtedness to the spirit of David Kaplan's treatment of demonstratives will be clear to readers familiar with his work. However, the current proposal is *not* that kind terms and the like are indexicals. You have to relativize narrow contents to contexts – roughly, to a world – to get *anything* that's semantically evaluable. But in the case of true indexicals you require a *further* relativization – roughly, to an occasion of utterance. So, according to this analysis, "water" isn't an indexical, but "I" and the like are. Which is just as it should be.

References

Burge, T (1986) "Individualism and psychology." *Philosophical Review*, 95: 3–45.

Davies, M (1986) "Externality, psychological explanation and narrow content." *Aristotelian Society Supplementary Volume*, 60: 263–83.

Dretske, F. (1981) *Knowledge and the Flow of Information*. Cambridge, MA: MIT Press.

Loar, B. (1988) "Social content and psychological content." In R. H. Grimm and D. D. Merill (eds), *Contents of Thought*. Tucson, AZ: University of Arizona Press.

Putnam, H. (1979) "The Meaning of 'Meaning'." In K. Gunderson (ed.), *Language, Mind, and Knowledge. Vol. 7, Minnesota Studies in the Philosophy of Science*. Minneapolis, MN: University of Minnesota Press.

Stich, S. P. (1983) *From Folk Psychology to Cognitive Science*. Cambridge, MA: MIT Press.

Ullman, S. (1979) *The Interpretation of Visual Motion*. Cambridge, MA: MIT Press.

White, S. (1982) "Partial character and the language of thought." *Pacific Philosophical Quarterly*, 63: 347–65.

An *a priori* Argument: The Argument from Causal Powers

Robert A. Wilson

In the Introduction we saw that much of the appeal of individualism derives from intuitive general views about explanation, causation, and causal powers. These views are the basis for an influential argument for individualism developed by Jerry Fodor (1987: ch. 2) that claims that individualism in psychology follows from the nature of scientific explanation. Its central claim is that scientific taxonomies satisfy a general constraint of which individualism in psychology is a particular instance.

1   Stating the Argument

The argument can be summarized as follows. Sciences typically individuate their explanatory categories and kinds by causal powers, and the causal powers that anything has supervene on that thing's intrinsic physical properties. So, if psychology is to be a science, mental states must supervene on the intrinsic physical properties of individuals; thus individualism is a constraint on psychology.

Both those who have criticized this argument as unsound (Braun 1991; Egan 1991; Van Gulick 1989) and those who have been more sympathetic to it (Crane 1991; McGinn 1991; Owens 1993; Williams 1990) have assumed that the argument is at least valid. I shall argue, by contrast, that this argument for individualism equivocates on "causal powers," and that this equivocation is not simply inherent in a particular formulation of the argument. Rather, the equivocation points to a deep and recurrent problem for those who claim that individualism in psychology follows from generally acceptable claims about explanation, causation, and causal powers. The appeal to the notion of causal powers itself is at the heart of the problem. In terms I shall explain, there is a distinction between an *extended* and a *restricted* notion of causal powers that, once drawn, makes it difficult to see how individualism could be a consequence of the purported scientific nature of psychology. This point about causal powers has implications for related arguments for individualism.

Let us be more precise. Consider the following explicit argument for individualism, which I shall refer to as the *argument from causal powers*:

1 Taxonomic properties and entities in the sciences must be individuated by their causal powers.
2 The cognitive sciences, particularly psychology, purport to identify taxonomic *mental* causes and formulate generalizations about those causes.
3 In the cognitive sciences, both the mental causes of an individual's behavior and that behavior itself must be individuated in terms of the causal powers of that individual.

So, since

4 The causal powers of anything are determined or fixed by that thing's intrinsic physical properties,
5 Any causes of behavior that are to be taxonomic in the cognitive sciences must be determined or fixed by the intrinsic physical properties of the individual. Thus,
6 The cognitive sciences, particularly psychology, should concern themselves only with states and processes that themselves are determined by the instrinsic physical properties of the individual.

Despite the argument's apparent validity, in §4 I argue that (1) and (4) require different notions of "causal powers"; in §§5–7 I defend my claim that this equivocation in the argument constitutes a deep and recurrent problem.

As a grounding for these claims, I focus in the next two sections on Premise (1) and the reasons that have been given for accepting it. This premise articulates a form of *global individualism*, that is, a generalization of the constraint that individualism imposes on psychology. Fodor appeals to what he claims to be general facts about causation and

causal explanation, particularly in the sciences, in arguing for global individualism. I make two points about Fodor's argument for (1). First, in the next section, I argue that (1) does not follow from such general facts about causal explanation. Second, in §3, I argue that the most plausible way of defending (1) is by invoking a general claim about the *revisability* of causal explanations and taxonomies. Far from following from uncontroversial claims about causation and causal explanation, (1) rests on an interesting but controversial claim about the nature of scientific explanation.

2 An Argument for Global Individualism: Powers and Properties

Fodor makes two relatively uncontroversial general claims about causal explanation in support of global individualism. He says:

> We want science to give causal explanations of such things (events, whatever) in nature as can be causally explained. Giving such explanations essentially involves projecting and confirming causal generalizations. And causal generalizations subsume the things they apply to in virtue of the causal properties of the things they apply to. Of course.
>
> In short, what you need in order to do science is a taxonomic apparatus that distinguishes between things insofar as they have *different* causal properties, and that groups things together insofar as they have the *same* causal properties. (1987: 34, footnote omitted)

The first claim is that scientific explanation is causal. The second is that the taxonomies that classify the *explanantia* in causal explanations must do so according to causal similarities and causal differences. Hence, Fodor argues, if we are to develop a scientific explanation for some phenomenon, we must taxonomize by causal similarities. The causal nature of scientific explanation *requires* individuation by causal powers.

This final conclusion does not follow, since individuation by sameness or similarity of causal *properties* is not the same thing as individuation by causal *powers*. The concept of a causal property is broader than the concept of a causal power: Powers are essentially forward-looking in a way that properties in general are not. The relevant causal similarities between two phenomena in a given discipline may involve the *causes* of those phenomena or the causal relations they stand in, rather than what those phenomena are capable of causing. The historical and relational properties that two entities share may well explain why those entities share many other properties, and there is no reason to regard explanations citing such properties as noncausal. Entities taxonomized by historical and relational causal properties can feature as both *explanantia* and *explananda* in causal explanations, and, as I shall argue in some detail in §4, the taxonomy of entities by their historical and relational causal properties is pervasive across the sciences. The fact that sciences offer causal explanations and individuate by causal properties does not entail that they must always individuate by causal powers.

Although I assume a fairly broad notion of causal property in what follows, one that does not rule out *a priori* either relational or historical properties as causal properties, this does not imply that I take *any* relational or historical predicate to name a causal property. Even on a narrower notion of causal property, which allows only intrinsic and extrinsic causal powers to be causal properties, the distinction between intrinsic powers and properties more generally still points to what is wrong in Fodor's argument for (1), as well as to an inherent tension in the argument from causal powers. Since the notion of a causal property must include at least the extrinsic causal powers that an entity instantiates, and since these do not supervene on that entity's intrinsic physical properties, my reliance on the broad notion of causal property is inessential to the form of my argument.

To illustrate the invalidity of Fodor's inference in his argument for global individualism, consider a nonscientific case. If individuation in science is individuation by causal powers *because* scientific explanation is causal, then the causal nature of other types of explanation should entail that the entities they refer to must be individuated by their causal powers. Suppose we pick out a group of individuals with the predicate "is a victim of the Hiroshima bombing." What determines whether someone belongs to this group are facts about that person's history, or perhaps even facts about that person's parents' history, not facts about that person's causal powers; an individual's causal powers do not constitute the individuative criteria that determine whether she is a victim of the Hir-

oshima bombing. Still, this way of classifying people proceeds by identifying a causal *property* that certain people share, and I take it as obvious that all sorts of causal generalizations are true of people who are classified together by this predicate. In virtue of having been present in Hiroshima at a certain time (or of having had parents who were present), certain people suffered cell degeneration, cancerous growths, and genetic diseases that were caused by the American nuclear attack on Hiroshima. The various generalizations true of these people are systematic, and it is explanatory to point out that some individual was a victim of the Hiroshima bombing in response to a query about aspects of her current bodily state.

This sort of relational individuation is ubiquitous in talk about groups of people (e.g., university graduates, divorcees, pensioners) and the individuals constituting those groups. The existence of a causal explanation for a given phenomenon does not entail that either the entities constituting the phenomenon or those referred to in the causal explanation must be individuated by their causal powers. Therefore, the ubiquity of causal explanation and individuation by causal *properties* across the sciences does not entail a commitment to explanation and individuation by causal *powers*.

3 The Preliminary Character of Relational Taxonomies

Despite the invalidity of Fodor's argument for (1), that argument rests on persistent intuitions about the nature of causation and causal explanation that warrant more careful consideration. Even granting some distinction between powers and properties, reflection on the nature of causal explanation brings out an intuitive distinction between relational and historical properties, on the one hand, and intrinsic properties, on the other. Though relational and historical kinds may feature in causal explanations, the properties that individuate such kinds do not play an appropriate explanatory role: Such kinds and properties are not *themselves* the ultimate bases of causal responsibility. If we are interested in entities *qua* causes or *qua explanantia*, there must be something about those entities themselves that our explanations strive to identify; a category can be genuinely taxonomic only insofar as it groups entities that share causal powers. Such intrinsic properties are causally responsible for the effects we ascribe in causal explanations, and therefore entities must be taxonomized in causal explanations in virtue of sharing them. Whether or not we insist on axonomy being by causal "powers," causal taxonomies must at least be by properties that supervene on the intrinsic properties that some entity instantiates.[1]

I have already said that the appeal to causal powers is at the core of the problem with the argument from causal powers; in this respect, what we call a "causal power" is not a verbal issue, as the previous point perhaps suggests. However, I want to bracket discussion of this issue for a moment in order to point to a prior problem for a proponent of global individualism, even one who claims only that individuation in science must be "by intrinsic causal properties" rather than "by causal powers." The problem stems from the fact that there are many causal explanations that, like the one in the example I introduced in the previous section, *do* feature kinds individuated by relational and historical properties, and such explanations violate the constraint of global individualism. Given the prima facie conflict between the constraint of global individualism and our explanatory practices, how does the proponent of global individualism explain away the appearances?

A focus on the "victim of the Hiroshima bombing" example might suggest the following response to this problem. Showing that there are *commonsense* causal explanations of human traits and actions that taxonomize people by something other than their intrinsic causal powers does not show anything about *scientific* causal explanation. After all, our everyday causal talk is not solely aimed at providing causal explanations, and one should expect such talk to be shaped by the other roles it plays in our lives. Perhaps because of this, commonsense causal explanations do not presuppose individuation by causal powers. By contrast, there is something special about the causal nature of *scientific* explanation that entails that scientific explanation presupposes individuation by causal powers.

If one thinks that (1) makes a point not about causal explanation in general but about scientific causal explanation, one needs some criterion distinguishing scientific from ordinary causal explanation. There are a number of closely related and familiar criteria that have been claimed to mark off scientific explanations from other types of explana-

tions. For example, scientific explanations are projectible, law-instantiating, and quantify over natural kinds in a way that other explanations need not. If it is only explanations with these properties – scientific explanations – of which (1) is true, then the existence of ordinary causal explanations that feature relational and historical kinds is irrelevant.

One serious problem with this proposal is that it is notoriously difficult to articulate these notions in such a way that they serve as criteria that demarcate scientific explanations as a class from nonscientific explanations. For example, part of what it is for scientific explanations to be projectible is for them to be *counterfactually rigorous*: In nearby possible worlds, entities of the kinds specified in the explanation also have the properties ascribed in the explanation. However, ordinary causal explanations that form no part of any science are counterfactually rigorous in precisely the same way; much the same is true of the criteria, such as degree of naturalness, entrenchment, or simplicity, that have been offered for marking off projectible from nonprojectible predicates. More pointedly, generalizations about historically or relationally individuated entities are no less projectible or scientific than any other types of causal generalizations. Indeed, as we will see in the next section, explanations that feature such kinds are widespread in existing sciences.[2]

Taking on the burden of demarcating scientific from ordinary causal explanation in order to defend global individualism is not a promising way for the proponent of global individualism to discount our liberal appeals to kinds individuated by historical and relational properties. More plausibly, such a proponent could concede that although both scientific and nonscientific causal explanations do feature relational and historical kinds, these are always *preliminary* to taxonomies that conform to global individualism. The preliminary character of relational and historical taxonomies reflects the fact that relational and historical properties are not *themselves* ultimately causally responsible for what entities instantiating such properties do and can do. Relational individuation plays a *reference-fixing* rather than an *essence-identifying* role in causal explanation (*sensu* Kripke 1980). Although many causal taxonomies do not individuate entities by their causal powers, they correspond to taxonomies that do; relational kinds feature in causal explanations because the classification of entities by readily observable, relational properties allows one to investigate further the intrinsic causal powers that these entities instantiate. And it is these causal powers that our scientific taxonomies aspire to identify.

A variation on our victim example illustrates what these claims about historical and relational kinds amount to. Suppose that the following generalization is true: that most victims of the Hiroshima bombing suffered from radiation effects of a specific type, say, some specific form of cancer. Though we might use the historical predicate "is a victim of the Hiroshima bombing" to pick out a particular group of people, what determines whether the preceding generalization is true of *particular individuals* is something about those individuals themselves, not something about their causal histories. The generalization applies to particular individuals in virtue of some intrinsic, physical feature, such as the mutation of a particular gene or the destruction of certain cells. What *really* explains why people with a historical, relational property – being in a certain spatiotemporal region – have a specific type of cancer is that these people now have the intrinsic physical property that *causes* the cancer. This claim about the causal (and thus explanatory) priority of such an intrinsic causal power is plausible because the possession of a certain gene or damage to certain cells partitions the class of people initially taxonomized as victims by the historical-relational property: Those with the gene (say) have the cancer, and those without it do not have the cancer. This allows us, at least in principle, to revise our initial taxonomic scheme. In the new taxonomy, people *are* taxonomized by some intrinsic causal power they have, and their sharing this causal power provides the basis for our causal generalizations about them. We thus arrive at an individualistic taxonomy that *does* form the basis for true causal generalizations; our historical classification is a preliminary guide to or approximation of this taxonomy. Relational taxonomies are sometimes revised in science in this way, as exemplified by the narrowing of the concept of *weight* to that of *mass* in Newtonian mechanics (Stalnaker 1989: 291): We begin with an extrinsic property (weight) and decompose it into an intrinsic property (mass) plus a relation (gravitational force). Importantly, we arrive at a property, an intrinsic causal power of an entity, that itself is ultimately causally responsible.

The claim that relational scientific taxonomies have a preliminary and revisable character – a claim needed to defend Fodor's argument for global individualism – rests on some variation of the

following view: *Any* category that features in a causal explanation must do so ultimately in virtue of the intrinsic causal powers of its instances. One could determine the plausibility of these general views of scientific taxonomy and explanation by examining a variety of accepted explanations in different sciences, and should some of these fail to taxonomize by intrinsic causal powers, one could determine whether such taxonomies are revisable in the appropriate way. I shall argue that there are such scientific explanations and taxonomies (§4) and that they are not revisable in the prescribed manner (§5). There are kinds and explanations in a variety of sciences for which global individualism is simply false. Or it is false if one gives "causal powers" what I think is its usual sense. As I hope to show in the next section, however, the argument from causal powers relies on *more than* this sense of "causal powers."

4 Causal Powers and Scientific Explanation

In summarizing his discussion of the sort of argument for individualism that we are considering, Fodor identifies two main points:

> *Methodological point*: Categorization in science is characteristically taxonomy by causal powers. Identity of causal powers is identity of causal consequences across nomologically possible contexts.

> *Metaphysical point*: Causal powers supervene on local microstructure. In the psychological case, they supervene on local neural structure. (1987: 44)

There is no understanding of "causal powers" that satisfies both of Fodor's points here; the same is true of (1) and (4) in the argument from causal powers.[3] If Fodor's methodological point is to be true of sciences as they are actually practiced, then causal powers do not always supervene on local microstructure. If his metaphysical point is to specify a truth about causal powers, then scientific taxonomies do not, as a matter of fact, always individuate in terms of causal powers (cf. Braun 1991: 380; Egan 1991: 187; Van Gulick 1989: 157).

To take this latter point first, assume that Fodor's metaphysical point, and so (4) in the argument from causal powers, are true. Burge (1986a:

14–20; 1989: 309–10) has claimed that when we examine patterns of individuation in a range of sciences, we find that individuation is not always solely or even primarily in terms of an individual entity's intrinsic causal powers. Burge's particular examples (battles, continents, plates, organs, species) are in no way special cases. Evolutionary paleontology offers reconstructive hypotheses about skeletal and other structures of past creatures based on the fossil record. In no real sense could it be said to taxonomize exclusively in terms of the causal powers of past creatures. Many of the geosciences are concerned with how certain formations, such as volcanos and mountains, came about, not with those entities' causal powers; volcanos and mountains are not classified in these sciences by their causal powers. Epidemiology sometimes taxonomizes diseases by how they are caused. For example, viral diseases, though varied in their particular causal powers, are grouped together because they are caused by viruses. The same is true of many particular diseases: syphilis, lead poisioning, and birth trauma are diseases or conditions that are typed in terms of their respective causes, not by what they themselves have the power to cause. For example, syphilis is a disease caused by the *Treponema pallidum* bacterium, which infects the blood vessels. This is how it is distinguished from closely related diseases, such as yaws and pinta (Schofield 1979: ch. 5).

The revisability claim sketched in the previous section makes a point about entities insofar as they are to be considered *as causes* or *as explanantia* for a given phenomenon. It might be thought that the previous examples invoke entities only as *explananda* rather than as *explanantia*; although entities that are not taxonomized by their intrinsic causal powers may be cited in causal explanations, they feature only as the *explananda* to which the generalizations apply. There *are* causal generalizations about continents, volcanos, mountains, skeletal structures, and viruses, but, the objection goes, none of these generalizations feature such kinds as causes or *explanantia*. And it is only *qua explanantia* that scientific kinds must be taxonomized by intrinsic causal powers.

Although intuitive, this claim is difficult to maintain once one acknowledges the ubiquity of explanations in the sciences in which there are kinds that do not conform to the constraint of global individualism. For such explanations do not refer to these kinds only as *explananda*, and the claim that they do is at best the sort of recon-

structive claim about the nature of scientific explanation of which one should be wary. Explanations of the form "Because it is an *x*," and "Because it has *x*," where *x* designates some non-individualistic kind or property, are common in the sciences. For example, the relational property of being highly specialized is causally responsible for the extinction of a species during rapid or catastrophic evolutionary change: "Because it is specialized" or "because it's a hedgehog" (i.e., a highly specialized organism) are both explanatory claims within evolutionary biology. Yet the property of being specialized and the properties that individuate species kinds are not individualistic. A particular virus can be cited as a cause of illness even though that kind of virus is taxonomized relationally. Entities taxonomized under historical or relational kinds themselves are often cited as causes in scientific explanations. Relationally individuated kinds play the role of both *explanans* and *explanandum* in explanatory practice, and such practice should be the ultimate arbiter for claims about constraints on scientific explanation.

Let me clarify this response and emphasize the importance of my methodological appeal to explanatory practice before moving on. The question of whether relational kinds can feature as causes in explanations, to which the answer is "Yes," is one question. Whether the relational properties that individuate those kinds are themselves causally responsible for the events, processes, and states being explained is another question, a question whose answer depends in part on broader and more controversial metaphysical issues, such as whether relations themselves can be causally efficacious. My claim is that one *must* accept an affirmative answer to the first question in light of explanatory practice in the sciences. Given this, however, a negative answer to the second question becomes more difficult to maintain. The most plausible way in which the "Yes–No" option can be defended is by accepting the view I described in the previous section, according to which relational taxonomies are always preliminary and lead to revised, individualistic taxonomies. As I shall argue *in passim*, this general revisability claim should also be rejected once one attends to explanations in the range of disciplines constituting the sciences. There may be *a priori* considerations that entail that historical and relational taxonomies are not "properly scientific," but the focus on explanatory practice in science must function as a check on such claims about the nature of scientific explanation.

If the causal powers of an entity supervene on the local microstructure of that entity, then global individualism is false. The intrinsic causal powers of individual entities are not all that important in some types of scientific causal explanation. Many sciences are not primarily concerned with what a thing can do. In some cases, the relevant discipline concentrates not so much on abilities as on the *history* or the *structure* of the entity or phenomenon of interest. This is true particularly in the social and biological sciences, where there is significant interest in *processes* and *systems*, rather than in the individual things constituting those processes and systems. This does not make these sciences any less scientific or entail that they are not concerned with formulating causal explanations for the phenomena in their respective domains.

To consolidate the preceding claim about global individualism I shall discuss three particular examples of nonindividualistic taxonomic kinds. The diversity of these examples together with those already mentioned suggests that it will be difficult for one simply to restrict the thesis of global individualism to some subset of scientific disciplines of which psychology is clearly a member. The details of the accompanying discussion not only address particular objections to my denial of global individualism, they also illustrate why there is an *inherent* tension in the use to which the notion of causal powers is put in the argument from causal powers.

Anthropologists are often interested in understanding a set of actions or practices in a particular culture. Those actions or practices are frequently taxonomized at a relatively abstract level by understanding the role of the practices in the larger social context. For example, incest is forbidden in many cultures and is often considered a paradigm *taboo*. The concept of a taboo is central to many explanations in anthropology, taboos being social attitudes or beliefs. Though different types of activities are considered taboo across cultures, practices are not taxonomized as taboos by their intrinsic causal powers. In classifying certain actions or practices as taboos, one is not concerned with the "local microstructure" of those actions or practices. Rather, one locates the practice amongst a complex network of other social and moral practices. Taboos are nonindividualistic; taxonomy in anthropology is not, or not *entirely*, individualistic.

The same is true of central categories in many other social sciences: gender and categories of sex-

ual preference in various fields of sociology, class in economics and history, criminal in social psychology and sociology. To take one of these, consider the social kind *criminal*. Being a criminal is a relational property that some people instantiate: A person is a criminal if he or she breaks any of a number of laws in a certain class. Whether a particular individual can be properly classified as a criminal is a function of the relations that that person has entered into; it is not determined by that individual's intrinsic causal powers. Still, there are many generalizations in sociology (and perhaps even in social psychology) about criminals as a social kind, and it is explanatory to appeal to an individual's criminal status to explain some of her behavior.

In order to clarify what someone who denies global individualism must accept, consider two related objections to my claims about the category criminal. The first objection is that I must be supposing that certain types of theories about criminality (e.g., Lombroso's theory of criminal man; see Gould 1981: ch. 4) are false, since these theories *would* provide some intrinsic causal power of an individual that determined whether he or she was a criminal. Now, although there are various theories about why some people are criminals, it should be clear that these are primarily accounts of what is causally responsible for criminal behavior in particular individuals; they need not supply criteria for individuating the kind criminal. Of course, *some* such theories might purport to identify the "underlying essence" of criminality. Yet it is compatible with the social kind criminal being a scientifically interesting kind that such theories be mistaken, or that they account for only some kinds of criminal behavior. So, although I do think that such theories are unlikely to be true, their truth is irrelevant to my claim about the taxonomic individuation of the category criminal.

The second objection is that without the existence of *some* intrinsic causal factor causally responsible for criminal behavior the category must be empty, like the category witch: Either there is some intrinsic property that criminals share *as* criminals, or the category can be of no theoretical interest at all. How else could being a criminal be an explanatory causal property of an individual? There are two problems with this objection. First, unlike being a witch, being a criminal is *not* a property deeply embedded in a theoretical framework in such a way that the falsity of the theory would render the corresponding category empty. Even if no theory could adequately explain criminal behavior, this would imply neither that there were no criminals nor that there were no theoretically interesting generalizations about criminals. Second, all that causation requires is that there be some causal factor that results in criminal behavior in each particular instance. Yet these factors may vary interpersonally and even intrapersonally over time; they need not be shared by individuals instantiating the kind and so constitute criteria for the category criminal.

In both of these cases, taboo and criminal, the properties that make an entity the kind of thing it is are not intrinsic to that individual entity. An entity falls under either of these concepts because of the relations that entity enters into. Central taxonomic properties in the biological sciences are also, like taboo and criminal, relational. In evolutionary biology, the concept of *species* is a central (perhaps *the* central) taxonomic concept. There are various causal generalizations true of members of a particular species, some of these concerning genetic and morphological properties, properties that *are* individualistic. Yet a species is taxonomized relationally as "a reproductive community of populations (reproductively isolated from others) that occupies a specific niche in nature" (Mayr 1982: 273). Although there is some variation in the precise definition of the species concept in evolutionary biology,[4] the *essentialist* conception of species, whereby species are defined exclusively in terms of the intrinsic genetic or even morphological characteristics that their members possess, is inadequate for explanation in the discipline. Species are taxonomized relationally, not by the intrinsic causal powers of individuals.

In saying that species are not individuated by intrinsic causal powers but relationally, I mean two things: The first is that an individual organism's species membership is not fixed by that organism's intrinsic properties but rather by the relations it bears to other individuals. To take the most extreme case, two individual organisms could be physically identical (or, more pertinently, *biochemically* identical) in composition and structure and still belong to different species. This is because two organisms identical in their intrinsic causal powers could be reproductively isolated and have independent phylogenies. The pattern of individuation in evolutionary biology as it is practiced does not abstract away from actual history.

Second, as biological kinds, species are not individuated from one another by their intrinsic causal powers. This is because species are individuated from one another, in part, by their phylogenetic history. Furthermore, if Mayr is right in thinking of species as populations, it is difficult to make sense of the claim that the causal powers of a species, considered as a population, distinguish that species from some other species. As populations, species don't seem to be the right type of thing to be individuated by intrinsic causal powers.

As a related aside, note the common misconception that both an individual organism's species membership and the individuation of species from one another are determined by the genotypes and phenotypes that individuals possess. Coupled with the claim – equally misleading, in my view – that an individual's genes fix her intrinsic causal powers, this view about taxonomy in evolutionary biology might be taken to support the claim that species *are* individuated by their intrinsic causal powers. Yet this view of species membership is mistaken. Both genotypes and phenotypes may vary across individuals belonging to the same species. Moreover, as Elliott Sober (1980, 1984: ch. 5) has convincingly argued, evolutionary thinking that recognizes the reality of populations and the inherent variability among their members offers explanations that are incompatible with what Sober calls the "natural state" explanations that essentialists offer. The sort of essentialism we are considering should be rejected because it presupposes a type of explanation of variation that is implausible.

Assuming that causal powers supervene on an individual's intrinsic physical properties, taxonomy in science as it is actually practiced is not exclusively individuation by intrinsic causal powers. Consider, now, the other conditional that is part of my claim that (1) and (4) are incompatible: that if we assume (1) and so Fodor's "methodological point" to be true, (4) and so Fodor's "metaphysical point" must be false. That is, if categorization in science typically *is* taxonomy by causal powers, then causal powers do not always supervene on local microstructure.

One way of explaining how historical and relational individuation is compatible with individuation by causal powers would be to broaden the notion of a causal power so as to allow an individual's causal *properties* more generally to constitute causal powers. Such a conception of causal powers would be an extension of that which we have been considering thus far, and though we might reasonably question how inclusive such a notion of causal powers need be, note that it must include at least *some* historical and relational properties if (1) is to be true. If one were to reconsider each of the examples I have given, supposing some appropriately extended notion of causal powers, then none of them would constitute a counterexample to my claim that (1) is false. For example, if one considered the phylogenetic lineage of an organism, one of its historical causal properties, to be one of its causal powers, then the criteria used for taxonomizing species *would* be cast in terms of the causal powers of individual entities (or at least this would become a more plausible view to hold). However, this wouldn't do for the individualist, since clearly on this view (4) would be false. If "causal power" is understood to mean causal *property*, then causal powers don't supervene on internal physical states. Some scientifically taxonomic, causal properties are historical and relational; such properties *can't* supervene on an individual's intrinsic physical state.

Here is a diagnosis of the problem in the argument from causal powers. For (1) to be true, "causal powers of *x*" must refer to a notion of causal powers that includes not only the intrinsic and the extrinsic causal powers of *x*, but all the causal properties of *x*, including at least some of its historical and relational causal properties: "causal powers" must be used in what I shall call its *extended sense*. For (4) to be true, "causal powers" can refer only to an entity's intrinsic causal powers: "Causal powers" must be used in what I shall call its *restricted sense*. The extended and restricted senses of "causal powers" are different, and so (1) and (4) cannot both be true on a common understanding of causal powers. Hence, (5) cannot be concluded in the argument from causal powers. Whether there is or ought to be solely individuation by causal powers in psychology is not something to be decided by an appeal to the *causal* nature of psychological explanation.

Although I have been assuming a relatively broad notion of causal property throughout this section, the basic point I have made is true even assuming the more minimal notion of a causal property that I mentioned in §2, which counts only intrinsic and extrinsic powers as causal powers. An individual's extrinsic causal powers, in contrast to her intrinsic causal powers (but like causal properties in general), do not supervene on that individual's intrinsic physical properties. Kinds taxonomized in terms of forward-looking properties (powers) that are extrinsic are not glob-

ally individualistic. If extrinsic causal powers play taxonomic and explanatory roles in the sciences, as I believe they frequently do, then the conclusion I have drawn could be reached assuming the narrower notion of a causal property. The argument would proceed in much the same way that my argument has proceeded, namely, by focusing on taxonomic practice in a range of sciences. Though such an argument would warrant a somewhat stronger conclusion than the one I have drawn, and would allow one to see that it is the attention to actual taxonomic practice rather than an excessively broad notion of a causal property that provides the backbone of my argument, its articulation requires a careful discussion of the distinction between intrinsic and extrinsic causal powers, as well as an examination of a different set of examples from the sciences. It is, I think, sufficiently clear in outline how such an argument would proceed; I leave its development for others.

5 Relational Taxonomies and Individualism

My argument in the previous section appealed to the relational nature of individuation in a variety of sciences to show that those sciences were not individualistic. This argument presupposes that there is an incompatibility between relational and individualistic taxonomies, a presupposition that a proponent of global individualism is likely to reject. Indeed, Fodor himself has claimed that the prevalence of relational taxonomies in science does not show global individualism, his "methodological point," to be false. In this section I defend the claim that relational and individualistic taxonomies are incompatible. Here we will return to the revisability claim about relational taxonomies introduced in §3.

Consider, first, the following argument for the incompatibility of relational individuation and individuation by intrinsic causal powers. Relational individuation involves taxonomizing an entity at least partly in terms of the relations that entity enters into. The relations that any entity enters into are determined partly by properties extrinsic to that entity. To individuate by intrinsic causal powers, as the individualist has stressed, is to taxonomize an entity *wholly* in terms of that entity's intrinsic physical properties. But no one type of thing can be partly individuated by properties that are extrinsic to it and wholly individuated by properties intrinsic to it. Hence no one *type* of thing can be both relational and individualistic.

Fodor has challenged this incompatibilist view of relational and individualistic taxonomies:

> Just as you'd expect, relational properties can count taxonomically whenever they affect causal powers. Thus "being a planet" is a relational property par excellence, but it's one that individualism permits to operate in astronomical taxonomy. For whether you are a planet affects your trajectory, and your trajectory determines what you can bump into; so whether you're a planet affects your causal powers, which is all [that] individualism asks for. (1987: 43)

This way of reconciling global individualism with the prevalence of relational taxonomies in the sciences is also manifest in Fodor's comments on the distinction between methodological *individualism* and methodological *solipsism*: "Methodological individualism is the doctrine that psychological states are individuated *with respect to their causal powers*. Methodological solipsism is the doctrine that psychological states are individuated *without respect to their semantic evaluation*" (1987: 42). Having drawn this distinction and conceded that solipsistic individuation *is* incompatible with relational individuation, Fodor continues: "there is nothing to stop principles of individuation from being simultaneously relational and individualistic. *Individualism does not prohibit the relational individuation of mental states*; it just says that no property of mental states, relational or otherwise, counts taxonomically unless it affects causal powers" (1987: 42).

The claim here is this: The idea at the core of global individualism is that an entity's causal powers are crucial to ways in which that entity is taxonomized in science. Yet the claim that taxonomy in science is "by causal powers" should not be construed too narrowly. One can preserve the core idea by taking global individualism to say that properties that *affect* an entity's causal powers in the same way can make no difference to scientific taxonomy. A relational property must make a difference to an entity's causal powers if it is to provide the basis for taxonomizing that entity scientifically.

Stalnaker (1989: 307–8) has pointed out that the reformulation of individualism proposed by Fodor here contrasts in a nontrivial way with standard characterizations of that view. Individualism is the view that taxonomy is by causal powers, not, as Fodor implies here, by what *causally affects* causal powers. The fact that being a planet affects the causal powers that a large blob of matter has is simply not relevant to the question of whether individualism is true. As Stalnaker goes on to argue, were individualism the thesis that individuation in psychology must be individuation by what affects causal powers, individualism would be compatible with *wide* individuation in psychology, since environmental facts clearly causally affect the causal powers that objects have, including their *intrinsic* causal powers. Stalnaker's point is that Fodor's compatibilism requires a construal of global individualism that is too liberal for global individualism to be the basis for individualism in psychology. I want to defend Stalnaker's claim and show how it relates to my own criticisms of the argument from causal powers. Since talk of "affecting" causal powers is somewhat vague and lumps together a variety of cases, let me first distinguish two different ways in which something can causally affect an entity's causal powers. (I am indebted to Sydney Shoemaker here.)

An entity's causal powers can be causally affected by the *relations* that that entity actually enters into: What that entity can do at a time is partially a function of what it is related to at that time. It is in this sense that a given entity's causal powers are affected by its being a planet and so by its having the relational property of orbiting a star. In this same sense, the causal powers that an organism has are causally affected by that organism's being a member of one species rather than another. Call this way in which an entity's relational properties affect its causal powers *contemporaneous* affecting: The relations that an entity stands in at a given time causally affect what powers it has at that time.

A second way in which the causal powers an entity has can be causally affected is historically: Events that form part of the history of the entity can be causally responsible for that entity's having certain causal powers rather than others. For example, the causal powers that a person has at a given time might be affected because she was present in Hiroshima in 1945, took a particular drug, or underwent special training. An event, process, relation, and so on *historically* affects an entity's causal powers only if that event made a difference to those causal powers at some earlier time.

I focus subsequently on contemporaneous affecting, partly because the case that Fodor considers is of this type but also because it is this case in which the problem with broadening global individualism to allow for properties that affect an entity's causal powers is most evident. Could we take global individualism to be the view that taxonomy in science must be either by causal powers or by what contemporaneously affects causal powers? I think not. Suppose that (1) in the argument from causal powers is extended in this way: This is how one should understand the claim that sciences taxonomize "by causal powers"; I shall refer to (1) so extended as (1*). The problem is that on such an understanding of taxonomy being "by causal powers," those properties in terms of which one must taxonomize do not supervene on intrinsic physical properties, and the argument does not allow one to infer either (5) or (6); precisely the same is true of "historical affecting," appealed to in this way. This is because either the fourth premise is false, if we modify it in the way we modified (1) to (1*), or although it is true [keeping it as (4) in the original argument], (1*) and (4) do not together allow one to infer (5). We thus arrive at the same conclusion I drew in §4: There is no single constraint on taxonomy, its having to be "by causal powers," which is reflected in actual taxonomic practice in science *and* which specifies properties that supervene on the intrinsic physical properties of the entities in the extensions of the resulting kinds.

We can understand what is wrong-headed about the general idea of modifying the argument from casual powers throughout to allow for taxonomy by what contemporaneously affects an entity's causal powers by considering what (5) and (6) in such an argument would have to say. Making the appropriate modifications would give us (5*) instead of (5):

(5*) Any causes of behavior that are to be taxonomic in the cognitive sciences must be determined or fixed by the intrinsic physical properties of the individual *or must contemporaneously affect those properties.*

Premise (6), the statement of individualism in psychology, would also need to be modified appropriately to include the emphasized disjunct. Yet an individualist should resist this modification of her view because individualism so construed would no longer imply that doppelgängers *must* be taxonomized under the same psychological kinds. Since molecularly identical individuals may be subject to different contemporaneous effects, they may be taxonomized differentially, even supposing these reformulated versions of global individualism and so individualism in psychology to be true. Recall

that the intuition that a properly scientific psychology must treat doppelgängers in the same way motivates individualism in psychology in the first place; this same intuition gives the individualist a prima facie reason to think that the taxonomy of mental states offered by folk psychology is objectionable. The proposed reformulation of the argument from causal powers does not allow one to derive a version of individualism in psychology worth deriving.

So Fodor's attempt to account for relational individuation by weakening or extending global individualism fails for much the same reason that the initial argument from causal powers fails: No single sense of "causal powers" makes both (1) and (4) true. Consider a second way in which an individualist could attempt to reconcile global individualism with the prevalence of relational taxonomies in science. The claim that historical and relational taxonomies have a *preliminary* character and the revisionary claim that often accompanies it are relevant here. Although an entity's history and its relations affect what causal powers it has at a time, this should not be taken to imply that its historical and relational properties are themselves taxonomic. Only causal powers (or properties that supervene on causal powers) can be taxonomic in science, even if historical and relational properties serve as a reliable guide to what causal powers it has. When an entity's history or its relations make a relevant difference to that entity's behavior, the corresponding historical or relational kinds are at best an approximation of or a proxy for taxonomic kinds individuated by causal powers.

To see how problematic these claims about relational taxonomies are, consider Fodor's own example of a putatively relational but individualistic concept, that of a *planet*. Something is a planet in virtue of facts about that thing's constitution (since comets are not planets) *and* facts about that thing's motion relative to a particular star (since meteors are not planets). The concept planet is relational. A physical duplicate of the Earth, say, that does not bear the relation to a star constitutive of being a planet is not a planet, even though that duplicate must, *ex hypothesi*, possess the same intrinsic causal powers as the Earth. Even a physical replica of the Earth that moved with exactly the same velocity as the Earth due to some complex combination of forces would not be a planet unless it orbited a star. Nevertheless, the concept of a planet *as it is* features in explanations in astronomy. It at least appears to be a perfectly acceptable concept in itself and does not seem to be preliminary in any way. Moreover, one cannot simply abstract away from an entity's actual relations in determining whether or not that entity is a planet. Because of these facts about taxonomic practice in astronomy, it is implausible to think that the concept planet is in any way preliminary or must be revised in some way in order to form a proper scientific kind. In fact, the concept appears to be *essentially* relational in that if we attempt to revise the concept planet in the required way, we lose the concept of a planet altogether. This suggests that it is neither necessary nor even possible in general to offer an individualistic revision of relational, scientific kinds.

Likewise, it is implausible to view the concept of a *species* as preliminary or as being revisable in the specified way. Reproductive isolation and niche occupation in an actual environment are two relational features that are part of the species concept (see § 4). Neither of these components of the species concept is or could be fixed by the intrinsic causal powers that an individual has; the relations that individual organisms instantiate play a crucial role in determining which species they belong to. Taxonomic practice in evolutionary biology does not appear to view the species concept as in any way preliminary, and as with the case of planet, I suggest taking the appearances at face value. Reflection on this example also suggests that it is neither necessary nor even possible in general to offer an individualistic revision of relational, scientific kinds.

The problems for the individualist's claim about the preliminary character of relational taxonomies and her subsequent revisability claim about the concepts of planet and species stem from two important differences between these cases and the paradigm case of a successful revision, that of the revision from weight to mass. In the latter case, there is a clear way in which the concept of weight can be factored into distinct internal and external components, and it is a trivial matter to show how these novel factors (mass and gravitational attraction, respectively) are to operate within Newtonian mechanics. The cases of planets and species have neither of these features. This is an *a posteriori*, contingent difference between the cases, depending as it does on how the concepts are embedded in the corresponding scientific theories. A more detailed discussion of the similarities and differences between these types of cases would, I think, help in determining whether *psychological* kinds are likely to be revisable in the required way. But to recognize that not all scientific kinds must be

revisable is already to acknowledge the failure of the argument from causal powers as an argument based on global individualism.

6 Causal Powers, One More Time[5]

Fodor (1991a) has offered a renewed and somewhat revised defence of his own position in *Psychosemantics* that is of interest not only because it expresses the tensions in the individualist's appeal to the notion of causal powers that I have identified, but also because it reflects more starkly the *a priori* character of Fodor's own commitment to global individualism. For these reasons and for the sake of completeness, I conclude my substantive discussion in this chapter by considering Fodor's more recent argument.

Fodor focuses on the ubiquity of relational individuation in the sciences, a fact that he takes to entail that certain relational properties, properties such as being a planet and being a member of a particular species, are causally and explanatorily adequate in themselves. In this respect, these relational kinds contrast with other relational properties, such as being a brother or having siblings. Even if there is some sense in which individuals have causal powers in virtue of instantiating this latter type of relational property, there is an intuitive sense in which an appeal to these causal powers is not truly explanatory. Given that properties like being a planet and being a member of a particular species are, as Fodor puts it, "relational properties in good standing" (p. 12) but that not *all* ascriptions of relational properties are explanatory, what is needed is some criterion distinguishing the two. Fodor takes the intuitive differences between the examples he presents as reason to develop a necessary condition "for when a difference in the properties of causes constitutes a difference in their causal powers" (p. 10). When is a relational property that an entity instantiates itself causally responsible for some effect?

Fodor thinks that there is an *a priori* answer to this question, an answer that provides a criterion for distinguishing two types of relational properties. Those concepts or kinds that satisfy this constraint or criterion can be taxonomic and so explanatory in the sciences; those that do not satisfy it cannot be taxonomic or explanatory. Fodor organizes his discussion around the claim that *wide* contents do not constitute causal powers satisfying the general condition he develops; hence, they are not to be taxonomic or explanatory in psychology. Fodor's argument for individualism in psychology here, like the argument from causal powers, utilizes a more general claim about scientific taxonomies.

Before examining Fodor's criterion itself, I want to express my doubts about Fodor's way of stating the problem that the prevalence of relational taxonomies poses for an individualist. For Fodor, the question that needs answering is this: When can the (relational) property of a cause count as what he calls a *real causal power*, where only real causal powers feature in scientific taxonomies and generalizations? Like the "methodological point" that Fodor made in *Psychosemantics* discussed in § 4, the relation that Fodor presumes to hold between causal powers and scientific explanation holds only if causal powers are conceived of as violating the constraint of supervenience specified in Fodor's "metaphysical point." Fodor relies on what I have called the *extended sense* of "causal powers" even in stating the problem in the way that he does.

Fodor presupposes the extended sense of "causal powers" throughout much of the paper. Consider the following two passages:

Taxonomy by relational properties is ubiquitous in the sciences, and it is not in dispute that properties like *being a meteor or being a planet* — properties which could, notice, distinguish molecularly identical chunks of rock — constitute causal powers. (p. 12)

And the intuition about features of causal history is that some of them *are* causal powers (e.g., having been dropped in transit; having been inoculated for smallpox) and some of them are not .... (p. 18; emphasis added)

If molecular duplicates can differ in some property, then that property cannot supervene on the internal physical properties that those duplicates share. Fodor is here abandoning the "metaphysical point" he made in *Psychosemantics*, the claim that causal powers supervene on local microstructure. As I argued in § 5, however, this metaphysical point is not an optional extra for an individualist defending the view that individualism in psychology follows from global individualism. In fact, elsewhere (e.g., pp. 16–17, 25), Fodor himself identifies the central claim of individualism as the claim that psychological kinds are locally supervenient.

Like Fodor's version of the argument from causal powers, his argument here shifts between two different and incompatible notions of causal

powers. In accord with the first, the extended sense, taxonomy in science *is* taxonomy by causal powers; in accord with the second, the restricted sense, causal powers supervene on intrinsic physical properties. The dilemma here can be stated in the terms that Fodor uses in "A modal argument". If real causal powers must supervene on intrinsic physical properties, it is false that *only* real causal powers taxonomize scientific kinds. And if it is true that only real causal powers are used to taxonomize scientific kinds, then real causal powers do not supervene on intrinsic physical properties, and so there is no reason for the properties of a scientific *psychology* to be locally supervenient.

Consider, now, Fodor's criterion, which he states in terms of what he calls *cause properties* (CP), the properties that a cause has:

For the difference between being CP1 and being CP2 to be a difference of causal powers, it must at least be that the effects of being CP1 differ from the effects of being CP2. But, I claim, it is further required that this difference between the effects be *nonconceptually* related to the difference between the causes. (p. 24)

In keeping with the spirit of the original argument from causal powers, this general criterion applies to scientific taxonomies *per se*. Properties that, intuitively, do not seem to endow their bearers with real causal powers include being a brother, having siblings, being an *H*-particle (defined in Fodor 1987: ch.2), and having water thoughts. Fodor claims that what the inadmissable cases have in common is that statements ascribing the effects that such powers have are conceptual truths. So, for example, if you are a sibling, you have the "power" to have sons who are nephews. But this is true in virtue of the meanings of "sibling," "son," and "nephew"; it is a conceptual truth that siblings have the power to have sons who are nephews. This is not true of the causal powers used in scientific taxonomies. As Fodor says of one's real causal powers, "to put it roughly, your causal powers are a function of your *contingent* connections, not of your conceptual connections" (p. 19). Relational taxonomies are genuinely explanatory kinds (i.e., they classify entities by their real causal powers) only if some of the statements that describe the effects that putative powers have are not conceptual truths.

Note that this criterion presupposes the analytic–synthetic distinction, since conceptual truths are just analytic truths, even if in some cases unobvious ones. The introduction of the notion of analyticity here to delineate real causal powers from what one might think of as *mere-Cambridge* causal powers (*sensu* Shoemaker 1980) would be enough for some of us to think that something had gone wrong. Whatever else one resurrects to save an argument for individualism, let it not be the analytic–synthetic distinction! Even those who disagree here about the general value of the analytic–synthetic distinction in the philosophy of science should have doubts about Fodor's reliance on it in this context, and not only because of Fodor's own explicit criticisms (Fodor 1987: ch. 3; Fodor and Lepore 1992) of views that, he claims, are committed to it. As I shall argue, the analytic–synthetic distinction simply cannot do the work that Fodor requires that it do in distinguishing real causal powers from mere-Cambridge causal powers. I shall focus specifically on the case of psychology, though the objection I want to make can be generalized unproblematically.

Fodor claims (pp. 23–4; cf. pp. 20–1) that each of the following statements is conceptually necessary:

If B is property that water thoughts have, then if I am connected to water in the right way, then B is a property that my thoughts have.

If B is a property that water behaviors have, then if my thoughts are water thoughts, then my behaviors have B.

Being connected to water rather than twater leads to water thinking rather than twater thinking.

For these statements to be conceptually necessary, they must both be necessary truths and be true in virtue solely of the meanings of the words they contain. I think that the analytic status of even these three statements can be reasonably questioned, though I shall not defend this claim here. Even if these statements *are* analytic, this is not sufficient to show that the property of having a particular wide content is not a real causal power; to show that, *every* statement ascribing an effect to the wide content of a mental state must be analytic, and this is an extremely implausible claim *whatever* one thinks of this type of appeal to the analytic–synthetic distinction. For example, consider each of the following statements:

Stella turned on the tap because she wanted water.

Archie called his mother because he was worried about her.

Joan walked because she thought she needed the exercise.

Each of these statements offers a commonsense, psychological explanation of a behavioral effect, and none of them is analytic. There are *many* effects that having mental states with a particular content have, and it is implausible to see *every statement* reporting a causal effect of an agent's beliefs and desires as analytic. Even if intuitions about analyticity are shared to a large extent for some core cases, there is a potentially infinite number of cases to consider, and very few of them will be analytic.

There are more details to Fodor's argument than I have discussed here. But I do not intend this section to function as a comprehensive discussion of Fodor's paper, and rather than focus on the specifics, I want instead to return to the broader issue of why Fodor's general approach here is mistaken by relating my discussion in this section to that in §4 and §5.

In §5 I argued that the existence of relational taxonomies in the sciences constitutes a general problem for the argument from causal powers, since the properties in terms of which such taxonomies are individuated do not supervene on the intrinsic properties of an individual. Fodor does not seem to think that there is a *general* problem here, I think, because he primarily uses the extended sense of "causal powers." A central criticism of both the argument from causal powers and Fodor's defense of it in "A modal argument" has been that the extended sense of "causal powers" will not allow you to derive individualism in psychology.

Since Fodor does not consider there to be a general problem for global individualism concerning relational individuation, he formulates a weak necessary condition for being a real causal power. All that the condition needs to do is to rule out, in a principled way, mere-Cambridge causal powers as genuinely explanatory. Yet, general worries about the appeal to analyticity to one side, we have seen that it is doubtful whether *on its own terms* Fodor's criterion rules out an explanatory appeal to wide content in psychology. Because his criterion does not apply to kinds in themselves but rather to the causal generalizations that they feature in, it cannot rule out an appeal to a given relational kind unless *every* causal generalization that it features in is analytic.

At the end of §5 I suggested that the question of when relational properties are revisable into narrow properties has only an *a posteriori* answer: It depends on whether there is (or is likely to be) a theoretical framework for expressing the resulting narrow property. The same is true of the question that Fodor attempts to answer with his *a priori* criterion, the question of when a relational property is itself causally responsible for some effect. This is why his criterion *cannot* rule out appeals to wide content in psychological explanations.

The need for an *a posteriori* answer to this question is implicit in several places in Fodor's own discussion. For example, he says:

> The question we are raising is not whether the difference between having CP1 and having CP2 is a difference in causal powers; rather, it is whether the difference between having CP1 and having CP2 is a difference in causal powers in virtue of its being responsible for a certain difference between E1 and E2 [effects], namely, in virtue of its being responsible for E1's having EP1 rather than EP2 and for E2's having EP2 rather than EP1. The point I am wanting to emphasize is that a cause property might fail to count as a causal power in virtue of its responsibility for one effect property, but still might constitute a causal power in virtue of its responsibility for some other effect property. (pp. 12–13)

Fodor illustrates his point here by considering the possibility of having *sibling's disease*, a disease that "causes people who have siblings to break out in a rash" (p. 13). If there were such a disease, then having it would be instantiating a real causal power, since the effects it has are contingent, not conceptual. This implies that any of the properties that Fodor would like to place together under the heading "relational properties not in good standing," properties like being a sibling, having a brother, being an *H*-particle, and having water thoughts, could be real causal powers were the world a certain way. All that one would have to do is to formulate some contingently true statement ascribing an effect that, say, having water thoughts has in order for water thoughts to count as real causal powers.

There is nothing about these relational properties *themselves* that makes them unsuitable for scientific taxonomies: Whether they are suitable or not depends on which effects you attribute to them *and* on how the world is. Precisely the same is true of the categories and kinds that feature in our existing sciences. There is no intrinsic difference between the relational properties of being a sibling and being a planet that makes only the latter suitable for scientific explanation. The relational properties of being a sibling and being a planet, as a matter of fact, do differ in the role that each plays in scientific taxonomies, but this is not because only one of them is of a special kind suitable for taxonomy in science. Determining an answer to the question Fodor has posed, the question of when a relational property that an entity instantiates is itself causally responsible for some effect, requires an *a posteriori* approach.

There is no *type* of relational property that plays an individuative role in scientific taxonomies, and so any *a priori* criterion attempting to capture what it is about certain relational properties that allows them to be taxonomic in science is not only mistaken but reflects a mistaken approach to issues concerning the nature of scientific taxonomies and explanations. This, in turn, brings us back to one of the key intuitions that motivates the argument from causal powers, the idea that it must be the intrinsic properties of entities that are taxonomic in science. For just as relational properties cannot be divided *a priori* into those that are and those that are not suitable for scientific taxonomy, neither can properties be divided into two groups, intrinsic and relational properties, only the first of which can be taxonomic in science.

7 Conclusion

The causal nature of psychology provides one with no reason to think that individuation in psychology, or indeed in any science concerned with developing causal generalizations, must abide by the constraint of individualism. It would be very interesting were some global analogue to individualism in psychology to function as a constraint on scientific explanation as it is practiced, or were there compelling arguments for thinking that it should serve as a regulative norm in science. The argument throughout this chapter has been that an examination of the patterns of individuation in sciences as they are practiced supports neither of these claims.

Central to my argument has been the claim that the individualist defending the argument from causal powers must employ an extended sense of "causal powers" to make global individualism true, whereas she must use "causal powers" in a restricted sense in order for causal powers to supervene on intrinsic physical properties. In § 3 we saw that the proponent of the argument from causal powers might accept the view that any relational, scientific concept can be factored into one that individuates the entities in its extension by their intrinsic causal powers. Towards the end of § 5, I suggested that the possibility of such revisions did not look plausible, but I have offered no *general* argument to show that this option is not defensible. Although I see no way that the ambitious revisability claim I have discussed can be successfully defended, a less ambitious claim about revisability might provide a suitable basis for a closely related argument for individualism. The argument I have in mind would require establishing what it is, if anything, about certain relational concepts in science that allows them to be revised narrowly and showing that relational concepts in psychology also have this property.

It would be a mistake to view my argument as showing (or even as trying to show) that causal powers have nothing to do with scientific taxonomy or that they are unimportant in scientific explanation. Many scientific taxonomies do individuate by causal powers, and in pointing out that there are many scientific taxonomies that do *not* individuate in this way, I do not mean to deny the interest that the former fact has. I have been concerned primarily with addressing a mistaken view about the consequences of adopting a "scientifically respectable" view of psychology; a properly scientific psychology need not be individualistic.

Finally, I claimed in the introduction to this chapter that the argument from causal powers relied on a number of intuitions about explanation, causation, and causal powers. Although the argument from causal powers should be rejected, working out which of these intuitions should be rejected along with it, or which inferences from these intuitions to the premises of the argument are invalid, is a task I shall not undertake now. Those swayed both by the intuitions about causation and explanation and by my critique of the argument from causal powers need a positive view of causation and explanation that allows them to understand why psychology need not be individualistic in order to be properly scientific. I begin to articulate such a view in Part II, where I re-examine some of the persistent intuitions about causal powers and explanation more closely. Isn't there some *other* argument from the intuition that the notion of causal powers is central to explanation to the claim that individualism is a constraint on psychology? In Chapter 5 I consider two such arguments, one based on a view of the nature of *properties*, the other on a view of the nature of *causation*, and explore the metaphysical conception that underlies these arguments, as well as the argument from causal powers.

So, as extended as the discussion of the argument from causal powers in this chapter has been, we are not yet finished with the issues it raises. But let us not get ahead of the game. There are a number of other arguments for individualism that we must first examine. The first of these is the *computational* argument for individualism.

Notes

1   These intuitions about the characterization of an entity *qua* cause in a causal explanation have been expressed to me independently and in various forms by Carl Ginet, Terence Horgan, Terence Irwin, and Sydney Shoemaker. They will be focal in much of the remaining discussion in this chapter.

2   What I say about projectibility goes also for appeals to laws and natural kinds as criteria of demarcation. Thus, recent discussions of psychological laws (Fodor 1987: ch. 1; 1991b; Horgan and Tienson 1990; Schiffer 1991) are not really relevant to the argument from causal powers.

3   These were, respectively: (1) Taxonomic properties and entities in the sciences must be individuated by their causal powers. (4) The causal powers of any-

thing are determined or fixed by that thing's intrinsic physical properties.

4   For example, this definition differs from Mayr's own earlier definition (1942); see Mayr (1982: ch. 6) for an overview. Note that even phenetic conceptions of species (Sokal and Crovello 1970) individuate species in terms of relational properties, such as behavioral and ecological properties. Richard Boyd's (1988, 1989, 1990) discussions of homeostatic property-cluster definitions indicate, I think, why species are not individuated by their intrinsic causal powers.

5   Even one more time will be one too many for some readers, who may prefer to go straight to the conclusion to this chapter. All quotations in this section are from Fodor's "A model argument for narrow content," as are all page number references.

16

Self-Knowledge

Knowing One's Own Mind

Donald Davidson

There is no secret about the nature of the evidence we use to decide what other people think: we observe their acts, read their letters, study their expressions, listen to their words, learn their histories, and note their relations to society. How we are able to assemble such material into a convincing picture of a mind is another matter; we know how to do it without necessarily knowing how we do it. Sometimes I learn what I believe in much the same way someone else does, by noticing what I say and do. There may be times when this is my only access to my own thoughts. According to Graham Wallas.

> The little girl had the making of a poet in her who, being told to be sure of her meaning before she spoke, said "How can I know what I think till I see what I say?"[1]

A similar thought was expressed by Robert Motherwell: "I would say that most good painters don't know what they think until they paint it."

Gilbert Ryle was with the poet and the painter all the way in this matter; he stoutly maintained that we know our own minds in exactly the same way we know the minds of others, by observing what we say, do, and paint. Ryle was wrong. It is seldom the case that I need or appeal to evidence or observation in order to find out what I believe; normally I know what I think before I speak or act. Even when I have evidence, I seldom make use of it. I can be wrong about my own thoughts, and so the appeal to what can be publicly determined is

not irrelevant. But the possibility that one may be mistaken about one's own thoughts cannot defeat the overriding presumption that a person knows what he or she believes; in general, the belief that one has a thought is enough to justify that belief. But though this is true, and even obvious to most of us, the fact has, so far as I can see, no easy explanation. While it is clear enough, at least in outline, what we have to go on in trying to fathom the thoughts of others, it is obscure why, in our own case, we can so often know what we think without appeal to evidence or recourse to observation.

Because we usually know what we believe (and desire and doubt and intend) without needing or using evidence (even when it is available), our sincere avowals concerning our present states of mind are not subject to the failings of conclusions based on evidence. Thus sincere first person present-tense claims about thoughts, while neither infallible nor incorrigible, have an authority no second or third person claim, or first person other-tense claim, can have. To recognize this fact is not, however, to explain it.

Since Wittgenstein it has become routine to try to relieve worries about "our knowledge of other minds" by remarking that it is an essential aspect of our use of certain mental predicates that we apply them to others on the basis of behavioral evidence but to ourselves without benefit of such aid. The remark is true, and when properly elaborated, it ought to answer someone who wonders how we can know the minds of others. But as a response to the skeptic, Wittgenstein's insight (if it is Wittgenstein's) should give little satisfaction. For, first, it is a strange idea that claims made without evidential or observational support should be favored over claims with such support. Of course, if evidence is not cited in support of a claim, the claim cannot be impugned by questioning the truth or relevance of the evidence. But these points hardly suffice to suggest that in general claims without evidential support are more trustworthy than those with. The second, and chief, difficulty is this. One would normally say that what counts as evidence for the application of a concept helps define the concept, or at least places constraints on its identification. If two concepts regularly depend for their application on different criteria or ranges of evidential support, they must be different concepts. So if what is apparently the same expression is sometimes correctly employed on the basis of a certain range of evidential support and sometimes on the basis of another range of evidential support (or none), the obvious conclusion would seem to be that the expression is ambiguous. Why then should we suppose that a predicate like "*x* believes that Ras Dashan is the highest mountain in Ethiopia," which is applied sometimes on the basis of behavioral evidence and sometimes not, is unambiguous? If it is ambiguous, then there is no reason to suppose it has the same meaning when applied to oneself that it has when applied to another. If we grant (as we should) that the necessarily public and interpersonal character of language guarantees that we often correctly apply these predicates to others, and that therefore we often do know what *others* think, then the question must be raised what grounds each of us has for thinking he knows what (in the same sense) *he* thinks. The Wittgensteinian style of answer may solve the problem of other minds, but it creates a corresponding problem about knowledge of one's own mind. The correspondence is not quite complete, however. The original problem of other minds invited the question how one knows others have minds at all. The problem we now face must be put this way: I know what to look for in attributing thoughts to others. Using quite different criteria (or none), I apply the same predicates to myself; so the skeptical question arises why I should think it is *thoughts* I am attributing to myself. But since the evidence I use in the case of others is open to the public, there is no reason why I shouldn't attribute thoughts to myself in the same way I do to others,

in the mode of Graham Wallace, Robert Motherwell, and Gilbert Ryle. In other words, I don't, but I could, treat my own mental states in the same way I do those of others. No such strategy is available to someone who seeks the same sort of authority with respect to the thoughts of others as he apparently has in dealing with his own thoughts. So the asymmetry between the cases remains a problem, and it is first person authority that creates the problem.

I have suggested an answer to this problem in another paper.[2] In that paper I argued that attention to how we attribute thoughts and meanings to others would explain first person authority without inviting skeptical doubts. In recent years, however, some of the very facts about the attribution of attitudes on which I relied to defend first person authority have been employed to attack that authority: it has been argued, on what are thought to be new grounds, that while the methods of the third person interpreter determine what we usually deem to be the contents of an agent's mind, the contents so determined may be unknown to the agent. In the present essay I consider some of these arguments, and urge that they do not constitute a genuine threat to first person authority. The explanation I offered in my earlier paper of the asymmetry between first and other-person attributions of attitudes seems to me if anything to be strengthened by the new considerations, or those of them that seem valid.

It should be stressed again that the problem I am concerned with does not require that our beliefs about our own contemporary states of mind be infallible or incorrigible. We can and do make mistakes about what we believe, desire, approve, and intend; there is also the possibility of self-deceit. But such cases, though not infrequent, are not and could not be standard; I do not argue for this now, but take it as one of the facts to be explained.

Setting aside, then, self-deception and other anomalous or borderline phenomena, the question is whether we can, without irrationality, inconsistency, or confusion, simply and straightforwardly think we have a belief we do not have, or think we do not have a belief we do have. A number of philosophers and philosophically minded psychologists have recently entertained views that entail or suggest that this could easily happen – indeed, that it must happen all the time.

The threat was there in Russell's idea of propositions that could be known to be true even though they contained "ingredients" with which the mind of the knower was not acquainted; and as the study of the *de re* attitudes evolved the peril grew more acute.

But it was Hilary Putnam who pulled the plug. Consider Putnam's 1975 argument to show that meanings, as he put it, "just ain't in the head."[3] Putnam argues persuasively that what words mean depends on more than "what is in the head." He tells a number of stories the moral of which is that aspects of the natural history of how someone learned the use of a word necessarily make a difference to what the word means. It seems to follow that two people might be in physically identical states, and yet mean different things by the same words.

The consequences are far-reaching. For if people can (usually) express their thoughts correctly in words, then their thoughts – their beliefs, desires, intentions, hopes, expectations – also must in part be identified by events and objects outside the person. If meanings ain't in the head, then neither, it would seem, are beliefs and desires and the rest.

Since some of you may be a little weary of Putnam's doppelganger on Twin Earth, let me tell my own science fiction story – if that is what it is. My story avoids some irrelevant difficulties in Putnam's story, though it introduces some new problems of its own.[4] (I'll come back to Earth, and Twin Earth, a little later.) Suppose lightning strikes a dead tree in a swamp; I am standing nearby. My body is reduced to its elements, while entirely by coincidence (and out of different molecules) the tree is turned into my physical replica. My replica, The Swampman, moves exactly as I did; according to its nature it departs the swamp, encounters and seems to recognize my friends, and appears to return their greetings in English. It moves into my house and seems to write articles on radical interpretation. No one can tell the difference.

But there *is* a difference. My replica can't recognize my friends; it can't *re*cognize anything, since it never cognized anything in the first place. It can't know my friends' names (though of course it seems to), it can't remember my house. It can't mean what I do by the word "house," for example, since the sound "house" it makes was not learned in a context that would give it the right meaning – or any meaning at all. Indeed, I don't see how my replica can be said to mean anything by the sounds it makes, nor to have any thoughts.

Putnam might not go along with this last claim, for he says that if two people (or objects) are in relevantly similar physical states, it is "absurd" to think their psychological states are "one bit different."[5] It would be a mistake to be sure that Putnam and I disagree on this point, however, since it is not yet clear how the phrase "psychological state" is being used.

Putnam holds that many philosophers have wrongly assumed that psychological states like belief and knowing the meaning of a word are both (I) "inner" in the sense that they do not presuppose the existence of any individual other than the subject to whom the state is ascribed, and (II) that these are the very states which we normally identify and individuate as we do beliefs and the other propositional attitudes. Since we normally identify and individuate mental states and meanings in terms partly of relations to objects and events other than the subject, Putnam believes (I) and (II) come apart: in his opinion, no states can satisfy both conditions.

Putnam calls psychological states satisfying condition (I) "narrow." He thinks of such states as solipsistic, and associates them with Descartes's view of the mental. Putnam may consider these states to be the only "true" psychological states; in much of his paper he omits the qualifier "narrow," despite the fact that narrow psychological states (so called) do not correspond to the propositional attitudes as normally identified. Not everyone has been persuaded that there is an intelligible distinction to be drawn between narrow (or inner, or Cartesian, or individualistic – all these terms are current) psychological states and psychological states identified (if any are) in terms of external facts (social or otherwise). Thus John Searle has claimed that our ordinary propositional attitudes satisfy condition (I), and so there is no need of states satisfying condition (II), while Tyler Burge has denied that there are, in any interesting sense, propositional attitudes that satisfy condition (I).[6] But there seems to be universal agreement that no states satisfy both conditions.

The thesis of this essay is that there is no reason to suppose that ordinary mental states do not satisfy both conditions (I) and (II): I think such states are "inner," in the sense of being identical with states of the body, and so identifiable without reference to objects or events outside the body; they are at the same time "nonindividualistic" in the sense that they can be, and usually are, identified in part by their causal relations to events and objects outside the subject whose states they are. A corollary of this thesis will turn out to be that contrary to what is often assumed, first person authority can without contradiction apply to states that are regularly identified by their relations to events and objects outside the person.

I begin with the corollary. Why is it natural to assume that states that satisfy condition (II) may not be known to the person who is in those states?

Now I must talk about Putnam's Twin Earth. He asks us to imagine two people exactly alike physically and (therefore) alike with respect to all "narrow" psychological states. One of the two people, an inhabitant of Earth, has learned to use the word water by being shown water, reading and hearing about it, etc. The other, an inhabitant of Twin Earth, has learned to use the word "water" under conditions not observably different, but the substance to which she has been exposed is not water but a lookalike substance we may call "twater." Under the circumstances, Putnam claims, the first speaker refers to water when she uses the word "water"; her twin refers to twater when *she* uses the word "water." So we seem to have a case where "narrow" psychological states are identical, and yet the speakers mean different things by the same word.

How about the thoughts of these two speakers? The first says to herself, when facing a glass of water, "Here's a glass of water"; the second mutters exactly the same sounds to herself when facing a glass of twater. Each speaks the truth, since their words mean different things. And since each is sincere, it is natural to suppose they believe different things, the first believing there is a glass of water in front of her, the second believing there is a glass of twater in front of *her*. But do they know what they believe? If the meanings of their words, and thus the beliefs expressed by using those words, are partly determined by external factors about which the agents are ignorant, their beliefs and meanings are not narrow in Putnam's sense. There is therefore nothing on the basis of which either speaker can tell which state she is in, for there is no internal or external clue to the difference available. We ought, it seems, to conclude that neither speaker knows what she means or thinks. The conclusion has been drawn explicitly by a number of philosophers, among them Putnam. Putnam declares that he "totally abandons the idea that if there is a difference in meaning...then there *must* be some difference in our concepts (or in our psychological state). What

determines meaning and extension "is not, in general, fully known to the speaker."[7] Here "psychological state" means *narrow* psychological state, and it is assumed that only such states are "fully known." Jerry Fodor believes that ordinary propositional attitudes are (pretty nearly) "in the head," but he agrees with Putnam that *if* propositional attitudes were partly identified by factors outside the agent, they would not be in the head, and would not necessarily be known to the agent.[8] John Searle also, though his reasons are not Fodor's, holds that meanings are in the head ("there is nowhere else for them to be"), but seems to accept the inference that if this were not the case, first person authority would be lost.[9] Perhaps the plainest statement of the position appears in Andrew Woodfield's introduction to a book of essays on the objects of thought. Referring to the claim that the contents of the mind are often determined by facts external to and perhaps unknown to the person whose mind it is, he says:

> Because the external relation is not determined subjectively, the subject is not authoritative about that. A third person might well be in a better position than the subject to know which object the subject is thinking about, hence be better placed to know which thought it was.[10]

Those who accept the thesis that the contents of propositional attitudes are partly identified in terms of external factors seem to have a problem similar to the problem of the skeptic who finds we may be altogether mistaken about the "outside" world. In the present case, ordinary scepticism of the senses is avoided by supposing the world itself more or less correctly determines the contents of thoughts about the world. (The speaker who thinks it is water is probably right, for he learned the use of the word "water" in a watery environment; the speaker who thinks twater is probably right, for he learned the word "water" in a twatery environment.) But skepticism is not defeated; it is only displaced onto knowledge of our own minds. Our ordinary beliefs about the external world are (on this view) directed onto the world, but we don't know what we believe.

There is, of course, a difference between water and twater, and it can be discovered by normal means, whether it is discovered or not. So a person might find out what he believes by discovering the difference between water and twater, and finding out enough about his own relations both to determine which one his talk and beliefs are about. The skeptical conclusion we seem to have reached concerns the extent of first person authority: it is far more limited than we supposed. Our beliefs about the world are mostly true, but we may easily be wrong about what we think. It is a transposed image of Cartesian skepticism.

Those who hold that the contents of our thoughts and the meanings of our words are often fixed by factors of which we are ignorant have not been much concerned with the apparent consequence of their views which I have been emphasizing. They have, of course, realized that if they were right, the Cartesian idea that the one thing we can be certain of is the contents of our own minds, and the Fregean notion of meanings fully "grasped," must be wrong. But they have not made much of an attempt, so far as I know, to resolve the seeming conflict between their views and the strong intuition that first person authority exists.

One reason for the lack of concern may be that some seem to see the problem as confined to a fairly limited range of cases, cases where concepts or words latch on to objects that are picked out or referred to using proper names, indexicals, and words for natural kinds. Others, though, argue that the ties between language and thought on the one hand and external affairs on the other are so pervasive that no aspect of thought as usually conceived is untouched. In this vein Daniel Dennett remarks that "one must be richly informed about, intimately connected with, the world at large, its occupants and properties, in order to be said with any propriety to have beliefs."[11] He goes on to claim that the identification of *all* beliefs is infected by the outside, nonsubjective factors that are recognized to operate in the sort of case we have been discussing. Burge also emphasizes the extent to which our beliefs are affected by external factors, though for reasons he does not explain, he apparently does not view this as a threat to first person authority.[12]

The subject has taken a disquieting turn. At one time behaviorism was invoked to show how it was possible for one person to know what was in another's mind; behaviorism was then rejected in part because it could not explain one of the most obvious aspects of mental states: the fact that they are in general known to the person who has them without appeal to behavioristic evidence. The recent fashion, though not strictly behavioristic, once more identifies mental states partly in terms of social and other external factors, thus making

them to that extent publicly discoverable. But at the same time it reinstates the problem of accounting for first person authority.

Those who are convinced of the external dimension of the contents of thoughts as ordinarily identified and individuated have reacted in different ways. One response has been to make a distinction between the contents of the mind as subjectively and internally determined, on the one hand, and ordinary beliefs, desires, and intentions, as we normally attribute them on the basis of social and other outward connections, on the other. This is clearly the trend of Putnam's argument (although the word "water" has different meanings, and is used to express different beliefs when it is used to refer to water and to twater, people using the word for these different purposes may be in "the same psychological state"). Jerry Fodor accepts the distinction for certain purposes, but argues that psychology should adopt the stance of "methodological solipsism" (Putnam's phrase) – that is, it should deal exclusively with inner states, the truly subjective psychological states which owe nothing to their relations to the outside world.[13]

Stephen Stich makes essentially the same distinction, but draws a sterner moral: where Fodor thinks we merely need to tinker a bit with propositional attitudes as usually conceived to separate out the purely subjective element, Stich holds that psychological states as we now think of them belong to a crude and confused "folk psychology" which must be replaced by a yet to be invented "cognitive science." The subtitle of his recent book is "The Case Against Belief."[14]

Clearly those who draw such a distinction have ensured that the problem of first person authority, at least as I have posed it, cannot be solved. For the problem I have set is how to explain the asymmetry between the way in which a person knows about his contemporary mental states and the way in which others know about them. The mental states in question are beliefs, desires, intentions, and so on, as ordinarily conceived. Those who accept something like Putnam's distinction do not even try to explain first person authority with respect to these states; if there is first person authority at all, it attaches to quite different states. (In Stich's case, it is not obvious that it can attach to anything.)

I think Putnam, Burge, Dennett, Fodor, Stich, and others are right in calling attention to the fact that ordinary mental states, at least the propositional attitudes, are partly identified by relations to society and the rest of the environment, relations which may in some respects not be known to the person in those states. They are also right, in my opinion, in holding that for this reason (if for no other), the concepts of "folk psychology" cannot be incorporated into a coherent and comprehensive system of laws of the sort for which physics strives. These concepts are part of a commonsense theory for describing, interpreting, and explaining human behavior which is a bit freestyle, but (so I think) indispensable. I can imagine a science concerned with people and purged of "folk psychology," but I cannot think in what its interest would consist. This is not, however, the topic of this essay.

I am here concerned with the puzzling discovery that we apparently do not know what we think – at least in the way we think we do. This is a real puzzle if, like me, you believe it is true that external factors partly determine the contents of thoughts, and also believe that in general we do know, and in a way others do not, what we think. The problem arises because admitting the identifying and individuating role of external factors seems to lead to the conclusion that our thoughts may not be known to us.

But does this conclusion follow? The answer depends, I believe, on the way in which one thinks the identification of mental contents depends on external factors.

The conclusion does follow, for example, for any theory which holds that propositional attitudes are identified by objects (such as propositions, tokens of propositions, or representations) which are in or "before" the mind, and which contain or incorporate (as "ingredients") objects or events outside the agent; for it is obvious that everyone is ignorant of endless features of every external object. That the conclusion follows from these assumptions is generally conceded.[15] However, for reasons I shall mention below, I reject the assumptions on which the conclusion is in this case based.

Tyler Burge has suggested that there is another way in which external factors enter into the determination of the contents of speech and thought. One of his "thought experiments" happens pretty well to fit me. Until recently I believed arthritis was an inflammation of the joints caused by calcium deposits; I did not know that any inflammation of the joints, for example gout, also counted as arthritis. So when a doctor told me (falsely as it turned out) that I had gout, I believed I had gout

but I did not believe I had arthritis. At this point Burge asks us to imagine a world in which I was physically the same but in which the word "arthritis" happened actually to apply only to inflammation of the joints caused by calcium deposits. Then the sentence "Gout is not a form of arthritis" would have been true, not false, and the belief that I expressed by this sentence would not have been the false belief that gout is not a form of arthritis but a true belief about some disease other than arthritis. Yet in the imagined world all my physical states, my "internal qualitative experiences", my behavior and dispositions to behave, are the same as they are in this world. My *belief* would have changed, but I would have no reason to suppose that it had, and so could not be said to know what I believed.

Burge stresses the fact that his argument depends on

> the possibility of someone's having a propositional attitude despite an incomplete mastery of some notion in its content ... *if* the thought experiment is to work, one must at some stage find the subject believing (or having some attitude characterized by) a content, despite an incomplete understanding or misapplication.[16]

It seems to follow that if Burge is right, whenever a person is wrong, confused, or partially misinformed about the meaning of a word, he is wrong, confused, or partially misinformed about any of his beliefs that is (or would be?) expressed by using that word. Since such "partial understanding" is "common or even normal in the case of a large number of expressions in our vocabularies" according to Burge, it must be equally common or normal for us to be wrong about what we believe (and, of course, fear, hope for, wish were the case, doubt, and so on).

Burge apparently accepts this conclusion; at least so I interpret his denial that "full understanding of a content is in general a necessary condition for believing the content." He explicitly rejects "the old model according to which a person must be directly acquainted with, or must immediately apprehend, the contents of his thoughts ... a person's thought *content* is not fixed by what goes on in him, or by what is accessible to him simply by careful reflection."[17]

I am uncertain how to understand these claims, since I am uncertain how seriously to take the talk of "direct acquaintance" with, and of "immediately apprehending," a content. But in any case I am convinced that if what we mean and think is determined by the linguistic habits of those around us in the way Burge believes they are, then first person authority is very seriously compromised. Since the degree and character of the compromise seem to me incompatible with what we know about the kind of knowledge we have of our own minds, I must reject some premise of Burge's. I agree that what I mean and think is not "fixed" (exclusively) by what goes on in me, so what I must reject is Burge's account of how social and other external factors control the contents of a person's mind.

For a number of reasons, I am inclined to discount the importance of the features of our attributions of attitudes to which Burge points. Suppose that I, who think the word "arthritis" applies to inflammation of the joints only if caused by calcium deposits, and my friend Arthur, who knows better, both sincerely utter to Smith the words "Carl has arthritis." According to Burge, if other things are more or less equal (Arthur and I are both generally competent speakers of English, both have often applied the word "arthritis" to genuine cases of arthritis, etc.) then our words on this occasion mean the same thing, Arthur and I mean the same thing by our words, and we express the same belief. My error about the dictionary meaning of the word (or about what arthritis is) makes no difference to what I meant or thought on this occasion. Burge's evidence for this claim seems to rest on his conviction that this is what anyone (unspoiled by philosophy) would report about Arthur and me. I doubt that Burge is right about this, but even if he is, I don't think it proves his claim. Ordinary attributions of meanings and attitudes rest on vast and vague assumptions about what is and is not shared (linguistically and otherwise) by the attributer, the person to whom the attribution is made, and the attributer's intended audience. When some of these assumptions prove false, we may alter the words we use to make the report, often in substantial ways. When nothing much hinges on it, we tend to choose the lazy way: we take someone at his word, even if this does not quite reflect some aspect of the speaker's thought or meaning. But this is not because we are bound (outside of a law court, anyway) to be legalistic about it. And often we aren't. If Smith (unspoiled by philosophy) reports to still another party (perhaps a distant doctor attempting a diagnosis on the basis of a telephone report) that Arthur and I both have said, and believe, that Carl has arthritis, he

may actively mislead *his* hearer. If this danger were to arise, Smith, alert to the facts, would not simply say "Arthur and Davidson both believe Carl has arthritis"; he would add something like, "But Davidson thinks arthritis must be caused by calcium deposits." The need to make this addition I take to show that the simple attribution was not quite right; there was a relevant difference in the thoughts Arthur and I expressed when we said "Carl has arthritis." Burge does not have to be budged by this argument, of course, since he can insist that the report is literally correct, but could, like any report, be misleading. I think, on the other hand, that this reply would overlook the extent to which the contents of one belief necessarily depend on the contents of others. Thoughts are not independent atoms, and so there can be no simple, rigid, rule for the correct attribution of a single thought.[18]

Though I reject Burge's insistence that we are bound to give a person's words the meaning they have in his linguistic community, and to interpret his propositional attitudes on the same basis, I think there is a somewhat different, but very important, sense in which social factors do control what a speaker can mean by his words. If a speaker wishes to be understood, he must intend his words to be interpreted in a certain way, and so must intend to provide his audience with the clues they need to arrive at the intended interpretation. This holds whether the hearer is sophisticated in the use of a language the speaker knows or is the learner of a first language. It is the requirement of learnability, interpretability, that provides the irreducible social factor, and that shows why someone can't mean something by his words that can't be correctly deciphered by another. (Burge seems to make this point himself in a later paper.)[19]

Now I would like to return to Putnam's Twin Earth example, which does not depend on the idea that social linguistic usage dictates (under more or less standard conditions) what speakers mean by their words, nor, of course, what their (narrow) psychological states are. I am, as I said, persuaded that Putnam is right; what our words mean is fixed in part by the circumstances in which we learned, and used, the words. Putnam's single example (water) is not enough, perhaps, to nail down this point, since it is possible to insist that "water" doesn't apply just to stuff with the same molecular structure as water but also to stuff enough like water in structure to be odorless, potable, to support swimming and sailing, etc. (I realize that this remark, like many others in this piece, may show that I don't know a rigid designator when I see one.) The issue does not depend on such special cases nor on how we do or should resolve them. The issue depends simply on how the basic connection between words and things, or thoughts and things, is established. I hold, along with Burge and Putnam if I understand them, that it is established by causal interactions between people and parts and aspects of the world. The dispositions to react differentially to objects and events thus set up are central to the correct interpretation of a person's thoughts and speech. If this were not the case, we would have no way of discovering what others think, or what they mean by their words. The principle is as simple and obvious as this: a sentence someone is inspired (caused) to hold true by and only by sightings of the moon is apt to mean something like "There's the moon"; the thought expressed is apt to be that the moon is there; the thought inspired by and only by sightings of the moon is apt to be the thought that the moon is there. Apt to be, allowing for intelligible error, second hand reports, and so on. Not that all words and sentences are this directly conditioned to what they are about; we can perfectly well learn to use the word "moon" without ever seeing it. The claim is that all thought and language must have a foundation in such direct historical connections, and these connections constrain the interpretation of thoughts and speech. Perhaps I should stress that the arguments for this claim do not rest on intuitions concerning what we would say if certain counterfactuals were true. No science fiction or thought experiments are required.[20]

I agree with Putnam and Burge, then, that

the intentional content of ordinary propositional attitudes . . . cannot be accounted for in terms of physical, phenomenal, causal-functional, computational, or syntactical states or process that are specified nonintentionally and are defined purely on the individual in isolation from his physical and social environment.[21]

The question remains whether this fact is a threat to first person authority, as Burge seems to think, and Putnam and others certainly think. I have rejected one of Burge's arguments which, if it were right, would pose such a threat. But there is the position described in the previous paragraph, and which I hold whether or not others do, since I think this much "externalism" is required to

explain how language can be learned, and how words and attitudes can be identified by an interpreter.

Why does Putnam think that if the reference of a word is (sometimes) fixed by the natural history of how the word was acquired, a user of the word may lose first person authority? Putnam claims (correctly, in my view) that two people can be in all relevant physical (chemical, physiological, etc.) respects the same and yet mean different things by their words and have different propositional attitudes (as these are normally identified). The differences are due to environmental differences about which the two agents may, in some respects, be ignorant. Why, under these circumstances, should we suppose these agents may not know what they mean and think? Talking with them will not easily show this. As we have noted, each, when faced with a glass of water or twater says honestly, "Here's a glass of water." If they are in their home environments, each is right; if they have switched earths, each is wrong. If we ask each one what he means by the word "water," he gives the right answer, using the same words, of course. If we ask each one what he believes, he gives the right answer. These answers are right because though verbally identical, they must be interpreted differently. And what is it that they do not know (in the usual authoritative way) about their own states? As we have seen, Putnam distinguishes the states we have just been discussing from "narrow" psychological states which do not presuppose the existence of any individual other than the subject in that state. We may now start to wonder why Putnam is interested in narrow psychological states. Part of the answer is, of course, that it is these states that he thinks have the "Cartesian" property of being known in a special way by the person who is in them. (The other part of the answer has to do with constructing a "scientific psychology"; this does not concern us here.)

The reasoning depends, I think, on two largely unquestioned assumptions. These are:

1 If a thought is identified by a relation to something outside the head, it isn't wholly in the head. (It ain't in the head.)
2 If a thought isn't wholly in the head, it can't be "grasped" by the mind in the way required by first person authority.

That this is Putnam's reasoning is suggested by his claim that if two heads are the same, narrow psychological states must be the same. Thus if we suppose two people are "molecule for molecule" the same ("in the sense in which two neckties can be 'identical' "; you may add, if you wish, that each of the two people "thinks the same verbalized thoughts . . . , has the same sense data, the same dispositions, etc."), then "it is absured to think [one] psychological state is one bit different from" the other. These are, of course, narrow psychological states, not the ones we normally attribute, which ain't in the head.[22]

It is not easy to say in exactly what way the verbalized thoughts, sense data, and dispositions can be identical without reverting to the neckties, so let us revert. Then the idea is this: the narrow psychological states of two people are identical when their physical states cannot be distinguished. There would be no point in disputing this, since narrow psychological states are Putnam's to define; what I wish to question is assumption (1) above which led to the conclusion that ordinary propositional attitudes aren't in the head, and that therefore first person authority doesn't apply to them.

It should be clear that it doesn't follow, simply from the fact that meanings are identified in part by relations to objects outside the head, that meanings aren't in the head. To suppose this would be as bad as to argue that because my being sunburned presupposes the existence of the sun, my sunburn isn't a condition of my skin. My sunburned skin may be indistinguishable from someone else's skin that achieved its burn by other means (our skins may be identical in "the necktie sense"); yet one of us is really sunburned and the other not. This is enough to show that an appreciation of the external factors that enter into our common ways of identifying mental states does not discredit an identity theory of the mental and the physical. Andrew Woodfield seems to think it does. He writes:

> No *de re* state about an object that is external to the person's brain can possibly be identical with a state of that brain, since no brain state presupposes the existence of an external object.[23]

Individual states and events don't *conceptually* presuppose anything in themselves; some of their *descriptions* may, however. My paternal grandfather didn't presuppose me, but if someone can be described as my paternal grandfather, several people besides my grandfather, including me, must exist.

Burge may make a similar mistake in the following passage:

> . . . no occurrence of a thought . . . could have a different content and be the very same token event . . . [T]hen . . . a person's thought event is not *identical* with any event in him that is described by physiology, biology, chemistry, or physics. For let *b* be any given event described in terms of one of the physical sciences that occurs in the subject while he thinks the relevant thought. Let "*b*" be such that it denotes the same physical event occurring in the subject in our counterfactual situation . . . *b* need not be affected by counterfactual differences [that do not change the contents of the thought event]. Thus . . . *b* [the physical event] is not identical with the subject's occurrent thought.[24]

Burge does not claim to have established the premise of this argument, and so not its conclusion. But he holds that the denial of the premise is "intuitively very implausible". He goes on, "materialist identity theories have schooled the imagination to picture the content of a mental event as varying while the event remains fixed. But whether such imaginings are possible fact or just philosophical fancy is a separate question." It is because he thinks the denial of the premise to be very improbable that he holds that "materialist identity theories" are themselves "rendered implausible by the non-individualistic thought experiments".[25]

I accept Burge's premise; I think its denial not merely implausible but absurd. If two mental events have different contents they are surely different events. What I take Burge's and Putnam's imagined cases to show (and what I think The Swampman example shows more directly) is that people who are in all relevant physical respects similar (or "identical" in the necktie sense) can differ in what they mean or think, just as they can differ in being grandfathers or being sunburned. But of course there is *something* different about them, even in the physical world; their causal histories are different.

I conclude that the mere fact that ordinary mental states and events are individuated in terms of relations to the outside world has no tendency to discredit mental–physical identity theories as such. In conjunction with a number of further (plausible) assumptions, the "externalism" of certain mental states and events can be used, I think, to discredit type-type identity theories; but if anything it supports token-token identity theories. (I see no good reason for calling all identity theories "materialist"; if some mental events are physical events, this makes them no more physical than mental. Identity is a symmetrical relation.)

Putnam and Woodfield are wrong, then, in claiming that it is "absurd" to think two people could be physically identical (in the "necktie" sense) and yet differ in their ordinary psychological states. Burge, unless he is willing to make far stronger play than he has with essentialist assumptions, is wrong in thinking he has shown all identity theories implausible. We are therefore free to hold that people can be in all relevant physical respects identical while differing psychologically: this is in fact the position of "anomalous monism" for which I have argued elsewhere.[26]

One obstacle to non-evidential knowledge of our own ordinary propositional attitudes has now been removed. For if ordinary beliefs and the other attitudes can be "in the head" even though they are identified as the attitudes they are partly in terms of what is not in the head, then the threat to first person authority cannot come simply from the fact that external factors are relevant to the identification of the attitudes.

But an apparent difficulty remains. True, my sunburn, though describable as such only in relation to the sun, is identical with a condition of my skin which can (I assume) be described without reference to such "external" factors. Still, if, as a scientist skilled in all the physical sciences, I have access only to my skin, and am denied knowledge of the history of its condition, then by hypothesis there is no way for me to tell that I am sunburned. Perhaps, then, someone has first person authority with respect to the contents of his mind only as those contents can be described or discovered without reference to external factors. Insofar as the contents are identified in terms of external factors, first person authority necessarily lapses. I can tell by examining my skin what my private or "narrow" condition is, but nothing I can learn in this restricted realm will tell me that I am sunburned. The difference between referring to and thinking of water and referring to and thinking of twater is like the difference between being sunburned and one's skin being in exactly the same condition through another cause. The semantic difference lies in the outside world, beyond the reach of subjective or sublunar knowledge. So the argument might run.

This analogy, between the limited view of the skin doctor and the tunnel vision of the mind's eye, is fundamentally flawed. It depends for its appeal on a faulty picture of the mind, a picture which those who have been attacking the subjective character of ordinary psychological states share with those they attack. If we can bring ourselves to give up this picture, first person authority will no longer be seen as a problem; indeed, it will turn out that first person authority is dependent on, and explained by, the social and public factors that were supposed to undermine that authority.

There is a picture of the mind which has become so ingrained in our philosophical tradition that it is almost impossible to escape its influence even when its worst faults are recognized and repudiated. In one crude, but familiar, version, it goes like this: the mind is a theater in which the conscious self watches a passing show (the shadows on the wall). The show consists of "appearances," sense data, qualia, what is given in experience. What appear on the stage are not the ordinary objects of the world that the outer eye registers and the heart loves, but their purported representatives. Whatever we know about the world outside depends on what we can glean from the inner clues.

The difficulty that has been apparent from the start with this description of the mental is to see how it is possible to beat a track from the inside to the outside. Another conspicuous, though perhaps less appreciated, difficulty is to locate the self in the picture. For the self seems on the one hand to include theater, stage, actors, and audience; on the other hand, what is known and registered pertains to the audience alone. This second problem could be as well stated as the problem of the location of the objects of the mind: are they *in* the mind, or simply viewed *by* it?

I am not now concerned with such (now largely disavowed) objects of the mind as sense-data, but with their judgmental cousins, the supposed objects of the propositional attitudes, whether thought of as propositions, tokens of propositions, representations, or fragments of "mentalese." The central idea I wish to attack is that these are entities that the mind can "entertain," "grasp," "have before it," or be "acquainted" with. (These metaphors are probably instructive: voyeurs merely want to have representations before the mind's eye, while the more aggressive grasp them; the English may be merely acquainted with the contents of the mind, while more friendly types will actually entertain them.)

It is easy to see how the discovery that external facts enter into the individuation of states of mind disturbs the picture of the mind I have been describing. For if to be in a state of mind is for the mind to be in some relation like grasping to an object, then whatever helps determine what object it is must equally be grasped if the mind is to know what state it is in. This is particularly evident if an external object is an "ingredient" in the object before the mind. But in either case, the person who is in the state of mind may not know what state of mind he is in.

It is at this point that the concept of the subjective – of a state of mind – seems to come apart. On the one hand, there are the true inner states, with respect to which the mind retains its authority; on the other hand there are the ordinary states of belief, desire, intention, and meaning, which are polluted by their necessary connections with the social and public world.

In analogy, there is the problem of the sunburn expert who cannot tell by inspecting the skin whether it is a case of sunburn or merely an identical condition with another cause. We can solve the sunburn problem by distinguishing between sunburn and sunnishburn; sunnishburn is just like sunburn except that the sun need not be involved. The expert can spot a case of sunnishburn just by looking, but not a case of sunburn. This solution works because skin conditions, unlike objects of the mind, are not required to be such that there be a special someone who can tell, just by looking, whether or not the condition obtains.

The solution in the case of mental states is different, and simpler; it is to get rid of the metaphor of objects before the mind. Most of us long ago gave up the idea of perceptions, sense data, the flow of experience, as things "given" to the mind; we should treat propositional objects in the same way. Of course people have beliefs, wishes, doubts, and so forth; but to allow this is not to suggest that beliefs, wishes and doubts are *entities* in or before the mind, or that being in such states requires there to be corresponding mental objects.

This has been said before, in various tones of voice, but for different reasons. Ontological scruples, for example, are no part of my interest. We will always need an infinite supply of objects to help describe and identify attitudes like belief; I am not suggesting for a moment that belief sentences, and sentences that attribute the other attitudes, are not relational in nature. What I am

suggesting is that the objects to which we relate people in order to describe their attitudes need not in any sense be *psychological* objects, objects to be grasped, known, or entertained by the person whose attitudes are described.

This point, too, is familiar; Quine makes it when he suggests that we may use our own sentences to keep track of the thoughts of people who do not know our language. Quine's interest is semantical, and he says nothing in this context about the epistemological and psychological aspects of the attitudes. We need to bring these various concerns together. Sentences about the attitudes are relational; for *semantic* reasons there must therefore be objects to which to relate those who have attitudes. But having an attitude is not having an entity before the mind; for compelling *psychological* and *epistemological* reasons we should deny that there are objects of the mind.

The source of the trouble is the dogma that to have a thought is to have an object before the mind. Putnam and Fodor (and many others) have distinguished two sorts of objects, those that are truly inner and thus "before the mind" or "grasped" by it, and those that identify the thought in the usual way. I agree that no objects can serve these two purposes. Putnam (and some of the other philosophers I have mentioned) think the difficulty springs from the fact that an object partly identified in terms of external relations cannot be counted on to coincide with an object before the mind because the mind may be ignorant of the external relation. Perhaps this is so. But it does not follow that we can find *other* objects which will ensure the desired coincidence. For if the object *isn't* connected with the world, we can never learn about the world by having that object before the mind; and for reciprocal reasons, it would be impossible to detect such a thought in another. So it seems that what is before the mind cannot include its outside connections – its semantics. On the other hand, if the object *is* connected with the world, then it cannot be fully "before the mind" in the relevant sense. Yet unless a *semantic* object can be before the mind *in its semantic aspect*, thought, conceived in terms of such objects, cannot escape the fate of sense data.

The basic difficulty is simple: if to have a thought is to have an object "before the mind," and the identity of the object determines what the thought is, then it must always be possible to be mistaken about what one is thinking. For unless one knows *everything* about the object, there will always be senses in which one does not know what object it is. Many attempts have been made to find a relation between a person and an object which will in all contexts hold if and only if the person can intuitively be said to know what object it is. But none of these attempts has succeeded, and I think the reason is clear. The only object that would satisfy the twin requirements of being "before the mind" and also such that it determines what the content of a thought must, like Hume's ideas and impressions, "be what it seems and seem what it is." There are no such objects, public or private, abstract or concrete.

The arguments of Burge, Putnam, Dennett, Fodor, Stich, Kaplan, Evans, and many others to show that propositions can't *both* determine the contents of our thoughts *and* be subjectively assured are, in my opinion, so many variants on the simple and general argument I have just sketched. It is not just propositions that can't do the job; no objects could.

When we have freed ourselves from the assumption that thoughts must have mysterious objects, we can see how the fact that mental states as we commonly conceive them are identified in part by their natural history not only fails to touch the internal character of such states or to threaten first person authority; it also opens the way to an explanation of first person authority. The explana-

tion comes with the realization that what a person's words mean depends in the most basic cases on the kinds of objects and events that have caused the person to hold the words to be applicable; similarly for what the person's thoughts are about. An interpreter of another's words and thoughts must depend on scattered information, fortunate training, and imaginative surmise in coming to understand the other. The agent herself, however, is not in a position to wonder whether she is generally using her own words to apply to the right objects and events, since whatever she regularly does apply them to gives her words the meaning they have and her thoughts the contents they have. Of course, in any particular case, she may be wrong in what she believes about the world; what is impossible is that she should be wrong most of the time. The reason is apparent: unless there is a presumption that the speaker knows what she means, i.e., is getting her own language right, there would be nothing for an interpreter to interpret. To put the matter another way, nothing could count as someone regularly misapplying her own words. First person authority, the social character of language, and the external determinants of thought and meaning go naturally together, once we give up the myth of the subjective, the idea that thoughts require mental objects.

Notes

Presidential Address delivered before the Sixtieth Annual Pacific Division Meeting of the American Philosophical Association in Los Angeles, California, March 28, 1986.

1 Graham Wallas, *The Art of Thought.*
2 Donald Davidson, "First person authority," *Dialectica*, 38 (1984), pp. 101–11.
3 Hilary Putnam, "The meaning of 'meaning'," reprinted in *Philosophical Papers, Vol. II: Mind, Language, and Reality*, Cambridge University Press, 1975, p. 227.
4 I make no claim for originality here; Stephen Stich has used a very similar example in "Autonomous psychology and the belief–desire thesis," *The Monist*, 61 (1978), pp. 573ff. I should emphasize that I am not suggesting that an object accidentally or artificially created could not think; The Swampman simply needs time in which to acquire a causal history that would make sense of the claim that he is speaking of, remembering, identifying, or thinking of items in the world. (I return to this point later.)

5 Hilary Putnam, "The meaning of 'meaning'," p. 144.
6 See John Searle, *Intentionality*, Cambridge University Press, 1983, and Tyler Burge, "Individualism and psychology," *The Philosophical Review*, 95 (1986), pp. 3–45.
7 Hilary Putnam, "The meaning of 'meaning'," pp. 164–5.
8 Jerry Fodor, "Cognitive science and the Twin Earth problem," *Notre Dame Journal of Formal Logic*, 23 (1982), p. 103. Also see his "Methodological solipsism considered as a research strategy in cognitive psychology," *The Behavioral and Brain Sciences*, 3 (1980).
9 John Searle, *Intentionality*, chapter 8.
10 *Thought and Object*, Andrew Woodfield, ed., Clarendon Press, 1982, p. viii.
11 Daniel Dennett, "Beyond belief," in *Thought and Object*, p. 76.
12 Tyler Burge, "Other bodies," in *Thought and Object*; "Individualism and the mental," in *Midwest Studies*

in *Philosophy, Volume 4*, Peter French, Theodore Uehling, Howard Wettstein, eds, University of Minnesota Press, 1979; "Two thought experiments reviewed," *Notre Dame Journal of Formal Logic*, 23 (1982), pp. 284–93; "Individualism and psychology."

13 Jerry Fodor, "Methodological solipsism considered as a research strategy in cognitive psychology."

14 Stephen Stich, *From Folk Psychology to Cognitive Science*, MIT Press, 1983.

15 See, for example, Gareth Evans, *The Varieties of Reference*, Oxford University Press, 1982, pp. 45, 199, 201.

16 Tyler Burge, "Individualism and the mental," p. 83.

17 Ibid., pp. 90, 102, 104.

18 Burge suggests that the reason we normally take a person to mean by his words what others in his linguistic community mean, whether or not the speaker knows what others mean, is that "People are frequently held, and hold themselves, to the standards of the community when misuse or misunderstanding are at issue." He also says such cases "depend on a certain responsibility to communal practice" ("Individualism and the mental," p. 90). I don't doubt the phenomenon, but its bearing on what it is supposed to show. (a) It is often reasonable to hold people responsible for knowing what their words mean; in such cases we may treat them as committed to positions they did not know or believe they were committed to. This has nothing (directly) to do with what they meant by their words, nor what they believed. (b) As good citizens and parents we want to encourage practices that enhance the chances for communication; using words as we think others do may enhance communication. This thought (whether or not justified) may help explain why some people tend to attribute meanings and beliefs in a legalistic way; they hope to encourage conformity. (c) A speaker who wishes to be understood must intend his words to be interpreted (and hence interpretable) along certai[...] tion may be served by using [...] (though often this is not the [...] hearer who wishes to understa[...] intend to interpret the speak[...] speaker intended (whether or no[...] is "standard"). These reciprocal intentions become morally important in endless situations which have no necessary connection with the determination of what someone had in mind.

19 See, for example, "Two thought experiments reviewed," p. 289.

20 Burge has described "thought experiments" which do not involve language at all; one of these experiments prompts him to claim that someone brought up in an environment without aluminum could not have "aluminum thoughts" ("Individualism and psychology," p. 5). Burge does not say why he thinks this, but it is by no means obvious that counterfactual assumptions are needed to make the point. In any case, the new thought experiments seem to rest on intuitions quite different from the intuitions invoked in "Individualism and the mental"; it is not clear how social norms feature in the new experiments, and the linguistic habits of the community are apparently irrelevant. At this point it may be that Burge's position is close to mine.

21 "Two thought experiments reviewed," p. 288.

22 "The meaning of 'meaning'," p. 227.

23 Andrew Woodfield, in *Thought and Object*, p. viii.

24 "Individualism and the mental," p. 111.

25 "Individualism and psychology," p. 15, note 7. Cf. "Individualism and the mental," p. 111.

26 "Mental events," in Donald Davidson, *Essays on Actions and Events*, Oxford University Press, 1982.

I am greatly indebted to Akeel Bilgrami and Ernie LePore for criticism and advice. Tyler Burge generously tried to correct my understanding of his work.

Privileged Access[1]

John Heil

Epistemic Privilege

Philosophical tradition has it that one's own mental life enjoys a privileged epistemic standing. I know my own states of mind immediately and with confidence. You may discover what I am thinking, of course, but you are liable to err in your assessment of my thoughts in ways that I cannot. Asymmetry of access evidently lies close to the centre of our conception of mentality. A theory of intentionality that failed to square with this aspect of the mental must be regarded with suspicion. What, however, are we to make of the notion of epistemic privilege?[2]

Descartes promoted the view that access to one's own mental states is infallible and incorrigible. In the third *Meditation*, for instance, he remarks that "for certainly, if I considered the ideas only as certain modes of my thought, without intending them to refer to some other exterior object, they uld hardly offer me a chance of making a mistake". Conveniently, *ideas* – that is, generic mental contents considered just in themselves, and not as representatives of outer things – have all and only the properties we take them to have.

For most of us, however, there are times when we are uncertain what we really want or believe. We are prone to myriad forms and degrees of self-deception. Infallibility with respect to the mental requires that whenever we exemplify a given mental property we know that we do so. But the ease with which we engage in talk of repression and the unconscious, together with our willingness to admit that we can fail to know our deepest preferences and opinions, suggest that infallibility is not part of the ordinary conception of mentality. Similar considerations tell against incorrigibility, the doctrine that beliefs we harbour concerning our own states of mind cannot fail to be true. If our aim is to capture some plausible conception of privileged access, then, it seems likely that both infallibility and incorrigibility are best left behind.

Direct Knowledge

One aspect of epistemic privilege is manifested in our conviction that we possess a capacity to *know directly* the contents of our own minds. Direct knowledge, I shall suppose, is knowledge not based on evidence. This cannot be all there is to privileged access, however. It is unlikely either that the scope of direct knowledge is limited to one's mental states, or that one's mental states are knowable only directly. In general, whatever can be known directly could be known as well on the basis of evidence. I know, perhaps, at least some of my own mental states directly. Your knowledge of them is indirect, mediated by your observation of what I say and do. Like you, however, I may know nothing of certain of my states of mind. And to the extent that I know my unconscious thoughts, I know them exclusively on the basis of evidence, evidence perhaps supplied by others – most especially by those who are acute observers of my behaviour.

It is important to be clear on what is and is not required for something to be directly known. The directness in question is, of course, epistemological, not causal. Direct knowledge is not to be confused with Russellian *knowledge by acquaintance*. What I know by acquaintance I know directly. But what, if anything, I can know directly

is a contingent matter. My knowledge that a certain shrub is a Toyon may be based on evidence concerning the shape of its leaves, the character of its bark, and the colour of the blossoms it produces. If you are a botanist, your knowledge may, in contrast, be direct. I can know directly what a blind person knows only by inference. If mute creatures can be said to possess knowledge, then some of these – pigeons, for instance, or honeybees – can know directly things I know exclusively on the basis of evidence.

Although, in general, claims to direct knowledge can be supplemented by appeals to evidence, this seems not to be so when the objects of knowledge are one's own mental states. I may know directly that I harbour some thought, or I may know this only indirectly, perhaps by means of some elaborate process of self-analysis. When my knowledge is direct, however, it is unlikely that, when prompted, I could produce relevant supporting evidence. Compare this with the case of a botanist who can tell at a glance that the shrub I am looking at is a Toyon. If I express doubts, the botanist can appeal to evidence of the sort I should need were I to make the identification.[3]

The asymmetry exhibited by such cases is undoubtedly important. It is difficult, however, to know what to make of it. I know directly – without evidence – that the vegetables I am eating are green and that my legs are crossed as I sit at my desk. If you insist that I produce evidence, I should not know what to do beyond indicating the items in question. It will not do, then, to imagine that privileged access can be explicated simply by an appeal to what can be known directly. The relation is not nearly so straightforward.

Is it, then, merely a contingent fact about my own mental states that I can know them directly? Although it is contingently true that on a given occasion I know myself to be in a certain mental state, it is plausible to suppose that such states are *essentially* such that they are directly knowable by agents to whom they belong. This may seem too weak to be helpful. After all, things other than states of mind can be known directly.[4] It is, nevertheless, not obviously an essential property of such things that they are directly knowable.

This, however, even if correct, is scarcely illuminating. We have noted already that my enjoying privileged access cannot be a matter of my knowing *all* of my thoughts directly. Nor can it be that, for every thought I *do* know myself to possess, my knowledge of it is direct. Once we embrace a modest view of epistemic privilege, however, we encounter immodest prospects. If, for instance, it is possible that I fail to know *some* of my thoughts directly, then might not I fail to know most (or *all*) of them directly – or, indeed, fail to know them *at all*, directly or otherwise? The possibility seems ridiculous. Once it is admitted that I might fail to know some of my thoughts, however, what entitles me to suppose that I am, in general, in a better position than others to assess their character? The supposition apparently requires that I be aware of two classes of thought – those I do and those I do not know about – and that I recognize the latter class to be much smaller than the former. But of course I cannot compare two classes, one of which is known to me and the other of which I am ignorant.

Consider now my knowledge of *your* thoughts. This is not, in typical cases, direct. Nevertheless it is at least conceivable that I could come to know your states of mind directly, without, that is, inferring them in the usual ways. I might, for instance, be wired to you in such a way that I share your nervous system. Science fiction aside, most of us learn to read the thoughts of colleagues and loved-ones just as a botanist learns to read the flora of the surrounding countryside. Given a measure of ignorance about my own thoughts, then, it is conceivable that I could know your mind better than my own.[5]

A characterization of privileged access based exclusively on what is directly known is anaemic, hence unsatisfactory: I know some of my thoughts directly (but know some of them only by inference); I know some of your thoughts by inference (although there is nothing to prevent me from knowing some of them directly). Asymmetry survives only quantitatively: the proportion of my thoughts that I know directly appears invariably to be greater than the proportion of yours I know directly. One may, however, wonder why there could not be cases in which the proportion is reversed. Something has gone wrong surely. A conception of privileged access that takes us along our present path must somewhere have taken the wrong turning. We should do well, then, to backtrack and look more carefully at the terrain.

Direct Knowability and Intentional Content

Intentional states, by and large, exhibit two components, a particular content and an attitude or disposition of some sort toward that content. In the case of beliefs, desires, and other propositional attitudes, content is specifiable sententially and attitudes are characterizable as acceptings, withholdings, wantings, and the like. Contents and attitudes can vary independently. This suggests that knowledge of intentional states incorporates a pair of distinguishable aspects, one pertaining to the content of the state, the other to its place in an agent's psychological economy. It suggests, as well, that in so far as we can be wrong about such things, we can be wrong in different ways – as when we fail to get the attitude right while being clear about the content, or grasp the attitude but misapprehend its object. And if we can be mistaken about each, it must be possible as well to be in the dark about both at once.

Until recently, doubts about infallible and incorrigible access to mental items have mostly been focused on considerations of the attitudes involved. A climber may wonder whether he really *believes* that his rope is safe or merely *hopes* that it is. He is, however, unlikely to be similarly puzzled about the content of the thought that concerns him. One may wonder whether such puzzlement is intelligible. Perhaps it is. A physicist reflecting on his belief that electrons carry observers with them into superposition may do so without having any very satisfactory conception of what this comes to.[6]

Psychological theorizing in this century has provided ammunition for sceptics about attitudes. Recent work in the philosophy of mind may abet another sort of sceptic, one who doubts that we ever know for certain the *contents* of our own states of mind. For reasons I shall take up presently, the most promising accounts of mental content lend themselves to this form of radical scepticism. Before attempting to plumb those depths, however, we should be clear about what is included in the ordinary conception of privileged access.

Two points bear emphasizing. First, direct knowability of mental states holds, it at all, only for "occurrent" states, those entertained at the time they are considered, and not, say, for those once, but no longer, possessed. My access to repressed states of mind or to those present only at some earlier time may be highly indirect. Second, beliefs we have about mental states and processes are neither infallible nor incorrigible. I may fail to know, directly or otherwise, what thoughts I harbour. And I may err in various ways in assessing their character. A plausible conception of direct knowability requires only that my mental states and processes be essentially such that they are directly knowable by me, not that they are, in every case directly known.

Some such conception of direct knowability is required by our ordinary notion of mentality. We can accept this, I think, while remaining agnostic about its realization, whatever it may be in virtue of which it obtains when and if it does obtain. Direct knowability constrains accounts of intentionality weakly but non-trivially. The point may be illustrated by reflecting on externalist theories of mental content.

Scepticism About Content

To focus the discussion, let us consider one important class of cognitive system, a class incorporating the capacity for something like *self-awareness*.[7] I have in mind systems capable of second- as well as first-order intentionality. Systems of this sort might, for instance, entertain beliefs about their own beliefs, desires, and intentions. More generally, such systems are capable of harbouring intentional states that include in their content the content of other intentional states. Self-awareness, when it is veridical, affords direct knowledge of mental contents.

Ordinary human beings count as self-aware systems in this sense. Whether other, non-human, creatures might achieve self-awareness is controversial. Differing intuitions concerning the reasonableness of ascribing intentional properties to mute creatures, or to computing machines, or to thermostats, hinge partly on differences in one's willingness to regard systems lacking in self-awareness as properly intentional at all. The notion that a system possesses first-order intentional states only if it recognizes (or is capable of recognizing) its possession of these states is interesting and worth exploring in detail.[8] I shall be concerned here, however, only with the *phenomenon* of self-awareness. My immediate aim is to show that one may consistently accept a relational or externalist explication of intentional content and retain the conviction that access to one's own states of mind is epistemically privileged.

The matter is important, I think, because the conviction that intentional content must depend on environmental circumstances of agents whose states possess that content appears to eliminate entirely the possibility of privileged access. We are faced with a dilemma. On the one hand, when we consider introspection, it seems patent that we have something like a direct Cartesian entrée to the contents of our own thoughts. We have seen that this need not be taken to imply that we are infallible or incorrigible concerning the mental. It requires only that to the extent that we do comprehend our own thoughts, we typically do so directly – that is, without relying on inference or evidence. On the other hand, if we suppose that the content of a given state of one's mind is determined in part by complicated features of one's circumstances, features of which one is mostly unaware, it would seem that, in order to grasp the content of that state, one would first have to get at those external circumstances.

The prospect is doubly unsettling. First, it seems to oblige me to base beliefs about the contents of my own thoughts on evidence. This flies in the face of the ordinary conviction that our knowledge of such things is, on the whole, epistemologically direct, not founded on evidence. Second, if beliefs I entertain about my own states of mind depend on evidential backing, then I might, with fair frequency, *make mistakes* about those states. I might have evidence, for instance, that a particular belief I harbour is the belief that p, the belief, say, that snow is white. But I could be wrong. My belief *might*, for all I know, be a belief about something altogether different – that the sky is blue or even that snow is *not* white. My getting its content right apparently requires that I get the determinants of that content right, and, so long as these are epistemically mediated, I may easily fail to do so. Worse, I seem open to sceptical worries about whether I am *ever* right about the content of my own thoughts.

Reflections on such things produce a variety of responses. Thus, one may be inclined to reject out of hand any conception of mentality that leads in this direction. If there are any intentional states with content, these must be, typically anyway, self-intimating, our access to them direct and unproblematic. In contrast, one may regard these consequences not as counterexamples to the theory in question, but as interesting, though perhaps startling, *discoveries* about the epistemic status of mind. They force us to abandon discredited superstitions about access to our own thoughts.[9] Alternatively, we may follow Putnam and embrace anti-realism hoping thereby to salvage self-awareness and disarm the sceptic.[10]

It is possible, however, to reconcile direct access to mental content with both externalism and common-sense realism. At least this is what I shall contend. An ulterior motive stems from a conviction that it is important to make a place for intentional contents as legitimate psychological *phenomena*, *data*, items about which one might reasonably expect theories of intelligent behaviour to have something to say.

Externalist Accounts of Content

Let us begin by pretending that the contents of one's mental states are determined, not by intrinsic features of those states, but by their *circumstances*, by goings-on external to them. We may suppose, further, that the circumstances in question include a good deal that is outside the agent to whom the states belong. Let us call theories that explicate intentionality this way *externalist* theories.

Imagine, then, that some particular mental state of mine, M, has the content that p in virtue of the obtaining of some state of affairs, A, that includes states or events outside M, occurrences in my environment. On a very simple externalist theory M might have the content that *this is a tree* in virtue of being caused in me by a tree. Here the state of affairs, A, M's being caused by a tree, has, as it were, one foot inside me, in M, and another anchored in the outside world. Of course different versions of externalism will provide different accounts of A, whatever it is in virtue of which states of mind have their particular content. In some instances A will be a causal relation of a certain sort. In others it might be something else entirely.

Suppose now that I pause to consider the content of M, I *introspect* on my own state of mind. Let us dub this introspective state M', and let us call the external state of affairs in virtue of which M' has whatever content it has, A'. What can be said about the content of M'? Is it plausible to suppose that its content *includes* that of M, my first-order mental state? And, even if this is so, is there any reason to think *either* that M's content, whatever it is, could be accurately preserved in my introspective thought, M', *or* that my access to the content of M could be in any sense epistemically *direct*?

It might seem at first blush that access to the contents of first-order states like M would necessitate my somehow coming to recognize the obtaining of states of affairs like A, those responsible for first-order content. In our simplified example this would mean that for me to come to know that M was a state with the content that *this is a tree*, I should first have to discover that M was *caused by* a tree. This is not something I could discover simply by getting at M. I should need, it seems, *evidence* about the circumstances in which M was produced, evidence that could easily fall short of conclusiveness. Thus, even if I happened to be right about what caused M, hence about M's intentional content, my access to that content would hardly be direct or privileged. It would be based on clues I assembled, and inferences I drew from these. In general, my beliefs about the content of my own thoughts might depend on the results of delicate tests and experiments.

It goes without saying that, under these circumstances, I might err in identifying the cause of M, hence err in my assessment of M's content. And in cases where I did not take the trouble to investigate the aetiology of my thoughts, my beliefs about their contents would be scarcely more than shots in the dark. After all, if externalism were true, one could not discover a state's intentional properties merely by inspecting that state. A particular mental item, just in itself, might have any content whatever, or none at all.

Externalism Without Scepticism

The emerging picture belies the ordinary conception of self-awareness. More seriously, we have seen that it portends an especially pernicious form of scepticism. A traditional sceptic seeks reasons for supposing that the world is as we think it is. We appear now to be faced with the prospect of a nastier sceptic, one who questions the presumption that we think what we think we think.[11]

This altogether bleak outlook is, however, founded on a fundamental mischaracterization of externalism. Consider again my second-order introspective state M'. We are supposing that externalism is correct, hence that the content of M' is determined by some state of affairs, A', that is at least partly distinct from M'. What, now, is to prevent A' from determining an intentional content for M' that *includes* the content of M? What, for instance, keeps our simplified theory from allowing that a causal relation of a certain sort endows my introspective thought with a content encompassing the content of the thought on which I am introspecting? The envisaged causal relation might plausibly be taken to include as a component the causal relation required to establish the content of the state on which I am introspecting, and it might include much more as well.

To see the point, it is important to keep in mind that externalist theories of the sort under discussion require only that certain conditions *obtain* in order for a given state to have a particular intentional content. They do not, or anyhow need not, require in addition that one know or believe these states to obtain.[12] Thus the content of M, that p, was determined by its being the case that A, not by my knowing or believing that A obtains. In our simplified externalist theory, my thought concerns a tree because it was prompted by a tree, not because I know or believe it was so prompted. The same must be true for second-order states of mind. When I introspect, the content of my introspection will be determined by its being caused in an appropriate way, not by my discovering that it was caused in that way.

One may be suspicious of the last move. It might be granted that my introspective thought could be about my thought that p, without thereby granting that the content of my introspection includes the *content* of the introspected thought. Just as a thought of George Herman Ruth need not include the Sultan of Swat in its content, even though George Herman Ruth *is* the Sultan of Swat, so it seems perfectly possible for me to introspect my thought that p without comprehending it as the thought *that p*. If externalism were true, my introspections would seem *typically* to have this character. This, at any rate, appears to follow from the view that the determinants of the content of an intentional state are external to that state.

It is possible, certainly, for me to entertain a second-order thought about the thought that p, without *that p*, occurring as part of the content of the second-order thought. I may think, for instance, of a complicated idea I had yesterday, without having a very clear notion of what that idea included. Similarly, I may apprehend an expression of the thought that p (in Urdu, say) without recognizing it to express the thought that p. The case we are considering, however, is the familiar one in which I introspect my own occurrent thought.

The contents of ordinary intentional goings-on, according to externalism, are determined by the obtaining of states of affairs that include components distinct from those goings-on. Contents, so determined, need not, and almost certainly will not, reflect important aspects of those external components. Similarly, the contents of introspective states need not, and almost certainly will not, reflect features of the external determinants of either those states themselves or the introspected states. My second-order introspective awareness of a particular intentional state can incorporate the latter's content without having to include (as part of *its* content) the conditions ultimately responsible for fixing the sense of the introspected thought. The content of *both* thoughts is generated externally. The content of second-order thoughts – introspections – would be determined, I have suggested, by a complex condition that included, perhaps, the condition responsible for the content of corresponding first-order states.

Privileged Access and the Mind's Eye

I have been discussing externalist theories of content as though only these could motivate doubts about the possibility of privileged access. We worry that, if the determinants of content are not, or not exclusively, "in the head", our access to content will be a chancy thing. But why should *proximity* be thought to matter? If the contents of one's thoughts were determined entirely by the state of one's brain, why should this fact alone make our access to them any less indirect or difficult? Nor is it clear that a Cartesian is in any better position to account for epistemic privilege. A thought's occurring in a non-physical substance does not, by itself, afford a reason for supposing that one's apprehension of it is unproblematic. Considerations of this sort suggest that worries about access to mental contents associated with externalism are misplaced. Precisely the same worries can be generated for non-externalist, even Cartesian, theories. Difficulties arise, if at all, not from the external or relational character of whatever fixes content, but from some other source.

The culprit, according to Donald Davidson, is not externalism but a certain "picture of the mind" in which beliefs about the contents of one's mental states are taken to be based on inward glimpses of those states or on the grasping of particular entities (*contents*, perhaps, or *propositions*, or *sentences in mentalese*). He recommends that we abandon the notion that knowledge of mental contents requires our inwardly perceiving in this way. Once we do so, we remove at least one of the reasons for supposing that externalism undermines privileged access.

Although our discussion has focused on propositional attitudes, it will be useful to reflect briefly on a distinct class of mental occurrence, the entertaining of visual images. I say to you: "Form an image of your grandmother", and you comply. Suppose I now ask: "How do you know that the image is of your *grandmother* – and not, say, someone *just like* her?' The question is ill-conceived. It is not that you cannot be wrong about what it is you imagine. If the person whom you had been raised to regard as your grandmother were an imposter, then you would be wrong in supposing that the image you now form is of your grandmother. It is an image of an imposter. This, however, seems not to be a mistake you make about the image. You mislabel that image because you are mistaken about your grandmother.

Imagining, at least in this respect, resembles drawing – as distinct from observing – a picture. In the course of a lecture on the battle of Borodino, you make *X*s on the blackboard to mark the location of Napoleon's forces and *O*s to mark the disposition of Kutuzov's army. I enquire: "How do you know the *X*s stand for Napoleon's troops and not Kutuzov's?" The question misfires no less than the corresponding question about an image you form of your grandmother. You may be wrong in many ways about Borodino, of course, in which case you will be wrong in supposing that your diagram depicts things as they were on the day of the battle. But the diagram is yours, and there cannot be any question of its failing to mean what you intend it to mean. As an observer, my situation is different. I could well be wrong or confused about your *X*s and *O*s. The asymmetry here is instructive. You and I are differently related to what you have drawn. I am an observer and, like any observer, may err in understanding or describing what I see. You, however, are not, or at any rate, not essentially an observer. I must take your word concerning what you have drawn, not because you have a better, more proximate view of it, but because the drawing is yours.

The privileged status we enjoy with respect to the contents of our own minds is analogous. That is, in introspecting and describing our thoughts, we are not reporting episodes that appear before our mind's eye. Were that so, we should be at a loss to account for the privileged status such reports are routinely accorded. The access I enjoy to my own mental contents would be superior to what is available to you, perhaps, but only accidentally so. Its superiority would be like that I enjoy with respect to the contents of my trouser pockets.

Consider the following description of visual imagining:

> Visual images might be like displays produced on a cathode ray tube (CRT) by a computer program operating on stored data. That is, ... images are temporary spatial displays in active memory that are generated from more abstract representations in long-term memory. Interpretive mechanisms (the "mind's eye") work over ("look at") these internal displays and classify them in terms of semantic categories (as would be involved in realizing that a particular spatial configuration corresponds to a dog's ear, for example).[13]

An account of this sort, whatever its empirical credentials, exudes an aura of implausibility at least in part because it promotes a conception of mental access that threatens to undermine epistemic privilege. If the conception were apt, then whatever asymmetry we find in the beliefs you and I have about your states of mind is purely fortuitous. If I could look over your mind's shoulder, then my epistemological position would be no different from yours as you gazed inwardly. Indeed I might see clearly what you apprehend only darkly.

Davidson holds that we are bound to misconstrue privileged access – what he calls first-person authority – so long as we persist in depicting the mind in this way.

> There is a picture of the mind which has become so ingrained in our philosophical tradition that it is almost impossible to escape its influence even when its worst faults are recognized and repudiated. In one crude, but familiar, version, it goes like this: the mind is a theatre in which the conscious self watches a passing show.... The show consists of "appearances", sense data, qualia, what is given in experience. What appear on the stage are not the ordinary objects of the world that the outer eye registers and the heart loves, but their purported representatives. Whatever we know about the world outside depends on what we can glean from the inner clues.[14]

Although Davidson's point is intended to apply, not to mental images, but to propositional attitudes, the moral is the same.

> Most of us long ago gave up the idea of perceptions, sense data, the flow of experience, as things "given" to the mind; we should treat propositional objects in the same way. Of course people have beliefs, wishes, doubts, and so forth; but to allow this is not to suggest that beliefs, wishes, and doubts are *entities* in or before the mind, or that being in such states requires there to be corresponding mental objects.... Sentences about the attitudes are relational; for *semantic* reasons there must therefore be objects to which to relate those who have attitudes. But having an attitude is not having an entity before the mind; for compelling *psychological* and *epistemological* reasons we should deny that there are objects of the mind.[15]

Davidson is convinced that worries about privileged access can be dispelled provided we abandon the notion that our awareness of mental contents is best regarded as the apprehension of content-bearing entities or episodes. In the case of mental images, this requires that we let go of the traditional conception of images as pictures or picture-like copies of external things gazed at inwardly. In the case of beliefs, desires, and other propositional attitudes, we are to turn away from the notion that, in introspecting, we encounter propositions, mental sentences, senses, or contents.

If this were so, and I am inclined to believe it is so, then we should have a way of defusing worries about privileged access that might otherwise to be thought to arise from externalist or naturalistic accounts of mental contents. We should be able to see how something like a Cartesian entrée to the contents of one's own mind does not depend on the Cartesian conception of mental substance. Indeed the picture of introspection encouraged by that conception is precisely the source of the difficulties we have been considering.

Concluding Remarks

Davidson's suggestion requires that we jettison the notion that content-bearing states of mind are usefully regarded as entities – Cartesian ideas, sentences in mentalese, neural inscriptions, pictures on an interior television screen. Such entities

might exist. Indeed we may be obliged to mention them in ascriptions and descriptions of thoughts, images, and the like. The point, then, is not one issuing from considerations of parsimony. It is founded, rather, on the notion that the *having* of a thought or image "is not the having of an object before the mind".

> If to have a thought is to have an object "before the mind," and the identity of the object determines what the thought is, then it must always be possible to be mistaken about what one is thinking. For unless one knows *everything* about the object, there will always be senses in which one does not know what the object is. Many attempts have been made to find a relation between a person and an object which will in all contexts hold if and only if the person can intuitively be said to know what the object is. But none of these attempts has succeeded, and I think the reason is clear. The only object that would satisfy the twin requirements of being "before the mind" and also such that it determines...the content of a thought, must, like Hume's ideas and impressions, "be what it seems and seem what it is". There are no such objects, public or private, abstract or concrete.[16]

If we imagined that introspecting were a matter of inwardly scrutinizing a mental object, then we should have to suppose that our ability to appreciate the content of introspected thoughts depends on a capacity to "read off" a thought's content from an inspection of the thought itself. Externalism poses obvious difficulties for such a picture. I have suggested, however, that non-externalist, even Cartesian, accounts of content are equally ill-suited to its requirements. We must understand theories of content as setting out conditions that agents must satisfy if they are to have contentful states of mind. Their satisfying these conditions need not be a matter of their recognizing them to be satisfied. This, I think is, or ought to be, uncontroversial. Anyone who questions it is faced with the spectre of a regress: if my thought's having a particular content requires that I recognize the obtaining of certain conditions, then it requires my having some *other* thought with a particular content, one, namely, corresponding to this recognition. But, of course, *this* thought would require its own corresponding recognition of the obtaining of appropriate conditions for *its* content, and we are off on a regress.[17]

If we are willing to allow the regress-blocking manoeuvre in the case of ordinary, first-order thoughts, there is no reason to balk at its application to second-order thoughts, introspections. Beliefs about the contents of one's own thoughts, then, need not be based on beliefs about whatever it is that fixes the contents of those thoughts. The contents of second-order thoughts are fixed, just as are the contents of first-order thoughts, by the obtaining of appropriate conditions.

This simple point will be difficult to appreciate, however, so long as we cling to what Davidson calls "a faulty picture of the mind", a picture in which knowledge of the contents of one's thoughts is caricatured as a species of inner perception. The conception of the mind as a place where specialized mental objects are housed ceased long ago to carry philosophical conviction. It survives, however, at least implicitly, in conceptions of the access we have to our own mental contents. My aim has been to show that it need not.

Notes

1 Work on this essay was supported by the National Endowment for Humanities.
2 The concept of privileged access is discussed usefully and at length in W. P. Alston, "Varieties of privileged access," *American Philosophical Quarterly*, 1971, pp. 223–41.
3 Evidence thus produced would bear on the character of the botanist's knowledge *claim*. It need not, however, figure in his *knowing*.
4 I mean by this that *if* they are known, they can be so known. The claim is not that we in fact possess knowledge, only that, if there is knowledge, some of it is direct. For stylistic reasons I shall omit the qualification in what follows.
5 Thus breathing new life into the old joke about two behaviourists meeting on the street. One says to the other: "You're fine, how am I?"
6 Tyler Burge has argued that such cases are common. See, e.g., "Intellectual norms and the foundations of mind", *Journal of Philosophy*, 1986, pp. 697–720.
7 I shall use the expression "self-awareness" in what is perhaps a non-standard way. I am concerned here only with the capacity to "introspect" on mental states and goings-on, not anything more elaborate. I shall not address, for instance, the ability sometimes ascribed to human beings to focus inwardly on an ego, self, or other mental substrate.
8 It meshes, certainly, in obvious ways with the notion that mental goings-on are essentially directly knowable. See, e.g., John R. Searle, *Minds, Brains, and Science*, Cambridge, Mass., Harvard University Press, 1985; and Donald Davidson, "Thought and talk," in *Inquiries Into Truth and Interpretation*, Oxford, Oxford University Press, 1984, pp. 155–70. Searle and Davidson differ importantly, however. Searle emphasizes the role of *consciousness*; Davidson focuses on the capacity for entertaining thoughts in which beliefs figure, thoughts about thoughts. The latter capacity is neither necessary nor sufficient for the possession of consciousness as it is ordinarily understood. Conscious thoughts are not – or not

typically – thoughts about thoughts; and if first-order thoughts can be unconscious, there is nothing to prevent thoughts about thoughts from being similarly unconscious.
9 See, e.g., Ruth Garrett Millikan, *Language, Thought and Other Biological Categories*, Cambridge, Mass., Bradford Books/MIT Press, 1984.
10 See, e.g., Hilary Putnam, *Reason, Truth, and History*, Cambridge, Cambridge University Press, 1981, ch. 1. See also J. Heil, "The epistemic route to anti-realism", *Australasian Journal of Philosophy*, forthcoming.
11 Similar concerns have been voiced by Donald Davidson whose position on this matter is discussed below. See, e.g., his "Knowing one's own mind," *Proceedings and Addresses of the American Philosophical Association*, 1987, pp. 441–58. Difficulties one encounters in attempting to formulate a coherent version of scepticism about the contents of one's thoughts suggest, in any case, underlying incoherencies in theories of content inspiring such scepticism.
12 An externalist theory that did so would incorporate an epistemic component. I doubt that anything is to be gained by such an emendation, but even if an epistemic condition is added the point at issue here remains unaffected provided we also allow the epistemic condition itself to be externally satisfiable, that is, provided we allow that I might know, for instance, that *p* just in virtue of certain, possibly external, conditions obtaining. The matter is discussed in more detail in "The epistemic route to anti-realism". See also Wittgenstein's remark in the *Tractatus*, §4.002.
13 S. Kosslyn, S. Pinker, G. Smith, and S. Schwartz, "The demystification of mental imagery", *The Behavioral and Brain Sciences*, 1979, pp. 535–81. A discussion of the liabilities of this conception of imagery may be found in J. Heil, "What does the mind's eye look at?", *Journal of Mind and Behavior*, 1982, pp. 143–9.

14 "Knowing one's own mind", p. 453.
15 Ibid., pp. 454–5.
16 Ibid., p. 455.
17 An account of content with an epistemic component can perhaps avoid a regress, though only by incor-porating a commitment to an externalist account of knowing, one that enables agents to know that something is so even when they are not, in the usual sense, justified in believing that it is so. See n. 12.

17

The Simulation Theory

Folk Psychology as Simulation
Robert M. Gordon

Recently I made a series of predictions of human behavior, using the meager resources allotted to a nonscientist. Having nothing to rely on but "common-sense" or "folk" psychology and being well forewarned of the infirmities of that so-called theory, I had reason to anticipate at best a very modest rate of success.

These were the predictions:

I shall now pour some coffee.
I shall now pick up the cup.
I shall now drink the coffee.
I shall now switch on the word processor.
I shall now draft the opening paragraphs of a paper on folk psychology.

My predictions, as I think no one will be surprised to learn, proved true in every instance. Should anyone doubt this, I recommend spending a few minutes predicting from one moment to another what you are "about to do." Such predictions, if not quite as reliable as "night will follow day" or "this chair will hold my weight," are at least among the most reliable one is likely to make. Of course, one would have to allow for unforeseen interventions by "nature" (sudden paralysis, a coffee cup glued to the table) and for ignorance (the stuff you pour and drink isn't coffee). But that seems a realistic limitation on any *psychological* basis for prediction.

This essay offers an account of the nature of folk psychology. Sections 1 and 2 focus on the prediction of behavior, beginning with reflections on my little experiment in prediction. Section 3 concerns the interaction of explanation and prediction in what I call hypothetico-practical reasoning. Finally, a new account of belief attribution is proposed and briefly defended in section 4.

1 Predicting One's Own Behavior

At least one lesson can be drawn from my prediction experiment. Discussions of the nature of "folk psychology" and of its own adequacy, particularly as a basis for predictions of overt human behavior, ought to begin by dividing the question: *one's own* behavior or *another's*; behavior in the *immediate* or in the *distant* future; behavior under *existing* conditions or under specified *hypothetical* conditions? For such a division uncovers a little-known and unappreciated success story: our prodigious ability to foretell what we ourselves are "about to do" in the (actual) immediate future. We have in this department a success rate that surely would be the envy of any behavioral or neurobehavioral science.

The trick, of course, is not to predict until one has "made up one's mind" what to do: then one simply declares what one "intends" to do. We display our confidence in the *predictive reliability* of these declarations by the way we formulate them: one typically says, not "I intend now to...," but simply "I shall now..." or "I will now..." Somehow, in learning to "express our (immediate) intention" we learn to utter sentences that, construed as statements about our own future behavior, prove to be extremely reliable.[1] (Normally, apart from the conditions mentioned earlier, the only errors occur when something "makes us change our mind": the telephone rings before we have poured the coffee, we see that the stuff isn't coffee, and so on.) A plausible explanation of this reliability is that our declarations of immediate intention are causally tied to some actual precursor of behavior: perhaps tapping into the brain's updated behavioral "plans" or into "executive commands" that are about to guide the relevant motor sequences.[2] In any case, these everyday predictions of behavior seem to have an anchor in psychological reality.

One might have thought all predictions of human behavior to be inferences from theoretical premises about beliefs, desires, and emotions, together with laws connecting these with behavior: laws of the form: "if A is in states S1, S2, S3, etc., and conditions C1, C2, C3 obtain, then A will (or will probably) do X." Thus one would have a *deductive-nomological* or *inductive-nomological* basis for prediction. This is plainly not so: declarations of immediate intention – "I shall now X" – are not products of inference from such premises.

Moreover, if they were, one could not account for either their predictive reliability or our *confidence* in their predictive reliability. We are not self-omniscient: we do not keep tabs on all of the relevant beliefs and attitudes, and *a fortiori* we do not keep a *reliable* inventory of these. But even if we knew all the relevant beliefs and attitudes, our predictions would at best be qualified and chancy. Folk psychology, on most accounts, doesn't specify a deterministic system; it specifies only the probable or "typical" effects of mental states. Using it as my basis I should have to qualify my predictions by saying, e.g., "*Typically*, I would now pick up the cup." And actions that are *atypical, exceptional*, or *out of character* – my wearing a tie to class, or my heckling the commencement speaker – would defy prediction altogether, even seconds before I take action. Whereas in fact I feel confident that I can predict what I am about to do now, whether the act is typical or not; and my confidence seems well-founded: I predict imminent atypical actions about as reliably as any others.

Although they are not based on nomological reasoning, declarations of immediate intention – these ultra-reliable predictors of behavior – are often products of *practical* reasoning: reasoning that provides the basis for a decision *to do* something.[3] "I shall now write a letter" may express a decision based on certain salient facts (a student asked me to write a letter of recommendation), salient norms and values (I have a duty to write letters for good students who request letters, and she's a good student), and a background of other facts, norms, and values that I am unable to list exhaustively. The important point is that declarations of the form: "I shall now do X" offer a bridge between such practical reasoning and prediction.

This bridge introduces a very interesting possibility: that of using *simulated* practical reasoning as a *predictive* device. First of all, it is easy to see how, by simulating the appropriate practical reasoning, we can extend our capacity for self-prediction in a way that would enable us to predict *our own behavior in hypothetical situations*. Thus I might predict, for example, what I would do if, right now, the screen of the word processor I am working on were to go blank; or what I would do if I were now to hear footsteps coming from the basement.

To simulate the appropriate practical reasoning I can engage in a kind of *pretend-play*: pretend that the indicated conditions *actually obtain*, with all other conditions remaining (so far as is logically possible and physically probable) as they presently stand; then – continuing the make-believe – try to "make up my mind" what to do given these (modified) conditions. I imagine, for instance, a lone modification of the actual world: the sound of footsteps from the basement.[4] Then I ask, in effect, "what shall I do now?" And I answer with a declaration of immediate intention, "I shall now..." This too is only feigned. But it is not feigned on a *tabula rasa*, as if at random: rather, the declaration of immediate intention appears to be formed in the way a *decision* is formed, *constrained* by the (pretended) "fact" that there is the sound of footsteps from the basement, the (*un*pretended) fact that such a sound would now be unlikely if there weren't an intruder in the basement, the (*un*pretended) awfulness of there being an intruder in the basement, and so forth.

What I have performed is a kind of *practical simulation*, a simulated deciding *what to do*. Some simulated decisions in hypothetical situations include acting out: e.g., rehearsals and drills. The kind I am interested in, however, suppress the behavioral output. One reports the simulated decision as a *hypothetical prediction*: a prediction of what I would do in the specified hypothetical circumstances, other things being as they are. For example: if I were now to hear footsteps from the basement, (probably) I would reach for the telephone and call an emergency number.[5]

I noted earlier that one could not account for either the *confidence* or the *reliability* with which I predict what I am about to do now, if such predictions were based on attributions of beliefs, desires, etc., together with laws. The same holds for *hypothetical* self-predictions. Once again I don't know enough about my beliefs and desires; and the laws would at best yield only the *typical* effects of those states, anyway.[6] In real life we sometimes surprise ourselves with *atypical* responses: "I certainly wouldn't have thought I'd react that way!" Practical simulation imitates real life in this respect, giving us the capacity to surprise ourselves *before* we confront the actual situation. If I pretend *realistically* that there is an intruder in the house I *might* find myself surprisingly brave – or cowardly.[7]

2 Predicting the Behavior of Others

In one type of hypothetical *self*-prediction the hypothetical situation is one that some *other* person has actually been in, or at least is described as having been in. The task is to answer the question, "What would *I* do in *that* person's situation?" For example, chess players report that, playing against a human opponent or even against a computer, they visualize the board from the other side, taking the opposing pieces for their own and vice versa. Further, they pretend that their *reasons for action* have shifted accordingly: whereas previously the fact that a move would make White's Queen vulnerable would constitute a reason *for* making the move, it now becomes a reason *against*; and so on. Thus transported in imagination, they "make up their mind what to do." *That*, they conclude, is what *I* would do (have done). They are "putting themselves in the other's shoes" in one sense of that expression: that is, they project themselves into the other's *situation*, but without any attempt to project themselves into, as we say, the other's "mind."

A prediction of how I would act in the other's situation is not, of course, a prediction of how the other will act – unless, of course, the other should happen to be, in causally relevant respects, a *replica* of me. But people claim also that by "putting themselves in the other's shoes," in a somewhat different sense of that expression, they can predict the *other*'s behavior. As in the case of hypothetical

self-prediction, the methodology essentially involves *deciding what to do*; but, extended to people of "minds" different from one's own, this is not the same as deciding *what I myself would do*. One tries to make *adjustments for relevant differences*. In chess, for example, a player would make not only the imaginative shifts required for predicting "what *I* would do in his shoes," but the further shifts required for predicting what *he* will do in his shoes. To this purpose the player might, e.g., simulate a lower level of play, trade one set of idiosyncrasies for another, and above all pretend ignorance of *his own* (actual) intentions. Army generals, salespeople, and detectives claim to do this sort of thing. Sherlock Holmes expresses the point with characteristic modesty:

> You know my methods in such cases, Watson. I put myself in the man's place, and, having first gauged his intelligence, I try to imagine how I should myself have proceeded under the same circumstances. In this case the matter was simplified by Brunton's intelligence being quite first-rate, so that it was unnecessary to make any allowance for the personal equation, as the astronomers have dubbed it. (Doyle 1894)

The procedure serves cooperative as well as competitive ends: not to go far afield, bridge players claim they can project themselves into their *partner's* shoes.

Several earlier philosophers claimed that interpersonal understanding depends on a procedure resembling what I call simulation. Precursors of simulation include historical reenactment (Collingwood 1946) and *Verstehen* or "empathetic understanding" (Schutz 1962, 1967; von Wright 1971, ch. 1).[8] But little attention has been given to prediction. Nor have these authors appreciated the methodological importance of hypothesis-testing and experimentation in practical simulation: the fact that at its heart is a type of reasoning I characterize as *hypothetico-practical*. Finally, they have not tried to explain the very concept of belief in terms of practical simulation, as I shall.

3 Hypothetico-practical Reasoning

Let me illustrate with an extended example of hypothetico-practical reasoning. A friend and I have sat down at a table in a fashionable international restaurant in New York. The waiter approaches. He greets me effusively in what strikes me as a Slavic language. He says nothing to my friend. I do not speak any Slavic language.

I wish to understand the waiter's behavior. I wish also to predict his future behavior, given various responses I might make to his greeting. As a first step, I shift spatiotemporal perspectives – I am standing over there now, where the waiter is, not sitting here. In some cases, shifting spatio-temporal perspectives might be enough: e.g., for predicting, or explaining, the behavior of a person I see in the path of an oncoming car. This would be woefully inadequate for the restaurant example, of course. As a further experiment, I might switch institutional roles. I suppose (and perhaps imagine) myself to be a waiter, waiting on a customer sitting here in this restaurant. Such counterfactual suppositions raise difficult questions: for example, shall I suppose myself to be a waiter who has read Quine (as I have)? Shall I suppose the *customer* to have read Quine?[9] Fortunately, I do not ordinarily have to ask these questions, since they would make no difference in my behavior in this situation; and when they do make a difference, the situation is likely to alert me to their relevance.

Donning my waiter's uniform is clearly not enough: to have what I see as a basis for greeting the customer in a Slavic language, supposing I could, I shall have to alter other facts. As a first stab, I might see myself as an *emigré* from a Slavic country, working as a waiter. I seem to recognize the customer: he is a countryman of mine who used to eat at the restaurant many years ago. It pleases him, as I recall, to be greeted in our native tongue. That would be a reason for doing so. There being no reason not to, that is what I shall do.

Other modifications of the world would lead to the same decision. Suppose that, before the restaurant episode, I had read a cheap spy thriller. Under its corrosive influence I hypothesize as follows: I am a counterintelligence agent posing as a waiter. The customer I am waiting on is a known spy from a Slavic country, and there is good reason to get him to reveal that he knows the language of this country. One way to do this is to watch his reaction as I address him in the language of his country. Given this background, I would indeed address him in that language, if I could.

To choose between the two hypotheses would require further tests. Suppose that in my real role of customer, I look puzzled and respond: "I don't

understand that language. You must be making a mistake." On the countryman hypothesis, the waiter will probably apologize – in English – and explain that he had mistaken me for someone else. On the counterspy hypothesis, he may either persist in speaking in the foreign tongue or turn to more subtle devices for getting the customer to reveal his knowledge of the language. If in fact the waiter apologizes, then the counterspy hypothesis will have suffered one perhaps small defeat.

Ideally, the hypothesis-testing would continue until the subject appeared to be, as it were, *the puppet of my (simulated) intentions*. In actuality, when I persist in my effort to find a pretend-world in which the other's behavior would accord with my intentions, I usually find myself, after a number of errors, "tracking" the other person fairly well, forming a fairly stable pretend-world for that person. Of course, I cannot predict or anticipate exactly what he will do, to any fine-grained description. But, by and large, I will not be very much surprised very often, at least in matters that are important to interpersonal co-ordination.

No matter how long I go on testing hypotheses, I will not have tried out all candidate explanations of the waiter's behavior. Perhaps some of the unexamined candidates would have done at least as well as the one I settle for, if I settle: perhaps indefinitely many of them would have. But these would be "far-fetched," I say intuitively. Therein I exhibit my inertial bias: the less "fetching" (or "stretching," as actors say) I have to do to track the other's behavior, the better. I tend to *feign* only when necessary, only when something in the other's behavior doesn't fit. This inertial bias may be thought of as a "least effort" principle: the "principle of least pretending." It explains why, other things being equal, I will prefer the less radical departure from the "real" world – i.e., from what I myself take to be the world.

Within a close-knit community, where people have a vast common fund of "facts" as well as shared norms and values, only a minimum of pretending would be called for. (In the limit case – a replica – the distinction noted earlier between "what I would do in the other's situation" and "what *the other will* do in his situation" would indeed vanish, except as a formal or conceptual distinction: what *I would* do and what *the other will* do would invariably coincide.) A person transplanted into an alien culture might have to do a great deal of pretending to explain and predict the behavior of those around him. Indeed, one might eventually learn to *begin* all attempts at explanation and prediction with a stereotypic set of adjustments: pretending that dancing causes rain, that grasshoppers taste better than beefsteak, that blue-eyed should never marry brown-eyed, and so on. This "default" set of world-modifications might be said to constitute one's "generalizations" about the alien culture.

Whether or not practical simulation begins with such stereotypes, it does not essentially involve (as one might think) an implicit *comparison to oneself.* Although it does essentially involve *deciding what to do,* that, as I have noted, is not the same as deciding *what I myself would do.* To predict another's behavior I may have to pretend that there is an Aryan race, that it is metaphysically the master race, and that I belong to it; finally, that I was born in Germany of German stock between 1900 and 1920. To make decisions within such a pretend-world is not to decide what *I myself* would do, much less to reliably know what *I myself* would do "in that situation." First, it is not possible for *me* to be in that situation, if indeed it is a *possible* situation (for anyone); second, it is not possible for me even to *believe* myself to be in that situation – not, at least, without such vast changes in my beliefs and attitudes as to make all prediction unreliable. Hence in such a case I cannot be making an implicit *comparison to myself.*[10]

4 Attributions of Beliefs

I do not deny that explanations are often couched in terms of *beliefs, desires,* and other propositional attitudes; or that predictions, particularly predictions of the behavior of others, are often made on the basis of attributions of such states. Moreover, as functionalist accounts of folk psychology have emphasized, common discourse about beliefs and other mental states presupposes that they enter into a multitude of causal and nomological relations. I don't want to deny this either. A particular instance or "token" of belief, such as Smith's belief that Dewey won the election, may be (given a background of other beliefs, desires, etc.) *a cause of* Smith's doing something (joining the Republican party) or undergoing something (being glad, being upset); it may have been *caused by* his reading in the newspapers that Dewey won and his believing that newspapers are reliable in such matters, or by his having taken a hallucinogenic drug.

There are in addition certain formally describable regularities that might be formulated as laws of typical causation: e.g., a belief that *p* and a belief that (if *p* then *q*) will typically cause a belief that *q*; a desire that *p* and a belief that (*p* if and only if I bring it about that *q*) will typically cause a desire to bring it about that *q*. And there are more specific regularities that obtain for particular individuals, classes, communities, or cultures: e.g., when some tennis players believe their opponents aren't playing at their best they typically get angry; when members of a certain tribe see a cloud they think inhabited by an animal spirit they typically prepare for the hunt. Sometimes it helps to remember such regularities when predicting or explaining behavior – even one's own.

One mustn't apply such generalizations too mechanically, however. For there are indefinitely many circumstances, not exhaustively specifiable in advance, in which these general or specific regularities fail to hold. Those generalizations that do not explicitly concern only "typical" instances should be understood to contain implicit *ceteris paribus* clauses. (This point is developed, along with much else that is congenial, in Putnam (1978, lecture VI).) How does one know how to recognize atypical situations or to expand the *ceteris paribus* clause? An answer is ready at hand. As long as one applies these generalizations *in the context of practical simulation,* the unspecifiable constraints on *one's own* practical reasoning would enable one to delimit the application of these rules. This gives one something to start with: as one learns more about others, of course, one learns how to modify these constraints in applying generalizations to them.

Moreover, the *interpretation* of such generalizations, as indeed of all common discourse about beliefs and other mental states, remains open to question. In the remainder of this essay I sketch and at least begin to defend a way of interpreting ordinary discourse about beliefs in terms of pretend play and practical simulation. The idea isn't wholly new. In *Word and Object,* Quine explained indirect quotation and the ascription of propositional attitudes in terms of what he called "an essentially dramatic act":

We project ourselves into what, from his remarks and other indications, we imagine the speaker's state of mind to have been, and then we say what, in our language, is natural and relevant for us in the state thus feigned. (1960, p. 92)

That is, we first try to stimulate, by a sort of pretending, another's state of mind; then we just "speak our mind." In Quine's view, this is essentially an exercise in translation and heir to all its problems. Stephen Stich develops the idea further, using a device introduced by Davidson: in saying, e.g., "Smith believes that Dewey won," one utters the content sentence "Dewey won," pretending to be asserting it oneself, as if performing a little skit (Stich 1983). To ascribe such a belief to Smith is to say that he is in a state *similar* to the one that might typically be expected to underlie that utterance – had it not been produced by way of play-acting.

As Stich portrays the play-acting device, it is merely a device for producing a specimen utterance which in turn is used to specify a particular theoretical state. The attribution of such a state is supposed to play a role in nomological reasoning roughly analogous to that of attributions of theoretical states in the physical sciences, and in that role to serve in the tasks of explaining and predicting the object's behavior.[11] Rather than treating the observer as an *agent* in his own right, as one who might form intentions to *act* on the basis of pretend inputs, it calls upon him merely to *speak* as he would given those inputs.

Stich's assumption that the methodological context for such attributions is nomological reasoning leads him, I believe, to misrepresent the role of pretending in folk psychology. I shall sketch very briefly a different role for pretending in belief attribution. On this account, the methodological context for such attributions is not nomological reasoning but practical simulation.

A chess player who visualizes the board from his opponent's point of view might find it helpful to *verbalize* from that point of view – to assert, for example, "my Queen is in danger." Stepping into Smith's shoes I might say: "Dewey won the election." Such assertions may then be used as premises of simulated practical inference. But wouldn't it be a great advantage to us practical simulators if we could *pool our resources*? We'll simulate Smith *together*, cooperatively, advising one another as to what premises or inputs to practical reasoning would work best for a simulation of Smith. That is, give the best predictions and the most stable explanations, explanations that won't have to be revised in the light of new evidence. Of course, I couldn't come *straight out* with the utter-

ance: "Dewey won." I need to flag the utterance as one that is being uttered *from within a Smith-simulation mode* and addressed to *your* Smith-simulation mode. I might do this by saying something like the following:

1 Let's do a Smith simulation. Ready? *Dewey won the election.*

The same task might be accomplished by saying:

2 *Smith believes that* Dewey won the election.

My suggestion is that (2) be read as saying the same thing as (1), though less explicitly.

It is worth noting that unlike Stich I am not characterizing belief as a relation to any linguistic entity or speech act, e.g., a sentence or an assertion. Nor, as far as I can see, does my suggestion involve explicating the contents of belief in terms of possible worlds. Rather than specifying *in a standard nonpretending mode of speech* a set of possible worlds, one says something about the *actual* world, albeit *in a nonstandard, pretending mode of speech*. Needless to say, the exposition and defense of this account of belief are much in need of further development. But it is interesting to note that, given the "principle of least pretending" mentioned earlier, our belief attributions would be in accord with something like the "principle of charity" put forward by Quine and Davidson: roughly, that one should prefer a translation that maximizes truth and rationality. More precisely, our attributions would conform to an improved version of this principle: Grandy's more general "principle of humanity" according to which one should prefer a translation on which "the imputed pattern of relations among beliefs, desires, and the world be as similar to our own as possible" (Grandy 1973, p. 443).

If I am right, to attribute a belief to another person is to make an assertion, to state something as a fact, *within the context of practical simulation*. Acquisition of the capacity to attribute beliefs is acquisition of the capacity to make assertions in such a context. There is some experimental support for this view. Very young children give verbal expression to predictions and explanations of the behavior of others. Yet up to about the age of four they evidently lack the concept of belief, or at least the capacity to make allowances for false or differing beliefs. Evidence of this can be teased out by presenting children with stories and dramatizations that involve dramatic irony: where we the audience know something important the protagonist doesn't know (Wimmer and Perner 1983).[12]

In one such story (illustrated with puppets) the puppet-child Maxi puts his chocolate in the box and goes out to play. While he is out, his mother transfers the chocolate to the cupboard. Where will Maxi look for the chocolate when he comes back? In the box, says the five-year-old, pointing to the miniature box on the puppet stage: a good prediction of a sort we ordinarily take for granted. (That is, after all, where the chocolate had been before it was, without Maxi's knowledge, transferred to the cupboard.) But the child of three to four years has a different response: verbally or by pointing the child indicates the cupboard. (That is, after all, where the chocolate is to be found, isn't it?) Suppose Maxi wants to mislead his gluttonous big brother to the *wrong* place, where will he lead him? The five-year-old indicates the cupboard, where (unbeknownst to Maxi) the chocolate actually is; often accompanying the response with what is described as "an ironical smile." The *younger* child indicates, incorrectly, the box.[13]

From this and other experiments it appears that normal children around age four or five vastly increase their capacity to predict the behavior of others. The child develops the ability to make allowances for what the other isn't in a position to know. She can predict behavioral failures, e.g., failure to look in the right place, failure to mislead another to the wrong place, that result from *cognitive* failures, i.e., *false beliefs*. At an earlier age she makes all predictions in an egocentric way, basing them all on *the actual facts*, i.e., the facts as she herself sees them. She either lacks the concept of belief altogether or at least lacks the ability to employ it in the prediction of behavior. One may even say that the young child attributes knowledge – by default – before she has learned to attribute belief.

It is the position of many philosophers that common-sense terms such as "believes" are *theoretical* terms, the meanings of which are fixed in the same way as theoretical terms in general: by the set of laws and generalizations in which they figure. This view is widely (but not universally) assumed in functionalist accounts of folk psychology. (It is the offspring of the dispositional theories that were popular in the days of philosophical behaviorism.) Presumably, mastery of the concept of belief would then be a matter of internalizing a sufficiently large number of laws or generalizations

in which the term "belief" (and related verb forms) occurs. The term "belief" would be used in something like the way biologists used the term "gene" before the discovery of DNA.[14]

But suppose that mastery of the concept of belief did consist in learning or in some manner internalizing a system of laws and generalizations concerning belief. One would in that case expect that *before* internalizing this system, the child would simply be unable to predict or explain human action. And *after* internalizing the system the child could deal indifferently with actions caused by *true* beliefs and actions caused by *false* beliefs. It is hard to see how the semantic question could be relevant.

Suppose on the other hand that the child of four develops the ability to make assertions, to state something as fact, *within the context of practical simulation*. That would give her the capacity to overcome an initial egocentric limitation to the *actual facts* (i.e., as *she* sees them). One would *expect* a change of just the sort we find in these experiments.

There is further evidence. Practical simulation involves the capacity for a certain kind of systematic pretending. It is well known that *autistic* children suffer a striking deficit in the capacity for pretend play. In addition they are often said to "treat people and objects alike"; they fail to treat others as subjects, as having "points of view" distinct from their own. This failure is confirmed by their performance in prediction tests like the one I have just described. A version of the Wimmer–Perner test was administered to autistic children of ages *six to sixteen* by a team of psychologists (Baron-Cohen, Leslie, and Frith 1985). *Almost all* these children gave the wrong answer, the three-year-old's answer. This indicates a highly specific deficit, not one in general intelligence. Although many autistic children are also mentally retarded, those tested were mostly in the average or borderline IQ range. Yet children with Down's syndrome, with IQ levels substantially below that range, suffered no deficit: almost all gave the right answer. My account of belief would predict that only those children who can engage in pretend play can master the concept of belief.[15] It is worth noting that autistic children do at least as well as normals in their comprehension of *mechanical* operations – a distinct blow to any functionalists who might think mastery of the concept of belief to consist in the acquisition of a theory of the functional organization of a mechanism.

I suspect that, once acquired, the capacity for practical simulation operates primarily at a subverbal level, enabling us to *anticipate* in our own actions the behavior of others, though we are unable to say *what* it is that we anticipate or *why*. The *self-reported* pretending I have described would then only be the tip of the iceberg. Something like it may happen quite regularly and without our knowledge: our decision-making or practical reasoning system gets partially disengaged from its "natural" inputs and fed instead with suppositions and images (or their "subpersonal" or "subdoxastic" counterparts). Given these artificial pretend inputs the system then "makes up its mind" what to do. Since the system is being run off-line, as it were, disengaged also from its natural output systems, its "decision" isn't actually executed but rather ends up as an anticipation, perhaps just an unconscious *motor* anticipation, of the other's behavior.

One interesting possibility is that the readiness for practical simulation is a prepackaged "module" called upon automatically in the perception of other human beings. One might even speculate that such a module makes its first appearance in the useful tendency many mammals have of turning their eyes toward the target of another's gaze. Thus the very sight of human eyes might *require* us to simulate at least their spatial perspective – and to this extent, at least, to put ourselves in the other's shoes. This would give substance to the notion that we perceive one another primarily as *subjects*: as world-centers rather than as objects in the world. It is pleasant to speculate that the phenomenology of *the Other* – particularly the Sartrean idea that consciousness of the Other robs us of our own perspective – might have such humble beginnings.

It remains the prevailing view of philosophers and cognitive scientists that mental states, as conceived by naive folk psychology, are constructs belonging to a prescientific theory of the inner workings of the human behavior control system housed, as we now know, in the brain. One problem with this conception of folk psychology is that mastery of its concepts would seem to demand a highly developed theoretical intellect and a methodological sophistication rivaling that of modern-day cognitive scientists. That is an awful lot to impute to the four-year-old, or to our savage ancestors. It is also uncanny that folk psychology hasn't changed very much over the millennia. Paul Churchland writes:

> The [folk psychology] of the Greeks is essentially the [folk psychology] we use today, and we are negligibly better at explaining human behavior in its terms than was Sophocles. That is a very long period of stagnation and infertility for any theory to display. (1981, p. 75)

Churchland thinks this a sign that folk psychology is a bad theory; but it could be a sign that it is no theory at all, not, at least, in the accepted sense of (roughly) a system of laws implicitly defining a set of terms. Instead it might be just the capacity for practical reasoning, supplemented by a special use of a childish and primitive capacity for pretend play. I hope that I have shown that to be a plausible and refreshing alternative.[16]

Notes

1 The qualifying phrase is added because I am concerned with *assertive* reliability, not *commissive* reliability: that of predictions, rather than that of promises, vows, and expressions of intention. Construing "I shall now X" as a mere expression of intention, if the speaker does not X he will have "failed to carry out" his intention: his *action* would in a (nonmoral) sense be "at fault." Construing it as a mere prediction, on the other hand, it would be the *prediction* that is "at fault," not the *action*. To use Seale's distinction (derived from Anscombe), declarations of intention have a world-to-word "direction of fit," whereas predictions and other "assertive" speech acts have a word-to-world direction of fit (Searle 1983). This distinction does not affect the essential point being made here.

2 A further possibility is that a degree of normative commitment is added by the *declaration* of an intention, even if it is announced only to oneself: one is then motivated to *mold* one's behavior to the declared intention. This was suggested to me by Brian McLaughlin.

3 More precisely, *what is expressed* by these declarations are often products of practical reasoning.

4 Imagery is not always needed in such simulations. For example, I need no imagery to simulate having a million dollars in the bank. Mere *supposition* would be enough.

5 Contrast, "I would (if such a situation were now to arise) reach for the telephone and dial an emergency

number" uttered as a declaration of *conditional intention*. The difference can be partially explicated in terms of "direction of fit."

6 Granted, if one were to do some of the pretending out loud, one might say, e.g., "I believe someone has broken into the house." But such a verbalization has a role in practical not nomological reasoning: one is articulating a possible basis for action, not giving a state description that is to be plugged into laws that bridge between internal states and behavior.

7 Needless to say, like any attempt to explain or predict one's own behavior, this may be corrupted by prejudice or self-deception.

8 Closer to my own view is Morton (1980, ch. 3) on the uses of imagination in understanding another's behavior.

9 As Quine has noted: "Casting our real selves thus in unreal roles, we do not generally know how much reality to hold constant" (1960, p. 92).

10 Nozick seems to miss this point in his account of *Verstehen* as "a special form of inference by analogy, in that I am the thing to which he is analogous." He argues that the inference depends on two empirical correlations: "that he acts as I would, and that I would as I (on the basis of imaginative projection) think I would" (1981, p. 636). Nozick's mistake is to think it relevant to ask, and indeed essential as the inferential link, how I would *in fact* behave in the other's shoes.

11 To do *this* job properly, it would have to meet certain standards of objectivity. And Stich argues with considerable force that it cannot. For it never frees itself fully from the subjectivity it necessarily begins with, the speaker-relativity that is built into the ascription of content.

12 The psychologists who conducted this study credit three philosophers (J. Bennett, D. Dennett, and G. Harman) with suggesting the experimental paradigm, each independently, in commentaries published with Premack and Woodruff, 1978.

13 My account simplifies the experiment and the results; but not, I think, unconscionably.

14 But a functionalist might wish to say that, whereas the correct *explication* of the concept requires that one cite such laws, *mastery* of the concept, i.e., capacity to *use* it, does not require that one have internalized such laws. Thus some functionalists might even be prepared to embrace something like my account of belief attributions. This possibility (or something close to it) was pointed out to me independently by Larry Davis and Sydney Shoemaker. I am inclined to think that this would be an uneasy alliance, but I confess I don't (as yet) have the arguments to persuade anybody who might think otherwise.

15 My account is close in many respects to the theory the investigators were themselves testing in the autism experiment. This is presented in Leslie (1987).

16 I have benefited enormously from the advice and criticism of Stephen Stich, in correspondence and conversation. I am indebted to Fred Adams and Larry Davis for much help in seeing through the murk, and have benefited further from comments by Robert Audi, John Barker, Hartry Field, Brain McLaughlin, Sydney Shoemaker, Raimo Tuomela, and (no doubt) others.

References

Baron-Cohen, S., Leslie, A. M., and Frith, U. (1985) "Does the autistic child have a 'theory of mind'?" *Cognition*, 21, 37–46.

Churchland, P. M. (1981) "Eliminative materialism and the propositional attitudes." *Journal of Philosophy*, 78, 67–90.

Collingwood, R. G. (1946) *The Idea of History*. New York: Oxford University Press.

Doyle, A. Conan (1894) "The Musgrave ritual." In *The Memoirs of Sherlock Holmes*. New York: Harper Bros.

Grandy, R. (1973) "Reference, meaning, and belief." *Journal of Philosophy*, 70, 439–52.

Leslie, A. M. (1987) "Pretense and representation: the origins of 'theory of mind'." *Psychological Review*, 94, 412–26.

Morton, A. (1980) *Frames of Mind*. Oxford: Oxford University Press.

Nozick, R. (1981) *Philosophical Explanations*. Cambridge, Mass.: Harvard University Press.

Premack, D. and Woodruff, G. (1978) "Does the chimpanzee have a theory of mind?" *Behavioral and Brain Sciences*, 1, 515–26.

Putnam, H. (1978) *Meaning and The Moral Sciences*. Boston: Routledge & Kegan Paul.

Quine, W. V. O. (1960) *Word and Object*. Cambridge, Mass.: MIT Press.

Schutz, A. (1962) *Collected Papers*. The Hague: Nijhoff.

Schutz, A. (1967) *Phenomenology and the Social World*. Evanston, Ill.: Northwestern University Press.

Searle, J. R. (1983) *Intentionality*. Cambridge: Cambridge University Press.

Stich, S. (1983) *From Folk Psychology to Cognitive Science: The Case Against Belief*. Cambridge, Mass.: MIT Press.

Wimmer, H. and Perner, J. (1983) "Beliefs about beliefs: representation and constraining function of wrong beliefs in young children's understanding of deception." *Cognition*, 13, 103–28.

Von Wright, G. H. (1971) *Explanation and Understanding*. Ithaca, NY: Cornell University Press.

The Mental Simulation Debate

Martin Davies

Introduction

In a well-known section from chapter 3 of *Individuals*, Strawson (1959, pp. 99–100) says:

> it is a necessary condition of one's ascribing states of consciousness, experiences, to oneself, in the way one does, that one should also ascribe them, or be prepared to ascribe them, to others who are not oneself.
> ...the ascribing phrases are used in just the same sense when the subject is another as when the subject is oneself.
> [But] how could the sense be the same when the method of verification was so different in the two cases...

Strawson's example is the predicate "is in pain"; but what he says goes equally for "believes that penguins waddle". It is a necessary condition of self-ascription:

> I believe that penguins waddle

that I can also ascribe beliefs to others:

> She believes that penguins waddle.

The predicate is used in the same sense in both cases – it is a single concept that has been mastered – despite the fact that the grounds for attribution are liable to be very different. In the first-person case, Strawson says (1959, p. 100), we would scarcely speak of there being a "method of verification"; but in the third-person case, it is natural to say, the grounds for attribution are provided by the observable situation and behaviour of the other.

This difference between the first-person and third-person cases, as regards grounds of attribution (or "method of verification") might show up in a philosophically fundamental account of our ascriptions of beliefs – in an account of what constitutes mastery of the concept of belief – as a difference between two clauses in that account. But the account as a whole should honour the idea that it is just the same thing that is being predicated in the two cases. In particular, the account should guarantee, somehow, that where first-person and third-person attributions converge upon a single subject of predication the two attributions are true under just the same conditions. For it would be impossible to maintain that the predicate "believes that penguins waddle" retains the same sense in both first-person and third-person attributions, if we could not rule out the possibility that

> I believe that penguins waddle

might be true, say, in my mouth, while

> He believes that penguins waddle

could be false when said of me.

This requirement – which Peacocke (1992, p. 171) calls the requirement of *referential coherence* – is surely a constraint upon any philosophically fundamental account of belief attribution (of our deployment of the concept of belief).

In an oft-quoted passage in *Word and Object*, Quine recommends the idea that third-person attributions of belief involve a kind of dramatic re-enactment (1960, p. 92):

> We project ourselves into what, from his remarks and other indications, we imagine the speaker's state of mind to have been, and then we say what, in our language, is natural and relevant for us in the state thus feigned.

This is the idea – with its stress upon the ability to imagine the state of mind of the other – that has been developed into the claim that a fundamental account of belief attributions should be cast in terms of mental simulation: simulating in imagination the state of mind of the other.

Quine's idea and Strawson's constraint date from 1960 and 1959 respectively. As we shall see, the question whether it is possible to meet the constraint while adopting the idea is still – over thirty years later – in need of an answer.

The idea of mental simulation – understanding another by imagining his or her state of mind – is not a new idea. Around the middle of this century – in the work of Collingwood (1946), for example – it had its home in disputes in the philosophy of social sciences and of history. These were disputes about whether the methods that were successful in explaining and predicting the physical world of material objects would also be appropriate to explanations and predictions of the human world.

The current form of the debate can be dated, not entirely arbitrarily, to 1986. For in that year, two key papers appeared: "Replication and functionalism" by Jane Heal, and "Folk psychology as simulation" by Robert Gordon.

The present essay has four parts. First, I shall sketch the two opposed positions in the current form of the mental simulation debate: the *theory theory* and the *simulation alternative*. Second, I shall give a brief review of some of the empirical literature – though it has to be said at the outset that, in my view, the empirical strand of the debate is at a rather inconclusive stage. In the third section, I shall focus upon the particular development of the simulation theory that has been offered by Alvin Goldman (1989; 1992). I shall use this exposition both as a way of motivating a particular way of delineating the two opposed views, and as a way of introducing the idea that simulation cannot be employed to give a philosophically fundamental account of our use of mental concepts. In the final section, I shall raise the question whether Robert Gordon's (1986; 1992a; 1992b; 1992; in press) development of the simulation view presents a more promising prospect.

1 The Debate in Outline

The friends of mental simulation are united by what they oppose; namely, the so-called "theory theory" about commonsense (or "folk") psychology. Let us begin there.

1.1 The theory theory

Suppose we ask: How are normal adult human beings able to negotiate a particular psychological task domain? How, for example, is a normal adult able to judge whether a sentence of his or her natural language is grammatical? One strategy for answering this kind of question is to postulate that human beings are in possession of a theory – in the linguistic case, a grammar – and that they deploy this theory (grammar) in order to solve the problems that the task domain presents.

It is not reckoned to be any block on this strategy that the person who is supposed to be deploying the theory is unaware of the theory, nor that – in the vast majority of cases – the deployer of the theory will never be conversant with the conceptual resources that are required to state the theory explicitly. The normal adult's relationship to the theory is said to be that of "tacit" or "implicit" knowledge. This "tacit theory" strategy is certainly one of the dominant paradigms in contemporary cognitive science.

Now, one impressive fact about human beings is that, with little or no formal training, they develop the capacity to deploy psychological concepts such as *belief* and *desire* in predictions and explanations of the actions and mental states of other members of the species. These predictions and explanations are said to *rationalize* the subject's actions or mental states; they present the subject's beliefs and desires as providing him or her with reasons for acting and thinking in certain ways. What is the nature of the basis of this ability?

In line with that dominant paradigm in cognitive science, many philosophers and psychologists argue that this everyday ability reflects the fact that normal adult human beings possess a primitive or "folk" psychological theory. This theory, just like its less primitive cousins in more developed domains, postulates theoretical entities – in this case, mental states – and contains laws which relate the mental states to one another and to external stimuli (on the input side) and actions (on the output side). When I predict what someone will do, or explain why they have done something, I do so by deploying this theory. Most of us are, of course, quite unaware that this is what we are doing; but, as with grammatical theory, that fact is reckoned to be unimportant. Our relationship to the psychological theory is allowed to be "tacit" or "implicit" knowledge.

This view about our actual practice of predicting and explaining mental states – a very general empirical claim about the basis of that ability – is one strand of what has come to be known as the *theory theory* about the propositional attitudes of commonsense psychology. But the theory theory has other strands too – clearly empirical psychological strands, and also more narrowly philosophical strands.

One of these strands is the claim that the best philosophical elucidation of the nature of the propositional attitudes is provided by a psychological theory's specification of the interconnected roles of the various attitudes (their causal or functional roles according to that theory). A further philosophical strand is the claim that an individual's mastery of the concepts of the propositional attitudes is precisely constituted by his or her tacit knowledge of such a theory embedding those notions. It is important to distinguish these two strands: one concerns mental states while the other concerns our concepts of mental states.

There are other empirical psychological strands, too – alongside the initial claim about our normal adult predictive and explanatory practices. Most importantly, these concern the nature of the psychological development that leads to the attained state of tacit mastery of a folk psychological theory. The theory theorist says that – by learning or by maturation – the various principles of an increasingly sophisticated psychological theory become available for deployment in prediction and explanation.

There may be yet further strands, but it is worth keeping in mind at least these four:

Psychological
- a strand that concerns the attained state of normal adults;
- a strand that concerns the course of development;

Philosophical
- a strand that concerns the elucidation of the nature of mental states;
- a strand that concerns the mastery of mental concepts.

1.2   The simulation alternative

Robert Gordon – in a series of papers beginning with the one that we have already mentioned: "Folk psychology as simulation" (1986) – and Alvin Goldman – in a series beginning with "Interpretation psychologized" (1989) – have mounted a challenge to the idea that folk psychology is best seen as a theory. These philosophers deny that our understanding of one another primarily proceeds by deployment of a theory, whether folk or otherwise. Rather, they claim that human beings are able to predict and explain each others' actions by using the resources of their own minds to simulate the

psychological aetiology of the actions of others. So, instead of being theorizers, we are *simulators*. We are mental simulators, not in the sense that we merely simulate mentation, but in the sense that we understand others by using our own mentation in a process of simulation.

Gordon begins by noting the prodigious ability we have to predict our own actions. He notes that before I act I often engage in practical reasoning, and suggests that to predict what I might do in a hypothetical situation I can "simulate the appropriate practical reasoning" by engaging "in a kind of pretend play". Gordon fills this out with the following example (1986, p. 161):

> I imagine, for instance, a lone modification of the actual world: the sound of footsteps from the basement. Then I ask, in effect, "what shall I do now?" And I answer with a declaration of immediate intention, "I shall now . . ." This too is only feigned. But it is not feigned on a *tabula rasa*, as if at random: rather, the declaration of immediate intention appears to be formed in the way a *decision* is formed, *constrained* by the (pretended) "fact" that there is a sound of footsteps from the basement, the (*un*pretended) fact that such a sound would now be unlikely if there weren't an intruder in the basement, the (*un*pretended) awfulness of there being an intruder in the basement, and so forth.

Gordon then extends this strategy to the third person case, where he says (p. 162):

> As in the case of hypothetical self-prediction, the methodology essentially involves *deciding what to do*; but, extended to people of "minds" different from one's own, this is not the same as deciding *what I myself would do*. One tries to make *adjustments for relevant differences*.

So, according to Gordon, my ability successfully to predict the actions of another relies upon the ability to engage in simulation. And this is not merely to simulate that *I* am in the other's situation, but to simulate *being* in that situation, having those psychological traits, and so on; in short, to simulate *being the other*.

It is important to note that the outcome of the pretence or simulation is not supposed to be determined by any theory that I hold; if it were then the gap between the theory theory and the simulation alternative would be narrow indeed. Rather – on one plausible elaboration of the basic idea of simulation – I feed the pretend inputs into my own decision-making processes and let those processes run "off-line," so that no action is actually produced. I then announce the decision that is produced as output by those "off-line" processes. Goldman spells out the idea of a process-driven (rather than a theory-driven) simulation quite clearly (1989, p. 173):

> But must all mental simulations be theory-driven in order to succeed? I think not. A simulation of some target systems might be accurate even if the agent lacks such a theory. This can happen if (1) the *process* that drives the simulation is the same as (or relevantly similar to) the process that drives the system, and (2) the initial states of the simulating agent are the same as, or relevantly similar to, those of the target system. Thus, if one person simulates a sequence of mental states of another, they will wind up in the same (or isomorphic) final states as long as (A) they began in the same (or isomorphic) initial states, and (B) both sequences were driven by the same cognitive process or routine. It is not necessary that the simulating agent have a theory of what the routine is, or how it works.

This idea of a system of decision processes that can be operated "off-line" is integral to Goldman's version of the simulation view. Gordon, in contrast, regards it as an "ancillary hypothesis", though a "very plausible" one (1992b, p. 87), and chooses to focus upon the less scientific-sounding idea of imaginative identification. These differences within the simulation camp are not un-important; but at this introductory stage perhaps we can fairly say that, so far as the mechanisms of prediction and explanation go, the basic proposals of Gordon and Goldman are fairly similar.

It is crucial, however, even at this introductory stage, to impose upon the simulation view a differentiation of various strands, corresponding to the several distinct strands in the theory theory. For a friend of simulation might or might not move from a claim about normal adult processes of prediction and explanation to more purely philosophical claims about the elucidation of the nature of mental states, or about the conditions for the possession of mental concepts.

All manner of hybrid positions are at least prima facie possible. For example, suppose someone holds that mental simulation provides a useful –

generally reliable – heuristic for the generation of hypotheses about how someone will behave, or about why someone has acted in a particular way. It is quite consistent to combine that view with the claim that mastery of the mental concepts used in those hypotheses is a matter of tacit knowledge of a theory, which in turn provides the resources for normative evaluation of the generated hypotheses.

Gordon's position is that simulation provides much more than an effective heuristic. Indeed, he enters the bold suggestion that the simulation view will yield an alternative to the theory theorist's understanding of mental states themselves; or rather, as he puts it (1986, p. 166), will provide "a way of interpreting ordinary discourse about beliefs."

In contrast, Goldman is not optimistic about the prospects of the simulation view yielding a constitutive account either of mental states or of the possession conditions for mental concepts. However, Goldman does not see this as calling for the re-introduction of strands of the theory theory, for what the theory theory offers is essentially a third-person account of mental states. The simulation view already addresses the case of third-person attribution of mental states, but only by taking for granted the first-person case. So, Goldman concludes (1989, p. 183), "If the simulation theory is right . . . it looks as if the main elements of the grasp of mental concepts must be located in the first-person sphere."

I shall return to Goldman in section 3, and to Gordon in section 4. In the meantime, however, we should take account of the empirical strands of the mental simulation debate – particularly, the strand that concerns the course of development. There too, as we shall see, there has been a kind of devolution upon the first-person case.

2 The Developmental Evidence

One of the four strands that we discerned within the theory theory concerns the developmental course leading up to the normal adult's attained state of possession of a folk psychological theory. In a version that most closely parallels the case of linguistic theory, this strand would say that tacit knowledge of the theory is innate, that it is embodied in a special-purpose module of the mind, and that development is predominantly a matter of maturation rather than of learning. Of course, other versions are certainly conceivable: someone might deny the nativism; someone else might reject the idea of a task-specific system.

It is strictly speaking consistent to combine a theory theorist's account of the attained state with a mainly simulation theoretic account of the course of development. For example, the principles of the theory might be extracted, by some kind of overseeing system, from the operation of a developed system for off-line simulation (cf. Goldman 1989, p. 176). But, despite that possibility, it is natural to start out with a simplifying background assumption to the effect that there is more continuity between the stages of development and the attained state. Given such a working hypothesis, a simulation theorist or a theory theorist can use empirical evidence in favour of the developmental strand of his or her overall view in order to reinforce the strand that concerns the attained state.

There is a very considerable body of research in developmental psychology, addressing the question whether the child's development of the capacity to deploy psychological concepts such as belief and desire to predict and explain human actions reflects the gradual development of a theory or the development of some different kind of ability. Does the child develop a theory of the mind or, rather, develop the ability to imagine what it is like to be in another person's shoes: to pretend or to simulate? Both Gordon and Goldman call upon this research in support of the simulation view. Indeed, they both cite two classic studies involving false beliefs (Wimmer and Perner 1983; Baron-Cohen, Leslie and Frith 1985).

2.1 The false belief task

Gordon gives a simple description of the task used by Wimmer and Perner (Gordon 1986, p. 168):

> The puppet-child Maxi puts his chocolate in the box and goes out to play. While he is out, his mother transfers the chocolate to the cupboard. Where will Maxi look for the chocolate when he comes back?

and of the key result:

> In the box, says the five-year-old, pointing to the miniature box on the puppet stage: a good prediction of the sort we ordinarily take for granted.... But the child of three to four years

has a different response: verbally or by pointing the child indicates the cupboard.

The simulation theorist's account of the difference between the performance of the younger and the older children is, of course, that the younger children as yet lack, while the older children have attained, the ability to engage in a kind of pretend play that involves simulating being someone whose cognitive position is substantially different from one's own. This account is then fortified by the finding of Baron-Cohen, Leslie and Frith that autistic children – who are typically poor at pretend play – make the same error as the younger children in the Wimmer and Perner study.

Gordon and Goldman are joined in their defence of the simulation view by Paul Harris (1989; 1991a; 1992), who offers a range of support for its developmental strand. Harris also notes (1992, pp. 121–4) that the false belief task – used in the experiments reported by Wimmer and Perner (1983) and much subsequent work – was originally introduced to make it impossible for a subject using a very simple simulation strategy to achieve predictive success. The simple simulation strategy – which Gordon (1992a, p. 13) calls "total projection" – is the one that does not make "adjustments for relevant differences" – particularly, for relevant cognitive differences. If a task – involving the prediction of behaviour, for example – can be performed by using that simple strategy then, of course, a creature's success on that task does not constitute evidence of the creature's possession of a psychological theory – a "theory of mind". Researchers seeking evidence of a "theory of mind" therefore began using the false belief task; for success on that task certainly requires *something* more sophisticated than total projection.

Now, whether the extra that is needed is deployment of a theory, or just more sophisticated simulation, is controversial. So, success on the false belief task is not clinching evidence on behalf of the theory theory. But, Harris's point is that, given the original motivation for the false belief paradigm, we should not really expect it to be the starting point for results that are especially congenial to the simulation theory and problematic for the theory theory.

It seems fair to say that both the advocates of the theory theory (Perner 1991; Perner and Howes 1992; Gopnik and Wellman 1992) and the friends of mental simulation (Harris 1989; 1991a; 1992) can provide acceptably principled accounts of the developmental data from the third-person false belief task. According to the theory theory, children undergo "a change from one mentalistic psychological theory to another somewhere between $2\frac{1}{2}$ and around 4" (Gopnik and Wellman 1992, p. 149). According to the simulation account, "the changes... stem from changes in the child's imaginative flexibility, rather than from a change in the child's so-called theory of mind" (Harris 1992, p. 131).

In order to make further progress with the empirical, developmental strand of the debate, we need to look elsewhere, and the obvious place to look is the first person. This case holds out the prospect of distinguishing empirically between the two theories, since here they seem bound to yield different predictions. For the theory theory, the first-person case is just one case among others; but the mental simulation account of third-person attribution of mental states works by taking first-person attributions for granted. Thus it seems that the theory theory predicts similar errors in both first-person and third-person attributions, while the simulation account predicts distinctive errors introduced by the use of simulation to cantilever out to the third person from the first person. (In fact, to be a little more accurate, we should say that the empirical psychological strands of the two theories seem bound to yield different predictions about actual attributions. The more purely philosophical strands – concerning the nature of mental states and the mastery of mental concepts – do not obviously yield any distinctive predictions about the actual practice of attribution.)

Harris himself suggests (1992, pp. 139–41) that what would be embarrassing for the theory theory would be results demonstrating a marked difference in accuracy as between first-person and third-person reports. And he notes that there are results – even in the work of those advocating the theory theory – that seem to reveal the crucial asymmetry between the first-person and third-person cases. Even very young children are very accurate, for example, at reporting what they are currently thinking, pretending, seeing, or wanting.

2.2 Focus on the first person

Alison Gopnik and Henry Wellman are advocates of the theory theory, and recommend that the course of development should be understood as a series of changes in the child's theory of mind. Some of the advantages that they claim for the theory theory relate to the absence of an asymmetry between first-person and third-person attributions which – they say, apparently in agreement with Harris – would be predicted by the simulation theory.

The assumption shared by Gopnik and Wellman, on the one hand, and Harris, on the other, is that the simulation theory is introspectionist about first-person attributions. In particular, the simulation theory predicts that reading off one's own mental states should be relatively easy, while attributing to a third person mental states different from one's own should be relatively difficult. In contrast, the theory theory predicts that the difficulty of the attribution task should correlate with a difference between kinds of mental state, which cross-cuts the first-person vs. third-person distinction. This is the difference in theoretical complexity between rudimentary notions of desire and perception, and the fully representational notion of belief.

Gopnik and Wellman review evidence that suggests that children who fail on the third-person version of the false belief task also fail on a first-person version of the task. They offer this as evidence that is problematic for the simulation theory, since it reveals no asymmetry between first-person and third-person attributions.

However, Harris (1992, p. 132) comments that this first kind of evidence does not really threaten the simulation theory. For Gopnik and Wellman's first-person version of the false belief task involves a past-tense attribution. And – whatever may be the appeal of introspection as a method for present-tense first-person attributions – it is quite consistent for a simulation theorist to group past-tense first-person attributions with the third-person case, since the simulation would involve the subject having to set aside his or her own *present* beliefs. Once again, it is hard to find anything decisive, one way or the other, in the developmental data.

This is not the end of the empirical story. There are other findings that have been offered in support of the theory theory, and as problematic for the simulation view. For example, Gopnik and Wellman also describe evidence that suggests that children who fail when asked to make first-person attributions of past beliefs are nevertheless able to make correct first-person attributions of other past mental states, such as desires and perceptions. The challenge to the simulation theory is to explain this difference between mental states. Why is a child who is unable to set aside his or her present beliefs nevertheless able to set aside his or her present desires?

The simulation view also comes under attack from developmental data presented by Josef Perner and Deborrah Howes. In their experiment, children are presented with a story much like that in the earlier experiments of Wimmer and Perner. But, instead of asking, "Where will [the puppet-child] look for the chocolate when he comes back?", the experimenters now ask, "Where does [the puppet-child] think the chocolates are?" The children in the experiment are old enough to answer this question correctly; but many of them give the wrong answer to a further question:

What if we go over to the park and ask John [the puppet-child]: "John, do you know where the chocolates are?" What will he say?

That is, many of the children answer, "No", to this question. Perner and Howes argue that this finding is difficult for the simulation view. If the first question is answered correctly as a result of the children simulating John, then the second ("self-reflective") question should be answered correctly, too, "since it is part and parcel of a belief to be convinced that one knows where the object is" (1992, p. 76), or again, since "the believer's reflective conviction that he is right is simply part and parcel of a conscious belief" (1992, p. 81).

These findings are suggestive, to be sure; but it is difficult to be convinced that the friend of simulation is totally devoid of a response to them. For example, the friend of simulation might raise a query about the precise questions that Perner and Howes asked the children in their experiment. The question that the children tend to answer incorrectly:

What if we go over to the park and ask John [the puppet-child]: "John, do you know where the chocolates are?" What will he say?

asks the experimental subject to imagine him- or herself going over to the park and talking to John. By explicitly placing the subject in the imagined scene, the question may make it more difficult for the subject to engage in a simulation of John. This difficulty is not present in the question that the same children can answer correctly:

Where does John think the chocolates are?

So, a better comparison would be with the question:

What if we go over to the park and ask John: "John, where are the chocolates?" What will he say?

This question was not asked in the experiment reported by Perner and Howes (1992).

There are other complications, too. We need to consider the inevitable role of theory where questions about knowledge are concerned. Even the most minimal grasp upon the concept of knowledge requires this much theory:

If it is not the case that p, then x (here, John) does not know that p.

A full evaluation would need to consider the possibility that this little piece of theory may introduce some confusion into an attempt to use simulation to answer questions involving knowledge.

Furthermore, we need to take into account that not every advocate of the simulation view shares the assumption that seems to condition this aspect of the debate; the assumption, namely, that the simulation theory must be introspectionist (or "Cartesian"; see Perner and Howes 1992, p. 75) about (present-tense) first-person attribution. A full evaluation would need to assess whether the predictions attributed to the simulation view really do depend upon the assumption of introspectionism. (I return briefly to the issue of introspectionism in section 4.1 below.)

3 Goldman and the Interpretation Strategy

Goldman's initial development of the simulation alternative to the theory theory takes place within a broader dialectical context: evaluating what he calls the "interpretation strategy". This is the strategy of studying our actual practice of interpretation – of attributing propositional attitudes and predicting and explaining actions in terms of attitudes – in order to extract the conditions of mentality. The idea behind the interpretation strategy is that a philosophically fundamental account – either of the nature of mental states, or of the conditions for possessing concepts of mental states – can be wrung from a description of our actual practice of attributing mental states.

The question with which the proponent of the strategy begins is then (Goldman 1989, p. 162):

> How does the (naive) interpreter arrive at his/her judgements about the mental attitudes of others?

Goldman considers three possible answers to this question:

1 theories of "radical interpretation" based upon principles of charity and rationality – in the style of Davidson or Dennett;
2 the "folk theory" approach to interpretation; and
3 the simulation alternative.

His overall argument is that the first two possible answers are inadequate; a simulation account of interpretation is to be preferred. But, whereas either the "radical interpretation" or the "folk theory" account of the actual practice of attribution could be reconfigured into a putative account of mental states themselves, the simulation alternative cannot – Goldman argues – be incorporated into a philosophically fundamental account of mentality. Thus, the interpretation strategy runs into the sand.

This broader dialectical context is not my main concern in this essay; so I shall leave aside Goldman's concerns about principles of charity and rationality, and ask about his grounds for ruling out the "folk theory" account of our interpretive practice. He launches three objections against this account. First (1989, pp. 166–7):

> Attempts by philosophers to articulate the putative laws or "platitudes" that comprise our folk-theory have been notably weak.

Second (p. 167):

> Why, one wonders, should it be so difficult to articulate laws if we appeal to them all the time in our interpretive practice?

Third, there is a worry about children's acquisition of knowledge of the putative folk theory (p. 167):

> Are such children [at the age of four, five, or six] sophisticated enough to represent such principles? And how, exactly, would they acquire them?

It is, of course, very striking that exactly analogous objections could be raised against the idea that our judgements of grammaticality are subserved by our having knowledge of a theory. Articulating the principles of universal grammar and the rules of particular languages is a far from easy task: doubtless some early attempts were "weak" and characterized by vagueness and inaccuracy. We can ask why it is so hard to spell out these principles if we are using them all the time as we perceive and produce linguistic items. And we can also ask whether young children are sufficiently sophisticated to represent such principles, and how children could come to acquire such knowledge. But very few people would regard those objections as doing serious damage to the credentials of the "theory theory" of grammaticality judgements, since in that domain the theory theory is a *tacit theory* theory.

The natural response, then, to Goldman's reasons for ruling out the "folk theory" account of our interpretive practice is to allow that the "folk theory" may be a tacitly known theory. Indeed, this is the way that I introduced the theory theory side of the debate (in line with what I described as a dominant paradigm in cognitive science). To be sure, this way of responding to Goldman's three objections carries with it an obligation: to give an account of tacit knowledge of theories which is not trivial. In particular, tacit knowledge must be a notion that discriminates more finely than "extensional equivalence". But work in the philosophy of linguistics gives us some grounds for optimism here (Evans 1981; Davies 1986, 1987, 1989; Peacocke 1986, 1989). So, let us suppose that we can meet the obligation to give an account of tacit knowledge of theories, so that the tacit theory theory can remain as a candidate account of our actual practice of interpretation.

Now consider the simulation alternative as that is described by Goldman (1989, p. 168):

> They ascribe mental states to others by pretending or imagining themselves to be in the other's shoes, constructing or generating the (further) state that they would then be in, and ascribing that state to the other.

I would like to suggest that there is more than one way to construe this proposal. In fact, I want to distinguish two construals corresponding to two rather different imaginative processes, and then to point out that one construal of the simulation alternative places it under more threat of collapse into the theory theory than does the other. This, of course, is intended to provide some motivation for pursuing that other construal of the simulation alternative.

3.1 The threat of collapse

The first construal of the simulation alternative has it that the simulator (pretending or imagining him- or herself to be in the other's shoes) imaginatively entertains hypotheses concerning mental states:

I believe that p
I desire that q

and then proceeds to a conclusion about a further mental state, or about an action, or about an intention to act:

I believe that r; or
I V; or
I intend to V

(which mental state, action, or intention to act is then ascribed to the other).

If we recall Goldman's distinction between "theory-driven" and "process-driven" simulation, we can see that this use of the imagination can count as a process-driven simulation provided that a certain condition is met. This condition is that the processing in the simulator (leading from the entertainment in imagination of the hypothesis to the arrival in imagination at the conclusion) is the same as, or relevantly similar to, or isomorphic to – let us say, follows the contours of – the process being simulated (that is, the process in the other that leads from mental states to further mental states, actions, or intentions to act).

This construal of the simulation alternative places it under some threat of collapse into the tacit theory theory. The crucial point to notice is that the processing in the simulator could *also* follow the contours of the derivational structure of a proof of a conclusion about, say, an intention to act from premises about, say, the agent's beliefs and desires – a proof cast in a psychological theory. This matching of structure between simulation process and deductive derivation could be quite general. Wherever, for example, two proofs draw upon a common axiom in the theory, the two pieces of simulation might draw upon a corre-

spondingly common cognitive mechanism. The threat of a collapse ensues because it is just this idea of matching of structure between a causal process and a derivational process that is used in some accounts of what it is for a cognitive processing system to embody tacit knowledge of a particular theory of the task domain. Roughly speaking, a component processing mechanism embodies tacit knowledge of a particular rule or axiom if it plays a role in mediating causally between representational states that is structurally analogous to the role that the rule or axiom itself plays in mediating derivationally between premises and conclusions (see again Evans 1981; Davies 1986, 1987, 1989; Peacocke 1986, 1989).

In brief, the upshot is that on the first construal of the simulation alternative there is some threat of collapse of the debate, since a cognitive system for process-driven simulation might yet embody tacit knowledge of a psychological theory.

When I say that there is some threat of collapse of the distinction between the theory theory and the simulation alternative on this first construal, I do not mean to suggest that there is absolutely nothing that could be said to reinforce the distinction. For example, it might be that the theory theory could distinguish itself by insisting that the psychological information that is drawn upon in the attribution, prediction and explanation process should have a particular nomological status. This is, in fact, what Goldman himself suggests (1992, p. 110):

> The crucial characteristic of the theory-theory is its postulation of the possession and employment of *nomological* information, information about causal generalizations.

Another possibility is that the theory theory might take on a commitment, not about the content of the psychological principles that are deployed, but about their representational format. The theory theory might distinguish itself by going beyond the account of tacit knowledge that I sketched, and insisting that the psychological information should be encoded in some specially favoured – perhaps sentential – format.

These tactics could serve to reduce the threat of collapse, though they would not eliminate it altogether. But, more importantly, they would disturb the shape of the debate. Many of the arguments for either the theory theory or the simulation alternative proceed by arguing against the other contender. We could already have reservations about this style of argument, since there appear to be intermediate positions worthy of exploration. But, if the theory theory takes on the highly specific commitments that we have just countenanced then, as Stephen Stich and Shaun Nichols point out (1992, p. 47; emphasis added), "the falsity of the theory-theory (narrowly construed) is *no comfort at all* to the . . . simulation theorist".

Stich and Nichols themselves take the heroic step (as friends of the theory theory) of proclaiming the kind of collapse that we have just been contemplating to be a victory for the simulation alternative. Their idea is that, if attribution of mental states to others proceeds by deployment of a psychological theory which is also deployed in one's own decision-taking processes (and in self-attribution of mental states), then the simulation alternative is correct. The theory theory is thus committed to other attribution of mental states drawing upon a theory that is not also implicated in one's own decision-taking; or, as they put it (1992, p. 47, n. 7):

> So, as we construe the controversy, it pits those who advocate any version of the off-line simulation account against those who think that prediction, explanation and interpretation are subserved by a tacit theory *stored somewhere other than in the Practical Reasoning System.*

On this construal of the controversy, it might turn out that the theory theorist has to defend the claim that we make use of two "copies" of the very same theory: one copy for use in our own decision-taking and the other for use in interpreting others.

As an alternative to all of these moves, I want to suggest a more general response to the threat of collapse – a response based upon appeal to an imaginative process that is rather different from the entertainment in imagination of hypotheses concerning mental states. The imaginative process that figures in the first construal of the simulation alternative is that of entertaining hypotheses of the form:

I believe that p
I desire that q.

Since these hypotheses exhibit the general form:

x believes that p
x desires that q

the states of entertaining them are appropriate inputs to a mechanism that embodies tacit knowledge of a psychological theory. The alternative that I have in mind is a process in which the simulator imaginatively adopts those mental states themselves. The simulator imagines believing that p and desiring that q. This process seems to deserve the title "imaginative identification".

Given this imaginative process, we have a second construal of the simulation alternative. I recommend that we set up the mental simulation debate by allowing the theory theory to make use of the notion of tacit theory, and to construe "theory" itself in an inclusive way, to include any body of information. A psychological theory is then a body of information about psychological states.

If a processing system is to embody tacit knowledge of such a theory – a psychological theory – then it must mediate "inference-like" transitions amongst representational states whose contents themselves concern mental states. Such contents might be of the forms:

I believe that p
I believe that q.

If, though, the proponent of the simulation alternative makes use of the idea of imaginative identification then the states of the simulator do not have contents such as these. Rather, they are "pretend belief" and "pretend desire" states, whose contents are simply that p or that q. Thus, the threat of collapse is avoided, since processing mechanisms that mediate transitions amongst states with such contents are not going to be embodiments of tacit knowledge of the principles of a psychological theory.

I said that I would use the exposition of Goldman's development of the simulation theory to motivate a particular way of delineating the theory theory and the simulation alternative. This is what I have just been doing – without suggesting that this is how Goldman himself would see the debate as best being conducted. Now, I return to the main thread of Goldman's own argument, in order to reach the second idea that I want to motivate.

3.2 Mental simulation and what is philosophically fundamental

Goldman's overall project was, you recall, an investigation of the interpretation strategy. At the stage of his argument that we have now reached, two putative accounts of our actual practice of attributing mental states – the "radical interpretation" account and the "folk theory" account – have been rejected (though we did not accept Goldman's reasons for ruling out the "folk theory" account, and did not even consider his reasons for finding the "radical interpretation" account wanting). Thus, by Goldman's lights, the simulation account of our interpretive practice is the last remaining candidate. But now, the simulation alternative itself faces an objection (Goldman 1989, p. 176):

> The simulation approach ostensibly makes this emphatic attitude the standard mode of interpretation. Is that not difficult to accept?

To this objection, Goldman offers two lines of reply. First, simulation need not be "introspectively vivid". If the theory theorist is allowed to appeal to tacit theory, then surely the friend of mental simulation may appeal to introspectively bland simulation. Second, simulation need not be our only method of making mental attributions. "In many cases", Goldman says (1989, p. 176), "the interpreter relies solely (at the time of interpretation) on inductively acquired information."

The importance of this second line of reply is that it points up the fact that, where there are different grounds available for making a judgement, one set of grounds may offer a philosophically fundamental account of our practice of making judgements of that kind, while another set of grounds does not. Thus, for example, it might be that inductively based attributions are conceived as ultimately answerable to judgements based upon mental simulation. Equally, it might be that attributions made by way of mental simulation – however natural and heuristically important they may be – are conceived as ultimately answerable to some other set of grounds for judgement.

So, the question to be asked is whether mental simulation can enter a philosophically fundamental account of propositional attitude attribution. Can simulation figure in a philosophical account of our most basic mastery of mental concepts? Goldman's answer to this question is that it cannot; and consequently he reaches his final assessment of the interpretation strategy, namely, that it cannot be carried through. The conditions of mentality cannot be wrung from a description of our practice of attributing mental states.

The "radical interpretation" account of our interpretive practice can be reconfigured into a constitutive account of mental states. We can say that what it is for a subject to believe that p is for the attribution of that belief to figure in an overall interpretation that makes the best sense possible of that subject's total life and conduct (Wiggins 1980, p. 199). Similarly, the "folk theory" account of mental state attribution can be reconfigured into a functionalist account of what mental states are. But these two accounts have been found wanting (says Goldman) as descriptions of our actual practice. The simulation alternative fares better by the standards of realistic description, but it cannot be transposed into an account of the truth conditions of mental attributions.

The reason given for this negative assessment of the prospects for a constitutive account of mental states based upon the idea of mental simulation is that simulation is too fallible (1989, p. 182):

> Since simulation is such a fallible procedure, there is little hope of treating "M is ascribed (or ascribable) to S on the basis of simulation" as constitutive of "S is in M."

A similar reason could be offered for casting doubt upon the prospects for an account of the conditions for mastery of mental concepts based upon the idea of simulation. For suppose we said that what is fundamentally required for a thinker to possess the concept of belief is – so far as third-person attributions are concerned – that the thinker should judge another to believe that p just in case the thinker arrives at the "pretend belief" that p as a result of simulating the other (putting him- or herself in the other's shoes). Then the fallibility of the simulation process would leave us with the unintuitive result that a thinker's judgements made in perfect accordance with the fundamental conditions for possession of the concept of belief could yet turn out to be false.

Here is the promised motivation for the idea that mental simulation cannot be employed to give a fundamental account of our use of mental concepts. But although the idea has now been motivated, it is not clear that the motivation is absolutely watertight.

Let us consider, first, whether the fallibility of mental simulation provides a conclusive reason for not using simulation in a constitutive account of the nature of mental states. In a constitutive account wrung from the "radical interpretation" account of our actual practice, we do not say that what it is for a subject to believe that *p* is for that attribution to be made by an eminently fallible interpreter trying to make the best sense possible of the subject's total life and conduct. Likewise, when we reconfigure the "folk theory" account as a functionalist proposal about the nature of mental states, we do not say that a belief state is a state that plays exactly the role specified by our presumably flawed current folk theory. So, it is reasonable to wonder whether we might not be able to employ an idealized notion of simulation in a constitutive account of the nature of mental states. Such an account might be open to other kinds of objections – circularity problems certainly threaten – and it might be excess to requirements in the context of some larger project. But it would not be ruled out simply by the fact that our actual ability to simulate others is a limited and flawed ability.

Whether this idea of idealized simulation can, in the end, be legitimately appealed to is a question that I shall not pursue here (though it arises again, briefly, at the end of section 4.2). Any further consideration might begin from the case of "radical interpretation". A constitutive account of the nature of mental states that is based upon the idea of "radical interpretation" does not allow that an attribution might be wrong even though it really does contribute to making the best sense possible of the subject's total life and conduct. But that constitutive account allows that in an actual empirical attribution based upon "radical interpretation" fallibility inevitably enters, since what is available to the interpreter are mere snippets of the subject's total life and conduct. Thus, on the "radical interpretation" approach, the constitutive account explains the fallibility of the empirical attribution process. The question that faces the simulation approach is whether it can provide a constitutive account that similarly explains the fallibility of the empirical process of attribution by simulation. More specifically, the question is whether the notion of idealized simulation can figure in such an account.

Leaving those questions aside for the time being, we might consider, second, whether an idealized notion of simulation could figure in an account of mastery of mental concepts – whether such a notion could play a part in the specification of possession conditions for the concept of belief, for example. In an account of the conditions for mastery of mental concepts, circularity problems are likely to be less acute than they would be in an

account of the nature of mental states, since there is no objection on grounds of circularity to the use of a concept in an account of its own possession conditions (Peacocke 1992, p. 9). Thus, for example, there would be no objection on the grounds of circularity to an account of mastery of the concept *square* that said that in order to master the concept square a thinker must judge to fall under that concept those objects that are in fact *square*. (Of course, there would be other objections to that putative account.)

3.3 Review

In this section, I have used an exposition of Goldman's development of the simulation theory in order to do two things.

First (3.1), I have used the threat of collapse of the distinction between the theory theory and the simulation alternative to motivate a particular way of delineating the two opposed views in this debate. On the one hand, I recommend a fairly inclusive version of the theory theory. On the other hand, I suggest that we regard the simulation process as the adoption in imagination of (pretend) beliefs and desires rather than the imaginative entertainment of hypotheses about beliefs and desires.

Second (3.2), I have used the undoubted fallibility of the simulation process to motivate the idea that mental simulation cannot figure in a philosophically fundamental account of the nature of mental states, or the conditions for mastery of mental concepts. But, having motivated that idea, I have – in the last few paragraphs of section 3.2 – entered the suggestion that the possibility of a simulation theoretic account of the mastery of mental concepts has not quite been ruled out.

4   Gordon and Our Discourse About Beliefs

There are at least two important ways in which Gordon's development of the simulation view differs from Goldman's. One difference is that Goldman sees himself as giving a "processing" version of the simulation view, in terms of the "off-line" operation of a system of decision processes. Gordon, in contrast, takes the unscientized notion of imaginative identification as the fundamental primitive notion.

A second difference arises from the fact that Goldman – as we have just seen – is not optimistic about the prospects of the simulation view yielding an account of our mastery of mental concepts. There are really two components to this pessimism about mental simulation's contribution to constitutive accounts. One component – as we noted at the end of section 1 – is that the simulation view addresses the case of third-person attribution of mental states by taking the first-person case for granted. It is this component that moves Goldman to say (1989, p. 183):

> If the simulation theory is right ... it looks as if the main elements of the grasp of mental concepts must be located in the first-person sphere.

The simulation view needs to be augmented, and Goldman (1993) seeks the needed further elucidation of the nature of mental states and of our grasp of the concepts of those states in the idea that mental states like belief have intrinsic, introspectible qualities – qualia. The other component is the fallibility of mental simulation, which presents a problem for the use of simulation even to cantilever out from the first-person case to the third-person case.

4.1   First person and third person

Gordon differs over both the first-person and the third-person case. In the first-person case, Gordon agrees that the simulation view needs to be augmented; but he disagrees about the nature of the augumentation that is required. In particular, Gordon rejects a certain kind of introspectionism.

Suppose that you are asked whether you believe that the planet Neptune has rings. According to the introspectionism that Goldman favours, the canonical way to answer this question is to look inwards and discern the intrinsic and introspectible qualities of inner states. Gordon (in press), in contrast, denies that there is any introspective identification of a state as a belief that the planet Neptune has rings. Rather, you simply ask yourself whether Neptune has rings. If you answer, "Yes, Neptune does have rings," then you report yourself as believing that Neptune has rings.

In this, Gordon explicitly follows Evans, who said (1982, pp. 225–6):

> We can encapsulate this procedure for answering questions about what one believes in the following simple rule: whenever you are in a

position to assert that p, you are *ipso facto* in a position to assert "I believe that p."

But, Evans went on to say (p. 226):

> But it seems pretty clear that mastery of this procedure cannot constitute a full understanding of the content of the judgment "I believe that p." Understanding of the content of the judgement must involve possession of the psychological concept expressed by "ξ believes that p," which the subject must conceive as capable of being instantiated otherwise than by himself.

And, in a similar spirit, Gordon (in press) distinguishes between *comprehending* and *uncomprehending* ascriptions. Someone who mechanically prefaces her assertions with "I believe that" is making only uncomprehending ascriptions. So, the account of the first-person case must be coupled with an account of third-person attributions of belief, in such a way as to make clear that it is the very same concept that is applied in the two cases.

In the third-person case, Gordon maintains that the simulation view offers a radical alternative account of our mental talk – "a way of interpreting ordinary discourse about beliefs" (1986, p. 166). Thus (Gordon, in press):

> To ascribe to O a belief that p is to assert that p within the context of a simulation of O.

This is certainly a use of simulation to cantilever out to the third-person case; but it is explicitly cast as an account of our "discourse about beliefs" – it tells us how to play the language game, but it does not immediately yield any statement of the truth conditions of "O believes that p." And because he is not directly concerned with truth conditions, Gordon is untroubled by the fallibility of simulation.

As Jane Heal (in press) notes, there is a potential problem for Gordon's account at just this point. For, to the extent that he does not award truth conditions to ascriptions of beliefs, but instead casts his account in terms of a certain kind of speech act – assertion within the context of simulation – he faces an obligation to explain how ascriptions of belief can occur in embedded contexts, for example, in the antecedents of conditionals ("If O believes that p, then ..."). Gordon (in press) makes some initial moves in response to this objection, by considering conditionals of the form:

If O believes that p, then she will do X.

Thus (Gordon, in press):

> Where I am supposing another person, Mary, to believe that p, I embed the supposition that p within a simulation of Mary and, using my *adjusted* motivational and other resources, "decide" whether or not to do X.

But, as he acknowledges, what he says about that kind of conditional does not generalize; the problem of embedded belief ascriptions is left open.

However, I do not want to press this objection, since it does not seem obvious that the problem of embedded contexts is insoluble. Gordon can perhaps draw some encouragement from the case of metaphor. If someone says, "Metaphorically, p," then he does not straightforwardly assert that p. But nor (on, say Davidson's [1984] account of metaphor) is there some other proposition, q, which the speaker advances with assertoric force. It is not that the operator "Metaphorically" converts the proposition that p into another proposition with which the speaker does the familiar assertoric thing. Rather, the only proposition involved is the proposition that p; but with this proposition, the speaker does a less familiar thing. The analogy with belief ascriptions is clear enough. If someone says, "O believes that p," then he does not straightforwardly assert that p. But nor (on Gordon's account of belief ascriptions) is there some other proposition, q, which the speaker advances with assertoric force – since "O believes that p" is not truth conditioned. The only proposition involved is the proposition that p; but with this proposition, the speaker does a less familiar thing: he asserts it within the context of a simulation of O. The reason why Gordon might draw some comfort from this analogy is, of course, that there seems to be no doubt that "Metaphorically, p" can occur embedded, for example, in the antecedent of a conditional. Whatever account is given if this occurrence of "Metaphorically, p" can, perhaps, be transposed to the case of "O believes that p".

Thus, Gordon's development of the simulation alternative as an account of our discourse about beliefs may survive the objection from embedded contexts. But, as it stands, it does not deliver an answer to the question with which we began.

4.2 The concept of belief

Strawson's constraint upon first-person and third-person attributions of mental states begins from the idea that "is in pain" and "believes that penguins waddle" are predicates – expressions that go together with names of individuals (here, of persons) to form sentences that are evaluable as true or false. It is the idea that these expressions are predicates that motivates the constraint. If someone claims that to say "I am in pain" is tantamount to saying "Ouch", and extends his claim to the third person by adding that to say "O is in pain" is to say "Ouch" within the context of a simulation of O, then he has achieved some conformity with a requirement of univocality. But he can hardly be said to have measured up to Strawson's constraint.

Likewise, if someone claims that to say "I believe that penguins waddle" is tantamount to saying "Penguins waddle" and extends this claim to the third person by adding that to say "O believes that penguins waddle" is to say "Penguins waddle" within the context of a simulation of O, then Strawson's constraint has been by-passed rather than met. For this account of our "discourse about beliefs" does not treat "believes that penguins waddle" as a genuine predicate.

The theory that I have just sketched (the "Ouch" theory of belief attribution) is not Gordon's. In fact, Gordon is very sensitive to the need to give an adequate account of *comprehending* first-person belief ascriptions, which "require conceptually prising one's own present beliefs apart from the facts, so that, like the beliefs of another, they may be false or at variance with the facts" (in press). But the "Ouch" theory serves well enough to highlight the fact that what Gordon gives us is not cast in the form of an account of "possession of the psychological concept expressed by "ξ believes that p'."

We can see easily enough what a simulation-based account of possession of that psychological concept would be like. Roughly, the first-person clause would say that a thinker judges "I believe that p" when she has the (conscious) belief that p (and so is ready to assert that p). The third-person clause would then cantilever out using the notion of simulation. Such a clause can be modelled upon a third-person clause offered by Peacocke (1992, p. 163) which does not make use of the notion of simulation. In outline, what Peacocke offers is:

> If a thinker judges "O believes that p," then the thinker incurs a commitment; namely, a commitment to O being in an internal state with a certain "functional role". The thinker does not, however, have to know what the functional role associated with believing that p is. The commitment is simply that O should be in an internal state with the same "functional role" as the internal state that the thinker would herself be in, were she herself to believe that p.

This clause presumes upon the first-person clause in that the thinker's commitment embeds the thought that the thinker herself believes that p. And the cantilever depends upon the idea of a relation between the first-person and the third-person; namely, the relation of having internal states with the same "functional role". Following the contours of this clause, we can offer an alternative, with mental simulation as the first-person/third-person relation upon which the cantilever depends:

> If a thinker judges "O believes that p," then the thinker incurs a commitment; namely, a commitment to believe (judge, assert) that p (within the scope of a simulation) if she were to simulate O.

The fallibility of ordinary everyday attempts at simulation poses a problem for this account of the possession conditions for the concept "ξ believes that p" – particularly, for the appropriate connections between the incurred commitments being met and the original judgement being true. A thinker's judgement "O believes that p" may be true, even though within the scope of her best – but flawed – effort at simulating O, the thinker would not, in fact, believe, judge or assert that p. (Cf. Peacocke 1992, pp. 169–70.)

The next move to make would be to introduce an idealized notion of simulation, as suggested at the end of section 3.2. That move would – more or less by stipulation – avoid the problem of fallibility. But, it is a further question whether it could contribute to a philosophically fundamental, and distinctive, account of mastery of the concept of belief, while also providing an explanation of the way that fallibility enters the empirical process of attribution. Answering that question might involve us in following out analogies, for example, between ideal simulation and ideal verification, and between simulation and spatial relocation. It might also cause us to reflect more upon the fallible and the fundamental. Clearly, these are not matters to embark upon now. But until the question is answered, we still do not know whether it is possible to meet Strawson's constraint while adopting Quine's idea.

As I remarked at the outset, the constraint and the idea date from 1959 and 1960, respectively. Here – as in so many other areas of philosophy – progress is slow. But what makes the progress slow is also what makes the mental simulation debate so fascinating. For it brings us up against much that is genuinely difficult in our conception of our own mentality.

Note

Early versions of this material were presented in talks at Harvard University, McGill University, Washington University St Louis, and the University of Alberta, during the autumn of 1992. I learned much from those occasions, and especially from discussions with Robert Gordon. Comments by Christopher Peacocke on the penultimate draft were very helpful in the preparation of this final version. Special thanks to Tony Stone for his advice and assistance.

PART VI

Consciousness, "Qualia," and Subjectivity

Introduction

"The" problem of consciousness or qualia is familiar. Indeed it is so familiar that we tend to overlook the most important thing about it: that its name is Legion, for it is many. There is no *single* problem of consciousness; there are at least the following nine quite distinct objections that have been brought against Functionalism and (in some cases) against materialism generally.

1 Early critics of the Identity Theory argued that our immediate mental access to qualia militates against their being features of any purely neurophysiological item.

2 Saul Kripke (1972) made ingenious use of modal distinctions against type or even token identity, arguing that unless mental items are necessarily identical with neurophysiological ones, which they are not, they cannot be identical with them at all. Kripke's close reasoning has attracted considerable critical attention. More sophisticated versions have been formulated as well, by (e.g.) Hart (1988) and Chalmers (1996).

3 As we saw in the introduction to Part II, philosophers such as Block ("Troubles with functionalism") have urged various counterexample cases against various materialist views – examples which seem to satisfy all the right materialist conditions but which lack mentality or one of its crucial aspects.

4 Farrell (1950), Gunderson (1970, 1974), and Nagel (1974) have worried over first-person/ third-person asymmetries and the perspectivalness or subjective point-of-view-iness of consciousness.

5 Nagel (1974) and Jackson (this volume) argue for the existence of a special, intrinsically perspectival kind of *fact*, the fact of "what it is like" to have a mental experience of such-and-such a kind, which intractably and in principle cannot be captured by physical science.

6 Levine (1983, 1993) contends that the qualitative character of experience is separated from all scientific fact by an "explanatory gap," a gap that distinguishes the case of mind and brain from any standard scientific reduction.

7 Jackson (1977) and others have defended the claim that in consciousness we are presented with mental individuals that themselves bear phenomenal, qualitative properties. For example, when a red flash bulb goes off in your face, your visual field exhibits a green blotch, an "after-image," a *thing* that is really green and has a fairly definite shape and exists for a few seconds before disappearing. If there are such things, they are entirely different from anything physical to be found in the brain of a (healthy) human subject. Belief in such "phenomenal individuals" as genuinely green afterimages has been unpopular among philosophers for some years, but it can be powerfully motivated (besides Jackson, see Lycan (1987b)).

8 A number of philosophers, most notably Sellars (1963), have stressed the ultra-smoothness, homogeneity, or grainlessness of phenomenal

feels, and contended for this reason that those feels cannot peacefully be dissolved into a metaphysic of little brute particles and their erratic motion through the void.

9 If human beings are functionally (even teleologically) organized systems of physical components and nothing more, then their "behavior" is only the mechanical, physically determined outcome of physical inputs and internal energy transformations. The inputs were themselves only the physical impacts of environmental causes, which causes were themselves the results of events completely external to us. We are merely automata. (It is no accident that Putnam's original inspiration was the Turing Machine.) But we know from the inside that this is false. Our conscious choices and our deliberate actions are entirely up to us; they feel entirely free. If I simply wish to raise my hand, then nothing can stop me from doing so unless quite externally and by making news (for example, a madman suddenly pinning me to the floor or a Phantom Jet hurtling through the wall of the building).

This is a formidable array of objections, and each is plausible on its face. Materialists and particularly Functionalists must respond in turn and in detail. Needless to say, materialists have responded at length.

Armstrong (1981) and Lycan (1996) have offered theories of conscious awareness, arguing that such awareness is a matter of "inner sense" or internal monitoring. Rosenthal (1993, 1997) contends that awareness is not thus perception-like, but only a matter of having thoughts about the mental states of which we are aware. However, none of these theories is aimed at accounting for the mental states' phenomenal properties.

Lewis (this volume) repudiates Nagel's and Jackson's funny facts, by denying a key premise of their "knowledge argument." Van Gulick too (this volume) rebuts that argument, as well as Block's "absent qualia" cases and Levine's appeal to the explanatory gap. Harman (this volume) addresses the problem of phenomenal individuals, taking what has come to be called the "representationalist" line: that such individuals and their qualia or phenomenal properties are really only representata, intentional objects of their containing experiences. Block ("Inverted Earth") objects to the latter claim and to the representationalist strategy generally.

Surprisingly or not, recent years have seen an increased reaction against the prevailing materialism. Further "mysterian" arguments (as Flanagan (1992) calls them) have been given for Nagel's thesis that even if one remains confident that materialism is true, we will never be able to understand how it can be true; see, e.g., McGinn (1991). There has even been a reemergence of some neo-Dualist views, as in Robinson (1988), Hart (1988), Strawson (1994), and Chalmers (1996).

Further Reading

On Kripkean modal arguments

Kripke, S. (1972) "Naming and necessity," in D. Davidson and G. Harman (eds), *Semantics of Natural Language*, D. Reidel.

Levin, M. (1975) "Kripke's argument against the identity thesis," *Journal of Philosophy* 72, 149–67.

Hill, C. S. (1981) "Why Cartesian intuitions are compatible with the identity thesis," *Philosophy and Phenomenological Research* 42, 254–65.

Leplin, J. (1979) "Theoretical explanation and the mind–body problem," *Philosophia* 8, 673–88.

Sher, G. (1977) "Kripke, Cartesian intuitions, and materialism," *Canadian Journal of Philosophy* 7, 227–38.

Levine, J. (1983) "Materialism and qualia: the explanatory gap," *Pacific Philosophical Quarterly* 64, 354–61.

Lycan, W. (1987) *Consciousness*, Bradford Books/MIT Press, ch. 2.

Hart, W. D. (1988) *Engines of the Soul*, Cambridge University Press.

Jackson, F. (1993) "Armchair metaphysics," in J. O'Leary-Hawthorne and M. Michael (eds), *Philosophy in Mind*, Kluwer Academic Publishing.

Chalmers, D. (1996) *The Conscious Mind*, Oxford University Press.

Puzzle cases

Shoemaker, S. (1975) "Functionalism and qualia," *Philosophical Studies* 27, 291–315.

Kirk, R. (1974) "Zombies v. Materialists," *Aristotelian Society Supplementary Volume* 48, 135–52.

Searle, J. (1980) "Minds, brains and programs," *Behavioral and Brain Sciences* 3, 417–24. [Officially about intentionality rather than qualia, but is easily adapted.]

Churchland, P. M. and Churchland, P. S. (1981) "Functionalism, qualia, and intentionality," *Philosophical Topics* 12, 121–45.

Davis, L. (1982) "Functionalism and absent qualia," *Philosophical Studies* 41, 231–49.

Lycan, W. (1987) *Consciousness*, Bradford Books/MIT Press, ch. 3.

Conscious awareness

Armstrong, D. M. (1980) "What is consciousness?," in *The Nature of Mind and Other Essays*, Cornell University Press.

Rosenthal, D. (1993) "Thinking that one thinks," in Davies and Humphreys (1993).

Rosenthal, D. (1997) "A theory of consciousness," in Block, Flanagan, and Güzeldere (1997).

Güzeldere, G. (1997) "Is consciousness the perception of what passes in one's own mind?," in Block, Flanagan, and Güzeldere (1997).

Subjectivity and/or "perspectival facts"

Farrell, B. (1950) "Experience," *Mind* 50, 170–98.

Gunderson, K. (1970) "Asymmetries and mind–body perplexities," in M. Radner and S. Winokur (eds), *Minnesota Studies in the Philosophy of Science*, vol. IV, University of Minnesota Press.

McGinn, C. (1983) *The Subjective View*, Oxford University Press.

McMullen, C. (1985) " 'Knowing what it's like' and the essential indexical," *Philosophical Studies* 48, 211–34.

Nagel, T. (1974) "What is it like to be a bat?," *Philosophical Review* 83, 435–50.

Rosenthal, D. (1983) "Reductionism and knowledge," in L. S. Cauman et al. (eds), *How Many Questions?* Hackett Publishing.

Churchland, P. M. (1985) "Reduction, qualia, and the direct introspection of brain states," *Journal of Philosophy* 82, 8–28.

Tye, M. (1986) "The subjective character of experience," *Mind* 95, 1–17.

Levin, J. (1986) "Could love be like a heat wave?; physicalism and the subjectivel character of experience," *Philosophical Studies* 49, 245–61; reprinted in the 1990 first edition of this anthology.

Lycan, W. (1990) "What is the 'subjectivity' of the mental?" in J. Tomberlin (ed.), *Philosophical Perspectives*, vol. 4, Ridgeview Publishing.

Nemirow, L. (1990). "Physicalism and the cognitive role of acquaintance," in the 1990 first edition of this anthology.

Loar, B. (1990) "Phenomenal states," in J. E. Tomberlin (ed.), *Philosophical Perspectives, 4: Action Theory and Philosophy of Mind*, Ridgeview Publishing.

Dennett, D. C. (1991) *Consciousness Explained*, Little, Brown.

Rey, G. (1991) "Sensations in a language of thought," in Villaneuva (1991).

Rey, G. (1992a) "Sensational sentences," in Davies and Humphreys (1992).

Flanagan, O. (1992) *Consciousness Reconsidered*, Bradford Books/MIT Press.

Searle, J. (1992) *The Rediscovery of the Mind*, MIT Press.

Levine, J. (1993) "On leaving out what it's like," in Davies and Humphreys (1993).

Kirk (1994) *Raw Feeling*, Oxford University Press.

Nelkin, N. (1996) *Consciousness and the Origins of Thought*, Cambridge University Press.

Lycan, W. G. (1996) *Consciousness and Experience*, Bradford Books/MIT Press, ch. 5.

Phenomenal individuals and representationalism

Hintikka, K. J. J. (1969) "On the logic of perception," in N. S. Care and R. H. Grimm (eds), *Perception and Personal Identity*, Case Western Reserve University Press.

Jackson F. (1977) *Perception*, Cambridge University Press.

Lycan, W. (1987) "Phenomenal objects: a backhanded defense," in J. Tomberlin (ed.), *Philosophical Perspectives, 1: Metaphysics*, Ridgeview Publishing.

Peacocke, C. (1983) *Sense and Content*, Oxford University Press.

Shoemaker, S. (1990) "Qualities and qualia: what's in the mind?" *Philosophy and Phenomenological Research* 50 (Supplementary Volume): 109–31.

Shoemaker, S. (1994) "Phenomenal character," *Noûs* 28: 21–38.

Dretske, F. (1995) *Naturalizing the Mind*, Bradford Books/MIT Press.

Lycan, W. G. (1996) *Consciousness and Experience*, Bradford Books/MIT Press, chs 4, 6, 7.

Tye, M. (1996) *Ten Problems of Consciousness*, Bradford Books/MIT Press.

Homogeneity or grainlessness

Gunderson, K. (1974) "The texture of mentality," in R. Bambrough (ed.), *Wisdom – Twelve Essays*, Oxford University Press.

Sellars, W. (1963) *Science, Perception, and Reality*, Routledge & Kegan Paul.

Green, M. (1979) "The grain objection," *Philosophy of Science*, 46, 559–89.

Richardson, R. and Muilenburg, G. (1982) "Sellars and sense impressions," *Erkenntnis* 17, 171–212.

Lycan, W. G. (1987) *Consciousness*, Bradford Books/MIT Press, ch. 7.

Freedom of the will

Levin, M. (1979) *Metaphysics and the Mind–Body Problem*, Oxford University Press, ch. VII.

Dennett, D. C. (1984) *Elbow Room*, Bradford Books/MIT Press.

Lycan, W. (1987) *Consciousness*, Bradford Books/MIT Press, ch. 9.

Neo-Dualisms

Robinson, H. (1982) *Matter and Sense*, Cambridge University Press.

Introduction

Robinson, W. S. (1988) *Brains and People*, Temple University Press.

Lockwood, M. (1989) *Mind, Brain, and the Quantum*, Blackwell Publishers.

Strawson, G. (1994) *Mental Reality*, Bradford Books/MIT Press.

Bealer, G. (1997) "Self-consciousness," *Philosophical Review* 106, 69–117.

Stubenberg, L. (1998) *Consciousness and Qualia*, John Benjamins.

Useful collections

Villanueva, E. (ed.) (1991) *Philosophical Issues, I: Consciousness*, Ridgeview Publishing.

Davies, M., and Humphries, G. W. (eds) (1993) *Consciousness*, Blackwell Publishers.

Metzinger, T. (ed.) (1995) *Conscious Experience*, Ferdinand Schöningh.

Block, N., Flanagan, O., and Güzeldere, G. (eds) (1997) *The Nature of Consciousness*, Bradford Books/MIT Press.

18

"Qualia"-Based Objections to Functionalism

An excerpt from "Troubles with Functionalism"

Ned Block

1.2 Homunculi-Headed Robots

In this section I shall describe a class of devices that are prima facie embarrassments for all versions of functionalism in that they indicate functionalism is guilty of liberalism – classifying systems that lack mentality as having mentality.

Consider the simple version of machine functionalism already described. It says that each system having mental states is described by at least one Turing-machine table of a certain kind, and each mental state of the system is identical to one of the machine-table states specified by the machine table. I shall consider inputs and outputs to be specified by descriptions of neural impulses in sense organs and motor-output neurons. This assumption should not be regarded as restricting what will be said to Psychofunctionalism rather than Functionalism. As already mentioned, every version of functionalism assumes *some* specification of inputs and outputs. A Functionalist specification would do as well for the purposes of what follows.

Imagine a body externally like a human body, say yours, but internally quite different. The neurons from sensory organs are connected to a bank of lights in a hollow cavity in the head. A set of buttons connects to the motor-output neurons. Inside the cavity resides a group of little men. Each has a very simple task: to implement a "square" of an adequate machine table that describes you. On one wall is a bulletin board on which is posted a state card; that is, a card that bears a symbol designating one of the states specified in the machine table. Here is what the little men do: Suppose the posted card has a "G" on it. This alerts the little men who implement G squares – "G-men" they call themselves. Suppose the light representing input I_{17} goes on. One of the G-men has the following as his sole task: when the card reads "G" and the I_{17} light goes on, he presses output button O_{191} and changes the state card to "M." This G-man is called upon to exercise his task only rarely. In spite of the low level of intelligence required of each little man, the system as a whole manages to simulate you because the functional organization they have been trained to realize is yours. A Turing machine can be represented as a finite set of quadruples (or quintuples, if the output is divided into two parts): current state, current input; next state, next output. Each little man has the task corresponding to a single quadruple. Through the efforts of the little men, the system realizes the same (reasonably adequate) machine table as you do and is thus functionally equivalent to you.[1]

I shall describe a version of the homunculi-headed simulation, which has more chance of being nomologically possible. How many homunculi are required? Perhaps a billion are enough.

Suppose we convert the government of China to functionalism, and we convince its officials...to realize a human mind for an hour. We provide each of the billion people in China (I chose China because it has a billion inhabitants) with a specially designed two-way radio that connects them in the appropriate way to other persons and to the artificial body mentioned in the previous example. We replace each of the little men with a citizen of China plus his or her radio. Instead of a bulletin board, we arrange to have letters displayed on a series of satellites placed so that they can be seen from anywhere in China.

The system of a billion people communicating with one another plus satellites plays the role of an external "brain" connected to the artificial body by radio. There is nothing absurd about a person being connected to his brain by radio. Perhaps the day will come when our brains will be periodically removed for cleaning and repairs. Imagine that this is done initially by treating neurons attaching the brain to the body with a chemical that allows them to stretch like rubber bands, thereby assuring that no brain–body connections are disrupted. Soon clever businessmen discover that they can attract more customers by replacing the stretched neurons with radio links so that brains can be cleaned without inconveniencing the customer by immobilizing his body.

It is not at all obvious that the China-body system is physically impossible. It could be functionally equivalent to you for a short time, say an hour.

"But," you may object, "how could something be functionally equivalent to me for *an hour*? Doesn't my functional organization determine, say, how I would react to doing nothing for a week but reading the *Reader's Digest*?" Remember that a machine table specifies a set of conditionals of the form: if the machine is in S_i and receives input I_j, it emits output O_k and goes into S_l. These conditionals are to be understood *subjunctively*. What gives a system a functional organization at a time is not just what it *does* at that time, but also the counterfactuals true of it at that time: what it *would* have done (and what its state transitions would have been) had it had a different input or been in a different state. If it is true of a system at time t that it *would* obey a given machine table no matter which of the states it is in and no matter which of the inputs it receives, then the system is described at t by the machine table (and realizes at t the abstract automaton specified by the table), even if it exists for only an instant. For the hour the Chinese system is "on," it *does* have a set of

inputs, outputs, and states of which such subjunctive conditionals are true. This is what makes any computer realize the abstract automaton that it realizes.

Of course, there are signals the system would respond to that you would not respond to – for example, massive radio interference or a flood of the Yangtze River. Such events might cause a malfunction, scotching the simulation, just as a bomb in a computer can make it fail to realize the machine table it was built to realize. But just as the computer *without* the bomb *can* realize the machine table, the system consisting of the people and artificial body can realize the machine table so long as there are no catastrophic interferences, such as floods, etc.

"But," someone may object, "there is a difference between a bomb in a computer and a bomb in the Chinese system, for in the case of the latter (unlike the former), inputs as specified in the machine table can be the cause of the malfunction. Unusual neural activity in the sense organs of residents of Chungking Province caused by a bomb or by a flood of the Yangtze can cause the system to go haywire."

Reply: The person who says what system he or she is talking about gets to say what signals count as inputs and outputs. I count as inputs and outputs only neural activity in the artificial body connected by radio to the people of China. Neural signals in the people of Chungking count no more as inputs to this system than input tape jammed by a saboteur between the relay contacts in the innards of a computer counts as an input to the computer.

Of course, the object consisting of the people of China + the artificial body has *other* Turing-machine descriptions under which neural signals in the inhabitants of Chungking *would* count as inputs. Such a new system (that is, the object under such a new Turing-machine description) would not be functionally equivalent to you. Likewise, any commercial computer can be redescribed in a way that allows tape jammed into its innards to count as inputs. In describing an object as a Turing machine, one draws a line between the inside and the outside. (If we count only neural impulses as inputs and outputs, we draw that line inside the body; if we count only peripheral stimulations as inputs, ... we draw that line at the skin.) In describing the Chinese system as a Turing machine, I have drawn the line in such a way that it satisfies a certain type of functional description – one that you *also* satisfy, and one that, according to functionalism, justifies attributions of mentality. Functionalism does not claim that every mental system has a machine table of a sort that justifies attributions of mentality with respect to *every* specification of inputs and outputs, but rather, only with respect to *some* specification.

Objection: The Chinese system would work too slowly. The kind of events and processes with which we normally have contact would pass by far too quickly for the system to detect them. Thus, we would be unable to converse with it, play bridge with it, etc.

Reply: It is hard to see why the system's time scale should matter. . . . Is it really contradictory or nonsensical to suppose we could meet a race of intelligent beings with whom we could communicate only by devices such as time-lapse photography? When we observe these creatures, they seem almost inanimate. But when we view the time-lapse movies, we see them conversing with one another. Indeed, we find they are saying that the only way they can make any sense of us is by viewing movies greatly slowed down. To take time scale as all important seems crudely behavioristic. . . .

What makes the homunculi-headed system (count the two systems as variants of a single system) just described a prima facie counterexample to (machine) functionalism is that there is prima facie doubt whether it has any mental states at all – especially whether it has what philosophers have variously called "qualitative states," "raw feels," or "immediate phenomenological qualities." (You ask: What is it that philosophers have called qualitative states? I answer, only half in jest: As Louis Armstrong said when asked what jazz is, "If you got to ask, you ain't never gonna get to know.") In Nagel's terms (1974), there is a prima facie doubt whether there is anything which it is like to be the homunculi-headed system.[2] . . .

3.1 The Problem of the Inputs and the Outputs

I have been supposing all along (as Psychofunctionalists often do – see Putnam 1967) that inputs and outputs can be specified by neural impulse descriptions. But this is a chauvinist claim, since it precludes organisms without neurons (such as machines) from having functional descriptions. How can one avoid chauvinism with respect to

specification of inputs and outputs? One way would be to characterize the inputs and outputs *only as* inputs and outputs. So the functional description of a person might list outputs by number: output$_1$, output$_2$, . . . Then a system could be functionally equivalent to you if it had a set of states, inputs, and outputs causally related to one another in the way yours are, no matter what the states, inputs, and outputs were like. Indeed, though this approach violates the demand of some functionalists that inputs and outputs be physically specified, other functionalists – those who insist only that input and output descriptions be *nonmental* – may have had something like this in mind. This version of functionalism does not "tack down" functional descriptions at the periphery with relatively specific descriptions of inputs and outputs: rather, this version of functionalism treats inputs and outputs just as all versions of functionalism treat internal states. That is, this version specifies states, inputs, and outputs only by requiring that they *be* states, inputs, and outputs.

The trouble with this version of functionalism is that it is wildly liberal. Economic systems have inputs and outputs, such as influx and outflux of credits and debits. And economic systems also have a rich variety of internal states, such as having a rate of increase of GNP equal to double the Prime Rate. It does not seem impossible that a wealthy sheik could gain control of the economy of a small country, for example Bolivia, and manipulate its financial system to make it functionally equivalent to a person, for example himself. If this seems implausible, remember that the economic states, inputs, and outputs designated by the sheik to correspond to his mental states, inputs, and outputs need not be "natural" economic magnitudes. Our hypothetical sheik could pick *any* economic magnitudes at all – for example, the fifth time derivative of the balance of payments. His only constraint is that the magnitudes he picks be economic, that their having such-and-such values be inputs, outputs, and states, and that he be able to set up a financial structure which can be made to fit the intended formal mold. The mapping from psychological magnitudes to economic magnitudes could be as bizarre as the sheik requires.

This version of functionalism is far too liberal and must therefore be rejected. If there are any fixed points when discussing the mind–body problem, one of them is that the economy of Bolivia could not have mental states, no matter how it is distorted by powerful hobbyists. Obviously, we must be more specific in our descriptions of inputs and outputs. The question is: is there a description of inputs and outputs specific enough to avoid liberalism, yet general enough to avoid chauvinism? I doubt that there is.

Every proposal for a description of inputs and outputs I have seen or thought of is guilty of either liberalism or chauvinism. Though this essay has concentrated on liberalism, chauvinism is the more pervasive problem. Consider standard Functional and Psychofunctional descriptions. Functionalists tend to specify inputs and outputs in the manner of behaviorists: outputs in terms of movements of arms and legs, sound emitted and the like; inputs in terms of light and sound falling on the eyes and ears.... Such descriptions are blatantly *species-specific*. Humans have arms and legs, but snakes do not – and whether or not snakes have mentality, one can easily imagine snake-like creatures that do. Indeed, one can imagine creatures with all manner of input–output devices, for example creatures that communicate and manipulate by emitting strong magnetic fields. Of course, one could formulate Functional descriptions for each such species, and somewhere in disjunctive heaven there is a disjunctive description which will handle all species that ever actually exist in the universe (the description may be infinitely long). But even an appeal to such suspicious entities as infinite disjunctions will not bail out Functionalism, since even the amended view will not tell us what there is in common to pain-feeling organisms in virtue of which they all have pain. And it will not allow the ascription of pain to some hypothetical (but non-existent) pain-feeling creatures. Further, these are just the grounds on which functionalists typically acerbically reject the disjunctive theories sometimes advanced by desperate physicalists. If functionalists suddenly smile on wildly disjunctive states to save themselves from chauvinism they will have no way of defending themselves from physicalism.

Standard Psychofunctional descriptions of inputs and outputs are also species-specific (for example in terms of neural activity) and hence chauvinist as well.

The chauvinism of standard input–output descriptions is not hard to explain. The variety of possible intelligent life is enormous. Given any fairly specific descriptions of inputs and outputs, any high-school-age science-fiction buff will be able to describe a sapient sentient being whose inputs and outputs fail to satisfy that description.

I shall argue that *any physical description* of inputs and outputs (recall that many functionalists have insisted on physical descriptions) yields a version of functionalism that is inevitably chauvinist or liberal. Imagine yourself so badly burned in a fire that your optimal way of communicating with the outside world is via modulations of your EEG pattern in Morse Code. You find that thinking an exciting thought produces a pattern that your audience agrees to interpret as a dot, and a dull thought produces a "dash." Indeed, this fantasy is not so far from reality. According to a recent newspaper article (*Boston Globe*, March 21, 1976), "at UCLA scientists are working on the use of EEG to control machines.... A subject puts electrodes on his scalp, and thinks an object through a maze." The "reverse" process is also presumably possible: others communicating with you in Morse Code by producing bursts of electrical activity that affect your brain (for example causing a long or short afterimage). Alternatively, if the cerebroscopes that philosophers often fancy become a reality, your thoughts will be readable directly from your brain. Again, the reverse process also seems possible. In these cases, *the brain itself becomes an essential part of one's input and output devices*. This possibility has embarrassing consequences for functionalists. You will recall that functionalists pointed out that physicalism is false because a single mental state can be realized by an indefinitely large variety of physical states that have no necessary and sufficient physical characterization. But if this functionalist point against physicalism is right *the same point applies to inputs and outputs*, since the physical realization of mental states can serve as an essential part of the input and output devices. That is, on any sense of "physical" in which the functionalist criticism of physicalism is correct, *there will be no physical characterization that applies to all and only mental systems' inputs and outputs*. Hence, any attempt to formulate a functional description with physical characterizations of inputs and outputs will inevitably either exclude some systems with mentality or include some systems without mentality. Hence, ...*functionalists cannot avoid both chauvinism and liberalism*.

So physical specifications of inputs and outputs will not do. Moreover, mental or "action" terminology (such as "punching the offending person") cannot be used either, since to use such specifications of inputs or outputs would be to give up the functionalist program of characterizing mentality in nonmental terms. On the other hand, as you will recall, characterizing inputs and outputs simply *as* inputs and outputs is inevitably liberal. I, for one, do not see how there can be a vocabulary for describing inputs and outputs that avoids both liberalism and chauvinism. I do not claim that this is a conclusive argument against functionalism. Rather, like the functionalist argument against physicalism, it is best construed as a burden-of-proof argument. The functionalist says to the physicalist: "It is very hard to see how there could be a single physical characterization of the internal states of all and only creatures with mentality." I say to the functionalist: "It is very hard to see how there could be a single physical characterization of the inputs and outputs of all and only creatures with mentality." In both cases, enough has been said to make it the responsibility of those who think there could be such characterizations to sketch how they could be possible.[3]

Notes

1   The basic idea for this example derives from Putnam (1967). I am indebted to many conversations with Hartry Field on the topic. Putnam's attempt to defend functionalism from the problem posed by such examples is discussed in section 1.3 of this essay.

2   Shoemaker (1975) argues (in reply to Block and Fodor 1972) that absent qualia are logically impossible; that is, that it is logically impossible that two systems be in the same functional state yet one's state have and the other's state lack qualitative content....

3   I am indebted to Sylvain Bromberger, Hartry Field, Jerry Fodor, David Hills, Paul Horwich, Bill Lycan, Georges Rey, and David Rosenthal for their detailed comments on one or another earlier draft of this paper. Beginning in the fall of 1975, parts of earlier versions were read at Tufts University, Princeton University, the University of North Carolina at Greensboro, and the State University of New York at Binghamton.

References

Armstrong, D. (1968) *A Materialist Theory of Mind*. London: Routledge & Kegan Paul.

Bever, T. (1970) "The cognitive basis for linguistic structures", in J. R. Hayes (ed.), *Cognition and the Development of Language*. New York: Wiley.

Block, N. (1980) "Are absent qualia impossible?" *Philosophical Review*, 89 (2).

Block, N. and Fodor, J. (1972) "What psychological states are not," *Philosophical Review*, 81, 159–81.

Chisholm, Roderick (1957) *Perceiving*. Ithaca, NY: Cornell University Press.

Cummins, R. (1975) "Functional analysis," *Journal of Philosophy*, 72, 741–64.

Davidson, D. (1970) "Mental events," in L. Swanson and J. W. Foster (eds), *Experience and Theory*. Amherst: University of Massachusetts Press.

Dennett, D. (1969) *Content and Consciousness*. London: Routledge & Kegan Paul.

Dennett, D. (1975) "Why the law of effect won't go away," *Journal for the Theory of Social Behavior*, 5, 169–87.

Dennett, D. (1978a) "Why a computer can't feel pain," *Synthese*, 38, 3.

Dennett, D. (1978b) *Brainstorms*, Montgomery, Vt.: Bradford.

Feldman, F. (1973) "Kripke's argument against materialism," *Philosophical Studies*, 416–19.

Fodor, J. (1965) "Explanations in psychology," in M. Black (ed.), *Philosophy in America*. London: Routledge & Kegan Paul.

Fodor, J. (1968) "The appeal to tacit knowledge in psychological explanation," *Journal of Philosophy*, 65, 627–40.

Fodor, J. (1974) "Special sciences," *Synthese*, 28, 97–115.

Fodor, J. (1975) *The Language of Thought*. New York: Crowell.

Fodor, J., Bever, T., and Garrett, M. (1974) *The Psychology of Language*. New York: McGraw-Hill.

Fodor, J. and Garrett, M. (1967) "Some syntactic determinants of sentential complexity," *Perception and Psychophysics*, 2, 289–96.

Geach, P. (1957) *Mental Acts*. London: Routledge & Kegan Paul.

Gendron, B. (1971) "On the relation of neurological and psychological theories: a critique of the hardware thesis," in R. C. Buck and R. S. Cohen (eds), *Boston Studies in the Philosophy of Science VIII*. Dordrecht: Reidel.

Grice, H. P. (1975) "Method in philosophical psychology (from the banal to the bizarre)," *Proceedings and Addresses of the American Philosophical Association*.

Gunderson, K. (1971) *Mentality and Machines*. Garden City: Doubleday Anchor.

Harman, G. (1973) *Thought*. Princeton: Princeton University Press.

Hempel, C. (1970) "Reduction: ontological and linguistic facets," in S. Morgenbesser, P. Suppes, and M. White (eds), *Essays in Honor of Ernest Nagel*. New York: St Martins Press.

Kalke, W. (1969) "What is wrong with Fodor and Putnam's functionalism?" *Noûs*, 3, 83–93.

Kim, J. (1972) "Phenomenal properties, psychophysical laws, and the identity theory," *The Monist*, 56 (2), 177–92.

Lewis, D. (1972) "Psychophysical and theoretical identifications," *Australasian Journal of Philosophy*, 50 (3), 249–58.

Locke, D. (1968) *Myself and Others*, Oxford: Oxford University Press.

Melzack, R. (1973) *The Puzzle of Pain*. New York: Basic Books.

Minsky, M. (1967) *Computation*. Englewood Cliffs, NJ: Prentice-Hall.

Mucciolo, L. F. (1974) "The identity thesis and neuropsychology," *Noûs*, 8, 327–42.

Nagel, T. (1969) "The boundaries of inner space," *Journal of Philosophy*, 66, 452–8.

Nagel, T. (1970) "Armstrong on the mind," *Philosophical Review*, 79, 394–403.

Nagel, T. (1972) Review of Dennett's *Content and Consciousness*, *Journal of Philosophy*, 50, 220–34.

Nagel, T. (1974) "What is it like to be a bat?" *Philosophical Review*, 83, 435–50.

Nelson, R. J. (1969) "Behaviorism is false," *Journal of Philosophy*, 66, 417–52.

Nelson, R. J. (1975) "Behaviorism, finite automata and stimulus response theory," *Theory and Decision*, 6, 249–67.

Nelson, R. J. (1976) "Mechanism, functionalism, and the identity theory," *Journal of Philosophy*, 73, 365–86.

Oppenheim, P. and Putnam, H. (1958) "Unity of science as a working hypothesis," in H. Feigl, M. Scriven, and G. Maxwell (eds), *Minnesota Studies in the Philosophy of Science II*. Minneapolis: University of Minnesota Press.

Pitcher, G. (1971) *A Theory of Perception*. Princeton: Princeton University Press.

Putnam, H. (1963) "Brains and behavior"; reprinted as are all Putnam's articles referred to here (except "On properties") in *Mind, Language and Reality: Philosophical Papers*, vol. 2. London: Cambridge University Press, 1975.

Putnam, H. (1966) "The mental life of some machines."

Putnam, H. (1967) "The nature of mental states" (originally published under the title "Psychological predicates").

Putnam, H. (1970) "On properties," in *Mathematics, Matter and Method: Philosophical Papers*, vol. 1. London: Cambridge University Press.

Putnam, H. (1975a) "Philosophy and our mental life."

Putnam, H. (1975b) "The meaning of 'meaning'."

Rorty, R. (1972) "Functionalism, machines and incorrigibility," *Journal of Philosophy*, 69, 203–20.

Scriven, M. (1966) *Primary Philosophy*. New York: McGraw-Hill.

Sellars, W. (1956) "Empiricism and the philosophy of mind," in H. Feigl and M. Scriven (eds), *Minnesota Studies in Philosophy of Science I*, Minneapolis: University of Minnesota Press.

Sellars, W. (1968) *Science and Metaphysics* (ch. 6). London: Routledge & Kegan Paul.

Shallice, T. (1972) "Dual functions of consciousness," *Psychological Review*, 79, 383–93.

Shoemaker, S. (1975) "Functionalism and qualia," *Philosophical Studies*, 27, 271–315.

Shoemaker, S. (1976) "Embodiment and behavior," in A. Rorty (ed.), *The Identities of Persons*. Berkeley: University of California Press.

Smart, J. J. C. (1971) "Reports of immediate experience," *Synthese*, 22, 346–59.

Wiggins, D. (1975) "Identity, designation, essentialism, and physicalism," *Philosophia*, 5, 1–30.

Epiphenomenal Qualia

Frank Jackson

It is undeniable that the physical, chemical and biological sciences have provided a great deal of information about the world we live in and about ourselves. I will use the label "physical information" for this kind of information, and also for information that automatically comes along with it. For example, if a medical scientist tells me enough about the processes that go on in my nervous system, and about how they relate to happenings in the world around me, to what has happened in the past and is likely to happen in the future, to what happens to other similar and dissimilar organisms, and the like, he or she tells me – if I am clever enough to fit it together appropriately – about what is often called the functional role of those states in me (and in organisms in general in similar cases). This information, and its kin, I also label "physical."

I do not mean these sketchy remarks to constitute a definition of "physical information," and of the correlative notions of physical property, process, and so on, but to indicate what I have in mind here. It is well known that there are problems with giving a precise definition of these notions, and so of the thesis of Physicalism that all (correct) information is physical information.[1] But – unlike some – I take the question of definition to cut across the central problems I want to discuss in this essay.

I am what is sometimes known as a "qualia freak." I think that there are certain features of the bodily sensations especially, but also of certain perceptual experiences, which no amount of purely physical information includes. Tell me everything physical there is to tell about what is going on in a living brain, the kind of states, their functional role, their relation to what goes on at other times and in other brains, and so on and so forth, and be I as clever as can be in fitting it all together, you won't have told me about the hurtfulness of pains, the itchiness of itches, pangs of jealousy, or about the characteristic experience of tasting a lemon, smelling a rose, hearing a loud noise, or seeing the sky.

There are many qualia freaks, and some of them say that their rejection of Physicalism is an unargued intuition.[2] I think that they are being unfair to themselves. They have the following argument. Nothing you could tell of a physical sort captures the smell of a rose, for instance. Therefore, Physicalism is false. By our lights this is a perfectly good argument. It is obviously not to the point to question its validity, and the premise is intuitively obviously true both to them and to me.

I must, however, admit that it is weak from a polemical point of view. There are, unfortunately for us, many who do not find the premise intuitively obvious. The task then is to present an argument whose premises are obvious to all, or at least to as many as possible. This I try to do in section 1 with what I will call "the Knowledge argument." In section 2 I contrast the Knowledge argument with the modal argument and in section 3 with the "What is it like to be" argument. In section 4 I tackle the question of the causal role of qualia. The major factor in stopping people from admitting qualia is the belief that they would have to be given a causal role with respect to the physical world and especially the brain;[3] and it is hard to do this without sounding like someone who believes in fairies. I seek in section 4 to turn this objection by arguing that the view

that qualia are epiphenomenal is a perfectly possible one.

1 The Knowledge Argument for Qualia

People vary considerably in their ability to discriminate colors. Suppose that in an experiment to catalog this variation Fred is discovered. Fred has better color vision than anyone else on record; he makes every discrimination that anyone has ever made, and moreover he makes one that we cannot even begin to make. Show him a batch of ripe tomatoes and he sorts them into two roughly equal groups and does so with complete consistency. That is, if you blindfold him, shuffle the tomatoes up, and then remove the blindfold and ask him to sort them out again, he sorts them into exactly the same two groups.

We ask Fred how he does it. He explains that all ripe tomatoes do not look the same color to him, and in fact that this is true of a great many objects that we classify together as red. He sees two colors where we see one, and he has in consequence developed for his own use two words "red$_1$" and "red$_2$" to mark the difference. Perhaps he tells us that he has often tried to teach the difference between red$_1$ and red$_2$ to his friends but has got nowhere and has concluded that the rest of the world is red$_1$–red$_2$ color-blind – or perhaps he has had partial success with his children; it doesn't matter. In any case he explains to us that it would be quite wrong to think that because "red" appears in both "red$_1$" and "red$_2$" that the two colors are shades of the one color. He only uses the common term "red" to fit more easily into our restricted usage. To him red$_1$ and red$_2$ are as different from each other and all the other colors as yellow is from blue. And his discriminatory behavior bears this out: he sorts red$_1$ from red$_2$ tomatoes with the greatest of ease in a wide variety of viewing circumstances. Moreover, an investigation of the physiological basis of Fred's exceptional ability reveals that Fred's optical system is able to separate out two groups of wavelengths in the red spectrum as sharply as we are able to sort out yellow from blue.[4]

I think that we should admit that Fred can see, really see, at least one more color than we can; red$_1$ is a different color from red$_2$. We are to Fred as a totally red–green color-blind person is to us. H. G. Wells's story *The country of the blind* is about a sighted person in a totally blind community.[5] This person never manages to convince them that he can see, that he has an extra sense. They ridicule this sense as quite inconceivable, and treat his capacity to avoid falling into ditches, to win fights, and so on as precisely that capacity and nothing more. We would be making their mistake if we refused to allow that Fred can see one more color than we can.

What kind of experience does Fred have when he sees red$_1$ and red$_2$? What is the new color or colors like? We would dearly like to know but do not; and it seems that no amount of physical information about Fred's brain and optical system tells us. We find out perhaps that Fred's cones respond differentially to certain light waves in the red section of the spectrum that make no difference to ours (or perhaps he has an extra cone) and that this leads in Fred to a wider range of those brain states responsible for visual discriminatory behavior. But none of this tells us what we really want to know about his color experience. There is something about it we don't know. But we know, we may suppose, everything about Fred's body, his behavior and dispositions to behavior and about his internal physiology, and everything about his history and relation to others that can be given in physical accounts of persons. We have all the physical information. Therefore, knowing all this is *not* knowing everything about Fred. It follows that Physicalism leaves something out.

To reinforce this conclusion, imagine that as a result of our investigations into the internal workings of Fred we find out how to make everyone's physiology like Fred's in the relevant respects; or perhaps Fred donates his body to science and on his death we are able to transplant his optical system into someone else – again the fine detail doesn't matter. The important point is that such a happening would create enormous interest. People would say "At last we will know what it is like to see the extra color, at last we will know how Fred has differed from us in the way he has struggled to tell us about for so long." Then it cannot be that we knew all along all about Fred. But *ex hypothesi* we did know all along everything about Fred that features in the physicalist scheme; hence the physicalist scheme leaves something out.

Put it this way. *After* the operation, we will know *more* about Fred and especially about his color experiences. But beforehand we had all the physical information we could desire about his body and brain, and indeed everything that has ever featured in physicalist accounts of mind and consciousness. Hence there is more to know than all that. Hence Physicalism is incomplete.

Fred and the new color(s) are of course essentially rhetorical devices. The same point can be made with normal people and familiar colors. Mary is a brilliant scientist who is, for whatever reason, forced to investigate the world from a black and white room *via* a black and white television monitor. She specializes in the neurophysiology of vision and acquires, let us suppose, all the physical information there is to obtain about what goes on when we see ripe tomatoes, or the sky, and use terms like "red," "blue," and so on. She discovers, for example, just which wavelength combinations from the sky stimulate the retina, and exactly how this produces *via* the central nervous system the contraction of the vocal cords and expulsion of air from the lungs that results in the uttering of the sentence "The sky is blue." (It can hardly be denied that it is in principle possible to obtain all this physical information from black and white television, otherwise the Open University would *of necessity* need to use color television.)

What will happen when Mary is released from her black and white room or is given a color television monitor? Will she *learn* anything or not? It seems just obvious that she will learn something about the world and our visual experience of it. But then it is inescapable that her previous knowledge was incomplete. But she had *all* the physical information. *Ergo* there is more to have than that, and Physicalism is false.

Clearly the same style of Knowledge argument could be deployed for taste, hearing, the bodily sensations, and generally speaking for the various mental states which are said to have (as it is variously put) raw feels, phenomenal features, or qualia. The conclusion in each case is that the qualia are left out of the physicalist story. And the polemical strength of the Knowledge argument is that it is so hard to deny the central claim that one can have all the physical information without having all the information there is to have.

2 The Modal Argument

By the Modal argument I mean an argument of the following style.[6] Skeptics about other minds are not making a mistake in deductive logic, whatever else may be wrong with their position. No amount of physical information about another *logically entails* that he or she is conscious or feels anything at all. Consequently there is a possible world with organisms exactly like us in every physical respect (and remember that includes functional states, physical history, et al.) but which differ from us profoundly in that they have no conscious mental life at all. But then what is it that we have and they lack? Not anything physical *ex hypothesi*. In all physical regards we and they are exactly alike. Consequently there is more to us than the purely physical. Thus Physicalism is false.[7]

It is sometimes objected that the Modal argument misconceives Physicalism on the ground that that doctrine is advanced as a *contingent* truth.[8] But to say this is only to say that physicalists restrict their claim to *some* possible worlds, including especially ours; and the Modal argument is only directed against this lesser claim. If we in *our* world, let alone beings in any others, have features additional to those of our physical replicas in other possible worlds, then we have nonphysical features or qualia.

The trouble rather with the Modal argument is that it rests on a disputable modal intuition. Disputable because it is disputed. Some sincerely deny that there can be physical replicas of us in other possible worlds which nevertheless lack consciousness. Moreover, at least one person who once had the intuition now has doubts.[9]

Head-counting may seem a poor approach to a discussion of the Modal argument. But frequently we can do no better when modal intuitions are in question, and remember our initial goal was to find the argument with the greatest polemical utility.

Of course, *qua* protagonists of the Knowledge argument we may well accept the modal intuition in question; but this will be a *consequence* of our already having an argument to the conclusion that qualia are left out of the physicalist story, not our ground for that conclusion. Moreover, the matter is complicated by the possibility that the connection between matters physical and qualia is like that sometimes held to obtain between esthetic qualities and natural ones. Two possible worlds which agree in all "natural" respects (including the experiences of sentient creatures) must agree in all esthetic qualities also, but it is plausibly held that the esthetic qualities cannot be reduced to the natural.

3 The "What is it like to be" Argument

In "What is it like to be a bat?" Thomas Nagel argues that no amount of physical information can tell us what it is like to be a bat, and indeed that

we, human beings, cannot imagine what it is like to be a bat.[10] His reason is that what this is like can only be understood from a bat's point of view, which is not our point of view and is not something capturable in physical terms which are essentially terms understandable equally from many points of view.

It is important to distinguish this argument from the Knowledge argument. When I complained that all the physical knowledge about Fred was not enough to tell us what his special color experience was like, I was not complaining that we weren't finding out what it is like to *be* Fred. I was complaining that there is something *about* his experience, a property of it, of which we were left ignorant. And if and when we come to know what this property is we still will not know what it is like to *be* Fred, but we will know more *about* him. No amount of knowledge about Fred, be it physical or not, amounts to knowledge "from the inside" considering Fred. We are not Fred. There is thus a whole set of items of knowledge expressed by forms of words like "that is *I myself* who is . . ." which Fred has and we simply cannot have because we are not him.[11]

When Fred sees the color he alone can see, one thing he knows is the way his experience of it differs from his experience of seeing red and so on; *another* is that he himself is seeing it. Physicalist and qualia freaks alike should acknowledge that no amount of information of whatever kind that *others* have *about* Fred amounts to knowledge of the second. My complaint though concerned the first and was that the special quality of his experience is certainly a fact about it, and one which Physicalism leaves out because no amount of physical information told us what it is.

Nagel speaks as if the problem he is raising is one of extrapolating from knowledge of one experience to another, of imagining what an unfamiliar experience would be like on the basis of familiar ones. In terms of Hume's example, from knowledge of some shades of blue we can work out what it would be like to see other shades of blue. Nagel argues that the trouble with bats et al. is that they are too unlike us. It is hard to see an objection to Physicalism here. Physicalism makes no special claims about the imaginative or extrapolative powers of human beings, and it is hard to see why it need do so.[12]

Anyway, our Knowledge argument makes no assumptions on this point. If Physicalism were true, enough physical information about Fred

Frank Jackson

would obviate any need to extrapolate or to perform special feats of imagination or understanding in order to know all about his special color experience. *The information would already be in our possession.* But it clearly isn't. That was the nub of the argument.

4 The Bogey of Epiphenomenalism

Is there any really *good* reason for refusing to countenance the idea that qualia are causally impotent with respect to the physical world? I will argue for the answer no, but in doing this I will say nothing about two views associated with the classical epiphenomenalist position. The first is that mental *states* are inefficacious with respect to the physical world. All I will be concerned to defend is that it is possible to hold that certain *properties* of certain mental states, namely those I've called qualia, are such that their possession or absence makes no difference to the physical world. The second is that the mental is *totally* causally inefficacious. For all I will say it may be that you have to hold that the instantiation of *qualia* makes a difference to *other mental states* though not to anything physical. Indeed general considerations to do with how you could come to be aware of the instantiation of qualia suggest such a position.[13]

Three reasons are standardly given for holding that a quale like the hurtfulness of a pain must be causally efficacious in the physical world, and so, for instance, that its instantiation must sometimes make a difference to what happens in the brain. None, I will argue, has any real force. (I am much indebted to Alec Hyslop and John Lucas for convincing me of this.)

(i) It is supposed to be just obvious that the hurtfulness of pain is partly responsible for the subject seeking to avoid pain, saying "It hurts" and so on. But, to reverse Hume, anything can fail to cause anything. No matter how often *B* follows *A*, and no matter how initially obvious the causality of the connection seems, the hypothesis that *A* causes *B* can be overturned by an overarching theory which shows the two as distinct effects of a common underlying causal process.

To the untutored the image on the screen of Lee Marvin's fist moving from left to right immediately followed by the image of John Wayne's head moving in the same general direction looks as causal as anything.[14] And of course throughout countless Westerns images similar to the first are

followed by images similar to the second. All this counts for precisely nothing when we know the over-arching theory concerning how the relevant images are both effects of an underlying causal process involving the projector and the film. The epiphenomenalist can say exactly the same about the connection between, for example, hurtfulness and behavior. It is simply a consequence of the fact that certain happenings in the brain cause both.

(ii) The second objection relates to Darwin's Theory of Evolution. According to natural selection the traits that evolve over time are those conducive to physical survival. We may assume that qualia evolved over time – we have them, the earliest forms of life do not – and so we should expect qualia to be conducive to survival. The objection is that they could hardly help us to survive if they do nothing to the physical world.

The appeal of this argument is undeniable, but there is a good reply to it. Polar bears have particularly thick, warm coats. The Theory of Evolution explains this (we suppose) by pointing out that having a thick warm coat is conducive to survival in the Arctic. But having a thick coat goes along with having a heavy coat, and having a heavy coat is *not* conducive to survival. It slows the animal down.

Does this mean that we have refuted Darwin because we have found an evolved trait – having a heavy coat – which is not conducive to survival? Clearly not. Having a heavy coat is an unavoidable concomitant of having a warm coat (in the context, modern insulation was not available), and the advantages for survival of having a warm coat outweighed the disadvantages of having a heavy one. The point is that all we can extract from Darwin's theory is that we should expect any evolved characteristic to be *either* conducive to survival *or* a by-product of one that is so conducive. The epiphenomenalist holds that qualia fall into the latter category. They are a by-product of certain brain processes that are highly conducive to survival.

(iii) The third objection is based on a point about how we come to know about other minds. We know about other minds by knowing about other behavior, at least in part. The nature of the inference is a matter of some controversy, but it is not a matter of controversy that it proceeds from behavior. That is why we think that stones do not feel and dogs do feel. But, runs the objection, how can a person's behavior provide any reason for believing he has qualia like mine, or indeed any qualia at all, unless this behavior can be regarded as the *outcome* of the qualia. Man Friday's footprint was evidence of Man Friday because footprints are causal outcomes of feet attached to people. And an epiphenomenalist cannot regard behavior, or indeed anything physical, as an outcome of qualia.

But consider my reading in *The Times* that Spurs won. This provides excellent evidence that the *Telegraph* has also reported that Spurs won, despite the fact that (I trust) the *Telegraph* does not get the results from *The Times*. They each send their own reporters to the game. The *Telegraph*'s report is in no sense an outcome of *The Times*'s, but the latter provides good evidence for the former nevertheless.

The reasoning involved can be reconstructed thus. I read in *The Times* that Spurs won. This gives me reason to think that Spurs won because I know that Spurs' winning is the most likely candidate to be what caused the report in *The Times*. But I also know that Spurs' winning would have had many effects, including almost certainly a report in the *Telegraph*.

I am arguing from one effect back to its cause and out again to another effect. The fact that neither effect causes the other is irrelevant. Now the epiphenomenalist allows that qualia are effects of what goes on in the brain. Qualia cause nothing physical but are caused by something physical. Hence the epiphenomenalist can argue from the behavior of others to the qualia of others by arguing from the behavior of others back to its causes in the brains of others and out again to their qualia.

You may well feel for one reason or another that this is a more dubious chain of reasoning than its model in the case of newspaper reports. You are right. The problem of other minds is a major philosophical problem, the problem of other newspaper reports is not. But there is no special problem for Epiphenomenalism as opposed to, say, Interactionism here.

There is a very understandable response to the three replies I have just made. "All right, there is no knockdown refutation of the existence of epiphenomenal qualia. But the fact remains that they are an excrescence. They *do* nothing, they *explain* nothing, they serve merely to soothe the intuitions of dualists, and it is left a total mystery how they fit into the worldview of science. In short we do not and cannot understand the how and why of them."

This is perfectly true; but is no objection to qualia, for it rests on an overly optimistic view of the human animal, and its powers. We are the products of Evolution. We understand and sense what we need to understand and sense in order to survive. Epiphenomenal qualia are totally irrelevant to survival. At no stage of our evolution did natural selection favor those who could make sense of how they are caused and the laws governing them, or in fact why they exist at all. And that is why we can't.

It is not sufficiently appreciated that Physicalism is an extremely optimistic view of our powers. If it is true, we have, in very broad outline admittedly, a grasp of our place in the scheme of things. Certain matters of sheer complexity defeat us – there are an awful lot of neurons – but in principle we have it all. But consider the antecedent probability that everything in the Universe be of a kind that is relevant in some way or other to the survival of *Homo sapiens*. It is very low surely. But then one must admit that it is very likely that there is a part of the whole scheme of things, maybe a big part, which no amount of evolution will ever bring us near to knowledge about or understanding of. For the simple reason that such knowledge and understanding is irrelevant to survival.

Physicalists typically emphasize that we are a part of nature on their view, which is fair enough. But if we are a part of nature, we are as nature has left us after however many years of evolution it is, and each step in that evolutionary progression has been a matter of chance constrained just by the need to preserve or increase survival value. The wonder is that we understand as much as we do, and there is no wonder that there should be matters which fall quite outside our comprehension. Perhaps exactly how epiphenomenal qualia fit into the scheme of things is one such.

This may seem an unduly pessimistic view of our capacity to articulate a truly comprehensive picture of our world and our place in it. But suppose we discovered living on the bottom of the deepest oceans a sort of sea slug which manifested intelligence. Perhaps survival in the conditions required rational powers. Despite their intelligence, these sea slugs have only a very restricted conception of the world by comparison with ours, the explanation for this being the nature of their immediate environment. Nevertheless they have developed sciences which work surprisingly well in these restricted terms. They also have philosophers, called slugists. Some call themselves

Frank Jackson

tough-minded slugists, others confess to being soft-minded slugists.

The tough-minded slugists hold that the restricted terms (or ones pretty like them which may be introduced as their sciences progress) suffice in principle to describe everything without remainder. These tough-minded slugists admit in moments of weakness to a feeling that their theory leaves something out. They resist this feeling and their opponents, the soft-minded slugists, by pointing out – absolutely correctly – that no slugist

has ever succeeded in spelling out how this mysterious residue fits into the highly successful view that their sciences have and are developing of how their world works.

Our sea slugs don't exist, but they might. And there might also exist super beings which stand to us as we stand to these slugs. We cannot adopt the perspective of these super beings, because we are not them, but the possibility of such a perspective is, I think, an antidote to excessive optimism.[15]

Notes

1 See, e.g., D. H. Mellor, "Materialism and phenomenal qualities," *Aristotelian Society Supp. Vol.* 47 (1973), 107–19; and J. W. Cornman, *Materialism and Sensations*, New Haven and London, 1971.

2 Particularly in discussion, but see, e.g., Keith Campbell, *Metaphysics*, Belmont, 1976, p. 67.

3 See, e.g., D. C. Dennett, "Current issues in the philosophy of mind," *American Philosophical Quarterly* 15 (1978), 249–61.

4 Put this, and similar specifications below, in terms of Land's theory if you prefer. See, e.g., Edwin H. Land, "Experiments in color vision," *Scientific American* 200 (May 5, 1959), 84–99.

5 H. G. Wells, *The Country of the Blind and Other Stories*, London, n.d.

6 See, e.g., Keith Campbell, *Body and Mind*, New York, 1970; and Robert Kirk, "Sentience and behavior," *Mind* 83 (1974), 43–60.

7 I have presented the argument in an interworld rather than the more usual intraworld fashion to avoid inessential complications to do with supervenience, causal anomalies and the like.

8 See, e.g., W. G. Lycan, "A new Lilliputian argument against machine functionalism," *Philosophical Studies* 35 (1979), 279–87, p. 280; and Don Locke, "Zombies, schizophrenics and purely physical objects," *Mind* 85 (1976), 97–9.

9 See R. Kirk, "From physical explicability to full-blooded materialism," *Philosophical Quarterly* 29 (1979), 229–37. See also the arguments against the

modal intuition in, e.g., Sydney Shoemaker, "Functionalism and qualia," *Philosophical Studies* 27 (1975), 291–315.

10 *Philosophical Review* 83 (1974), 435–50. Two things need to be said about this article. One is that, despite my dissociations to come, I am much indebted to it. The other is that the emphasis changes through the article, and by the end Nagel is objecting not so much to Physicalism as to all extant theories of mind for ignoring points of view, including those that admit (irreducible) qualia.

11 Knowledge *de se* in the terms of David Lewis, "Attitudes de dicto and de se," *Philosophical Review* 88 (1979), 513–43.

12 See Laurence Nemirow's comments on "What it is..." in his review of T. Nagel *Mortal Questions* in *Philosophical Review* 89 (1980), 473–7. I am indebted here in particular to a discussion with David Lewis.

13 See my review of K. Campbell, *Body and Mind*, in *Australasian Journal of Philosophy* 50 (1972), 77–80.

14 Cf. Jean Piaget, "The child's conception of physical causality," reprinted in *The Essential Piaget*, London, 1977.

15 I am indebted to Robert Pargetter for a number of comments and, despite his dissent, to section IV of Paul E. Meehl's "The complete autocerebroscopist," in Paul Feyerabend and Grover Maxwell (eds), *Mind, Matter and Method*, Minneapolis, 1966.

19

Functionalist Responses

What Experience Teaches

David Lewis

Experience the Best Teacher

They say that experience is the best teacher, and the classroom is no substitute for Real Life. There's truth to this. If you want to know what some new and different experience is like, you can learn it by going out and really *having* that experience. You can't learn it by being told about the experience, however thorough your lessons may be.

Does this prove much of anything about the metaphysics of mind and the limits of science? I think not.

Example: Skunks and Vegemite. I have smelled skunks, so I know what it's like to smell skunks. But skunks live only in some parts of the world, so you may never have smelled a skunk. If you haven't smelled a skunk, then you don't know what it's like. You never will, unless someday you smell a skunk for yourself. On the other hand, you may have tasted Vegemite, that famous Australian substance; and I never have. So you may know what it's like to taste Vegemite. I don't, and unless I taste Vegemite (what, and spoil a good example!), I never will. It won't help at all to take lessons on the chemical composition of skunk scent or Vegemite, the physiology of the nostrils or the taste-buds, and the neurophysiology of the sensory nerves and the brain.

Example: The Captive Scientist.[1] Mary, a brilliant scientist, has lived from birth in a cell where every-thing is black or white. (Even she herself is painted all over.) She views the world on black-and-white television. By television she reads books, she joins in discussion, she watches the results of experiments done under her direction. In this way she becomes the world's leading expert on color and color vision and the brain states produced by exposure to colors. But she doesn't know what it's like to see color. And she never will, unless she escapes from her cell.

Example: The Bat.[2] The bat is an alien creature, with a sonar sense quite unlike any sense of ours. We can never have the experiences of a bat; because we could not become bat-like enough to have those experiences and still be ourselves. We will never know what it's like to be a bat. Not even if we come to know all the facts there are about the bat's behavior and behavioral dispositions, about the bat's physical structure and processes, about the bat's functional organization. Not even if we come to know all the same sort of physical facts about all the other bats, or about other creatures, or about ourselves. Not even if we come to possess all physical facts whatever. Not even if we become able to recognize all the mathematical and logical implications of all these facts, no matter how complicated and how far beyond the reach of finite deduction.

Experience is the best teacher, in this sense: having an experience is the best way or perhaps the only way, of coming to know what that experience is like. No amount of scientific information about the stimuli that produce that experience and the process that goes on in you when you have that experience will enable you to know what it's like to have the experience.

...But Not Necessarily

Having an experience is surely one good way, and surely the only practical way, of coming to know what that experience is like. Can we say, flatly, that it is the only *possible* way? Probably not. There is a change that takes place in you when you have the experience and thereby come to know what it's like. Perhaps the exact same change could in principle be produced in you by precise neurosurgery, very far beyond the limits of present-day technique. Or it could possibly be produced in you by magic. If we ignore the laws of nature, which are after all contingent, then there is no necessary connection between cause and effect: anything could cause anything. For instance, the casting of a spell could do to you exactly what your first smell of skunk would do. We might quibble about whether a state produced in this artificial fashion would deserve the *name* "knowing what it's like to smell a skunk," but we can imagine that so far as what goes on within you is concerned, it would differ not at all.[3]

Just as we can imagine that a spell might produce the same change as a smell, so likewise we can imagine that science lessons might cause that same change. Even that is possible, in the broadest sense of the word. If we ignored all we know about how the world really works, we could not say what might happen to someone if he were taught about the chemistry of scent and the physiology of the nose. There might have been a causal mechanism that transforms science lessons into whatever it is that experience gives us. But there isn't. It is not an absolutely necessary truth that experience is the best teacher about what a new experience is like. It's a contingent truth. But we have good reason to think it's true.

We have good reason to think that something of this kind is true, anyway, but less reason to be sure exactly what. Maybe some way of giving the lessons that hasn't yet been invented, and some way of taking them in that hasn't yet been practiced, could give us a big surprise. Consider sight-reading: a trained musician can read the score and know what it would be like to hear the music. If I'd never heard that some people can sight-read, I

would never have thought it humanly possible. Of course the moral is that new music isn't altogether new – the big new experience is a rearrangement of lots of little old experiences. It just might turn out the same for new smells and tastes *vis-à-vis* old ones; or even for color vision *vis-à-vis* black and white;[4] or even for sonar sense experience *vis-à-vis* the sort we enjoy. The thing we can say with some confidence is that we have no faculty for knowing on the basis of mere science lessons what some *new enough* experience would be like. But how new is "new enough"? – There, we just might be in for surprises.

Three Ways to Miss the Point

The First Way. A literalist might see the phrase "know what it's like" and take that to mean: "know what it resembles." Then he might ask: what's so hard about that? Why can't you just be told which experiences resemble one another? You needn't have had the experiences – all you need, to be taught your lessons, is some way of referring to them. You could be told: the smell of skunk somewhat resembles the smell of burning rubber. I have been told: the taste of Vegemite somewhat resembles that of Marmite. Black-and-white Mary might know more than most of us about the resemblances among color-experiences. She might know which ones are spontaneously called "similar" by subjects who have them; which gradual changes from one to another tend to escape notice; which ones get conflated with which in memory; which ones involve roughly the same neurons firing in similar rhythms; and so forth. We could even know what the bat's sonar experiences resemble just by knowing that they do not at all resemble any experiences of humans, but do resemble – as it might be – certain experiences that occur in certain fish. This misses the point. *Pace* the literalist, "know what it's like" does not mean "know what it resembles." The most that's true is that knowing what it resembles *may* help you to know what it's like. If you are taught that experience A resembles B and C closely, D less, E not at all, that will help you know what A is like – *if* you know already what B and C and D and E are like. Otherwise, it helps you not at all. I don't know any better what it's like to taste Vegemite when I'm told that it tastes like Marmite, because I don't know what Marmite tastes like either. (Nor do I know any better what Marmite tastes like for being told it tastes like

Vegemite.) Maybe Mary knows enough to triangulate each color experience exactly in a network of resemblances, or in many networks of resemblance in different respects, while never knowing what any node of any network is like. Maybe we could do the same for bat experiences. But no amount of information about resemblances, just by itself, does anything to help us know what an experience is like.

The Second Way. Insofar as I don't know what it would be like to drive a steam locomotive fast on a cold, stormy night, part of my problem is just that I don't know what experiences I would have. The firebox puts out a lot of heat, especially when the fireman opens the door to throw on more coal; on the other hand, the cab is drafty and gives poor protection from the weather. Would I be too hot or too cold? Or both by turns? Or would it be chilled face and scorched legs? If I knew the answers to such questions, I'd know much better what it would be like to drive the locomotive. So maybe "know what it's like" just means "know what experiences one has." Then again: what's the problem? Why can't you just be told what experiences you would have if, say, you tasted Vegemite? Again, you needn't have had the experiences – all you need, to be taught your lessons, is some way of referring to them. We have ways to refer to experiences we haven't had. We can refer to them in terms of their causes: the experience one has upon tasting Vegemite, the experience one has upon tasting a substance of such-and-such chemical composition. Or we can refer to them in terms of their effects: the experience that just caused Fred to say "Yeeuch!" Or we can refer to them in terms of the physical states of the nervous system that mediate between those causes and effects: the experience one has when one's nerves are firing in such-and-such pattern. (According to some materialists, I myself for one, this means the experience which is identical with such-and-such firing pattern. According to other materialists it means the experience which is realized by such-and-such firing pattern. According to many dualists, it means the experience which is merely the lawful companion of such-and-such firing pattern. But whichever it is, we get a way of referring to the experience.) Black-and-white Mary is in a position to refer to color-experiences in all these ways. Therefore you should have no problem in telling her exactly what experiences one has upon seeing the colors. Or rather, your only problem is that

you'd be telling her what she knows very well already! In general, to know what is the X is to know that the X is the Y, where it's not too obvious that the X is the Y. (Just knowing that the X is the X won't do, of course, because it is too obvious.) If Mary knows that the experience of seeing green is the experience associated with such-and-such pattern of nerve firings, then she knows the right sort of unobvious identity. So she knows what experience one has upon seeing green.

(Sometimes it's suggested that you need a "rigid designator": you know what is the X by knowing that the X is the Y only if "the Y" is a term whose referent does not depend on any contingent matter of fact. In the first place, this suggestion is false. You can know who is the man on the balcony by knowing that the man on the balcony is the Prime Minister even if neither "the Prime Minister" nor any other phrase available to you rigidly designates the man who is, in fact, the Prime Minister. In the second place, according to one version of Materialism (the one I accept) a description of the form "the state of having nerves firing in such-and-such a pattern" *is* a rigid designator, and what it designates is in fact an experience; and according to another version of Materialism, a description of the form "having some or other state which occupies so-and-so functional role" is a rigid designator of an experience. So even if the false suggestion were granted, still it hasn't been shown, without begging the question against Materialism, that Mary could not know what experience one has upon seeing red.)

Since Mary *does* know what experiences she would have if she saw the colors, but she *doesn't* know what it would be like to see the colors, we'd better conclude that "know what it's like" does not after all mean "know what experiences one has." The locomotive example was misleading. Yes, by learning what experiences the driver would have, I can know what driving the locomotive would be like; but only because I already know what those experiences are like. (It matters that I know what they're like under the appropriate descriptions – as it might be, the description "chilled face and scorched legs." This is something we'll return to later.) Mary may know as well as I do that when the driver leans out into the storm to watch the signals, he will have the experience of seeing sometimes green lights and sometimes red. She knows better than I what experiences he has when signals come into view. She can give many more unobviously equivalent descriptions of those experiences than I can. But knowing what color-experiences the driver has won't help Mary to know what his job is like. It will help me.

The Third Way. Until Mary sees green, here is one thing she will never know: she will never know that she is seeing green. The reason why is just that until she sees green, it will never be true that she is seeing green. Some knowledge is irreducibly egocentric, or *de se*.[5] It is not just knowledge about what goes on in the world; it is knowledge of who and when in the world one is. Knowledge of what goes on in the world will be true alike for all who live in that world; whereas egocentric knowledge may be true for one and false for another, or true for one at one time and false for the same one at another time. Maybe Mary knows in advance, as she plots her escape, that 9 a.m. on the 13th of May, 1997, is the moment when someone previously confined in a black-and-white cell sees color for the first time. But until that moment comes, she will never know that she herself is then seeing color – because she isn't. What isn't true isn't knowledge. This goes as much for egocentric knowledge as for the rest. So only those of whom an egocentric proposition is true can know it, and only at times when it is true of them can they know it. That one is then seeing color is an egocentric proposition. So we've found a proposition which Mary can never know until she sees color – which, as it happens, is the very moment when she will first know what it's like to see color! Have we discovered the reason why experience is the best teacher? And not contingently after all, but as a necessary consequence of the logic of egocentric knowledge?

No; we have two separate phenomena here, and only some bewitchment about the "first-person perspective" could make us miss the difference. In the first place, Mary will probably go on knowing what it's like to see green after she stops knowing the egocentric proposition that she's then seeing green. Since what isn't true isn't known she must stop knowing that proposition the moment she stops seeing green. (Does that only mean that we should have taken a different egocentric proposition: that one *has* seen green? No; for in that case Mary could go on knowing the proposition even after she forgets what it's like to see green, as might happen if she were soon recaptured.) In the second place, Mary might come to know what it's like to see green even if she didn't know the egocentric proposition. She

might not have known in advance that her escape route would take her across a green meadow, and it might take her a little while to recognize grass by its shape. So at first she might know only that she was seeing some colors or other, and thereby finding out what some color-experiences or other were like, without being able to put a name either to the colors or to the experiences. She would then know what it was like to see green, though not under that description, indeed not under any description more useful than "the color-experience I'm having now"; but she would not know the egocentric proposition that she is then seeing green, since she wouldn't know which color she was seeing. In the third place, the gaining of egocentric knowledge may have prerequisites that have nothing to do with experience. Just as mary can't know she's seeing green until she *does* see green, she can't know she's turning 50 until she *does* turn 50. But – I hope! – turning 50 does not involve some special experience. In short, though indeed one can gain egocentric knowledge that one is in some situation only when one is in it, that is not the same as finding out what an experience is like only when one has that experience.

We've just rejected two suggestions that don't work separately, and we may note that they don't work any better when put together. One knows what is the X by knowing that the X is the Y, where the identity is not too obvious; and "the Y" might be an egocentric description. So knowledge that the X is the Y might be irreducibly egocentric knowledge, therefore knowledge that cannot be had until it is true of one that the X is the Y. So one way of knowing what is the X will remain unavailable until it comes true of one that the X is the Y. One way that I could gain an unobvious identity concerning the taste of Vegemite would be for it to come true that the taste of Vegemite was the taste I was having at that very moment – and that would come true at the very moment I tasted Vegemite and found out what it was like! Is this why experience is the best teacher? – No; cases of gaining an unobvious egocentric identity are a dime a dozen, and most of them do not result in finding out what an experience is like. Suppose I plan ahead that I will finally break down and taste Vegemite next Thursday noon. Then on Wednesday noon, if I watch the clock, I first gain the unobvious egocentric knowledge that the taste of Vegemite is the taste I shall be having in exactly 24 hours, and thereby I have a new way of knowing what is the taste of Vegemite. But on Wednesday noon I don't yet know what it's like. Another example: from time to time I find myself next to a Vegemite-taster. On those occasions, and only those, I know what is the taste of Vegemite by knowing that it is the taste being had by the person next to me. But on no such occasion has it ever yet happened that I knew what it was like to taste Vegemite.

The Hypothesis of Phenomenal Information

No amount of the physical information that black-and-white Mary gathers could help her know what it was like to see colors; no amount of the physical information that we might gather about bats could help us know what it's like to have their experiences; and likewise in other cases. There is a natural and tempting explanation of why physical information does not help. That is the hypothesis that besides physical information there is an irreducibly different kind of information to be had: *phenomenal information*. The two are independent. Two possible cases might be exactly alike physically, yet differ phenomenally. When we get physical information we narrow down the physical possibilities, and perhaps we narrow them down all the way to one, but we leave open a range of phenomenal possibilities. When we have an experience, on the other hand, we acquire phenomenal information; possibilities previously open are eliminated; and that is what it is to learn what the experience is like.

(Analogy. Suppose the question concerned the location of a point within a certain region of the x-y plane. We might be told that its x-coordinate lies in certain intervals, and outside certain others. We might even get enough of this information to fix the x-coordinate exactly. But no amount of x-information would tell us anything about the y-coordinate; any amount of x-information leaves open all the y-possibilities. But when at last we make a y-measurement, we acquire a new kind of information; possibilities previously open are eliminated; and that is how we learn where the point is in the y-direction.)

What might the subject matter of phenomenal information be? *If* the Hypothesis of Phenomenal Information is true, then you have an easy answer: it is information about experience. More specifically, it is information about a certain part or aspect or feature of experience. But if the Hypothesis is false, then there is still experience (complete with all its parts and aspects and features) and yet no information about experience is phenomenal information. So it cannot be said in a neutral way, without presupposing the Hypothesis, that information about experience is phenomenal information. For if the Hypothesis is false and Materialism is true, it may be that all the information there is about experience is physical information, and can very well be presented in lessons for the inexperienced.

It makes no difference to put some fashionable new phrase in place of "experience." If instead of "experience" you say "raw feel" (or just "feeling"), or "way it feels," or "what it's like," then I submit that you mean nothing different. Is there anything it's like to be this robot? Does this robot have experiences? – I can tell no difference between the new question and the old. Does sunburn feel the same way to you that it does to me? Do we have the same raw feel? Do we have the same experience when sunburned? – Again, same question. "Know the feeling," "know what it's like" – interchangeable. (Except that the former may hint at an alternative to the Hypothesis of Phenomenal Information.) So if the friend of phenomenal information says that its subject matter is raw feels, or ways to feel, or what it's like, then I respond just as I do if he says that the subject matter is experience. Maybe so, *if* the Hypothesis of Phenomenal Information is true; but if the Hypothesis is false and Materialism is true, nevertheless there is still information about raw feels, ways to feel or what it's like; but in that case it is physical information and can be conveyed in lessons.

We might get a candidate for the subject matter of phenomenal information that is not just experience renamed, but is still tendentious. For instance, we might be told that phenomenal information concerns the intrinsic character of experience. A friend of phenomenal information might indeed believe that it reveals certain special, nonphysical intrinsic properties of experience. He might even believe that it reveals the existence of some special nonphysical thing or process, *all* of whose intrinsic properties are nonphysical. But he is by no means alone in saying that experience has an intrinsic character. Plenty of us materialists say so too. We say that a certain color-experience is whatever state occupies a certain functional role. So if the occupant of that role (universally, or in the case of humans, or in the case of certain humans) is a certain pattern of neural firing, then that pattern of firing *is* the experience (in the case in question). Therefore the intrinsic character of the experience is the intrinsic character of the firing pattern. For instance, a frequency of firing is part of the intrinsic character of the experience. If we materialists are right about what experience is, then black-and-white Mary knows all about the intrinsic character of color-experience; whereas most people who know what color-experience is like remain totally ignorant about its intrinsic character.[6]

To say that phenomenal information concerns "qualia" would be tendentious in much the same way. For how was this notion introduced? Often thus. We are told to imagine someone who, when he sees red things, has just the sort of experiences that we have when we see green things, and vice versa; and we are told to call this a case of "inverted qualia." And then we are told to imagine someone queerer still, who sees red and responds to it appropriately, and indeed has entirely the same functional organization of inner states as we do and yet has no experiences at all; and we are told to call this a case of "absent qualia." Now a friend of phenomenal information might well think that these deficiencies have something to do with the nonphysical subject matter of phenomenal information. But others can understand them otherwise. Some materialists will reject the cases outright, but others, and I for one, will make sense of them as best we can. Maybe the point is that the states that occupy the roles of experiences, and therefore *are* the experiences, in normal people are inverted or absent in victims of inverted or absent qualia. (This presupposes, what might be false, that most people are enough alike). Experience of red – the state that occupies that role in normal people – occurs also in the victim of "inverted qualia," but in him it occupies the role of experience of green; whereas the state that occupies in him the role of experience of red is the state that occupies in normal people the role of experience of green. Experience of red and of green – that is, the occupants of those roles for normal people – do not occur at all in the victim of "absent qualia"; the occupants of those roles for him are states that don't occur at all in the normal. Thus we make good sense of inverted and absent qualia; but in such a way that "qualia" is just the word for role-occupying states taken *per se* rather than *qua* occupants of roles. Qualia, so understood, could not be the subject matter of phenomenal

information. Mary knows all about them. We who have them mostly don't.[7]

It is best to rest content with an unhelpful name and a *via negativa*. Stipulate that "the phenomenal aspect of the world" is to name whatever is the subject matter of phenomenal information, if there is any such thing; the phenomenal aspect, if such there be, is that which we can become informed about by having new experiences but never by taking lessons. Having said this, it will be safe to say that information about the phenomenal aspect of the world can only be phenomenal information. But all we really know, after thus closing the circle, is that phenomenal information is supposed to reveal the presence of some sort of nonphysical things or processes within experience, or else it is supposed to reveal that certain physical things or processes within experience have some sort of nonphysical properties.

The Knowledge Argument

If we invoke the Hypothesis of Phenomenal Information to explain why no amount of physical information suffices to teach us what a new experience is like, then we have a powerful argument to refute any materialist theory of the mind. Frank Jackson (see note 1) calls it the "Knowledge Argument." Arguments against one materialist theory or another are never very conclusive. It is always possible to adjust the details. But the Knowledge Argument, if it worked, would directly refute the bare minimum that is common to *all* materialist theories.

It goes as follows. First in a simplified form; afterward we'll do it properly. Minimal Materialism is a supervenience thesis: no difference without physical difference. That is: any two possibilities that are just alike physically are just alike *simpliciter*. If two possibilities are just alike physically, then no physical information can eliminate one but not both of them. If two possibilities are just alike *simpliciter* (if that is possible) then no information whatsoever can eliminate one but not both of them. So if there is a kind of information – namely, phenomenal information – that can eliminate possibilities that any amount of physical information leaves open, then there must be possibilities that are just alike physically, but not just alike *simpliciter*. That is just what Minimal Materialism denies.

(Analogy. If two possible locations in our region agree in their *x*-coordinate, then no amount of *x*-

information can eliminate one but not both. If, *per impossibile*, two possible locations agreed in all their coordinates, then no information whatsoever could eliminate one but not both. So if there is a kind of information – namely, *y*-information – that can eliminate locations that any amount of *x*-information leaves open, then there must be locations in the region that agree in their *x*-coordinate but not in all their coordinates.)

Now to remove the simplification. What we saw so far was the Knowledge Argument against Materialism taken as a necessary truth, applying unrestrictedly to all possible worlds. But we materialists usually think that Materialism is a contingent truth. We grant that there are spooky possible worlds where Materialism is false, but we insist that our actual world isn't one of them. If so, then there might after all be two possibilities that are alike physically but not alike *simpliciter*; but one or both of the two would have to be possibilities where Materialism was false. Spooky worlds could differ with respect to their spooks without differing physically. Our Minimal Materialism must be a *restricted* supervenience thesis: within a certain class of worlds, which includes our actual world, there is no difference without physical difference. Within that class, any two possibilities just alike physically are just alike *simpliciter*. But what delineates the relevant class? (It is trivial that our world belongs to *some* class wherein there is no difference without physical difference. That will be so however spooky our world may be. The unit class of our world is one such class, for instance. And so is any class that contains our world, and contains no two physical duplicates.) I think the relevant class should consist of the worlds that have nothing wholly alien to this world. The inhabitants of such a non-alien world could be made from the inhabitants of ours, so to speak, by a process of division and recombination. That will make no wholly different kinds of things, and no wholly different fundamental properties of things.[8] Our restricted materialist supervenience thesis should go as follows: throughout the non-alien worlds, there is no difference without physical difference.

If the Hypothesis of Phenomenal Information be granted, then the Knowledge Argument refutes this restricted supervenience nearly as decisively as it refutes the unrestricted version. Consider a possibility that is eliminated by phenomenal information, but not by any amount of physical information. There are two cases. Maybe this possibility has nothing that is alien to our world. In that case the argument goes as before: actuality and the eliminated possibility are just alike physically, they are not just alike *simpliciter*; furthermore, both of them fall within the restriction to non-alien worlds, so we have a counterexample even to restricted supervenience. Or maybe instead the eliminated possibility does have something X which is alien to this world – an alien kind of thing, or maybe an alien fundamental property of non-alien things. Then the phenomenal information gained by having a new experience has revealed something negative: at least in part, it is the information that X is *not* present. How can that be? If there is such a thing as phenomenal information, presumably what it reveals is positive: the presence of something hitherto unknown. Not, of course, something alien from actuality itself; but something alien from actuality as it is inadequately represented by the inexperienced and by the materialists. If Mary learns something when she finds out what it's like to see the colors, presumably she learns that there's *more* to the world than she knew before – not *less*. It's easy to think that phenomenal information might eliminate possibilities that are impoverished by comparison with actuality, but that would make a counterexample to the restricted supervenience thesis. To eliminate possibilities without making a counterexample, phenomenal information would have to eliminate possibilities less impoverished than actuality. And how can phenomenal information do that? Compare ordinary perceptual information. Maybe Jean-Paul can just *see* that Pierre is absent from the café, at least if it's a small café. But how can he just see that Pierre is absent from Paris, let alone from the whole of actuality?

(Is there a third case? What if the eliminated possibility is in one respect richer than actuality, in another respect poorer? Suppose the eliminated possibility has X, which is alien from actuality, but also it lacks Y. Then phenomenal information might eliminate it by revealing the actual presence of Y, without having to reveal the actual absence of X – but then I say there ought to be a third possibility, one with neither X nor Y, poorer and in no respect richer than actuality, and again without any physical difference from actuality. For why should taking away X automatically restore Y? Why can't they vary independently?[9] But this third possibility differs *simpliciter* from actuality without differing physically. Further, it has nothing alien from actuality. So we regain a counterexample to the restricted supervenience thesis.)

The Knowledge Argument works. There is no way to grant the Hypothesis of Phenomenal Information and still uphold Materialism. Therefore I deny the Hypothesis. I cannot refute it outright. But later I shall argue, first, that it is more peculiar, and therefore less tempting, that it may at first seem; and, second, that we are not forced to accept it, since an alternative hypothesis does justice to the way experience best teaches us what it's like.

Three More Ways to Miss the Point

The Hypothesis of Phenomenal Information characterizes information in terms of eliminated possibilities. But there are other conceptions of "information." Therefore the Hypothesis has look-alikes: hypotheses which say that experience produces "information" which could not be gained otherwise, but do not characterize this "information" in terms of eliminated possibilities. These look-alikes do not work as premises for the Knowledge Argument. They do not say that phenomenal information eliminates possibilities that differ, but do not differ physically, from uneliminated possibilities. The look-alike hypotheses of phenomenal "information" are consistent with Materialism, and may very well be true. But they don't make the Knowledge Argument go away. Whatever harmless look-alikes may or may not be true, and whatever conception may or may not deserve the name "information," the only way to save Materialism is fix our attention squarely on the genuine Hypothesis of Phenomenal Information, and deny it. To avert our eyes, and attend to something else, is no substitute for that denial.

Might a look-alike help at least to this extent: by giving us something true that well might have been confused with the genuine Hypothesis, thereby explaining how we might have believed the Hypothesis although it was false? I think not. Each of the look-alikes turns out to imply not only that experience can give us "information" that no amount of lessons can give, but also that lessons in Russian can give us "information" that no amount of lessons in English can give (and vice versa). I doubt that any friend of phenomenal information ever thought that the special role of experience in teaching what it's like was on a par with the special role of Russian! I will have to say before I'm done that phenomenal information is an illusion, but I think I must look elsewhere for a credible hypothesis about what sort of illusion it might be.

The Fourth Way. If a hidden camera takes photographs of a room, the film ends up bearing traces of what went on in the room. The traces are distinctive: that is, the details of the traces depend on the details of what went on, and if what went on had been different in any of many ways, the traces would have been correspondingly different. So we can say that the traces bear information, and that he who has the film has the information. That might be said because the traces, plus the way they depend on what went on, suffice to eliminate possibilities; but instead we might say "information" and just mean "distinctive traces." If so, it's certainly true that new experience imparts "information" unlike any that can be gained from lessons. Experience and lessons leave different kinds of traces. That is so whether or not the experience eliminates possibilities that the lessons leave open. It is equally true, of course, that lessons in Russian leave traces unlike any that are left by lessons in English, regardless of whether the lessons cover the same ground and eliminate the same possibilities.

The Fifth Way. When we speak of transmission of "information," we often mean transmission of text. Repositories of "information," such as libraries, are storehouses of text. Whether the text is empty verbiage or highly informative is beside the point. Maybe we too contain information by being storehouses of text. Maybe there is a language of thought, and maybe the way we believe things is to store sentences of this language in some special way, or in some special part of our brains. In that case, we could say that storing away a new sentence was storing away a new piece of "information," whether or not that new piece eliminated any possibilities not already eliminated by the sentences stored previously. Maybe, also, the language of thought is not fixed once and for all, but can gain new words. Maybe, for instance, it borrows words from public language. And maybe, when one has a new experience, that causes one's language of thought to gain a new word which denotes that experience – a word which could not have been added to the language by any other means. If all this is so, then when Mary sees colors, her language of thought gains new words, allowing her to store away new sentences and thereby gain "information." All this about the language of thought, the storing of sentences, and the gaining of words is speculation. But it is plausible speculation, even if no longer the only game in town. If it is all true, then we have another look-alike hypothesis of phenomenal "information." When Mary gains new words and stores new sentences, that is "information" that she never had before, regardless of whether it eliminates any possibilities that she had not eliminated already.

But again, the special role of experience turns out to be on a par with the special role of Russian. If the language of thought picks up new words by borrowing from public language, then lessons in Russian add new words, and result in the storing of new sentences, and thereby impart "information" that never could have been had from lessons in English. (You might say that the new Russian words are mere synonyms of old words, or at least old phrases, that were there already; and synonyms don't count. But no reason has been given why the new inner words created by experience may not also be synonyms of old phrases, perhaps of long descriptions in the language of neurophysiology.)

The Sixth Way. A philosopher who is skeptical about possibility, as so many are, may wish to replace possibilities themselves with linguistic *ersatz* possibilities: maximal consistent sets of sentences. And he may be content to take "consistent" in a narrowly logical sense, so that a set with "Fred is married" and "Fred is a bachelor" may count as consistent, and only an overt contradiction like "Fred is married" and "Fred is not married" will be ruled out.[10] The *ersatz* possibilities might also be taken as sets of sentences of the language of thought, if the philosopher believes in it. Then if someone's language of thought gains new words, whether as a result of new experience or as a result of being taught in Russian, the *ersatz* possibilities become richer and more numerous. The sets of sentences that were maximal before are no longer maximal after new words are added. So when Mary sees colors and her language of thought gains new words, there are new *ersatz* possibilities; and she can straightway eliminate some of them. Suppose she knows beforehand that she is about to see green, and that the experience of seeing green is associated with neural firing pattern F. So when she sees green and gains the new word G for her experience, then straightway there are new, enriched *ersatz* possibilities with sentences saying that she has G without F, and straightway she knows

enough to eliminate these *ersatz* possibilities. (Even if she does not know beforehand what she is about to see, straightway she can eliminate at least those of her new-found *ersatz* possibilities with sentences denying that she then has G.) Just as we can characterize information in terms of elimination of possibilities, so we can characterize *ersatz* "information" in terms of elimination of *ersatz* "possibilities." So here we have the closest look-alike hypothesis of all, provided that language-of-thoughtism is true. But we still do not have the genuine Hypothesis of Phenomenal Information, since the eliminated *ersatz* possibility of G without F may not have been a genuine possibility at all. It may have been like the *ersatz* possibility of married bachelors.

Curiouser and Curiouser

The Hypothesis of Phenomenal Information is more peculiar than it may at first seem. For one thing, because it is opposed to more than just Materialism. Some of you may have welcomed the Knowledge Argument because you thought all along that physical information was inadequate to explain the phenomena of mind. You may have been convinced all along that the mind could do things that no physical system could do: bend spoons, invent new jokes, demonstrate the consistency of arithmetic, reduce the wave packet, or what have you. You may have been convinced that the full causal story of how the deeds of mind are accomplished involves the causal interactions not only of material bodies but also of astral bodies; not only the vibrations of the electromagnetic field but also the good or bad vibes of the psionic field; not only protoplasm but ectoplasm. I doubt it, but never mind. It's irrelevant to our topic. The Knowledge Argument is targeted against you no less than it is against Materialism itself.

Let *parapsychology* be the science of all the nonphysical things, properties, causal processes, laws of nature, and so forth that may be required to explain the things we do. Let us suppose that we learn ever so much parapsychology. It will make no difference. Black-and-white Mary may study all the parapsychology as well as all the psychophysics of color vision, but she still won't know what it's like. Lessons on the aura of Vegemite will do no more for us than lessons on its chemical composition. And so it goes. Our intuitive starting point wasn't just that *physics* lessons couldn't help the inexperienced to know what it's like. It was that *lessons* couldn't help. If there is such a thing as phenomenal information, it isn't just independent of physical information. It's independent of every sort of information that could be served up in lessons for the inexperienced. For it is supposed to eliminate possibilities that any amount of lessons leave open. Therefore phenomenal information is not just parapsychological information, if such there be. It's something very much stranger.

The genuine Hypothesis of Phenomenal Information, as distinguished from its look-alikes, treats information in terms of the elimination of possibilities. When we lack information, several alternative possibilities are open, when we get the information some of the alternatives are excluded. But a second peculiar thing about phenomenal information is that it resists this treatment. (So does logical or mathematical "information." However, phenomenal information cannot be logical or mathematical, because lessons in logic and mathematics no more teach us what a new experience is like than lessons in physics or parapsychology do.) When someone doesn't know what it's like to have an experience, where are the alternative open possibilities? I cannot present to myself in thought a range of alternative possibilities about what it might be like to taste Vegemite. That is because I cannot imagine either what it *is* like to taste Vegemite, or any alternative way that it *might* be like but in fact isn't. (I could perfectly well imagine that Vegemite tastes just like peanut butter, or something else familiar to me, but let's suppose I've been told authoritatively that this isn't so.) I can't even pose the question that phenomenal information is supposed to answer: is it this way or that? It seems that the alternative possibilities must be unthinkable beforehand; and afterward too, except for the one that turns out to be actualized. I don't say there's anything altogether impossible about a range of unthinkable alternatives; only something peculiar. But it's peculiar enough to suggest that we may somehow have gone astray.

From Phenomenal to Epiphenomenal

A third peculiar thing about phenomenal information is that it is strangely isolated from all other sorts of information; and this is so regardless of whether the mind works on physical or parapsychological principles. The phenomenal aspect of the world has nothing to do with explaining why people seemingly talk about the phenomenal aspect of the world. For instance, it plays no part in explaining the movements of the pens of philosophers writing treatises about phenomenal information and the way experience has provided them with it.

When Mary gets out of her black-and-white cell, her jaw drops. She says "At last! So this is what it's like to see colors!" Afterward she does things she couldn't do before, such as recognizing a new sample of the first color she ever saw. She may also do other things she didn't do before: unfortunate things, like writing about phenomenal information and the poverty of Materialism. One might think she said what she said and did what she did because she came to know what it's like to see colors. Not so, if the Hypothesis of Phenomenal Information is right. For suppose the phenomenal aspect of the world had been otherwise, so that she gained different phenomenal information. Or suppose the phenomenal aspect of the world had been absent altogether, as we materialists think it is. Would that have made the slightest difference to what she did or said then or later? I think not. Making a difference to what she does or says means, at least in part, making a difference to the motions of the particles of which she is composed. (Or better: making a difference to the spatiotemporal shape of the wave-function of those particles. But let that pass.) For how could she do or say anything different, if none of her particles moved any differently? But if something nonphysical sometimes makes a difference to the motions of physical particles, then physics as we know it is wrong. Not just silent, not just incomplete – wrong. Either the particles are caused to change their motion without benefit of any force, or else there is some extra force that works very differently from the usual four. To believe in the phenomenal aspect of the world, but deny that it is epiphenomenal, is to bet against the truth of physics. Given the success of physics hitherto, and even with due allowance for the foundational ailments of quantum mechanics, such betting is rash! A friend of the phenomenal aspect would be safer to join Jackson in defense of *epiphenomenal* qualia.

But there is more to the case than just an empirical bet in favor of physics. Suppose there is a phenomenal aspect of the world, and suppose it does make some difference to the motions of Mary's jaw or the noises out of her mouth. Then we can describe the phenomenal aspect, if we know enough, in terms of its physical effects. It is that on which physical phenomena depend in such-and-such way. This descriptive handle will enable us to give lessons on it to the inexperienced. But insofar as we can give lessons on it, what we have is just parapsychology. That whereof we cannot learn except by having the experience still eludes us. I do not argue that *everything* about the alleged distinctive subject matter of phenomenal information must be epiphenomenal. Part of it may be parapsychological instead. But I insist that *some* aspect of it must be epiphenomenal.

Suppose that the Hypothesis of Phenomenal Information is true and suppose that V_1 and V_2 are all of the maximally specific phenomenal possibilities concerning what it's like to taste Vegemite; anyone who tastes Vegemite will find out which one obtains, and no one else can. And suppose that P_1 and P_2 are all the maximally specific physical possibilities. (Of course we really need far more than two Ps, and maybe a friend of phenomenal information would want more than two Vs, but absurdly small numbers will do for an example.) Then we have four alternative hypotheses about the causal independence or dependence of the Ps on the Vs. Each one can be expressed as a pair of counterfactual conditionals. Two hypotheses are patterns of dependence.

K_1: if V_1 then P_1, if V_2 then P_2
K_2: if V_1 then P_2, if V_2 then P_1

The other two are patterns of independence.

K_3: if V_1 then P_1, if V_2 then P_1
K_4: if V_1 then P_2, if V_2 then P_2

These dependency hypotheses are, I take it, contingent propositions. They are made true, if they are, by some contingent feature of the world, though it's indeed a vexed question what sort of feature it is.[11] Now we have eight joint possibilities.

$K_1V_1P_1$ $K_3V_1P_1$ $K_3V_2P_1$ $K_2V_2P_1$
$K_2V_1P_2$ $K_4V_1P_2$ $K_4V_2P_2$ $K_1V_2P_2$

Between the four on the top row and the four on the bottom row, there is the physical difference between P_1 and P_2. Between the four on the left and the four on the right, there is the phenomenal difference between V_1 and V_2. And between the four on the edges and the four in the middle there

is a parapsychological difference. It is the difference between dependence and independence of the physical on the phenomenal; between efficacy and epiphenomenalism, so far as this one example is concerned. There's nothing ineffable about that. Whether or not you've tasted Vegemite, and whether or not you can conceive of the alleged difference between V_1 and V_2, you can still be told whether the physical difference between P_1 and P_2 does or doesn't depend on some part of the phenomenal aspect of the world.

Lessons can teach the inexperienced which parapsychological possibility obtains, dependence or independence. Let it be dependence: we have either K_1 or K_2. For if we had independence, then already we would have found our epiphenomenal difference: namely, the difference between V_1 and V_2. And lessons can teach the inexperienced which of the two physical possibilities obtains. Without loss of generality let it be P_1. Now two of our original eight joint possibilities remain open: $K_1V_1P_1$ and $K_2V_2P_1$. The difference between those is not at all physical, and not at all parapsychological: it's P_1, and it's dependence, in both cases. The difference is entirely phenomenal. And also it is entirely epiphenomenal. Nothing physical, and nothing parapsychological, depends on the difference between $K_1V_1P_1$ and $K_2V_2P_1$. We have the same sort of pattern of dependence either way; it's just that the phenomenal possibilities have been swapped. Whether it's independence or whether it's dependence, therefore, we have found an epiphenomenal part of the phenomenal aspect of the world. It is the residue left behind when we remove the parapsychological part.

Suppose that someday I taste Vegemite, and hold forth about how I know at last what it's like. The sound of my holding forth is a physical effect, part of the realized physical possibility P_1. This physical effect is exactly the same whether it's part of the joint possibility $K_1V_1P_1$ or part of its alternative $K_2V_2P_1$. It may be caused by V_1 in accordance with K_1, or it may instead be caused by V_2 in accordance with K_2, but it's the same either way. So it does not occur because we have K_1V_1 rather than K_2V_2 or vice versa. The alleged difference between these two possibilities does nothing to explain the alleged physical manifestation of my finding out which one of them is realized. It is in that way that the difference is epiphenomenal. That makes it very queer, and repugnant to good sense.

The Ability Hypothesis

So the Hypothesis of Phenomenal Information turns out to be very peculiar indeed. It would be nice, and not only for materialists, if we could reject it. For materialists, it is essential to reject it. And we can. There is an alternative hypothesis about what it is to learn what an experience is like: the *Ability Hypothesis*. Laurence Nemirow summarizes it thus:

> some modes of understanding consist, not in the grasping of facts, but in the acquisition of abilities.... As for understanding an experience, we may construe that as an ability to place oneself, at will, in a state representative of the experience. I understand the experience of seeing red if I can at will visualize red. Now it is perfectly clear why there must be a special connection between the ability to place oneself in a state representative of a given experience and the point of view of experiencer: exercising the ability just *is* what we call "adopting the point of view of experiencer." ... We can, then, come to terms with the subjectivity of our understanding of experience without positing subjective facts as the objects of our understanding. This account explains, incidentally, the linguistic incommunicability of our subjective understanding of experience (a phenomenon which might seem to support the hypothesis of subjective facts). The latter is explained as a special case of the linguistic incommunicability of abilities to place oneself at will in a given state, such as the state of having lowered blood pressure, and the state of having wiggling ears.[12]

If you have a new experience, you gain abilities to remember and to imagine. After you taste Vegemite, and you learn what it's like, you can afterward remember the experience you had. By remembering how it once was, you can afterward imagine such an experience. Indeed, even if you eventually forget the occasion itself, you will very likely retain your ability to imagine such an experience.

Further, you gain an ability to recognize the same experience if it comes again. If you taste Vegemite on another day, you will probably know that you have met the taste once before. And if, while tasting Vegemite, you know that it is Vegemite you are tasting, then you will be able to put the name to the experience if you have it again. Or if you are told nothing at the time, but later you somehow know that it is Vegemite that you are then remembering or imagining tasting, again you can put the name to the experience, or to the memory, or to the experience of imagining, if it comes again. Here, the ability you gain is an ability to gain information if given other information. Nevertheless, the information gained is not phenomenal, and the ability to gain information is not the same thing as information itself.

Earlier, I mentioned "knowing what an experience is like under a description." Now I can say that what I meant by this was having the ability to remember or imagine an experience while also knowing the egocentric proposition that what one is then imagining is the experience of such-and-such description. One might well know what an experience is like under one description, but not under another. One might even know what some experience is like, but not under any description whatever – unless it be some rather trivial description like "that queer taste that I'm imagining right now." That is what would happen if you slipped a dab of Vegemite into my food without telling me what it was: afterward, I would know what it was like to taste Vegemite, but not under that description, and not under any other nontrivial description. It might be suggested that "knowing what it's like to taste Vegemite" really means what I'd call "knowing what it's like to taste Vegemite under the description 'tasting Vegemite'"; and if so, knowing what it's like would involve both ability and information. I disagree. For surely it would make sense to say: "I know this experience well, I've long known what it's like, but only today have I found out that it's the experience of tasting Vegemite." But this verbal question is unimportant. For the information involved in knowing what it's like under a description, and allegedly involved in knowing what it's like, is anyhow not the queer phenomenal information that needs rejecting.

(Is there a problem here for the friend of phenomenal information? Suppose he says that knowing what it's like to taste Vegemite means knowing that the taste of Vegemite has a certain "phenomenal character." This requires putting the name to the taste, so clearly it corresponds to our notion of knowing what it's like to taste Vegemite under the description "tasting Vegemite." But we also have our notion of knowing what it's like *simpliciter*, and what can he offer that corresponds to that? Perhaps he should answer by appeal to a trivial description, as follows: knowing what it's like *simpliciter* means knowing what it's like under the trivial description "taste I'm imagining now," and that means knowing that the taste one is imagining now has a certain phenomenal character.)

As well as gaining the ability to remember and imagine the experience you had, you also gain the ability to imagine related experiences that you never had. After tasting Vegemite, you might for instance become able to imagine tasting Vegemite ice cream. By performing imaginative experiments, you can predict with some confidence what you would do in circumstances that have never arisen – whether you'd ask for a second helping of Vegemite ice cream, for example.

These abilities to remember and imagine and recognize are abilities you cannot gain (unless by super-neurosurgery, or by magic) except by tasting Vegemite and learning what it's like. You can't get them by taking lessons on the physics or the parapsychology of the experience, or even by taking comprehensive lessons that cover the whole of physics and parapsychology. The Ability Hypothesis says that knowing what an experience is like just *is* the possession of these abilities to remember, imagine, and recognize. It isn't the possession of any kind of information, ordinary or peculiar. It isn't knowing that certain possibilities aren't actualized. It isn't knowing-that. It's knowing-how. Therefore it should be no surprise that lessons won't teach you what an experience is like. Lessons impart information; ability is something else. Knowledge-that does not automatically provide know-how.

There are parallel cases. Some know how to wiggle their ears; others don't. If you can't do it, no amount of information will help. Some know how to eat with chopsticks, others don't. Information will help up to a point – for instance, if your trouble is that you hold one chopstick in each hand – but no amount of information, by itself, will bring you to a very high level of know-how. Some know how to recognize a C-38 locomotive by sight, others don't. If you don't, it won't much help if you memorize a detailed geometrical description of its shape, even though that does all the eliminating of possibilities that there is to be done. (Conversely, knowing the shape by sight doesn't enable you to write down the geometrical description.) Information very often contributes to know-how, but often it doesn't contribute enough. That's why music students have to practice.

Know-how is ability. But of course some aspects of ability are in no sense knowledge: strength, sufficient funds. Other aspects of ability are, purely and simply, a matter of information. If you want to know how to open the combination lock on the bank vault, information is all you need. It remains that there are aspects of ability that do *not* consist simply of possession of information, and that we *do* call knowledge. The Ability Hypothesis holds that knowing what an experience is like is that sort of knowledge.

If the Ability Hypothesis is the correct analysis of knowing what an experience is like, then phenomenal information is an illusion. We ought to explain that illusion. It would be feeble, I think, just to say that we're fooled by the ambiguity of the word "know": we confuse ability with information because we confuse knowledge in the sense of knowing-how with knowledge in the sense of knowing-that. There may be two senses of the word "know," but they are well and truly entangled. They mark the two pure endpoints of a range of mixed cases. The usual thing is that we gain information and ability together. If so, it should be no surprise if we apply to pure cases of gaining ability, or to pure cases of gaining information, the same word "know" that we apply to all the mixed cases.

Along with information and ability, acquaintance is a third element of the mixture. If Lloyd George died too soon, there's a sense in which Father never can know him. Information won't do it, even if Father is a most thorough biographer and the archives are very complete. (And the trouble isn't that there's some very special information about someone that you can only get by being in his presence.) Know-how won't do it either, no matter how good Father may be at imagining Lloyd George, seemingly remembering him, and recognizing him. (Father may be able to recognize Lloyd George even if there's no longer any Lloyd George to recognize – if *per impossible* he did turn up, Father could tell it was him.) Again, what we have is not just a third separate sense of "know." Meeting someone, gaining a lot of information about him that would be hard to gain otherwise, and gaining abilities regarding him usually go together. The pure cases are exceptions.

A friend of phenomenal information will agree, of course, that when we learn what an experience is like, we gain abilities to remember, imagine, and recognize. But he will say that it is because we gain phenomenal information that we gain the abilities.

He might even say the same about other cases of gaining know-how: you can recognize the C-38 when you have phenomenal information about what it's like to see that shape, you can eat with chopsticks or wiggle your ears when you gain phenomenal information about the experience of doing so, and so on. What should friends of the Ability Hypothesis make of this? Is he offering a conjecture, which we must reject, about the causal origin of abilities? I think not. He thinks, as we do, that experiences leave distinctive traces in people, and that these traces enable us to do things. Likewise being taught to recognize a C-38 or to eat with chopsticks, or whatever happens on first wiggling the ears, leave traces that enable us to do things afterward. That much is common ground. He also interprets these enabling traces as representations that bear information about their causes. (If the same traces had been caused in some deviant way they might perhaps have carried misinformation.) We might even be able to accept that too. The time for us to quarrel comes only when he says that these traces represent special phenomenal facts, facts which cannot be represented in any other way, and therefore which cannot be taught in physics lessons or even in parapsychology lessons. That is the part, and the *only* part, which we must reject. But that is no part of his psychological story about how we gain abilities. It is just a gratuitous metaphysical gloss on that story.

We say that learning what an experience is like means gaining certain abilities. If the causal basis for those abilities turns out also to be a special kind of representation of some sort of information, so be it. We need only deny that it represents a special kind of information about a special subject matter. Apart from that it's up for grabs what, if anything, it may represent. The details of stimuli: the chemical composition of Vegemite, reflectances of surfaces, the motions of well-handled chopsticks or of ears? The details of inner states produced by those stimuli: patterns of firings of nerves? We could agree to either, so long as we did not confuse "having information" represented in this special way with having the same information in the form of knowledge or belief. Or we could disagree. Treating the ability-conferring trace as a representation is optional. What's essential is that when we learn what an experience is like by having it, we gain abilities to remember, imagine, and recognize.

Acknowledgment

Part of this paper derives from a lecture at LaTrobe University in 1981. I thank LaTrobe for support in 1981, Harvard University for support under a Santayana Fellowship in 1988, and Frank Jackson for very helpful discussion.

Notes

1   See Frank Jackson, "Epiphenomenal qualia," *Philosophical Quarterly* 32 (1982), pp. 127–36, and reprinted in this volume; "What Mary didn't know," *Journal of Philosophy* 83 (1986), pp. 291–5.

2   See B. A. Farrell, "Experience," *Mind* 59 (1950), pp. 170–98; and Thomas Nagel, "What is it like to be a bat?" *Philosophical Review* 83 (1974), pp. 435–50, also in Thomas Nagel, *Mortal Questions* (Cambridge: Cambridge University Press, 1979).

3   See Peter Unger, "On experience and the development of the understanding," *American Philosophical Quarterly* 3 (1966), pp. 1–9.

4   For such speculation, see Paul M. Churchland, "Reduction, qualia, and the direct introspection of brain states," *Journal of Philosophy* 82 (1985), pp. 8–28.

5   See my "Attitudes *de dicto* and *de se*," *Philosophical Review* 88 (1979), pp. 513–43, also in my *Philosophical Papers*, vol. 1 (New York: Oxford University Press, 1983); and Roderick Chisholm, *The First Person: An Essay on Reference and Intentionality* (Minneapolis: University of Minnesota Press, 1981).

6   See Gilbert Harman, "The intrinsic quality of experience," *Philosophical Perspectives* 4 (1990).

7   See Ned Block and Jerry A. Fodor, "What psychological states are not," *Philosophical Review* 81 (1972), pp. 159–81, also in Ned Block (ed.), *Readings in Philosophy of Psychology*, vol. I (Cambridge, Mass.: Harvard University Press, 1980); and my "Mad pain and Martian pain," in *Readings in Philosophy of Psychology*, vol. I, and in my *Philosophical Papers*, vol. I.

8   See my "New work for a theory of universals," *Australasian Journal of Philosophy* 61 (1983), pp. 343–77, especially pp. 361–4. For a different view

about how to state minimal Materialism, see Terence Horgan, "Supervenience and microphysics," *Pacific Philosophical Quarterly* 63 (1982), pp. 29–43.

9 On recombination of possibilities, see my *On the Plurality of Worlds* (Oxford: Blackwell Publishers, 1986), pp. 87–92. The present argument may call for a principle that also allows recombination of properties; I now think that would not necessarily require treating properties as non-spatiotemporal parts of their instances. On recombination of properties, see also D. M. Armstrong, *A Combinatorial Theory of Possibility* (Cambridge: Cambridge University Press 1989).

10 See *On the Plurality of Worlds*, pp. 142–65, on linguistic *ersatz* possibilities.

11 On dependency hypotheses, see my "Causal decision theory," *Australasian Journal of Philosophy* 59 (1981), pp. 5–30, reprinted in my *Philosophical Papers*, vol. II (New York: Oxford University Press, 1986).

12 Laurence Nemirow, review of Nagel's *Mortal Questions*, *Philosophical Review* 89 (1980), pp. 475–6. For a fuller statement, see Nemirow, "Physicalism and the cognitive role of acquaintance;" and *Functionalism and the Subjective Quality of Experience* (doctoral dissertation, Stanford, 1979). See also Michael Tye, "The subjective qualities of experience," *Mind* 95 (1986), pp. 1–17.

I should record a disagreement with Nemirow on one very small point. We agree that the phrase "what experience E is like" does not denote some "subjective quality" of E, something which supposedly would be part of the subject matter of the phenomenal information gained by having E. But whereas I have taken the phrase to denote E itself, Nemirow takes it to be a syncategorematic part of the expression "know what experience E is like." See "Physicalism and the cognitive role of acquaintance" section III.

Understanding the Phenomenal Mind: Are We All Just Armadillos?

Robert Van Gulick

Do phenomenal mental states pose a special obstacle to materialism or functionalism? Three main families of arguments in the recent philosophical literature may seem to show that they do: the "knowledge argument", the "explanatory gap argument" and the various versions of the "inverted and absent qualia argument". However, as I shall show, none of the three in fact presents an insurmountable barrier to materialistic functionalism.

Before turning to the arguments, let me issue one caveat about the use of the word "phenomenal". In much of the recent philosophical literature it has been used to refer exclusively to sensory qualia or so-called raw feels, such as the redness of which one is immediately aware when viewing a ripe tomato, or the taste of a fresh mango. Although I will myself spend some time discussing just such sensory qualia, I none the less believe it is a serious mistake to equate the phenomenal aspect of mind solely with such properties. We should not forget that the idea of the phenomenal structure of experience entered philosophical thought through Kant, who introduced it in the context of rejecting the sensational theory of experience associated with traditional empiricism. Phenomenal experience is not merely a succession of qualitatively distinguished sensory ideas, but rather the organized cognitive experience of a world of objects and of ourselves as subjects within that world.

Any adequate theory of the phenomenal aspect of mentality should take this richer Kantian concept into account. To focus exclusively on raw feels would be a mistake in at least two respects. First, it would provide too narrow a definition of what needs to be explained; and, second, I doubt that qualia and raw feels can themselves be understood in isolation from the roles they play within the richer Kantian structure of phenomenal experience.

The Knowledge Argument

Let us turn then to the "knowledge argument". Its basic underlying assumption is that there is some knowledge about experience that can be acquired *only* by undergoing the relevant experience oneself. In the paradigm case, one can come to know what the character of phenomenal red is only by having a red experience. No *physical* knowledge of what goes on in the brain when one has a red experience will suffice. It is for this reason that Thomas Nagel (1974) believes that no human can ever know what it is like to be a bat. Given our human inability to undergo experiences of the sort the bat has when sensing its surroundings by echo location, the relevant knowledge about bat-type experience is forever beyond us. The relevant facts about what it is like to be a bat are cognitively inaccessible to us in the sense that we are incapable of even understanding them.

To see how this is supposed to lead to an anti-materialist conclusion, let us consider the knowledge argument as presented by Frank Jackson (this volume, 1986), certainly the most widely discussed anti-physicalist argument in the American philosophical world during the 1980s. Jackson offers the hypothetical case of Mary the super colour scientist who has spent her entire life within a strictly black and white (and grey) environment. Mary none the less (via television) has become the world's greatest expert on colour perception and *ex hypothesi* she is said to know *everything physical* there is to know about what goes on in a normal perceiver when he perceives something red. Yet, Jackson argues, Mary does not know *everything* there is to know about having a red experience, a fact that he believes is obvious if we consider what would happen if Mary were released from her achromatic isolation and shown a ripe tomato for the first time. Jackson's claim is that Mary would come to know something that she didn't know before. But since *ex hypothesi* she already knew *everything physical* there was to know about seeing red, the knowledge or information she gains must be non-physical phenomenal information.

A1   *The knowledge argument*

P1   Mary (before her release) knows *everything physical* there is to know about seeing red.

P2   Mary (before her release) does not know *everything* there is to know about seeing red because she learns something about it on her release.

Therefore:

C3   There are some truths about seeing red that escape the physicalist story.

C4   Physicalism is false and phenomenal properties cannot be explained as (or identified with) physical properties.

This argument has been regarded as a serious threat to physicalism. Indeed, so ardent a physicalist and formidable a philosopher as David Lewis (this volume) has held that if we admit that Mary really gains information when she first experiences red, then physicalism must be false. However, being regarded as a serious threat is not the same as being regarded as a sound argument, and a wide variety of critical objections have been raised against the knowledge argument. We can classify them into groups by use of a few diagnostic questions about Mary (figure 19.1). They are all variants of the question that riveted the Watergate investigations of Richard Nixon: *what* did she know and *when* did she know it?

Question 1: Does Mary in fact learn anything or gain any knowledge when she first experiences red?

Most philosophers have been willing to concede that Mary does learn something, but Paul Churchland (1985) has argued that the claim is open to reasonable doubt. Remember that *ex hypothesi* Mary knows *everything physical* there is to know about what goes on in people's brains when they experience red. Since our present knowledge of the brain is so far short of what Mary would know, it is difficult to say what she would or would not be able to understand or anticipate. It seems at least possible that when Mary sees her first tomato (rather than expressing surprise) she might remark, "Ah yes, it is just as I expected it would be." Thus there is the possibility of undercutting the argument right at the start by simply rejecting its second premise.

But let us follow most philosophers in conceding that Mary gains at least some knowledge and push on to question 2.

Question 2: What sort of knowledge does Mary gain? Is it strictly *know-how* or does it include new *knowledge* of *facts*, *propositions* or *information*?

One reply to the knowledge argument, originally proposed by Laurence Nemirow (1980, 1990) and championed by David Lewis (1983, this volume), is to hold that the only knowledge Mary gains is *know-how*; she gains no new knowledge of facts or propositions. According to this so-called "*ability reply*", she gains only new practical abilities to recognize and imagine the relevant phenomenal

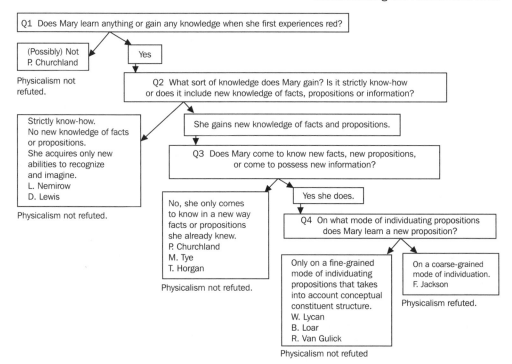

Figure 19.1 Classification of critical objections raised against the knowledge argument.

properties. If the argument's second premise P2 is thus read as saying only that Mary gains new abilities (new know-how) then its conclusion C3 no longer follows. There need be no truths or information left out of the physicalist story nor out of Mary's prior knowledge. The ability reply thus promises a quick and clean solution to the knowledge argument. But its viability depends on the plausibility of the claim that Mary gains no new knowledge of facts or propositions and, like many other philosophers, I find that claim not very plausible. Part of what Mary gains is know-how, but that does not seem to be all she gains. There seems to be a fact about how phenomenal red appears that she apprehends only after her release. Let us thus turn to a *similar* sounding but *importantly different* question:

Question 3: Does Mary come to know *new facts, new propositions* or come to possess *new information?*

The difference between questions 2 and 3 is a change in the scope of the word "new". In question 2 it qualifies knowledge (new *knowledge*), but in question 3 it qualifies the *object of knowledge* (knowledge of new propositions or new facts).

The difference can be significant since there are philosophers who hold that Mary gains new knowledge only in the sense that she comes to know *in a new way* facts and propositions that she already knew (Churchland 1985; Tye 1986). There are various options for unpacking the notion of knowing an old fact in a new way. Mary now knows directly by introspection what she knew before only indirectly by inference. Mary is now able to represent such facts to herself using a basic biological and probably pre-linguistic system of representation quite distinct from the linguistic representations she had to use to represent such facts in the past. Such differences in *mode of access* or *system of representation* might justify us in saying that Mary was now in a new epistemic state and might suffice to explain our inclination to accept the claim that Mary gains new knowledge. Read in this way, P2 again fails to support the argument's conclusion; there need be no facts or propositions that Mary failed to know before her release and thus none that was left out by the physicalist story.

David Lewis (this volume) has recently criticized such approaches as inadequate to account for the intuitive appeal of the knowledge argument. He argues that they make the sense in which Mary gains new knowledge from experiencing red no different from that in which she gains new knowledge about her brain when she learns Russian or Urdu and thus acquires a new system of representation. He finds it uncharitable to suppose that the proponents of the knowledge argument have confused so innocuous a sense of "new knowledge" with any that would support their conclusion. Lewis's criticism strikes me as a bit unfair in so far as the differences between Mary's linguistic and biological non-linguistic systems for representing experiential states seem far greater than those between English and Russian and thus better able to account for our sense that Mary has gained new knowledge *even if* she has not come to know a new proposition.

There is, however, one last question we need to ask, one which can allow us to concede even the strong claim that Mary learns a new proposition without being forced to an anti-physicalist conclusion.

Question 4: On what mode of individuating propositions does Mary learn a new proposition? (That is, what counts here as a new proposition?)

Propositions, like beliefs, can be individuated in a variety of fine- or coarse-grained ways. Coarse-grained propositions might be taken as functions from possible worlds to truth values. On such a mode of individuation, the proposition that $5 + 7 = 12$ is the same proposition as the proposition that 38 is the square root of 1,444, they are both true in every possible world. And the proposition that water freezes at 32°F is the same proposition as the proposition that H_2O freezes at 32°F. However, one can use a more fine-grained scheme of individuation which treats propositions as having *constituent structure* composed of such things as *concepts* that must also match up if two propositions are to be identified.

Thus, *even if* Mary has come to know a new proposition, that in itself need not undercut materialism *as long as* propositions are being individuated in a sufficiently fine-grained way (Loar 1990; Lycan 1990b). I find this reply to the knowledge argument quite attractive, especially as developed in a recent paper by Brian Loar (1990). Indeed, I have made a similar argument in the past in a reply to Thomas Nagel's argument regarding the individuation of facts (Van Gulick 1985). Loar argues that Mary acquires a new concept, a concept that enters her cognitive repertoire in part on the basis

of her newly acquired discriminative abilities. Thus, using this new concept, she is able to apprehend the truth of new propositions. Yet the addition of such a new proposition to her store of knowledge need not cause any concern to the physicalist in so far as the *property* to which her new concept refers can be just some property she referred to in the past by use of a *purely physical concept*, i.e. a concept constructed within the resources of the physical sciences.

What then is the bottom line on the knowledge argument? Despite its widespread intuitive appeal and the air of mystification it produces about the explanatory elusiveness of phenomenal qualities, I think it's pretty clearly a loser as an argument against the possibility of giving a materialist explanation of phenomenal mentality. There are any number of points at which one can cut off the argument. Though I favour a Loar-type solution, I think each of the other replies provides a plausible place at which to draw the line against the anti-materialist attack. Please choose your favourite.

The Explanatory Gap Argument

Let us turn then to our second argument, the "explanatory gap argument". It aims at a more modest, though still substantive, result. It does not try to show that materialism is false, but only that with respect to the phenomenal aspect of mind, materialism is in an important sense unintelligible or incapable of being adequately comprehended, at least by us humans. Thus Thomas Nagel writes, "We have at present no conception of how a single event or thing could have both physical and phenomenological aspects or how if it did they might be related" (1986, p. 47). Joseph Levine puts the point like this:

> there is more to our concept of pain than its causal role, there is how it feels; and what is left unexplained by the discovery of C-fiber firing (the standard philosophical candidate for the neural basis of pain, despite its total empirical implausibility) is why pain should feel the way it does! For there seems to be nothing about C-fiber firing that makes it naturally "fit" the phenomenal properties of pain, any more than it would fit some other set of phenomenal properties. Unlike its functional role, the identification of the qualitative side of pain with C-fiber

firing (or some property of C-fiber firing) leaves the connection between it and what we identify it with completely mysterious. One might say it makes the way pain feels into merely a brute fact. (Levine 1983, p. 358)

Levine maintains that psychophysical statements asserting such brute fact identities are unintelligible, they leave an explanatory gap that we have no idea how to fill.

Colin McGinn (1989) has argued that making the psychophysical link intelligible may be beyond our conceptual capacities. We humans should not with hubris assume that every fact about the natural world is within our cognitive capacity to comprehend. Just as monkeys are unable to comprehend the concept of an electron, and armadillos (those ugly armoured ant-eating survivors of an earlier biological era that still inhabit Texas and points south) are not even up to the task of doing elementary arithmetic. So, too, we may all be armadillos when it comes to understanding the link between brain and phenomenal mentality. Or so McGinn suggests.

The explanatory gap argument is not an argument in the sense that the knowledge argument is. Its strength derives not from any path of deductive reasoning but rather from the intuitive appeal of its conclusion, which speaks to our bewilderment about how any physical story about the brain could ever explain phenomenal consciousness. Recall Wittgenstein holding his head in the *Philosophical Investigations* and saying, "THIS is supposed to be produced by a process in the brain!" (1953, p. 412). None the less, I want to consider one deductive reconstruction of the argument because I think it will help us see what needs to be done to defuse the intuitive appeal of the position. At one point, Joe Levine makes an approving reference to John Locke's seventeenth-century claim that sensory qualia are *arbitrary*:

The point I am trying to make was captured by Locke in his discussion of the relation between primary and secondary qualities. He states that the simple ideas which we experience in response to impingements from the external world bear no intelligible relation to the corpuscular processes underlying impingement and response. Rather the two sets of phenomena are stuck together in an arbitrary manner. (Levine 1983, p. 359)

Immediately following this passage Levine attempts to support his point by appeal to a standard philosophical case of hypothetical spectrum inversion with red and green qualia switching causal roles in an otherwise normal subject. What is important here is the suggestion that basic ideas, such as colour qualia, are *simples*. They have *no structure*, and since each one is what it is *sui generis*, it is hard to see how their connection to anything could be anything but arbitrary. We might reconstruct the explanatory gap argument as A2:

A2 *The explanatory gap argument*
P1 Qualia such as phenomenal hues are basic simples; they have no structure.

Thus:

C2 Any links between such qualia and the organizational structure of their neural substrates must be arbitrary.

Thus:

C3 The links between qualia and their neural bases are unintelligible and present us with an unfillable explanatory gap.

Formulating the argument in this way suggests a possible line of reply, one that has been made by Larry Hardin (1988). It is the first premise of A2 that we must reject. Hardin argues that the phenomenal hues that philosophers such as Locke and Levine regard as *sui generis simples* are not in fact such, but rather elements within a highly organized and structured colour space. Any attempt to invert them or interchange them *in undetectable ways* would have to preserve that structural organization. More importantly, the articulation of an organized structure among colour qualia provides the basis for establishing *explanatory connections* between them and their neural substrates. The method is the familiar one of explaining higher-order organization in terms of underlying structure. Consider a few brief examples.

1   Some colour qualia are phenomenally experienced as binary (e.g. orange and purple) and others as unary (e.g. red and blue) while other combinations are phenomenally impossible (e.g. a colour that is both red and green in the way purple is both red and blue). This phenomenal organization is explained by appeal to the existence of two underlying opponent colour channels, one subserving red/green discrimination and the other

yellow/blue. Since red and green are mutually exclusive extreme outputs of the red/green channel, they cannot be combined; binaries are always combinations of the outputs of the two distinct channels.

2 Some hues are experienced as warm, positive and advancing (red and yellow) and others as cool, negative and receding (green and blue). They have an affective dimension. The warm hues are those that result from increased stimulation in their respective channel, while the cool hues result from decreased stimulation.

3 Phenomenal yellow tends to be "captured" by phenomenal green in the sense that hues intermediate between yellow and green tend to be perceived as shades of green (rather than of yellow) far more quickly as one moves away from unary yellow than when one moves away from any other unary hue. This phenomenon has as yet no neural explanation. (All examples are from Hardin 1988, pp. 134–42)

The three examples allow us to make our two points. First, most (perhaps even all) of the hypothetical spectrum inversions considered by philosophers would disrupt the organization of the phenomenal colour space in detectable ways. One cannot preserve structure while interchanging red with orange or with any other binary hue, nor by interchanging red with the cool hues of green or blue, nor red with yellow given the phenomenon of capture. Second, and of more immediate relevance to the explanatory gap argument, the phenomenal colour space is revealed to have a *complex organizational structure* that allows us to establish *explanatory* rather than simply brute fact connections between it and underlying neural processes.

Our critic may still reply that any explanations we produce will still leave something essentially qualitative unexplained. No matter how much structural organization we can find in the phenomenal realm and explain neurophysiologically, she will insist that the distinct redness of phenomenal red will not have been captured or explained by our theory. For though it may be impossible to map the hues of *our* colour space in a way that rearranges them, while making the change behaviourally undetectable by preserving all their organizational relations, it seems there could be other non-human creatures who had *alien qualia* quite unlike our own, but whose interrelations exactly mirrored those among our phenomenal hues (Shoemaker 1981a). Red*, their correlate of red,

would bear to green* and orange* the same relations that red bears to our phenomenal greens and oranges; yet red* would not be the same as red. If so, then something essentially qualitative would seem to have escaped our explanation (Shoemaker 1975, 1981b). We might have explained why a given brain process is identical with experiencing red rather than with experiencing orange but not why it is a case of experiencing red rather than red*.

This countercharge needs to be taken seriously, but I think we have altered the nature of the debate. The more one can articulate structure within the phenomenal realm, the greater the chances for physical explanation; without structure we have no place to attach our explanatory "hooks". There is indeed a residue that continues to escape explanation, but the more we can explain relationally about the phenomenal realm, the more the leftover residue shrinks towards zero. Though I admit that we are as yet a long way from that.

The Absent Qualia Argument

These considerations bring us to our third family of arguments, those that appeal to the alleged possibility of absent qualia. Such arguments are typically directed against the functionalist thesis that mental states can be type-individuated on the basis of the causal functional relations they bear to each other and to the inputs and outputs of the relevant system. The standard and by now all too familiar absent qualia claim is that given *any* functionally specified organizational structure, it is always possible (at least in principle) to construct realizations of that structure which we have every reason to believe possess *no qualia*: realizations such as Ned Block's nation of China example in which the functional role of each state is filled by a distinct member of the population of China (Block 1978). It is claimed that the bizarre construction would realize the relevant functional organization, though it is absurd to believe that the overall construction, as opposed to its individual personal parts, actually has any qualia or phenomenal properties.

This line of argument has been much discussed and criticized, at times in subtle and successful ways (e.g. by Sydney Shoemaker 1975, 1981a). But I wish to offer a not very subtle criticism: the argument is *question begging*. Consider how it might look on reconstruction.

A3 *The absent qualia argument*

P1 Any functional model of mental organization will be capable of being realized by systems lacking qualia (or phenomenal properties): the absent qualia claim.

P2 A model M of some feature of the world F explains F (or what F is) only if nothing could be a realization of M without being F.

Therefore:

C3 Functionalism cannot explain (what) phenomenal mentality (is).

The reasoning is valid, but its premises are problematic. One might object to the claim of its second premise that nothing short of a logically or metaphysically sufficient condition counts as an adequate explanation. But the real problem is premise 1. How can the anti-functionalist know *a priori* that *any future* functionalist theory will allow for absent qualia realization? The absent qualia claim is made plausible only by construing functionalism as restricted to a highly abstract sort of *computationalism*, which requires of its realizations only that they mirror in the temporal or causal order of their states the sequence relations specified in the functional model. There is a widespread but mistaken belief that in constructing his model the functionalist cannot appeal to any relations among states other than that of *simple causation* (by which I mean causing, inhibiting or contributing to the joint causation of). So construed, it would seem that a realization by the population of China would always be possible, all we need to do is make sure that each person goes "on" and "off" in a way that mirrors the sequence of states in the model. But the functionalist need not and should not accept any such restriction on his theorizing; his job is to characterize the relations that hold among mental states, processes and properties without regard for the austere constraints of purely computational relations or relations of simple causation.

Once such constraints are rejected, the absent qualia claim no longer seems obvious. What we need to determine is whether there are functional relations into which phenomenal states can enter but non-phenomenal states cannot. The burden of proof may lie with the functionalist to show that there are such relations by coming forward with a specific theory about the roles played by phenomenal states, but his attempts cannot be rendered

dead before arrival by *a priori* appeals to inevitable absent qualia realizations.

The Functional Role of Phenomenal States: A First Attempt

One way to investigate this question is to consider the psychological roles played by phenomenal states in humans (Van Gulick 1989). Which of our human psychological abilities, if any, are dependent on our having conscious phenomenal experience? This way of asking the question has its limits. Even if it should be that certain psychological processes cannot operate *in humans* in the absence of experience, it would not follow that phenomenal experience is a necessary condition *in general* for those psychological processes or abilities. The "necessity" may be only a contingent fact about how those processes are realized in us and nothing more.

That said, let us consider a few abilities that seem *de facto* to require conscious phenomenal experience in humans. Tony Marcel (1988) mentions at least four such abilities. Two concern respects in which human subjects suffer a total (or nearly total) loss of function as the result of losing some aspect of their capacity for phenomenal experience:

1 Loss of the ability to initiate actions with respect to parts of the world lost from conscious experience though still in some sense perceived (as in cases of blindsight with respect to objects located within the blind field of a hemianopic patient).

2 Loss of the ability to form an integrated self-concept in amnesic patients as the result of losing the capacity for episodic memory (i.e. memory of past conscious experiences as such).

Two others concern less pathological limitations:

3 The inability to learn new non-habitual tasks without conscious awareness of task instructions.

4 The inability to form plans of action without conscious thought.

One might ask, "What, if anything, do these various cases of dependency on phenomenal experience have in common?" A sceptical or deflationary answer would be that they share nothing in common, or nothing more than the brute fact that the particular human representation systems that underlie or subserve those abilities just happen *accidentally* to involve representations with phenomenal content. I think we should resist such a deflationary strategy; at least we should not embrace it until we have made a thorough effort to find some psychologically interesting explanation of *why* the relevant abilities seem to require conscious phenomenal experience in humans.

In his discussion, Marcel at least implicitly suggests that all four abilities require not merely consciousness but some form of *self-consciousness* since the mental states that figure in the relevant psychological processes are all *reflexive* and *meta-cognitive in content*. That is, all the relevant processes require awareness or knowledge about some aspect of one's own mental or psychological organization or activity.

Ability 4: Both planning and control of plan execution require knowledge of one's goals and their relative priority, as well as knowledge of one's mental capacities and resources and the ability to monitor the ongoing operation of those resources in the course of execution. All of which, as Philip Johnson-Laird (1983, 1988) has argued, involves having a model of oneself.
Ability 2: The lack of personal integration noted in amnesic patients could well result from the inability to construct and update such a self-model.
Ability 3: The inability to acquire new non-habitual task behaviours might be a result of the failure of the same systems involved in action planning.
Ability 1: And even the fact that hemianopic patients do not initiate voluntary actions towards objects in the blind field might be explained on this basis as a deficit in the representation of the *world-in-relation-to-self* that is employed by the action planning system.

While I think that there may be something interestingly right about this suggestion, I find it less than satisfying as an answer to the question of *why* the relevant abilities in humans all seem to require conscious phenomenal experience. The proposed explanation is that they all involve reflexive meta-cognition (or meta-psychological knowledge.) But left unanswered is the question of why such meta-cognition should require phenomenal awareness. Meta-cognitive awareness is a straightforwardly functional process, and one should be able to build such self-directed control

and its associated iterative mental states into an organized system without having to give it anything like phenomenal awareness.

One could fall back on a *unitary version* of the *brute fact explanation* by arguing that all the relevant abilities involve higher order meta-cognition and its associated model of the self, and then claiming that it is *just a brute fact* that the self-model in humans involves phenomenal awareness. The final explanation would still terminate in a brute fact, but it would replace four independent brute fact terminations with one making it less *ad hoc*.

I am still inclined to hope for more. The account in terms of functionally defined self-monitoring and self-control offers both too little and too much to explain the role of phenomenal consciousness. Too little because it seems one could get the higher-order cognition without phenomenal experience; too much because it is doubtful that such sophisticated meta-cognitive processes are present in all the non-human animals which we believe to have some form of phenomenal consciousness (see Nelkin, 1993).

The Functional Role of Phenomenal States: A Second and More Speculative Attempt

We may gain some insight if we take a somewhat different perspective on the proposal to analyse self-consciousness in terms of reflexive meta-cognition. Most accounts of meta-cognition postulate a set of explicit higher-order processes that are distinct from the lower-level cognitive processes they monitor and control. However, as I have argued elsewhere (Van Gulick 1988a, b), meta-cognitive understanding can also be implicitly embodied in the very processes that operate on lower-level representations. In particular, a system can be said to possess information about (or understand) the intentional content of its own internal representations, in so far as its internal operations with respect to those representations are specifically adapted to their content.

In brief, this involves two steps. First, one gives a basically functionalist account of what it is to possess information (or understand) some fact in terms of having a capacity specifically to modify one's behaviour in a way which adapts it to that fact, and then one applies that general account of understanding to the special case of understanding facts about the intentional content of one's own internal system of representation (Van Gulick 1988a, b).

If we expand our account of meta-cognition to cover such cases, we can introduce a notion which may help explain what is special about phenomenal representations. The notion is that of *semantic transparency* and concerns the extent to which a system can be said to understand the content of the internal symbols or representations on which it operates. The basic idea is that the greater the extent to which the system's use of a representation reflects an understanding of its content, the more the representation can be said to be semantically transparent to the system. The relevant behaviour by the system will consist in part of behaviours connecting the symbols with the outside world through input and output relations, but will also include behaviours relating symbols to each other in ways sensitive to their content. The important point is that the understanding is embedded in the organization of the system, that is, in how it is organized to relate symbols to its input, output and each other.

Phenomenal representations, of the sort associated with normal conscious experience, involve a very high degree of semantic transparency. Indeed, they are so transparent that we typically "look" right through them. Our experience is the experience of a world of familiar objects – of desks, chairs, coffee cups and beech trees. Moreover, this transparency is to some extent an *immediately experienced feature of our conscious life*. On the whole, when we have a conscious experience, we know what we are conscious of (though there are exceptions such as infants, persons newly sighted after a lifetime of congenital blindness or patients suffering from visual agnosia). The phenomenal representations that are constructed or activated in conscious experience are normally transparent to us. We know what they represent in virtue of our capacity instantaneously and effortlessly to connect those representations with other semantically related representations.

My understanding that part of my visual field represents the presence of a telephone is in part a matter of my ability rapidly to connect that representation with a host of others concerning the structure, function and use of a telephone. It is the awareness of these transitions among representations in the seemingly continuous flow of experience that provides the phenomenal or subjective experience of understanding, our conscious feeling that we know what we are thinking about.

A bit of care is needed here. I am not claiming that a system's being able to make such automatic and rapid transitions is in itself sufficient to guarantee that it has a subjective phenomenal life and that there is *something that it is like to be* that system. I am *assuming* that human beings have a subjective life and making the more modest claim that our *subjective experience of understanding* is to be accounted for in terms of the connections and transitions that our underlying organization allows us to make within our experience.

We are now in a position to pose two last *why* questions, which are perhaps the most interesting and the most difficult, though I can at present supply only some sketchy and speculative suggestions in answer. The questions are these:

1 Why do phenomenal representations (normally) involve a high degree of semantic transparency?
2 Why do we humans use representations with phenomenal properties to construct our self-model?

I suggest we take quite seriously the Kantian notion that our conscious phenomenal experience is the experience of a world – a world of objects. Conscious experience involves more than just being in states that represent or refer to objects and their properties. In some sense, which is hard to articulate, it involves there *being* a world of objects *inherent* in the representation. Or perhaps one should say it inherently involves an interdependent structure of conscious subject and world of objects set over against one another since, as Kant taught us, the notions of subject and object are interdependent correlatives within the structure of experience. One might say that conscious phenomenal experience involves the construction of a model of the world that in some sense itself *is a world*, but is so only from the subjective perspective of the self, which in turn exists only as a feature of the organization of experience. The problem is to give some account of the objectivity and concreteness of phenomenal objects, i.e. to give some account of the fact that we *experience* them as concrete, independent and objective. How might trying to solve this problem help with our two questions?

With respect to our first question, the semantic transparency of phenomenal representation might be explained as a consequence of the fact that such representations are *of a world* in the strong sense we have been considering. Part of what makes a world a world in that sense is the density of relations and connections among the objects which are simultaneously the *constituents* of which that world is composed and also *constituted as* the objects that they are by their relations within that world. Put another way, the (experienced) objectivity of phenomenal objects consists in part of the enormous diversity of the perspectives from which they are accessible from within the representation. Any phenomenal object is delimited and defined within the representation in large part through the relations that it bears to other objects, which are in turn defined in part by the relations that they bear to it. It is in part the density of these interdefining relations that gives phenomenal objects their "thickness", their objectivity. The fact that the phenomenal representation of objects involves such dense and interdependent relations might help to account for its high degree of semantic transparency; any phenomenal representation of an object would of necessity also be a representation of its myriad relations within its world.

Solving our problem and explaining the sense in which conscious phenomenal representations are objective and *of a world* may also help to explain the importance and role of qualia such as colours. As we learned long ago from *The Critique of Pure Reason* (1781), conscious experience requires the presence of an *intuition* in the Kantian sense of the term, that is, a *continuous sensuous manifold*, whether it be the spatial manifold of perception or the merely temporal manifold of inner sense. Without such a particular manifold there is no way in which objects can be present as particular things. Thus the "thing-liness" of phenomenal experience, the sense in which objects are present to us in experience as real and concrete, requires that there be such an intuition or sensuous manifold within the structure of experience. Indeed, in clinical cases in which there is a loss of part of the sensuous manifold, reports of patients indicate (directly, or indirectly by omission) that it is subjectively as if a portion of *the world itself* has been lost. Consider this autobiographical comment by Oliver Sacks:

I didn't care to tell Nurse Sulu that she was bisected and half of her was missing. And then suddenly with a most enormous and wonderful relief, I realized I was having one of my migraines. I had completely lost my visual field to the left, and with this as would sometimes happen, the sense that there was (or ever

had been, or could be) any world on the left. (Sacks 1984, p. 98)

Qualia might then be understood as properties by which regions of such manifolds are differentiated and by which objects as particulars are delimited and located within them.

We can thus begin to see a route by which qualia might be connected with semantic transparency via the fact that phenomenal representations are *of a world* in the strong sense we have been discussing. As we noted just above, part of what makes a representation *of a world* in the relevant sense is the density of relations among objects that it specifies. In particular, such a representation should specify in very great detail the spatiotemporal relations holding among arbitrary pairs of objects within the represented world, i.e. it should carry a rich and easily accessed store of information about how any represented object is spatiotemporally related to other objects in the represented world, with perhaps some falling off of detail or precision as we move from an object's immediate neighbours to objects at a greater distance.

Sensuous manifolds provide a medium well suited for the representation of such rich and easily accessed spatiotemporal information. They have a continuous structure isomorphic to the spatiotemporal domains they are used to represent. Thus, by using qualia to delimit regions of such manifolds as representing objects, it is possible to implicitly represent a large stock of information about the relative spatiotemporal relations of those objects.

Indeed, following a suggestion by the ethologist Konrad Lorenz (1973), it is plausible to suppose that the phenomenal representation of space appeared evolutionarily with the transition from organisms whose system of spatial representation was linked to the guidance of specific behaviour patterns (such as taxes) to those with a general representation of space capable of being used to guide a wide range of behaviours in flexible and open-ended ways. Both ants and birds acquire and make use of spatial information. In so far as the ability of ants to acquire and make use of spatial information is restricted to a fairly narrow range of stimulus/response mechanisms, there is little reason to think that they have a general and central representation of space; in contrast, it is hard to imagine how birds could do without one.

What, then, have we shown with respect to our first question? I hope to have shown that in so far as the phenomenal mode of representation is *of a world* in the strong sense and involves a sensuous manifold of representation, it is particularly well suited for the construction of representations with a high degree of semantic transparency. I have not argued that phenomenal representation is either necessary or sufficient for a high degree of semantic transparency. It may be possible for active representational systems to achieve a high degree of semantic transparency using non-phenomenal representations; though phenomenal representations provide *one* design solution to the problem of achieving high semantic transparency, they need not be the *only* solution. And, conversely, it seems possible for phenomenal representations to lack a high degree of semantic transparency as seems to be the case with the visual experiences of those with visual agnosia. Such agnosia appears to result from damage to the association cortex which prevents the establishment of a normal rich network of connections to representations in other modalities; the fact that the agnosic cannot connect the representations in his visual system with those in other systems leaves him in a state of not understanding his visual experiences. For him they become semantically opaque.

Consider in this regard the hypothesis offered by Baars (1988) that one of the functions of consciousness is to "broadcast" information throughout the nervous system and make that information widely available. Here again there are possibilities for explaining in a more than brute fact way *why* phenomenal representations play the functional roles they do. As we noted above, part of the objectivity of phenomenal representation consists in the density and diversity of ways in which objects are represented. Objects within the phenomenal model are represented from many perspectives and in many different modalities which none the less harmonize and "agree". Conscious phenomenal awareness thus likely involves large-scale higher-order patterns of brain activity spanning many different sensory and representational modalities providing a very rich set of active associative links. Thus it becomes quite reasonable to think of conscious awareness as identical with (or at least part of) the process by which information is broadcast. Because of their highly integrated and multimodal content, conscious phenomenal representations require rich associative networks of activation as their basis. Thus, any type of brain activity able to serve as the neural substrate for phenomenal representations would seem of

necessity also able to fulfil the function of "broadcasting information". Some recent hypotheses about the neurological substrate of consciousness (Flohr 1991) seem to support just such a link.

With respect to our second question let me make three very brief suggestions.

1 Phenomenal representation probably predates the advent of meta-cognitive self-models in evolutionary development. Since it has the high degree of semantic transparency that is desirable in constructing a self-model, it may have been "recruited" for that application.

2 We should not forget the Kantian point that the conscious self is implicitly represented in the structure of conscious experience. Thus constructing a model of the self of the sort used in meta-cognitive process is in part a matter of making *explicit* what is at least partly *implicit* in the phenomenal mode of representation.

3 Third is the fact that having a model of the self of the sort that is lost in amnesics seems to require the presence of an intuition in the Kantian sense, that is a sensuous manifold, within which the self can be constructed or located as a self. It need not be a spatial intuition; for Kant it was merely temporal. But it seems that some sort of intuition is required, some structure with particularity, within which the isolated units of experience can be unified into the experiences of a single self. Again, the phenomenal mode of representation satisfies the design requirement for the self-model. The intuition of continuous time associated with phenomenal experience provides the required intuition within which to carry out the construction of a unified self. For amnesics it is not merely the self that is truncated and compressed into the present moment; it is time itself that shrinks.

Conclusion

None of the three families of arguments we have considered succeeds in giving a sound *a priori* reason for concluding that the phenomenal aspect of mind cannot be adequately explained in physical or functional terms. First, the *knowledge argument* turns out to be vulnerable in a wide variety of ways. Second, as long as phenomenal properties are not thought of as basic simples, filling the *explanatory gap* between the phenomenal and the physical (or functional) remains an option by continuing the step-by-step process of articulating structure within the phenomenal realm and mapping it onto the structure of underlying non-phenomenal processes. And, third, only when we have such theories will we be in a position to say without begging the question whether or not non-phenomenal representations (*absent qualia*) can play the same functional roles as phenomenal representations. The ultimate outcome of such theorizing remains an empirical question not open to *a priori* answer. As we saw above, there are reasonable prospects for articulating the structure of the phenomenal colour space, for linking semantic transparency with phenomenal objectivity and for showing why phenomenal representations serve an information-broadcasting role within the nervous system. Thus, there is at least some reason to think that future theorizing will fill the gaps and banish absent qualia.

Acknowledgements

An earlier version of this chapter was presented at the conference on "The Phenomenal Mind: How is it Possible? Why is it Necessary?" held at the Center for Interdisciplinary Studies (ZiF), Bielefeld University, Bielefeld, Germany, May 1990. The final two sections of the chapter are revised versions of material originally published in Van Gulick (1989); I am grateful to Martin Davies who encouraged me to include them and offered many acute criticisms from which I have benefited in making the revisions.

References

Baars, B. (1988) A *Cognitive Theory of Consciousness*. Cambridge: Cambridge University Press.

Block, N. J. (1978) "Troubles with functionalism." In W. Savage (ed.), *Perception and Cognition: Minnesota Studies in the Philosophy of Science, vol. IX*. Minneapolis, MN: University of Minnesota Press.

Churchland, P. M. (1985) "Reduction, qualia, and the direct introspection of brain states." *Journal of Philosophy*, 82: 8–28.

Flohr, H. (1991) "Brain processes and consciousness: a new and specific hypothesis." *Theory and Psychology*, 1: 245–62.

Hardin, C. L. (1988) *Color for Philosophers*. Indianapolis: Hackett Publishing.

Horgan, T. (1984) "Jackson on physical information and qualia. "Philosophical Quarterly, 34: 147–52.

Jackson, F. (1986) "What Mary didn't know." *Journal of Philosophy*, 83: 291–5.

Johnson-Laird, P. (1983) *Mental Models*. Cambridge: Cambridge University Press.

Johnson-Laird, P. (1988) "A computational analysis of consciousness." In Marcel and Bisiach (1988).

Kant, I. (1781) [1929] *Critique of Pure Reason*. Second edition 1787. Translated by N. Kemp Smith. New York: St. Martin's Press.

Lewis, D. (1983) "Postscript to Mad pain and Martian pain'." In *Philosophical Papers, Vol. I*. Oxford: Oxford University Press.

Levine, J. (1983) "Materialism and qualia: the Explanatory gap." *Pacific Philosophical Quarterly*, 64: 356 61.

Loar, B. (1990) "Phenomenal states." In Tomberlin (1990).

Lorenz, K. (1973) *Behind the Mirror*. New York: Harcourt Brace Jovanovich.

Lycan, W. G. (ed.) (1990a) *Mind and Cognition: A Reader*, 1st edn. Oxford: Blackwell Publishers.

Lycan, W. G. (1990b) "What is the subjectivity' of the mental?" In Tomberlin (1990).

McGinn, C. (1989) "Can we solve the mind–body problem?" *Mind*, 98: 349–66.

Marcel, A. J. (1988) "Phenomenal experience and functionalism." In Marcel and Bisiach (1988).

Marcel, A. J. and Bisiach, E. (eds), *Consciousness in Contemporary Science*. Oxford: Oxford University Press.

Nagel, T. (1974) "What is it like to be a bat?" *Philosophical Review*, 82:435–56.

Nagel, T. (1986) *The View from Nowhere*. Oxford: Oxford University Press.

Nelkin, N. (1993) "The connection between internationality and consciousness." In M. Davies and G. W. Humphreys (eds), *Consciousness*. Oxford: Blackwell Publishers.

Nemirow, L. (1980) Review of Nagel's *Mortal Questions*. *Philosophical Review*, 89: 473–7.

Nemirow, L. (1990) "Physicalism and the cognitive role of acquaintance." In Lycan (1990a).

Sacks, O. (1984) *A Leg to Stand On*. New York: Summit Books.

Shoemaker, S. (1975) "Functionalism and qualia." *Philosophical Studies*, 27: 291–315.

Shoemaker, S. (1981a) "The inverted spectrum." *Journal of Philosophy*, 74: 357–81.

Shoemaker, S. (1991b) "Absent qualia are impossible – a reply to Block." *Philosophical Review*, 90: 581–99.

Tomberlin, J. (ed.) (1990) *Philosophical Perspectives, 4: Action Theory and Philosophy of Mind*. Atascadero, CA: Ridgeview Publishing.

Tye, M. (1986) "The subjective qualities of experience." *Mind*, 95: 1–17.

Van Gulick, R. (1985) "Physicalism and the subjectivity of the mental." *Philosophical Topics*, 13: 51–70.

Van Gulick, R. (1988a) "A Functionalist plea for self-consciousness." *Philosophical Review*, 97: 149–81.

Van Gulick, R. (1988b) "Consciousness, intrinsic intentionality and self-understanding machines." In Marcel and Bisiach (1988).

Van Gulick, R. (1989). "What difference does consciousness make?" *Philosophical Topics*, 17: 211–30.

Wittgenstein, L. (1953) *Philosophical Investigations*. Translated by G. E. M. Anscombe. Oxford: Blackwell Publishers.

20

The Representationalism Debate

The Intrinsic Quality of Experience

Gilbert Harman

The Problem

Many philosophers, psychologists, and artificial intelligence researchers accept a broadly functionalist view of the relation between mind and body, for example, viewing the mind in the body as something like a computer in a robot, perhaps with massively parallel processing (as in Rumelhart and McClelland 1986). But this view of the mind has not gone unchallenged. Some philosophers and others object strenuously that functionalism must inevitably fail to account for the most important part of mental life, namely, the subjective feel of conscious experience.

The computer model of mind represents one version of functionalism, although it is not the only version. In its most general form, functionalism defines mental states and processes by their causal or functional relations to each other and to perceptual inputs from the world outside and behavioral outputs expressed in action. According to functionalism, it is the functional relations that are important, not the intrinsic qualities of the stuff in which these relations are instanced. Just as the same computer programs can be run on different computers made out of different materials, so functionalism allows for the same mental states and events in beings with very different physical constitutions, since the very same functional relations might be instantiated in beings with very different physical makeups. According to functionalism, beliefs, desires, thoughts, and feelings are not limited to beings that are materi-

ally like ourselves. Such psychological states and events might also occur, for example, in silicon based beings, as long as the right functional relations obtained.

Functionalism can allow for the possibility that something about silicon makes it impossible for the relevant relations to obtain in silicon based beings, perhaps because the relevant events could not occur fast enough in silicon. It is even conceivable that the relevant functional relations might obtain only in the sort of material that makes up human brains (Thagard 1986; Dennett 1987, chapter 9). Functionalism implies that in such a case the material is important only because it is needed for the relevant functional relations and not because of some other more mysterious or magical connection between that sort of matter and a certain sort of consciousness.

Various issues arise within the general functionalist approach. For one thing, there is a dispute about how to identify the inputs to a functional system. Should inputs be identified with events in the external environment (Harman 1988) or should they instead be identified with events that are more internal such as the stimulation of an organism's sensory organs (Block 1986)? There is also the possibility of disagreement as to how deterministic the relevant functional relations have to be. Do they have to be completely deterministic, or can they be merely probabilistic? Or might they even be simply nondeterministic, not even associated with definite probabilities (Harman 1973, pp. 51–3)?

I will not be concerned with these issues here. Instead, I will concentrate on the different and more basic issue that I have already mentioned, namely, whether this sort of functionalism, no matter how elaborated, can account for the subjective feel of experience, for "what it is like" (Nagel 1974) to undergo this or that experience. Furthermore, I will not consider the general challenge, "How does functionalism account for X?" for this or that X. Nor will I consider negative arguments against particular functionalist analyses. I will instead consider three related arguments that purport to demonstrate that functionalism cannot account for this aspect of experience. I will argue that all three arguments are fallacious. I will say little that is original and will for the most part merely elaborate points made many years ago (Quine 1960, p. 235; Anscombe 1965; Armstrong 1961, 1962, and especially 1968; Pitcher 1971), points that I do not think have been properly appreciated. The three arguments are these:

First, when you attend to a pain in your leg or to your experience of the redness of an apple, you are aware of an intrinsic quality of your experience, where an intrinsic quality is a quality something has in itself, apart from its relations to other things. This quality of experience cannot be captured in a functional definition, since such a definition is concerned entirely with relations, relations between mental states and perceptual input, relations among mental states, and relations between mental states and behavioral output. For example, "An essential feature of [Armstrong's functionalist] analysis is that it tells us nothing about the intrinsic nature of mental states . . . He never takes seriously the natural objection that we must know the intrinsic nature of our own mental states since we experience them directly" (Nagel 1970).

Second, a person blind from birth could know all about the physical and functional facts of color perception without knowing what it is like to see something red. So, what it is like to see something red cannot be explicated in purely functional terms (Nagel 1974; Jackson 1982, 1986).

Third, it is conceivable that two people should have similarly functioning visual systems despite the fact that things that look red to one person look green to the other, things that look orange to the first person look blue to the second, and so forth (Lycan 1973; Shoemaker 1982). This sort of spectrum inversion in the way things look is possible but cannot be given a purely functional description, since by hypothesis there are no functional differences between the people in question. Since the way things look to a person is an aspect of that person's mental life, this means that an important aspect of a person's mental life cannot be explicated in purely functional terms.

Intentionality

In order to assess these arguments, I begin by remarking on what is sometimes called the intentionality of experience. Our experience of the world has content – that is, it represents things as being in a certain way. In particular, perceptual experience represents a perceiver as in a particular environment, for example, as facing a tree with brown bark and green leaves fluttering in a slight breeze.

One thing that philosophers mean when they refer to this as the intentional content of experience is that the content of the experience may not reflect what is really there. Although it looks to me as if I am seeing a tree, that may be a clever illusion produced with tilted mirrors and painted backdrops. Or it may be a hallucination produced by a drug in my coffee.

There are many other examples of intentionality. Ponce de Leon searched Florida for the Fountain of Youth. What he was looking for was a fountain whose waters would give eternal youth to whoever would drink them. In fact, there is no such thing as a Fountain of Youth, but that does not mean Ponce de Leon wasn't looking for anything. He was looking for something. We can therefore say that his search had an intentional object. But the thing that he was looking for, the intentional object of his search, did not (and does not) exist.

A painting of a unicorn is a painting of something; it has a certain content. But the content does not correspond to anything actual; the thing that the painting represents does not exist. The painting has an intentional content in the relevant sense of "intentional."

Imagining or mentally picturing a unicorn is usefully compared with a painting of a unicorn. In both cases the content is not actual; the object pictured, the intentional object of the picturing, does not exist. It is only an intentional object.

This is not to suppose that mentally picturing a unicorn involves an awareness of a mental picture of a unicorn. I am comparing mentally picturing something with a picture of something, not with a perception of a picture. An awareness of a picture has as its intentional object a picture. The picture has as its intentional object a unicorn. Imagining a unicorn is different from imagining a picture of a unicorn. The intentional object of the imagining is a unicorn, not a picture of a unicorn.

It is very important to distinguish between the properties of a represented object and the properties of a representation of that object. Clearly, these properties can be very different. The unicorn is pictured as having four legs and a single horn. The painting of the unicorn does not have four legs and a single horn. The painting is flat and covered with paint. The unicorn is not pictured as flat or covered with paint. Similarly, an imagined unicorn is imagined as having legs and a horn. The imagining of the unicorn has no legs or horn. The imagining of the unicorn is a mental activity. The unicorn is not imagined as either an activity or anything mental.

The notorious sense datum theory of perception arises through failing to keep these elementary points straight. According to that ancient theory, perception of external objects in the environment is always indirect and mediated by a more direct awareness of a mental sense datum. Defenders of the sense datum theory argue for it by appealing to the so-called argument from illusion. This argument begins with the uncontroversial premise that the way things are presented in perception is not always the way they are. Eloise sees some brown and green. But there is nothing brown and green before her; it is all an illusion or hallucination. From this the argument fallaciously infers that the brown and green Eloise sees is not external to her and so must be internal or mental. Since veridical, nonillusory, nonhallucinatory perception can be qualitatively indistinguishable from illusory or hallucinatory perception, the argument concludes that in all cases of perception Eloise is directly aware of something inner and mental and only indirectly aware of external objects like trees and leaves.

An analogous argument about paintings would start from the premise that a painting can be a painting of a unicorn even though there are no unicorns. From this it might be concluded that the painting is "in the first instance" a painting of something else that is actual, for example, the painter's idea of a unicorn.

In order to see that such arguments are fallacious, consider the corresponding argument applied to searches: "Ponce de Leon was searching for the Fountain of Youth. But there is no such thing. So he must have been searching for something mental." This is just a mistake. From the fact that there is no Fountain of Youth, it does not follow that Ponce de Leon was searching for something mental. In particular, he was not looking for an idea of the Fountain of Youth. He already had the idea. What he wanted was a real Fountain of Youth, not just the idea of such a thing.

The painter has painted a picture of a unicorn. The picture painted is not a picture of an idea of a unicorn. The painter might be at a loss to paint a picture of an idea, especially if he is not familiar with conceptual art. It may be that the painter has an idea of a unicorn and tries to capture that idea in his painting. But that is to say his painting is a painting of the same thing that his idea is an idea of. The painting is not a painting of the idea, but a painting of what the idea is about.

In the same way, what Eloise sees before her is a tree, whether or not it is a hallucination. That is to say, the content of her visual experience is that she is presented with a tree, not with an idea of a tree. Perhaps, Eloise's visual experience involves some sort of mental picture of the environment. It does not follow that she is aware of a mental picture. If there is a mental picture, it may be that what she is aware of is whatever is represented by that mental picture; but then that mental picture represents something in the world, not something in the mind.

Now, we sometimes count someone as perceiving something only if that thing exists. So, if there is no tree before her and Eloise is suffering from a hallucination, we might describe this either by saying that Eloise sees something that is not really there or by saying that she does not really see anything at all but only seems to see something. There is not a use of "search for" corresponding to this second use of "see" that would allow us to say that, because there was and is no such thing as the Fountain of Youth, Ponce de Leon was not really searching for anything at all.

But this ambiguity in perceptual verbs does not affect the point I am trying to make. To see that it does not, let us use "see†" ("see-dagger") for the sense of "see" in which the object seen might not exist, as when Macbeth saw a dagger before him.[1] And let us use "see*" ("see-star") for the sense of "see" in which only things that exist can be seen.

Macbeth saw† a dagger but he did not see* a dagger.

The argument from illusion starts from a case in which Eloise "sees" something brown and green before her, although there is nothing brown and green before her in the external physical world. From this, the argument infers that the brown and green she sees must be internal and mental. Now, if "see" is "see†" here, this is the fallacy already noted, like that of concluding that Ponce de Leon was searching for something mental from the fact that there is no Fountain of Youth in the external world. On the other hand, if "see" is "see*" here, then the premise of the argument simply begs the question. No reason at all has so far been given for the claim that Eloise sees* something brown and green in this case. It is true that her perceptual experience represents her as visually presented with something brown and green; but that is to say merely that she sees† something brown and green, not that she sees* anything at all. (From now on I will suppress the † and * modification of perceptual verbs unless indication of which sense is meant is crucial to the discussion.)

Here, some philosophers (e.g., Jackson 1977) would object as follows:

> You agree that there is a sense in which Eloise sees something green and brown when there is nothing green and brown before her in the external world. You are able to deny that this brown and green thing is mental by taking it to be a nonexistent and merely intentional object. But it is surely more reasonable to suppose that one is in this case aware of something mental than to suppose that one is aware of something that does not exist. How can there be anything that does not exist? The very suggestion is a contradiction in terms, since "be" simply means "exist," so that you are really saying that there exists something that does not exist (Quine 1948). There are no such things as nonexistent objects!

In reply, let me concede immediately that I do not have a well worked out theory of intentional objects. Parsons (1980) offers one such theory, although I do not mean to express an opinion as to the success of Parson's approach. Indeed, I am quite willing to believe that there are not really any nonexistent objects and that apparent talk of such objects should be analyzed away somehow. I do not see that it is my job to resolve this issue.

However this issue is resolved, the theory that results had better end up agreeing that Ponce de Leon was looking for something when he was looking for the Fountain of Youth, even though there is no Fountain of Youth, and the theory had better *not* have the consequence that Ponce de Leon was looking for something mental. If a logical theory can account for searches for things that do not, as it happens, exist, it can presumably also allow for a sense of "see" in which Macbeth can see something that does not really exist.

Another point is that Eloise's visual experience does not just present a tree. It presents a tree as viewed from a certain place. Various features that the tree is presented as having are presented as relations between the viewer and the tree, for example, features the tree has from here. The tree is presented as "in front of" and "hiding" certain other trees. It is presented as fuller on "the right." It is presented as the same size "from here" as a closer smaller tree, which is not to say that it really looks the same in size, only that it is presented as subtending roughly the same angle from here as the smaller tree. To be presented as the same in size from here is not to be presented as the same in size, period.

I do not mean to suggest that the way the tree is visually presented as being from here is something that is easily expressed in words. In particular, I do not mean to suggest that the tree can thus be presented as subtending a certain visual angle only to someone who understands words like "subtend" and "angle" (as is assumed in Peacocke 1983, chapter 1). I mean only that this feature of a tree from here is an objective feature of the tree in relation to here, a feature to which perceivers are sensitive and which their visual experience can somehow represent things as having from here.

Now, perhaps, Eloise's visual experience even presents a tree as seen by her, that is, as an object of her visual experience. If so, there is a sense after all in which Eloise's visual experience represents something mental: it represents objects in the world as objects of visual experience. But this does not mean that Eloise's visual experience in any way reveals to her the intrinsic properties of that experience by virtue of which it has the content it has.

I want to stress this point, because it is very important. Eloise is aware of the tree as a tree that she is now seeing. So, we can suppose she is aware of some features of her current visual experience. In particular, she is aware that her visual experience has the feature of being an experience of seeing a tree. That is to be aware of an intentional feature of her experience; she is aware that her experience has a certain content. On the other hand, I want to argue that she is not aware of those intrinsic features of her experience by virtue of which it has that content. Indeed, I believe that she has no access at all to the intrinsic features of her mental representation that make it a mental representation of seeing a tree.

Things are different with paintings. In the case of a painting Eloise can be aware of those features of the painting that are responsible for its being a painting of a unicorn. That is, she can turn her attention to the pattern of the paint on the canvas by virtue of which the painting represents a unicorn. But in the case of her visual experience of a tree, I want to say that she is not aware of, as it were, the mental paint by virtue of which her experience is an experience of seeing a tree. She is aware only of the intentional or relational features of her experience, not of its intrinsic non-intentional features.

Some sense datum theorists will object that Eloise is indeed aware of the relevant mental paint when she is aware of an arrangement of color, because these sense datum theorists assert that the color she is aware of is inner and mental and not a property of external objects. But this sense datum claim is counter to ordinary visual experience. When Eloise sees a tree before her, the colors she experiences are all experienced as features of the tree and its surroundings. None of them are experienced as intrinsic features of her experience. Nor does she experience any features of anything as intrinsic features of her experience. And that is true of you too. There is nothing special about Eloise's visual experience. When you see a tree, you do not experience any features as intrinsic features of your experience. Look at a tree and try to turn your attention to intrinsic features of your visual experience. I predict you will find that the only features there to turn your attention to will be features of the presented tree, including relational features of the tree "from here."

The sense datum theorists' view about our immediate experience of color is definitely not the naive view; it does not represent the viewpoint of ordinary perception. The sense datum theory is not the result of phenomenological study; it is rather the result of an argument, namely, the argument from illusion. But that argument is either invalid or question-begging, as we have seen.

It is very important to distinguish what are experienced as intrinsic features of the intentional object of experience from intrinsic features of the experience itself. It is not always easy to distinguish these things, but they can be distinguished. Consider the experience of having a pain in your right leg. It is very tempting to confuse features of what you experience as happening in your leg with intrinsic features of your experience. But the happening in your leg that you are presented with is the intentional object of your experience; it is not the experience itself. The content of your experience is that there is a disturbance of a certain specific sort in your right leg. The intentional object of the experience is an event located in your right leg. The experience itself is not located in your right leg. If the experience is anywhere specific, it is somewhere in your brain.

Notice that the content of your experience may not be true to what is actually happening. A slipped disc in your back may press against your sciatic nerve making it appear that there is a disturbance in your right leg when there really is not. The intentional object of your painful experience may not exist. Of course, that is not to say there is no pain in your leg. You do feel something there. But there is a sense in which what you feel in your leg is an illusion or hallucination.

It is true that, if Melvin hallucinates a pink elephant, the elephant that Melvin sees does not exist. But the pain in your leg resulting from a slipped disc in your back certainly does exist.[2] The pain is not an intentional object in quite the way the elephant is. The pain in your leg caused by the slipped disc in your back is more like the afterimage of a bright light. If you look at a blank wall, you see the image on the wall. The image is on the wall, the pain is in your leg. There is no physical spot on the wall, there is no physical disturbance in your leg. The afterimage exists, the pain exists. When we talk about afterimages or referred pains, some of what we say is about our experience and some of what we say is about the intentional object of that experience. When we say the pain or afterimage exists, we mean that the experience exists. When we say that the afterimage is on the wall or that the pain is in your leg, we are talking about the location of the intentional object of that experience.

Assessment of the First Objection

We are now in a position to reject the first of the three arguments against functionalism which I now repeat:

> When you attend to a pain in your leg or to your experience of the redness of an apple, you are aware of an intrinsic quality of your experience, where an intrinsic quality is a quality something has in itself, apart from its relations to other things. This quality of experience cannot be captured in a functional definition, since such a definition is concerned entirely with relations, relations between mental states and perceptual input, relations among mental states, and relations between mental states and behavioral output.

We can now see that this argument fails through confounding a quality of the intentional object of an experience with a quality of the experience itself. When you attend to a pain in your leg or to your experience of the redness of an apple, you are attending to a quality of an occurrence in your leg or a quality of the apple. Perhaps this quality is presented to you as an intrinsic quality of the occurrence in your leg or as an intrinsic quality of the surface of the apple. But it is not at all presented as an intrinsic quality of your experience. And, since you are not aware of the intrinsic character of your experience, the fact that functionalism abstracts from the intrinsic character of experience does not show it leaves out anything you are aware of.

To be sure, there are possible complications. Suppose David undergoes brain surgery which he watches in a mirror. Suppose that he sees certain intrinsic features of the firing of certain neurons in his brain and suppose that the firing of these neurons is the realization of part of the experience he is having at that moment. In that case, David is aware of intrinsic features of his experience. But that way of being aware of intrinsic features of experience is not incompatible with functionalism. Given a functionalist account of David's perception of trees, tables, and the brain processes of other people, the same account applies when the object perceived happens to be David's own brain processes. The awareness David has of his own brain processes is psychologically similar to the awareness any other sighted perceiver might have of those same brain processes, including perceivers constructed in a very different way from the way in which David is constructed.

According to functionalism, the psychologically relevant properties of an internal process are all functional properties. The intrinsic nature of the process is relevant only inasmuch as it is responsible for the process's having the functional properties it has. I have been considering the objection that certain intrinsic features of experience must be psychologically relevant properties apart from their contribution to function, since these are properties we are or can be aware of. The objection is not just that we can become aware of intrinsic features of certain mental processes in the way just mentioned, that is, by perceiving in a mirror the underlying physical processes that realize those mental processes. That would not be an objection to functionalism. The objection is rather that all or most conscious experience has intrinsic aspects of which we are or can be aware in such a way that these aspects of the experience are psychologically significant over and above the contribution they make to function.

Of course, to say that these aspects are psychologically significant is not to claim that they are or ought to be significant for the science of psychology. Rather, they are supposed to be psychologically significant in the sense of mentally significant, whether or not this aspect of experience is susceptible of scientific understanding. The objection is that any account of our mental life that does not count these intrinsic properties as mental or psychological properties leaves out a crucial aspect of our experience.

My reply to this objection is that it cannot be defended without confusing intrinsic features of the intentional object of experience with intrinsic features of the experience. Apart from that confusion, there is no reason to think that we are ever aware of the relevant intrinsic features of our experiences.

There are other ways in which one might be aware of intrinsic features of our experience without that casting any doubt on functionalism. For example, one might be aware of intrinsic features of experience without being aware of them as intrinsic features of experience, just as Ortcutt can be aware of a man who, as it happens, is a spy without being aware of the man as a spy. When Eloise sees a tree, she is aware of her perceptual experience as an experience with a certain intentional content. Suppose that her experience is realized by a particular physical event and that certain intrinsic features of the event are in this case responsible for certain intentional features of Eloise's experience. Perhaps there is then a sense in which Eloise is aware of this physical process and aware of those intrinsic features, although she is not aware of them as the intrinsic features that they are.

Even if that is so, it is no objection to functionalism. The intrinsic features that Eloise is aware of in that case are no more psychologically significant than is the property of being a spy to Ortcutt's perception of a man who happens to be a spy. The case gives no reason to think that there is a psychologically significant difference between Eloise's experience and the experience of any functional duplicate of Eloise that is made of different stuff from what Eloise is made of.

Similarly, if Eloise undertakes the sort of education recommended by Paul Churchland (1985) so that she automatically thinks of the intentional aspects of her experience in terms of their neurophysiological causes, then she may be aware of intrinsic features of her experience as the very features that they are. But again that would be no objection to functionalism, since it gives no reason to think that there is a psychological difference between Eloise after such training and a robot who is Eloise's functional duplicate and who has been given similar training (Shoemaker 1985). The duplicate now wrongly thinks of certain aspects of its experience as certain features of certain neurological processes – wrongly, because the relevant processes in the duplicate are not neurological processes at all.

Observe, by the way, that I am not offering any sort of positive argument that Eloise and her duplicate must have experiences that are psychologically similar in all respects. I am only observing that the cases just considered are compatible with the functionalist claim that their experiences are similar.

The objections to functionalism that I am considering in this essay claim that certain intrinsic properties of experience so inform the experience that any experience with different intrinsic properties would have a different psychological character. What I have argued so far is that this objection is not established by simple inspection of our experience.

Perception and Understanding

Now, let me turn to the second objection, which I repeat:

A person blind from birth could know all about the physical and functional facts of color perception without knowing what it is like to see something red. So, what it is like to see something red cannot be explicated in purely functional terms.

In order to address this objection, I have to say something about the functionalist theory of the content of mental representations and, more particularly, something about the functionalist theory of concepts. I have to do this because to know what it is like to see something red is to be capable of representing to yourself something's being red. You can represent that to yourself only if you have the relevant concept of what it is for something to be red. The blind person lacks the full concept of redness that a sighted person has; so the blind person cannot fully represent what it is for a sighted person to see something red. Therefore, the blind person cannot be said to know what it is like to see something red.

One kind of functionalist account of mental representation supposes that mental representations are constructed from concepts, where the content of a representation is determined by the concepts it contains and the way these concepts are put together to form that representation (Harman 1987). In this view, what it is to have a given concept is functionally determined. Someone has the appropriate concept of something's being red if and only if the person has available a concept that functions in the appropriate way. The relevant functioning may involve connections with the use of other concepts, connections to perceptual input, and/or connections to behavioral output. In this case, connections to perceptual input are crucial. If the concept is to function in such a way that the person has the full concept of something's being red, the person must be disposed to form representations involving that concept as the natural and immediate consequence of seeing something red. Since the blind person lacks any concept of this sort, the blind person lacks the full concept of something's being red. Therefore, the blind person does not know what it is like to see something red.

It is not easy to specify the relevant functional relation precisely. Someone who goes blind later in life will normally retain the relevant concept of something's being red. Such a person has a concept that he or she would be able to use in forming such immediate visual representations except for the condition that interferes in his or her case with normal visual perception. So, the right functional relation holds for such a person. I am supposing that the person blind from birth has no such concept; that is, the person has no concept of something's being red that could be immediately brought into service in visual representations of the environment if the person were suddenly to acquire sight.

We are now in a position to assess the claim that the person blind from birth could know all the physical and functional facts about color perception without knowing what it is like to see something red. I claim that there is one important functional fact about color perception that the blind person cannot know, namely, that there is a concept R such that when a normal perceiver sees something red in good lighting conditions, the perceiver has visual experience with a representational structure containing this concept R. The person blind from birth does not know that fact, because in order to know it the person needs to be able to represent that fact to him or herself, which requires having the relevant concepts. A key concept needed to represent that fact is the concept of something's being red, because the fact in question is a fact about what happens when a normal perceiver sees something red. Since the person blind from birth does not have the full concept of something's being red, the person cannot fully understand that fact and so cannot know that fact.

The blind person might know something resembling this, for example, that there is a concept R such that, when a normal perceiver sees something that reflects light of such and such a frequency, the perceiver has visual experience with a representational structure containing this concept R. But that is to know something different.

The person blind from birth fails to know what it is like to see something red because he or she does not fully understand what it is for something to be red, that is, because he or she does not have the full concept of something's being red. So, contrary to what is assumed in the second objection, the person blind from birth does not know all the functional facts, since he or she does not know how the concept R functions with respect to the perception of things that are red.

This response to the second objection appeals to a functionalism that refers to the functions of concepts, not just to the functions of overall mental states. There are other versions of functionalism that try to make do with references to the functions of overall mental states, without appeal to con-

cepts. Some of these versions identify the contents of such states with sets of possible worlds (or centered possible worlds). These versions of functionalism cannot respond to the objection in the way that I have responded. It is unclear to me whether any satisfactory response is possible on behalf of such theories. For example, Lewis (1983) is forced to say that although the person blind from birth lacks certain skills, e.g., the ability to recognize red objects just by looking at them in the way that sighted people can, this person lacks no information about visual perception. I am not happy with that response, since it is clearly false to say that the person blind from birth does not lack any information.

Inverted Spectrum

I now turn to the third objection to functionalism, which I repeat:

> It is conceivable that two people should have similarly functioning visual systems despite the fact that things that look red to one person look green to the other, things that look orange to the first person look blue to the second, and so forth. This sort of spectrum inversion in the way things look is possible but cannot be given a purely functional description, since by hypothesis there are no functional differences between the people in question. Since the way things look to a person is an aspect of that person's mental life, this means that there is an important aspect of a person's mental life that cannot be explicated in purely functional terms.

In order to discuss this objection, I need to say something more about how perceptual states function. In particular, I have to say something about how perceptual states function in relation to belief.

Perceptual experience represents a particular environment of the perceiver. Normally, a perceiver uses this representation as his or her representation of the environment. That is to say, the perceiver uses it in order to negotiate the furniture. In still other words, this representation is used as the perceiver's belief about the environment. This sort of use of perceptual representations is the normal case, although there are exceptions when a perceiver inhibits his or her natural tendency and refrains from using a perceptual representation (or certain aspects of that representation) as a guide to the environment, as a belief about the surroundings. The content of perceptual representation is functionally defined in part by the ways in which this representation normally arises in perception and in part by the ways in which the representation is normally used to guide actions (Armstrong 1961, 1968; Dennett 1969; Harman 1973).

The objection has us consider two people, call them Alice and Fred, with similarly functioning visual systems but with inverted spectra with respect to each other. Things that look red to Alice look green to Fred, things that look blue to Alice look orange to Fred, and so on. We are to imagine that this difference between Alice and Fred is not reflected in their behavior in any way. They both call ripe strawberries "red" and call grass "green" and they do this in the effortless ways in which normal perceivers do who have learned English in the usual ways.

Consider what this means for Alice in a normal case of perception. She looks at a ripe strawberry. Perceptual processing results in a perceptual representation of that strawberry, including a representation of its color. She uses this representation as her guide to the environment, that is, as her belief about the strawberry, in particular, her belief about its color. She expresses her belief about the color of the strawberry by using the words, "it is red." Similarly, for Fred. His perception of the strawberry results in a perceptual representation of the color of the strawberry that he uses as his belief about the color and expresses with the same words, "it is red."

Now, in the normal case of perception, there can be no distinction between how things look and how they are believed to be, since how things look is given by the content of one's perceptual representation and in the normal case one's perceptual representation is used as one's belief about the environment. The hypothesis of the inverted spectrum objection is that the strawberry looks different in color to Alice and to Fred. Since everything is supposed to be functioning in them in the normal way, it follows that they must have different beliefs about the color of the strawberry. If they had the same beliefs while having perceptual representations that differed in content, then at least one of them would have a perceptual representation that was not functioning as his or her belief about the color of the strawberry, which is to say that it would not be functioning in what we are assuming is the normal way.

A further consequence of the inverted spectrum hypothesis is that, since in the normal case Alice and Fred express their beliefs about the color of strawberries and grass by saying "it is red" and "it is green," they must mean something different by their color words. By "red" Fred means the way ripe strawberries look to him. Since that is the way grass looks to Alice, what Fred means by "red" is what she means by "green."

It is important to see that these really are consequences of the inverted spectrum hypothesis. If Alice and Fred meant the same thing by their color terms, then either (a) one of them would not be using these words to express his or her beliefs about color or (b) one of them would not be using his or her perceptual representations of color as his or her beliefs about color. In either case, there would be a failure of normal functioning, contrary to the hypothesis of the inverted spectrum objection.

According to functionalism, if Alice and Fred use words in the same way with respect to the same things, then they mean the same things by those words (assuming also that they are members of the same linguistic community and their words are taken from the common language). But this is just common sense. Suppose Alice and Humphrey are both members of the same linguistic community, using words in the same way, etc. Alice is an ordinary human being and Humphrey is a humanoid robot made of quite a different material from Alice. Common sense would attribute the same meanings to Humphrey's words as to Alice's, given that they use words in the same way. Some sort of philosophical argument is needed to argue otherwise. No such argument has been provided by defenders of the inverted spectrum objection.

Shoemaker (1982) offers a different version of the inverted spectrum objection. He has us consider a single person, call him Harry, at two different times, at an initial time of normal color perception and at a later time after Harry has suffered through a highly noticeable spectrum inversion (perhaps as the result of the sort of brain operation described in Lycan (1973), in which nerves are switched around so that red things now have the perceptual consequences that green things used to have, etc.) and has finally completely adapted his responses so as to restore normal functioning. Shoemaker agrees that Harry now has the same beliefs about color as before and means the same things by his color words, and he agrees that there is a sense in which strawberries now look to Harry the same as they looked before Harry's spectrum inversion. But Shoemaker takes it to be evident that there is another sense of "looks" in which it may very well be true that things do not look the same as they looked before, so that in this second sense of "looks" red things look the way green things used to look.

In other words, Shoemaker thinks it is evident that there may be a psychologically relevant difference between the sort of experience Harry had on looking at a ripe strawberry at the initial stage and the experience he has on looking at a ripe strawberry at the final stage (after he has completely adapted to his operation). That is, he thinks it is evident that there may be a psychologically relevant difference between these experiences even though there is no functional difference and no difference in the content of the experiences.

Now, this may seem evident to anyone who has fallen victim to the sense datum fallacy, which holds that one's awareness of the color of a strawberry is mediated by one's awareness of an intrinsic feature of a perceptual representation. But why should anyone else agree? Two perceptual experiences with the same intentional content must be psychologically the same. In particular, there can be nothing one is aware of in having the one experience that one is not aware of in having the other, since the intentional content of an experience comprises everything one is aware of in having that experience.

I suggest that Shoemaker's inverted spectrum hypothesis will seem evident only to someone who *begins* with the prior assumption that people have an immediate and direct awareness of intrinsic features of their experience, including those intrinsic features that function to represent color. Such a person can then go on to suppose that the intrinsic feature of experience that represents red for Alice is the intrinsic feature of experience that represents green for Fred, and so forth. This prior assumption is exactly the view behind the first objection, which I have argued is contrary to ordinary experience and can be defended only by confusing qualities of the intentional objects of experience with qualities of the experience itself. Shoemaker's inverted spectrum hypothesis therefore offers no independent argument against functionalism.[3]

Conclusion

To summarize briefly, I have described and replied to three related objections to functionalism. The first claims that we are directly aware of intrinsic features of our experience and argues that there is no way to account for this awareness in a functional view. To this, I reply that when we clearly distinguish properties of the object of experience from properties of the experience, we see that we are not aware of the relevant intrinsic features of the experience. The second objection claims that a person blind from birth can know all about the functional role of visual experience without knowing what it is like to see something red. To this I reply that the blind person does not know all about the functional role of visual experience; in particular, the blind person does not know how such experience functions in relation to the perception of red objects. The third objection claims that functionalism cannot account for the possibility of an inverted spectrum. To this I reply that someone with the relevant sort of inverted spectrum would have to have beliefs about the colors of things that are different from the beliefs others have and would have to mean something different by his or her color terms, despite being a functionally normal color perceiver who sorts things by color in exactly the way others do and who uses color terminology in the same way that others do. Functionalism's rejection of this possibility is commonsensical and is certainly not so utterly implausible or counter-intuitive that these cases present an objection to functionalism. On the other hand, to imagine that there could be relevant cases of inverted spectrum without inversion of belief and meaning is to fall back onto the first objection and not to offer any additional consideration against functionalism.

Notes

The preparation of this essay was supported in part by research grants to Princeton University from the James S. McDonnell Foundation and the National Science Foundation.

1 W. Shakespeare, *Macbeth*, Act II, Scene I: Is this a dagger which I see before me, The handle toward my hand? Come let me clutch thee. I have thee not, and yet I see thee still. Art thou not, fatal vision, sensible

To feeling as to sight? or art thou but A dagger of the mind, a false creating, Proceeding from the heat oppressed brain? ... see thee still; And on thy blade and dudgeon gouts of blood, Which was not so before. There's no such thing; it is the bloody business which informs Thus to mine eyes.

2   I am indebted to Sydney Shoemaker for emphasizing this to me.

3   I should say that Shoemaker himself does not offer his case as an objection to what he calls functionalism. He claims that his version of functionalism is compatible with his case. But I am considering a version of functionalism that is defined in a way that makes it incompatible with such a case.

References

Anscombe, G. E. M. (1965) "The intentionality of sensation: a grammatical feature," *Analytical Philosophy*, second series, edited by R. J. Butler (Oxford, Blackwell); reprinted in Anscombe, G. E. M., *Metaphysics and the Philosophy of Mind: Collected Philosophical Papers, Volume II* (Minneapolis: University of Minnesota Press, 1981), pp. 3–20.

Armstrong, David M. (1961) *Perception and the Physical World* (London: Routledge and Kegan Paul).

Armstrong, David M. (1962) *Bodily Sensations* (London: Routledge and Kegan Paul).

Armstrong, David M. (1968) *The Materialist Theory of Mind* (London: Routledge and Kegan Paul).

Block, Ned (1986) "Advertisement for a semantics for psychology," *Midwest Studies in Philosophy* 10: 615–78.

Churchland, Paul (1985) "Reduction, qualia, and the direct introspection of mental states," *Journal of Philosophy* 82: 8–28.

Dennett, Daniel C. (1969) *Content and Consciousness* (London: Routledge and Kegan Paul).

Dennett, Daniel C. (1987) *The Intentional Stance* (Cambridge, Mass.: MIT Press).

Harman, Gilbert (1973) *Thought* (Princeton, NJ: Princeton University Press).

Harman, Gilbert (1987) "(Nonsolipsistic) conceptual role semantics," *New Directions in Semantics*, edited by Ernest LePore, London, Academic Press, pp. 55–81.

Harman, Gilbert (1988) "Wide functionalism," *Cognition and Representation*, edited by Stephen Schiffer and Susan Steele (Boulder, Col.: Westview Press), pp. 11–20.

Jackson, Frank (1977) *Perception: A Representative Theory* (Cambridge: Cambridge University Press).

Jackson, Frank (1982) "Epiphenomenal qualia," *Philosophical Quarterly* 32: 127–32.

Jackson, Frank (1986) "What Mary didn't know," *Journal of Philosophy* 83: 291–5.

Lewis, David K. (1983) "Postscript to 'Mad pain and martian pain'," *Philosophical Papers*, Vol. 1 (New York: Oxford University Press), pp. 130–2.

Lycan, William G. (1973) "Inverted spectrum," *Ratio* 15.

Nagel, Thomas (1970) "Armstrong on the mind," *Philosophical Review* 79, reprinted in *Reading in the Philosophy of Psychology Volume 1*, edited by Ned Block (Cambridge, Mass.: Harvard University Press).

Nagel, Thomas (1974) "What is it like to be a bat?" *Philosophical Review* 83: 435–50.

Parsons, Terence (1980) *Nonexistent Objects* (New Haven: Yale University Press).

Peacocke, Christopher (1983) *Sense and Content* (Oxford: Oxford University Press).

Pitcher, George (1971) *A Theory of Perception* (Princeton, NJ: Princeton University Press).

Quine, W. V. (1948) "On what there is," *Review of Metaphysics*, reprinted in *From a Logical Point of View* (Cambridge, Mass.: Harvard University Press, 1953).

Quine, W. V. (1960) *World and Object* (Cambridge, Mass.: MIT Press).

Rumelhart, David E. and McClelland, James L. (1986) *Parallel Distributed Processing*, 2 volumes (Cambridge, Mass.: MIT Press).

Shoemaker, Sydney (1982) "The inverted spectrum," *Journal of Philosophy* 79: 357–81.

Shoemaker, Sydney (1985) "Churchland on reduction, qualia, and introspection," *PSA 1984*, Volume 2 (Philosophy of Science Association), pp. 799–809.

Thagard, Paul T. (1986) "Parallel computation and the mind–body problem," *Cognitive Science* 10: 301–18.

Inverted Earth

Ned Block

This essay started life as a response to Gilbert Harman's "The intrinsic quality of experience" in this volume, and it retains that format even though the aim of the essay is to argue that there is an "inversion" argument for qualia realism and against functionalism that is better than the traditional inverted spectrum argument.[1] (Qualia realism in the sense that I will be using the term is the view that there are intrinsic mental features of our experience.) Those who have not read Harman's essay may want to skip the last section of this essay.

The Fallacy of Intentionalizing Qualia

To a first approximation, the inverted spectrum hypothesis is that things we agree are red look to you the way things we agree are green look to me (and we are functionally identical). There is a simple argument from the possibility of an inverted spectrum to the falsity of functionalism: if two different mental states can play exactly the same functional role, then there is an aspect of mentality (the "qualitative" aspect) that eludes characterization in terms of functional role. In terms of the machine version of functionalism: even if we are computers, if nonetheless you and I could be computationally exactly alike though mentally different (in what it is like to see something red), then the mental outruns the computational.

The "containment response"[2] to the inverted spectrum would be to give up on functionalism as a theory of experience (or at least of its qualitative aspect), retaining functionalism as a theory of the cognitive aspect of the mind. I favor this approach, but I will not pursue it here. This essay is directed against the thoroughgoing functionalist who insists on functionalism as a theory of the whole of the mind.[3] The drawback of the containment response is that it arguably commits its proponents to the possibility of a "zombie," a being that is like us in cognitive states but totally lacking in qualia.[4]

I gave a first approximation to the inverted spectrum hypothesis above. But a proper statement of it must make use of a distinction between two kinds of content of experience, one of which is a matter of the way the experience represents the world, the other of which is a matter of "what it is like" (in Tom Nagel's phrase) to have it. The former has been called intentional or representational content; the latter qualitative or sensational content.[5] In terms of this distinction, the inverted spectrum hypothesis is this: when you and I have experiences that have the intentional content look-

ing red, your qualitative content is the same as the qualitative content that I have when my experience has the intentional content looking green (and we are functionally identical). This essay will be concerned with this rather dramatic version of the claim that there is a gap between intentional and qualitative contents of experience. But the emphasis here and in the literature on this dramatic case should not make us forget that if the functionalist theory of qualia were correct, it would also preclude less systematic qualitative differences among functionally identical people, differences the hypothesizing of which though hard to work out in detail is also less vulnerable to the abuse that has been heaped on the inverted spectrum hypothesis.

If blood looks red to both of us, then in the *intentional* sense of "looks the same," blood looks the same to us. (In respect of color, that is. I will leave out this qualification from now on, and I will also ignore the fact of different shades of red for simplicity.) The *qualitative* sense of "looks the same" can be defined via appeal to such notions as "what it's like," or alternatively, by direct appeal to the inverted spectrum hypothesis itself. If your spectrum is inverted with respect to mine, then red things look the same to you – in the qualitative sense – as green things look to me.

As Shoemaker points out, it is easy to go from these senses of "looks" to kinds of content. If blood looks the same to us in the intentional sense, then the intentional contents of our experiences of it are the same. If blood looks the same to you in the qualitative sense as grass looks to me, then the qualitative contents of our experiences are the same.[6]

Now that the intentional/qualitative distinction has been introduced I can correct a vital error made by both sides of the inverted spectrum debate. My point is that if an inverted spectrum is possible, then experiential contents *that can be expressed in public language* (for example, *looking red*) are not qualitative contents, but rather intentional contents. *For suppose that spectrum inversion is rife*: there is no spectrum of the vast majority, despite widespread functional similarity in relevant respects. How could I justify the claim that red things look red to me but not to you? How could I claim that the qualitative content of my experience as of red things is *looking red*, whereas yours is, say, *looking blue*? Any argument I could use against you could equally well be used by you against me. And it will not do to say we are both right, each with our own sense of "red." "Red" is a public language word, not a word that means one thing in your mouth and another thing in mine.

Since I will be appealing to this point later it will be useful to have a name for it. I will tendentiously describe the supposition that experiential contents that can be expressed in public language such as *looking red* are qualitative contents as the fallacy of intentionalizing qualia.[7]

Note that the intentional contents of color experience must be referentially based – these contents are "Californian," not neo-Fregean. The reason is that "modes of presentation" of color experiences are qualitative contents, and qualitative contents are precisely that in which our experiences as of red things – our contents of *looking red* – can differ. What gives an experience the content of *looking red* is its relation to red things, not its qualitative content. One way to put the point would be that each of us may have our own "concept" of the look of red, where a concept is a qualitative content, but such differences in "concept" of red make no difference to whether something looks red to us. Whether something looks red to us depends on whether we are having an experience as of something red, not on our different "concepts" of red. (Recall that I am ignoring the fact of different shades of a single color.)[8]

I want to note two points about the argument against intentionalizing qualia. First, the argument is not really directed against qualia skeptics like Harman and Dennett, since they don't accept the inverted spectrum premise. Also, they already believe the conclusion on one formulation of it, namely that *looking red* is an intentional content.[9] The second point is that although I hope qualia realists are convinced, I do not intend to go into the matter in much detail here. I mentioned above that the point could be avoided by supposing that "red" and hence "looking red" is ambiguous, being privately defined by each of us in terms of his own qualitative content. I scoffed, saying that "red" is a univocal public language word. But of course the matter need not end here. And there are other more sophisticated ploys the determined defender of a qualitative definition of "red" might make. I will not pursue the matter because since this essay is directed against the qualia skeptics, a rear-guard action against other members of my team would not be good strategy. Qualia realists who are tempted to intentionalize qualia should note the power of the view that *looking red* is an intentional content in defending qualia realism in the face of the functionalist challenge.

One route to the fallacy of intentionalizing qualia among qualia realists is to define secondary quality terms in terms of the qualitative contents of the experiences they normally produce, a view shared (despite many differences of opinion) by McGinn (op. cit.) and Peacocke (op. cit.). Peacocke defines "red" in terms of "red", "red" being the name he gives to "the" quale produced by red things. Since the semantic content of "looks red" is given by that of "looks" and "red," the meaning of "looks red" is given in terms of 'red'. Such a view would not be very attractive if there is no "the" quale produced by red things.

McGinn considers the possibility that things to which we and Martians both apply "red" look to us the way things we and the Martians agree are "green" look to them. Though he remains agnostic on whether such Martians could be totally functionally identical to us (and thus agnostic on the possibility of an inverted spectrum), he concludes that in such a case, things that are red relative to us (e.g., ripe tomatoes) are green relative to them, even though both groups apply "red" to things that are the color of ripe tomatoes. Thus according to McGinn, the Martians might have always spoken a language in which "red" is applied to things just as we apply it, but nonetheless they mean green by it. But if we are willing to consider such a possibility, why not consider the possibility that those of us with short ear-lobes bear a relation to those of us with long ear-lobes that McGinn's Earthians bear to McGinn's Martians? This is not as absurd as might appear, given that there are enormous differences among normal people in the physiological machinery of color vision (see Hardin, op. cit.). Why should we try to define "red" in terms of a quale that red things are supposed to produce in all of us when we don't have any good reason to believe that there is any such thing?

My argument is not based on the idea that spectrum inversion is merely possible (though not actual). I claim that we simply do not know if spectrum inversion obtains or not. Further, even if we were to find good evidence against spectrum inversion actually obtaining, there could be a race of people otherwise very like us who have color vision, color sensations, and color terms for whom spectrum inversion does obtain. Presumably, any good theory of the semantics of color terms will apply to them as well as us.[10]

A defender of a McGinn–Peacocke analysis of color in terms of qualia might wish to allow the possibility of spectrum inversion, but insist that nonetheless our color concepts preclude spectrum inversion. The reasoning might go like this: prior to general relativity, the concept of a straight line presupposed the axioms of Euclidean Geometry, along with the idea that a straight line is the shortest distance between two points, the path of a stretched string or a light ray, the path along which travel uses up the least fuel, and the like. But general relativity plus observations revealed that Euclidean straight lines were not the paths that had the other properties just listed – those properties accompanied Riemmanian straight lines – hence the generally accepted view that space is Riemmanian. The point of the story is that before the development of general relativity and alternative geometries, the unsticking of the notion of a Euclidean straight line from the cluster of other properties was precluded by our concepts – literally inconceivable, though not actually impossible. To conceive of it required a conceptual revolution.

The application of the model to spectrum inversion is this: the application of "red" to red things, and the production by red things of the same quale in all of us, are joined by our concepts, conceptual revision being required for their unsticking. The analogy is not persuasive. In wondering whether the sunset looks to you as it does to me, I may be imagining you with an experience qualitatively like mine. In daily life, we do not usually take the possibility of spectrum inversion into account. But it would be a mistake to jump from this fact about practice to the idea that spectrum inversion is precluded by our concepts. Spectrum inversion can be understood easily by children (assuming it can be understood at all). Try it out on the next eight-year old you encounter. Indeed, they sometimes come up with the idea themselves. (My eleven-year-old daughter offered spectrum inversion as an explanation of why people seem to have different favorite colors.)

My brand of qualia realism is quasi-functional. According to me, the *intentional* content of experience is functional. An experience has the intentional content of looking red if it functions in the right way – if it is caused by red things in the right circumstances, and used in thought about red things and action with respect to red things rightly.[11] The functional roles I am talking about are what I call "long-arm" roles, roles that include real things in the world as the inputs and outputs. They are to be distinguished from the "short-arm" roles that functionalists sometimes prefer, roles that stop at the skin. It is essential to the functional role that characterizes the intentional content of *looking red* that it be caused (appropriately) by red things and cause appropriate thought about and action on red things.

So this is why my brand of qualia realism is quasi-*functional*; here is why it is *quasi*-functional: the *qualitative* content of experience is *not* functionally characterizable. Two experiences can differ functionally, hence have different intentional contents, but have the same qualitative content, that is, be alike in "what it is like" to have them. Further, two experiences can be alike in function (and hence have the same intentional content), but have different qualitative contents.

So quasi-functional qualia realism is functionalist about the intentional content of experience. And it is also functionalist about the belief that blood is red, the concept of red, and the meaning of "red."[12]

But didn't I identify color "concepts" with qualitative contents earlier? Yes, and this is certainly one reasonable way to use the concept of a concept, but one can equally well individuate concepts in line with public language meanings, as Harman does. Harman says that what makes a concept the concept of red is its production in a natural and immediate way by red things, its role in thinking about and manipulating red things, in causing the subject to judge that two things are the same color, and the like. This is something about which the quasi-functional qualia realist may as well agree with Harman. So let it be common ground that possession of the concept of red is a matter of how our experiences function, not their intrinsic qualitative properties.[13]

Harman's refutation of the inverted spectrum depends on rejecting the distinction I've been talking about between qualitative and intentional content. He claims that experience has only one kind of content: intentional content. According to Harman, two experiences with the same intentional content must be the same in all mental respects. His rejection of the distinction leads him to state and refute a version of the inverted spectrum hypothesis that involves only intentional content. His version of the inverted spectrum hypothesis is: "things that look red to one person look green to the other, things that look orange to the first person look blue to the second, and so forth," where the people referred to are functionally the same.[14] But this inverted spectrum hypothesis is made of straw. According to this straw inverted spectrum hypothesis, the experience you get on looking at red things, your experience as of red, the one that produces sincere utterances like "This is red," in the normal way – this experience might be one whose intentional content is *looking green*. But no proponent of the inverted spectrum should accept *this* inverted spectrum hypothesis. The proponent of the inverted spectrum hypothesizes inverted qualitative contents, not inverted *intentional* contents.

Perhaps misunderstanding on this matter is partly responsible for the fact that both sides of the inverted spectrum argument tend to see nothing at all in the other side. To quote Harman on the inverted spectrum from an earlier paper, "I speak of an 'argument' here, although (as D. Lewis has observed in a similar context), the 'argument' really comes down simply to denying the functionalist account of the content of concepts and thoughts without actually offering any reason for that denial."[15] The straw inverted spectrum hypothesis does indeed have this question-begging flavor, supposing as it does that there could be inverted intentional contents. The supposition that there could be inverted intentional contents amounts to the supposition that someone's concept of red might function as a concept of green without thereby being a concept of green. And that does just deny the functionalist account of concepts.

The Inverted Spectrum and Inverted Earth

Let us consider positive arguments for the possibility of an inverted spectrum. If the proponent of the inverted spectrum could establish that the burden of proof is on those who deny the possibility, then positive arguments would be unnecessary. But since no one has succeeded in establishing the burden of proof, the emphasis in the literature has been *epistemic*: science fiction cases which (allegedly) would be *evidence* for an inverted spectrum are produced and discussed.[16] The idea is that if there could be evidence for an inverted spectrum, then it is possible. For example, imagine genetically identical twins one of whom has had color inverting lenses placed in its eyes at birth.[17]

Both twins are raised normally, and as adults, they both apply "red" to red things in the normal way. But though the twins are functionally identical in the relevant respects, we may suppose that the internal physiological state that mediates between red things and "red" utterances in one is the same as the internal physiological state that mediates between green things and "green" utterances in the other. And one can argue from this to the claim that things that they both call red look to one the way things they both call green look to the other. There is much to be said on both sides of this debate. I do not wish to enter into the argument here.

Interpersonal inverted spectrum cases such as the one just mentioned have not been taken very seriously by the opposition. They suppose (as does Harman) that there is no reason to think that the different physiological realizations of the experience of red things involves any *experiential* difference. Like any mental state, the experience of red has alternative physiological realizations, and this is held to be just a case of alternative realizations of the very same experience.

The qualia realist reply to Harman is that when *we* put on the inverting lenses, grass looks red, ripe strawberries green, the sky yellow, and the like. So shouldn't we suppose that the same is true of the twin who wears the inverting lenses? Here, as elsewhere in the disputes about qualia we would do well to follow Searle's (op. cit.) advice of looking to the first person point of view. This appeal to what happens when we ourselves put on the inverting lenses suggests a version of the inverted spectrum example that involves just such a case – the *intra*personal inverted spectrum.[18]

I think it is best to treat the intrapersonal inverted spectrum as having four stages. First, we have a functionally normal person. Second, inverting lenses are placed in his eyes and he says grass looks red and blood looks green.[19] Third, after a period of confused use of color terms, he finally adapts to the point where he uses color language normally. That is, he naturally and immediately describes blood as "red" and grass as "green." At the third stage, he is functionally normal except in one important respect: he recalls the period before the insertion of the lenses as a period in which "grass looked to me the way blood now looks." Fourth, he has amnesia about the period before the lenses were inserted and is functionally totally normal – just as in the first period. The crucial stage is the third. Here we have the evidence of the victim's testimony that grass used to look to him the way blood now looks. Note that as I have described it there is no use of "quale" or other technical terms in what he says – he's just talking about the way red things look and used to look as compared with green things. At this point, he is functionally abnormal precisely because he is saying such odd things. But if we are prepared to believe him, then when he gets amnesia and is functionally normal, why should we think that his qualia have re-inverted?

The main advantage of the intrapersonal case over the interpersonal case is the availability of the subject's introspective report at stage 3. Suppose the subject is *you*. By hypothesis, you recall what grass used to look like, and you realize that it used to look to you the way ripe tomatoes now look. Is there anything incoherent about this? Dennett and Rey say yes. Dennett insists that your inclinations to say such things reflect a memory malfunction, and Rey says that we don't know what to make of what you say.[20] I concede that there is some justice in these complaints (though I disagree with them). After all, the adapted subject is not a normal person. Perhaps it can be shown that the hypothesis of confusion will always be more plausible than the hypothesis of spectrum inversion. Certainly if you think the distinction between intentional and qualitative content is a confusion, it will be natural to look for some way of avoiding taking the subject's memory reports at stage 3 at face value.

I believe that these criticisms can be defeated on their own terms, but instead of trying to do that here, I propose to take a different tack. I will describe a case that is the "converse" of the usual inverted spectrum case, a case of inverted *intentional* content and functional inversion combined with identical qualitative content. In the usual inverted spectrum case, we have two persons (or stages of the same person) whose experiences are functionally and intentionally the same but qualitatively inverted. I will describe a case of two persons/stages whose experiences are qualitatively the same but intentionally and functionally inverted. If I am right about this case, the distinction between the intentional and qualitative content of experience is vindicated, and the functionalist theory of qualitative content is refuted.

As with the usual inverted spectrum argument, mine hinges on a science fiction example. (The fancifulness of my example could be much reduced. E.g., imagine rooms to which our subjects are confined for their whole lives instead of whole planets.) I will make use of an example of

Harman's: Inverted Earth.[21] Inverted Earth differs from Earth in two respects. Firstly, everything has the complementary color of the color on Earth. The sky is yellow, grass is red, fire hydrants are green, etc. I mean everything *really* has these oddball colors. If you visited Inverted Earth along with a team of scientists from your university, you would all agree that on this planet, the sky is yellow, grass is red, etc. Secondly, the vocabulary of the residents of Inverted Earth is also inverted: If you ask what color the (yellow) sky is, they (truthfully) say "Blue!" If you ask what color the (red) grass is, they say "Green." If you brought a speaker of the Inverted Earth dialect to a neutral place (with unknown sky color, unfamiliar vegetation, and the like) and employed a team of linguists using any reasonable methods to plumb his language, you would have to come to the conclusion that he uses "red" to mean what we mean by "green," "blue" to mean what we mean by "yellow," etc. You would have to come to the conclusion that the Inverted Earth dialect differs from ours in "inverted meanings" of color words. If commerce develops between the two planets and painters on Inverted Earth order paint from one of our paint stores, we shall have to translate their order for "green paint" into an order to our stockboy to get red paint. Inverted Earth differs from earth in switched words and switched stimuli.

Further, the intentional contents of attitudes and experiences of Inverted Earthlings are also inverted. If a foreigner misreads a phrasebook and comes to the conclusion that "trash-can" means a type of sandwich, despite what he says, he does not actually want a trash-can for lunch – he wants a sandwich. Similarly, when a resident of Inverted Earth wonders, as he would put it, "why the sky is blue," he is wondering not why the sky is blue, but why it is yellow. And when he looks at the sky (in normal circumstances for Inverted Earth), the experience he has that he would describe as the sky looking "blue" is actually the experience of the sky looking yellow. There is no mystery or asymmetry here. I am using our language to describe his intentional contents; if he used his language to describe ours, he would correctly describe us as inverted in just the same way.

These two differences that I have mentioned "cancel out" in the sense that the talk on Inverted Earth will *sound* just like talk on Earth. Radio programs from Inverted Earth sound to us like radio programs from far away places where English is spoken, like New Zealand. Children on both planets ask their parents "Why is the sky blue?" "Why is grass green?"

Now let's have the analog of the intrasubjective inverted spectrum example. A team of mad scientists knock you out. While you are out cold, they insert color inverting lenses in your eyes, and change your body pigments so you don't have a nasty shock when you wake up and look at your feet. They transport you to Inverted Earth, where you are substituted for a counterpart who has occupied a niche on Inverted Earth that corresponds exactly (except for colors of things) with your niche at home. You wake up, and since the inverting lenses cancel out the inverted colors, you notice no difference at all. "What it's like" for you to interact with the world and with other people does not change at all. For example, the yellow sky looks blue to you, and all the people around you describe yellow objects such as the sky as "blue." As far as the qualitative aspect of your mental life is concerned, nothing is any different from the way it would have been had you stayed home. Further, we may suppose that your brain is exactly the same in its physiological properties as it would have been had you stayed at home. (Of course, the statements in the science of color would have to be different on both planets. Pure light of 577 nm is described by us as "yellow" and by them as "blue." So let us suppose that you and the twins in the examples to follow know nothing of the science of color, and hence these scientific differences make no difference to you.)[22]

There you are on Inverted Earth. The qualitative content of your experience of the (local) sky is just the same as the day before, when you looked at the sky at home. What about the intentional content of this experience? Here there may be some disagreement. The causal rooting of your color words is virtually entirely at home; your use of "blue" is grounded in references to blue things and to the uses of "blue" by other people to refer to blue things. For this reason, I would say that on your first day on Inverted Earth, your intentional contents remain the same as they were – that is different from the natives. At first, when you look at the sky, thinking the thought that you would express as "It is as blue as ever," you are expressing the same thought that you would have been expressing yesterday at home, only today you are *wrong*. Also, your thought is not the same as the one a native of Inverted Earth would express with the same words. Nonetheless, according to me, after enough time has passed on Inverted Earth,

your embedding in the physical and linguistic environment of Inverted Earth would dominate, and so your intentional contents would shift so as to be the same as those of the natives. Consider an analogy (supplied by Martin Davies): if you had a Margaret Thatcher recognitional capacity before your journey to Inverted Earth, and on arriving misidentify twin MT as MT, you are mistaken. But eventually your "That's MT" judgments get to be about twin MT, and so become right having started out wrong. If you were kidnapped at age 15, by the time 50 years have passed, you use "red" to mean green, just as the natives do. Once your intentional contents have inverted, so do your functional states. The state that is now *normally* caused by blue things is the same state that earlier was normally caused by yellow things. So once 50 years have passed, you and your earlier stage at home would exemplify what I want, namely a case of functional and intentional inversion together with the same qualitative contents – the converse of the inverted spectrum case. This is enough to refute the functionalist theory of qualitative content and at the same time to establish the intentional/qualitative distinction.

But what if the facts of human physiology get in the way of the case as I described it? My response is the same as the one mentioned earlier (based on Shoemaker's rebuttal of Harrison), namely that it is possible for there to be a race of people very much like us, with color vision, and color sensations, but whose physiology does not rule out the case described (or spectrum inversion). The functionalist can hardly be satisfied with the claim that our experiences are functional states but the other race's experiences are not.

The functionalist theory that I have in mind is a functional state identity theory, a theory that says that each and every mental state *is* some functional state. If mental state M = functional state F, then any instance of M must also be an instance of F. But in the Inverted Earth case just described, two instances of the same qualitative state – yours and Twin's – have different functional roles. And the qualitative state that you share with Twin cannot be identical to *both* your functional state and Twin's functional state, since that would be a case of $Q = F_1$, $Q = F_2$ and $\sim (F_1 = F_2)$, which contravenes transitivity of identity. There is still one loose end to the argument: the existence of one sort of functional description on which the two qualitative states are functionally different does not rule out the possibility of another sort of functional description on which they are the same. I will return to this matter when I consider objections to the Inverted Earth argument later.

Note that this intrapersonal Inverted Earth case does not have the weakness that we saw in the intrapersonal inverted spectrum case. In the latter case, the subject's internal disturbance renders his first person reports vulnerable to doubt. But you, the subject of the Inverted Earth case, have had no internal disturbance. Your move to Inverted Earth was accomplished without your noticing it – there was no period of confusion or adaptation. All the inversion went on outside your brain – in your inverting lenses, and in your physical and linguistic environment. The intrapersonal case has the considerable advantage of testimony for Inverted Earth as for the inverted spectrum case. But some readers may feel some doubt about the claim that after 50 years your intentional contents and language are the same as that of the Inverted Earth natives. For this reason, it may be helpful to move briefly to the interpersonal Inverted Earth case. I will be talking in terms of the interpersonal case later, but I hope the reader will refer back from time to time to the first person point of view that is better captured in the intrapersonal case.

Imagine a pair of genetically identical twins, one of whom is adopted on Inverted Earth after having had inverting lenses inserted into his eyes and body pigment changes, the other of whom grows up normally on Earth (without special lenses). To try to bring in the first person point of view, let the home twin be you. When you two look at your respective skies, you both hear "blue," and the same retinal stimulation occurs. We may suppose that you and Twin are in relevant respects neurologically the same. (We could even suppose that your brains are molecular duplicates.) But then you two are the same in the qualitative contents of your experiences, just as in the intrasubjective example, your qualitative contents were the same before and after your trip to Inverted Earth. For qualitative contents supervene on physical constitution, and your physical constitutions are relevantly the same.

Though you and Twin have the same qualitative contents at every moment, you are inverted functionally and with respect to intentional contents of experience. For in his intentional contents, Twin is the same as his friends on Inverted Earth. When Twin or any other resident of Inverted Earth thinks the thought that he would express as "The blue of the sky is very saturated," his

thought is about *yellow*. Thus your intentional contents of experience are inverted with respect to Twin's. What about functional inversion?

One's mental representation of blue – one's concept of blue, in the psychologists' sense of the term "concept" – plays a familiar role in being produced in a natural and immediate way by blue things, and in controlling one's behavior towards blue things. (Harman assumes that one's experience of blue *is* one's concept of blue; I am happy to go along; the issue is not relevant to the controversy discussed here.) I speak of the familiar role of one's concept of blue. Perhaps it would help here to think of you and Twin of both being engaged in a game. You are shown something of a certain color, and your task is to find something of the same color. I show you a ripe strawberry, and you look around, finding a matching English double-decker bus. Twin, in his corresponding situation, matches his green strawberries with a green bus.

There you and Twin are, looking at your respective skies, having experiences with just the same qualitative contents. At this very moment, you are in a state produced in a natural and immediate way by blue things, one that plays the aforementioned familiar functional role in controlling your responses to blue things. At the same time, Twin is in a state produced by yellow things, one that plays the same familiar functional role in controlling his responses to yellow things, so you are functionally inverted with respect to Twin. Think of the color matching game. The qualitative state that functions so as to guide you in matching blue target with blue sample also functions so as to guide Twin in matching yellow target with yellow sample. Of course there is considerable functional similarity between you and Twin; indeed you are functionally exactly alike if we take the border between the inside and the outside to be at the skin, including your production of the same noise "Blue again!" when you see the sky. Later I will take up the matter of whether this internal functional description can be used to avoid the criticism of functionalism that I am making.

Further, your perceptual state is about blue things whereas Twin's is about yellow things, so you are intentionally inverted. (The "inversion" has to do with the fact that yellow and blue are simply examples of complementary colors.)

Notice that I am not saying that if you and Twin were brought together into my study, you would then be intentionally or functionally inverted. (If shown a red thing and asked its color, you would produce different noises but mean the same thing by them.) The Inverted Earth case *depends* on your not being together in my study. The environmental inversion is crucial to the case, so it is no help to imagine it gone. In this respect, the Inverted Earth case gets a bit less of a grip on the imagination than the inverted spectrum case. *Those* twins can be imagined in *any* old environment, still retaining the same functional identity and qualitative inversion. But this is no real argumentative disadvantage to Inverted Earth. The reader must simply remember that the environmental inversion is part of what makes the example work, so it must be maintained.

The upshot is that if you and Twin are looking at your respective skies, saying "Still blue," you have experiences that have the same qualitative content, but inverted intentional content, and they are functionally inverted. Conclusion: the distinction between intentional and qualitative content is vindicated, and the functional theory of qualia is refuted.

The Inverted Earth argument just given can be attacked in a variety of ways. I will examine a few of them shortly, but first I want to make some comparisons with the more traditional inverted spectrum argument.

The Inverted Earth case is meant to exemplify qualitative identity plus functional and intentional inversion, whereas the inverted spectrum case is meant to exemplify the converse, qualitative inversion plus functional and intentional identity. As I mentioned earlier, the qualitative difference in the best version of the inverted spectrum case (the intrasubjective inversion) is meant to be established by the testimony of the inverted subject. As I also mentioned, the weakness of the case is that unusual things have happened inside this subject (the "adaptation" period), and so there is some doubt (taken more seriously by some philosophers than by others) that the subject's words can simply be taken at face value. The contrast with the Inverted Earth case is strong. When you are kidnapped and wake up on Inverted Earth, there is no difference at all in what it is like for you. In this case unlike the intrasubjective inverted spectrum, there is no internal disturbance to throw doubt on the subject's testimony. (Of course, any subject may miss a series of small changes, but there is no reason to suspect these in the Inverted Earth case.) Further, in the intersubjective Inverted Earth case, we have supervenience on our side. Your brain is a molecular doppelganger of Twin's,

and since intrinsic properties such as qualitative content are presumably supervenient on physical properties, we can conclude that you are qualitatively identical to Twin. Note that supervenience is asymmetrical with respect to sameness and difference. That is, the molecule-for-molecule identity of your brain with Twin's establishes that intrinsic properties like qualia are the same. But the physical difference between the brains of the inverted spectrum twins does not establish any qualitative difference between them, because the critic can always allege (as Harman does) that the physical difference is just a matter of alternative realizations of the same mental state.

The advantage of the Inverted Earth case is that there is no *internal* switch as in the inverted spectrum case. The switching goes on outside the brain. So far, the Inverted Earth argument is a better argument against functionalism than the inverted spectrum argument. But does it fare as well with respect to objections?

The first objection I want to consider is that Twin does not have the same intentional contents as his friends on Inverted Earth because when he looks at the sky he has a qualitatively different experience from the one his friends have (because he has inverting lenses and they don't). And his color judgments are answerable to the qualitative contents of his experiences. So when he says and his friends echo "The sky looks blue," what they say is true whereas what he says is false because the sky does not look blue to *him*.[23]

The first thing to note about this objection is that it assumes an inverted spectrum; it claims that Twin's spectrum is inverted with respect to that of his friends, and it uses that claim to argue that Twin's intentional contents are not the same as those of his friends. For this reason, no functionalist can accept this objection, least of all Harman. Harman insists (as I have) that the intentional content of the experience as of yellow consists in its natural and immediate production by yellow things, its role in manipulating yellow things and the like. And since Twin is the same as his friends in this respect, Harman cannot suppose he differs from them in intentional content.

Further, those of us who accept the possibility of an inverted spectrum cannot accept the objection either, since it commits the fallacy of intentionalizing qualia. If inverted spectra are possible, then the natives of Inverted Earth may differ from one another in the qualitative content produced by the sky. No one of them can be singled out as the one whose qualitative content on looking at the sky is *really* that of *looking yellow*. Intentional content cannot be reduced to qualitative content.

Note that I have not used the possibility of an inverted spectrum to defend Inverted Earth. The objection assumes an inverted spectrum, and I simply pointed out the consequences of that assumption.

Now onto a more serious objection. I have said that you are qualitatively identical to but functionally inverted with respect to Twin. At the moment when each of you are looking at your respective skies, you are in a state produced by blue things that controls manipulation of blue things, whereas Twin is in a state produced by yellow things that controls manipulation of yellow things. (Recall the example of the color matching game.) My reasoning involves thinking of inputs and outputs as involving objects in the world. But this is just one way of thinking of inputs and outputs according to one type of functional description. The existence of one functional description according to which you are an invert of Twin does not preclude other functional descriptions according to which you and Twin are functionally the same. If there are other functional descriptions according to which you and Twin are functionally the same, how can I claim to have refuted functionalism?

Indeed, there are a variety of functional descriptions according to which you are functionally the same as Twin. For example, your brain is physically identical to Twin's, so any functional description that draws the line between the inside and the outside at the surface of the brain will be a functional description according to which you and Twin are functionally the same. For internal functional organization is just as supervenient on internal physical state as is qualitative state.

But brain-internal functional states cannot capture the intentional content of experience. For that content depends on the colors in the outside world. Here is a way of dramatizing the point. The inverting lenses (and the post-retinal inverter as well) invert the color solid 180 degrees.[24] But one can just as well imagine inverters that invert the color solid by smaller amounts, e.g., 90 degrees. Imagine a series of clones of yours (and Twin's) whose lenses contain a series of different inverters. Imagine each of these clones confronted with a color patch so chosen as to produce exactly the same neural signal in each of the identical brains. If your brain is confronted with a red patch, another will be confronted with a yellow patch, another with a blue patch, etc. But you will all be having exactly the same qualitative content. If * is the neural signal that we are counting as input to your brain, * would be produced by red in your brain, by yellow in one of your clones, and by blue in another clone. So neither * nor any brain-internal functional state triggered by it can correspond to any single color in the world. The intentional content of your experience is *looking red*, whereas that of your clones are *looking yellow*, *looking blue*, etc.[25] Your intentional contents are all different, but since your brains are exactly the same (by hypothesis), and since internal functional organization is supervenient on the brain, *all* internal functional descriptions will be shared by all of you. So no purely brain-internal functional description can capture the intentional content of experience.[26]

What I have just argued is that no brain-internal functional state could be suitable for identification with an intentional content of experience. If intentional contents of experience are functional states, they are "long-arm" functional states that reach out into the world of things and their colors. But though Harman commits himself to recognizing *only* long-arm functional states, there is no good reason why the functionalist cannot recognize *both* these long-arm functional roles *and* short-arm functional roles that are purely internal. Why can't the functionalist identify intentional contents with long-arm functional states and qualitative content with short-arm functional states? The result would be a kind of "dualist" or "two factor" version of functionalism.[27]

My response: perhaps such a two factor theory is workable, but the burden of proof is on the functionalist to tell us what the short-arm functional states might be. Without some indication of what these functional states would be like we have no reason to believe in such a functional theory of qualia.[28] In terms of machine versions of functionalism, the responsibility of the functionalist is to find a characterization of qualia in terms of the "program" of the mind. Good luck to him.[29]

I have conceded that *if* there is some functional characterization of qualia, that will sink the Inverted Earth Argument. But this concession does not yield any superiority of the inverted spectrum over Inverted Earth. For the same possibility would sink the inverted spectrum argument as well. The inverted spectrum twins are supposed to be qualitatively different but functionally identical. And that is supposed to show that qualitative states are not functional states. But if there is a functional theory of qualia, it will be one on which the inverted spectrum twins are functionally different after all.

Perhaps a physiological theory of qualia is possible. If there is a physiological theory of qualia, it can be functionalized.[30] Such a move is changing the subject in the context of the inverted spectrum argument, however. Functionalism in that context is linked to the computer model of the mind. The idea is rather as if two machines with different hardware might have different qualia despite computational identity: having the same computational structure and running all the same programs. Since the issue is whether qualia are computational states, you can't legitimately defend a computationalist theory by appealing to the hardware difference itself.

Let us now turn to what is the most plausible candidate for an alternative functional description designed to make you functionally identical to Twin, namely one that exploits the fact of the inverting lenses. Let's focus on the version in which the inverting lens is installed inside the lens of the eye. Then it may be objected that when you and Twin are looking at your respective skies, you have the *same* inputs. There is blue light in *both* of your eyes, despite the fact that Twin is looking at a yellow sky. So there is no functional inversion.

I've been using a functional description (as does Harman) in which the inputs relevant to experiences as of red are red objects in the world. The objection I am considering is that the boundary between the inside and the outside should be moved inwards, and inputs should be thought of in terms of the color of the light hitting the retina, not in terms of colored objects. Here is a first approximation to my reply: you give me an independently motivated conception of the boundary between the inside and the outside of the system, and I will tailor an inverted earth example to suit. In this case the tailoring is done. You will recall that I mentioned an alternative to the inverting lenses, one that seems to me more physically plausible than the lenses, namely a neural inverter behind the retina. The retina reacts in a well understood way to triples of light wavelengths, transforming them into impulses in the optic nerve. I don't know any reason why it shouldn't be in principle possible for a miniaturized silicon chip to register those impulses and substitute transformed impulses for them.

Sensation is generally the product of the action of the world on a transducer that registers some feature of the world and outputs some corresponding signal that conveys information to the brain. The visual apparatus registers light, the auditory apparatus sound, and so forth. The natural way of thinking of inputs and outputs is in terms of impingements on such transducers. With any real transducer, there is often indeterminacy as to exactly where transduction starts or finishes. The lens of the eye could be thought of as the visual transducer, or alternatively the visual transducer could be thought of as ending at the rods and cones or one of the other layers of the retina, or in the optic nerve, or in the lateral geniculate nucleus. I could locate my inverter at any of those places. However, I suppose it could be discovered that there is a "visual sensorium" in the brain with a sharp natural boundary such that any change within it changes qualia and any change outside it does not (except by affecting its inputs). In that case, the choice of the boundary of the sensorium as the border between inside and outside would require placement of the inverter in a place that would change qualia. My response to this possibility is to note as I did in the section on the fallacy of intentionalizing qualia that there could be a type of person otherwise very like us who has color vision and color sensations but no sharp sensorium boundary. Thus I can run my thought experiments on a sort of being (perhaps hypothetical, perhaps us) that has color experience but no sharply bounded sensorium.

Awareness of Intrinsic Properties

Thus far, I have been arguing against Harman's objections to the inverted spectrum, and giving my own argument in terms of Inverted Earth for accepting the qualitative/intentional distinction, and the falsity of a functionalist theory of qualia. But there is one consideration raised by Harman that I have not yet mentioned. He says that the qualitative/intentional distinction depends on the view that we are aware of intrinsic properties of our experience. This latter view is one that he spends more than half the essay arguing against. So in order fully to examine his objection to the inverted spectrum hypothesis, we shall have to turn to his objection to the view that we are aware of intrinsic features of our experience.

Harman's primary argument is, as far as I can see, an appeal to – of all things – introspection. He says that the idea that we are aware of the "mental paint" is "counter to ordinary visual experience." Here is the main passage where the argument is given.

When Eloise sees a tree before her, the colors she experiences are all experienced as features of the tree and its surroundings. None of them are experienced as intrinsic features of her experience. Nor does she experience any features of anything as intrinsic features of her experience. And that is true of you too . . . Look at a tree and try to turn your attention to intrinsic features of your visual experience. I predict you will find that the only features there to turn your attention to will be features of the presented tree.

In my view, Harman's appeal to introspection here is an error in philosophical method. When I look at my blue wall, I *think* that in addition to being aware of the color I can also make myself aware of what it is like for me to be aware of the color. I'm sure others will disagree. The one thing we should all agree on is that this is no way to do philosophy. Our intuitions can tell us something about our concepts and our experiences so long as we use them rightly. One principle is: *Elicit simple intuitions about complex cases rather than complex intuitions about simple cases.* Looking at a blue wall is easy to do, but it is not easy (perhaps not possible) to answer on the basis of introspection alone the highly theoretical question of whether in so doing I am aware of intrinsic properties of my experience. The point of the complicated science fiction stories described above is to produce complex cases about which one can consult simple intuitions. Harman hopes to argue against the inverted spectrum by appealing to the introspective judgment that we are not aware of intrinsic features of our experience. I think he proceeds the wrong way around. If arguments such as the one I gave convince us that it is possible for qualitative content to remain the same while intentional content is inverted (or conversely), then that will settle the issue of whether we are aware of intrinsic features of our experience. Or at any rate, it will settle the matter that is really at stake: whether *there are* intrinsic mental features of our experience.

Finally, let me turn to Harman's critique of Jackson. Let us put the issue in terms of Jackson's Mary, the scientist who knows all the physical and functional facts about color perception that can be learned in a black and white environment. The issue Jackson poses is this: does Mary acquire new knowledge on seeing red? The qualia realist says she acquires genuine knowledge *that*, genuine new information, viz., knowledge that this is what it is like to see red. Lewis, Nemirow, Shoemaker, and other critics have said that what Mary acquires is something more like knowledge *how*, new skills not new information. Harman's line is that Mary *does* genuinely acquire new information, genuine knowledge that – and here he appears (misleadingly) to accommodate the qualia realist intuition – but he goes on to say that functionalism is not refuted because Mary did not know all the functional facts before seeing red. Harman says that knowledge of all the functional facts requires possession of the full concept of red, and that is a matter of being in a certain functional state. More specifically, the full concept of red must be produced in a natural and immediate way by red things and must play a certain role in thought and action with respect to red things. While she is still locked in the black and white room, Mary has no state that is produced in a natural and immediate way by red things, and plays the appropriate role in thought and action. So Mary had no such functional state before seeing red; hence she did not know all the functional facts. When she sees a red thing for the first time she acquires the concept of red, and with it the functional facts that she lacked for lack of that concept. Further, she now can be said to know that blood is red, apples are red, and the like, whereas earlier she could mouth those words, but lacking the concept of red, she did not really possess the knowledge.

In sum: Jackson says that Mary knows all the functional facts before she sees anything red, yet she learns a new fact, so the functional facts do not include all the facts. Some of Jackson's critics deny that Mary learns a new fact. Harman, by contrast, allows that Mary learns new facts on seeing red, but he denies that Mary knew all the functional facts before she saw anything red. He says she acquires a new functional fact as well, in acquiring the concept of red itself.

If Harman is right about all this – and for the sake of argument, let's suppose that he is – he has provided no argument against qualia realism; rather, he has shown that the Jackson argument does not serve very well as a locus of controversy between the qualia realist and the qualia skeptic.

The knowledge that Harman shows Mary lacks in the black and white room has little to do with the real issues about qualia. Until Mary sees green for the first time, she cannot have the full concept of green, and so she cannot have the knowledge that some olives are green. Indeed, she can't even have the false belief that all olives are green. This fact has little to do with the disagreement between the qualia skeptic and the qualia realist.

If one accepts Harman's claim that Mary can't have any beliefs about the colors of things until she leaves the black and white room, then the real issue between the qualia realist and the qualia skeptic about Mary is that the qualia realist says Mary acquires *two* types of knowledge *that* when she sees colors for the first time, whereas the qualia skeptic says she acquires only one. All can agree (assuming Harman is right about concepts) that she acquires knowledge involving *intentional* contents. For example, she acquires the concept of green and having already read the *Encyclopaedia Britannica*, she acquires the knowledge that olives are green. However, the qualia realist says she acquires knowledge involving qualitative contents in addition to the intentional contents. This is the crux of the matter, and on this, Harman's reply to Jackson is silent.

Notes

1   The reply was delivered at the Chapel Hill Colloquium, October 17, 1987. A later version of this paper was delivered at the Universities of Oxford, Cambridge, and Edinburgh; at Birkbeck College and Kings College London; and at a meeting of the Anglo-French Philosophy Group. I am grateful for support to the American Council of Learned Societies and to the National Science Foundation (DIR88 12559). I am also grateful to Martin Davies and Christopher Peacocke for comments on an earlier version, and I am grateful for useful discussions on these matters with Davies and with Sam Guttenplan.

2   Cf. John Haugeland, "The nature and plausibility of cognitivism," *The behavioral and Brain Sciences* 1/215–26, 1978.

3   In "Functionalism and qualia," *Philosophical Studies* 27/291–315, 1975 (reprinted in my *Readings in Philosophy of Psychology*, Vol. 1, Harvard University Press, 1980) Sydney Shoemaker shows how functionalism can provide identity conditions for qualia even if it abandons an attempt to characterize particular qualiatative states. Shoemaker's technique does, however, assume that "absent" qualia are impossible, an assumption that I dispute.

4   For arguments against the possibility of such a zombie, see Shoemaker, op. cit.; Colin McGinn, *The Subjective View*, Oxford University Press: Oxford, 1983; and John Searle, *What's Wrong with the Philosophy of Mind*, MIT Press: Cambridge, Mass., forthcoming. I reply to Shoemaker in "Are absent qualia impossible?" *The Philosophical Review* 89/257–74, 1980. Shoemaker responds in "Absent qualia are impossible – a reply to Block," *The Philosophical Review* 90, 4/581–99, 1981.

5   The intentional/qualitative terminology is from Shoemaker's, "The inverted spectrum," *The Journal of Philosophy* 74, 7, 1981, 357–81. This essay is reprinted with a new postscript together with other papers of Shoemaker's on the same topic (including "Functionalism and qualia") in *Identity, Cause and Mind: Philosophical Essays*, Cambridge University Press: Cambridge, 1984. The representational/sensational terminology is from Christopher Peacocke, *Sense and Content*, Oxford University Press: Oxford, 1983, chapters 1 and 2. Peacocke uses "what it is like" in a way that includes both representational and sensational content. Frank Jackson's distinction between comparative and phenomenal senses of "looks" comes to much the same thing. See chapter 2 of *Perception*, Cambridge University Press: Cambridge, 1977.

6   Peacocke, op. cit., uses a number of intriguing examples to argue for the representational/sensational distinction without any commitment to an inverted spectrum. For example, he argues that in looking at a room through one eye, one has an experience with a representational content that is the same as that of the experience one gets on looking with two eyes (the same objects are represented to be the same distances away), but the sensational contents differ. If he is right, then there is a much greater distance between the representation/sensational distinction and the inverted spectrum than I suppose. I will sidestep the issue by individuating intentional contents *functionally*. So the monocular and binocular intentional contents will be different because they function differently. For example, since we are fully aware of the difference, and can make use of it in our verbal reports of our experiences, the binocular experience can produce different reports from those produced by the monocular experience. See Michael Tye's review of Peacocke's book in *Canadian Philosophical Reviews* V/173–5, 1985, for a discussion of another of Peacocke's examples from the same point of view.

7   One qualification: It is useful to have some terms to refer to that content of experience that is mental

without being intentional. I have used "what it is like" and "qualitative content" in this way, and so I do not wish to regard these terms as referring to intentional contents.

8 The point I have been making does assume that it is often the case that objects have colors, e.g., the book I am now looking at is blue. It does not assume that questions of what color something is always have a determinate answer, nor does it deny that what color an object is is relative to all sorts of things, for example, the position of the perceiver. An expanse of color in a comic strip may be orange from a distance yet also be red and yellow from close up. If this is objectivism, I am happy to be an objectivist. See C. L. Hardin, *Color for Philosophers: Unweaving the Rainbow*, Indianapolis: Hackett Publishing, 1988, for a forceful argument against objectivism (and subjectivism).

9 Some qualia skeptics hold that there is no such thing as qualitative content whereas others believe that there is such a thing but that it is identical to intentional content. Dan Dennett seems to me to have vacillated on this issue. In "Quining qualia," forthcoming in A. Marcel and E. Bisiach, eds, *Consciousness in Contemporary Society*, Oxford University Press: Oxford, he takes a functionalist view of qualia, as he does in "Toward a cognitive theory of consciousness" in *Brainstorms: Philosophical Essays on Mind and Psychology*, MIT Press: Cambridge, Mass., 1978, 149–73. But in other papers he has been more of an eliminativist about qualia. See especially "On the absence of phenomenology," in *Body, Mind and Method: Essays in Honor of Virgil Aldrich*, D. Gustafson and B. Tapscott, eds, D. Reidel: Dordrecht, 93–113, 1979; and "Why you can't make a computer that feels pain," *Synthese* 38.3, 1978, reprinted in *Brainstorms*, 190–229. The answer to the title question (why you can't make a computer that feels pain) is that there isn't any such thing as pain.

10 This point is stimulated by Shoemaker's (op. cit.) argument against Harrison.

11 Note that I've said that the function of *an experience* is what gives it the intentional content of *looking red*; I did not say that anything at all (even something that isn't an experience) that has that function has that content. This issue – the issue of "absent qualia" – is not taken up in this essay.

12 But it is not functionalist, for reasons mentioned earlier, about the meaning of "what it is like" and "qualitative content." The view I'm defending of the semantics of color terms is similar to Paul Churchland's in *Scientific Realism and the Plasticity of Mind*, Cambridge University Press: Cambridge, 1979, ch. 2.

13 So long as the experience has *some* qualitative content or other – which it must have, being an experience. As I said in the last note, whether a non-experience could have the functional role of an experience is a matter I do not intend to discuss here.

14 W. Lycan, *Consciousness*, MIT Press: Cambridge, 1987 also puts the inverted spectrum hypothesis in this way.

15 "Conceptual role semantics," *The Notre Dame Journal of Formal Logic* 23, 2, 1982, p. 250. Lycan, op. cit., p. 60 says that proponents of the inverted spectrum hypothesis "simply ... deny the truth of Functionalism ... without argument."

16 See, for example, Sydney Shoemaker, "The inverted spectrum," op. cit., and William Lycan, "inverted spectrum," *Ratio* 15, 1973.

17 A perhaps more realistic possibility would be that of a miniature computer placed in a sinus cavity hooked into the optic nerve behind the retina that registers the output of the retina and changes the signals that represent red to signals that represent green, and so forth, feeding the transformed signals to the lateral geniculate nucleus. Many of the objections to the empirical possibility of an inverted spectrum by Harrison and Hardin are also objections to the possibility of a color inverter. See Bernard Harrison, *Form and Content*, Oxford University Press: Oxford, and C. L. Hardin, op. cit. See also Shoemaker's comment on Harrison in the paper referred to earlier (p.336 of *Identity, Cause and Mind*). Harrison and Hardin both argue in different ways that the color solid has asymmetries that prevent indetectable color inversion. As will become clear later, the main claim of this essay is one that would not be damaged if they are right, for I am claiming only that the "Inverted Earth" argument to be presented is a better argument against functionalism than the inverted spectrum argument. (Further, both arguments can avoid inverting spectacles.) However, I cannot resist mentioning that neither Harrison's nor Hardin's objections work. Hardin points out the main problems with Harrison. For example, Harrison argues that there may be more shades between some unique (primary) colors than others, rendering an inversion detectable. Hardin points out that the number of shades seen between any two colors is a highly variable matter among people with perfectly normal color vision. Hardin's own objection is that some colors (red and yellow) are warm whereas others (blue and green) are cool. But he gives no argument against the possibility of warm/cool inversion. That is, he gives no argument against the possibility that things we agree have a warm color produce the same qualitative character in you that things we agree have a cool color produce in me.

Hardin also argues that if the color-inverted person sees blood as green plus cool, epiphenomenalism would have to be true, whereas supposing he sees blood as green plus warm verges on incoherence. These claims – at least the first – draw their plausibility from the fallacy of intentionalizing qualia. The reason that the possibility of seeing blood as green plus cool is supposed to involve epiphenomenalism is that it is supposed that seeing blood as cool-colored would lead to saying and acting as if it were cool-colored, which is incompatible with the functional (and therefore behavioral) identity presupposed in the inverted spectrum hypothesis. But this claim depends on thinking of the inverted spectrum as intentional inversion. Suppose that the qualitative property that leads you to say something is red and leads me to say something is green is Q_a whereas Q_b has the opposite effect. And suppose that the qualitative property that leads you to say something is warm-colored and leads me to say something is cool-colored is Q_x, whereas Q_y has the opposite effect. There is no threat of epiphenomenalism in my experiencing red things via the qualitative content $Q_b + Q_y$. The appearance of an epiphenomenalism problem comes only from the fallacy of intentionalizing qualia via thinking of $Q_b + Q_y$ as having an intentional content involving coolness.

18 I said that when we put on the inverting lenses, grass looks red, so am I not committed to the claim that for the inverted twin as well grass looks red? No. Grass looks to the *temporary* wearer of the lenses the way red things normally look. But the inverted twin is not a temporary wearer: grass looks to him the way green things normally look.

19 This stage is broken into parts in a way that adds to its power to convince in Shoemaker, op. cit.

20 See Dennett's "Quining qualia," op. cit., and Rey's *Mind without Consciousness: A Discrepancy between Explanatory and Moral Psychology*, forthcoming from MIT Press.

21 "Conceptual role semantics," op. cit., p. 251. I have an earlier but clumsier example to the same effect, in "Troubles with functionalism," pp. 302–3 (n. 21), in my *Readings in Philosophy of Psychology*, Vol. 1. Harvard University Press: Cambridge, Mass., 1980. See also Ron McClamrock's use of Harman's example for a different purpose in his 1984 Ph.D. thesis, MIT.

22 In my clumsier example (mentioned in the last note) I had the inverting lenses and the switched color words, but instead of the yellow sky and the like on Inverted Earth, I had my events take place in a remote arctic village where (I supposed) the people had no standing beliefs about the colors of things.

23 This objection is suggested by the McGinn–Peacocke view mentioned earlier according to which the intentional content ("representational content" in Peacocke's terminology) of an experience as of red is defined in terms of its qualitative content (sensational content).

24 I am thinking of an inversion of the constant brightness hue-saturation wheel.

25 Since your qualitative contents are the same but your intentional contents are all different, *looking red* is not a qualitative content. Thus we see that the Inverted Earth case can be used to unmask the fallacy of intentionalizing qualia, just as the inverted spectrum case can.

26 What makes the difference between the intentional content of the experience of *looking red* and *looking blue* is the connection between these experiences and the colored objects in the world. Therefore any conception of content that leaves out the connection between experience and the world will have no way of distinguishing between these different intentional contents. "Narrow content," the aspect of content that is "inside the head" is just such a conception of content, and so it is not hard to see that the "narrow content" of *looking red* and *looking green* must be the same. In my "Functional role and truth conditions," *Proceedings of the Aristotelian Society*: Supplementary Volume LXI/157–81, I argue that a theory that uses Harman's "long-arm" functional roles (the ones that I have adopted here) is equivalent to a "two-factor" theory utilizing "short-arm" functional roles plus a referential component.

27 See the paper referred to in the last note for a discussion of such a two-factor theory in the context of propositional attitudes.

28 I also think an "absent qualia" argument would doom any such proposal; but I cannot go into that here.

29 I take the view that thought is functional, but that the best bet for a theory of qualia lies in neurophysiology. See my "Troubles with functionalism," op. cit.

30 As advocated by Lycan, op. cit., 1987. I described this idea as "physio-functionalism" in my "Troubles with functionalism," op. cit.

PART VII

Emotion

Introduction

As we saw in the Introduction to Part I, most philosophical research on the emotions has tried to understand them as complexes of more commonplace propositional attitudes. This is usually called the "cognitive" approach, though that term misleadingly suggests that the research has attended closely to cognitive science. Until recently, philosophers of the emotions have all but ignored related work in cognitive psychology, ethology, evolutionary biology, and neuroscience.

Griffiths (1997) argues that "the emotions" do not constitute a single kind. Rather, they break up into three kinds, that are only very loosely related to each other: affect-program responses, which are biology-based, culturally invariant short-term states of fear, anger, lust, and the like; the higher cognitive emotions that are culturally influenced, such as shame and vengefulness; and what Griffiths calls "socially sustained pretenses," such as "the vapors." There is no reason to think that a single theory of "the emotions" should or could cover all three of these domains.

Nash (this volume) presents a fairly sophisticated cognitive theory. It draws nothing essential from any natural science, but it does suggest an evolutionary explanation for the motivational phenomena that are Nash's focus. Griffiths (this volume) advances a psychoevolutionary theory of affect-program responses, and tries to explain why common sense might have erroneously assimilated other "emotions" to these.

Further Reading

Philosophical works

Ben-Ze'ev, A. (1987) "The nature of emotions," *Philosophical Studies*, 52, 393–409.

de Sousa, R. (1987) *The Rationality of Emotion*, Bradford Books/MIT Press.

Gordon, R. M. (1987) *The Structure of Emotions*, Cambridge University Press.

Greenspan, P. (1988) *Emotions and Reasons*, Routledge.

Griffiths, P. (1997) *What Emotions Really Are*, University of Chicago Press.

Harré, R. (ed.) (1986) *The Social Construction of the Emotions*, Oxford University Press.

Lyons, W. (1980) *Emotion*, Cambridge University Press.

Marks, J. (1982) "A theory of emotions," *Philosophical Studies*, 42, 227–42.

Rey, G. (1980) "Functionalism and the emotions," in A. Rorty (ed.) *Explaining Emotions*, University of California Press.

Rorty, A. (ed.) (1980) *Explaining Emotions*, University of California Press.

Solomon, R. (1977) *The Passions*, Doubleday.

Stocker, M. (1987) "Emotional thoughts," *American Philosophical Quarterly*, 24, 59–69.

Scientific works

Clark, M. S. and Fiske, S. (eds) (1982) *Affect and Cognition*, Lawrence Erlbaum Associates.

Lewis, M. and Rosenblum, L. (eds) (1978) *The Development of Affect*, Plenum Press.

McNaughton, N. (1989) *Biology and Emotion*, Cambridge University Press.

Plutchik, R. (1980) *Emotion: A Psychoevolutionary Synthesis*, Harper and Row.

Plutchik, R. and Kellerman, H. (eds) (1980) *Emotion: Theory, Research and Experience, vol. 1: Theories of Emotion*, Academic Press.

Scherer, K. R. and Ekman, P. (eds) (1984) *Approaches to Emotion*, Lawrence Erlbaum Associates.

21

Two Theories

Cognitive Theories of Emotion
Ronald Alan Nash

There is widespread agreement in philosophy that an adequate theory of emotion must be a cognitive theory. There is rather less agreement on the general form such a theory should take. Yet there is evidence of a growing consensus that a *purely* cognitive theory is inadequate, even when such a theory is broadly construed to include conative as well as cognitive conditions.[1] The chief objection to the Pure Cognitive Theory is that it fails to do justice to the *passive* aspect of emotion: the sense in which a person in an occurrent emotional state is upset, perturbed, agitated, or moved.[2] William Alston put the point succinctly in a well-known article:

> we cannot identify emotions with evaluations alone, without completely losing contact with such phrases as "emotional reaction," "getting emotional over it," and "controlling one's emotions." An evaluation can be either emotional or unemotional. Two people can see a snake as equally dangerous, and yet one is gripped with fear while the other is calm. (Alston 1967, p. 485)

On Alston's view, only a theory which is in part noncognitive – in short, a Hybrid Cognitive Theory – can account for the passivity of emotion. The difference between emotional and unemotional evaluations, he goes on to suggest, is that an emotional evaluation causes (in the evaluator) typical bodily disturbances and sensations (Alston 1967, p. 486). To be emotionally upset or perturbed is,

for example, to tremble or quiver or shudder with fear.

Proponents of the Pure Cognitive Theory go astray, according to William Lyons, because they ignore a rich tradition of physiological research:

> Excepting their denial that emotions are feelings, philosophers have had very little to say about the "bodily motions" part of emotions, particularly in recent times, even though, somewhat ironically, it is this very aspect of emotions which distinguishes them from being just beliefs and desires of certain sorts.[3]

I think Alston and Lyons are right in demanding an account of the passivity of emotion. But we should be wary of accepting the "bodily motions" thesis, despite the supporting empirical data. For that thesis rests on two assumptions, neither of which bears close scrutiny. The first assumption is that, since physiological changes (and sensations) accompany emotion, and since these changes clearly count as a way of being affected, then being emotionally upset (perturbed, agitated, moved) essentially consists in undergoing such changes. The second assumption is that the Pure Cognitive Theory, given the resources at its disposal, is incapable of providing an account of emotional affect. The first assumption, I shall argue, involves a fallacy; the second, a misconception.

I consider the first assumption in section 2. Alston and Lyons largely ignore the question of the significance of "bodily motions," and I show that an inquiry into the functional role of these phenomena does not reveal clear and important effects on intentional action (as opposed to mere behavior). I present my positive thesis in Section 3 in connection with the second assumption. The Hybrid Theory, I argue, underestimates the power of its rival; and I show how a version of the Pure Theory can offer a better account of the passivity of emotion. My thesis (in its unqualified form) is that what makes some evaluation/desire complex emotional is not its association with typical physiological changes, though such changes may accompany all or most emotions; it is rather the presence of a focused attention of a particular sort on the object of emotion, resulting in the agent's overvaluation of that object (relative to his dispassionate evaluation of it). This cognitive account of passivity, I note, has considerable power: it can explain why emotional action is sometimes unreasonable, ill-advised, or impetuous; and why controlling one's emotions is thought to be a worthwhile project, at least on some occasions.

1 Cognitive Theories: Pure and Hybrid

What I call a Pure Cognitive Theory is one that analyzes an emotion solely in terms of beliefs, desires, and other intentional states.[4] Its chief contemporary proponent is Robert Solomon. In his book *The Passions* he claims that an emotion is an "evaluative (or normative) judgment, a judgment about my situation and/or about all other people" (Solomon 1976, p. 187). However, Solomon's slogan, "emotions are judgments," is only a battle cry; his theory implicitly includes reference to an agent's desires and goals. My anger at John for stealing my car, he notes, is not identical with my judgment that John has wronged me; for I might make such a judgment in an impersonal and uninvolved way, without caring one way or the other (Solomon 1980, pp. 258, 276). What is distinctive about emotional judgments is that they are "self-involved and relatively intense evaluative judgments.... The judgments and objects that constitute our emotions are those which are especially important to us, meaningful to us, concerning matters in which we have invested our Selves" (Solomon 1976, p. 188).

At first sight, Solomon appears to have a solution to the problem of distinguishing emotional from unemotional evaluations. But his answer,

while suggestive, is unsatisfactory in two respects. First, it is an important fact about emotions that they are in some sense "intense" experiences. But judgments – unlike desires and sensations – do not appear to be the sorts of things that admit of degrees of intensity. Beliefs admit of degrees of *certainty* (or confidence) of course, and perhaps that is what we have in mind when we say "S has a passionate belief (believes passionately) in (that) *p*." On the other hand, if "passionate belief" is taken to indicate a disposition to emotion when, for example, the belief is contradicted, then "passionate belief" must be analyzed in terms of emotion and not the other way round. Second, as one of Solomon's critics has pointed out, judgments which are especially meaningful to us are not *ipso facto* emotional: in a clear-sighted moment a woman may make the dispassionate judgment that her adored husband is a drunkard and a liar (Robinson 1983, p. 733).

Another move open to Solomon (which he doesn't explore) is to characterize the intensity of an emotion in terms of strength of desire. But this too is problematic. It is not just that one would then face the difficult task of specifying the threshold that a desire must exceed in order for some evaluation/desire complex to count as emotional. A more serious objection is that there are (or could be) strong desires which are not part of, or connected to, an emotion. An agent may want something very badly – say, to visit Paris this summer – yet his desire may not be an emotional one. That is, he may have this desire yet have no tendency to feel joy if his desire is satisfied and disappointment if it is not. His visiting Paris this summer simply figures high on his list of preferences, and receives due consideration in his future planning.

Perhaps this sounds strange, even pathological. What sort of desire must this be if its satisfaction or frustration is not the occasion for emotions like joy or disappointment? Such a desire, I concede, is unlike the strong desires of typical humans, which do lead to emotion in relevant circumstances. My point here is that *the concept* of a desire (or a strong desire) does not *entail* a disposition to emotion, given relevant beliefs. It is not implausible to suppose that there could be intelligent beings, more or less like us, who lacked emotion altogether. I see no reason to think that, in virtue of their tepid temperaments, such beings must lack strong desires as well. A phlegmatic agent need not be an apathetic one.

Emotional states thus appear to involve more than evaluative judgments and desires, however strong. The Hybrid Cognitive Theory promises to supply the additional conditions. Its starting point is the language we use to describe occurrent emotions, language which is clearly inappropriate in connection with dispassionate states of mind. Consider Alston's example of fear. Though two agents evaluate a snake as dangerous, want to avoid harm, and take steps to avoid the danger, one is gripped with fear while the other remains calm. The frightened man, we say, is upset or disturbed; he is distracted or perturbed. We say he trembles or quivers or shudders with fear. The linguistic data do not, of course, present us with a ready-made theory. Exactly what these expressions refer to – and whether they refer to the same phenomena – is an open question. The Hybrid Theory, as I understand it, takes some of these descriptions as fundamental and analyzes the others in terms of them.

The fundamental descriptions refer to bodily disturbances: trembling, blushing, perspiring, and so on. There is a corresponding set of descriptions from the first-person point of view: emotional subjects undergoing such disturbances report experiencing pangs, throbs, tingles, burnings, and other sensations. The exact nature of these bodily disturbances is a subject for empirical investigation. Experimental psychologists have identified a number of peripheral effects of neurological changes like adrenaline secretion; these effects include increases in heart and respiratory rates, alterations in blood flow to various parts of the body, and changes in blood pressure and digestive processes. These effects, it appears, regularly accompany emotional behavior in higher mammals; that is, behavior like flight, attack, foraging, distress vocalization, and so on. Similar effects are noticed in humans in connection with a much wider but roughly analogous range of behavior (see, e.g., Panksepp 1982). The fact that experimental psychologists have intensively studied these phenomena is taken by the Hybrid Theory as a definite point in its favor. It suggests, if not confirms, the hypothesis that, to be emotionally upset or perturbed, is to be affected by peripheral bodily disturbances.[5]

Insofar as the Hybrid Theory focuses on these phenomena it can be seen as a descendant of William James's theory of emotion (James 1892). But where James *identified* an emotion like fear with a certain pattern of physiological changes and bodily sensations, the Hybrid Theory regards these phenomena as only a component – albeit an essential component – of an emotion. Where James was committed to the claim that each of the different emotion-types – fear, anger, jealousy, grief, etc. – is distinguished by a unique pattern of bodily disturbances and feelings, the Hybrid Theory follows the Pure Theory in individuating the various emotions according to types of judgments or beliefs. What makes a certain psychological state anger, for example, is that an appropriate causal chain of mental and bodily states begins with: (a) the evaluation that someone has been treated unjustly; and (b) the desire that people (or at least some people, namely, this one) not be treated unjustly. These states then give rise to: (c) some distinctive sort of bodily disturbance, the exact nature of which is to be determined by scientific investigation; (d) certain sensations which are the subjective experience of some or all of the bodily disturbances; and (e) a desire to act in some characteristic way (e.g., rectify the injustice, seek revenge). Now it could turn out that each emotion-type has, as James thought, a unique pattern of physiological changes and sensations associated with it. But thus far neither introspection nor experimental psychology has tended to confirm James's view. It may be instead that there are only a few different types of bodily disturbance (and sensation) associated with emotion, such that several emotion-types – say, shame and embarrassment or disappointment and depression – have as a component the same sort of bodily disturbance. Or it could be that the bodily disturbances associated with some emotions also occur in the absence of emotion; say, as a result of illness or drugs. The Hybrid Theory hedges its bets by individuating the various emotion-types solely in terms of evaluative beliefs and dispositional wants.

2 Objections to the Hybrid Theory

The Hybrid Theory looks to be an ideal marriage of cognitive and feeling theories. Yet in crucial respects it is essentially an orthodox (i.e., pure) cognitive theory that makes only token concessions to the Jamesian view. For according to Lyons, evaluations not only serve to individuate emotions, they also explain the desires to act typical of many emotions: "the evaluation of the object, event or situation, which the subject of an emotion makes, leads [him] both rationally and causally to certain specific desires, which in turn lead to behavior in suitable circumstances" (Lyons 1980, p. 49). For example, the urge to flee typical of fear arises, in Lyons's view, as the rational product of the agent's evaluation of danger and his desire to avoid harm.

It is here, I believe, that the Hybrid Theory runs into trouble. The problem is not, however, the use of the term "rational" to describe emotional behavior; for there is still plenty of room for irrationality on this account, since emotional action is regarded as rational given the agent's beliefs and desires, which may not themselves be rational. Rather my objection concerns the role that bodily disturbances and feelings are supposed to play in emotion. For if emotional desires are explained by antecedent evaluations and desires (which need not be emotional), what difference does it make if the subject of the emotion also undergoes certain bodily disturbances and sensations? These phenomena will, no doubt, make a difference in a person's subjective experience and, to some extent, in his appearance; but they do not, according to the Hybrid Theory, have any appreciable effect on his intentional actions or tendencies to action.[6]

Suppose for example that a human being lacked the neurological mechanisms that give rise to these bodily disturbances; and suppose the mechanisms in question have no other causal role. Would this defective human lack emotion? According to the Hybrid Theory he would, despite the fact that he may nonetheless flee from danger, seek revenge when insulted, attempt to avoid embarrassing situations, and in general exhibit a wide range of typically "emotional" behavior. He would not, of course, blush with embarrassment or tremble with fear; he would not display typical *signs* of emotion. But why suppose that these signs or symptoms are necessary to emotion? After all, a patient may have a disease yet exhibit none of the typical symptoms.

Now there is no reason, perhaps, why bodily changes and sensations *must* have some causal role (e.g., in producing action) in order to be essential components of emotion. It may be sufficient that they are part of some whole (constituting an emotion) in which some parts (e.g., beliefs and desires) do have such causal roles. However, these other parts of emotion (the beliefs and desires) may occur in the absence of emotion, and this leaves the problem of understanding how emotions function as distinctive explanations of action.

So my objection to the Hybrid Theory may not be a fatal objection; it may be that certain bodily disturbances are not merely symptoms of emotion

but (in part) constitute emotion. My present point is that the objection is nevertheless an unanswered objection and that the problem of distinguishing emotional from unemotional evaluations really involves two questions. The first asks for an account of emotion sufficient to distinguish, e.g., the terrified man who flees out of fear from the fearless man who flees out of prudence. That is: what conditions must obtain, in addition to the presence of relevant beliefs and desires, in order for an emotional state to be the case? The second question concerns the significance of the additional conditions: what do they help us to explain, given that emotions have some explanatory role? Alston and Lyons have quite a lot to say about the first question, but neither addresses the second.

To answer the second question we need to look more carefully at the differences between emotional and dispassionate action. It is of course true that emotions do not always lead to action. Sometimes they only lead to tendencies to action; tendencies which may be inhibited or controlled. In other cases an emotion may lead to inaction; a person suffering from depression, for example, tends to neglect his typical interests and activities. In yet other cases there may be no tendency to action or inaction; but the subject of the emotion is nonetheless perturbed or upset or moved: his emotion has produced certain alterations in his typical (i.e., nonemotional) mental life. An account of the passivity of emotion ought to shed some light on all these cases. I shall begin with an example where an emotion issues in action; in section 3 I offer an account of that example which is applicable to the other cases.

Before presenting that example let me note a methodological point. As mentioned above, emotions admit of degrees of intensity. Fear, for example, embraces a range of cases extending from mild apprehension to absolute terror; and anger includes the spectrum from slight petulance to full-blown rage. At the low end of the scale emotions converge with dispassionate attitudes; and in some cases it may be difficult to tell whether some particular mental state (or states) is (are) an emotion. But this vagueness needn't stand in the way of attempts to define the concept of emotion; what is needed is an account of the characteristics which become increasingly predominant as we move up the scale of intensity. (We also need an account of why those particular characteristics are essential.) In accordance with this view I think it is worthwhile beginning with a case of intense emotion where such characteristics should be clearly evident.

My example concerns the differences in behavior of two individuals, Pat and Ray. Pat is a passionate person who is subject to strong emotions, and who often acts on the basis of those emotions. Ray is a mostly rational agent who usually acts on the basis of his considered judgments. I shall imagine that Pat and Ray make the same evaluation of a situation, and have the same attitudes or preferences with respect to that situation. But where Pat's evaluation leads to an intense occurrent emotion, Ray remains cool and composed. I then compare their respective actions given these assumptions, and consider how Pat's emotion explains his actions. Imagine the following case:

Pat and Ray go to see a film at their local cinema. They have been there many times before, since the cinema is showing a series on the political situation in Central America, and both Pat and Ray hold strong views on human rights. There is a large crowd and they take seats near the back of the theater. Part way through the film they smell smoke and soon the cry of "Fire!" echoes through the hall. Smoke begins to waft into the theater, apparently coming from the direction of the lobby (the oil in the popcorn machine has ignited). Both Pat and Ray take the situation to be dangerous, though it is not yet difficult to breathe. But where Ray remains cool, Pat becomes very frightened: he feels terror-stricken and looks around anxiously for a route to escape. He leaps from his seat and rushes for what he takes to be the nearest exit – the lobby – and tramples a small boy and his mother who are standing in the aisle. Fortunately for Pat, Ray has surveyed the situation and has realized that everyone can be evacuated safely if they proceed in an orderly fashion through the two exits at the front of the theater. Ray helps up the boy and his mother, and goes to the lobby to assist Pat, who is nearly overcome by smoke. They go back into the theater and join the line of patrons filing patiently to safety through the exits near the screen.

Aside from the fact that I imagine the majority of movie-goers in the example as more closely resembling Ray than Pat, I think the scenario is a plausible one. Consider now the differences in action between Pat and Ray.

Ordinarily, we would explain those differences by saying, "Pat acted as he did because he was frightened; Ray was not." But we need to be more precise than that; what exactly does it mean to say that Pat was frightened, and how does his fear explain his actions? We cannot reply simply that Pat evaluated the situation as dangerous and wanted to avoid harm. For as I imagine the case, Ray shares those beliefs and desires yet is not in a state of fear.

It might be argued that, though Pat and Ray share certain beliefs and desires, they differ with respect to other antecedent beliefs and desires. Pat, it might be said, rushes for the lobby to escape the fire because he is unaware of other possible exits; and he tramples the people in the aisle in his urge to reach safety because he lacks concern for the welfare of others.

But I have constructed the example to rule out these possibilities. Pat and Ray have been to the theater many times before, and it is assumed they are equally familiar with its layout (they have stared at the two exit lights many times while waiting for a film to begin). And since both hold strong views on human rights, it is assumed they have an equal concern for the welfare of others. But it is consistent with these shared beliefs, attitudes, and desires, I think, that Pat, under the influence of fear, is led to act just as he does.

Pat's fear might be summed up in terms of the thought "*I must get out of here now*." I am not suggesting that Pat necessarily says this to himself (though he may) or that he even has a conscious thought which approximates it. Rather his actions seem to assume a desire of this sort; it explains why he rushes for the nearest exit (a poor choice as it turns out), and why his concern for the welfare of others takes a back seat to his concern for his own safety. This desire in part distinguishes his case from that of Ray, who does not have such a desire. Ray has a slightly different desire; his desire might be expressed by the thought "I must get out of here now." Unlike Pat, Ray does not desire only his own safety; he is concerned for himself (perhaps above all) but not only for himself. And where Pat's "now" is a virtually unqualified immediate "now," Ray's "now" is more in the order of "as soon as possible, consistent with the reasonable satisfaction of the needs of others."

But how is it that Pat finds himself seized with the desire "*I must get out of here now*" and Ray does not? One answer is that explanation terminates at this point; that our answer cannot go beyond "Because he (Pat) is afraid." Or perhaps we can say a little more; we can say:

1 Pat differs from Ray insofar as Pat has some dispositional state such that, when he finds himself in a situation resembling the present one, he is likely to be seized with a desire like "*I* must get out of here *now*".

A second answer is one that the Hybrid Theory might give. Lyons's view, as noted above, is that emotional desires are the rational product of antecedent beliefs and desires. But this is clearly inadequate. It is true that Pat's desire to flee is supported by his evaluation of danger and desire to avoid harm. But these states are not alone sufficient to explain the peculiar *urgency* of his desire; after all, Ray shares these states but his desire to flee is rather different. We thus expect the Hybrid Theory will complement this account with some reference to Pat's bodily disturbances and sensations. But how do these bodily changes contribute to Pat's desire and subsequent action? As I see it, the Hybrid Theory has two possible responses.[7] Both, however, seem to me unsatisfactory.

One response is that bodily feelings are motivational insofar as they are pleasant or painful. If Pat is motivated by certain bodily sensations – caused by constriction of the chest, rapid heartbeat, perspiring palms, and so on – it must be because

2a Pat finds his sensations unpleasant and his actions are designed to eliminate or relieve those sensations; or
2b Pat's sensations directly cause his urgent desire to flee.

I will set aside (2b); it is a version of the terminal explanation response: it says that emotional desires are caused by state *S* and that this fact is brute and inexplicable. There may be nothing wrong with this general answer. However it is unlikely, in humans, that the sensations directly cause desires; desires appear to be "central," sensations "peripheral." It is more likely that the sensations *and* the desire are caused by some third state. This then leaves open the question why we should regard the sensations and corresponding bodily disturbances as essential to, rather than by-products of, emotion.

Response (2a) is more interesting. Does Pat flee because he wishes to avoid having certain present sensations? He might, if we attribute certain other beliefs to him: namely, a causal hypothesis about

the origin of his unpleasant feelings. For Pat does not, on the face of it, appear to take steps to eliminate his feelings; rather he seems bent on avoiding the danger presented by the fire. If his feelings are indirectly connected to his desire to flee the theater, a plausible explanation would need to posit a bridge between this desire and the aversion to certain feelings, i.e., the belief that the feelings are caused by the present situation and that eliminating the cause will eliminate the effect.

But do we need to attribute these beliefs to Pat? Do we have any reason to do so? Pat could, of course, have such beliefs as the (partial) cause of his actions. Or his fleeing could be motivated by his desire to escape danger *and* his desire to eliminate his present unpleasant sensations. (This might explain why Pat's desire is more urgent than Ray's; Pat has two reasons to flee). What counts for theoretical purposes is first, whether Pat's actions (or desires) *must* have this sort of causal history (i.e., involving aversion to feelings); and second, if not, whether this causal history is *typical* of emotion (or at least of fear).

I think it is obvious that this causal history is not a necessary condition for the desire to flee. Pat may simply want to avoid the dangerous situation in the theater. A cast of other possibilities (avoiding his ex-wife, preventing his car from being towed, etc.) wait in the wings for confirming evidence. Indeed, the causal history in question, though not recherché, is rather special; in relatively few cases are sensations the (or an) object of emotion. The sort of aversion-behavior characteristic of disgust, for example, may centrally involve the desire to avoid certain unpleasant feelings. But it is implausible to take this sort of case as standard. Perhaps it gives us grounds for recognizing the role of bodily disturbances in *some* emotions.

The fact that bodily disturbances are typically associated with many emotions needn't guarantee that they play a central role in action; Pat, for example, may have such disturbances, yet only be dimly aware of them. It would not be surprising, for example, to hear Pat say, in recounting his adventure, that "only after I reached safety did I become aware that my heart was pounding, that I was trembling..." Such an admission strongly suggests that Pat may have an urgent desire to flee in the absence of any aversion to his present sensations. Response (2a) is thus unsatisfactory as a general account.

Another response consists in positing a different indirect role for the bodily disturbances. It might be argued that Pat's actions – choosing a poor escape route despite his knowledge of the environment, and trampling bystanders despite his concern for the welfare of others – are not the result of an especially urgent desire for his own safety. Rather we could say that Pat's desire to escape is exactly similar to Ray's, but the disparity in their actions is due to additional influences on Pat which effect the execution or satisfaction of his desire. Pat's bodily disturbances, the response runs, interfere with his process of decision; they somehow inhibit cool calculation and balanced judgment. How do they do this? A plausible answer is

3 Pat *is distracted* or diverted by his experience of profound changes taking place in his body, changes over which he has little or no control.[8]

The result is not that Pat loses his concern for the welfare of others; rather he simply doesn't notice his trampling of the woman and her son. Similarly, he chooses to escape via the lobby not because he is concerned to find the nearest exit, but because the lobby is the only exit that comes to mind. To this might be added the hypothesis that Pat also fails to examine his own beliefs and decisions; he neglects, or is unable, to ask himself the right questions.

I find (3) intriguing, though it too is problematic. First, as I noted in connection with (2a), at the moment of decision Pat may only be dimly aware of the disturbances in his body, and this makes it unlikely that he is distracted by them. Second, the distraction argument would work only for emotions where the bodily disturbances are fairly intense; but not all emotions fall into this category. Third, and most importantly, it is decidedly more plausible to suppose that Pat's attention is focused on the danger rather than on his sensations. For one thing, this is a *simpler* explanation. We know, *ex hypothesi*, that Pat evaluates his situation as dangerous and wants to avoid harm. If his attention is concentrated exclusively on the contents of these states, it might explain his actions, given his other, apparently contradictory, states of mind (his geographical knowledge and other-directed concerns).[9]

I develop this explanation in the next section. Before abandoning the Hybrid Theory, however, there is an objection that deserves to be answered. It might be thought that my survey of possible connections between physiological changes and emotional action ignores some plausible candidates. The release of adrenaline (and other hormo-

nal changes) are seen by ethologists as having adaptive functions for different organisms in life-challenging circumstances. One such function is preparing the body for action: increases in heart and respiratory rates, for instance, serve to marshal an organism's resources for flight or fight. Another function is communicative: the resulting changes in appearance alert others to the organism's state of mind and may succeed in, e.g., deterring an attacker or drawing aid.

I don't wish to underestimate the role that physiological changes may play in emotion. But it should be noticed that neither of these functions speak to the issue at hand. Though Pat may indeed be energized by a rush of adrenaline, the resulting peripheral changes contribute to the *efficiency* of actions performed in satisfaction of his emotional desire, and not to the formation of the desire itself.[10] Perhaps Pat's bodily changes enable him to trample the boy and his mother (or do a "better" job of trampling them); but, for all we know, he would still try to do so in the absence of such changes. His ill-advised rush to the lobby might be less energetic if he were not affected physiologically; but this is not to say that he would thereby opt for another route of escape. Similar arguments, I take it, apply to the communicative function: the informational content of Pat's terrified appearance is undoubtedly important; but it has no apparent effect on his intentional actions (except via the effect of the actions of others on Pat's subsequent intentional actions, where the actions of others are modified by Pat's terrified appearance).

Let me sum up the gist of the argument thus far. The Pure Cognitive Theory (or at least Solomon's version of it) seems unable to account for the sense in which a subject is affected emotionally. The Hybrid Theory tries to fill this gap by analyzing affect in terms of peripheral bodily changes and sensations, where these phenomena are causal effects of evaluations. However, one may wonder whether these bodily disturbances are merely signs or symptoms of emotion rather than essential components. Alston and Lyons say little to allay these suspicions. An inquiry into the functional role of these bodily phenomena shows there is in fact little to say; these phenomena have important effects on *behavior*, but not on *intentional action*, except for the rather special case where sensations are the object of emotion. This conclusion, combined with two plausible assumptions, leads to the verdict that the Hybrid Theory is on the wrong track. The first assumption is that emotional action frequently has distinctive features not shared by dispassionate action. My example, I trust, makes that claim plausible. The second is that an emotional agent acts as he does because he is upset or perturbed. If that thesis were false, emotions would not play the explanatory role they do in our commonsense psychology.

The Hybrid Theory's first mistake is that it underestimates the Pure Cognitive Theory. To show this will be the burden of the next section. The mistake is, I think, an easy one to make; for the Pure Theory has not been well defended by its supporters. Once that mistake is made, it is natural to commit a second error: to adopt the bodily motions thesis without careful examination of its explanatory potential. For that thesis is not only the best available alternative, it comes certified with the seal of scientific research.

3   A New Cognitive Theory

The principal difference between Pat and Ray, I have argued, is that Pat's desire to act is especially *urgent*. His desire is not merely a strong desire, however; Ray may want just as badly to escape the danger. Pat has a special and immediate concern for his own safety: his desire can be summarized in terms of the thought "*I must get out of here now.*" The challenge is to explain how is it that Pat is seized with this desire and Ray is not, given that both evaluate the situation as dangerous and want to avoid harm. One answer, which I have labeled the terminal explanation response, posits a direct and inexplicable causal link between this desire and some dispositional state of Pat (operating in tandem with his other beliefs and desires). Thus far I have not objected to that answer. But I believe it is less than satisfactory. For one thing, it is not very informative. For another, it does not promise a unified (or relatively unified) theory of emotion.

Though the particular example of fear I discuss clearly involves an urgent desire to act, that is not the case with every occurrent emotion or even every intense occurrent emotion. Suppose Diane is severely disappointed that she has not been accepted to medical school. Her disappointment need not give rise to some urgent desire to act. Indeed, she may be rendered incapable of action; she may be hurt and confused, muddled and bewildered. She is nonetheless emotionally upset and perturbed. The terminal explanation response would need to posit a number of different states, each giving rise to a different form of affect (urgent desire, bewilderment, etc.). Or, perhaps, it could posit some single state which has different effects depending on the agent's evaluation of his situation. But such a theory would be pluralistic; it would not offer a unified account of emotion, except (perhaps) at the physiological level.[11] As I note in section 4, some degree of pluralism is inevitable in the theory of emotion. But I think we can do better than the terminal explanation response; I think a Pure Theory can offer an account which can illuminate the cases of both Pat and Diane, as well as numerous others.

The central concepts of the New (Pure) Cognitive Theory are *focus of attention* and *overvaluation*. In the remainder of this section I offer a sketch of the theory and show how it can be applied to a range of cases. In the following section I consider what the theory does and does not entail, reply to several objections and note some of the theory's limitations.

Applied to the example of fear, the New Theory proposes the following account. Though Pat and Ray are in similar psychological situations, Pat also has some dispositional state E that is activated by this situation. (Ray may have a functionally similar state that is "kicked in" by different inputs). One output of E is an intensification of attention on the content of certain states: typically, the beliefs and desires which trigger E. As a result, Pat fails to access relevant information in his possession and he neglects considerations which would normally have a role in his decisions.

The beliefs and desires which trigger E are Pat's evaluation of danger and his desire to avoid harm. As a result of E (and these other states) he is completely absorbed with thoughts of danger and concern for his own safety, though the situation is not yet a crisis; this preoccupation leads to, or is implicit in, the desire "*I must get out of here now.*" Though in possession of relevant knowledge – the location of the various exits – he does not stop to reflect on the best route of escape: he follows the first stratagem that comes to mind. Unluckily, he flees towards the smoke-filled lobby, a poor choice. His preoccupation also leads him to neglect considerations which would normally figure in his planning: his concern for the well-being of others is pushed into the background, and he callously tramples others in his desperate urge to escape.

Pat's emotional desire need not be the outcome of some explicit chain of reasoning. Once he perceives the danger he is quickly seized with the urgent desire to flee. It may be that he forms this desire as the result of some rapid but unconscious computation, distinguished by the focus of attention described above. But I needn't make that (plausible) assumption in order to distinguish my view from the terminal explanation response. For even if Pat's desire is a direct effect of the hypothetical state I call E (in conjunction with relevant evaluations and desires), the New Theory differs from the terminal explanation response in identifying certain essential features that are implicit in that desire; it involves an *obsessive overvaluation*: a focus of attention on particular aspects of the situation, resulting in a disproportionate weighting of the facts. As I shall argue, it is these features which are applicable to cases of emotional passivity not characterized by especially urgent desires.

In an important sense Pat's actions are irrational; it is just this sort of case that lends credence to the popular view that an emotional response is not a rational response. At the same time, there is a sense in which Pat acts rationally, given his (irrational) overvaluation; if his life is in imminent danger (as it appears to him), it makes sense to escape through the nearest exit, leaving others to fend for themselves. However, not every case of an urgent emotional desire to act can be rationally reconstructed in this way. Consider a case of anger. Ira has been overlooked for a choice assignment; a co-worker with less seniority has been handed the job. Ira sees himself as the victim of an injustice, and he finds himself preoccupied with thoughts of revenge. The desire for revenge is arguably a classic case of irrationality; not only is revenge unlikely to correct the apparent injustice, it may lead to further injustice. (It is true that revenge may sometimes have a deterrent effect; but the vengeful person typically has retribution, not deterrence, in mind).

Now Ira forms the desire for revenge in part because he is entirely preoccupied with the injustice. He tends to overvalue certain facts – namely, the injustice he perceives himself as suffering – because he is unable, or finds it difficult, to consider other facts bearing on the situation. It may be that the co-worker has relevant talents that he does not; or perhaps the employer is saving an even choicer assignment for Ira. But these possibilities do not even occur to him. His anger has become a criterion of salience; he only perceives his own talents, the defects of his rival, and the animosity of his employer. Though the injustice, if genuine,

is relatively minor, Ira tends to blow it out of proportion; he regards it as disgraceful and criminal.

How does this tendency to overvaluation contribute to the desire for revenge? The explanation here is not as obvious as in the example of fear; Ira's desire is not the rational outcome of his overvaluation of injustice and his desire not to be a victim of it. The tendency for aggressive counterattack may be instinctual or "hard-wired"; a complete explanation may require an evolutionary account of emotion. Thus the terminal explanation response has some currency. But the obsessive overvaluation is nonetheless relevant; it serves as a trigger for the aggressive reaction: the more extreme the evaluation, it seems, the greater the tendency to seek revenge.

The notion of an obsessive overvaluation applies equally to cases of emotion not distinguished by an urgent desire. Consider the case of Diane, disappointed at her failure to be accepted to medical school. Her fondest hope has been frustrated and she is hurt and bewildered. She doesn't know where to turn; she finds herself brooding over her failure and her uncertain future. But things are not as bad as they appear; she is young and bright and a world of possibilities await her. Were she not emotionally affected she would sit down calmly and map out her options: she could take a graduate degree in biology or reapply to medical school or pursue her interests in medical ethics. But these possibilities receive little weight in her reflections. For her attention is focused squarely on her failure; she sees her years of work as wasted, her ideals an illusion, the encouragement of her teachers a cruel joke. Fortunately this emotionally induced loss of perspective is usually temporary; when the shock of disappointment passes she will likely be in a better position to make rational plans for her future.

Diane may also be affected physiologically as the result of her evaluation. She may feel "down" or "blue"; she may have little energy and no appetite. These bodily changes, perhaps, make it even more difficult for her to deal with her situation in a rational and constructive way. I do not deny that physiological changes of the sort proposed by the Hybrid Theory have some role in emotion. What I deny is that bodily changes *constitute* being emotionally upset or perturbed, or are even necessary to such a state. For imagine that Diane is *not* affected by peripheral physiological changes; it would nonetheless be fair to describe her as emotionally affected on the basis of her obsessive overvaluation. On the other hand, if she were affected bodily but not cognitively we might describe her as "moved"; but such a description would have little point: it would not connect up in any interesting way with her beliefs and goals.

The explanatory power of the New Theory should be evident from these examples. I note some of the limits of the theory in the next section. By way of concluding this sketch of the theory let me mention one of its other virtues. Solomon's version of the Pure Theory seems unable to account for the intensity of emotion; beliefs and judgments do not seem to be the sorts of things which admit of degrees of intensity. The New Theory shows that there are in fact two parameters of belief that allow us to measure the intensity of an emotional state. First, attentional focus itself admits of degrees; a person may be mildly interested in or completely absorbed by some state of affairs. Another mode of intensity is a typical product of attentional focus: overvaluation. Though beliefs do not admit of degrees (except along the scale of certainty or confidence), evaluation terms do admit of such degrees: an agent may evaluate a situation as better or worse, less or more dangerous, unjust, disappointing, embarrassing, etc. Since an emotional agent's evaluation of a situation tends to be more extreme than it would be in the absence of emotion, we can measure the intensity of his state according to the degree to which his evaluation diverges from his dispassionate norm.

I call this account a "new" cognitive theory. Its central idea is hardly new, however; it can be traced back at least to Descartes, who remarked that the passions "almost always cause the good things, as well as the evil, to seem much greater and more important than they are; so that they incite us to seek after the one and flee from the others with more ardor and care than is desirable" (Descartes 1911, sec. 138). A number of contemporary writers have also alluded to concepts like attention and salience (Rorty 1980; Calhoun 1984). But this view has not, to my knowledge, been systematically developed; most importantly, it has not been developed as an alternative to the Hybrid Theory's analysis of passivity.

4 Objections and Limits

The chief objections to my theory concern attentional focus and overvaluation. Does the theory commit us to regarding every instance of attentional focus as an emotion? Since attention is always directed to something or other (at least during waking life), does this mean every conscious person is always in some emotional state? Or, if focus of attention entails some minimum period of attention, does this mean that we are not in some emotional state only when our attention flits rapidly from one thing to another? With respect to overvaluation: does the theory make it a matter of definition that emotions are irrational or unreasonable? If so, how does it rule out the existence of plausible cases like appropriate anger or shame? Why is it impossible to have an emotional judgement which is proportionate to its object?

As far as attentional focus is concerned, the questions above rest on a misunderstanding of my use of the phrase. We can distinguish between *active* and *passive* attention; the difference between, say, my thoughts of tomorrow's session with the dentist, and my dentist's thoughts of that same session. Where the dentist carries out a prior intention to plan for tomorrow's appointments – she sits down at four o'clock and reviews the next day's cases – I find myself at four o'clock dwelling on the impending experience of being in the dentist's chair, despite my earlier intention to avoid thinking about it. When the dentist finishes her planning, her attention turns elsewhere; mine, however, remains on the dreaded future prospect, thought it may occasionally shift elsewhere. I require considerable effort to avoid thoughts of the dentist's drill; for her the shift in topic is effortless.

It is not so much that I think *longer* about tomorrow's appointment, though I probably do. My case may present difficulties, and the dentist may spend considerable time examining X-rays, checking reference works, and so on. (Her reflections may also include thoughts of me as a person, not just a set of molars). It is rather that I am *prepossessed* by (or with) certain thoughts; her psychological life at four o'clock is best described with active verbs like "reflecting" and "deliberating."

I use the phrase "attentional focus" to indicate this passive sort of attention. Though it is probably true that a significant portion of mental life consists in thoughts and images that are not deliberate – that simply occur, randomly, by association or as a result of perception – only a minority of these are emotional. The emotional thoughts are, in the first place, evaluative. They also tend to be powerful and persistent: unlike many nondeliberate thoughts, emotional ones have important links with desire and action.

The objections to overvaluation are more challenging. Isn't it possible for a person to be in an occurrent state of anger–even an intense state of anger–yet his anger be in just proportion to its object? Moreover, aren't there situations where it is right or appropriate for a person to be angry? Similarly, does it follow from the fact that a man is in love that his attitude towards the beloved is disproportionate or unreasonable?

To answer these objections we should first distinguish questions about the universality of overvaluation in emotion from questions about the value of such overvaluation. It could be that anger is sometimes right or appropriate *because of* the tendency to overvaluation. (Perhaps this tendency helps to ensure active opposition to injustice). I will set the normative issue aside and consider whether it is fair to assume that all emotions involve overvaluation.

Three characteristics of emotion should be kept in mind when reflecting on this question. First, emotions admit of degrees of intensity; and this intensity (I have argued) is proportional to the degree of attentional focus and overvaluation. So it is possible for a person to be angry while exhibiting only a subtle degree of overvaluation. Second, I claim only that emotions involve a *tendency* to overvaluation; and this tendency may be overridden by other beliefs and desires. So a person may be angry, yet betray no obsessive overvaluation. Third (and most importantly), my concept of overvaluation should be understood in relative terms; not in terms of some objective standard of rationality, but rather in terms of the emotional subject's everyday dispassionate attitudes. For obviously a person's dispassionate judgments may be over- (or under-) valuations; in the absence of emotion he may have an inflated sense of his self-worth or believe that the injustice in South Africa is real but minor. Emotion has no monopoly on unreason. But what emotions tend to do is *amplify* judgments and attitudes: when this same person is in the relevant emotional states his sense of self-worth expands to massive proportions (pride) and his evaluation of racial injustice moves up the scale from minor to serious (anger or indignation). Though both emotional judgments are overvaluations relative to the agent's dispassionate beliefs, the second is nonetheless a fair and appropriate evaluation from the point of view of normative reason. So it is possible, within the framework of the New Theory, for an instance of anger (or any other emotion) to involve judgments which are objectively in just proportion to their objects.[12]

There may be cases, however, where attention (of the passive sort) is concentrated on some situation and an overvaluation is virtually impossible. A grief-stricken parent who views the death of her young child as tragic and catastrophic can hardly be regarded as guilty of an overvaluation; and indeed, it is hard to imagine that her dispassionate evaluation (were she able to view the situation dispassionately) would be any different. Yet the New Theory can still distinguish her emotional state from a dispassionate state involving the same judgment: while grief-stricken she finds it difficult to think of anything but her loss. Notice also that, if her grief were so intense that it persisted beyond a decent interval, it would be appropriate to offer her the gentle reminder that life does, and must, go on.

I turn now to the case of love. That case seems at first a fairly weak counterexample to my theory, since the process of "falling" in love is so often represented by poets as a (wonderful) sort of irrationality. But ecstatic passionate love is of course not the only sort of love; there is also the case of steady and durable devotion. And it doesn't seem that loving devotion necessarily involves overvaluation. Such a case presents a problem because we cannot say that the emotional attitude is sensible because the emotion is weak; for the beloved in this case cannot fairly charge her lover with not loving her deeply enough.

A better answer, I think, is that loving devotion is largely dispositional. It counts as an emotion because it involves a disposition to experience other emotions in typical circumstances, e.g., anxiety and sympathy when the beloved is ill. These emotions typically involve the sorts of obsessive overvaluations I have discussed. If the devoted lover did not tend to experience these emotions in relevant circumstances, we could still label his attitude "love." But we would not describe him as "emotional." "Love" in this case would denote a dispassionate evaluative judgment rather than an emotion. Emotion-terms do not always denote emotions: I may fear it is going to rain or regret leaving the party early, yet "fear" and "regret" may not refer to emotional states.

Finally, let me acknowledge some of the limitations of the New Theory. Though the theory can, I believe, illuminate a wide range of cases, it cannot handle every case. There are momentary emotions

– cases of surprise and irritation, for example – that are too fleeting to involve the sort of focus of attention I have described. Perhaps emotional affect, in these cases, is best described in terms of bodily changes and sensations. There are other cases like joy where the emotion begins with a focus on some particular object – a financial windfall, say – but then develops into a generally joyful mood where relatively many things are seen as in a rosy glow. This sort of case is at least partly amenable to analysis by the New Theory: the focus of attention is not on a particular object, but on *aspects* of the world in general. Certain features of the world – namely, the positive ones – stand out, and others recede. But in this case, unlike the momentary cases, the agent's cognitive state – his general point of view – has undergone a transformation. Relative to his dispassionate state (and, sadly, the world) his perspective constitutes an overvaluation.

It is unrealistic, I think, to expect any theory of emotion to capture every case; emotional phenomena are simply too diverse. Any theory bold enough to attempt a thoroughly unified account of emotion is inevitably sentenced to death by counterexample. Yet there are cases and there are cases. The momentary emotions that give the New Theory trouble are, I think, fairly trivial. One of the merits of the New Theory is that it addresses the morally interesting cases: those in which emotion leads to action (or inaction or cognitive transformation) that cries out for explanation. One of the glaring weaknesses of the Hybrid Theory is that it has most to say about the trivial cases. Let me conclude by mentioning a final example: a nontrivial case that poses problems for the New Theory and which one would expect the Hybrid Theory to handle nicely. However, I am not convinced that the Hybrid Theory can in fact illuminate this case; and this suggests the alternative to the New Theory may lie elsewhere.

Consider the rather curious emotion of embarrassment. Embarrassment involves the subject's evaluation that he is the object of the attention of others, and a desire not to be such an object. But embarrassment is selective; not even very shy people have a universal aversion to being the object of attention. Why then this aversion in some situations? We cannot say that the relevant features of embarrassing situations always involve others noticing one's defects or inadequacies, for a person can be embarrassed by (justified) compliments as

well as by criticisms. One can be embarrassed without being ashamed.

It may be possible to explain the aversion-behavior typical of embarrassment without solving the mystery of why people get embarrassed. For the fact is, embarrassment is an unpleasant experience; the subject of embarrassment is bothered by feelings of self-consciousness. He might not mind being an object of attention – many people don't – if the attention didn't make him feel awkward and uneasy. In order to minimize these feelings he tries to shift attention to another topic or in some way make himself inconspicuous. Or at least he has a tendency to do so; he may just grin and bear it while at the same time wishing he were elsewhere.

An organism that lacked feelings might have no reason to avoid or minimize the embarrassing situation; it would not *feel* embarrassed. It is tempting to conclude from this that the Hybrid Theory is, after all, on the right track: a full-blown theory of emotion should include feelings as well as evaluations and desires, at least with respect to some emotions. But there is a problem about the nature of (some) emotional feelings that the Hybrid Theory may be ill-equipped to handle. According to that theory, emotional feelings are bodily sensations caused by disturbances in the periphery of the body. These sensations (or the bodily changes which give rise to them) are caused by, *inter alia*, certain evaluations. But the sensations themselves have no intentionality; they are mere throbs, pangs, and tingles. They count as feelings *of* fear or anger or embarrassment insofar as they bear the right sort of causal connection with the relevant evaluations. But the example of embarrassment should make us suspicious of this account. It seems to me that the experience of the embarrassed person cannot be divided into an evaluation *and* certain feelings. However, we can make such a distinction in the case of bodily feelings. One can imagine having all the bodily symptoms associated with fear in the absence of any evaluation of danger. (Apparently injections of adrenaline can produce such symptoms.) But can we imagine feelings of self-consciousness without some reference to the attention of others? It seems to me we cannot. Feeling self-conscious is the experience of the unwelcome attention of others, not just a feeling caused by (the perception of) such attention. The feeling itself appears to be an intentional state or an aspect of an intentional state. The bodily sensation account of feelings is unable to capture what may be an "intimate" relation between emotional feelings (or some emotional feelings) and evaluations. So the Hybrid Theory not only neglects the cognitive approach to affect, its account of (some) emotional feelings may also be suspect.[13]

Notes

1 Those who explicitly defend this view include Alston (1967), Lyons (1980), Rey (1980), and Schaffer (1983).

2 This is usually what philosophers have in mind when they refer to the "passivity" of emotion. For a more minimal sense see Gordon (1986). I express doubts about Gordon's approach in Nash (1987).

3 Lyons (1980), p. 115. That Lyons intends to analyze "being emotionally upset" in terms of bodily motions is made clear elsewhere in the same work (e.g., p. 58).

4 I thus use the term "cognitive" rather broadly, as embracing a good deal more than knowledge or belief. Such a theory might be more accurately labeled purely cognitive/conative or purely intentional. I adopt the broader usage primarily for convenience. Still, my use of the term does not diverge widely from that of the so-called cognitive sciences, which concern themselves with wants, goals, and intentions as well as beliefs.

5 Alston uses the terms "bodily disturbance" and "bodily upset"; Lyons prefers "unusual bodily changes," so as to allow for decreased pulse and respiratory rates associated with emotions like depression or ennui (Lyons 1980, pp. 116–17). The distinction is not crucial for my discussion in this essay and I often ignore it.

6 Neither Lyons nor Alston explicitly makes this claim. Since they are silent on the effects of bodily disturbances on action, I attribute the claim to them by default. Jerome Schaffer, however, does make the point explicit; noting the "irrelevance of emotion to belief and desire on the one hand and action on the other," he concludes that emotions are "superfluous" (Schaffer 1983, p. 163).

7 As noted earlier, Alston and Lyons do not address the present question; the responses I attribute to the Hybrid Theory are thus speculative.

8 Alston alludes to this point in passing (1967, p. 482).

9 Another possibility is that the bodily disturbances disrupt or interfere with the agent's intentional actions whether or not he is clearly aware of those disturbances. This possibility falls under the terminal explanation response, which I discuss in section 3. See also n. 10.

10 If the release of adrenaline is responsible for the desire itself, then we return to the terminal explanation response. As noted earlier, there may be nothing wrong with that answer. It cannot be the Hybrid Theory's answer, however, for in that case the relevant physiological changes would be central rather than peripheral.

11 The empirical data do not appear to support the single state hypothesis, however. There appear to be at least four different neural circuits involved in emotion, though even this reduction is controversial. See Panskepp (1982) and the commentary in the same volume.

12 It might also be possible for an agent to have similar (disproportionate) attitudes in both emotional and dispassionate states. It is conceivable that Ira could continue to overvalue the injustice, his merits and his colleague's demerits, though now he is no longer angry but resigned. However, such a case would arise, I suspect, as the result of a sort of cognitive inertia; if Ira had not first been angry, he would not now regard the matter in this light.

13 I wish to thank the following individuals and institutions. For helpful comments on one or more generations of this essay: John G. Bennett, Michael Bratman, Carl Ginet, Sydney Shoemaker, and the anonymous referees for *Noûs*. For a post-doctoral grant: The Social Sciences and Humanities Research Council of Canada. For sanctuary: The Center for the Study of Language and Information, Stanford University.

References

Alston, William (1967) "Emotion and feeling," *Encyclopedia of Philosophy*, ed. Paul Edwards, New York: Macmillan, vol. 2, 479–86.

Calhoun, Cheshire (1984) "Cognitive emotions?" in *What is An Emotion?* ed. C. Calhoun and R. Solomon, New York: Oxford University Press, 327–42.

Descartes, René (1911) *The Passions of the Soul, in Philosophical Words of Descartes*, trans. by E. S. Haldane and G. R. T. Ross, Cambridge: Cambridge University Press, vol. 1, 329–427.

Gordon, Robert M. (1986) "The passivity of emotions," *Philosophical Review* 95: 371–92.

James, William (1892) *Psychology*, New York: Henry Holt.

Lyons, William (1980) *Emotion*, Cambridge: Cambridge University Press, 1980.

Nash, Ronald Alan (1987) "Passivity and responsibility," manuscript.

Panskeep, Jaak (1982) "Toward a general psychobiological theory of emotions," *The Behavioral and Brain Sciences* 5: 407–22.

Rey, Georges (1980) "Functionalism and the emotions," in *Explaining Emotions*, ed. A. O. Rorty, Berkeley: University of California Press, 163–95.

Robinson, Jenefer (1983) "Emotion, judgment and desire," *Journal of Philosophy* 80: 731–41.

Rorty, Amélie (1980) "Explaining emotions," in *Explaining Emotions*, ed. A. O. Rorty, Berkeley: University of California Press 103–26.

Schaffer, Jerome (1983) "An assessment of emotion," *American Philosophical Quarterly* 20: 161–73.

Solomon, Robert C. (1976) *The Passions*, New York: Doubleday.

Solomon, Robert C. (1980) "Emotions and choice," in *Explaining Emotions*, ed. A. O. Rorty, Berkeley: University of California Press, 251–81.

Modularity, and the Psychoevolutionary Theory of Emotion

P. E. Griffiths

1 Introduction

Everyday discourse classes emotions into kinds like fear, anger, love, disgust and sadness. It would be a mistake to assume that this is the best classification for all scientific purposes. First, even the most superficial conversation about emotion soon leads to a wish to distinguish more kinds of emotion than we have names for. It is not difficult to find counterexamples to even the most mundane assertions about love or anger. The next conversational step is to insist that what we say is true of one kind of love, or anger, or whatever, but not of others. So even in casual conversation, we do not take the standard emotion vocabulary to be definitive.

Secondly, members of other cultures seem to experience emotions that are unknown to us. The Japanese experience called "amae" is not one which Westerners can readily imagine, and certainly not one most Westerners would claim to have experienced.[1] It follows that the emotion vocabulary of English is at least incomplete. Other facts about the cultural diversity of emotional experience suggest that even for the domain of emotions it describes, our vocabulary may not capture the definitive distinctions between one emotion and another. Heelas (1986) introduces the notions of "hyper-" and "hypocognition." A particular emotion category may be central to a culture. In consequence, a larger segment of the emotional experience of individuals in that culture may be conceptualized in that category. Alternatively, a category may be squeezed into insignificance, or even nonexistence, by the expansion of other categories, or by the direct hostility of the culture to that category. In current Western culture, "love" may be hypercognized in comparison with other cultures, and "piety" hypocognized in comparison with previous stages of our own culture. States that were classified under one head in one time or place are now classified under another.

These facts about emotion make it unwise to assume that our current vocabulary draws all and only those distinctions which will be required for the scientific study of emotion.[2]

There are two main strands to our everyday discourse about emotion. The first strand contrasts emotion with rational thought and action. Emotions are conceived as "passive", or involuntary. They are intrusive elements in our motivation, interfering with rational action based upon justified beliefs and stable desires. This element of everyday discourse also links emotions to various physiological events. Emotions take over systems whose operation is usually voluntary, causing behaviors such as flinching and orienting. They also divert from their usual paths systems whose operation is characteristically involuntary, such as the beating of the heart, or sweat glands. It is this strand of our thought that motivates philosophers like William Lyons (1980), who believe that a mental state cannot count as an emotion unless it causes physiological disturbance.

The second, contrasting strand of everyday discourse treats emotions as intentional states, embodying judgements of various kinds. Fear is an attitude we have to certain kinds of objects. It somehow embodies the judgement that those objects are threats to us. This strand of our thought lies behind the major philosophical approach to emotion of the last 25 years – the cognitive theory. Philosophical cognitivism centres around two claims. First, that the occurrence of propositional attitudes is essential to the occurrence of emotions. Second, that the identity of particular emotions depends upon the kinds of propositional attitudes they involve. The philosophical cognitivist claims that it is a necessary condition of fearing something that you believe it to be dangerous, and desire to avoid the danger. An extensive philosophical literature defends this position against various counterexamples, and relates the cognitivist orthodoxy to questions concerning the rationality and moral status of emotions.[3]

There are a number of problems with the idea that having an emotion involves having appropriate beliefs and desires. The content of some emotions blatantly contradicts the contents of our beliefs, as when a person is afraid of what they are sure is a harmless earthworm. The cognitive contents associated with some emotions are also liable to occur without the emotion occurring. For example, people face terrible dangers, and with no apparent death wish, remain unafraid, and take sensible decisions.

A number of authors have suggested more or less *ad hoc* additions to the theory in the hope of making it extensionally adequate. Among the more notable suggestions, William Lyons (1980) suggests that the cognitive state must cause physiological disturbances of some kind if it is to count as an emotion. Michael Stocker (1987) has suggested that the cognitive contents must be held "emotionally," as well "evidentially." The contents must be "entered into," or "lived." As Stocker admits, these notions are "difficult to characterize".

I have argued elsewhere (Griffiths 1989b) that none of the sophisticated versions of cognitivism succeed in overcoming the original array of difficulties. In the same article I show that even if cognitivism were able to provide an extensionally adequate taxonomy of emotions, this would fail to fulfil many of the desiderata for a theory of emotions.

One of the continuing attractions of the cognitive approach is that it promises a theory of emotion that preserves the categories used in our everyday discourse. I have suggested, however, that there is good reason to doubt whether these categories are definitive. The alternative approach which I describe in this essay – the psychoevolutionary theory – will not preserve the traditional categories. First, it does not pretend to be a theory of

all the things which can properly be called "emotions" in English. Secondly, it revises those emotion categories which it does attempt to explain. I shall defend this revisionary approach in two ways. First, I show that the new categories of emotion are far more theoretically fruitful than the old in ethology, evolutionary theory and in the neurosciences. Thus, even if we were to retain the old vocabulary, we would need the new vocabulary in order to state a body of important generalizations about emotional phenomena. Secondly, I shall show that using the new vocabulary we can give a partial account of the origins of the old vocabulary, and explain why theories which use that old vocabulary encounter characteristic difficulties.

2 The Psychoevolutionary Theory of Emotion

The psychoevolutionary approach to emotions was pioneered by Darwin (1872). Darwin used the French anatomist Duchenne's data on facial musculature, obtained by electrical stimulation of the facial muscle groups, to put forward *component analyses* of particular emotional expressions. He also pioneered the *judgement test*, in which a subject's ability to recognize emotion on the basis of photographed faces is assessed.

These two techniques have remained the most important tools in the investigation of facial expressions. In this section I outline some of the most telling of those modern experiments. I describe a judgement test with isolated New Guinean subjects, a comparative component analysis carried out on American and Japanese subjects, and some work on facial expression in deaf and blind born infants. The tendency of all this work is to show that there are some patterns of emotive response, which occur in all cultures. These results contradict the orthodoxy which prevailed before the 1960s. Previously, authors like La Barre (1947) and R. L. Birdwhistell (1963) had popularized the view that emotions are expressed in a culture-specific, learnt code, akin to a language. This view was made tenable by a reliance upon anecdotal evidence, a conflation of facial expression with other behaviours, such as gestures, and the phenomenon of display rules, which we discuss below. This position still seems to be favoured by authors such as Rom Harré (1986).

Ekman and Friesen (1971) conducted an experiment with subjects from the Fore language group in New Guinea. These subjects had seen no movies or magazines, they neither spoke nor understood English or pidgin, they had not lived in any Western settlement or government town, and they had never worked for a white man. Forty photographs were used in experiments with 189 adults and 130 children from the Fore.

Ekman and Friesen utilized a judgement task originally designed for work with children. The subject was given three photographs at once, each showing a face. The faces were selected, on the basis of a previously devised component theory, to be clear expressions of one basic emotion. The subject was then told a story which was designed to involve one of these emotions. Finally, they were asked to say which photograph showed the person described in the story. The stories described situations with emotional significance in the life of the Fore speakers, such as the death of a child, or an unarmed encounter with a wild pig. This method has the advantage of avoiding the necessity of translating emotion terms from one language to another.

High degrees of agreement were observed between the categories which the pictures were intended to represent and the categories which they were chosen as representing by the Fore. For example, photographs intended to represent sadness, anger and surprise were shown to the New Guineans, who were asked to select which picture represented the face of a man whose child had just died: 79 per cent of adults and 81 per cent of children selected the face intended to represent sadness. These results confirm the view that similar facial behaviour is selected for the same emotion in visually isolated preliterate cultures. Ekman and Friesen also conducted a reverse test using their New Guinean subjects. They asked members of this culture to show how their face would appear if they were the person described in one of the emotion stories that had been used in the judgement test. Video tapes of nine New Guineans were shown to thirty-four US college students. Except for the poses of fear and surprise (which the New Guineans had difficulty in discriminating), the students, who had never seen anyone from New Guinea, accurately judged the emotion intended by their poses. This reverse test further confirms the results of the study.

Ekman and Friesen (1980) also conducted a component analysis of spontaneous facial expression. Twenty-five subjects from the University of Berkeley and twenty-five subjects from the Waseda University, Tokyo, watched a neutral and a stress-inducing film whilst alone in a room.[4] They were aware that skin conductance and heart-rate measures were being taken but unaware that a video tape of their facial behaviour was being made. The facial behaviour of both groups during the stress film was radically different from that during the neutral film. When the repertoire of facial behaviours shown during the stress phase by the two sets of subjects was compared it was very similar.[5] Correlations between the facial behaviour shown by Japanese and American subjects in relation to the stress film ranged from 0.72 to 0.96, depending upon whether a particular facial area was compared or the movement of the entire face.

Perhaps the most interesting result from this experiment was that when an authority figure was introduced into the room and asked questions about the subject's emotions as the stress film was shown again the facial behaviour of the Japanese differed radically from that of the Americans. The characteristic difference was that the Japanese showed more positive emotion than the Americans and less negative emotion. The Japanese appeared to have masked their negative feelings by politely smiling. Slow-motion videotape analysis showed the micro-momentary occurrence of characteristic negative emotional expressions, and then showed them being replaced with a polite smile. This behaviour appears to have been unconscious and relatively automatic on the part of the Japanese. This is a classic example of so-called "display rules" in operation. A display rule is a means whereby an individual, or more often a whole society, habitually mask or suppress a natural emotional response in order to conform more closely to some norm or ideal. The existence of display rules may have played a role in making plausible the view of La Barre and others that even basic emotional expressions are culture specific.

Finally, we can turn to component analyses on the deaf and blind born. Eibl-Eibesfeldt (1973) analysed the facial movements of infants born deaf and blind and of normal infants when exposed to the same stimuli. He discovered that the same patterns of muscular activity were used to display the same kinds of emotions in both groups. This finding confirms the results of Thompson (1941) and Fulcher (1942), both of whom discovered the same patterns of muscular activity in the blind and seeing for each type of emotional behaviour. This result seems to have been fairly well confirmed and has extremely important implications for our theory of emotion.

3   Are Emotional Responses Innate?

The evidence just reviewed will be used below to support the idea that certain emotional displays are controlled by "affect-programs". An affect-program is a neural circuit, probably in the hypothalamus and associated regions. When triggered, it initiates the complex series of reactions which make up an emotional response. These are generally thought to include facial expression, vocalization and expressive vocal changes, skeletal muscular reactions, such as orienting or flinching, and changes in autonomic nervous system activity, leading to alterations in heart rate, skin temperature and so on.

However, the issue of whether affect-programs exist must not be confused with the issue of whether they are innate. In principle, an affect-program may be entirely innate, entirely learnt, or a mixture of the two. These are questions about how the circuitry gets built, not about whether it exists. It is not possible to argue from the fact that emotions are controlled by affect-programs to the fact that they are innate.

There is, however, an argument in the other direction. If emotional responses are innate, this would provide support for the view that there are affect-programs. The argument is something like this. If there are complex, co-ordinated responses, involving many different physiological systems, and these depend upon an innate factor, our present scientific understanding makes a circuit in the central nervous system just about the only mechanism that could be built by the genes and then lead to the production of these complex sequences of behaviour. In this section I assess the evidence for the innateness of the various elements of the affect-program response.

The results on facial expressions gathered by Ekman and Friesen are evidence for the innateness of those expressions. They are particularly good evidence because facial expresions are mostly arbitrary behaviours. In humans, the fact that the fear expression expresses fear and the joy expression expresses joy, cannot be explained by any intrinsic appropriateness of those expressions. Only surprise retains its utilitarian purpose (it serves to

increase uptake of visual information). If these arbitrary expressions were the results of learning or social training, the use of the same expression for the same purpose in different cultures would be inexplicable.[6]

The data gathered by Eibl-Eibesfeldt is also good evidence for innateness. It is implausible to suppose that deaf and blind born infants have learnt the correct facial expression for joy or disgust from those around them.

Unfortunately, the research on the innateness or otherwise of other postulated affect-program elements is not as decisive. We know that orienting to the stimulus is part of the surprise response, other than that I am not aware of any studies of muscular/skeletal response in humans. Panksepp (1982) has worked on affect-program controlled muscular/skeletal responses in animals, and claims to have isolated a number of behaviour sequences. I doubt, however, whether these results can be carried over to humans. I discuss my reservations on this point in section 6. I also know of no solid data on vocal responses.

Turning to ANS responses, there is a massive body of research, dating back to W. B. Cannon in the interwar years. Unfortunately, most of it is addressed to the question of the specificity of ANS arousal to particular emotions, not to the innateness of that arousal (the two issues are connected, but in a way too complex to go into here). Anecdotally, it seems plausible that adrenaline release and the accompanying heart rate and other changes accompany fear in the New Guineans, as well as in Westerners, but there are no studies that I know of. A further problem is raised for such research by the direct utility of some such ANS responses. Studies would have to rule out the possibility that adrenaline release is a learnt response which occurs in all cultures because it is always useful. Studies on infants, as well as cross-cultural studies, would be necessary to ascertain this.[7]

As a consequence of the lack of research on these topics, it must be concluded that if there are affect-programs their contents are at least partly innate, but that the boundary between the innate and the learnt is unclear.

4   The Affect-Program Theory

The idea that there are affect-programs controlling the various pancultural emotional responses received some support from the fact that those responses are at least partly innate. But the main argument for the existence of affect-programs is the following argument to the best explanation. There are a number of important characteristics of emotional responses that seem to stand in need of explanation. They are often brief, quick, complex, organized and to a greater or lesser extent involuntary. Let us consider these characteristics in a little more detail. If emotions are distinguished from moods (Griffiths 1989a) they are typically *brief*, they may last as little as a few seconds. The onset of an emotion may be so *quick* as to be regarded as near instantaneous. An emotional response is both *complex* and *organized*. It typically involves at least four kinds of co-ordinated changes. Firstly, there are skeletal/muscular changes such as flinching, orienting or relaxing. Secondly, there are changes in the facial musculature, leading to emotional expressions. Thirdly, there are vocalizations and more general changes in the vocal muscles leading to expressive tones of voice. Fourthly, there are autonomic nervous system responses, such as sweating, secretion of adrenaline and changes in heart rate. The characteristic sensations of the various emotions might also be mentioned. Perhaps the most important feature of emotional responses is that they are typically *involuntary*. They occur without the conscious instigation of the subject. In this they are rather like reflexes, but they are unlike reflexes in being more complex and organized. The argument for the existence of affect-programs is simply that the features of emotion just described, and particularly the last feature, can best be explained on the hypothesis that a neural program stores a predetermined set of responses which are activated in a co-ordinated fashion in rapid response to some external stimuli. This argument has been advanced forcibly in a number of works by Paul Ekman (1972, 1973, 1980).

The existence of neural circuits that are partially innately specified, and which control the rapid responses uncovered by the psychoevolutionary theory is the best evidenced part of the affect-program theory. In addition to the data and arguments already given, there is a body of neuroscientific work which has attempted to map such circuits in the limbic system. This is reviewed in section 6. These neural circuits, and their surface manifestations, may be regarded as the "output side" of the psychoevolutionary/affect-program theory, dealing with what happens when an emotional response is triggered. The "input side", dealing with the events that trigger the emotional response, is in a somewhat less developed state.

The fact that the elements of the affect-program responses are at least partially innate tells us nothing about whether there are any stimuli to which the affect-programs are innately sensitive. But there is a considerable amount of research which throws light on this question. J. B. Watson (1925) found that new-born babies are afraid of loud sounds and loss of balance, but almost nothing else. More recent research has suggested that the new born are sensitive to one further class of stimuli, namely the facial expressions of caregivers (Trevarthen 1984). It might, therefore, be concluded that the system which triggers the affect-programs has very few innate elements. But this makes no allowance for responses which emerge during maturation, or for the possibility of learning preparedness (Seligman 1970). Experience may be needed to produce a response, but if less experience is needed to produce a response to one object than to another, the explanation of this "preparedness" to learn may involve genetic factors.

There is experimental evidence for learning preparedness in the cases of fear and disgust. Seligman (1971) has argued that phobias are best understood as cases of highly prepared (often one-trial) learning of fear responses. He suggests that the stimuli for which humans are predisposed to acquire fear are those which would have been prevalent sources of danger during human evolution. Ohman et al. (1976) conducted conditioning experiments on human beings in an attempt to test a similar proposal. They found that associations between classic phobic stimuli, such as snakes, and aversive stimuli, in this case electric shock, were more resistant to extinction than associations established with a similar number of trials between shock and neutral stimuli, such as flowers, or arbitrary stimuli, such as shapes. They were also more resistant than associations between phobic stimuli and non-aversive stimuli, in this case, sounds. They concluded that the association of certain classic phobic stimuli with danger is a prepared association in humans.

Disgust responses have been widely studied in animals under the heading of "taste aversion". Many species exhibit a marked inability to associate anything but ingested substances with nausea, and have remarkable capacities to identify and avoid noxious substances in their diet. Various authors have suggested the existence of specialized mechanisms for associating illness with tastes (Rozin and Kalat 1971; Garcia et al. 1974). Logue et al. (1981) attempted to show that the same phenomenon is found in humans. It appears that in humans, as in other animals, there is a strong tendency to acquire disgust for a taste which has been followed by illness, even where higher-level cognitive systems are aware that no causal connection exists between the food and the illness.

The data suggests that affect-program responses are innately sensitive to very few stimuli. Most of the contents of the triggering system are learnt. There is, however, considerable evidence that this learning mechanism is biased. It is not a general-purpose mechanism, equally capable of learning any facts that the world may embody. Some kinds of fact are easier to learn, and some harder. Although the organism does not arrive in the world with a preconceived map of what is emotionally significant, it does bring with it some preconceived ideas about what is *likely* to be emotionally significant.

This picture of the triggering of affect-programs makes considerable evolutionary sense. Affect-programs are adaptive responses to events that have a particular ecological significance for the organism. The fear response is adapted to dangers, the disgust response to noxious stimuli, the anger response to challenges, the surprise response to novel stimuli. The local events which possess the properties of being dangerous, noxious or novel may be very different from one environment to the other. If affect-programs are to be of significant adaptive advantage to an organism over an evolutionarily significant time period, it would be advantageous for them to be linked to some mechanism which can interpret the broad ecological categories of danger, novelty and so forth, in the light of local conditions, and equate them with detectable features of the local environment. So it comes as no surprise that organisms have to learn which events in their particular environment should trigger the affect-programs.

There are, however, certain constancies in the environment which a learning system can be pre-programmed to take account of. The disgust response is designed to prevent the ingestion of noxious substances. It would be extremely ineffi-cient if the disgust response were to be elicited by non-gustatory stimuli, however well those stimuli might correlate with illness. Such responses would be useless, and probably counterproductive. A constraint on the learning mechanism which helps to restrict disgust to gustatory stimuli would be advantageous.

The other sort of constraint on learning discussed above, a preparedness to associate particular stimuli with danger, has obvious adaptive advantages. A prepared learning mechanism of this sort makes it possible to compromise between the advantages of flexibility in the face of environmental variation, and of inheriting the experience of past generations.

There may be another adaptive advantage to the neonate's apparently innate sensitivity to the facial expressions of caregivers. Learning the significance of the facial expressions of conspecifics would be a complex and probably lengthy task, and it would be highly advantageous to have this data available as early as possible. Responding appropriately to the emotional state of caregivers may well be directly advantageous to the infant. Furthermore, the significance of events in the current environment can be very rapidly assessed by noting the assessment of those who have already lived in that environment. Very few children have been hurt by snakes, or spiders, or the dark, but it seems that only a slight demonstration of revulsion or anxiety by adults is needed to produce a powerful aversion to these things in the young. An innate capacity to interpret the emotional responses of conspecifics would facilitate learning of this kind.

Finally, it may be possible to give an evolutionary explanation of the irrational persistence of judgements about the emotional significance of the environment. A single display of fear by a caregiver may result in a fear of the dark that will be retained despite any amount of information about the harmlessness of darkness. Emotional responses do not seem to adjust themselves as readily as beliefs when new information is acquired about the environment. Sustained counter-conditioning seems to be needed to delete an assessment once it has become linked to an affect-program response. This could be due to the evolutionary advantages of "false-positive" responses. The costs of failing to respond to dangers, challenges, noxious stimuli, and so on may well outweigh the costs of responding unnecessarily. Failing to respond to danger may lead to death, while responding unnecessarily merely wastes a little energy. In evolutionary terms, phobias and irrational distastes may have much to recommend them.

5 Affect-Programs and Modularity

I have argued that the systems which trigger affect-programs must learn the emotional significance of features of the local environment. This learning is constrained in various ways which may have evolutionary explanations. In this section, I want to argue that at least some of the systems which trigger affect-programs are distinct from the systems that create the model of the world which guides rational action, that is, from the system of beliefs and desires.

The main reason for supposing that there is such a separate system is the need to explain the ways in which emotional responses can conflict with other cognitive activity. There is some sense in which fear embodies the judgement that something is dangerous. But it is common for a person to display the symptoms of fear when confronted by a stimuli they know to be harmless. The same is true of the other affect-program responses. They frequently occur when their occurrence is irrational in the light of our beliefs and desires. This suggests that there is a process which is capable of evaluating stimuli and triggering the appropriate affect-program, but which is separate from the process which leads to the fixation of belief.

This process would be "modular", in something like the sense popularized by Fodor (1983). Fodor was primarily concerned to argue that there are modules responsible for processing sensory data to the point where it becomes a conscious perception. Perception, he argues, is informationally encapsulated. We know that a complex process of interpretation is required in order to construct, say, a visual image. The process has access to information which allows it to establish prior probabilities for various possible interpretations of the data, but it does not have access to everything known to the subject. The fact that the mask in the concave mask illusion feels concave does not affect the visual perception of a convex mask. This process's operation is also mandatory. We cannot decide whether to process visual data in this way. Finally, the process is opaque to introspection. There is no conscious awareness of the complex act of interpretation that gives rise to the perception.

The way in which certain kinds of emotional response, notably those dealt with by affect-pro-

gram theory, can conflict with other cognitive processes would be neatly explained if there are processes that trigger affect-programs which are "informationally encapsulated". In that case, there would not be a free flow of information between them and the rest of the mind. It is possible for a modular system to respond as if a certain state of affairs obtains although the organism as a whole believes that state of affairs does not obtain. Informational encapsulation is perhaps the most important feature of modular systems. It captures what we mean when we say that modular processes are "separate" from the rest of the mind. The system(s) which triggers affect-programs has other features which Fodor thinks characteristic of modular systems. Its operation is mandatory. We do not choose to respond with fear or anger to a given stimulus. The system is largely opaque to our central cognitive processes. We are aware of its outputs, which are the affect-program responses themselves, but not aware of the processes that lead to them.

The suggestion that the affect-program triggering system is a module fits neatly into the evolutionary perspective on emotion that gave rise to the affect-program view. Fodor, drawing on Rozin (1976) and others, gives a psychoevolutionary account of the existence of modules in minds such as ours which are capable of more general intelligence. Modules, argues Fodor, originated in phylogenetic predecessors who did not have this general-purpose intelligence. They provide relatively unintelligent but effective ways of performing certain low-level cognitive processes such as perception, and, I am suggesting, immediate response to certain important kinds of stimuli. We have retained these modules, Fodor argues, because the very unintelligence of modular systems gives them a number of advantages. Among these are the very short response times that can be obtained by having a mandatory system and a limited data base. If a system is mandatory there is no decision time incorporated in the response time. If the system operates on a limited data base, which is chosen for its relevance to the question in hand, the procedures through which it must go in order to make its decision may be more rapid. Finally, and most interestingly, Fodor suggests that there are penalties to allowing our general cognitive processes to interfere too freely with certain areas of mental activity. He points out that, in the case of perception, it is vital for an organism to be able to accept data which contradicts even its most firmly held beliefs. If perception were an entirely top-down process then the perception of novelty would be impossible. The modularity of our perceptual processes means that we are compelled to consider data hostile to our present beliefs even if eventually we decide not to change them on the basis of that data.

Similarly, the modularity of affect-program responses can be seen as a mechanism for saving us from our own intelligence. Consider the startle response experienced when confronted with novel stimuli. No matter how much we may want to appear blasé, we are forced to gather as much information as possible from the novel stimulus. The affect-program causes us to orient towards the stimulus, to open our eyes widely and to direct our attention largely towards the stimulus. It also triggers preliminary elements of a flight or fight response in case this should be necessary when the stimulus has been evaluated. Similar observations can be made about the fear response. No matter what our higher cognitive processes tell us about the situation, if we have experienced an object as harmful in some past segment of our learning history, the appraisal mechanism will trigger our fear affect-program and this will initiate expressive facial changes and the necessary autonomic nervous system changes for a flight or fight response. When it comes to dangers, false positives are usually preferable to false negatives!

It is, of course, not necessary to the argument that any particular modular process, or even modular processes generally, are useful to us today. It is only necessary that in some previous state, preserving our modular responses may have been more useful than incorporating those areas of our activity into general intelligence.

The modularity of the systems which trigger affect-programs differs in one important respect from that of perceptual input systems. The output of perceptual systems is a mental event, a perception, whereas that of the emotion system is behavioural. But this does not conflict with the Fodorean approach to modularity. Fordor establishes the notion of a modular system by analogy with reflexes, which, of course, have a behavioural output. Fodor draws the analogy in the following, typically Fodorean, words:

> ... reflexes are informationally encapsulated with bells on ... you have come to know perfectly well that under no conceivable circumstances would I stick my finger in your eye. ... Still, if I jab my finger near enough to your eye, you'll blink. To say, as we did above, that the blink reflex is mandatory is to say, inter alia, that it has no access to what you know about my character or, for that matter, to any other of your beliefs, utilities and expectations. For this reason the blink reflex is often produced when sober reflection would show it to be uncalled for ... it is prepared to trade false positives for speed.

> That is what it is like for a system to be informationally encapsulated. If you now imagine a system that is encapsulated in the way that reflexes are, but also computational in the way that reflexes are not, you will have some idea of what I'm proposing that input systems are like. (1983, pp. 71–2)

Given the data that I have reviewed about the triggering of affect-programs, a great deal would be explained by considering the proprietary appraisal mechanism for the affect-programs as a module of this sort – a system akin to a reflex in its encapsulation and mandatory operation, but with relatively sophisticated information-processing arrangements for the interpretation of the stimulus.

It may be the case that affect-programs can be triggered by other routes, in addition to this modular one. The existence of a relatively unintelligent, dedicated mechanism does not imply that higher-level cognitive processes cannot initiate the same events. Perhaps affect-programs can be triggered voluntarily as well as involuntarily, in something like the way that heart rate can be brought under voluntary control by the use of bio-feedback devices. Even if this is not possible, there may be certain higher-level processes, such as the imaginative representation of emotion-inducing stimuli, that can trigger the affect-programs.

6 The Neural Basis of the Affect-Programs

Research on the neural substrate of the affect-programs suggests that they are subserved by neural circuits in the limbic system, the phylogenetically old portion of the cortex which surrounds the brainstem, or in associated brainstem structures. The hypothalamus in particular is a plausible locus for many of these responses. The central role of the hypothalamus in emotion was first stressed in the classic work of W. D. Cannon in the 1920s, and has been reiterated by many later authors.

The role of these sub-cortical structures in emotion has led P. D. MacLean, in a long series of papers (MacLean 1952, 1969, 1970, 1980), to argue that emotions represent a phylogenetically more primitive way of processing important information and directing our responses to that information, than that localized in the neo-cortex. This idea is supported by Fodor's explanation of the retention of modular systems in animals equipped with higher cognition. Modules evolved in our fore-bears for want of a powerful general-purpose cognitive mechanism to bring to bear. They were retained because of their efficiency as dedicated systems for those tasks. If such an account is accepted, the natural place to look for the localization of such brain functions is in the parts of our own brains equivalent to the brains of our evolutionary forebears. It is by no means safe to assume that inheritance of structure carries with it inheritance of function, but it does provide a rational basis for a research strategy, and evidence such as MacLean's which supports this approach should be taken seriously.

A recent attempt to locate the neural circuits subserving emotional responses is to be found in Panksepp (1982). Panksepp suggests that four circuits can be found in the hypothalamus in certain animals. He calls these the "expectancy", "fear", "rage" and "panic" pathways. His main technique for locating such pathways is direct stimulation of cells in the hypothalamus, evoking various sorts of behaviour. The aim is to find areas which trigger a substantial series of connected behaviours in order to demonstrate the existence of a hard-wired basis for complex behaviour sequences which could be triggered relatively automatically by major life-challenges, such as danger or the presence of a potential fulfiller of a basic need. Panksepp's approach has met with some success, enough to lead him to propose his four pathways. He is also admirably conservative in refusing to posit any hypothalamic emotions for which he is unable to locate a pathway and specify a set of resultant behaviours. But I do have certain reservations about his methodology. I suspect that Panksepp's concentration on longer-term responses, such as sequences of movements, will make his results less applicable to humans than might otherwise have been the case. It seems plausible that in humans, only short-term responses are controlled by the

affect-program, longer-term responses, such as attack or flight, being predominantly under the control of higher cognitive processes. The predominant features in the human response seems to be the expressive and ANS elements. The expressive responses are present in animals, as Darwin showed, and attempts to evoke expressive responses in other primates might reveal pathways that would be directly relevant to the realization of the affect-programs in humans.

7 The Significance of the Psychoevolutionary Theory

The psychoevolutionary theory describes a set of well-defined physiological responses that can be used to create a new classification of emotional responses. Ekman and his co-workers call the responses they have isolated fear, anger, joy, surprise, disgust and sadness. They use these traditional labels because the new categories coincide more or less well with the occurrent, phenomenologically salient instances of these traditional categories. I shall refer to these six categories as the affect-program responses.

This new way of classifying emotions abstracts away from causes. The identity of an emotion depends upon the character of the response, not on the nature of the stimuli. This puts it on one side of a dichotomy which has been nicely characterized by Paul Rozin:

If one focuses on traditional definitions of emotion, which emphasize visceral and expressive responses, disgust can be viewed as an extension of the set of stimuli or contexts that elicit a fundamental rejection (distaste-disgust) emotion. In the same manner, we typically describe both the negative response to a looming object in infants and the response to the threat of nuclear war in adults as fear, presuming that the same underlying internal response is generated by different situations at different levels of cognitive sophistication. We [*Rozin and his co-worker*] prefer a conception in which the interaction of the subject with the object or context is a critical part of the definition of emotion. (Rozin 1987, p. 35)

I advocate abstracting away from the objects or contexts that cause emotion, because they vary enormously in response to local culture and individual learning. Concentrating on the response makes it possible to discern what is common to emotions in all humans, and even in related species. Once we have these response-based categories, it becomes possible to provide an evolutionary explanation of them. Furthermore, the new classifications appear to link up with some promising work in the neurosciences. This is surely ample theoretical justification for introducing an "output side" classification.

Although the new categories are defined in terms of the emotional response itself, the new theory does provide insights into the causes of emotion. The psychoevolutionary perspective, as I have tried to show, gives us the rationale of the way in which affect-program responses are triggered, and the way in which the contents of the triggering mechanism are sensitized to certain stimuli.

I have no desire to ban the kind of "input side" taxonomy Rozin suggests. Viewed as a total account of emotional phenomena the psychoevolutionary perspective is seriously incomplete. Clearly, in addition to the affect-program responses, the traditionally defined realm of emotion involves higher-level cognitive phenomena. It also, and very importantly, involves learnt, culture-specific elements. In understanding an emotion like romantic love, it is vital to understand that it is culturally prescribed for certain classes of objects. The nature of the response, in such a case, may not be the most important characteristic of the emotion, and may alter so as to reflect societies' changing attitude to the prescribed object.

Accepting the affect-program taxonomy does not exclude the delineation of more complex states, involving cognitive and cultural factors, and perhaps building in one or more of the affect-program responses. Attention to the input-side may well be important in deriving such a taxonomy. But the introduction of these states must have some theoretical utility. It is not enough that the new category achieve a rough extensional equivalence with one of the prescientific categories. The temptation to reconstruct the traditional categories of prescientific English without any other theoretical payoff should be resisted. An analogy may help to show why such a salvage job would not be useful. Consider the prescientific concept of heat. What was called "heat" turned out to be a complex phenomenon, derived from our sensory experience of several genuine physical properties. Prominent amongst these are temperature (mean molecular kinetic energy), quantity of heat (total molecular

kinetic energy), and conductivity (a matter of the relative ease with which electrons are detached from atoms of different elements). An understanding of the folk concept of heat involves all these factors. What is more, the folk concept is less a useful amalgam of these factors than a misleading conflation of them! Using the folk concept we have no means of explaining how a person can touch a very hot piece of aluminium foil and remain unharmed. Similarly, it must have seemed to Wenceslaus's peasant, as he gathered winter fuel, that the handle of his axe was warmer than the blade, simply because wood is less conductive than metal. The folk concept is a liability when it comes to physical theory. It is of (limited) utility only in certain practical applications.

To continue the analogy, it may be possible to describe a complex property which answers to the prescientific concept of heat. But this property does not have much theoretical utility. Quite simply, you can't do physics with it, whereas you can do physics with the concepts of atom, molecule, electron and kinetic energy. The only thing the complex property might be needed for is to explain how the prescientific notion of heat arises, and why it is useful in a limited range of everyday applications.

I suggest that emotion is a complex phenomenon like heat. Emotional phenomena involve psychoevolved adaptive responses, cognitive factors and cultural factors. All of these are needed to give an adequate account of what underlies folk discourse about emotion. It is also possible, as we shall see below, to give an account of the origin, and limited utility, of the folk taxonomy, much as we can give an account of the origin, and limited utility, of the folk conception of heat. I also suggest that emotion and the folk categories of emotion, are not kinds that will be of interest to a developed science. For the purposes of psychology and the philosophy of mind, a new taxonomy is required, and the affect-program states are a contribution to that.

In the final section of the essay I want to show how the psychoevolutionary theory can be used to illuminate the prescientific conception of emotion, and explain its characteristic strengths and weaknesses.

8   Exploring the Folk Conception

I said in my introduction that there were two strands to the prescientific conception of emotion.

The first emphasizes the involuntary and disruptive effects of emotion, both physiological and motivational. The second stresses their intentionality. In everyday discourse, emotional responses are assigned intentional objects, with assertions such as "They are afraid of that spider". The cognitivist claims that this emotion embodies the judgement that spiders are dangerous. This claim is firmly grounded in the everyday conception of emotion. It is intuitively paradoxical to say "I don't think it's dangerous, but I'm afraid of it". However, if the theory I have outlined is correct, the relationship between emotions and cognitive states is more complicated than in the prescientific conception. People often experience so-called "irrational" emotions.

The affect-program theory can account for the occurrence of irrational emotional responses, and also for their appearance of paradox. The judgement that the current stimulus is dangerous can occur in two ways. First, it can arise through the normal processes of belief fixation. Secondly, the modular triggering system may class a stimulus as falling into one of the emotion-evoking categories, and trigger the affect-program response. If these processes run in tandem, as they often do, the subject will both exhibit the symptoms of fear, and assert that the cause of his fear is dangerous. In this situation, both elements of the folk-conception of emotion are satisfied. A cognitive state is present, and an involuntary response is evoked. If, however, only the affect-program system classes the stimulus as a danger, the subject will exhibit the symptoms of fear, but will deny making the judgements which folk theory supposes to be implicit in the emotion. Conversely, if only the belief system classes the object as a danger, the subject may take steps to avoid it, but will not have any of the symptoms of fear, and may hotly deny being afraid.

The ability to draw this distinction is a considerable advance, as it avoids the paradoxes which have dogged the cognitive theory of emotions. Emotions radically at odds with our beliefs and desires are in fact commonplace. Other traditional problems for cognitivism also become more tractable. It has traditionally been thought paradoxical that fictional presentations can evoke emotional responses, or that imagined events can evoke real emotions. In both cases, the cognitive factors required by standard theories are, *ex hypothesi*, absent. Michael Stocker (1987) has argued that this paradox can only be resolved by allowing the

cognitive content of emotions to be different in kind from the cognitive content of beliefs. The present proposal allows us to flesh out this suggestion, not by positing a new and mysterious class of mental states, but by utilizing notions like modularity and informational encapsulation that are already deployed elsewhere in psychology. The occurrence of emotions in the absence of suitable beliefs is converted from a philosophers' paradox into a practical subject for psychological investigation.

As well as explaining some of the paradoxes generated by the prescientific conception of emotion, the psychoevolutionary and affect-program accounts allow us to explain the origins of that conception. Affect-program responses can be seen as paradigmatic mental events around which other relevantly similar events are gathered. Jerome Schaffer (1983) has pointed out that, if emotions were merely collections of beliefs and desires, it would be hard to account for the distinctions we draw between emotional and rational action, and for the deep-seated belief that emotions are disruptive events that are often at odds with other sources of motivation. The nature of the affect-program responses makes these elements of our concept of emotion easier to understand.

The affect-program system is precisely a source of disruptive motivations not integrated into the system of rational action on the basis of beliefs and desires. It is the characteristic properties of the affect-program states, their informational encapsulation, and their involuntariness, which necessitate the introduction of something other than belief and desire into our conception of ourselves.

If we take the affect-program responses as the paradigm emotional events, there are two ways in which higher cognitive elements might be introduced into our conception of an emotion. First, there is the fact that in many cases, central belief formation and affect-program triggering run side by side. It would be understandable if these cognitive elements were to be regarded as part of the emotional response. The emotion term might then be applied to the cognitive elements even when they occur in isolation, as it is to the affect-program element occurring in isolation. Furthermore, it seems plausible that the use of an intentional content-based classification of mental states is a basic element of our prescientific understanding of ourselves. If this is correct, our everyday discourse lacks the resources to make the distinctions between fear as it occurs in "John was afraid of the spider" and as it occurs in "John is afraid we will be a little late for the meeting."

If some of our traditional emotion categories are derived from affect-program responses in this way, this will make it possible to explain the way in which folk psychology selectively parcels up cognitive states, and labels some of these parcels, but not others, "emotions".

Emotion types which don't correspond to known types of affect-programs cannot be explained in this way. Jealousy, hope and envy, all of which which may be such types, seem to be based on more or less common arrangements of desires. The idea that an emotion is an isolated source of motivation may help here. Perhaps it is the common occurrence and relative isolation of these sets of desires that leads us to class them as emotions. The irruption of such strong desires for particular outcomes is relatively involuntary, and disruptive of our pursuit of more general, long-term projects, in much the same way as the occurrence of affect-program responses.

It might seem that states of this kind are just what the cognitivist originally promised us. A purely cognitive specification picks out an emotion type. Even in this case, however, the cognitivist is unable to provide us with much of a *theory* of these states. We want, above all, to know why it is these sets of desires occur so commonly, and not some of the myriad others that the cognitive taxonomy makes room for (Griffiths 1989b). Perhaps psy-

choevolutionary factors are at work in creating common patterns of human motivation such as these. This idea, however, is highly speculative. If these largely cognitive emotion types turn out to be culture-specific, there will be a very different etiological story to be told.

The nature of the affect-programs may also be of the first importance in understanding the social construction of emotion categories, and emotional responses. The role of the affect-programs would be akin to that of the real physiological or mental disorders upon which certain societies model mythical diseases (Newman 1960). Similarly, the construction of social models of emotional response proceeds in accordance with the societies' understanding of emotion. It is often the special status which emotions have in virtue of being thought involuntary that constructed-emotions seek to share. It may be that socially constructed emotions, such as romantic love, mimic the general features of affect-program phenomena, and perhaps of those cognitive states that resemble affect-program states in their motivational isolation and involuntariness. Such constructed emotions purport to be urgent, involuntary aberrations from the usual patterns of action rationalized by beliefs and stable desires, whereas they are, in fact, subconsciously directed intentional actions, reflecting roles available in a culture, and assisting the individual to achieve various social ends. Some authors have provocatively compared such emotions to hysterical illnesses (Averill 1980a, 1980b).

Notes

1 It is sometimes described as taking moral satisfaction in one's childlike dependency on someone. The Japanese are said to experience this as a basic emotion.

2 This argument will have less force for social constructionist theorists, such as Claire Armon-Jones (1985, 1986a, 1986b), who believe that emotions can be exhaustively understood as learnt behaviours reflecting surrounding social norms. On such a picture, our emotion vocabulary is a critical part of the apparatus by which people are taught to have the emotions of the local culture. This makes it more likely that the local vocabulary will reflect the psychological reality of emotion in that culture.

I have argued elsewhere (Griffiths 1988) that social constructionist ideas can shed light upon some emotional phenomena, and upon some ways that emotions are classified. However, the view that all emotions are learnt behaviours reflecting local social

norms is not credible. One of the largest problems for this view is the body of data on the evolution of emotion that is summarized in this essay.

3 A seminal cognitivist work is Kenny (1963), classic presentations include Solomon (1977) and Lyons (1980).

4 Previous research in Japan had established that having subjects watch certain stress-inducing films led to self-reports of similar emotions in both Japanese and United States subjects.

5 Judgements as to similarity in facial expression are made using FAST (facial affect scoring technique). FAST is an atlas of pictures of three areas of the total face. Judges are asked to class a picture of one area of a subject's face, by comparing a photograph of that area to the standard samples in the atlas. Their judgements collectively determine a classification of the expression as one, or none, of the known responses.

6   In Darwin's own words: "Whenever the same movements...express the same emotions in the several distinct races of man, we may infer with much probability that such expressions are true ones – that is, are innate or instinctive. Conventional expressions...would probably have differed in different races, in the same manner as do their languages" (Darwin 1872, p. 15). Darwin also pioneered the explanatory scheme which is now used to account for the form of the various emotional expressions. He tried to show that these responses are relics of functional responses, tooth-baring in human anger, for example, being a relic of tooth-baring in preparation for attack. Darwin stressed the similarities between the emotional responses of man and of allied, primate species, suggesting an origin for the response in a common ancestor. In humans, these responses are retained because they have acquired a role in intra-specific communication.

7   The idea that ANS response differs from one emotion to another is the subject of considerable controversy. It would be congenial to the psychoevolutionary perspective if they did differ, as this would allow them to be adaptations to particular kinds of emotion-inducing situation. The debate is widely thought to have been settled by S. Schachter and J. E. Singer (1962). Schachter and Singer showed that subjects could be induced to label the same drug-induced physiological disturbance as one emotion or another depending on the available cognitive cues. They concluded that the feelings caused by physiological disturbance were the same for the various emotions, and that cognitive factors identified the emotions. But this result is less conclusive than has been claimed. First, it is well established that subjects who are unable to account for their current introspective state will invent an explanation that allows them to make sense of their condition, and claim that the explanation is the result of direct knowledge of their own mental processes (the phenomenon of "confabulation"; Gazzaniga and Smylie (1984), Nisbett and Wilson (1977). Schachter and Singer's subjects may have been doing this, rather than experiencing emotion in any normal sense. Secondly, contradictory results have been obtained elsewhere by using what are arguably more sensitive experimental techniques (Ekman 1983).

References

Armon-Jones, C. (1985) "Prescription, explication and the social construction of emotion", *Journal for the Theory of Social Behaviour* 15, 1–22.

Armon-Jones, C. (1986a) "The thesis of constructionism", in R. Harré (ed.), *The Social Construction of Emotions*, OUP, Oxford.

Armon-Jones, C. (1986b) "The social functions of emotions", in R. Harré (ed.), *The Social Construction of Emotions*, OUP, Oxford.

Averill, J. R. (1980a) "Emotion and anxiety: sociocultural, biological and psychological determinants", in A. O. Rorty (ed.), *Explaining Emotions*, University of California Press.

Averill, J. R. (1980b) "A constructionist view of emotion", in R. Plutchik and H. Kellerman (eds), *Emotion: Theory, Research and Experience*, Vol. 1, Academic Press, New York.

Birdwhistell, R. L. (1963) "The kinesic level in the investigation of the emotions", in P. H. Knapp (ed.), *Expression of the Emotions in Man*, International Universities Press, New York.

Darwin, C. (1955) (1872) *The Expression of Emotion in Man and Animals*, Philosophical Library, New York.

Eibl-Eibesfeldt, I. (1973) "The expressive behaviour of the deaf and blind born", in M. V. Cranach and I. Vine (eds), *Social Communication and Movement*, Academic Press, New York.

Ekman, P. (1972) *Emotions in the Human Face*, Pergamon Press, New York.

Ekman, P. (ed.) (1973) *Darwin and Facial Expression*, Academic Press, New York.

Ekman, P. (1980) "Biological and cultural contributions to body and facial movements in the expression of emotions", in A. O. Rorty (ed.), *Explaining Emotions*, University of California Press.

Ekman, P. (1983) "Autonomic nervous system activity distinguishes among emotions", *Science* 221, 1208–10.

Ekman, P. and Friesen, W. V. (1971) "Constants across cultures in the face and emotion", *Journal of Personality and Social Psychology* 17(2), 124–9.

Fodor, J. (1983) *The Modularity of Mind*, Bradford Books.

Fuicher, J. S. (1942) "'Voluntary' facial expression in blind and seeing children", *Archives of Psychology* 38, No. 272.

Garcia, J., Walter, G. H., and Rusiniak, K. W. (1974) "Behavioural regularities in the milieu interne in man and rat", *Science* 185, 824–31.

Gazzaniga, M. S. and Smylie, C. S. (1984) "What does language do for a right hemisphere?" in M. S. Gazzaniga (ed.), *Handbook of Cognitive Neuroscience*, Plenum Press, pp. 199–202.

Griffiths, P. E. (1988) "Emotion and evolution", unpublished Ph.D. thesis submitted to Australian National University, June 1988.

Griffiths, P. E. (1989a) "Folk, functional and neurochemical aspects of mood", *Philosophical Psychology* 2, 1989.

Griffiths, P. E. (1989b) "The degeneration of the cognitive theory of emotion", *Philosophical Psychology* **2**, 1989.

Harré, R. (ed.) (1986) *The Social Construction of Emotions*, OUP, Oxford.

Heelas, P. (1986) "Emotions across cultures", in R. Harré (ed.), *The Social Construction of Emotions*, OUP, Oxford.

Kenny, A. (1963) *Action, Emotion and Will*, Routledge & Kegan Paul, London.

La Barre, W. (1947) "The cultural basis of emotions and gestures", *Journal of Personality* **16**, 49–68.

Logue, A. W., Ophir, I. and Strauss, K. E. (1981) "The acquisition of taste aversions in humans", *Behavior Research and Therapy* **19**, 319–33.

Lyons, W. (1980) *Emotion*, Cambridge University Press.

MacLean, P. D. (1952) "Some psychiatric implications of physiological studies on frontotemporal portions of the limbic system", *Electroencephalography and Clinical Neurophysiology* **4**, 407–418.

MacLean, P. D. (1969) "The hypothalamus and emotional behavior", in W. Haymaker et al. (eds), *The Hypothalamus*, Charles C. Thomas, Springfield, Illinois.

MacLean, P. D. (1970) "The triune brain, emotion and scientific bias", in F. O. Schmitt et al. (eds), *The Neurosciences*, Rockefeller University Press, New York.

MacLean, P. D. (1980) "Sensory and perceptive factors in emotional functions of the triune brain", in A. O. Rorty (ed.), *Explaining Emotions*, University of California Press.

Newman, P. L. (1960) " 'Wild man' behaviour in a New Guinean Highland community", *American Anthropologist* **66**, 1–19.

Nisbett, R. E. and Wilson, T. DeCamp (1977) "Telling more than we can know: verbal reports on mental processes", *Psychological Review* **84**, 233.

Ohman, A., Fredrikson, M., Hugdahl, K. and Rimmo, P. (1976) "The premise of equipotentiality in human classical conditioning", *Journal of Experimental Psychology: General* **105**, 313–37.

Panksepp, J. (1982) "Towards a general psychological theory of emotions", *Behaviour and Brain Sciences* **5**, 407–67.

Rozin, P. (1976) "The evolution of intelligence and access to the cognitive unconscious", in *Progress in Psychobiology and Physiological Psychology*, Vol. 6, Academic Press, New York.

Rozin, P. and Fallon, A. (1987) "A perspective on disgust", *Psychological Review* **94**, 23–41.

Rozin, P. and Kalat, J. W. (1971) "Specific hungers and poison avoidance as adaptive specializations of learning", *Psychological Review* **78**, 459–86.

Schachter, S. and Singer, J. E. (1962) "Cognitive, social and psychological determinants of emotional state", *Psychological Review* **69**, 379–99.

Schaffer, J. A. (1983) "An assessment of emotion", *American Philosophical Quarterly* **20**, 161–73.

Seligman, M. E. P. (1970) "On the generality of the laws of learning", *Psychological Review* **77**, 407–18.

Seligman, M. E. P. (1971) "Phobias and preparedness", *Behaviour Therapy* **2**, 307–20.

Solomon, R. (1977) *The Passions*, Anchor Books.

Stocker, M. (1987) "Emotional thoughts", *American Philosophical Quarterly* **24**(1).

Thompson, J. (1941) "Development of facial expression of emotion in blind and seeing children", *Archives of Psychology* **37**, No. 264.

Trevarthen, C. (1984) "Emotions in infancy: regulators of contact and relationships with persons", in P. Ekman and K. R. Scherer (eds), *Approaches to Emotion*, Lawrence Erlbaum Associates, Hillsdale, New Jersey.

Watson, J. B. (1925) *Behaviourism*, Kegan Paul, Trench, Trubner & Co., London.

Weinrich, J. D. (1980) "Towards a sociobiological theory of the emotions", in R. Plutchik and H. Kellerman (eds), *Emotion: Theory, Research and Experience*, Vol. 1, Academic Press, New York.

Subject Index

Names Index